ENCYCLOPÆDIA
OF
NEW ORLEANS
ARTISTS
1718~1918

ENCYCLOPÆDIA
OF
NEW ORLEANS
ARTISTS
1718~1918

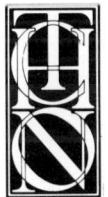

THE HISTORIC
NEW ORLEANS
COLLECTION

By special direction of the board of the Kemper and Leila Williams Foundation, this work is gratefully and lovingly dedicated to Boyd Cruise, in recognition of his original concept and his years of early work on the project, and, more importantly, his devoted service to the Williamses in the establishment of the Historic New Orleans Collection itself.

Joanne P. Platou, Director
The Historic New Orleans Collection
533 Royal Street
New Orleans, Louisiana 70130

International Standard Book Number: 0–917860–23–3
Library of Congress Catalog Card Number: 87–80477
© 1987 by the Historic New Orleans Collection
All rights reserved
First edition. 2,000 copies
Printed in the United States of America
Jacket and book design by Michael Ledet Designs, New Orleans
Typography and production by Impressions, Inc., Madison, Wisconsin

FOREWORD

The inception of this volume can be traced to the 1940s when Boyd Cruise, a distinguished watercolorist and the curator for General and Mrs. L. Kemper Williams's growing collection of Louisiana material, began research on artists and art of Louisiana. After the death of Mrs. Williams in December 1966 and the formal establishment of the Kemper and Leila Williams Foundation, Boyd Cruise became the first director of the Historic New Orleans Collection. Over the years, he continued to expand his files and started to write what he planned would be an encyclopaedia of Louisiana artists and artisans. He remained undaunted by the magnitude of the task he had set for himself.

Meantime, in 1976, the Collection's curators created study files of Louisiana artists in response to the growing number of inquiries regarding this subject. Boyd Cruise, now in retirement, placed his extensive research at the Collection, to be made available to the public, and gave his encouragement to carry on with the book. He had already set the time frame of the book, 1718–1918. The alphabetical format was retained, for as the introduction to the 11th edition of the *Encyclopaedia Britannica* succinctly states, "The convenience of an arrangement of material based on a single alphabetization of subject words and proper names has established itself in the common sense of mankind . . ."

In response to the growing interest in American art, and more recently in Southern art, the board of the Williams Foundation agreed that a publication of artists, itinerant or residents of New Orleans, would be a valuable research resource. Alberta Collier, art critic for a New Orleans newspaper, became the first editor. Upon her retirement in 1982, the work was turned over to Collection staff members.

With staff teams assigned to untapped sources of information, other artists' names and large quantities of material were added. It became increasingly apparent to the editors, curators John Mahé and Rosanne McCaffrey, that the artisans, architects, and photographers would have to be dropped so as to make a volume of manageable size.

Though works of this kind, dealing with a limited subject and geographic area, are dwarfed by the immensity and complexity of the great dictionaries and encyclopaedias, many of the same problems had to be addressed. What to include and how to make it intelligible called for consistency and constant refinement of the initial system of entry as the amount of data grew. Enormous hours of staff time were dedicated to completing the task as quickly as possible. The final thrust came between 1982 and 1986 with a manuscript ready for publication at the beginning of 1987. The task was completed.

This encyclopaedia is but one product of the joint effort. By its nature, the length of entries is necessarily limited. The supporting research, as well as additional unpublished information on the listed artists, is available at the Collection along with files of over 15,000 artists and artisans of all periods.

It is hoped by the many contributors to this volume that it will serve as the basis for further research on the subject and that facts and resources not available to the Collection at this time will be shared by those who have the knowledge.

Joanne P. Platou
Director

ACKNOWLEDGMENTS

The compilation and production of the *Encyclopaedia of New Orleans Artists, 1718–1918* has been a collaborative effort calling upon the cooperation and expertise of many people throughout the country. The Historic New Orleans Collection sponsored the project from its beginnings to the final product. Few institutions have been able to devote the requisite time and staff to such an endeavor, and it is to the credit of the board of directors of the Kemper and Leila Williams Foundation that the project continued through its years of research, development, editing, and production.

Acknowledgment for the initial research for the book must be given to Boyd Cruise, director emeritus of the Historic New Orleans Collection. Beginning in the 1940s, Mr. Cruise, as the sole curator to the Collection's founders, General and Mrs. L. Kemper Williams, researched from diverse sources the items acquired by the Williamses for their private collection. As the historical references grew, the Williamses suggested the need for compiling the available information on local and itinerant artists into one published volume as a framework for further study by future scholars. Mr. Cruise pursued this mission with exemplary perseverance for nearly 30 years as curator and then as director of the Collection, and into his retirement as director emeritus.

Many local historians and collectors were interested in the proposed publication and generously supplied the Williamses and Mr. Cruise with the background material relating to artists which they had acquired during their years of research. Don Didier was particularly cooperative in sending information that he had gathered for a similar publication he had been considering. H. Parrot Bacot, Leonard V. Huber, Samuel Wilson, Jr., and Richard Koch have made significant contributions to the study of Louisiana art, and they offered information and copies of their articles and publications about local artists. Among other individuals who furnished references were Albert L. Lieutaud, Connie G. Griffith, William R. Cullison III, Ruth R. Fontenot, D. Clive Hardy, Zuma Y. Salaun, J. Raymond Samuel, Sidney L. Villeré, Arthur Scully, Jr., Richard R. Dixon, and Harold Schilke. Certain past Collection staff members supplied Mr. Cruise with translations: Robert D. Bush, Maria Ybor, Renée Peck, Carrie Davis, and Chislane Pleasanton. The staffs at several institutions throughout the country were most accommodating to Mr. Cruise's inquiries during his research trips and through correspondence: Esther Sparks, Art Institute of Chicago; Chicago Historical Society; Douglas Marshall, William L. Clements Library, University of Michigan; Daniel H. Woodward, Huntington Library; Sidney Kaplin, National Portrait Gallery; Frank C. Mevers, New Hampshire Historical Society; William G. Duprey, New–York Historical Society; Anthony Cardillo, George Freedley, H. Ward Jandl, Leo M. J. Manglaviti, Elizabeth E. Roth, Paul R. Rugen, New York Public Library; John Aubrey and Paul Banks, Newberry Library; Joyce H. Lamont, University of Alabama. Others who shared with him their knowledge included Milton P. Adler, Reverend F. P. Prucha, Mrs. J. C. Rathbone, and Robert J. Woodward.

Stanton M. Frazar, as director of the Historic New Orleans Collection from 1975 until 1986, guided the project after Mr. Cruise finished his first draft of the manuscript. Without his active interest in the value and worth of the project, it would have been impossible to achieve the necessary support of coordinating a most diverse staff behind so monumental an undertaking.

The editors owe a great debt to the succession of staff members of the Historic New Orleans Collection who have contributed their time over the years. Joanne Platou, as Mr. Frazar's successor as director, continued the commitment to the book during the months of production and proferred her encouragement. In the curatorial division, John H. Lawrence gave valuable editorial assistance in the final stages; and the curatorial research staff, including Patricia A. McWhorter, Kellye Magee, and Kitty Farley, as well as past staff members Wayne Lempka, Eloise Gamble, Raimund Berchtold, Richard Marvin, and Ashley Scott, assisted in compiling data and confirming pictorial references.

Special thanks are due to the Collection's library staff, Florence M. Jumonville, Pamela D. Arceneaux, Jessica Travis, Adrienne E. Duffy, Edith N. Haupt, and former librarians Marie Kambur, Elizabeth Polchow, and Judith MacMillan for assisting the researchers and editors in locating the many familiar and obscure citations. They took on the task of combing the thousands of books, pamphlets, and pieces of sheet music in the library collections for lost references and helped in assembling and editing the bibliography. Miss Jumonville brought many new pieces of information to our attention and, with Mrs. Arceneaux and Mrs. Travis, assisted in the arduous task of proofreading copy.

Within the manuscripts division, Ralph Draughon, Jr. gave the benefit of his comprehensive background in American history; Alfred

E. Lemmon, Catherine C. Kahn, Taronda Spencer, Angelita Rosal, and Donald R. Gaylord provided research assistance from their areas of specialty, as did Susan T. Cole, Victor McGee, and Mark Luccioni earlier.

The Collection's education department supplied a daily reservoir of personnel who confirmed thousands of reference citations in newspapers, city directories, and other literary sources. This important task was diligently supervised by Elsa L. Schneider and assistant Patricia S. Cromiller, with Roberta Berry, Noreen B. Lapeyre, Edye Conkerton, Marla Morris, and Naomi R. Lowrey among the always accommodating docents. Edward Ross, of the publications department, assisted in the final stages of getting the book ready for press.

During the early days of the project, well–known local art columnist Alberta Collier was given responsibility for the preparation of Mr. Cruise's first draft for publication. She was ably assisted by John M. Collier, Jr., Laura Cole Rosenthal, and Christine Lathrop. Merle Harton contributed editorial assistance during the next phase and accomplished much of the preliminary research in New Orleans city directories.

Outside of the Collection staff, we owe lasting gratitude to the many individuals and institutions who generously shared their time, knowledge, and innumerable services to assist us in the encyclopaedia's production. The Collection has been fortunate in receiving a number of university interns who provided valuable assistance to the professional staff while themselves learning museum operations. Several contributed their talents to researching this book, including Edwin Foster Blair II, Mary Borgen, Mirian D. Carter, Catherine Gardner, David Gourgues, Ellen Holmes, David Hunkel, Donna Kelly, Colin Kemmerly, Susan Leal, Glenn Mackie, Mary Mackie, Elizabeth McCarron, Molly Stewart, and Laura Uhl. Jessie Poesch, an outstanding scholar on the arts in the South, graciously scheduled students from Tulane University as interns, and she shared her vast resources and editorial experience from her numerous publications.

Special thanks are extended to the volunteers who freely gave their time to various parts of the project: William P. Farrington, Bronwen Fitzpatrick, and Nancy Piston.

Essential to the final preparation of the encyclopaedia have been the comments and criticisms from colleagues who read the completed manuscript. George E. Jordan, in his capacity as a local art historian, tendered valuable information and led us to many citations that became incorporated in the text. Charles L. Mackie added to our knowledge of local genealogy and of new source materials in notarial records. Warren M. Billings reviewed our editorial plans and contributed his expertise.

ACKNOWLEDGMENTS

Numerous institutions aided the researchers and the editors in the preparation of this book. The valuable resources of the Louisiana Division of the New Orleans Public Library were freely opened to us throughout the project. The head of the division, Collin B. Hamer, Jr., was most cooperative and understanding during our many searches through his collections and went far beyond the normal response to provide every conceivable assistance. Wayne M. Everard displayed particular patience with our constant telephone calls to confirm information and citations. We wish also to thank their bright and attentive staff: Jean M. Jones, Ernest J. Brin, David W. Deakle, and Suhad Khalaf.

The holdings of the Louisiana Collection, in the Howard-Tilton Memorial Library at Tulane University, were always conveniently accessible to our staff. The Collection's head, Jane Stevens, and her associate, Gay Gomez Craft, were unfailingly helpful and generously shared their knowledge and their holdings. They, as well as Jane Johnson and Leslie Palmer, made the task of research a consistently pleasant one. The staff of Special Collections/University Archives in the library was also helpful in providing information: Wilbur E. Meneray, Sue McGrady Woodward, Mary Lachin LeBlanc, Joan G. Caldwell, Guillermo Nañez Falcón, Doris H. Antin, and Linda Poe. Other library staff of assistance at Tulane included Kelly Brewin, Helen Burkes, Philip Jones, Geoffrey Kimball, Susan McClellan, Betty Mailhes, Eva Martinez, Sylvia Metzinger, Buford M. Myers, Katie Nachod, and Martha Barton Robertson.

The editors wish to single out Rose Lambert, of the Louisiana Historical Center of the Louisiana State Museum, for her cooperation, interest, and tireless assistance in the project from its beginnings with Mr. Cruise. When she had heard of the Williamses' interest in compiling information on artists, Miss Lambert scanned hundreds of newspapers and made note of any artists mentioned. Three other librarians at the museum, Josie Cerf, Rose Oliver, and Aline Morris, also helped Mr. Cruise in his research. Edward F. Haas, the Center's director, also aided our work, as did J. B. Harter of the museum, who shared his considerable knowledge and his office space while allowing our researchers access to that institution's artists files.

We are indebted to individuals at other local institutions who shared their knowledge and interests: Charles E. Nolan, Archives of the Archdiocese of New Orleans; staff, Troy H. Middleton Memorial Library, Louisiana State University; William A. Fagaly, Jeanette Downing, Elise Hamilton, Winston Lill, and Paul Riley, New Orleans Museum of Art; Marie E. Windell, Earl K. Long Library, University of New Orleans.

Information and services were provided on specific artists by many other people and organizations including: August Alfaro; Archivist of Dôle; Mrs. Beauregard Bassich; Jack Belsom; Barbara Boger; Central Michigan University Library; Alanna Chesebro, Richard York Gallery; Mrs. William Coke, Ladies' Hermitage Association; Nathaniel Cortlandt Curtis, Jr.; Detroit Public Library; Mrs. John T. Farnsworth; Catherine B. Foss; John Fowler; Frick Art Reference Library; John Geiser III; Harry T. Howard; Liza Kirwin, Archives of American Art; Mrs. Edmond Le Breton; Jacob V. Mancuso; Minnesota Historical Society; Monroe County Library System; Harold D. Moser and Sharon Macpherson, Papers of Andrew Jackson; Asta Muir, Royal Scottish Academy; Olen A. Nance; New York Public Library; Nina Nichols Pugh; Richard Relf; J. Richard Rivoire; George H. Schroeter, Mobile Public Library; Thomas Byrne Memorial Library, Spring Hill College; Philip Werlein IV; Rosemary Challoner Wilkinson; Peter M. Wolf. Others, although not mentioned by name, undoubtedly added to the wealth of information which was gathered and which will continue to enrich the Collection's holdings and files.

To all of our associates, colleagues, and friends who contributed to the preparation and production of this book, we extend our deepest appreciation and utmost thanks.

John A. Mahé II
Rosanne McCaffrey

INTRODUCTION

In a city with a long history of identification with the arts, the lack of a comprehensive reference work on New Orleans artists has been striking. The present volume fills the gap: it is an inclusive listing of all artists active in New Orleans during a time span of two hundred years, from 1718, when the city was founded, through 1918.

An artist is defined as one whose work takes visual form and is practiced in conscious pursuit of beauty or aesthetic pleasure, that is, fine art. To produce a comprehensive reference tool, we have interpreted this definition broadly. Those who listed themselves as "artists" or "painters" have been assumed to meet the criterion for inclusion unless further research showed that they were actually performing artists or house painters. Arbitrary exclusion could only hamper the usefulness of the book.

This volume presents biographical data on over 2,700 artists and art organizations, both major and minor, who were associated with New Orleans. Its purpose is to illuminate the careers of forgotten artists and to consider established artists in the light of their New Orleans careers. Most of them pursued their vocations in the city, but other artists have also been included. In addition to artists active in New Orleans, the following categories were included: artists, born in New Orleans, whose artistic work was done elsewhere, and the artists or firms that created historically significant prints depicting New Orleans subjects when information about the artist of the original artwork was lacking. The latter entries are abbreviated since their only function is to comment on a New Orleans artwork. In a few cases, artists who portrayed New Orleans scenes or citizens have been included. For example, an important nineteenth–century portrait painter, Thomas Sully, has been listed even though he never worked in New Orleans. Because Sully painted so many important New Orleanians, it has frequently been asserted that he visited the city; it seemed important to state definitively that he had not worked here.

The cutoff date for inclusion in the encyclopaedia is January 1, 1919. An artist must have exhibited or sold a work or otherwise given evidence of serious artistic activity before that date. Studying art during that period is not acceptable for inclusion. Because of this dating, some important twentieth–century artists who were students at the time have been excluded; others who had shown a few pieces, such as Josephine Crawford and Caroline Durieux, are included.

The arrangement is alphabetical. The standard word–by–word system of alphabetization is used. "Mc" and "M'" and "St." are alphabetized as though they were spelled out "Mac" and "Saint." Company names such as "F. G. Koeckert & Co." are alphabetized by surname and then by first names or initials. So that it will be readily apparent to the reader the manner in which the firm's name appeared, first and last names are not inverted. Company names with no first name or initials, such as "Smith Brothers," are alphabetized after all entries which contain given names.

Within each entry a format has been followed which makes pertinent information quickly accessible. The possible components of an entry are name, places/dates of birth/death, race, occupation/active New Orleans dates, associated crafts and occupations, firm or organization officers, studied, contemporary listings, exhibited, awarded, memberships/positions, prose, and references. Information in all categories was not available for every artist: the minimum information for an entry consists of name, occupation or prose, and references. Cross–references appear in small capitals.

NAME. Artists are listed under their most commonly used names or the names they employed professionally. Alternate forms of these names which appeared in contemporary sources are presented in parentheses; clearly random alterations in spelling, mere translations from one language to another, or shortened forms of names have not been included as alternate forms. Married women artists are listed under the surname they used for most of their artistic careers, and then cross–referenced from their married or maiden names. This is the first reference book on New Orleans to identify and include women artists in a comprehensive manner.

For artists whose gender, but not a complete given name, is known, the honorifics, when ascertainable, "Mr.," "Mrs.," "Mme.," or "Miss" are used. The names of companies and organizations are transcribed as they appeared in contemporary citations, including abbreviations and ampersands.

PLACES/DATES OF BIRTH/DEATH. Place is presented as given in the sources. Birth and death dates were frequently arrived at by inference or subtraction; in these cases, the date is preceded by "ca." For example, when age is given in an obituary or a census, subtraction provided an approximate birthdate. Or, when a man appears in a city directory one year and the following year his widow is listed, he was presumed to have died the previous year even if no death certificate or obituary has been found. When conflicting information for month and day is present, alternatives are listed. When alternative years are reported, an inclusive circa date is given.

RACE. Racial identifications have been taken only from contemporary sources, such as city directories, newspapers, censuses, and birth and death certificates; generally it has been possible to identify the race of an artist because racial designations were, with few exceptions, reported by contemporary sources.

The definitive history of black artists in New Orleans has yet to be written; information on the more famous, such as lithographer Jules Lion, is available, but the careers of other black artists and craftsmen are still obscure. Research for this volume has uncovered many of these previously unknown artists. Twenty–two black artists, largely sculptors and painters, have been identified; additional racial information from contemporary sources, such as "free man of color" or "mulatto" is supplied in parentheses. There is one artist who has been identified as an American Indian; all other artists are either known to be or presumed to be white.

OCCUPATION/ACTIVE DATES: This line indicates the artistic métier; if the person worked in more than one medium, each occupation is listed in order of its importance in that individual's New Orleans career. Certain occupations have been designated as representing the visual arts: a person must have practiced one of these to be included in this volume. Artisans and craftsmen have not been included, unless they also practiced one of these professions. The following are the occupations acceptable for inclusion:

art association
art craftsman: pottery
    decorator, metal craftsman,
    pottery designer, or art
    jeweler
art dealer
art school
art teacher
artist: designation with no
    evidence of medium
bookbinder: artistic
    bookbinding
cartoonist
colorer: of prints or
    photographs
commercial artist
designer: of carnival parades,
    flags, banners, emblems, or
    stained glass; fancy paper
    cutter or model maker

engraver: in any medium,
    including bank notes,
    jewelry, steel, mezzotint,
    photo, copper, stone, wood,
    aquatint
etcher
hair worker
illustrator
lithographer
museum
painter: in any medium on any
    support
potter: art potter
restorer
sculptor: in any medium,
    including stone, metal, clay,
    wood, artificial flowers, glass,
    and wax
silhouettist
sketch artist

Active dates are the dates of known activity in New Orleans, not of an artist's total career activity in other cities. For certain well–known artists, these dates will constitute a very small portion of their artistic careers. Active dates are inclusive from the first mention of an individual or firm's artistic activity in the city until the last, even when they extend beyond the 1918 cutoff date. Itinerant artists were not continuously in residence, but the inclusive dates enable one to identify possible works. In a few cases an artist came to New Orleans on a few specifically dated occasions and is positively known not to have been in the city in the interim; then, the active dates are given as distinct dates, separated by a semicolon.

ASSOCIATED OCCUPATIONS. Crafts or professions which are closely associated with the arts are also given as part of the occupational information. Although considered associated occupations, practitioners of these crafts without fine arts activity are not included. Many architects made fine drawings in conjunction with their architectural practice, but, unless they produced artwork for exhibition or sale, they have not been included. Photographers are included only if they were also colorers because, in the early years of the profession, it was not generally considered to be an art form.

If known, the relationship between the craft and the art are given: for example, "sculptor, also stone carver" indicates someone who considered himself an artist, but also worked at a craft, whereas "sculptor, primarily stone carver" indicates a craftsman who devoted less time to mainly artistic activity. Associated crafts and occupations include the following:

architect
art store proprietor
builder
cabinetmaker
calligrapher
carpenter
cartographer
carver
copyist
decorator
draftsman
engineer
furniture maker
geographer
gilder
glazier
goldsmith

grainer
ivory/wood turner
jeweler
marble carver/worker
molder
museum proprietor
needleworker
ornamental painter
photographer
pressman
printer
publisher
sign painter
silversmith
stained–glass worker
stationer
stencil cutter

stereotyper

stone carver/worker

surveyor

taxidermist

topographical engineer

watchmaker

FIRM OR ORGANIZATION OFFICERS. On the occupation line, owners or partners in a business or officers of an organization are listed with their positions. Those with separate artistic activities are cross–referenced to an individual entry; those who were primarily businessmen in an art–related firm are merely listed, along with place and date of birth and death when known. Years of association with the firm are sometimes given in parentheses.

STUDIED. The art schools and masters with whom artists studied are given, as well as place and years studied; sometimes only a city or country is known. The cutoff date for listings in this category is January 1, 1919. Information, particularly about foreign academies and teachers, is taken from both contemporary New Orleans sources and secondary sources; it is as accurate as those sources. Primary research on teachers and schools has not been done, nor have the claims of artists about their studies been independently verified.

CONTEMPORARY LISTINGS. These give artistic occupations as they appeared in contemporary sources, along with New Orleans business addresses where available. Spellings of occupations are generally given as they appear in the sources; the addresses are also as they appear in the sources except that foreign words have been translated into English. Addresses were changed several times in the eighteenth and nineteenth centuries, the last major change taking place in 1893–94; no attempt has been made to translate old addresses into modern terms so the researcher using these addresses should be wary. Designations such as "street," "avenue," and so forth have not been used, except in cases of possible confusion, such as "Exchange Place" and "Exchange Alley." Non–artistic occupations and crafts are not listed, nor are home addresses, unless it appears that the artist used his residence as a studio. The usual sources for contemporary listings are city directories, newspapers, magazines, censuses, journals, diaries, artworks, trade cards, and advertisements. Dates given in parentheses are the dates of the sources. The cutoff date for this category is January 1, 1919.

EXHIBITED. Exhibitions include expositions, art school shows, one–man and group exhibitions, galleries, salons, museums, art associations, and exhibitions at business establishments. If other than New Orleans, the place of exhibition is also given. They are arranged in chronological order if the dates are known or can be surmised from other facts. The cutoff date for this category is January 1, 1919.

AWARDED. Awards received by an artist at fairs, expositions, competitions, and juried shows are recorded in chronological order, with the title of the competition; the sponsoring organization or patron; place, if other than New Orleans; award won; and year. The cutoff date for this category is January 1, 1919.

MEMBERSHIPS/POSITIONS. This category includes only artistic organizations, such as art leagues or museum boards. The name of the organization is followed by position held; arrangement is chronological. Cutoff date is January 1, 1919.

PROSE. Prose sections are provided for more important artists, summarizing their careers. In the case of nationally or internationally known artists who worked in New Orleans only briefly, such as Audubon or Degas, the outlines of their careers are presented in prose, but the emphasis is on information as detailed as possible about their New Orleans activities. For less important artists, this section is a catch–all category for information which does not fit into any of the previous sections. Prose may include activities outside New Orleans, important aspects of their careers not related to the arts, relationships to other artists, and events in their careers after 1918. Also in this section, when it appears possible that two separate entries might be the same artist, but conclusive evidence has not been found, the reader is referred from one entry to another by "*cf.*" to compare the information available.

REFERENCES. Each entry is followed by a list of sources used in preparing that entry. Each artist appearing in the book has a file in the curatorial division of the Historic New Orleans Collection, containing all information accumulated about his or her life and career. Materials which merely duplicate information, sales catalogues, and outdated sources have been consulted, but have not generally been cited.

References in the entry appear in shortened form; those frequently cited are abbreviated. Full citations to all references appear in the bibliography. The order of references is as follows: New Orleans directories (city, business, and suburban), newspapers and contemporary periodicals, all other primary and secondary sources.

New Orleans directories, the earliest dated 1805, were combed by researchers for artists. They provided occupations, employers, business addresses, and a timeline for the artist's moves from job to job and place to place.

At times, a directory listing of an individual as an artist was the original source for the inclusion of that person. In other cases, an artist's name was discovered in other sources. Directories were searched for three editions prior to the earliest year the artist was known to have practiced, and continued another three beyond the last listing. Gaps in the running dates for the twentieth–century listings occurred because directories were not published every year and because only the directories at the Collection were used. The latest directories consulted were the 1979 city directory and the 1980 suburban directory.

In city directories the artist's name may appear in the alphabetical residential listings, in the groupings by business in the back of the book, and/or in an advertisement; in business directories the artist may appear as a business listing and/or in an advertisement. Occasionally there are two directories available for the same year. In 1856 and 1867 there are two separate city directories, published by different companies. Similarly, there are two business directories for 1858 and 1858–59 and two for 1860 and 1860–61. The reference entry for this encyclopaedia does not specify in these cases since only the year is given. Both directories should be checked by a researcher in those four cases. The artist may be listed in either or both.

Despite the importance of directory information, there are certain problems in using them. They appeared sporadically before 1850. Full names are not always provided, and spellings of a particular name may vary widely, with striking inaccuracy, from year to year. Rarely, an artist may appear twice in a single directory under different spellings. Entries printed in a directory reflect information gathered the previous year and could have changed by the date of publication. The date in parentheses given in the entry reflects the publication date of the directories.

Newspapers and contemporary periodicals are arranged in alphabetical order, with several citations to the same publication in chronological order. Titles of most newspapers are abbreviated, but full citations appear in the bibliography. Advertisements for the services of an artist or company often run consecutively through several issues of a periodical without a change in the advertising copy.

News reports, articles, and advertisements provided invaluable information. In the 1930s the Works Progress Administration Artists Project at the then Delgado Museum of Art undertook the monumental task of searching thousands of issues of local newspapers for any mention of New Orleans artists; this work, along with additional research, was brought together as two typewritten manuscripts, "Lives, New Orleans Artists" and "N.O. Artists Directory, 1805–1940." A copy of these manuscripts was made available to the Collection by the New Orleans Museum of Art and formed the basis for much of the newspaper research for this project. Additional newspapers, magazines, and journals were also searched, however, and all earlier citations were verified. This work, incredibly time–consuming, was done primarily from microfilm, most of which is in the manuscripts division of the Historic New Orleans Collection. Important newspaper holdings at the Louisiana State Museum, Tulane University, and the New Orleans Public Library, as well as the large collection of New Orleans magazines and journals at Tulane, supplemented the Collection's own resources.

The obituary file and news index at the New Orleans Public Library were essential in providing leads to further newspaper research. Modern newspapers were not run in their entirety, although their comprehensive dates are provided in the bibliography. They were used selectively to find obituaries and important post–1918 articles about the artists.

In the reference section for each entry, all sources other than directories and periodicals are grouped alphabetically. Many books and articles were checked, but do not appear in the references because information is available elsewhere or because they are inaccurate or outdated. They are retained, however, as part of the bibliography for New Orleans art. Manuscript material is listed in a separate section of the bibliography, under "Special Collections."

Catalogues yielded important information, especially those of the Artists' Association and its successor, the Art Association; however, a complete run of these catalogues was not available. Also helpful were the Mechanics' and Agricultural Fair Association reports listing award–winning entries in many artistic fields. Nineteenth– and twentieth–century auction catalogues sometimes provided information on artworks not available elsewhere.

United States census records for Louisiana from 1810 through 1910 were searched for New Orleans artists; the 1890 census, however, is unavailable because the original records were destroyed. From 1810 through 1840 the names of specific artists already on the list were checked, because occupation was not included on the census. Beginning in 1850, a thorough search for artistic occupations was made, resulting in the addition of many artists to the book. Research concentrated on Orleans Parish, Algiers, Jefferson City, Lafayette, and Carrollton, all parts of present–day New Orleans. The original records are housed at the National Archives; microfilm copies at the Collection were used for this project.

The Historic New Orleans Collection's Survey of Historic New Orleans Cemeteries includes inscriptions from nine local cemeteries. It was used for birth and death dates and other pertinent data, such as country of origin.

The standard artistic reference works were consulted for all artists active in New Orleans; they provided essential information on the careers of artists whose careers were largely outside the city. However, since these publications are national or international in scope, information on local artists is often sketchy and sometimes contains inaccuracies or discrepancies. Primary sources were preferred to these compendia.

Special collections at local repositories contain very important material, such as maps, scrapbooks, letters, records of local governmental agencies, death records, court proceedings, sheet music, and original works by artists. Sometimes the only material available about an artist is an extant artwork. When an artwork is cited as a source, the abbreviation for the institution holding the piece is given, followed by an accession number, for example, THNOC 1959.1.

The accuracy of entries was checked and re–checked at every stage of preparation: from research, through filling out worksheets and checking files against manuscript, to several stages of editing and proofreading. This volume is as accurate as possible at this time. No further information, sources, or additions were incorporated after January 1, 1987. Any further information uncovered will be added to the artists files available to researchers in the curatorial division of the Historic New Orleans Collection.

ABBREVIATIONS

AK	Alaska	MT	Montana
AL	Alabama	NC	North Carolina
AR	Arkansas	ND	North Dakota
AZ	Arizona	NE	Nebraska
CA	California	NH	New Hampshire
CO	Colorado	NJ	New Jersey
CT	Connecticut	NM	New Mexico
DC	District of Columbia	NV	Nevada
DE	Delaware	NY	New York
FL	Florida	OH	Ohio
GA	Georgia	OK	Oklahoma
HI	Hawaii	OR	Oregon
IA	Iowa	PA	Pennsylvania
ID	Idaho	RI	Rhode Island
IL	Illinois	SC	South Carolina
IN	Indiana	SD	South Dakota
KS	Kansas	TN	Tennessee
KY	Kentucky	TX	Texas
LA	Louisiana	UT	Utah
MA	Massachusetts	VA	Virginia
MD	Maryland	VT	Vermont
ME	Maine	WA	Washington
MI	Michigan	WI	Wisconsin
MN	Minnesota	WV	West Virginia
MO	Missouri	WY	Wyoming
MS	Mississippi		

AANO	Artists' Association of New Orleans	oppos.	opposite
al.	alley	pl.	place
botw.	between	pres.	president
ca.	circa	prof.	professor
cor.	corner	prop.	proprietor
LHS	Louisiana Historical Society	secy.	secretary
LSM	Louisiana State Museum	supt.	superintendent
LSU	Louisiana State University	THNOC	The Historic New Orleans Collection
mgr.	manager	treas.	treasurer
N.O.	New Orleans	TU	Tulane University
NOBD	New Orleans business directory	U.S.	United States
		v. pres.	vice president
NOCD	New Orleans city directory	WICCE	World's Industrial and Cotton Centennial Exposition
NOPL	New Orleans Public Library		
NOSD	New Orleans suburban directory		
N.Y.C.	New York City	WPA	Works Progress Administration

The usual abbreviations and contractions in general use

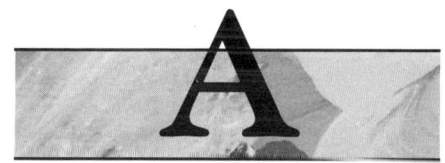

AAMOND, PHILIP
Lithographer, active N.O. 1851.
Contemporary listings: lithographer, Laurel betw. Josephine and Jackson (1851).
References: NOCD 1851–54.

AARON, FREDERICK S. *See* VON EHREN, SUSUS FREDERICK

ABBOT, JOSEPH
Sketch artist, active N.O. 1887.
Studied: with WILLIAM JENNINGS WARRINGTON (1887).
Exhibited: studio and art rooms of William Jennings Warrington (1887).
References: *T. Demo.*, Oct. 13, 1887.

ABRAMS, WILLIAM H.
Painter, active N.O. 1857–58; primarily photographer.
Contemporary listings: ambrotype, daguerreotype, photograph, melainotype, and portrait painting saloon, 74 Chartres (1857–58).
Possibly William Abrams, born MA ca. 1825, listed as a painter in the 1850 census.
References: NOCD 1858, 1860–61, 1866; NOBD 1857–58; Smith and Tucker, 152; U.S. Census (1850), roll 234.

ACADEMIE DE DESSIN ET DE PEINTURE
(Academie de Dessin et de Peinture d'Orleans)
Art school, active N.O. 1826–27; TOUSSAINT FRANÇOIS BIGOT, teacher and probably owner.
Contemporary listings: drawing and painting school, 76 Orleans (1826); drawing and painting school, St. Peter betw. Royal and Bourbon (1827).
References: *Argus*, June 1, 1826, Mar. 7, 1827.

ACADEMIE DE DESSIN ET DE PEINTURE DE LA NOUVELLE ORLEANS (New Orleans Drawing & Painting Academy)
Art school, active N.O. 1845–46; TOUSSAINT FRANÇOIS BIGOT, teacher and owner.
Contemporary listings: 43 St. Philip (1845–46).

Offered all kinds of drawing, particularly architecture and marine.
References: NOCD 1846; *Courier*, Nov. 10, 1845.

ACADEMIE DE DESSIN ET DE PEINTURE POUR LES PERSONNES DE COULEUR
Art school, active N.O. 1827; WILLIAM BALDWIN, teacher.
Contemporary listings: drawing and painting school, Burgundy betw. St. Peter and Orleans (1827).
References: *Argus*, Feb. 19, 1827.

ACADEMY OF DESIGN
Art school, active N.O. 1857–58.
Contemporary listings: 51 St. Peter (1857); Clinton cor. St. Peter (1858).
References: NOCD 1857–58.

ACADEMY OF FINE ARTS
Art school, active N.O. ca. 1886–89; WILLIAM JENNINGS WARRINGTON, director.
Contemporary listings: 169 St. Charles (1889).
References: NOCD 1889; *D. Pic.*, Jan. 22, 1889; *T. Demo.*, Jan. 22, 1889.

ADAM, CAPT. LOUIS A.
Born N.O. ca. 1832–34; died N.O. Aug. 9, 1905.
Designer, active N.O. 1884.
Member of the Washington Artillery who designed a memorial picture with the motto of the battalion, battle scenes, and photographic portraits of its members (1884).
References: NOCD 1857–60, 1866–73, 1875–86, 1889–90, 1893–94, 1896–1905; *D. Pic.*, Aug. 10, 1905; *D. States*, May 20, 1884; *T. Demo.*, Aug. 10, 1905; U.S. Census (1860), roll 420.

ADAMS, CARL C.
Sketch artist, active N.O. 1905; primarily draftsman.
Awarded: *Architectural Art and Its Allies*, second prize for cover design (1906).
Memberships/positions: T–Square Club (1905), v. pres. (1906).

Submitted a design in a T–Square Club emblem competition (1905). In 1906 Adams left his position with the N.O. architectural firm of Stone Brothers and moved to N.Y.C., where he worked and also became a finalist for a prize from the Societé des Beaux Arts, Paris (1908).
References: NOCD 1904–1906; *Architectural Art*, 1(Aug. 1905):14, 1(June 1906):5, 7, 9, 3(June 1908):6.

ADAMS, NORA D.
Painter, active N.O. 1909–15.
Contemporary listings: artist (1909, 1911); china painter, 2263 Carondelet (1910); china painter (1912); china studio, 717 Nashville (1914); china painting, 717 Nashville (1915).
References: NOCD 1909–12, 1914–16.

ADEVENSE, GEORGE
Sculptor, active N.O. 1882–83.
Contemporary listings: sculptor (1882); sculptor, 228 Chartres (1883).
References: NOCD 1882–83.

ADORCI, OCTAVE
Born France ca. 1814–18; died N.O. Aug. 22, 1892.
Sketch artist, active N.O. 1865–91.
Contemporary listings: artist, 255 Burgundy (1867); artist, French Opera (1868); artist (1871–72, 1891). Signed his only known drawing "1865/N.O./O. adorci." Listed as a chorist (1887) and as a doorkeeper (1890) at the French Opera House; and as an actor (1892).
References: NOCD 1867–68, 1871–72, 1887–91; N.O. Death Certificate (1892), 102:611, NOPL; U.S. Census (1870), roll 523; Wiesendanger, 1.

AHLE, JOHN F.
Born at sea Apr. 1857.
Engraver, active N.O. 1900–1902.
Contemporary listings: photo engraver, *Item* (1900); engraver, *D. Item* (1901–1902).
References: NOCD 1900–1902; U.S. Census (1900), roll 570.

AHREN, SUSA F. *See* VON EHREN, SUSUS FREDERICK

AIBLE, JACOB
Born Germany ca. 1807.
Engraver, active N.O. 1860.

Contemporary listings: engraver (1860).
References: U.S. Census (1860), roll 418.

AICKLEN, JOHN ARTHUR
Born N.O. Feb. 20, 1875; died N.O. May 10, 1928.
Sculptor, active N.O. 1910; primarily stone cutter.
Contemporary listings: marble sculptor (1910).
References: NOCD 1896–97, 1899–1901, 1903–1904, 1907, 1909, 1911, 1913, 1915, 1918, 1923, 1925, 1927; N.O. Board of Health, Death Index 1927–29, NOPL; Orleans Parish Registrar of Voters, NOPL; U.S. Census (1910), roll 521.

AIENA, JOSEPH
Born N.O. Dec. 23, 1877; died N.O. Sept. 25, 1951.
Commercial artist, painter, active N.O. 1897–1951.
Contemporary listings: artist, PHOTO–ENGRAVING CO. (1897–99, 1901–1905); artist, NEW ORLEANS ENGRAVING & ELECTROTYPE CO., LTD. (1906, 1908–1909, 1911, 1916, 1918); painter (1907); artist (1910, 1917); secy., SLATTERY–SMITH CO. LTD. (1912); v. pres., Slattery–Smith Co. Ltd. (1913); v. pres. and secy., Slattery–Smith Co. Ltd. (1914–15). Worked as an artist for the New Orleans Engraving & Electrotype Co., Ltd., until 1920, then as a commercial artist until his death.
References: NOCD 1897–99, 1901–33, 1935, 1938, 1940, 1942, 1945–47, 1949; *T. Pic.*, Sept. 26, 1951; Orleans Parish Registrar of Voters, NOPL; THNOC 00.19.

AIKMAN, HELEN
Painter, active N.O. ca. 1889.
Exhibited: Cotton Palace (1889).
References: *T. Demo.*, Feb. 19, 1889.

AIRNS, JOHN A.
Engraver, active N.O. 1876.
Contemporary listings: engraver, 101 Canal (1876).
References: *Demo.*, Apr. 20, 1876.

AITKENS, ADRIAN F. *See* AITKENS & GILLIN; GENSLINGER & AITKENS

AITKENS & GILLIN
Lithographers, active N.O. 1894; also stationers, printers; Adrian F. Ait-

kens (died N.O. Dec. 25, 1926), THOMAS GILLIN, partners. Contemporary listings: lithographers, 68 Camp (1894). References: NOCD 1894; *T. Pic.*, Dec. 26, 1926.

ALAUX, ALEXANDRE
Born Commercy, France Mar. 28, 1851; died N.O. Aug. 9, 1932.
Painter, restorer, active N.O. 1869–1932.
Studied: with FRANÇOIS BERNARD (ca. 1865); with ERNEST CICERI and EUGENE PHILASTRE; Académie Royale des Beaux Arts, Brussels, Belgium (diploma 1878).
Contemporary listings: painter (1900); artist (1902, 1911–12, 1918); portrait painter, 418 Bourbon (1904–1905); portrait painter, 613 Royal (1906); portrait painter, 1145 Esplanade (1907); portrait painter, 619 Esplanade (1908–1909); miniaturist (1910); artist, 1828 Magazine (1913–16); artist, 1807 Magazine (1917).
Exhibited: Académie Royale des Beaux Arts; L'Exposition de la Miniature, Brussels (1912).
Awarded: Académie Royale des Beaux Arts, laurel crown (ca. 1878); Leopold II of Brussels, gold medal (1880).
Memberships/positions: Cercle des Arts Réunis; Société Artistique, Arlon, Belgium; Cercle Artistique et Littéraire, Arlon and Brussels; ART ASSOCIATION OF NEW ORLEANS (1905).
Shortly after his birth, Alaux's mother took him to N.Y.C., then to N.O. (1855). Sent to school in France, he returned to N.O. where he studied with Bernard and received his first recognition as an artist when he was awarded four silver medals at an exposition he is said to have entered at the fair grounds in 1869. Alaux went to Belgium to study art further and earned a diploma from the Académie Royale. After marrying in Brussels, he worked there as an artist and as a professor at the Cours Sainte Marguerite. Alaux returned to N.O. (1899) where he excelled at miniatures, portraits, and historical tab

leaux, as well as marine, still life, genre, and religious painting. He is especially known for his copies of late 18th– and 19th–century portraits made for LA families. Two of his children were artists, LOUIS ALBERT S. ALAUX and MARIE FERNANDE ALAUX.
References: NOCD 1902, 1904–1909, 1911–22, 1924–25, 1928, 1930–32; *Item–Trib.*, Jan. 4, 1925; *T. Demo.*, May 8, Oct. 24, 1904; *T. Pic.*, May 1, 1916, May 13, 1923, May 5, 1929, Oct. 12, 1930, Aug. 10, 28, 1932, Aug. 8, 1948; Collier, "Work of Artistic Historical Value," *T. Pic.*, Aug. 20, 1967; Collier, "World of Art," *T. Pic.*, May 21, 1970; Art Asso., *Catalogue* (1905); Bruns, 309; Glenk, 45, 51, 54, 56, 72, 167; Information courtesy George E. Jordan; LSM, *Annual Report for 1918*, 59; LSM, *Biennial Report for 1922–23*, 28, 75, 104; Orleans Parish Registrar of Voters, NOPL; Thompson, "Checklist"; U.S. Census (1900), roll 572, (1910), roll 520; WPA, "Lives."

ALAUX, LOUIS ALBERT S.
Born Belgium; died Mandeville LA Aug. 10, 1904.
Sketch artist, active N.O. ca. 1903–1904.
Alaux studied in a Belgian primary school and arrived in N.O. soon after his father, ALEXANDRE ALAUX, returned to N.O. (1899). Louis Alaux studied architecture at the College of the Immaculate Conception. He frequently sketched, and his drawing of a drowning man appealing to the Virgin and Child was made the day before he himself drowned. The drawing was copied by his father as a large painting that was given to the Church of Our Lady of the Lake as a memorial to the son. Brother of MARIE FERNANDE ALAUX.
References: *T. Demo.*, Aug. 13, Oct. 24, 1904; *T. Pic.*, Aug. 8, 1948.

ALAUX, MARIE FERNANDE
Born Brussels, Belgium May 9, 1883; died N.O. Aug. 16, 1958.
Painter, active N.O. 1908–49.
Contemporary listings: artist (1908, 1916, 1918),

Studied with and assisted her father, ALEXANDRE ALAUX. Sister of LOUIS ALBERT S. ALAUX.
References: NOCD 1908, 1918, 1931–33, 1935, 1938, 1942, 1945–47, 1949, 1952–55; *T. Demo.*, Oct. 24, 1904; *T. Pic.*, May 1, 1916, May 5, 1929, Aug. 28, 1932, Feb. 5, 1933, Aug. 18, 1958; Orleans Parish Registrar of Voters, NOPL; U.S. Census (1900), roll 572, (1910), roll 520.

ALBERT, ERNEST
Painter, active N.O. 1892–98.
Contemporary listings: theatrical scene painter, St. Charles Theatre (1892); theatrical scene painter, Tulane Theatre (1898).
References: *D. States*, Oct. 16, 1892, Oct. 9, 1898.

ALBERT, JOSEPH
Artist, active N.O. 1887.
Contemporary listings: artist (1887).
References: NOCD 1887.

ALBERT, MARTIN
Born LA ca. 1887.
Engraver, lithographer, active N.O. 1905–18; also printer, photographer.
Contemporary listings: photo engraver (1905); lithographer (1906); photo engraver, NEW ORLEANS ENGRAVING AND ELECTROTYPE CO. LTD. (1908, 1912); engraver (1910, 1915, 1918).
References: NOCD 1899, 1901, 1903, 1905–1908, 1910, 1912–13, 1915, 1918; U.S. Census (1910), roll 520.

ALCANTARA, JESUS
Born Mexico July 1866; died before 1955.
Painter, engraver, active N.O. 1898–1901; also photographer.
Contemporary listings: portrait painter (1898); photo engraver (1901).
References: NOCD 1896–98, 1900–1902; *T. Pic.*, May 18, 1955; U.S. Census (1900), roll 572.

ALCIATORE, ANTOINE GASTON
Born N.O. Mar. 22, 1896.
Painter, active N.O. ca. 1915.
Exhibited: ART ASSOCIATION OF NEW ORLEANS (1915).

A grandson of Antoine Alciatore, founder of Antoine's Restaurant.
References: NOCD 1917–20; Art Asso., *Special Exhibition*; Kendall, *History*, 3:898–99; Orleans Parish Registrar of Voters, NOPL.

ALDRIDGE, E. L.
Engraver, active N.O. 1868.
Contemporary listings: engraver (1868).
References: NOCD 1868.

ALEXANDER, CENEILLA BOWER (Mrs. William McFadden Alexander)
Born Bainbridge GA ca. 1865; died N.O. Mar. 23, 1966.
Painter, designer, active N.O. ca. 1902–45.
Studied: New York School of Art, N.Y.C.
Designed the parade floats for the Rex carnival organization (ca. 1902–45).
References: NOCD 1945–47, 1949, 1952–56, 1958, 1961–62, 1964–66; *States–Item*, Mar. 24, 1966; *T. Pic.*, Mar. 24, 1966; THNOC 1974.25.19-.414, 1981.331.16–.82, 1982.24.1, 1982.24.3–.12, 1982.44.1–.4.

ALEXANDER, SIR JAMES EDWARD
Born England Oct. 16, 1803; died Apr. 2, 1885.
Illustrator, active N.O. 1831.
British author and illustrator who traveled throughout the Americas. He visited N.O. (1831) and made a pencil and ink drawing of the site of the Battle of N.O.
References: J. E. Alexander, 2:21–23; *Encyclopaedia Britannica*; THNOC 1965.96.

ALFARO, LUCY. *See* ROSADO, LUCY ALFONSO

ALFONSO, CONCEPCION VARGAS. *See* VARGAS, CONCEPCION

ALFONSO, LUCY. *See* ROSADO, LUCY ALFONSO

ALLAIN, ARMANTINE PITOT (Mrs. J. Valerien Allain)
Born LA Feb. 1809; died N.O. Oct. 8, 1897.
Painter, active N.O. ca. 1885–86.
Exhibited: American Exposition (1885–86).
Miniaturist and daughter of Jacques François (James) Pitot, mayor of N.O. (1804–1805).

References: *D. Pic.*, Oct. 9, 1897; Creole Exhibit, 36; LHS (1900), items 61–62, 168; Pitot, xx-xxi; U.S. Census (1850), roll 235.

ALLAUZE, MONSUITE. *See* LUISSI, MANSUETTO

ALLEN, MR. _____
Painter, active N.O. 1842.
Contemporary listings: portrait painter, Royal near Customhouse (1842).
References: *D. Pic.*, Mar. 20, 1842.

ALLEN, W. A.
Sketch artist, active N.O. 1905.
Submitted a design in a T–Square Club emblem competition (1905).
References: *Architectural Art*, 1(Aug. 1905):14.

ALLERMANN, JOHN, JR.
Born LA June 1866; died N.O. Apr. 17, 1902.
Engraver, lithographer, active N.O. 1884–1902; also pressman, engineer.
Contemporary listings: apprentice, SOUTHERN LITHOGRAPHIC CO. (1884); engraver, Southern Lithographic Co. (1885); lithographer (1888, 1893–1901); lithographer, M. F. DUNN & BRO. (1889–92); lithographer, H. WEHRMANN & CO. (1902).
References: NOCD 1884–85, 1887–1902; *D. Pic.*, Apr. 18, 20, 1902; U.S. Census (1900), roll 572.

ALLFREE, ESTHER L.
Painter, active N.O. 1913–15.
Contemporary listings: ARTS & CRAFTS STUDIO (1913); china painter, 921 Canal (1914); art studio, 921 Canal (1914–15).
References: NOCD 1913–15.

ALLINZI, MANJUETO. *See* LUISSI, MANSUETTO

ALLISON, ELIZABETH
Born London, England ca. 1812.
Art teacher, active N.O. 1842–49.
Contemporary listings: teacher of oil painting, watercolor and drawing, Institution for Young Ladies (1847); drawing teacher, High School for Young Ladies (1848–49).
With her sister, MARIA ALLISON, established a girls' high school in 1842 at which they taught art classes. Pos-

sibly Elizabeth Allison, born ca. 1792; died N.O. Oct. 14, 1872.
References: NOCD 1843–44, 1849–60; *Bee*, Oct. 7–Nov. 10, 1847 (advs.); *D. Crescent*, Nov. 28, 1848–Sept. 8, 1849 (advs.); *D. Delta*, Mar. 20, 1847; *D. Pic.*, Nov. 13, 1848–Jan. 2, 1849 (advs.), Oct. 15, 1872; Mobley, 857–58; Thompson, "Checklist"; U.S. Census (1850), roll 237, (1860), roll 416.

ALLISON, MARIA. *See also* BOUDET, MARGARET J.
Born London, England ca. 1810–14.
Art teacher, active N.O. 1842–60.
Contemporary listings: teacher of oil painting, watercolor and drawing, Institution for Young Ladies (1847); drawing teacher, High School for Young Ladies (1848–49); teacher of pencil drawing, flower, watercolor and oil painting, Miss Allison's Institution for Young Ladies (1855–56); drawing and painting teacher, Miss Allison's Institution for Young Ladies (1857); teacher of drawing, flower and oil painting, Institution for Young Ladies (1859–60).
With her sister, ELIZABETH ALLISON, established a girls' high school in 1842 at which they taught art classes.
References: NOCD 1843–44, 1849–61; *Bee*, Oct. 7–Nov. 10, 1847 (advs.); *D. Crescent*, Nov. 28, 1848–Sept. 8, 1849 (advs.); *D. Delta*, Mar. 20, 1847; *D. Pic.*, Nov. 13, 1848–Jan. 2, 1849 (advs.), Oct. 30, 1855–Apr. 12, 1856 (advs.), Sept. 27–Nov. 18, 1857 (advs.), Sept. 13, 1859–Feb. 12, 1860 (advs.); Mobley, 857–58; Thompson, "Checklist"; U.S. Census (1850), roll 237, (1860), roll 416.

ALLISON, MISSES. *See* ALLISON, ELIZABETH; ALLISON, MARIA

ALMY, JOSEPH A.
Painter, active N.O. 1860.
Contemporary listings: scenic artist, Varieties Theatre (1860).
References: *D. True Delta*, Nov. 18, 1860.

ALMY, OSCAR F.
Born West Indies ca. 1818.
Painter, active N.O. 1860.

Contemporary listings: scenic artist, Varieties Theatre (1860).
Also worked in N.Y.C. (1850, 1859).
References: *D. True Delta*, Nov. 18, 1860; Groce and Wallace.

ALUEJE, MANSUETE. *See* LUISSI, MANSUETTO

ALUISE, M. *See* LUISSI, MANSUETTO

ALVEZ, LOLA
Commercial artist, active N.O. 1896.
Contemporary listings: staff artist, *Figaro* (1896).
References: NOCD 1896.

AMANS, JACQUES GUILLAUME LUCIEN
Born Maastricht, Netherlands 1801; died Paris, France Jan. 10, 1888.
Painter, active N.O. 1836–ca. 1856–58.
Studied: France.
Contemporary listings: portrait painter, Royal betw. Toulouse and St. Peter (1837, 1844–45); portrait painter, 184 Royal (1840–42); miniature painter, 184 Royal (1843–44); portrait painter, 110 Bourbon (1845–46, 1850–52); artist, Bourbon betw. Bienville and Customhouse (1853–54); artist and portrait painter, Bourbon near Bienville (1855–58).
Exhibited: Salon, Paris (1831–37); American Exposition (1885–86).
Considered the most important portrait painter in N.O. during the 1840s and early 1850s, Amans's only known works are his LA portraits. Painting in a style showing the influence of the French painter Jean–Auguste–Dominique Ingres, he favored a three–quarter length seated figure with emphasis on the head and hands. Amans probably studied at the Ecole des Beaux Arts, Paris, before exhibiting in the Paris salons from 1831 to 1837. His arrival in N.O. is recorded in 1836, the date he supposedly bought the sugar plantation, Trinity, on Bayou Lafourche and the date of his earliest known LA portrait. Amans may have come to N.O. at the suggestion of JEAN JOSEPH VAUDECHAMP. Both exhibited at the same Paris salons, traveled to N.O. on the same ships (1836, 1837), and occupied studios in the same block of Royal (1837). Amans's first local newspaper advertisement, in the *Bee* (Dec. 2, 1837), reported his "having returned to New Orleans." He spent the winter months in the city, painting the portraits of many prominent New Orleanians; to avoid the yellow fever season, he usually left the city in summer to visit his plantation, those of other LA planters, or France. His important works include seated portraits of Andrew Jackson (1840), painted for the 25th anniversary of the Battle of N.O.; an equestrian portrait of Jackson (1844), painted with THEODORE MOISE, which won a $1000 prize from the city's second municipality; *Ascension of St. Joseph* (ca. 1846) for St. Augustine Church; and a seated portrait of Zachary Taylor (1848), painted from life in Baton Rouge LA. Amans and his wife, Marguerite Azoline Landreaux, left LA in 1856, placing their real estate and finances in the hands of agents. They moved to La Cour Levy, near Versailles, France. Amans was living in Paris when his wife died in 1878.
References: NOCD 1838, 1841–44, 1846, 1850–56, 1858; NOBD 1857–58; *Bee*, Dec. 2, 1837, Nov. 23, 1840, June 22, Dec. 27, 1844; *Courier*, Sept. 7, 1841, July 3, 1843, Mar. 2, Dec. 26, 1844, Jan. 3, Nov. 10, 1845, Jan. 17, 1846, Jan. 2, 1847, Dec. 1, 1849, Feb. 1, 1850; *Current Topics*, Aug. 1891, 19; *D. Crescent*, Dec. 25, 1857; *D. Pic.*, Jan. 15, 1888, July 1, 1891; *Revue Louisianaise* 1(Aug. 2, 1846):440–41; *Wkly. Delta*, Feb. 27, 1848; Bénézit; Bringier Family Genealogy, Hermitage Foundation Papers, THNOC; Bruns, 309; Creole Exhibit, 10; Fielding, *Dictionary*; Groce and Wallace; Harter and Tucker, 118; Information courtesy George E. Jordan; *Mallett's*; Orleans Parish Notarial Archives, Felix Grima, Mar. 18, 1844, 40:70; Poesch, *Art of the Old South*, 266–68; THNOC 1986.193; Thompson, "Checklist"; Tucker; WPA, "Lives."

AMARI, MME. ___
Painter, art teacher, active N.O. ca. 1857.

Contemporary listings: portrait painter and teacher of painting, 175 Carondelet (1857).
Exhibited: Norman's bookstore (1857).
References: *D. Pic.*, Nov. 18, 1857; *D. True Delta*, Nov. 22, 1857.

AMENDT, PHILIP
Lithographer, active N.O. 1854–61.
Contemporary listings: lithographer, Villere near St. Louis (1854); MEY & AMENDT (1857); lithographer, 59 Exchange (1858); lithographer, cor. Goodchildren and Union (1858–61); lithographer, 65 Union (1861).
Cf. HERMANDT, PH.
References: NOCD 1854, 1859–61; NOBD 1858, 1858–59, 1860–61; Groce and Wallace; "Si J'Etais Roi," Sheet Music Collection, LA Coll., TU.

AMERICAN ART STUDIO
Painters, active N.O. 1907.
Contemporary listings: portrait painters, 124 St. Charles (1907).
References: NOCD 1907.

AMERICAN BANK NOTE COMPANY. *See also* RAWDON, WRIGHT, HATCH AND EDSON
Engravers, active N.O. 1860–85; also printers; Charles R. Benton, agent, George W. Hatch, pres., SALOMON SCHMIDT, mgr., IMANUEL ALBERT SCHMIDT, mgr.
Contemporary listings: 10, late 12, Royal (1860); 12 Royal (1861); 36 Natchez (1866–80); 10 Union (1884); 48 Carondelet (1885).
Bank note engravers, organized in 1858, with offices in N.Y.C., Philadelphia, and a branch in N.O. by 1860. The N.O. office engraved and printed bank notes for the city (1867), contracted to furnish bonds with coupons to the Board of Liquidation for issue (1882), and advertised that they executed steel–plate engravings for stock and bond certificates (1884).
References: NOCD 1860–61, 1867–80, 1885; *D. Pic.*, Oct. 20, 1867; *Repub.*, Sept. 26, 1867; *T. Demo.*, Jan. 7, 1884; Boyd, 158; Dunlap, 3:258; Groce and Wallace; *Louisiana State Gazetteer*, 123, Orleans Parish No-

tarial Archives, Samuel Flower, Aug. 23, 1882, 2:96.

AMERICAN LITHOGRAPHIC CO. OF N.Y.
Lithographers, active N.O. 1895–1901; JOHN G. WALLASTER, mgr.
Contemporary listings: 131 Camp (1895–1901).
References: NOCD 1895–1901.

AMUEDO, ANTHONY J., JR.
Artist, active N.O. 1897.
Contemporary listings: artist (1897).
References: NOCD 1897, 1899–1903, 1905–24, 1927.

ANDERSON, _____
Painter, active N.O. ca. 1883.
Exhibited: LILIENTHAL's art gallery (1883).
References: *Lilienthal's*, 6.

ANDERSON, A.
Painter, active N.O. ca. 1907.
Exhibited: ART ASSOCIATION OF NEW ORLEANS (1907).
Possibly Adele Anderson listed as an associate member of the Art Association in 1905.
References: *T. Demo.*, Jan. 6, 1907; Art Asso., *Catalogue* (1905).

ANDERSON, ALBERT C.
Painter, active N.O. 1832–34; also sign painter, glazier, gilder.
Contemporary listings: painter, 213 Common (1832); ANDERSON & CLEAL, and landscape, herald, military flag and banner painter, 64 Bienville (1834).
References: NOCD 1832, 1834–35; *Advertiser*, May 19, July 23, 1834.

ANDERSON, ANNETTE McCONNELL
(Mrs. George W. Anderson)
Born N.O. Dec. 16, 1867; died Ocean Springs MS Jan. 25, 1964.
Painter, active N.O. 1889–1920.
Studied: ARTISTS' ASSOCIATION OF NEW ORLEANS (1890); NEWCOMB COLLEGE; Art Students League, N.Y.C.; with Alden Weir, CT; Philadelphia.
Exhibited: Artists' Association of New Orleans (1889–90, 1899); ART ASSOCIATION OF NEW ORLEANS (1907, 1910–11).
Memberships/positions: Artists' Association of New Orleans (1890).
Fourth painter to be invited for a solo exhibition at DELGADO MUSEUM OF ART (1920). Mother of MS painter Walter

Anderson; with her family founded the Shearwater Pottery in Ocean Springs MS.
References: *Current Topics*, Jan. 1891, 24; *D. Pic.*, Dec. 17, 1889, Nov. 13, Dec. 17, 1890; *D. States*, Dec. 17, 1890; *Harlequin*, Dec. 6, 1899, 5; *T. Demo.*, May 16, 1890; *T. Pic.*, Jan. 26, 28, 1964; AANO, *Catalogue* (1890, 1899); Art Asso., *Catalogue* (1907, 1910, 1911); WPA, "Lives."

ANDERSON, CHARLES A.
Artist, active N.O. 1874.
Contemporary listings: artist, 90 Baronne (1874).
References: NOCD 1874.

ANDERSON, FREDERICK TANQUERAY
Born Jefferson County AR July 1, 1846; died Larchmont NY Nov. 14, 1926.
Painter.
Studied: with Camille Pissarro, France (ca. 1889–94).
Noted for watercolors of Mississippi River scenes and steamboats. Anderson made several trips to N.O. as a child (1850–57). His family moved to the city ca. 1856, but he was living in AR again by 1860. He moved to Memphis TN (1870) and four years later received public recognition as an artist. He traveled to Europe to study art seriously (ca. 1889–94); he returned to Memphis (1894), where he became a contributor to *Harper's Weekly*, *Leslie's*, and other illustrated magazines. At Pres. Theodore Roosevelt's request, Anderson painted the steamboat *New Orleans*.
References: Glenk, 141, 274; LSM, *Annual Report for 1918*, 58; Southeast Arkansas Arts and Science Center; THNOC 1958.17, 1967.15.

ANDERSON, MR. M.
Born LA ca. 1825.
Artist, active N.O. 1860.
Contemporary listings: artist (1860).
References: U.S. Census (1860), roll 417.

ANDERSON, SAMUEL. *See also* ANDERSON & BLESSING; ANDERSON & TURNER
Born PA ca. 1823.
Colorer, art teacher, engraver, painter, art dealer, active N.O. 1865–72; primarily photographer.

Contemporary listings: colorer, 61 Camp (1865, 1867); painter and teacher of drawing, painting and coloring photographs, 61 Camp (1866); colorer, 183 Canal (1869–72); engraver (1872).
Awarded: Grand State Fair, diploma, $10 for best photograph in oil, and one dollar for best India ink pictures (1867); Fifth Louisiana State Fair, best colored photographs in oil (1871).
References: NOCD 1858, 1860–61, 1866–82; *Bee*, Aug. 23, 1865, Jan. 5, May 18, 1866, Oct. 30, 1869, Apr. 3, 1870; *D. Pic.*, Nov. 1, 1863, Aug. 11, 1865, June 26, 1866, Dec. 3, 1871; *Our Home Journal*, Feb. 25, 1871, 107, May 11, 1872, 296; *Repub.*, Jan. 7, 1871; *Times*, Apr. 22, 1866; *Almanach de la Louisiane* (1867):137; Mechanics' and Agricultural Fair Asso., *Report* (1867):28; Smith and Tucker, 152; U.S. Census (1870), roll 521.

ANDERSON & BLESSING
Colorers, active N.O. 1858–59; primarily photographers; SAMUEL ANDERSON, Samuel T. Blessing, partners.
Contemporary listings: colorers, 134 Canal (1858); colorers, 61 Camp (1859).
References: NOCD 1858–61; NOBD, 1857–58; *Bee*, Apr. 25, 1860; *D. Pic.*, Dec. 2, 1856, Oct. 30, 1859, Sept. 11, 1863.

ANDERSON & CLEAL
Painters, active N.O. 1834; also glaziers, sign painters, gilders; ALBERT C. ANDERSON, M. D. Cleal, partners.
Contemporary listings: landscape, herald, military flag and banner painters, 64 Bienville (1834).
References: NOCD 1834–35; *Advertiser*, May 19, 1834.

ANDERSON & TURNER
Colorers, active N.O. 1864; primarily photographers; SAMUEL ANDERSON, AUSTIN AUGUSTUS TURNER, partners.
Contemporary listings: colorers, 61 Camp (1864).
References: NOBD 1865; *D. Pic.*, Nov. 19, 1864; Smith and Tucker, 118–20, 152, 170.

ANDREE, C.
Born Italy Oct. 1862.
Sculptor, active N.O. 1900.
Contemporary listings: sculptor (1900).
References: U.S. Census (1900), roll 572.

ANDREWS, AMBROSE
Painter, active N.O. 1841–42.
Studied: National Academy of Design, N.Y.C. (1824).
Contemporary listings: miniature painter, 44 Canal (1841); portrait and miniature painter, 8 St. Charles (1841–42).
Exhibited: St. Louis MO (1844); Pennsylvania Academy of Fine Arts, Philadelphia (1848); American Art Union, National Academy of Design, N.Y.C. (1849); American Institute (1856); Royal Academy, London (1859).
Itinerant portrait, miniature, and landscape painter, active throughout the U.S. (1824–59): Schuylerville NY (1824), Troy NY (1829–31), Stockbridge MA (1836), New Haven CT (1837), Houston TX (1837–41), St. Louis (1844), N.Y.C. (1847–53), Buffalo NY (1856–59). Possibly Ambrose Andrus, born West Stockbridge MA July 19, 1801.
References: D. Pic., June 24, Nov. 11, 1841, Apr. 29–Aug. 17, 1842 (advs.); Lafayette City Advertiser, Jan. 1, 1842; Bénézit; Bolton, Painters in Miniature; Fielding, Dictionary; Groce and Wallace; Mallett's; Pinckney, 17, 27–29.

ANDREWS, JOHN
Born N.O. Dec. 1848; died N.O. Mar. 29, 1932.
Engraver, active N.O. 1870–72.
Contemporary listings: engraver (1870, 1872).
References: NOCD 1869–85, 1887–1922, 1925–27, 1929, 1931–32; T. Pic., Mar. 30, 1932.

ANDRIEU, ALPH.
Sketch artist, active N.O. 1846.
Contemporary listings: artist, 5 Camp (1846).
A lithograph published of a scene he drew from The Three Musketeers sold for 50 cents for the benefit of scene

painter LOUIS DOMINIQUE GRANDJEAN DEVELLE (1846).
References: Bee, Apr. 27, 1846; Courier, Apr. 17, 1846; Revue Louisianaise, 1(Apr. 19, 1846):68; T. Demo., June 13, 1910; Groce and Wallace.

ANDRIEU, C.
Painter, active N.O. 1841.
Contemporary listings: portrait painter, 150 Chartres (1841).
References: NOCD 1841; Glenk, 72; Groce and Wallace; WPA "Lives."

ANDRIEU, EUGENE A.
Born N.O. Jan. 14, 1872; died N.O. Aug. 16, 1951.
Painter, sculptor, active N.O.
Studied: with his father, JULES FRANK ANDRIEU; with ELLSWORTH WOODWARD.
Exhibited: ART ASSOCIATION OF NEW ORLEANS.
Real estate agent and broker, and amateur artist who painted in his spare time and specialized in landscapes in watercolor and pastel. He also did woodcarving.
References: NOCD 1893–95, 1898–1901, 1903–28, 1931; Morn. Trib., Nov. 29, 1926; T. Pic., Aug. 17, 1951; WPA, "Lives."

ANDRIEU, JULES FRANK
Born N.O. Mar. 4, 1844; died N.O. Feb. 12, 1923.
Painter, sculptor, active N.O. 1887–1921.
Studied: with ERNEST CICERI, Paris.
Contemporary listings: artist (1913).
Exhibited: ARTISTS' ASSOCIATION OF NEW ORLEANS (1887, 1889–94, 1896); ART ASSOCIATION OF NEW ORLEANS (1907).
Memberships/positions: Artists' Association of New Orleans (1896–97).
Businessman who exhibited landscapes at the Artists' Association. Andrieu executed a medal of Abraham Lincoln which was exhibited by the New York Affiliate Society and a bust of N.O. businessman and philanthropist Julien Poydras. He painted in Pass Christian MS ca. 1903–11.
Father of EUGENE A. ANDRIEU.
References: NOCD 1860–61, 1866, 1868–77, 1879–1902, 1911–23; Art

9

and Letters, 1(Dec. 1887):228; *Current Topics*, Jan. 1892, 24, Jan. 1893, 11; *D. City Item*, Dec. 17, 1891; *D. Pic.*, Dec. 17, 29, 1887, Dec. 17, 1889, Nov. 13, Dec. 17, 1890; *Item*, Feb. 3, 6, 14, 1921; *T. Demo.*, Dec. 13, 1892, Dec. 14, 1894, Jan. 6, 1907; *T. Pic.*, Feb. 14, 1923; AANO, *Catalogue* (1890, 1891, 1896, 1897); Art Asso., *Catalogue* (1907); Bénézit; *Mallett's*; Thompson, "Checklist"; WPA, "Lives."

ANDRIEU, MATHUREN ARTHUR
Born France; died Providence RI 1896.
Painter, active N.O. 1840.
Studied: Royal Academy, Paris.
Contemporary listings: portrait painter, 150 Chartres (1840).
Exhibited: Exchange Saloon (1850); Montgomery AL (1850); Charleston SC (1851); St. Louis MO (1853).
Itinerant portrait, landscape, scenery, and panorama painter who settled in Providence in 1862.
References: *Courier*, Apr. 15, 1848; *D. Crescent*, Mar. 30, 1850; *D. Pic.*, Apr. 22, 1840; Groce and Wallace; Little, "Indigenous Painting," 456.

ANGELIN, ANTOINE (Angelain)
Born LA ca. 1793–1800; died N.O. Aug. 30, 1860.
Painter, active N.O. 1837–60.
Contemporary listings: artist, 254 Burgundy (1837); portrait painter, 263 Burgundy (1841); miniature painter, 248 Burgundy (1843–44, 1846).
References: NOCD 1822–23, 1832, 1834, 1837, 1841, 1843–44, 1846, 1851–54, 1856, 1858–60; *Bee*, Aug. 31, 1860; Glenk, 72; Groce and Wallace; U.S. Census (1840), roll 132, (1850), roll 235, (1860), roll 418; WPA, "Lives."

ANGELUS, FATHER
Painter, active N.O. 1891.
Monk from the Calceated Order, Munich, Germany, who, with FATHER MYSSEN, frescoed the interior of the mortuary chapel built in the St. Roch Cemetery (1891).
References: *D. Pic.*, Aug. 23, 1891.

ANGUENEULLE, A.
Artist, restorer, active N.O. 1884–85.

Contemporary listings: artist, 83 Exchange Al. (1884); repairer porcelain, 83 Exchange Al. (1885).
References: NOCD 1885; *D. States*, Oct. 8, 1884.

ANSELMI, DOMINICK
Born N.O. Nov. 11, 1854.
Engraver, lithographer, active N.O. 1885–1905; primarily printer.
Contemporary listings: engraver, SOUTHERN LITHOGRAPHIC CO. (1885); stone artist, T. FITZWILLIAM & CO. (1900); lithographer, T. Fitzwilliam & Co., Ltd. (1902, 1905).
References: NOCD 1875, 1877–96, 1898–1902, 1905–18, 1920–25; Orleans Parish Registrar of Voters, NOPL.

ANTOGNILLI, DAVID
Sculptor, active N.O. 1853.
Contemporary listings: sculptor, 67 Conti (1853).
References: NOCD 1853; Groce and Wallace.

ANTROBUS, JOHN
Born Staffordshire or Warwickshire, England 1831; died Detroit MI Oct. 18, 1907.
Painter, active N.O. 1859–60.
Studied: Paris.
Exhibited: St. Charles Hotel (1859); Hoffman's (1860).
Awarded: Michigan State Fair, silver medal (1878).
Itinerant portrait, landscape, and genre painter; also poet and journalist. Antrobus arrived in Philadelphia from England in 1850, and three years later was living in Savannah GA. In 1855–56 he painted portraits in Montgomery AL and then traveled through the American West and Mexico. He opened a studio in N.O. (1859) and planned a series of 12 large paintings intended as a panorama of southern life and nature. Two of these he completed while living in Carroll Parish (1860–61): a plantation slave funeral and a Bayou Macon cotton plantation scene. Antrobus briefly joined the Confederate Army as a lieutenant in 1861 with the intention of illustrating the war in VA. After apparently changing allegiance, he opened a studio in 1862

with the Chicago sculptor Leonard W. Volk. Antrobus was the first artist to paint a portrait of Gen. Ulysses S. Grant and designed the Grant medal authorized by Congress in 1863. He married in LA before 1860 when he was listed in the U.S. census with his wife Jennie and four-month-old daughter. He then lived in Chicago and traveled through the northern and central U.S. for commissions as a painter. He settled in Detroit (1875–1907), where he became one of the city's leading painters.
References: *D. Crescent*, Jan. 26, 1859; *D. Pic.*, July 9, 1861; *D. True Delta*, Apr. 22, 29, 1860; *Demo.*, Apr. 4, 1877; *Detroit Free Press*, July 4, 1878, Oct. 19, 1907; *Detroit News*, Oct. 18, 1907; Bruns, 309; Creole Exhibit, 8; Grant, 9:406–7, 409, 542–43; Groce and Wallace; *Mallett's*; THNOC 1960.46; Thompson, "Checklist"; U.S. Census (1860), roll 409; WPA, *Illinois*, 110; Yeager, "Antrobus."

ANTZ, GEORGE
Born Bavaria ca. 1814–15; died N.O. Sept. 29, 1881.
Engraver, active N.O. 1838–77; also silversmith, gilder, jeweler, watchmaker.
Contemporary listings: engraver, 28 Conti (1838); engraver, 77 Magazine (1842, 1846); engraver, cor. Poydras and Camp (1849–50); engraver, cor. Conti and Exchange Al. (1850–51); engraver, 159 Poydras (1852); LUND & ANTZ (1853–56); engraver, 16 Exchange Al. (1865–68); ANTZ & BOHNE (1870–74); Himmel & Antz (1875); engraver, 186 Poydras (1875–77).
References: NOCD 1838, 1842–44, 1846, 1849–56, 1866–81; NOBD 1865; *D. Crescent*, Nov. 13, 1850–Jan. 4, 1851 (advs.); *D. Pic.*, Sept. 30, 1881; *Repub.*, June 22, 1875; Groce and Wallace; N.O. Death Certificate (1881), 79:632, NOPL; Thompson, "Checklist"; U.S. Census (1870), roll 519.

ANTZ & BOHNE
Engravers, active N.O. 1870–71; primarily jewelers, watchmakers;

GEORGE ANTZ, Frederick H. Bohne, partners.
Contemporary listings: engravers, 12 Exchange Pl. (1870–71).
References: NOCD 1870–74; Boyd, 158.

APPLEGATE, PLINY
Born IA ca. 1858.
Painter, active N.O. 1893–1910.
Contemporary listings: artist (1909–10); painter (1910).
Mentioned as "a talented and well known artist of St. Louis," when his painting of the Southern Athletic clubhouse was shown (1893).
References: NOCD 1909; *D. Item*, Aug. 14, 1893; U.S. Census (1910), roll 524.

AREU, RAMON
Artist, active N.O. 1877.
Contemporary listings: artist (1877).
References: NOCD 1877.

ARIGONE, FERDINAND
Painter, active N.O. 1870.
Contemporary listings: miniature painter (1870).
Cf. ARRIGONI, MR. F.
References: NOCD 1870.

ARION, A.
Painter, active N.O. 1901–1902.
Contemporary listings: portrait painter, 725 Poydras (1901); artist, 725 Poydras (1902).
References: NOCD 1901–1902.

ARMAND, G.
Artist, active N.O. 1822.
Contemporary listings: artist of the theater, 35 St. Philip (1822).
References: NOCD 1822; Groce and Wallace.

ARMANDO, JOHN
Born ca. 1780–90.
Sculptor, active N.O. 1823–24.
Contemporary listings: artist in plaster of Paris, 131 Delord (1823); artist in plaster of Paris, 277 Camp (1824).
References: NOCD 1823–24, 1834, 1837–38, 1841; U.S. Census (1830), roll 45.

ARMS, JOHN L.
Born Fulton County NY ca. 1838; died N.O. Oct. 13, 1898.
Sculptor, active N.O. 1873; primarily carpenter.

Contemporary listings: woodcarver (1873).
References: NOCD 1873–81, 1884–98; *D. Pic.*, Oct. 14, 1898.

ARMSTRONG, CHARLES RICE
Born N.O. Aug. 22, 1888; died N.O. Nov. 28, 1947.
Painter, active N.O. ca. 1915–16; primarily architect.
Exhibited: ART ASSOCIATION OF NEW ORLEANS (1915–16).
Partner, with RICHARD KOCH, in the architectural firm of Armstrong & Koch (1916–33).
References: NOCD 1914–17, 1919–33, 1935, 1938, 1940, 1942, 1945–47; *T. Pic.*, Nov. 29, 1947; Art Asso., *Catalogue* (1915, 1916); Art Asso., *Special Exhibition*; Orleans Parish Registrar of Voters, NOPL.

ARNOLD, EDWARD EVERARD
Born Heilbronn, Württemberg ca. 1816–28; died N.O. Oct. 14, 1866.
Painter, lithographer, active N.O. ca. 1846–66; also sign painter.
Contemporary listings: EVANS & ARNOLD, artist and painter (1850); portrait, marine, and landscape painter (1851–52); artist, painter, 7 Mandeville (1853–54); artist, painter, 66 Louisa (1855–56); portrait painter, 103 Poydras (1857); artist, painter, 103 Poydras (1858–59); artist, painter, 74 Mandeville, and marine painter, 29 Royal, and lithographer, 88 Gravier (1860); artist, painter, and marine painter, Royal cor. Bienville (1861); portrait and fancy painter, 58 Frenchman (1865); marine painter, 68 Bienville (1866–67).
Came to N.O. ca. 1846 and was a portrait and landscape painter who specialized in portraits of ships. In 1850 Arnold planned a painted view of N.O. with his partner, JAMES GUY EVANS, and a lithographic scene with R. W. FISHBOURNE. Apparently neither project was carried out.
References: NOCD 1853–61, 1866–67; NOBD 1865; *D. Orleanian*, Sept. 22, Oct. 13, Nov. 9, 1850, Mar. 14, 23, 28, Apr. 1–2, 22, 1851, Apr. 4, 1852; *D. Pic.*, June 27, 1860; *Times*, Oct. 15, 1866; Collier, "The World of Art: Historic New Orleans Collec-

tion Adds 1850 Era Marine Painting," *T. Pic.*, July 20, 1975; Glenk, 273; Groce and Wallace; N.O. Death Certificate (1866), 35:166, NOPL; Thompson, "Checklist"; Toledano, "Marine Painters," 874–78; U.S. Census (1850), roll 238, (1860), roll 419; WPA, "Lives."

ARNOLD, T. H.
Designer, active N.O. ca. 1866.
Signed the artwork on sheet music covers lithographed by T. FITZWILLIAM & CO.
References: "The Blacksmith in the Woods," "Trades Assembly March," Sheet Music Collection, Hogan Jazz Archives, TU.

ARRES, JOHN
Born LA ca. 1880.
Engraver, active N.O. 1910.
Contemporary listings: photo engraver, newspapers (1910).
References: U.S. Census (1910), roll 520.

ARRIGONI, MR. F.
Born Italy.
Painter, active N.O. 1867–68.
Contemporary listings: scenic artist, Clio Theatre (1867); decorative painter, Academy of Music (1868).
Executed the drop curtain for the New Galveston (TX) Theatre (ca. 1870). *Cf.* ARIGONE, FERDINAND.
References: *D. Crescent*, Oct. 4, 1867; *D. Pic.*, Jan. 24, 1907; *Repub.*, Sept. 9, 1868; Gallegly, *Footlights*, 101.

ART ASSOCIATION OF NEW ORLEANS
Art association, active N.O. 1903–59.
Organized in 1903 by the merging of the ARTISTS' ASSOCIATION OF NEW ORLEANS and the ARTS EXHIBITION CLUB. Its primary objective was to develop art and a taste for artistic culture, and its chief aim was to create a public museum of art. The association is credited with having influenced Isaac Delgado in donating money to build the DELGADO MUSEUM OF ART in 1910. The association's original membership was 313 and included the city's most notable artists. Judge W. W. Howe presided over the first meeting on Dec. 10, 1903, and

G. R. Westfeldt was the first elected president. The annual exhibitions featured work by local and European artists. Its first exhibition took place at the Athenaeum, Feb. 27–Mar. 12, 1904; in later years (1912–59), exhibitions were held at the Delgado Museum.
References: NOCD 1917–29, 1931–33, 1935, 1938, 1940, 1942, 1945–47, 1949; *D. Pic.*, Dec. 6, 11, 1903, Feb. 21, 1904, Mar. 15, 1908; *Harlequin*, 1904, 3; *Item–Trib.*, Feb. 14, 1926, Feb. 7, 1937; *Morn. Trib.*, Mar. 6, 1933; *T. Demo.*, Feb. 28, 1904, Mar. 5, 11, Dec. 27, 1905, Jan. 6–7, 1907, Mar. 15, 1908; *T. Pic.*, May 2, 1915, Mar. 3, 16, 1936, Mar. 10, 1937, Mar. 4, 1938, Feb. 25, Mar. 4, 1951; *Town Talk*, Feb. 1905, 46; Art Asso., *Catalogue* (1904, 1905, 1907, 1910, 1911, 1913, 1914, 1915, 1916, 1917, 1918, 1919, 1921, 1922, 1924, 1925, 1926, 1927, 1928, 1929, 1930, 1931, 1932, 1933, 1934, 1935, 1936, 1937, 1938, 1939, 1940, 1941, 1942, 1943, 1945, 1946, 1947, 1949, 1950, 1951, 1952, 1953, 1954, 1955, 1956, 1957); Art Asso., *Charter* (1916); Art Asso., *Charter* (1928); Art Asso., *Membership, 1913*; Art Asso., *Special Exhibition*; Kendall, *History*, 2:659–60; New Orleans Museum of Art, *1977 Artists Biennial*; Reeves, 107, 123.

ART DESIGNING AND ENGRAVING CO.
Engravers, active N.O. 1898; HENRY G. GRELLE, mgr.
Contemporary listings: chalk plate engraving, Hennen bldg. (1898).
References: *Men and Matters*, June 1898 (adv.).

ART LEAGUE OF NEW ORLEANS
Art association, active N.O. 1889–91.
Contemporary listings: 249 Baronne (1889–91).
Membership association that transformed a residential building into workshops, studios, and art salesrooms for advanced students to pursue industrial and pictorial arts. Most of the members had already studied art at NEWCOMB COLLEGE or Tulane

University. Their exhibitions included pottery, needlework, architectural drawings, oil paintings, and watercolors. In 1890 the league met monthly at Tulane Hall.
References: *D. Pic.*, Mar. 10, 1889, June 15, 1890; Kendall, *History*, 2:661; Soards, 321.

ART LEAGUE POTTERY CLUB
Art association, active N.O. ca. 1890–92.
Contemporary listings: 249 Baronne (1890).
Exhibited: Christian Woman's Exchange (1890).
Successor to the NEW ORLEANS ART POTTERY COMPANY, organized to give clay workers a place to continue their art. WILLIAM WOODWARD was its president in 1890.
References: *D. Pic.*, Jan. 5, 1890, Mar. 3, 1892; *T. Demo.*, Jan. 6, 1890.

ART LITHOGRAPH CO. (Art Lithographing Co.)
Lithographers, active N.O. 1897–99; José G. Curado, mgr., Joseph Weckerling, owner, secy.–treas.
Contemporary listings: 514 Natchez (1897–99).
References: NOCD 1897–99.

ART MATERIAL & PHOTO SUPPLY CO., LTD.
Engravers, active N.O. 1903; R. De Montluzin, pres., JULIAN EMILE RIVOIRE, mgr.
Contemporary listings: engravers, 157 Baronne (1903).
References: NOCD 1903.

ART POTTERY COMPANY. See NEW ORLEANS ART POTTERY COMPANY

ARTER, J. CHARLES
Died Alliance OH 1923.
Painter, restorer, active N.O. 1907. NY portrait painter who also had studios in Venice and London. Arter visited N.O. in 1907, when his portrait of Pope Pius X was exhibited at the ART ASSOCIATION OF NEW ORLEANS. While in the city, he painted portraits of N.O. Archbishop James H. Blenk and LA Gov. Newton C. Blanchard, made copies of portraits of Bienville and La Salle, and restored the painting *The Battle of New Orleans* by Eugene Louis Lami. He in-

tended to leave N.O. for Mexico and then England.
References: *D. Pic.*, Jan. 15, Apr. 2, June 16, 1907; *T. Demo.*, Apr. 29, 1908; Fielding, *Dictionary*; Glenk, 40, 72; *Mallett's*; *Picayune's Guide* (1913):43, 59.

ARTISTS' ASSOCIATION OF NEW ORLEANS
Art association, art school, active N.O. 1885–1903.
Contemporary listings: 31 Camp (1886); 31 and 33 Camp (1887–89); 59 Carondelet (1890); 203 Camp (1891–94); school of art, 836 Canal (1895); 618 Commercial (1896, 1900–1908); school of art, 315 Carondelet (1897).
Formed in 1885 after almost all artists had resigned from the SOUTHERN ART UNION. The association, incorporated in 1886, was intended to promote the study of the fine arts, to give free instruction to those in need, to publish an art journal, and to establish a school of art. The school opened Oct. 5, 1885, at the association's rented spaces on the third floor of the State National Bank building, 31–33 Camp. Elementary and advanced courses were taught by local artists CHARLES WELLINGTON BOYLE, GEORGE DAVID COULON, ANDRES MOLINARY, AUGUST NOLTE, PAUL POINCY, and BROR ANDERS WIKSTROM. Public school teachers paid half–rates to attend, and pupils donated one picture each to an art auction to raise additional funds. The first annual exhibition was held Nov. 5–7, 1886, with 89 works by 17 artists. The association's journal, *Art and Letters*, an illustrated bi–monthly magazine, was first issued in Feb. 1887, with a cover design by Wikstrom and with illustrations by other members. Views of the association's building at 203 Camp and of its interior were printed in an article in the *Daily Picayune* (Nov. 13, 1890). In 1903, it merged with the ARTS EXHIBITION CLUB to form the ART ASSOCIATION OF NEW ORLEANS.
References: NOCD 1886–97, 1900–1908; *Current Topics*, Nov. 1890, 22–23, Jan. 1891, 23–25, June 1891, 22–23, Oct. 1891, 18, 27, Jan. 1893, 10, Feb. 1893, vii, July 1893, xv; *D. City Item*, Mar. 4, 1892; *D. Item*, Jan. 18, Feb. 14, 1893; *D. Pic.*, Sept. 26, 1885, Nov. 6–7, 1886, May 7, Dec. 29, 1887, Dec. 17, 21, 1889, Nov. 13, Dec. 17, 1890, May 22, 24, 1891, Mar. 3, 6, Dec. 13, 1892, Feb. 19, Nov. 27, 1893, Jan. 21, 1900, Dec. 9, 1902, Dec. 6, 1903; *D. States*, Oct. 29, 1886, Mar. 18, 1888, May 16–17, Nov. 13, 1890, Dec. 17, 1891; *Down in Dixie*, July 15, 1896, 10; *Harlequin*, Dec. 6, 1899, 4–5; *Lantern*, 1886, 6; *T. Demo.*, May 16, Nov. 13, Dec. 17, 1890, Mar. 3, Dec. 18, 1892, Jan. 18, Feb. 15, 1893, Dec. 14, 1894, Dec. 3, 1901; *Woman's World*, Dec. 20, 1890, 4; AANO, *Catalogue* (1886, 1890, 1891, 1893, 1896, 1897, 1899, 1901, 1901–1902, 1902–1903); AANO, *Charter*; AANO, *School of Art*, 1886–87, 1892–93; New Orleans Museum of Art, *1977 Artists Biennial*; Orleans Parish Notarial Archives, Bussière Rouen, Mar. 29, 1886, 2:75; Reeves, 125, 128, 131–32.

ARTISTS' MUTUAL ASSISTANCE SOCIETY
Art association, active N.O. 1894–95.
Contemporary listings: 332 N. Derbigny (1894–95).
References: NOCD 1894–95.

ARTS & CRAFTS STUDIO
Painters, active N.O. 1913; MISS E. L. ALLFREE, LILLY FAHEY, BERTHA FRICKESSEN, partners.
Contemporary listings: china painting, 921 Canal (1913).
References: NOCD 1913.

ARTS EXHIBITION CLUB
Art association, active N.O. 1901–1903.
Exhibited: NEWCOMB COLLEGE (1902); Tulane University (1903).
Organized by WILLIAM WOODWARD in Mar. 1901 as an association similar to the arts and crafts societies in other U.S. cities. The club was incorporated on May 16, 1901, to promote the love and practice of the fine arts and culture, to establish a library of art literature, and to encourage ed-

ucation in the fine arts. It planned annual exhibitions of contemporary artists from throughout the world in painting, sculpture, architectural design, and art crafts, and was to purchase at least one artwork to be kept for a public gallery (*See* DELGADO MUSEUM OF ART). It was considered a rival art club by the older ARTISTS' ASSOCIATION OF NEW ORLEANS, with which it merged in 1903 to form the ART ASSOCIATION OF NEW ORLEANS. References: *D. Pic.*, Dec. 6, 1903; *T. Demo.*, Mar. 12, 23, 1901, Apr. 6, 12, 1902; *Arts Exhibition Club*; Coulon MS, Scrapbook 100, LSM; Orleans Parish Notarial Archives, George Covington Preot, May 16, 1901, 16:218.

ASTRUC, _____
Artist, active N.O. 1838.
Contemporary listings: artist, Orleans Theatre (1838).
References: NOCD 1838.

ATWOOD, JESSE
Born NH ca. 1802.
Painter, engraver, active N.O. 1847.
Exhibited: 30 St. Charles (1847).
Itinerant portrait painter in RI (ca. 1828), PA (ca. 1830), Deerfield MA (1832), Philadelphia PA (1840–1841, 1843, 1847, 1849–54), and Richmond VA (1841). Atwood was in N.O. in Apr. 1847 en route to Monterrey, Mexico, to paint a portrait of Gen. Zachary Taylor. He returned to the city in June 1847 and exhibited the finished work at 30 St. Charles for 50 cents admission. It was reported to be the first portrait of Taylor by an artist, but it was ridiculed in the *Daily Delta* (Aug. 21, 1847) as "stupid pumpkin–skinned libel." Atwood left N.O. with plans to exhibit the painting in St. Louis MO, Louisville KY, Cincinnati OH, and Philadelphia.
References: *Comm. Times*, June 18, 21, 26, 1847; *D. Delta*, Apr. 22, June 18, 20–22 (advs.), Aug. 6, 21, 1847; *D. Pic.*, Apr. 29, 1847; Brainerd Dyer, 185–86; Groce and Wallace; Harry Peters, *America on Stone*, 81; Thompson, "Checklist."

AUDEBERT, WILLIAM AMANT
Born ca. 1780–90.
Art teacher, active N.O. 1809–32.
Contemporary listings: teacher, Lyceum of the Youth, 56 Toulouse (1809); teacher, 56 Toulouse (1811); teacher (1819); teacher, 125 St. Peter (1823–24, 1827, 1830); teacher, 241 Bourbon (1832).
His school offered instructions in drawing within a curriculum including foreign languages, mathematics, and writing.
References: NOCD 1811, 1823–24, 1827, 1830, 1832; *Bee*, July 22, 1832; *Courier*, June 14, 1809, May 17, 1819; *Moniteur*, June 14–July 5, 1809 (advs.); Arthur, *Old New Orleans*, 226; Groce and Wallace; U.S. Census (1830), roll 45.

AUDERER, FREDERICK
Lithographer, active N.O. 1871–73.
Contemporary listings: lithographer, with CHARLES W. CLARK (1871); lithographer, with HUGH LEWIS (1873).
References: NOCD 1871, 1873.

AUDIBERT, LOUIS
Born France ca. 1818.
Painter, lithographer, active N.O. 1850–51.
Contemporary listings: portrait painter, lithographer (1850); lithographer, artist, 111 Chartres (1851).
Editor of the *Album Louisianais*, a N.O. weekly literary journal in French, first published in Apr. 1851. Alternate issues of the journal featured a piece of music and a lithograph of a prominent N.O. public building. Audibert also designed and lithographed the print *St. Charles Hotel's Ruins* (1851) and did the artwork for sheet music covers with LOUIS XAVIER MAGNY.
References: *Courier*, Nov. 30, 1850, Jan. 24, 1851; *D. Delta*, Apr. 6, 1851; *D. Pic.*, Apr. 5, 1851; *T. Deutsche Zeitung*, Apr. 6, 1851; "The Crescent Mazurka," "Golden Bird of Hope," Sheet Music Collection, LA Coll., TU; Dichter and Shapiro, 252; Groce and Wallace; *Mallett's Supplement*; Harry Peters, *America on Stone*, 81; "Sea Serpent," Sheet Music Col-

lection, THNOC; THNOC 1945.5.1; U.S. Census (1850), roll 235.

AUDIBERT, PAUL R.
Commercial artist, engraver, active N.O. 1894.
Contemporary listings: artist, ELECTRIC ENGRAVING CO., PHOTO–ENGRAVING CO. (1894).
Worked for Moss Engraving Co. in N.Y.C. before joining the Electric Engraving Co. in partnership with GEORGE FRANÇOIS MUGNIER (1894). Their commercial partnership dissolved late in 1894.
References: NOCD 1894; Orleans Parish Notarial Archives, William C. Dufour, Nov. 3, 1894, 1:9; *Washington Artillery Souvenir*, 28.

AUDUBON, JOHN JAMES (Jean Jacques Fougere Audubon)
Born Les Cayes, Saint–Domingue (Haiti) Apr. 26, 1785; died Minnie's Land NY Jan. 27, 1851.
Painter, art teacher, active N.O. 1821–37.
Studied: with John Stein, Natchez MS (1822); with THOMAS SULLY, Philadelphia PA (1824).
Exhibited: Manchester, England (1826); Royal Institution, Edinburgh (1826–27); Linnaean Society, Royal Society, London (1827).
Memberships/positions: Lyceum of Natural History, NY (1824); Royal Society, Edinburgh (1827); fellow, Royal Society, London (1830).
Wildlife and portrait painter. Audubon was the illegitimate son of Mlle. Rabin and Jean Audubon, who brought their son to France to be reared. The boy demonstrated an interest in wildlife, especially in drawing birds, after he was sent to his father's estate near Nantes (1791). He came to the U.S. to run his father's farm, Mill Grove, PA (1803), married Lucy Bakewell (1808), and worked in unsuccessful business enterprises in MO, KY, and OH. Audubon's early contact with N.O. was through his brother–in–law, Thomas Woodhouse Bakewell, of Audubon & Bakewell, a N.O. commission house for goods imported from England (1811–12). The artist, who was living in KY at the time, would have joined Bakewell in N.O., but the business failed as a result of the War of 1812. Audubon came to N.O. in pursuit of money owed him from another business deal (1819), but returned to KY immediately. In 1820 he was in Cincinnati where he opened an art school. There, Audubon conceived the idea of making life–size watercolor drawings of all species of American birds and left for LA with one of his students, JOSEPH ROBERT MASON, to begin the project. Carrying letters of introduction, they arrived in N.O. by keelboat on Jan. 7, 1821 with the intention of staying only seven or eight months before joining an expedition to the western U.S. to draw birds. They lived on the boat until Feb. 22 when they began renting a room on Barracks near Royal. Audubon hunted birds for his drawings with the help of Mason, who drew the flowers for the backgrounds of the paintings. While Audubon was desperately looking for work, an Italian painter, probably JEAN BAPTISTE FOGLIARDI, offered him $100 a month to paint scenery at a N.O. theater, but he refused. Audubon then applied to assist portrait painter JOHN WESLEY JARVIS to paint clothing and backgrounds, but was rejected. Audubon met other artists and personalities while in N.O. RALPH E. W. EARL was in the city to sell his portrait of Andrew Jackson to the City Council. Jackson himself passed through N.O. (Apr. 22–28, 1821) on his way to assume the governorship of Florida and sat for a portrait by JOHN VANDERLYN. Audubon met both artists and saw the portraits. Vanderlyn gave Audubon a written endorsement for his watercolors and drawings. Audubon also met the miniature painter AMBROSE DUVAL and another identified in his journal as "Hetchberger the painter." Eventually, Audubon received commissions for portraits executed in black chalk for $25 each, and he began giving art lessons to friends and acquaintances. Because prospects for

work were not good in N.O., Audubon, with Mason, left the city on June 16, 1821, to spend the summer and fall at Oakley plantation, near St. Francisville LA, as an instructor to the owner's daughter. He also painted the birds he found in that area. He returned to N.O. by Nov. 1821 to a rented room on St. Ann and a steady income from teaching private students; he applied unsuccessfully to teach at N.O. schools. Audubon had become well-known among the hunters in the area who procured birds for him from the lakes and region around N.O. He also continued to meet other artists in the city, including painters named Brutter, Jany or Janin, and SELLE. The scene painter BASTEROT unsuccessfully tried to convince Audubon to assist him in painting a panoramic view of N.O. On Dec. 18, Audubon's family arrived in N.O. and moved into a rented house on Dauphine. His wife worked as a governess for a friend and the two sons, JOHN WOODHOUSE AUDUBON and VICTOR GIFFORD AUDUBON, attended school. Audubon again left N.O., with Mason, on Mar. 16, 1822, for Natchez MS, where his family eventually joined him. He met the itinerant portrait painter John Stein, from whom he learned to paint in oil, and the two artists made a portrait painting tour as far as Jackson MS. Audubon's wife remained at Beech Woods plantation near St. Francisville LA, where she taught the children of neighboring plantations. After his tour with Stein, Audubon also gave art lessons and sought commissions in the area. Audubon had acquired a significant portfolio of bird paintings during his stay in LA, and he decided to seek a patron for their publication. In Oct. 1823, he left Beech Woods with his son Victor whom he left in Louisville to work as a clerk in his in-laws' store. His trip to Philadelphia and to N.Y.C. to find a publisher for his drawings was unsuccessful, and he returned to Beech Woods in 1824. On May 26, 1826, Audubon left N.O. for Europe with the money he and his wife had saved. In Great Britain he exhibited his drawings with great success and obtained subscriptions to his projected publication. The establishment of William Howe Lizars, of Edinburgh, engraved, printed, and colored the first 10 plates in 1826–27, and Robert Havell, Jr., and his son, of London, published the other 425 plates between 1828 and 1838 under the title *The Birds of America.* After spending over three years away from his family, Audubon returned to Bayou Sara in Nov. 1829 for his wife, and they left N.O. in Jan. 1830 for Louisville, where they were reunited with Victor and John. Audubon made more bird expeditions to NJ and PA (1830), to FL (1831–32), and to Labrador, Canada (1833). On a collecting expedition along the southern coast of the U.S., Audubon arrived in N.O. sometime before Mar. 3, 1837; during his stay in the city, he met another artist and naturalist, CHARLES ALEXANDER LESUEUR. The Audubon party boarded their ship Mar. 29, 1837 and went on to explore the bayous and shorelines of LA and TX. Throughout the years of making bird drawings, Audubon had been assisted in painting the backgrounds by his son Victor, John R. Mason, George Lehman, and Maria Martin. Audubon's home, Minnie's Land, was built in 1841–42 on the Hudson River in NY, where he died. His other publications include *Ornithological Biography*, *A Synopsis of the Birds of America*, *The Viviparous Quadrupeds of North America*, and smaller editions of *Birds* and *Quadrupeds.*

References: *Bee*, Sept. 14, 1841, Mar. 24, 1843; *Comm. Bull.*, Feb. 8, 1843, Feb. 7, 1851; *Courier*, Jan. 1, 1821; July 5, 1831, Mar. 11, 1837, Mar. 25, 1843; *D. Pic.*, Aug. 10, Nov. 1, 1842, June 22, Oct. 28, 1843, May 25, 1844, Jan. 7, 1873; Alexander Adams; *Appleton's CAB*; J. J. Audubon, *Birds*; J. J. Audubon, *Journal*, 111–227; J. J. Audubon, *Letters*, 2:148–57; Bénézit; Bruns, 309;

Chancellor; *DAB*; Fielding, *Dictionary*; Ford; Friends of the Cabildo, *Audubon*; Glenk, 72, 179; Groce and Wallace; Herrick; Lafayette Natural History Museum; Lindsey, 2–16, 101, 168–69; LSM, *Audubon in Louisiana*; *Mallett's*; McDermott, "Audubon's Earliest Oil Portraits," 434–35; McDermott, "Likeness by Audubon"; Peterson, ix–xi; Thompson, "Checklist."

AUDUBON, JOHN WOODHOUSE

Born Henderson KY Nov. 30, 1812; died N.Y.C. Feb. 18 or 21, 1862. Painter, active N.O. 1837, 1845, 1853?

Exhibited: Apollo Association; American Art–Union; National Academy of Design, N.Y.C.

Memberships/positions: National Academy of Design, N.Y.C. (1847). Portrait and wildlife painter. He was the younger son of JOHN JAMES AUDUBON, who trained him to assist in his work on American birds and wildlife. The son lived with his family during their short stay in N.O. (1821–22), and traveled with his father on a bird expedition to Labrador, Canada (1833). He went to England (1834) with his parents to join his brother, VICTOR GIFFORD AUDUBON. While there, he worked professionally as a portrait painter and helped in the publication of his father's book, *The Birds of America*. He accompanied his father on a collecting expedition along the southern coast of the U.S. in 1837, spending nearly a month in N.O. From 1839, N.Y.C. was his home. Because of his father's failing health, the son painted 72 of the 150 plates for the elder Audubon's next publication, *The Viviparous Quadrupeds of North America*. According to most sources, the son made an animal–painting expedition to TX for specimens for the book (1845–46); but the *Daily Picayune* (Dec. 3, 1845) reported that his brother Victor was in N.O. on his way to western TX to paint animals and also mentioned his return (Mar. 15, 1846) but only as "young Audubon." He stopped in N.O. briefly (Feb. 1849) to buy supplies for a gold–hunting expedition to CA. One of the brothers returned to N.O. in Apr. 1853 to solicit subscriptions to *Quadrupeds*. Both sons continued publishing editions of their father's work after his death.

References: *Courier*, Sept. 15, 1846; *D. Pic.*, Dec. 3, 1845, Mar. 15, 1846; *T. Pic.*, Dec. 2, 1945; Alexander Adams, 424–25, 466; J. J. Audubon, *Letters*, 2:148–57; J. W. Audubon, 15, 48–49; Bannon and Clark, 65; Bénézit; Cahalane, xii–xiii; Groce and Wallace; Jones, 254; *Mallett's*; Thompson, "Checklist."

AUDUBON, VICTOR GIFFORD

Born Louisville KY June 12 or 29, 1809; died N.Y.C. Aug. 17, 1860. Painter, active N.O. ca. 1845–46, 1853?

Exhibited: Royal Academy, London (1832–39); National Academy of Design, N.Y.C.; Apollo Association; American Art–Union.

Memberships/positions: National Academy of Design, N.Y.C. (1864). Landscape, wildlife, and miniature painter. He was the older son of JOHN JAMES AUDUBON, who trained him to assist in his work on American birds, having him paint many of the backgrounds and settings. He lived with his family in N.O. (1821–22), and was sent by his father to England (1834) as his business representative for the publication of *Birds of America*, until the rest of the Audubon family joined him. He supervised the printing of the plates until his return to the U.S. (1836). According to the *Daily Picayune*, it was Victor Audubon who came through N.O. in Dec. 1845 and Mar. 1846 on his way to and from an expedition to western TX to gather specimens for his father's next book, *The Viviparous Quadrupeds of North America*. On this project, the son also painted backgrounds, supervised the lithographers and printers, and edited text. Either Victor Audubon, or his brother, JOHN WOODHOUSE AUDUBON, returned to N.O. in Apr. 1853 to solicit subscriptions to *Quadrupeds*. Both brothers contin-

ued publishing editions of their father's work after his death.
References: *Comm. Bull.*, Aug. 25, 1860; *D. Pic.*, Dec. 3, 1845, Mar. 15, 1846, Apr. 24, 1853; Alexander Adams, 401; Bannon and Clark, 100, 103, 105–8; Bénézit; Cahalane, xii–xiii; Fielding, *Dictionary*; Groce and Wallace; *Mallett's*; Thompson, "Checklist"; WPA, "Lives."

AUDUBON PORTRAIT HOUSE
Art dealers, active N.O. 1900–1901; RICHARD W. ORTTE, mgr.
Contemporary listings: 1806 Magazine (1900–1901).
References: NOCD 1900–1901.

AUFDEMORTE, ALBERT GEORGE
Born N.O. Sept. 16, 1880; died N.O. Aug. 21, 1969.
Painter, active N.O. 1898–1969.
Contemporary listings: artist (1898, 1903, 1909, 1911–12, 1918); scenic painter (1899–1902, 1906, 1908, 1913–14, 1916); scenic artist, Tulane & Crescent Theatres (1910); scenic artist (1915, 1917).
Aufdemorte began his career as an apprentice at the French Opera House (ca. 1898) and continued to be listed as a scenic painter or artist through 1946. He is recorded as producing scenic effects for a carnival organization as early as 1902 and designed scenery, painted stage sets, and managed the dens for carnival organizations until his death. He was also listed as manager of the CRESCENT SCENIC STUDIO (1922–24) and as a painter (1940, 1952–53, 1958).
References: NOCD 1898–1903, 1906, 1908–28, 1930–33, 1935, 1938, 1940, 1942, 1945–47, 1949, 1952–55, 1958, 1960, 1965–68; *T. Pic.*, Aug. 22, 1969; *Comus Diamond Jubilee*; La Cour, 203; U.S. Census (1910), roll 520.

AUGUSTE, GUSTAVE
Born N.O. ca. 1846; died N.O. Oct. 3, 1906; black.
Sculptor, active N.O. 1890–1906; primarily marble worker, also architect.
Contemporary listings: sculptor (1890–91, 1906)

References: NOCD 1868, 1870–72, 1874–78, 1880–83, 1885–88, 1890–91, 1893–94, 1898–1900, 1902, 1904; N.O. Death Certificate (1906), 139:106, NOPL.

AUGUSTIN, LEON
Artist, active N.O. 1892–97.
Contemporary listings: artist (1892–93); artist, with John C. Norton (1897).
References: NOCD 1892–93, 1895, 1897.

AUROY, HENRY
Painter, active N.O. 1880–88; primarily gilder.
Contemporary listings: fresco painter (1880); painter (1887–88).
References: NOCD 1880–88.

AUSTIN, ELIZA A. (Mrs. William S. Austin)
Sculptor, active N.O. 1869–78.
Contemporary listings: artist, 112 Canal (1878).
Awarded: Grand State Fair, bronze medal for best specimen of wax work (1869).
References: NOCD 1872, 1878; Mechanics' and Agricultural Fair Asso., *Report* (1869):66.

AVERY, KATE BUCKNER. *See* BUCKNER, KATE

AVET, LOUIS
Born N.O.
Engraver, sculptor, active N.O. 1849, 1881–84.
Studied: with Michelini, Rome.
Contemporary listings: cameo miniature engraver, cor. Chartres and Toulouse (1849); artist in cameo portraits, LILIENTHAL's (1881, 1884); cameo portraits, A. B. Griswold's jewelry store (1881).
Avet advertised that he engraved cameo portraits from daguerreotypes (1849). He worked for many years in N.Y.C. with Ball, Black & Co. and with Tiffany & Co. In 1881 he announced his two–month return to N.O., where he created cameo portraits from photographs and from life. When the visit ended, he went to his studio in Cincinnati, but continued arrangements for portraits through a local agent, Alphonse Walz, 26 Conti. In Mar. 1884, Avet

was in N.O. again, making cameos and plaster medallions. He returned to Cincinnati in June, but was back in N.O. by Nov., cutting cameos and planning a display at the World's Industrial and Cotton Centennial Exposition.

References: *Bee*, Apr. 21–May 24, 1849 (advs.), Mar. 9, Apr. 17, May 8, 1881; *D. Pic.*, Mar. 20, 27, 1881, Nov. 2, 1884; *D. States*, Mar. 16, May 2, 1884; *T. Demo.*, Mar. 2, May 14, 1884.

AYLWARD, WILLIAM JAMES
Born Milwaukee WI Sept. 5, 1875. Painter.
Studied: with Howard Pyle.
Illustrator and landscape painter who was possibly in N.O., to paint the watercolor *Loading Cotton on the Levee at New Orleans* (ca. 1910). He later exhibited at the Paris salon (1924) and the National Academy of Design, N.Y.C. (1925).
References: Bénézit; Fielding, *Dictionary*; *Mallett's*; *Old Print Shop Portfolio* (Oct. 1946).

AYRES, REV. NELSON
Born Mar. 20, 1848; died KS Dec. 8, 1918.

Artist, engraver, designer, active N.O. 1889–95.
Contemporary listings: designer, engraver (1889–90); artist, *Picayune* (1891–95).
Ayres advertised in N.O. that he created woodcuts, book illustrations, and artistic designs (1889–90). He worked for the *Daily Picayune* (1891–95), while living in Bay St. Louis MS (1891) and then N.O. (1891–99). At the newspaper he was employed as an artist (1891–95) and literary critic (1892, 1896–99). Following the deaths of his wife (1894) and his son (1895), he was ordained a Catholic priest (1896) and became assistant rector of St. Peter and Paul Catholic Church (1898). He was also assigned to LA church parishes in Kenner, St. Francisville, and Mandeville. In 1912 he requested a removal to NY, due to ill health, to live with his daughter.
References: NOCD 1891–99; *D. Pic.*, Dec. 8, 12, 1889, Feb. 28, Nov. 13, 1890, Aug. 7, 28, Nov. 20, 1892, Apr. 11, 1895; Priests' Biographical File, Archives of the Archdiocese of N.O.

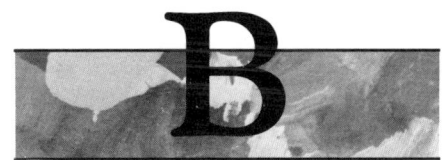

B., MR. E. C.
Painter, active N.O. 1839.
Contemporary listings: portrait painter (1839).
Advertised as a gentleman who wanted to transfer his professional services from the city to the country to restore his health.
References: *Comm. Bull.*, Jan. 3, 1839.

B., J.
Sketch artist, active N.O. 1887.
Signed a pencil sketch of Tante Zoe, praline seller, in 1887, which was probably done in N.O.
References: LSM, *Annual Report for 1918*, 60.

BABLED, CHARLES LUCIEN C.
Born N.O. ca. July 1870; died Bogalusa LA Sept. 24, 1911.
Painter, sculptor, active N.O. 1897–98, also publisher.
Studied: linear drawing with COL. LEON JOSEPH FREMAUX (1883).
Contemporary listings: painter (1897); sculptor (1898).
Listed as sporting editor (1892) and, with Louis P. Bouby, as publisher (1893), of *L'Orleanais*.
References: NOCD 1886–90, 1892–93, 1895, 1897–98, 1900; *D. Pic.*, Sept. 26, Oct. 1, 1911; *T. Demo.*, May 8, 1883.

BACHE, WILLIAM
Born Bromsgrove, Worcestershire, England Dec. 22, 1771; died 1845.
Silhouettist.
Itinerant silhouettist and profilist who worked in Philadelphia (1793, 1812), Richmond VA (1804), Salem MA (1810), and Hartford and New Haven CT (1810). In 1811 Bache married and settled in Wellsboro PA, where he became a successful businessman and land owner; he ended his silhouette–making career when he lost the use of his right hand in an accident. It has been suggested that he worked in LA (1804) and the West Indies, it seems likely that he was the senior partner in BACHE & TODD, silhouettists, who advertised in N.O. in Nov. 1804.
References: Groce and Wallace; London, 15.

BACHE & TODD
Silhouettists, active N.O. 1804; probably WILLIAM BACHE.
Contemporary listings: silhouettists, Royal near St. Ann (1804).
Advertised as the patentees of the "physiognotrace" for taking profile likenesses.
References: *Gazette*, Nov. 16, 1804; Arthur, *Old New Orleans*, 125–26.

BACHMAN, JOHN
Sketch artist, active N.O. 1851, 1861.
Artist, lithographer, and publisher, active in N.Y.C. and vicinity. Working on his own and with others (ca. 1849–79), he drew a *Birds' Eye View of New-Orleans* (1851) and *Panorama of the Seat of War*, (1861) which showed the LA coast and which he claimed to have drawn from nature and lithographed.
References: Groce and Wallace; Harry Peters, *America on Stone*, 82–84; Reps, 311; Stokes and Haskell, 179, plate 80a; THNOC 1956.50, 1971.54.

BACKUS, MRS. A[LCIDE]. V.
Designer, active N.O. ca. 1888; also decorator.
Exhibited: TULANE DECORATIVE ART LEAGUE FOR WOMEN (1888).
References: NOCD 1887; *D. Pic.*, Feb. 12, 1888; Tulane Decorative Art League, 4.

BADER, OTTO F. W.
Born N.O. Nov. 21, 1872; died N.O. June 4, 1931.
Lithographer, engraver, active N.O. 1891–1931; also pressman.
Contemporary listings: lithographer, KOECKERT & WALLE (1891); lithographer (1892–93, 1896, 1904, 1907, 1910, 1913–14, 1916–17); engraver (1894); foreman, WALLE & CO.

(1899, 1901), transferer, Walle & Co. (1900, 1902); transferer, WALLE & CO. LTD. (1909–11, 1915); lithographer, Walle & Co. Ltd. (1912); Walle & Co. Ltd. (1918).
Also listed as a lithographer (1919–20, 1923, 1927, 1929–31)and transferer, Walle & Co. (1922).
References: NOCD 1889, 1891–94, 1896, 1899–1907, 1909–23, 1927–31; *T. Pic.*, June 5, 1931; Orleans Parish Registrar of Voters, NOPL; U.S. Census (1910), roll 520.

BADGER, CHARLES J., SR.
Born N.O. May 21, 1865; died N.O. Jan. 18, 1934.
Engraver, designer, active N.O. 1886–1931; also marble cutter.
Contemporary listings: engraver, with J. F. Birchmeier (1886); engraver (1907, 1909, 1913, 1915–16); marble engraver (1908, 1910); marble designer, with F. G. Birchmeier (1911).
Also listed with Washington Marble Works (1890, 1892–93) and with various Birchmeier marble companies up to 1911. Later listed as engraver (1921–27, 1929) and engraver with Samuel Gately Marble & Granite Works (1931).
References: NOCD 1881–84, 1886–87, 1890–1904, 1906–11, 1913, 1915–16, 1919–29, 1931–33; *T. Pic.*, Jan. 19, 1934; Orleans Parish Registrar of Voters, NOPL.

BAENZIGER, EMILE F.
Designer, active N.O. 1895.
Contemporary listings: model maker, 804 Poydras (1895).
References: NOCD 1895.

BAGNETTO, ANTHONY R. (Antonio)
Born Italy Nov. 1850; died N.O. Jan. 23, 1907.
Painter, designer, active N.O. 1866–1907; also decorator.
Studied: with FERDINAND ARIGONE.
Contemporary listings: scenic artist, Academy of Music (1873, 1882–83); artist (1874, 1878, 1891, 1897–98, 1900–1904); scenic artist, Globe Theatre (1875); scenic artist (1876–77, 1879, 1881, 1905–1907); scene painter (1880); scenic artist, Grand Opera House (1883–84); scenic art-

ist, Spanish Fort (1884); scenic artist, St. Charles Theatre (1884).
Bagnetto's career as a scenic artist began in 1866 in the employ of David Bidwell of the St. Charles Theatre; he continued as a scenic artist at local theaters through 1884. In 1876 he began designing for some of the carnival organizations and, from 1878 through 1907, worked exclusively for the Rex organization. He also devised carnival pageants for the Order of Caliphs, Dallas TX (1900), for Saratoga Springs NY (1901), and for Buffalo NY. Father of JAMES C. BAGNETTO and JOSEPH SAMUEL BAGNETTO.
References: NOCD 1867, 1873–88, 1890–91, 1893–95, 1897–1907; *D. Pic.*, Jan. 24, 1907, Sept. 19, 1913; *D. States*, Aug. 19, 1883, June 23, July 21, Aug. 20, 1884, Oct. 24, 1897, Feb. 19, 1900; *Eve. Chronicle*, Oct. 2, 1884; *Spanish Fort D. Herald*, Sept. 1, 1883; *T. Demo.*, Nov. 19, 1905; U.S. Census (1900), roll 570.

BAGNETTO, CHARLES
Born LA July 26, 1859; died N.O. Feb. 14, 1939.
Painter, active N.O. 1884–1931.
Contemporary listings: scenic artist, Academy of Music (1884, 1886–87); scenic artist, with WILLIAM W. FETTERS, St. Charles Theatre (1884); scenic artist, Grand Opera House (1887); painter (1903); artist (1905–13, 1916–17); scenic artist (1914–15).
During the late 1800s, he worked with members of the DEUTSCHMANN family designing and building parade floats for carnival organizations.
References: NOCD 1886–87, 1889, 1892–1903, 1905–33; *D. Pic.*, Sept. 19, 1887; *Eve. Chronicle*, Sept. 15, Oct. 2, 1884; *T. Pic.*, Feb. 16, 1939; Information courtesy Catherine B. Foss, May 9, 1986; Orleans Parish Registrar of Voters, NOPL; U.S. Census (1910), roll 520.

BAGNETTO, JAMES C.
Born N.O. Apr. 1882; died N.O. Aug. 25, 1917.
Artist, active N.O. 1895–1905.
Contemporary listings: artist (1895, 1900–1903); artist, with Antonio R. Bagnetto (1905).

Son of ANTHONY R. BAGNETTO; brother of JOSEPH SAMUEL BAGNETTO.
References: NOCD 1895, 1900–1903, 1905, 1908–12, 1913–17; *D. Pic.*, Sept. 19, 1913; *T. Pic.*, Aug. 26, 1917; U.S. Census (1900), roll 570.

BAGNETTO, JOSEPH SAMUEL
Born LA Oct. 1890.
Artist, active N.O. 1897–1910.
Contemporary listings: artist (1897–99, 1903, 1905, 1910); painter (1900); artist, 712 Baronne (1901); artist, 546 S. Roman (1902, 1904).
Son of ANTHONY R. BAGNETTO; brother of JAMES C. BAGNETTO.
References: NOCD 1897–1910, 1914–19; *D. Pic.*, Sept. 19, 1913.

BAHIN, LOUIS JOSEPH
Born Marseilles, France.
Painter, active N.O. 1854.
Portrait, genre, and history painter who worked in Natchez MS (ca. 1850) and filed a declaration for American citizenship in N.O. (1854).
References: *Courier*, Jan. 29, 1852; Anglo–American Art Museum, *American Folk Art*, item 4; Barker, 522, 525; Bruns, 283, 309; Croce and Wallace.

BAILEY, GEORGE W. R. *See* BAYLEY, GEORGE W. R.

BAILEY, HENRIETTA DAVIDSON
Born N.O. Feb. 27, 1874; died N.O. Nov. 10, 1950.
Art craftsman, designer, potter, painter, art teacher, active N.O. 1904–38; also printer.
Studied: NEWCOMB COLLEGE (1901–1909); with Arthur Dow, Ipswich MA (1905).
Contemporary listings: teacher, Home Institute (1914–15, 1917–18); teacher, Katherine School (1916).
Exhibited: ART ASSOCIATION OF NEW ORLEANS (1910, 1913–14, 1916–18); Panama–Pacific International Exposition, San Francisco (1915).
Memberships/positions: Art Association of New Orleans; Newcomb Art Alumnae Association.
Listed at Newcomb College as a substitute teacher (1908–26), as an art craftsman (1909–27), and on the art faculty (1926–38). Bailey also decorated pottery at Newcomb (1904–38). Bailey exhibited ceramics at the Museum of Fine Arts, Houston (1930), and block prints at an exhibit of Newcomb art school alumnae (1931). She received first prizes from the Southern Art League for a collection of decorated pottery (1931) and for a block print (1932). She continued to exhibit in N.O. until her retirement in 1938.
References: NOCD 1914–33, 1935, 1938, 1940, 1942, 1945–46, 1949; *Item*, Feb. 6, 1921; *T. Pic.*, July 17, 24, 31, 1932, Jan. 14, 1934, Jan. 13, 1935, Nov. 11, 1950; Art Asso., *Catalogue* (1910, 1913, 1914, 1916, 1917, 1918); Art Asso., *Exhibition of Silversmithing*; Ormond and Irvine, 150, 151, 179; Poesch, *Newcomb Pottery*, 97, 157; THNOC Cemetery Survey; *Who's Who in American Art*, 1938–39.

BAILEY, LOUISE MARIE (Mrs. Harry Shannon)
Born N.O.; died N.O. Feb. 8, 1922.
Artist, active N.O. 1895–99.
Contemporary listings: artist (1895–96, 1898–99).
References: NOCD 1895–96, 1898–1900; *T. Pic.*, Feb. 9, 1922; THNOC Cemetery Survey.

BAILEY, SALLIE. *See* TEBAULT, SALLIE BAILEY

BAILEY, SAMUEL A.
Engraver, designer, active N.O. 1897–1900.
Contemporary listings: designer (1897); engraver, with Maurice Scooler (1899); engraver (1900).
References: NOCD 1895, 1897–1900.

BAILLY, A.
Sculptor, active N.O. 1850.
Contemporary listings: sculptor, 31 Exchange Al. (1850).
Possibly Joseph Alexis Bailly, born Paris, France Jan. 21, 1825; died Philadelphia PA June 15, 1883. He came to the U.S. in 1848, settled in Philadelphia by 1850 where he worked as a wood carver, wax modeler, and portrait sculptor.
References: NOCD 1850; *Courier*, Oct. 3, 1838; Groce and Wallace.

BAISLEY, CHARLES T.
Born Boston MA.
Painter, active N.O. ca. 1907.
Exhibited: ART ASSOCIATION OF NEW ORLEANS (1907).
Amateur painter who was listed as an officer with the Whitney–Central National Bank.
References: NOCD 1907–10, 1915–16; *D. Pic.*, Jan. 15, 1907; *T. Demo.*, Jan. 6, 1907; Art Asso., *Catalogue* (1907).

BAJATA, GASPAR
Sculptor, active N.O. 1884–1902.
Contemporary listings: sculptor, DE-GIORGI & BAJATA (1884); sculptor (1887); artist (1902).
References: NOCD 1884, 1887, 1902.

BAKER, ALDEN HEIRN
Born N.O. Nov. 1874; died N.O. Sept. 10, 1953.
Commercial artist, active N.O. 1900; also stereotyper.
Contemporary listings: artist (1900).
Worked as a clerk, foreman, and stereotyper at the N.O. *Times Democrat* (1890–1914) and as a circulation manager and department manager at the *Times–Picayune* (1915–32). He retired to a farm near Hammond LA (1932).
References: NOCD 1891–1900, 1903–32; *States*, Sept. 11, 1953; *T. Pic.*, Sept. 11, 1953; U.S. Census (1900), roll 575.

BAKER, MARY FRANCES
Born N.O. Oct. 28, 1879; died N.O. Aug. 23, 1943.
Painter, designer, art teacher, active N.O. 1901–40.
Studied: Pennsylvania Academy of Fine Arts, Philadelphia; with William Chase; NEWCOMB COLLEGE (1897–1902, 1905–1906).
Contemporary listings: portrait painter, 2263 Carondelet (1908–1909); artist, 2263 Carondelet (1910, 1914); artist (1911); portrait painter, 2262 Carondelet (1912); teacher (1913, 1917); portrait painter, 300 Audubon (1915); teacher, Francis T. Nicholls Industrial School (1916, 1918).

Exhibited: ARTISTS' ASSOCIATION OF NEW ORLEANS (1901); ART ASSOCIATION OF NEW ORLEANS (1902, 1905, 1907, 1910, 1913–14, 1917–18); Tercentenary Exposition, Jamestown VA (1907).
Awarded: Newcomb, Mary L. S. Neill medal for watercolor; Woodbury Summer School, Ogunquit ME, traveling scholarship (1902); Art Association of New Orleans, silver medal (1908).
Memberships/positions: ARTS EXHIBITION CLUB (1901); Art Association of New Orleans.
Continued to exhibit in the 1920s and to teach at N.O. public and vocational schools until her retirement in 1941. She also designed floats and souvenirs for carnival organizations.
References: NOCD 1908–33, 1935, 1938, 1940, 1942; *Item*, Jan. 16, 27, Feb. 3, 18, 1921; *States*, Aug. 25, 1943; *T. Demo.*, Jan. 6, 1907, Feb. 25, 1910, Jan. 14, 1913; *T. Pic.*, Dec. 3, 1923, Aug. 25–26, 1943; AANO, *Catalogue* (1901); Art Asso., *Catalogue* (1902, 1905, 1907, 1910, 1913, 1914, 1917, 1918); Arts Exhibition Club, 16; Cline, *Contemporary Art*, 6; Ormond and Irvine, 151; Poesch, *Newcomb Pottery*, 97, 157; Smithsonian, *Newcomb Pottery*, 3; U.S. Census (1910), roll 523; *Who's Who in American Art*, 1938–39.

BAKER, WILLIAM H.
Born NY 1825; died Brooklyn NY Mar. 29, 1875.
Painter, active N.O. 1848–61.
Studied: with ENOCH WOOD PERRY, JR.
Contemporary listings: portrait painter and artist, 11 St. Charles (1848); portrait painter, 11 St. Charles (1849); artist and portrait painter, 13 St. Charles and 71 Canal (1850); artist, portrait and landscape painter, 71 Canal (1852); portrait painter, 123 Canal (1853–58); portrait painter, 126 Canal (1859–60); portrait painter, Carondelet cor. Canal (1861).
Exhibited: Hall's store (1850); Tyler & Hewitt store (1851); Capitol, Nashville TN (ca. 1858); National

Academy of Design, N.Y.C. (1866, 1869, 1871); Brooklyn Art Association (1870–73, 1875).

Baker came to N.O. from Nashville, perhaps working as a merchant or clerk in the city as early as 1845 and continuing to 1850. He first occupied an art studio in the fall of 1848 continuing his career as a portrait painter in N.O. until the Civil War. During that time he left the city for considerable periods. In 1854 he spent some months in the North; in the summer and fall of 1855 he left to visit the galleries of France and England; and in 1858 he was exhibiting in Nashville. By 1865 Baker was in N.Y.C. as a portrait and genre painter and in 1869 became the principal of a free school of design of the Brooklyn Art Association.

References: NOCD 1846, 1849–61; *D. Crescent*, Dec. 8, 1848, Nov. 21, 1849, Feb. 11, May 20, Dec. 2, 1850, Nov. 26, 1855; *D. Delta*, Apr. 30, 1852, Dec. 2, 1855; *D. Pic.*, Aug. 15, 1851, Dec. 16, 1854, Nov. 14, 1858, June 6, 1875; *D. Times*, Feb. 2, 18, 1852; *Mercantile Advertiser*, Dec. 17, 1851; *Appleton's CAB*; Bruns, 309; Clement and Hutton; Creole Art Gallery, 7; Fielding, *Dictionary*; Glenk, 66, 72; Groce and Wallace; Harter and Tucker, 118; LSM, *Biennial Report for 1920–21*, 27–28, 65, 91; Marlor, 112; Seebold, 1:24; Thieme and Becker; U.S. Census (1850), roll 234.

BALDWIN, WILLIAM
Born LA ca. 1808.
Painter, art teacher, active N.O. 1827–50.
Contemporary listings: miniature painter, 199 Burgundy, and proprietor and professor of drawing, ACADEMIE DE DESSIN ET DE PEINTURE POUR LES PERSONNES DE COULEUR (1827); miniature painter, 43 Bayou (1830, 1832); portrait painter, 285 Dauphine (1834–35); miniature and oil painter and teacher of painting and drawing, 125 Barracks betw. Dauphine and Burgundy (1837); portrait painter, Villere near St. Philip (1841–42); miniature painter, Villere near St. Philip (1843–44); portrait painter, cor. Claiborne and St. Ann (1846); portrait painter (1850).
References: NOCD 1827, 1830, 1832, 1834–35, 1841–44, 1846; *Argus*, Feb. 19, 1827; *Bee*, June 6, 1837; Glenk, 72; Groce and Wallace; U.S. Census (1840), roll 131, (1850), roll 236.

BALIGANT, CHARLES M.
Art teacher, sculptor, painter, active N.O. 1803–1808.
Contemporary listings: proprietor, drawing school, and drawing teacher (1803); drawing professor, 63 St. Louis (1806); teacher of drawing and painting, proprietor, school of drawing, 65 St. Louis, and proprietor, school of drawing and painting, cor. St. Peter and the Church (1808).
Advertised, in 1803, as the former professor of drawing and sculptor-in-chief of the port of Brest, France. He taught figure drawing and landscape, ornamental, and miniature painting at his studio or at clients' houses. By 1816, he may have been living in Bay St. Louis MS.
References: *Courier*, Mar. 11, 1808, Sept. 2, 1811, Aug. 2, 1816; *Moniteur*, Apr. 30, June 4, July 30, 1803, June 21, 1806, Aug. 10, Nov. 30, 1808; Fortier, *Louisiana*, 2:225; Groce and Wallace.

BALLARD, LUCIA
Painter, active N.O. ca. 1892–94.
Exhibited: ARTISTS' ASSOCIATION OF NEW ORLEANS (1892, 1894).
References: *D. Pic.*, Dec. 14, 1892; *T. Demo.*, Dec. 13, 1892, Dec. 14, 1894.

BALLARD, MARY (Mrs. Allen Tupper)
Born Ascension Parish LA Mar. 2, 1871; died Hunibeck–bie–Thun, Switzerland Jan. 19, 1964.
Sketch artist, painter, art craftsman, active N.O. 1890–94.
Studied: NEWCOMB COLLEGE (1889–91).
Exhibited: ARTISTS' ASSOCIATION OF NEW ORLEANS (1890–92, 1894); FIVE OR MORE CLUB, Tulane Hall (1893).
Awarded: Artists' Association of New Orleans, first prize for antique draw-

ing, first prize for sketching from nature (1890).

Ballard moved to Switzerland after the death of her husband in the early 1930s, came back to N.O. during World War II, but returned to Europe thereafter.

References: *Current Topics*, Jan. 1891, 24, Jan. 1892, 24; *D. Pic.*, Dec. 17, 1890, Dec. 17, 1891, Dec. 14, 1892, Feb. 14, 1893; *D. States*, May 16, 1890; *T. Demo.*, May 16, 1890, Dec. 14, 1894; *T. Pic.*, Jan. 22, 1964; AANO, *Catalogue* (1890, 1891); Orleans Parish Registrar of Voters, NOPL; Ormond and Irvine, 80, 151; Thompson, "Checklist."

BANVARD, JOHN

Born N.Y.C. Nov. 15, 1815; died Watertown SD May 16, 1891.

Sketch artist, painter, active N.O. 1842.

Self–taught panorama, landscape, portrait, ornamental, and scenic painter. He traveled along the Mississippi River in 1833 as the scenic artist on the *Floating Theatre*, the first showboat in America; with another troupe in 1834–35; and made paintings along the route to N.O., Natchez MS, Cincinnati OH, and Louisville KY. In 1840, Banvard decided to be the first artist to portray the grandeur of America's scenery in a huge panorama. He made sketches and drawings along the course of the Missouri and Mississippi rivers while floating downriver in a skiff in 1842, reaching N.O. in the summer. He again sketched along the Mississippi River in 1843. The resulting panorama, about 425 yards long and wound on rollers, was painted during 1844–46 in Louisville, where it was first exhibited. It then traveled to Boston, N.Y.C., Washington DC, and London, with Banvard sometimes acting as narrator of the accompanying descriptive text; this text was published as *Description of Banvard's Panorama of the Mississippi River* (1847). He retired a wealthy man to Long Island NY and then to Watertown SD, where he continued to paint.

References: *D. Crescent*, Mar. 7–8, 1848; *D. Orleanian*, July 3, 1850; *Illustrated London News*, July 7, 1849; Barker, 448–49; *DAB*; Groce and Wallace; Hanners, "Adventures"; Hanners, "John Banvard"; Henry Lewis, 3–6; McCracken, *Portrait*, 218; McDermott, *Lost Panoramas*, 18–46; McGinnis, 102–31; Pinckney, 70–71; Rathbone, *Mississippi Panorama*, 53–54.

BANZ, LOUIS

Lithographer, active N.O. 1886.

Contemporary listings: lithographer, M. F. DUNN & BRO. (1886).

References: NOCD 1886.

BARBELET, CHARLES

Painter, active N.O. 1896.

Contemporary listings: fresco painter (1896).

References: NOCD 1896.

BARBIER, MR. _____

Painter, active N.O. 1819–20; also decorator.

Contemporary listings: scenic artist, Orleans Theatre (1819–20).

A *Courier* (Nov. 26, 1819) announcement for a play at the Orleans Theatre called Barbier "a pupil of the Royal school." He worked with DAGUERRE on scenery at the Orleans (1820). Possibly Andre F. Barbier listed as a builder, 44 Ursuline (1822) and 118 Ursuline (1823).

References: NOCD 1822–23; *L'Ami des Lois*, June 7, 1820; *Courier*, Nov. 19, 26, Dec. 6, 1819, Feb. 16, June 5, 1820; *Gazette*, Nov. 15, 1819; Groce and Wallace.

BARGES, FRANK

Sculptor, active N.O. 1900.

Contemporary listings: sculptor (1900).

References: NOCD 1900.

BARKER, JOHN R.

Born New Brunswick, Canada ca. 1836; died N.O. Nov. 19, 1870.

Artist, active N.O. 1870.

Contemporary listings: artist, 189 Royal (1870).

At the time of his death from yellow fever, he was listed as having arrived in N.O. 10 weeks before from St. Joseph or St. Louis MO.

References: Louisiana Charity Hospital, Death Records, NOPL.

BARNETT, ZELIA M.
Born LA ca. 1888.
Designer, active N.O. 1910–16; primarily decorator.
Contemporary listings: artist (1910, 1916).
Listed as either decorator or designer with Schwartz–Eustis Co., Ltd. (1907, 1909, 1912–15, 1917–20, 1923–25).
References: NOCD 1907, 1909–10, 1912–20, 1923–25; U.S. Census (1910), roll 519.

BARNEY, SAMUEL C.
Artist, active N.O. 1861–69.
Contemporary listings: artist, Gravier cor. Tchoupitoulas (1861); artist, Orleans House (1868); artist, the Green Room (1869).
Possibly Samuel Barney, born Ireland ca. 1810, listed as a merchant in the 1850 census, or, born Ireland ca. 1834, listed in the 1860 census.
References: NOCD 1861, 1868–70; U.S. Census (1850), roll 234, (1860), roll 417.

BARON, CLEMIRE
Engraver, active N.O. 1834–35.
Contemporary listings: engraver, 143 Goodchildren (1834–35).
References: NOCD 1834–35; Groce and Wallace.

BARR, ARTHUR
Painter, active N.O. 1905.
Contemporary listings: scenic artist, designer, Grand Opera House (1905).
Before coming to N.O., he was head scenic artist and designer for the Shuberts in N.Y.C., but was forced to leave that city for health reasons.
References: D. Pic., Nov. 19, 1905; T. Demo., Sept. 12, 1905.

BARRETT, ANTHONY
Born Germany ca. 1804.
Sculptor, active N.O. 1850–53; also marble cutter, marble worker.
Contemporary listings: proprietor, JUNJEL & BARRET (1850–51); sculptor, 111 St. Charles (1852–53).
Tomb builder and sculptor of cemetery statuary. He was the senior partner with Frederick Barrett in A.

Barrett & Co. (1861, 1867) and probably associated with WILLIAM BARRETT, sculptor.
References: NOCD 1849–56, 1858–61, 1866 74; D. Southern Star, Dec. 7, 1865; D. True Delta, Apr. 26, 1857; T. Deutsche Zeitung, May 1, 1853; Friends of the Cabildo, N.O. Architecture, 3:121; Groce and Wallace; U.S. Census (1850), roll 234.

BARRETT, WILLIAM
Born Denmark ca. 1815–20; died N.O. June 19, 1881.
Lithographer, engraver, active N.O. 1870–71; also stationer, printer.
Contemporary listings: lithographer, engraver, 60 Camp (1870); proprietor, BARRETT, SEYMOUR & CO. (1870–71).
References: NOCD 1867–72, 1875–81; D. Pic., June 20, 1881; THNOC 76–29–L; U.S. Census (1860), roll 415.

BARRETT, WILLIAM
Sculptor, active N.O. 1869.
Contemporary listings: sculptor, 111 St. Charles (1869).
His bust of Alexander von Humboldt was unveiled at Turners' Hall at the centennial festival of the scientist's birth (1869). Barrett was probably associated with ANTHONY BARRETT.
References: Bee, Aug. 28–29, 1869; Repub., Sept. 15, 1869.

BARRETT, SEYMOUR & CO.
Lithographers, active N.O. 1870–71; also stationers, printers; WILLIAM BARRETT, James W. Seymour, Eugene H. Angamar, partners.
Contemporary listings: lithographers, 60 Camp (1870–71).
References: NOCD 1871; Green Room, Dec. 16, 1870.

BARROW, IDA MARY
Born N.O. Jan. 21, 1868; died Covington LA June 22, 1947.
Art teacher, active N.O. 1891–1932.
Studied: George Peabody College, Nashville TN; Art Institute, Chicago; Columbia School of Art; with Thomas Anshutz and Hugh Breckenridge.
Contemporary listings: teacher, McDonogh H.S. No. 2 (1891–94, 1896–98, 1902, 1904–1905, 1907–1909); teacher, McDonogh H.S. No.

3 (1895, 1900); teacher, Normal School (1899, 1901); teacher (1910, 1915); teacher, McDonogh School No. 1 (1911); drawing teacher (1913).

Memberships/positions: Fine Arts Association of N.O., honorary life member.

Taught art for 45 years, including 15 years at Jackson Street Girls' High School and 15 years at Tulane University summer schools. She retired from teaching in 1929, but continued her appointment as supervisor/ director of drawing for the Orleans Parish public schools (ca. 1923–32).

References: NOCD 1891–1902, 1904–1905, 1907–11, 1915, 1918–19, 1922–33, 1935, 1938, 1940; *T. Demo.*, Jan. 14, 1913; *T. Pic.*, June 23, 1947; Orleans Parish Registrar of Voters, NOPL; WPA "Lives."

BARROW, ROBERT J.

Lithographer, active N.O. 1894–98. Contemporary listings: lithographer (1894, 1896, 1898).

Possibly Robert James Barrow III, born May 10, 1871; died Dec. 14, 1931.

References: NOCD 1894, 1896–98, 1902–1903; Floyd, *Barrow Family*, 104.

BARRY, BERNARD

Born Clarendon NY Apr. 5, 1876; died N.O. July 5, 1929.

Engraver, designer, active N.O. 1894–1929.

Contemporary listings: engraver, A. B. Griswold & Co. (1894–99, 1901–18).

He designed the official flag of N.O. with GUSTAVE J. COURET (1918). Barry continued with A. B. Griswold & Co. as an engraver (1919–22) and designer (1923–24), then with Hausmann, Inc., as an engraver (1925, 1927–29).

References: NOCD 1891, 1894–1929; *T. Pic.*, Feb. 6, 1918, July 6, 1929; Orleans Parish Registrar of Voters, NOPL.

BARTHELEMY, CHARLES L.

Born N.O. Oct. 1878; died Covington LA Dec. 25, 1918.

Sculptor, active N.O. 1901–1905; also carver, furniture maker, cabinet maker.

Contemporary listings: sculptor (1901); wood carver, 2030 Ursulines (1905).

References: NOCD 1897–98, 1901–1903, 1905–10; *T. Pic.*, Dec. 26, 1918.

BARTHELEMY, LEON

Sculptor, active N.O. 1906.

Contemporary listings: wood carver (1906).

References: NOCD 1897, 1899, 1901, 1905–11.

BARTNEY, JOHN (Bartley)

Born Ireland ca. 1821–23.

Artist, active N.O. 1860–61.

Contemporary listings: artist, 55 St. Thomas (1860–61).

References: NOCD 1854–61; Groce and Wallace; U.S. Census (1850), roll 234, (1860), roll 415.

BASTEROT, MR. _____. *See also* AUDUBON, JOHN JAMES

Painter, art teacher, active N.O. 1821–23.

Contemporary listings: portrait painter, teacher of drawing and painting, St. Ann (1821); portrait painter, miniature painter, 63 St. Ann (1823).

Describing himself in the *Courier* as "a pupil of the French school," Basterot advertised as teaching figure and landscape painting and drawing in oil, watercolor, and pencil. At the time, he planned to paint a panoramic view of the city.

References: NOCD 1823; *Courier*, Oct. 24, 1821; Adams, 247; Glenk, 72; Groce and Wallace.

BATTIER, ANTONINE (Mrs. William Battier)

Painter, art teacher, active N.O. 1851–60.

Contemporary listings: portrait and miniature painter, teacher of drawing and painting, 162 Conti (1851); portrait painter, drawing and painting academy for young ladies, 164 Conti (1854); miniature portrait painter, drawing and painting academy for young ladies, 164 Conti (1855); miniature portrait painter,

drawing and painting academy for young ladies, 316 Chartres (1860).
References: *Bee*, Nov. 4, 1851; *D. Pic.*, Jan. 18–22, 1854 (advs.), Nov. 29, 1854–Mar. 17, 1855 (advs.), Jan. 16, 1860; Groce and Wallace; U.S. Census (1860), roll 419.

BATZ, ALEXANDRE DE. *See* DE BATZ, ALEXANDRE

BAUER, HENRY
Artist, active N.O. 1896.
Contemporary listings: artist (1896).
Possibly Henry R. Bauer, born N.O. ca. 1879; died N.O. Dec. 29, 1910.
References: NOCD 1896, 1898–99, 1903–11; *D. Pic.*, Dec. 30, 1910.

BAUMGARTNER, N. A.
Artist, active N.O. 1860–61.
Contemporary listings: artist, 82 Race (1860–61).
References: NOCD 1858–61; Groce and Wallace.

BAYLAT, MR. _____
Painter, restorer, art teacher, active N.O. 1817; also architect, engineer.
Studied: Paris Academy of Painting; with Jacques–Louis David.
Contemporary listings: miniature and portrait painter, teacher of drawing and painting, Dauphine betw. St. Louis and Conti (1817).
In 1817, Baylat advertised as having arrived from Paris, where he had been a civil and military engineer for the French government. In N.O., he offered to draw portraits in oil and pastel, correct poor likenesses, alter the dress in portraits by other artists, repair and decorate houses "in the latest Paris style," execute plans, and oversee construction. Baylat taught the drawing and painting of portraits, figures, architecture, ornament, flowers, landscape, and animals. He had brought with him portraits he had painted in Paris, many of which were copies of works in the Louvre, including David's portrait of Napoleon in imperial attire.
References: *Courier*, May 30, 1817; Groce and Wallace

BAYLEY, GEORGE W. R.
Born NY ca. 1821; died N.O. Dec. 14, 1876.

Sketch artist, active N.O. 1849; primarily surveyor, engineer.
Exhibited: J.B. Steel's (1849).
Exhibited the charter of the Templar Lodge No. 16 I.O.O.F., decorated with drawings of knights templars, battle scenes, and allegorical figures of Charity, Truth, and Time (1849); compiled surveys for a *New Map of Louisiana*, published 1853.
References: NOCD 1849–50, 1860–61, 1866–67, 1870–76; *D. Crescent*, Mar. 7, 1853; *D. Pic.*, Oct. 14, 1849, Jan. 11, 1851, Mar. 8, 1868, Dec. 15, 1876; THNOC Cemetery Survey.

BAYNE, MARY A. *See* VAUGHT, MARY BAYNE

BEALE, MRS. MARIA
Artist, active N.O. ca. 1892.
Exhibited: ARTISTS' ASSOCIATION OF NEW ORLEANS (1892).
References: *T. Demo.*, Dec. 13, 1892.

BEARD, JAMES CARTER
Born Cincinnati OH June 6, 1837; died N.O. Nov. 15, 1913.
Illustrator, active N.O. 1910–13.
Studied with his father, JAMES HENRY BEARD.
Contemporary listings: artist (1910, 1913).
Attorney who served in the Civil War, after which he turned to art and writing. Beard became famous as a draftsman of plant and animal life. His illustrations appeared in dictionaries, encyclopedias, books on natural history, and books he authored, as well as in magazines such as *Harper's* and *Century*. After the death of his wife, he moved to N.O. to live with his son and contributed drawings and articles to the *Daily Picayune*.
References: NOCD 1910, 1913–14; *D. Pic.*, June 11, 1911, Nov. 16, 1913; *DAB*; Groce and Wallace; McCracken, *Portrait*, 218; N.O. Death Certificate (1913), 159:43, NOPL; U.S. Census (1910), roll 524; WPA, "Lives."

BEARD, JAMES HENRY
Born Buffalo NY May 20, 1814; died Flushing NY, Apr. 4, 1893.
Painter, active N.O. 1838?–52.

Contemporary listings: painter, with THEODORE SIDNEY MOISE (1843); artist, 13 St. Charles (1850); artist, 95 Camp (1851); artist (1852).

Exhibited: studio of Theodore Sidney Moise (1843); National Academy of Design, N.Y.C. (1846); J. B. Steel's store (1848); Hall's store (1851); Centennial Exhibition, Philadelphia (1876); SOUTHERN ART UNION (1882); Creole Art Gallery (1892).

Memberships/positions: National Academy of Design, honorary member (1848), academician (1872); Century Club, N.Y.C.

Portrait, animal, landscape, and genre painter. At the age of 17 he became an itinerant painter, settling in Cincinnati OH (ca. 1834); in 1870 he moved to N.Y.C. and finally to Flushing NY. He continued to travel during these years and may have been J. H. Beard listed in the NOCD 1838. He is known to have maintained N.O. studios during the winters of 1843 and 1850–52. Paintings of LA subjects by Beard dated 1847 and 1858 indicate that he was probably in the state at other times. His four sons, including JAMES CARTER BEARD, were artists.

References: NOCD 1838; *D. Crescent*, July 24, 1849, Mar. 15, 1851; *D. Delta*, Jan. 29, Mar. 30, 1851; *D. Pic.*, Apr. 6, 1843, Jan. 31, 1877, Oct. 19, 1879, Feb. 15, 1882; *Demo.*, Nov. 22, 1876; *New York Times*, Apr. 5, 1893; *Repub.*, Apr. 6, 1875; *D. Times*, Feb. 18, 1852; *Wkly. Delta*, Feb. 21, 1848, Feb. 4, 1850; Bénézit; Bruns, 310; Clement and Hutton, 43; Creole Art Gallery, 16, 23–24; *DAB*; Glenk, 72; Groce and Wallace; LSM, *Biennial Report for 1922–23*, 58; McCracken, *Portrait*, 218; Moise, 31; Rutledge, *Catalogue*; Tuckerman, 436.

BEARMANN, ROBERT E. L.
Born LA ca. 1886.
Lithographer, active N.O. 1910–19; also printer.
Contemporary listings: lithographer (1910–12).
References: NOCD 1905–1909, 1911–14, 1916–19; U.S. Census (1910), roll 520.

BEAUCE, ——
Artist, active N.O. 1842.
Contemporary listings: artist, Orleans Theatre (1842).
References: NOCD 1842; Groce and Wallace.

BEAUDEAU, MR. ——
Art teacher, active N.O. 1844.
Contemporary listings: drawing teacher, Garreau's Seminary for the Two Sexes (1844).
Also a mathematics teacher who was a former professor of the Normal School of Paris, France.
References: *Bee*, Sept. 27, 1884.

BEAUREGARD, ALICE TOUTANT (Mrs. Edward C. Morse)
Born N.O.; died Washington DC May 4, 1956.
Art craftsman, active N.O. 1916–17.
Studied: NEWCOMB COLLEGE (1908–12, 1914–17).
Granddaughter of Gen. P. G. T. Beauregard, she was an art craftsman during the 1916–17 session at Newcomb College.
References: NOCD 1945–47, 1949, 1952–56, 1958; *T. Pic.*, May 5, 1956; Ormond and Irvine, 151; Poesch, *Newcomb Pottery*, 97.

BEAUREGARD, ED
Born LA ca. 1890.
Engraver, active N.O. 1910.
Contemporary listings: jewelry engraver (1910).
References: U.S. Census (1910), roll 520.

BECK, F. & CO.
Lithographers, active N.O. 1843; also printers.
Contemporary listings: lithographers, printers, Bayou Road and cor. Greatmen and History (1843).
Issued and printed *La Lorgnette*, a journal of theater and art.
References: *Lorgnette*, Jan. 15–Apr. 20, 1843.

BECKER, GEORGE J.
Lithographer, active N.O. 1841; also printer.
Contemporary listings: proprietor of Becker's Writing Academy, 44 Canal (1840–41); P. SNELL & BECKER, 44 Canal and 36 Camp (1841).

References: NOCD 1841; *D. Pic.*, Nov. 10–Dec. 4, 1840 (advs.), Dec. 4, 1840–Jan. 26, 1841 (advs.), Jan. 19, 26, 1841.

BEEKER, CHARLES, JR.
Born LA Sept. 1880.
Artist, active N.O. 1900.
Contemporary listings: artist (1900).
References: U.S. Census (1900), roll 576.

BEGUE, MR. A.
Artist, active N.O. 1882.
An artist from Paris who opened a business in which he painted flowers on quill pens.
References: *Bee*, July 27, 1882.

BEHAN, JOHN HENRY
Born N.O. Sept. 22, 1839; died N.O. Feb. 2, 1894.
Designer, active N.O. ca. 1882–94; also carpenter, builder.
Businessman, principally with cotton presses, who also designed carnival pageants, notably those of the Krewe of Momus (1882–83) and of the Atlanteans, an organiazation of which he was a founder in 1891. He also designed for carnival organizations in other cities.
References: NOCD 1851–61, 1866–67, 1869–94; *D. Pic.*, Feb. 3, 1894; U.S. Census (1860), roll 415; Waldo, 218–19; Samuel Wilson, *Guide*, 35; Perry Young, 177.

BEHR, THEODORE
Painter, active N.O. ca. 1885–1903.
Mentioned as the noted mural painter who attended meetings of the ARTISTS' ASSOCIATION OF NEW ORLEANS.
References: Seebold, 1:316.

BELAUME, JACQUES
Born Havana, Cuba.
Engraver, active N.O. 1807–26; also jeweler.
Studied: with a French engraver, Havana (before 1807).
Contemporary listings: engraver, 2 Royal (1807); engraver, St. Louis (1808–1809); engraver, Delarue's silversmith shop (1812); engraver, 104 Royal (1826).
Advertised that he engraved on all metals, made seals and bas–reliefs, and set and repaired gold and silver jewelry. Belaumé was in Havana sometime between Apr. 1808 and Feb. 1809 to handle family affairs. In 1826 he advertised that all claims and debts to him should be settled, because he planned to leave the country.
References: NOCD 1811; *Argus*, June 20, Sept. 7, 1826; *Courier*, Oct. 14, Dec. 16, 1807, Apr. 6, 1808, Feb. 27, 1809, July 27, 1812; Fielding, *American Engravers*; Fielding, *Dictionary*; Groce and Wallace; Tinker, *Creole City*, 57; U.S. Census (1810), roll 10.

BELDEN, ARABELLA TREAT (Mrs. James G. Belden)
Born Palmyra NY ca. 1833–34; died Mandeville LA July 21, 1896.
Painter, active N.O. 1880–89.
Exhibited: World's Industrial and Cotton Centennial Exposition (1884–85); ARTISTS' ASSOCIATION OF NEW ORLEANS (1887); ART LEAGUE OF NEW ORLEANS (1889).
Memberships/positions: SOUTHERN ART UNION, committee of art (1880–81).
Came to N.O. as a child with her parents, but probably trained in art in the North. She painted landscapes, flower subjects, and portraits. Three of her children studied art: DR. HENRY EVELYN BELDEN, DR. JAMES WEBSTER BELDEN, and Mrs. Walter B. Jackson.
References: *Art and Letters* 1(Dec. 1887):227; *Bee*, May 27, 1880, May 4, 1881; *D. Pic.*, Dec. 29, 1887, Mar. 10, 1889, July 22–23, 26, 1896; *Demo.*, May 12, 1881; Harter and Tucker, 118; Mount, 193–94; Thompson, "Checklist"; U.S. Census (1860), roll 416; WPA "Lives."

BELDEN, AUGUSTUS
Painter, active N.O. 1840.
Contemporary listings: 17 Bourbon (1841).
References: NOCD 1841; Glenk, 73; WPA "Lives."

BELDEN, FRANCES MARSDEN (Mrs. Charles F. Belden)
Died N.O. Aug. 7, 1923.
Sculptor, active N.O. ca. 1888.
Studied: NEWCOMB COLLEGE (1885–88, 1890–91).

Exhibited: TULANE DECORATIVE ART LEAGUE FOR WOMEN (1888).
References: NOCD 1910–11, 1913–19, 1921; *D. Pic.*, Feb. 12, 1888; *T. Pic.*, Aug. 8, 1923; Poesch, *Newcomb Pottery*, 97; Tulane Decorative Art League, 3.

BELDEN, DR. HENRY EVELYN
Born N.O. May 14, 1859; died N.O. Jan. 9, 1930.
Sculptor, active N.O. 1896; also jeweler.
Dentist, amateur woodcarver, and jeweler who made gold buckles, pins, and ornaments and set them with jewels. Son of ARABELLA TREAT BELDEN; brother of DR. JAMES WEBSTER BELDEN.
References: NOCD 1880–1920, 1922–30; *T. Pic*, Jan. 10, 1930; Mount, 194; Orleans Parish Registrar of Voters, NOPL; WPA "Lives."

BELDEN, DR. JAMES WEBSTER
Born N.O. Oct. 10, 1856; died N.O. Nov. 7, 1914.
Sculptor, active N.O. 1876–87.
Studied: with Thompson; with John Lafarge, John Quincy Adams Ward, and Augustus St. Gaudens, NY.
Contemporary listings: sculptor (1876); artist, sculptor (1877); artist (1886–87).
Noted for his portrait busts, in particular one of Rutherford B. Hayes, presented to the President (ca. 1877). While in N.Y.C. working under Moses Lafaye, Belden designed and modeled the frieze and ceiling of the dining room of the Vanderbilt house and assisted in work on the Astor house. He returned to N.O. in 1884, an accomplished artist specializing in bas–reliefs. He eventually abandoned art, to study medicine. From about 1890 to 1895, he practiced medicine with his father, after which he practiced on his own. Son of ARABELLA TREAT BELDEN; brother of DR. HENRY EVELYN BELDEN.
References: NOCD 1873, 1875–77, 1886–1914; *Bull.*, May 26, 1876; *Demo.*, June 13, 1877; *T. Demo.*, Feb. 24, 1884; *T. Pic*, Nov. 8, 1914; Fortier, *Louisiana*, 3:42; Mount, 193–

94; Simms, 29; U.S. Census (1860), roll 416.

BELKNAP, JACKSON OGDEN
Born AL ca. 1829.
Painter, designer, active N.O. 1870–73; also gilder.
Contemporary listings: artist (1871).
Awarded: Grand State Fair, silver medal for best gilding on glass (1867), silver medal for best painting and gilding on reverse of glass (1868).
Listed in 1854 as a sign and ornamental painter in Mobile AL where he lived through 1868. In 1871, while living in N.O., Belknap patented an iron pagoda and public fountain, adorned with advertisements painted on glass. One pagoda, standing 27 feet tall, was constructed on the Canal Street median at Camp. Also in 1871, examples of his paintings on glass were incorporated into a 12–foot–high desk and advertising table displayed at the St. Charles Hotel.
References: NOCD 1871–73; *Comm. Bull.*, Jan. 23, 1871; *D. Pic.*, Jan. 19, 1868, Apr. 2, June 25, 1871; *Repub.*, Sept. 2, 1870, Feb. 8, 1871, May 12, 1872; Mechanics' and Agricultural Fair Asso., *Report* (1867):28, (1868):42; *Southern Business Directory, 1854*, 31; U.S. Census (1870), roll 519; U.S. Patent Office, *Specifications*, July 11, 1871.

BELL, JESSIE MARGARET
Born N.O. ca. 1871; died N.O. Sept. 11, 1895.
Painter, sketch artist, active N.O. ca. 1890–94.
Studied: ARTISTS' ASSOCIATION OF NEW ORLEANS (1890).
Exhibited: Artists' Association of New Orleans (1890, 1892, 1894); Tulane University (1893).
References: *D. Pic.*, Nov. 13, 1890, Dec. 14, 1892, Feb. 14, 1893, Sept. 12, 1895; *D. States*, May 16, 1890; *T. Demo.*, Dec. 14, 1894.

BELLENOT, CHARLES
Born Switzerland ca. 1825.
Engraver, active N.O. 1851–61; also stencil cutter.
Contemporary listings: engraver, cor. Bienville and Exchange Al. (1851–61).

Advertised as a die sinker, engraver, and embosser of cards and envelopes (1855). At the outbreak of the Civil War, he advertised as a manufacturer of emblems and buttons for military uniforms.
References: NOCD 1851–61; *Bee*, May 6–9, 1861; *D. Crescent*, Sept. 6, 1855, Oct. 24, 1861; U.S. Census (1860), roll 421.

BELLEW, FRANK HENRY TEMPLE
Born Cawnpore, Hindustan, India Apr. 18, 1828; died Long Island NY June 29, 1888.
Illustrator, cartoonist, active N.O. ca. 1855.
Caricaturist, cartoonist, and illustrator for books and for periodicals such as *Harper's Weekly*, *Scribner's Monthly*, and *Vanity Fair*, and considered an important early influence in the evolution of the modern comic strip. Probably "Bellew" whose name appears in the wood engraving *Street Railroad, New Orleans*, published in *Ballou's Pictorial Drawing Room Companion* (Sept. 1855). The *Daily Picayune* (Aug. 31, 1860) reported that Bellew had previously spent some time in the city.
References: *Ballou's Pictorial Drawing Room Companion*, Sept. 1855, 156; *D. Crescent*, July 19, 1855; *D. Pic.*, Aug. 31, 1860; *New York Times*, June 30, 1888; *DAB*; Fielding, *Dictionary*; Groce and Wallace; Hamilton, 1:71; Reinders, 129.

BELLOTT, MISS _____
Painter, active N.O. ca. 1884–85.
Exhibited: Woman's Department, World's Industrial and Cotton Centennial Exposition (1884–85).
References: Woman's Department of the World's Exposition, 160.

BELMONT, MELVILLE
Painter, active N.O. 1912–13.
Studied: Boston MA.
Contemporary listings: fresco artist, 749 Baronne (1913).
Painted a copy of Murillo's *Immaculate Conception* for St. Patrick's Church which was installed in 1912.
References: NOCD 1913; *Item*, Sept. 8, 1912.

BELNEAU, C.
Born France ca. 1822.
Engraver, active N.O. 1850.
Contemporary listings: engraver (1850).
Name had been previously misinterpreted as Belucan.
References: Groce and Wallace; U.S. Census (1850), roll 235.

BELZONS, JOSEPH
Art teacher, active N.O. 1805–1806.
Contemporary listings: 63 Bourbon (1805); proprietor, school of drawing, 63 Bourbon (1806).
References: NOCD 1805; *Moniteur*, Oct. 1, 1806; LSM, *Annual Report for 1918*, 60.

BEMISS, AMY
Painter, sketch artist, active N.O. ca. 1883–97.
Studied: with ANDRES MOLINARY.
Exhibited: WAGENER's gallery (1883, 1885).
Portrait and flower painter and sketch artist whose work was illustrated in *Art and Letters* (1887) and *Men and Matters* (1897).
References: *Art and Letters* 1(Aug. 1887):129, 131; *D. Pic.*, July 26, 1885; *Men and Matters*, Sept. 1897, 51, 67; *T. Demo.*, July 17, 1883.

BENDERNAGEL, ALBERT
Born June 9, 1873; died N.O. July 6, 1951.
Painter, active N.O. 1893–1905; primarily architect.
Exhibited: ARTISTS' ASSOCIATION OF NEW ORLEANS (1897).
Memberships/positions: Artists' Association of New Orleans (1897); ARTS EXHIBITION CLUB (1901); ART ASSOCIATION OF NEW ORLEANS (1905).
As a practicing architect, Bendernagel worked on his own and in association with the following architectural firms: Sully and Toledano (1893); Thomas Sully and Co. (1894); Harrod, Andry and Bendernagel (1898); Andry and Bendernagel (1901–13); Burton and Bendernagel (1914–22); Emile Weil (1924–32); and Bendernagel and Cazalé (ca. 1937–38). In association with Paul Andry, he designed two of his most notable buildings: Tilton Memorial

Library (1901) and the N.O. Stock Exchange (1906).
References: NOCD 1892–1929, 1931–33, 1935, 1938, 1940, 1942, 1945–47, 1949; *Architectural Art*, 1(Oct. 1905):11; *D. Pic.*, Mar. 30, 1897; *T. Demo.*, Mar. 14, 1901; *T. Pic.*, July 7, 1951; AANO, *Catalogue* (1897); *Arts Exhibition Club*, 16; Friends of the Cabildo, *N.O. Architecture*, 2:222, 3:54; Gebhard and Nevins, items 69–70; O'Connor, 562; Orleans Parish Registrar of Voters, NOPL; Reeves, 130; THNOC 1979.325.2501; Samuel Wilson, *Guide*, 64, 75.

BENDIX, CHARLES L., JR.
Born N.O. ca. 1888; died N.Y.C. Dec. 5, 1944.
Engraver, etcher, active N.O. 1907–10.
Contemporary listings: engraver (1907); etcher (1908); photo–engraver, *Times–Democrat* (1909–10).
References: NOCD 1904–1905, 1907–10, 1917–18, 1920–23; *T. Pic.*, Dec. 7, 1944; U.S. Census (1910), roll 525.

BENITO, F.
Artist, active N.O. 1849.
Contemporary listings: artist, 289 Marais (1849).
Possibly F. Benit[o?], mulatto, born LA ca. 1820, listed as a painter in the 1850 census; or F[rançois?]. Benito, born LA ca. 1815, listed as a bricklayer in the 1850 census and in the NOCD 1850–54.
References: NOCD 1849, 1851–54; Groce and Wallace; U.S. Census (1850), rolls 235, 236.

BENNETT, SMITH W.
Born Monroe LA ca. 1844–50; died N.O. May 18, 1907.
Engraver, designer, illustrator, active N.O. 1876–1907; also printer.
Contemporary listings: designer, wood engraver, 61 Camp (1878); wood engraver, 61 Camp (1879–80); proprietor, BENNETT & ZENNECK (1881); proprietor, BENNETT & PATTERSON (1882–84); proprietor, SMITH W. BENNETT & CO. (1885); engraver (1886, 1895); engraver, *The Lantern* (1888); engraver, 46 Camp (1889);

proprietor, BENNETT & KOENIG (1890); wood engraver, 26 Commercial (1891–94); wood engraver, 205 Exchange Al. (1896); wood engraver, 614 Commercial (1897–1900); engraver, 334 Magazine (1901–1907). Name appeared in illustrations in *New Orleans Democrat* (1876), *Frank Leslie's Illustrated Newspaper* (1876), and *Illustrated Visitors' Guide to New Orleans* (1879).
References: NOCD 1878–1907; *D. Pic.*, May 19, 1907; *Demo.*, May 7–Dec. 31, 1876 (advs.), Feb. 22, 1877; *Leslie's*, Dec. 2, 1876; *Lantern*, Sept. 22, 1886, Jan. 15, 1887; *Mascot*, Apr. 29, Sept. 23, 1882; N.O. Death Certificate (1907), 140: 1198, NOPL; Waldo.

SMITH W. BENNETT & CO.
Engravers, designers, active N.O. 1884–85; also printers; SMITH W. BENNETT, owner.
Contemporary listings: job printing, wood engraving and designing, 20 Natchez (1884).
References: NOCD 1885; *Mascot*, June 7, 1884.

BENNETT & KOENIG
Engravers, active N.O. 1890; SMITH W. BENNETT, Charles A. Koenig, partners.
Contemporary listings: wood engravers, 46 Camp (1890).
References: NOCD 1890.

BENNETT & PATTERSON
Engravers, designers, active N.O. 1882–84; also printers; SMITH W. BENNETT, ROBERT L. PATTERSON, partners.
Contemporary listings: wood engravers, designers, 61 Camp (1882); wood engravers, 12 Commercial (1883); wood engravers, 12 Union (1884).
Names appeared in the masthead of the *Mascot*, May 13, 1882–Oct. 6, 1883 and Feb. 23, 1884–July 25, 1885.
References: NOCD 1882–84; *Mascot*, May 13, 1882–Oct. 6, 1883, Feb. 23, 1884–July 25, 1885.

BENNETT & ZENNECK
Engravers, commercial artists, active N.O. 1880–81; SMITH W. BENNETT, ADOLPH ZENNECK, partners.

Contemporary listings: artists, engravers (1880); wood engravers, 61 Camp (1881).
References: NOCD 1881; *D. Pic.*, June 10, 1880; Tinker, *Lafcadio Hearn*, 86–89.

BENOIST, MME. A.
Hair worker, active N.O. 1858–59.
Contemporary listings: ornamental hair manufacturer, 205 Bourbon (1858–59).
References: NOBD 1858–59.

BENSADON, JUDAH
Born PA ca. 1822; died N.O. July 16, 1852.
Sculptor, active N.O. 1851–52; also stonecutter.
Contemporary listings: sculptor, 224 Camp (1851); sculptor, 227 Camp (1852).
References: NOCD 1851–52; *D. Pic.*, July 17, 1852; U.S. Census (1850), roll 237.

BENSON, JOHN
Born England ca. 1827.
Painter, active N.O. 1849–59; primarily sign painter, glazier.
Contemporary listings: painter, Live Oak betw. Philip and First (1849–51); painter (1857); BENSON & BRO. (1858–59).
May have been in NY where his daughter was born (ca. 1852).
Brother of JOSEPH BENSON.
References: NOCD 1849–51, 1854–60; *D. True Delta*, Nov. 21, 1860; Apr. 7, 1861; Groce and Wallace; U.S. Census (1860), roll 416.

BENSON, JOSEPH
Born Manchester, England ca. 1818–19; died N.O. Sept. 18, 1860.
Painter, active N.O. 1848–60; primarily sign and ornamental painter, glazier.
Contemporary listings: painter, 132 Camp (1848–51); painter (1857, 1860); BENSON & BRO. (1858–59).
Brother of JOHN BENSON.
References: NOCD 1849–60; *D. Crescent*, Mar. 16, 1850, Jan. 7, 1851, Sept. 19, 1860; *D. True Delta*, Sept. 19, 1860, Apr. 7, 1861; *Miscellany*, Jan. 1848, 104.

BENSON, MARIE LEVERING
Art craftsman, potter, art teacher, active N.O. ca. 1905–1908.

Studied: NEWCOMB COLLEGE (1904–1906); Dow Summer school, Ipswich MA (1906).
Contemporary listings: teacher (1907).
Exhibited: Panama–Pacific International Exposition, San Francisco (1915).
Listed as a pottery worker in Newcomb catalogue (1906–1908). She left N.O. in 1908 for Washington DC to head a department at the National Arts and Crafts School.
References: NOCD 1907; *D. Pic.*, Oct. 1, 1908; Ormond and Irvine, 45, 151; Poesch, *Newcomb Pottery*, 27, 52, 97.

BENSON & BRO. (Benson Bros.)
Painters, active N.O. 1856–57; primarily ornamental and sign painters, glaziers; JOHN BENSON, JOSEPH BENSON, partners.
Contemporary listings: painters, 132 Camp (1857).
Painted scenes from the life of St. Joseph on the ceiling of St. Joseph's Church (1856).
References: NOCD 1857–59; *D. Creole*, Sept. 25, 1856; *D. True Delta*, July 6, 1856, Jan. 3, 1857; *Semi-Wkly. Creole*, Feb. 16, Apr. 19, 1856; Groce and Wallace.

BEORCI, ACHILLE
Artist, designer, active N.O. (1882–86); also decorator.
Contemporary listings: artist (1882, 1886).
With RAYMOND II. MASSARINI, designed and decorated a triumphal arch at the West End railroad terminus (1883).
References: NOCD 1882, 1886; *D. States*, July 14, 1883.

BERCOLI, AUGUST
Born Baden, Germany ca. 1832.
Lithographer, active N.O. 1860.
Contemporary listings: lithographer (1860).
Listed in the same household with HENRY FLICORN and BENEDICT SIMON (1860).
References: Groce and Wallace; U.S. Census (1860), roll 421.

BERGER, MR. _____
Born France.
Painter, active N.O. 1889; also decorator.
Contemporary listings: scenic artist, with HARRY H. DRESSEL, French Opera House (1889); painter (1891).
References: NOCD 1891; *D. States*, Oct. 5, 17, 20, 1889.

BERGER, AUGUST
Painter, active N.O. 1896.
Contemporary listings: portrait painter, 419 Natchez (1896).
References: NOCD 1896.

BERINGER, PETER
Art teacher, active N.O. 1868.
Contemporary listings: optician, 93 Exchange Pl., and drawing school, 94 Exchange Pl. (1868).
References: NOCD 1859, 1868.

BERJOT, DR. MARIE EUGENE
Born Valence or Paris, France May 1816; died N.O. Nov. 26, 1898.
Painter, active N.O. ca. 1871–72.
Awarded: Grand State Fair, first prize for best historical painting in the U.S. (1871).
Physician, author, and amateur artist who painted a banner for the annual festival of the Lusitanian Portuguese Benevolent Association (1872).
References: NOCD 1867–69, 1871–78, 1885–89, 1891–98; *D. Pic.*, Dec. 3, 1871, Nov. 27–28, 1898; *Repub.*, June 11, 1872; Caulfeild, 198; Tinker, *Ecrits*, 36–37.

BERNARD, FRANÇOIS
Born France ca. 1812.
Painter, art teacher, active N.O. ca. 1856–75.
Studied: with Paul Delaroche.
Contemporary listings: portrait painter, 105 Canal (1856–58); portrait painter, cor. Carondelet and Canal (1859); portrait painter, 146 Customhouse (1860, 1866, 1868–69); portrait and photograph painter, 146 Customhouse (1867); portrait painter (1870–72).
Exhibited: WAGENER's (1867); Grand State Fair (1868); WAGENER & MEYER's (1869–71); American Exposition (1885–86).
Awarded: Grand State Fair, silver medal for best head in oil (1869).

Portrait, landscape, and genre painter. Bernard is known in LA primarily for his portraits in oil, pastel, and watercolor. His portraits of LA residents are dated as early as 1848, but he is first recorded in N.O. during an 1856 visit. Bernard returned in Dec. 1856 to settle in N.O., supposedly at the invitation of a group of sugar planters who wanted him to paint their portraits. He worked in N.O. during the winter months and traveled as an itinerant painter in the summer. It is probable that Bernard returned to France during these travels, since his children were born there (ca. 1857 and ca. 1862). He seems to have left N.O. during the Civil War and traveled, especially around Mandeville LA where he painted local Indians. In Feb. 1867 it was reported that he had returned to the city. He taught drawing to ALEXANDRE ALAUX and advised the continuation of his studies in Europe. Bernard left N.O. for Peru (ca. 1875). Possibly François Bernard born Nîmes, France Feb. 8, 1814; studied at the Ecole des Beaux Arts at Paris and Collin; and exhibited in the Paris salon between 1842 and 1849.
References: NOCD 1866–72; NOBD 1858; *Bee*, Dec. 9, 1856, Nov. 2–3, 1859, Nov. 9, 1860, Dec. 8, 1867, Dec. 19, 1869; *D. Pic.*, Feb. 10, Mar. 22, 1857, Dec. 22, 1867, Jan. 10, 1868, Apr. 11, 1869, Nov. 6, 1870; *Present Age*, Feb. 1871, 22; *Times*, Feb. 3, 1867; *T. Pic.*, May 13, 1923, May 1, June 26, 1938; Barker, 400; Bénézit; Bruns, 310; Coulon MS; Scrapbook 100, LSM; Creole Exhibit, 10, 13; Glenk, 46, 73; Groce and Wallace; Harter and Tucker, 118; LeBreton, 385; LSM, *Annual Report for 1918*, 16; LSM, *Biennial Report for 1918*, 100–1; LSM, *Biennial Report for 1920–21*, 90; LSM, *Biennial Report for 1924–25*, 26; LSM, *Biennial Report for 1926–27*, 28; LSM, *Biennial Report for 1928–29*, 70; Mechanics' and Agricultural Fair Asso., *Report* (1869):98; Norton Art Gallery, 4; Orr; Seebold, 1:22, 29; U.S.

Census (1870), roll 521; Wiesendanger, 10–12.

BERNARD, HERBERT
Painter, active N.O. 1904–1905.
Contemporary listings: scenic artist, with LOUIS F. FETT, Greenwall Theatre (1904–1905).
References: NOCD 1905–1907, 1909–14, 1917–25, 1927–33, 1935, 1938, 1940, 1942, 1945–47, 1949; *T. Demo.*, Oct. 21, 1904.

BERNARDET, _____
Artist, active N.O. 1842.
Contemporary listings: artist, Orleans Theatre (1842).
References: NOCD 1842.

BERNINGHAUS, OSCAR E.
Born St. Louis MO Oct. 2, 1874; died Apr. 27, 1952.
Painter, illustrator, active N.O. ca. 1896.
Studied: St. Louis School of Fine Art, MO.
Awarded: St. Louis, Dolph prize (1907); share of Chicago Fine Arts Bldg. prize; Chamber of Commerce prize.
Memberships/positions: Taos Students' Association, NM.
Illustrated a souvenir packet with scenes of N.O. for the Sunset Limited Railroad (ca. 1896).
References: Fielding,*Dictionary*; THNOC 1985.27.1–.2.

BERT.
Illustrator, cartoonist, active N.O. 1884
The abbreviated name appears in five lithographic cartoons in the N.O. *Figaro* (1884).
References: *Figaro*, June 21, 1884, cover, June 28, 1884, 12, July 19, 1884, cover, 6–7, 12.

BERTIERI, MR. _____
Painter, active N.O. 1880.
Contemporary listings: scenic artist, Théâtre de L'Opéra (1880).
References: *Demo.*, Dec. 23, 1880; *D. Pic.*, Dec. 20, 1880; *D. States*, Dec. 17, 1880.

BERTON, C.
Born France ca. 1824.
Artist, active N.O. 1850.
Contemporary listings: artist (1850),

References: U.S. Census (1850), roll 235; Groce and Wallace.

BESANÇON, _____
Born Geneva, Switzerland.
Engraver, active N.O. 1842; primarily watchmaker.
Studied: with Breguet.
Contemporary listings: engraver, 105 Royal (1842).
Possibly Justin J. Besançon, in Louisville KY (1859).
References: NOCD 1842; *Bee*, Jan. 14, 1842; Groce and Wallace.

BETTZ, CHARLES
Lithographer, active N.O. 1876–77.
Contemporary listings: lithographer, with H. WEHRMANN (1876); lithographer (1877).
References: NOCD 1876–77.

BEUST, ANTON VON. *See* VON BEUST, ANTON

BEYER, FRANK D.
Painter, active N.O. 1896–99.
Contemporary listings: portraits (1896); artist (1897); portrait painter, 1210 Camp (1898); artist, 1372 Camp (1899).
References: NOCD 1896–97, 1899; NOBD 1897.

BIGOT, STEPHANIE WILKINSON (Mrs. TOUSSAINT FRANÇOIS BIGOT)
Born N.O. ca. 1816–18; died N.O. Aug. 17, 1871.
Art teacher, active N.O. 1855.
Contemporary listings: drawing and painting teacher, Ecole Supérieure (1855).
Teacher and principal in N.O. public schools (1844–70). Daughter of Gen. James Wilkinson, LA's first military governor.
References: NOCD 1846, 1850–61, 1866–70; *Bee*, Nov. 5, 1855; *Times*, Aug. 20, 1871; Jordan, "Request: La. Artists of 1800s," *T. Pic.*, Jan. 12, 1975; Castellanos, 25, 26; N.O. Death Certificate (1871), 52:100, NOPL; U.S. Census (1850), roll 235, (1860), roll 417.

BIGOT, THEODORE M.
Artist, active N.O. 1861–66.
Contemporary listings: artist, 203 Marais (1861, 1866).
References: NOCD 1861, 1866.

BIGOT, TOUSSAINT FRANÇOIS
Born Rennes, France 1794; died N.O.
Mar. 14, 1869.
Art teacher, sketch artist, painter,
active N.O. ca. 1816–69.
Studied: with Baron Watelet and
Jacques–Louis David, Paris, France.
Contemporary listings: drawing and
painting teacher, ACADEMIE DE DES-
SIN ET DE PEINTURE (1826); drawing
and painting teacher, ACADEMIE DE
DESSIN ET DE PEINTURE D'ORLEANS
(1827); professor of drawing, Central School (1827, 1830); drawing
master, 145 Ursuline (1832); drawing master, Ursuline Academy
(1834–35); professor of the primary
and drawing schools (1841); co–director, Gratuitous School (1842);
professor of drawing, public school
(1843–44); teacher of drawing, NEW
ORLEANS DRAWING & PAINTING ACAD-
EMY (1845–46); drawing professor,
43 St. Philip (1846); portrait painter,
39 St. Philip (1849); drawing master,
39 St. Philip (1850); drawing master,
143 St. Philip (1851–52); drawing
master, Canal betw. Villere and Marais (1853).
Exhibited: Cosmorama, cor. Orleans
and Bourbon (1826–27).
Landscape, history, and portrait
painter. Before coming to N.O. (ca.
1816), Bigot taught at the "écoles de
marines" of France, according to the
Argus (June 1, 1826). In N.O. he exhibited paintings and opened a drawing and painting academy (1826–27);
became professor of the primary and
drawing departments of the central
public school, located in the old Ursuline Convent (1827–41); and continued to serve as drawing master for
the public schools of the first municipality until 1845. He then advertised
a private drawing and painting academy which operated at various lo-
cations through 1853. Apparently he
visited CA in the 1850s; he, or perhaps one of his children, probably
painted the five LA scenes attributed
to "C. E. Bigot" in Mississippi Panorama. His wife, STEPHANIE WILKIN-
SON BIGOT, was also an art teacher
and artist.

References: NOCD 1827, 1830,
1832, 1834–35, 1841–44, 1846,
1849–54, 1857–58; Argus, Mar. 20,
June 1, 1826, Feb. 16, 1827; Bee,
May 30, 1836, Mar. 17, 1869; Cour-
ier, Apr. 6, May 1, 1827, June 10,
1841, July 2, 1842, Nov. 10, 1845;
D. Pic., May 17, 1897; Jordan, "Re-
quest: La. Artists of 1800s," T. Pic.,
Jan. 12, 1975; Castellanos, 25–26;
Creole Exhibit, 9; Fulton and Tole-
dano, "Landscape Painting," 504–5;
Glenk, 73; Groce and Wallace; N.O.
Death Certificate (1869), 44:432,
NOPL; Rathbone, Mississippi Pano-
rama, 54–57; Toledano, "Marine
Painters," 874–75; U.S. Census
(1840), roll 132, (1850), roll 235.

BILDSTEIN, FRANÇOIS
Born Nancy, France ca. 1856; died
N.O. Aug. 10, 1935.
Illustrator, lithographer, engraver,
commercial artist, active N.O. 1883–
1930.
Contemporary listings: artist, Mascot
(1885); BILDSTEIN & HOFFMAN, and
artist, Mascot Publishing Co. (1887);
designer, Mascot Publishing Co.
(1888); mgr., PHOTO–ENGRAVING CO.
(1893–1905); NEW ORLEANS ENGRAV-
ING AND ELECTROTYPE CO., LTD.
(1906); secy., New Orleans Engraving and Electrotype Co., Ltd. (1907–
10); pres. and mgr., New Orleans
Engraving and Electrotype Co., Ltd.
(1911–18).
Moved to N.Y.C. from France (1881)
and then to N.O. (ca. 1883). His name
appeared on the masthead and illustrations in the Mascot (1883–95) and
on illustrations and cartoons in Figaro (1884) and the Jolly Joker
(1899). Founder of the New Orleans
Engraving and Electrotype Co., Ltd.,
he served as its president until 1923,
after which he became superintendent of the French Hospital in N.O.
until 1928.
References: NOCD 1885, 1887–
1927, 1929–31, 1933, 1935; D. Pic.,
Sept. 1, 1901, Sept. 1, 1902, Mar.
28, 1905; Figaro, Mar. 29–June 28,
1884 (illus.); Jolly Joker, Sept. 1,
1899, cover; Mascot, Oct. 6, 1883–
Feb. 2, 1895, masthead; T. Pic., Aug.

11, 13, 1935; *Wkly. Pelican*, Nov. 12, 1887; Kendall, *History*, 2:843.

BILDSTEIN & HOFFMAN
Engravers, active N.O. 1887; FRANÇOIS BILDSTEIN, GEORGE B. HOFFMAN, partners.
Contemporary listings: engravers, Mascot office (1887).
Name appeared on the masthead of the *Mascot* (1887–95), probably as the engravers.
References: *Mascot*, Oct. 15, 1887, masthead, 6; Nov. 5, 1887–Feb. 2, 1895, mastheads.

BILFELDT, JEAN JOSEPH
Born Avignon, France Dec. 31, 1792; died Paris, France ca. 1849.
Painter, active N.O. 1836–42.
Studied: with Pierre Raspay, France.
Contemporary listings: portrait painter, 147 Royal (1837–38); miniature painter, 64 Bienville (1841); portrait painter, artist, 64 Bienville (1842).
Exhibited: Salon, Paris (1822–44).
With AIMABLE DESIRE LANSOT, he exhibited the *Panorama of Paris*, executed by Philastre and Cambon, "scene painters to the grand opera" (*Bee*, Jan. 5, 1839). The work was displayed in St. Anthony Square, Royal, at the rear of St. Louis Cathedral.
References: NOCD 1838, 1842; *Bee*, Nov. 11, 1837, Jan. 5, 1839; *Comm. Bull.*, Dec. 18, 1841; Bénézit; Bruns, 56, 285, 310; Glenk, 73; Groce and Wallace; LSM, *Biennial Report for 1916–17*, 100; Thieme and Becker; Thompson, "Checklist"; WPA, "Lives."

BILLINGS, GEORGE F.
Born Linden MI July 30, 1870; died N.O. July 1, 1933.
Commercial artist, active N.O. 1893–1931; also photographer.
Contemporary listings: artist, with WILLIAM W. WASHBURN (1896); artist, 612 Commercial (1901); art dept. mgr., COMMERCIAL ART STUDIO (1902); artist (1903); Commercial Art Studio (1906); mgr., Commercial Art Studio (1907–1908).
Came to N.O. (1893) where he worked in various art and photographic studios until 1931.

References: NOCD 1896, 1901–1903, 1906–12, 1918–33; *T. Pic.*, July 3, 1933; Orleans Parish Registrar of Voters, NOPL.

BIORSI, A. *See* BEORCI, ACHILLE

BIRCH, G.
Sketch artist, active N.O. ca. 1806.
Drew *The Seat of Mr. Duplantier near New Orleans & Lately Occupied as Headquarters by Genl. J. Wilkinson*, engraved and published by William Russell Birch in Philadelphia PA (1806). Possibly George Birch, Philadelphia landscape painter (1807–10).
References: Groce and Wallace; Huber et al., 63, 92; THNOC 1960.12.

BIRDSALL, ELMER J.
Painter, active N.O. 1902–1906.
Contemporary listings: artist (1902–1903); portrait painter, 1232 Baronne (1904); artist, 1232 Baronne (1905); artist, with Junius Garlick, 620 Commercial Pl. (1906).
References: NOCD 1902–1907.

BLACK, JOHN
Designer, active N.O. 1894–95; primarily stained glass worker.
Contemporary listings: Black and Heagy, glass, 623 Baronne (1895); glass, 623 Baronne (1896).
Came to N.O. in 1894 to open a southern branch of the stained glass factory he operated in Indianapolis IN, which made colored glass, figures, and landscapes in lead, and also produced metal sashes.
References: NOCD 1895–96; *D. Pic.*, Sept. 9, 1894.

BLACK AND WHITE CLUB
Art school, active N.O. 1887–90.
Sketch club of the ARTISTS' ASSOCIATION OF NEW ORLEANS art school.
References: *D. Pic.*, May 7, 1887, Nov. 13, 1890.

BLACKMAN, FANNIE (Mrs. Edward H. Ludlow)
Art craftsman, active N.O. 1886–87.
Studied: ARTISTS' ASSOCIATION OF NEW ORLEANS (1886); with WILLIAM J. WARRINGTON (1887).
Contemporary listings: artist, Chestnut cor. Antonine (1887).

Exhibited: Artists' Association of New Orleans (1886); William J. Warrington's studio (1887).
References: NOCD 1887; *D. Pic.*, Nov. 7, 1886; *D. States*, Oct. 12, 1887; *T. Demo.*, Nov. 8, 1891.

BLAIR, MR. _____
Painter, active N.O. ca. 1848.
Exhibited: Armory Hall (1848).
Itinerant panoramist who was commissioned to paint *Reception of Gen. Taylor at New Orleans*, which was exhibited at Armory Hall (1848). Blair later exhibited a panorama of geology and biblical history in St. Louis MO and Milwaukee WI (1852).
References: *D. Delta*, Mar. 24, 1848; *Wkly. Delta*, Mar. 27, 1848; Groce and Wallace; William Young.

BLAKELY, DOROTHY LEOTA
Born NJ; died N.O. Aug. 14, 1921.
Painter, active N.O. ca. 1918.
Exhibited: ART ASSOCIATION OF NEW ORLEANS (1918).
Reported to have moved to N.O. ca. 1909.
References: NOCD 1919–21; *T. Pic.*, Aug. 14, 1921; Art Asso., *Catalogue* (1918).

BLAKESLEY, HORACE
Born N.Y.C. Sept. 16, 1796; died Padre Island TX Oct. 7, 1867.
Sculptor, active N.O. 1853; primarily stone and marble cutter.
Contemporary listings: sculptor, cor. Girod and St. Paul (1853).
References: NOCD 1832, 1838, 1842–44, 1846, 1849–61, 1866–67; Friends of the Cabildo, *N.O. Architecture*, 3:131; Huber and Bernard, 28–29; THNOC Cemetery Survey; U.S. Census (1840), roll 133, (1850), roll 234, (1860), roll 417.

BLANCHARD, BLANCHE VIRGINIA (Mrs. Charles Milo Williams)
Born N.O. 1866; died N.O. Dec. 6, 1959.
Painter, active N.O. ca. 1884–94.
Studied: Academy of the Daughters of Charity, Emmetsburg MD; Corcoran Gallery, Washington DC (1888); with CHARLES GIROUX; with WILLIAM AIKEN WALKER.
Exhibited: Exhibit of Woman's Work, LA State Department, World's Industrial and Cotton Centennial Exposition (1884–85); Grunewald's music store (1890); NEWCOMB COLLEGE (1893); ARTISTS' ASSOCIATION OF NEW ORLEANS (1899).
Memberships/positions: Artists' Association of New Orleans (1893).
Portrait, landscape, and genre painter; also a noted harpist, vocalist, actress, and poet. After her schooling, Blanchard moved to Washington DC where she was well-known among literary and art circles there and in Baltimore. She became a protégé of Pres. Grover Cleveland and painted an official portrait of him for the White House. In N.O. she painted with and collected works by her artist friends. She admired her teacher, William Aiken Walker, and copied his genre subjects and painting style. Her husband was a prominent N.O. architect, engineer, and photographer. Their home at 1035 Carrollton attracted the leading figures in the city's art, music, and literary circles.
References: NOCD 1954–56, 1958; *D. Pic.*, Feb. 14, 1893, Apr. 23, 1894; *T. Demo.*, May 11, 1890; *T. Pic.*, Dec. 7, 1959; Delgado, *New Orleans*, items 11–12; Norton Art Gallery, 5; Soniat du Fossat, 86; Trovaioli and Toledano, 56, 58, 60–61, 83; Wiesendanger, 14–15.

BLANCHARD, VIRGINIA A.
Sketch artist, active N.O. ca. 1891–99.
Exhibited: ARTISTS' ASSOCIATION OF NEW ORLEANS (1891–92, 1899).
References: *Current Topics*, June 1891, 22; *D. Pic.*, Apr. 7, Dec. 14, 1892; AANO, *Catalogue* (1899); Trovaioli and Toledano, 58.

BLANCQ, HENRY ARISTIDE
Born N.O. July 18, 1878; died N.O. June 22, 1966.
Artist, active N.O. 1900–1905.
Contemporary listings: scenic artist (1900–1901, 1903); artist (1902, 1905).
Listed with the U.S. Customs Service (1906–47).
References: NOCD 1896–1933, 1935, 1938, 1940, 1942, 1945–47, 1949, 1952–56, 1958, 1960; *T. Pic.*,

June 23, 1966; Orleans Parish Registrar of Voters, NOPL.

BLANJEAN, L. EDWARD (E. J.)
Art teacher, active N.O. ca. 1889.
Contemporary listings: French and drawing teacher, A. S. Leche's Graded Institute for Boys (ca. 1889).
References: NOCD 1886–88; NOBD 1889.

BLELOCK & CO.
Lithographers, active N.O. 1866–68; primarily stationers; William H. Blelock, G. H. Blelock, A. Eyrich, C. S. W. Titcomb, partners.
Contemporary listings: stationers and news dealers, 130 Canal (1866–68).
Lithographed and published the portrait *Jefferson Davis* (ca. 1862–68).
References: NOCD 1866–68; *D. Pic.*, Feb. 4, 1866; Harry Peters, *America on Stone*; THNOC 1954.22.

BLETHEN, GRACE (Mrs. James Frederick Dunn)
Born Minneapolis MN May 16, 1885; died N.O. Sept. 22, 1970.
Art craftsman, active N.O. ca. 1908–1939.
Studied: NEWCOMB COLLEGE (1900–1908).
An art craftsman at Newcomb College (1908–1909); listed as an artist in 1939.
References: NOCD 1931, 1935, 1954–56, 1958, 1960–62, 1964–69, 1971; *T. Pic.*, Sept. 24, 1970; Orleans Parish Registrar of Voters, NOPL; Ormond and Irvine, 151; Poesch, *Newcomb Pottery*, 97.

BLIGNY, LOUIS M.
Born France ca. 1828.
Sculptor, active N.O. 1870–84; primarily carver.
Contemporary listings: sculptor (1870, 1882–84); wood carver, 68 St. Peter (1871).
With PETER B. PETIT, carved a statue, *Madonna and Child* (1872).
References: NOCD 1871–74, 1882–84, 1886–95; Arthur, *LSM Guide Book*, 99; Glenk, 97, 229; U.S. Census (1870), roll 521.

BLITH, JAMES W.
Born Scotland ca. 1844.
Artist, active N.O. 1880.
Contemporary listings: artist (1880).

References: U.S. Census (1880), roll 463.

BLOCK, MRS. M.
Sculptor, active N.O. ca. 1870.
Awarded: Grand State Fair, best and largest display of wax work (1870).
References: NOCD 1866–67; Mechanics' and Agricultural Fair Asso., *Report* (1870):28.

BLOHORN, JOHN
Painter, active N.O. 1908.
Partner with HENRY STANG in SOUTHERN ART COMPANY.
References: NOCD 1908.

BLONDELET, JEANNE
Artist, active N.O. 1872.
Contemporary listings: artist (1872).
References: NOCD 1869, 1871–72.

BLOOD, HANNIBAL S.
Born Lake George NY ca. 1810–13; died N.O. Apr. 10, 1873.
Sketch artist, active N.O. ca. 1847.
Arrived in N.O. ca. 1837; later listed as a steamboat captain, agent, and grocer. Three of his sketches of steamboats were published by FISHBOURNE's Lithography (ca. 1847).
References: NOCD 1846, 1849–61, 1866–67, 1870–73; *D. Pic.*, Apr. 11, 1873; Anglo–American Art Museum, *Sail and Steam*, item 7; Friends of the Cabildo, *250 Years*, 39, 52; Rathbone, *Mississippi Panorama*, 162–63; U.S. Census (1860), rolls 415–17.

B. BLOOMFIELD & CO.
Lithographers, engravers, active N.O. 1874; primarily stationers, printers; Benjamin Bloomfield (born N.O. ca. 1824–25; died Opelousas LA Mar. 17, 1903), Thomas M. Anderson, partners.
Contemporary listings: lithographers, engravers, 47 Chartres (1874).
References: NOCD 1868, 1875–77; *Bee*, Sept. 10, 1874; *Repub.*, Dec. 23, 1874; *T. Demo.*, Mar. 18, 1903; U.S. Census (1860), roll 415.

BLOOMFIELD, JAMES
Painter, designer, active N.O. 1897; also stained glass worker.
Contemporary listings: design and painting, NEW ORLEANS ART GLASS COMPANY (1897).

Exhibited: ARTISTS' ASSOCIATION OF NEW ORLEANS (1897).
Designed and executed stained glass for St. Patrick's Church.
References: *D. Pic.*, Mar. 30, 1897; *Men and Matters*, Sept. 1897, 55; AANO, *Catalogue* (1897); Davies, 55.

BLOOMFIELD & STEEL
Lithographers, engravers, active N.O. 1867; primarily stationers, printers; Benjamin Bloomfield (born N.O. ca. 1824–25; died Opelousas LA Mar. 17, 1903), Edgar Steel, partners.
Contemporary listings: lithographers, engravers, 60 Camp (1867).
References: NOCD 1860–61, 1866–68; *Repub.*, Apr. 11, 1867; *T. Demo.*, Mar. 18, 1903.

BLOWER, PHILIP
Born ca. 1770–80.
Engraver, active N.O. 1834–35.
Contemporary listings: engraver, 211 St. Charles (1834–35).
References: NOCD 1834–35; U.S. Census (1830), roll 45; WPA, "Lives."

BLUM, MRS. STANFORD KOHN
Painter, active N.O. ca. 1915.
Exhibited: ART ASSOCIATION OF NEW ORLEANS (1915).
References: Art Asso., *Special Exhibition*.

BLUMENSCHEIN, ERNEST LEONARD
Born Pittsburgh PA May 26, 1874.
Illustrator, painter, active N.O. 1898.
Studied: Cincinnati Art Academy; Art Students League, N.Y.C.; with Jean–Paul Laurens and Collin, Paris, France.
Memberships/positions: Association of American Artists, Paris; Salmagundi Club, N.Y.C.
Illustrator whose work appeared in *Scribner's* and other American magazines. Blumenschein probably visited N.O. during the 1898 carnival season on an assignment to draw the scenes published in *Harper's Weekly* (May 12, 1898). His paintings of American Indian life were exhibited at the DELGADO MUSEUM OF ART in 1930.
References: *T. Pic.*, Feb. 3, 1930; Bénézit; Norman Walker, 249, 253–54.

BLYTHE, WILSON
Artist, active N.O. 1884.
Contemporary listings: artist (1884).
References: NOCD 1884.

BODMER, KARL
Born Reisbach, Switzerland Feb. 6, 1809; died Barbizon, France Oct. 30, 1893.
Painter, active N.O. 1833–34.
Studied: with his uncle, Johann Jakob Meyer, Paris; with Cornu, Paris (1831).
After arriving in Boston July 4, 1832, on an expedition with amateur naturalist Prince Alexander Philip Maximilian of Weid–Neuweid, Germany, they traveled along the Missouri River where Bodmer painted landscapes and Indians. Bodmer came to N.O. alone in Dec. 1833 and stayed until Jan. 1834, painting full–length portraits of Choctaw Indians. When he rejoined Maximilian in 1834, they returned to Europe where Maximilian's journal, illustrated with Bodmer's drawings, was published.
References: Anglo–American Art Museum, *Sail and Steam*, item 6; Curry, 33, 185; Ewers, 76–97; Groce and Wallace; McCracken, *Portrait*, 72–76; Rathbone, *Westward*, 72, 96–97, 274; WPA, "Lives."

BOEDEWIG, GEORGE
Colorer, active N.O. 1886.
Contemporary listings: artist, 205 Canal (1886).
He colored enlarged photos in India ink, pastel, and watercolors.
References: *T. Demo.*, Mar. 23, 1886.

BOEHLER, EMILE R.
Born N.O. ca. 1846; died N.O. Nov. 8, 1902.
Lithographer, painter, designer, active N.O. 1872–1902; also draftsman, printer.
Contemporary listings: with JOHN E. BOEHLER (1872); lithographer, 128 and 130 Exchange Al. (1873); lithographer (1878, 1887–89, 1891–93, 1895); lithographer, BOEHLER & TUTTLE (1881); lithographer, 68 Camp (1883–84); lithographer, 17 Commercial (1885); lithographer, 517 Customhouse (1890); artist

(1896, 1898, 1900–1902); artist, 2539 Customhouse (1897, 1899); portrait painter, 2539 Customhouse (1898).

Also drew the plates for the pageants of several carnival organizations. Son of CAPT. JOHN E. BOEHLER; brother of JOHN E. BOEHLER, JR.

References: NOCD 1869–70, 1872–81, 1883–93, 1895–1903; NOBD 1898; *D. Pic.*, Nov. 9, 1902; *Repub.*, Sept. 2–3, 4, 10–11, 1870, June 11, Aug. 9, 1872; U.S. Census (1870), roll 521.

BOEHLER, CAPT. JOHN E.
Born Baden, Germany ca. 1811–17. Lithographer, active N.O. 1840–75; also printer.

Contemporary listings: lithographic printer (1840); lithographic printing office, 134 Chartres (1841); lithographer, 276 Bourbon (1846); lithographer, 27 Exchange Al. (1849–52); lithographer, 116 Exchange Pl. (1853–57); lithographer, 115 and 116 Exchange Pl. (1858); lithographer, 115 Exchange Pl. and 118 St. Louis (1859); lithographer, 115 Exchange Pl. (1860); lithographer, 117 Exchange Pl. (1861, 1865–66); lithographer, 30 Camp (1867); lithographer, 115 and 117 Exchange Pl. (1868–70); lithographer, 93 and 115 Exchange Al. (1871); lithographer, 128 and 130 Exchange Al. (1872–73); lithographer, 130 Exchange Al. (1874–75).

Awarded: Grand State Fair, best lithography (1867), best colored lithograph and best desplay of lithographic views (1868).

Lithographed sheet music covers (1866–67) for the N.O. music publisher Louis Grunewald. Father of EMILE R. BOEHLER and JOHN E. BOEHLER, JR.

References: NOBD 1857–58; *Bee*, May 27, 1854, Sept. 16, 1876; *Courier*, July 18, 1840; *D. Crescent*, Jan. 22, 1866; *D. Pic.*, Jan. 19, 1868; "Crescent Hall Polka," "Grunewald's Latest Publications," Sheet Music Collection, THNOC; Groce and Wallace; Mechanics' and Agricultural Fair Asso., *Report* (1867):27,

(1868):40, 42; THNOC 1966.81, 1984.11.10, 59–202–L; THNOC Cemetery Survey; U.S. Census (1850), roll 235, (1870), roll 521.

BOEHLER, JOHN E., JR.
Born N.O. ca. 1854–56; died N.O. Aug. 30, 1920.

Lithographer, active N.O. 1880–89; also printer.

Contemporary listings: lithographer (1880–81, 1889).

Son of CAPT. JOHN E. BOEHLER; brother of EMILE R. BOEHLER.

References: NOCD 1870, 1872–73, 1875–78, 1881–83, 1885–86, 1888–89, 1891–96, 1898–1918, 1920; *Item*, Aug. 30, 1920; U.S. Census (1870), roll 521, (1880), roll 462.

BOEHLER & TUTTLE
Engravers, active N.O. 1881; EMILE R. BOEHLER, CHARLES F. TUTTLE, partners.

Contemporary listings: engravers, 26 Commercial (1881).

References. NOCD 1881.

BOESEL, GEORGE J.
Born N.O. ca. 1886; died N.Y.C. Nov. 11, 1951.

Painter, active N.O. 1905–27.

Contemporary listings: artist (1905, 1909); scenic artist (1908).

Also listed as artist (1927).

References: NOCD 1905, 1908–1909, 1927; *T. Pic.*, Nov. 15, 1951.

BOGER, FREDERICK
Born Baltimore MD Oct. 12, 1856 or 1857; died Cincinnati OH Oct. 12, 1940.

Painter, sketch artist, active N.O. ca. 1875–90; also photographer.

Studied: with Frank Duveneck, Cincinnati OH.

Contemporary listings: artist, T. FITZWILLIAM & CO. (1888–89).

Exhibited: Savannah GA (1911).

Memberships/positions: Cincinnati Art Club.

Tutored in art as a youth in Baltimore, Boger came to N.O. (ca. 1875) to pursue a career in art. He worked in oil, watercolor, pastel, and pencil. At times, Boger booked passage on a riverboat to sketch passengers' portraits in pencil. His career as an

artist was primarily in Cincinnati (ca. 1890–1936). He exhibited at the Clauson Galleries, Cincinnati (1920s).
References: NOCD 1888–89; Bénézit; Fielding, *Dictionary*; Information courtesy Miss Barbara Boger, Dec. 13, 1986; THNOC 1987.3.1–.14.

BOGLE, ROBERT
Born Georgetown SC ca. 1817–20.
Painter, active N.O. 1844.
Contemporary listings: portrait painter, oppos. Verandah Hotel, St. Charles (1844).
Exhibited: Washington Armory (1844–45); Armstrong's Exchange (1851).
Itinerant portrait painter who worked with his twin brother James in N.Y.C. (1840), Charleston (1840–41, 1843), and Baltimore (1842). Robert Bogle came to N.O. in 1844 to work as a portrait painter and to exhibit two large narrative paintings which the brothers had executed in 1840 and had exhibited throughout the country for sale. The paintings were again on view and offered for sale in N.O. in Nov. 1845 and in Feb. 1851, but neither artist was in the city. Robert Bogle continued to travel, to SC, MD, and Washington DC.
References: *D. Pic.*, Jan. 7, 1844; *D. Delta*, Feb. 5, 1851; *Wkly. Delta*, Nov. 17, 1845; Bruns, 45, 310; Groce and Wallace.

BOH, JOHN P.
Born LA Apr. 18, 1854; died N.O. Mar. 24, 1927.
Sculptor, active N.O. 1870–89; also carver.
Contemporary listings: apprentice sculptor (1870); apprentice with LOUIS M. BLIGNY (1872); wood carver, PETIT & BOH (1886–87); wood carver and sculptor, PETIT & BOH (1888–89).
References: NOCD 1872–73, 1880–1920, 1922–27; *T. Pic.*, Mar. 26, 1927; Orleans Parish Registrar of Voters, NOPL; U.S. Census (1870), roll 521.

BOHHURD, EMILE
Born N.O. ca. 1846.
Engraver, active N.O. 1860.

Contemporary listings: engraver (1860).
Son of G. A. BOHHURD.
References: Groce and Wallace; U.S. Census (1860), roll 421.

BOHHURD, G. A.
Born Baden, Germany ca. 1810.
Lithographer, active N.O. 1860.
Contemporary listings: lithographer (1860).
Father of EMILE BOHHURD.
References: Groce and Wallace; U.S. Census (1860), roll 421.

BOHM, LOUIS, JR.
Born N.O. ca. 1869.
Painter, active N.O. 1886.
Contemporary listings: asst. scenic artist, St. Charles Theatre (1886).
Probably brother of ROBERT W. BOHM.
References: NOCD 1886; *D. Pic.*, Jan. 13, 1903.

BOHM, ROBERT W.
Born N.O. Jan. 1868; died N.O. June 2, 1901.
Painter, active N.O. 1885–1901.
Contemporary listings: painter (1885–86, 1899); scenic artist (1886, 1898, 1900); scenic artist, Academy of Music (1888); artist, St. Charles Theatre and Academy of Music (1889–90); artist, Bidwell's Theatres and People's Theatre (1891); scenic artist, St. Charles Theatre (1892); scenic artist, French Opera House (1896); artist (1901).
In 1886 Bohm formed a partnership with ROBERT STRUVE, which lasted until the latter's death in 1900. They painted scenery for N.O. and Mobile AL theaters and scenery and other artwork for N.O. carnival parades, including the unique 1900 electrical parade of the Krewe of Nereus. Bohm worked with EMILE NIPPERT and CLARK COX or FRANK COX in painting curtains at the French Opera House (1896). Probably brother of LOUIS BOHM, JR.
References: NOCD 1885–86, 1888–93, 1898–1901; *D. Pic.*, June 3, 1901; *D. States*, Oct. 1, 1888, Feb. 19, 1900; *Lantern*, Nov. 10, 1886, 6; *Mascot*, Sept. 19, 1891, 4; *T. Demo.*, Sept. 22, 1896; La Cour, 203; U.S. Census (1900), roll 573.

BOHUNEK, RUDOLF
Born Bohemia ca. 1875.
Painter, etcher, active N.O. ca. 1909–13.
Studied: School of Art, Prague.
Contemporary listings: portrait and history painter, etcher, 940 Gravier (1909); portrait painter, etcher, 921 Canal (1910).
Exhibited: 940 Gravier (1909); ART ASSOCIATION OF NEW ORLEANS (1910).
Memberships/positions: Royal Imperial Academy, Prague.
Came to the U.S. in 1907; left N.O. (ca. 1911–13) to return to Prague. After coming back to the U.S., he opened an art school in Chicago.
References: NOCD 1910; D. States, Feb. 20, 1909; Art Asso, Catalogue (1910); Bruns, 55, 310; Glenk, 40, 48, 51; LSM artists files; U.S. Census (1910), roll 525; WPA, "Notes," 77.

BOILEAU, LOUIS
Born Switzerland ca. 1821; died N.O. Nov. 20, 1851.
Painter, active N.O. 1850–51.
Contemporary listings: portrait painter (1850–51).
Arrived in N.O. ca. May 1850 from Havre, France.
References: Louisiana Charity Hospital, Death Records, NOPL.

BOIS, WILLIAM
Artist, active N.O. 1882–84.
Contemporary listings: artist (1882–84).
References: NOCD 1882–84.

BOISSEAU, ALFRED L.
Born Paris, France, Feb. 28, 1823.
Painter, art teacher, art dealer, active N.O. 1845–46; also photographer.
Studied: with Paul Delaroche, Paris.
Contemporary listings: portrait painter, 102 and 104 Royal (1845); portrait painter, 104 Royal (1846).
Exhibited: Salon, Paris (1842–48); National Academy of Design, N.Y.C. (1849); American Art Union, N.Y.C. (1852).
Itinerant portrait and genre painter. Boisseau worked in N.O. (1845–46) and later exhibited two paintings with LA subjects at the 1848 Paris salon; La Creole and Marche d'Indiens de la

Louisiane. He probably returned to LA since three portraits of LA residents (dated 1849, 1859, and 1865 respectively) were signed by him. Boisseau advertised in Cleveland in Dec. 1852 and Jan. 1853 as a portrait and landscape painter, teacher of drawing and painting, and art dealer, and in 1855 as a daguerrean; he was in that city as late as 1859.
References: NOCD 1846; Bee, Jan. 3, Dec. 22, 1845; Jordan, "Painting Has Puzzle to It," T. Pic., July 11, 1976; Anglo–American Art Museum, Catalogue, plate 4; Anglo–American Art Museum, Louisiana Landscape, item 10; Bénézit; Bruns, 56, 128, 295, 310; Groce and Wallace; Montreal Museum, item 298; Rathbone, "Mississippi Panorama," 67; Rinhart, 113; Salam, 49–61; Wiesendanger, 16–17; WPA Louisiana, 164.

BOISSONNEAU, MARGUERITE
Sketch artist, active N.O. ca. 1890–99.
Studied: ARTISTS' ASSOCIATION OF NEW ORLEANS (1890).
Exhibited: Artists' Association of New Orleans (1890–91, 1894, 1896–97, 1899).
Memberships/positions: Artists' Association of New Orleans (1890).
References: NOCD 1887, 1889–93; D. States, May 16, 1890; D. Pic., Nov. 13, Dec. 17, 1890; T. Demo., Dec. 14, 1894; AANO, Catalogue (1890–91, 1896, 1897, 1899).

BONER, EDWIN R.
Artist, active N.O. 1873.
Contemporary listings: artist (1873).
References: NOCD 1871–74.

BONNECAZE, CARLOTTA MARIE
Born N.O. Mar. 22, 1887; died N.O. Mar. 5, 1930.
Art teacher, designer, active N.O. ca. 1908–13.
Contemporary listings: teacher (1908, 1911, 1913–14); drawing teacher (1913).
Designed costumes and parade floats for N.O. carnival organizations, including Proteus and Comus.
References: NOCD 1908, 1911, 1913–14, 1919–30; T. Demo., Jan.

14, 1913; *T. Pic.*, Mar. 6, 1930; Dufour, *Krewe of Proteus*, 14–15; Glenk, 211; LSM, *Biennial Report for 1920–21*, 90; Orleans Parish Registrar of Voters, NOPL.

BONNET, ANTHONY E.
Painter, active N.O. 1889–91.
Contemporary listings: painter (1889); artist (1891).
References: NOCD 1889, 1891.

BONNO, PIERRE
Sculptor, active N.O. 1832–35.
Contemporary listings: sculptor, cor. St. Ann and Dauphine (1832, 1834–35).
Cf. BONNOT, PIERRE.
References: NOCD 1832, 1834–35; Groce and Wallace.

BONNOT, PIERRE
Born France ca. 1813.
Sculptor, active N.O. 1870–72; primarily carver, also builder.
Contemporary listings: woodcarver, with Dubuc & Bonnot (1870); woodcarver (1872).
Cf. BONNO, PIERRE.
References: NOCD 1850, 1852–61, 1866–68, 1870, 1872–78; Friends of the Cabildo, *N.O. Architecture*, 3:121; U.S. Census (1850), roll 236.

BONQUOIS, OSCAR S.
Lithographer, active N.O 1884–86.
Contemporary listings: lithographer (1884); lithographer, SOUTHERN LITHOGRAPHIC COMPANY (1885); lithographer, M. F. DUNN & BRO. (1886).
References: NOCD 1880, 1884–86.

BOONE, ISAAC WILLIAM
Born PA ca. 1812.
Engraver, active N.O. 1877; also stencil cutter, jeweler.
Contemporary listings: GRAHAM & BOONE (1877).
References: NOCD 1866–67, 1870–81; U.S. Census (1860), roll 417.

BOQUETA DE WOISERI, JOHN L.
Painter, engraver, hair worker, art teacher, active N.O. 1803; also geographer, engineer.
Contemporary listings: painter, engraver, hair worker, and teacher of drawing and painting, Burgundy (1803).
Itinerant artist who announced his arrival in N.O. on May 28, 1803. He was probably in the city during the ceremonies that transferred the colony of LA from Spain to France to the U.S. during Nov.–Dec. 1803. His *A View of New Orleans Taken From The Plantation Of Marigny* (signed and dated Nov. 5, 1803) is the first known painting of N.O. as an American city. Boqueta de Woiseri probably left the city shortly after; he announced, in the Philadelphia *Aurora* (Feb. 21, 1804), his progress in printing an engraving of N.O. from his painting and of a plan of N.O. He claimed to have been in N.O. during a number of years and to have worked on the project for over six years. He also painted views of Philadelphia and Boston and made an engraving with vignettes of six American cities. He is listed in N.Y.C. (1807–11) as a painter and engraver.
References: *Moniteur*, May 28–June 4, 1803 (advs.); Philadelphia *Aurora General Advertiser*, Feb. 21, 1804; Bénézit; Davidson, *Antiques*, 20–21; Davidson, *Life in America*, 2:110; Fielding, *American Engravers*; Fielding, *Dictionary*; Groce and Wallace; Huber et al., 57, 92; THNOC 1958.41–.42; Wunderlich, 114.

BORNET, CHARLES ETIENNE
Born France ca. 1829–31.
Hair worker, active N.O. 1850–61.
Contemporary listings: hair work maker (1850); hair worker, 299 Royal (1854); hair worker, 50 Conti and 195 Bourbon (1856); ornamental hair manufacturer, 201 Bourbon (1858); hair worker, 138 Orleans (1860–61).
Son of FRANÇOIS BORNET.
References: NOCD 1854, 1856, 1860–61; NOBD 1858; U.S. Census (1850), roll 235, (1860), roll 418.

BORNET, FRANÇOIS
Born France ca. 1805.
Hair worker, active N.O. 1850–58.
Contemporary listings: hair work maker (1850); hair worker, 74 Main (1851); hair worker, 132 Burgundy (1852).
Father of CHARLES ETIENNE BORNET.
References: NOCD 1851–52, 1858; U.S. Census (1850), roll 235.

BORNET, P.
Hair worker, active N.O. 1853–54.
Contemporary listings: hair worker,
155 Chartres (1853); hair worker, 99
Chartres (1854).
References: NOCD 1853–54.
BORNET, PAUL V.
Died after Jan. 20, 1883.
Hair worker, active N.O. 1875–78.
Contemporary listings: hair worker
(1875); hair worker, 196 Canal
(1878).
References: NOCD 1870, 1873,
1875–80, 1883–84; Bee, Jan. 21,
1883.
BORRA, JH.
Art teacher, active N.O. 1845.
Contemporary listings: music and
drawing teacher, Louisiana High
School (1845).
References: Bee, Nov. 15, 1845;
Courier, Nov. 17, 1845.
BORRIE, ARMAND
Artist, active N.O. 1887.
Contemporary listings: artist (1887).
References: NOCD 1887.
BOSCH, ARCHIBALD
Born LA ca. 1892.
Commercial artist, engraver, lithog-
rapher, active N.O. 1908–11.
Contemporary listings: engraver,
DAMERON-PIERSON CO., LTD. (1908);
lithographer (1910); artist, WALLE &
CO. (1911).
References: NOCD 1908, 1911; U.S.
Census (1910), roll 524.
BOTTCHER, JOHN A.
Painter, active N.O. ca. 1823.
Exhibited: Academy of Fine Arts
(1823).
Possibly an itinerant artist, he exhib-
ited a collection of transparent paint-
ings of European views and of Na-
poleonic battle scenes at his Academy
of Fine Arts, 64 St. Ann.
References: Gazette, Dec. 25, 1823;
New Orleans City Council, Proceed-
ings, Dec. 20, 1823, NOPL; Groce
and Wallace.
BOUCHARD, ADOLPHE
Born ca. 1826–29; died St. Elmo AL
Sept. 23, 1904.
Sculptor, active N.O. 1857–61.
Contemporary listings: sculptor, 319
St. Peter (1857); sculptor in wood or

in plaster, 97 Rampart (1858); sculptor, 97 Rampart (1858–59); sculptor, St. Philip near Prieur (1859);
sculptor, 308 St. Philip (1860–61).
Advertised that he also did ship and
ornamental house work, pattern-
making, and block cuts (1858).
References: NOCD 1851–61, 1866–
69, 1871–74; NOBD 1858–59; T.
Demo., Sept. 30, 1904; Groce and
Wallace; U.S. Census (1850), roll
231, (1860), roll 418.
BOUCHER, AUGUSTUS
Born ca. 1866; died N.O. Apr. 9,
1895.
Painter, active N.O. ca.1892–94.
Exhibited: FIVE OR MORE CLUB, Tu-
lane University (1892); ARTISTS' AS-
SOCIATION OF NEW ORLEANS (1894).
References: D. Pic., Mar. 3, 1892,
Apr. 10, 1895; T. Demo., Dec. 14,
1894.
BOUCHEREAU, LIONEL SIDNEY
Born N.O. Oct. 25, 1892; died N.O.
Nov. 19, 1945.
Lithographer, active N.O. 1910–15.
Contemporary listings: can factory
lithographer (1910); lithographer
(1913–15).
References: NOCD 1911–15, 1920–
21, 1923, 1925–26, 1928–33, 1935,
1938, 1940, 1942, 1945–46; T. Pic.,
Nov. 20, 1945; Orleans Parish Re-
gistrar of Voters, NOPL; U.S. Census
(1910), roll 521.
BOUDET, DOMINIC W.
Born France; died Baltimore MD Oct.
1845.
Painter, active N.O. 1833.
Studied: with his father, Nicholas
Vincent Boudet.
Contemporary listings: portrait and
miniature painter (1833).
Exhibited: 93 Chartres (1833); National Academy of Design, N.Y.C.
(1831).
Itinerant portrait, miniature, and historical painter from Paris, who
worked with his father (1805–20) in
Richmond VA, Baltimore, Washington DC, and Philadelphia. Boudet
worked alone in Charleston SC
(1820, 1838), N.Y.C. (1825, 1827–
28, 1830–33, 1837), Frederick MD
(1833), and Baltimore (1845). He

exhibited his most famous painting, *La Belle Nature*, throughout the country, including N.O. (Dec. 1833). References: *Courier*, Dec. 24, 1833; Groce and Wallace; Lay, 401; New-York Historical Society, 920.

BOUDET, MARGARET J. *See also* ALLISON, MARIA
Painter, artist, art teacher, active N.O. 1855–60.
Contemporary listings: teacher of pencil drawing, watercolor and oil painting, and the painting of flowers, Miss Allison's Institution for Young Ladies (1855–56); teacher of drawing, oil painting, and the painting of flowers, Institution for Young Ladies (1859–60).
References: NOCD 1861; *D. Pic.*, Nov. 8, 1855–Apr. 12, 1856 (advs.), Sept. 12, 1859–Feb. 12, 1860 (advs.); Mobley, 857–58; U.S. Census (1860), roll 416.

BOUDET, NUMA H.
Born France; died before 1913.
Sculptor, active N.O. 1861–67.
Contemporary listings: sculptor, 142 Orleans (1861); sculptor, 208 Main (1866); sculptor, 71 St. Ann (1867).
References: NOCD 1861, 1866–67; *D. Pic.*, Mar. 17, 1913.

BOUDOUSQUIE, PAUL CHARLES
Born N.O. Aug. 18, 1847; died Mobile AL 1925.
Painter, lithographer, engraver, active N.O. 1866–70; primarily architect.
Studied: Spring Hill College, Mobile AL; Chaptal College of Engineers, Paris, France; drawing with Cassagne, France; painting with THEODORE SIDNEY MOISE; architecture with Jacques Nicolas Bussière de Pouilly.
Contemporary listings: artist, 93 Exchange Pl. (1869); artist, lithographer, engraver, 56 Exchange Al. (1870).
Memberships/positions: Iberville Historical Society of Mobile (1902).
Painted watercolors of N.O. buildings and sites for real estate transactions (1866–69). He was listed in the NOCD 1870 for "artistic Plans, Drawings of machinery, inventions, landscapes, views, oil paintings, lithography, engraving, etc." He left N.O. to supervise work sites along the Gulf Coast for the U.S. Engineer Department and had a long career as an instructor of drawing, painting, and penmanship at Spring Hill College, Mobile (1871–1925).
References: NOCD 1867–70; Kenny, 354–55; LSM, *Biennial Report for 1926-27*, 57; Friends of the Cabildo, *N.O. Architecture*, 4:128; Orleans Parish Notarial Archives, Plan Books; Spring Hill College, 116–18.

BOULDEN, GEORGE (Bowland)
Painter, active N.O. 1904.
Chattanooga TN artist hired to decorate with frescoes the interior of the Greenwall Theatre when it was built (1904).
References: *D. Pic.*, Oct. 20, 1904; *Item*, Oct. 20, 1904.

BOULET, ALEXANDER
Born Italy ca. 1818.
Painter, active N.O. 1850–66; also decorator.
Contemporary listings: artist painter (1850); artist, fresco and scene painter, and decorator (1851); painter, 94 St. Peter (1852); painter, 69 Chartres (1853); scenic artist, Gaiety Theatre (1855); scenic artist, Gaiety Theatre, and Spaulding and Rodgers' Amphitheatre and Museum (1856); scenic artist, Crisp's Gaiety Theatre (1857); scenic artist, St. Charles Theatre (1857–59); fresco painter and scenic artist, Varieties Theatre (1860); artist, 259 Bourbon (1861, 1866).
Exhibited: MAGNY's (1851).
Scenic artist and fresco painter, assisted by JEAN BAPTISTE ROSSI, who executed the paintings and decorations, presumably in fresco, in the newly reconstructed St. Louis Cathedral (1851). The paintings included images of Louis, King of France; the biblical quotation "Let there be light"; figures of Faith, Hope, and Charity; the four Evangelists; and St. Cecilia attended by musical figures. Designed borders enclosed the paintings, and imitation mosaic completed the decoration. The artworks were apparently re-

placed by the redecoration of the cathedral's interior by ERASME HUMBRECHT (1872–73). Boulet also worked with ANTOINE MONDELLI in painting a classically styled cenotaph for American statesmen John C. Calhoun, Henry Clay, and Daniel Webster, which was temporarily constructed for special memorial ceremonies in Lafayette Square (1852). He also painted frescoes for the remodeled interior of the St. Charles Theatre (1857), the ballroom in the Masonic Hall (1860), the hall and parlors of the Campbell mansion, cor. Julia and St. Charles (1860), and the ceiling of the Varieties Theatre (1860).
References: NOCD 1852–53, 1860–61, 1866; *Bee*, Oct. 10, 1851; *Courier*, Jan. 15, July 25, 1851; Nov. 30, 1855; *D. Creole*, Jan. 1, 8, Feb. 28, 1857; *D. Crescent*, Dec. 11, 1856, Jan. 26, 1857, Nov. 3, 1858, Nov. 26, 1859, Dec. 10, 1860; *D. Delta*, Aug. 21, 27, Dec. 9, 1851, Dec. 11, 1852, Oct. 21, 1856, July 15, Sept. 30, 1860; *D. Pic.*, Apr. 22, Nov. 4, 6, 1856, Sept. 10, 1857; *T. Pic.*, Mar. 11, 1951; Coulon MS, Scrapbook 100, LSM; Groce and Wallace; Huber and Wilson, *Basilica*, 34, 40; U.S. Census (1850), roll 235, (1860), roll 419.

BOURGOIN, AUGUSTE
Artist, active N.O. 1872.
Contemporary listings: artist (1872).
References: NOCD 1872.

BOURK, RAYMOND A.
Born N.O. Mar. 29, 1856; died N.O. Dec. 20, 1928.
Engraver, lithographer, commercial artist, active N.O. 1885–95.
Contemporary listings: engraver, T. FITZWILLIAM & CO. (1885, 1888–89); artist, T. Fitzwilliam & Co. (1886–87); lithographic artist, T. Fitzwilliam & Co. (1890–91); lithographer (1892, 1894–95).
References: NOCD 1876–77, 1879–80, 1882–92, 1894–1922, 1924–29; *T. Pic.*, Dec. 21, 1928; Orleans Parish Registrar of Voters, NOPL.

BOWA, PETER
Sculptor, active N.O. 1823.
Contemporary listings: artist in plaster of Paris, 277 Camp (1823).
References: NOCD 1823; Groce and Wallace.

BOWEN, O. F.
Painter, active N.O. 1854.
Contemporary listings: PHILLIPS AND BOWEN (1854).
References: *Semi-Wkly. Creole*, Dec. 16, 1854.

BOWER, CENEILLA. See ALEXANDER, CENEILLA BOWER

BOWERS, LAURA FLORIAN. See FLORIAN, LAURA EUGENIE

BOWES, J. V.
Painter, active N.O. 1865.
Contemporary listings: scenic artist, with LOUIS DOMINIQUE GRANDJEAN DEVELLE, Varieties Theatre (1865).
References: *D. Southern Star*, Sept. 27, 1865; *Times*, Dec. 6, 30, 1865.

BOWLING, LOUISE
Sketch artist, active N.O. ca. 1884–85.
Exhibited: World's Industrial and Cotton Centennial Exposition (1884–85).
References: Woman's Department of the World's Exposition, 157.

BOWMAN, M. J.
Painter, active N.O. ca. 1902.
Exhibited: G. MOSES and Sons (1902).
References: Moses, item 26.

BOYD, JOHN RUTHERFORD
Born Philadelphia PA 1884; died 1951.
Sketch artist, active N.O. 1909.
Studied: Pennsylvania Academy of Fine Arts, Philadelphia.
Began his career as an illustrator, then became a painter, designer, sculptor, and teacher. His works appeared in a number of major magazines. He signed a pencil drawing entitled *New Orleans Market* (1909).
References: Fielding, *Dictionary*; Hirschl & Adler Galleries, Inc. to George E. Jordan, Feb. 22, 1983.

BOYER, FREDERICK
Lithographer, active N.O. 1888.
Contemporary listings: lithographer (1888).
References: NOCD 1888.

BOYLE, CHARLES WELLINGTON
Born Lewisburg LA Mar. 9, 1861; died N.O. Feb. 9, 1925.
Art teacher, painter, restorer, active N.O. 1883–1925.
Studied: Art Students League, N.Y.C., with Robert Henri and Frank V. DuMond; with Chase (probably William Merritt Chase, N.Y.C.); with PAUL POINCY and ANDRES MOLINARY.
Contemporary listings: artist (1885, 1891); elementary class instructor, ARTISTS' ASSOCIATION OF NEW ORLEANS (1886–87); artist, 9 Commercial (1889); portrait painter, 9 Commercial (1890); drawing teacher, Artists' Association of New Orleans (1891); drawing teacher, Valence Institute (1892); prof., Home Institute (1900–1908, 1910–12).
Exhibited: LILIENTHAL's (1883); Ellis's store (1885); American Exposition (1885–86); Artists' Association of New Orleans (1886–87, 1889–92, 1894, 1899, 1901–1903); FIVE OR MORE CLUB, NEWCOMB COLLEGE (1890); Amateur Art League (1891); G. MOSES & Son (1902); ART ASSOCIATION OF NEW ORLEANS (1904, 1910–11); National Association of Newspaper Artists, Hotel Bruno (1905); Home Institute (1905–1906); Newcomb College (1905); Farish's art store (1907).
Memberships/positions: National Arts Club of New York; Southern States Art League; Louisiana State Fair, art and science committee, chairman; Artists' Association of New Orleans, secy. (1886–90, 1892).
Primarily an art teacher, Boyle was known as a painter for his N.O. views and LA landscapes; he also painted portraits. He was a founder of the SOUTHERN ART UNION (1880) and the Artists' Association of New Orleans (1885), where he taught the elementary class for some years. He also taught art at Ruston (LA) College, the Louisiana Valence Institute, Ferrels' School for Boys, and the Home Institute, the latter three in N.O. Boyle was the first curator of the DELGADO MUSEUM OF ART (1911–22) and then acted as director from 1922 until his death. His work was exhibited at the museum in a one–man show in 1919.
References: NOCD 1885–92, 1900–1908, 1910–24; Architectural Art 2(Mar. 1907):7; Art and Letters 1(Dec. 1887):227; Current Topics, Jan. 1893, 11; D. Pic., May 31, July 26, Oct. 25, 1885, Nov. 6, 1886, May 7, Dec. 17, 1887, Dec. 17, 1889, Feb. 14, Nov. 13, Dec. 17, 1890, Apr. 29, May 22, Dec. 17, 1891, Sept. 27, 1903, Mar. 20, 1905, May 12, 1907, Dec. 12, 1909, Nov. 30, 1911; D. States, Oct. 29, 1886, Dec. 17, 1890, Sept. 20, 1903; Item, Feb. 6, 1921; Lantern, Oct. 1886, 6; T. Demo., Dec. 14, 1894, Mar. 15, Dec. 28, 1908; T. Pic., Mar. 16, 1919, Feb. 10, 1925; Town Talk, July 1904, 25, Feb. 1905, 46; AANO, Catalogue (1886, 1890, 1891, 1899, 1901, 1901–1902, 1902–1903); Anglo–American Art Museum, Sail and Steam, item 19; Art Asso., Catalogue (1904, 1910, 1911); Cline, Contemporary Art, 5–6; Creole Exhibit, 14; Delgado, Catalogue of Paintings, Sculpture, 16; Glenk, 73; Lilienthal's, 7; LSU, Louisiana Artists; LSM, Biennial Report for 1928–29, 67; Scrapbook 100, 71–73, LSM; Moses, item 34; Orleans Parish Registrar of Voters, NOPL; Sutton, 86; Thompson, "Checklist"; U.S. Census (1910), roll 519; Wiesendanger, 18–19; WPA, "Lives."

BRADFORD, KATE
Sketch artist, active N.O. 1889–90.
Contemporary listings: artist (1889–90).
Exhibited: Cotton Palace, Lafayette Square (1889).
Possibly Katherine Bradford, born ca. 1860; died N.O. Nov. 22, 1943.
References: NOCD 1890; T. Demo., Feb. 19, 1889.

BRADLEY, HORACE. See GRAHAM, CHARLES

BRADY, ALICE THORNTON
Died Atlanta GA May 31, 1913.
Painter, active N.O. 1906–13.
Contemporary listings: painter, 2024 Coliseum (1913).
Exhibited: ART ASSOCIATION OF NEW ORLEANS (1910–11, 1913).

Submitted a design in the competition for a new cover of *Architectural Art & Its Allies* (1906). When her work was exhibited in N.O. in 1910–11, she was living in San José, Costa Rica.
References: *Architectural Art* 1(June 1906):9; *D. Pic.*, June 3, 1913; Art Asso., *Catalogue* (1910, 1911, 1913); THNOC Cemetery Survey.

BRAMMER, ROBERT
Born Waterford, Ireland ca. 1811; died Biloxi MS June 29, 1853.
Painter, active N.O. 1842–53.
Contemporary listings: BRAMMER & VON SMITH (1842); with THEODORE SIDNEY MOISE and JAMES HENRY BEARD (1843); landscape painter, St. Charles above Canal (1844); landscape painter, cor. Camp and Canal (1847); landscape painter (1851, 1853).
Exhibited: studio of Theodore Sidney Moise (1843).
Itinerant painter who was in Louisville KY in 1839 and 1841, the latter year with a partner, Augustus A. Von Smith. In 1842 the two artists opened a studio in N.O. as portrait painters. Although Von Smith was not listed again, Brammer returned to N.O. for extended stays over the next 10 years. He advertised as a landscape painter, especially of scenery along the American rivers, and was perhaps the earliest such specialist to live in N.O. He periodically left the city, mostly during the summer months, and visited the northern states, as well as the Gulf Coast, where he died.
References: NOCD 1842; *Comm. Times*, Nov. 25, 1847; *D. Delta*, July 3, 1853; *D. Orleanian*, Apr. 16, 1851, June 11, 16, Aug. 6, 1853; *D. Pic.*, Apr. 6, 1843, Nov. 20, 1844; *Times*, Oct. 4, 1866; Creole Art Gallery, 35; Groce and Wallace; Norton Art Gallery, 7; Sterns' Auction Co. (1916); Thompson, "Checklist"; Virginia Museum, 78, 230.

BRAMMER, T. N.
Painter, active N.O. 1860–61.
Mentioned as a landscape painter; possibly T.W. Brammer listed at 97 Exchange Pl. (1860–61).

References: NOCD 1860–61; WPA, "Lives."

BRAMMER & VON SMITH
Painters, active N.O. 1842; ROBERT BRAMMER, Augustus A. Von Smith, partners.
Contemporary listings: portrait painters, 10 St. Charles (1842).
References: NOCD 1842.

BRAND, R.
Sketch artist, active N.O. 1840.
Made a pencil sketch of Andrew Jackson, dated Jan. 8, 1840, when Jackson was in the city for the 25th anniversary of the Battle of N.O.
References: Glenk, 201; LSM, *Biennial Report for 1922–23*, 59.

BRANNAN, WILLIAM PENN
Died Cincinnati OH Aug. 9, 1866.
Painter, active N.O. 1852–53.
Contemporary listings: artist, 92 Camp (1853).
Exhibited: National Academy of Design, N.Y.C. (1847); Hall's (1852).
Portrait painter who lived in Cincinnati (ca. 1840–47) and Louisville KY (1859). Brannan went back to Cincinnati (ca. 1860) and wrote for the daily press under various assumed names, the most common of which was "Vandyke Brown." He authored two published works, *Vagaries of Vandyke Brown* (1865) and *The Harp of a Thousand Strings or Laughter for a Lifetime*.
References: NOCD 1853; *D. Times*, Feb. 18, 1852; *Appleton's CAB*; Groce and Wallace.

BRAUN, CHARLES E.
Commercial artist, active N.O. 1898.
Contemporary listings: artist, ART LITHOGRAPH CO. (1898).
References: NOCD 1898, 1900–1901, 1903, 1905–23, 1925–26.

BRAUN, HENRY AUGUST
Born N.O. Aug. 5, 1869; died N.O. Jan. 4, 1939.
Lithographer, active N.O. 1889–1918; also printer, pressman.
Contemporary listings: lithographer (1889, 1891–92, 1896–1901, 1903–1905, 1908, 1910–12, 1914–17); lithographic printer, WALLE & CO., LTD. (1906); lithographic pressman, Walle & Co., Ltd. (1907); lithogra-

pher, Walle & Co., Ltd. (1912, 1915–16).

Son of JOSEPH BRAUN; brother of WILLIAM J. BRAUN.
References: NOCD 1889–93, 1896–1901, 1903–23, 1925–26, 1928, 1931–33, 1938; *T. Pic.*, Jan. 5, 1939; Orleans Parish Registrar of Voters, NOPL; U.S. Census (1910), roll 520.

BRAUN, JOSEPH
Died before 1939.
Lithographer, active N.O. 1885; also pressman.
Contemporary listings: lithographer (1885).
Father of HENRY AUGUST BRAUN and WILLIAM J. BRAUN.
References: NOCD 1885–86; *T. Pic.*, Jan. 5, 1939.

BRAUN, LOUIS. *See* LOHR, AUGUST

BRAUN, WILLIAM J.
Lithographer, active N.O. 1891–99; also pressman, printer.
Contemporary listings: lithographer (1891–92, 1897–99).
Son of JOSEPH BRAUN; brother of HENRY AUGUST BRAUN. *Cf.* BROWN, WILLIAM J.
References: NOCD 1889, 1895, 1897–99.

BREEN, JOHN
Born Ireland ca. 1820.
Painter, active N.O. 1870; also ornamental painter, glazier.
Frescoed the gentlemen's parlor at the St. Charles Hotel (1870).
References: NOCD 1850–61, 1866–76, 1878–85; *D. Pic.*, Dec. 15, 1870; U.S. Census (1870), roll 524.

BREFLCHL, _____ (J. M. Breffeihl)
Died ca. 1839–42.
Engraver, active N.O. 1832.
Contemporary listings: engraver, 38 Conti (1832).
References: NOCD 1832, 1834–35, 1837–38, 1842; Groce and Wallace.

BREMER, CORA E.
Died N.O. Aug. 11, 1934.
Painter, active N.O. 1890–1900.
Contemporary listings: artist (1890, 1892–93, 1896–97, 1900); artist, Pine cor. Carrollton (1894).
Exhibited: SEEBOLD'S (1890); ARTISTS' ASSOCIATION OF NEW ORLEANS (1892, 1905); ART ASSOCIATION OF NEW ORLEANS (1905).
References: NOCD 1893–94, 1896–97, 1900–1901, 1904–1905, 1907, 1909–11, 1917; *D. States*, July 20, 1890; *D. Pic.*, Dec. 13–14, 1892; *T. Demo.*, Dec. 13, 1892; *T. Pic.*, Aug. 13, 1934; Art Asso., *Catalogue* (1905); Arts Exhibition Club, 16; Thompson, "Checklist."

BREMER, FREDRIKA
Born Abö, Finland Aug. 17, 1801; died Arsta, Sweden Dec. 31, 1865.
Painter, sketch artist, active N.O. 1854.
Noted Swedish novelist, reformer, and champion of women's rights, who sketched and painted in N.O. during a visit to the U.S.
References: Bremer, 2:209–10; *Encyclopaedia Britannica.*

BRENNAN, JOSEPH
Painter, active N.O. 1857.
Mentioned as a landscape painter.
References: WPA, "Lives."

BRENNAN, MICHAEL
Engraver, active N.O. 1866–74.
Contemporary listings: engraver, Tonti near Main (1866); engraver (1874).
References: NOCD 1866, 1874.

BRES, SELINA ELIZABETH (Mrs. William Benjamin Gregory)
Born N.O. Jan. 1, 1870; died Neuilly–sur–Seine, France Nov. 6, 1953.
Art craftsman, active N.O. 1896–1935.
Studied: with ELLSWORTH WOODWARD (1884); TULANE FREE DRAWING CLASSES (1886–87); NEWCOMB COLLEGE (graduated 1896; 1896–1902).
Contemporary listings: Art craftsman, Newcomb (1908–1909).
Exhibited: ARTISTS' ASSOCIATION OF NEW ORLEANS (1897).
Memberships/positions: Le Petit Salon.
Bres was a member of the first class at Newcomb College in pottery decoration (1895), which became her specialty; she reportedly sold the first piece of Newcomb pottery. She continued at Newcomb as a student and art craftsman through 1910 and also

studied voice and piano. Bres was listed as an artist in the NOCD 1924–35 and exhibited during that time at the Artist's Guild and the Arts and Crafts Club, the latter which, as a charter member, she helped to organize. She is credited with the publication of the first souvenir postcard in the South. Mother of renowned N.O. sculptor Angela Gregory.
References: NOCD 1912–15, 1917, 1919–20, 1922, 1924–25, 1929–30, 1932–33, 1935, 1945–47, 1949, 1952–53; *D. States*, Jan. 23, 1898; *Item*, Apr. 16, 1921; *Item–Trib.*, Feb. 26, 1933; *States*, Nov. 7, 1953; *T. Pic.*, Feb. 29, 1924, Feb. 26, 1933, Nov. 7, 1953; AANO, *Catalogue* (1897); Foote, 26; Friends of the Cabildo, *N.O. Architecture*, 3:inside cover; Newcomb College, 8–10; Orleans Parish Registrar of Voters, NOPL; Ormond and Irvine, 33, 152; Poesch, *Newcomb Pottery*, 19, 20, 98; U.S. Census (1910), roll 524.

BRETON, HENRY
Hair worker, active N.O. 1875.
Contemporary listings: hairworker (1875).
References: NOCD 1875.

BRETT, JOHN A.
Born N.O.; died N.O. ca. 1888.
Painter, active N.O. 1873.
Painted a diorama of N.O., including a picture of the federal fleet as it came up the river in 1862.
References: NOCD 1874–78, 1880–81, 1884, 1880–95, *D. Pic.*, Feb. 28, 1895; *Repub.*, May 28, 1873.

BRETTE, JULES
Born Autun, France ca. 1830–32; died N.O. Apr. 6, 1894.
Art teacher, painter, active N.O. 1852–53.
Studied: with Horace Vernet.
Contemporary listings: proprietor, NATIONAL DRAWING ACADEMY (1852–53).
Brette arrived in N.O. in 1852 with a troupe to perform as a singer at the French Opera House. He remained in the city, opening a drawing and painting academy; subsequently he became the owner of a popular school for young women where he was listed

as a French teacher (1855–61). From 1864 to 1894, he was a money–broker and stockbroker.
References: NOCD 1855–61, 1866–67, 1869–94; *D. Crescent*, Apr. 18, 1853; *D. Delta*, Feb. 20, 1853; *D. Pic.*, Dec. 28, 1852, Jan. 9, 30, Feb. 1, 1853, Aug. 7, 1891, Apr. 7, 1894; Groce and Wallace; N.O. Death Certificate (1894), 106: 72, NOPL; U.S. Census (1860), roll 417.

BREWER, GEORGE ST. P.
Born England Mar. 1814; died St. Louis MO Dec. 26 or 28, 1852.
Painter, active N.O. 1850.
Exhibited: Armory Hall (1850).
Itinerant panoramist who arrived in the U.S. (ca. 1830s) and lived in IL, MO, and KY. His most famous work was a panorama that included views of the Mammoth Cave, Niagara Falls, the Nile River, and other natural wonders. From 1848 to 1851 he exhibited it in Louisville KY, Philadelphia, N.O. (1850), Cincinnati, and Boston.
References: *Courier*, Jan. 9, 1853; *D. Crescent*, Jan. 28, Mar. 2, 1850; *D. Delta*, Jan. 22, 29, Feb. 11, 1850; *Wkly. Delta*, Jan. 20, 1850; Bruns, 278, 310; Groce and Wallace; McDermott, *Lost Panoramas*, 15.

BREWSTER, EDMUND
Born ca. 1784–94.
Painter, engraver, active N.O. 1819–24.
Contemporary listings: portrait painter, 18 Customhouse (1819); engraver (1821); engraver and portrait painter, 16 Conti (1822); engraver and portrait and miniature painter (1823); portrait painter, 93 Chartres (1824).
Exhibited: Maspero's Coffee–house (1819).
Portrait and landscape painter and engraver who worked in Philadelphia (1818, 1828–49). During the interim (1819–24), Brewster was recognized in N.O. as a talented young artist, and his copy of Gilbert Stuart's Landsdowne portrait of George Washington, one of the artist's first paintings done in N.O., was purchased for the session hall of the

City Council (Apr. 1819). His bust portrait of Father Antoine de Sedella was used as a prototype for engravings he made of the celebrated N.O. priest and is one of the earliest known portraits printed in N.O. Brewster also painted a life–size portrait of *Père Antoine*, commissioned for the priest's parish church, now St. Louis Cathedral (1822).
References: NOCD 1822–24; *Courier*, Mar. 1, July 28, 1820, Feb. 18, 1824, May 11, 1829; *Gazette*, Apr. 6, 10, 1819, Mar. 13, 17, 1824; *T. Demo.*, May 8, 1904; Collier, "Portrait Is Gift of Mrs. Francis," *T. Pic.*, June 6, 1971; Dunlap, 2:173, 3:284; Glenk, 73, 229–31; Groce and Wallace; LSM, *Annual Report for 1918*, betw. 56 and 57; LSM, *Biennial Report for 1916–17*, 49; New Orleans City Council, Proceedings, Apr. 17, Nov. 24, 1821, NOPL; Harry Peters, *America on Stone*, 109; THNOC 1982.43; U.S. Census (1820), roll 32; WPA, "Lives."

BRICE, MARY B. (1. Mrs. Mary B. Prague; 2. Mrs. Albert G. Brice)
Born N.O. ca. 1830; died N.O. Mar. 12, 1923.
Painter, sketch artist, active N.O. 1866–94; also needleworker.
Studied: with WILLIAM HENRY BUCK; San Francisco (1891).
Exhibited: LILIENTHAL's (1884); ARTISTS' ASSOCIATION OF NEW ORLEANS (1887, 1894); Cotton Palace, Lafayette Square (1889); Camp St. (1891).
Awarded: Grand State Fair, best fruit painting in watercolor (1867), best specimen of Lepidoptera in watercolor (1868).
Occasional landscape, still life, and genre painter who devoted some time each year to painting and sketching from nature.
References: NOCD 1913–19, 1921–23; *D. Pic.*, Nov. 11, 1884, Dec. 29, 1887, Apr. 12, 1891; *D. States*, Jan. 23, 1898; *Times*, Dec. 3, 1866; *T. Demo.*, Feb. 19, 1889, Dec. 14, 1894; *T. Pic.*, Mar. 13, 1923; Cline, *Contemporary Art*, 6; Mechanics' and Agricultural Fair Asso., *Report* (1867):28, (1868):40; Mount, 162;

U.S. Census (1860), roll 416; WPA, "Lives."

BRIDGES, WILLIAM
Lithographer, active N.O. 1897.
Contemporary listings: lithographer (1897).
References: NOCD 1896–97.

BRIES, _____
Painter, active N.O. ca. 1867.
Decorated the library ceiling of a residence on First Street (present address 1331 First).
References: Collier, "The World of Art: Ceiling Work Found in Old House," *T. Pic.*, July 28, 1968.

BRIGGS, CHARLES L.
Painter, art dealer, active N.O. 1870–72.
Contemporary listings: picture dealer (1871–72).
Awarded: Grand State Fair, best marine painting (1870).
References: NOCD 1871–72; Mechanics' and Agricultural Fair Asso., *Report* (1870):28.

BRIGHAM, W. E.
Engraver, active N.O. 1871.
Contemporary listings: designer and engraver on wood, 106 Camp (1871).
References: *Our Home Journal*, Jan. 14, 1871, 13, Jan. 21, 1871, 24.

BRIGNONE, MICHEL J.
Born France ca. 1819.
Sculptor, active N.O. 1859–85.
Contemporary listings: sculptor, 289 Orleans (1859–60); sculptor, Tonti near Roman (1861, 1866); woodcarver (1869, 1871); sculptor on wood, 105 Liberty (1870); woodcarver, 105 Liberty (1872–73); carver, 105 N. Liberty (1874–79); carver (1880, 1884); carver, with J.E. Behan (1881); carver, 284 Magazine (1882–83); carver, with A. Samuels (1885).
References: NOCD 1859–61, 1866, 1869–85; U.S. Census (1870), roll 521.

BRINFORT, MISS _____
Art craftsman, art teacher, active N.O. 1888.
Contemporary listings: art potter and instructor in clay modeling on pottery, NEW ORLEANS ART POTTERY COMPANY (1888).

Exhibited: Exchange, Lafayette Square (1888).
References: *D. States*, Dec. 23, 1888.
BRINGHARD, MIKE
Engraver, active N.O. 1857.
Contemporary listings: engraver (1857).
References: NOCD 1857.
BRINGIER, MISS _____
Painter, active N.O. 1885–86.
Exhibited: American Exposition (1885–86).
Described as a "Creole of New Orleans."
References: Creole Exhibit, 8.
BRISBI, JULES
Sculptor, active N.O. 1868–69; also carpenter, cabinetmaker.
Contemporary listings: carver in wood, 94 Main (1868–69).
References: NOCD 1868–69, 1871–77, 1879–83.
BRISSET, EUGENE
Art teacher, lithographer, active N.O. 1821–42.
Contemporary listings: drawing teacher, school for colored children, Bourbon near Toulouse (1821); teacher and lithographic printer, 72 Bourbon (1822).
His school's curriculum, perhaps the earliest program in the South for black children, included writing, French, arithmetic, and geography, as well as drawing. In 1842, his lithographic press and stones were advertised for sale.
References: NOCD 1822, *Courier*, Dec. 8, 1842; *Gazette*, Dec. 14, 1821.
BRISTOW, HOWARD
Sketch artist, active N.O. 1861.
Made a pen–and–ink allegorical drawing, depicting health and sickness (1861).
References: *D. Crescent*, Mar. 30, 1861.
BRITON, CHARLES
Born Gothenburg, Sweden ca. May 1840; died N.O. July 1, 1884.
Lithographer, engraver, designer, active N.O. ca. 1864–84.
Contemporary listings: artist, 115 Exchange Pl. (1869); lithographer, with JOHN E. BOEHLER (1870); lithog-

rapher, 26 Commercial (1876, 1878); engraver, with ADOLPHE ZENNECK (1877); lithographer, with Adolphe Zenneck (1879); lithographer, 17 Commercial, and engraver (1880); lithographer, 17 Commercial (1881–84).
In Mexico and NY before coming to N.O. (ca. 1864), he was the first of the known carnival artists, and designed costumes and tableau floats for the principal pageants during the 1870s and the first half of the 1880s. Perhaps his most noted designs were for the costumes of the 1873 tableau of the Comus organization, *Origin of Species*, where local and national politicians were satirically lampooned by maskers dressed as Darwinian creatures. He also did work for carnival celebrations held in Cincinnati and Baltimore.
References: NOCD 1868–70, 1876–84; *D. Pic.*, July 2–3, 1884; *D. States*, July 2, 1884; *T. Demo.*, July 3, 1884; La Cour, 200; N.O. Death Certificate (1884), 85:447, NOPL; U.S. Census (1880), roll 460; Perry Young, 127, 215, plates III, V.
BROCARD, AUGUSTE
Born ca. 1802; died N.O. May 25, 1855.
Artist, active N.O. 1849–52.
Contemporary listings: artist, Johnson cor. Hospital (1849–52).
References: NOCD 1837–38, 1841–44, 1846, 1849–52, 1854–56; *Courier*, May 26, 1855; Crocc and Wallace.
BRODOWSKI, STANISLAUS CHARLES
Born France June 11, 1842; died N.O. July 22, 1910.
Sculptor, active N.O. 1884–85.
Exhibited: *Daily Picayune* office (1884); *Times–Democrat* office (1885).
Amateur wood carver who was primarily a sales clerk and warehouseman.
References: NOCD 1867–1910; *D. Pic.*, Apr. 29, 1884, July 23, 1910; *T. Demo.*, Dec. 27, 1885; U.S. Census (1860), roll 418.
BRONSON, _____
Artist, active N.O. 1852.
References: *D. Times*, Feb. 18, 1852.

BROOK, HENRY T. (Brooke, Brooks)
Born England ca. 1827.
Artist, active N.O. 1860; also printer.
Contemporary listings: artist (1860).
References: NOCD 1852–53, 1857–
61, 1866–67, 1869; U.S. Census
(1860), roll 416.

BROOK, MISS M.
Artist, active N.O. ca. 1800.
Signed two pin–prick watercolor
portraits in N.O. (ca. 1800).
References: Bishop, 159.

BROWN, CHARLES
Lithographer, active N.O. 1896.
Contemporary listings: lithographer
(1896).
References: NOCD 1896.

BROWN, DILLON HENRY
Painter, active N.O. 1859; primarily
decorator.
Came to N.O. from NY and deco-
rated the interior of the St. Charles
Hotel (1859).
References: Bee, Oct. 31, 1859.

BROWN, HENRY F.
Artist, active N.O. 1885.
Contemporary listings: artist (1885).
References: NOCD 1885.

BROWN, JOHN R.
Engraver, active N.O. 1887.
Studied: G. KOECKERT & CO. (1886).
Contemporary listings: engraver, M.
F. DUNN & BRO. (1887).
References: NOCD 1886–87.

BROWN, MRS. LEE JEFFREYS GARRETT.
See GARRETT–BROWN, MRS. LEE
JEFFREYS

BROWN, LYDIA M.
Born NY ca. 1875.
Sketch artist, painter, designer, ac-
tive N.O. ca. 1910–26.
Studied: Art Students' League,
N.Y.C.; with Frank V. DuMond, C.
Hawthorne.
Contemporary listings: artist (1910).
Exhibited: ART ASSOCIATION OF NEW
ORLEANS (1910–11, 1913–15, 1917–
18).
Memberships/positions: Artists'
Guild, treas., chairman, hanging
committee.
Portrait, genre, and landscape painter
formerly of Albany NY, who lived in
the N.O. French Quarter. She was
one of the founders of the Arts and
Crafts Club, chairman of its house
committee (1921), and designed cos-
tumes for Le Petit Théâtre du Vieux
Carré.
References: NOCD 1923–26; Item,
Jan. 16, Feb. 6, Mar. 13, June 12,
June 25, 1922; Item–Trib., Jan. 4,
1925; States, Feb. 14, 1926; T. Pic.,
Jan. 2, 1923, Jan. 25, 1937; Art Asso.,
Catalogue (1910, 1911, 1913, 1914,
1915, 1917, 1918); Art Asso., Special Exhibition; U.S. Census (1910),
roll 523.

BROWN, MISS M. S.
Sculptor, active N.O. ca. 1870.
Awarded: Grand State Fair, best
specimen of wax work (1870).
Listed as a teacher at Girls' High
School (1872–75).
References: NOCD 1872–75, 1881;
Mechanics' and Agricultural Fair
Asso., Report (1870):28.

BROWN, WILLIAM HENRY
Born Charleston SC May 22, 1808;
died Charleston SC Sept 16, 1883.
Silhouettist, active N.O. ca. 1842.
Itinerant silhouettist of portraits and
historical subjects. Brown was an engineer by profession who also worked
as an artist in the 1830s while living
in Philadelphia. He traveled across
New England and the South cutting
profiles (ca. 1841–59) and was recorded in N.O. and Natchez MS (ca.
1842). He may have been Wm. H.
Brown listed as an engineer in Algiers, in the NOCD 1842–43. During his travels, he produced silhouettes of many famous Americans: 26
of them were printed as lithographic
plates in Portrait Gallery of Distinguished American Citizens (1846).
Brown gave up his art career when
public demand waned and returned
to his original profession in 1859.
References: Jordan, "Rare Pastie
'Silhouettes' Come to New Orleans," T. Pic., Oct. 26, 1975; Jordan, "The World of Art: Rare 'Pasties' Visiting New York," T. Pic., Nov.
27, 1977; Bishop, item 258; Groce
and Wallace; Charles Hart, "Last of
the Silhouettists," 332–35; Mississippi State Historical Museum, Made
By Hand, 105–6; Sotheby, American

Folk Art, item 97; THNOC 1975.93.1–.5.

BROWN, WILLIAM J.
Lithographer, active N.O. 1884–96.
Contemporary listings: lithographer (1884, 1894, 1896).
Cf. BRAUN, WILLIAM J.
References: NOCD 1874, 1884, 1894, 1896.

BROWNE, MR. _____
Sketch artist, active N.O. 1860.
Reported in N.O. (1860) to be sketching scenery, localities, and public buildings, as illustrations to contrast the old and new sectors of the city for *Frank Leslie's Illustrated Newspaper*.
References: *D. Pic.*, July 15, 1860.

BRUGNIENS, CLAUDE
Born LA ca. 1840.
Artist, active N.O. 1870; also photographer, marble worker.
Contemporary listings: artist, with Mrs. C. Seligman (1870).
References: NOCD 1860–61, 1866, 1870–71; U.S. Census (1850), roll 234.

BRUNET, MR. _____
Sketch artist, active N.O. ca. 1880.
Raffled his crayon drawing of the late Col. Charles Didier Dreux, first LA officer killed in the Civil War, at Renaud's grocery (1880).
References: *D. States*, June 12, 1880.

BRUNET, ADRIEN
Engraver, active N.O. 1886; primarily jeweler.
Contemporary listings: engraver, 134 Royal (1886).
Created the gold prize medals for the victors of the four–oared shell race at Spanish Fort (1886).
References: NOCD 1882–85, 1887, 1891; *D. States*, July 7, 1886.

BRUNIG, GEORGE (Gottlieb)
Born N.O. ca. 1834; died N.O. Dec. 22, 1890.
Hairworker, active N.O. 1866–78; also jeweler.
Contemporary listings: artist in hair jewelry and hair worker, 118 Canal (1866–70); hair artist, with M. Scooler (1872); hair jeweler, 73 Royal (1873–75, 1878); hair braider,

with W. Kappes (1876); hair braider, 73 Royal (1877).
References: NOCD 1866–90; *Denson and Nelson*, 10; *Louisiana State Gazetteer*; THNOC Cemetery Survey.

BRUNNEL, ROBERT
Artist, active N.O. 1870.
Contemporary listings: artist, with William H. Phelps, card and sign painter (1870).
References: NOCD 1870.

BRUTTER. *See* AUDUBON, JOHN JAMES.

BUCHNER, CHARLES G.
Engraver, active N.O. 1893.
Contemporary listings: engraver, Frantz & Opitz (1893).
References: NOCD 1893.

BUCK, LAWRENCE H.
Born ca. 1865–75; died 1929.
Painter, active N.O. 1881; primarily architect.
Studied: with ANDRES MOLINARY (1881).
Exhibited: SOUTHERN ART UNION (1881).
Architect and watercolorist who practiced in N.Y.C. and Chicago. Son of WILLIAM HENRY BUCK.
References: *D. Pic.*, May 28, 1881; WPA, "Lives."

BUCK, WILLIAM HENRY
Born Bergen or Tromsøo, Norway 1840; died N.O. Sept. 5, 1888.
Painter, restorer, active N.O. 1869–88.
Studied: Boston; with ERNEST CICERI, RICHARD CLAGUE, ANDRES MOLINARY, ACHILLE PERELLI (1860).
Contemporary listings: artist, 26 Carondelet (1881–88).
Exhibited: Goupil's, N.Y.C. (1877); W. E. SEEBOLD's (1877–78, 1883–85); WAGENER's (1877–78, 1880, 1885); LILIENTHAL's (1880–81); SOUTHERN ART UNION (1881); World's Industrial and Cotton Centennial Exposition (1884–85); Creole Exhibit, American Exposition (1885–86); ARTISTS' ASSOCIATION OF NEW ORLEANS (1886–87).
Awarded: Grand State Fair, silver medals for best landscape in oil, best painting in watercolors, and best pas-

tel painting (1869), and diploma for best drawing in pastel (1870). Memberships/positions: Southern Art Union (1880–82).

Buck emigrated from Norway to Boston, where he first studied painting, and spent some time in New England. He came to N.O. (ca. 1860), and during the next 20 years, he was listed successively as a clerk, commission merchant, cotton weigher, and cotton broker. Throughout that time, he also studied with the leading artists in N.O., exhibited his work in the city, and won awards for paintings in oil, watercolor, and pastel. Around 1880, Buck left the cotton business to work full–time as an artist. He shared studios with Molinary, Perelli, and PAUL POINCY, until he moved into his own studio at 26 Carondelet. He was the popular successor to Clague as the leading landscape painter in LA. Live oak trees became his typical subject, and he traveled throughout the state painting scenes of the Teche and Attakapas regions. He also restored paintings, made pictures in cut paper, and helped to organize the Southern Art Union (1880), which he served as director (1882). He showed his works at the city's two major expositions (1884–86) and in the early exhibitions of the Artists' Association, until his death in 1888.

References: NOCD 1860–61, 1866–68, 1870, 1873–88; Art and Letters 1(Dec. 1887):211, 227; Bee, May 27, 1880, May 4, 1881, D. Pic., May 4, 1865, Apr. 11, 1869, July 22, Sept. 29, Nov. 27, Dec. 2, 1877, Mar. 24, May 26, 1881, Feb. 6, 17, 1882, Oct. 30, Nov. 30, Dec. 3, 1884, July 26, 1885, Nov. 6, 1886, Dec. 17, 29, 1887, Sept. 6, 1888; D. States, May 13, June 12, Dec. 21, 1880, Mar. 19, May 21, 25, 1883, Apr. 13, 1884, Nov. 5, 1886; Demo., Sept. 25, 1877, Nov. 24, 1878, Feb. 27, May 12, 1881; Harlequin, Oct. 25, 1899, 9, Nov. 1, 1899, 3; T. Demo., Apr. 23, July 30, 1883; Bartlett, "On the Gallery," T. Pic., Mar. 9, 1980; AANO, Catalogue (1886); Anglo–American Art Museum, Louisiana Landscape, item 18; Anglo–American Art Museum, Sail and Steam, items 19–20; Creole Exhibit, 10, 13, 18; Fulton and Toledano, "Landscape Painting," 505; Glenk, 73, 87; Lilienthal's, 5–8; LSM, Biennial Report for 1919, 27, 57; LSM, Biennial Report for 1922-23, 60; Mechanics' and Agricultural Fair Asso., Report (1869):71, (1870):28; N.O. Death Certificate (1888), 93:890, NOPL; Norton Art Gallery, 7–13; THNOC Cemetery Project; Thompson, "Checklist"; WICCE, Catalogue, 36; Wiesendanger, 20–21; WPA, "Lives."

BUCKINGHAM, J. L. R.
Engraver, commercial artist, active N.O. 1873–75.
Contemporary listings: artist, NEW ORLEANS ENGRAVING COMPANY (1873); proprietor, ZENNECK & BUCKINGHAM (1873–75).
References: NOCD 1875; D. Pic., Jan. 5, 15–16, 19, 26, Feb. 2, 9, 16, 23, Mar. 2, 9, 30, Apr. 27, 1873, Oct. 15, Nov. 6, Dec. 9, 1874; Repub., Feb. 15, 1874; Tinker, Creole City, 327.

BUCKLEY, JOHN P.
Painter, active N.O. 1885–88.
Contemporary listings: artist (1885, 1887); painter (1888).
References: NOCD 1885, 1887–92, 1897–98.

BUCKNER, KATE (Mrs. Daniel Dudley Avery)
Born N.O. Sept. 4, 1869; died Avery Island LA Jan. 9, 1968.
Painter, active N.O. ca. 1891–93.
Exhibited: ARTISTS' ASSOCIATION OF NEW ORLEANS (1891); FIVE OR MORE CLUB, Tulane University (1892–93). Probably Mrs. Avery who studied pottery at NEWCOMB COLLEGE (1895–97).
References: Current Topics, Jan. 1892, 24; D. Pic., Dec. 17, 1891, Mar. 3, 1892, Jan. 15, Feb. 14, 1893; T. Demo., Mar. 3, 1892; T. Pic., Jan. 10, 1968; AANO, Catalogue (1891); Information courtesy Mrs. Beauregard Bassich, July 2, 1986; Poesch, Newcomb Pottery, 96.

BUECHNER, DANIEL ANTON
Born N.O. June 30, 1856; died N.O. July 18, 1937.
Engraver, lithographer, etcher, commercial artist, designer, sculptor, active N.O. 1877–1937; also calligrapher.
Studied: McMicken School of Design, University of Cincinnati, with Thomas Satterwhite Noble, Benn Pittman, Lois T. Rebisso, R. Russell Whittemore, William H. Humphreys, Mattie J. Keller (1870–76).
Contemporary listings: lithographer, with HENRY KLUNG (1878); designer (1879, 1883–84); designer and lithographer, T. FITZWILLIAM & CO. (1881); engraver, T. Fitzwilliam & Co. (1885); artist, T. Fitzwilliam & Co. (1886–87); lithographer (1889, 1895, 1898–1900, 1905, 1912–13, 1915, 1917–18); engraver, 61 Camp (1891–94); lithographer, 325 Camp (1896); engraver, 325 Camp (1897); engraver (1911).
Exhibited: McMicken School of Design (1874, 1876); Ohio Mechanics Institute (1875).
Buechner moved with his family to Cincinnati (1858), where he studied art (1870–76) and first worked as a professional artist (1872–73). In 1876 he traveled down the Ohio and Mississippi rivers. In Memphis TN (1877) he is credited as that city's first lithographer when he worked for S. C. Toof and Co. Buechner reached N.O. (1877) and began his career as one of the leading lithographic artists in the city, with a brief residence in Galveston TX (1880) with M. Strickland and Co. Buechner is most often associated with designs and printing for N.O. carnival activities and has been considered a leading producer of Mardi Gras art. He was the first American artist to design a carnival ball invitation for the Rex organization (1879); he also designed the lithographs of carnival parades printed by the firm of T. Fitzwilliam & Co. where he was the premier designer and chromolithographer (1885–1918). As a commercial artist with his own studio,

Buechner made product designs for the World's Industrial and Cotton Centennial Exposition (1884–85) and for product labels for the American Can and Continental Can companies (from 1909).
References: NOCD 1878, 1885–87, 1889, 1891–1900, 1905, 1911–13, 1915, 1917–19, 1923, 1925–28, 1930, 1933; T. Pic., July 19, 1937; Buechner, Buechner.

BUHLER, VIOLA VOLCKMANN. See
VOLCKMANN, VIOLA ADELAIDE

BUJAC, ALFRED
Artist, active N.O. 1849–51.
Contemporary listings: artist, Jefferson Parish near Gretna LA (1849–50); artist, Chestnut betw. Alix and Eliza (1851).
References: NOCD 1849–51; Groce and Wallace.

BURDGE, ERNEST WATSON
Born N.O. Apr. 4, 1851; died N.O. Sept. 23, 1917.
Lithographer, active N.O. 1870–77.
Contemporary listings: lithographer, MANOUVRIER & SIMON (1870); lithographic printer, with DAVID WEIL (1871); lithographer (1876–77).
References: NOCD 1868, 1870–71, 1873–74, 1876–81, 1886–1917; T. Pic., Sept. 24, 1917.

BURGEON, ADELBERT J.
Engraver, active N.O. 1874–75.
Contemporary listings: engraver on glass, 8 St. Charles (1874–75).
References: NOCD 1874–75.

BURGER, MORTIMER M.
Cartoonist, art teacher, active N.O. 1908–12.
Contemporary listings: art mgr., cartoonist, Morning World (1908); cartoonist, Harlequin (1909); director, BURGER SCHOOL OF ART (1909–12).
References: NOCD 1908, 1910–12; Harlequin, May 27, 1909, 1, 12, June 3, 1909, 1, 10, 12.

BURGER SCHOOL OF ART
Art school, active N.O. 1909–12; MORTIMER M. BURGER, director.
Contemporary listings: 317 Carondelet (1909–12).
References: NOCD 1910–12; Harlequin, June 3, 1909, 10.

BURGESS, EMMA RUTH (Mrs. Charles R. Higbee)
Born Fall River MA ca. 1882.
Art craftsman, active N.O. ca. 1900–11.
Studied: NEWCOMB COLLEGE (1900–1902, 1904–1907).
Exhibited: ART ASSOCIATION OF NEW ORLEANS (1907).
Awarded: Newcomb College, Mary L. S. Neill Book Club medal, excellence in watercolor painting.
Came to N.O. (1900) with her uncle, ELLSWORTH WOODWARD. Specialized in embroidery on tablerunners, book covers, and wall hangings; also did metalwork, especially silver and perforated brass lampshades, and pottery designs.
References: *T. Demo.*, Jan. 6, 1907; Art Asso., *Catalogue* (1907); Ormond and Irvine, 152; Poesch, *Newcomb Pottery*, 37, 40, 98.

BURGESS, FRANK
Born LA Jan. 8, 1868.
Artist, active N.O. 1900.
Contemporary listings: artist (1900).
References: U.S. Census (1900), roll 570.

BURK, MR. _____
Painter, active N.O. 1876.
Contemporary listings: scenic artist, St. Charles Theatre (1876).
References: *Times*, Oct. 29, 1876.

BURKE, ALMA MASON. *See* MASON, ALMA FLORENCE

BURKE, G.
Engraver, active N.O. 1838.
Contemporary listings: engraver, Puff Store in the St. Charles Arcade (1838).
References: *D. Pic.*, Oct. 7, 1838.

BURKE, GEORGE F.
Born Cook County IL May 1, 1869.
Lithographer, active N.O. 1909–13; also printer.
Contemporary listings: lithographer (1909–11, 1913); lithographer, can factory (1910).
References: NOCD 1909–33, 1935, 1938, 1940; Orleans Parish Registrar of Voters, NOPL; U.S. Census (1910), roll 520.

BURKE, THOMAS B.
Born England ca. 1847.
Painter, active N.O. 1870–80; also sign painter.
Contemporary listings: BURKE & STAMP (1870–73); scenic painter, Gaiety Theatre (1875); painter (1876–80).
References: NOCD 1870–80; U.S. Census (1880), roll 456.

BURKE, MRS. V. C.
Sketch artist, active N.O. ca. 1869.
Awarded: Grand State Fair, bronze medal for best drawing in pastel, crayon, stump, or pencil (1869).
References: *D. Pic.*, Apr. 13, 1869; Mechanics' and Agricultural Fair Asso., *Report* (1869):67.

BURKE, WILLIAM. *See* NATIONAL PUBLISHING & PORTRAIT CO.

BURKE & STAMP
Painters, active N.O. 1870–73; THOMAS B. BURKE, Thomas Stamp, owners.
Contemporary listings: painters (1870); sign and fresco painters, 80 Rampart (1872); house and sign painters (1873).
References: NOCD 1870–73.

BURTHE, LEOPOLD
Born N.O. ca. 1823.
Painter, active N.O. 1850.
Contemporary listings: artist (1850).
His painting of Ophelia from *Hamlet* was selected from over 5,000 paintings by artists residing in Paris to be published in the June 1852 issue of the publication *L'Artiste*.
References: NOCD 1849–52; *D. Crescent*, Oct. 21, 1852; U.S. Census (1850), roll 232.

BUSH, JOSEPH HENRY
Born Frankfort KY ca. 1794–1800; died Lexington KY Jan. 11, 1865.
Painter, active N.O. 1831–45.
Studied: with THOMAS SULLY, Philadelphia (ca. 1814–17).
Contemporary listings: portrait painter, cor. Chartres and St. Louis (1831); portrait painter, cor. Camp and Common (1841); portrait painter, St. Charles north of Lafayette Square (1845).
Exhibited: Pennsylvania Academy of Fine Arts, Philadelphia (1815).

After studying in Philadelphia under the patronage of Henry Clay, Bush lived in Louisville KY much of his life. He spent most of the year with portrait commissions throughout KY, especially Frankfort, Lexington, and Louisville, and in Cincinnati OH. In 1831 Bush was reported in N.O. with a studio adjoining that of JAMES G. SAWKINS. During the winter months he painted portraits of planters, especially in N.O. (1831, 1841, 1845), in Baton Rouge LA (1848) where he painted Gen. Zachary Taylor, and in Vicksburg and Natchez MS (ca. 1845).

References: *Bee*, Jan. 29, 1841; *Bull Frog*, Feb. 12, 1841; *D. Pic.*, Jan. 28, 1845; *Mercantile Advertiser*, Nov. 24, 1831; *Wkly. Delta*, Mar. 13, 1848; Barker, 402; Bruns, 188, 205, 243, 310; Floyd, *Jouett–Bush–Frazer*, 83–123; Groce and Wallace; LSM, *Annual Report for 1919*, 58.

BUTLER, B. F.
Lithographer, active N.O. 1841; also printer.
Contemporary listings: lithographic printer, Exchange Al. betw. Conti and St. Louis (1841).
Possibly Benjamin F. Butler, a lithographer in N.Y.C. (1846–48) and in San Francisco (1852–59).
References: NOCD 1841; Groce and Wallace.

BUTLER, CELIA A. *See* DEL'ISLE, CELIA A. BUTLER

BUTLER, MARY WILLIAMS
Born N.O. Mar. 15, 1873; died N.O. Oct. 20, 1937.
Art teacher, art craftsman, active N.O. 1898–1937; also jeweler.
Studied: NEWCOMB COLLEGE (1898–1904); with Prof. Denman Ross, Boston (1908).
Contemporary listings: assistant teacher, Newcomb Art School (1901–1902); prof., Newcomb (1903); drawing instructor, Newcomb (1904–1905); independent designer, Newcomb (1906); assistant prof. in drawing and design, Newcomb (1907–18).
Exhibited: ART ASSOCIATION OF NEW ORLEANS (1905, 1910 11), crafts show, Newcomb (1911).

Memberships/positions: ARTS EXHIBITION CLUB (1901); Art Association of New Orleans (1910).
Continued as assistant professor in drawing and design at Newcomb College until 1934 when she was made a full professor, a position she held until her death.
References: NOCD 1903–1908, 1910–19, 1921–30, 1932–33, 1935; *Item*, Oct. 21, 1937; *T. Pic.*, Oct. 21–22, 1937; Art Asso., *Catalogue* (1905, 1910, 1911); *Arts Exhibition Club*, 16; Ormond and Irvine, 152; Poesch, *Newcomb Pottery*, 98; Radcliffe, 12; THNOC Cemetery Survey.

BYRD, HENRY
Born Ireland ca. 1805–1806; died N.O. Sept. 26, 1884.
Painter, active N.O. 1841, 1858, 1866–84.
Contemporary listings: portrait painter, Royal near Customhouse (1841); portrait painter, 4 Perdido (1841–42); portrait painter, Poydras betw. St. Charles and Carondelet (1866); painter, artist, LILIENTHAL's photographic gallery (1867); portrait painter and artist, 131 Poydras (1868); portrait painter, 1 Camp (1869–79); artist (1879–80); portrait painter, Hillary cor. Commercial (1881–83); portrait painter (1884).
Exhibited: WAGENER's (1866); WASHBURN's (1880); S. T. Blessing's gallery (1880–82).
Awarded: Louisiana State Fair, medal, best oil painting on canvas (1839).
Portrait painter who was first recorded in the U.S. in N.Y.C. (1832–38). Byrd lived in N.O. early in 1841, but moved to Little Rock AR by Aug. 1841. He worked throughout AR during the 1840s and settled with his family in El Dorado (1851–66), where he became the state's most prolific antebellum portrait painter. Byrd visited N.O. early in 1858, returning after the Civil War to make the city his home until his death (1866–84).
References: NOCD 1841–42, 1867–83; *Bull Frog*, Feb. 12, Mar. 31,

1841; *D. Pic.*, Mar. 18, 1841, Apr. 23, June 11, 1882, Sept. 27–28, 1884; *D. States*, Apr. 17, June 12, 1880; *Demo.*, Sept. 5, 1880, May 31, 1881; *Harlequin*, Nov. 1, 1899, 3; *Times*, Apr. 22, 1866, Jan. 1–10, 1867 (advs.); Boyd, 200; Bruns, 310; Fagg; Glenk, 73; Groce and Wallace; Harter and Tucker, 119; LSM, *Biennial Report for 1924–25*, 27, 57; N.O. Death Certificate (1884), 85:1055, NOPL; U.S. Census (1840), roll 133, (1870), roll 515.

BYRNE, P.
Painter, active N.O. 1830; also sign and ornamental painter.
Contemporary listings: fresco painter, 78 Dauphine and 28 Customhouse (1830).
References: NOCD 1830.

BYRNE, GERALDINE MAUBERRET. *See* MAUBERRET, GERALDINE REGIS

If you have further information about New Orleans artists (1718–present), please make it available for the artists files at the Historic New Orleans Collection.

Artist: _____

Information:

Your Name: _____

Address: _____

City, State, Zip: _____

Please pass on this order form:

_____ *Encyclopaedia of New Orleans Artists, 1718–1918* @ $39.95
_____ Shipping & handling $2.50 per book
_____ 9% tax, Orleans Parish
_____ 4% tax, Louisiana
_____ TOTAL AMOUNT DUE

☐ Check or money order   ☐ Visa   ☐ MasterCard

Exp. date: _____

Signature: _____

Name: _____

Address: _____

City, State, Zip: _____

Curatorial Division
The Historic New Orleans Collection
533 Royal Street
New Orleans, Louisiana 70130

The Shop
The Historic New Orleans Collection
533 Royal Street
New Orleans, Louisiana 70130

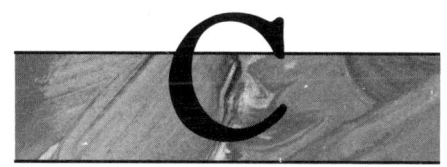

C., H. C., JR.
Sketch artist, active N.O. ca. 1895.
Initials appeared on the illustrations of five early public buildings appearing in *New Orleans As It Was* (1895), by Henry C. Castellanos. Probably Henry Charles Castellanos, Jr., born N.O. ca. 1877; died N.O. Apr. 7, 1953.
References: *T. Pic.*, Apr. 8, 1953; Castellanos, following 304.

C., R.
Sketch artist, active N.O. 1843.
Initials appeared on several drawings in *La Lorgnette* in the style of French artist Honoré Daumier.
References: *Lorgnette*, Jan. 12, 19, 22, 26, 1843.

CABLE, JAMES B.
Lithographer, active N.O. 1876; also printer.
Contemporary listings: lithographer, 73 Carondelet (1876).
References: NOCD 1876–78.

CADY, REBECCA
Born Washington DC ca. 1831.
Art teacher, active N.O. 1855.
Contemporary listings: teacher of papier maché, with MRS. HOUGHTON, 128 Canal (1855).
Also taught other subjects and did dressmaking.
References: NOCD 1857–61; *D. Delta*, Apr. 1, 1855; U.S. Census (1860), roll 421.

CAIFASSI, MARCAUS
Sculptor, active N.O. 1870–71.
Contemporary listings: sculptor, 107 St. Charles (1870–71).
References: Boyd, 205.

CAIRNS, JOHN A.
Born NY ca. 1843 or LA Oct. 1845; died N.O. July 9, 1903.
Engraver, active N.O. 1870–1903.
Contemporary listings: engraver, with FREDERICK HOLYLAND (1870, 1873–75); engraver, 101 Canal (1876–79, 1881); engraver, 13 St. Charles (1880); engraver (1886, 1888, 1895, 1897, 1899–1900); engraver, Koch & Dreyfus (1887); engraver, 55 Chartres (1890); engraver, T. Hausmann & Sons (1896); engraver, with Alvin M. Hill (1898); engraver, 130 Exchange Pl. (1901–1903).
Probably a jewelry engraver since all firms listed were jewelers.
References: NOCD 1868–71, 1873–81, 1884, 1886–90, 1895–1903; *D. Demo.*, May 3, 1876; *D. Pic.*, Jan. 29, 1875, July 10, 1903; U.S. Census (1900), roll 574.

CAIRNS, RALPH WATSON
Born N.O. July 26, 1887.
Engraver, active N.O. 1905–40.
Contemporary listings: engraver (1905); engraver, with OTTO J. LAUTERBACH (1908–11); engraver, 130 Exchange Pl. (1912); engraver, 126 Exchange Pl. (1913–18).
References: NOCD 1905–33, 1935, 1938, 1940; Orleans Parish Registrar of Voters, NOPL.

CAKE, DAVID
Born PA ca. 1812; died N.O. Nov. 19, 1847.
Artist.
"Portrait maker" who died in Charity Hospital six hours after arriving in N.O. from Cincinnati OH.
References: Louisiana Charity Hospital, Death Records, NOPL.

CALDWELL, G. H. (Mrs. Charles Caldwell)
Art teacher, active N.O. 1868–69.
Contemporary listings: teacher of drawing, landscape, and portraiture, Strangers' Hotel (1868–69).
References: NOCD 1860–61, 1866, 1871; *D. Crescent*, Nov. 17, 1868, Jan. 1, 1869.

CALLENDER, F. ARTHUR
Born Boston MA; died after 1917.
Painter, active N.O. 1892–93.
Studied: with Boulanger and Lefebvre, Paris.
Contemporary listings: landscape painter (1892–93).

Exhibited: ARTISTS' ASSOCIATION OF NEW ORLEANS (1892); Tulane University (1892–93).

Visiting artist at Tulane University, Callender came from Boston to paint scenes of the state for the LA department at the 1893 Columbian Exposition in Chicago.

References: *Current Topics*, Jan. 1893, 11; *D. Pic.*, Mar. 3, 6, Dec. 13, 1892, Feb. 14, 1893; *T. Demo.*, Mar. 3, 1892, Feb. 15, 1893; *American Art Annual*, 1915.

CALLICO, JOSEPH FREDERIC

Born ca. 1828; died N.O. Aug. 29, 1885.

Sculptor, active N.O. 1855; also marblecutter.

Contemporary listings: sculptor, 288 St. Louis (1855).

References: NOCD 1849–61, 1866–73, 1875–77, 1881–85; *Bee*, Aug. 30, 1885; *National*, Oct. 1, 1855; *Almanach de la Louisiane* (1867), 17; Groce and Wallace.

CALYO, NICOLINO V.

Born Naples, Italy 1799; died N.Y.C. Dec. 9, 1884.

Painter, sculptor.

Studied: Academy of Naples.

Exhibited: Western Exchange (1837); Commercial Hall (1852).

Portrait, landscape, historical, miniature, and panoramic painter who came to the U.S. in the 1830s, worked in Baltimore and N.Y.C. and traveled extensively. Calyo may have come to N.O. when two of his works were exhibited: a panorama of the 1835 great fire in N.Y.C. (1837) and dioramas with wax figures of the Mexican War (1852). It is reported that Calyo painted watercolors of FL, LA, and Cuba.

References: *D. Crescent*, Nov. 12, 13, 1852; *D. Pic.*, Nov. 11, 1852; *True Amer.*, Mar. 6–23, 1837 (advs.); Friends of the Cabildo, *250 Years*, 37; Groce and Wallace; Montreal Museum.

CAMILLE, MR. P.

Born France ca. 1832.

Artist, active N.O. 1860; also photographer.

Contemporary listings: photographic artist (1860); CAMILLE'S GALLERY OF ART (1860–61).

References: NOCD 1858–59, 1867; *Bee*, June 22, 1860; *La Renaissance Louisianaise*, 1(Nov. 10, 1861): 275; Smith and Tucker, 154; U.S. Census (1860), roll 419.

CAMILLE'S GALLERY OF FINE ART

Art dealer; active N.O. 1860–61; P. CAMILLE, owner.

Contemporary listings: Old Levee cor. Hospital (1860–61).

Advertised "all kinds of Daguerreotypes, Graphs, or Types, of the smallest sizes, copied in life size, on paper or on canvas prepared to be painted in Oil or Water Colors" (1860–61).

References: NOCD 1860–61.

CAMPBELL, _____

Artist, active N.O. 1863.

Made new scenery for the Varieties Theatre with LOUIS DOMINIQUE GRANDJEAN DEVELLE and ERNEST CICERI (1863).

References: *Era*, Dec. 24, 1863.

CAMPBELL, FRANCES

Painter, active N.O.

Studied: with GEORGE PETER ALEXANDER HEALY.

Nineteenth-century painter who did portraits of Louisianians including Mrs. Thomas J. Semmes, Mrs. Sylvester P. Walmsley, and Mrs. Frederick W. Tilton; also painted Theodore Roosevelt.

References: Seebold, 1:335.

CAMPBELL, GEORGINE

Born N.O. ca. 1848; died Washington DC Aug. 1931.

Painter, active N.O. ca. 1884–85.

Studied: 12 years abroad, mostly Paris.

Exhibited: World's Industrial and Cotton Centennial Exposition (1884–85).

Awarded: World's Industrial and Cotton Centennial Exposition, blue ribbon (1884–85).

Portrait and miniature painter of prominent people in N.Y.C., where she had moved ca. 1883, and later in Washington DC. She probably returned to N.O. while her work was exhibited at the exposition.

References: *D. States*, Jan. 16, 1887; *T. Demo.*, June 8, 1890; *T. Pic.*, Aug. 13, 1931; WICCE, *Catalogue*, 26.

CAMPBELL, J.
Designer, active N.O. 1848–49.
Contemporary listings: glass staining, 195 Gravier (1848); glass staining and painting, 195 Gravier (1849).
References: NOCD 1849, 1851; *D. Crescent*, June 12, 1848.

CAMPBELL, ROBERT
Engraver, active N.O. 1879.
Contemporary listings: engraver, with Meyer L. Navra (1879).
References: NOCD 1873–74, 1876–80.

CAMPILLO, C.
Born Italy ca. 1827.
Artist, active N.O. 1850.
Contemporary listings: artist (1850).
Lived at the same boarding house as G. CAMPILLO.
References: U.S. Census (1850), roll 235.

CAMPILLO, G.
Born Italy ca. 1822.
Artist, active N.O. 1850.
Contemporary listings: artist (1850).
Lived at the same boarding house as C. CAMPILLO.
References: U.S. Census (1850), roll 235.

CANFIELD, L.
Born MA ca. 1824.
Painter, active N.O. 1850–52.
Contemporary listings: importer of French china, china gilded and painted to order, 99 Chartres St. (1850–52).
References: NOCD 1850–52, 1854–56, 1858–61; U.S. Census (1850), roll 235.

CANOVA, DOMINIQUE
Born Milan, Italy 1800; died N.O. Apr. 7, 1868.
Painter, art teacher, lithographer, active N.O. 1838–68; also decorator, ornamental painter.
Contemporary listings: portrait painter, 80 Royal (1838–39, 1841); teacher of drawing, 80 Royal (1839–40); portrait painter (1842); teacher of drawing, Louisiana College, *Institution pour les Jeunes Demoiselles* and Classical and Commercial Institution (1844); teacher of drawing, De Villers's Lyceum (1845); teacher of drawing, Franklin High School (1846, 1850–52); teacher of drawing and painting, with JULES LION, 1 Exchange Passage (1848); artist painter, 8 Annette (1849–50); lithographer (1850, ca. 1854–59); artist–painter, 6 Annette (1851–53); teacher of drawing and painting, *Institution de Jeunes Demoiselles* (1852); artist painter, 243 Canal (1854); artiste, Derbigny cor. Bayou Rd. (1859–60); artist, Lapeyrouse near Claiborne (1861, 1866).
Probably Dominico Canova who worked in N.Y.C. (1825) for lithographer Anthony Imbert. Canova was first recorded in LA as the professor of drawing and painting at Jefferson College in Convent LA, from ca. 1837–39. He first advertised in N.O. in 1838 as a portrait painter available during the Christmas holidays when he was free from his teaching duties. He returned to N.O., apparently permanently, in 1840 and earned a reputation for ornamental painting, murals, and frescoes. His first known major commission was, with A. PINOLI, for frescoes in the rotunda and the dining room of the St. Louis Exchange Hotel (1841), after it had been damaged by fire. Other dateable commissions included paintings on the ceiling of the bishop's church (now Our Lady of Victory Church) and interior decorations done there with ANTOINE MONDELLI (1846); with JEAN ROSSI and PERACHI, frescoes in St. Alphonsus Church (1866); and frescoes for Pierre Soulé house on St. Louis (present address 720 St. Louis) (before 1866). Canova collaborated with local Italian artists in decorating the rotunda of the St. Louis Exchange Hotel as a temporary monument to the martyrs of Italian liberty (1846), and with other local artists in suggesting the site for the Henry Clay monument on Canal at Royal (1860). Work attributed to Canova on stylistic or other grounds, but without contemporary references includes: decorating the ceil-

ing and walls of the dining room of the Verandah Hotel; doors and ceiling in San Francisco plantation; the walls and ceiling of the Mirror Room in the James Robb house; the John Watt house; the ceiling of the Robinson–Jordan house; and the ceiling, proscenium arch, and drop curtain of the French Opera House. Canova was the lithographic artist for a cartoon about N.O. philanthropist John McDonogh (1850) and for a sheet music cover printed by JOHN E. BOEHLER (ca. 1854–59). He is often credited with the painting and fresco work in St. Louis Cathedral, and as being the nephew of the Italian sculptor and painter Antonio Canova (1757–1822), but neither claim is documented.
References: NOCD 1841–42, 1849–56, 1859–61, 1866; *Bee*, Dec. 19, 1838, Jan. 5, 1839, Dec. 19, 1839–Mar. 4, 1840 (advs.), Sept. 28, Oct. 24, 1844, Jan. 24, 1845, Oct. 13, 1846, Nov. 30, 1848, Oct. 31, 1850, Jan. 22, Aug. 5, 1852, Apr. 14, 1868; *Comm. Bull.*, May 24, 1841, Jan. 10, 1842; *Courier*, July 12, Aug. 1, Sept. 30, 1844, Jan. 11, 29, 1845, Sept. 26, 1846, Nov. 30, 1848, Oct. 21, 1850, Jan. 2, 1851, Aug. 5, 1852, Jan. 18, 1857; *D. Pic.*, July 20, 1841, Jan. 17, 1852, Feb. 12, 1860, Apr. 8, 1868; *D. Tropic*, Jan. 13, 1845; *Item*, July 5, 1954; *Revue Louisianaise*, 1(Aug. 2, 1846):441, 587, 1(Aug. 16, 1846):514, 2(Nov. 8, 1846):149; *States*, July 3, 1954; *T. Deutsche Zeitung*, Dec. 2, 1866; *Times*, Sept. 9, 23, Nov. 30, 1866; *T. Pic.*, Aug. 15, 1926, July 6, 1954; Mary Cable, 47, 89, 118, 120; Caldwell, 207–19; Chambon, 45; "La Dernière Heure du Condamné," Sheet Music Collection, THNOC; Glenk, 73; Groce and Wallace; Kendall, *History*, 2:656, 687; Laughlin, plate 80; LSM *Biennial Report for 1922–23*, 63; N.O. Death Certificate (1868), 42:170, NOPL; Norman, 158; Overdyke, 177; Scully, 56; Second District Court, Succession of Dominique Canova, 32061, NOPL; THNOC 59–202–L; U.S. Census (1840), roll 132, (1850), roll 238; Samuel Wilson, *Guide to Architecture*, 37, 55; WPA, "Lives."

CANTON, RICHARD
Born TN ca. 1838.
Artist, active N.O. 1850.
Contemporary listings: artist (1850).
Probably the son of THOMAS CANTON.
References: Groce and Wallace; U.S. Census (1850), roll 234.

CANTON, THOMAS
Born TN ca. 1815.
Artist, active N.O. 1850.
Contemporary listings: artist (1850).
Probably the father of RICHARD CANTON.
References: Groce and Wallace; U.S. Census (1850), roll 234.

CAPO, MICHEL
Born Minorca, Spain ca. 1844; died N.O. Mar. 27, 1912.
Lithographer, active N.O. 1880–95; primarily printer, also stationer.
Contemporary listings: lithographer, 113 Royal (1882–84); lithographer, 19 Decatur (1885–92); lithographer, 133 Decatur (1895).
Operated, at 113 Royal, what he claimed was N.O.'s first steam chromo-lithographing machine, imported from Paris (1880).
References: NOCD 1872–1912; *D. Pic.*, Oct. 18, 1895, Mar. 28, 1912; *Demo.*, Dec. 25, 1880; N.O. Death Certificate (1912), 154:743, NOPL; U.S. Census (1880), roll 461.

CAPONE, GAETANO
Born Maori, Italy 1845.
Painter, active N.O. 1918–19.
Studied: Academy of Naples, Italy; with César Fracassini, Naples and Rome; with Palizzi and Morelli, Italy.
NY resident who made courtyard studies in N.O. in the winter of 1918–19. Capone returned Oct. 11, 1919, for one month to make additional studies and to paint portraits and exhibited his work that year at the Louisiana State Museum.
References: *T. Pic.*, Oct. 12, 1919; Bénézit; LSM, *Annual Report for 1919*, 28, 57; LSM, *Biennial Report for 1920–21*, 69.

CARDELI, C.
Art teacher, active N.O. 1822.
Contemporary listings: drawing master, Lancastrian School (1822).
References: NOCD 1822.

CARDELLI, PIETRO
Born Rome, Italy 1791; died N.O. Oct. 1822.
Sculptor, art teacher, active N.O. 1820–22.
Contemporary listings: sculptor (1821); sculptor, teacher of drawing, 67 Conti (1822).
Exhibited: Salon, Paris (1804, 1810, 1812); Royal Academy, London (1815–16).
Worked in Paris (1806–10) on the bas–reliefs of the Vendôme column; in London (1815–16); and in Washington DC (1818), where he did decorative carving for the U.S. Capitol and portrait busts of distinguished Americans. Cardelli came to N.O. in 1820, probably at the suggestion of architect BENJAMIN HENRY LATROBE; in 1821, he contracted with the N.O. City Council to design and execute the bas–relief for the pediment of City Hall (now the Cabildo).
References: NOCD 1822; *Gazette*, July 25, 1821, Oct. 7, 1822; Bénézit; Fairman, 46; Friends of the Cabildo, *250 Years*, 39–40; Groce and Wallace; New Orleans City Council, Mayor's Office Messages, Feb. 24, July 7, 1821, May 25, 1822, NOPL; New Orleans City Council, Records, Oct. 14, Nov. 11, 1820, Feb. 17, 24, July 7, 21, 1821, May 25, 1822, NOPL; Seebold, 1:22; Wilson and Huber, *Cabildo*, 59–60.

CARDONA, ANTONIO C., SR.
Born Mahm, Balearic Islands, Spain ca. Jan. 1835; died N.O. Oct. 4, 1899.
Painter, active N.O. 1875–99.
Studied: Europe (ca. 1863–75).
Exhibited: Werlein's music store (1895).
Music teacher, also educated as a painter, who gained experience in Europe for 10–12 years before coming to N.O. He was painting in N.O. by 1875, but devoted little time to it again until 1895. Cardona exe-

cuted portraits, but excelled in painting fruits and other still lifes.
References: NOCD 1866, 1868–69, 1871, 1873–77, 1879–1901; *T. Demo.*, Nov. 17, 1895; N.O. Death Certificate (1899), 120:639, NOPL.

CARL, KATHERINE AUGUSTA
Born N.O. 1854; died N.Y.C. Dec. 8, 1938.
Painter.
Studied: Academie Julian, Paris; with Jean–Paul Laurens, Gustave Courtois, and William Adolphe Bouguereau, Paris.
Exhibited: Tennessee Centennial Exposition, Nashville (1897); Salon, Paris (1902); Louisiana Purchase Exposition, St. Louis MO (1904); London; Berlin.
Awarded: Salon, Paris, honorable mention (1890); Chevalier of the Legion of Honor (1896); International Exposition, Paris, honorable mention (1900); Order of the Double Dragon and Order of the Manchu Flaming Pearl, China.
Memberships/positions: Société Nationale des Beaux Arts, Paris; International Society of Women Painters, London; Louisiana Purchase Exposition, St. Louis, International Jury of Applied Arts and International Jury of Fine Arts (1904); National Society of French Artists; Société des Beaux–Arts du Champs–de–Mars, France.
Left N.O. permanently ca. 1859 to live in Paris, China, and N.Y.C. Carl was noted for her portrait of the Empress Dowager Tze Hsi of China and was the author and illustrator of *With the Empress Dowager of China* (1905).
References: *T. Pic.*, July 20, 1930, Dec. 9, 1938; Bénézit; Clara Clement, *Women in the Fine Arts*, 71–72; Fielding, *Dictionary*; Tennessee Centennial Exposition, 18, 140; *Who's Who in America*, 1938–39; *Who's Who in America*, 1903–1905; *Who's Who in American Art*, 1938–39; WPA, "Lives."

CARLIN, ETIENNE CONSTANT
Born Clermont, France 1808; died Paris, France June 16, 1869.
Painter.

Painted portraits of LA residents dating from ca. 1840 and from 1853–54 and made exact copies of earlier portraits. Carlin may have been in N.O. in 1851–52.
References: *Courier*, July 3, 1851, Mar. 19, 1852; Jordan, "Carlin is Noted for Details," *T. Pic.*, Mar. 30, 1975; Bénézit; Bruns, 310; Glenk, 73; LSM, *Biennial Report for 1916–17*, following 40.

CARLOS, C.
Painter, active N.O. 1870.
Awarded: Grand State Fair, diploma for best landscape painting (1870).
Possibly Clement Carlos, listed in the NOCD 1867–1902.
References: NOCD 1867–81, 1884, 1886, 1888–89, 1892, 1894–96, 1899, 1901–1903; Mechanics' and Agricultural Fair Asso., *Report* (1870):31.

CARNAHAN, CHARLES
Lithographer, active N.O. 1856–78; also printer.
Contemporary listings: TOLTI & CARNAHAN (1856, 1858–60); lithographer, 119 Exchange Al. (1857); lithographer, with JOHN DOUGLAS (1878).
References: NOCD 1856–60, 1867, 1877–78; Groce and Wallace.

CARNEY, ANN SHEEN. *See* SHEEN, ANN EVELYN

CARON, MAY
Born N.O. Sept. 15, 1880; died N.O. June 13, 1939.
Painter, active N.O. ca. 1915.
Exhibited: ART ASSOCIATION OF NEW ORLEANS (1915).
Listed as a dressmaker (1895–97, 1904–1905, 1909) and later as a landlady (1927).
References: NOCD 1895–97, 1901–1905, 1909, 1915, 1935, 1938; *T. Pic.*, June 14, 1939; Art Asso., *Special Exhibition*; Orleans Parish Registrar of Voters, NOPL.

CARPANTIER, MR. _____
Art teacher, active N.O. 1846.
Contemporary listings: teacher of drawing and sketching, 22 Jefferson (1846).
References: *La Patria*, Mar. 15, 1846.

CARPENTER, HORACE
Born Port Gibson MS Mar. 17, 1837; died N.O. Feb. 15, 1906.
Artist, active N.O. ca. 1880–87.
Exhibited: ARTISTS' ASSOCIATION OF NEW ORLEANS (1886–87).
Memberships/positions: SOUTHERN ART UNION (1880–81); Artists' Association of New Orleans (1886–87); New Orleans Camera Club, pres. (1891).
Amateur artist who lived in N.O. about 65 years and worked with the Sun Mutual Insurance Co. (1868–91).
References: NOCD 1860–61, 1868–92, 1894–95, 1897–98, 1900, 1903; *Art and Letters*, 1(Dec. 1887):228; *Bee*, May 27, 1880, May 4, 1881; *Current Topics*, Nov. 1891, 22; *D. Pic.*, Nov. 6, 1886, Dec. 17, 1887, Feb. 17, 1906; *D. States*, Nov. 5, 1886; AANO, *Catalogue* (1886); THNOC Cemetery Survey.

CARPENTER, JEROME E.
Engraver, active N.O. 1886; also printer.
Contemporary listings: engraver (1886).
References: NOCD 1884–87, 1890–92.

CARR, ROBERT D.
Artist, active N.O. 1917.
Contemporary listings: artist, 606 Commercial (1917).
Probably Carr who with WILLIAM K. PATRICK signed cartoons in *Club Men of Louisiana in Caricature* (1917).
References: NOCD 1917; Patrick, 210, 225, 325, 327, 348.

CARRAU, JOSEPH
Painter, active N.O. 1904–1907.
Contemporary listings: scenic artist (1904–1905); painter (1907).
References: NOCD 1904–1905, 1907.

CARREDES, JOSEPH
Lithographer, active N.O. 1871.
Contemporary listings: lithographer (1871).
References: NOCD 1871.

CARRIERE, LAURE JOSEPHINE
Born N.O. Mar. 1, 1876; died N.O. Apr. 28, 1925.
Artist, active N.O. ca. 1901.

Exhibited: ARTISTS' ASSOCIATION OF NEW ORLEANS (1901).
References: NOCD 1921, 1924; *T. Pic.*, Apr. 29, 1925; AANO, *Catalogue*, 1901; Orleans Parish, Office of the Recorder of Births, Marriages and Deaths, Birth Certificate (May 9, 1876), 66:573; LSM, *Biennial Report for 1926-27*, 29.

CARRUTH, ROBERTA BEVERLY KENNON.
See KENNON, ROBERTA BEVERLY

CARTER, DENNIS MALONE
Born Ireland ca. 1818-27; died N.Y.C. July 6, 1881.
Painter, active N.O. 1845-46.
Contemporary listings: portrait painter, 32 St. Charles (1845); portrait painter, 13 St. Charles (1846).
Exhibited: NATIONAL GALLERY OF PAINTINGS (1845); National Academy of Design, N.Y.C. (1848-81); American Art Union, N.Y.C. (1848-49); Pennsylvania Academy of Fine Arts, Philadelphia (1855-67); Boston Athanaeum (1857-61); Washington Art Association, Washington DC (1857).
Memberships/positions: Artists' Fund Society (1859).
Carter came to the U.S. in 1839 and spent most of his life in NY. In N.O. he painted a portrait of Rev. Theodore Clapp of the First Unitarian Church (1845). Later, in N.Y.C., he painted one of his most famous works, *Battle of New Orleans* (1856), which was copied for prints and illustrations. He also painted other historical pictures and portraits of distinguished men from life.
References: NOCD 1846; *D. Tropic*, Feb. 22, Mar. 1, May 2, 1845; *Revue Louisianaise*, 1(Aug. 2, 1846):441; Bénézit; Bruns, 310; Clement and Hutton, 122; Foote, 25; Glenk, 237; Groce and Wallace; THNOC 1954.12, 1958.43.1, 1958.83, 1959.183.2, 1959.184.1, 1960.22, 1964.6.

CARTER, JAMES S.
Painter, active N.O. 1905.
Contemporary listings: portraits (1905).
References: NOCD 1897, 1902-1905, 1907-33, 1935.

CARTER, LINCOLN J.
Born ca. 1865.
Painter, active N.O. 1891.
Contemporary listings: scene painter (1891).
References: *States*, Nov. 8, 1891, Apr. 6, 1896.

CARVER, O.
Engraver, active N.O. 1867.
Contemporary listings: engraver, 136 Port (1867).
References: NOCD 1867.

CASANOVA, FRANCISCO
Painter, active N.O. 1876-77; also photographer.
Contemporary listings: portrait painter, 183 Canal (1876-77).
References: NOCD 1875-78.

CASE & GREEN
Lithographers; Lucius Case, WILLIAM GREEN, partners.
Hartford CT lithography firm, which issued a Battle of N.O. lithograph (ca. 1849-52) copied from an aquatint engraved by Philibert Louis Debucourt after JEAN HYACINTHE LACLOTTE.
References: Groce and Wallace; THNOC 1971.53.

CASEY, ROBERT JAMES
Born N.O. Nov. 22, 1880 or 1881; died N.O. May 25, 1962.
Lithographer, active N.O. 1898-99; also printer.
Contemporary listings: lithographer (1898-99).
References: NOCD 1898-1921, 1923-33, 1935, 1938, 1940, 1942, 1945-47, 1949, 1952-56, 1958, 1960-62; *T. Pic.*, May 26, 1962; Orleans Parish Registrar of Voters, NOPL.

CASHEN, HENRY
Born England ca. 1831.
Painter, active N.O. 1860-61.
Contemporary listings: portrait painter, 197 Camp (1860); portrait painter, 175 St. Charles (1861).
Possibly Cashen who was a portrait painter in Cincinnati OH in 1853.
References: NOCD 1861; *D. Crescent*, Dec. 10, 1860; Groce and Wallace; U.S. Census (1860), roll 416.

CASSE, BERNARD
Born N.O. Jan. 1866; died N.O. Feb. 4, 1909.

Engraver, active N.O. 1896; primarily stone cutter, also decorator.
Contemporary listings: engraver (1896).
Brother of JULES CASSE.
References: NOCD 1880–87, 1890–92, 1894–97, 1899–1901, 1905–1907; *D. Pic.*, Feb. 5, 7, 1909; U.S. Census (1870), roll 522.

CASSE, JULES
Born N.O. June 1861; died N.O. Mar. 15, 1914.
Sculptor, active N.O. 1876–85; primarily marble and stone carver.
Contemporary listings: sculptor (1876–77); sculptor, with Peter Casse (1885).
Learned marble cutting from his father, Peter Casse, one of the pioneers in the business in N.O.
Brother of BERNARD CASSE.
References: NOCD 1876–77, 1880–1914; *D. Pic.*, Mar. 16, 1914; N.O. Death Certificate (1914), 160:58, NOPL; THNOC Cemetery Survey; U.S. Census (1870), roll 522.

CASTELLANOS, HENRY CHARLES, JR. *See* C., H. C., JR.

CASTELLANOS, DR. JOHN JOSEPH
Born N.O. Nov. 4, 1835; died N.O. Oct. 29, 1914.
Sketch artist, active N.O. ca. 1856–1913.
Professor at Charity Hospital who illustrated lectures with anatomical drawings on thin sheets of overlaid paper picturing the various layers of the human body. However, his favorite style of drawing was caricature. Father of JOHN JOSEPH CASTELLANOS, JR., and CORINNE CASTELLANOS MELLEN.
References: NOCD 1857–61, 1866–1915; *T. Pic.*, Oct. 30, 1914; Caulfeild, 206; A. E. Fossier, 37; Mount, 108; Tinker, *Ecrits*, 74; U.S. Census (1860), roll 418.

CASTELLANOS, JOHN JOSEPH, JR.
Artist, active N.O. 1899.
Contemporary listings: artist (1899).
Son of DR. JOHN JOSEPH CASTELLANOS and brother of CORINNE CASTELLANOS MELLEN.
References: NOCD 1897, 1899, 1901; Mount, 108.

CASTILLION, AUGUST
Engraver, active N.O. 1905.
Contemporary listings: engraver, 838 Royal (1905).
References: NOCD 1904, 1905.

CASTLEDEN, GEORGE FREDERICK
Born Canterbury, England Dec. 4, 1861; died Abingdon VA Dec. 1945.
Etcher, painter, active N.O. 1911, ca. 1917–36.
Studied: with Thomas Sidney Cooper, Cooper Gallery, Canterbury.
Awarded: Cooper Gallery, Canterbury, first prize for landscape painting; Territorial Exposition, Regina, Canada, first prize for landscape in oil and for collections of oil paintings and watercolors (1896); Winnipeg, Canada, gold medal for etching, four first prizes and two second prizes (1896); Exhibition of Canadian Artists, Toronto, Canada, first prize.
Memberships/positions: ART LEAGUE OF NEW ORLEANS, charter member.
Etcher and painter who moved first to Canada (1888), then to the U.S. (ca. 1903). He traveled throughout the U.S. as a scenic painter, visiting N.O. in 1911. He returned in either 1917 or 1920, and remained until 1936 when he moved to Charleston SC. Castleden was noted for his paintings and illustrations of French Quarter courtyards; he exhibited locally through the Arts and Crafts Club and the Art League of New Orleans. With Mazie Howell, he executed landscapes for the N.O. department store D. H. Holmes.
References: NOCD 1924–33, 1935; *Item-Trib.*, Jan. 4, 1925, Oct. 14, 1928; *Morn. Trib.*, Nov. 29, 1926; *States*, Dec. 4, 1927, Aug. 12, 1935; *T. Pic.*, Oct. 29, 1922, Dec. 3, 1923, Feb. 29, 1924, Oct. 25, 1925, Dec. 6, 1927, Apr. 1, 1934, Apr. 12, 1936, Jan. 1, 1946; Looney, 385; Scrapbook 100, LSM; *Who's Who in American Art*, 1938–39; WPA Guide to Louisiana, 170; WPA, "Lives."

CATLIN, GEORGE
Born Wilkes–Barre PA July 26, 1796; died Jersey City NJ Dec. 23, 1872.
Painter, active N.O. 1835.

Exhibited: Pittsburgh (1833); 78 Chartres (1835); Stuyvesant Institute, NY (1837); Washington DC, Philadelphia, Boston (ca. 1838); Egyptian Hall, London (1839); London (ca. 1840–44); Louvre, Paris (ca. 1845).

Memberships/positions: Pennsylvania Academy of Fine Arts, Philadelphia (1824); National Academy of Design, N.Y.C. (1826); American Academy of Fine Arts, N.Y.C.

Portrait painter, miniaturist, and writer renowned for his paintings of American Indians. Catlin studied and practiced law while he taught himself to paint. He became a miniaturist in Philadelphia (1823–25) and while there, saw the delegation of Indians which first inspired him to paint and record all the native American tribes in the country. He worked in PA, NY, VA, and MO (1823–30). For the next eight years he traveled around the U.S.: he visited 48 tribes, painted about 500 canvases, and exhibited and lectured on Indian life and customs. He exhibited 200 portraits, paintings of ceremonies, landscapes, and hunting scenes in N.O. (Mar. 25– Apr. 11, 1835). Each painting was shown individually while Catlin explained the clothing and traditions of each tribe to the audience. He took his "Indian Gallery" to Europe and toured until 1852 when he lost the collection to creditors. He then undertook additional journeys to South America, the western U.S., and Alaska, but spent most of his time traveling in Europe and publishing. He returned to America in 1870. Catlin's published works included *Letters and Notes on the Manners, Customs and Conditions of the North American Indian,* which came out in 20 editions from 1841 to 1860; *North American Indians Portfolio of Hunting Scenes and Amusements* (1844); and *North American Indian Collection* (1848).

References: *Bee,* Mar. 24, 1835–Apr. 8, 1835 (advs.), Mar. 24, 26, Apr. 3, 8, 1835, May 19, 1840; *Comm. Bull.,* Feb. 10, 1846; *Courier,* Jan. 27, Apr.

2, 6, 11, 1835, Dec. 30, 1836, Mar. 29, 1837; *D. Delta,* July 24, 1847; *D. Orleanian,* Jan. 26, 1849; *D. True Delta,* Mar. 15, 1855, Feb. 7, 1864; *Mercantile Advertiser,* May 15, 1834; *Repub.,* Jan. 19, 1873; Barker, 451– 52; Clement and Hutton, 125; Corcoran Gallery, 33; Curry, 34–35, 186; Ewers, 56–73; Groce and Wallace; McCracken, *Catlin;* Mc-Cracken, *Portrait,* 47–56, 72–73, 96–98, 116, 148; Museum of Fine Arts, 1:97–98; Rathbone, *Mississippi Panorama,* 70–82; Rathbone, *Westward,* 274.

CAUCHE, JOSEPH E.

Born LA Mar. 1882.

Lithographer, active N.O. 1900–18; also printer, pressman.

Contemporary listings: lithographer (1900, 1910, 1912–13, 1917–18); lithographer, with HENRIETTA TER-MIER WEHRMANN (1901).

References: NOCD 1901–1902, 1910 18; U.S. Census (1900), roll 571, (1910), roll 521.

CAVAILLER, PAUL

Born France ca. 1813.

Sketch artist, lithographer, active N.O. 1842–54.

Contemporary listings: lithographer, Laharpe cor. Claiborne (1846); lithographer (1850); lithographer, near St. Ann cor. Prieur (1851–53); lithographer, St. Peter cor. Miro (1854).

Noted for his lithographed riverfront views of the first, second, and third municipalities of N.O. (1842), and of the Tivoli Gardens. He also did artwork for sheet music covers. *Cf.* CAV-ALIER, _____.

References: NOCD 1843–44, 1846, 1851–56, 1858; Groce and Wallace; Reps, 311; THNOC 1950.61.39–.40, 1978.42; U.S. Census (1850), roll 236; "Valse de Tivoli," Sheet Music Collection, THNOC.

CAVALIER,

Art teacher, active N.O. 1846.

Contemporary listings: professor of drawing, Institution Garreau (1846). *Cf.* CAVAILLER, PAUL.

References: *Bee,* Feb. 7, 1846.

CAVANAUGH, JOHN
Born Ireland ca. 1818–27.
Sculptor, active N.O. 1853–55; primarily stonecutter.
Contemporary listings: marble and stone sculptor, 224 Camp (1853–54); marble and stone sculptor, 21 St. Joseph (1855).
Possibly John Cavanaugh, born ca. 1813; died Mobile AL May 25, 1865.
References: NOCD 1849–61; *D. Delta*, Sept. 30, 1847; *Times*, May 31, 1865; Groce and Wallace; N.O. Death Certificate (1865), 29:608, NOPL; U.S. Census (1860), roll 415.

CAVITO, ANGELO
Engraver, active N.O. 1891.
Contemporary listings: engraver (1891).
References: NOCD 1891.

CAZELLES, FRANÇOIS
Sculptor, active N.O. 1892–98; also jeweler.
Studied: Ecole des Beaux Arts, Paris.
Contemporary listings: sculptor (1892, 1896–98); artist (1894).
Began career as a sculptor but later turned to the stage and theatrical management.
References: NOCD 1885–89, 1892, 1894, 1896–1906; *Item*, Oct. 16, 1904.

CECILIUS, FATHER
Art teacher, active N.O. 1728.
Capuchin schoolmaster who possibly taught drawing in N.O. (1728) at an early educational institution in the Mississippi valley.
References: Fortier, *Louisiana*, 1:187; Rowland and Sanders, 2:507–9.

CELLI, ROMEO
Born Rome, Italy Nov. 20, 1877; died N.O. June 24, 1935.
Painter, sculptor, active N.O. 1904–35; also decorator, carver.
Studied: Colegio Rosi, L. Apollinare di Roma, Accademia dei Belle Arti; Museo Artistico Industriale, Istituto degli Artigianelli; with Professor Moneti.
Contemporary listings: wood sculptor (1910); wood carver (1911, 1913).

While in Italy, Celli carved wood professionally (ca. 1892–93), then served in the Italian navy (ca. 1895–1904) until he came to N.O. (Apr. 1904). Immediately after his arrival, he began working as a wood carver. He was noted for his carved plaques, particularly portraits; carved furniture; and a carved altar for St. Mary's Assumption Church. He also did interior decorative plaster work for homes in N.O. and N.Y.C.; he remained active as a sculptor until his death.
References: NOCD 1907, 1909, 1911, 1913–33; *Item–Trib.*, Aug. 23, 1931, Oct. 2, 23, 1932; *Morn. Trib.*, July 23–24, 1932; *T. Pic.*, Oct. 14, 1923, Oct. 15, 1929, June 25, 1935; Cline, *Contemporary Art*, 7; U.S. Census (1910), roll 521; WPA, "Lives."

CERESA AND PINOLI
Painters, active N.O. 1838; ———.
Ceresa, A. PINOLI, partners.
Contemporary listings: historical and portrait painters, Exchange Al. betw. Conti and St. Louis (1838).
Italian artists who painted a new curtain for the Camp Street Theatre (1838).
References: NOCD 1838; *True Amer.*, Oct. 23, 1838; Groce and Wallace; Kendall, *Golden Age*, 162.

CERVEAU, JOSEPH LOUIS FIRMIN
Born Smyrna, Asia Minor ca. 1812; died Natchez MS 1896.
Painter, active N.O. 1839.
Exhibited: Plough's Museum, St. Charles (1839).
With ——— VALENTINE, exhibited their dioramas, including the *Fairy Grotto*.
References: *Courier*, June 7, 1839; Hemperley, 460; Waring, 1.

CHALL, ALFRED
Born France ca. 1826.
Artist, active N.O. 1850.
Contemporary listings: artist of the French Theatre (1850).
References: Groce and Wallace; U.S. Census (1850), roll 236.

CHALLONER, CAPT. WILLIAM LINDSAY
Born Bedminster, England 1852; died Baltimore MD Oct. 19, 1901.

Painter, active N.O. ca. 1882–87. Contemporary listings: artist and marine painter (1887).

Exhibited: Grunewald's music store and the Sazeracs (1887); Twenty-third Exhibition of the Mechanics' Institute, San Francisco (1888); Creole Art Gallery (1892).

Ship captain and painter of historical harbor scenes and ships who studied at the York Naval Academy. He commanded fruit trade ships out of N.Y.C., N.O. (1882–87), and San Francisco, and served in the Spanish–American War (1898). Notable among his paintings are Confederate steamers and scenes of N.O. and the West Coast. While in N.O. he executed several paintings of ships and port scenes, many dated 1885. In 1887 he painted and exhibited a Civil War scene entitled, *Confederate Steamboat "Webb" Passing Through the Union Blockade in New Orleans.* References: NOCD 1885, 1887, 1891–98, 1900–1901; *States*, Mar. 27, 1887; *T. Demo.*, Feb. 27, 1887; Collier, "The World of Art: Historic Civil War Painting Restored," *T. Pic.*, Aug. 4, 1968; Creole Art Gallery, 11; Glenk, 73, 273; Information from Rosemary Challoner Wilkinson; LSM, *Biennial Report for 1926–27*, 66; Rathbone, *Mississippi Panorama*, 82.

CHAMBAUD, T.
Painter, active N.O. 1827.
Contemporary listings: miniature painter, 137 Chartres (1827).
References: NOCD 1827; Groce and Wallace.

CHAMPNEY, JAMES WELLS
Born Boston, MA July 16, 1843; died N.Y.C. May 1, 1903.
Painter, illustrator, sketch artist, engraver, art teacher, active N.O. 1873–74.
Studied: Lowell Institute, MA; with Edward Frère, Ecouen, France (1866); Académie d'Anvers, France; with Van Lerius, Royal Academy, Antwerp, Belgium (1868).
Exhibited: Salon, Paris (1869, 1875); Centennial Exposition, Philadelphia (1876); SOUTHERN ART UNION (1882); Columbian Exposition, Chicago (1893); Tennessee Centennial Exposition, Nashville (1897).
Awarded: Royal Academy, Antwerp, first prize in drawing (1868).
Memberships/positions: National Academy of Design, N.Y.C. (1882); American Society of Painters in Watercolors, N.Y.C.
Apprenticed to a wood engraver at age 16, Champney studied and made many sketching tours in Europe. He was sent to N.O. by *Scribner's Monthly* (1873–74) with journalist Edward King to portray the South in a series of illustrated articles entitled "The Great South," which was eventually republished as *The Southern States of North America* (1875). He maintained studios in Deerfield MA and N.Y.C. He specialized in genre painting and was one of the first Americans to apply Impressionist theories to his work.
References: *D. Pic.*, Feb. 15, 1882; *Appleton's CAB*; Bénézit; *DAB*; Kelly, 7, 29, 87; Edward King, *The Great South*; Edward King, *Southern States*; Museum of Fine Arts, 1:98–99; Tennessee Centennial Exposition, 19.

CHAPEL, GUY
Born Detroit MI 1871; died after 1934.
Painter, active N.O. 1902.
Studied with G. G. Hopkins and R. S. Robbins; Smith Academy, Chicago; Art Institute, Chicago.
Painted scenes in and around N.O., one dated "3/11/02."
References: Bénézit; Fielding, *Dictionary*; *Mallett's*; Morton's Auction Exchange (Mar. 13, 1979): 20, (Oct. 29–30, 1982): no. 686, (Dec. 10–11, 1982): no. 274, (May 20, 1983): no. 1105.

CHAPERON, _____. *See* RUBE, CHAPERON AND JAMBON

CHAPIN, CHARLES H.
Died N.Y.C. Mar. 1889.
Painter, art teacher, active N.O. ca. 1882–85.
Contemporary listings: artist (1883); portrait and landscape painter, 16 Dryades, and artist and teacher of painting, 12 Dryades (1884); por-

trait and landscape painter, 12 Dryades (1885).
Exhibited: SEEBOLD's (1884–85).
Memberships/positions: Lotus Club, N.Y.C., founder.
N.Y.C. artist who spent some winters in N.O. (ca. 1882–83). Chapin kept a studio on Dryades St. (1884–85). He was noted for his portrait of the Polish actress Helena Modjeska, in her role as Mary, Queen of Scots, and also for his landscapes in oil and in watercolor. He mysteriously disappeared in Dec. 1888. In Mar. 1889, a body identified as his was recovered from the North River.
References: NOCD 1885; D. Pic., Jan. 6, Nov. 30, Dec. 3, 1884, July 26, 1885, Jan 29, Mar. 15, 1889; D. States, Aug. 17, 1883, Jan. 6, Apr. 13, 1884; T. Demo., Dec. 1, 1883, Jan. 7, Nov. 29, 30, 1884, Feb. 1, 1885; Seebold, 1:315.

CHAPOTEL, CHARLES B.
Born LA Oct. 1879.
Sculptor, active N.O. 1899–1900.
Contemporary listings: sculptor (1899–1900).
References: NOCD 1899; U.S. Census (1900), roll 572.

CHAPSKY AND TEETZEL. See also
TEETZEL & CHAPSKY
Engravers, active N.O. 1871; also stencil cutters; Robert Chapsky (born Prussia ca. 1842; died N.O. Mar. 8, 1900), GEORGE E. TEETZEL, partners.
Contemporary listings: engravers, 74 St. Charles (1871).
References: NOCD 1871–72; Comm. Bull., Dec. 29, 1870–Feb. 20, 1871 (advs.); D. Pic., Mar. 9, 1900; THNOC 85–75–L.

CHARBONNET, MARIE NATHALIE LOEW
(Mrs. James Alfred Charbonnet)
Born N.O. 1845; died N.O. Nov. 20, 1924.
Painter, active N.O.
Studied: with GEORGE COULON.
Amateur artist who gave her paintings to family and friends as gifts.
References: NOCD 1882–92, 1895–1902, 1905; T. Pic., Nov. 22, 1924; WPA, "Lives."

CHARLES, JOHN, JR.
Engraver, active N.O. 1878.
Contemporary listings: engraver (1878).
References: NOCD 1878.

CHARTON, EDWARD
Died ca. 1895–1902.
Artist, active N.O. 1891–95.
Contemporary listings: artist (1891, 1895).
Possibly Edouard Charton, still life painter, born Paris 1800s and student of Justin Lequien and Bourgogne, who exhibited at the salon in 1881.
References: NOCD 1870, 1873–75, 1877–79, 1884–85, 1889, 1891, 1893–95, 1903; D. Pic., Sept. 2, 1910; Bénézit.

CHATEAU, R.
Born Metz, France ca. 1857.
Painter, active N.O. 1897.
Studied: with Jean–Léon Gérome, Paris.
Contemporary listings: portrait painter, 439 Chartres (1897).
References: D. States, June 20, 1897.

CHATILLON, JOSEPH AUGUSTE DE. See
DE CHATILLON, JOSEPH AUGUSTE
CHATRY, AUGUST (Gustave)
Painter, active N.O. 1896–97.
Contemporary listings: portrait painter, 941 Canal (1896); artist (1897).
References: NOCD 1891, 1893, 1896–97, 1899, 1901, 1903, 1905–1906.

CHAUCHON, LOUIS
Born N.O. ca. 1815.
Painter, active N.O. 1880.
Contemporary listings: portrait painter, 26 St. Charles (1880).
References: NOCD 1873–74, 1878, 1880; U.S. Census (1860), roll 418.

CHAUVIERE, ETIENNE MARIE JOSEPH
Born Nantes, France 1870; died N.O. May 30, 1939.
Designer, etcher, painter, active N.O. 1905–39.
Studied: Academie Julien, Paris; with Benjamin Constant, Luc Olivier Merson, Lefebvre, and Jean–Paul Laurens, France.
Contemporary listings: portrait painter (1906); artist, 620 Canal

(1909); portrait painter, 620 Canal (1910); artist, NEW ORLEANS ENGRAVING & ELECTROTYPE CO., LTD. (1911, 1914, 1917); artist (1916, 1918).
Exhibited: Salon, Paris (before 1905); ART ASSOCIATION OF NEW ORLEANS (1913, 1915).
Memberships/positions: ART LEAGUE OF NEW ORLEANS; Louisiana Society of Etchers.
Influenced by the French painter P. L. N. Grolleron, Chauvière worked as an illustrator and designed stained glass windows and mosaics while in France where he won prizes for portraiture and composition. In N.O. he drew sketches depicting carnival parades for various publications and was employed as an artist with GRELLE-EGERTON ENGRAVING CO. (1924–39). He exhibited with the Art League of New Orleans, Arts and Crafts Club, and won a prize for etching at the Mid–South Fair, Memphis TN (1938). At the time of his death, he was a student at the Reinike Academy of Art.
References: NOCD 1909–11, 1914, 1916–18, 1920–25, 1931–32; *Arts and Antiques*, 1(Nov. 1938):17–18; *Item–Trib.*, Jan. 16, Nov. 20, 1938; *T. Demo.*, May 27, 1906; *T. Pic.*, May 31, 1939; Art Asso., *Catalogue* (1913, 1915); Art Asso., *Special Exhibition*; THNOC 1974.49; WPA, "Lives."

CHAUVIERE, STEPHEN. *See* CHAUVIERE, ETIENNE MARIE

CHAVIN, FRANÇOIS
Born France ca. 1799.
Lithographer, active N.O. 1843–50; also printer.
Contemporary listings: J. MANOUVRIER & CHAVIN (1843–44); lithographic printer, 85 Toulouse (1849–50).
References: NOCD 1843–44, 1846, 1849–54, 1857; Groce and Wallace; U.S. Census (1850), roll 235.

CHERARE, JOSEPH
Born France ca. 1877.
Artist, active N.O. 1910.
Contemporary listings: artist/photograph (1910).
References: U.S. Census (1910), roll 519.

CHERET. *See* LACHAUME DE GAVAUX, JEAN LOUIS

CHERY, LOUIS
Born France ca. 1829.
Engraver, active N.O. 1860.
Contemporary listings: engraver (1860).
References: Groce and Wallace; U.S. Census (1860), roll 421.

CHESSE, ROSEMOND GEORGE
Engraver, active N.O. 1893–1901.
Contemporary listings: engraver, Frantz & Opitz (1893); engraver, 529 Royal (1895); engraver (1896, 1898–99, 1901).
References: NOCD 1893, 1895–96, 1898–99, 1901.

CHEVAL, JULIEN
Painter, active N.O. 1892–95.
Contemporary listings: artist (1892–93); painter (1895).
References: NOCD 1892–93, 1895.

CHEVALERET, AUGUSTE
Painter, active N.O. 1850.
Contemporary listings: studio, Bourbon near Toulouse (1850).
References: *D. Crescent*, June 4, 1850.

CHEVALLIE, MARIE ROSALIE
Born Philadelphia PA ca. 1837; died N.O. Jan. 12, 1919.
Art teacher, active N.O. 1889.
Contemporary listings: public school drawing teacher (1889).
Came to N.O. (ca. 1841) and taught in the public schools for 55 years, although listed as an art teacher only one year.
References: NOCD 1870, 1872–1018; *D. Pic.*, Feb. 21, 1889, *T. Pic.*, Jan. 13–14, 1919.

CHILDS, JOHN V. *See also* CHILDS, CLARK & CO.
Born NY ca. 1812–17; died N.O. Jan. 17, 1872.
Engraver, active N.O. 1836–72; also printer.
Contemporary listings: engraver, 3 Camp (1837–40, 1842); engraver, 79 Common (1842); engraver, 79 Gravier (1843–44); engraver, 5 Camp (1845–46); engraver, 9 Camp (1849–52); engraver, 10 Camp (1853–55, 1857–61); CHILDS & HAMMOND (1855–57); engraver, LILIEN-

THAL's (1862); engraver, 28 Camp (1862, 1865); engraver, 118 Canal (1866); engraver, 161 Common (1866–67); engraver (1868–70); engraver, 90 Camp (1872).
Awarded: Grand State Fair, first premium for copperplate engraving (1846).
Established an engraving and printing office in 1836. He also engraved copperplates, silver, jewelry, door plates, bank notes, bills of exchange and lading, diplomas, mercantile and visiting cards, and notarial, consular, and counting house seals. Childs printed the first N.O. provisional stamp and a series of fractional currency notes for making change, after the postal system of the Confederate states began on June 1, 1861.
References: NOCD 1837–38, 1842–44, 1846, 1849–61, 1866–70, 1872; NOBD 1857–58, 1865; *Courier*, June 25, 1845; *D. Crescent*, Nov. 12, 1850, Oct. 25, 1858; *D. Delta*, Feb. 9, 1862; *D. Pic.*, Dec. 30, 1838–Jan. 9, 1839 (advs.), Jan. 19, 1840, Aug. 7, 1842, May 1, 1859, Mar. 23, 25, 1862, Sept 2, 1866, Jan. 19, 1872; *D. True Delta*, Nov. 27, 1862; *De Bow's Review*, Feb. 1846, 166; *Jeffersonian*, Nov. 29, 1845; *Times*, Nov. 25, 1866; *Wkly. Delta*, Jan. 12, 1846; *Edwards' Descriptive Gazetteer*; *Louisiana State Gazetteer*; Huber and Wagner, 143; U.S. Census (1870), roll 524; *The World in Miniature*, cover.

CHILDS, CLARK & CO.
Engravers, active N.O. 1838; possibly JOHN V. CHILDS, J. R. CLARK, partners.
Signed the engravings included in one edition of the 1838 NOCD.
References: NOCD 1838 (THNOC 52–5).

CHILDS & HAMMOND
Engravers, active N.O. 1855–57; also printers; JOHN V. CHILDS, JOHN T. HAMMOND, partners.
Contemporary listings: engravers, 10 Camp (1855–57).
References: NOCD 1856–57; *D. Creole*, July 19, 1856; *D. Delta*, Apr. 22, June 3, July 21, 1855.

CHOL, A.
Artist, active N.O. 1851–56.
Contemporary listings: artist, 301 Royal (1851–54); artist, 245 Royal (1855–56).
References: NOCD 1850–56, 1858–61; Groce and Wallace.

CHRETIEN, EUGENE JOHN
Born N.O. Oct. 13, 1892; died ca. 1974.
Lithographer, active N.O. 1910–53; also pressman.
Contemporary listings: lithographer (1910); feeder, WALLE & CO. (1915–16); Walle & Co. (1918).
Worked for Walle & Co. as a pressman and lithographer (1919–60).
References: NOCD 1914–16, 1918–24, 1926, 1929–33, 1935, 1938, 1940, 1942, 1945–47, 1949, 1952–56, 1958, 1960–61, 1965–69, 1971–74; Orleans Parish Registrar of Voters, NOPL; U.S. Census (1910), roll 521.

MISS JEANNETTE CHRISTIE & CO.
Art teacher, active N.O. 1884–85.
Contemporary listings: teacher in watercolor, 147 Canal (1884–85).
Christie was from Chicago; she also sold art supplies.
References: *Eve. Chronicle*, Apr. 11, 1885.

CHRISTMAS, WHITNEY
Artist, active N.O. 1891.
Contemporary listings: artist (1891).
References: NOCD 1891.

CHRISTY, ELIZABETH
Born LA Aug. 1861.
Artist, active N.O. 1900.
Contemporary listings: artist (1900).
References: U.S. Census (1900), roll 574.

CHURCH, FREDERIC EDWIN
Born Hartford CT May 4, 1826; died N.Y.C. Apr. 7, 1900.
Painter, active N.O. 1880, 1891.
Studied: with Benjamin A. Coe and A. H. Emmons, Hartford CT; with Thomas Cole, Catskill NY (1844–48).
Exhibited: National Academy of Design, N.Y.C. (1845); American Art Union, N.Y.C. (1847–52); Bloomfield, Steel & Co. (1859).
Memberships/positions: National Academy of Design (1848).

Renowned American landscape painter who in 1853 and 1857 traveled to South America for artistic inspiration. He also visited Labrador, the West Indies, Europe, and the Near East on sketching expeditions. His most famous painting, *Niagara*, was exhibited in N.O. in 1859. In 1877 Church became crippled by rheumatism and had difficulty painting. He visited N.O. in 1880 and again in 1891.
References: *D. Crescent*, Mar. 5, 7, 1859; *D. Pic.*, Mar. 4–23, 1859 (advs.), Mar. 30, Apr. 5, 1859; *D. States*, Apr. 17, 1880; Champlin; Groce and Wallace; Grace King, *Memories*, 101.

CHURCHILL, FRANCIS GORTON
Born Natchez MS Feb. 12, 1876; died N.O. Mar. 6, 1924.
Painter, sketch artist, etcher, active N.O. 1910–24; primarily architect.
Studied: Tulane University (1891–96); Cincinnati Academy of Art (1897–98).
Exhibited: ART ASSOCIATION OF NEW ORLEANS (1910, 1915–17).
Memberships/positions: Art Association of New Orleans; National Art Club, N.Y.C.
Architect with the firms Favrot & Livaudais; DeBuys, Levy & Co., Ltd.; and DeBuys, Churchill & Labouisse. The latter firm designed buildings for Loyola University (1910–16). Churchill published *Pen Drawings of Old New Orleans* (1916), which contained illustrations of the city's historic streets and buildings. He was one of the founders of the Arts and Crafts Club and a member of the American Institute of Architects.
References: NOCD 1900, 1903–24; *T. Pic.*, Feb. 15, 1920, Mar. 7, Sept. 20, 1924, Mar. 3, 1951; *Tulane News Bulletin*, 1(Oct. 1920):112–13; Art Asso., *Catalogue* (1910, 1916, 1917); Art Asso., *Special Exhibition*; Churchill; Fielding, *Dictionary*; Kendall, *History*, 2:865–66; U.S. Census (1910), roll 519; Samuel Wilson, *Guide to Architecture*, 74,

CICERI, CHARLES
Born Milan, Italy.
Painter, active N.O. 1811.

Studied: Paris.
Contemporary listings: scenic painter (1811).
References: *Moniteur*, May 4, 11, 23, June 22, 1811; Groce and Wallace; Hornblow, 1:201; Odell, 2:6, 8, 18, 39, 84, 181.

CICERI, ERNEST
Born Paris, France ca. 1817; died N.O. July 5, 1866.
Painter, art teacher, active N.O. ca. 1859–66.
Contemporary listings: painter (1866).
Exhibited: L. UTER's (1861).
Decorative painter, initially employed by the Louvre, Paris, who came to N.O. by invitation of the Opera House Association to paint the decorations and scenery of the New French Opera House with LOUIS DOMINIQUE GRANDJEAN DEVELLE (1859). He also made new scenery for the Varieties Theatre with Develle and CAMPBELL (1863) and taught art classes in gouache and pastel to many LA artists. He painted miniatures and some LA scenes, but seems to have preferred making fantastic European landscapes. Possibly a son of the French painter and decorator Pierre–Luc–Charles Ciceri and grandson of the French miniaturist Jean–Baptiste Isabey.
References: *Bee*, Dec. 28, 1861, July 6, 1866; *D. Pic.*, July 22, Dec. 2, 1877; *D. States*, Jan. 20, 1882; *Era*, Dec. 24, 1863; *T. Demo.*, Dec. 29, 1901; *Trib.*, Dec. 8, 1867; Bénézit; Creole Art Gallery, 19, Davies, 53, Glenk, 73; Information courtesy George E. Jordan; Looney, 384; Righter, 382.

CIPRIANI, LORENZO
Born Toscana, Italy ca. 1838–40; died N.O. July 14, 1911.
Painter, active N.O. 1880–1911.
Contemporary listings: painter (1880–83, 1886, 1889, 1897, 1905, 1907, 1910); painter, 125 Ursuline (1894); painter, 933 Ursuline (1895); painter, 934 Ursuline (1896, 1898–1902, 1906, 1908, 1911); artist (1903).
Father of LOUIS L. CIPRIANI.

References: NOCD 1877, 1880–83, 1886, 1889, 1894–1908, 1910–11, 1914; N.O. Death Certificate (1911), 152:800, NOPL; U.S. Census (1910), roll 521.

CIPRIANI, LOUIS L.
Born N.O. ca. 1874; died N.O. Mar. 17, 1953.
Painter, active N.O. 1896–1925.
Contemporary listings: painter, 934 Ursuline (1896, 1913); painter (1897, 1899, 1901, 1903, 1906); fresco artist (1905); artist (1908, 1910–11); portrait artist (1910); painter, 1140 N. Rampart (1916–17); painter, 4226 Dumaine (1918).
Son of LORENZO CIPRIANI.
References: NOCD 1895–99, 1901, 1903–1908, 1910–18, 1920–21, 1923–33, 1935, 1938, 1940, 1942, 1945–46, 1949, 1952–53; T. Pic., Mar. 19, 1953; U.S. Census (1910), roll 521.

CLABBON, CHARLES
Born Engalnd ca. 1877.
Lithographer, active N.O. 1910.
Contemporary listings: lithographer (1910).
References: U.S. Census (1910), roll 521.

CLAGUE, RICHARD, JR.
Born Paris, France May 11, 1821; died Algiers LA Nov. 29, 1873.
Painter, art teacher, active N.O. 1850–73.
Studied: with Jean Charles Ferdinand Humbert, Geneva, Switzerland (1836–37); with LEON POMAREDE (ca. 1842–43); with François Edouard Picot, Paris (ca. 1849); Ecole des Beaux Arts, Paris (1849); probably with Horace Vernet, Ernest Hébert, and Jean–Auguste–Dominique Ingres, Paris.
Contemporary listings: painter, 40 Camp (1850); artist, teacher of painting, 102 Royal (1851); painter, Johnson cor. St. Louis (1867); journeyman painter (1868); landscape painter (1869, 1871); portrait painter (1870); landscape painter, 439 Rampart (1872); portrait painter, 30 Orleans (1873).
Exhibited: Salon, Paris (1848–49, 1853); St. Charles and St. Louis Exchanges (1850); WAGENER's (1867); WAGENER & MEYER's (1870–71); Grand State Fair (1871).
Awarded: Grand State Fairs, silver medal for best southern landscape in oil, diploma and $20 for best head in oil, diploma and $20 for best compostion in oil (1867), and gold medal for best landscape in oil (1868).
First major LA landscape painter of the 19th century; helped introduce European painting traditions, particularly those of the Barbizon school. Although his parents were New Orleanians, he was born in Paris, and in his early years lived intermittently in each of the two cities. Upon the death of his father (1836), he received a substantial inheritance which provided him with the funds for extensive travel and study. He served as a draftsman on an expedition sponsored by Napoleon III to Algeria, in search of the source of the Nile (Nov. 1856–Mar. 1857). By late 1857, he was in N.O. to stay, opening a studio with PAUL POINCY on Camp. In July 1861, he joined the 10th Louisiana Infantry of the Confederate army, resigning his commission within a few months (Feb. 1862). He lost most of his money during the Civil War, afterward living frugally, painting and teaching his craft for a living. Clague is credited with establishing the LA landscape school: among his pupils were N.O. artists WILLIAM H. BUCK and MARSHALL J. SMITH, JR. In his later years, Clague painted in summer resort areas of southern LA, the Gulf Coast, and Spring Hill AL. Internationally known for his scenes of bayous, swamps, and the lakeshores, Clague was also an accomplished portrait painter.
References: NOCD 1842, 1853, 1867–73; Bee, Dec. 13, 1850, Apr. 15, 1851, June 21, 1861, Jan. 22, 1871, Nov. 30, 1873; Comm. Bull., Jan. 21, 1871; Courier, Jan. 15, 1852; D. Pic., Feb. 20, Mar. 23, May 3, 1867, Jan. 10, 19, 1868, Nov. 6, 1870, Mar. 12, 1871, Dec. 2, 1873, Sept. 25, 1875, Mar. 16, 1876, Nov. 15, 1877, May 26, 1881, Feb. 14,

1890, Feb. 14, 1893, Dec. 18, 1903; *D. States*, Apr. 17, 1880, May 26, 1881, Jan. 20, 1882, Apr. 13, 1884; *Demo.*, Nov. 4, 1877, Jan. 13, 1878; Collier, "A Romantic Classicist," *Dixie*, Oct. 27, 1974; *Repub.*, Nov. 23, 1871, Dec. 2, 1873, May 17, 1874; *Times*, Mar. 12, 1871; *T. Demo.*, July 30, 1883, Jan. 24, 1884, Dec. 29, 1901; Jordan, "Clague Seen in Retrospective," *T. Pic.*, Nov. 25, 1974; Booth, 2:336; Bruns, 311; Coulon MS, Scrapbook 100, LSM; Groce and Wallace; Glenk, 69, 74; Harter and Tucker, 119; LSM, *Biennial Report for 1922-23*, 58; LSM, *Biennial Report for 1924-25*, 50; Mechanics' and Agricultural Fair Asso., *Report* (1867):29, (1868):42; N.O. Death Certificate (1873), 59:937, NOPL; "Roster of Artists," Special Collections, TU; Thompson, "Checklist"; Toledano, *Clague*; *Present Age*, Feb. 1871, 23; St. Louis Cemetery II, Interment Book, Archives of the Archdiocese of New Orleans; U.S. Census (1870), roll 522.

CLARET, E.
Sculptor, active N.O. 1851; also builder.
Contemporary listings: sculptor, St. Philip betw. Dauphine and Burgundy (1851).
Possibly Etienne Claret (called "Larose"), born St.–Marcelin (Isère), France ca. 1808; died N.O. Sept. 11, 1860.
References: NOCD 1851-55, 1857-58; *Bee*, Sept. 12, 1860.

CLARK, CHARLES W. *See also* HOFELINE, ALBERT D.
Born Harrisonburg VA ca. 1820-24; died N.O. Dec. 19, 1907.
Lithographer, active N.O. 1869-70; primarily printer.
Contemporary listings: lithographer, 106 Gravier (1869-70).
Awarded: Grand State Fair, silver medal for best specimen of lithography (1870).
Arrived in N.O. ca. 1849; partner in Clark & Brisbin, printers (1857-61), and in Clark & Hofeline, printers (1874-82).

References: NOCD 1857-61, 1870-83, 1888-93, 1895-96, 1898-1901, 1903-1907; *D. Pic.*, Dec. 20, 1907; *Item*, Dec. 20, 1907; *Repub.*, Oct. 17, 1869; Groce and Wallace; Mechanics' and Agricultural Fair Asso., *Report* (1870):31; U.S. Census (1860), roll 416.

CLARK, GEORGE
Born ca. 1810-20.
Painter, active N.O. 1840.
Contemporary listings: portrait painter, artist (1840).
References: *D. Pic.*, Dec. 3, 1840; U.S. Census (1840), roll 133.

CLARK, J. R. *See also* CHILDS, CLARK & CO.
Born ca. 1800-20.
Engraver, active N.O. 1841-43.
Contemporary listings: CLARK & CO. (1841-42); note engraver, cor. Common and St. Charles (1842); engraver, cor. St. Charles and Common (1843).
References: NOCD 1841-43; *D. Pic.*, Nov. 23, 1841, June 23-Aug. 12, 1842 (advs.); Groce and Wallace; U.S. Census (1840), roll 133.

CLARK & CO.
Engravers, active N.O. 1841-42; also printers; J. R. CLARK, owner.
Contemporary listings: engravers, cor. St. Charles and Common (1841-42).
Primarily engravers of southern bank notes.
References: NOCD 1841; *D. Pic.*, Nov. 23, 1841, June 23-Aug. 12, 1842 (advs.).

CLARKE, MISS A.
Sketch artist, art teacher, painter, active N.O. 1882.
Studied: with Professor G. A. Gilbert of Toronto, Canada, and N.Y.C.
Contemporary listings: artist and teacher of drawing and painting, 50 Robertson (1882).
Awarded: Art Exhibition of British North America, Toronto, first and second prizes for drawing (1870).
References: *D. Pic.*, Mar. 3, 1882.

CLARKE, JOHN HAWLEY
Born DE ca. 1831-32; died N.O. July 15, 1911.

Colorer, sketch artist, active N.O. 1856–85; primarily photographer.
Contemporary listings: CLARKE & HEDRICK (1856); colorer of photographs, 101 Canal (1872, 1879–82); colorer of photographs, 99 and 101 Canal (1875); colorer of photographs, 151 Canal (1885).
Exhibited: Baton Rouge LA fair (1860).
Awarded: Louisiana State Fair, honorable mention for best drawing in pastel (1870).
Secured the services of GEORGE DAVID COULON to color photographs (1872). His business at 101 Canal was also an art gallery and painting studio.
References: NOCD 1857, 1860–61, 1869–1907, 1911–14; *Bee*, Mar. 28, 1875; *D. Pic.*, Nov. 24, 1872, July 17, 1914; *National Repub.*, Dec. 11, 1872; *Repub.*, May 6, 1876; Land, 79; Mechanics' and Agricultural Fair Asso., *Report* (1870):31; Morrison, *Industries*, 160; Smith and Tucker, 74–79, 154–55; THNOC 1981.369-.64; U.S. Census (1860), roll 421.

CLARKE & HEDRICK
Colorers, active N.O. 1856; primarily photographers; JOHN HAWLEY CLARKE, F. S. HEDRICK, partners.
Contemporary listings: photographic colorers, 94 Canal (1856).
References: NOCD 1857; *D. Orleanian*, Dec. 21, 1856; Smith and Tucker, 77–78.

CLASSEN, JAMES M.
Engraver, active N.O. 1843; also printer.
Contemporary listings: engraver, 52 Canal (1843).
In N.Y.C. (1844–50).
References: *D. Pic.*, Mar. 8, 1843; Groce and Wallace.

CLAUDE, ADRIENNE
Born N.O. ca. 1859; died N.O. Jan. 24, 1920.
Painter, active N.O. 1892–1919.
Contemporary listings: artist (1892, 1898, 1905, 1907, 1909, 1912, 1914, 1917); portrait painter, 914 Marigny (1904); portrait painter, 2478 Dauphine (1916).
References: NOCD 1891–92, 1895, 1898, 1904–1907, 1909–19; *T. Pic.*, Jan. 25, 1920.

CLAYTON, GEORGE
Painter, active N.O. 1888.
Contemporary listings: scenic painter, Eden Theatre (1888).
References: NOCD 1888–89, 1891, 1893; *Mascot*, Jan. 7, Feb. 18, 1888.

CLEAL, M. D. *See* ANDERSON & CLEAL

CLEARY, EDWARD P.
Born LA Apr. 1853; black.
Painter, active N.O. 1872–1901; also sign and ornamental painter.
Contemporary listings: painter (1872, 1886, 1888–89, 1891–92, 1897–1901); painter, 182 St. Mary (1878); artist, Peniston cor. Perrier (1887); portrait painter (1890, 1900); artist (1893–96).
Exhibited: Colored People's Exhibit, World's Industrial and Cotton Centennial Exhibition (1884–85).
Painted portraits and still lifes, and also did japanning and ornamentation of objects.
References: NOCD 1872–1901; *D. Pic.*, Feb. 24, 1885; U.S. Census (1900), roll 575.

CLEBURNE, REV. ROBERT C.
Born Bellville, Ireland ca. 1828; died N.O. May 10, 1891.
Sketch artist, active N.O. 1867.
Bookkeeper for the U.S. Custom House when he drew a vignette representing the process of unloading vessels and warehousing goods and the seal of the state of LA (1867). Later he served the Episcopal Church in Cheneyville LA until 1889, when he returned to N.O. to become the pastor of St. John's Episcopal Church.
References: NOCD 1870–76, 1890–91; *D. City Item*, May 11, 1891; *Repub.*, May 30, 1867.

CLEMENTS, GEORGE HENRY
Born N.O. ca. 1855; died 1935.
Painter, active N.O. ca. 1870–87.
Studied: Union Art League, N.Y.C.; Julien's Academy, Paris (1881); Colarossi's (ca. 1881–82); Paris (1883); Florence (ca. 1884).
Contemporary listings: portrait painter (1875); artist, 19 Commercial (1879); artist, 3 Carondelet (1880).
Exhibited: FRANK WAGENER's (1882–83, 1885); J. Eastman Chase's, Bos-

ton (1887); ARTISTS' ASSOCIATION OF
NEW ORLEANS (1899); ART ASSOCIA-
TION OF NEW ORLEANS (1904, 1914);
Salon, Paris; Dudley Gallery, London.
Memberships/positions: New York
Water Color Club; Boston Society of
Water Color Painters; Boston Water
Color Club; Salmagundi Club, N.Y.C.
(1904).
While working in a cotton buyer's
office, Clements began painting portraits in oil (ca. 1870). In 1875 he
was praised as having a remarkable
talent for portrait painting. The
Commercial Bulletin (Nov. 5, 1875)
reported that he was only 20 years
old and had "never taken a lesson in
drawing, painting, or in the mixing
of colors, . . ." In 1880, Clements left
N.O. to begin his formal art instruction. He went to TX, then to N.Y.C.
to study art at the Union Art League.
He made sketches in the Catskill
Mountains with Benjamin B. G. Stone
(1880); and toured France, Switzerland, and Italy (1883–84), making
sketches and etchings from nature
and copying paintings and frescoes;
and went to Rome (May 1884). He
opened a studio in Boston (Jan.
1887), and spent the summer of 1887
painting in N.O. and on a cotton
plantation near Opelousas LA. Later
Clements became a resident of
Flushing NY (ca. 1900, 1904), and
then N.Y.C. (1914, 1926).
References: NOCD 1879–80; *Bull.*,
Nov. 5, 1875; *D. Pic.*, June 21, Nov
1, 1885, Mar. 13, 1887; *D. States*,
Nov. 12, 1880, Jan. 20, 1882, Jan.
16, 1887; *Harlequin*, Dec. 6, 1899,
4; *T. Demo.*, July 17, 1883, Mar. 2,
1914; AANO, *Catalogue* (1899); Art
Asso, *Catalogue* (1904, 1914); Clements, 146–50; Cline, *Art and Artists*,
6; Fielding, *Dictionary*; Information
courtesy the Archives of American
Art; Rightor, 385; Seebold, 1:315.

CLIFFORD, JOHN
Born Sweden ca. 1848.
Lithographer, active N.O. 1870; pri-
marily pressman, printer.
Contemporary listings: lithographer
(1870).

References: NOCD 1866–68, 1870–
93; U.S. Census (1870), roll 519.

CLINE, DR. ISAAC MONROE
Born Madisonville TN Oct. 13, 1861;
died N.O. Aug. 3, 1955.
Restorer, art dealer, active N.O.
1901–54.
Memberships/positions: Art Club,
Washington DC; National Arts Club,
N.Y.C.
Meteorologist, author, and art collector who came to N.O. in Aug.
1901. Cline was head of the U.S.
weather bureau station at N.O. until
1935; upon retirement, he opened
an art dealership, the Art House. He
collected art extensively throughout
his life and was the first in N.O. to
give a focused attention to local antique art. As the honorary curator of
the Louisiana State Museum, two of
his biennial reports were important
histories of the N.O. art scene and
were subsequently published: *Art
and Artists in New Orleans During the
Last Century* (1922) and *Contemporary Art and Artists in New Orleans*
(1924). His interest and example
started a second generation of col
lectors in acquiring and saving 19th-
century LA art. Father–in–law of
CAPT. ERNEST E. BONNAR DRAKE.
References: NOCD 1902–33, 1935,
1938, 1940, 1942, 1945–47, 1949,
1952–55; *D. Pic.*, Jan. 23, 1910, Nov.
12, 1913; *States*, July 9, 1945; *T. Pic.*,
Jan. 28, 1934, Aug. 4, 1955; Cline,
Art and Artists; Cline, *Contemporary
Art*; Cline, *Storms, Floods and Sunshine*; Freeman; Kendall, *History*,
2:790–93; LSM, *Biennial Report for
1934–35*, 70–71; NCAB; Stern's
Auction Co., *Catalogue* (1911);
Who's Who in America, 1936–37.

CLIPP, MICHAEL
Sculptor, active N.O. 1873.
Contemporary listings: sculptor
(1873).
References: NOCD 1873.

COATES, ALICE SCUDDER. *See* SCUDDER,
ALICE RAYMOND

COCKE, FRANCES LAWRENCE HOWE.
See HOWE, FRANCES LAWRENCE

COHEN, ISAAC
Artist, active N.O. 1878–93; also
photographer.

Contemporary listings: artist (1878, 1880, 1893).

Possibly Isaac Cohen, died Covington LA Sept. 28, 1899.

References: NOCD 1878–80, 1882–83, 1889, 1891–93; *D. Pic.*, Sept. 30, 1899.

COLAC, DENIS

Sculptor, active N.O. 1841–42.

Contemporary listings: marble sculptor, 83 Basin (1841–42).

References: NOCD 1841–42; Groce and Wallace.

COLE, CHARLES OCTAVIUS

Born Newburyport MA July 1, 1814.

Painter, active N.O. 1838–42.

Contemporary listings: portrait painter, 15 Merchants Exchange and cor. Exchange and Canal (1838); portrait painter, cor. Exchange and Canal and 9 Royal (1839); portrait painter, 9 Royal and cor. Royal and Bienville (1840); portrait painter, cor. Royal and Bienville (1841); portrait painter, oppos. St. Charles Hotel (1842).

Exhibited: Exchange Hotel (1839).

Cole lived in Portland ME during the summer of 1839 and moved back there from at least 1850–56.

References: NOCD 1838, 1841–42; *D. Pic.*, Dec. 15, 1838–Jan. 2, 1839 (advs.), Jan. 3, 1839–Jan. 3, 1840 (advs.), Feb. 9, Nov. 19, 1839, Feb. 4–Aug. 25, 1840 (advs.); *T. Pic.*, Mar. 15, 1967; Glenk, 74; Groce and Wallace; U.S. Census (1840), roll 132.

COLE, NANCY M.

Artist, active N.O. 1885.

Contemporary listings: artist, 159 Lafayette (1885).

References: NOCD 1885.

COLEMANN, BROWNING

Art craftsman, active N.O. 1903.

Studied: NEWCOMB COLLEGE (1901–1903).

References: NOCD 1906–1907; Poesch, *Newcomb Pottery*, 46, 98, 112, 116, 118.

COLLARD, _____

Sketch artist, active N.O. 1824.

Made two hand–colored drawings of the interior of St. Mary's Church, Chartres (1824).

References: LSM, *Biennial Report for 1920–21*, 77.

COLLAS, LOUIS ANTOINE

Born Bordeaux, France 1775; died 1856.

Painter, active N.O. 1822–29.

Studied: with François André Vincent, Paris.

Contemporary listings: portrait and miniature painter, 35 St. Peter (1822); portrait and miniature painter, 87 St. Peter (1823); portrait and miniature painter, 81 St. Peter and 83 St. Peter (1824); portrait and miniature painter, cor. Royal and St. Ann (1826); oil and miniature portrait painter, Orleans (1827); oil and miniature portrait painter, cor. Royal and St. Peter (1828); oil and miniature portrait painter, 244 Royal (1829).

Exhibited: Salon, Paris (1798–99, 1812, 1831, 1833); St. Petersburg, Russia (1808–11); American Academy of Fine Arts, N.Y.C. (1816, 1820); American Academy, Philadelphia (1816); Elkin's Exchange (1823).

French miniaturist and portrait painter who traveled to Russia and painted members of the czar's court. He came to the U.S. and was listed in N.Y.C. as "Lewis Collers" (1816). Collas painted there, in Charleston SC, in Philadelphia, and along the eastern seaboard. His residence in 1820 was in N.Y.C., but by 1822 he had moved to N.O. where he lived and painted intermittently until 1829, while continuing frequent visits to the North. Collas returned to Paris in 1831–32.

References: NOCD 1822–24; *Courier*, Apr. 22–24, 1826 (advs.), Apr. 5–7, 1827 (advs.), Apr. 5–7, 1828 (advs.), Mar. 7–16, 1829 (advs.); *Gazette*, Jan. 20, 1823, Jan. 28, 1824; Bénézit; Bruns, 311; Carolina Art Association, 45–49; Friends of the Cabildo, *250 Years*, 40, 49; Glenk, 50, 68, 74; Groce and Wallace; Harter and Tucker, 119; LSM, *Biennial Report for 1920–21*, 28–29, 34, 62; LSM, *Biennial Report for 1916–1917*, 100; Metropolitan Museum,

24; Salam, 18–22; U.S. Census, (1840), roll 132; WPA, "Lives."

COLLINS, CHARLES
Born London, England ca. 1818–20; died N.O. Mar. 8, 1899.
Engraver, active N.O. 1842–50; primarily printer.
Contemporary listings: SHIELDS & COLLINS (1842, 1848–50); engraver (1850).
Arrived N.O. ca. 1836, according to his obituary.
References: NOCD 1842, 1846, 1855–61, 1867–68, 1870–84, 1886–98; *D. Pic.*, Mar. 9, 1899; Groce and Wallace; U.S. Census (1850), roll 237, (1870), roll 522.

COLOMB, CHRISTOPHE
Painter, active N.O. 1814.
Contemporary listings: scenic painter, Orleans Theatre (1814).
Painter of *White Hall Plantation* (ca. 1800), the home of the Bringier family, whose daughter, Fanny, Colomb married.
References: Anglo–American Art Museum, *Louisiana Landscape*, item 1; Groce and Wallace; Kane, *Plantation*, 89–96; Laussat, 65; Orleans Parish Notarial Archives, Marc Lafitte, Feb. 28, 1814, 4:66; Seebold, 1:129, 131.

COLON, A.
Artist, active N.O. 1849; also sign painter.
Contemporary listings: artist, 3 Dauphine (1849).
References: NOCD 1849–50, 1854; Groce and Wallace.

COLSON, CHARLES
Painter, active N.O. 1837.
Painted three extant portraits.
References: Collier, "The World of Art: 'Operation Paintings' Project Cited," *T. Pic.*, June 21, 1964; Glenk, 74.

COLUMBIO, SPALDIME
Born KY Jan. 1871.
Artist, active N.O. 1900.
Contemporary listings: artist (1900).
References: U.S. Census (1900), roll 574.

COMFORD, EDWARD P. *See* THOMAS & COMFORD

COMMERCIAL ART STUDIO
Art dealers, painters, active N.O. 1902–1908, GEORGE F. BILLINGS, N. D. Burke, Arthur B. Tebetts, mgrs,

Contemporary listings: 606 Commercial (1902); 311 Baronne (1906–1908).
Specialized in portraits in pastel, crayon, and watercolor.
References: NOCD 1902, 1906–1908; *D. States*, Feb. 10, 1902.

COMMERCIAL LITHOGRAPHY. *See* AUDIBERT, LOUIS

CONEIO, JOSEPH
Painter, active N.O. 1893–1900.
Contemporary listings: artist (1893); painter (1900).
References: NOCD 1893, 1900.

CONNER, SAMUEL A.
Born ca. 1860; died N.O. April 17, 1915.
Lithographer, active N.O. 1878; primarily photographer, also printer.
Contemporary listings: lithographer (1878).
References: NOCD 1872, 1875, 1877–1916; *Town Talk*, July 1904, 31; N.O. Death Certificate (1915), 163:323; NOPL.

CONNORS, JOHN M.
Born IL ca. 1888.
Lithographer, active N.O. 1910.
Contemporary listings: lithographer (1910).
References: U.S. Census (1910), roll 524.

CONRAD, CHARLES JAMES
Born N.O. Dec. 1, 1881; died N.O. Apr. 24, 1950.
Engraver, active N.O. 1900–47; also photographer.
Contemporary listings: engraver (1900, 1905, 1907, 1911); engraver, PHOTO-ENGRAVING CO. (1904), photo–engraving dept., *Times–Democrat* (1906, 1908–10); foreman, photo–engraving dept., *Times–Democrat* (1912–16); engraving dept., *Times–Picayune* (1917); foreman, photo–engraving dept., *Times–Picayune* (1918).
Left school at age 12 to become a copy boy for the *Daily Picayune*; then worked as an engraver with his uncle, FRANÇOIS BILDSTEIN (ca. 1894–98). Conrad worked in various supervisory capacities as a photoengraver at the *Times–Picayune* (1919–49).

References: NOCD 1900–1901, 1904–33, 1935, 1938, 1940, 1942, 1945–47, 1949; *T. Pic.*, Jan. 25, 1937, Apr. 25, 1950; Orleans Parish Registrar of Voters, NOPL; U.S. Census (1900), roll 572, (1910), roll 521.

CONRAD, FRANK B.
Painter, active N.O. 1893–1947.
Contemporary listings: CONRAD & JONES (1893–94); painter (1907–18). Listed in various capacities as a clerk or laborer (1894–1905) and painter (1919–47).
References: NOCD 1884–86, 1888, 1890, 1892–1905, 1907–33, 1935, 1938, 1942, 1945–47, 1949, 1952–56.

CONRAD & JONES
Painters, active N.O. 1893–94; FRANK B. CONRAD, John D. Jones, partners.
Contemporary listings: portraits, 134 S. Rampart (1893); portrait painters, 252 S. Rampart (1894).
References: NOCD 1893–94.

CONROY, DENNIS W.
Art teacher, active N.O. 1850.
Contemporary listings: teacher of cromatic painting (1850).
References: NOCD 1846; *D. Delta*, Jan. 15, 1850.

CONS, JOHN
Engraver, active N.O. 1881.
Contemporary listings: engraver (1881).
References: NOCD 1881.

A. CONSTANT & CO.
Painters, active N.O. 1861; primarily photographers.
Contemporary listings: portrait painters (1861).
References: NOCD 1861; *Bee*, Jan. 1, 1861; *La Renaissance Louisianaise* 1(Nov. 10, 1861):375; Smith and Tucker, 155.

CONSTANTINE, JOHN
Born Athens, Greece Dec. 31, 1866; died N.O. Jan. 5, 1940.
Painter, active N.O. 1905–38; also decorator.
Contemporary listings: scenic artist (1905, 1918); scenic artist, 603 S. Telemachus (1906–1907); artist (1908); scenic artist, 607 S. Tele-

machus (1909–12); scenic artist, 609 S. Telemachus (1913–14); proprietor, CRESCENT SCENIC STUDIO (1915–17).
Listed as an artist (1920–21, 1928–30, 1938), painter (1923–27), commercial artist (1932), and interior decorator (1935).
References: NOCD 1904–18, 1920–21, 1923–33, 1935, 1938, 1940; *T. Pic.*, Jan. 6, 1940; Orleans Parish Registrar of Voters, NOPL; U.S. Census (1910), roll 520.

CONTINENTAL BANK NOTE COMPANY
Engravers, active N.O. 1872.
Contemporary listings: engravers, 27 Carondelet (1872).
A branch of the N.Y.C. firm; J. L. Meserve was the local agent.
References: *National Repub.*, Feb. 6, 1872; *Repub.*, Jan. 30, 1872.

CONVERSO, RAFFAELE
Born Italy.
Painter, active N.O. 1885.
Contemporary listings: panel and fresco painter (1885).
References: *D. States*, Aug. 5, 1885.

COOK, FREDERICK C.
Born London, England ca. 1829; died N.O. Feb. 26, 1899.
Painter, active N.O. ca. 1851–99.
Contemporary listings: artist (1887).
Businessman who came to N.O. (ca. 1851) where he was the owner of Belleville Iron Works, Algiers LA. Cook invented over 60 patented mechanical devices and studied science and art in his spare time.
References: NOCD 1887, 1893–98; *D. Pic.*, Feb. 27, Mar. 5, 1899.

COOKE, GEORGE
Born St. Mary's County MD Mar. 17, 1793; died N.O. Mar. 26, 1849.
Art dealer, painter, active N.O. 1844–49.
Contemporary listings: painter, (1844–47); proprietor, National Gallery of Paintings (1844–49); portrait painter, 13 St. Charles (1846); artist (1849).
Exhibited: Globe Theatre, Richmond VA (1829, 1833); Pennsylvania Academy of Fine Arts, Philadelphia, American Academy of Fine Arts, N.Y.C. (1833); National Academy of

Design, N.Y.C. (1834); Boston Athenaeum (1835); Charleston SC (1836); Charles Bird King's Gallery, Washington DC (1837); Apollo Gallery, N.Y.C. (1838–39, 1844); American Art Union, N.Y.C. (1839); Royal oppos. the Post Office (1844); National Gallery of Paintings (1845–46).

Memberships/positions: American Academy of Fine Arts (1832), director (1834–35).

Portrait, historical, and landscape painter, and author. He began painting professionally in 1819; then traveled in Europe, studying the works of the old masters and painting many original scenes (1826–31). By 1838 he had returned to the U.S. when his view of Charleston SC was engraved by W. J. Bennett and published in N.Y.C. During 1842–43 he resided in Columbus GA, before moving to Athens GA and then AL. In 1844, Cooke had arrived in N.O. where he met Daniel Pratt, millionaire industrialist and art collector from AL. Pratt outfitted the third and fourth stories of his new warehouse at 13 St. Charles as the National Gallery of Paintings and made Cooke its proprietor. Its purpose was to display and sell the works of celebrated artists, both foreign and American; many of the works displayed were from the collection of N.O. businessman James Robb. It continued until Cooke's death and was replaced the following year by CHARLES GALVANI's gallery.

References: NOCD 1846; *Bee*, Jan. 20–27, 1845 (advs.), Mar. 24, 27, 1847; *Comm. Bull.*, Jan. 7–8, 1847 (advs.), Mar. 25, 1847, Mar. 31–Apr. 7, 1847 (advs.), Apr. 14, 1847; *Comm. Times*, Jan. 29, 1848; *Courier*, Dec. 16, 1844, Jan. 20, Apr. 2, Dec. 2, 1845; *D. Crescent*, Mar. 28, 1849, Mar. 14–16, 1850 (advs.); *D. Delta*, Dec. 24, 1845, Apr. 13, 25, 26, 1847, Apr. 30, 1850; *D. Pic.*, Apr. 26, Dec. 17, 1844, Jan. 17, Feb. 13, Mar. 4, 1845, Oct. 17, 1850; *D. Tropic*, Dec. 17, 1844, Jan. 15, 30, Feb. 12, 17–18, 20, 22, 26, Mar. 1, 6, 17, Apr. 10, May 20, Dec. 3, 22,

1845, Jan. 21, Feb. 11, 1846; *De-Bow's Review*, Mar. 1846, 287; Richmond *Standard*, Oct. 1, 8, 1881; *Wkly. Delta*, Apr. 9, 1849; Banks, 449–54; Dunlap, 2:346–47; Groce and Wallace; Information courtesy George E. Jordan; N.O. Death Certificate (1849), 11:1401, NOPL; Norman, 169–72; Rudolph, 117–53; Waugh, 3.

COOKE, MARIA AMELIA (Mrs. Singleton Jones Cooke)
Born ca. 1808; died Summerville AL Feb. 19, 1888.
Painter, art teacher, active N.O. 1859.
Contemporary listings: painter and teacher of painting and drawing, cor. Prytania and Thalia (1859).
Before N.O., she taught in Philadelphia and parts of the South, including Vicksburg MS.
References: *D. Pic.*, Oct. 14, 1859, Feb. 26, 1888.

COOPER, WASHINGTON BOGART
Born near Jonesboro TN 1802; died Nashville TN Apr. 19, 1889.
Painter, active N.O. 1838–39.
Contemporary listings: portrait painter, cor. Canal and Exchange Pl. (1838–39).
Portrait painter who worked with his younger brother WILLIAM BROWN COOPER, in Chattanooga, Memphis, and Knoxville TN. They made a tour down the Mississippi River to Natchez and N.O. and advertised together in N.O. as "W. Cooper," (1838–39). They also painted in Selma AL (1840s).
References: *D. Pic.*, Dec. 6, 1838–Aug. 22, 1839 (advs.); Groce and Wallace; Lay, 402; U.S. Census (1840), roll 133.

COOPER, WILLIAM BROWN
Born Smith County TN 1811; died Chattanooga TN 1900.
Painter, active N.O. 1838–39.
Studied: National Academy of Design, N.Y.C. (1832); Europe.
Contemporary listings: portrait painter, cor. Canal and Exchange Place (1838–39).
Portrait painter who worked with his elder brother WASHINGTON BOGART COOPER.

References: *D. Pic.*, Dec. 6, 1838–
Aug. 22, 1839 (advs.); Bruns, 311;
Groce and Wallace; Lay, 402; U.S.
Census (1840), roll 133.

COPMANN, PETER
Born Rudköbing, Denmark Feb. 25,
1794; died Basseterre, Guadeloupe
1850.
Painter, active N.O. 1837.
Studied: l'Académie (1818).
Contemporary listings: portrait
painter, 22 Chartres (1837).
Exhibited: l'Académie (1819–20);
Copenhagen (1832); National Academy of Design, N.Y.C. (1834).
Itinerant portrait and landscape
painter who worked in Hamburg and
Dresden (1821). He immigrated to
the U.S. and worked in Brooklyn NY
(1834), Charleston SC (1834–35),
and Louisville KY (1848). Copmann
invented a fixative for pastel pictures.
References: NOCD 1837; Bénézit;
Groce and Wallace.

COQUET, ROSE
Born ca. 1797.
Painter, active N.O. 1817.
References: Ludlow, 137–38.

COQUILLE, JOHN HIPPOLYTE
Born Donaldsonville LA ca. 1883;
died Chicago IL Sept. 12, 1931.
Engraver, active N.O. 1901–1907;
primarily photographer.
Contemporary listings: engraver,
Daily Item (1901); engraver (1902–
1907).
References: NOCD 1900–16, 1918–
23; *T. Pic.*, Sept. 13–14, 1931; U.S.
Census (1910), roll 523.

CORADI, L.
Born France ca 1813.
Artist, active N.O. 1850.
Contemporary listings: artist (1850).
Lived in the same house as C. BERTON.
References: Groce and Wallace; U.S.
Census (1850), roll 235.

CORDTZ, ROBERT
Painter, active N.O. 1883.
Came to N.O. from Chicago to paint
life-size oil paintings representing
sports of all kinds for the walls of the
Baronne Street Pit where cock fights
were held.

References: *D. States*, Jan. 21, 1883;
T. Demo., Jan. 19, 1883.

CORNEBOIRE, THEODORE
Artist, active N.O. 1824.
Contemporary listings: artist, 145
Orleans (1824).
References: NOCD 1822, 1824;
Glenk, 74; WPA, "Lives."

CORNELL, J. V.
Born CT ca. 1815.
Painter, active N.O. 1859–66.
Contemporary listings: scenic
painter, Spalding and Rogers' Amphitheatre (1859–60); painter (1861,
1866); with Cornell & Gourly, painters (1861).
References: NOCD 1861, 1866; *D.
Pic.*, June 8, 1859; *D. True Delta*,
Feb. 5, 1860; U.S. Census (1860),
roll 416.

CORNIE, LOUIS
Sketch artist, active N.O. 1867.
Awarded: Grand State Fair, best colored crayon drawing (1867).
References: Mechanics' and Agricultural Fair Asso., *Report* (1867):28.

CORRADI, NESTORE
Born Italy.
Painter, active N.O. 1837.
Studied: Italy.
Contemporary listings: portrait and
miniature painter, 147 Old Levee
(1837).
References: *Bee*, Aug. 17–31, 1837
(advs.); Groce and Wallace.

CORVIN, JOSEPH C.
Born France ca. 1799.
Engraver, active N.O. 1820.
Arrived in N.O. on the brig *Gustave*
from Marseilles, France on Jan. 31,
1820.
References: Rieder, *New Orleans Ship
Lists*, 8.

COSSAS, _____
Artist, active N.O. 1842.
Contemporary listings: artist, Orleans Theatre (1842).
References: NOCD 1842.

COTTRELL, WILLIAM H.
Painter, active N.O. 1891.
Contemporary listings: portrait
painter, 286 Camp (1891).
References: NOCD 1876–84, 1886,
1889–92.

COULON, GEORGE DAVID
Born Seloncourt, France Nov. 14,
1822; died N.O. Feb. 28, 1904.
Painter, art teacher, restorer, co
lorer, active N.O. ca. 1838–1904.
Studied: with TOUSSAINT FRANÇOIS
BIGOT (1836, 1841); with ANTOINE
MONDELLI (ca. 1838–39); with LEON
POMAREDE (ca. 1839); with JULIEN
HUDSON (1840); with FRANÇOIS
FLEISCHBEIN; with JACQUES AMANS.
Contemporary listings: painter, 20
Jefferson (1843–44); portrait painter,
47 Conti (1846); portrait painter, 83
Conti (1849); portrait painter, 103
Conti (1850–56); portrait painter,
Claiborne cor. Laharpe (1857–58);
portrait painter, 94 Canal (1859);
portrait painter, cor. Canal and St.
Charles (1860); portrait painter
(1861, 1880, 1895, 1900); portrait
and fancy painter, 80 Camp (1865);
portrait painter, 80 Camp (1866–67);
portrait painter, 37 Camp (1868–79);
photograph colorer, with JOHN HAW-
LEY CLARKE (1872); painter (1896);
artist (1881, 1888, 1891–92); portrait painter, 378 N. Claiborne
(1882–84, 1889–90, 1894); artist,
378 N. Claiborne (1885–87); instructor of elementary class, ARTISTS'
ASSOCIATION OF NEW ORLEANS (1886–
87); artist, 1536 N. Claiborne (1897,
1904); portrait painter, 1536 N.
Claiborne (1898, 1901–1902); artist, 228 Exchange Pl. (1903).
Exhibited: Library of Lelièvre
(1860); John Hawley Clarke's gallery (1872); SOUTHERN ART UNION
(1881–82); THEODORE LILIENTHAL'S
(1883); FRANK WAGENER'S (1883);
Creole Exhibit, American Exposition
(1885–86); Artists' Association of
New Orleans (1889–90, 1894, 1896,
1899, 1901); Tulane University
(1892–93).
Memberships/positions: Southern Art
Union (1880–81); Artists' Association of New Orleans (1885–1903).
Notable portrait and landscape
painter who came to N.O. as a child
with his parents (1833). He studied
with many local artists and assisted
Léon Pomarède in painting the
Transfiguration in St. Patrick's

Church (ca. 1839). Coulon painted
his first portrait in 1841 and began
painting landscapes, still lifes, and
animals; by 1845 he had added con-
servation work to his career, handling the relining and restoring of
canvases. He also taught drawing and
painting at schools for young ladies
in N.O. (1851–65) and later gave
private art lessons. He gained commissions for decorations in public
buildings such as for the frescoing of
the ceiling of the Old Criminal Court
in the Cabildo and for paintings for
religious and charitable institutions.
Coulon painted from nature and from
death masks; after 1853 he is also
believed to have painted portraits
from photographs. Many of his blue–
and–green–toned landscape paintings were also taken from photographs and prints. He worked with
photographer John Hawley Clarke,
coloring photographs with pastels
and oils (1872); and as his interest in
photography grew, so did his tech-
nical skill in capturing minute details, especially in the clothing and
jewelry in his portraits. He earned a
comfortable living as a painter and
was long a prominent figure in N.O.
Coulon was one of the founders of
the Southern Art Union (1880) and
of the Artists' Association of New Orleans (1885), in which he remained
active throughout his later years. An
autobiographical letter was written
late in Coulon's life (Mar. 24, 1901)
for his friend BROR ANDERS WIKSTROM
and contains a brief, and often in
accurate, annotated list of the painters who lived and worked in N.O.
during his long career in the city.
Husband of MARIE-PAOLINE CAS-
BERGUE COULON; father of GEORGE JO-
SEPH AMEDE COULON and MARY ELIZ-
ABETH EMMA COULON.
References: NOCD 1843–44, 1846,
1849–61, 1866–1904; NOBD 1865;
Bee, Oct. 8, 1860, Nov. 24, 1872,
May 27, 1880, May 4, Nov. 16, 1881;
Courier, Mar. 5, 1854; Current Top-
ics, Jan. 1891, 24; D. Pic., Jan. 12,
1871, Nov. 24, 1872, May 26, 1881,
Mar. 19, 1882, Nov. 1, 1885, May

7, 1887, Dec. 17, 1889, Dec. 17, 1890, Mar. 3, 1892, Feb. 14, 1893, May 17, 1897, Feb. 29, 1904; *D. States*, Oct. 29, Nov. 5, 1886, Dec. 17, 1890; *Demo.*, Feb. 27, May 12, 1881; *Item*, Feb. 29, 1904; *National Repub.*, Nov. 24, Dec. 11, 1872; *T. Demo.*, July 17, 30, 1883, Dec. 17, 1890, June 11, 1893, Dec. 14, 1894, Feb. 29, 1904; AANO, *Catalogue* (1890, 1899, 1901); Bonner, *Southern Quarterly*; Bonner, thesis; Bruns, 311; *The City of New Orleans*, 43; Coulon MS, Scrapbook 100, LSM; Creole Exhibit, 12; Fielding, *Dictionary*; Glenk, 74; Groce and Wallace; LSM *Biennial Report for 1924–25*, 27; LSM *Biennial Report for 1926–27*, 29; LSM *Biennial Report for 1928–29*, 35, 69, 71; Mount 135–36; U.S. Census (1850), roll 236, (1870), roll 522, (1880), roll 462, (1900), roll 572.

COULON, GEORGE JOSEPH AMEDE
Born N.O. July 28, 1854; died ca. 1922.
Painter, active N.O. 1874–1908; also photographer.
Contemporary listings: portrait painter, with his father GEORGE DAVID COULON (1874–75, 1879); portrait painter (1876–78, 1880); artist (1881, 1889–90, 1893–94, 1897); portrait painter, 378 N.Claiborne (1882–84); artist, 228 Exchange Pl. (1898–1902, 1904–1905, 1907–1908); portrait painter, 228 Exchange Pl. (1906).
Exhibited: SOUTHERN ART UNION (1881).
In 1888 he published *350 Miles in a Skiff Through the Louisiana Swamps*, an illustrated diary of his travels, which included his drawings and photographs of the Atchafalaya Basin. Known for his portraits and still lifes, he created a 28–panel pastel and oil decoration of fruit, fish, and game for Fabacher's restaurant, 137 Royal (1894). Son of MARIE–PAOLINE CASBERGUE COULON; brother of MARY ELIZABETH EMMA COULON.
References: NOCD 1872, 1874–85, 1889–90, 1893–94, 1897–1902, 1904–1908; *D. Pic.*, May 26, 28,

1881; *Demo.*, Feb. 27, 1881; *D. States*, Nov. 4, 1888; Bonner, *Southern Quarterly*, 41, 48, 57, 61; Bonner, thesis; *The City of New Orleans*; Coulon MS, Scrapbook 100, LSM; Coulon, *350 Miles*; Glenk, 50; LHS (1903); U.S. Census (1870), roll 522, (1880), roll 462; Wiesendanger, 38–41.

COULON, MARIE–PAOLINE CASBERGUE
(Mrs. GEORGE DAVID COULON)
Born N.O. June 14, 1831; died N.O. July 3, 1914.
Sketch artist, painter, active N.O. ca. 1867–1901.
Exhibited: Peck's store (1867).
Awarded: Grand State Fair, best pastel drawing (1867).
Painted still lifes of birds and game, but gave up painting sometime before 1901 due to poor health. Mother of GEORGE JOSEPH AMEDE COULON and MARY ELIZABETH EMMA COULON.
References: NOCD 1906–1908, 1912; *Times*, Feb. 3, 1867; Bonner, *Southern Quarterly*, 41, 47, 61; Bonner, thesis; Coulon MS, Scrapbook 100, LSM; Mechanics' and Agricultural Fair Asso., *Report* (1867):28; U.S. Census (1870), roll 522, (1880), roll 462, (1900), roll 572.

COULON, MARY ELIZABETH EMMA
Born N.O. May 11, 1859; died N.O. Apr. 1, 1928.
Painter, active N.O. 1900–20.
Contemporary listings: portrait painter (1904); artist (1915).
Exhibited: Grunewald's music store (1904).
Portrait, landscape, and still life painter who signed her works and was generally referred to as Emma Coulon. Daughter of GEORGE DAVID COULON and MARIE–PAOLINE CASBERGUE COULON; sister of GEORGE JOSEPH AMEDE COULON.
References: NOCD 1915–16, 1920–21; *D. States*, Sept. 18, 1904; *T. Pic.*, Apr. 3, 1928; Bonner, *Southern Quarterly*, 41, 48, 61; Bonner, thesis; Coulon MS, Scrapbook 100, LSM; Glenk, 74; LSM, *Biennial Report for 1928–29*, 34–35, 71; Morton's Auction Exchange (Mar. 13, 1979); U.S.

Census (1870), roll 522, (1880), roll 462, (1900), roll 572.

COURET, GUSTAVE J.
Born N.O. Jan. 3, 1883; died N.O. Mar. 28, 1972.
Sketch artist, active N.O. 1915–22; primarily draftsman, architect.
Exhibited: ART ASSOCIATION OF NEW ORLEANS (1915).
With BERNARD BARRY he designed the official flag of N.O. (1918). Brother of JOHN P. COURET.
References: NOCD 1906–1909, 1912–16, 1920–25, 1927–33, 1935, 1938, 1940, 1942, 1947, 1949, 1952–55, 1973; NOSD 1959, 1963–66; *T. Pic.*, Feb. 6, 1918, Mar. 30, 1972; Art Asso., *Special Exhibition*; Orleans Parish Registrar of Voters, NOPL.

COURET, JOHN P.
Born N.O. Nov. 16, 1881; died Apr. 27, 1967.
Painter, active N.O. ca. 1915.
Exhibited: ART ASSOCIATION OF NEW ORLEANS (1915).
Amateur artist who was a bank employee and then cotton broker. He served on the N.O. Cotton Exchange (1924–56). Brother of GUSTAVE J. COURET.
References: NOCD 1901–15, 1917–33, 1935, 1938, 1940, 1942, 1947, 1949, 1952–56, 1958, 1960–62, 1965–67; *T. Pic.*, Apr. 28, 1967; Art Asso., *Special Exhibition*.

COUTANT, WILLIAM H.
Painter, active N.O. 1832.
Contemporary listings: miniature painter, 89 Customhouse (1832).
References: *Courier*, Nov. 14–16, 1832 (advs.); Bruns, 311; Glenk, 74; Groce and Wallace.

COWAN, DOCIE
Lithographer, active N.O. 1890.
Contemporary listings: lithographer (1890).
References: NOCD 1889–90.

COWELL, _____
Sketch artist, active N.O. ca. 1845.
Engravings of French Quarter buildings in Norman's *New Orleans and Environs* (1845) were made from his original drawings. *Cf.* COWELL, JO-SEPH LEATHLEY, JR.; COWELL, JOSEPH S.
References: Norman.

COWELL, JOSEPH LEATHLEY, JR.
Painter, active N.O. 1835–46; also decorator.
Contemporary listings: assistant scenic artist, with ANTOINE MONDELLI, St. Charles Theatre (1835); chief scenic artist, Camp Street Theater (1836–37); scenic artist, American Theatre (1846).
Son of JOSEPH LEATHLEY COWELL, SR.
Cf. COWELL, _____; COWELL, JOSEPH S.
References: *D. Delta*, Oct. 30, 1846; Groce and Wallace; Kendall, *Golden Age*, 102–3, 121; Ludlow, 515.

COWELL, JOSEPH LEATHLEY, SR.
Born near Torquay, England Aug. 7, 1792; died London, England Nov. 13, 1863.
Painter, active N.O. 1837–38.
Contemporary listings: scenic painter, Camp Street Theater (1837–38).
Exhibited: Pennsylvania Academy of Fine Arts, Philadelphia (1828); National Academy of Design, N.Y.C. (1829).
Actor, author, and painter who began his career in portrait painting, but gave it up for the N.Y.C. stage (1812). He worked in England as an actor and scene painter, later returning to the U.S. (1821). He appeared in N.O. theaters (1829–47) and occasionally designed and painted the sets. Father of JOSEPH LEATHLEY COWELL, JR.
References: NOCD 1830; *Courier*, Mar. 20, 1837; *D. Delta*, Oct. 30, 1846; *True Amer.*, Oct. 20, 23, 1838; Groce and Wallace; Kendall, *Golden Age*, passim.

COWELL, JOSEPH S.
Born England ca. 1815; died N.O. Feb. 18, 1848.
Painter, active N.O. 1847.
Painter who came to N.O. from Memphis and lived in the city 10 months, the last five of which were spent in the hospital. *Cf.* COWELL, _____; COWELL, JOSEPH LEATHLEY, JR.
References: Louisiana Charity Hospital Death Records, 1847–50, NOPL; Groce and Wallace.

COX, CLARK

Painter, active N.O. 1891–1904.
Contemporary listings: with FRANK COX's scenic studio, Grand Opera House (1891); artist (1892–93, 1895–96, 1898); artist, Grand Opera House (1899); chief scenic artist, Elysium Theatre (1904).
Exhibited: ARTISTS' ASSOCIATION OF NEW ORLEANS (1892, 1894).
Scenic artist and fresco painter who worked with EMILE E. NIPPERT in TX and N.O. for Frank Cox's studio (1891). He was associated with COX BROTHERS, and then with French scenic artist BERGER in the decoration of the French Opera House (1903). He later moved to Dallas TX from N.O. and after almost 60 years of scenic work devoted himself to painting landscapes of the western U.S. He was probably the brother of EUGENE COX and Frank Cox.
References: NOCD 1892–93, 1895–96, 1898–99; *Current Topics*, Jan. 1893, 11; *D. Pic.*, Apr. 18, May 9, 1904; *D. States*, Sept. 27, 1891; *Item*, Apr. 27, May 15, 19, 1904; *T. Demo.*, Dec. 14, 1894, Sept. 22, 1896; Fisk, 107–8; THNOC artists files.

COX, EUGENE

Painter, active N.O. 1895–99.
Contemporary listings: artist (1895–96, 1899).
Scenic artist and fresco painter who was associated with COX BROTHERS. Probably the brother of CLARK COX and FRANK COX.
References: NOCD 1895–99; *T. Demo.*, Sept. 22, 1896; Seebold, 1:316; THNOC artists files.

COX, FRANCES A.

Painter, active N.O. ca. 1880–84.
Studied: with ANDRES MOLINARY (1881).
Exhibited: SEEBOLD's (1884).
Memberships/positions: SOUTHERN ART UNION (1880–81).
Sister of N.O. author George Washington Cable.
References: NOCD 1880, 1882–83; *D. Pic.*, Mar. 23–24, May 4, 1881, Nov. 30, 1884; *Demo.*, May 27, 1880, May 12, 1881; Thompson, "Checklist."

COX, FRANK

Painter, active N.O. 1890–99; also architect.
Contemporary listings: scenic artist, French Opera House (1890); scenic studio, Grand Opera House (1891); scenic artist, St. Charles Theatre (1891–92); artist (1893, 1897, 1899); COX BROTHERS (1895).
Exhibited: ARTISTS' ASSOCIATION OF NEW ORLEANS (1891–92, 1894, 1898–99).
Memberships/positions: Artists' Association of New Orleans, v. pres. (1899).
N.Y.C. scenic artist and theatrical architect who designed, built, and remodeled interiors of theaters across the U.S., including TX, AL, IL, and LA. He set up a branch of his business in N.O., painted scenery for numerous productions, held contracts for several southern theaters, and maintained a studio in the Grand Opera House, with CLARK COX and EMILE E. NIPPERT as employees (1891). He designed the New Crescent Theatre on the site of Grunewald Hall (1893), although it was never built. As the architect, builder, and designer for the new Grand Opera House interior, he had Cox Brothers paint the curtain and do the frescoing for the Jan. 3, 1895 opening. Cox also painted and exhibited landscapes from his travels around the U.S. Probably the brother of Clark Cox and EUGENE COX.
References: NOCD 1891–99; *Current Topics*, Jan. 1892, 24, 26, Jan. 1893, 11; *D. City Item*, Dec. 13, 1892; *D. Pic.*, July 20, 1890, Jan. 20, 1893, Apr. 29, 1894, Sept. 1, 22, 1895; *D. States*, Mar. 22, Sept. 27, 1891, Sept. 18, 1892, Jan. 9, 1893; *Item*, Dec. 17, 1891; *T. Demo.*, Dec. 13, 1892, Jan. 8–9, Feb. 1, 1893, Dec. 14, 1894, Sept. 22, 1896; AANO, *Catalogue* (1891, 1898, 1899); Gallegly, *Footlights*, 145; La Cour, 203; Seebold, 1:316.

COX BROTHERS

Painters, active N.O. 1895; CLARK COX, EUGENE COX, FRANK COX, probably brothers.

Contemporary listings: scenic artists and frescoers, Grand Opera House (1895).

Scenic artists and fresco painters who worked in many southern theaters, particularly in TX and LA. They painted the curtain and did the frescoes for the new Grand Opera House (1895) and produced pageants and scenery for the Comus carnival organization for several years.
References: *D. Pic.*, Sept. 1, 22, 1895; *T. Pic.*, July 5, 1914; Gallegly, *Footlights*, 140; La Cour, 203; THNOC artists files.

CRAGER, SIDONIA LOEB. *See* LOEB, SIDONIA

CRAIG, FANNY ESHLEMAN (1. Mrs. Fountain Barksdale Craig; 2. Mrs. Jacques Ventadour)
Born N.O. June 9, 1875; died N.O. Dec. 30, 1969.
Painter, active N.O. 1918–34.
Studied: Pennsylvania Academy of Fine Arts, Philadelphia.
Exhibited: ART ASSOCIATION OF NEW ORLEANS (1918).
Studied with Andre Lohte (ca. 1924) and continued to exhibit in the 1920s and 1930s with the Art Association of New Orleans, Arts and Crafts Club, and Artists' Guild.
References: NOCD 1907–1908, 1910–15, 1917–21, 1923–33; *Item–Trib.*, Oct. 31, 1926; *Morn. Trib.*, Jan. 26, 1927, Mar. 30, 1934; *Item*, Jan. 16, Feb. 6, 18, Apr. 1, June 12, 1921, Feb. 18, 1923, Dufour, "A La Mode: Former Orleanian's Poems Full of Color and Imagery, If Obscure," *States–Item*, June 16, 1966; *T. Pic.*, Apr. 1, 1934, Dec. 31, 1969; Art Asso., *Catalogue* (1918, 1919); Orleans Parish Registrar of Voters, NOPL.

CRAPPUS, JEAN
Born Baden, Germany ca. 1828.
Artist, active N.O. 1860.
Contemporary listings: artist (1860).
References: U.S. Census (1860), roll 418.

CRASSONS, HARRY WILLIAM
Born N.O. Mar. 25, 1883; died N.O. Sept. 30, 1953.

Painter, active N.O. 1906–49; also draftsman.
Contemporary listings: artist (1906, 1909–11, 1914, 1916); scenic artist (1907); portrait painter (1910); scenic artist, Tulane & Crescent Theatres (1912); artist, 1430 Chartres (1913, 1915); painter (1918).
As an apprentice, Crassons designed scenery at the French Opera House before 1900. He was a partner in Soulie & Crassons (from 1922), maker of carnival parade floats for the major organizations.
References: NOCD 1906–16, 1918–31, 1933, 1935, 1940, 1942, 1945–47, 1949, 1952–53; *T. Pic.*, Oct. 1, 2, 1953; La Cour, 201, 203; Orleans Parish Registrar of Voters, NOPL; THNOC 1974.25.19.418–.420; U.S. Census (1910), roll 521.

CRASSONS, HOWARD M.
Born N.O. Jan. 6, 1888.
Painter, active N.O. 1910; primarily sign painter.
Contemporary listings: scenic painter (1910).
Listed as a sign painter (1907–24) and then owner of his own sign shop (1924–60).
References: NOCD 1907–1908, 1912–15, 1917, 1920, 1924–33, 1935, 1938, 1940, 1942, 1945–47, 1949, 1952–56, 1958, 1960–62, 1964–69, 1971–74, 1977; Orleans Parish Registrar of Voters, NOPL; U.S. Census (1910), roll 521.

CRAWFORD, JOSEPHINE MARIEN
Born N.O. Dec. 31, 1878; died N.O. Mar. 25, 1952.
Painter, sketch artist, active N.O. 1895–1941.
Initially a self–taught artist, Crawford did sketches as a hobby; her earliest works date to 1896. In 1922 she began studying art at the New Orleans Art School, run by the Arts and Crafts Club. She continued her artistic education with André L'Hôte in Paris (1927–28). In N.O. she had her first one–man show at the Arts and Crafts Club (1928) and regularly exhibited at the club throughout her career. Other exhibitions included the Montross Gallery, N.Y.C. (1929);

NEWCOMB COLLEGE; Louisiana State University; Boyer Galleries, Philadelphia (1935); Central American Art Circuit (1941); and a retrospective exhibition at the DELGADO MUSEUM OF ART (1965). She was awarded the Blanche S. Benjamin prize for an outstanding LA scene for her painting *Rue Kerlerec* (1934). Her paintings were usually portraits, landscapes, and still lifes executed with a simplicity of line to produce strong compositions and an economy of color.
References: NOCD 1931–33, 1935, 1947, 1949; *Item–Trib.*, Dec. 9, 1928, Apr. 19, 1935; *States*, Feb. 9, 1934, Mar. 26, 1952; *T. Pic.*, Jan. 28, Feb. 11, Apr. 1, 1934, May 5, 1935, Mar. 4, 1941, Mar. 26, 1952; Collier, "Gallery Sets First Fall Exhibition," *T. Pic.*, Sept. 19, 1965; Jordan, "Crawford Bequest," *T. Pic.*, Apr. 2, 1978; Delgado, *World*; Orleans Parish Registrar of Voters, NOPL; THNOC, Josephine Crawford Papers; THNOC 1978.23.1–.389.

CRAWFORD, PETER
Lithographer, active N.O. 1894.
Contemporary listings: lithographer, Academy of Music (1894).
References: NOCD 1894.

CREMONA, PETER
Sculptor, active N.O. 1814.
Contemporary listings: sculptor in wax (1814).
References: *Courier*, Aug. 1, 1814; *Gazette*, July 28, 1814, Apr. 25, July 8, 1815; WPA, "Lives."

CRESCENT ART STUDIO
Painters, active N.O. 1905; Samuel Jochelson, mgr.
Contemporary listings: portrait painters, 316 Baronne (1905).
References: NOCD 1905.

CRESCENT BUREAU OF ILLUSTRATION
Engravers, designers, active N.O. 1884; also printers.
Contemporary listings: 68 Camp (1884).
Advertised "Illuminated printing, artistic engraving on wood, stone, or metal. Lithographic designing a specialty."
References: *Mascot*, Mar. 29, 1884.

CRESCENT CITY ART STAINED GLASS WORKS
Designers, active N.O. 1897–1902; JACOB JULIUS LIPS, owner.
Contemporary listings: 338 Baronne (1897); 618 Baronne (1898–1900); 419 Carondelet (1901–1902).
References: NOCD 1897–1902.

CRESCENT LITHOGRAPHY (Crescent Lithograph Office)
Lithographers, active N.O. 1869.
Contemporary listings: lithographers, 94 Camp (1869).
Listed under HUGH LEWIS. The firm lithographed a letterhead of the Southern Hospital Association for Disabled Soldiers after a drawing by DOUGLAS E. JERROLD, SR.
References: NOCD 1869; THNOC 1953.146.

CRESCENT PHOTOGRAPHIC GALLERY
Colorers, active N.O. 1866; primarily photographers; M. J. Hinton, owner.
Contemporary listings: colorers, 99 Camp (1866).
References: *D. Pic.*, Apr. 18, 1866; Smith and Tucker, 160.

CRESCENT SCENIC STUDIO
Painters?, active N.O. 1915–25; JOHN CONSTANTINE, owner (1915, 1917), ALBERT G. AUFDEMORTE, mgr. (1922–24).
Contemporary listings: 607 S. Telemachus (1915, 1917).
Listed as Crescent Scenic Studio and Papier Maché Works in 1915 and as Crescent Scenic Studio in 1919, 1922–25.
References: NOCD 1915, 1917, 1919, 1922–25.

CROEGAERT, GEORGE
Born Anvers, France 1848.
Painter, active N.O. 1869–71.
Contemporary listings: portrait painter (1871).
Exhibited: Salon des Artistes Français (1914).
Awarded: Grand State Fair, silver medal for flower painting in oil (1869).
References: NOCD 1871; *D. Pic.*, Apr. 11, 1869; Bénézit; Mechanics' and Agricultural Fair Asso., *Report* (1869):72.

CROFT, EDWARD J.
Born Austria or Prussia ca. 1827–35.
Painter, active N.O. 1870–81; also
sign and ornamental painter.
Contemporary listings: artist (1870–
72, 1878, 1880); painter (1874,
1879–81); fresco painter (1875).
References: NOCD 1871–72, 1874–
75, 1878–81; T. Deutsche Zeitung,
Feb. 2, 1867; U.S. Census (1870),
roll 519, (1880), roll 463.

CROUCH, EMILY
Painter, active N.O. 1897.
Assisted LILLIE JONTE in painting a
temperance union banner which was
designed by MARY CROUCH (1897).
References: D. Pic., Apr. 10, 1897.

CROUCH, MARY
Designer, active N.O. 1897.
Designed a temperance union ban-
ner which was painted by LILLIE
JONTE with the assistance of EMILY
CROUCH (1897). Possibly Mary
Haughton Crouch (Mrs. Walter V.
Crouch), born Jackson MS Sept. 19,
1846; died N.O. July 22, 1899.
References: D. Pic., Apr. 10, 1897;
N.O. Death Certificate (1899),
120:62, NOPL; THNOC Cemetery
Survey.

CROWLEY, JOSEPH
Lithographer, active N.O. 1890–95.
Contemporary listings: lithographer
(1890, 1893, 1895).
References: NOCD 1890, 1893–95.

CRUISIN, C.
Born VA ca. 1812.
Engraver, active N.O. 1860.
Contemporary listings: engraver
(1860).
References: Groce and Wallace; U.S.
Census (1860), roll 421.

CRUMB, LEE H.
Engraver, designer, active N.O.
1870–73.
Contemporary listings: wood and
metal engraver, 106 Camp, and designer (1870); engraver, 68 Camp
(1870–71).
Awarded: Grand State Fair, best
specimen of engraving on wood
(1870).
References: NOCD 1870, 1873; D.
Pic., Apr. 27, 1870; Baroncelli-Ja-
von, 191; Boyd, 158, Mechanics' and

Agricultural Fair Asso., Report
(1870):31.

CULVER, JEREMIAH E.
Born N.O. Sept. 25, 1891; died N.O.
Apr. 1, 1959.
Lithographer, active N.O. 1909–33;
also pressman, printer.
Contemporary listings: lithographer
(1909); lithographer, WALLE & CO.,
LTD. (1910, 1912).
References: NOCD 1909, 1912–25,
1928–29, 1931, 1933, 1945–47,
1949, 1952–55; States-Item, Apr. 2,
1959; Orleans Parish Registrar of
Voters, NOPL; U.S. Census (1910),
roll 525.

CUNGMAN, MR. _____
Colorer, active N.O. 1855.
Contemporary listings: photograph
colorer, with EDWARD JACOBS (1855).
References: D. Delta, Apr. 8, 1855.

CUP AND SAUCER CLUB
Art association, active N.O. ca. 1879.
Informal art and literary circle organized by ANDRES MOLINARY at 3
Carondelet, the former studio of EV-
ERETT B. D. JULIO. Perhaps the first art
club in N.O., its name came from a
requirement that members bring
their own cup and saucer for their
refreshments.
References: Seebold, 1:127; Tallant,
315; WPA, "Lives."

CURADO, JOSEPH G.
Artist, active N.O. 1895–99.
Contemporary listings: artist (1895–
96); F. G. KOECKERT & CO. (1897);
mgr., ART LITHOGRAPH CO. (1898);
supt. and mgr., Art Lithograph Co.
(1899).
References: NOCD 1895–99.

CURLEY, JACOB
Artist, active N.O. 1905.
Contemporary listings: artist, SOUTH-
ERN ART STUDIO (1905).
References: NOCD 1905.

CURRIER, NATHANIEL
Born Roxbury MA Mar. 27, 1813;
died N.Y.C. Nov. 20, 1888.
Lithographer; also printer.
Lithographer, printer, and publisher
whose N.O.-related prints included
Ruins of Planters' Hotel, New Orleans
(1835), Gen: Andrew Jackson. The
Hero Of New-Orleans, General An-

drew Jackson. At New–Orleans Jan: 8th. 1815 (ca. 1840s), and *The Battle Of New–Orleans, Fought Jany. 8th. 1815* (1842). He became a partner in the nationally known lithographic firm of CURRIER AND IVES and worked there until his retirement (1857–80). References: Beall, 144; *DAB*; Fielding, *Dictionary*; Groce and Wallace; THNOC 1950.24, 1950.27, 1975-.100; David Woodward, 109.

CURRIER AND IVES
Noted N.Y.C. lithography firm which began with partners NATHANIEL CURRIER and James Merritt Ives, and designed, printed, and sold popular prints of American scenes and events (1857–1907). N.O.–related images included *The City Of New Orleans* (ca. 1872–74), *The Levee–New Orleans* (1884), and *The City of New Orleans, And The Mississippi River. Lake Pontchartrain in Distance* (1885). References: *Encyclopaedia Brittanica*; Groce and Wallace; Pratt; THNOC 00.35, 1941.1, 1950.47.

CURTAIN, MISS M. A.
Art teacher, active N.O. 1873.
Contemporary listings: teacher of drawing and painting, 339 Carondelet (1873).
References: NOCD 1873; *D. Pic.*, Jan. 26, 1873.

CURTIS, CHARLES ANTHONY
Born N.O.; died N.O. Nov. 27, 1960. Engraver, active N.O. 1900–12; primarily jeweler, watchmaker.
Contemporary listings: artist (1900); engraver, 2256 Dryades (1912).
References: NOCD 1900–1901, 1903–13, 1915–16, 1918–26, 1928–33, 1935, 1940, 1942, 1945–47, 1949, 1952–56, 1958, 1960; *T. Pic.*, Nov. 30, 1960; Woods, *Directory* (1912):79.

CURTIS, NATHANIEL CORTLANDT
Born Smithville NC Feb. 8, 1881; died N.O. Apr. 15, 1953.
Sketch artist, painter, active N.O. 1912–53; primarily architect.
Exhibited: ART ASSOCIATION OF NEW ORLEANS (1915–17).
Architect, professor, artist, and author. With WILLIAM and ELLSWORTH WOODWARD, he helped found the school of architecture at Tulane University. By 1921 he joined the architectural firm of Moise H. Goldstein, later Goldstein, Parham, and Labouisse (1921–53) as chief designer. At Tulane he was professor of architecture (1912–17), lecturer (1921–37), and associate professor (1937–53). Curtis was an active member and instructor at the Arts and Crafts Club and exhibited watercolors and sketches there (1921, 1927). He designed a map, *The Creole City of New Orleans*, (1930) and wrote *New Orleans Its Old Houses, Shops and Public Buildings* (1933) which he illustrated with drawings he had done from 1914 to 1932 of local architecture and street scenes. References: NOCD 1913–17, 1921–33, 1935, 1938, 1940, 1942, 1945–47, 1949, 1952–53; *Item*, Aug. 14, 1921, Apr. 16, 1953; *Morn. Trib.*, Oct. 19, 1927; Art Asso., *Catalogue* (1916, 1917); Art Asso., *Special Exhibition*; Curtis; Information courtesy Nathaniel Cortlandt Curtis, Jr., Sept. 16, 1986; Orleans Parish Registrar of Voters, NOPL; THNOC 1958.74.

CUSACHS, PHILIP G.
Born N.O. July 21, 1841.
Illustrator, sketch artist, active N.O. 1870–84.
Studied: Leipzig, Germany.
Contemporary listings: pen and ink artist (1874).
Exhibited: N.O. (ca. 1874); N.Y.C. (1876).
Memberships/positions: Art League, N.Y.C. (1884).
Artist who visited studios in Spain and later set up his own studio at his father's store in N.O. (1870). His pen-and-ink drawings were used in the N.Y.C. *Daily Graphic*: these included the procession and tableau of the Comus carnival organization (Feb. 24, 1874) and of McComb City MS (Apr. 2, 1874). Following work in Chattanooga TN (1874), Cusachs obtained employment on the art staff of the *Daily Graphic* (1874). He later did sketches of the floats for the Momus carnival parade (1876). He be-

came a resident of N.Y.C. and was distinguished there as a cartoonist, newspaper artist, and one of the founders of the Art League. He visited N.O. in June 1874 and in April 1884 and his illustrations appeared in the city's *Figaro* later in 1884.

References: NOCD 1872–74; *D. Pic.*, May 31, 1884; *D. States*, Apr. 18, 23, 1884, Jan. 16, 1887; *Figaro*, Apr. 19, 26, May 17, 1884; *Repub.*, Feb. 21, Mar. 1, 8, Apr. 8, 23, June 27, 1874, Jan. 23, Feb. 5–6, 1876; THNOC 1979.235.118–.136.

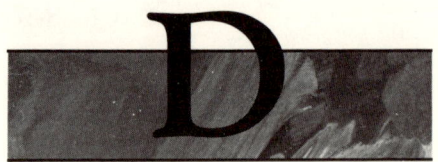

D

D'ABNOUR, RICHARD
Artist, active N.O. 1811.
Miniature artist who stencilled and inked on ivory a commemorative mourning piece associated with Mrs. W. C. C. Claiborne, wife of LA's first American governor.
References: NOCD 1811; Huber et al. 90; THNOC 1975.143.2.

DAHMER, GEORGE
Lithographer, active N.O. 1895.
Contemporary listings: lithographer (1895).
References: NOCD 1893, 1895–97.

DAKIN, CECILIA VIETS. *See* JAMISON, CECILIA VIETS DAKIN HAMILTON

DALE, ARTHUR C.
Engraver, active N.O. 1902–30.
Contemporary listings: photo–engraver, PHOTO–ENGRAVING CO. (1902); engraver, Photo–Engraving Co. (1903–1904); engraver (1905–1907, 1914–18).
References: NOCD 1901–1907, 1912–27, 1929–31, 1933, 1935.

DALLAS, JACOB A.
Born Philadelphia PA 1825; died N.Y.C. Sept. 9, 1857.
Illustrator, painter, active N.O. 1852.
Studied: with Bass Otis, Pennsylvania Academy of Fine Arts, Philadelphia.
Exhibited: Arcade (1852); Armory Hall (1855).
Memberships/positions: National Academy of Design, N.Y.C.
From ca. 1850, Dallas lived in N.Y.C. where he worked as an artist for *Harper's* and with other artists on panoramas. He and JOSEPH KYLE were in N.O. in Feb. 1852 to make sketches for a panorama of the Mississippi River. While in the city, they exhibited an oil painting of a view of Canal Street seen from the levee. Dallas is not recorded again in N.O., but he did contribute to an exhibition of a series of paintings by 10 prominent American artists illustrating John Bunyan's *Pilgrim's Progress*. They were shown in N.O. (Mar.–May 1855), and then in Baton Rouge LA, and Natchez and Vicksburg MS. Some of Dallas's N.O. sketches from 1852 were published in *Emerson's Magazine and Putnam's Monthly* in Oct. 1857, the month after his death.
References: *Courier*, Mar. 6, 1855; *D. Delta*, Jan. 24, 1860; *D. Pic.*, Apr. 1, 13, 1855, Oct. 18, 1857; *D. Times*, Feb. 18, 1852; Bénézit; Groce and Wallace; Hamilton, 100.

DALY, JOHN J., JR.
Artist, active N.O. 1900; primarily photographer.
Contemporary listings: artist (1900).
References: NOCD 1898–1900, 1903–1908, 1910, 1912–14, 1916.

DAMERON–PIERSON CO., LTD.
Engravers, lithographers, active N.O. 1904–present; primarily printers, stationers; Frank Dameron (born 1861; died 1938), Joseph Ogden Pierson (born ca. 1875; died 1953), partners.
Contemporary listings: lithographers, 317 Camp (1905–1907); lithographers., 317–321 Camp (1908, 1910); lithographers, 400–404 Camp (1910–18).
Founded in 1904 as printers, blank book makers, stationers, and lithographers. Beginning 1908, the firm also sold office supplies; it moved to its present location at 400 Camp (1910) where it continues in operation.
References: NOCD 1905–33, 1935, 1938, 1940, 1942, 1945–47, 1949, 1952–56, 1958, 1960–62, 1964–69, 1971–79; *T. Pic.*, June 1, 1925, Dec. 5–6, 1938, May 25, 1953; Kendall, *History*, 3:932.

DANGERFIELD, FRED
Painter, active N.O. 1895.
Contemporary listings: scenic artist, Grand Opera House (1895).
References: *D. States*, Oct. 20, 1895.

DANNEMAN, L.
Sculptor, active N.O. 1849–51.
Contemporary listings: sculptor, 182
Toulouse (1849–51).
References: NOCD 1849–51; Groce
and Wallace.

DANTONET, EMILE J.
Died N.O. Dec. 4, 1933.
Painter, active N.O. 1882–92.
Studied: SOUTHERN ART UNION (1882).
Exhibited: Southern Art Union
(1882); ARTISTS' ASSOCIATION OF NEW
ORLEANS (1886–87, 1889–92).
Memberships/positions: Artists' Association of New Orleans, financial
secy. (1886–90), treas. (1890).
Probably an amateur artist, he was
listed as a clerk (1884–93), a bookkeeper (1894–1902), and with Louisiana Red Cypress Co. (1908–31).
References: NOCD 1876–1933;
Current Topics, Jan. 1891, 24; *D. Pic.*,
May 2, 1882, Nov. 6, 1886, Dec. 17,
1887, Dec. 17, 1889, Nov. 13, Dec.
17, 1890, Dec. 13, 1892; *D. States*,
Nov. 5, 1886; *T. Demo.*, Dec. 13,
1892, *T. Pic.*, Dec. 5, 1933; AANO,
Catalogue (1886, 1890, 1891); Kendall, *History*, 2:659.

DA PONTE, CORNELIA E. DURANT
Died N.O. Oct. 6, 1865.
Art teacher, active N.O. 1848–62.
Contemporary listings: teacher,
drawing and painting (1848);
teacher, drawing and painting, Mrs.
Hurd's, Camp (1851–52); teacher,
drawing and painting, 159 Poydras
(1859–60); teacher, drawing and
painting, 197 Camp (1861–62).
Mother of DURANT DA PONTE.
References: *D. Crescent*, July 14,
1848, Mar. 24, 1851; *D. Delta*, May
9, 1847, Oct. 21, 1859, Jan. 12,
1860, June 13, 1861; *D. Pic.*, Mar.
28, 1851, Jan. 3, 1852, Oct. 7, 1865;
D. States, Jan. 8–Mar. 13, 1862
(advs.).

DA PONTE, DURANT
Born ca. 1826; died Alameda CA
Aug. 6, 1894.
Painter, active N.O. 1883–93.
Exhibited: ARTISTS' ASSOCIATION OF
NEW ORLEANS (1887); Tulane University (1893)

Memberships/positions: Artists' Association of New Orleans (1888,
1890).
Amateur artist who was a social and
political leader, prominent journalist, newspaper editor, and lawyer. Da
Ponte began his career at the *Daily
Crescent* (ca. 1844) and was later
listed with the *Daily Picayune* (1850–
52, 1870), the *Louisiana Courier*
(1853–55), and the *New Orleans
Democrat* (1877). He worked as a
broker and financier during his later
years. Many of the paintings he exhibited were made during his travels
in the U.S., particularly in the West.
Son of CORNELIA E. DURANT DA PONTE.
References: NOCD 1850–57, 1859–
61, 1866–68, 1871, 1877, 1879,
1881–94; *Art and Letters*, 1(Dec.
1887):228; *D. Item*, Aug. 8, 1894;
D. Pic., Dec. 29, 1887, Feb. 24,
1888, Nov. 13, 1890, Feb. 14, 1893,
Aug. 18, Sept. 9, Dec. 30, 1894; *T.
Demo.*, Apr. 26, 1883, Oct. 8, 13,
1887, Feb. 15, 1893, Aug. 8, 1894;
Mount, 110–11.

DAQUERRE, MR.
Painter, active N.O. 1820.
Contemporary listings: with BARBIER,
scenic painter, Orleans Theatre
(1820).
References: *Courier*, Feb. 16, 1820.

DARDIGNAC, BERNARD
Born France ca. 1820.
Sculptor, art teacher, active N.O.
1860–66.
Contemporary listings: artificial
flower manufacturer, 167 Bourbon
(1860); artificial flowers, 161 Royal
(1861); teacher and manufacturer of
flowers, 161 Royal and 155 Royal
(1863); artificial flowers, 120 Carondelet (1866).
References: NOCD 1860–61, 1866;
Bee, Apr. 8, 1863; U.S. Census
(1860), roll 418.

DARLING, JAMES
Artist, active N.O. 1895.
Contemporary listings: artist (1895).
References: NOCD 1895.

DARODE, MR. _____
Painter, active N.O. 1819
Contemporary listings: miniature
painter, 44 Main (1819)

Advertised as being from Paris and a pupil of "the celebrated Isabat [Isabey]."
References: *Gazette*, Jan. 5, 1819; Bénézit.

DAVENOUS, MR. _____
Art teacher, active N.O. 1814.
Contemporary listings: drawing teacher, U. Dibart's Boarding School, Royal (1814).
References: *Courier*, May 6, 1814.

DAVENPORT, H. GEORGE
Illustrator, cartoonist, commercial artist, active N.O. 1912–14; black.
Contemporary listings: illustrator, cartoonist, 2723 Baronne (1912); illustrator, cartoonist, designer, 1819 Delachaise (1914).
Possibly Davenport who signed a drawing on the cover of *Harlequin* (Nov. 1, 1906).
References: *Harlequin*, Nov. 1, 1906, cover; Woods (1912), 16, (1914), 66.

DAVID, DR. GEORGE PHILIP PERCIVAL
Born N.O. ca. 1857; died N.O. Sept. 18, 1904.
Sculptor, active N.O. ca. 1873–97.
Studied: with Linniere, Paris.
Socially prominent N.O. physician who was also an amateur actor and singer. David studied sculpture while taking medical courses in Paris. Sculpting later became his favorite pastime, and he worked in marble and clay that was cast in bronze.
References: NOCD 1873, 1875–84, 1886–97; *D. Pic.*, Sept. 19, 1904; Mount, 171–72.

DAVID, LOUIS
Commercial artist, active N.O. 1890–93.
Contemporary listings: artist, with WILLIAM WATSON WASHBURN (1890); artist, NATIONAL PUBLISHING & PORTRAIT CO. (1892); artist (1893).
References: NOCD 1890, 1892–93.

DAVID, LOUIS P.
Born Cuba or N.O. ca. 1804–1808.
Painter, sketch artist, active N.O. 1837–71; also photographer, sign and ornamental painter.
Contemporary listings: painter (1837–38, 1841–42, 1866–70); portrait painter, 80 Royal (1849); portrait painter and drawing master, 80 Royal (1850–54); portrait and fresco painter, 50 St. Peter (1871).
References: NOCD 1837–38, 1841–44, 1846, 1849–61, 1866–71, 1874; Groce and Wallace; U.S. Census (1850), roll 235, (1860), roll 418, (1870), roll 521.

DAVID-PASCIN, MME. HERMINE
Artist, active N.O. ca. 1918.
Contemporary listings: 530 Royal (1918).
Exhibited: ART ASSOCIATION OF NEW ORLEANS (1918).
References: Art Asso., *Catalogue* (1918).

DAVIDSON, J. O.
Sketch artist, painter, active N.O 1883–84.
Illustrator for periodicals and for juvenile books, as well as a painter noted for scenes of maritime and naval history. Davidson was sent to N.O. in 1883 by *Harper's Weekly* to select a local writer for the text for his series of illustrations of N.O. He collaborated with newspaper writer LAFCADIO HEARN on articles which were published in 1883–84. Davidson's illustrations of Civil War engagements for *Century* included depictions of the 1862 naval engagements in and around N.O.; they appeared during 1884–86.
References: Cohn, 166–67; Sears, 355–57; Tinker, *Lafcadio Hearn*, 183–84; Turner, 200, 233.

DAVIES, ELIZA
Born ca. 1877.
Sketch artist, active N.O. ca. 1889.
Exhibited: ACADEMY OF FINE ARTS (1889).
References: *D. Pic.*, June 22, 1889.

DAVIES, KATHERINE (Sister Francis de Chantal)
Art craftsman, pottery decorator, active N.O. ca. 1885–1900; also needleworker.
Studied: TULANE FREE DRAWING CLASSES (1886).
Exhibited: ART LEAGUE OF NEW ORLEANS (1889).
Memberships/positions: NEW ORLEANS ART POTTERY CO. (ca. 1885–90).
Sister of NELLIE MARCIA DAVIES.

References: *D. Pic.*, Mar. 10, 1889;
Eve. Chronicle, May 22, 1886; Glenk,
287; LSM, *Biennial Report for 1924–
25*, 51; Ormond and Irvine, 36–37.
DAVIES, NELLIE MARCIA
Died N.O. Apr. 7, 1942.
Art craftsman, active N.O. ca. 1888;
also decorator.
Exhibited: TULANE DECORATIVE ART
LEAGUE FOR WOMEN (1888).
Sister of KATHERINE DAVIES.
References: *D. Pic.*, Feb. 12, 1888;
T. Pic., Apr. 8, 1942; Tulane Deco-
rative Art League, 2–3.
D'AVIGNON, FRANCIS
Artist, active N.O. 1867.
Contemporary listings: artist, 43
Baronne (1867).
Possibly the lithographer, engraver,
and portrait painter, born St. Pe-
tersburg, Russia ca. 1814, or France,
who came to the U.S. in the early
1840s and was active in N.Y.C.
(1844–59) and in Boston (1859–60).
References: NOCD 1867; Groce and
Wallace.
DAVIS, GEORGE
Lithographer, active N.O. 1880–87.
Contemporary listings: lithographer
(1880); lithographer, G. KOECKERT &
CO. (1887).
References: NOCD 1880, 1886–87,
1889.
DAVIS, MILFORD
Lithographer, active N.O. 1887–90.
Contemporary listings: lithographer,
G. KOECKERT & CO. (1887); lithogra-
pher, with CHARLES KUMMEL (1890).
References: NOCD 1887, 1890
DAVIS, PETER
Born N.O. Mar. 1848; died N.O. July
20, 1921.
Lithographer, engraver, active N.O.
1871–1921; also printer.
Contemporary listings: lithographer,
with CHARLES W. CLARK (1871); li-
thographer, with HUGH LEWIS (1872–
74, 1879); lithographer (1877–78,
1898, 1911, 1913–14, 1916–18);
NEW ORLEANS LITHOGRAPHING & EN-
GRAVING COMPANY (1880); NEW OR-
LEANS LITHOGRAPHING COMPANY
(1882–84); engraver, SOUTHERN
LITHOGRAPHIC COMPANY (1885); G.
KOECKERT & CO. (1886–88); T. FITZ-

WILLIAM & CO. (1889); lithographer,
with CHARLES KUMMEL (1890); li-
thographer, ART LITHOGRAPH CO.
(1899); lithographer, with MICHEL
CAPO (1900–1902); lithographer, H.
WEHRMANN & SONS (1903–1904); li-
thographer, WEHRMANN'S SONS
(1907–10); lithographer, T. FITZWIL-
LIAM & CO., LTD. (1912).
References: NOCD 1870–74, 1877–
90, 1893–95, 1898–1920; *Mascot*,
Mar. 18, 1882; *T. Pic.*, July 22, 1921;
U.S. Census (1910), roll 520.
DAVIS, THEODORE RUSSELL
Born Boston MA 1840; died Asbury
Park NJ Nov. 10, 1894.
Sketch artist, illustrator, active N.O.
1861–62; 1866.
Artist and correspondent with *Harper's Weekly* (1861–84), Davis was
sent on his first important assignment
to the South at the start of the Civil
War. Beginning in May 1861, he
traveled as a neutral agent with William H. Russell, a correspondent for
the London *Times*. Davis reached
N.O. probably in June, but any drawings made of the city were never
published because Davis's early
sketches were confiscated by members of a Confederate vigilance committee in Memphis TN. He was in
N.O. again in Sept. 1862, after making drawings of Baton Rouge LA and
the lower Mississippi River which
were published in *Harper's* (Aug.
1862). In July 1866, Davis returned
to N.O. as one of two artists (*Cf.*
WAUD, ALFRED R.) traveling separately to record the results of the
Civil War in the South and its re-
covery for *Harper's* (published Aug.
25).
References: *Harper's Wkly.*, June 22,
1861, 394, 397, July 20, 1861, 450,
Aug. 16, 1862, 520–25, Aug. 30,
1862, 556–59, Aug. 25, 1866, 534–
37, Sept. 1, 1866, 556; Friends of
the Cabildo, *250 Years*, 61, 66, 73;
Groce and Wallace; Kelly, 33; Toledano, "Marine Painters," 877.
DAY, ROBERT SLARK
Born Stonington CT Aug. 4, 1855;
died N.O. Nov. 16, 1895.

Painter, sketch artist, active N.O. ca. 1887–95.
Exhibited: ARTISTS' ASSOCIATION OF NEW ORLEANS (1887).
Prominent cotton broker who exhibited one year and, as an amateur artist, made watercolors and pen–and ink–drawings for his friends.
References: NOCD 1873, 1875–95; *Art and Letters* 1(June 1887), 1(Dec. 1887):228; *D. Pic.*, Dec. 17, 29, 1887, Nov. 19, 1895; Kendall, *History*, 2:660.

DEACHELER, MICHEL
Artist, active N.O. 1900.
Contemporary listings: artist (1900).
References: NOCD 1900.

DEADLE, LOUIS
Lithographer, active N.O. 1878.
Contemporary listings: lithographer, with H. WEHRMANN (1878).
References: NOCD 1878.

DE ARMAS, ARTHUR M.
Born N.O. Apr. 1850; died N.O. Apr. 27, 1903.
Artist, active N.O. 1881; primarily surveyor.
Contemporary listings: artist (1881).
Son of CHARLES ARTHUR DE ARMAS.
References: NOCD 1873–75, 1877–79, 1881, 1883–85, 1887–1900, 1902–1903; *D. Pic.*, Apr. 28, 1903; U.S. Census (1850), roll 238, (1860), roll 418.

DE ARMAS, CHARLES ARTHUR
Born N.O. ca. 1824–25; died N.O. May 12, 1889.
Artist, active N.O. 1849–85; primarily architect, surveyor, civil engineer.
Painted watercolors of N.O. buildings and sites used in real estate transactions. Father of ARTHUR M. DE ARMAS.
References: NOCD 1850–61, 1866–67, 1869–74, 1876, 1878–83, 1885–89; *D. Pic.*, May 13, 1889; Friends of the Cabildo, *N.O. Architecture*, 1:20, 41, 67, 107, 2:37, 53, 82, 83, 84, 86, 97, 157, 163, 211, 222, 4:40, 78, 79, 82, 101, 117, 141, 145, 149, 6:47; Orleans Parish Notarial Archives, Plan Books; U.S. Census (1860), roll 418.

DE BATZ, ALEXANDRE
Died Fort de Chartres, Illinois country 1759.
Sketch artist, active N.O. 1732–35; primarily draftsman, engineer, architect.
By 1730 De Batz had come to N.O., probably from Montaterre, France, as a draftsman for the king's engineers. Between Dec. 1731 and Jan. 1732, he made architectural drawings of the buildings in N.O., probably for a government inventory. He also traveled to the nearby Indian villages to make surveys and sketches, and on June 22, 1732, in N.O., he made two drawings from the sketches. One shows a temple structure, the chief's cabin, and Indians of the Colapissa tribe, and the other shows the chief of the Tunica tribe; they are the earliest known views of Indian life in the lower Mississippi Valley. His other drawings show Indians from the Illinois, Fox, and Atakapas tribes of LA (1735) and of Choctaw warriors and a Natchez chief. By 1733 De Batz was using the title "Engineer for the King" and in 1735 was sent to Mobile as engineer. He returned to N.O. by 1740 and again made plans and drawings of buildings and worked as an architect. After a posting in AR, De Batz was sent to Fort Chartres (ca. 1757), where he worked as engineer and architect until his death.
References: Bushnell, "Drawings," 1–15; Délégation, 57–58; Detroit Institute, 78–79; Huber and Wilson, *Basilica*, 11; Huber et al., *Louisiana Purchase*, 13–14, 18, 87; Josephy, 158–59; Montreal Museum; Richardson, 20–21; Samuel Wilson, *Bienville*, 31, 32, 35, 36; Samuel Wilson, *Capuchin*, 23–27; Samuel Wilson, "Louisiana Drawings," 75–89; Samuel Wilson, "Religious Architecture," 65–66; WPA, "Lives."

DE BEAUVILLE, ANDRE
Sculptor, active N.O. 1859.
A noted French sculptor in his day, De Beauville visited N.O. in 1859. In the city he met the actress ADAH ISAACS MENKEN, and roused in her

what became a lifelong interest in carving stone figures.

References: Paul Lewis, 79–80.

DEBUCOURT, PHILIBERT-LOUIS. *See* LACLOTTE, JEAN HYACINTHE

DE BUSEIL, COMPTE CHARLES
Born Paris, France ca. 1829; died Lafayette LA Oct. 17, 1895.
Painter, active N.O. ca. 1890s.
French painter who worked at the N.O. French Opera House. De Buseil also painted on canvas the landscapes on the ceiling and walls of the dining room of Myrtle plantation, near Lafayette LA (ca. 1891), and was noted in that city for his decorations in several public places.
References: *D. Pic.*, Oct. 18, 1895; WPA, *Louisiana*, 403.

DE CHANTAL, SISTER FRANCIS. *See* DAVIES, KATHERINE

DE CALCINARA, MARIE ROUSSEL. *See* ROUSSEL, MARIE

DE CHATILLON, JOSEPH AUGUSTE
Born Paris, France Jan. 29, 1808; died Paris Mar. 26, 1881.
Painter, designer, sculptor, active N.O. 1845–49; also decorator.
Studied: Ecole des Beaux Arts, Paris (1827).
Contemporary listings: artist and portrait, historical, and genre painter, 163 Royal (1846).
Exhibited: Salon, Paris (1831, 1836–46, 1848, 1857, 1859, 1866); 95 St. Charles (1847); ballroom, St. Louis Exchange (1849).
Awarded: Musée Royal du Louvre, Paris, gold medal (1836–37).
Painter and poet associated with the Romantic and Realist movements in France, a friend of Victor Hugo, and a portraitist of the French royal family. De Chatillon was first recorded in N.O. in June 1845 with N.O. architect J. N. B. DePouilly when they made a sketch for a monument to Andrew Jackson for the Place d'Armes (now Jackson Square). He advertised in Jan. 1846 as a portrait and historical painter, a wall and ceiling decorator, and a costume designer. He left N.O. with the artist LOUIS DOMINIQUE GRANDJEAN DEVELLE on July 11, 1846, for the Rio Grande to make sketches of Gen. Zachary Taylor, his officers, and the battle sites of the Mexican War. They returned to the city in Aug. to work on a large painting, *Battle of Resaca de Palma*, based on the sketches. While working on the painting, through the fall of 1847, De Chatillon issued a lithographic portrait of Taylor printed by X. MAGNY and based upon his field drawings. By Oct. 1847, the huge battle painting, 12 by 29 feet, was exhibited and formally opened to the public at ceremonies attended by Taylor on Dec. 29. It was offered for sale to the N.O. City Council (Nov. 1849) and sent to Washington DC to be purchased for the White House (Dec. 1849). Eight of De Chatillon's poems were published in the *Courier* (Nov. 1848–Oct. 1849). He probably spent little time in N.O. and frequently traveled to France to participate in the annual salons in Paris. He is sometimes confused with Auguste Chatillon, a N.O. drayman, who was listed in N.O. 1843–58 and died Aug. 4, 1860.
References: NOCD 1846; *Bee*, Jan. 23, Aug. 7, 1846, May 4, Nov. 24, Dec. 6, 1847, Mar. 22, 1849, June 14, 1885; *Courier*, June 28, 1845, July 7, Aug. 6, 8, 1846, May 4, 27, 31, Oct. 25, Nov. 26, Dec. 1, 1847, Nov. 8, 1848, Jan. 31, Mar. 21, July 25, Aug. 9, 18, 30, Sept. 13, Oct. 24, 1849, Aug. 26, 1852; *D. Crescent*, Nov. 28, 1849; *D. Delta*, Nov. 30, 1847; *D. National*, Nov. 29, 1847; *D. Pic.*, Dec. 15, 1847; *Revue Louisianaise* 1(Aug. 9, 1846):465, 1(Aug. 30, 1846):537, 4(May 16, 1847): 161; *Wkly. Delta*, July 13, 1846; Bénézit; Caulfeild, 93–94; Glenk, 39, 73; Groce and Wallace; Salam, 45–49; Testut, 81; Thieme and Becker; Tinker, *Ecrits*, 92.

DECOMBES, J. M. C.
Lithographer, active N.O. 1851–53.
Contemporary listings: lithographer, 13 Exchange Al. (1851–53).
References: NOCD 1849–53; *Courier*, July 24, 1851; Groce and Wallace.

DECUIR, JOSEPH A[UGUST].
Born LA Aug. 1852; died N.O. May 22, 1928.
Painter, active N.O. 1880–1912.
Contemporary listings: portrait painter (1880–81, 1909); artist (1882–88, 1891–94, 1896–1903, 1906–1908, 1910–12); portrait painter, 195 Canal (1889); portrait painter, 168 Bayou Rd. (1890); portrait painter, 933 France (1904–1905).
References: NOCD 1875–94, 1896–1912; LSM, *Biennial Report for 1928–29*, 77; N.O. Board of Health, Death Index (1927–29), NOPL; U.S. Census (1880), roll 462, (1900), roll 573.

DEEVES, JOHN F.
Died before 1920.
Lithographer, designer, active N.O. 1885–91.
Contemporary listings: lithographer, KOECKERT AND DEEVES (1886); designer, 26 Commercial (1890–91).
References: NOCD 1875–86, 1889–91; *T. Pic.*, Feb. 2, 1920.

DEFRASSE, AUGUSTE
Born Ausierre, France ca. 1820–21; died N.O. Oct. 10, 1864.
Sculptor, active N.O. 1854–64; also carver.
Contemporary listings: sculptor, Gravier near Magdalen (1854–55); Defrasse & Co., Gravier near Magdalen (1856); sculptor, Gravier near Magnolia (1857–59); sculptor, 366 Gravier (1860–61); sculptor (1864).
Defrasse designed in plaster and sculpted in marble the large bas–relief for the main room, Marble Hall, of the U.S. Custom House at N.O. (1856). He also designed and carved patterns and cast–iron ornamentation for building exteriors, including work for the city waterworks (1861). With other artists, he suggested the selection of the site and the form of improvement for the Henry Clay monument (1860).
References: NOCD 1854–61; *Courier*, Apr. 23, 1856; *D. Crescent*, Dec. 5, 1859; *D. Pic.*, Apr. 24, 1856, May 17, 1857, Feb. 12, 1860, Oct. 11, 1864; *Repub.*, May 30, 1875; *T. Pic.*, Mar. 26, 1961; Friends of the Ca-bildo, *N.O. Architecture*, 2:90, 102; Groce and Wallace; N.O. Death Certificate (1864), 28:146, NOPL; U.S. Census (1850), roll 234, (1860), roll 417.

DEGAS, EDGAR GERMAIN HILAIRE
Born Paris, France July 19, 1834; died Paris Sept. 27, 1917.
Painter, active N.O. 1872–73.
Studied: Lycée Louis–Le–Grand; with Louis Lamothe, Ecole des Beaux Arts, Paris.
Renowned French painter, sketch artist, and sculptor linked with the Impressionist art movement. Degas's mother, Marie–Célestine Musson DeGas, and her siblings were born in N.O., but the family moved to Paris in 1819. Mme. DeGas's father, J. B. Germain Musson, and his son, Michel, returned to N.O. in the 1830s where the son became a successful cotton merchant. In 1865, Edgar Degas's brothers, René and Achille, also moved to N.O. where they established a cotton brokerage house, DeGas Brothers. Edgar Degas remained in Paris to study law, but abandoned that career to pursue painting. His talent brought him success as a portraitist, and he exhibited in the Paris salons (1865–70). He also altered the spelling of his surname. The N.O. relatives occasionally visited Paris, meeting Degas who painted their portraits. On a business trip to France (1872), René DeGas persuaded his brother to join him on the return trip. They docked in N.Y.C., taking a train which arrived in N.O. Oct. 28, 1872. During his visit, Degas stayed with the Musson family in a large rented house at 372 Esplanade. He spent most of his time with the family and their friends and made many sketches and painted their portraits. *Cotton Market in New Orleans* was one of Degas's favorites and, after being exhibited in the 1876 second Impressionists exhibition in Paris, became one of his most famous works. The painting includes portraits of Michel Musson, René and Achille DeGas, and some of their business associates in Musson's office

in the family's building at Canal and Royal. Degas remained in the city for four months and left for Paris on Mar. 4, 1873. He took with him the sketches and paintings he made during his visit, and, except for the *Cotton Market*, he kept possession throughout his life of all his N.O. work. Degas gradually turned from oil portraits and became famous for pastel and charcoal drawings of ballet dancers, café settings, and horse races.

References: Foster, "Degas' New Orleans Period: Impressionist Sojourned about Four Months in Crescent City," *Dixie*, May 2, 1965; *T. Pic.*, June 14, 1953, June 10, 1956; Collier, "The World of Art: Major Art Event of Year: 'Cotton Exchange' on View," *T. Pic.*, June 8, 1975; Bénézit; Byrnes, 664–68; Degas, 13–31; "Degas' American Cousins"; *Encyclopaedia Britannica*, Krebs, 63–72; Rewald et al.; WPA, *New Orleans*, 103.

DEGIORGI, PETER
Sculptor, active N.O. 1883–84; also decorator.
Contemporary listings: sculptor, French Opera House (1883); proprietor, DEGIORGI & BAJATA (1884).
References: NOCD 1884; *D. Pic.*, Nov. 1, 1883.

DEGIORGI & BAJATA
Sculptors, active N.O. 1884; PETER DEGIORGI, GASPAR BAJATA, partners.
Contemporary listings: sculptors, 157 Bourbon (1884).
References: NOCD 1884.

DE GIRARDIN, MLLE. ____
Art teacher, active N.O. 1849.
Contemporary listings: teacher of painting and drawing, Institution de Mme. Van–Nooten (1849).
References: *Bee*, Sept. 17, 1849.

DE JAHAM, MARIE THERESE BERNARD (Mrs. George de Jaham)
Born N.O. Oct. 3, 1869; died N.O. Oct. 4, 1916.
Painter, restorer, active N.O. 1900–16; also copyist.
Studied: with GEORGE DAVID COULON and ANDRES MOLINARY.

Contemporary listings: painter (1900); portrait painter, 2019 Burgundy (1903, 1909–12); portrait painter (1904–1908, 1913, 1916); artist (1910); artist, 2019 Burgundy (1914–15).
Portrait, still life, and religious painter who painted on canvas a copy of Murillo's *Assumption* and life–size figures of the four evangelists that were installed on the ceiling of St. Augustine's Church (1910). De Jaham also received commissions for frescoes, landscapes, mural decorations, restoration of damaged statuary, and stage scenery.
References: NOCD 1903–16; *D. Pic.*, Apr. 3, 1910; *Item*, Oct. 5, 1916; *States–Item*, Jan. 14, 1975; *T. Pic.*, Oct. 5, 1916; N.O. Death Certificate (1916), 167:406, NOPL; U.S. Census (1900), roll 572, (1910), roll 521.

DEJAN, MR. ____
Art teacher, active N.O. 1825.
Studied: LOUISIANA DRAWING ACADEMY.
Contemporary listings: assistant professor, Louisiana Drawing Academy (1825).
Possibly Camille Dejan listed as a teacher, 90 Champs Élysées (1830).
References: NOCD 1830; *Courier*, Nov. 1, 1825.

DELABOSTRIE, FRANCIS
Engraver, hair worker, active N.O. 1808.
Contemporary listings: engraver, hair worker, F. Delabostrie & Co., cor. Royal and St. Peter (1808).
References: NOCD 1805, 1811; *Courier*, Nov. 7, 1808.

DELACROIX, FELIX
Painter, active N.O. ca. 1815.
Reported as "the great French painter" whose Battle of N.O. scene was rediscovered and exhibited in 1878–79 in N.O. Delacroix had arrived in N.O. shortly after the battle and studied sketches made by artists who were eye witnesses.
References: *Demo.*, Feb. 24, 1878, Mar. 26, 1879.

DELAMORE, PETIT
Artist, active N.O. 1861.
Contemporary listings: artist, 138 St. Peter (1861).
References: NOCD 1861.

DE LAPOUYADE, ROBERT P[AUL].
Born Covington LA July 5, 1877;
died N.O. Mar. 17, 1937.
Painter, active N.O. 1897–1937; also
decorator.
Studied: with COX BROTHERS; with
HARRY H. DRESSEL (1892).
Contemporary listings: painter
(1897, 1900); scenic artist (1901–
1902, 1905–1907, 1910–12, 1915);
artist (1903); scenic artist, Winter
Garden (1908–1909); scenic artist,
French Opera House (1914); scenic
painter (1916–18).
Apprenticed to Dressel in 1892, de
Lapouyade reportedly began his own
career as a scenic artist during the
1901–1902 season at the Grand Opera House. He opened his studio in
1910 at 1417 Moss, where he painted
the backdrops for the sets he designed for operas and carnival balls.
Two of his most famous sets were for
the 1912 production of the opera
Madame Butterfly and for the tableaux for the 1912 ball of the carnival organization Elves of Oberon.
Before World War I, silent movies
were filmed on the stage erected in
the open lot behind de Lapouyade's
studio. Later in his career, he designed and built sets for elaborate
vaudeville shows and became scenic
artist for stage plays at theaters such
as the Greenwall, Dauphine, and St.
Charles. He did similar work for
clubs, schools, and businesses
throughout the South and was a window and store decorator for some of
N.O.'s large retail stores. He formed
the company R. de Lapouyade & Sons
(ca. 1933) where he worked until his
death. His son Robert Perret de Lapouyade continued as a decorator.
References: NOCD 1895–97, 1899,
1900–1903, 1905–12, 1914–33,
1935; *D. States*, Feb. 11, 1912; *T.
Pic.*, July 5, 1914, Mar. 5, 1916, Mar.
18, 1937; Harkey, "The End of the
Make–Believe House," *T. Pic.*, Dec.
21, 1941; La Cour, 203; THNOC
artists files; U.S. Census (1910), roll
521.

DELAQUIERT, JULES
Painter, active N.O. 1849–53.
Contemporary listings: artist, cor.
Bourbon and Orleans (1849–52);
artist, 80 Bourbon (1853).
References: NOCD 1849–53; Glenk,
74; Groce and Wallace.

DE LASSUS, JEAN PIERRE. *See* LASSUS,
JEAN PIERRE

DE LA VASSELAIS, CHARLES
Born Metz, France; died N.O. Apr.
3, 1926.
Commercial artist, active N.O. 1897–
1901.
Studied: France.
Contemporary listings: artist, *Picayune* (1897–98, 1900–1901).
French army officer and son of a
count, De la Vasselais was in N.O. by
1897 and for a few years assisted *Picayune* artist LOUIS A. WINTERHALDER
in making sketches of local events
that were published in the newspaper. He later traveled as a salesman
through southern LA.
References: NOCD 1897–98, 1900–
1901, 1903–1906, 1910–16, 1918–
24, 1926; *T. Pic.*, Apr. 4, 1926; Kendall, "Old Days," 328.

DE LA VEGA, THOMAS
Art teacher, painter, active N.O.
1832.
Contemporary listings: teacher of
drawing and of oil, miniature and
portrait painting, cor. Conti and Dumaine (1832).
Memberships/positions: Real Academia de Bellas Artes de San Fer-
nando, Madrid, Spain, honorary
member.
References: *Bee*, Mar. 16, 1832.

DELAVIGNE, MARIE ODELLE
Born N.O. Oct. 22, 1873; died N.O.
Feb. 25, 1963.
Art craftsmen, art teacher, active
N.O. 1892–1947.
Studied: NEWCOMB COLLEGE (1892–
99).
Contemporary listings: teacher
(1913, 1918).
Exhibited: Louisiana Purchase Ex-
position, St. Louis MO (1904); ART
ASSOCIATION OF NEW ORLEANS (1910–
11, 1913, 1915, 1917); Panama–Pa-

cific International Exposition, San Francisco (1915).
Memberships/positions: Louisiana Art Teachers' Association (1913).
Newcomb art craftsman (1901–25) who specialized in embroidery and was also a pottery decorator. She exhibited landscape paintings, was a member of the Art Guild by 1921, and was listed as an artist (1945–47).
References: NOCD 1913, 1918, 1923–24, 1926–27, 1930, 1932–33, 1942, 1945–47, 1956, 1962; *Item*, Jan. 30, Feb. 6, 1921; Art Asso., *Catalogue* (1910, 1911, 1913, 1915, 1917); Art Asso., *Special Exhibition*; Orleans Parish Registrar of Voters, NOPL; Ormond and Irvine, 153; Poesch, *Newcomb Pottery*, 98–99.

DELEL, MICHAEL
Born Germany May 1850.
Artist, active N.O. 1900.
Contemporary listings: artist (1900).
References: U.S. Census (1900), roll 575.

DE LESSEPS, CHARLES. *See* LESSEPS, CHARLES DE

DE LESSEPS, NUMA. *See* LESSEPS, CHARLES DE

DELGADO MUSEUM OF ART (Isaac Delgado Museum of Art)
Museum, active N.O. 1911–71.
The museum, designed by Samuel A. Marx of the Chicago firm of Lebenbaum & Marx, was constructed, with a donation of $150,000 from N.O. businessman Isaac Delgado in Feb. 1910, on land provided by the commissioners of the City Park Improvement Association. It opened to the public on Dec. 16, 1911, as the third art museum in the South. The directorship of the museum in the early days was on a rather informal basis. The first curator, CHARLES WELLINGTON BOYLE (1911–22), was later acting director (1922–25). Officers of the board of administrators were also acting directors; the most important of these was ELLSWORTH WOODWARD, who generally served as chairman of the art committee and acting director from 1925 until 1939. Woodward influenced early policies that established the museum's role to ed-

ucate the community in art and to promote southern artists and the sale of their work. The exhibition program was sponsored by local art organizations, especially the ART ASSOCIATION OF NEW ORLEANS. The acquisition of a permanent art collection was secondary during the early decades; it developed from the donations of several private collectors who gave paintings by LA artists, Chinese jades, American and European silver, Greek vases, ancient glass, and 19th–century French and German paintings. Funds for maintenance and acquisitions came from the City of N.O. The museum hired its first professionally–trained director in 1948. Three new wings (galleries, auditorium, and education) opened Nov. 1971 when the name was changed to New Orleans Museum of Art.
References: *T. Demo.*, Mar. 23, 1911; Dunbar, "Diamond Jubilee"; Dunbar, "Growth of the Art Collection"; New Orleans Museum of Art, 7–12; Tallant, 315.

DELIHIAS, VICTOR
Engraver, active N.O. 1868.
Contemporary listings: engraver, 158 Claiborne cor. St. Ann (1868).
References: NOCD 1868.

DEL'ISLE, CELIA A. BUTLER (Mrs. Victor Gaschet Del'Isle)
Painter, art teacher, active N.O. 1870–1907.
Contemporary listings: artist (1885, 1904, 1906–1907); artist, 5 Prytania (1887); artist, Soniat cor. Dryades (1888); art school, 206 Soniat (1894); artist, Soniat cor. Dryades (1895).
Exhibited: LILIENTHAL's (1883); Creole Exhibit, American Exposition (1885–86).
Awarded: Grand State Fair, diploma for best landscape painting, and diploma for best animal painting (1870).
References: NOCD 1874, 1885, 1887–88, 1892–95, 1897, 1901, 1903–1904, 1906–1907, 1910–12; *D. Pic.*, Oct. 1, 1910; Creole Exhibit, 13; Lilienthal's, 6–8; Mechanics' and

Agricultural Fair Asso., *Report* (1870):28.

DE LOS RIOS, MR. _____
Art teacher, active N.O. 1834.
Contemporary listings: Poonah painting and drawing teacher, cor. Dumaine and Royal, and 21 St. Philip (1834).
References: *Bee*, Sept. 15–29, 1834 (advs.); Oct. 18, 1834; Groce and Wallace.

DE MANCILAS, FLORES
Born Malaga, Spain ca. 1872.
Sculptor, designer, active N.O. 1902.
Studied: with De Savia, Rome; with Luigi Amici; Munich.
Contemporary listings: sculptor and designer, 234 Bourbon (1902).
Designed a model for the competition of a memorial arch to Jefferson Davis (1902).
References: *D. Pic.*, Nov. 10, 1902; *D. States*, Apr. 27, 1902.

DEMILLIERE, MISS _____
Art teacher, active N.O. 1808; also embroiderer.
Contemporary listings: teacher of drawing and embroidery, cor. St. Philip and Conti (1808).
In France she taught drawing and embroidery; after her arrival in N.O. she continued to give lessons, either in private homes or in the house of her father, AUGUSTE DEMILLIERE.
References: *Courier*, Aug. 26, 1808.

DEMILLIERE, AUGUSTE
Painter, silhouettist, active N.O. 1808–16.
Contemporary listings: portrait painter, cor. St. Philip and Conti (1808).
Arrived in N.Y.C. from France Jan. 1797. Later that year Demillière opened a drawing academy in Philadelphia (1802–1807), and worked with his son, AUGUSTE JR., as portrait and miniature painters and profilists in Charleston SC. He visited France in 1807–1808 before arriving in N.O., where he advertised the sale of his profile machine and about 100 paintings by various artists on several subjects. Father of MISS DEMILLIERE.
References: *Courier*, Aug. 26, 29, Sept. 9, 1808; June 3, 1811; *L'Ami*

des Lois, May 14, 1816; Groce and Wallace.

DEMILLIERE, AUGUSTE, JR.
Painter, active N.O. 1808–16.
Contemporary listings: miniature painter (1816).
Began his art career as a miniature painter and profilist in Charleston SC with his father AUGUSTE DEMILLIERE, with whom he probably came to N.O. (1808).
References: *L'Ami des Lois*, May 14, 1816; *Courier*, May 1, 1816; Groce and Wallace.

DE MONTULE, EDOUARD. *See* MONTULE, EDOUARD DE.

DE MORRILL, W.
Art teacher, active N.O. 1844.
Contemporary listings: drawing and painting teacher, 21 Royal (1844).
References: *D. Tropic*, Jan. 15, 1844.

DEMPSEY, MARTIN R., JR.
Born N.O. Aug. 24, 1882; died N.O. Mar. 25, 1950.
Lithographer, active N.O. 1905–10.
Contemporary listings: lithographer (1905, 1909–10).
References: NOCD 1904–1906, 1908–26, 1928, 1931–33, 1935, 1940, 1942, 1945–47, 1949; *D. Pic.*, Mar. 29, 1907; *T. Pic.*, Mar. 27, 1950; Orleans Parish Registrar of Voters, NOPL.

DENEGAN, SAMUEL
Sculptor, active N.O. 1841–42.
Contemporary listings: sculptor, 28 Basin (1841–42).
References: NOCD 1841–42; Groce and Wallace.

DE ORNELLAS, JOHN A.
Engraver, active N.O. 1867–71; primarily jeweler, watchmaker.
Contemporary listings: engraver, 89 Customhouse (1867); engraver, 236 Chartres (1870); engraver, 84 Chartres (1870–71).
References: NOCD 1866–70; Boyd, 158.

DE POMORSKI, CONSTANTINE P.
Painter, active N.O. 1897–1908.
Contemporary listings: painter (1897–98, 1908); artist (1900); fresco painter (1901); frescoer (1902).

References: NOCD 1897–98, 1900–1902, 1908.

DE POMORSKI, FELIX VICTOR
Born ca. 1873; died N.O. Nov. 11, 1948.
Painter, active N.O. 1902–29; also decorator.
Contemporary listings: artist (1902); painter (1903–10, 1912, 1914–16); fresco painter (1911).
Also listed as a painter, decorator, or interior decorator (1921–40).
References: NOCD 1898, 1902–12, 1914–16, 1921–29, 1932–33, 1935, 1940, 1942, 1945–47; *T. Pic.*, Nov. 13, 1948.

DE PONTALBA, GASTON. *See* PONTALBA, GASTON DE

DE PONTELLI, MR. L.
Painter, art teacher, active N.O. 1842–44.
Contemporary listings: portrait painter, teacher, 147 Royal (1842); portrait painter, 117 Royal (1843–44).
Reported in 1842 to have arrived in N.O. from Paris.
References: NOCD 1843–44; *Bee*, Dec. 10, 1842; Groce and Wallace.

DESCOMMES, GEORGE
Painter, active N.O. ca. 1894.
Exhibited: ARTISTS' ASSOCIATION OF NEW ORLEANS (1894).
References: *T. Demo.*, Dec. 14, 1894.

DESEAMUS, JOSEPH FRANK
Born Long Island NY Mar. 1818; died Algiers LA June 15, 1905.
Painter, active N.O. 1859–1904; primarily sign and ornamental painter.
Contemporary listings: painter (1859–60); painter, Patterson, Algiers (1861); painter, Delaronde (1866–67); painter, Delaronde betw. Seguin and Bartholomew (1868); painter (1870, 1875–81, 1885, 1887–91, 1896, 1898–99, 1901–1904); portrait painter (1873); scenic artist, St. Charles Hall (1874–78); artist (1882–84, 1886, 1893–95).
References: NOCD 1859–61, 1866–68, 1870, 1873, 1875–91, 1893–99, 1901–1904; *D. Pic.*, June 16, 1905; *T. Demo.*, June 16, 1905; *Louisiana*

State Gazetteer, 211; Seymour, 31; U.S. Census (1860), roll 415.

DE SEEFELD, C. MAIR
Painter, active N.O. 1835.
Contemporary listings: miniature painter, 41 Bienville (1835).
References: *Bee*, Jan. 14, 1835.

DES ESSARTS, D. D.
Born before 1765.
Art teacher, active N.O. ca. 1808–11.
Contemporary listings: art teacher, 43 Bourbon (1808).
References: NOCD 1809, 1811; *Moniteur*, Mar. 19, 1808; Groce and Wallace; U.S. Census (1810), roll 10.

DESSOMES, EDWARD E.
Born N.O. 1845; died N.O. Feb. 21, 1908.
Painter, art teacher, active N.O. 1888–1908.
Studied: Paris.
Exhibited: ARTISTS' ASSOCIATION OF NEW ORLEANS (1889–90).
Memberships/positions: Artists' Association of New Orleans (1890).
Portrait and landscape painter who was a member of a prominent N.O. family. Dessomes studied medicine in Paris but also visited art studios to study painting. After returning to N.O. (1888), he preferred working as an artist in rural Covington LA rather than as a physician. At the time of his death, he was living in N.O. at 1124 Burgundy.
References: NOCD 1890–94; *Bee*, Sept. 30, Oct. 3, 1888; *D. Pic.*, Dec. 17, 1889, Nov. 13, Dec. 17, 1890, Feb. 22, 1908; *Item*, Feb. 22, 1908; AANO, *Catalogue* (1890); THNOC Cemetery Survey.

DESTOR, ARTHUR
Painter, active N.O. 1904–1905.
Contemporary listings: fresco painter, 510 St. Peter (1904); fresco painter (1905).
References: NOCD 1882, 1902, 1904–1906, 1908.

DE THULSTRUP, THURE
Born Stockholm, Sweden Apr. 5, 1848; died N.Y.C. June 9, 1930.
Painter, active N.O. ca. 1902.
Studied: Paris.

Exhibited: Louisiana Historical Society (1903); ART ASSOCIATION OF NEW ORLEANS (1904); Louisiana Purchase Exposition, St. Louis MO (1904).

Memberships/positions: Society of Illustrators; American Water Color Society.

Known in the U.S. as Thure de Thulstrup, his full name was Bror Thure Thulstrup. He joined the French Foreign Legion, studied art in Paris, and emigrated to Canada. He moved to N.Y.C. by 1879 and, as a student of military history, specialized in painting war and naval scenes. De Thulstrup worked freelance for New York weekly magazines as an illustrator; his drawings were also published in books. He came to N.O. (ca. 1902) to make studies and sketches for the large historical painting *Hoisting American Colors, Louisiana Cession, 1803* which was exhibited in N.O. (1903) and St. Louis (1904).

References: *Item*, Feb. 23, 1921; *T. Demo.*, Dec. 17, 1903; Art Asso., *Catalogue* (1904); *DAB*; Edwin Davis, *Louisiana*, 29, 162; Fielding, *Dictionary*; Glenk, 190–91; LHS (1903); Johnson and Buel, 2:92, 94; LSM, *Biennial Report for 1932–33*, 46; Sears, 391–92.

DE TROBRIAND, PHILIPPE REGIS DENIS DE KEREDERN

Born Château des Rochettes, near Tours, France June 4, 1816; died Bayport NY July 15, 1897.

Sketch artist, painter, active N.O. 1879–97.

Amateur artist and member of a wealthy French family, his full name was Philippe Régis Denis de Keredern, Baron de Trobriand. He first came to the U.S. in 1841 and became a permanent resident in 1854. As colonel of the 55th NY Volunteers, he served in the Civil War and became the first Frenchman since Lafayette to be brevetted a Brigadier General in the U.S. Army. During Reconstruction, De Trobriand commanded the U.S. troops stationed in N.O. from the time of his appointment in Oct. 1874 until they were withdrawn in 1877. He was then stationed at Jackson Barracks until his retirement from the army on Mar. 20, 1879, when he chose to live in N.O. during the winter, at 276 Clouet, and to spend alternate summers with his daughters in France and on Long Island NY. In N.O. he painted landscapes of rural LA.

References: NOCD 1880–97; *D. Pic.*, July 18, 1897; *New York Times*, July 17, 1897; *Appleton's CAB*; *DAB*; Delgado, *New Orleans*, item 67; Morton's Auction Exchange (Aug. 29, 1967); Post; THNOC 1974.79.

DEUTSCHMAN, ADOLPH C.

Born N.O. Nov. 2, 1872; died N.O. July 30, 1925.

Artist, active N.O. 1897–98; primarily carpenter, builder, decorator.

Contemporary listings: artist (1897–98).

Builder of carnival parade floats (beginning ca. 1894) under his father, HENRY J. DEUTSCHMANN, and later with Deutschmann Bros. (1924–25) with his brother, JOHN HENRY DEUTSCHMAN. The brothers altered the spelling of their surname but maintained the original in their business.

References: NOCD 1894–1910, 1912–18, 1922–25; *T. Pic.*, Feb. 18, 1917, July 31, 1925; Orleans Parish Registrar of Voters, NOPL; U.S. Census (1910), roll 519.

DEUTSCHMAN, JOHN HENRY

Born N.O. Aug. 19, 1875; died N.O. May 6, 1938.

Artist, designer, active N.O. 1897–99; primarily carpenter, builder, decorator.

Contemporary listings: artist (1897); designer (1899).

Builder of carnival parade floats (beginning ca. 1887) under his father, HENRY J. DEUTSCHMANN, and later with Deutschmann Bros. (1924–25) with his brother, ADOLPH DEUTSCHMAN. His sons continued the business after his death.

References: NOCD 1895, 1897–1902, 1904, 1906–10, 1912–15, 1917–19, 1922–16, 1928–33, 1935; *T. Pic.*, Feb. 18, 1917; May 7, 1938; La Cour, 201; Orleans Parish Registrar of Voters, NOPL; WPA, *New Orleans*, 177.

DEUTSCHMANN, HENRY J.
Born N.O. Sept. 4, 1842; died N.O. Apr. 5, 1926.
Designer, active N.O. 1877–1918; also carpenter, decorator, builder.
First member of a family of artists who designed and built carnival parade floats and ball tableaux, primarily in N.O. but also in Kansas City MO, Louisville KY, Atlanta GA, and N.Y.C. He is credited with having designed the first floats used in a parade of the Rex carnival organization (1877). His sons, ADOLPH C. DEUTSCHMAN and JOHN HENRY DEUTSCHMAN, worked with and succeeded him in the business.
References: NOCD 1867, 1870–74, 1878, 1880–84, 1886–1905, 1907–10, 1913–19, 1922–24; *T. Pic.*, Feb. 18, 1917, Apr. 6, 1926; La Cour, 201; Orleans Parish Registrar of Voters, NOPL.

DE VAUDRICOURT, MR. A.
Art teacher, active N.O. 1835.
Contemporary listings: drawing teacher, E. Johns music store (1835). Later established himself as a lithographer and topographical draftsman in Boston, N.Y.C., and TX.
References: NOCD 1834–35, 1841; *Bee*, Feb. 9, 1835; *Courier*, Feb. 16, 1835; Groce and Wallace.

DEVELLE, DOMINIQUE LOUIS GRAND-JEAN. *See* FILBERT, DOMINIQUE LOUIS GRAND-JEAN

DEVELLE, LOUIS DOMINIQUE GRANDJEAN
Born Paris, France ca. 1799; died N.O. June 22, 1868.
Painter, art teacher, active N.O. 1829–68.
Studied: with Pierre Luc Charles Ciceri, Paris.
Contemporary listings: scene painter, Orleans Theatre (1829–36, 1838, 1841–57); teacher of drawing and painting, 78 St. Philip (1830); scene painter, 178 St. Philip (1837); scenic painter, Varieties Theatre (1844, 1863–65); scenic painter, Opera House (1861); teacher of painting and drawing, 195 St. Claude (1866).

Exhibited: 95 St. Charles (1847); ball room, St. Louis Exchange (1849).
According to family tradition, Develle was originally named after his father, DOMINIQUE LOUIS GRAND-JEAN FILBERT. Sources show that in LA, instead of Filbert, he used the surname Develle, his father's professional alias. At an early age, while still in France, Develle was sent to Rheims to work on the decorations of the cathedral for the coronation of Charles X (ca. 1824) and then spent three years working at the theater at LeHavre. Develle is first documented in N.O. for scenic work for an opera at the Orleans Theatre (Mar. 1829). For the next four years, he worked in N.O. probably only during the theater season in the fall and winter and returned to France for the summer. By 1834, Develle had a residential listing in N.O. and he was joined by his parents. For over 30 years, he worked primarily as the scene designer and painter at the Orleans Theatre until the Civil War interrupted operatic performances in N.O., the building burned in 1866. He was noted for the excellent details in his sets and rarely worked with assistants (*Cf.* ANTOINE MONDELLI). His local fame was such that his work was credited in newspaper announcements and advertisements of the operas. Develle also worked on other projects in N.O. and the U.S. He was selected in 1842 to make the decorations in St. Louis Cathedral for the mass honoring the death of Ferdinand, eldest son of Louis Philippe of France. In July–Aug. 1846, during the Mexican War, he joined N.O. artist JOSEPH AUGUSTE DE CHATILLON on a trip to the Rio Grande to make sketches of Zachary Taylor and his officers for an historical painting completed after their return to N.O. In 1848 he advertised as a painter of historical subjects and landscapes. With other artists, he suggested the selection of the site and form of improvement for the Henry Clay monument (1860), eventually erected on the neutral ground at Canal and

Royal. After his career at the Orleans Theatre and during the Civil War, Develle worked with VARNOUT at the French Opera House (1861) and from 1863 (with ERNEST CICERI and CAMPBELL) until 1865 at the Varieties Theatre where popular musical entertainment continued. In 1864 he decorated the proscenium and the drop curtain for the Academy of Music. Family tradition suggests that Develle's son, Louis Dominique Grandjean Develle (born Paris ca. 1820; died N.O. May 10, 1885), was also a scenic artist; however, the son was listed as a clerk (1851–60) and as a cotton broker and classer (1860–85), and no contemporary sources show him to have worked in theatrical design.

References: NOCD 1830, 1832, 1834–35, 1837, 1841–43, 1846, 1852–56, 1858–61, 1866; *Bee*, Nov. 18, 1830, May 3, 1831, May 10, 1836, Apr. 18, Aug. 7, 1846, Nov. 24, Dec. 6, 1847, Nov. 20, 1866, June 24, 1868; *Comm. Bull.*, Jan. 26, 1843; *Courier*, Mar. 24, June 29, Nov. 19, 1829, Nov. 11, 1830, Feb. 16, 26, 1833, Jan. 30, May 2, Sept. 3, 1838, Mar. 13, 1841, Aug. 19, Dec. 12, 1842, Nov. 2, 1843, Feb. 15, June 21, 22, Dec. 19, 1844, Feb. 26, 1845, Mar. 25, Apr. 17, July 7, Aug. 6, 8, Oct. 10, 1846, Apr. 12, Oct. 25, Nov. 26, Dec. 1, 1847, Jan. 26, May 6, 1848, Jan. 16, 1849, Jan. 16, 1850, Mar. 18, 1851, Feb. 16, 1852, Mar. 11, Oct. 11, 1853, Mar. 18, 1854, Apr. 6, July 27, 1856, Feb. 20, 1857; *D. Crescent*, Apr. 29, 1854; *D. Delta*, Apr. 17, 1847, Nov. 6, 1853, Apr. 28, 1854, Apr. 21, 1855, Jan. 30, 1861; *D. National*, Nov. 29, 1847; *D. Pic.*, Nov. 27, 1849, Apr. 11, 1852, Nov. 13, 1855, Feb. 12, 1860, Dec. 14, 1870; *D. Tropic*, Oct. 8, Nov. 18, 1845, May 26, 1846; *Era*, Dec. 24, 1863; *New York Clipper*, Sept. 24, 1864; *Revue Louisianaise* 1(Apr. 5, 1846): 21–22, 1(Aug. 9, 1846): 465, 1(Aug. 30, 1846): 537, 2(Jan. 10, 1847): 360; *Times*, Dec. 6, 1865; *T. Pic.*, May 30, 1956, July 14, 1957, Oct. 30, 1960; Collier, "The World of Art: Historic N.O. Collection Has Develle 'Red Store' on View," *T. Pic.*, Aug. 26, 1973; *Wkly. Delta*, July 13, 1846; Freeman, item 102; Groce and Wallace; Information courtesy Jack Belsom; Kmen, 118–19, 136–37, 160–61; Orleans Parish Notarial Archives, Plan Book, 34:36; U.S. Census (1840), roll 132, (1850), roll 235, (1860), roll 418.

DEVILLE, B. FELIX
Born Pensacola FL ca. 1817; died N.O. June 29, 1864; black ("mulatto").
Painter, active N.O. 1850–66.
Contemporary listings: painter, 94 Basin (1856); painter, Basin cor. Canal (1859); artist (1860); painter, 263 Chartres (1860); painter, Conti near Tremé (1861, 1866).
References: NOCD 1856, 1859–61, 1866; *Bee*, June 30, 1864; Groce and Wallace; N.O. Death Certificate (1864), 26:78, NOPL; U.S. Census (1850), roll 235, (1860), roll 419.

DEVINE, HENRY C.
Painter, active N.O. 1887–88.
Contemporary listings: portrait painter (1887); artist, 134 Camp (1888).
References: NOCD 1887–88.

DEVOTI, JEAN
Art teacher, active N.O. 1851.
Contemporary listings: teacher of landscape painting, 80 Royal (1851). Also listed at Devoti's Dancing Academy (1842–43, 1846). He claimed in his 1851 advertisement to be able to teach landscape painting in two colors in 15 lessons to amateurs of both sexes.
References: NOCD 1842–43, 1846; *Bee*, Apr. 22, 1851.

DE WOISERI, JOHN L. BOQUETA. *See* BOQUETA DE WOISERI, JOHN L.

DICKENSCHNEIDER, CHARLES
Born LA ca. 1892.
Engraver, active N.O. 1910.
Contemporary listings: printing house engraver (1910).
References: U.S. Census (1910), roll 521.

DICKS, ALFRED
Born NY ca. 1822.
Engraver, active N.O. 1860.

Contemporary listings: engraver (1860).
References: U.S. Census (1860), roll 417.

DIETRICH, F. F.
Born France ca. 1824.
Artist, active N.O. 1860.
Contemporary listings: artist (1860).
References: U.S. Census (1860), roll 418.

DODGE, JOHN WOOD
Born N.Y.C. Nov. 4, 1807; died Dec. 16, 1893.
Painter, active N.O. 1848–49.
Contemporary listings: miniature painter, 71 Canal (1848).
Exhibited: Armory Hall (1849); National Academy of Design, N.Y.C. (1862).
Memberships/positions: National Academy of Design (1832).
Portrait, miniature, and panorama painter active in N.Y.C. (1830–44), where he exhibited as an associate member of the National Academy. Dodge's miniature of Andrew Jackson was one of the last portraits for which the president sat. It was exhibited in Dodge's N.O. studio during his visit to the city in Feb. 1848 to paint miniatures.
References: *Bee*, Feb. 24, 1849; *Courier*, Apr. 25, 1843, Apr. 26, 1845; *D. Crescent*, Feb. 23, Mar. 6, 1849; *D. Delta*, Feb. 16, 1848, Feb. 23, 1849; *D. Pic.*, Feb. 20, 22, 27, Mar. 2, 1849; *T. Pic.*, Aug. 21, 1977; Bolton, *Painters in Miniature*; Bruns, 311; Fielding, *Dictionary*; Groce and Wallace; Harter and Tucker, 120; LSM, *Annual Report for 1919*, 28; LSM, *Biennial Report for 1924–25*, 52; WPA, "Lives."

DOERING, PAUL
Painter, art teacher, active N.O. 1889–90.
Contemporary listings: artist and teacher of crayon, watercolor, oil, and porcelain painting, 111 Carondelet (1889); portrait painter, 111 Carondelet (1890).
Exhibited: ARTISTS' ASSOCIATION OF NEW ORLEANS (1889); Tulane University (1890).

Memberships/positions: School of Arts, Munich and Dresden, Germany; Royal Porcelain Painting Academy, Meissen, Saxony.
References: NOCD 1890; *D. Pic.*, Dec. 17, 1889, Feb. 14, 1890; *D. States*, Dec. 1, 1889.

DOHRE, WILLIAM S. (Doehre)
Born LA ca. 1871; died ca. 1920.
Engraver, lithographer, commercial artist, active N.O. 1891–1919.
Contemporary listings: engraver, M. F. DUNN & BRO. (1891, 1901); engraver (1894, 1898–1900, 1902, 1904–1905, 1912, 1917); engraver, WALLE & CO., LTD. (1902, 1907–10, 1914–15); lithographer (1903, 1913, 1915); litho–engraver, Walle & Co., Ltd. (1906); artist, Walle & Co., Ltd. (1911, 1916); Walle & Co., Ltd. (1918).
References: NOCD 1891, 1894, 1896, 1898–1920; U.S. Census (1910), roll 521.

DOLBEAR, RUFUS LEVI
Sketch artist, active N.O. ca. 1868.
Exhibited: Grand State Fair (1868).
Penmenship expert, proprietor of a writing academy (1848–54), and president of Dolbear Commercial College (1854–88).
References: NOCD 1846, 1849, 1850–61, 1866–68, 1870–72; *D. Pic.*, Jan. 8, 1868.

DOLL, GEORGE WENDELEN
Born N.O. 1845; died N.O. Apr. 28, 1899.
Sketch artist, active N.O. 1881.
Signed black and white ink drawings for the float designs for the carnival parade of Phunny Phorty Phellows (1881); one of the originators of the Rex carnival organization.
References: NOCD 1867, 1870–74, 1876, 1881–87, 1890–96, 1898; *D. Pic.*, Apr. 29, 1899; *D. States*, Apr. 29, 1899; *T. Demo.*, Apr. 29, 1899; Friends of the Cabildo, *250 Years*, 79.

DOMENGET, JOSEPH
Born Chambery, France Nov. 1857; died N.O. Jan. 3, 1911.
Sculptor, engraver, active N.O. 1889–1911; also cabinetmaker, carver, decorator.

Contemporary listings: sculptor, 146 Chartres (1889); sculptor and engraver in wood and marble, 46 St. Ann (1890); sculptor (1891, 1906, 1911); sculptor, 82 Baronne (1893–94); woodcarver, 337 Baronne (1895); Domenget and Ledrut (1896); woodcarver (1908); sculptor, with James Trebuquet (1910). References: NOCD 1890–91, 1893–96, 1898–1911; NOBD 1889; *D. Pic.*, Jan. 8, 1911; Edwin Davis, *Louisiana*, 315; U.S. Census (1900), roll 570; WPA, *Louisiana*, 170–71.

DOMINIQUE, J[EAN].
Lithographer, active N.O. 1886–90.
Contemporary listings: lithographer, T. FITZWILLIAM & CO. (1886–90).
References: NOCD 1882–83, 1886–90.

DONALDSON, PETER M.
Painter, active N.O. 1897–1900.
Contemporary listings: painter (1897, 1899); painter, 2302 Calliope (1898); scenic artist (1900).
References: NOCD 1895, 1897–1900.

DONNELSON, J. L.
Sculptor, active N.O. 1852.
Exhibited: Norman's bookstore (1852).
References: *D. Pic.*, Mar. 16, 1852; Groce and Wallace.

DOREE. *See* GOLDSBOROUGH, ANNA FARRAR

DOUGHTY, THOMAS
Born Philadelphia PA July 19, 1793; died N.Y.C. July 22, 1856.
Painter, active N.O. 1844.
Exhibited: Casey's Music Saloon (1844).
One of the first American artists who devoted his career to landscape painting, Doughty's subjects were primarily the rivers and mountains of PA, NY, and New England. He lived mostly in Philadelphia, Boston, and N.Y.C., and traveled throughout the U.S. and to London and Paris to exhibit and sell his work. His brief exhibition in N.O. contained landscapes in oil of scenes in New England. Four of the paintings were purchased by the prominent N.O. art patron James Robb; they were displayed in GEORGE COOKE's National Gallery of Paintings (Feb. 1845).
References: *D. Pic.*, Jan. 12–13, Mar. 1, 1844, Feb. 22, 1845; Collier, "The World of Art: Hunt for Doughty Works Is Begun in New Orleans," *T. Pic.*, Jan. 3, 1972; *Appleton's CAB*; Bénézit; *Bryan's*; *DAB*; Fielding, *Dictionary*; Groce and Wallace; Norman, 171.

DOUGLAS, JOHN, JR.
Born N.O. May 19, 1860; died N.O. Nov. 4, 1936.
Engraver, active N.O. 1878–1917.
Contemporary listings: engraver (1878, 1917); engraver, John Douglas (1879–1900); engraver, 112 Camp (1901–1904, 1906–11).
Employed by his father, JOHN SR., as an engraver, he took over the business after the latter's death. After 1911, AUGUST KNOTZCH became the proprietor although Douglas kept an office at 112 Camp through 1924.
References: NOCD 1878–1904, 1906–1927, 1929–30, 1932–33; *T. Pic.*, Nov. 5, 1936; American Illustrating Company, 175; Orleans Parish Registrar of Voters, NOPL; U.S. Census (1860), roll 416, (1900), roll 575.

DOUGLAS, JOHN R.
Painter, active N.O. 1884.
Contemporary listings: landscape painter, 18 St. Charles, (1884).
Also listed as proprietor of the "Extra Dry" bar, 18 St. Charles (1883–85).
References: NOCD 1883–85; *Mascot*, Oct. 11, 1884.

DOUGLAS, JOHN, SR.
Born Dublin, Ireland 1827; died N.O. Aug. 30, 1900.
Engraver, lithographer, active N.O. 1852–1900; also printer.
Contemporary listings: engraver and lithographer, 17 St. Charles (1853–54, 1857–61); engraver, 17 St. Charles (1855–56, 1863, 1865); engraver and lithographer, 28 Camp (1865–66); engraver and lithographer, 10 Camp (1867–94); engraver and lithographer, 112 Camp (1895); engraver, 112 Camp (1896–1900).

Awarded: Grand State Fair, diploma and $10 for best engraving on copperplate (1867), silver medal for best specimen of engraving on copperplate (1868), bronze medal for best specimen of engraving on copperplate (1869), diploma for best specimen of engraving on copperplate (1870).

Apprentice with Waller & Co., engravers and printers in Dublin, Douglas was one of several young Irish engravers who immigrated to N.O. in 1848. Douglas specialized in printing engraved cards, especially visiting, wedding, and business cards. He was considered the finest steel and copperplate engraver in the city and introduced in N.O. the transferring of copperplate engraving to lithographic stone for printing. He also designed and engraved Confederate bonds and money (1861). His son, JOHN JR., worked with him and continued the business after his death.

References: NOCD 1851–61, 1866–1900; NOBD 1865, *Bee*, Nov. 27, 1866; *Bull.*, Aug. 30, 1874; *D. Crescent*, May 8, 1867; *D. Delta*, May 12, 1861; *D. Pic.*, July 26, 1857, June 19, 1863, June 10, 1866, Mar. 21, 1867, Jan. 19, 1868, Apr. 13, 1869, Jan. 7, 1872, Aug. 31, 1900; *D. States*, Aug. 5, 1891, Aug. 31, 1900; *D. True Delta*, Mar. 14, 1858, Dec. 23, 1860, Sept. 29, 1861, Sept. 3, 15, 1865; Groce and Wallace; *Land*, 192; Mechanics' and Agricultural Fair Asso., *Report* (1867):27, (1868):42, (1869):74, (1870):34; New Orleans City Council, Proceedings, June 26, 1852, NOPL; N.O. Death Certificate (1900), 123:134, NOPL; THNOC 1970.27, 76–29–L; U.S. Census (1860), roll 416.

DOUGLASS, A. G.
Born England ca. 1835.
Painter, active N.O. 1870.
Contemporary listings: portrait painter (1870).
References: U.S. Census (1870), roll 519.

DOUGLASS, DAVID BATES
Died Oct. 19, 1849.
Sketch artist, active N.O. 1815.

As a second lieutenant in the U.S. Army, he fought at the Battle of N.O. He made a sketch of the battle, later engraved in Philadelphia by John Vallance.
References: Groce and Wallace.

DOUVILLIER, LOUIS BOUCHER
Born Paris, France ca. 1761; died N.O. July 26, 1821.
Painter, active N.O. 1811.
Contemporary listings: scenic painter, St. Philip St. Theatre (1811).
French singer and actor who met his wife, SUZANNE THEODORE VAILLANDE DOUVILLIER, in Charleston SC (1796) and traveled with her in a performing troupe to Philadelphia (1797–98) and then to N.O. (by ca. 1799). They appeared on stage and painted scenery at the St. Philip St. Theatre, until Douvillier's accidental death.
References: NOCD 1805, 1811; *Courier*, May 20, 1811, July 2, 27, 1821; *Gazette*, June 5, 1817; *Moniteur*, Jan. 16, 1808; Ludlow, 145–49; Moore, 489; St. Louis Cathedral Funerals (July 26, 1821), 35:336, Archives of the Archdiocese of N.O.

DOUVILLIER, SUZANNE THEODORE VAILLANDE (Mrs. LOUIS BOUCHER DOUVILLIER)
Born Dôle, France before 1778; died N.O. Aug. 30, 1826.
Painter, active N.O. 1812–13.
Studied: Paris.
Contemporary listings: scenic painter, St. Philip St. Theatre (1812–13).
French dancer and pantomime actress who was in Santo Domingo by 1788 where she met Alexandre Placide, a noted French acrobat, actor, and theater manager. She accompanied him to the U.S., performing in N.Y.C. (1792), Baltimore, and Charleston (1794–96). In a major public scandal, she left Placide in Charleston for French singer Louis Boucher Douvillier, whom she married. The couple toured together in the U.S. including Philadelphia (1797–98) and N.O. (by ca. 1799). They apparently remained in the city for the remainder of their lives, performing and painting scenery at the

St. Philip St. Theatre. She retired in 1818.
References: NOCD 1823; *Courier*, Jan. 13, 1812, Mar. 17, 1813; *Moniteur*, Jan. 2, 1812, Mar. 20, 1813; Groce and Wallace; Hughes, 76; Information courtesy Archivist of Dôle, July 25, 1963; Ludlow, 145–49; Moore, 478–90; St. Louis Cathedral Funerals (Aug. 30, 1828), 140:630, Archives of the Archdiocese of N.O.

DOVENMUEHLE, CHRISTIAN M.
Lithographer, active N.O. 1890–91; primarily printer.
Contemporary listings: lithographer, KOECKERT & WALLE (1890–91).
References: NOCD 1890–91, 1893, 1895.

DOWLING, JAMES A.
Born LA June 1866.
Commercial artist, painter, active N.O. 1887–1902; also photographer.
Contemporary listings: artist (1887–91, 1899, 1901–1902); crayon artist (1893–94); artist, painter, 241 Olivier (1900).
References: NOCD 1887–95, 1897, 1899–1902; U.S. Census (1900), roll 575.

DOWLING, JOHN HARCOURT
Painter, engraver, active N.O. 1876–83.
Contemporary listings: portrait painter and general engraver, 81 Gravier (1876); portrait painter, 101 Royal (1877); artist, 180 Delord (1880); portrait painter, 251 St. Charles (1881); artist (1882–83).
References: NOCD 1876–83; *D. States*, Jan. 23, 1882; *Repub.*, Jan. 2, 1877; *Southern Business Guide*, 418.

DOYLE, ALEXANDER
Born Steubenville OH Jan. 28, 1857; died Boston MA Dec. 21, 1922.
Sculptor, active N.O. 1882–83.
Studied: National Academies at Carrara, Rome, and Florence; with Nicoli, Dupré, Pellicia.
Memberships/positions: Royal Raphael Academy, Urbino, Italy.
Noted sculptor who settled in N.Y.C. in 1878 and earned a broad reputation throughout the U.S. for commemorative monuments until his retirement in 1911. Doyle was in N.O. from June 1882 to May 1883. He designed the Robert E. Lee statue at Lee Circle, cast in bronze by a NY brass foundry and dedicated Feb. 22, 1884. He also designed the Margaret Haughery statue for Margaret Place which was sculpted in Italy from marble and dedicated July 9, 1884. Other works in N.O. include a statue of a Confederate soldier and an equestrian statue of Albert Sidney Johnston for the tomb of the Benevolent Association of Louisiana, Division of the Army of Tennessee, Metairie Cemetery (dedicated May 20, 1886); the figure on the monument of the Firemen's Charitable Association, Greenwood Cemetery (dedicated Oct. 23, 1887); and the statue of Gen. P. G. T. Beauregard at the entrance to City Park (unveiled Nov. 11, 1915). He also submitted designs for the John J. McDonogh monument and the Jefferson Davis monument, but these were rejected.
References: *D. Pic.*, May 17, Sept. 14, 1882, Jan. 10, 18, Apr. 6, May 22, June 9, Sept. 24, 1883, May 29, June 29, July 8–10, 1884, Nov. 13, 1886, Mar. 18, July 29, Oct. 24, Dec. 13, 1887, Feb. 22, 1888; *D. States*, Nov. 13, 1886, Oct. 17, 24, 1887, Jan. 24, 27, 1898, May 29–30, 1912; *Eve. Chronicle*, May 18, 21, 1886; *Lantern*, Apr. 9, 1887, 5; *T. Demo.*, Feb. 4, 1883, Feb. 22, 1884, Apr. 7, 1887, Jan. 27, 1898, Apr. 28, 1909; *T. Pic.*, Nov. 15, Dec. 6, 1925, Jan. 3, 1926; Roehl, "Follow–up: City's Monuments Showing Their Age," *T. Pic./States–Item*, Oct. 30, 1983; Bénézit; *DAB*; Fielding, *Dictionary*; Friends of the Cabildo, *N.O. Architecture*, 3:111, 115–17; *Historical Sketch Book*, 224–25; WPA, "Lives."

DOYLE, GEORGE
Sculptor, active N.O. ca. 1879–80.
Sculpted the granite statue for the Washington Artillery monument, Metairie Cemetery (dedicated Feb. 22, 1880).
References: *Bee*, Feb. 24, 1880; *D. Pic.*, Feb. 23, 1880; *T. Pic.*, Feb. 21,

1926; Friends of the Cabildo, *N.O. Architecture*, 3:117–19.

DOYLE, THOMAS
Born LA Nov. 1884.
Engraver, active N.O. 1900.
Contemporary listings: engraver (1900).
References: U.S. Census (1900), roll 572.

DRAKE, CAPT. ERNEST E. BONNAR
Born Devonshire, England June 22, 1881; died N.O. Oct. 21, 1943.
Painter, active N.O. ca. 1914.
Exhibited: ART ASSOCIATION OF NEW ORLEANS (1914).
Amateur artist who came to the U.S. in 1910. By 1914 Drake had arrived in N.O.; he became a navigation officer and port captain for shipping companies. Son–in–law of ISAAC MONROE CLINE.
References: NOCD 1914–19, 1921–23, 1925–33, 1935, 1938, 1940, 1942; *Item*, Oct. 23, 1943; *T. Pic.*, Oct. 23, 1943; Art Asso., *Catalogue* (1914); Kendall, *History*, 3:903–4; Orleans Parish Registrar of Voters, NOPL.

DRAWING ACADEMY OF LOUISIANA. *See* LOUISIANA DRAWING ACADEMY

DREIS, THEOBALD J.
Born Kiel, Germany July 1, 1867; died N.O. Sept. 22, 1936.
Painter, active N.O. 1897–1931; also decorator.
Contemporary listings: fresco artist (1897); fresco painter, 128 Exchange Pl. (1898), DREIS & GEISER (1902–1907); fresco and scenic artist, 2910 Palmyra (1908); fresco painter (1909); painter, 2910 Palmyra (1910–16); painter, 2906 Palmyra (1917); fresco painter, 2906 Palmyra (1918).
References: NOCD 1897–1923, 1927–33, 1935; *T. Pic.*, Sept. 24, 1936; Orleans Parish Registrar of Voters, NOPL.

DREIS & GEISER
Painters, active N.O. 1902–1907; THEOBALD J. DREIS, JOHN GEISER, partners.
Contemporary listings: fresco and scenic artists, 2021 Palmyra (1902–1906); fresco and scenic artists (1907).
References: NOCD 1902–1907.

DRENNAN, GEORGIA BERTHA
Born Lexington MS Apr. 26, 1882; died N.O. Aug. 24, 1967.
Artist, active N.O. 1907–1908.
Studied: NEWCOMB COLLEGE (1902–1907).
Exhibited: ART ASSOCIATION OF NEW ORLEANS (1907–1908).
Also listed as draftsman (1922–28), artist (1930), and government clerk (1942–55). Drennan was an architect for the Historic American Buildings Survey (1938).
References: NOCD 1922–25, 1927–30, 1932, 1938, 1940, 1942, 1945–47, 1949, 1952–55; *D. Pic.*, Mar. 15, 1908; *T. Demo.*, Jan. 6, 1907; *T. Pic.*, Aug. 26, 1967; Art Asso., *Catalogue* (1907); Orleans Parish Registrar of Voters, NOPL; Poesch, *Newcomb Pottery*, 99.

DRESSEL, HARRY H.
Born Hanover, Germany 1850; died N.O. May 29, 1905.
Painter, active N.O. 1875–1905; also decorator.
Studied: with his uncle, Royal Opera House, Hanover.
Contemporary listings: scenic artist, Varieties Theatre (1875–77); scenic artist, Bidwell's Academy of Music (1877, 1879–80); DRESSEL & EVANS (1880–82); scenic artist, Spanish Fort Opera House (1883); DRESSEL & WEST (1883); scenic artist, West End Opera House (1883–84); scenic artist, Grunewald Opera House (1884–85); scenic artist, Grand Opera House and Saiter's Opera House (1888); fresco artist, French Opera House (1889); artist (1890, 1904); scenic artist, Garden District Theatre (1893); DRESSEL & NIPPERT (1899–1900); scenic artist, Grand Opera House (1902); scenic artist (1905).
References: NOCD 1876–77, 1879–90, 1893, 1900, 1904–1905; *Bull.*, Oct. 31, Nov. 2, Dec. 2, 4, 1875; *D. Pic.*, Aug. 10, 1877, Sept. 8, 1884, May 1, 1888, Oct. 23, 1899, Oct. 26, 1902, May 30, 1905; *D. States*, Oct. 23, Nov. 20, Dec. 28, 1880, Apr. 22,

July 1, Aug. 28, 1883, May 20, June 28, July 20, Nov. 2, 1884, Oct. 30, 1886, Aug. 14, Oct. 5, 1888, July 22, Oct. 17, Nov. 30, 1889, Feb. 19, 1900, May 30, 1905; *Demo.*, Oct. 31, 1880; *Eve. Chronicle*, Aug. 26, 1884, Jan. 3, 1885; *Mascot*, July 28, 1883, Oct. 6, 1888, June 14, 1890; *New York Clipper*, Apr. 7, 1883; *Repub.*, Jan. 15, Feb. 1, 9, Mar. 1, Apr. 18, 21, 30, Nov. 14, 1876; *Times*, Oct. 14, 1877, Oct. 24, 1880; *T. Demo.*, May 10, 14, 21, 1883, Oct. 20, 1889, May 30, 1905; *T. Pic.*, Dec. 21, 1941; La Cour, 203; Orleans Parish Notarial Archives, John Bendernagel, Dec. 31, 1890, 32:636; THNOC artists files.

DRESSEL & EVANS
Painters, active N.O. 1880–82; HARRY H. DRESSEL, J. CHARLES EVANS, partners.
Contemporary listings: scenic artists, St. Charles Theatre (1880); scenic artists, 104 St. Charles (1881–82).
References: NOCD 1881–82; *Demo.*, Oct. 31, 1880; *Times*, Oct. 24, 1880.

DRESSEL & NIPPERT
Painters, active N.O. 1899–1900; HARRY H. DRESSEL, EMILE NIPPERT, partners.
Contemporary listings: scenic artists, Grand Opera House (1899–1900).
References: NOCD 1900; *D. Pic.*, Oct. 23, 1899.

DRESSEL & WEST
Painters, active N.O. 1883; HARRY H. DRESSEL, WILLIAM J. WEST, partners.
Painted the scenery and drop curtain for Gorman's Standard Novelty Co. (1883).
References: *D. States*, Apr. 22, 1883.

DREYFOUS, FELIX JULIUS
Born N.O. Oct. 21, 1896; died N.O. Jan. 24, 1975.
Painter, active N.O. ca. 1918; primarily architect.
Exhibited: ART ASSOCIATION OF NEW ORLEANS (1918).
Architect who, in association with Leon C. Weiss and Solis Seiferth, designed the LA State Capitol, Baton Rouge, and Charity Hospital. Member of the American Institute of Architects and the Louisiana Institute of Architects.
References: NOCD 1918–33, 1935, 1938, 1940, 1942, 1947, 1949, 1952–56, 1958, 1960–62, 1964, 1966–69, 1971–75; NOSD 1959, 1963; *T. Pic.*, Jan. 25–26, 1975; Green, "Architectural Trailblazers," *T. Pic./States–Item*, Feb. 11, 1984; Art Asso., *Catalogue* (1918); Looney, 393; Samuel Wilson, *Guide to Architecture*, 58, 63, 65, 70, 72, 74.

DROZ, A.
Engraver, lithographer, active N.O. 1833–38.
Contemporary listings: ZIMMER & DROZ (1833); engraver, 116 St. Ann (1834).
Signed the masthead of *Figaro* (July 3, 1838). Possibly Amez Droz, born ca. 1790–1800, living in Lafayette Parish (1830).
References: NOCD 1834; *Courier*, Jan. 25, 1833; Groce and Wallace; Scrapbook 39A, LSM; U.S. Census (1830), roll 44.

DRURY & PHILLIPS
Painters, active N.O. 1850–51; also sign and ornamental painters; N. L. Drury, A. L. PHILLIPS, partners.
Contemporary listings: portrait painters, 173 Carondelet (1850–51).
References: NOCD 1850–51; *D. Crescent*, Aug. 30, 1850, Jan. 7, 1851.

DRYSDALE, ALEXANDER JOHN
Born Marietta GA Mar. 2, 1870; died N.O. Feb. 9, 1934.
Painter, active N.O. 1889–1934.
Studied: with IDA HASKELL, SOUTHERN ART UNION (1883–86); with PAUL POINCY (1887); with Bryson Boroughs, Clifford Carleton, Charles C. Curran, and Frank V. DuMond, Art Students League, N.Y.C. (1901–1903).
Contemporary listings: portrait painter, 325 Camp (1905); portrait painter, 504 Magazine (1906–1907); studio, Board of Trade Building (1907); artist, 504 Magazine (1908–18).
Exhibited: ARTISTS' ASSOCIATION OF NEW ORLEANS (1889–92, 1894, 1896–97, 1899, 1901–1903); Tu-

lane University (1893); ART ASSOCI-
ATION OF NEW ORLEANS (1904–11,
1913, 1915–18); National Association of Newspaper Artists (1905);
DELGADO MUSEUM (1911).

Awarded: Art Association of New
Orleans, gold medal for best oil
painting (1909).

Memberships/positions: Artists' Association of New Orleans, v. pres.
(1899); Art Association of New Orleans.

Landscape painter with a unique
personal style for depicting calm hazy
scenes of LA marshes, bayous, and
large moss–laden oak trees. As a child
in Mobile AL (1875–82), he became
interested in painting. After the
Drysdales moved to N.O. (1883), he
studied accounting with a private tu-
tor and took art lessons at night at
the Southern Art Union. Drysdale
became a clerk at a hardware store
(1886–89), then a runner and teller
with the N.O. National Bank (1889–
1901). During his years as a banker,
he studied painting with the city's
leading artists, produced traditional
oil paintings on canvas, and exhibited at 13 consecutive exhibitions of
the Artists' Association. Having received considerable local acclaim for
his art, Drysdale gave up his banking
career for that of an artist and moved
to N.Y.C. For three years (1901–
1903), he studied and exhibited there
and came under the influence of such
American painters as GEORGE INNESS,
Robert Henri, and William Merritt
Chase, and of the work of J. B. C.
Corot and Claude Monet. Drysdale
returned to N.O. (1903) and listed
himself as a portrait painter, although he exhibited primarily landscapes at the annuals of the Art Association. His so–called "watercolor"
technique (developed by 1916) actually employed oil paint diluted in
kerosene that was applied to sized
board with brushes and cotton balls:
he considered the color and atmos-
phere of his paintings to be similar
to the Impressionists. His two largest
and most important commissions,
however, were oil paintings on canvas for the restaurant of the D. H.
Holmes department store (1927) and
for the administration building of the
Shushan Airport (1933). Drysdale
became one of the most sought–after
living artists in the city during the
1920s–30s; it is estimated that he
produced some 10,000 works.

References: NOCD 1888–1901,
1905–33; Current Topics, Jan. 1892,
24–25; D. Pic., Dec. 17, 1889, Nov.
13, 1890, Dec. 17, 1891, Feb. 14,
1893, Mar. 30, 1897, Mar. 20, 1905,
Mar. 15, 1908, Mar. 12, 1909, July
6, 1913; D. States, Sept. 1, 1886;
Item, Feb. 6, 1921; Item–Trib., Jan.
4, 1925, Feb. 28, 1932; Men and
Matters, Sept. 1897, cover, 41, Dec.
1897, cover, 33, 42, Jan. 1898,
cover, Feb. 1898, 12, Dec. 1904, 25–
30; Morn. Trib., Oct. 5, 1927, June
7, 1929; T. Demo., Dec. 13, 1892,
Dec. 14, 1894, Dec. 27, 1905, Jan.
6, 1907, Jan. 16, 1912; T. Pic., Feb.
10, 1934, July 3, 1953; Jordan,
"Drysdale Bayou Painting Adorns T.
Roosevelt's Sagamore Hill," T. Pic.,
Oct. 31, 1976; Town Talk, Feb. 1905,
46; AANO, Catalogue (1890, 1896,
1899, 1901, 1902, 1903); Anglo–
American Art Museum, Louisiana
Landscape, item 25; Art Asso., Catalogue (1904, 1905, 1907, 1910,
1911, 1913, 1915, 1916, 1917,
1918, 1919); Buechner, Drysdale;
Bruce Chambers, 88; Edwin Davis,
Louisiana, 315; Fielding, Dictionary;
Kelly, 37, 96; Mount, 50–52; Stern's
Auction Co. (1916):4, 5, (1925):10;
U.S. Census (1910), roll 524; Wie-
sendanger, 44–45; WPA, "Lives";
WPA, Louisiana, 167.

DUBARRY, ARMENIA

Painter, active N.O. 1894–98.

Contemporary listings: artist, 1630
Calliope (1897); portrait painter,
1630 Calliope (1898).

Exhibited: ARTISTS' ASSOCIATION OF
NEW ORLEANS (1894, 1896).

Memberships/positions: Artists' Association of New Orleans (1896).

References: NOCD 1897; NOBD
1898; T. Demo., Dec. 14, 1894,
AANO, Catalogue (1896).

DUBOIS, MR. _____
Painter, active N.O. 1869.
Contemporary listings: scenic artist, decorative painter, French Opera (1869).
References: *D. Pic.*, Oct. 13, 1869; *Repub.*, Oct. 17, 1869.

DUBOUSQUET, EUGÈNE
Engraver, active N.O. 1834–35.
Contemporary listings: engraver, 102 Poets (1834–35).
References: NOCD 1834–35; Groce and Wallace.

DUBUC, MAXIMILLIAN, JR.
Engraver, active N.O. 1905; also jeweler.
Contemporary listings: engraver (1905).
References: NOCD 1905, 1907–12.

DUCLARY, LEPELLETIER
Born Martinique ca. 1824.
Painter, active N.O. ca. 1849–52.
Studied: Paris?
Contemporary listings: portrait painter (1849); artist, 80 Chartres (1851).
Exhibited: St. Louis Exchange (1849); Armstrong's Cafe (1851).
References: *Bee*, Apr. 2, 1849, Sept. 10, Nov. 22, Dec. 13, 1851, May 29, 1852; *Courier*, Sept. 10, Nov. 22, 1851; Coulon MS, Scrapbook 100, LSM; Groce and Wallace; Reinders, 197; U.S. Census (1850), roll 235.

DUCLOS, LOUIS
Engraver, active N.O. 1811; also bookbinder, printer.
Contemporary listings: engraver, 53 St. Peter (1811).
References: NOCD 1811; *Courier*, Aug. 31, 1812; U.S. Census (1810), roll 10.

DUCOING, FRANK J., JR.
Painter, active N.O. 1888–93.
Contemporary listings: painter (1888); artist (1893).
References: NOCD 1888–93.

DUCOING, JOHN J.
Artist, active N.O. 1885.
Contemporary listings: artist, 140 Elysian Fields (1885).
References: NOCD 1875, 1878–85, 1887–91, 1893.

DUCOMMAN, BRUTUS
Born Denmark ca. 1854; died N.O. July 21, 1877.
Painter, active N.O. 1877.
Contemporary listings: portrait painter (1877).
Brother–in–law and partner of HAROLD RUDOLPH.
References: *D. Pic.*, July 22, 1877.

DUFORT, SARAH E.
Born LA Dec. 1862.
Painter, active N.O. 1899–1903.
Contemporary listings: artist (1899); portrait painter, 1116 Baronne and 1352 Magazine (1903).
Mother of VIRGIE DUFORT.
References: NOCD 1899, 1903–1906; U.S. Census (1900), roll 570.

DUFORT, VIRGIE
Born LA Aug. 1881.
Painter, active N.O. 1903–1905.
Contemporary listings: portrait painter, 1116 Baronne (1903); artist, 617 St. Joseph (1904–1905).
Daughter of SARAH E. DUFORT.
References: NOCD 1903–1905, 1907, 1909–10; U.S. Census (1900), roll 570.

DUFOUR, ALBERT
Painter, active N.O. 1867.
Contemporary listings: artist, Orleans Theatre (1867).
References: NOCD 1867.

DU GARRY, MR. _____
Art teacher, active N.O. 1826–34.
Contemporary listings: drawing teacher, 277 Bourbon or 59 Bienville (1826); drawing teacher, Mr. and Mrs. Montilly's Academy for Young Ladies (1834).
References: *Argus*, Feb. 15, 1826; *Bee*, Oct. 25, 1834; Groce and Wallace.

DUGGAN, EDITH BOXER
Born N.O. June 3, 1878; died N.O. Nov. 3, 1932.
Sketch artist, painter, active N.O. 1892.
Studied: with ANDRES MOLINARY; with PAUL POINCY; NEWCOMB COLLEGE; Chase Studio, N.Y.C.; with Frank V. DuMond, Art Students League, N.Y.C.
Created the drawings for the article "A Christmas Mamma" in the *Daily Picayune*. She also painted portraits of prominent members of N.O. society, including author Grace King.

References: *D. Pic.*, Dec. 25, 1892, Jan. 1, 1893; *T. Pic.*, Nov. 4, 1932; Seebold, 2:165, 168, 249; THNOC Cemetery Survey.

DUMAS, VALSIN
Sculptor, active N.O. 1841–44.
Contemporary listings: marble sculptor, 87 Basin (1841–44).
References: NOCD 1841–44, 1849–50; Groce and Wallace.

DUMONT DE MONTIGNY, LOUIS FRANÇOIS BENJAMIN
Sketch artist, active N.O. ca. 1719–37; also cartographer.
French soldier in LA who traveled throughout the Mississippi River valley and along the Gulf Coast. He served as a lieutenant and as engineer at Forts Rosalie and St. Claude and went up the Arkansas River (1721). He made maps and drawings to illustrate his journals which were published in Paris (1753).
References: Groce and Wallace; Samuel Wilson, *Bienville's New Orleans*, 20–21; WPA, *Louisiana*, 161.

DUMOULIN, ADOLPHE
Lithographer, active N.O. 1885.
Contemporary listings: lithographer, T. FITZWILLIAM & CO. (1885).
References: NOCD 1885.

DUNBAR, MOSES
Sculptor, active N.O. 1879; black.
Contemporary listings: woodcarver (1879).
References: NOCD 1867, 1871–74, 1876–79.

DUNCAN, JOSEPH
Born Scotland ca. 1825.
Artist, active N.O. 1850.
Contemporary listings: artist (1850).
References: Groce and Wallace; U.S. Census (1850), roll 234.

DUNLAP, JAMES BOLIVER
Born Indianapolis IN May 7, 1825; died Indianapolis Sept. 4, 1864.
Painter, active N.O. 1850.
Contemporary listings: portrait painter (1850).
Painter, sculptor, lithographer, wood engraver, and cartoonist who traveled from IN to CA by way of N.O. to open a studio in San Francisco. By 1860 he had returned to the eastern U.S.

References: Groce and Wallace; U.S. Census (1850), roll 234.

DUNLAP, VIRGINIA M.
Artist, active N.O. 1905–12.
Contemporary listings: artist (1905, 1907, 1912).
References: NOCD 1905, 1907, 1912.

DUNN, GRACE BLETHEN. *See* BLETHEN, GRACE

DUNN, DR. JOHN GIBSON
Born Lawrenceburg IN ca. 1826; died N.O. 1858.
Painter, active N.O. 1850.
Studied: with Jacob Cox, Indianapolis IN (ca. 1843).
Contemporary listings: painter, 13 St. Charles (1850).
References: *D. Delta*, Jan. 24, Apr. 1, 1850; *D. Pic.*, May 25, 1847; Groce and Wallace; Peat, 66–67.

DUNN, JOSEPH D.
Painter, active N.O. 1893.
Contemporary listings: portrait painter, 5 Carondelet (1893).
References: NOCD 1893.

M. F. DUNN & BRO.
Lithographers, engravers, active N.O. 1878–1903; primarily stationers, printers, bookbinders; Michael Fitzgerald Dunn, Dennis J. Dunn, partners.
Contemporary listings: lithographers, 70 Camp (1882, 1889–92); 70 Camp and 127 Gravier (1885); bookbinders, 76 Camp (1893); steam press lithographers, engravers, and bookbinders, 332 Camp (1895–96); lithographers, 332 Camp (1898).
Reported to have been a printer since 1863, Michael Dunn worked for T. FITWILLIAM & CO. (1868–78) before the partnership with his brother Dennis. Their firm was noted for its stationery and blank book manufacturing, and their lithographic presses printed black and white and color pictorial material, including sheet music. The firm was listed through 1903, and Michael Dunn continued as a stationer through 1913.
References: NOCD 1867–1903; NOBD, 1897; *D. Item*, Feb. 18, 1896; *D. Pic.*, Mar. 3, 1885, Sept. 1, 1895; *D. States*, Mar. 3, 8, 1885; *Eve.*

Chronicle, Mar. 3, 1885; *T. Demo.*, Jan. 12, 1893; Land, 157; Sheet Music Collection, THNOC.

DUNNING, JOHN N.
Lithographer, active N.O. 1885.
Contemporary listings: lithographer (1885).
References: NOCD 1885.

DUPERLY, ARMAND, JR.
Born ca. 1854.
Artist, active N.O. 1860.
Contemporary listings: artist, 408 Villere (1860).
Son of ARMAND DUPERLY, SR.
References: NOCD 1860–61, 1866; U.S. Census (1860), roll 419.

DUPERLY, ARMAND, SR.
Born Jamaica ca. 1833.
Artist, lithographer, active N.O. 1857–61.
Contemporary listings: artist, 66 St. Charles (1861).
Created a lithographic portrait of Archbishop Antoine Blanc (1857).
Father of ARMAND DUPERLY, JR.
References: NOCD 1858–61; *Bee*, Apr. 17, 1857; *D. Crescent*, Apr. 17, 1857; Groce and Wallace; U.S. Census (1860), roll 419.

DU PORTAIL, J. B. POINTEL. *See* POINTEL DU PORTAIL, J. B.

DU PRATZ, ANTOINE SIMON LE PAGE. *See* LE PAGE DU PRATZ, ANTOINE SIMON

DUQUESNAY, ALBERT
Sketch artist, painter, active N.O. 1870.
While in N.O., he executed drawings and watercolors, signed and dated 1870, of French Quarter scenes.
References: THNOC artists files.

DUREL, PAULIN
Born LA ca. 1816–17; died Mandeville LA June 20, 1882.
Engraver, lithographer, active N.O. 1870–73; primarily stationer, printer.
Contemporary listings: engraver, lithographer, 37 Chartres (1873).
References: NOCD 1841–43, 1846, 1849–61, 1866–82; *Bee*, June 21, 1882; *D. Pic.*, June 21, 1882; THNOC 76–29–L; U.S. Census (1880), roll 461.

DUREL, RENE NORBERT
Born N.O. Jan. 1880; died N.O. Dec. 22, 1946.
Commercial artist, engraver, active N.O. 1902–46.
Contemporary listings: artist, ROMANSKI Photo–Engraving Co., Ltd. (1902, 1907); engraver (1903); artist (1904–1906, 1910, 1915–17); artist, GRELLE–EGERTON ENGRAVING CO. (1908–1909, 1913–14, 1918); art dept. mgr., Grelle–Egerton Engraving Co. (1911–12).
Signed sheet music covers and 37 caricatures with WILLIAM K. PATRICK in *Club Men of Louisiana in Caricature* (1917). Durel was listed with Grelle–Egerton through 1932, then with NEW ORLEANS ENGRAVING & ELECTROTYPE CO. LTD. (1935, 1942, 1945–46).
References: NOCD 1897–1933, 1935, 1938, 1940, 1942, 1945–46; *T. Pic.*, Dec. 23, 1946; Jordan, "The World of Art: Sheet Music Covers," *T. Pic.*, Jan. 28, 1979; Orleans Parish Registrar of Voters, NOPL; Patrick; Sheet Music Collection, THNOC.

DURIEUX, CAROLINE SPELMAN WOGAN
(Mrs. Pierre Durieux)
Born N.O. Jan. 22, 1896.
Lithographer, painter, etcher, active N.O. 1913–43.
Studied: NEWCOMB COLLEGE (1913–17); with Henry McCarter and Arthur B. Carles, Pennsylvania Academy of Fine Arts, Philadelphia (1917–19).
Exhibited: ART ASSOCIATION OF NEW ORLEANS (1915–17).
Awarded: Newcomb College, Neill Medal.
Renowned as a 20th–century lithographer and satirist, Durieux drew obsessively, particularly caricatures, throughout grade school and began her serious art studies at Newcomb College. With her marriage in 1920 to an import–export dealer, she lived in and traveled through much of Central and South America and made bold paintings of the local landscape and of flowers. Beginning in 1926, Durieux resided in Mexico City for several years where she worked

closely with noted Mexican artists, particularly Diego Rivera, executed her first lithograph (1931), and held her first solo exhibition (1934). During these years, Durieux frequently visited her family in N.O. and exhibited at the Arts and Crafts Club. In 1936 she returned to N.O. and worked as an illustrator on the Federal Writers Project for eight months before becoming an assistant professor of design at Newcomb (1937–43). While at Newcomb, she continued her printmaking and made popular lithographs that humorously satirized N.O.'s Creole society. During some of these years, she also held the position of state director of the Federal Art Project (1939–43). In 1943 Durieux joined the faculty at Louisiana State University, Baton Rouge, where she taught printmaking, received her Master of Fine Arts degree (1949), and retired as Professor Emeritus of Fine Arts (1964). During her years at L.S.U., she created two new printmaking processes with the collaboration of L.S.U. scientists: electron printing and the addition of color to the 19th–century cliché verre technique. Durieux has held memberships in numerous art organizations but has retired and is living in Baton Rouge.

References: NOCD 1938, 1940, 1942; Baton Rouge State-Times, Oct. 12, 1981; Item, Jan. 28, 1931, Apr. 24, 1932, Feb. 10, 1935, Feb. 5, 12, Mar. 2, Nov. 9, 1939, Nov. 10, 1940, Jan. 6, 1941, Oct. 30, 1945; Morn. Trib., Oct. 27, Dec. 29, 1926, Jan. 26, Nov. 16, 1927, Dec. 19, 1932, Jan. 30, 1933, Dec. 28, 1934; Time, Jan. 20, 1941; T. Pic., May 4, 1924, Jan. 6, 1930, Jan. 6, 1935, Feb. 16, Mar. 8, 1936, Jan. 30, Dec. 11, 1938, Jan. 8, 22, Feb. 25, Apr. 2, 1939, Oct. 6, 1940, Nov. 7, 1943, Sept. 10, 1950, Dec. 6, 1959, Sept. 25, 1960, Oct. 28, 1971, Jan. 11, 1976; Anglo–American Art Museum, Catalogue; Art Asso., Catalogue (1916, 1917); Art Asso., Special Exhibition; Arts and Humanities Council; Richard Cox; Loyola University; LSU,

Caroline Durieux; Ormond and Irvine, 172; Saxon; THNOC, Caroline Durieux Retrospective Exhibition; Barbara Walker, 3, 9–11, 14; Wickiser et al.; WPA, "Lives."

DURKIN, JOHN
Born 1868; died N.Y.C. May 12, 1903.
Sketch artist, illustrator, active N.O. 1884; 1886.
Illustrator for Harper's Weekly. Durkin was sent to N.O. (1884) as an assistant to CHARLES GRAHAM, to make sketches of the World's Industrial and Cotton Centennial Exposition (published Dec. 20, 1884). Again assisting Graham, he returned to N.O. (1886), along with another artist assistant HORACE BRADLEY and other Harper's representatives on a tour of the southern states.
References: D. Pic., Nov. 29, 1886; D. States, Dec. 1, 1886; Harper's Wkly., Dec. 20, 1884, 838, Aug. 13, 1887, 570–71; Kelly, 38.

DUVAL, AMBROSE
Born ca. 1760–70.
Painter, art teacher, active N.O. 1803–35.
Contemporary listings: miniature portrait painter and painting teacher, Chaslan's or Labatut's house (1803); miniature painter and drawing master, 121 Bourbon (1823); miniature painter and drawing master, 129 Bourbon (1824, 1827); painter, 130 Bourbon (1829); miniature painter, 129 Bourbon (1830); portrait painter, 130 Bourbon (1832); portrait painter, 132 Bourbon (1834–35).
One of the first and the best of the early N.O. miniature painters who worked in a French style of portraiture. Duval advertised in Feb. 1803 his arrival from Europe and his services as a teacher of figures, landscapes, and flowers. His most important commission was the miniature portrait of William C. C. Claiborne (ca. 1805), LA's first American governor, which was used for a popular engraving by James Barton Longacre. Duval also called himself a nat-

uralist and exhibited his collection of preserved birds in N.O.

References: NOCD 1805, 1823–24, 1827, 1830, 1832, 1834–35; *Courier*, Aug. 5, 1811, Dec. 5, 1817, Aug. 3, 1829; *Moniteur*, Feb. 5, 1803; Bénézit; Bruns, 58, 260, 311; Fielding, *Dictionary*; Friends of the Cabildo, *250 Years*, 50; Glenk, 68, 74; Groce and Wallace; THNOC 1975.142, 1981.206; U.S. Census (1810), roll 10, (1830), roll 45; Wilson and Huber, *Cabildo*, 57; WPA, *Miniatures and Fans*; WPA, *New Orleans*, 99.

DUVAL, JULIEN

Born West Indies ca. 1786–90; died N.O. June 22, 1851.

Art teacher, active N.O. 1821–40.

Contemporary listings: drawing teacher, 21 Maine (1821); drawing teacher, 115 Conti (1832); drawing teacher, 107 Bourbon (1837); drawing teacher, 5 Bourbon (1840).

Primarily a professor of languages, especially French and English, who advertised that he also taught geography, arithmetic, drawing, and bookkeeping (1819, 1821, 1832, 1840).

References: NOCD 1822–24, 1827, 1830, 1832, 1834–35, 1837–38, 1841–43, 1846, 1849, 1851; *Bee*, June 23, 1851; *Courier*, June 14, 1819, Sept. 10, Oct. 29, 1821, Nov. 12, 1832, July 25, 1840; Groce and Wallace; U.S. Census (1830), roll 45, (1840), roll 132, (1850), roll 236.

DUVERGER, PAUL

Artist, active N.O. 1857.

Contemporary listings: artist, Orleans cor. Miro (1857).

References: NOCD 1857; Groce and Wallace.

DUZDEIN, JOHN A.

Born SC ca. 1815.

Engraver, active N.O. 1860.

Contemporary listings: engraver (1860).

References: Groce and Wallace; U.S. Census (1860), roll 416.

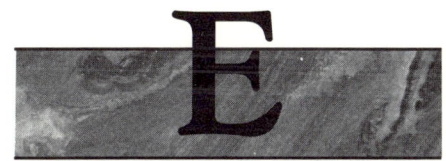

EACHES, JAMES M.
Born VA 1817; died 1847.
Painter, active N.O. 1842.
Contemporary listings: portrait painter, 1 St. Charles (1842).
Exhibited: National Academy of Design, N.Y.C. (1838).
Son of Joseph Eaches, mayor of Alexandria VA and older brother of portrait painter Hector Eaches.
References: NOCD 1842; *D. Pic.*, Feb. 2, 1842; Groce and Wallace.

EARL, RALPH ELEAZAR WHITESIDES
Born England 1788; died the Hermitage, near Nashville TN Sept. 16, 1838.
Painter, active N.O. 1821; 1828.
Studied: with his father, Ralph Earl, Northampton MA; England (ca. 1809–13); with Benjamin West, John Trumbull, London (1809); Paris, (1814).
Portrait and landscape painter who worked as an itinerant artist in GA, AL, TN, and along the Mississippi River. In 1816 Earl decided to record the heroes of the Battle of N.O. and painted Andrew Jackson in Nashville (1817). While there, Earl met Mrs. Jackson's niece, Jane Caffery, whom he married in 1818. That year, he painted a full–length portrait of Jackson, standing at the site of the Battle of N.O., which was exhibited at Earl's Tennessee Museum. A copy of the portrait was exhibited in Natchez MS in Feb. 1821, but the city could not raise the funds needed to purchase it. Earl took the portrait to N.O. to offer it to the mayor and the City Council (Mar. 1821), and the city bought it for $1,000 for the Council Hall. Earl returned to N.O. in 1828, when he accompanied the Jackson family to ceremonics commemorating the Battle of N.O. After Jackson became president (1829), Earl became a member of the Jackson household at the White House and at the Hermitage and painted many portraits of Jackson, his family, and his friends.
References: *T. Demo.*, May 9, 1885; Collier, "The World of Art: Museum May Get Portrait of Jackson," *T. Pic.*, Nov. 8, 1970; Barker, 279; Creole Art Gallery, 15; Fielding, *Dictionary*; Groce and Wallace; Information courtesy Mrs. William Coke, Ladies' Hermitage Association, Mar. 25, 1986; Kendall, *History*, 2:656; Ludlow, 179; MacBeth, 390; New Orleans City Council, Letters, Jan. 16, Mar. 9, 1821, doc. 661, NOPL; New Orleans City Council, Proceedings, Mar. 10, Apr. 14, 1821, NOPL; Warren, *Bayou Bend*, 147.

EARL & BURELL
Lithographers, active N.O. 1889; primarily printers, publishers; Samuel S. Earl (born St. Charles [MO] ca. 1842; died N.O. Mar. 3, 1920), Francis M. Burell, partners.
Contemporary listings: job printers, publishers and lithographers, 55 and 57 Magazine (1889).
Successors to Burell & Co., N.O. publishers.
References: NOCD 1890; NOBD 1889; *T. Pic.*, Mar. 5, 1920.

EASTMAN, SETH
Born Brunswick ME Jan. 24, 1808; died Washington DC Aug. 31, 1875.
Sketch artist, active N.O. 1848.
Army officer, topographical draftsman, and painter. Eastman attended the U.S. Military Academy at West Point NY (1824–29), where he later taught drawing (1833–40). His interest in Indian life and western scenery began while stationed in various posts in the West. Eastman was in LA on topographical duty (1831–32?) and made sketches in N.O. (1848) while traveling with the U.S. Army, 1st Infantry Division, en route to TX. Almost 300 plates in Henry R. Schoolcraft's *Indian Tribes of the United States* were made from his western drawings, and the U.S. Con-

gress commissioned him to paint Indian scenes and views of western forts (1867–70).

References: *Appleton's CAB*; Bénézit; Curry, 35; Delgado, *New Orleans*, items 31–35; Fielding, *Dictionary*; Groce and Wallace; McCracken, *Portrait*, 65–71; McDermott, *Art of Eastman*, 14; McNay Art Institute; Museum of Fine Arts, 1:144–45; Pinckney, 49.

EATON, JOSEPH ORIEL
Born Newark OH Feb. 8, 1829; died Yonkers NY Feb. 7, 1875.
Painter, active N.O. 1855; 1857.
Studied: N.Y.C.
Contemporary listings: portrait painter (1855).
Exhibited: A. Munroe's store (1857); National Academy of Design, N.Y.C. (1868–74).
Memberships/positions: National Academy of Design, N.Y.C., associate; Society of Painters in Watercolors; Artists' Fund Society.
Itinerant portrait, genre, and landscape painter in oil and watercolors. Eaton worked in Indianapolis (1846–48), Cincinnati (1850, 1853, 1857–60), N.O. (1855, 1857), and visited Europe (1873). He settled in N.Y.C. and was most successful late in his career as a painter of children's portraits.
References: *D. Crescent*, Jan. 29, 1857; *D. Delta*, Apr. 7, 1855; *Appleton's CAB*; Bénézit; *Bryan's*; Fielding, *Dictionary*; Groce and Wallace.

EBERHARDT, ALBERT
Born Switzerland ca. 1846; died N.O. Sept. 27, 1870.
Engraver, active N.O. 1870.
Died of yellow fever one month after arriving in N.O. from Cincinnati.
References: Louisiana Charity Hospital, Death Records, NOPL.

ECKERT, WILLIAM A.
Lithographer, active N.O. 1881–87; also pressman.
Contemporary listings: lithographer (1881–82, 1885–86); lithographer, NEW ORLEANS LITHOGRAPHIC CO. (1883–84); lithographer, G. KOECKERT & CO. (1887).

References: NOCD 1879–94, 1896–98, 1900–1901, 1903–10.

EDMONDS, A. E.
Painter, active N.O. ca. 1915.
Exhibited: ART ASSOCIATION OF NEW ORLEANS (1915).
References: *Item*, May 3, 1915; Art Asso., *Special Exhibition*.

EDMONDS, J. E.
Cartoonist, active N.O. ca. 1903.
Signed three cartoons published in the N.O. weekly, *Harlequin* (1903). Possibly James E. Edmonds who was a reporter for the N.O. *Times–Democrat* (1905–1906) and an editor with the N.O. *Item* (1914–16) and the *Times–Picayune* (1920–25).
References: NOCD 1905–1906, 1914–17, 1920–28, 1931–33, 1935, 1938, 1940; *Harlequin*, Mar. 19, 1903, 1, Apr. 16, 1903, 1, Apr. 23, 1903, 4.

EDMONDS, JOHN
Hair worker, active N.O. 1858–61; also watchmaker, jeweler.
Contemporary listings: hair (ornamental) manuf., 2 Carondelet (1858); hairworker, 1 Carondelet (1858–61).
References: NOCD 1859–61, 1866–67, 1871–78, 1880–81; NOBD 1858.

EDOUART, AUGUSTE (Augustin Amant Constance Fidèle)
Born Dunkerque, France 1789; died Guînes, France, 1861.
Silhouettist, painter, hair worker, active N.O. 1842; 1844.
Contemporary listings: silhouettist, cor. Royal and Conti (1844).
Exhibited: Royal Academy, London (1815–16); Exhibition of Works of Art, cor. Royal and Conti (1844).
After leaving the French army in 1813, Edouart went to England as a French teacher and later was occupied as a hair worker and as a painter. His interest in silhouettes began after he saw those made by machine and discovered that he could produce better ones cut by hand with scissors. He started his new career as a silhouettist in 1825 in England, then traveled to Scotland (1830–32) and Ireland (1833–39). His methods were published in his autobiograph-

ical book A Treatise on Silhouette Likenesses (1835). He made two images at the same time, one for the client and another for a portfolio of his work that he exhibited during his travels. From 1839 to 1849, Edouart worked throughout the U.S., including N.O. (1842, 1844). On his return to Europe (Dec. 1849), his ship wrecked, and though he survived, only 12,000 of the probable 100,000 portrait silhouettes he had with him were saved.
References: D. Pic., Mar. 19, 1844, Mar. 19–21, 1844 (advs.); Bénézit; Collection of American Silhouette Portraits, 5–8, 53–59; Groce and Wallace; Helfer, 64–68; Emily Jackson, Ancestors, 1–22; Emily Jackson, Silhouette, 96–101; Lister, 16, 22–28, 30–32, 57–58; London, 6, 55–57, 62–65, 68, 76, 139, 157; Megroz, 93–99; Ritchan, 392–93.

EDSON, TRACY ROBINSON
Born Otsego County NY 1809; died Nov. 29, 1881.
Engraver, active N.O. 1841–42.
Contemporary listings: engraver, 2 Royal (1841–42).
Engraver in N.Y.C. (1834–37, 1847–60) with RAWDON, WRIGHT, HATCH & EDSON (1835, 1847–58) and with the AMERICAN BANK NOTE COMPANY.
References: NOCD 1841–44; Boggs; Groce and Wallace.

EDWARDS, A. ESTHER
Sketch artist, active N.O. ca. 1916.
Exhibited: ART ASSOCIATION OF NEW ORLEANS (1916).
References: Art Asso., Catalogue (1916).

EDWARDS, THOMAS
Silhouettist, active N.O. 1825.
Exhibited: Boston Athenaeum.
Silhouettist, portrait and miniature painter, teacher, and lithographer. Edwards was active in Boston MA (1822–56) where he contributed drawings to the city's first lithographic press, established in 1825 by the Pendleton Brothers. He signed a pair of hollow–cut silhouettes of JOHN J. AUDUBON and his wife, Lucy B. Audubon, that are inscribed "New Orleans 1825."

References: Bénézit; Carrick, 13–14, 82; Fielding, Dictionary; Groce and Wallace; Sotheby, Americana (Nov. 1977), lot 625.

E. ENGRAVING CO. See ELECTRIC ENGRAVING CO.

EEPKE, HENRY
Lithographer, active N.O. 1891.
Contemporary listings: lithographer, T. FITZWILLIAM & CO. (1891).
References: NOCD 1891.

EGAN, ANNIE
Born LA ca. 1892.
Artist, active N.O. 1910.
Contemporary listings: artist, novelty company (1910).
References: U.S. Census (1910), roll 523.

EGERTON, WALTER WILLIAM
Born N.O. Oct. 22, 1880; died ca. 1948.
Engraver, active N.O. 1903–40.
Contemporary listings: engraver, PHOTO-ENGRAVING CO. (1903–1904); GRELLE-EGERTON ENGRAVING CO. (1907–18).
Remained with Grelle–Egerton until 1932; later listed with the NEW ORLEANS ENGRAVING & ELECTROTYPE CO., LTD. (1935, 1942).
References: NOCD 1898–1933, 1935, 1938, 1940, 1942, 1945–47, 1949.

EHREN, FREDERICK S., SUSIS T., or SUTER F. See VON EHREN, SUSUS FREDERICK

EIFFERT, FREDERICK
Designer, active N.O. 1858.
Contemporary listings: fancy paper cutter, Greatmen betw. Marigny and Mandeville (1858).
References: NOCD 1858–61.

EISENMANN, CHARLES L.
Artist, active N.O. 1874; primarily photographic printer.
Contemporary listings: artist, with WILLIAM WATSON WASHBURN (1874).
References: NOCD 1872–75.

ELECTRIC ENGRAVING CO.
Engravers, active N.O. 1894–1902; PAUL R. AUDIBERT, GEORGE FRANÇOIS MUGNIER, partners.
Contemporary listings: engravings and designing, 116 Exchange Pl. (1895); 116 Exchange Pl. (1895–

1900); engravers and photo–engraving, 116 Exchange Pl. (1898).

Commercial partnership of Audibert and Mugnier which advertised as the largest photoengraving establishment in the South (1894). The partnership dissolved in 1894: Audibert left the firm, and Mugnier remained as manager. The Company engraved illustrations for *Men and Matters* (1896, 1902).

References: NOCD 1895–1900; NOBD 1898; *Men and Matters*, Feb. 1896, cover, 8–13; June 1902, cover; Orleans Parish Notarial Archives, William C. Dufour, Nov. 3, 1894, 1:9; *Washington Artillery Souvenir*, 78.

ELLIOT, MRS. A.
Born CT ca. 1840.
Painter, active N.O. 1867–70.
Contemporary listings: figure and portrait painter, Canal St. (1867); portrait painter (1870).
Exhibited: Zimmerman's jewelry store (1867); E. A. Tyler's jewelry store (1869).
Cf. HARRIET T. ELLIOTT.
References: *D. Pic.*, Oct. 18, 1867, Feb. 12, 1869; *Times*, Feb. 3, 1867; U.S. Census (1870), roll 519.

ELLIOTT, ESTHER HUGER
Born Sewanee TN.
Art craftsman, potter, active N.O. 1895–1905.
Studied: NEWCOMB COLLEGE (1887, 1890–91, 1895).
Exhibited: ART ASSOCIATION OF NEW ORLEANS (1905).
In 1896–98 and 1900–1905, she was a special art student/pottery worker at Tulane University.
References: Art Asso., *Catalogue* (1905); Ormond & Irvine, 154; Poesch, *Newcomb Pottery*, 99.

ELLIOTT, HARRIET T. (Mrs. William R. Elliott)
Painter, colorer, active N.O. 1871–89.
Contemporary listings: artist, 6 Camp (1871–75, 1880, 1882–83); photograph colorer (1875); portrait painter, 6 Camp (1876–78, 1881); artist, 96 Canal (1884); artist, 195 Canal (1885); artist (1886–89).

Memberships/positions: SOUTHERN ART UNION, art committee (1880–81). *Cf.* ELLIOT, MRS. A.
References: NOCD 1869, 1871–78, 1880–92; *Bee*, May 27, 1880, May 4, 1881; *Bull.*, May 14, 29, Oct. 14, 1875; *Demo.*, May 27, 1880.

ELLIOTT, HENRY J.
Sculptor, active N.O. 1879; black.
Contemporary listings: sculptor (1879).
References: NOCD 1866, 1868, 1870–80, 1882–86.

ELLIOTT, HUGER
Painter, active N.O. ca. 1907.
Studied: Ecole des Beaux Arts, Paris.
Exhibited: ART ASSOCIATION OF NEW ORLEANS (1907).
Listed at the University of Pennsylvania (1907).
References: NOCD 1896; Art Asso., *Catalogue* (1907).

ELLIOTT, SARAH B. (Mrs. Joseph Elliott)
Painter, active N.O. 1883.
Contemporary listings: portrait painter, 96 Canal (1883).
Exhibited: Blessing's gallery (1883).
References: NOCD 1884–85; *D. Pic.*, Sept. 11, 1883; *D. States*, Sept. 2, 1883.

ELLIOTT, W. L.
Painter, active N.O. 1846.
Contemporary listings: painter (1846).
Mentioned (1938) among artists who worked in N.O. before 1865. Possibly Wyatt L. Elliott, born Louisville KY ca. 1825; died N.O. Nov. 9, 1856; listed in NOCD 1852–53.
References: NOCD 1846, 1852–53, 1857; *D. Pic.*, Nov. 9, 1856; *Item–Trib.*, Aug. 7, 1938.

ELLWOOD, ANNA E.
Born N.O. Nov. 13, 1878.
Artist, active N.O. 1910.
Contemporary listings: floral artist (1910).
References: Orleans Parish Registrar of Voters, NOPL; U.S. Census (1910), roll 524.

EMLING, LOUIS C.
Artist, active N.O. 1884.
Contemporary listings: artist (1884).
References: NOCD 1884.

ENDICOTT & CO.
Engravers, active N.O. 1840; George Endicott, J. R. CLARK, partners.
Contemporary listings: bank note engraving company office, cor. St. Charles and Common (1840). Purchased Casilear, Durand & Co. of N.Y.C. and moved it to N.O., under the new name, to furnish banking institutions in the South and West with bank notes, certificates, bonds, and checks.
References: D. Pic., Feb. 11–Apr. 11, 1840 (advs.).

ENGEL, ADOLPHE
Artist, active N.O. 1898–99.
Contemporary listings: artist (1898–99).
References: NOCD 1898–99.

ENGLISH, J.
Artist, active N.O. 1851–53.
Contemporary listings: artist, 32 Phillippa (1851–53).
References: NOCD 1851–53; Groce and Wallace.

ENNIS, JANIE BERT
Born GA ca. 1890.
Art craftsman, active N.O. 1910.
Contemporary listings: artist (1910).
Exhibited: ART ASSOCIATION OF NEW ORLEANS (1910).
References: Art Asso., Catalogue, (1910); U.S. Census (1910), roll 519.

ERARD, CHARLES ALBERT
Born N.O. ca. 1888; died N.O. Dec. 4, 1918.
Commercial artist, painter, active N.O. 1908–17; also decorator.
Contemporary listings: artist, NEW ORLEANS ENGRAVING & ELECTROTYPE CO., LTD. (1908–1909, 1911–17); scenic artist (1910).
References: NOCD 1906–17; T. Pic., Dec. 5, 1918; U.S. Census (1910), roll 521.

ERD, JOHN J. F[REDERICK]. (Jacob J. F.)
Born Mobile AL ca. 1868; died N.O. May 5, 1907.
Lithographer, active N.O. 1888–1905, also printer, pressman.
Contemporary listings: lithographer, KOECKERT & WALLE (1888–90); lithographer, T. FITZWILLIAM & CO. (1900); lithographer (1902–1905).

References: NOCD 1886, 1888–90, 1897, 1899–1905; D. Pic., May 6, 12, 1907.

ERDMANN, VAITINE
Sculptor, active N.O. 1905.
Contemporary listings: wood carver (1905).
References: NOCD 1905.

ERNEST, MR. _____
Art teacher, active N.O. 1820.
Contemporary listings: teacher of drawing and embroidery (1820).
Advertised the sale of painted fans and colored engravings.
References: Courier, Dec. 22, 1820; Gazette, Dec. 15, 1820.

ERNST, MR. _____
Artist, active N.O. 1861.
Contemporary listings: artist, 71 Magazine (1861).
References: D. Pic., Sept. 8, 1861.

ERTZ, EDWARD FREDERICK. See also NEW ORLEANS ETCHING CLUB
Born Canfield IL Mar. 1, 1862.
Engraver, etcher, painter, sketch artist, designer, active N.O. ca. 1881–90; also draftsman.
Studied: with Paul Louis Delance, Jules Lefebvre, and Benjamin Constant, Paris.
Contemporary listings: engraver, 116 Gravier (1883–84); engraver, 46 Camp (1885–87).
Exhibited: SEEBOLD's (1886); ARTISTS' ASSOCIATION OF NEW ORLEANS (1886, 1889–90, 1894); Tulane University Annual Art and Industrial Exhibition (1890); Tennessee Centennial and International Exposition, Nashville (1897).
Awarded: International Exposition, St. Etienne, diploma of honor; Exposition d'Angers, gold medal; Grand Prix International Exposition, Rouen, France; Société des Amis des Arts de la Somme, medal (1899); Ville d'Elboeuf, France, medal; Bristol Arts and Crafts, England, two awards; American Art Society, Philadelphia, medal (1902).
Memberships/positions: Artists' Association of New Orleans (1886, 1889–90); Royal Society of British Artists, London; Society of Arts, London, fellow; Imperial Arts

League; British Water Color Society; Essex Art Club; Aberdeen Artists Guild; Société Internationale d'Aquarellistes, Paris; Société des Cinquante; Union Internationale des Beaux–Arts; Chicago Society of Etchers; Chicago Artists Guild; California Society of Etchers.

Specialized in wood engraving, designing, and sketching from nature. Ertz served a five–year apprenticeship doing engraving in Chicago, and came to N.O. (ca. 1881). He began a business which extended over LA, TX, and MS by 1885. During that time he executed popular engraved and lithographed views of the World's Industrial and Cotton Centennial Exposition and was noted in *The Industries of New Orleans* as having "the largest establishment and really the only one of the kind in the South" with the first routing and ruling machines. He was the engraver for the vignette in the masthead of the N.O. *States* and for illustrations in newspapers and other printed publications. Although he left N.O. in 1890, he continued to send works for exhibition at the Artists' Association. From 1892 to 1898, Ertz was living in Paris as a teacher of watercolor at the Académie Delécluse; he later moved to England and in 1929 was living in Pulborough, Sussex.

References: NOCD 1883–87; *D. Pic.*, Nov. 6, 1886, Dec. 17, 1889, Feb. 14, Nov. 13, 1890; *D. States*, Nov. 5, 1886; *Eve. Chronicle*, July 9, 1885; *States*, May 25, 1884; *T. Demo.*, Jan. 3, 1886, Dec. 14, 1894; Bénézit; Fielding, *Dictionary*; Morrison, *Industries*, 18, 64, 148; Tennessee Centennial Exposition, 35, 262; THNOC 1982.223; Thompson, "Checklist."

ESCOSURA, IGNACIO LEON Y. *See* LEON Y ESCOSURA, IGNACIO

ESNARD, PAUL F.
Born N.O. Apr. 9, 1876; died Baton Rouge LA Mar. 22, 1953.
Engraver, active N.O. 1904–10; primarily watchmaker, jeweler.
Studied: Grandacto College; Horological School of Chicago (graduated 1894).

Contemporary listings: engraver (1904–1905); jewelry engraver (1910).
Worked in jewelry stores in Rockford IL, Bluefield WV, N.O., and Franklin LA. He established a store in Baton Rouge in 1915.
References: NOCD 1891–92, 1894, 1897–1900, 1902–1905, 1908–13; *T. Pic.*, Mar. 24, 1953; Ellis Davis, 400; U.S. Census (1910), roll 520.

ESSANG, AARON
Born Berlin, Prussia ca. 1829; died N.O. Aug. 19, 1858.
Painter, active N.O. 1858.
Contemporary listings: portrait painter (1858).
References: Louisiana Charity Hospital, Death Records, NOPL.

ESSANG, V.
Painter, active N.O. 1858.
Contemporary listings: artist, cor. St. Charles and Poydras (1858).
Advertised that he created likenesses in oil and pastel.
References: *D. Pic.*, Mar. 31, 1858.

ESTES, MISS E.
Colorer, active N.O. 1881.
Contemporary listings: retoucher, with WILLIAM WATSON WASHBURN (1881).
References: NOCD 1881.

ESTES, LUCY J. (Mrs. Thomas Estes)
Artist, active N.O. 1878.
Contemporary listings: artist (1878).
References: NOCD 1878–81, 1884–85.

EUSTIS, CELESTINE
Born N.O. ca. 1833; died Aiken SC Feb. 11, 1921.
Sketch artist, active N.O. ca. 1840s.
Amateur artist who did pencil sketches, including portraits.
References: *T. Pic.*, Feb. 13, 1921; Ripley, 11.

EUSTON, B. B.
Sketch artist, active N.O. 1867–89.
Contemporary listings: professor of penmanship (1867); professor of penmanship, Dolbear Commercial College (1868).
Exhibited: Philip Werlein's music store (1889).
Awarded: Grand State Fair, honorable mention for illuminated penmanship (1868).

References: NOCD 1867–68, 1887–91; *D. Pic.*, Jan. 19, 1868, Feb. 24, 1889. _____

EVANS, _____
Painter, active N.O. 1892.
Contemporary listings: scenic artist, Wenger's Theatre (1892).
References: *D. Pic.*, Nov. 6, 1892.

EVANS, BERNARD
Engraver, active N.O 1834–35.
Contemporary listings: engraver, 19 Bagatelle (1834–35).
References: NOCD 1834–35; Groce and Wallace.

EVANS, CHARLES
Born PA ca. 1825.
Artist, active N.O. 1860.
Contemporary listings: artist (1860).
References: U.S. Census (1860), roll 417.

EVANS, EDWARD
Lithographer, active N.O. 1884.
Contemporary listings: lithographer (1884).
References: NOCD 1884.

EVANS, HOMER T.
Painter, active N.O 1889.
Contemporary listings: scene painter, Grand Opera House (1889).
References: *D. States*, Sept. 22, 1889.

EVANS, J. CHARLES
Painter, active N.O. 1880–82; also ornamental painter.
Contemporary listings: artist (1880); DRESSEL & EVANS (1881–82).
Scenic artist from Galveston TX, who decorated the interior of the old Perkins' Opera House in Houston TX (1879). He arrived in N.O. on August 29, 1880, to make the city his home.
References: NOCD 1881–82; *Demo.*, Aug. 30, Oct. 31, 1880, July 15, 1881; *Times*, Oct. 24, 1880; Gallegly, *Plays and Players*, 43.

EVANS, JAMES GUY
Born England ca. 1810.
Painter, active N.O. 1843–53.
Contemporary listings: painter, 11 Levee (1843–44); artist (1846); historical and marine painter, 48 Canal (1848); marine painter, Seguir betw. Delaronde and Villere (1849); ship painter, Seguir betw. Delaronde and Villere (1850); painter, 210 Phil-

lippa (1850); marine painter, EVANS & ARNOLD (1850); painter, 69 Poet (1851–53); EVANS & JOHNSON (1852).
A self–taught itinerant marine painter, Evans was probably with his wife in Spain when their first child was born (ca. 1836); two children were born in AL, probably Mobile (ca. 1837 and ca. 1839); and two others were born in LA (ca. 1840 and ca. 1843). He was noted for portraits of ships, usually painted for the captains and owners of the vessels depicted. Evans also served as a Methodist preacher and missionary in the N.O. suburbs of Carrollton and Belleville (1850). With EDWARD EVERARD ARNOLD he proposed to paint a general view of N.O. (1850), but it was apparently never carried out.
References: NOCD 1842–44, 1846, 1849–56, 1858; *D. Orleanian*, Jan. 1–June 29, 1848, July 18, Aug. 20, 25, Sept. 1, 3, 8, 12, 15, 22, 26, 28, Oct. 9, 11–13, 19, Nov. 9, 1850, July 21, 1852; *D. Pic.*, Mar. 11, 1846; Groce and Wallace; Samuel et al., 2; Thompson, "Checklist"; U.S. Census (1850), roll 238.

EVANS, JOHN M.
Born LA. ca. 1874.
Painter, lithographer, active N.O. 1889–1914.
Contemporary listings: lithographer (1889); artist (1910, 1914); scenic artist (1911–12).
References: NOCD 1889–90, 1892, 1894–99, 1911–12, 1914; U.S. Census (1910), roll 520.

EVANS, WILLIAM HENRY
Born N.O. Dec. 1848; died N.O. Feb. 28, 1920; Indian (Natchez tribe).
Lithographer, active N.O 1886–95.
Contemporary listings: lithographer (1886–87, 1889–90, 1895); lithographer, Academy of Music (1888).
References: NOCD 1874–78, 1880–1904, 1906–1909, 1911–20; *T. Pic.*, Feb. 29, 1920.

EVANS & ARNOLD
Painters, active N.O. 1850; EDWARD EVERARD ARNOLD, JAMES GUY EVANS, partners.
Short–lived partnership in which Evans specialized in marine painting and

Arnold in landscapes and portraits. The *Daily Orleanian* (Sept. 22, 1850) reported that they intended to paint a view of N.O. from their Marigny studio. By Mar. 1851 the alliance had dissolved, and Arnold advertised by himself. Their paintings included *British Ship in a Storm* (ca. 1850–51) and *Towboat Towing Cotton Ships Up to New Orleans* (ca. 1850).
References: *D. Orleanian*, Sept. 22, 28, Oct. 13, 19, Nov. 9, 1850; Anglo–American Art Museum, *Sail and Steam*, items 10–12; Groce and Wallace; Rathbone, *Mississippi Panorama*, 93; Samuel et al., 61.

EVANS & JOHNSON
Painters, active N.O. 1852; also sign and ornamental painters; JAMES GUY EVANS, _____ Johnson, partners.
Contemporary listings: historical and marine painters (1852).
References: *D. Orleanian*, June 20, 1852.

EVEN, ANTOINE LUCAS
Born N.O. ca. 1826–31; died N.O. Jan. 30, 1897.
Lithographer, active N.O. 1858; primarily printer.
Contemporary listings: lithographer, 159 Dauphine (1858).
References: NOCD 1854–55, 1857–61, 1867–95; *D. Pic.*, Jan. 31, 1897; *D. States*, Jan. 31, 1897; Groce and Wallace; N.O. Death Certificate (1897), 113:32, NOPL; U.S. Census (1850), roll 235, (1860), roll 418.

EVERITE, G.
Born England ca. 1828.
Artist, active N.O. 1850.
Contemporary listings: artist (1850).
References: Groce and Wallace; U.S. Census (1850), roll 234.

EVERSHED, EMILIE GABRIELLE POULLALT DE GELBOIS (1. Mrs. Guesdon; 2. Mrs. Thomas Evershed).
Born Nantes, France July 1, 1800; died N.O. Jan. 18, 1879.
Art teacher, active N.O. 1825–35.
After coming to N.O. (ca. 1817) with Guesdon, Evershed's first husband abandoned her, and she married Thomas Evershed (ca. 1821) who died about two years later. She worked as a French and music teacher, then opened a school with Mr. Fiske (1825) and taught drawing, languages, and music. Evershed advertised her Female Seminary (1826), which included drawing and painting in the curriculum. Her Academy for Young Ladies (1827–34) also offered drawing lessons. After 1840, she wrote poems, essays, and books that were published in N.O. and Paris.
References: NOCD 1827, 1830, 1834–35; *Advertiser*, Dec. 12, 1826; *Argus*, Aug. 1, 1827; *Bee*, Jan. 21, 1879; *Gazette*, June 8, 1825; Caulfeild, 87–90; Tinker, *Ecrits*, 186–89; U.S. Census (1830), roll 45.

EXCELSIOR MEMORIAL & PORTRAIT HOUSE
Art dealer, active N.O. 1897–99; John C. Norton, owner.
Contemporary listings: 209 and 211 S. Claiborne (1897); 1633 Gasquet (1898–99).
References: NOCD 1897–99.

EXNARD, _____
Painter, active N.O. ca. 1883.
Exhibited: LILIENTHAL's art gallery (1883).
References: Lilienthal's, 6.

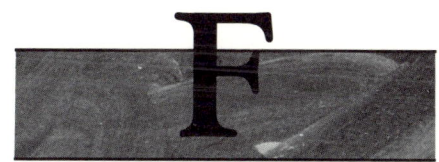

FABER, IOLA Y.
Artist, active N.O. 1905.
Contemporary listings: artist (1905).
References: NOCD 1905.

FAEFFERD, EDMUND
Engraver, active N.O. 1841–42.
Contemporary listings: engraver, 28
Royal (1841–42).
References: NOCD 1841–42; Groce
and Wallace.

FAHEY, LILLY
Art craftsman, active N.O. 1913.
Contemporary listings: ARTS & CRAFTS
STUDIO (1913).
References: NOCD 1913.

FAHRENBERG, ALBERT, SR.
Born Cologne, Prussia ca. 1825.
Painter, active N.O. 1860.
Contemporary listings: portrait
painter (1860).
References: Groce and Wallace;
Pinckney, 211; U.S. Census (1860),
roll 420.

FARRAN, MISS _____
Painter, active N.O. ca. 1881.
Exhibited: J. C. Eyrich's store (1881).
References: *Demo.*, Feb. 27, 1881.

FARWELL, MISS M.
Painter, sketch artist, active N.O.
1890–1901.
Studied: ARTISTS' ASSOCIATION OF NEW
ORLEANS (1890).
Exhibited: Artists' Association of New
Orleans (1890–91).
Memberships/positions: ARTS EXHI-
BITION CLUB (1901).
References: *D. Pic.*, Nov. 13, 1890,
May 22, 1891; *D. States*, May 16,
1890.

FASS, MISS _____
Painter, active N.O. ca. 1891.
Exhibited: ARTISTS' ASSOCIATION OF
NEW ORLEANS (1891).
References: *Current Topics*, Jan.
1892, 24; AANO, *Catalogue* (1891).

FASSWENBURG, FREDERICK
Painter, active N.O. 1841–42.
Contemporary listings: portrait
painter, 211 Royal (1841–42).
References: NOCD 1841–42.

FASSY, DR. MARIE BLANCHE
Born N.O. ca. 1871; died N.O. Jan.
31, 1934.
Artist, active N.O. 1890–91.
Contemporary listings: artist (1890–
91).
The first woman to graduate in den-
tistry in LA.
References: NOCD 1890–91; *T. Pic.*,
Feb. 1–2, 1934.

FAURE, ALCIDE
Born France ca. 1844.
Painter, active N.O. 1876–89; also
sign and ornamental painter.
Contemporary listings: painter
(1876–77, 1879–81, 1883–84,
1887, 1889); fresco painter (1880,
1888); frescoer (1885).
References: NOCD 1876–77, 1879–
85, 1887–89; U.S. Census (1880),
roll 460.

FAURE, MARIE ROSALBA
Born N.O. Nov. 11, 1865; died N.O
Feb. 27, 1927.
Painter, art teacher, active N.O.
1897–1927.
Contemporary listings: artist (1903–
1904, 1906, 1908); teacher, Guillot
Institute (1907); teacher, Mc-
Donogh High School 2 (1911);
teacher, Sophie B. Wright Girls' H.S.
(1912–14, 1916–18).
Exhibited: ARTISTS' ASSOCIATION OF
NEW ORLEANS (1896–97, 1901–
1902).
Memberships/positions: Artists' As-
sociation of New Orleans (1896); ART
ASSOCIATION OF NEW ORLEANS (1905).
References: NOCD 1903–1904,
1906–1908, 1911–14, 1916–27; *D.
Pic.*, Mar. 30, 1897, Dec. 9, 1902; *T.
Pic.*, Feb. 28, 1927; AANO, *Cata-
logue* (1896–97, 1901, 1902); Art
Asso., *Catalogue* (1905); Mount, 136;
Orleans Parish Registrar of Voters,
NOPL.

FEITEL, ARTHUR HENRY
Born N.O. June 3, 1891; died N.O.
Sept. 10, 1982.

Sketch artist, painter, art teacher, active N.O. 1915–32; primarily architect.

Studied: School of Architecture, Tulane University (1907–11); Ecole des Beaux Arts, Paris (1911–14).

Exhibited: ART ASSOCIATION OF NEW ORLEANS (1915–16).

Architect who traveled, studied, and sketched in Europe (1911–14) and worked as a draftsman with several U.S. government agencies. In N.O., he went into partnership with architect Paul Andry (1923). Feitel's architectural works included L.S.U. Medical School and additions to DePaul Sanitarium, Hotel Dieu Hospital, and Mercy Hospital. He exhibited architectural drawings at the Arts and Crafts Club (1924, 1938), served as chairman of the club's executive committee in charge of exhibits (1935–36), and was on the faculty of the club's New Orleans Art School where he taught architecture (1925–26, 1928–32). He was a member of the Art Association of New Orleans where he was on the Board of Directors (1928–38) and served as secy. (1924–27), exec. v. pres. (1939), pres. (1940–42, 1951), second v. pres. (1943) and first v. pres. (1945–47, 1949). He was on the Board of Directors of the DELGADO MUSEUM OF ART. He served as the museum's pres. and acting director (1927) and volunteer director (1957). He received the New Orleans Museum of Art's Isaac Delgado Memorial Award (1975).

References: NOCD 1916–19, 1923–33, 1935, 1938, 1940, 1942, 1945–47, 1949, 1952–56, 1958, 1960–62, 1964–69, 1971–77, 1979; *Item*, Oct. 4, 1932, Apr. 14, 1957; *Item–Trib.*, Sept. 29, 1929; *T. Pic.*, Jan. 20, 1924, May 24, 1925, July 15, Sept. 30, 1928, Oct. 8, 1929, Oct. 25, 1936, Apr. 10, 1938, June 18, 1975, Sept. 12, 1982; Art Asso., *Catalogue* (1915, 1916, 1924, 1925, 1926, 1927, 1928, 1929, 1930, 1931, 1932, 1933, 1934, 1935, 1936, 1937, 1938, 1939, 1940, 1941, 1942, 1943, 1945, 1946, 1947, 1949,

1951); Biographical and Professional Record of Arthur H. Feitel; Delgado, *Bulletin*, 1(Jan. 1927):2; New Orleans Art School, *Bulletin* (1929–30, 1930–31); New Orleans Art School, *Year Book* (1926).

FELLOWS, LUCIA RUSSELL (Mrs. George Emery Fellows)

Designer, active N.O. ca. 1886–88.

Studied: LADIES' DECORATIVE ART LEAGUE (1886).

Exhibited: TULANE DECORATIVE ART LEAGUE FOR WOMEN (1888).

Awarded: Ladies' Decorative Art Class, first honors (1886).

Memberships/positions: Tulane Decorative Art League for Women (1887–88), secy. (1887); FIVE OR MORE CLUB, v. pres. (1888).

References: *D. Pic.*, Feb. 12, 1888; *Eve. Chronicle*, May 22, 1886; *NCAB*, 1917; Tulane Decorative Art League.

FENN, HARRY

Born Richmond, England Sept. 14, 1838; died Montclair NJ Apr. 21, 1911.

Illustrator, active N.O. ca. 1900.

Exhibited: ART ASSOCIATION OF NEW ORLEANS (1904–1905).

Painter and illustrator who came to the U.S. in 1857. A founder of the American Water Color Society, Fenn made sketches for illustrations in *Picturesque America*, and he came to N.O. to illustrate in color Maurice Thompson's *My Winter Garden* (published 1900). While living in N.Y.C., he sent works to the Art Association exhibitions (1904–1905).

References: *Appleton's CAB*; Art Asso., *Catalogue* (1904, 1905); Fielding, *Dictionary*; Kouwenhoven, item 242; McCracken, *Portrait*, 220; Sears, 359–60; Maurice Thompson; WPA, *Louisiana*, 167.

FERDINAND, MADAM _____

Hair worker, active N.O. 1849–50.

Contemporary listings: hair worker, 160 Bourbon (1849–50).

References: NOCD 1849–50.

FERNANDEZ, MISS V.

Artist, active N.O. ca. 1890.

Exhibited: ARTISTS' ASSOCIATION OF NEW ORLEANS (1890).

References: *D. States*, May 16, 1890.

FERRERA, ADOLPH
Born Cuba ca. 1889.
Lithographer, active N.O. 1910.
Contemporary listings: lithographer,
printing office (1910).
Arrived in U.S. in 1902.
References: U.S. Census (1910), roll
521.
FESTE, ERNEST
Painter, active N.O. 1896–97; also
decorator.
Contemporary listings: artist (1896);
painter (1897).
References: NOCD 1896–97, 1902–
1903.
FETT, LOUIS F.
Born Detroit MI.
Painter, active N.O. ca. 1898–1905.
Contemporary listings: scenic artist,
Baldwin–Melville Stock Company,
Grand Opera House, and Audubon
Theater (1902); scenic artist, Bald-
win–Melville Stock Company,
Greenwall Theater (1904–1905).
References: NOCD 1904–1905; *D.
Item*, Jan. 3, 1902; *D. Pic.*, Jan. 12,
Sept. 2, Oct. 12, 26, 1902, *D. States*,
May 21, 1905; *Item*, Oct. 23, 1904;
T. Demo., May 23, 25, 1905.
FETTERS, WILLIAM W.
Painter, active N.O. 1884–88.
Contemporary listings: scenic artist,
Academy of Music (1884, 1887);
scenic artist, St. Charles Theatre
(1886–88); scenic artist, Grand Op-
era House (1887).
References: NOCD 1886–88; *D. Pic.*,
Sept. 19, 1887; *D. States*, Feb. 8,
Mar. 16, 1886; *Eve. Chronicle*, Sept.
10, 15, Oct. 2, 1884; *Mascot*, Dec.
24, 1887; *T. Demo.*, Oct. 21, 1886.
FETTLERS, H. M.
Painter, active N.O. 1866.
Contemporary listings: scenic artist,
St. Charles Theatre (1866).
References: *Times*, Oct. 2, 1866.
FEUILLE, MR. ____
Painter, active N.O. ca. 1834–41.
Contemporary listings: portrait and
miniature painter (1834); portrait
and miniature painter, 132 Chartres
(1835); portrait and miniature
painter, 164 Chartres (1835); painter
(1836).

Feuille (first name unknown), a portrait painter who also worked in other
parts of LA, is sometimes confused
with his brother, JEAN FRANÇOIS
FEUILLE, an engraver and printer.
Portraits that have been attributed to
the engraver were probably done by
the portrait painter.
References: *Bee*, Mar. 5, Oct. 13, 19,
1835; *Courier*, May 28, 31, June 6,
1834, Aug. 20, 1836, Apr. 6, 1841;
Bruns, 164, 290, 312; LSM, *Biennial
Report for 1926–27*, 29; Wiesendan-
ger, 46–47.
FEUILLE, JEAN FRANÇOIS
Engraver, active N.O. 1835–41; also
printer.
Contemporary listings: engraver and
printer on copper, 164 Chartres
(1835–36); engraver, 147 Chartres
(1837); engraver, 156 Chartres
(1838); engraver (1839); engraver,
Exchange Al. near St. Louis (1841).
Memberships/positions: National
Academy of Design, N.Y.C. (1832).
Sometimes confused with his brother,
FEUILLE (first name unknown), a por-
trait painter.
References: NOCD 1837–38, 1841;
Bee, Dec. 30, 1835, Jan. 5, 1836;
Courier, Oct. 8–9, 1835, Nov. 21,
1837, Feb. 4, 1839; Bruns, 164, 290,
312; Friends of the Cabildo, *250
Years*, 59; Groce and Wallace; Harter
and Tucker, 120; Wiesendanger, 46–
47.
FEUSIER, HOYLE & CO.
Lithographers, active N.O. 1866–67;
Auguste Fousier, possibly J. HOYLE,
partners.
Contemporary listings: lithogra-
phers, 9 Commercial (1866–67).
Printed sheet music covers.
References: "Les Folies du Carna-
val," Sheet Music Collection,
THNOC; *Louisiana State Gazetteer*,
155.
FEUSIER & TURBERG
Lithographers, active N.O. 1867;
Auguste Feusier, Pierre F. Turberg,
partners.
Contemporary listings: lithogra-
phers, 9 Commercial (1867).
Printed sheet music covers.

References: NOCD 1867; "The
Conquered Banner," "Santa Claus'
Music Satchel," Sheet Music Collec-
tion, LA Coll., TU.

FICKLEN, BESSIE ALEXANDER (Mrs.
John Rose Ficklen)
Born N.O. ca. 1861; died Savannah
GA Mar. 2, 1945.
Illustrator, active N.O. ca. 1890–
1921.
Studied: NEWCOMB COLLEGE (1889–
91, 1896–99, 1902–1904).
Exhibited: Tulane University (1892);
ART ASSOCIATION OF NEW ORLEANS
(1905).
Memberships/positions: Art Associ-
ation of New Orleans (1905).
Illustrated *Catterel Ratterel (Dog-
gerel)* (1890); member of the Artists'
Guild (1921).
References: NOCD 1908, 1912–13,
1916–17, 1920, 1922–28, 1930,
1932; *D. Pic.*, Mar. 3, 1892; *Item*,
Jan. 16, Feb. 6, 1921; *T. Pic.*, Mar.
8, 1945; Edward Alexander, *Catterel
Ratterel (Doggerel)*; Art Asso., *Cat-
alogue* (1905); Poesch, *Newcomb
Pottery*, 99.

FIENZES, F.
Born France ca. 1818.
Artist, active N.O. 1860.
Contemporary listings: artist (1860).
References: Groce and Wallace;
Thompson, "Checklist."

**FILBERT, DOMINIQUE LOUIS GRAND-
JEAN** (called Develle)
Born Paris, France ca. 1769; died
N.O. Nov. 11, 1836.
Painter, active N.O.? 1834–36.
Both Filbert and his father used the
pseudonym Develle as a professional
alias. According to family tradition,
the younger Filbert was a theater
scene designer and painter in France.
His death certificate stated that he
had come to N.O. with his wife two
years before and was living with his
son LOUIS DOMINIQUE GRANDJEAN DE-
VELLE. In LA, Develle and his des-
cendants had replaced the surname
Filbert with Develle. Although father and son may have worked together designing and painting scenery in N.O., Filbert moved to the
city probably to join his family after

his retirement from the French thea-
ter.
References: *T. Pic.*, May 30, 1956;
N.O. Death Certificate (1836), 7:67,
NOPL.

FINCH, _____
Artist, active N.O. 1852.
References: *D. Times*, Feb. 18, 1852.

FINKANEGLE, MR. _____
Painter, active N.O. 1859.
Contemporary listings: portrait and
landscape painter, E. Jacobs art gal-
lery (1859).
References: *D. Pic.*, Dec. 17, 1859;
Groce and Wallace.

FINLEY, EDWARD
Born NY ca. 1835–36.
Painter, active N.O. 1879–86.
Contemporary listings: portrait
painter (1879–80, 1886); artist
(1882–83).
References: NOCD 1871–73, 1879–
80, 1882–83, 1886; U.S. Census
(1870), roll 519, (1880), roll 460.

FINN, MR. _____
Sculptor, active N.O. 1832–42.
Contemporary listings: fancy glass
works, 115 Chartres (1832); fancy
glass blowing and spinning, 92
Chartres (1833); fancy glass working, blowing and spinning, 113
Chartres (1842).
Exhibited: over Muh's jewelry store,
115 Chartres (1832); 92 Chartres
(1833); 113 Chartres (1842).
References: *Bee*, Jan. 19, 1832;
Courier, Jan. 10, 1832, Jan. 19–Feb.
23, 1832 (advs.), Feb. 7, May 7,
1832, Feb. 26, Mar. 2, 1833.

FINN, ALEXANDER
Lithographer, active N.O. 1885.
Contemporary listings: lithographer,
T. FITZWILLIAM & CO. (1885).
References: NOCD 1885.

FINNEGAN, JOHN
Painter, active N.O. 1868.
Contemporary listings: scenic
painter, Harris & Finnegan (1868).
References: NOCD 1868–69, 1872,
1874; *Repub.*, Feb. 14, 1872.

FINSLY, JOHN
Painter, active N.O. 1884.
With JULIUS FRANCK, frescoed the
hall, parlor, and dining room of the

residence of Robert Roberts, St. Charles near Conery (1884).
References: *Eve. Chronicle*, Sept. 23, 1884.

FIRMAN, CAESAR
Born Germany ca. 1850; died N.O. Jan. 13, 1876.
Lithographer, active N.O. 1875–76. Died seven weeks after arriving in N.O. from St. Louis MO.
References: Louisiana Charity Hospital, Death Records, NOPL.

FISCHER, MARY ELLEN SIGSBEE (1. Mrs. William Balfour Ker; 2. Mrs. Anton Otto Fischer)
Born N.O. Feb. 26, 1876.
Illustrator.
Studied: Art Students League, Washington DC and N.Y.C.; Paris.
Magazine illustrator who lived in Woodstock NY (1940–44).
References: Collins and Opitz; *Who's Who in America*, 1940–41.

FISHBOURNE, R. W.
Lithographer, engraver, active N.O. 1838–50.
Contemporary listings: GREEN & FISHBOURNE (1840); lithographer, 53 Magazine (1840–41); lithographer and proprietor, ORLEANS LITHOGRAPHIC OFFICE (1841); SNELL & FISHBOURNE (1842); lithographer and engraver, 275 Poydras (1843–44); lithographer, Goodchildren betw. Cotton Press and St. Ferdinand (1846); 46 Canal (1846, ca. 1847, 1849–50); lithographer, 10 Banks Arcade (1850).
Worked with WILLIAM GREENE in N.Y.C. (1836) and again in N.O. when both his name and Greene's, as partners in the Orleans Lithographic Office, appeared in each plate of five engravings of public buildings published in the NOCD 1838. The partnership was also called GREEN & FISHBOURNE, one of the earliest printing firms in N.O. to introduce lithography as an affordable alternative to copperplate engraving. By Nov. 10, 1840, Fishbourne had bought out Green's interest in the firm and specialized in the lithographic printing of maps, plans, designs, billheads, circulars, and cards;

and after 1841, he added views of buildings and plans of machinery. He planned to make the first lithographic view of N.O., taken from St. Patrick's Church, from the design of EDWARD EVERARD ARNOLD, but it was never begun due to a lack of public support. After N.O., Fishbourne worked in San Francisco (ca. 1850–63).
References: NOCD 1838, 1841–44, 1846, 1849–50; *Courier*, July 9, 1846; *D. Orleanian*, Oct. 13, 1850; *D. Pic.*, Mar. 14–Nov. 21, 1840 (advs.), Nov. 11, 1840–May 18, 1841 (advs.), Jan. 27, 1841; *Wkly. Delta*, July 13, 1846, Jan. 28–29, 1848; Groce and Wallace; Harry Peters, *America on Stone*, 291–92; Harry Peters, *California on Stone*, 121–22; THNOC 1953.129.

FISHER, ALEXANDER
Born LA Dec. 1879.
Lithographer, active N.O. 1900.
Contemporary listings: lithographer (1900).
References: U.S. Census (1900), roll 572.

FISHER, CHARLES F.
Born Prussia ca. 1792; died N.O. Oct. 15, 1873.
Painter, designer, active N.O. ca. 1851–72.
Contemporary listings: artist (1851, 1854–56); portrait painter, 64 St. Ann (1852–53); artist, 157 Main (1857); artist, 59 Claiborne (1860); portrait painter, 321 Bienville (1867); artist (1870, 1872); artist painter (1871).
Exhibited: 100 Camp (1852); 77 St. Charles (1852–53); cor. St. Charles and Common (1855); Governor's antechamber, Dryades (1871).
Fisher received considerable attention in local newspapers as perhaps the first local artist since JEAN HYACINTHE LACLOTTE to paint the Battle of N.O. He claimed that the work, begun in 1841, took 11 years to complete. During those years he was probably working as a blacksmith (1842–44, 1846) and as a machinist (1850–51); he also patented his invention of a steam propeller for ships.

The painting was eight by six feet and was based on descriptions by the surviving officers and on published accounts. It was first seen publicly in N.O. from Nov. 1852 to Jan. 1853, then Sept. to Dec. 1855 and Oct. 1871, as well as in Cincinnati (July 1853) and in N.Y.C. (Sept. 1853). Fisher was probably looking for a purchaser during these exhibitions; he offered it for sale to the U.S. government (1854) and to the N.O. City Council (1854, 1868, 1873). He planned to send it to N.Y.C. again, after the 1871 N.O. showing, to exhibit and sell it to Grand Duke Alexis of Russia, who was visiting the U.S. The painting was probably the prototype for Fisher's lithograph of Andrew Jackson at the battle (1856). Newspaper articles mentioned that Fisher was struggling financially as an artist, especially after a fire in Oct. 1855 in which he lost all his possesions except the painting.
References: NOCD 1850–53, 1857, 1860–61, 1866–68, 1870, 1872–74; *Bee*, Oct. 3, 1855, Feb. 5, 1856; *Courier*, Apr. 8, 1851, Jan. 28, 30, 1853, Sept. 5–26, 1855; *D. Crescent*, Nov. 22, Dec. 28, 1852, Jan. 4, 8, 1853; *D. Delta*, Nov. 20, Dec. 9, 1852, June 21, 1854, Sept. 10, 1855, Feb. 5, 1856; *D. Pic.*, Oct. 10, Nov. 21, 1852, Jan. 8, 1853, Jan. 14, 1854, Sept. 2, 9, Oct. 28, 1855; *D. True Delta*, Feb. 6, 1856; *Repub.*, Feb. 20, 1868, Feb. 10, 1869, Oct. 12, 1871, Sept. 10, 1873; *Times*, Oct. 25, 1871; *T. Deutsche Zeitung*, Nov. 25, 28, Dec. 25, 1852, Oct. 27, 1855, Feb. 7, 1856; Fairman, 148; Groce and Wallace; LSM, *Annual Report for 1918*, 59; N.O. Death Certificate (1873), 59:602, NOPL; THNOC 1962.17; U.S. Census (1860), roll 421, (1870), roll 520.

FITZGERALD, ROBERT T.
Lithographer, active N.O. 1890–97; also bookbinder, pressman.
Contemporary listings: lithographer, KOECKERT & WALLE (1890–92); lithographer (1893–95, 1897).
References: NOCD 1886, 1888–95, 1897–1900.

T. FITZWILLIAM & CO., LTD.
Lithographers, engravers, active N.O. 1872–1932; primarily printers, stationers; Thomas W. Fitzwilliam (born Ireland 1834; died N.O. Dec. 22, 1917), pres.
Contemporary listings: lithographers, 76 Camp and 27 Bank Place (1872); engravers, 76 Camp (1878); lithographers, 76 Camp (1880); steam lithographers, 62 Camp and 15 Bank Place (1883); lithographers, 62 Camp (1885–94); lithographers, 324 Camp (1895–1918).
The owner, Thomas W. Fitzwilliam, came to N.O. in 1853 and learned the printing and bookbinding trades as a youth. He began his own business in 1860 at 76 Camp where the company remained until his death. The firm was first listed as "T. Fitzwilliam, stationer, printer & account book manufacturer" (1861, 1866–67). Its listing as "T. Fitzwilliam & Co." began in 1868, primarily as stationers and printers, with the addition of the partners M. F. DUNN (1868–78) and Joseph H. Kirkwood (1879–98). Lithographic printing was first advertised by the firm in 1872, and by 1885 they had a near monopoly on the lithographic printing of bonds, stocks, labels, cards, posters, and invitations in N.O. Lithography was considered the artistic specialty of the house, and they were noted for printing the chromolithographic supplements to the newspapers that illustrated the parades of the carnival organizations Proteus (1886–1911), Rex (1892–1901), Comus (1899–1903), Momus (1900–1901), and Nereus (1900). The firm was later listed as "T. Fitzwilliam & Co., Ltd." (1902–32), under four presidents: the founder (1902–17); his son, Thomas W. Fitzwilliam (1918–29); John B. Fitzwilliam (1930–31); and Killian Huger (1932).
References: NOCD 1868–1932; NOBD 1898; *D. Pic.*, Apr. 3, 1872, May 15, 1878, Nov. 11, 1885; *D. States*, Feb. 15, 1883; *Repub.*, Sept. 13, 1871; *T. Demo.*, Sept. 24, 1913; *T. Pic.*, Dec. 22–23, 1917; Glenk,

325–26; La Cour, 210; LSM, *Biennial Report for 1932–33*, 45; Morrison, *Industries*, 170.

FITZWILSON, GEORGE W.
Born VA ca. 1810.
Painter, active N.O. 1870–77.
Contemporary listings: oil painter (1870); portrait painter, with SAMUEL ANDERSON (1873); portrait painter (1876–77).
Before coming to N.O., he advertised as a portrait painter in Charleston SC in Dec. 1846 and July 1847.
References: NOCD 1873, 1876–77; Groce and Wallace; U.S. Census (1870), roll 521.

FIVE OR MORE CLUB
Art association, active N.O. 1888–93; ELLSWORTH WOODWARD, art director.
Contemporary listings: 249 Baronne (1888, 1890–91).
Art association with headquarters in the TULANE DECORATIVE ART LEAGUE FOR WOMEN (1888). Members did sketches in crayon, pen–and–ink, watercolor, and oil, and often worked from models and still lifes. By 1890 membership was mostly NEWCOMB COLLEGE art students. Its annual studio receptions, sometimes held with the Art League, Newcomb, and the NEW ORLEANS ART POTTERY COMPANY, are credited with introducing local art talent to the city's art patrons.
References: *D. Pic.*, Feb. 12, 1888, Feb. 14, 1890; *D. States*, June 10, 1888; *Down in Dixie*, July 15, 1896, 10; *T. Demo.*, May 11, 1891, Feb. 15, 1893; Brandt Dixon, 77; Soards, 322; Tulane Decorative Art League.

FLECHO, A.
Engraver, active N.O. 1834; also jeweler.
Contemporary listings: engraver, 25 Conti (1834).
References: NOCD 1834.

FLEISCHBEIN, EMMA ELIZABETH. *See* FLEISCHBEIN, FRANZ JOSEPH

FLEISCHBEIN, ERNEST. *See* FLEISCHBEIN, FRANZ JOSEPH

FLEISCHBEIN, FRANÇOIS
Born Godramstein, Bavaria ca. 1801–1805; died N.O. Nov. 16, 1868.
Painter, art teacher, active N.O. 1833–68.
Studied: Munich; with Girodet, Paris.
Contemporary listings: portrait painter, Hotel de la Marine (1833); portrait painter (1834); portrait painter, 164 Chartres (1836–37); portrait painter, 100 Royal (1838); portrait painter, 135 Conti (1841); portrait painter, 139 Barracks (1842); portrait painter, 283 Dauphine (1843); portrait painter, cor. Casacalvo and Race (1846); portrait painter, cor. Casacalvo and Peace (1850–54); painter, 25 Moreau (1857); daguerrian & ambrotype gallery, Frenchmen cor. Casacalvo (1858).
Full name Franz Joseph Fleischbein, but known in N.O. as François, a portrait painter and a painter of small historical and mythological paintings. Fleischbein first advertised his arrival from France in July 1833 as a portrait painter at the Hotel de la Marine on Levee. His four children were born in LA (ca. 1837, 1839, 1840, 1843), and he apparently resided in LA until his death. GEORGE DAVID COULON, one of his students, stated that Fleischbein had bad eyesight in his later years. Fleischbein's surviving sketchbooks include drawings made in Paris of classical sculpture and of a Jacques–Louis David painting. They also include two sketches by his younger son Ernest (dated 1857) and by his older daughter Emma Elizabeth.
References: NOCD 1837–38, 1841–43, 1846, 1850–61, 1866; NOBD 1858; *Bee*, July 8, 1833; *Courier*, Dec. 9–13, 1836 (advs.), Feb. 28, 1837, Dec. 6, 1839, Sept. 18, 1851; Jordan, "Old Sketch Books Recall Early N.O. Artist," *T. Pic.*, Apr. 4, 1976; *Whig*, Nov. 13, 1834; Bruns, 277, 296, 312; Coulon MS, Scrapbook 100, LSM; Fielding, *Dictionary*; Groce and Wallace; Glenk, 39, 74; Harter and Tucker, 120–21; LSM, *Biennial Report for 1916–17*, 100; LSM, *Biennial Report for 1928–29*, 79; N.O. Death Certificate (1867), 41:537, NOPL; Seebold,

1:23; Smith and Tucker, 157; U.S. Census (1840), roll 132, (1850), roll 238; Wiesendanger, 48–49; WPA, *American Portrait Inventory*, 99.

FLENTGE, FREDERICK
Painter, active N.O. 1875.
Contemporary listings: landscape painter (1875).
References: NOCD 1871, 1875.

FLETCHER, GRACE
Painter, active N.O. ca. 1890.
Exhibited: ARTISTS' ASSOCIATION OF NEW ORLEANS (1890).
References: *D. Pic.*, Nov. 13, 1890; *T. Demo.*, Nov. 13, 1890.

FLETCHER, WILLIAM
Painter, active N.O. 1848.
Contemporary listings: scene painter, Olympic Theatre (1848).
References: *D. Crescent*, May 15, 1848.

FLEURY, ALBERT
Born Le Havre, France Feb. 2, 1848.
Painter, active N.O. 1901–1902.
Professor at the Art Institute, Chicago, who came to N.O. to paint the mural decoration over the proscenium arch in the new St. Charles Theatre (1901–1902).
References: *D. Item*, Jan. 12, 1902; *T. Demo.*, Dec. 14, 1901; Bénézit; Fielding, *Dictionary*.

FLICORN, HENRY
Born Baden, Germany ca. 1842.
Lithographer, active N.O. 1860.
Contemporary listings: lithographer (1860).
Listed in the same household with AUGUST BERCOLI and BENEDICT SIMON.
References: Friends of the Cabildo, *250 Years*, 59; Groce and Wallace; U.S. Census (1860), roll 421.

FLOHR, OTTO
Born Berlin, Prussia Apr. 20, 1861; died N.O. Nov. 22, 1932.
Lithographer, active N.O. 1907–33; also printer, pressman.
Contemporary listings: lithographer (1908–1909, 1914–15, 1917–18).
Immigrated to U.S. in 1893 and came to N.O. in 1907.
References: NOCD 1908–18, 1920–21, 1923–33; *T. Pic.*, Nov. 23, 1932; Orleans Parish Registrar of Voters, NOPL; U.S. Census (1910), roll 520.

FLORENCE, GEORGE
Born LA ca. 1878.
Commercial artist, active N.O. 1910–11.
Contemporary listings: artist (1910); artist, HOME ART STUDIO (1911).
References: NOCD 1911; U.S. Census (1910), roll 519.

FLORES, FRANK
Painter, active N.O. 1900.
Contemporary listings: portrait painter and artist, 520 Royal (1900).
References: NOCD 1899–1900.

FLORES, S.
Sculptor, active N.O. 1903.
Contemporary listings: sculptor, 234 Bourbon (1903).
References: NOCD 1903.

FLORIAN, AZELIA. *See* FLORIAN, MARGUERITE MARIE LE DET DE SIGRAIS

FLORIAN, ELIZA. *See* FLORIAN, MARGUERITE MARIE LE DET DE SIGRAIS

FLORIAN, JEAN BAPTISTE
Born St. Mâlo, France May 15, 1767; died N.O. Sept. 26, 1811.
Artist, art teacher, active N.O. 1809–11.
Contemporary listings: Ladies Boarding School, Faubourg Lacourse (1811).
Titled the Comte de Pontcadeuc, Florian was an amateur artist who fled France for England in 1793 because of the Revolution. He was accompanied by his wife, MARGUERITE MARIE LE DET DE SIGRAIS FLORIAN, who was also an artist. The family, which eventually included four daughters, all of whom were artists, remained in England for 15 years. In 1808, Florian left for LA where he had invested in a plantation; he arrived in N.O. on Jan. 22, 1809. His wife and daughters arrived a year later with the artworks and books they had rescued from France. After some financial setbacks, he began a school for young ladies but died of yellow fever shortly after it opened. His extant paintings include landscapes and still lifes.
References: NOCD 1811; Groce and Wallace; E. Herndon Smith.

FLORIAN, LAURA EUGENIE (Mrs. George Phillips Bowers). *See* FLORIAN, MARGUERITE MARIE LE DET DE SIGRAIS

FLORIAN, MARGUERITE MARIE LE DET DE SIGRAIS
Born St. Mâlo, France Apr. 1, 1770; died N.O. Sept. 29, 1817.
Art teacher, active N.O. 1811–14.
After 12 years experience as a teacher in London, Mme. Florian, with her four daughters, Azelia (born Bath, England 1798; died Mobile AL 1860), Eliza (born Romney, England 1795), Laura Eugénie (born La Barre, France; died Mobile Jan. 1 or 2, 1857), and Virginia Josephine (born La Barre June 24, 1793; died Mobile ca. 1881), continued their school for young ladies in N.O. after the death of her husband, JEAN BAPTISTE FLORIAN, in 1811. The school included in its curriculum music, needlework, and painting and drawing landscapes, figures, and flowers. The daughters may have continued the school after their mother's death. They moved to Mobile with their husbands and families in 1830.
References: NOCD 1811; *Courier*, Dec. 25, 1811, Nov. 18, 1814; Groce and Wallace; E. Herndon Smith; Museum of Fine Arts, 1:163.

FLORIAN, VIRGINIA JOSEPHINE (Mrs. Gilbert Christian Russell). *See* FLORIAN, MARGUERITE MARIE LE DET DE SIGRAIS

FLORVILLE. *See* FOY, PROSPER FLORVILLE

FLYNN, EDWARD J.
Painter, art dealer, active N.O. 1889–1918.
Contemporary listings: portrait painter (1889–1891); artist (1890); artist, 128 S. Rampart (1892–94); artist, 411 S. Rampart (1895, 1897–1901); photo artist, 411 S. Rampart (1896); portrait painter, 411 S. Rampart (1898); pictures, 411 S. Rampart (1902–1903); portrait painter, 1212 Canal (1904); picture frames, 1212 Canal (1905–1906, 1910); pictures, 1212 Canal (1907–1909, 1911–15, 1917–18).

References: NOCD 1889–1918; NOBD, 1898.

FLYNN, WILLIAM
Lithographer, active N.O. 1894.
Contemporary listings: lithographer (1894).
References: NOCD 1894.

FOGLIARDI, JEAN BAPTISTE
Born Italy.
Painter, art teacher, active N.O. 1820–25.
Studied: Italy (before 1820).
Contemporary listings: scene painter, Orleans Theatre (1820–23, 1825); scene painter, St. Philip Theatre (1822); drawing master, LOUISIANA DRAWING ACADEMY (1824–25).
Noted scene painter for the Orleans Theatre, who also taught art and architecture at his drawing academy. Fogliardi is probably the Italian scene painter who offered JOHN JAMES AUDUBON a job in his theater as an assistant. Audubon's project may have been Fogliardi's inspiration for adding paintings of birds to the interior decorations of the Orleans Theatre when it was refurbished (1824). Fogliardi designed and executed the paintings on the cenotaph constructed for the funeral ceremony in honor of Napoleon in N.O. (1821) and on the triumphal arch, designed by JOSEPH PILIE, erected in the Place d'Armes (now Jackson Square) in honor of the visit of Gen. Lafayette to N.O. (1825). He employed one of his pupils, MR. DEJAN, as an assistant professor for his drawing academy (Nov. 1825).
References: NOCD 1824; *Argus*, Sept. 17, Nov. 8, 1824; *Courier*, Aug. 11, 14, 1820, Jan. 10, 15, May 4, 28, Oct. 26, Dec. 24, 1821, Jan. 30, Feb. 1, 27, Apr. 22, 1822, July 3, Aug. 31, Sept. 16–Oct. 1, 1824 (advs.), Jan. 14, June 13, Aug. 3, Oct. 21, 24–26, Oct. 31–Nov. 1, 1825 (advs.), Dec. 15, 22, 1825; *Gazette*, Aug. 19, 1820, June 1, Dec. 21, 1821, Dec. 6, 1823, Mar. 18, July 31, Sept. 17, 1824, Oct. 26, 1825; Arthur, *Audubon*, 152; Groce and Wallace; Levasseur, 2:91; Thompson, "Checklist"; Tinker, *Creole City*, 57.

FOLSOM, CHARLES L.
Lithographer, active N.O. 1875.
Contemporary listings: lithographer (1875).
References: NOCD 1875.

FOLTZER, EDWARD
Born France ca. 1863; died N.O. Apr. 22, 1917.
Engraver, active N.O. 1909; also calligrapher.
Contemporary listings: engraver (1909).
References: NOCD 1899–1911, 1913–14; *T. Pic.*, Apr. 23, 1917; Commercial File, THNOC.

FONDE, CHARLES H.
Born 1827; died 1881.
Lithographer, active N.O 1848.
Contemporary listings: lithographer (1848).
N.O. bookkeeper (1842) who became the professor of drawing at Mandeville College in St. Tammany Parish LA (1844–45). Fondé was listed again in N.O. (1849) and advertised the sale of his lithograph (1848) of Abbé Adrien Emmanuel Rouquette, the first native of LA to be ordained a Catholic priest. He was in Mobile AL (1851) in the firm of Fondé and Belknap (probably JACKSON OGDEN BELKNAP), which restored paintings and accepted commissions for landscapes, views of country houses, and other paintings.
References: NOCD 1842, 1846, 1849; *Bee*, Nov. 26, 1844, Jan. 7, 1845, Feb. 22, 1848; *D. Pic.*, Jan. 10–Feb. 5, 1845 (advs.), Jan. 30, 1845; *Courier*, Nov. 12, 1844, Jan. 6, 1845; *D. Tropic*, Jan. 13–Feb. 24, 1845 (advs.); Bruns, 224, 312; Groce and Wallace; Lay, 402; U.S. Census (1840), roll 133.

FONTANA, JULES
Commercial artist, engraver, active N.O. 1904–1909; also printer.
Contemporary listings: artist, PHOTO-ENGRAVING CO. (1904); artist (1905, 1909); artist, WALLE & CO., LTD. (1906); engraver, Walle & Co., Ltd. (1907–1908).
References: NOCD 1904–23, 1926–28, 1930–32, 1935, 1938.

FONTASSE, JEAN
Lithographer, active N.O. 1846.
Contemporary listings: lithographer, 81 St. Philip (1846).
References: NOCD 1846; Groce and Wallace.

FORBES, ELISHA
Engraver, painter, active N.O. 1830.
Contemporary listings: wood engraver, &c., and miniature painter, 121 Levee (1830).
References: NOCD 1830 (adv.); Friends of the Cabildo, *250 Years*, 59; Groce and Wallace; Hamilton, 1:81.

FORD, MR. _____
Painter, active N.O 1845.
Mentioned by ALFRED S. WAUGH in Jan. 1845 as an artist of talent from Dublin who had been a partner of THEODORE MOISE in N.O.
References: McDermott, "Alfred S. Waugh," 303.

FORMUSA, JOSEPH
Born N.O. Aug. 29, 1892; died N.O. Nov. 1, 1969.
Lithographer, active N.O. 1910–27.
Contemporary listings: lithographer (1910, 1916, 1918).
References: NOCD 1909, 1914–16, 1918–23, 1925–33, 1935, 1938, 1940, 1942, 1945–47, 1949, 1952–55; *T. Pic.*, Nov. 2, 1969; Orleans Parish Registrar of Voters, NOPL; U.S. Census (1910), roll 520.

FOROI, JEAN
Born LA ca. 1876.
Lithographer, active N.O. 1910.
Contemporary listings: lithographer (1910).
References: U.S. Census (1910), roll 520.

FORSHEY, CALEB GOLDSMITH. See FORSHEY, WILLIAM

FORSHEY, WILLIAM
Born OH ca. 1820.
Sculptor, active N.O. 1849–52; primarily surveyor.
Contemporary listings: marble sculptor (1849); sculptor, 13 St. Charles (1850–52).
In OH Forshey first carved wood and ivory, then turned to sculpting in 1847. After coming to N.O., he began working in marble. In May 1849,

he exhibited his second bust portrait which was to be cast and sold to help pay expenses for his art studies. By May 1850 he was working on the carved relief for the stone that the State of LA was sending to Washington DC to be used in the building of the Washington Monument. The sandstone block was taken from the hills of the Ouachita region of LA and was selected by the sculptor's brother, the N.O. civil engineer Caleb Goldsmith Forshey (born Somerset County PA July 18, 1812; died N.O. July 25, 1881), an amateur sculptor. William Forshey's sculpture, *Offering of Innocence*, was credited, when exhibited in Dec. 1850, as being the first full–length statue in marble in LA. In Feb. 1852 he modeled busts which were to be reproduced in marble in Italy during his trip there later in the year. Forshey may have continued as a sculptor but was listed as a surveyor (1854–56) and as city surveyor (1857).
References: NOCD 1850–61, 1866; *Comm. Bull.*, Nov. 21, 1850; *Courier*, Dec. 12–13, 1850; *D. Crescent*, May 16, 1850; *D. Delta*, May 3, 1849, May 18, 1850; *D. Times*, Feb. 18, 1852; *Wkly. Delta*, May 7, 1849; Groce and Wallace; Madwell, 394; Reinders, 200; U.S. Census (1850), roll 232.

FOSTER, JOSEPH A.
Painter, active N.O. 1838–44.
Studied: with ANTOINE MONDELLI.
Contemporary listings: scenic artist, Camp Street Theatre (1838); painter, 184 Julia (1842); scenic artist, with Mondelli, Poydras Street Theatre (1842); scenic artist, National Amphitheatre (1844).
References: NOCD 1842; *Courier*, Dec. 6, 1842; *D. Tropic*, Jan. 23, 1844; *True Amer.*, Oct. 20, 1838; Groce and Wallace.

FOSTER, CAPT. ROBERT W.
Painter, active N.O. 1870; primarily surveyor.
Sea captain, marine surveyor, port warden, and amateur painter whose picture of a steamer, *Cortes at Sea*,

was to be raffled at a Fête Champêtre at the Carrollton Gardens (1870).
References: NOCD 1867–74; *D. Pic.*, June 8, 1870.

FOURCADE, JOSEPH
Born before 1775.
Painter, art teacher, active N.O. 1818–20.
Contemporary listings: teacher of art, portrait and miniature painter, Bourbon (1818); teacher of art, portrait and miniature painter, 43 Conti (1820).
References: *Courier*, Feb. 13–Apr. 13, 1818 (advs.), Mar. 30, 1818; *Gazette*, Nov. 7–8, 1820; Friends of the Cabildo, *250 Years*, 37; Groce and Wallace.

FOURNIER, MRS. AUGUSTINE
Born France ca. 1822.
Art craftsman, active N.O. 1857–68.
Contemporary listings: artificial flowers, 70 Bourbon (1857–59); artificial flowers, 56 Bourbon (1860–61); artificial flower maker, 68 Bourbon (1865); artificial flowers, 86 Royal (1866–68).
Listed in the same household as EMELIE FOURNIER.
References: NOCD 1857–61, 1866–68; NOBD 1858, 1865; U.S. Census (1860), roll 421.

FOURNIER, EMELIE
Born France ca. 1832.
Art craftsman, active N.O. 1860.
Contemporary listings: artificial flower maker (1860).
Listed in same household as MRS. AUGUSTINE FOURNIER
References: U.S. Census (1860), roll 421.

FOWLER, DOROTHY
Painter, active N.O. ca. 1918.
Exhibited: ART ASSOCIATION OF NEW ORLEANS (1918).
References: Art Asso., *Catalogue* (1918).

FOWLER, TREVOR THOMAS
Born Dublin, Ireland 1800.
Painter, active N.O. 1840–52.
Studied: Royal Academy, London (ca. 1829), Royal Hibernian Academy, Dublin (ca. 1830–35); Paris (1842–43).

Contemporary listings: portrait painter, 49 Camp (1840–41); artist, oppos. St. Charles Hotel (1841); portrait painter, 8 St. Charles and 10 St. Charles (1842); portrait painter, St. Charles near Canal (1844); portrait painter, 127 Canal (1845); portrait painter, 11 St. Charles (1845–47); portrait painter, 51 Canal (1849); portrait and landscape painter, 57 Canal (1851); portrait painter, 137 Common (1852).

Exhibited: Royal Academy, London (1829); Royal Hibernian Academy, Dublin (1830–35); National Academy of Design, N.Y.C. (1837–38); Royal Irish Art Union, Dublin (1843–44); Pennsylvania Academy of Fine Arts, Philadelphia (betw. 1854 and 1869).

Itinerant portrait, landscape, and genre painter who was listed in N.Y.C. (1837–38). Fowler was in N.O. by Jan. 1840; at that time he accompanied Andrew Jackson on his return to Nashville from the 25th-anniversary celebration of the Battle of N.O. and, on board the steamer, painted a portrait of the former president. Fowler also executed portraits, commissioned by the Whig Tippecanoe Club of N.O., of Henry Clay and of William Henry Harrison, who was elected president later in the year. He sent the portrait of Harrison back to the city in Oct. 1840 when it was displayed and received favorable publicity. He returned to the city in Dec. 1840 with the portrait of Clay. Both portraits were acquired by the City of N.O. During the next 12 years, Fowler spent many winters in N.O., where he was regarded as one of the city's leading portraitists. Local newspapers reported his return in March 1842 and Nov. 1844 (when he shared a studio with THEODORE SIDNEY MOISE) and in Feb. and Nov. 1845, Nov. 1846, Dec. 1847, and Jan. 1852. Between 1854 and 1869, he lived in Germantown and Philadelphia PA. According to Fielding, he died in N.O. in 1871.

References: NOCD 1841–42; *Bull Frog*, Feb. 12, 1841; *Comm. Bull.*, June 17, Dec. 12, 1840, May 4, 1841; *D. Pic.*, Oct. 14, 16, 20, Dec. 8, 1840, Feb. 13, Mar. 27, 1842, Nov. 19–20, 1844, Feb. 28, June 10, Dec. 2, 1845–Feb. 25, 1847 (advs.), Nov. 29, 1846, Dec. 27, 1849, Jan. 30, 1852; *D. Times*, Feb. 18, 1852; *T. Pic.*, Feb. 1, 1942; Barker, 402; Bénézit; Bruns, 312; Fielding, *Dictionary*; Groce and Wallace; Huber and Wilson, *Pontalba*, 42; LSM, *Biennial Report for 1928–29*, 67; New York Historical Society, 2:837; "Paintings of Note," 286, 288; Wiesendanger, 50; WPA, *American Portrait Inventory*, 102; WPA, *Louisiana*, 164.

FOY, PROSPER FLORVILLE

Born N.O. June 29, 1820; died N.O. Mar. 16, 1903; black ("free man of color," "mulatto").

Sculptor, active N.O. 1843–69; primarily marble cutter.

Studied: France.

Contemporary listings: marble sculptor, St. Louis near Old Basin (1843–44); marble sculptor, 105 Rampart (1846); sculptor, 81 Rampart (1850–56, 1853–59); sculptor, 83 Rampart (1860–61, 1866–69).

Marble cutter and sculptor who never used his surname in designating his work, but instead used "Florville" as his signature. He was the illegitimate son of RENE PROSPER FOY and lived and worked in the same shop with his father on Rampart Street. He began his own business in 1836 and specialized in tombs, monuments, slabs, head and foot stones, tablets, and vases. Among his intimate friends was ACHILLE PERELLI, who carved a bust of Foy (1855) which Foy kept all his life. Between 1870 and 1903 he was listed at his marble works at 81–87 Rampart, which was conveniently located near St. Louis Cemeteries I and II for which he designed and built tombs, sculpture, and ornamentation. He also built many of the tombs designed by N.O. architect J. N. B. DePouilly and tombs for St. Bernard Cemetery. According to Jordan, Foy also worked in NC (ca. 1841–56), possibly during the summers.

References: NOCD 1841–44, 1846, 1849–61, 1866–1903; *Courier*, Aug. 1, 1844, Aug. 19, 1848, Feb. 1, 1849, May 1, 1850, May 22, Sept. 6, 1851; *D. Pic.*, Mar. 17, 1903; *D. States*, Dec. 10, 1880; Caldwell, 195; Curtis, 185–86; Friends of the Cabildo, *N.O. Architecture*, 3:75, 105–6, 130, 6:107; Glenk, 96; Groce and Wallace; Information courtesy George E. Jordan; Land, 78; LSM Cemetery File; N.O. Death Certificate (1903), 129:582, NOPL; Second District Court, Succession of Prosper Foy, 1854, docket 7355, NOPL; U.S. Census (1850), roll 235, (1870), roll 521; WPA, "Lives."

FOY, RENE PROSPER
Born Orléans, France July 3, 1787; died N.O. Feb. 7, 1854.
Sculptor, engraver, art teacher, active N.O. 1807–38; primarily marble cutter, stone carver, also gilder. Contemporary listings: sculptor, 21 Bourbon (1807); sculptor and engraver, cor. Esplanade and Rampart and cor. St. Louis and Basin (1825); sculptor and drawing teacher, 56 Basin (1827); sculptor, 56 Basin (1830); sculptor, cor. St. Louis and Basin (1835); sculptor, 128 Basin (1837–38).
Marble cutter, carver, and engraver who lived in Bordeaux, France, and Saint–Domingue before coming to N.O. A veteran of the Napoleonic Wars who also fought in the Battle of N.O., Foy first advertised in N.O. in 1807 as a sculptor in marble, stone, and plaster. In June 1817, he advertised that he could supply gravestones, sundials, chimney pieces, cornices, capitals, and medallions in either stucco or plaster. By Oct. of that year, his business required his going to Europe, and he put his tile and brick kiln up for sale. Two years later he fathered a son, PROSPER FLORVILLE FOY, who was born in N.O. (1820). By 1825 the elder Foy had returned permanently to the city, when he announced the opening of his studio where he worked as a marble cutter, engraver, sculptor, gilder, and maker of sun dials, as well as a

teacher of civil, military, and naval architecture. He executed and repaired mausoleums, mantelpieces, bas–reliefs and the like (1835); and his son lived and worked with him in a shop on Rampart. Foy also contributed articles and poems to N.O. newspapers.
References: NOCD 1811, 1830, 1834, 1837–38, 1843–44, 1849–55; *Argus*, Apr. 17, 1827; *Bee*, Aug. 6, 1835, Feb. 8, 1854; *Courier*, Apr. 30, 1813, May 16, 1814, June 20, Oct. 22–29, 1817 (advs.), July 1, 1854; *D. Pic.*, Mar. 17, 1903; *Gazette*, June 10, Nov. 8, 1825; *Moniteur*, July 11, 1807; Delery, 109, 163; Friends of the Cabildo, *N.O. Architecture*, 3:75, 6:20–21; Groce and Wallace; Prosper Foy Papers, TU; Second District Court, Succession of Prosper Foy, 1854, docket 7355, NOPL; Testut, 175–77; U.S. Census (1840), roll 1315.

FRAENKEL, THEODORE OSCAR
Born Chicago IL Mar. 17, 1857; died N.Y.C. 1924.
Painter, active N.O. 1899–1901; primarily architect.
Studied: Chicago.
Exhibited: ARTISTS' ASSOCIATION OF NEW ORLEANS (1899, 1901).
Awarded: International Exposition, Paris, gold medal for watercolors (1900).
Architect with the firm of Burton & Fraenkel (1900-1901), who painted and exhibited landscapes in N.O. He returned to Chicago, then moved to N.Y.C. in 1904.
References: NOCD 1900–1901; *Harlequin*, Dec. 6, 1899; AANO, *Catalogue* (1899, 1901); Bénézit; LSM, *Biennial Report for 1922-23*, 107; Withey, 218.

FRANCK, AUGUST
Painter, active N.O. 1888.
Contemporary listings: fresco painter (1888).
References: NOCD 1888.

FRANCK, JULIUS
Painter, active N.O. 1884–88.
Contemporary listings: fresco painter (1884); painter (1885); painter, 34

Toulouse (1886–87); fresco painter, with Joseph R. Schmide (1888).

With JOHN FINSLY, frescoed the hall, parlor, and dining room of the residence of Robert Roberts, St. Charles near Conery (1884).

References: NOCD 1884–88; *Eve. Chronicle*, Sept. 23, 1884.

FRANK, CHARLES LEE

Artist, active N.O. 1900–1903.

Contemporary listings: WYNNE & FRANK (1900); artist (1902–1903).

References: NOCD 1900, 1902–1904; Thomas Thompson, 64.

FRAZEE, JOHN L.

Painter, active N.O. 1895; primarily sign painter, also stained glass worker.

Contemporary listings: artist (1895).

References: NOCD 1887–89, 1891–95, 1903; Rossini (adv.); WPA, "Directory."

FRAZEE, ORIAN

Sculptor, active N.O. 1889.

Sent from Atlanta GA to N.O., with E. C. Bruffey of the Atlanta *Constitution*, to take a plaster of Paris cast of the face, right hand, and foot from the body of Jefferson Davis, who had died in N.O. Dec. 6, 1889. The casts were probably to be used in making a heroic–sized statue of Davis for the city of Atlanta.

References: *D. States*, Dec. 7–8, 1889.

FREDERICK, GEORGE

Sculptor, active N.O. 1905.

Contemporary listings: woodcarver (1905).

References: NOCD 1905.

FREDERICKS, JOHN

Painter, active N.O. 1881–84.

Contemporary listings: painter (1881); artist (1882–84).

References: NOCD 1881–84.

FREMAUX, COL. LEON JOSEPH

Born Paris, France Apr. 18, 1821; died N.O. May 3, 1898.

Sketch artist, art teacher, active N.O. 1875–83; primarily surveyor, engineer, also architect, draftsman.

Full name Napoléon Joseph Frémaux, he was brought to N.O. in 1830, but soon was sent to Paris to study. He returned to N.O. in 1839 where he worked as a civil engineer and an architect, then as assistant state engineer from 1855 until the Civil War. After the war he worked as an architect in Mobile AL; he returned to N.O. in 1866 as an architect with Frémaux & Bercegeay (1868), and later with the city surveyor's office (1870–78). In 1875, he made sketches of N.O. street merchants and vendors for the amusement of his family. A limited edition of the drawings was published by the N.O. printers Peychaud & Garcia from plates made by an engraver in the firm of jeweler A. B. Griswold. The prints were hand–tinted by Frémaux and his children and were bound as the book *New Orleans Characters* (1876; reprinted 1949). Frémaux also taught linear drawing at the SOUTHERN ART UNION (1882–83).

References: NOCD 1855–56, 1858, 1867–68, 1870–98; Baton Rouge *Advocate*, Jan. 26, 1861; *D. Pic.*, Apr. 14, 1868, Dec. 11, 1874, Nov. 11, 1882, May 20, 1883, May 4, 1898; *D. States*, May 5, 1898; *Men and Matters*, Nov. 1895, 12, 42, 44, 47; *Repub.*, Dec. 9, 1874; *T. Demo.*, May 8, 1883, May 4–5, 1898; *T. Pic.*, Oct. 25, 1936, Mar. 13, 1949; Booth, 2:929; Frémaux; Friends of the Cabildo, *N.O. Architecture*, 4:52; LHS, (1903); Mechanics' and Agricultural Fair, *Report* (1869):76; Murrell, 2:32, 34; Nelson; U.S. Census (1860), roll 408.

FRERET, EMILY M.

Sketch artist, art teacher, active N.O. 1911–18.

Contemporary listings: artist (1911–14, 1916, 1918); teacher (1915).

Exhibited: ART ASSOCIATION OF NEW ORLEANS (1915, 1917).

Awarded: American Electrical Association, poster art contest, second prize (1916).

References: NOCD 1911–16, 1918; *Item*, Aug. 8, 1916; Art Asso., *Catalogue* (1915, 1917).

FRETTE, JEAN BAPTISTE, JR.

Born ca. 1765; died N.O. June 21, 1842.

Painter, active N.O. 1811–35; primarily decorator, glazier.

Contemporary listings: painter, 19 Bourbon (1811); merchant painter, 92 Royal (1822); merchant painter, 214 Royal (1823–24, 1827, 1830); watercolor, oil and fresco painter, with assistant P. M. GURNIER (1829); painter, Main betw. Conti and Levee (1831); painter, 21 Main (1832); painter, 35 Conti (1834–35).

References: NOCD 1805, 1809, 1811, 1822–24, 1827, 1830, 1832, 1834–35, 1842; NOBD 1807; *Bee*, Apr. 19, 1831, June 22, 1842; *Courier*, June 4, 1829; *Gazette*, Sept. 30, 1806, Oct. 14, 1808; *Moniteur*, Dec. 26, 1807; Mayor's Office, Messages, May 3, 1823, 10:161, NOPL; U.S. Census (1820), roll 32, (1830), roll 45.

FRICKESSEN, BERTHA

Art craftsman, active N.O. 1913.

Contemporary listings: ARTS & CRAFTS STUDIO (1913).

References: NOCD 1913.

FRIEDAL, HARRY

Born Wurttembürg ca. 1827.

Painter, active N.O. 1860.

Contemporary listings: fresco painter (1860).

References: U.S. Census (1860), roll 415.

FRITCH, GUSTAVE A.

Painter, active N.O. 1897–1900.

Contemporary listings: fresco painter (1897, 1900); painter (1898–99).

References: NOCD 1897–1900.

FRITCH, LOUIS T.

Born N.O. Apr. 6, 1882; died N.O. Nov. 27, 1956.

Engraver, active N.O. 1903–1909; primarily photographer.

Contemporary listings: engraver (1903, 1905); photo–engraver (1904); engraver, ROMANSKI Photo–Engraving Co. Ltd. (1908); photo–engraver, Romanski Photo–Engraving Co. Ltd. (1909).

Listed as operator (1902) and foreman (1907) for Romanski Photo–Engraving Co., Ltd. and as photographer for the *Daily Picayune* and *Times–Picayune* (1908–1924).

References: NOCD 1901–33, 1935, 1938, 1940, 1942, 1945–47, 1949, 1952–56; *T. Pic.*, Nov. 28–29, 1956; Orleans Parish Registrar of Voters, NOPL; U.S. Census (1910), roll 521.

FROBUS, JOHN H. C. N.

Born N.O. ca. 1832–33.

Colorer, active N.O 1858–60; primarily photographer, printer.

Contemporary listings: colorer, 27 Customhouse (1858); portrait maker (1860).

Advertised as a daguerreotypist and an ambrotypist who specialized in hand–colored memorial portraits.

References: NOCD 1855–56, 1858–59, 1861, 1866; *Bee*, Jan. 1, 8, Mar. 26, 1857, Oct. 14, 1858, Jan. 17, 31, 1859, Sept. 24, 1863; *D. Pic.*, Feb. 11, 1851; *Wkly. Mirror*, Nov. 13, 1858; Smith and Tucker, 87, 114–15, 158; U.S. Census (1850), roll 235, (1860), roll 421.

FROMKES, MAURICE

Born Poland Feb. 19, 1872; died Paris, France Sept. 17, 1931.

Painter, active N.O. 1916–17.

Studied: with Ward and Low, National Academy of Design, N.Y.C. (1890); Cooper Union, N.Y.C. (1888); Holland and France (1899).

Exhibited: DELGADO MUSEUM OF ART (1917).

Awarded: Salmagundi Club, Isadore prize (1908).

Came to the U.S. (ca. 1880) where he became a leading American painter. He spent the winter of 1916–17 in N.O. and exhibited his oil and pastel paintings at the Delgado Museum, Jan. 13–Feb. 21, 1917. He moved to Madrid in 1921 and began a series of paintings of Spain and of prominent Spaniards. Awarded diploma of honor at the International Exposition of Fine Arts, Bordeaux, France (1927)

References: *American Art Annual*, 28:410; Delgado *Bulletin*, 1(Dec. 1927):4; *T. Pic.*, Jan. 26, 1917; Delgado *Catalogue*, 18; Fielding, *Dictionary*; LSM, *Biennial Report 1922–23*, 107; McGlauflin; *Who's Who in America, 1930–31*; WPA, "Lives."

FROST, MRS. G.
Painter, etcher, active N.O. 1886–91.
Studied: ARTISTS' ASSOCIATION OF NEW ORLEANS (1886–87, 1890).
Exhibited: Artists' Association of New Orleans (1886–87, 1890–91).
Possibly Mary Mathilda Frost (Mrs. George Hobart Frost), died N.O. Feb. 8, 1920.
References: *Current Topics*, Jan. 1892, 24; *D. Pic.*, Nov. 7, 1886, May 7, 1887, Dec. 17, 1891; *D. States*, May 16, 1890; *T. Demo.*, Nov. 13, 1890; AANO, *Catalogue* (1891).

FUCHS, FEODOR
Lithographer, active N.O. 1885.
Contemporary listings: lithographer, SOUTHERN LITHOGRAPHIC CO. (1885).
References: NOCD 1885.

FUDGE. *See* GIBSON, DAVID

FULLMER, HARRY
Artist, active N.O. 1890.
Contemporary listings: artist, LILIENTHAL & Co. (1890).
References: NOCD 1890.

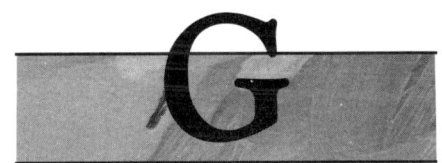

GABRY, JULES
Born France; died N.O.
Potter, active N.O. ca. 1894–97.
The first potter employed in the art department of NEWCOMB COLLEGE (1894–97). Gabry had come to N.O. via Brazil from Sèvres, France, where he had worked for Clement Massier at Golf Juan Pottery. Before Newcomb, he was with the Louisiana Porcelain Manufacturing Co. in N.O. Although it has been claimed that Gabry committed suicide by jumping into the Mississippi River in Dec. 1895, the year is probably inaccurate since his works are dated through 1897.
References: Paul Evans, 180–82; Ormond and Irvine, 24, 37, 145; Poesch, *Newcomb Pottery*, 17–18, 94, 108.

GACHOT, MRS. ___ . *See* LOUISIANA PAINTING & SCULPTURE ACADEMY

GACHOT, A. M.
Painter, art teacher, active N.O. 1817–21.
Studied: with Jacques–Louis David, Paris.
Contemporary listings: teacher of painting, portrait and miniature painter, Dumaine betw. Dauphine and Burgundy (1817).
References: *L'Ami des Lois*, Nov. 15, 1817; Groce and Wallace; Harter and Tucker, 121; LSM, *Biennial Report for 1922-23*, 59.

GALEPPI, ALEXANDRE
Born Dalpe, Switzerland ca. 1820; died Joinville–le–Pont, France, Oct. 3, 1874.
Engraver, sculptor, art dealer, active N.O. 1849–58.
Contemporary listings: sculptor, 36 Toulouse (1849); engraver of letters, plates, cor. Toulouse and Chartres (1850–53); engraver, 161 Chartres (1858).
Galeppi emigrated to the U.S. in 1848. In N.O. he advertised that he imported engravings, lithographs, paper hangings, frames, mirrors, and wallpaper from Paris. He left N.O. during the Civil War, returned for a short stay, and, after leaving his N.O. property in the hands of agents, settled with his family by the early 1870s in France.
References: NOCD 1849–61, 1866, 1870–71; *Courier*, July 24, 1851; Groce and Wallace; Second District Court, Succession of Alexandre Galeppi, 1875, docket 38026, NOPL; U.S. Census (1850), roll 235; William Young.

GALLAGHER, THOMAS
Engraver, active N.O. 1875.
Contemporary listings: engraver (1875).
Possibly Thomas Gallagher, born County Mayo, Ireland; died N.O. Oct. 26, 1881.
References: NOCD 1866–68, 1871–72, 1875–77; *D. Pic.*, Oct. 27, 1881.

GALLERY OF FINE ARTS
Art gallery, active N.O. 1842.
Contemporary listings: 89 Camp (1842).
The gallery held an exhibition of paintings by American, French, and English artists, some of them on loan from N.O. residents, for the purpose of improving the public taste.
References: *Bee*, Jan. 10, 1842; *D. Pic.*, Jan. 7, 1842.

GALLEY, FELIX
Painter, commercial artist, active N.O. 1890–92.
Contemporary listings: artist, Novelty Picture Co. (1890); fresco painter, Peoples Theatre and artist (1891); portrait painter, 114 St. Charles (1892).
References: NOCD 1890–92; *Mascot*, Sept. 19, 1891, 4.

GALLIER, JOSEPHINE BLANCHE
Born N.O. Jan. 2, 1856; died Nov. 7, 1933.
Painter, active N.O. ca. 1885.
Exhibited: Creole Exhibit, American Exposition (1885–86); Louisiana

Purchase Exposition, St. Louis MO (1904).
Amateur artist and daughter of N.O. architect James Gallier, Jr.
References: *T. Pic.*, Nov. 9, 1933; Comité de l'Exposition française, 26; Creole Exhibit, 14; Information Courtesy Charles L. Mackie, July 2, 1986; U.S. Census (1860), roll 419.

GALLOTTI, BARTHOLOMEW
Painter, active N.O. ca. 1916.
Exhibited: ART ASSOCIATION OF NEW ORLEANS (1916).
References: Art Asso., *Catalogue* (1916).

GALMICHE, EUGENE
Born LA ca. 1863.
Commercial artist, active N.O. 1905–13; also carpenter, molder.
Contemporary listings: artist (1905–1908, 1912–13); carnival artist (1910).
References: NOCD 1891, 1893–99, 1901–1902, 1904–14, 1916–17; U.S. Census (1910), roll 521.

GALVANI, CHARLES
Born Italy ca. 1805; died before June 21, 1866.
Painter, restorer, art dealer, active N.O. ca. 1848–59.
Contemporary listings: restorer, 71 Canal (1849); art dealer, artist, painter, 71 Canal (1850); artist painter, restorer, Union Gallery of Fine Arts, 13 St. Charles (1851); portrait painter, 10 Marais (1855); portrait painter, Apollo near Jackson (1856); Galvani Gallery of Paintings (1857–58); portrait painter, Canal near St. Charles (1857–58); portrait painter, 103 Canal (1856, 1858–59). Probably in Venice as a miniaturist and lithographer (ca. 1830), Galvani may have been in N.O. by 1848. Besides being a portrait painter, he became the city's leading art dealer during the 1850s. After spending his summers acquiring artworks in Europe and the U.S., Galvani would open his N.O. gallery in Oct. or Nov. and remain in the city through Mar. He was first recorded when he advertised the sale of a collection of Flemish and Italian paintings in Nov. 1849. He returned in Oct. 1850 with American and European art and opened the Union Gallery of Fine Arts (sometimes referred to as the Galvani Gallery of Paintings) at 13 St. Charles in rooms formerly occupied by the National Gallery of Paintings owned by GEORGE COOKE. As a working artist who traveled extensively, Galvani proposed to establish a public gallery of art and a school of design similar to those in the northeastern U.S. (Feb. 1851). He sought 500 backers, apparently without success, but opened his own gallery free to the public. For his winter art seasons of 1857–58 and 1858–59, Galvani opened at 53 St. Charles with oil paintings, watercolors, and prints, and from that location became a distributor of art throughout the southwestern U.S. During the 1850s, Galvani also sold art through local auction houses and sponsored his own weekly auctions to promote sales. His most important public auction was the internationally known art collection of the wealthy N.O. businessman James Robb (1859).
References: NOCD 1850–52, 1855–61; NOBD 1858–59; *Bee*, Nov. 19, 1850, Jan. 12, Mar. 15, 1858; *Comm. Bull.*, Feb. 21, 1857, Jan. 4, 1858; *D. Creole*, Mar. 4, 1857; *D. Crescent*, Nov. 3, 1849, Jan. 9, 1850, Feb. 21, 1851; *D. Delta*, Mar. 30, 1857; *D. Orleanian*, Jan. 1, 1858; *D. Pic.*, Nov. 23, 1849, Oct. 17, 1850, Jan. 2, 15, Feb. 16, 1851, Nov. 18, 1856, Jan. 25–Feb. 12, 1857 (advs.), Mar. 14, 1857, Feb. 12, 1860, June 21, 1866; *D. True Delta*, Feb. 1, Dec. 27, 1857; Galvani; Glenk, 74; Groce and Wallace; James Robb Collection, THNOC; U.S. Census (1850), roll 234.

GALVIN, EDWARD
Lithographer, active N.O. 1882–89; also printer.
Contemporary listings: lithographer (1882, 1884); lithographer, T. FITZWILLIAM & CO. (1883, 1888–89).
References: NOCD 1882–84, 1886, 1888–91.

GAMBERINI, DOMENICO
Born Ravenna, Italy.
Silhouettist, sketch artist, active N.O.
1848.
Contemporary listings: scissors–cut
paper, drawings & pictures, St. Louis
Exchange Hotel (1848).
References: *Bee*, Jan 27, 1848; *Courier*, Jan. 31, Feb. 2, 1848; *D. Delta*,
Feb. 1, 5, 1848; Groce and Wallace.

GAMOTIS, ALPHONSE J.
Born N.O. Mar. 9, 1842; died N.O.
Jan. 6, 1919.
Painter, active N.O. ca. 1882–94.
Exhibited: WAGENER's (1882);
SOUTHERN ART UNION (1882); American Exposition (1885–86); ARTISTS'
ASSOCIATION OF NEW ORLEANS (1886–87, 1894).
Memberships/positions: Artists' Association of New Orleans (1886–87).
Amateur artist, who specialized in
landscapes in watercolor; also listed
as a clerk (1867–72) and as a druggist (1873–1918).
References: NOCD 1867–70, 1872–77, 1879–84, 1886–1910, 1913–18;
Art and Letters, 1(Dec. 1887):228;
D. Pic., Mar. 19, 1882, Nov. 6, 1886,
Dec. 29, 1887; *D. States*, Jan. 20,
1882, Nov. 5, 1886; *T. Demo.*, Dec.
14, 1894; *T. Pic.*, Jan. 7, 1919; Collier, "The World of Art: Delgado
Adds 14 Oils to Its Collection," *T.
Pic.*, Mar. 14, 1971; AANO, *Catalogue* (1886); Creole Exhibit, 14;
LSM, *Biennial Report for 1922–23*,
60; THNOC Cemetery Survey; U.S.
Census (1860), roll 419; Wiesendanger, 51.

GANGLIONICS
Art association, active N.O. ca. 1885.
Club dedicated to artistic and literary study, which evolved into the
ARTISTS' ASSOCIATION OF NEW ORLEANS.
References: Seebold, 1:25; Tallant,
314–15.

GARBEILLE, PHILIPPE
Born France.
Sculptor, silhouettist, active N.O.
1842–48.
Studied: Academy of Fine Arts, Marseilles, France (1838); with Bertel
Thorvaldsen, Rome (ca. 1839); Paris,

Contemporary listings: sculptor
(1842, 1844); sculptor, 110 St. Peter
(1843); sculptor, Camp near Canal
(1845); sculptor, 7 Camp (1846);
sculptor, Camp (1847); sculptor, St.
Charles (1847).
Exhibited: Armory Hall (1847); Hebert's book store (1848); American
Exposition (1885–86).
One of the earliest portrait sculptors
in N.O. to receive public acclaim.
Garbeille was first listed in N.O. in
1842; he had his silhouette cut by
the visiting artist AUGUSTE EDOUART
on Jan. 26, 1844. By 1846 Garbeille
had gained a high reputation for his
portrait busts of businessmen, actors,
musicians, and famous visitors to the
city. Some were life–size marble
busts, but many were miniature statuettes in plaster or clay that were
caricatures of the sitters. The *Revue
Louisianaise*, a N.O. literary and art
publication, printed the drawings of
several of the statuettes between
Dec. 1846 and May 1848 as "Garbeille's Gallery." Garbeille received
two important commissions from St.
Louis Cathedral, marble statues of
St. Francis and the *Virgin and Child*
(ca. 1846). The N.O. City Council
requested a portrait bust of Gen.
Zachary Taylor, and Garbeille was
sent to Mexico (June–Oct. 1847) with
money raised through local subscription. Upon his return, he remained
in N.O. for several more months selling casts of his two busts of Taylor.
He apparently tried to form an artists
society and an art gallery in N.O.
Garbeille was next reported to be in
Washington DC working on a bust of
Pres. James K. Polk (May 1848), in
N.Y.C. (1849–50), and in Havana,
Cuba (1853).
References: NOCD 1843–44, 1846;
Bee, Oct. 4, 31, 1843, May 20, Oct.
19, 1847, Dec. 13, 1850; *Comm.
Times*, Feb. 25, Mar. 13, Apr. 2, 30,
May 20, June 10, 25, Oct. 18, Dec.
16, 1847, May 29, 1848; *Courier*,
July 11, 1842, May 22, 1844, July
1, 1845, Nov. 9, 1846, May 27, Aug.
30, 1847, May 26, June 2, 1848, Oct.
1, 1853, Aug. 28, 1856; *D. Delta*,

May 22, Oct. 19, 1847; *D. National*, Oct. 19, Dec. 14, 1847; *D. Pic.*, Oct. 22, 1845, Sept. 7, Nov. 30, 1847, May 17, 1897; *Revue Louisianaise*, 1(Apr. 2, 1846):440–41, 1(Apr. 12, 1846):46–47, 2(Dec. 27, 1846)–2(Apr. 4, 1847) (illus.), 4(May 2, 1847):116, 4(Apr. 4, 1847)–4(Aug. 22, 1847) (illus); *T. Demo.*, Jan. 12, 1913; *Wkly. Delta*, May 24, Oct. 25, 1847, Aug. 12, 1850; *Bénézit*; *Collection of American Silhouette Portraits*, 56; Coulon MS, Scrapbook 100, LSM; Creole Exhibit, 16; Glenk, 89, 92–93, 95; Groce and Wallace; LSM, *Biennial Report for 1920–21*, 81; LSM, *Biennial Report for 1924–25*, 50; LSM, *Biennial Report for 1932–33*, 62, 66; Roster of Artists, Special Collections, TU; Tinker, *Creole City*, 166; Tinker, *Pen, Pills and Pistols*; WPA, *Louisiana*, 164.

GARCIA, AUGUSTIN MARCELIN
Born ca. 1836; died N.O. Jan. 30, 1871.
Painter, active N.O. 1852–56.
Contemporary listings: scene painter, 241 Treme (1852); scene painter, Main near Prieur (1853–56).
References: NOCD 1852–61, 1866–67, 1870–71; *Bee*, Jan. 31, 1871; Groce and Wallace.

GARCIA, J.
Art teacher, active N.O. 1863.
Contemporary listings: professor of painting, 181 Camp (1863).
Also taught Spanish, music, and bookkeeping.
References: *Bee*, Dec. 2, 1876; *D. Pic.*, June 28, 1885; *Era*, Aug. 15, 1863.

GARCIA, PHILIP
Born Havana, Cuba ca. Apr. 1892; died N.O. Sept. 28, 1918.
Commercial artist, active N.O. 1910–18.
Contemporary listings: artist, ROMANSKI Photo–Engraving Co., Ltd. (1910); artist, SPENCER ENGRAVING CO., LTD. (1911); artist, SLATTERY-SMITH CO., LTD. (1912); artist, NEW ORLEANS ENGRAVING & ELECTROTYPE CO., LTD. (1913–14); artist, PANAMA PHOTO–ENGRAVING CO. (1916–18).

References: NOCD 1910–14, 1916–18; *T. Pic.*, Sept. 29, 1918; U.S. Census (1910), roll 521.

GARCIA AND FAUCHE
Lithographers, active N.O. 1882–83; primarily stationers, printers; Joseph Garcia (born N.O. ca. 1846; died N.O. Aug. 23, 1920), William A. Fauche, partners.
Contemporary listings: lithographers, 56 Camp (1882–83).
Also listed as stationers and printers, 56 Camp (1882–90) and later as Garcia Stationery Co. Limited (1891–1940).
References: NOCD 1882–1933, 1935, 1938, 1940.

GARDBERG, JACOB
Sculptor, active N.O. 1905–16.
Contemporary listings: woodcarver (1905–1906, 1911, 1913, 1916); woodcarver, with W. Feldman (1910).
References: NOCD 1905–1906, 1910–11, 1913–16, 1918.

GARDINA, JOSEPH
Born Italy ca. 1884.
Artist, active N.O. 1910.
Contemporary listings: picture artist (1910).
Immigrated to U.S. in 1890.
References: NOCD 1906–1909, 1912–13, 1915–16, 1918–21; U.S. Census (1910), roll 521.

GARDNER, PATRICK
Born Ballymahan, Longford, Ireland ca. 1813–14; died N.O. Jan. 8, 1861.
Painter, active N.O. 1841–61.
Contemporary listings: artist, 83 Conti (1841); painter, Villere near Bienville (1846); painter, Bienville betw. Treme and Marais (1849–54); painter, 241 Bienville (1855–59); painter, 216 Bienville (1860–61).
References: NOCD 1841–42, 1846, 1849–61; *D. True Delta*, Jan. 9, 13, 1861; Glenk, 75; Groce and Wallace; U.S. Census (1860), roll 421; WPA, "Lives."

GARIC, ELLEN
Art teacher, active N.O. 1913.
Contemporary listings: drawing teacher, Public School of N.O. (1913).

References: NOCD 1913–14; *T. Demo.*, Jan. 14, 1913.

GARIC, LILLIAN ANN GUEDRY (Mrs. Henry Garic).
Art craftsman, active N.O. ca. 1899–1905.
Studied: NEWCOMB COLLEGE (1899–1905).
Exhibited: Pan-American Exposition, Buffalo NY (1901).
Specialized in pottery decoration and china painting.
References: Art Asso., *Catalogue* (1910); Ormond & Irvine, 156; Poesch, *Newcomb Pottery*, 42, 99.

GARNER, DAVID E.
Born GA ca. 1879.
Painter, active N.O. 1910–16.
Contemporary listings: painter–artiste (1910); painter, 2014 Foucher (1911–12); painter, 2524 Cadiz (1913); painter (1915–16).
References: NOCD 1908–13, 1915–16, 1918; U.S. Census (1910), roll 524.

GARNERAY, AMBROISE-LOUIS
Born Paris, France Feb. 19, 1783; died Paris Sept. 11, 1857.
Painter.
French marine painter and designer who learned the aquatint process and engraved views of French and foreign ports (1821–32). Because his depiction of N.O. was geographically incorrect, Garneray probably did not come to the city, but used other sources to make the painting *Vue de la Nouvelle Orléans* that was engraved in Paris by Sigismond Himely.
References: Anglo–American Art Museum, *Sail and Steam*, item 4; Bénézit; *Bryan's*; Groce and Wallace; *Nouvelle Biographie Générale*; Edgar Smith, 217–18.

GARRETT-BROWN, MRS. LEE JEFFREYS
Born NC; died Denver CO 1898.
Sketch artist, painter, active N.O. 1890–97; also photographer.
Studied: ARTISTS' ASSOCIATION OF NEW ORLEANS (1890–91).
Exhibited: Artists' Association of New Orleans (1890–93, 1896–97).
Memberships/positions: Artists' Association of New Orleans (1896).

Amateur artist noted for her paintings of home interiors, still lifes, and landscapes; editor of the *Louisiana Review* (1894–96).
References: NOCD 1894–96; *Current Topics*, Jan. 1892, 24, Jan. 1893, 11, Nov. 1893, 198; *D. Pic.*, Dec. 17, 1891, Dec. 14, 1892, Mar. 30, 1897; *D. States*, May 16, 1890; *Louisiana Review*, May 27, 1891, 4; *T. Demo.*, Dec. 13, 1892; AANO, *Catalogue* (1891, 1896, 1897); LSM, *Biennial Report for 1922–23*, 105; Mount, 166–67; WPA, "Lives."

GARRISON, SYDNEY W.
Engraver, active N.O. 1867–70.
Contemporary listings: engraver, Royal cor. Canal (1867); engraver, 25 Royal (1869); engraver, with FRED HOLYLAND (1870).
References: NOCD 1867, 1869–71.

GASQUET, MARTHA. *See* WESTFELDT, MARTHA GASQUET

GASTAL, J.
Sculptor, active N.O. 1858.
Contemporary listings: shipcarver, Magazine cor. Calliope (1858).
References: NOCD 1858; NOBD 1858.

GAUDCHAUX, H.
Commercial artist, active N.O. ca. 1842.
Designed the engraved masthead of *La Lorgnette* (1842–43).
References: *Lorgnette*, Dec. 11, 1842, Jan. 6–Apr. 20, 1843 (masthead).

GAUMARD, _____
Sculptor, active N.O. 1837
Contemporary listings: sculptor, 488 Barracks (1837).
References: NOCD 1837.

GAUTIER, ALEXANDER W.
Born N.O. Feb. 1875; died N.O. Apr. 3, 1902.
Artist, active N.O. 1899.
Contemporary listings: artist (1899).
References: NOCD 1892–1902; *D. Pic.*, Apr. 4, 6, 1902; *D. States*, Apr. 6, 1902.

GAUTREAU, J. B.
Sculptor, active N.O. 1832.
Contemporary listings: sculptor, Adel cor. Rousseau (1832).

References: NOCD 1832; Groce and Wallace.

GAUVIN, J. D.
Art teacher, active N.O. 1860–61.
Contemporary listings: teacher of drawing, Louisiana Academy (1860–61).
References: *Bee*, Sept. 8, 10, Dec. 6, 1860, Jan. 3, 1861.

GAUX, ALPHONSE
Engraver, active N.O. 1873–74.
Contemporary listings: wood engraver (1873–74).
References: NOCD 1870, 1873–75, 1879–81.

GAUX, JULES A.
Born France ca. 1811.
Painter, art teacher, active N.O. 1834–46; also printer.
Contemporary listings: miniature painter and professor of drawing, 22 Toulouse (1834); miniature painter and professor of drawing, 127 St. Peter (ca. 1835); miniature painter, 22 Toulouse (1835); miniature painter, 104 Chartres (1837); portrait painter, 106 Chartres (1841, 1843–44); miniature painter, 112 Chartres (1846).
Perhaps in N.O. as early as 1832, he was founder and director of the tri-weekly N.O. journal *L'Indépendant* (begun 1834), printed by J. A. Gaux & Cie., 65 St. Louis.
References: NOCD 1834–35, 1837, 1841–44, 1846, 1851; *Courier*, Aug. 18, 1832, Sept. 29, 1836, Aug. 31, 1841, Nov. 4, 1842, Nov. 2, 1844; Bruns, 312; Glenk, 75; Groce and Wallace; McMullan, 133; Tinker, *Ecrits*, 218; U.S. Census (1850), roll 235; WPA, "Lives."

GAVIN, ROBERT
Born Leith, Scotland 1827; died Edinburgh, Scotland Oct. 5, 1883.
Painter, active N.O. 1868.
Studied: with Thomas Duncan, School of Design, Edinburgh.
Exhibited: Royal Scottish Academy (1846–82); Royal Academy, London.
Memberships/positions: Royal Scottish Academy, associate (1854–78), academician (1879–83).

Scottish genre and landscape painter who visited the southern U.S. (1868) where he took an interest in depicting the lives of blacks. Three of his oil studies, identified as a N.O. slave man, woman, and girl, were shown in the 1870 annual exhibition of the Royal Scottish Academy. Eleven paintings of mulattos, quadroons, and slaves, probably also done in N.O., were shown in the academy's 1871 and 1872 exhibitions, and two others were shown in London. Later in his career, Gavin painted Moorish pictures that he exhibited at the academy (1874–82).
References: Bénézit; Information courtesy Royal Scottish Academy, June 18, 1986.

GAVITO, ANGEL D.
Born Oviedo, Spain Nov. 23, 1866; died N.O. Aug. 30, 1931.
Engraver, active N.O. 1890–1892; also printer.
Contemporary listings: engraver, with Victor Mauberret (1890–92).
Also listed as manager, foreman, and superintendent with Mauberret's Printing House (1895–1922).
References: NOCD 1889–92, 1895–1930; *T. Pic.*, Aug. 31, 1931; Orleans Parish Registrar of Voters, NOPL.

GAY, EDWARD
Painter, active N.O. 1866.
Contemporary listings: artist, 309 Poydras (1866).
Possibly Edward B. Gay, born Dublin, Ireland Apr. 27, 1837; died NY 1928, who first came to the U.S. in 1848, studied art in Germany in the 1860s, and eventually opened a studio in N.Y.C. while residing in Mount Vernon NY. He specialized in landscape painting, for which he won a medal in N.O. (1885) and exhibited at the ART ASSOCIATION OF NEW ORLEANS.
References: NOCD 1866; *Art and Letters*, 1(Aug. 1887): 150–52; *T. Demo.*, Mar. 16, 1914; *Appleton's CAB*; Art Asso., *Catalogue* (1907); Bénézit; Fielding, *Dictionary*; Groce and Wallace.

GAY, GEORGE
Died 1914.
Painter, active N.O. 1884–97.

Contemporary listings: painter (1895, 1897); artist (1896).

Exhibited: World's Industrial and Cotton Centennial Exposition (1884–85).

Probably an amateur artist, Gay painted landscapes, usually of coastal scenes near N.O.

References: NOCD 1878, 1891, 1894–99, 1907; Anglo–American Art Museum, *Sail and Steam*, item 42; Glenk, 69, 274; Louisiana Art Commission Galleries, 2, 4; LSM, *Annual Report for 1918*, 59; LSM, *Biennial Report for 1922–23*, 58; LSM, *Biennial Report for 1932–33*, 54; Wiesendanger, 52.

GEISER, JOHN
Born Langenthal, Switzerland Feb. 19, 1869; died N.O. Nov. 3, 1943.

Painter, active N.O. 1898–1943; also decorator.

Contemporary listings: painter (1898–99, 1901); fresco painter (1900); DREIS & GEISER (1902–1907); painter, 2821 Palmyra (1908–18); fresco artist (1910).

Settled in N.O. in 1894 after arriving in the U.S. the year before. In 1918 Geiser was the contractor for decorating and painting the interior of St. Louis Cathedral, which included the restoration of the murals. He remained active as an artist and painter the rest of his life and exhibited at the Arts and Crafts Club (1932). His son and grandson continued the firm as John Geiser, Incorporated, Fresco Artists and Interior Decorators, until 1983.

References: NOCD 1898–1933, 1935, 1938, 1940, 1942; *States*, Dec. 4, 1932, Nov. 4, 1943; Amoss, "An Art Carried On," *States-Item*, Feb. 11, 1976; Collier, "Decorative Wall Paintings Reappear From Past," *T. Pic.*, Feb. 13, 1972; Information courtesy John Geiser III, Aug. 14, 1986; U.S. Census (1910), roll 520.

GEIST, L.
Artist, active N.O. 1846.

Painted *Orleans Artillery Leaving for the Mexican War* (1846).

References: Glenk, 132.

GEISTLICH, JOHN CHARLES
Sculptor, active N.O. 1859–60; primarily carpenter.

Contemporary listings: wax figures, 307 Ursulines (1859–60).

References: NOCD 1859–61, 1866, 1869–71; Groce and Wallace.

GENERALLY, FLEURY THEOTIME DE RINALDI
Born France Dec. 31, 1779; died N.O. May 14, 1849.

Painter, designer, engraver, active N.O. ca. 1814–20; also decorator, sign painter.

Contemporary listings: painter, designer, decorator, Jefferson (1818); painter, designer, decorator, engraver, Conti betw. Royal and Bourbon (1818).

Sent to Santo Domingo as chief accountant for the French government, then to Philadelphia, Générally arrived in N.O. on Dec. 14, 1814. Although listed as a bookkeeper and as an employee of the sheriff's office through 1850, he was mentioned as having artistic talent and made sketches during a river trip from N.O. to St. Louis MO (Feb. 1–Aug. 4, 1820).

References: NOCD 1823, 1827, 1832, 1834–35, 1837–38, 1841–43, 1846, 1849–50; *L'Ami des Lois*, July 23–Aug. 18, 1818 (advs.), Aug. 22–Sept. 12, 1818 (advs.); *D. Orleanian*, May 15, 1849; Anglo–American Art Museum, *Louisiana Landscape*; Anglo–American Art Museum, *Sail and Steam*; Delery, 82–85, 87, 89, 127–28; Fortier, *Louisiana*, 3:177; Groce and Wallace; Samuel et al., 165; U.S. Census (1830), roll 45.

GENIN, JOHN
Born Lyons, France 1830; died N.O. Oct. 19, 1895.

Painter, restorer, art teacher, active N.O. 1860–95.

Studied: with Léon Bonnat, Paris.

Contemporary listings: portrait and fancy painter, 6 Exchange Al. (1865); portrait painter, 23 Annette (1867); portrait painter, 82 Royal (1870); portrait painter, PIERSON & GENIN, 24 1/2 Carondelet (1872); portrait painter (1874); portrait painter, 150

Canal (1875–78, 1880–83); restorer (1882); artist, painter, 2 Carondelet (1883); artist (1878–79); portrait painter, 3 Carondelet (1884–86); portrait painter, 47 Royal (1887–94); portrait painter, 233 Royal (1895). Exhibited: L. UTER's (1870, 1875, ca. 1877, 1878–80, 1882–83, 1893); Athénée Louisianais (1880); LILIEN-THAL's (1883); Produce Exchange (1884); World's Industrial and Cotton Centennial Exposition (1884–85).

Awarded: Grand State Fair, diploma, best composition painting (1870, 1871).

Memberships/positions: SOUTHERN ART UNION, art instructor (1880–81); Athénée Louisianais (1880).

Primarily a portrait painter, but also a landscape, genre, and historical painter. Genin, among all 19th–century N.O. artists, was most continuously influenced by French painting because of his many summer trips to France. He was probably first recorded in N.O. in the 1860 U.S. census, as "Johanny Genin," age 30, born in France. He appeared only intermittently during the rest of the 1860s but received public acclaim for an historical painting (1865) and for his drawings published in the *Almanach de la Louisiane* (1866). In 1870, he was recognized for the first of at least three allegorical paintings of LA; in the other two (1879–80 and 1884), his second wife served as a model. In 1878, Genin visited Paris for the Universal Exposition, exhibited his paintings at the Champ de Mars and at private exhibitions, and visited the studios of Paris's prominent portrait painters, including Alexandre Cabanel. By 1881 he was ranked among the principal painters in N.O., and by the next year was considered the leading painter of N.O. families, especially of women, children, and the elderly. From 1870, Genin exhibited mostly at the store of Laurent Uter and by 1886 maintained his studio there.

References: NOCD 1867, 1870, 1872, 1874–1895; NOBD 1865; *Bee*, May 5, Dec. 10, 1870, Dec. 12, 1875, Apr. 1, 3, 1877, Mar. 17, Nov. 24, 1878, Nov. 9, 1879, Jan. 1, 11, May 27, 1880, May 4, 1881, Jan. 22, May 28, Oct. 11, Dec. 17, 1882, Mar. 18, Oct. 6–11, 1883 (advs.); *D. Item*, Feb. 15, 1893; *D. Pic.*, Dec. 3, 1871, Nov. 7, 1875, Oct. 13, 1877, Mar. 24, 1881; *D. States*, Apr. 17, 1880, Apr. 2, 1883, May 4, 1884; *Demo.*, Mar. 17, 1878, Jan. 18, May 27, 1880, May 12, 1881; *Times*, Dec. 21, 1865; *T. Demo.*, Oct. 20, 1895; Jordan, "Interest in Guard History Saves Fine Old Paintings," *T. Pic.*, Oct. 7, 1976; *Almanach de la Louisiane* (1866): frontis., 24, 144; Anglo–American Art Museum, *Louisiana Landscape*, item 16; Boyd, 200; Bruns, 312; Coulon MS, Scrapbook 100, LSM; Fielding, *Dictionary*; Fulton and Toledano, "Landscape Painting," 506; Glenk, 45, 47, 52, 55, 61, 65, 75, 216–217; Harter and Tucker, 121; Lilienthal's, 8; LSM, *Annual Report for 1918*, 59; LSM, *Biennial Report for 1920–21*, 28, 38, 91; LSM, *Biennial Report for 1922–23*, 54; LSM, *Biennial Report for 1924–25*, 49, 62; Mechanics' and Agricultural Fair Asso., *Report* (1870):39; N.O. Death Certificate (1895), 109:768, NOPL; Soniat du Fossat, 84; THNOC 83–32–L; U.S. Census (1860), roll 421; Wiesendanger, 52–53; WPA, "Lives."

GENSLINGER, CHARLES H.
Born OH ca. 1856; died ca. 1896. Engraver, lithographer, active N.O. 1880–91; also stationer, printer.
Contemporary listings: engraver (1880); HUNTER & GENSLINGER (1883–86); lithographer, 48 Camp (1891).
References: NOCD 1880–1892, 1896–97; *D. States*, June 8, 1891; U.S. Census (1880), roll 459.

GENSLINGER AND AITKENS
Lithographers, active N.O. 1892; also stationers, printers; L. Wallace Genslinger, Adrian F. Aitkens, partners.
Contemporary listings: lithographers, 48 Camp (1892).
References: NOCD 1892–93.

GERARD, _____
Engraver, designer, active N.O. 1855.

Contemporary listings: designer and engraver on wood, Sherman, Warton & Co. printers, 41 Camp (1855). Signed an engraving of a view of Louisiana College (1855). References: *Courier*, Aug. 15, 1850; *D. Pic.*, Jan. 21, 1855; Louisiana College.

GERARD, CHARLES
Born France ca. 1832.
Designer, sketch artist, active N.O. 1860–66.
Contemporary listings: drawing (1860); embroidery designer, 77 Bourbon (1860–61, 1866).
References: NOCD 1858–61, 1866; U.S. Census (1860), roll 421.

GERARD, MRS. EMILE
Art craftsman, active N.O. 1876–91.
Contemporary listings: artificial flowers, 34 Bourbon (1876–79, 1881–85), artificial flowers, 166 Royal (1886–91).
References: NOCD 1877–79, 1881–91; *Bee*, Oct. 22, 1876; *D. City Item*, Jan. 31, 1892.

GERHARDT, KARL
Born Boston MA Jan 7, 1853; died near Shreveport LA May 7, 1940.
Sculptor, painter, art teacher, active N.O. ca. 1883–1916; also decorator, draftsman, engineer.
Studied: Ecole des Beaux Arts, Paris (ca. 1884); with Falguierie and Dubois, Paris.
Contemporary listings: sculptor (1906, 1910–11, 1915).
Exhibited: Salon, Paris (1884); ART ASSOCIATION OF NEW ORLEANS (1913, 1915–16).
Sculptor and painter who was mainly self–taught, with a brief period of study in Paris. During the 1880s he became well–known and executed busts and statues of many famous Americans, including one of Mark Twain. His obituary reported that he had come to N.O. in 1883 and taught art for 12 years, but he was first listed in 1904 as a machinist and continued through 1918 in various occupations, including that of manager and president of his own tailoring company. Gerhardt moved to Blanchard

LA ca. 1930 and kept a studio there where he painted occasionally.
References: NOCD 1904–1909, 1911–13, 1915–18; *Item*, May 8, 1940; *Appleton's CAB*; Art Asso., *Catalogue* (1913, 1916); Art Asso., *Special Exhibition*; Fielding, *Dictionary*; LSM, *Biennial Report for 1916–17*, 102; U.S. Census (1910), roll 521.

GERSON, BERTHA
Painter, active N.O. ca. 1915.
Exhibited: ART ASSOCIATION OF NEW ORLEANS (1915).
References: NOCD 1919; Art Asso., *Catalogue* (1915).

GERY, JULES E. (Julius)
Born N.O. ca. 1856; died San Antonio TX Dec. 7, 1931.
Engraver, active N.O. 1876–92.
Contemporary listings: with JOHN A. CAIRNS (1876); engraver (1877, 1879, 1891–92); engraver, with FREDERICK HOLYLAND (1878); engraver, 12 Exchange Pl. (1880, 1882–84); engraver, 25 Exchange Pl. (1881); engraver, 113 Canal (1885–90).
References: NOCD 1876–92; *T. Pic.*, Dec. 16, 1931.

GERY, LOUIS F.
Born France ca. 1830.
Engraver, active N.O. 1850–90; also printer, engineer, stencil cutter.
Contemporary listings: engraver (1850, 1873); engraver, 60 Customhouse (1854); engraver, Gravier near St. Charles (1856, 1858–60); engraver, St. Ann betw. Rampart and Burgundy (1857); general engraver, 70 Chartres (1858), engraver, Camp cor. Canal (1861); engraver on metals, 113 Customhouse, and engraver, 106 Customhouse (1865); engraver, 113 Customhouse (1866–67); engraver on metals, jewels, etc., 107 Customhouse (1867); engraver, 70 St. Charles (1869, 1871); general engraver, 70 St. Charles (1870); GERY & LAUTERBACH (1872–73); engraver, 3 St. Charles (1874); engraver, 18 Royal and Exchange Al. (1875); engraver, 25 Exchange Pl. (1876–86); engraver, 24 Exchange Al. (1880, 1882); engraver, 39 Bourbon (1887–90).

Probably the father of LOUIS W. GERY. Also engraved sheet music covers. References: NOCD 1849, 1851–54, 1856–61, 1866–90; NOBD 1865; *Bee*, Oct. 2, Dec. 18, 1875, Feb. 3, 1880, July 22, 1882; *D. Pic.*, Apr. 27, 1870; *D. True Delta*, Oct. 7, 1865; *Almanach de la Louisiane* (1867):209; Boyd, 158; Groce and Wallace; *Louisiana State Gazetteer*; Sheet Music Collection, THNOC; U.S. Census (1850), roll 235.

GERY, LOUIS W.
Born N.O. ca. 1862; died N.O. Feb. 17, 1929.
Engraver, active N.O. 1884–1928.
Contemporary listings: engraver, with LOUIS F. GERY (1882–83); engraver (1884, 1897); engraver, 19 Camp (1886); engraver, Frantz & Opitz (1888); engraver, 115½ Common (1889); engraver, with Alvin M. Hill (1890, 1893–96); engraver, 39 Bourbon (1891–92); engraver, 130 Exchange Pl. (1898); engraver, 133 Exchange Pl. (1899–1901); engraver, with Leonard Krower (1902–1904); engraver, with M. Scooler (1905–1907); engraver, 131 Camp (1908–1909); engraver, 600 Godchaux Bldg., 527 Canal (1910–14); engraver, Thomas Hausmann & Sons, Ltd. (1916–18).
Also listed as an engraver (1919–23, 1927), engraver with Hausmann Inc. (1928), and superintendant of Hausmann's engraving department (1929).
References: NOCD 1882–84, 1887–1914, 1916–30; *Eve. Chronicle*, Mar. 23, 1886; *T. Pic.*, Feb. 19–21, 1929, Jan. 1, 1930.

GERY & LAUTERBACH
Engravers, active N.O. 1872–73; also stencil cutters; LOUIS F. GERY, T. J. LAUTERBACH, partners.
Contemporary listings: engravers and stencil cutters, 3 St. Charles (1872–73).
References: NOCD 1872–73.

GHILONI, PIETRO
Born Italy ca. 1864; died after 1932.
Sculptor, active N.O. 1903–14; also decorator, marble worker.

Studied: Royal Academy, Florence, Italy.
Contemporary listings: sculptor (1904); sculptor, 532–534 Julia (1905–1906); sculptor, 415 Dauphine (1907); sculptor, Ghiloni & Menconi (1908–1909); sculptor, 1059 Camp (1909); sculptor, 1029 Camp (1910); sculptor, 521 Baronne (1911); sculptor, Schwartz–Eustis Co. Ltd. (1914).
Exhibited: 1059 Camp (1908).
Awarded: Exposition of London, England, 1st diploma of honor (1888); Universal Exposition, Paris, bronze medal (1889).
Ghiloni emigrated in 1892 to N.Y.C. where he was employed by artists and architects and given commissions for private decorative work. He was brought to N.O. in 1903 by the architect Robert Palestine to do decorative work in the newly constructed Commercial Hotel. In 1905 he advertised as a sculptor, but also listed interior and exterior architectural decoration, stone and wood carving, imitation stone, and scale models as a speciality. By 1909 Ghiloni had completed the City Park Pavilion, the facade of the N.O. Stock Exchange, and reliefs for the interior of the annex of the New Grunewald Hotel. In 1932 he lent a marble bust to an exhibition at the DELGADO MUSEUM OF ART.
References: NOCD 1905–14; *Architectural Art* 1(Nov. 1905): 15; *D. News*, Mar. 15, 1909; *T. Demo.*, July 31, 1904; Bénézit; Blanchard, 82; Delgado, *Catalogue*, 11, 52; Glenk, 95; U.S. Census (1910), roll 524.

GIBBS, GEORGE
Born N.O. Mar. 8, 1870; died Philadelphia PA Oct. 8, 1942.
Illustrator.
Studied: Corcoran School of Art, Washington DC; Art Students' League, Washington DC.
Author and illustrator of over 35 books, Gibbs spent his last 50 years in Philadelphia.
References: *T. Pic.*, Oct. 11, 1942; Bénézit; Fielding, *Dictionary*.

GIBBS, JANE J.
Born MS ca. 1884.
Art teacher, active N.O. 1910.
Contemporary listings: art teacher, public school (1910).
Possibly Jane Gibbs of Lafayette LA who exhibited at the ART ASSOCIATION OF NEW ORLEANS (1916).
References: Art Asso., *Catalogue* (1916); U.S. Census (1910), roll 524.

GIBBS, LOUISE
Born IL ca. 1858.
Artist, active N.O. 1880.
Contemporary listings: artist (1880).
References: U.S. Census (1880), roll 463.

GIBERT, MRS. LEON C.
Painter, active N.O. ca. 1892–1905.
Exhibited: ARTISTS' ASSOCIATION OF NEW ORLEANS (1892); Tulane University (1893).
Memberships/positions: ARTS EXHIBITION CLUB (1901); ART ASSOCIATION OF NEW ORLEANS (1905).
References: *Current Topics*, Jan. 1893, 11; *D. Pic.*, Feb. 14, 1893; *T. Demo.*, Dec. 13, 1892, Art Asso, *Catalogue* (1905).

GIBSON, DAVID
Cartoonist, commercial artist, active N.O. 1883–85.
Contemporary listings: artist (1884–85).
Cartoonist for *Mascot* (1883) and *Figaro* (1883–84), who signed most of his drawings "Fudge."
References: NOCD 1876–79, 1884–85, 1888; *Figaro*, Dec. 8, 1883, 3–4, 6–8, Dec. 14, 1883, 1, 6–7, Dec. 24, 1883, 1, Feb. 23, 1884, 1, Mar. 1, 1884, 1, Apr. 5–July 19, 1884 (masthead), Apr. 19, 1884, 12, Apr. 26, 1884, 1, May 3, 1884, 12, May 31, 1884, 6–7, June 21, 1884, 6–7; *Mascot*, Aug. 18, 1883, 409, 412, 414, Aug. 25, 1883, 417, 421, Sept. 8, 1883, 436, Sept. 15, 1883, 448, Sept. 22, 1883, 453.

GIBSON, FRED J.
Painter, active N.O. 1902–1907.
Contemporary listings: scenic artist, St. Charles Orpheum theater (1902); scenic artist, Elysium Theatre (1903–1904, 1907).

References: NOCD 1903, 1905; *D. Pic.*, Jan. 19, 1902; *D. States*, Feb. 14, Mar. 18, 1904; *Item*, Jan. 19, 1902, Dec. 7, 1903.

GIBSON, WILLIAM HAMILTON
Born Sandy Hook CT Oct. 5, 1850; died Washington DC 1896.
Illustrator, active N.O. 1886.
Studied: Polytechnic Institute, Brooklyn NY.
Exhibited: N.Y.C. (regularly after 1872); First American Watercolor Exhibition, London (1873); Edinburgh (1873).
Memberships/positions: New York Watercolor Club (1885); Art Union.
Working primarily in N.Y.C., Gibson illustrated and/or wrote articles and books, primarily on natural history. He came to N.O. in 1886 to draw illustrations for Charles Dudley Warner's articles "New Orleans" and "The Acadian Land" published in *Harper's New Monthly Magazine* (Jan.–Feb. 1887).
References: *D. Pic.*, Jan. 23, 1887; *Appleton's CAB*; Fielding, *Dictionary*; *Harper's Monthly*, Jan., Feb. 1887; THNOC 1960.65; Charles D. Warner, "Acadian Land," 334, 337, 339, 342, 346, 348; Charles D. Warner, "New Orleans," 196, 199, 206; WPA, *Louisiana*, 167; WPA, *New Orleans*, 104.

GIESEN, GERTRUDE AGUSTA
Born N.O. ca. 1866; died Shreveport LA Sept. 26, 1953.
Art craftsman, active N.O. ca. 1888–89.
Exhibited: TULANE DECORATIVE ART LEAGUE FOR WOMEN (1888); ART LEAGUE OF NEW ORLEANS (1889).
Memberships/positions: Tulane Decorative Art League for Women, treas. (1888); Art League of New Orleans (1889).
References: *D. Pic.*, Feb. 12, 1888, Mar. 10, 1889; *T. Pic.*, Sept. 29, 1953; Tulane Decorative Art League.

GIESEN, LOUISE. See WOODWARD, LOUISE GIESEN

GILBERT, _____
Illustrator, active N.O. ca. 1870–87.
Signed illustrations in the 1870 *Almanach de la Renaissance* and in several issues of *Le Diamant* (1887).

References: *Diamant,* June 26, 1887, 69, July 10, 1887, 72–73, July 24, 1887, 79, 81; *Almanach de la Renaissance,* 132, 144, 146.

GILES, ALFRED E.
Born London, England ca. 1864; died N.O. Nov. 11, 1898.
Lithographer, active N.O. 1892–98; also printer.
Contemporary listings: lithographer, KOECKERT & WALLE (1892); lithographer (1898).
References: NOCD 1892–94, 1898; *D. Pic.,* Nov. 13, 20, 1898.

GILLIN, THOMAS
Born N.O.; died N.O. Sept. 17, 1921.
Lithographer, active N.O. 1894–95; primarily stationer, printer.
Contemporary listings: AITKENS & GILLIN (1894); lithographer, 330 Camp (1895).
References: NOCD 1880, 1882–1905, 1907–20; *T. Pic.,* Sept. 18, 1921, Dec. 26, 1926.

GIORGI, A. FREDERICO
Born Italy.
Painter, sculptor, active N.O. ca. 1907–11; also carver.
Studied: with Pio Ioris, Academia Delle Belle Arti, Rome.
Contemporary listings: artist, 620 Canal (1909); portrait painter (1910); artist (1911).
Exhibited: ART ASSOCIATION OF NEW ORLEANS (1910).
In 1910 Giorgi painted murals in the newly opened dining room of the Monteleone Hotel. At the time, it was reported that he was primarily a portrait painter who had been in N.O. for three years after working in St. Louis MO and Pittsburgh PA.
References: NOCD 1909, 1911; *D. Pic.,* Jan. 9, 1910; Art Asso., *Catalogue* (1910); Glenk, 75; LSM, *Biennial Report for 1920–21,* 85; WPA, "Lives."

GIRARDIN, FRANK J.
Born Louisville KY Oct. 6, 1856.
Painter, active N.O. ca. 1913–14.
Studied: with Noble, Art Academy, Cincinnati OH.
Awarded: Cincinnati Art Club, 1st prize (1903).

Memberships/positions: Cincinnati Art Club; Richmond Group of Painters, IN.
References: Bénézit; Fielding, *Dictionary;* LSM, *Biennial Report for 1922–23,* 107.

GIRAULT, LOUIS C.
Painter, active N.O. 1870–92.
Contemporary listings: artist (1870, 1890–92).
Exhibited: LILIENTHAL's (1883); ARTISTS' ASSOCIATION OF NEW ORLEANS (1886–87, 1889, 1892).
Memberships/positions: Artists' Association of New Orleans (1886, 1890).
Also listed as a cigar and tobacco merchant (1870–72, 1887–88) and as a cooper (1874–84). He painted landscapes of local scenery in oil, watercolor, and gouache and was an admirer of RICHARD CLAGUE.
References: NOCD 1870–72, 1874–93; *Art and Letters,* 1(Dec. 1887):228; *Current Topics,* Jan. 1893, 11; *D. Pic.,* Nov. 6, 1886, Dec. 29, 1887, Dec. 17, 1889, Nov. 13, 1890, Dec. 13, 1892; *D. States,* Nov. 5, 1886; *T. Demo.,* July 30, 1883, Dec. 13, 1892; AANO, *Catalogue* (1886); Lilienthal's, 5, 8; Trovaioli and Toledano, 62.

GIROUST, MRS. _____
Art teacher, art craftsman, active N.O. 1812.
Contemporary listings: teacher of embroidery and maker of paper flowers (1812).
References: *Courier,* Sept. 25, 1812.

GIROUX, CHARLES
Born France ca. 1828.
Painter, active N.O. 1868–85.
Contemporary listings: artist (1880); painter (1882–83).
Exhibited: Blessing's gallery (1883, 1885); LILIENTHAL's (1883–84).
Memberships/positions: SOUTHERN ART UNION (1880–81); ARTISTS' ASSOCIATION OF NEW ORLEANS (1885).
Primarily a landscape painter, whose subject was often Bayou Teche; also a genre painter. Many of his paintings are known to bear the signature of his friend and student, BLANCHE BLANCHARD. He may have been an

amateur artist; possibly C. Giroux, a cotton broker who was listed in the NOCD 1871–81.
References: NOCD 1871–73, 1875, 1878, 1880–83; *D. Pic.*, Oct. 25, 1885; *D. States*, Apr. 13, 1884; *Demo.*, May 27, 1880, May 12, 1881; *T. Demo.*, July 17, 30, 1883; Anglo–American Art Museum, *Louisiana Landscape*, item 17; Information courtesy George E. Jordan; Lilienthal's, 5, 7–8; Norton Art Gallery, 20–22; U.S. Census (1880), roll 459; Wiesendanger, 54–55.

GIROUX, CLAUDIUS
Sketch artist, active N.O. 1843.
Signed the pictorial lithographed covers of two pieces of sheet music; one is dated "N.O. 1843."
References: "Bateliere," "Reverie," "La Willis," Sheet Music Collection, LA Coll., TU; Trovaioli and Toledano, 58, 60.

GISSLER, FRANÇOIS XAVIER
Artist, active N.O. 1858–66; also watchmaker.
Contemporary listings: artist, 157 Main (1858); artist, 175 Main (1859); artist, 59 Claiborne (1860–61, 1866).
References: NOCD 1854, 1858–61, 1866, 1870–71, 1875–79, 1881; Groce and Wallace.

GLANZ, JULIUS
Art teacher, active N.O. 1860.
Contemporary listings: teacher of drawing and painting, Jefferson School (1860).
References: *Carrollton Sun*, Sept. 22, 1860.

GLENAT, LUCILE A.
Born IL ca. 1876.
Painter, art teacher, active N.O. 1909–12.
Contemporary listings: china painter, 151 Baronne (1909); artist–teacher (1910); art studio, 931 Canal (1910–11); artist, 931 Canal (1912).
References: NOCD 1909–12; U. S. Census (1910), roll 525.

CLENN, MISS G. S.
Art craftsman, active N.O. ca. 1888.
Exhibited: TULANE DECORATIVE ART LEAGUE FOR WOMEN (1888).

Memberships/positions: Tulane Decorative Art League for Women (1888).
Possibly Georgie S. Glenn, died N.Y.C. Nov. 19, 1905.
References: *D. Pic.*, Feb. 12, 1888, Nov. 22, 26, 1905; *T. Demo.*, Nov. 22, 26, 1905; Tulane Decorative Art League.

GLITCHMAN, A.
Lithographer, active N.O. 1849–50.
Contemporary listings: lithographer, Derbigny betw. Bienville and Customhouse (1849–50).
References: NOCD 1849–50; Groce and Wallace.

GLUCKSMAN, TOURO
Born N.O. May 22, 1884.
Lithographer, active N.O. 1905.
Contemporary listings: lithographer (1905).
Also listed as an electrician and as a projectionist.
References: NOCD 1900–1905, 1907–1908, 1910–22, 1924–25, 1927–33, 1935, 1938, 1940, 1942; Orleans Parish Registrar of Voters, NOPL.

GLUNG, HEINRICH
Lithographer, active N.O. 1874.
Contemporary listings: lithographer (1874).
References: NOCD 1874.

GOATER, JOHN H.
Engraver, commercial artist, active N.O. 1854–56.
Contemporary listings: artist and engraver (1854); designer and engraver, 105 Poydras (1855).
Worked in N.Y.C. (1851) and in Brooklyn NY after N.O. During the 1850s and 1860s, Goater worked for *Vanity Fair*.
References: NOCD 1855–56; *State Repub.*, Jan. 20, Feb. 7, 1855; *D. Delta*, Dec. 17, 1854, Jan. 28, 1855; Fielding, *Dictionary*; Groce and Wallace; Museum of Fine Arts, 1:171.

GODEFROID, MR. F. (Godefroy)
Born France.
Painter, art teacher, active N.O. 1807–20.
Studied: with Jacques–Louis David, Paris.

Contemporary listings: historical, portrait, animal, landscape, fresco, watercolor, and pastel painter, teacher of drawing, 13 Dauphine (1807); painter, Dauphine (1809).
Executed the standard of colors for the fifth anniversary of the Battle of N.O. (1820).
References: NOCD 1809; NOBD 1807; *Courier*, May 30, 1808, Jan. 10, 1820; *Moniteur*, Apr. 4, Oct. 24, 1807; Fielding, *Dictionary*; Glenk, 46, 61, 75, 240; Groce and Wallace.

GODEFROY, LOUIS
Born Port Louis Island, Guadaloupe ca. 1792; died N.O. Mar. 30, 1841.
Painter, active N.O. 1824–32.
Contemporary listings: painter, 139 Tchoupitoulas (1824); painter, 69 Tchoupitoulas (1827); painter, 31 Poydras (1827, 1830, 1832).
References: NOCD 1824, 1827, 1830, 1832, 1841; *Bee*, Mar. 31, 1841; Fielding, *Dictionary*; LSM, *Biennial Report for 1920–21*, 34; N.O. Death Certificate (1841), 8:720, NOPL; U.S. Census (1840), roll 132.

GODFROI, JEAN BAPTISTE (Godfrey)
Painter, active N.O. ca. 1862–69; black.
References: *Bee*, Nov. 30, 1869; *Repub.*, July 7, 1869.

GOESLING, ALPHONSE
Born LA Dec. 1879.
Lithographer, active N.O. 1899–1901.
Contemporary listings: lithographer (1899–1901).
References: NOCD 1899–1901; U.S. Census (1900), roll 574.

GOLDBERGER, JACOB
Lithographer, active N.O. 1897.
Contemporary listings: lithographer (1897).
References: NOCD 1897.

GOLDSBOROUGH, ANNA FARRAR
Died Newark NY Dec. 10, 1970.
Cartoonist, painter, active N.O. 1915–20s.
Exhibited: ART ASSOCIATION OF NEW ORLEANS (1915).
During the 1920s, cartoonist for the *Times–Picayune* who signed herself "Doree."

References: *T. Pic.*, Feb. 2, 1971; Art Asso., *Catalogue* (1915).

GOLDTHWAITE, FRANK JOSEPH
Born N.O. ca. 1887–88; died N.O. Jan. 7, 1929.
Lithographer, engraver, commercial artist, active N.O. 1907–28; also printer.
Contemporary listings: lithographer (1907); artist–painter (1910); lithographer, WALLE & CO. LTD. (1912); engraver, Walle & Co. Ltd. (1913–15); artist, Walle & Co. Ltd. (1916); designer (1917); Walle & Co. Ltd. (1918).
Continued to be listed with Walle & Co. as lithographer (1920–21, 1927–28) and as artist (1922–25).
References: NOCD 1907–25, 1927–28; *T. Pic.*, Jan. 8, 1929; U.S. Census (1910), roll 521.

GOMER, JOHN R.
Painter, active N.O. 1859–61.
Contemporary listings: portrait painter, 116 Royal (1859–61).
References: NOCD 1859–61; Groce and Wallace.

GOMEZ, JOSEPH
Painter, active N.O. ca. 1870.
Awarded: Grand State Fair, honorable mention for best painting in watercolors (1870).
References: Mechanics' and Agricultural Fair Asso., *Report* (1870):39.

GOODWANE, MRS. WILLIAM
Art teacher, active N.O. 1842.
Contemporary listings: teacher of drawing, painting, mezzotint and perspective, 40 Camp (1842).
References: *D. Pic.*, Jan. 30–Feb. 2, 1842 (advs.), Feb. 13, 1842; Groce and Wallace.

GORDILLO, FRANCISCA DE SALAZAR. *See* SALAZAR Y MAGAÑA, FRANCISCA DE

GORDON, GEORGE HUME
Born Edinburgh, Scotland ca. 1815; died N.O. Sept. 26, 1887.
Art teacher, active N.O. 1849–87.
Contemporary listings: teacher, 69 Elmire (1849–53); teacher of drawing, Public School for Young Ladies (1850); teacher of drawing, Public Schools (1854); teacher (1857–61, 1880–87); professor (1866–69); principal (1871–79).

References: NOCD 1849–53, 1857–61, 1866–87; *Courier*, Jan. 29, 1854; *D. Orleanian*, May 15–18, 1850 (advs.); *D.Pic.*, Sept. 27, 1887; N.O. Death Certificate (1887), 91:1034, NOPL; U.S. Census (1850), roll 238.

GORMAN, THOMAS F.
Artist, active N.O. 1898.
Contemporary listings: artist (1898). Primarily listed as a clerk.
References: NOCD 1890–92, 1894–98, 1900, 1902 1905, 1907–1908, 1910–15.

GOTTHEIL, EDWARD
Born Prussia ca. 1813; died N.O. Dec. 5, 1877.
Artist, active N.O. 1849; primarily architect.
Contemporary listings: artist, cor. Nayades and Felicity (1849).
Came to N.O. ca. 1847 and became an architect, a civil engineer, and an accomplished linguist. Gottheil was appointed by LA Gov. James Madison Wells as Chief Commissioner and General Agent of the State of LA to the Paris Exposition (1868).
References: NOCD 1849–56, 1858, 1861; *D. Pic.*, Oct. 2, Dec. 15, 1866, Dec. 6, 1877; *Times*, Sept. 13, 1866; Gottheil; Groce and Wallace; U.S. Census (1860), roll 419.

GOULD, THEODORE A.
Painter, active N.O. 1847–49.
Contemporary listings: painter (1847); portrait artist, cor. Baronne and Julia (1848); portrait artist, 244 Camp (1848); artist (1849).
Exhibited: Maguire's Daguerrean rooms (1847); Robert Hall's store (1849).
References: *Comm. Times*, June 15, Aug. 4, 1847, Aug. 30, 1848; *D. Crescent*, Apr. 1, May 4, 13, 18, June 24, July 14, 26, 1848; *D. Delta*, Feb. 17, July 26, 1848; *D. Pic.*, Dec. 12, 1849; Downs, 388; Glenk, 75; Groce and Wallace.

GOUTO, A.
Commercial artist, active N.O. ca. 1893–1903.
Contemporary listings: artist, with WILLIAM WATSON WASHBURN (ca. 1893–1903).
References: *T. Demo.*, Aug. 20, 1903,

GOUTTMANN, M. H.
Born Russia.
Painter, active N.O. 1905.
Studied: Russia; Ecole des Beaux Arts, Paris.
Contemporary listings: portrait painter (1905).
Portrait painter who had previously worked in Munich. In Apr. 1905 he had recently arrived in N.O., declaring his intention to become a U.S. citizen and to make N.O. his permanent home.
References: *T. Demo.*, Apr. 30, 1905.

GOUYT, THEODORE
Artist, active N.O. 1841–42.
Contemporary listings: artist, St. Ann near Robertson (1841–42).
References: NOCD 1841–42; Groce and Wallace.

GRABAU, HENRY
Born Prussia?
Commercial artist, engraver, active N.O. 1887–1902; primarily draughtsman.
Contemporary listings: artist, with J. F. Braun (1887); artist (1888); crayon portraits, patent drawings, photo engravings, 174 Clio (1889); artist, 14 Exchange Pl. (1890–91); artist, 105 Exchange Al. (1895–99); artist, 144 Carondelet (1900–1902).
Exhibited: American Exposition (1885–86); WILLIAM J. WARRINGTON's studio (1887).
References: NOCD 1882, 1885–1902; *D. States*, Oct. 12, 1887; *T. Demo.*, Oct. 18, 1887, June 1, 1890; Creole Exhibit, 16; THNOC 1950.61.35.

GRABER, EDWARD
Engraver, active N.O. 1882–83.
Contemporary listings: engraver (1882–83).
References: NOCD 1882–83.

GRAEF, JACOB
Born Bavaria ca. 1837.
Hair worker, active N.O. 1859–60.
Contemporary listings: hair work, Bourbon near Orleans (1859); hair work, 153 Bourbon (1860).
References: NOCD 1859–60; U.S. Census (1860), roll 418.

GRAFTON, ROBERT WADSWORTH
Born Chicago IL 1876; died Michigan City IN 1936.

Painter, active N.O. 1916–20. Studied: Art Institute, Chicago (1895–99); Académie Julian, Paris (1899); England; Holland. Contemporary listings: mural painter, St. Charles Hotel (1917); artist, 536 Dumaine (1920–21). Exhibited: Art Institute, Chicago (ca. 1907); Salon, Paris; Indiana Art Association, Fort Wayne (1908); ART ASSOCIATION OF NEW ORLEANS (1914, 1916–17); Thurber Art Galleries, Chicago (1917–18); Brooks Memorial Museum, Memphis TN. Awarded: Art Association of Richmond IN, Mary T. R. Foulke prize (1910); Hoosier Salon, Chicago, Leroy Goddard prize. Memberships/positions: Chicago Society of Artists, pres.; Palette and Chisel Club; Chicago Arts Club; Chicago Artists' Guild.

Landscape, genre, and portrait painter active mainly in Michigan City IN (ca. 1908–36) who visited N.O. during several winters. He was one of the organizers of the first art classes in the French Quarter (ca. 1919), the precursor of the Arts and Crafts Club. Grafton first exhibited in the city at the Art Association (1914), but probably did not come to N.O. until Jan. 1916. During that year he painted scenes of N.O. with his friend, LOUIS OSCAR GRIFFIN, and both received acclaim for two murals in the St. Charles Hotel (1917). His views of the city made up a one–man show in Chicago (1917–18) and were exhibited at and published by the St. Charles Hotel (1928). References: NOCD 1920; *American*, Sept. 27, 1916; *Item*, Feb. 16, 1921; *T. Pic.*, Feb. 18, 1917; AANO, *Catalogue* (1919); Art Asso., *Catalogue* (1914, 1916, 1917); Bénézit; Fielding, *Dictionary*; Friends of the Cabildo, *N.O. Architecture*, 3:67; Glenk, 69; Cathy Harvey, 68; LSM, *Biennial Report 1922–23*, 107; LSM, *Biennial Report for 1924–25*, 49; St. Charles Hotel, *New Orleans*; Thurber Art Galleries; Wiesendanger, 56; WPA, *New Orleans*, 108.

GRAHAM, CHARLES
Born Rock Island IL 1852; died N.Y.C. Aug. 9, 1911.
Sketch artist, illustrator, active N.O. ca. 1884; 1886.
Illustrator who was an itinerant artist for N.Y.C. publishers Harper & Brothers (ca. 1876–92). Graham's favorite subject was city views, and his drawings appeared in almost every issue of *Harper's Weekly* from 1880 to 1892. He was sent to N.O., probably in the fall of 1884, with JOHN DURKIN, and made the sketch (published Dec. 13, 1884) for his view of the city during the World's Industrial and Cotton Centennial Exposition. Graham returned to N.O. (1886) with two artist assistants, Durkin and Horace Bradley, on a tour of the southern states with other *Harper's* representatives. The trio arrived in N.O. by train from Mobile AL on Nov. 28, 1886, and were met and entertained during their stay by a committee of the city's prominent citizens. On Dec. 1, the artists sketched around the city. They were scheduled to leave N.O. on Dec. 2 by train and stop in Baton Rouge to sketch the Morganza levee under construction. Graham became a freelance illustrator after leaving *Harper's* and after 1900 worked in oil painting.
References: *D. Pic.*, Nov. 29, 1886; *Harper's Wkly.*, Sept. 15, 1888; Kelly, 8, 41, 103; McCracken, *Portrait*; Taft, 178; THNOC 1959.200.

GRAHAM, L. L.
Painter, active N.O. 1874–77.
Contemporary listings: scenic artist, Academy of Music (1874–77).
References: NOCD 1876–77; *Times*, Sept. 6, 1874, Dec. 22, 1875.

GRAHAM, LEWIS
Born St. Louis MO ca. 1821; died N.O. Dec. 24, 1905.
Lithographer, active N.O. ca. 1870–1903; primarily printer, publisher, bookbinder.
Graham's first listing was with the Crescent Job Office (1852–54). By 1855 he started his own printing company, which was the first of a

succession of firms bearing his name through 1924: L. Graham, 37 Gravier (1855–56, 1859–61), 76 Camp (1858), Planters Hotel (1866), 90 Camp (1866–68); L. Graham & Co., 73 Camp (1869–77); Lewis Graham, 73 Camp (1878–79); L. Graham & Son, 127 Gravier (1880–84), 99–103 Gravier (1885–93); L. Graham & Son Ltd., 44–46 Baronne (1893–94), 207–11 Baronne (1895–1902); L. Graham Co. Ltd., 715 Perdido (1903–1907), 430–32 Common (1908–20), 515 Magazine (1921–24). The firms were primarily job printers for stationery, letterheads, books (*Graham's Crescent City Directory for 1867*), pamphlets, and programs; and sometimes listed lithography among their work (ca. 1870, 1897–98, 1902–1903). By 1894 they claimed to be the largest printery and bindery in the South. His son, Lewis Spence Graham (born N.O. ca. 1857; died N.O. Sept. 12, 1908) was listed with his father's companies as printer (1875–78), bookkeeper (1879–80), and partner (1880–99).
References: NOCD 1852–61, 1866–1912, 1914–24; *D. Crescent*, Jan. 8, 1866; *D. Pic.*, Jan. 7, 1866; *Repub.*, Mar. 17, 1872; *Times*, Sept. 2, 1866; *French Opera*; N.O. Death Certificates (1905), 137:32, (1908), 143:988, NOPL; THNOC 58–90–L, 76–29–L.

GRAHAM & BOONE
Engravers, active N.O. 1877; Henry W. Graham, ISAAC WILLIAM BOONE, partners.
Contemporary listings: engravers, 176 Gravier (1877).
References: NOCD 1877.

GRAND, THOMAS
Sculptor, active N.O. 1818.
Contemporary listings: sculptor in marble, stone, and wood, Maine betw. Burgundy and Dauphine (1818).
References: *Gazette*, July 3, 6, 1818; Groce and Wallace.

GRANER, LUIS
Born Barcelona, Spain 1867; died 1929.

Painter, active N.O. ca. 1914–22.
Studied: Barcelona; Rome.
Contemporary listings: artist (1917).
Exhibited: Salon, Paris (ca. 1895–1910); DELGADO MUSEUM OF ART (1917); Copley Gallery, Boston (1917).
Awarded: Barcelona, Madrid, Berlin, Paris, medals.
Memberships/positions: Societé Nationale des Beaux Arts, France (1904).
Internationally known portrait, genre, and landscape painter who came to the U.S. in 1910. Graner worked in NY, CA, and in South America, but gained a reputation after 1914 for his scenes of rural LA and N.O. where he lived for several winters.
References: NOCD 1917; *T. Pic.*, Apr. 18, 1915, Feb. 25, 1917, Mar. 4, 1925; Cline, *Art and Artists*, 10; Copley Gallery; Edwin Davis, *Story of Louisiana*, 1:314; Delgado, *Bulletin*, 1(Dec. 1927):4; Delgado, *Catalogue of Paintings, Sculpture*, 19; Fielding, *Dictionary*; Freeman, 7–9; Glenk, 70; Kendall, *History*, 2:662; LSM, *Biennial Report for 1920–21*, 39; LSM, *Biennial Report for 1922–23*, 29; LSM *Biennial Report for 1928–29*, 34; Seebold, 1:316; WPA, *Louisiana*, 168.

GRANER, ROSA RAINOLD (Mrs. Leonard S. Murray)
Born 1904; died N.O. Aug. 16, 1962.
Art craftsman, sculptor, art teacher, active N.O. 1917–61.
Studied: NEWCOMB COLLEGE (1917 26).
Listed as a Newcomb arts craftsman specializing in pottery design (1917–29), Graner became a prominent local sculptor who was noted for her portrait busts, garden sculptures, and commissions for public buildings. She frequently exhibited with the Arts and Crafts Club (1920s–40s), where she also studied, taught, and won prizes (1928–29, 1945) for her crafts and sculpture.
References: NOCD 1924, 1928, 1931–32, 1935, 1940, 1942, 1945–47, 1949, 1952–53; *Item*, Oct. 30,

1945, July 22, 1948; *Item–Trib.*, Dec. 9, 1928, Feb. 7, 1937; *Morn. Trib.*, Dec. 18, 1928; *States*, Oct. 22, 1941, Nov. 14, 1943, Jan. 27, Sept. 24, 1948, July 7, 1954, Jan. 4, 1955; *States–Item*, Aug. 16, 1962; *T. Pic.*, Sept. 30, 1928, May 12, 1929, Apr. 3, 1930, May 24, 1935, Feb. 7, 14, Oct. 3, 1937, May 12, 1940, Oct. 23, 1941, Jan. 24, Nov. 14, 1943, May 4, 1945, Dec. 2, 1949, Aug. 18, 1954, Jan. 9, 1955; Collier, "The World of Art," *T. Pic.*, Mar. 13, 1955; Collier, "The World of Art: Newcomb to Feature Two Artists," *T. Pic.*, Nov. 4, 1956; Collier, "The World of Art," *T. Pic.*, Nov. 11, 1956; Collier, "The World of Art: Revival in Portraiture Noted," *T. Pic.*, Aug. 3, 1958; *T. Pic.*, Nov. 7, 1961, Aug. 17, 18, 1962; Poesch, *Newcomb Pottery*, 99.

GRANGER, JOHN H.
Born NY ca. 1846.
Engraver, commercial artist, active N.O. 1910–15.
Contemporary listings: engraver (1910, 1914–15); artist (1912).
References: NOCD 1910–15; U.S. Census (1910), roll 520.

GRANT, S. DIAMOND
Born TX ca. 1885.
Artist, active N.O. 1910.
Contemporary listings: artist (1910).
References: U.S. Census (1910), roll 519.

GRANZIN, ALBERT BISMARCK
Born N.O. Aug. 1866; died N.O. Feb. 29, 1932.
Engraver, active N.O. 1886–1929; also jeweler, watchmaker.
Contemporary listings: engraver, A. B. Griswold & Co. (1886–88, 1901, 1903–1904); engraver, with B. Kaufman (1898); engraver (1899–1900, 1911); engraver, with A. M. Hill (1905–1907); engraver, White Bros. (1912–16, 1919).
References: NOCD 1886–1909, 1911–32; *T. Pic.*, Mar. 1, 1932, Dec. 29, 1949; U.S. Census (1900), roll 570.

GRAVIER, _____
Artist, active N.O. 1870.
Contemporary listings: artist (1870).
References: NOCD 1870.

GRAY, CHARLES
Painter, active N.O. 1885.
Itinerant painter and musician who came to N.O. to show his paintings of LA scenes at a bookstore on Canal (1885).
References: *Eve. Chronicle*, Nov. 3, 1885.

GRAY, JOHN S.
Painter, active N.O. 1902.
Contemporary listings: portrait artist, Anchor Supply Co. (1902).
References: NOCD 1902.

GRAY, LEONIDAS W. P.
Born N.O. Sept. 1837; died N.O. Oct. 28, 1898.
Engraver, active N.O. 1898.
Contemporary listings: engraver, 130 Exchange (1898).
References: NOCD 1891, 1893–97, 1899; NOBD 1898; *D. Pic.*, Oct. 29, 1898.

GRAYSON, ROB.
Born LA Feb. 5, 1872.
Artist, active N.O. 1900.
Contemporary listings: artist (1900).
References: U.S. Census (1900), roll 570.

GREBNER, MAXIMILIAN
Art teacher, active N.O. 1873.
Contemporary listings: drawing academy, 112 St. Charles (1873).
References: NOCD 1873.

GREEN, R. H.
Engraver, active N.O. 1873.
Contemporary listings: engraver, with JOHN DOUGLAS (1873).
References: NOCD 1873.

GREEN, ROBERT S.
Lithographer, active N.O. 1867; also printer.
Contemporary listings: lithographer, 10 Camp (1867).
References: NOCD 1857, 1859–61, 1867–73, 1876–95, 1897, 1899.

GREEN & FISHBOURNE
Lithographers, active N.O. 1840; WILLIAM GREENE, R. W. FISHBOURNE, proprietors.
Contemporary listings: lithographers, 53 Magazine (1840).
Previously listed in N.Y.C. (1836) as "Greene & Pishbourne," the N.O. firm was noted for lithographic work with the detail of copperplate en-

graving, and specialized in the quick–printing of bills, notices, labels, and cards. The company operated only from Mar. until Nov. 1840 when Greene's interests were purchased by Fishbourne. In the firm's listings, Greene's name consistently appeared as "Green." References: NOCD 1842; *D. Pic.*, Mar. 14, 1840–Jan. 2, 1841 (advs.), Sept. 10, 1840; Groce and Wallace.

GREEND, ODBERT V.
Lithographer, commercial artist, active N.O. 1888–90.
Contemporary listings: STANDARD MUSIC AND PHOTO-LITHO COMPANY (1886–87); WEHRMANN & CO. (1887); artist (1888); lithographer (1889–90).
References: NOCD 1887–90; *T. Demo.*, Nov. 11, 1887.

GREENE, WILLIAM
Lithographer, active N.O. 1838–42.
Contemporary listings: lithographer, 53 Magazine (1838); lithographer, ORLEANS LITHOGRAPHIC OFFICE (1838–39); lithographer, CREEN & FISHBOURNE (1840–41).
Probably the itinerant lithographer who was active in N.Y.C. (1836–37, 1848), Albany NY (1843–45), and Hartford CT (1849–52). Greene advertised in N.O., in July 1838, that his office printed maps, drawings, circulars, cards, labels, and bank notes. With R. W. FISHBOURNE, he lithographed views of public buildings in N.O. that were published in the NOCD 1838. The next year he announced that his work was equal to copperplate engraving at half the cost. Greene was probably the partner in the Hartford lithographic firm of Case and Green, which issued a copy (ca. 1849–52) of the engraving of the Battle of N.O. after JEAN HYACINTHE LACLOTTE.
References: NOCD 1838, 1841–43; *True Amer.*, Nov. 5, 1839; *D. Pic.*, Dec. 18, 1839, Sept. 10, Nov. 11, 1840; Dufour, *Battle of New Orleans*, 2; Friends of the Cabildo, *250 Years*, 59; Groce and Wallace; LSM, *Biennial Report for 1928–29*, 37.

GREGORY, HENRY S.
Born AL ca. 1857.
Commercial artist, active N.O. 1878; primarily printer.
Contemporary listings: artist (1878).
Son of JOHN H. GREGORY.
References: NOCD 1875, 1878–81, 1883–84; U.S. Census (1870), roll 519.

GREGORY, JOHN H.
Born GA ca. 1829.
Commercial artist, active N.O. 1871–74; primarily printer.
Contemporary listings: artist (1871, 1874).
Father of HENRY S. GREGORY.
References: NOCD 1870–78; U.S. Census (1870), roll 519.

GREGORY, SELINA BRES. *See* BRES, SELINA ELIZABETH

GRELLE, HENRY G.
Born LA ca. 1878; died ca. 1946.
Commercial artist, active N.O. 1893–1938; also draftsman.
Contemporary listings: artist (1893, 1903–1904, 1906); ROMANSKI & Grelle, proprietors, SOUTHERN BUREAU OF ENGRAVING (1895), artist, *Daily Picayune* (1896); artist, *Daily Item* (1897–1900); ART DESIGNING & ENGRAVING CO. (1898); artist, PHOTO-ENGRAVING CO. (1899, 1901); artist, with JACOB JULIUS LIPS (1902); GRELLE-EGERTON ENGRAVING CO. (1907–32).
Signed the cover and masthead of the *Jolly Joker* (1899, 1900) and the cover of the *Pioneer* (1908). Grelle continued with Grelle-Egerton (through 1932) and as a commercial artist (1935, 1938).
References: NOCD 1893–1933, 1935, 1938, 1940, 1942, 1945–46; *D. Pic.*, Aug. 17–18, 1895; *Jolly Joker*, Apr. 1, 1899, cover, Jan. 27, 1900, cover; *Men and Matters*, June 1898, (adv.); *Pioneer*, July 15, 1908, cover; *Picayune's Guide* (1897), 33, 50, 107; U.S. Census (1910), roll 520.

GRELLE-EGERTON ENGRAVING CO.
Engravers, active N.O. 1907–1932; W. C. Tebault, pres. (1907); HENRY G. GRELLE, secy. and mgr. (1907), mgr. (1908–1909), pres. and mgr.

(1910–32); WALTER W. EGERTON, V. pres. (1908–1909), secy. (1910–32). Contemporary listings: 105 Decatur (1907); 210 Camp (1908–11); 604 Canal (1912); 316 St. Charles (1913–18).
The firm did the photoengraving work for the *Item* and the *States*.
References: NOCD 1907–32; *States–Item*, Apr. 13, 1961.

GRENIER, FRANK F.
Born MI ca. 1863.
Colorer, active N.O. 1910.
Contemporary listings: artist (colorer and stainer) (1910).
References: U.S. Census (1910), roll 520.

GRIFFIN, ISAAC
Painter, active N.O. ca. 1864.
Awarded: American Arts Association, prize (1864).
References: *Grand Celebration*, 31.

GRIFFITH, LOUIS OSCAR
Born Greencastle IN Oct. 10, 1875; died 1956.
Etcher, painter, active N.O. 1916–17.
Studied: with Frank Reaugh, Dallas TX; St. Louis Academy of Fine Arts; Chicago Art Institute; National Academy of Design, N.Y.C.
Exhibited: ART ASSOCIATION OF NEW ORLEANS (1916–17).
Awarded: Pan–American Exposition, Buffalo NY, gold medal; Panama–Pacific International Exposition, San Francisco, bronze medal for etching.
Memberships/positions: Salon, Paris; Chicago Galleries Association; Boston Artists Guild; Chicago Society of Painters and Sculptors; Chicago Society of Etchers, founder.
With ROBERT WADSWORTH GRAFTON, painted murals for the St. Charles Hotel (1917). Griffith's etching "The Old Morphy House" (N.O.) was selected by the American Federation of Arts to be included in the Second International Exhibition of Modern Engravings, Florence, Italy (1927).
References: *American*, Sept. 27, 1916; *T. Pic.*, Feb. 18, 1917; Art Asso., *Catalogue* (1916, 1917); Bénézit; Fielding, *Dictionary*; Fisk, 97–100; St. Charles Hotel, *New Orleans*.

GRIMALDI, JOHN B.
Born N.O. ca. 1894; died Sulphur LA July 2, 1950.
Engraver, active N.O. 1909–16.
Contemporary listings: engraver, 130 Exchange Pl. (1909); engraver (1910); engraver, with C. E. Adler (1911–15); engraver, T. Hausmann & Sons (1916).
References: NOCD 1909–16; *T. Pic.*, July 4–5, 1950; U.S. Census (1910), roll 521.

GRISAFFI, JOSEPH
Artist, active N.O. 1892.
Contemporary listings: artist (1892).
References: NOCD 1892.

GROSZ, LOUIS ANTHONY
Born N.O. ca. 1883; died N.O. Mar. 29, 1948.
Sketch artist, active N.O. 1905; primarily draughtsman, architect.
Submitted a design in a T–Square Club emblem competition (1905). Partner in the N.O. architectural firm of Rosenthal and Grosz (ca. 1916–40).
References: NOCD 1899–1901, 1903–1906, 1912–13, 1915–18, 1920; *Architectural Art*, 1(1905):14.

GROVES, HIRAM
Lithographer, active N.O. 1836–38.
Contemporary listings: H. Groves & Co., ORLEANS LITHOGRAPHIC OFFICE (1836); lithographer, 112 Chartres (1838).
References: NOCD 1838, 1842; *Bee*, Dec. 30, 1836; Groce and Wallace.

GRUNEBOROUGH, MISS H.
Hair worker, active N.O. ca. 1868.
Awarded: Grand State Fair, certificate for best specimen of hair work for jewelry (1868).
References: Mechanics' and Agricultural Fair Asso., *Report* (1868):47.

GSCHWINDT, ROBERT
Born Hungary?
Painter, art dealer, restorer, art teacher, active N.O. 1854–67; also photographer.
Studied: Academy of Arts, Vienna; Academy of Rome; with Thomas Couture, Paris.
Contemporary listings: portrait painter, 87 Chartres (1854–55); portrait painter, 50 Chartres (1856);

portrait painter, 132 Canal (1856–58); school of painting, 132 Canal (1857); gallery of oil paintings, 3 Carondelet (1859); portrait painter, 82 Camp (1859–61); portrait painter, 126 Customhouse (1866); artist's studio, 126 Customhouse (1867); portrait painter, 113 Canal (1867).
Exhibited: LAURENT UTER's store (1854–55); Todd's carpet store (1856); A. E. Blackmar's music store (1866–67); Salon, Paris (before 1854, 1879–80).
Awarded: Grand State Fair, diploma for best head in oil (1866).
Memberships/positions: Union of German Artists; Imperial Academy, St. Petersburg, Russia (1862).
Portrait painter who spent several winters in N.O. and was noted for the delicate touch and color he gave to portraits of women. Gschwindt first advertised in N.O. (Dec. 1854–Feb. 1855) as a portrait painter who could copy old paintings, restore faded ones, and reproduce portraits from daguerreotypes. He had arrived with a collection of paintings he brought from Rome and Paris and opened his gallery/studio for their exhibition and sale. Each spring between 1856 and 1859, Gschwindt would travel north through the U.S. or go to Europe and return to N.O. in the winter to paint portraits and sell the paintings and engravings he had acquired during his travels. After leaving N.O. in the spring of 1859, Gschwindt spent the Civil War years in St. Petersburg and Moscow, painting portraits of the Russian court, and in Paris. He returned to N.O. by Nov. 1866 for the state fair and opened a gallery of original paintings by old and modern masters he had collected in Europe. It was considered the rarest collection of paintings ever offered for sale in N.O. and was reported to include original works by such European masters as Van Dyke, Tintoretto, Poussin, Rosa, and Jourdan. It was eventually auctioned in Mar. 1867 when Gschwindt was preparing to leave N.O., apparently for the last time. He returned to Europe and later exhibited genre paintings in the Paris salons.
References: NOCD 1858–61, 1867–68; NOBD 1857–58; *Bee*, Dec. 29, 1854, Dec. 29, 1854–Feb. 5, 1855 (advs.); Feb. 5, 1855, Jan. 7, Feb. 22, Mar. 11, 1856, Nov. 15, 1856, Nov. 23–Dec. 8, 1857 (advs.); *D. Crescent*, Feb. 6, 1856, Dec. 5, 1857, Mar. 21, 1859; *D. Delta*, Jan. 6, Feb. 7, 1855, Dec. 14, 1856, Feb. 15, 1857; *D. Orleanian*, Dec. 31, 1854; *D. Pic.*, Nov. 18. 1856, Dec. 5, 1866; *Times*, Dec. 5, 1866, Jan. 8, Feb. 3, Mar. 10, 1867; *T. Deutsche Zeitung*, Jan. 27, 1867; Bénézit; Coulon MS, Scrapbook 100, LSM; Fielding, *Dictionary*; Glenk; Groce and Wallace; Mechanics' and Agricultural Fair Asso., *Report* (1867):27.

GUALDI, PIETRO
Born Carpi, Italy July 22, 1808; died N.O. Jan. 4, 1857.
Painter, active N.O. 1852–57; also architect.
Contemporary listings: panorama painter (1854); artist (1857).
Studied: Academy of Arts, Milan (ca. 1834–35).
Painter who worked at LaScala, Milan, probably as a scene painter, before entering the academy. Gualdi went to Mexico in 1835 where he is supposed to have designed theater sets and is known to have painted scenes in Mexico City, including a view of the cathedral. He came to N.O., perhaps as early as Dec. 1851, and by Mar. 1854 received public notice for his large panorama of N.O. taken from the tower of St. Patrick's Church during Jan.–Mar. 1853. The oil painting, 20 x 128 feet, was exhibited in an octagonal building designed by Gualdi for that purpose. He was the artist for the new First Presbyterian Church (1855) and painted watercolors of N.O. buildings and sites in real estate transactions (1855–56). His last commission was probably the design for the circular marble tomb for the Italian Mutual Benevolent Society in St. Louis Cemetery I. Gualdi died shortly after

its completion and was the first person to be buried in the tomb.
References: NOCD 1852–57; *Bee*, Mar. 13, 16, 1854; *Courier*, Dec. 4, 1851; *D. Delta*, Mar. 14–Apr. 28, 1854 (advs.); *D. Pic.*, Mar. 14–15, 16, 1854, Oct. 22, 1855, Jan. 5, 1857, May 17, 1897; *State Rep.*, Apr. 5, 1854; *T. Deutsche Zeitung*, Mar. 14, 1854; *T. Pic.*, Feb. 23, 1938, Aug. 6, 1972; Collier, "The World of Art: State Museum's Gualdi Painting Has Near Twin in New Hampshire," *T. Pic.*, July 13, 1975; Bacot, "Pietro Gualdi," 242; Creole Exhibit, 8; Friends of the Cabildo, *N.O. Architecture*, 2:226, 3:9, 97; Groce and Wallace; P. Gualdi to James Robb, Oct. 1, 1855, James Robb Collection, THNOC; Information courtesy H. Parrott Bacot, Apr. 16, 1980; Jewell, 36.

GUAY, EDWARD
Born Canada ca. 1832; died ca. 1878.
Artist, active N.O. 1871; primarily photographer.
Contemporary listings: artist (1871).
References: NOCD 1859–61, 1867, 1871–73, 1875, 1877, 1879; Smith and Tucker, 158; U.S. Census (1860), roll 417.

GUEDRY, LILLIAN ANN. *See* GARIC, LILLIAN ANN GUEDRY

GUENARD, G. WASHINGTON (Guesnard)
Born N.O. ca. 1839; died N.O. Feb. 8, 1894.
Painter, active N.O. 1872–94.
Contemporary listings: painter (1872–79, 1884–87, 1889–94); portrait painter (1880); painter, Morgan's Louisiana & Texas Railroad (1880–83); painter, So. Pacific Co. (1888).
References: NOCD 1869, 1872–94; *D. Pic.*, Feb. 11, 1894; N.O. Death Certificate (1894), 105:923, NOPL; U.S. Census (1880), roll 462.

GUENARD, HORTAIRE J.
Born N.O. ca. 1827; died June 12, 1899.
Painter, active N.O. 1850–99.
Contemporary listings: portrait painter (1850); portrait painter, with JUST. TRUDEAU, 234 Camp (1851); artist, 48 Casacalvo (1857); painter,

124 Clouet (1867); painter (1872–73, 1875–76, 1879–80, 1882–87, 1889–93, 1897, 1899); painter, So. Pacific Co. (1888); artist (1898).
References: NOCD 1857, 1860–61, 1866–67, 1870, 1872–73, 1875–76, 1879–80, 1882–94, 1896–99; *Spectator*, Feb. 14, 1851; Groce and Wallace; N.O. Death Certificate (1899), 119:878, NOPL; U.S. Census (1850), roll 238; Wiesendanger, 57.

GUERIN, EMILE
Hair worker, active N.O. 1855–66; primarily jeweler, watchmaker.
Contemporary listings: ornamental hair work, GUERIN & KELLER (1855–57); ornamental hair manufacturer, 109 Canal (1858); hair worker, 120 Canal (1866).
References: NOCD 1854–61, 1866; NOBD 1858; *Bee*, Oct. 29, 1855, Jan. 4, 1856; *Courier*, Oct. 23, 1853, Jan. 22, 1854; *D. Delta*, Dec. 6, 1855; *D. Pic.*, Oct. 23, 1853, Jan. 20, 1854, Jan. 3, 1857; *D. Southern Star*, Jan. 20, Feb. 7, 1866.

GUERIN, JULES
Born St. Louis MO Nov. 18, 1866; died 1946.
Painter, sketch artist, active N.O. ca. 1890s.
Studied: with Benjamin Constant and Jean Paul Laurens, Paris.
Awarded: International Exposition, Paris, honorable mention (1900); Louisiana Purchase Exposition, St. Louis MO, silver medal (1904); Buffalo NY, honorable mention (1910); Chicago, Yerkes medal.
Memberships/positions: American Watercolor Society.
As a young man, Guerin lived in N.O. on Royal (present address 1140 Royal); he claimed that his early work was inspired by the ironwork of French Quarter balconies. He eventually became internationally known as a free–lance renderer of presentation drawings for architectural firms and city planners. Guerin also became a mural painter: he returned to LA in 1932 to install two frescoes, entitled *The Abundance of the Earth*, in Memorial Hall, the entrance to the Senate chamber in the new state cap-

itol in Baton Rouge. At that time, he divided his time among his studios in N.Y.C., Paris, London, and Cairo.
References: NOCD 1897–1910; *Item–Trib.*, Feb. 28, 1932; Bénézit; Brooklyn Museum, 21, 72, 95, 99, 101, 177, figs. 5, 14, 50; Kubly, 34.

GUERIN & KELLER
Hair workers, active N.O. 1855–57; EMILE GUERIN, T. A. Keller (born Germany ca. 1811), partners.
Contemporary listings: hair work, 119 Canal (1855, 1857); hair work and hair jewelry, 119 Canal (1856).
References: NOCD 1856, 1858; *Bee*, Oct. 29, 1855–Jan. 4, 1856 (advs.); *Courier*, Oct. 23, 1853–Jan. 22, 1854 (advs.); *D. Delta*, Dec. 6, 1855; *D. Pic.*, Jan. 20, 1854, Jan. 3, 1857; U.S. Census (1860), roll 417.

GUGENHEIM, JACOB
Died ca. 1959.
Painter, active N.O. 1897–1903; primarily decorator.
Contemporary listings: fresco painter (1897); painter (1898–99, 1901, 1903).
Also listed as decorator (1909, 1912, 1917–18, 1921, 1924, 1926–28, 1933, 1942).
References: NOCD 1897–1933, 1935, 1938, 1940, 1942, 1945–47, 1949, 1952–56, 1958, 1960.

GUIBET, JEAN BAPTISTE
Born Rochefort, France ca. 1806; died N.O. Feb. 19, 1876.
Painter, art teacher, active N.O. 1865–76; also architect.
Contemporary listings: drawing master, 61 Royal (1865); portrait painter, 390 St. Claude, and painter, lessons in drawing, oil painting, watercolor, and pastel, 62 Bourbon (1867); professor of drawing, 390 St. Claude (1868); professor of drawing (1869, 1875–76); drawing teacher (1870); portrait painter (1870, 1874); artist (1871); drawing master, Jesuit's College (1872); professor (1876–77).
References: NOCD 1854–56, 1858, 1867–71, 1874–77; NOBD 1865; *Courier*, Aug. 15, 1850, May 8, 1851, May 6, 1852, Feb. 11, 1853, July 23, 1854, July 15, 1855; *Repub.*, July 27, 1872, *Almanach de la Louisiane*

(1867):224; U. S. Census (1860), roll 418, (1870), roll 522.

GUICHARD, RALPH JOSEPH
Born Mar. 15, 1871; died Nov. 24, 1939.
Artist, active N.O. 1905–19.
Contemporary listings: artist (1905–1908); artist, 2626 Laharpe (1910–13).
Also listed as artist (1919).
References: NOCD 1891–94, 1896–1917, 1919–21, 1923–25, 1928–33, 1935, 1938, 1940; THNOC Cemetery Survey.

GUIGNON, JOBSON
Artist, active N.O. 1850–51.
Advertised himself as "the celebrated mechanician" and the inventor of a new pageant, the *Grand Mechanical Panorama*, which he exhibited at 52 St. Charles (Dec. 1850–Jan. 1851). The panorama was a series of moving tableaux of views in CA, the port of N.O., the explosion of the steamboat *Louisiana*, and George Washington.
References: *D. Delta*, Dec. 18, 1850–Jan. 8, 1851 (advs.).

GUILLAUME, ADOLPH
Sculptor, active N.O. 1885.
Contemporary listings: sculptor, with Pierre Casse (1885).
References: NOCD 1885.

GUILLAUME, PIERRE
Restorer, active N.O. 1834–37.
Contemporary listings: restorer, 117 Chartres (1834–35, 1837).
References: NOCD 1834–35, 1837.

GUILMETTE, CHARLES
Born Scotland ca. 1815.
Artist, active N.O. 1850.
Contemporary listings: artist (1850).
References: Groce and Wallace; U.S. Census (1850), roll 235.

GUION, LULU
Artist, active N.O. 1895–96.
Contemporary listings: artist (1895–96).
Probably sister of SARAH GUION.
References: NOCD 1895–96.

GUION, SARAH
Artist, active N.O. 1895–96.
Contemporary listings: artist (1895–96).

Probably sister of LULU GUION.
References: NOCD 1895–96.

GUMBO
Cartoonist, active N.O. 1893–94.
Signed nine front–page cartoons in
the *Mascot* (1893–94).
References: *Mascot,* July 1, 8, 15,
Sept. 30, Oct, 7, 14, 21, Nov. 4,
1893, Dec. 29, 1894.

GUNGEL, B.
Sculptor, active N.O. 1857.
Contemporary listings: sculptor
(1857).
References: NOCD 1857, 1866;
Groce and Wallace.

GUNSBURG, CHARLES
Painter, active N.O. 1887–99; also
decorator.
Contemporary listings: painter
(1887, 1898); portrait painter
(1890); artist (1899).

References: NOCD 1887, 1890,
1897–1900.

GURNIER, P. M.
Painter, active N.O. 1829; also decorator.
Contemporary listings: painter and
decorator in watercolor, oil, and
fresco, with JEAN BAPTISTE FRETTE, JR.
(1829).
Listed as a decorator, 114 St. Ann
(1830).
References: NOCD 1830; *Courier,*
June 4, 1829.

GUSSET, CHRISTIAN (Charles)
Sculptor, active N.O. 1869; also carpenter, carver.
Contemporary listings: wood carver
(1869); carver, 142 Bienville (1870,
1872–73).
References: NOCD 1868–73.

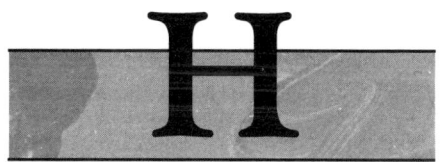

HAAS, MRS. _____
Artist, active N.O. ca. 1878.
Exhibited: SEEBOLD's (1878).
References: *Demo.*, June 14, 1878.

HABER, EMILE A.
Born St. Louis MO ca. 1872; died
N.O. Nov. 28, 1927.
Lithographer, active N.O. 1910–23;
also printer.
Contemporary listings: lithographer
(1910, 1917).
References: NOCD 1911, 1917–27;
T. Pic., Nov. 29, 1927; U.S. Census
(1910), roll 519.

HACHARD, MARIE MADELEINE
Born Rouen, France ca. 1704; died
N.O. Aug. 9, 1760.
Sketch artist, active N.O. 1727.
Came to N.O. in 1727 with the first
group of Ursuline nuns from France
and made a pencil sketch of Gov.
Bienville's house that year.
References: Fortier, *Louisiana*,
1:484; Glenk, 240; Hachard.

HAGEDORN, H. C.
Painter, active N.O. 1842.
Contemporary listings: portrait
painter, 91 Orleans (1842).
Possibly Hermann Conrad Hagedorn, German painter and architect
who exhibited at the Berlin Academy
in 1828, 1830, 1832, and 1838.
References: NOCD 1842; Bénézit;
Groce and Wallace; U.S. Census
(1840), roll 132; William Young.

HAGEN, DOROTHY
Painter, active N.O. ca. 1918.
Exhibited: ART ASSOCIATION OF NEW
ORLEANS (1918).
References: NOCD 1921, 1923; Art
Asso., *Catalogue* (1918).

HALDER, RODOLPH
Born Switzerland ca. 1798; died N.O.
Dec. 15, 1850.
Lithographer, active N.O. 1850.
Contemporary listings: lithographer
(1850).
References: Groce and Wallace;
Louisiana Charity Hospital, Death

Records, NOPL; U.S. Census (1850),
roll 234.

HALE, ELLEN DAY
Born Worcester MA Feb. 11, 1855;
died Brookline MA Feb. 11, 1940.
Sketch artist, active N.O. 1876.
Studied: with William Rimmer, Bos-
ton (1873–79); with William Morris
Hunt and Helen Knowlton, Boston
(1874–79); Pennsylvania Academy
of Fine Arts, Philadelphia (1878);
with Emmanuel Fremiet, Jardin des
Plantes (1881); with Louis Joseph–
Raphael Collin and Gustave Claude–
Etienne Courtois, Academie Cola-
rossi (1881); with Carolus–Duran,
Paris (1882); with Tony Robert–
Fleury, Rodolphe Julian, William–
Adolphe Bouguereau, and Jean–
Jacques Henner, Académie Julian
(1882); Académie Julian (1885).
Exhibited: Centennial Exposition,
Philadelphia (1876); Boston Art Club
(1878, 1884, 1886); Pennsylvania
Academy of Fine Arts (1883, 1889,
1891, 1894–95, 1898); American
Exposition (1885–86); Salon, Paris
(1885); St. Botolphe Club, Boston
(1886); Williams & Everett, Boston
(1888); World's Columbian Exposi-
tion, Chicago (1893); Corcoran Gal-
lery, Washington DC (1907);
Worcester Museum of Art (1915).
Awarded: Society of Washington
Artists, Washington DC, 1st prize
(1910).
Memberships/positions: Washington
Watercolor Club (1914); Chicago
Society of Etchers; North Shore Art
Asso.; Washington Art Club.
Portrait and landscape painter, print-
maker, and writer who traveled
through LA in 1876 and made a
charcoal sketch of the N.O. French
Market.
References: Fielding, *Dictionary*; In-
formation courtesy Alanna Chese-
bro, Richard York Gallery, Nov. 17,
1981; THNOC 1981.323.

HALE, WALTER
Born Chicago IL Aug. 4, 1869; died France 1917.
Sketch artist, painter, active N.O. 1897–1901.
Exhibited: Nationale des Beaux Arts, Paris (1911).
Signed and dated several illustrations of Vieux Carré landmarks and streets which accompanied his article "George W. Cable's New Orleans."
References: Bénézit; Hale.

HALL, MRS. ALFRED S.
Painter, active N.O. ca. 1897.
Exhibited: ARTISTS' ASSOCIATION OF NEW ORLEANS (1897).
References: *D. Pic.*, Mar. 30, 1897; AANO, *Catalogue* (1897); Arts Exhibition Club, 14.

HALL, ANDREW VAN
Born Terrebonne Parish LA Sept. 8, 1880; died N.O. Feb. 23, 1948.
Commercial artist, painter, active N.O. 1900–48.
Contemporary listings: artist, with George A. Simms (1902–1903); artist, Dugazon & Co., Ltd. (1905); artist, *Times–Democrat* (1906–12, 1914); artist, 320 St. Charles (1913); artist, *Times–Picayune* (1915–16); artist (1917); artist, 539 Bienville (1918).
Made illustrations, some in watercolor and India ink, for *Harlequin* (1900–1906); continued as an artist with the *Times–Picayune* until 1929 when he became a commercial artist.
References: NOCD 1898–99, 1901–1903, 1905–24, 1926–31, 1933, 1938; *Harlequin*, Oct. 27, 1900–June 21, 1906; *T. Pic.*, Feb. 25, 1948; Orleans Parish Registrar of Voters, NOPL; U.S. Census (1910), roll 519.

HALL, CAPT. BASIL
Born Scotland Dec. 31, 1788; died England Sept. 11, 1844.
Sketch artist, active N.O. ca. 1827–28.
Memberships/positions: National Academy of Design, N.Y.C. (1828–30).
British naval officer and author who traveled through the U.S. and Canada making numerous sketches, including views of N.O., published in his *Forty Etchings from Sketches Made with the Camera Lucida in North America in the Years 1827 and 1828.*
References: *Appleton's CAB*; Davidson, *Life in America*, 1:183; Gernsheim, 116; Groce and Wallace; Hall; Larsen, 138–39; LHS (1903).

HALL, EDITH
Painter, active N.O. ca. 1891–93.
Exhibited: ARTISTS' ASSOCIATION OF NEW ORLEANS (1891); Tulane University (1893).
Memberships/positions: FIVE OR MORE CLUB (1893).
References: *D. City Item*, Dec. 17, 1891; *D. Pic.*, Dec. 17, 1891, Feb. 14, 1893.

HALL, ELLERY A.
Artist, active N.O. 1896–98.
Contemporary listings: artist (1896–98).
References: NOCD 1896–98.

HALL, FRANCES DEVEREUX JONES (Mrs. Harry Usher Hall)
Born N.O. May 1872; died PA Dec. 6, 1941.
Art craftsman, art teacher, active N.O. ca. 1892–1904.
Studied: NEWCOMB COLLEGE (1889–94); Pennsylvania Academy of Fine Arts, Philadelphia; with Henry McCarter, Howard Pyle, Charles Grafly, and John Henry Twachtman.
Contemporary listings: drawing teacher, Newcomb College (1895–1901); artist (1900).
Exhibited: Tulane University (1892–93); ARTISTS' ASSOCIATION OF NEW ORLEANS (1892, 1896, 1901); ART ASSOCIATION OF NEW ORLEANS (1904–1905, 1907).
Memberships/positions: Art Alliance of Philadelphia; National Association of Women Painters and Sculptors, N.Y.C.; Artists' Association of New Orleans (1896); Art Association of New Orleans (1905).
Designed calendars in 1896 (with CAROLINE OGDEN, KATHARINE KOPMAN, and FRANCES HOWE), 1898, and 1900 (with Kopman) and illustrated N.O. author Grace King's *New Orleans: The Place and the People*

(1907). Hall moved to Philadelphia between 1904 and 1907.
References: NOCD 1897–1902; *Current Topics*, Jan. 1893, 11; *D. Pic.*, Mar. 3, Dec. 13, 1892, Feb. 14, 1893; *D. States*, Dec. 15, 1897, Jan. 23, 1898; *Harlequin*, Dec. 6, 1899, 2; *Men and Matters*, Sept. 1897, 48; *T. Demo.*, Mar. 3, Dec. 13, 1892; *T. Pic.*, Dec. 8, 1941; AANO, *Catalogue* (1896, 1901, 1903); Art Asso., *Catalogue* (1904, 1905, 1907); Collins and Opitz; Fielding, *Dictionary*; Grace King, *New Orleans*; Mc-Glauflin, 226; Poesch, *Newcomb Pottery*, 100; Thompson, "Checklist"; U.S. Census (1900), roll 574.

HALL, JOHN
Artist, active N.O. 1885.
Contemporary listings: scenic artist, Lyceum Pavilion (1885).
References: *New York Clipper*, Mar. 21, 1885.

HALL, MARJORIE
Bookbinder, active N.O. ca. 1917.
Exhibited: ART ASSOCIATION OF NEW ORLEANS (1917).
References: Art Asso., *Catalogue* (1917).

HALLER, PAUL J.
Born LA ca. 1890.
Engraver, etcher, active N.O. 1908–21.
Contemporary listings: engraver, ROMANSKI Photo Engraving Co. Ltd. (1908); photo–engraver, 705 Louisiana (1910); engraver, GRELLE-EGERTON ENGRAVING CO. (1911); etcher, Grelle–Egerton Engraving Co. (1913); photo engraver, 4321 Laurel (1914); engraver, 608 Sixth (1915); engraver, 421 Joseph (1916); engraver, 817 Pleasant (1917); photo–engraver, Grelle–Egerton Engraving Co. (1918).
References: NOCD 1906–11, 1913–21; U.S. Census (1910), roll 524.

HALLIDAY, CORA
Born St. Louis MO Feb. 27, 1859; died N.O. Apr. 3, 1937.
Painter, active N.O. 1887–89.
Studied: with WILLIAM JENNINGS WARRINGTON (1888); ACADEMY OF FINE ARTS (1889).

Exhibited: William Jennings Warrington's studio (1887); Werlein's music store (1888); Academy of Fine Arts (1889).
Flower and animal painter. Daughter of JOHN HALLIDAY.
References: NOCD 1923–24, 1926, 1931–33, 1935; *D. Pic.*, Jan. 15, 1888, Jan. 22, 1889; *D. States*, Oct. 12, 1887, Jan. 14, 1888; *T. Demo.*, Oct. 13, 1887; *T. Pic.*, Apr. 4, 1937; Orleans Parish Registrar of Voters, NOPL; U.S. Census (1870), roll 525.

HALLIDAY, JOHN
Born Ireland ca. 1824; died ca. 1883–84.
Sculptor, active N.O. 1866–77; also marble worker, engineer.
Contemporary listings: sculptor, 143 St. Charles (1868); sculptor (1870, 1873, 1876–77).
Exhibited: Grunewald's music store (1873).
Halliday's first appearance in N.O. was as a lecturer at the Academy of Sciences on the subjects of sculpture, painting, and architecture. Father of CORA HALLIDAY.
References: NOCD 1868, 1870, 1872–77, 1879–83; *D. Pic.*, Nov. 6, 1866; *Repub.*, June 29, 1873; U.S. Census (1870), roll 525.

HAMEY, E. T.
Painter, active N.O. 1868–69.
Mentioned as the chief scenic artist for the Varieties Theatre (1868–69).
References: Kendall, *Golden Age*, 412.

HAMILTON, CECILIA VIETS DAKIN. *See* JAMISON, CECILIA VIETS DAKIN HAMILTON

HAMILTON, JOHN R.
Sketch artist, active N.O. 1863.
Correspondent and artist for *Harper's Weekly*, who reported on Gen. Nathaniel P. Banks's activities in N.O. (1863).
References: *Harper's Wkly.*, Mar. 7, 1863, 157, Apr. 4, 1863, 221–22; Museum of Fine Arts, 2:70–71.

HAMMERSMITH, PAUL
Born Naperville IL Mar. 17, 1857; died 1937.
Etcher, painter, active N.O. 1891; also photographer.

Awarded: St. Paul Art Institute, bronze medal (1918).

Memberships/positions: California Society of Etchers; Chicago Society of Etchers; Wisconsin Painters and Sculptors, pres.; Etching Society of San Francisco.

Milwaukee WI watchmaker and engraver who sketched and painted landscapes as an avocation, especially during his travels. Hammersmith's watercolors and etchings of N.O. were made in WI from the photographs taken during his visit to the city in Feb. 1891.

References: *Milwaukee Journal*, Feb. 27, 1934; Jordan, "Artist Recorded Charms of New Orleans," *T. Pic.*, July 31, 1977; Fielding, *Dictionary*; Hammersmith; THNOC 1977.79.1–.25; 1977.82.1–.3.

HAMMOND, JOHN T.
Born NY ca. 1820.

Engraver, lithographer, colorer, active N.O. 1844–61; also printer.

Contemporary listings: engraver, 14 Exchange Pl. (1844); SHIELDS & HAMMOND (1845); engraver, 9 Camp (1846, 1854–55, 1860); engraver, 13 Camp (1849–51); engraver, 3 Camp, and HAMMOND & PHILBRICK (1852); engraver (1853); CHILDS & HAMMOND (1855–57); engraver, lithographer, 9 Camp (1858–59); engraver, 28 Camp (1861).

Engraver of landscapes and subjects in Philadelphia (1839) and later in St. Louis MO. Hammond arrived in N.O. by Sept. 1844 from Cincinnati OH where he had been with Durand & Co., bank note engravers. He advertised in N.O. as a general engraver, particularly of visiting cards, jewelry, and silverware, and as a printer. In the 1850s he claimed to be the only engraver on metal of pictorial subjects in the South, including portraits, landscapes, documents, and book illustrations. Hammond also received public notice for an engraving of the race horse Lecomte, after a painting by THEODORE SIDNEY MOISE (1854), and for his illustrations of N.O. buildings printed in the NOBD 1858–59.

References: NOCD 1846, 1849–61; NOBD 1857–58, 1858–59 (illus.); *Courier*, Nov. 9, 1854; *D. Crescent*, Nov. 9, 1854, July 2, 1858–Jan. 1, 1859 (advs.); *D. Pic.*, Oct. 22, Nov. 9, 1854; *D. Tropic*, Sept. 5, 1844; *Wkly. Delta*, Apr. 18, 1850; Groce and Wallace; Stauffer, 1:118; Thompson, "Checklist"; U.S. Census (1860), roll 420.

HAMMOND & PHILBRICK
Engravers, active N.O. 1852–54; also jewelers; JOHN T. HAMMOND, George Philbrick, partners.

Contemporary listings: engravers, 86 Canal (1852).

References: NOCD 1853–54; *D. Pic.*, Apr. 30, 1852.

HANINGTON, MR. ____
Painter, active N.O. 1832–56.

Exhibited: Orleans Ballroom (1839); cor. Camp and Poydras (1841); National Amphitheatre (1845); Armory Hall (1856).

Itinerant painter of transparencies and dioramas who was in N.O. to show the use of microscopes, to sell painted transparencies (1832), and to exhibit dioramas (1839, 1841, 1845, 1856). Hanington was either one of or both of brothers, Henry and William J., who painted moving dioramas of spectacular historical events lighted by special illumination which were exhibited throughout the country. Henry was listed in N.Y.C. 1832–45 and appeared in the advertisements for the 1839 N.O. exhibit. William J. was listed in N.Y.C. 1836–70 and was mentioned by Groce and Wallace as being a partner with his brother from the 1830s through the 1856 N.O. exhibit.

References: *Bee*, Feb. 17, 24, Mar. 17, 21, 1832; *Comm. Bull.*, Dec. 31, 1841; *Courier*, May 10–31, 1839 (advs.); *D. Crescent*, Feb. 11, 1856; *D. Delta*, Feb. 7, 1856; *D. Pic.*, Feb. 13, 1845; Mar. 1, 1856; Groce and Wallace; Thompson, "Checklist."

HANKES, MASTER ____
Born ca. 1813.

Silhouettist, active N.O. 1827–30.

Contemporary listings: silhouettist, 60 Chartres (1827); silhouettist, 113 Chartres (1830).

Exhibited: Grand Promenade (1827); 113 Chartres (1830).

References: *Advertiser*, Apr. 2, 1830; *Argus*, Mar. 7, 16, Apr. 13, 17, 21, 1827, Jan. 20, Feb. 2, 1830; *Courier*, Apr. 24, 1827, Apr. 12, 1830; Emily Jackson, *Silhouette*, 113.

HANNAN, JOHN J.
Sculptor, active N.O. 1880; primarily marble cutter, stone cutter, carver.
Contemporary listings: sculptor, KURSHEEDT & BIENVENU (1880).
References: NOCD 1874–75, 1877–81, 1890–1919; *D. States*, Oct. 21, 1884.

HARBY, MRS. _____
Art teacher, active N.O. 1831–35.
Contemporary listings: teacher of painting on velvet, HARBY'S DAY & BOARDING ACADEMY (1835).
References: *Advertiser*, Jan. 19, 1835; U.S. Census (1830), roll 45.

HARBY'S DAY & BOARDING ACADEMY
School, active N.O. ca. 1830–38.
Contemporary listings: instruction in painting on velvet, satin, silk, and paper (1831); instruction in painting on velvet, satin, ivory, silk, and paper, 84 St. Charles (1832).
School, owned by George W. Harby (born N.O. ca. 1797; died N.O. June 22, 1862), which offered instruction primarily in languages and the classics. In spring and summer 1831–32, the school gave special courses in painting, separate from the regular academy hours, probably taught by MRS. HARBY.
References: *Advertiser*, June 21, 1832; *Emporium*, Sept. 25, 1832; *Mercantile Advertiser*, June 6, 1831.

HARDING, MR. _____
Painter, active N.O. 1839.
Contemporary listings: portrait painter, 21 Camp (1839).
Cf. HARDING, CHESTER; HARDING, HORACE.
References: *True Amer.*, Dec. 13, 1839.

HARDING, CHESTER
Born Conway MA Sept. 1, 1792; died Boston MA Apr. 1, 1866.
Painter, active N.O. 1841.

Studied: Pennsylvania Academy of Fine Arts, Philadelphia (ca. 1818); London (1823–26).
Contemporary listings: portrait painter, cor. Camp and Canal (1841).
Memberships/positions: National Academy of Design, N.Y.C. (1828).
Itinerant portrait painter who worked in Baltimore, Washington DC, Richmond VA, St. Louis, Boston, and London. Harding painted portraits of James Madison, James Monroe, John Quincy Adams, and Henry Clay, and the only known portrait of Daniel Boone. He advertised his services as a portrait painter in N.O. at the corner of Canal and Camp (1841). Brother of HORACE HARDING. *Cf.* HARDING, MR. _____.
References: *Bee*, Feb. 11–Mar. 1, 1841 (advs.); *D. Pic.*, Apr. 22, 1866; *Appleton's CAB*, 79; Bruns, 313; *DAB*; *Encyclopaedia Britannica*; Fielding, *Dictionary*; Flexner, *Light*, 205–7, 227, 261; Glenk, 75; Groce and Wallace; Lipton, 34, 45–50; LSM, *Biennial Report for 1922–23*, 58; Ludlow, 194; Thompson, "Checklist."

HARDING, HARVEY A.
Painter, sculptor, active N.O. 1856–91; also printer, sign painter, ornamental painter, carver.
Contemporary listings: sculptor, 12 Commercial (1856); painter and sculptor, 12 Commercial, and 121 Poydras (1858–59); sculptor, 12 Commercial (1859); painter, 167 Carondelet (1866); painter, 180 Girod (1867); painter, 173 Lafayette (1868); painter, 134 1/2 Baronne (1869–70); painter (1872–73, 1879, 1881, 1885, 1890–91); painter, 403 Baronne (1874); painter, 208 Julia (1875–78); painter, 143 Baronne (1889).
References: NOCD 1856–61, 1866–91; NOBD 1865; *D. Creole*, July 1–2, Oct. 17, 1856; *D. Pic.*, Feb. 7, 1913; *Semi-Wkly. Creole*, Jan. 30, 1856; Groce and Wallace.

HARDING, HORACE
Born Conway MA 1794; died Woodville MS ca. 1857.
Painter, active N.O. 1835–57.

Contemporary listings: portrait painter, Banks Arcade, 60 Magazine (1835–36); portrait painter, oppos. the Arcade on Magazine (1837); portrait painter, 74 Chartres (1856–57). Itinerant portrait painter who lived in Paris KY (ca. 1815–20), where he was joined by his brother CHESTER HARDING. He also worked in Vincennes IN (1820) and Cincinnati OH (1834–50). *Cf.* HARDING, MR. _____.

References: *Bee*, Nov. 10, 1856, Jan. 1–29, 1857 (advs.); *Pic.*, May 26, 1837; *True Amer.*, May 3, 1836; *Union*, Oct. 5, 1835; Groce and Wallace.

HARMAN, GEORGE W.

Commercial artist, art teacher, active N.O. ca. 1888–97.

Studied: Wittemberg College.

Contemporary listings: teacher, Soulé's Commercial College (1888–94); principal, Classical and Commercial Institute (1894–95); penmanship teacher, University School (1895–97).

Signed pen sketches on cover of sheet music and on cover of 1896 catalogue for University School and for Commercial Institute.

References: NOCD 1888–97; "Song of the Picture on the Wall," Sheet Music Collection, LA Coll., TU; THNOC 1984.114.

HARNEY, PAUL E.

Born N.O. 1850; died St. Louis MO 1915.

Painter.

Landscape painter who was a native New Orleanian.

References: Schwarz, item 24; Morton's Auction Exchange (May 1983): item 1107.

HARPER, NINA

Born N.O.; died Houston TX Feb. 23, 1931.

Painter, active N.O. 1908–24.

Studied: NEWCOMB COLLEGE (1909).

Exhibited: ART ASSOCIATION OF NEW ORLEANS (1908, 1910–11, 1913–14); DELGADO MUSEUM OF ART, Inaugural Exhibition (1911).

Memberships/positions: Art Association of New Orleans (1910, 1912–14).

References: NOCD 1916, 1920–21; *D. Pic.*, Dec. 26, 1909; *Item*, Jan. 16, Feb. 6, 18, 27, 1921; *T. Demo.*, Mar. 15, 1908; *T. Pic.*, Feb. 29, 1924, Feb. 24, 1931; Art Asso., *Catalogue* (1910, 1911, 1913, 1914); Delgado, *Inaugural Exhibition*.

HARRIS, E. R. *See* IDEAL ART CO.

HARRIS, T. B.

Sketch artist, active N.O. 1880.

Contemporary listings: crayon portraitist, 98 Prytania (1880).

Exhibited: E. Heath's store (1880).

Possibly Thomas Harris, painter, listed 1874–94.

References: NOCD 1874, 1876–79, 1881, 1884–94; *D. Pic.*, May 7, 1880.

HARRIS, THOMAS B.

Born ca. 1822; died N.O. Jan. 1, 1896.

Engraver, active N.O. 1870–77; also silversmith, watchmaker, jeweler.

Contemporary listings: engraver, 152 Julia (1870–71); engraver, 170 Julia (1872, 1876–77).

References: NOCD 1860–61, 1866–67, 1870–82, 1884, 1886, 1891; *D. Pic.*, Jan. 2, 1896.

HARRIS, WILLIAM. *See* D. J. WALLACE & HARRIS

HARRISON, G. F.

Engraver, active N.O. 1850.

Contemporary listings: engraver, 31 Exchange Al. (1850).

References: NOCD 1850, 1854.

HART, MR. _____

Painter, active N.O. 1854.

Contemporary listings: scenic painter, Dan Rice's Amphitheatre (1854).

References: *D. Crescent*, May 13, 1854.

HART, ALFRED

Born Norwich CT Mar. 28, 1816.

Painter, active N.O. 1855, 1860.

Exhibited: Armory Hall (1855, 1860).

Painted a panorama of John Bunyan's *Pilgrim's Progress*, after settling in Hartford CT in 1848. He was its proprietor when it was exhibited in N.O. in 1855, although the individual scenes were listed as being by other artists. When it returned to the city in 1860, he was sole manager and

proprietor and was credited with painting some of its scenes.
References: *D. Delta*, May 6, 1855, Jan. 24, 1860; *D. Pic.*, Mar. 6, 1855, Feb. 12, 1860; Groce and Wallace.

HART, BEMIS SHARP. *See* SHARP, BEMIS

HART, MRS. G.
Art teacher, active N.O. 1897.
Contemporary listings: drawing teacher, McDonogh School 23 (1897).
References: NOCD 1897.

HART, HENRY D.
Born England ca. 1820.
Engraver, active N.O. 1850.
Contemporary listings: engraver (1850).
References: Groce and Wallace; U.S. Census (1850), roll 234.

HART, JOEL TANNER
Born near Winchester KY Feb. 10, 1810; died Florence, Italy Mar. 2, 1877.
Sculptor, active N.O. 1860.
American portrait sculptor who lived permanently in Florence after 1849. Hart was commissioned by the Clay Monumental Association (N.O.) to execute a full-length statue of Henry Clay for a public monument. Hart made a plaster model in Florence, sent it to Munich to be cast in bronze by Z. Muller, and shipped it to N.O. On a rare visit to the U.S., Hart was present when the statue was unveiled on Canal at Royal on April 12, 1860.
References: *Bee*, Apr. 11, 13, 1860; *Courier*, Sept 30, 1845; *Crescent Monthly*, Mar. 1867, 233; *D. Crescent*, June 4, 1859; *D. Delta*, Sept. 2, 1855, Mar. 18, 1860; *D. Orleanian*, May 13, 1857; *D. Pic.*, Sept. 19, 1858, Feb. 18, May 20, 1859; *D. Tropic*, Sept. 29, Nov. 25, 1845; *Times*, Feb. 3, 1867; *T. Pic.*, Dec. 20, 1925; *Appleton's CAB*; Coleman, 3–23; Craven, 197–200, 313; *DAB*; Groce and Wallace.

HART, TOBY
Born Newberry SC Aug. 29, 1835; died N.O. Dec. 17, 1907.
Painter, active N.O. 1871–1905, also sign, banner, and ornamental painter, decorator.

Contemporary listings: painter, 20 Commercial (1871–72, 1874–76); painter, 23 Commercial (1877–81); scenic painter, 23 Commercial (1880); painter, 21 Commercial (1882–94); painter, 628 Commercial (1895–1901); fresco painter, 628 Commercial (1904–1905).
References: NOCD 1860–61, 1867–68, 1870–1908; *D. Crescent*, Dec. 3, 1861; *D. Pic.*, Mar. 11, 1891, Dec. 18, 1907; *D. States*, Feb. 10, 1902; *Demo.*, Sept. 7, 1880; *Item*, Dec. 18, 1907; *Mascot*, Sept. 1, 1883, 432; *Repub.*, Nov. 14, 1869, Mar. 31, Aug. 6, 1872, Feb. 26, 1873, Sept. 3, 1876; *Town Talk*, July 1904, Feb. 1905; *Wkly. States*, Mar. 19, 1886; U.S. Census (1870), roll 524.

HART, W. A.
Painter, active N.O. 1854–61; also sign and ornamental painter.
Contemporary listings: painter, 56 Carondelet (1854); fancy painter, 56 Carondelet (1856); fancy painter, 109 Poydras (1857); painter, 109 Poydras (1858); painter, 305 Poydras (1859–61).
First reported in N.O. as Hart & Marding in the *Daily Times* (Feb. 18, 1852). He also painted watercolors of N.O. buildings and sites used in real estate transactions (1858).
References: NOCD 1854, 1856, 1857–61; *D. Times*, Feb. 18, 1852; Orleans Parish Notarial Archives, Plan Book 52:5.

HARTRATH, JOSEPH
Engraver, active N.O. 1860–61.
Contemporary listings: engraver, 205 Conti (1860–61).
References: NOCD 1860–61; Groce and Wallace.

HARVEY, E. T.
Born ca. 1848.
Painter, active N.O. 1869.
Contemporary listings: scene painter, Varieties Theatre (1869).
References: *Times*, Mar. 18, 1869; TIINOC artists files.

HASKELL, IDA C.
Born ca. 1861; died 1932.
Art teacher, active N.O. 1884–86.
Studied: Philadelphia Art Museum; Chicago Art Institute; Pennsylvania

Academy of Fine Arts, Philadelphia; Paris.

Contemporary listings: drawing and painting teacher, SOUTHERN ART UNION (1884); teacher, Southern Art Union (1886).

Memberships/positions: New York Art League; Chicago Art Institute; National Association of Women Painters and Sculptors, N.Y.C.

References: NOCD 1886; *D. Pic.*, Nov. 26, 1884; *T. Demo.*, Nov. 23, 28, Dec. 14, 1884; Fielding, *Dictionary*; Mount, 50.

HASTINGS, EUGENE

Painter, sculptor, active N.O. ca. 1868.

Awarded: Grand State Fair, honorable mentions, best watercolor painting and best bronze bust (1868).

References: *D. Pic.*, Jan. 19, 1868; Mechanics' and Agricultural Asso., *Report* (1868):43.

HAUG, FIDEL (Frederick)

Born Würtemburg, Germany Sept. 1829; died N.O. Apr. 16, 1909.

Painter, active N.O. 1860–1909.

Contemporary listings: painter, 409 Liberty (1860, 1867); fresco painter (1861, 1876–77, 1885, 1887, 1893–94, 1900–1901, 1903–1906, 1908); painter (1869–70, 1872–75, 1878–84, 1886, 1888–92, 1895–99, 1902, 1907, 1909).

Painted murals for the New Orleans Savings Institute and frescoes for the Exposition Building on St. Charles (1872), Ames Methodist Episcopal Church (1876), and Trinity Church with ERASMUS HUMBRECHT (1883).

References: NOCD 1860–61, 1867, 1869–70, 1872–1909; *D. Pic.*, Oct. 28, 1883, Apr. 17, 1909; *Repub.*, Apr. 30, 1876; Jewell, 65; U.S. Census (1880), roll 458, (1900), roll 570; WPA, *Louisiana*, 165.

HAUSMANN, GABRIEL

Born N.O. May 8, 1872; died N.O. Jan. 31, 1945.

Engraver, active N.O. 1888–93; primarily jeweler.

Contemporary listings: engraver, with FREDERICK HOLYLAND (1888); engraver, Leonard Krower & Co.

(1890); engraver, T. Hausmann & Son (1891–93).

Listed with T. Hausmann & Sons (1894–1917), then with Hausmann, Inc. (1918–35).

References: NOCD 1888, 1890–1903, 1905–33, 1935; *T. Pic.*, Feb. 1, 1945; Orleans Parish Registrar of Voters, NOPL.

HAWKINS, EZEKIEL C.

Colorer, active N.O. 1845, 1856; primarily photographer.

Contemporary listings: Hawkins' Photographic Gallery and colored miniatures, cor. Canal and Exchange Pl. (1845); colorer, Dobyns & Harrington photographers (1856).

Landscape and portrait painter and commercial artist, active in Cincinnati OH intermittently between 1843 and 1860 when he was also a partner with other daguerreotypists in various cities. It is said that he perfected the collodion photographic process. His N.O. gallery (1845) produced colored miniatures, probably hand–colored, from a refracting achromatic camera. He may have been Hawkins who was a portrait and miniature painter in N.O. in 1834.

References: *D. Pic.*, Dec. 2, 1845; *Semi–Wkly. Creole*, Mar. 1, 1856; Groce and Wallace; Rinhart, 120; Smith and Tucker, 159.

HAWTHORNE, MRS. C. C.

Designer, active N.O. ca. 1888–98.

Studied: Tulane University (1886–87); NEWCOMB COLLEGE (1889–98).

Exhibited: TULANE DECORATIVE ART LEAGUE FOR WOMEN (1888).

References: NOCD 1894; *D. Pic.*, Feb. 12, 1888, Feb. 14, 1893; Ormond and Irvine, 156; Poesch, *Newcomb Pottery*, 99–100; Tulane Decorative Art League.

HAYS, WILLIAM H.

Born VA ca. 1800; died N.O. Sept. 3, 1828.

Painter, silhouettist, art dealer, active N.O. 1815–22; also sign and ornamental painter, glazier, gilder.

Contemporary listings: portrait and landscape painter, Chartres betw. Bienville and Conti (1815); painter and art dealer, Chartres betw. Bienville and Conti (1817–18); painter, 4 Chartres (1821); silhouettist and portrait painter, 4 Chartres (1822). References: NOCD 1822; *Bee,* Apr. 7, 1829; *Courier,* Jan. 23, Apr. 17, 1822, Sept. 4, 6, Oct. 18, 1828; *Gazette,* Apr. 15, Dec. 19, 1815, May 31–June 5, 1817 (advs.), Jan. 29, 1818, June 14, 1821; Groce and Wallace; Thompson, "Checklist."

HEAD, SAMUEL
Born England ca. 1815.
Sculptor, active N.O. 1851–53; also marble cutter.
Contemporary listings: sculptor, 239 Carondelet (1851–53).
References: NOCD 1838, 1849–54; Groce and Wallace; U.S. Census (1850), roll 237; William Young.

HEALY, GEORGE PETER ALEXANDER
Born Boston MA July 15, 1813; died Chicago IL June 24, 1894.
Painter, active N.O. 1860–61.
Studied: with Baron Antoine Jean Gros, Paris (1834–35).
Contemporary listings: portrait painter (1860–61).
Exhibited: World's Industrial and Cotton Centennial Exposition (1884–85); Salon, Paris (1840, 1878).
Awarded: Salon, Paris, third medal (1840); Paris International Exhibition, gold medal (1855); Grand State Fair, honorable mention for the display of portraits, with THOMAS CANTWELL HEALY (1868).
Memberships/positions: Chicago Academy of Design, founder; National Academy of Design, N.Y.C. (ca. 1857).
Portrait and historical painter, patronized by American statesmen and English and French royalty, who worked in the U.S. and Europe (1830–55). Healy then settled in Chicago (1855–67). Previously thought to have been active in N.O. in 1843 as well as in 1845, it now seems that this artist was his brother, Thomas Cantwell Healy. Family information indicates that he may have been in N.O. in the winters of 1857–59. During intermittent stays in N.O. in 1860 and 1861, he painted a large number of portraits and possibly re-

sided at the St. Charles Hotel. Healy returned to Europe (1867–92) and established a home and studio in Rome, then Paris.
References: *Bee,* June 24, Sept. 22, 1842, Dec. 5, 1850, Apr. 3, 1852; *Comm. Bull.,* Sept. 18, 23, 1851; *Courier,* June 28, 1845, Mar. 16, 1855; *D. Crescent,* Jan. 4, 1851; *D. Pic.,* Apr. 8, 12, 1841, June 24, 1842, July 13, 1844, May 18, July 2, 15, Oct. 23, 1845, Aug. 8, 1846, Sept. 19, 1849, Sept. 18, 1851, Nov. 27, 1855, Sept. 29, 1859, Feb. 26, May 14, July 17, 1861, Jan. 19, 1868; *D. Tropic,* July 24, 1845; *D. True Delta,* Aug. 8, Sept. 21, 1851, Mar. 18, 1860, May 27, 1864; *Wkly. Delta,* Oct. 27, 1851; *Appleton's CAB*; Bénézit; Bruns, 313; *DAB*; De Mare; Glasgow; Glenk, 75; Groce and Wallace; LSM, *Healy*; Mechanics' and Agricultural Fair, *Report* (1868):42; WICCE, *Catalogue,* 16, 20.

HEALY, THOMAS CANTWELL
Born Albany NY Dec. 7, 1820; died Claiborne County MS Dec. 10, 1889.
Painter, active N.O. 1843–72.
Studied: with his brother, GEORGE PETER ALEXANDER HEALY, Paris (1838).
Contemporary listings: portrait painter, 127 Canal (1843); portrait painter, cor. St. Charles and Common (1845); portrait painter, 12 Union (1862); portrait painter (1867, 1869); artist, 131 Poydras (1868).
Exhibited: Athenaeum, Boston (1832, 1840); National Academy of Design, N.Y.C. (1839, 1842); National Gallery of Paintings (1845); FRANK WAGENER's (1869).
Awarded: Grand State Fair, silver medal for best head in oil and honorable mention for the display of portraits, the latter with George Peter Alexander Healy (1868).
Itinerant portrait painter who returned from Paris to the U.S. (1839) and settled in Lowell MA. By 1843 he was working in MS, particularly in Claiborne Co. and Port Gibson, where he spent the rest of his life, with occasional stays in N.O. (1858, 1861) and elsewhere.

References: NOCD 1868; *D. Pic.*, Feb. 21, 1843, Mar. 22, 1862, Jan. 8, 1867, Jan. 19, 1868, Apr. 27, 1869; *D. Tropic*, Feb. 22, Apr. 10, 1845; Bruns, 313; Glasgow; Groce and Wallace; McDermott, "Alfred S. Waugh," 303; Mechanics, and Agricultural Fair Asso., *Report* (1868):42; Mississippi Museum.

HEANEY, MISS _____
Art teacher, active N.O. 1829–30.
Contemporary listings: teacher of drawing and painting, Young Ladies Seminary (1829–30).
References: NOCD 1830; *Courier*, June 25, Nov. 2, 1829.

HEARN, LAFCADIO (Patricio Lafcadio Tessima Carlos Hearn)
Born Santa Maura, Ionian Archipelago, Greece June 27, 1850; died Okubo, Japan Sept. 26, 1904.
Illustrator, active N.O. 1879–80.
Renowned author and journalist who immigrated to the U.S. in 1869 and spent his formative years with N.O. newspapers (1877–87), with the *Item*, as columnist, reviewer, and translator, and with the *Times–Democrat*, as editor and translator. He also illustrated his articles for the *Item* with his own cartoons and sketches which were cut onto wood blocks by the engravers BENNETT & ZENNECK. In 1890 Hearn was sent on assignment to Japan and remained there as a teacher and writer for the rest of his life.
References: NOCD 1880, 1886–87; *D. Pic.*, Sept. 29, Nov. 9, 1904; *T. Demo.*, Sept. 29, 1904; *DAB*; *Encyclopaedia Britannica*; Frost; Hearn, xvii–xxv; Jumonville, 43–44, 66–67; Tinker, *Creole City*, 253; Tinker, *Hearn*, 50–96.

HEARSEY, JAMES P.
Painter, active N.O. 1827–30.
Studied: with JOHN WESLEY JARVIS.
Contemporary listings: portrait painter, 3 St. Charles (1827); portrait painter (1829); portrait painter, Nayades near Erato (1830).
References: NOCD 1827, 1830, 1832, 1834–35; *Courier*, Apr. 23, 1829; Groce and Wallace; William Young.

HEATON, AUGUSTUS GOODYEAR
Born Philadelphia PA Apr. 28, 1844; died 1931.
Painter, active N.O. 1892, 1930.
Studied: with Alexandre Cabanel, Ecole des Beaux Arts, Paris (1863); with Léon Joseph Florentin Bonnat, Paris (1879).
Exhibited: Tulane University (1892).
Awarded: Columbian Exposition, Chicago, bronze medal (1893).
Memberships/positions: Philadelphia Sketch Club; Society of Independent Artists; Salmagundi Club, N.Y.C. (1908).
Artist and poet who, during his visit to the city in 1892, painted portraits of a number of prominent New Orleanians, including Varina Anne Davis as queen of Comus. He returned in Mar. 1930 for ten days to give three lectures on art.
References: *D. Pic.*, Mar. 3, 1892; *T. Pic.*, Mar. 18, 1930; Jordan, "The World of Art: Carnival Visitors' Work," *T. Pic.*, Feb. 5, 1978; Fielding, *Dictionary*; Glenk, 75.

HEDRICK, F. S.
Born MD ca. 1820.
Colorer, active N.O. 1856; primarily photographer.
Contemporary listings: photographic colorer, 26 Camp, and partner, CLARKE & HEDRICK (1856).
References: NOCD 1857–60; *Bee*, Mar. 17, Apr. 10, 1856; *D. Pic.*, Feb. 10, 14, 1856; U.S. Census (1860), roll 421.

HEILL, CARL
Born Germany ca. 1829.
Artist, active N.O. 1850.
Contemporary listings: artist (1850).
Boarded at the same address with GEORGE, JACOB, and PHI[LIP]. HEILL, probably his brothers.
References: Groce and Wallace; U.S. Census (1850), roll 235.

HEILL, GEORGE
Born Germany ca. 1823.
Artist, active N.O. 1850.
Contemporary listings: artist (1850).
Boarded at the same address with CARL, JACOB, and PHI[LIP]. HEILL, probably his brothers.

References: Groce and Wallace; U.S. Census (1850), roll 235.

HEILL, JACOB
Born Germany ca. 1826.
Artist, active N.O. 1850.
Contemporary listings: artist (1850). Boarded at the same address with CARL, GEORGE, and PHI[LIP]. HEILL, probably his brothers.
References: Groce and Wallace; U.S. Census (1850), roll 235.

HEILL, PHI[LIP].
Born Germany ca. 1820.
Artist, active N.O. 1850.
Contemporary listings: artist (1850). Boarded at the same address with CARL, GEORGE, and JACOB HEILL, probably his brothers.
References: Groce and Wallace; U.S. Census (1850), roll 235.

HELLMAN, BERNARD
Born Wurstburg, Germany May 7, 1827; died N.O. May 13, 1895.
Commercial artist, active N.O. 1885.
Contemporary listings: artist, SOUTHERN LITHOGRAPHIC CO. (1885).
References: NOCD 1867–68, 1870–93, 1895; D. Pic., May 14, 1895.

HELM, KATHERINE HARDING
Born KY.
Painter, active N.O. ca. 1896–1904.
Exhibited: ARTISTS' ASSOCIATION OF NEW ORLEANS (1896).
Memberships/positions: Artists' Association of New Orleans (1896).
Painted a portrait of Jefferson Davis for the Ladies Confederate Memorial Association which presented it to the Louisiana Historical Association (1904).
References: D. Pic., Feb. 19, 1904; Item, Feb. 19, 1904; T. Demo., Feb. 17, 1904; AANO, Catalogue (1896); Mount, 136.

HELMAN, ZEB
Born Russia Dec. 1858 or 1861; died N.O. Apr. 18, 1947.
Painter, active N.O. 1895–1906.
Contemporary listings: painter (1895); painter, 1228 Dryades (1895–96); fresco painter, 1228 Dryades (1897); fresco painter (1898–1904, 1906).
References: NOCD 1895–1904, 1906–1917, 1920–23, 1930, T. Pic.,

Apr. 20, 1947; U.S. Census (1900), roll 570.

HEMENWAY, MARY LOUISE JORDAN LIDDELL. See LIDDELL, MARY LOUISE JORDAN

HENDERSON, MRS. L. M.
Painter, active N.O. ca. 1897.
Exhibited: ARTISTS' ASSOCIATION OF NEW ORLEANS (1897).
References: D. Pic., Mar. 30, 1897; AANO, Catalogue (1897).

HENDERSON, WILLIAM PENHALLOW
Born Medford MA June 4, 1877; died Tesuque NM Oct. 15, 1943.
Painter, sketch artist, active N.O. 1912.
Studied: Massachusetts Normal Art School (1891); School of Drawing and Painting, Museum of Fine Arts, Boston (1899–1901).
Exhibited: Boston, N.Y.C., Chicago, San Diego, San Francisco, Omaha NE, Milwaukee WI, and Santa Fe NM.
Awarded: Paige Traveling Scholarship (1901).
Memberships/positions: Denver Art Association; Santa Fe–Taos Art Colony.
Artist, illustrator, and designer who taught at Chicago's Academy of Fine Arts (1904–10) and moved to Santa Fe (1916) where he became a member of the Santa Fe–Taos Art Colony. He executed in pastel "Old Spanish Church on the Rampart, New Orleans" during a visit in 1912.
References: Feldman; Fielding, Dictionary.

HENNESSY, HUGH
Born N.O. ca. 1870; died N.O. July 14, 1910.
Lithographer, active N.O. 1886–87.
Contemporary listings: lithographer, T. FITZWILLIAM & CO. (1886–87).
Son of PATRICK RYAN HENNESSY.
References: NOCD 1886–89; D. Pic., July 15, 1910.

HENNESSY, PATRICK RYAN
Died N.O. Nov. 24, 1896.
Lithographer, active N.O. 1885–86.
Contemporary listings: lithographer, T. FITZWILLIAM & CO. (1885); lithographer (1886).
Father of HUGH HENNESSY.

References: NOCD 1874–93; *D. Pic.*, Nov. 25, 1896.

HENRI, PIERRE
Born France.
Painter, active N.O. ca. 1812–17.
Contemporary listings: miniature painter, Royal near Bienville, and miniature painter, 26 St. Peter (1812).
Exhibited: Columbianum, Philadelphia (1795).
Itinerant miniature painter who arrived in N.Y.C. from France in May 1788. Henri worked in Philadelphia (1789–90, 1795, 1799–1802, 1804, 1808–14), Charleston SC (1790–93), N.Y.C. (1794, 1807, 1818), Baltimore (1803–1804), Richmond VA (1804), and N.O. (1812).
References: *Courier*, June 3, Oct. 5, 1812, Sept. 10, 1813, Aug. 2, 1816, July 2, 1817; Dunlap, 3:20; Glenk, 75; Groce and Wallace; WPA, "Lives."

HENRY, ALPHONSE
Artist, active N.O. 1867.
Contemporary listings: artist, 257 Robertson (1867).
References: NOCD 1866–67; U.S. Census (1860), roll 419.

HENRY, VINCENT
Engraver, active N.O. 1838.
Contemporary listings: engraver, 86 Girod (1838).
References: NOCD 1838; Groce and Wallace; William Young.

HENRY, WILLIAM F. *See* ORTTE & HENRY

HEREDIN, FRANCISCO
Born Mexico ca. 1829; died N.O. August 21, 1850.
Lithographer, active N.O. 1850.
Contemporary listings: lithographer (1850).
References: Louisiana Charity Hospital, Death Records, NOPL; Groce and Wallace; U.S. Census (1850), roll 234.

HERMANDT, PH.
Born Darmstadt, Germany ca. 1825.
Lithographer, active N.O. 1860.
Contemporary listings: lithographer (1860).
Cf. AMENDT, PHILIP.
References: Groce and Wallace; U.S. Census (1860), roll 421.

HERMITAGE, WILLIAM A.
Painter, active N.O. 1872–88; primarily sign and ornamental painter.
Contemporary listings: painter, 168 Girod (1873); Hermitage & Shaw, painters, 14 Perdido (1877); painter, 14 Perdido (1879); painter, 78 Carondelet (1880–81); painter, 7 Carroll (1882); painter, 76 Carondelet (1883); painter, 134 Carondelet (1884–85); painter, 200 St. Charles (1886); painter, 150 St. Joseph (1887–88).
Painted several transparencies for the Penn Guards, one of which bore a picture of Horace Greeley on one side and a picture of D. P. Penn, a candidate for LA governor, on the reverse (1872).
References: NOCD 1873–88; *Repub.*, Aug. 23, 1872.

HERR, MERCEDES
Born N.O. ca. 1869–70; died N.O. Sept. 22, 1956.
Painter, active N.O. 1904.
Studied: with Mrs. E. Maguier; Dykers Institute.
Contemporary listings: portrait painter (1904).
Primarily a music teacher (1903–29), she also painted china and was mentioned as having worked in oil, pastel, and watercolor.
References: NOCD 1903–1904, 1906–1907, 1913–19, 1923, 1925–29, 1931, 1933; *T. Pic.*, Sept. 25, 1956; Peeler, 50.

HERRERA, JOSEPH
Painter, active N.O. 1791.
Contemporary listings: painter (1791).
References: Spanish Census of N.O., NOPL.

HERRICK, MRS. S. S.
Painter, active N.O. ca. 1885.
Exhibited: Grunewald's music store (1885).
References: *D. States*, July 27, 1885; *T. Demo.*, July 3, 1885.

HERRING, LEWIS
Painter, colorer, active N.O. 1868–69.
Contemporary listings: portrait painting, 455 Burgundy (1868).

Exhibited: National Academy of Design, N.Y.C. (1859).

Awarded: Grand State Fair, silver medal for best marine painting, bronze medal for best colored photograph in oil, certificate for best painting on silk (1869).

References: NOCD 1868; *D. Pic.*, Apr. 11, 1869; Groce and Wallace; Mechanics' and Agricultural Fair Asso., *Report* (1869):79.

HERRON, FRANK J.

Born Mexico ca. 1840.

Painter, active N.O. 1868–1901; also sign and ornamental painter.

Contemporary listings: painter, 141 Gravier (1868); banner painting, 115 Lafayette (1869); painter (1875, 1889); sketch painter (1884).

Exhibited: Continental saloon (1884).

A Civil War veteran, Herron designed and painted a banner to represent the Louisiana Confederate Veterans for the Confederate reunion in Memphis TN (1901).

References: NOCD 1868–80, 1882–86, 1888–89, 1892–93, 1902; *D. Pic.*, Apr. 16, 1901; *D. States*, Aug. 24, 1884; *Eve. Chronicle*, Aug. 20, 1884; THNOC Cemetery Survey, 1981; United Confederate Veterans, 9; U.S. Census (1870), roll 522.

HERTZOG, PAUL

Painter, active N.O. 1872.

Contemporary listings: fresco painter (1872).

References: NOCD 1872.

HERVE, MRS. F.

Art teacher, art craftsman, active N.O. 1853–54.

Contemporary listings: teacher of the manufacture of paper flowers, wax fruits, embroideries in relief, oil painting, painting on glass, etc., 170 Bourbon and 164 Treme (1853); artificial flowers, 164 Treme (1854).

References: NOCD 1854; *Bee*, June 2, 1853; *D. Pic.*, Jan. 5–Feb. 1, 1853 (advs.); Groce and Wallace; U.S. Census (1850), roll 236.

HERVIEU, AUGUSTE JEAN JACQUES

Born St. Germain–en–Laye, France 1794; died 1858.

Sketch artist, active N.O. 1827.

Studied: with Girodet and Anne Louis Gros, France; with Sir Thomas Lawrence, England.

Exhibited: Royal Academy, London (intermittently 1819–58).

Memberships/positions: Société des Beaux Arts, Lille, France (1825).

French artist and miniature and portrait painter who accompanied Mrs. Frances Trollope to the U.S. from England in 1827 with the intention of becoming a drawing teacher in a settlement in TN. They arrived in the U.S. at N.O. during Christmas 1827 and left on New Year's Day 1828 for Memphis. Instead of remaining in TN, Hervieu became Mrs. Trollope's companion and protégé during her tour to other American cities, settled with the Trollopes in Cincinnati OH, and drew the 24 illustrations for the book about her travels, *Domestic Manners of the Americans* (1832). Two of the illustrations were made from sketches in N.O.: "Philosphical Millinery Store" and "New Orleans Steam Boat." Hervieu returned to Europe in 1831 and exhibited in London until his death.

References: Bénézit; Bolton, *Painters in Miniature*, 82; Fielding, *Dictionary*; Groce and Wallace; McDermott, "Mrs. Trollope"; Trollope; WPA, "Passenger Lists", Jan.–Dec. 1827.

HESTER, MISS HARRISON P.

Born N.O. Mar. 19, 1897.

Painter, bookbinder, active N.O. ca. 1918.

Exhibited: ART ASSOCIATION OF NEW ORLEANS (1918).

Hester was a teacher in the N.O. public school system (1923–53) and in private schools (1954–56). She served in varying capacities as a librarian (1958–62, 1967–74).

References: NOCD 1912, 1918–20, 1923–33, 1935, 1938, 1940, 1942, 1945–47, 1949, 1952–56, 1958, 1960–62, 1964–69, 1971–74; *T. Pic.*, Nov. 21, 1971; Art Asso., *Catalogue* (1918); Orleans Parish Registrar of Voters, NOPL.

HETCHBERGER, _____. _See_ AUDUBON, JOHN JAMES

HEULAN, MR. J. J.
Art teacher, active N.O. 1811.
Contemporary listings: drawing teacher St. Philip betw. Burgundy and Rampart (1811).
References: _Courier_, Feb. 18, 1811; Groce and Wallace.

HEULLANT, MAURICE
Born Paris, France Dec. 2, 1883.
Sculptor, active N.O. 1910–74; also cabinetmaker.
Contemporary listings: woodcarver (1910, 1914–15); woodcarver, Waldhorn Co. (1916–18).
Selected to be one of five N.O. sculptors to design the 34 carved stone panels for the exterior of the Lapeyre Miltenberger Home for Convalescents at Charity Hospital (1932). By 1938 Heullant claimed to have worked on most of the buildings recently constructed in N.O. and he was listed as a sculptor from 1942 to 1978. In 1962 he was presented an award for excellence in craftsmanship in wood carving by the American Association of Architects.
References: NOCD 1910, 1913–19, 1922–30, 1932–33, 1935, 1938, 1940, 1942, 1945–47, 1949, 1952–56, 1958, 1960–62, 1964–69, 1971–78; _Morn. Trib._, Nov. 9, 1932; _T. Pic._, May 15, 1938, Dec. 7, 1962; Orleans Parish Registrar of Voters, NOPL.

HEUSTIS, LOUISE LYONS
Born Mobile AL.
Painter, active N.O. 1881–1930.
Studied: Philadelphia Life School; Académie Julian and with William–Adolphe Bouguereau, Fleury, Charles Lasar, and Frederick William MacMonnies, Paris (ca. 1887); with William Merritt Chase and Kenyon Cox, Art Students League, N.Y.C.
Exhibited: SOUTHERN ART UNION (1881); ARTISTS' ASSOCIATION OF NEW ORLEANS (1892, 1894, 1899, 1902); ART ASSOCIATION OF NEW ORLEANS (1904, 1907–1908, 1918).
Memberships/positions: Art Students League and Woman's Art Club, N.Y.C. (1904).

After returning from her European studies in 1890, Heustis settled permanently in N.Y.C. as a portrait painter and visited N.O. often. In the 1920s she continued exhibiting periodically in N.O. at the Arts and Crafts Club, Southern States Art League, and the Art Association of New Orleans.
References: _Current Topics_, Jan. 1893, 11; _D. Pic._, May 26, 1881, Nov. 4, 1894; _Harlequin_, Dec. 6, 1899, 4; _T. Demo._, Dec. 14, 1894, Mar. 15, 1908; _T. Pic._, Mar. 14, 1918, Mar. 16, 1930; _Wkly. T. Demo._, Oct. 23, 1908; AANO, _Catalogue_ (1899, 1902); Art Asso., _Catalogue_ (1904, 1907).

HEWLETT, MR. FLORENCE
Sculptor, active N.O. ca. 1864.
Awarded: American Arts Association of New Orleans, prize for bronze bust (1864).
References: _Grand Celebration_, 30.

HEWLETT, FLORIAN
Painter, active N.O. 1867–79.
Contemporary listings: artist, 324 Burgundy (1867); painter, 178 Rampart (1870–71, 1873); painter (1872, 1875, 1878–79).
References: NOCD 1867, 1870–73, 1875, 1878–79.

HEYER, WILLIAM D.
Born ca. Mar. 1823; died N.O. Aug. 23, 1901.
Art teacher, active N.O. 1865–66.
Contemporary listings: drawing teacher, Central High School for Boys (1865–66).
Listed as a dry goods operator (1878–81, 1885–86), variety store operator (1882–84), and solicitor (1901).
References: NOCD 1858, 1866–68, 1872, 1878–86, 1888, 1890–93, 1895–98, 1901; _D. Pic._, Jan. 15, 1865, Aug. 24, 1901; _Repub._, June 29, 1867.

HEYMAN, CHARLES
Artist, active N.O. 1837.
Contemporary listings: artist, 172 Bourbon (1837).
References: NOCD 1837; Groce and Wallace.

HEZEAU, LOUIS FRANÇOIS
Born Corbeil, France Mar. 1796 or 1798; died N.O. May 12, 1865.

Art craftsman, active N.O. 1837–59.
Contemporary listings: artificial flower maker, 86 St. Ann (1837–38); artificial flower manufacturer, 74 Royal (1841); artificial flower factory, 74 Royal (1843, 1846); artificial flower manufacturer, 74 Royal (1849–50); artificial flower manufacturer, 71 Royal (1851); artificial flowers, 186 Royal (1856, 1858–59).
Husband of VICTOIRE HEZEAU.
References: NOCD 1838, 1842–43, 1846, 1849–56, 1858–61; Bee, May 8, 1837, Aug. 7, 1841, May 13, 1865; D. Pic., Oct. 10, 1866; N.O. Death Certificate (1865), 29:507, NOPL; U.S. Census (1850), roll 235.

HEZEAU, VICTOIRE (Mrs. LOUIS FRANÇOIS HEZEAU)
Born France ca. 1806.
Art craftsman, active N.O. 1837–42.
Contemporary listings: artificial flower maker, 86 St. Ann (1837); artificial flower maker, 76 Royal (1842).
References: NOCD 1842, 1866–68; Bee, May 8, 1837; U.S. Census (1850), roll 235.

HIGBEE, EMMA RUTH BURGESS. See BURGESS, EMMA RUTH

HILL, ALBERT D.
Artist, active N.O. 1897–98.
Contemporary listings: artist (1897–98).
References: NOCD 1897–98.

HILL, CHARLES A.
Artist, active N.O. 1889.
Contemporary listings: artist (1889).
References: NOCD 1889.

HILL, JOHN WILLIAM
Born London, England Jan. 13, 1812; died near West Nyack NY Sept. 24, 1879.
Artist, active N.O. 1852.
Studied: with his father, John Hill.
Exhibited: Pennsylvania Academy of Fine Arts, Philadelphia, and National Academy of Design, N.Y.C. (intermittently 1828–73); American Society of Painters in Water Colors (1867).
Memberships/positions: National Academy of Design (1833).
Brought to the U.S. in 1819, Hill was apprenticed to his father John Hill,

an engraver. From the late 1840s until 1855, he worked as a topographical artist and drew views of U.S. cities for a series of lithographs and engravings by Smith Bros. of N.Y.C. On two of these views, he collaborated with BENJAMIN F. SMITH, JR.: New Orleans from St. Patrick's Church 1852 and New Orleans from the Lower Cotton Press 1852. Later, Hill became the leading artist of the American Pre–Raphaelites and focused on landscape painting and watercolor studies of birds and flowers.
References: Bénézit; Dufour; St. Patrick's, 53; Fielding, Dictionary; Groce and Wallace; Kelly, 42; Reps, 312; THNOC 1947.20, 1954.3.

HINCK, HENRY
Lithographer, active N.O. 1872–73; also stationer, printer.
Contemporary listings: HINCK & COMPANY (1872); lithographer, 118 Common (1873).
References: NOCD 1871–78.

HINCK & COMPANY
Lithographers, active N.O. 1872; also stationers, printers, bookbinders; HENRY HINCK, Ferdinand J. Kuhnholz, partners.
Contemporary listings: 60 Camp (1872).
References: NOCD 1872.

HINCKS, LEDA. See PLAUCHE, LEDA HINCKS

HINCKS, MRS. W.
Painter, active N.O. ca. 1894.
Exhibited: ARTISTS' ASSOCIATION OF NEW ORLEANS (1894).
References: T. Demo., Dec. 14, 1894.

HIRSCH, MR. _____
Colorer, active N.O. 1856.
Contemporary listings: colorer, Giroux & Hirsch photographers (1856).
References: Bee, Mar. 3, 1856; Smith and Tucker, 160.

HIRSCH, HANS
Born Berlin, Prussia ca. June 1855; died N.O. Sept. 6, 1924.
Sculptor, art teacher, active N.O. 1915–24.
Contemporary listings: sculptor, 1024 St. Charles (1915); sculptor, fine artstone, garden furniture, and lighting stands, 1140 Carondelet

(1916); sculptor, fine artstone, garden furniture, and lighting stands, instructions in modeling and wood carving, 1140 Carondelet (1917); sculptor, 1140 Carondelet (1918). Exhibited: ART ASSOCIATION OF NEW ORLEANS (1915).
References: NOCD 1907–23; *Item*, May 3, 1915; *T. Pic.*, Sept. 8, 1924; Art Asso., *Special Exhibition*.

HIRT, L.
Art teacher, sketch artist, active N.O. 1841; also architect, engineer.
Studied: Ecole des Beaux Arts, Paris.
Contemporary listings: drawing academy, 204 Tchoupitoulas (1841). Hirt taught the drawing of architecture, machinery, surveys, and decoration. He also offered to execute plans for property dealers and builders, demonstrating his abilities by designing a map of N.O., with views of the city's major buildings, which was lithographed by JULES MANOUVRIER (1841).
References: *Bee*, July 28, 1841; *D. Pic.*, Apr. 11, 1841; Groce and Wallace; THNOC 1952.4.

HITE, GEORGE HARRISON
Born Urbana OH; died ca. 1880.
Painter, active N.O. 1844.
Contemporary listings: miniature painter, cor. Lafayette Square and St. Charles (1844).
References: *D. Pic.*, Nov. 19–20, 30, 1844; Fielding, *Dictionary*; Groce and Wallace.

HOBSON-CROSSMAN, ROTHSAY STEWART
Painter, active N.O. ca. 1915.
Exhibited: ART ASSOCIATION OF NEW ORLEANS (1915).
References: Art Asso., *Special Exhibition*.

HOEFFLER, ADOLF
Born Frankfurt–am–Main, Germany 1825; died 1898.
Painter, active N.O. 1848.
Studied: Municipal Institute of Frankfurt and the Academies of Munich and Dusseldorf, Germany.
Landscape and portrait painter who came to the U.S. via N.O. in Dec. 1848 and painted and sketched in the Mississippi River valley in 1849.

References: Bénézit; Groce and Wallace.

HOEGEN, ANTHONY
Artist, active N.O. 1895.
Contemporary listings: artist (1895).
References: NOCD 1895.

HOENING, JULIUS ROBERT
Born Elberfeld, Germany May 30, 1835; died Covington LA May 24, 1904.
Painter, art teacher, colorer, active N.O. 1860–1904; also ornamental painter, photographer.
Studied: Dusseldorf (before 1860).
Contemporary listings: teacher of drawing and painting, and portrait painter, 46 Camp and 61 Common (1860); artist painter, 61 Common (1861); portrait and fancy painter, and teacher of drawing and painting, 145 Canal and 167 Poydras (1865); portrait painter, Carondelet cor. Fourth (1867); portrait painter, 113 Carondelet (1868); portrait painter, 113 Canal (1869); portrait painter, 132 Canal and 157 Poydras (1870); portrait painter, 157 Poydras and 167 Canal (1871); portrait painter, 82 Camp (1872); artist, with THEODORE LILIENTHAL, and portrait painter, 112 St. Charles (1873); portrait painter, 441 Baronne (1876); portrait painter, 178 Canal (1877); portrait painter (1878, 1893); portrait painter, 165 Canal (1879); portrait and fresco painter and colorer, 287 Camp and 77 Calliope (1880); portrait painter, 77 Calliope (1881); artist, 133 Royal (1882–83); artist (1884, 1895, 1897–99, 1902, 1904); portrait painter, 196 Canal (1885); portrait painter, 19 Commercial (1886–91).
Exhibited: Heath & Lara importers (1873); Lilienthal's art gallery (1883).
Awarded: Grand State Fair, silver medal for best colored photographs in oil, and bronze medal for best photographs in India ink (1870).
Having immigrated to the U.S. in 1858, Hoening first advertised in N.O. in Jan. 1860 as a former pupil of the Dusseldorf School. He offered to teach drawing in India ink and crayon, painting in watercolor, pas-

tel, and oil, for beginning and advanced students, at their homes or at the studio he shared with B. & G. MOSES, photographers. His association with photography affected his portrait painting; throughout his career and as early as 1865, he was advertising copies of daguerreotypes, ambrotypes, or cartes–de–visite, enlarged and painted in oil, watercolor, or India ink. Furthermore, his 1870 awards were also for work in painted photographs. Known for his portraits, Hoening was also a painter of landscapes and animals. In 1880 he first advertised as a fresco and ornamental painter and was commissioned to paint in fresco 12 portraits on the ceiling of the French Opera House. He was also credited, at the time of his death, with frescoes in the Grand Opera House and in many private homes. In Oct. 1885 Hoening, ANDRES MOLINARY, and PAUL POINCY were the founders of the art school opened by the ARTISTS' ASSOCIATION OF NEW ORLEANS.
References: NOCD 1861, 1867–73, 1875–91, 1893, 1895, 1897–99, 1902–1904; NOBD 1865; Bee, Sept. 27, 1885; D. Delta, Jan. 22, 1860; D. Pic., Feb. 12, Oct. 13, 1860, Apr. 12, 1873, May 25–26, 1904; D. States, Oct. 20, 1880; Repub., Nov. 16, 1873; Times, Feb. 14, 1865; T. Demo., May 25, 1904; Boyd, 200; Bruns; Caldwell, 204; Glenk, 76; Lilienthal's, 6; LSM, Biennial Report for 1916–17, 100–1, LSM, Biennial Report for 1924–25, 47; Mechanics' and Agricultural Fair Asso., Report (1870):42; U.S. Census (1870), roll 524, (1880), roll 459; WPA, "Lives."

HOEPPNER, ERNEST
Born Germany ca. 1863; died New Braunfels TX Oct. 20, 1898.
Illustator, active N.O. 1888–96.
Contemporary listings: artist (1889–91, 1895).
Came to the U.S. when quite young. While living in NY, Hoeppner was employed by Puck, Life, and other pictorial publications. During his years in N.O. he worked for the Times–Democrat, Daily Delta, Daily Picayune, and Item. A colorful character, Hoeppner is credited with providing author William Sydney Porter with the pseudonym O. Henry, when the two were in N.O. He left for TX ca. 1896, on the advice of his physician.
References: NOCD 1888–91, 1893, 1895; D. Pic., Oct. 22, 1898; Kendall, "Old Days," 328–30; Kendall, "Who Killa de Chief?" 499.

HOERNER, WILLIAM J.
Born N.O. Feb. 12, 1874; died N.O. Oct. 26, 1965.
Engraver, lithographer, commercial artist, active N.O. 1891–1965.
Contemporary listings: engraver, T. FITZWILLIAM & CO. (1891, 1911); engraver (1898–1901, 1904–1906, 1908–10, 1912–16); engraver, DAMERON–PIERSON CO., LTD. (1918).
Continued as an engraver, litho–artist, and artist with Dameron–Pierson Co., Ltd. until his death.
References: NOCD 1889, 1891, 1898–1902, 1904–1906, 1908–16, 1918–33, 1935, 1938, 1940, 1942, 1945–47, 1949, 1952–56, 1958, 1960–62, 1964–68; T. Pic., Oct. 27, 1965; Orleans Parish Registrar of Voters, NOPL.

HOFELINE, ALBERT D.
Born N.O. Jan. 15, 1848 or 1849; died N.O. Dec. 29, 1928.
Engraver, active N.O. 1888–1908; primarily printer.
Contemporary listings: partner, Clark & Hofeline (1874–82); with JAMES S. RIVERS (1883–84); partner, MALUS & HOFELINE (1888–98); engraver and printer, 305 Chartres (1899–1908).
References: NOCD 1871–84, 1887–1929; T. Pic., Dec. 30, 1928; U.S. Census (1870), roll 522.

HOFFMAN, CHARLES
Sculptor, active N.O. 1884; primarily marble and stone cutter.
Exhibited: Ferdinand Lascar's store (1884).
Possibly Charles Hoffmann, born Bavaria, Germany ca. 1835; died N.O. Oct. 1, 1891.
References: NOCD 1877, 1879–89; D. Pic., May 23, 1884, Oct. 15, 1891.

HOFFMAN, GEORGE B.
Engraver, active N.O. 1884–88.
Contemporary listings: engraver, HUNTER & GENSLINGER (1884); engraver, with EDWARD F. ERTZ (1885–86); engraver and partner, BILDSTEIN & HOFFMAN (1887); engraver, Mascot Publishing Co. (1888).
Signed numerous engravings for the *Mascot* (1887–88).
References: NOCD 1884–88; *Mascot*, Aug. 20, 27, Sept. 3, 24, Oct. 15, Nov. 26, Dec. 3, 1887, Jan. 7, 1888.

HOFFMANN, LOUIS
Painter, active N.O. ca. 1883.
Mentioned as the painter whose works depicting incidents in LA history adorned the ceiling of the exchange room at the N.O. Cotton Exchange. Possibly Louis Hoffman, born Algiers LA Apr. 1860; died June 8, 1910; listed as a painter in Algiers, 1890–1910. *Cf.* HOPKIN, ROBERT.
References: NOCD 1890, 1892, 1894, 1896–1910; *D. Pic.*, June 9, 1910; *Picayune's Guide* (1913):124; U.S. Census (1900), roll 575.

HOFLE, EMILE
Artist, active N.O. 1895.
Contemporary listings: artist (1895).
References: NOCD 1895.

HOHENBERG, BARON VON. *See*
WÜRTTEMBERG, PRINCE PAUL OF

HOLDEN, JOHN
Born England ca. 1810–11; died N.O. Oct. 30, 1855.
Sculptor, active N.O. 1850–51; also stone and marble cutter.
Contemporary listings: stone and marble sculptor, St. Louis betw. Robertson and Villere (1850–51).
References: NOCD 1849–54; *Comm. Bull.*, Oct. 31, 1855; *Courier*, Oct. 31, 1855; *D. Crescent*, Oct. 31, 1855; *D. Pic.*, Oct. 31, 1855; *T. Deutsche Zeitung*, Nov. 1, 1855; Groce and Wallace; U.S. Census (1850), roll 235.

HOLMES, RALPH WILLIAM
Born Chicago or La Grange IL 1877.
Commercial artist, active N.O. 1904.
Studied: Art Institute, Chicago; with Gari Melchers.

Contemporary listings: artist, with H. M. Goddard (1904).
Exhibited: ART ASSOCIATION OF NEW ORLEANS (1904).
Awarded: Associated Artists of Pittsburgh, Carnegie Institute, silver medal (1915).
Memberships/positions: Art Students League; California Art Club; Los Angeles Painters and Sculptors.
References: NOCD 1904; Art Asso., *Catalogue* (1904); Fielding, *Dictionary*.

HOLSBURG, CLARENCE
Born LA ca. 1888.
Engraver, active N.O. 1910.
Contemporary listings: engraver (1910).
References: U.S. Census (1910), roll 524.

HOLT, MISS ____
Painter, active N.O. ca. 1881.
Exhibited: LILIENTHAL's art gallery and Werlein's music store (1881).
Cf. HOLT, SARAH BARTON.
References: *Demo.*, Feb. 27, 1881.

HOLT, SALLY SHEPHERD
Born Mobile AL June 15, 1873; died N.O. Aug. 20, 1965.
Art craftsman, active N.O. 1895–1939.
Studied: NEWCOMB COLLEGE (1895, 1902–1905, 1907–1909); art craftsman, Newcomb (1910–13, 1915–29).
Contemporary listings: artist (1910).
Exhibited: ART ASSOCIATION OF NEW ORLEANS (1910); Newcomb Art Alumnae Association show (1910, 1913).
Distinguished in the media of pottery decoration, bookbinding, beaded lampshades, and stained glass.
References: NOCD 1910, 1922–23, 1928, 1931–32, 1938, 1940, 1949, 1952–53, 1956; *T. Pic.*, Aug. 21, 1965; Art Asso., *Catalogue* (1910); N.O. Death Certificate (1906), 137:595, NOPL; Orleans Parish Registrar of Voters, NOPL; Ormond and Irvine, 157; Poesch, *Newcomb Pottery*, 40, 100; U.S. Census (1910), roll 523.

HOLT, SARAH BARTON
Born MS ca. 1831; died N.O. Feb. 24, 1906.

Artist, active N.O. ca. 1885–86.
Exhibited: American Exposition
(1885–86).
Cf. HOLT, MISS ———.
References: *D. Pic.*, Mar. 4, 1906;
Creole Exhibit, 12, 16.
HOLT, WILLIAM A.
Engraver, active N.O. 1888; primarily printer.
Contemporary listings: engraver, 163
Lafayette (1888).
References: NOCD 1872, 1874–
1901.
HOLYLAND, EDWARD T.
Born N.O. Apr. 1862; died N.O. July
24, 1917.
Engraver, active N.O. 1885–1905.
Contemporary listings: engraver
(1885, 1888, 1890, 1892, 1903–
1905); engraver, 18 Chartres (1894);
engraver, with T. Hausmann (1900–
1902).
References: NOCD 1885, 1887–88,
1890–1915, 1917; *T. Pic.*, July 25,
1917.
HOLYLAND, FREDERICK
Born N.Y.C. ca. 1832–34; died
Hammond LA June 27, 1894
Engraver, active N.O. 1860–94; also
printer.
Contemporary listings: engraver
(1860); engraver, 115 Canal (1861,
1867); engraver, 96 Customhouse
(1868); engraver, 25 Royal (1869–
71); engraver, 25 Royal (1870); engraver, 12 St. Charles (1872); engraver, 18 St. Charles (1872–75);
engraver, 8 St. Charles (1876–88);
engraver, 31 Chartres (1889–90,
1892–93); engraver, Leonard
Krower & Co. (1891); engraver, 18
Chartres (1894); engraver, 122
Chartres (1895).
Awarded: Grand State Fair, blue ribbon for best specimen of engraving
on metal (1869).
During the Civil War he was commissioned by the Confederate government to engrave bonds and notes
in Richmond VA and Columbia SC.
References: NOCD 1861, 1867–69,
1871–95; *D. Pic.*, Apr. 13, 18, 1869,
Mar. 5, 1872, Nov. 4, 1874, Jan. 15,
1875; *D. States*, May 1, 1883, Oct.
30, 1888; *National Republican*, Mar.

10, Sept. 15, 1872; *Repub.*, Feb. 12,
Nov. 22, 1871, June 22, Sept. 10,
1873, Dec. 15, 1874, May 6, 1876;
T. Demo., June 28, 1894; Boyd, 158;
Mechanics' and Agricultural Fair
Asso., *Report* (1869):79; U.S. Census
(1870), roll 524, (1860), roll 415.
HOME ART STUDIO. *See* ORTTE, RICHARD
HOMO, ALEXANDER
Born France ca. 1851.
Painter, sketch artist, active N.O.
1870, 1881.
Contemporary listings: landscape
drawer (1870).
Exhibited: SOUTHERN ART UNION
(1881).
Awarded: Grand State Fair, silver
medals for best drawing in stump or
pencil and best drawing in crayon
(1870).
Possibly Alexander Homo, died Paris
July 22, 1889, and exhibited at the
Paris salon beginning in 1877.
References: *D. Pic.*, May 26, 1881;
Bénézit; Mechanics' and Agricultural Fair Asso., *Report* (1870):42;
U.S. Census (1870), roll 522.
HONFLEUR, MR. ———
Art teacher, painter, active N.O.
1842; also daguerreotypist.
Contemporary listings: teacher of
drawing, painting, and perspective,
40 Camp (1842).
References: *Courier*, Mar. 2, 1856;
D. Pic., Mar. 15, June 18, 1842.
HOOPER, MRS. ———
Sculptor, active N.O. 1870.
Awarded: Grand State Fair, best
specimen of wax fruit (1870).
References: Mechanics' and Agricultural Fair Asso., *Report* (1870):42.
HOOPER, JOSEPH J.
Lithographer, active N.O. 1875–
1904; primarily stationer, printer.
Contemporary listings: lithographer,
69 Canal (1875–76); lithographer,
340 and 342 Carondelet (1894); lithographer, 612 Gravier (1904).
References: NOCD 1868, 1870–
1912, 1914–23; *Town Talk*, Sept.
1904, 26; *Washington Artillery Souvenir*, 47.
HOPF, WILLIAM
Sketch artist, lithographer, active
N.O. 1873–74; also engineer.

Contemporary listings: sketch artist, 31 Royal (1873); lithographer, 2 Carondelet (1874).

Made sketches to illustrate Thomas Jefferson Spear's historical work on N.O.

References: NOCD 1873–76; *Bee*, Oct. 4, 1874; *Repub.*, Aug. 9, 1872, Sept. 12, Oct. 2, 1873, Mar. 28, 1876.

HOPKIN, ROBERT

Born Glasgow, Scotland Jan. 3, 1832; died Detroit MI Mar. 21, 1909.

Painter, active N.O. ca. 1883.

Historical, landscape, marine, scene, and animal painter of Chicago, who was commissioned by J. B. Sullivan & Bro. to produce four mural paintings depicting the exploration of the Mississippi River for the ceiling of the N.O. Cotton Exchange (1883). *Cf.* HOFFMANN, LOUIS.

References: *D. Pic.*, May 9, 1883; Bénézit; Fielding, *Dictionary*; Glenk, 71, 76, 331; Groce and Wallace; LSM, *Annual Report for 1918*, 27, 60.

HOPKINS, I.

Silhouettist, active N.O. 1805.

Contemporary listings: silhouettist, 7 Bienville (1805).

References: *Gazette*, Oct. 8, 1805; Groce and Wallace.

HOPKINS, JOHN D.

Painter, active N.O. 1873–81.

Contemporary listings: painter (1873, 1881); painter, with Hugh Williams (1875); artist (1877).

References: NOCD 1873–75, 1877, 1881; *Repub.*, Mar. 5, 1875.

HORLZ, _____

Painter, active N.O. 1857.

An exhibition of the Horlz Panorama at 145 Baronne included scenes of the Mexican War, the War of Napoleon, Perry's Expedition to Japan, and the Battles of the Crimea, as well as views of N.O., Paris, Genoa, Geneva, and Lucerne.

References: *D. Creole*, Feb. 14–26, 1857.

HORNIKEL, EMILE F.

Born Germany ca. 1862.

Engraver, active N.O. 1907–10.

Contemporary listings: engraver, with C. E. Adler (1907–1909); stationery engraver (1910).

References: NOCD 1907–1909; U.S. Census (1910), roll 519.

HORSCHER, HENRY

Hair worker, active N.O. 1860–66.

Contemporary listings: hair worker, Prytania near Polymnia (1860–61); hair worker (1866).

References: NOCD 1860–61, 1866.

HORTON, CHARLES

Artist, active N.O. 1859–61.

Contemporary listings: artist, 134 Canal (1859–61).

References: NOCD 1859–61; Groce and Wallace.

HORTON, JOSEPH

Sketch artist, active N.O. ca. 1880–81.

Sketched *Louisiana–The Business Boom in the South–A Scene on the Levee at New Orleans* published in *Frank Leslie's Illustrated Newspaper* (Jan. 8, 1881).

References: *Leslie's*, Jan. 8, 1881, 320.

HOUGHTON, MRS. _____

Art teacher, active N.O. 1855.

Contemporary listings: teacher of papier maché, with REBECCA CADY (1855).

References: *D. Delta*, Apr. 1, 1855.

HOUGHTON, JOHN H.

Painter, active N.O. 1858–70.

Contemporary listings: partner, Houghton & Dabin, painters, 61 Exchange Pl. (1858); painter, 392 Baronne (1859–61); portrait and fancy painter, 47 Perdido (1865); painter, Perdido near Baronne (1866); painter, 76 Perdido (1868); painter (1869); painter, 317 Dryades (1870).

References: NOCD 1858–61, 1866, 1868–70; NOBD 1865.

HOUGUENAGUE, JEAN

Born ca. 1800–10.

Lithographer, active N.O. 1840–46; also printer.

Contemporary listings: lithographic printer, Exchange Al. near St. Louis (1841–42); lithographer, Exchange Al. betw. St. Louis and Conti (1843–44); lithographic printer, 10 Exchange Al. (1846).

Also printed sheet music covers.

References: NOCD 1841–44, 1846; "Grand Tippecanoe March," "Jackson's Grand March," Sheet Music Collection, LA Coll., TU; THNOC 1970.11.48; U.S. Census (1840), roll 132.

HOWARD, MRS. HARRY
Sketch artist, active N.O. ca. 1892–93.
Studied: ARTISTS' ASSOCIATION OF NEW ORLEANS (1893).
Exhibited: Artists' Association of New Orleans (1892).
References: *Current Topics*, Jan. 1893, 11, Nov. 1893, 198; *D. Pic.*, Dec. 18, 1892.

HOWARD, LOUIS C.
Painter, active N.O. ca. 1915.
Exhibited: ART ASSOCIATION OF NEW ORLEANS (1915).
Amateur landscape painter and N.O. businessman who in 1915 was president of the Union Hat Manufacturing Co.
References: NOCD 1910–24, 1926, 1928–30; Art Asso., *Special Exhibition*; Patrick, 252.

HOWE, FRANCES LAWRENCE (Mrs. Charles Pollard Cocke)
Died Jan. 16, 1951.
Art craftsman, painter, sketch artist, active N.O. 1891–1907.
Studied: NEWCOMB COLLEGE (1889–94, 1906–1907).
Exhibited: ARTISTS' ASSOCIATION OF NEW ORLEANS (1891–92, 1894); Tulane University (1892–93).
Memberships/positions: ARTS EXHIBITION CLUB (1901).
Painted landscapes, still lifes, and figures; listed as a pottery designer (1906–1907).
References: *Current Topics*, Jan. 1892, 24, Jan. 1893, 10; *D. Pic.*, Dec. 17, 1891, Mar. 3, Dec. 14, 1892, Feb. 14, 1893; *Men and Matters*, Sept. 1897, 48; *T. Demo.*, Mar. 3, Dec. 13, 1892, Dec. 14, 1894; Ogden et al.; Ormond and Irvine, 149, 153; Poesch, *Newcomb Pottery*, 50, 98, 124.

HOWE, LOUISE E.
Art teacher, active N.O. ca. 1909–15.
Contemporary listings: teacher, N.C. Maguire school (1909); drawing teacher, N.O. public schools (1913);

teacher, McDonogh #11 school (1915).
References: NOCD 1909–10, 1913, 1915, 1917, 1919–20, 1923; *T. Demo.*, Jan. 14, 1913.

HOWE, WILLIAM HENRY.
Born Ravenna OH 1846; died Bronxville NY 1929.
Painter, active N.O. 1890.
Studied: Royal Academy, Dusseldorf, Germany (1880–82); with Otto de Thoren and F. de Vuillefroy, Paris (1882–83).
Exhibited: Salon, Paris (1883, 1890); Europe (ca. 1883–93); World's Industrial and Cotton Centennial Exposition (1884–85); ART ASSOCIATION OF NEW ORLEANS (1907).
Awarded: World's Industrial and Cotton Centennial Exposition, honorable mention (1885); Salon, Paris, medals (1888–89); London, gold medal (1890); Pennsylvania Academy of Fine Arts, Philadelphia, Temple gold medal (1890); Boston, gold medal (1890); Columbian Exposition, Chicago, medal (1893); San Francisco, gold medal (1894); Atlanta GA, gold medal (1895); Buffalo NY, silver medal (1901).
Memberships/positions: Academie, Paris, officer (1896); National Academy of Design, N.Y.C. (1897); Society of American Artists (1899); Chevalier, Legion of Honor (1899).
Itinerant landscape, animal, and genre painter who submitted paintings to exhibitions in N.O. at the exposition (1884–85) and at the Art Association (1907). Howe visited the city in 1890; one of his paintings, *Farm Scene with Negro Boy*, is inscribed "1890 New Orleans."
References: Art Asso., *Catalogue* (1907); Bénézit; Fielding, *Dictionary*; Tennessee Centennial, 54; WICCE, *Catalogue*, 21; William Young.

HOWELL, ELIZA HILTON
Born N.O.
Painter, active N.O. 1890–97.
Studied: with ACHILLE PERELLI, SOUTHERN ART UNION; with ANDRES MOLINARY; with PAUL POINCY; ART-

ISTS' ASSOCIATION OF NEW ORLEANS
(1890).
Exhibited: Artists' Association of New
Orleans (1890, 1892, 1896–97); FIVE
OR MORE CLUB (1893).
Memberships/positions: Five or More
Club; BLACK AND WHITE CLUB.
References: *Current Topics*, Jan.
1893, 10–11; *D. Pic.*, Nov. 13, 1890,
Dec. 14, 1892, Feb. 14, 1893; *D.
States*, May 16, 1890; AANO, *Catalogue* (1896, 1897); Information
courtesy Mrs. John T. Farnsworth,
Nov. 16, 1985; Mount, 98–99.

HOWES, N. S.
Painter, active N.O. ca. 1868.
Awarded: Grand State Fair, silver
medal for best composition in oil
(1868).
References: *D. Pic.*, Jan. 19, 1868.

HOY, LEE
Born China ca. 1854.
Sculptor, active N.O. 1880.
Contemporary listings: wood carver
(1880).
References: U.S. Census (1880), roll
460.

HOYLE, GEORGE
Born England ca. 1830–35.
Lithographer, active N.O. 1868–81;
also printer.
Contemporary listings: lithographer,
with JOHN DOUGLAS (1868, 1871,
1875); lithographer (1870); lithographic printer, with John Douglas
(1870, 1881); lithographer, with
HUGH LEWIS (1876–78).
References: NOCD 1868, 1870–81;
U.S. Census (1870), roll 522, (1880),
roll 461.

HOYLE, J. *See also* FEUSIER, HOYLE & CO.
Born England ca. 1827.
Lithographer, active N.O. 1866; also
printer.
Contemporary listings: lithographer,
324 Bayou (1866).
References: NOCD 1866; U.S. Census (1860), roll 417.

HOYT, CHARLES
Lithographer, active N.O. 1894.
Contemporary listings: lithographer,
12 N. Broad (1894).
References: NOCD 1894.

HOYT, FRANK T.
Painter, active N.O. 1872–73.
Contemporary listings: scenic artist,
Academy of Music (1872–73).
References: NOCD 1873; *Repub.*,
Sept. 1, 1872.

HOYT, HARRY E.
Painter, active N.O. 1872–85.
Contemporary listings: scenic artist,
Academy of Music (1872–73); scenic painter, Academy of Music
(1884); scenic painter, St. Charles
Theatre (1884–85).
References: *D. Pic.*, Jan. 19, 1887;
D. States, Sept. 19, Nov. 3, 1884; *Eve.
Chronicle*, Sept. 10, 15, 1884, Nov.
11, 1885; *Repub.*, Sept. 8, Dec. 1, 8,
1872, Feb. 2, June 15, 21, 1873.

HUBER, GUSTAVE, JR.
Lithographer, active N.O. 1887.
Contemporary listings: lithographer
(1887).
References: NOCD 1885, 1887.

HUBER, VICTOR
Born Vienna, Austria June 8, 1875;
died N.O. Apr. 24, 1941.
Engraver, sculptor, active N.O.
1891–1941; primarily marble and
stone cutter; also draftsman.
Contemporary listings: engraver
(1892).
Came to N.O. in 1885 with his family
and attended school. In 1889 Huber
returned to Vienna where he worked
as a wood engraver for two years. He
returned to N.O. in 1891 and worked
as a wood engraver with the NEW ORLEANS ENGRAVING COMPANY, then with
HENRY GRABAU, and then as a draftsman with ALBERT WEIBLEN. From
Weiblen he learned marble cutting
and in 1894 left to work in N.Y.C.
as a marble worker, mainly as a carver
for Brooklyn monument and cemetery builders. By 1897 he returned
to N.O., after losing the sight in one
eye from an accident while working,
and became a music teacher and performer. Huber eventually returned
to Weiblen as a stone cutter, until he
opened his own business (ca. 1906)
for cemetery work, statuary, mantels, and stone work for building. His
company contracted to complete the
marble work on the Chalmette Mon-

ument to the Battle of N.O. (1910). In 1911 he began the firm Victor Huber Marble and Granite Company on St. Louis and Scott and later was the founder of Hope Mausoleum.
References: NOCD 1892–94, 1899–1904, 1906–33, 1935, 1938, 1940; *T. Pic.*, Apr. 25, 1941; Victor Huber; Orleans Parish Registrar of Voters, NOPL.

HUDSON, JULIEN (Jules)
Born N.O.; died 1844; black?
Painter, art teacher, active N.O. 1831–40.
Studied: with Abdel de Pujol, Paris (1837); with ANTHONY MEUCCI (ca. 1831).
Contemporary listings: miniature painter and drawing teacher, 117 Bienville (1831); miniature painter, 117 Bienville (1832); portrait painter, 120 Bienville (1837–38).
GEORGE DAVID COULON wrote that he studied in N.O. in 1840 under Hudson. Contemporary evidence does not mention Hudson's race: his identification as a black rests on the portrait of a man (dated 1839), apparently a mulatto, which has traditionally been considered a self-portrait.
References: NOCD 1837–38; *Bee*, June 6, 1831; *Courier*, Dec. 3, 1831–Jan. 10, 1832; Bruns, 313; Coulon MS, Scrapbook 100, LSM; Fine, 30; Glenk, 45, 76; Groce and Wallace; O'Neill, 73; THNOC artists files.

HUDSON, SAMUEL ADAMS
Born Brimfield MA Feb. 13, 1813; died Springfield IL Feb. 19, 1877.
Sketch artist, painter, active N.O. ca. 1838–48.
Boston tailor who painted in his spare time until 1847 when he began, in Louisville KY, a gigantic panorama of the Mississippi and Ohio rivers, based on sketches and drawings made during four trips between 1838 and 1848. The last scenes of the canvas were of N.O. with its ships and public buildings prominently displayed. The panorama was exhibited in 1848–49 in the North but was destroyed by fire in 1849. Hudson then returned to tailoring.

References: *D. Orleanian*, Apr. 20, 1848; Arrington, "Samuel A. Hudson's Panorama"; Groce and Wallace.

HUGER, EMILY HAMILTON
Born N.O. Jan. 11, 1881; died Feb. 3, 1946.
Painter, active N.O. 1897–1918.
Studied: NEWCOMB COLLEGE (1897–1902); with William Merritt Chase, John Connah, William A. Bell, N.Y.C.; with Hugh Breckenridge, Philadelphia; with ELLSWORTH WOODWARD.
Exhibited: Louisiana Purchase Exposition, St. Louis MO (1904); ART ASSOCIATION OF NEW ORLEANS (1917–18).
Memberships/positions: ARTS EXHIBITION CLUB (1901); Art Association of New Orleans; American Federation of the Arts; College Art Association; Western Arts Asso.
She was a member in N.O. of the Southern States Art League, Artists' Guild, and the Arts and Crafts Club.
References: NOCD 1903, 1905, 1907–18; *D. States*, Dec. 6, 1903; *Item*, Jan. 16, 1921; Art Asso., *Catalogue* (1917, 1918):4; Arts Exhibition Club, 14; Fielding, *Dictionary*; Ormond and Irvine, 157; U.S. Census (1910), roll 524; *Who's Who in American Art*, 1938–39.

HUGHES, MISS M. M.
Painter, active N.O. 1889–90.
Studied: ARTISTS' ASSOCIATION OF NEW ORLEANS (1890).
Exhibited: ACADEMY OF FINE ARTS (1889); Artists' Association of New Orleans (1890).
References: *D. Pic.*, Jan. 22, 1889; *D. States*, May 16, 1890.

HULTBERG, CHARLES EVALD
Born Sweden 1874; died Biloxi MS Nov. 19, 1948.
Painter, active N.O. ca. 1908–18.
Studied: with Algernon M. Talmage, Cornwall, England.
Exhibited: ART ASSOCIATION OF NEW ORLEANS (1908, 1917–18).
References: NOCD 1910–11, 1917; *D. Pic.*, Mar. 15, 1908; *T. Pic.*, Nov. 21, 1948; Art Asso., *Catalogue* (1917, 1918); THNOC artists files.

HUMBRECHT, ERASMUS
Born Alsace ca. 1849.
Painter, active N.O. 1872–93.
Studied: Switzerland.
Contemporary listings: artist (1873); painter (1874–84, 1893).
After leaving Europe, Humbrecht stopped in Martinique to decorate a monastery. In 1872 he arrived in N.O. and was commissioned to paint murals in fresco for the St. Louis Cathedral, completed in 1873. In 1893 he was commissioned to retouch some of the paintings in the cathedral and to replace others with his own compositions. During the same period, he completed commissions in the Mississippi Valley for portraits and for buildings, including in N.O. Holy Trinity Catholic Church (1874), the American Drug Store (1880), and Trinity Church with FIDEL HAUG (1883).
References: NOCD 1873–84, 1893; *Bull.*, June 27, 1874; *D. States*, Sept. 7, 1880; *T. Pic.*, Apr. 24, 1938; Glenk, 76; Huber and Wilson, *Basilica*, 41–42; WPA, *Louisiana*, 166.

HUNTER, A.
Lithographer, painter, art dealer, active N.O. 1844–46; also printer.
Contemporary listings: lithographer, in the Arcade (1844); print–dealer, Exchange Pl. (1846).
Exhibited: American Institute, N.Y.C. (1845).
Possibly Alfred Hunter, listed as having a bookstore (1849–51).
References: NOCD 1849–51; *D. Pic.*, Nov. 19, 1844, Sept. 13, 1846; Groce and Wallace.

HUNTER & GENSLINGER
Engravers, active N.O. 1883–86; also stencil cutters, stationers, printers; Eugene W. Hunter (born ca. 1846; died Feb. 2, 1898), CHARLES H. GENSLINGER, partners.
Contemporary listings: engravers, 116 Gravier (1883–86).
References: NOCD 1880–90; *D. Pic.*, Feb. 4, 1898.

HUTCHISON, LOUISE L. (Mrs. Joseph Hutchison)
Art craftsman, active N.O. 1879–85.
Contemporary listings: artist (1879); artificial flowers, 194 Canal (1880–85).

References: NOCD 1875–77, 1879–85.

HUTSON, CHARLES WOODWARD
Born McPhersonville SC Sept. 23, 1840; died N.O. May 27, 1936.
Painter, active N.O. 1908–36.
Studied: with his daughter, ETHEL HUTSON.
Exhibited: ART ASSOCIATION OF NEW ORLEANS (1911, 1913–16); Independent's Show, N.Y.C. (1917).
Scholar, author, and teacher who was admitted to the SC bar (1865) but turned instead to a teaching career. Hutson taught languages and the classics at universities in nearly all the southern states between 1873 and his retirement in 1908, including Louisiana State University (1869–73). He had begun sketching in pastel while in TX in 1905 but not seriously until his retirement, when he moved to N.O. His earliest N.O. subjects were pastel studies of French Quarter buildings, but he eventually turned to nature studies, particularly landscapes and coastal scenes, and to representations of historical and classical themes. Hutson's early work progressed from pastels to watercolors, and he began to paint in oils in 1923 with a series of "Fantasies," based on subjects from the Bible and the classics. He exhibited regularly in N.O. until his death, and had three one–man exhibitions at the DELGADO MUSEUM OF ART (1931, 1948, 1965, the last a major retrospective). In 1924, Hutson received the Blanche Benjamin prize in landscape painting. He began to establish a national reputation when one of his works was shown at the New York Independent's Show (1917) with other pioneers of modern American painting, and after his death, his reputation grew with exhibitions in N.Y.C., Washington DC, and throughout the South. Self–described as an amateur, Hutson is considered by art historians to be an exponent of modern abstract primitivism.
References: NOCD 1910–13, 1915–27, 1929–31, 1933, 1935; Arts and Crafts Club, *Bulletin* (1929–30):14;

Item, Jan. 16, Feb. 6, Apr. 6, 1921, Nov. 13, 1948; *Item–Trib.*, Apr. 27, 1927, Aug. 30, 1931; *Morn. Trib.*, May 11, Oct. 5, 1927, Mar. 22, 1935; *States*, Feb. 14, 1926, Dec. 4, 1932, Apr. 12, 1936; *T. Pic.*, Apr. 3, 1921, Feb. 29, 1924, Dec. 20, 1925, Oct. 20, 1926, Mar. 3, June 15, 1930, July 9, Sept. 24, 1933, Mar. 25, 1935, Jan. 19, 1938; Art Asso., *Catalogue* (1911, 1913, 1914, 1915, 1916); Art Asso., *Catalogue of Oil Paintings by Charles W. Hutson*; Art Asso., *Paintings by Charles W. Hutson*; Art Asso., *Special Exhibition*; Delgado, *Catalogue of Oil Paintings by Charles W. Hutson*; Delgado, *Charles W. Hutson, 1840–1936*; Janis, 160–65; Kendall, *History*, 3:1187–90; U.S. Census (1910), roll 524.

HUTSON, ETHEL
Born Baton Rouge LA Apr. 19, 1872; died Gulfport MS June 12, 1951.
Painter, pottery decorator, active N.O. 1904–47.
Studied: NEWCOMB COLLEGE; Pratt Institute, Brooklyn NY; National Academy of Design, N.Y.C.; Art Students League, N.Y.C.; Cooper Institute, N.Y.C.; with Bessie Cary Lemly, ELLSWORTH WOODWARD, MARY GIVEN SHEERER; with Mrs. J. P. McAuley, Galveston TX; with Howard Chandler Christy, Arthur W. Dow, Francis C. Jones, G. Maynard, Luis Mora, and G. R. Smith.
Contemporary listings: artist (1910).
Exhibited: ART ASSOCIATION OF NEW ORLEANS (1904, 1911, 1913–15).
Memberships/positions: Art Association of New Orleans; Mississippi Art Association (1913–14).
Landscape and nature painter, teacher, writer, and daughter of CHARLES WOODWARD HUTSON. She continued to exhibit in N.O. into the 1940s, particularly with the Arts and Crafts Club, and was secretary to the director at the DELGADO MUSEUM OF ART (1925–45) where she supervised the WPA art project, and secretary–treasurer at the Southern States Art League (1925–47). She lived on the Gulf Coast in her last years.

References: NOCD 1909–11, 1913–28, 1930–33, 1935, 1938, 1940, 1942, 1945–47, 1949; *Item*, Jan. 16, Feb. 3, 6, 1921; *Item–Trib.*, Oct. 20, 1940; *Morn. Trib.*, Oct. 5, 1927; *States*, Feb. 9, 14, 1926; *T. Pic.*, Oct. 4, 1925, Mar. 3, 1930, Oct. 25, 1936, Feb. 23, 1938, Oct. 23, 1941, June 14–15, 1951; Art Asso., *Catalogue* (1904, 1911, 1913, 1914, 1915, 1945); Art Asso., *Special Exhibition*; Cline, *Contemporary Art*; Fielding, *Dictionary*; Orleans Parish Registrar of Voters, NOPL; Poesch, *Newcomb Pottery*, 52; U.S. Census (1910), roll 524; *Who's Who in American Art*, 1938–39.

A. W. HYATT STATIONERY MNFG. CO. LTD.
Lithographers, active N.O. 1892–1915; also stationers and printers, ARTHUR WILLIAM HYATT, pres.
Contemporary listings: lithographers, 73 Camp (1892–94); lithographers, 409 Camp (1895–98); lithographers, 407 Camp (1899–1915).
Although their last ad for lithographic work appeared in 1915, the company continued as printers until 1947 when the name changed until Hyatt, Inc. By 1975 the firm had changed to its present name, Hyatt Corporation, and was specializing in architectural and engineering supplies.
References: NOCD 1892–1933, 1935, 1938, 1940, 1942, 1945–47; O'Connor.

HYATT, ARTHUR WILLIAM
Born Brighton, England Oct. 26, 1832; died N.O. Jan. 24, 1900.
Lithographer, active N.O. 1871–1900; also printer, stationer.
Contemporary listings: lithographer, 38 Camp (1874–80); lithographer, 73 Camp (1881–91).
Having worked in TX on the *Galveston News* beginning in 1843, Hyatt arrived in N.O. ca. 1849 and was first listed in 1860. He worked for other printers and stationers before going into partnership as Christian & Hyatt in 1869 and taking over as sole proprietor in 1871. The company, un-

der his name alone, served as stationers, printers, lithographers, engravers, bookbinders, and blank book manufacturers. In 1882 it claimed to be the largest printing office and bindery in the South. By 1892 the business had become A. W. HYATT STATIONERY MNFG. CO. LTD. with Hyatt acting as its president until his death.
References: NOCD 1860–61, 1867–1900; *Bull.*, Apr. 10, 1874; *Demo.*, July 6, 1876; *T. Demo.*, Jan. 25, 27, 1900; Land, 198; N.O. Death Certificate (1900), 121:491, NOPL; *Photographic Album of the City of N.O.*; U.S. Census (1850), roll 123, (1860), roll 420.

HYDE, EDWARD H.
Designer, engraver, active N.O. 1871.
Contemporary listings: designer and wood engraver, 61 Camp (1871).
Advertised that he executed wood cuts, designs, and ornamental drawings (1871).
References: NOCD 1870–71.

HYDE, MRS. G. W.
Hair worker, active N.O. ca. 1885–86.
Exhibited: American Exposition (1885–86).
References: Creole Exhibit, 18.

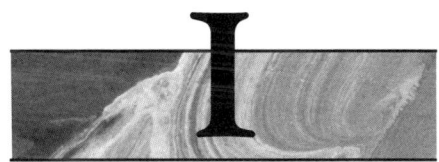

IANET, H.
Sculptor, active N.O. 1851.
Contemporary listings: sculptor
(1851).
Cf. JANET, HENRI.
References: *Courier*, Apr. 24, 1851.

IDEAL ART COMPANY
Art dealers, active N.O. 1895;
Charles B. Buckley, E. R. Harris,
Louis Thomas, partners.
Contemporary listings: portraits, 703
Camp (1895).
References: NOCD 1895.

INGLES, MARGOT LABARRE (Mrs.
Sidney Lee Ingles)
Born N.O. Sept. 5, 1882; died N.O.
Oct. 31, 1962.
Artist, active N.O. 1910.
Contemporary listings: artist (1910).
References: *T. Pic.*, Nov. 2, 1962;
Orleans Parish Registrar of Voters,
NOPL; U.S. Census (1910), roll 519.

INMAN, HENRY
Born Utica NY Oct. 28, 1801; died
N.Y.C. Jan. 17, 1846.
Painter, active N.O. ca. 1820–21.
Primarily a portrait and miniature
painter, as well as genre, landscape,
and historical painter. During his apprenticeship to JOHN WESLEY JARVIS,
Inman painted the backgrounds and
draperies of Jarvis's portraits (1814–
22). He probably accompanied Jarvis
on his first trip to N.O. during the
winter of 1820–21 and perhaps again
during 1821–22. Inman later lived in
N.Y.C., where he was one of the
founders of the National Academy of
Design (1826); he was one of the first
to introduce lithography to the U.S.
(ca. 1828). He became one of the
leading portraitists of his time, working in N.Y.C., Philadelphia, and England.
References: *Bee*, Jan. 10, 1840, Jan.
7, 1842, Jan. 29, 1846; *Comm. Bull.*,
July 26, 1841; *D. Delta*, Dec. 21,
1845, Jan. 29, 1846; *D. Pic.*, Jan. 29,
1846, Oct. 27, 1847; *Jeffersonian*,
Jan. 29, 1846; *Appleton's CAB*; Bé-

nézit; Bolton, *Draughtsmen*, 37; Bol-
ton, "Inman," 117; Cline, *Art and
Artists*; *DAB*; Dunlap, 2:219–20,
3:137; Edward Fenno to his sister,
May 12, 1822, Clements Library;
Groce and Wallace; Lipton, 44;
Longaker, 118; Thompson, "Check-
list"; Tuckerman, 235–44.

INNESS, GEORGE
Born near Newburgh NY May 1,
1825; died Bridge of Allan, Scotland
Aug. 3, 1894.
Painter, active N.O. 1884; 1890.
Studied: with Régis F. Gignoux,
Brooklyn NY (ca. 1843).
Exhibited: World's Industrial and
Cotton Centennial Exposition (1884–
85); SEEBOLD's (1890).
Associated with the art of the Hudson River school after the Civil War,
Inness was considered, during his
lifetime, one of the foremost American painters, especially in landscapes. He traveled throughout Europe and the U.S. and settled in
Montclair NJ by 1878. He visited
N.O. in 1884 when three of his
paintings were exhibited at the art
gallery of the exposition. However,
the *Daily Picayune* described his
Mount Washington as "an ugly picture . . . only a combination of paint
and canvas." Inness returned to N.O.
in 1890, at the invitation of BROR AN-
DERS WIKSTROM; he exhibited work at
the art gallery of F. W. E. Seebold
and gave a talk on Impressionistic art
at the Seebold home.
References: *Crescent Monthly*, Feb.
1867, 153; *D. Pic.*, Apr. 13, 1885;
Appleton's CAB; Art Asso., *Catalogue*
(1907); *DAB*; *Encyclopaedia Britannica*; Groce and Wallace; Ireland,
445, 447; Klitgaard, 102; Seebold,
1:315–16.

IRISH, T. T.
Engraver, active N.O. 1849.
Contemporary listings: copper en-
graver, Andrew near Jersey (1849).

197

References: NOCD 1849–50; Groce and Wallace.

IRMA, _____
Artist, active N.O. 1841.
Contemporary listings: artist, St. Ann near Villere (1841).
Possibly Mr. P. Irma, born ca. 1800–10, listed in the 1840 census.
References: NOCD 1841; U.S. Census (1840), roll 131.

IRVINE, SARAH AGNES ESTELLE (Sadie)
Born N.O. July 21, 1887; died N.O. Sept. 4, 1970.
Art craftsman, painter, art teacher, active N.O. ca. 1903–67.
Studied: NEWCOMB COLLEGE (1903–1906); Art Students League, N.Y.C. (after 1906).
Contemporary listings: artist (1910); watercolor painter (1918).
Exhibited: ART ASSOCIATION OF NEW ORLEANS (1907–1908, 1910, 1913, 1917–18); Tercentenary Exposition, Jamestown VA (1907); Panama–Pacific International Exposition, San Francisco (1915).
Awarded: Byron Holley Medal for watercolor (1905); Mary L. S. Neill Medal (1907); traveling scholarship (1908); Art Association of New Orleans (1908); Pennsylvania Academy of the Fine Arts, Philadelphia, scholarship (1914).
One of the most noted artists of the Newcomb style, especially in her pottery decorations, watercolors, and block prints. Irvine was associated with Newcomb College in its guild and as a faculty member until 1952, then taught at the Academy of the Sacred Heart until 1967. She exhibited with the Art Association of New Orleans and the Southern States Art League and received the ELLSWORTH WOODWARD prize for pottery (1930).
References: NOCD 1928–33, 1935, 1938, 1940, 1942, 1945–47, 1949, 1952–56, 1958, 1960–62, 1964–69, 1971; D. Pic., Oct. 17, 1908; Item–Trib., Mar. 12, 1933; Morn. Trib., May 4, 1927; States–Item, Sept. 5, 1970; T. Pic., Mar. 14, 1918, May 5, 1929, Mar. 6, 1932, Mar. 12, 1933, Jan. 7, 14, 28, Feb. 4, 1934, Jan. 6, 13, 1935, Mar. 8, 1936, Mar. 10, 1937, Mar. 4, 1938, Feb. 20, 1949, Sept. 21, 1952; Collier, "The World of Art," T. Pic., Sept. 22, 1968; T. Pic., Sept. 7, 1970; Art Asso., Catalogue (1907, 1910, 1913, 1917, 1918, 1934, 1943); Blasberg, "Sadie Irvine," 250–51; Fairbanks, 590; Louisiana Crafts Council; Ormond and Irvine, 77, 130–31, 134, 136–37, 157–58; Poesch, Newcomb Pottery, 100; Smithsonian, Newcomb, 13, 15, 19, 24; U.S. Census (1910), roll 524.

ISABELLE, MRS. JAMES
Painter, active N.O. 1870.
Made a silk banner, with representations of LA's Gov. Henry C. Warmoth and Lt. Gov. Oscar J. Dunn, for the Second Ward Radical Republican Club (1870).
References: Repub., Oct. 12, 1870.

ISNARD, JEAN JACQUES
Born N.O. ca. 1798; died N.O. Aug. 14, 1859.
Sculptor, engraver, active N.O. 1818–46; also stone carver, marble carver, cabinetmaker, gilder.
Contemporary listings: engraver, St. Peter (1818); sculptor (1819); marble sculptor, cor. St. Louis and Rampart (1841, 1843); marble sculptor, 170 Canal (1846).
In partnership with J. F. ST. GEES (1817–18), they advertised all types of stone work and carving, including naval carving, paving in marble, and the manufacture of architectural elements and sundials. He was commissioned by the City of N.O. to make repairs to the W. C. C. Claiborne cemetery monument (1819).
References: NOCD 1822–24, 1827, 1830, 1832, 1834–35, 1837–38, 1841–43, 1846; L'Ami Des Lois, Mar. 10–14, 1818 (advs.); Bee, Aug. 16, 1859; Courier, Oct. 10, 22, 1817, Mar. 13, 1818; D. Pic., Aug. 16, 1859; Groce and Wallace; Mayor's Office, Messages Jan. 3, 1818–Dec. 31, 1819, 8:111–12, NOPL; N.O. Death Certificate (1859), 20: 379, NOPL; U.S. Census (1850), roll 235.

IVORY, LOUIS
Engraver, active N.O. 1882–84.
Contemporary listings: engraver (1882–84).
References: NOCD 1882–86.

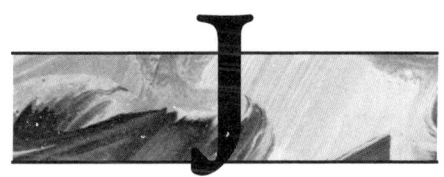

JACKSON, CLAUDE D.
Painter, active N.O. 1917–20.
Contemporary listings: painter, 1121 Henry Clay (1917).
Exhibited: ART ASSOCIATION OF NEW ORLEANS (1917).
Listed as an artist in 1920.
References: NOCD 1917–18, 1920; Art Asso., *Catalogue* (1917, 1919).

JACKSON, LEO
Born N.O. ca. 1895; died St. Florentine, France ca. Nov. 1920.
Engraver, active N.O. 1910–17.
Contemporary listings: engraver, William Frantz & Co. (1910–13); engraver (1915); engraver, with C. E. Adler (1916–17).
References: NOCD 1908, 1910–13, 1915–19; *Item*, Nov. 18, 1920.

JACKSON, THOMAS J.
Died NY Nov. 1842.
Painter, active N.O. 1840–42.
Contemporary listings: portrait and miniature painter, 21 Camp (1840–41); portrait and miniature painter, 8 St. Charles (1841–42).
Exhibited: American Academy (1833).
References: NOCD 1841–42; *Bull Frog*, Feb. 12, 1841; *D. Pic.*, Oct. 13, Nov. 11, 1840, Jan. 2, 31, Feb. 5, Nov. 28, 1841, Aug. 12, Dec. 1, 1842; Groce and Wallace.

JACOBS, EDWARD
Born England ca. 1810; died N.O. Jan. 11, 1892.
Colorer, art dealer, active N.O. 1855–64; primarily photographer.
Contemporary listings: artist (1850); photographic paintings in oil colors (1856–57); photographs in oil, water colors, or pastel, 93 Camp (1859); auctioneer (1873, 1876–77, 1885).
Established in N.O. as a daguerreotypist in 1842, Jacobs also sold daguerreotype equipment and taught the process in his studio at Canal and Camp At the end of 1850 he moved to 93 Camp where in Jan. 1855 he first advertised a gallery of fine art where he sold paintings, drawings, prints, and marble and bronze statuettes. In Jan. 1856 Jacobs advertised that he could color photographic portraits by hand to give them the value and durability of oil paintings. During his career as a pioneer photographer in N.O., Jacobs was among the first to offer new techniques as they developed: calotypes, ambrotypes, and ivorytypes. He continued to work at the same studio, sometimes associated with other photographers, until his retirement in 1864, and was listed sporadically as an auctioneer from 1873 until his death in 1892.
References: NOCD 1846, 1849–61, 1873, 1876–77, 1885; *Bee*, Jan. 11, 1851, Oct. 17, 1855, Jan. 18, Mar. 10, 1856, Nov. 5, 1859, Jan. 2, 1860; *D. Crescent*, Mar. 19, 1860; *D. Pic.*, July 27, 1844, Dec. 4, 1845, Dec. 24, 1850, Jan. 2, 21, 1851, Jan. 3, Apr. 28, 1855, Oct. 12, Nov. 21, 1856, Feb. 7, 1857, July 17, 1861; *D. True Delta*, Nov. 4, 1860; *De Bow's Review*, Nov. 1859; *Parlor Magazine*, Jan. 1857, 8, Feb. 1857, 7; *State Repub.*, Apr. 8, 1854; *T. Demo.*, Jan. 12, 1892; Groce and Wallace; N.O. Death Certificate (1892), 100:1137, NOPL; Rinhart, 122; U.S. Census (1850), roll 234, (1860), roll 421.

JACOBSEN, ANTONIO NICOLO GASPARO
Born Copenhagen, Denmark Nov. 2, 1850; died West Hoboken NJ Feb. 2, 1921.
Painter.
Studied: Royal Academy, Copenhagen.
Noted American marine painter who immigrated to the U.S. in 1871, settling in N.Y.C. where he earned his reputation as a painter of portraits of clipper ships and steam vessels. Jacobsen moved to West Hoboken NJ in 1880 and, sometimes assisted by his two sons, made numerous paint-

ings of ships taken from sketches, pictures, or blueprints supplied by his clients. Between 1876 and 1909, he received commissions to paint portraits of the vessels of three steamer lines located in N.O.: the Morgan Line, the New Orleans Belize Royal Mail, and the Central American Steamship Company. It has been asserted that Jacobsen came to N.O. once to make sketches for his painting *Towboat R. W. Wilmot*, dated 1899, but he probably never did visit the city.

References: Collier, "The World of Art," *T. Pic.*, Sept. 23, 1973; Anglo–American Art Museum, *Sail and Steam*, items 38–40; Freeman; Friends of the Cabildo, *250 Years*, 61; Glenk, 76, 273; Jacobsen; LSM, *Biennial Report for 1920–21*, 81; LSM, *Biennial Report for 1922–23*, 58, 75; LSM, *Biennial Report for 1924–25*, 61; LSM, *Biennial Report for 1928–29*, appendix; LSM, *Biennial Report for 1932–33*, 33; Toledano, "Marine Painters," 874–78; Wiesendanger, 60–61.

JACONA, ALBERT
Born Italy ca. 1882.
Engraver, active N.O. 1910.
Contemporary listings: engraver (1910).
References: U.S. Census (1910), roll 521.

JACONO, HUMBERT J.
Born Italy ca. 1881; died N.O. Jan. 26, 1919.
Engraver, active N.O. 1898–1919; also jeweler.
Contemporary listings: engraver, Schaffnit & Walter jewelers (1898); engraver (1901, 1903); engraver, with M. Scooler jeweler (1904–1908); engraver, 223 Bourbon (1909–12); engraver, 221 Bourbon (1913); engraver, 237 Bourbon (1914–18).
References: NOCD 1898, 1900–1901, 1903–19; *T. Pic.*, Jan. 27, 1919; U.S. Census (1910), roll 521.

JACQUET, ADOLPHE J.
Born France ca. 1825; died N.O. Jan. 17, 1892.

Sketch artist, art teacher, active N.O. 1870–77.
Contemporary listings: teacher of drawing, N.O. Central High School (1870); teacher of drawing, Boys Central High School (1874–77).
References: NOCD 1870–77, 1879–81, 1884–92; *Bee*, June 25, 1876; *D. Pic.*, Jan. 18, 1892; N.O. Death Certificate (1892), 100:1188, NOPL; Thompson, "Checklist."

JAHAM, MARIE DE. *See* DE JAHAM, MARIE
JAMBON, _____. *See* RUBE, CHAPERON AND JAMBON

JAMES, CHARLES H.
Artist, active N.O. 1873–92; also sign painter.
Contemporary listings: painter (1873–74, 1876–78, 1880, 1882–86, 1888–89, 1891–92); artist (1881).
References: NOCD 1861, 1866–67, 1869–70, 1872–86, 1888–89, 1891–92; NOBD 1889.

JAMISON, CECILIA VIETS DAKIN HAMILTON (1. Mrs. George Hamilton; 2. Mrs. Samuel Jamison)
Born Yarmouth, Nova Scotia, Canada 1837; died Roxbury MA Apr. 11, 1909.
Sketch artist, painter, active N.O. 1887–1902.
Studied: Rome.
Noted writer of juvenile literature and adult romances, who early in her career was also an artist. Shortly after marrying Hamilton in Boston MA (ca. 1860), she went alone to Rome to study portrait painting and remained there for three years. After returning to the U.S., she set up portrait studios in N.Y.C. and Boston and began having her writings published. After her second marriage to N.O. lawyer Samuel Jamison in 1878, the couple moved to Live Oak plantation, near Thibodaux LA, where she wrote her most successful books, many of them popular children's stories, and contributed articles and serials to national periodicals. The Jamisons left Live Oak in 1887 and lived in N.O. until 1902, where she continued her writing, was involved in the city's literary circles, and be-

came an advocate of social welfare. She continued to paint, and her home was adorned with many of her own artworks. After her husband's death in 1902, she left N.O. to reside permanently in MA.
References: *D. Pic.*, Apr. 13, 1909; *DAB*; Fielding, *Dictionary*; Knight, 221; Kunitz and Haycraft, 414–15; *Who Was Who in America*, 490; WPA, "Lives"; WPA, *New Orleans*, 114.

JANET, HENRI
Sculptor, active N.O. 1856.
Contemporary listings: sculptor, 107 Chartres (1856).
Cf. IANET, H.
References: *Courier*, Feb. 29, Apr. 8, 1856; Groce and Wallace; William Young.

JANIN. See JEANNIN, JEAN BAPTISTE

JANSEN, EMILE CHARLES
Born N.O. Dec. 20, 1872; died N.O. July 20, 1962.
Engraver, active N.O. 1891–1928; also engineer, jeweler.
Contemporary listings: engraver (1891, 1896); engraver, 79 Customhouse (1893–94); engraver, 613 Customhouse (1897–99, 1901–1902); engraver, 611 Customhouse (1900); engraver, 613 Iberville (1903–1904); engraver, 328 Chartres (1905–12); engraver, 239 Chartres (1913–14).
Later listed as an engraver (1927–28); and for many years as a smoking pipe repairman.
References: NOCD 1891, 1893–1919, 1921–33, 1935, 1938, 1940, 1942, 1945–47, 1949, 1952–53, 1958, 1960–62; NOBD 1898; *T. Pic.*, June 3, 1928, July 21, 1962; Orleans Parish Registrar of Voters, NOPL; U.S. Census (1910), roll 520.

JANVIER, CHARLES A.
Born Baltimore MD ca. 1832; died N.O. Feb. 23, 1897.
Sketch artist, painter, active N.O. ca. 1854–97.
Exhibited: ARTISTS' ASSOCIATION OF NEW ORLEANS (1892).
An amateur artist, Janvier came to N.O. ca. 1854 and eventually became a partner in two insurance

agencies and a member of the N.O. Stock Exchange.
References: NOCD 1877–97; *D. Pic.*, Mar. 3, 1892, Feb. 24, 1897; Dufour and Huber, 42; N.O. Death Certificate (1897), 113:255, NOPL; Thompson, "Checklist."

JANY. See AUDUBON, JOHN JAMES

JARDET, FLORENCE M.
Sketch artist, painter, active N.O. 1911–24.
Studied: NEWCOMB COLLEGE (1905).
Contemporary listings: artist, 321 Hennen Bldg. (1911–12, 1914–18).
Exhibited: ART ASSOCIATION OF NEW ORLEANS (1911, 1915).
Awarded: Newcomb Art School, Home Study prize (1907); Neill Medal (1908).
Continued to be listed as an artist (1919–24).
References: NOCD 1911–12, 1914–20, 1923–24; *T. Pic.*, May 2, 1915; Art Asso., *Catalogue* (1911); Art Asso., *Special Exhibition*; Ormond and Irvine, 158.

JARLEY, MRS. ____
Sculptor, active N.O. 1871–72, 1887.
Exhibited: Opera House (1871); Idlewild (1872); Lafayette Presbyterian Church (1887).
Visited the city to exhibit her artworks made of wax.
References: *D. Pic.*, May 23, 1871; *Repub.*, June 5, 8, 1872; *T. Demo.*, Apr. 30, May 4, 1887.

JARVIS, JOHN WESLEY
Born South Shields, England 1780; died N.Y.C. Jan. 12, 1840.
Painter, active N.O. 1821–34.
Studied: with Edward Savage, Philadelphia (1796–1801).
Contemporary listings: painting rooms, Conti betw. Chartres and Levee (1821–22); portrait painter, 9 Customhouse (1822); portrait and miniature painter, 48 Canal (1830).
One of the outstanding American portrait painters of the early 19th century. Brought to the U.S. ca. 1785, Jarvis began his career as an apprentice to the Philadelphia engraver Edward Savage (1796) and moved with him to N.Y.C. (1801).

Jarvis continued as an engraver in that city on his own, then as a partner in portrait and miniature painting with Joseph Wood. Jarvis moved to Baltimore in 1810 but returned to N.Y.C. in 1813; for the next 20 years he was the foremost portrait painter in the city. In 1814 he was commissioned to paint portraits of the heroes of the War of 1812 for the N.Y.C. city hall and hired HENRY INMAN as his assistant. Because he painted a portrait of Andrew Jackson for the series, many sources place the two artists in N.O. in Jan. 1815. It is unlikely that Jarvis was in N.O. at that time; the portrait was probably painted in N.Y.C. in 1819. It is often asserted that Jarvis regularly spent most winters in N.O. between 1816 and 1834 while maintaining a permanent studio in N.Y.C. However, contemporary sources record him in N.O. only during five winters: 1820–21, 1821–22, 1828–29, 1829–30, 1833–34. Edward Fenno, a Philadelphia merchant who settled in N.O. in 1819, mentioned that Jarvis, accompanied by his assistant, Inman, was in the city in Dec. 1820 and Mar. 1821. In Jan. 1821, JOHN JAMES AUDUBON approached Jarvis for employment as an assistant to paint clothing and backgrounds, but was not hired. Despite this rejection, Audubon often visited Jarvis in his N.O. studio in Jan., Apr., and Dec. 1821. Audubon's journal contains several descriptions of the portrait painter, including "an Original, and a Craked [sic] Man." Jarvis earned $6,000 during his successful first season in the city. Jarvis's first known local advertisement placed him in N.O. Dec. 1821; another ad was dated Mar. 1822; he was also listed in the NOCD 1822. Dickson states that Jarvis was in Cincinnati en route to N.O. in Aug. 1828 and was in the city until Apr. 1829. Jarvis was recorded again in the NOCD 1830, indicating that he probably spent the winter of 1829–30 in the city. An eccentric who was known for a flamboyant lifestyle and heavy drinking, Jarvis suffered a stroke in N.O. early in 1834 and was partially paralyzed. He went back to N.Y.C., where he spent the rest of his life, never returning to N.O.

References: NOCD 1822, 1830; *D. Crescent,* July 9, 1849; *D. Delta,* May 29, 1855; *D. Pic.,* June 15, 1841, June 28, 30, 1845, July 4, 1849; *Gazette,* Dec. 20, 1821, Mar. 7, 1822; *Item–Trib.,* July 17, 1938; Alexander Adams, 225–27; Arthur, *Old New Orleans,* facing 32; Barker, 271; Bénézit; Bolton, *Draughtsmen,* 37; Bolton and Groce, 299–321; Bruns, 313; *Bryan's;* Cline, *Art and Artists,* 6; *DAB;* Dickson; Edward Fenno Papers, E. Fenno to James Fenno, Dec. 27, 1820, May 5, 1821; William L. Clements Library; Fielding, *Dictionary;* Fulton and Toledano, "Portrait Painting," 792–94; Glenk, 39, 59, 61, 76, 144, 146; Groce and Wallace; Emily Jackson, *Silhouette,* 119; James, *Border Captain,* 176; Kendall, *History,* 2:653; Kendall, "Old New Orleans Houses," 800–1; Lay, 408; Lipton, 44; Looney, 384; LSM, *Biennial Report for 1922–23,* 29, 59; LSU, *Louisiana Paintings,* item 29; Murrell, 1:74, 76; Museum of Fine Arts, 1:202–4; Neal, 649–50; Nott, 28–29, 44; Rinhart, 122; Rutledge, "Paintings," 794–98; Soniat du Fossat, 85; Tallant, 314; Wehle, 53–56, 90; WPA, *American Portrait Inventory,* 144; WPA, "Lives"; WPA, *Louisiana,* 162; WPA, *New Orleans,* 98.

JAUFROID, DORA
Art teacher, active N.O. 1913–19.
Contemporary listings: drawing teacher, N.O. Public Schools (1913).
References: NOCD 1914, 1919; *T. Demo.,* Jan. 14, 1913.

JAUME, ALEXANDER CHARLES
Born France ca. 1813–14; died N.O. Jan. 19, 1858.
Painter, sketch artist, art teacher, restorer, active N.O. 1837–58.
Contemporary listings: teacher of drawing and painting, 137 Royal, and miniature painter, 235 Bourbon (1837); professor of drawing, 135 Royal (1838); teacher of drawing, Burgundy betw. St. Peter and Toulouse, and Charles Cuvellier's insti-

tution (1839); portrait painter, Basin near Customhouse (1841); portrait painter, Royal and St. Peter (1841); portrait painter, 196 Royal (1842); teacher of drawing, the Louisiana Institution, and Orleans High School (1843); miniature painter, 196 Royal (1843–44); teacher of drawing, Orleans High School (1844–45); miniature painter, 212 Royal (1846); portrait painter, teacher of drawing, 212 Royal (1849–50); portrait painter, St. Peter betw. Claiborne and Derbigny (1851–53); teacher of drawing, college directed by Mr. Jegon (1853); portrait painter, St. Peter near Derbigny (1854–56); teacher of drawing and painting, College of New Orleans (1855–56); teacher of drawing and painting, 104 Royal and 323 St. Peter (1855); teacher of drawing and painting, Southern Institute (1856); portrait painter, 104 Royal (1858).
References: NOCD 1837–38, 1841–44, 1846, 1849–56, 1858; *Bee*, Nov. 22, 1837, Nov. 7, 1839, Nov. 15, 1843, Jan. 7, 1845, Dec. 3, 1849, Jan. 30, Apr. 23, 1850, Apr. 14, 1853, Oct. 6, Nov. 10, 1855, Jan. 4, Mar. 13, 1856, Jan. 20, 1858; *Courier*, Oct. 4, 1841, Oct. 3, 1842, May 3, Oct. 31, Dec. 7, 1843, May 23, 1844, Apr. 2, 1846, Mar. 16, 1847, June 1, 15, 1850, July 17, 1851, Sept. 7, 1856, Jan. 20, 1858; *D. Pic.*, Oct. 15, 1843; Glenk, 39, 76; Groce and Wallace; Harter and Tucker, 122; N.O. Death Certificate (1858), 18:645, NOPL; U.S. Census (1840), roll 131, (1850), roll 236.

JAUME, J.
Artist, active N.O. 1842.
Contemporary listings: artist, 23 Basin (1842).
References: NOCD 1842; Groce and Wallace.

JEANEY, JOHN
Artist, active N.O. 1888.
Contemporary listings: artist (1888).
References: NOCD 1888.

JEANNIN, JEAN BAPTISTE
Born France ca. 1792; died N.O. Sept. 8, 1863.

Sketch artist, art teacher, active N.O. 1820–22.
Studied: Arts and Sciences School, Paris.
Contemporary listings: teacher of drawing, 52 Dauphine (1820); teacher of drawing, 48 Toulouse (1822).
Arrived in the U.S. (ca. 1818), taught in Charleston SC (1820), then settled in N.O. as a teacher of languages, drawing, mathematics, and geography (Nov. 1820). JOHN JAMES AUDUBON in his journal incorrectly spelled Janin. He continued teaching liberal arts through 1858, when he was director of the Orleans Central Lyceum.
References: NOCD 1827, 1830, 1832, 1837–38, 1841–44, 1846, 1849–58; *Bee*, Aug. 21, 1856, Sept. 9, 1863; *Gazette*, Nov. 30, 1820, Dec. 2, 1822; Groce and Wallace; N.O. Death Certificate (1863), 24:126, NOPL.

JEFFERSON, JOSEPH
Born Philadelphia PA Feb. 20, 1829; died Palm Beach FL Apr. 23, 1905.
Painter, active N.O. ca. 1870–1905.
Exhibited: Pennsylvania Academy of Fine Arts, Philadelphia (1868); World's Industrial and Cotton Centennial Exposition (1884–85); American Exposition (1885–86); National Academy of Design, N.Y.C. (1890); Washington, DC (1899).
Memberships/positions: American Academy of Arts and Letters.
A skilled and prominent actor, Jefferson was from a family of actors and the last of three generations with that name. He was trained early in what became his dual careers, acting and painting. He performed throughout his childhood, and he worked as an assistant artist for his father who was primarily a manager and scenic artist rather than an actor. Probably Jefferson's first appearance in N.O. was at the St. Charles Theatre (1844–45). By the 1860s he had become one of America's most noted actors for his character portrayals; in 1865 he debuted in England in a new version of the play *Rip Van Winkle*, a role that

gave him international fame and that he reprised for the rest of his life. Jefferson often came to LA on hunting expeditions and in 1869 bought Orange Island, a 600–acre salt dome within marshland in Iberia Parish, a few miles from the Gulf of Mexico. There he built a home that he used as one of his retreats between acting tours. His favorite recreation was painting, and his favorite subjects were picturesque studies taken from nature: the swamps in the South, the waterfalls and forests in the East, and the mountains in the West. Jefferson traveled frequently for his acting tours and always brought along his art supplies. To achieve his distinctive painting style, Jefferson used brushes to lay in the colors, but then worked with his fingers, a palette knife, rags, feathers, or blotting paper. In addition to traditional oil painting on canvas, Jefferson also produced monotypes, in which the painting was made on tin and the image transferred to paper or other material by rolling the two through a wringer. Jefferson was also an art connoisseur and had a notable collection of modern Dutch masters, as well as works by Rembrandt, Gainsborough, Corot, and Diaz. He felt that he had risen from the ranks of amateur after his first solo exhibition in 1899 of 16 of his paintings. At the time, he received some critical acclaim for his paintings, but the value of the works was based more on his fame as an actor than on his skill as an artist.
References: *D. Pic.*, Dec. 22, 1875, Apr. 13, 1885, June 8, 1890, Oct. 12, 1902, Dec. 21, 1894; *Dixie*, May 23, 1971, 11; *Every Saturday*, Feb. 18, 1871; *T. Demo.*, Feb. 28, 1884, Mar. 27, 1890; *Appleton's CAB*; Bénézit; Creole Exhibit, 13; *DAB*; Fielding, *Dictionary*; Fischer Galleries; Groce and Wallace; Eugénie Jefferson; Joseph Jefferson, 63–65, 343–51, 464–76; Kendall, *Golden Age*, 416–17, 422–23, 560–61; Kendall, "Old New Orleans Houses," 804–5; Louisiana Bicentennial Commission, 21; Seébold, 1:43, 315, facing 324; Francis Wilson; Winter; WICCE, *Catalogue*, 42; WPA, *Louisiana*, 173, 438–39; WPA, *New Orleans*, 105.

JENKINS, GEORGE W.
Painter, active N.O. 1847.
Amateur artist who exhibited a collection of paintings by other artists at the St. Charles Exchange (1847). In Jan. 1848, it was reported that he had been successful in N.O. as an artist, but had taken up daguerreotypes and had gone to Natchez MS permanently. Possibly George Washington Allston Jenkins (1816–1907), portrait and genre painter who exhibited at the National Academy of Design, N.Y.C. (1842–65).
References: *Comm. Times*, Mar. 6, 1847; *Wkly. Delta*, Jan. 3, 1848.

JENKINS, J. S., SR.
Painter, active N.O. 1840–42.
Contemporary listings: profile painter, 95 Common (1840–42). Itinerant artist and profile miniaturist who arrived in N.O. from Havana, Cuba in Aug. 1840 and advertised that his profiles were made on ivory paper so that they could be sent in mailed letters. He left N.O. after Jan. 1841 and returned by Dec. of the same year.
References: NOCD 1842; *D. Pic.*, Aug. 25, 1840–Jan. 2, 1841 (advs.), Jan. 30, June 23, Dec. 7, 1842; Groce and Wallace; William Young.

JENKS, B. W.
Painter, active N.O. 1843–44.
Contemporary listings: portrait painter, 34 St. Charles (1843–44).
References: NOCD 1843–44; Groce and Wallace; William Young.

JENNINGS, _____
Painter, active N.O. 1883.
Contemporary listings: portrait painter (1883).
Exhibited: LILIENTHAL's (1883).
References: *T. Demo.*, July 30, 1883.

JERROLD, DOUGLAS E., SR.
Sketch artist, painter, cartoonist, active N.O. ca. 1864–72.
Contemporary listings: pen artist (1870).

Awarded: Grand State Fair, silver medal for best drawing with pen (1870).
Painted a watercolor (1864) inscribed "Douglas Jerrold Sr. late Capt: 3rd Md. Cavy. & Ag. Sig. Officer. N.O." He also drew the vignette on the membership form of the Southern Hospital Association for Disabled Soldiers which was lithographed by CRESCENT LITHOGRAPHY (ca. 1869). In 1870 Jerrold lived in Mandeville LA and his cartoon of LA Gov. Henry C. Warmouth appeared in *Bizarre* (1872).
References: *Repub.*, Aug. 7–8, 1872; Mechanics' and Agricultural Fair, *Report* (1870):44; THNOC Artists Files.

JERRY, LOUIS W.
Born LA Apr. 1862.
Engraver, active N.O. 1900.
Contemporary listings: engraver (1900).
References: U.S. Census (1900), roll 570.

JOUHELSON, SOLOMON. *See* CRESCENT ART STUDIO

JOHNSON, ____. *See* EVANS & JOHNSON

JOHNSON, ARTHUR E.
Painter, active N.O. 1885; primarily sign painter; black.
Contemporary listings: portrait painter (1885); painter (1887–98).
Exhibited: Colored People's Exhibit, World's Industrial and Cotton Centennial Exposition (1884–85).
Primarily a house and sign painter; he was noted in newspapers for his portrait of E. A. Burke, director-general of the exposition.
References: NOCD 1887–94, 1896–98; NOBD 1889; *D. Pic.*, Feb. 24, 1885; *Eve. Chronicle*, Jan. 19, 1885.

JOHNSON, D. G.
Engraver, active N.O. 1835–43.
Contemporary listings: steel and copper plate engraver, cor. Camp and Canal (1838).
Listed as a portrait painter and engraver in N.Y.C. (1831–35, 1843–45), Johnson was in N.O. between 1835 and 1843 at which time he engraved the *Topographical Map of the City & Environs of New-Orleans*

(1839), which included views of the city's major buildings. In Dec. 1840 he wrote from N.O. to artist/inventor Samuel F. B. Morse that he was experimenting with taking daguerreotype portraits.
References: NOCD 1838; *Bee*, Jan. 24, 1840; Groce and Wallace; Smith and Tucker, 161.

JOHNSON, EUGENIA
Artist, active N.O. 1874–80.
Contemporary listings: artist, with SAMUEL ANDERSON (1874); artist (1880).
Memberships/positions: SOUTHERN ART UNION (1880).
References: NOCD 1874; *Bee*, May 27, 1880; *Demo.*, May 27, 1880.

JOHNSON, MARY BELLE. *See* WOODWARD, MARY BELLE JOHNSON

JOHNSON, PETER
Born Denmark Feb. 1843; died N.O. Apr. 6, 1917.
Engraver, active N.O. 1900.
Contemporary listings: engraver (1900).
References: *T. Pic.*, Apr. 7, 1917; U.S. Census (1900), roll 574.

JOHNSON, PETER
Artist, active N.O. 1877.
Artist who was commissioned by a N.O. merchant to create the Pelican Pavilion for the garden of his Lake Pontchartrain establishment. Johnson designed a glass fountain and two rural scenes with windmills, balloons, towers, churches, and grazing herds, with components that were set in motion mechanically.
References: *Bee*, May 13, 1877.

JOHNSON & YOUNG
Painters, active N.O. 1887.
Painted the drop curtain for Faranta's Theatre (1887).
References: *T. Demo.*, Sept. 14, 1887.

JONES, MR. ____
Artist, active N.O. 1817.
Contemporary listings: scenic artist, St. Philip Street Theatre, and Olympic Circus (1817).
References: *Courier*, May 30, July 2, 16, 1817; *Gazette*, June 21, Dec. 9, 1817; Ludlow, 146.

JONES, F. H.
Painter, active N.O. 1870.
Contemporary listings: portrait painter (1870).
References: NOCD 1870.
JONES, FRANCES DEVEREUX. *See* HALL, FRANCES DEVEREUX JONES
JONES, JOHN D. *See* CONRAD & JONES
JONES, RICHARD
Artist, active N.O. 1817.
Scenic artist in N.O. (1817). Possibly the same Richard Jones who was active as a scenic artist in Mobile AL in 1835.
References: Ludlow, 120, 138–39, 434.
JONTE, LILLIE
Born N.O.; died N.O. Sept. 21, 1943.
Painter, art teacher, active N.O. 1887–1920s.
Studied: with GEORGE DAVID COULON (1887–88).
Contemporary listings: painter (1888); artist (1897).
Exhibited: Philip Werlein's music store (1888); Tulane University (1893).
References: NOCD 1887; *D. Pic.*, Mar. 25, 1888, Apr. 10, 1897; *T. Demo.*, Feb. 15, 1893; *T. Pic.*, Sept. 22, 1943; Information courtesy Charles L. Mackie.
JOOR, DAISY THEODOSIA
Art teacher, sketch artist, active N.O. 1910–13.
Contemporary listings: artist (1910); art teacher (1910–11); drawing teacher (1913).
Exhibited: ART ASSOCIATION OF NEW ORLEANS (1910).
References: NOCD 1909–12; *T. Demo.*, Jan. 14, 1913; Art Asso., *Catalogue* (1910).
JOOR, HARRIET COULTER
Died Mar. 28, 1965.
Art craftsman, painter, active N.O. ca. 1902–1905.
Studied: NEWCOMB COLLEGE (1896–1901); Dow Summer School, Ipswich MA (1900–1901).
Exhibited: Louisiana Purchase Exposition, St. Louis MO (1904); ART ASSOCIATION OF NEW ORLEANS (1910).
Awarded: Neill medal for proficiency in watercolor painting (1904).

Memberships/positions: Art Association of New Orleans (1905).
One of the nine members of the first ceramic art class at Newcomb (1895), Joor's pottery designs were simplified naturalistic forms. Her work was among the prize–winning pieces at a Paris exhibition (1900) where Newcomb pottery won a bronze medal. In 1905 she left N.O. to teach at Chicago University and worked as a free–lance writer and designer. Among her published writings are her reminiscences of the formative years of Newcomb's art program. During the 1930s Joor taught art at Southwestern Louisiana Institute, Lafayette LA.
References: *Harlequin*, June 23, 1904, 8; Art Asso., *Catalogue* (1905, 1910); Ormond and Irvine, 68, 158; Poesch, *Newcomb Pottery*, 17, 29, 47, 48, 54, 100, 108, 113, 116; Radcliffe, 35; Smithsonian Institution, *Newcomb Pottery*, 13, 14, 19.
JORDAN, MABLE PAUL (Mrs. George Grant Woodbridge)
Born Atlanta GA; died N.O. May 21, 1962.
Art craftsman, active N.O. 1914–15.
Received a Bachelor of Arts degree in 1905 and a Master of Arts degree in 1932, possibly from NEWCOMB COLLEGE.
References: *T. Pic.*, May 22, 1962; Ormond and Irvine, 158.
JOUETT, MATTHEW HARRIS
Born Mercer County KY Apr. 22, 1788; died Lexington KY Aug. 10, 1827.
Painter, active N.O. ca. 1817–27.
Studied: with Gilbert Stuart, Boston (ca. 1816–17).
Contemporary listings: portrait and miniature painter, 19 Magazine (1823); portrait and miniature painter, 9 or 49 Canal (1824).
Educated for the law, Jouett was a mainly self–taught portrait and miniature painter who, after the War of 1812, devoted his full career to art. He was considered one of the best painters west of the Allegheny mountains during his lifetime. He practiced law in Lexington KY, and between 1817 and his death spent

his winters painting portraits in N.O., Natchez MS, and other towns along the Mississippi River.
References: NOCD 1823–24; *Gazette*, Mar. 12, 1824, May 16, 1825; *Appleton's CAB*; Barker, 281; Bénézit; Bruns, 313; *Bryan's*; *DAB*; Dunlap 3:100–1; Fielding, *Dictionary*; Floyd, *Jouett*; Glenk, 58, 76; Groce and Wallace; Harter and Tucker 1:122; Huber et al., 93; Kendall, *History*, 2:653; Kendall, "Old New Orleans Houses," 800–1; Lay, 408; LSM, *Biennial Report for 1920-21*, 35; Poesch, *Art of the Old South*, 168–69; Tuckerman, 68; WPA, *Louisiana, 163*; WPA, *New Orleans*, 98; William Young.

JOUNG, JULIUS
Sketch artist, active N.O. ca. 1863–64.
Soldier whose unit, 20th Wisconsin Volunteers, was in the N.O. area in Aug. 1863 and Aug. 1864. Joung made the sketch for *Intirior [sic] View Of The U.S. Barracks General Hospital New Orleans La*, one of the vignettes on a series of printed letterheads published in N.O. by Louis Schwarz (ca. 1867–78).
References: Frederick Dyer, 2:1682; THNOC 1953.133.1.

JOURDAN, JOHN J.
Born CA 1842; died N.O. June 19, 1912.
Painter, active N.O. 1889–90.
Contemporary listings: portrait painter, 40 Royal (1889–90).
Exhibited: Werlein's music store (1889).
Businessman who painted portraits as a pastime and briefly set up a full–time studio during 1889–90.
References: NOCD 1884–96, 1898–1913; *D. Pic.*, June 9, 1889; N.O. Death Certificate (1912), 155:243, NOPL.

JOVANNIS, MR. _____
Lithographer, active N.O. 1849.
Lithographer employed by the Spanish Literary Society of N.O. to lithograph portraits of the principal modern Spanish writers. One lithograph would accompany each part of *La Risa*, a series published in Ma-

drid, and made available in N.O. through the society. The completed volume was intended to be available by May 1849 and was to contain 550 pages and 30–32 illustrations by the best artists in N.O.
References: *Patria*, Jan. 7, Feb. 2, 1849.

JULIO, EVERETT B. D.
Born St. Helena 1843; died Kingston GA Sept. 15, 1879.
Painter, art teacher, art dealer, active N.O. 1870–78.
Studied: with Dr. William Rimmer, Boston; Lowell Institute, Boston; with Leon Bonnat, Paris (1873–75).
Contemporary listings: historical painter (1870–71); portrait painter, artist, 23 Exchange Pl. (1872); portrait and landscape painter, 166 Canal (1873); artist, 60 Carondelet (1875–76); painter, teacher of drawing, 3 Carondelet (1876); artist, portrait and landscape painter, drawing and painting teacher, 3 Carondelet (1877); artist, landscape painter, 3½ Carondelet (1878).
Exhibited: Grand State Fair (1870); WAGENER & MEYER's (1870–71); Salon, Paris (1874–75); Centennial Exposition, Philadelphia (1876); 20 Camp (1877–78).
Portrait, historical, landscape, and genre painter, Julio received his formal education in Paris. He came to the U.S. (ca. 1861) and first settled in Boston, where he studied art under Rimmer, and then lived in St. Louis MO (ca. 1864). His first notice in N.O. (Jan. 1870) was the exhibition of his most important historical painting, *The Last Meeting of Lee and Jackson* (completed ca. 1869), a life-size portrait of the Civil War generals Robert E. Lee and Stonewall Jackson and their horses. Julio intended to sell the painting by subscription for presentation to the chapel at Washington and Lee University (VA) where the generals were buried. The painting brought him national fame: it was copied by him for other patrons and was made into an engraving in N.Y.C. by Halpin. Julio planned a series of paintings of

Confederate soldiers, but left for Europe (Sept. 1873) where he studied with Bonnat, considered the best colorist of the modern French artists, and traveled in Normandy and Italy. After returning to N.O. (Nov. 1875), he opened a drawing academy with a collection of casts of antique statuary; he hoped to attract art teachers and students from throughout the U.S. His plans for a grand school of painting and drawing failed, and he turned to a more profitable career as a portrait painter in oil, watercolor, and crayon, taking likenesses from life or from pictures of the dead. He also continued to exhibit and sell at his studio the work of other artists, particularly that of RICHARD CLAGUE. During 1878 Julio made a tour of TX and the West. He returned to N.O. by Dec. but tuberculosis curtailed his painting career. In July 1878, he left for GA in an unsuccessful attempt to recover. Following his death, Julio's studio and gallery containing his art collection was taken over by ANDRES MOLINARY. Julio's name is often given in later sources as E. B. D. Fabrino Julio; this form appears as early as the 1887 edition of *Appleton's Cyclopaedia of American Biography*. "Fabrino," however, was not listed as part of Julio's name in N.O. references during his lifetime.

References: NOCD 1872–73, 1877–78; *Bee*, Feb. 20, 1870, Jan. 14, 1871, Apr. 5, 30, 1876, Feb. 2, 1878; *Bull.*, July 14, 1875; *D. Pic.*, Jan. 20, Apr. 27, 1870, Jan. 6, 15, June 18, 1871, Apr. 13, 20, May 14, 1873, Nov. 28, Dec. 30, 1875, Mar. 19, 31, 1876, July 19, Aug. 26, Dec. 27, 1877, Jan. 13, 1878, Sept. 17, 1879, May 26, 1881; *D. States*, Nov. 12, 1880; *Demo.*, Dec. 17, 1876, Feb. 23, Mar. 31, Dec. 18, 1877, Jan. 13, Feb. 21, Dec. 22, 1878, Mar. 16, Oct. 5, 1879; *Elite*, Feb. 28, 1900; *National Repub.*, June 2, Aug. 8, 1872; *Present Age*, Feb. 1871, 22; *Repub.*, Dec. 5, 8, 15, 1872, Feb. 16, Sept. 9, 1873, Jan. 3, 1874, Jan. 2, Feb. 29, Apr. 16, 20, 30, July 2, 1876; *Spanish Fort Daily Herald*, Aug. 18,

1883; *States*, Feb. 17, 1924; *T. Deutsche Zeitung*, Jan. 30, 1870; *Times*, Jan. 6, 15, 1871, Jan. 7, Feb. 2, 24, Mar. 3, 1878, Sept. 17, 1879; *T. Demo.*, July 30, 1883, Dec. 29, 1901; *T. Pic.*, Jan. 16, 23, 1949; Anglo–American Art Museum, *Louisiana Landscape*, item 14; *Appleton's CAB*; Coulon MS, Scrapbook 100, LSM; Creole Exhibit, 13; Edwin Davis, *Louisiana*, 314–15; Fielding, *Dictionary*; Fleming, 409–11; Fulton and Toledano, "New Orleans Landscape," 504–10; Glenk, 64, 70, 76, 135; Kendall, *History*, 2:658; Kendall, "Old New Orleans Houses," 801; Lilienthal's, 4–5; LSM, *Biennial Report for 1922–23*, 28–29, 58, 76; Norton Art Gallery, 23; Rathbone, *Mississippi Panorama*, 95–96; *Washington Artillery Souvenir*, 1; Wiesendanger, 62–63; Wilkerson, 84–85; WPA, "Lives."

JUMP, EDWARD
Born Paris, France ca. 1831–38; died Chicago IL Apr. 21, 1883.
Sketch artist, caricaturist, active N.O. 1878.
Exhibited: Crescent Hall (1878).
Artist who was famous for cartoons and caricatures. Jump came to the U.S. as a young man and lived in CA until he returned to Paris. He came back to the U.S. in 1868 and, after marrying in Washington DC, worked for *Frank Leslie's Illustrated Newspaper* in N.Y.C. and for an illustrated newspaper in Montreal, Canada. Jump visited cities throughout the West and South where he made cartoons of local citizens. In N.O. (Mar. 1878) he exhibited one of his large pictures, a composite of watercolor sketches, photographs, and caricatures of New Orleanians.
References: *Chicago Tribune*, Apr. 21, 1883; *D. Pic.*, Oct. 25, 1878, Apr. 24, 1883; *Demo.*, Mar. 24, 1878; Glenk, 86, 285; Hamilton, 1:163; LSM, *Biennial Report for 1920–21*, 84–85; Murrell, 1:235, 2:7–9.

JUNCA, T. M.
Painter, active N.O. 1857.
Contemporary listings: painter (1857).

Exhibited: Librairie Nouvelle (1857). A singer at the Orleans Theatre in 1857, Junca painted two scenes of naval battles from the War of 1812. His name was misinterpreted by Groce and Wallace as "Mousx Junca," instead of "Mons. Junca." References: *D. Pic.*, Apr. 17, 1857; Creole Art Gallery, 3, 14; Friends of the Cabildo, *250 Years*, 61; Groce and Wallace.

JUNGEL, BARTHOLOMEW
Born Germany ca. Jan. 1819; died N.O. Apr. 6, 1880.
Sculptor, active N.O. 1850–80; primarily marble cutter, stone cutter, carver.
Contemporary listings: marble and stone sculptors, JUNJEL & BARRET (1850–51); marble sculptor, 295 Conti (1867); marble sculptor, 260 St. Louis (1879–80).
References: NOCD 1850–51, 1856–61, 1866, 1868, 1871–73, 1875–80; *Almanuch de la Louisiane* (1867):217; Groce and Wallace; N.O.

Death Certificate (1880), 76:491, NOPL; *Southern Business Guide*, 428.

JUNJEL & BARRET
Sculptors, active N.O. 1850–51; BARTHOLOMEW JUNGEL, ANTHONY BAR-RETT, partners.
Contemporary listings: marble and stone sculptors, 109 St. Charles (1850–51).
Apparently Jungel and Barrett's names were misspelled in the firm's listings.
References: NOCD 1850–51; Groce and Wallace.

JUNOD, JULES L.
Born Switzerland ca. 1860–62; died N.O. Feb. 21, 1913.
Sculptor, painter, active N.O. 1888–1913; also carver, decorator.
Contemporary listings: painter (1888–90); sculptor (1892–93, 1897–1900, 1903–1904, 1906–11, 1913); sculptor, 287 Dumaine (1894).
References: NOCD 1888–90, 1892–1913; *D. Pic.*, Feb. 22, 1913; U.S. Census (1910), roll 521.

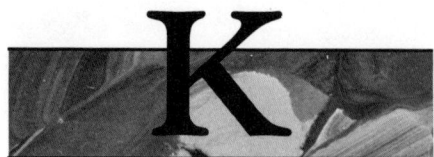

KAISER, CHARLES WILLARD
Painter, active N.O. 1889–1904; also sign painter.
Contemporary listings: scenic painter, Lee Hall, Gretna (1889); painter (1889–90); artist (1899); artist, 215 Carondelet (1902–1904).
References: NOCD 1885, 1889–94, 1896, 1899–1904; *D. States*, Feb. 25, 1889; THNOC Cemetery Survey.

KALINSKI, ACHILLE
Born Brussels, Belgium ca. Oct. 1842; died N.O. May 26, 1891.
Sketch artist, active N.O. 1868.
Awarded: Grand State Fair, best specimen of drawing with pencil, silver medal (1868).
References: NOCD 1868–78, 1880–91; Mechanics' and Agricultural Fair Asso., *Report* (1868):42; N.O. Death Certificate (1891), 99:633, NOPL; THNOC Cemetery Survey.

KALISKI, HENRY
Artist, active N.O. 1885–86.
Contemporary listings: artist, SOUTHERN LITHOGRAPHIC CO. (1885); artist, M. F. DUNN & BRO. (1886).
References: NOCD 1885–86.

KANE, PAUL
Born Mallow, County Cork, Ireland Sept. 3, 1810; died Toronto, Canada Feb. 20, 1871.
Painter, active N.O. 1838.
Studied: with Thomas Drury, Upper Canada College (1830); Rome, Genoa, Naples, Florence, Venice, Bologna, Italy, and the Louvre, Paris (1841–45).
Portrait, landscape, and Indian painter. Author and illustrator of *Wanderings of an Artist among the Indians of North America*, Kane was brought to York (now Toronto), Canada in 1819, but left there for the U.S. ca. 1836. He painted a few portraits in N.O. (1838) to earn enough money to get to Mobile AL where he worked for two years before going to Italy to study. He returned to Toronto in 1845 and then traveled throughout the Canadian wilderness making sketches for a series of paintings of Indian life (1845–48).
References: *Appleton's CAB*; Groce and Wallace; Harper, 391–99; Paul Kane; "Literary and Artistic Celebrities," 401–6; McCracken, *Portrait*, 100–4.

KAPPELER, ROBERT
Lithographer, active N.O. 1871.
Contemporary listings: lithographer, with BENEDICT SIMON (1871).
References: NOCD 1871.

KAUFMAN, JULIUS J.
Born LA ca. 1852.
Engraver, active N.O. 1870–71; also stencil cutter.
Contemporary listings: engraver (1870); engraver, 69 Canal (1871).
References: NOCD 1871–72; U.S. Census (1870), roll 521.

KEARNEY, MRS. W.
Painter, active N.O. 1868.
Awarded: Grand State Fair, silver medal for best painting in water colors (1868).
References: *D. Pic.*, Jan. 19, 1868; Mechanics' and Agricultural Fair Asso., *Report* (1868):43.

KEATING, JOHN
Born LA ca. 1846.
Lithographer, active N.O. 1870.
Contemporary listings: lithographer (1870).
References: U.S. Census (1870), roll 522.

KEEN, CHARLES
Lithographer, active N.O. 1885.
Contemporary listings: lithographer, T. FITZWILLIAM & CO. (1885).
Possibly Charles B. Keen, born N.O. ca. 1870; died N.O. June 3, 1943.
References: NOCD 1885–86; *T. Pic.*, June 4, 1943.

KEENER, MARY A.
Artist, active N.O. ca. 1868.
Awarded: Grand State Fair, four honorable mentions for four best landscape cuttings (1868).

Exhibited the landscapes, *Deer Scene, Log Cabin Life, Crossing the Branch,* and *Parent and Child* (1868). Possibly Mary Ann Keener Wilkinson, born AL Feb. 13, 1843; died N.O. May 11, 1894, buried in Lafayette Cemetery I.
References: Mechanics' and Agricultural Fair Asso., *Report* (1868):41; N.O. Death Certificate (1894), 106:307, NOPL; THNOC Cemetery Survey.

KEEP, IRENE BORDEN
Born LA Nov. 1876.
Art craftsman, active N.O. 1900–1904.
Studied: NEWCOMB COLLEGE (1897–1904).
Contemporary listings: artist (1900, 1902).
References: NOCD 1902; Ormond and Irvine, 158; Poesch, *Newcomb Pottery*, 100; U.S. Census (1900), roll 575.

KEITH, GEORGE A.
Born NY ca. 1824.
Artist, active N.O. 1850.
Contemporary listings: artiste (1850).
References: Groce and Wallace; U.S. Census (1850), roll 234.

KELLER, FIDEL
Born Canton Aargau, Switzerland ca. 1818; died N.O. June 2, 1875.
Hair worker, active N.O. 1844–46.
Contemporary listings: hair braiding and plaiting for necklaces, bracelets, etc., American Theatre (1844); hair braiding, under St. Charles Hotel (1846).
Keller ran a bookstore most of his life, and it was there that he advertised hair braiding for jewelry pieces "Sacred to the Memory both of the Living and Dead" (*Daily Delta*, 1846). In 1862 he was sentenced to two years at hard labor on Ship Island for exhibiting a human skeleton in his store window and claiming that it was the bones of a slain Yankee soldier.
References: NOCD 1846, 1850–61, 1866–68, 1870–75; *D. Delta*, July 10, 1846, July 2–3, 1862; *D. Pic.*, Feb. 4, 1844, June 3, 1875.

KELLER, L.
Painter, active N.O. 1856.
Exhibited: Pelican Theater (1856).
Keller's gigantic ciglorama featuring views around the world was presented in N.O. in Feb. 1856.
References: *D. Crescent*, Feb. 11–12, 1856.

KELLER, T. A. *See* GUERIN & KELLER

KELLOGG, MINOR KILBOURNE
Born Manlius Square NY Aug. 22, 1814; died 1889.
Painter, restorer, active N.O. 1849.
Studied: Italy (1841–45).
Exhibited: Pennsylvania Academy of Fine Arts, Philadelphia.
Memberships/positions: National Academy of Design, N.Y.C. (1851).
Portrait and miniature painter who worked in Cincinnati (1840), N.Y.C. (1851), Europe (1854–58), Baltimore (1867–70), and again N.Y.C. (1878–79). He was in N.O. in Apr. 1849 and may have restored an Italian painting and completed his portrait of Maj. Gen. Worth while in the city.
References: *D. Delta*, May 9, 1847, Apr. 17, 1849; *Wkly. Delta*, Apr. 2, 1849, Dec. 8, 1851; Bolton, *Painters in Miniature*; Groce and Wallace.

KELLY, FLORENCE
Painter, active N.O. 1870.
Awarded: Grand State Fair, silver medal for best composition painting by a person under 16 years of age (1870).
References: Mechanics' and Agricultural Fair Asso., *Report* (1870):45.

KEMBLE, EDWARD WINDSOR
Born Sacramento CA Jan. 18, 1861; died 1933.
Illustrator, active N.O. ca. 1885–97.
Kemble, a self–taught artist, was noted for his depiction of blacks. He illustrated a number of books during his career and, after 1881, was connected with magazines such as *Harper's, Century,* and *Leslie's* as an illustrator and cartoonist. His drawings of N.O. and LA appeared in all three of these periodicals on various occasions (ca. 1885–97).
References: *Century Magazine*, Apr. 1886, 807–23, Nov. 1887, 100–20;

Harper's Wkly., Feb. 18, Oct. 13, Nov. 3, 1888; *Biographical Sketches of American Artists* (1915), 135; Fielding, *Dictionary*; THNOC 1954.30, 1957.61.1–.2, 1978.209, 1979.338, 1979.349.

KEMMIS, J. A.
Engraver, active N.O. 1866–67; also stencil cutter.
Contemporary listings: engraver, 134 Exchange Pl. (1866); engraver, 127 Gravier (1867).
References: NOCD 1866–67, 1869.

KEMPER, MISS N.
Hair worker, active N.O. 1869.
Awarded: Grand State Fair, silver butter knife prize for best specimen of hair flowers wreath (1869).
References: Mechanics' and Agricultural Fair Asso., *Report* (1869):82.

KENDALL, GEORGE
Engraver, active N.O. 1885.
Contemporary listings: engraver (1885).
References: NOCD 1885.

JAMES S. KENDALL & SONS
Painters, active N.O. 1878–83; also sign painters; James S. Kendall, Shelby R. Kendall, partners.
Contemporary listings: painters, 34 Union (1878); scenic painters, 3 Carondelet (1882); scenic painters, 83 Carondelet (1883).
References: NOCD 1878, 1882; *Mascot*, Feb. 3, 1883.

JAMES S. KENDALL'S SONS
Painters, active N.O. 1883–85; also sign painters; Shelby R. Kendall, William P. Kendall, partners.
Contemporary listings: painters, 83 Carondelet (1883); painters, 76 Carondelet (1884–85); scenic painters, 99 Baronne (1885).
References: NOCD 1883–85; *Mascot*, Dec. 19, 1885.

KENNEDY, MRS. FRANCIS M.
Painter, active N.O. 1914.
Contemporary listings: tapestry painter (1914).
References: NOCD 1915–16; *T. Pic.*, June 28, 1914.

KENNEY, MARY A.
Painter, active N.O. 1889–90.
Contemporary listings: portrait painter, Exposition betw. Constance

and Magazine (1889); landscape painter (1889–90).
References: NOCD 1881, 1885, 1889–90.

KENNON, ROBERTA BEVERLY (Mrs. Luther E. Carruth)
Died N.O. Nov. 8, 1931.
Art craftsman, active N.O. 1901–10.
Studied: NEWCOMB COLLEGE (1896–1905); Dow Summer School, Ipswich MA (1902).
Exhibited: Louisiana Purchase Exposition, St. Louis MO (1904); ART ASSOCIATION OF NEW ORLEANS (1910).
References: *T. Pic.*, Nov. 9, 1931; Art Asso., *Catalogue* (1910); Ormond & Irvine, 70, 84, 89, 92, 158; Poesch, *Newcomb Pottery*, 8, 27, 49, 100–1, 111–12, 115.

KEPPLER, ADOLPH M.
Born N.O. May 10, 1873; died N.O. July 26, 1943.
Engraver, active N.O. 1886–1942.
Contemporary listings: engraver, with J. E. Gery (1886, 1889–90); engraver (1891, 1896, 1903, 1915); engraver, 113 Canal (1892–94); engraver, with J. C. Meyer (1895); engraver, John C. Meyer & Son (1902, 1907–1908, 1917).
References: NOCD 1886, 1889–1933, 1935, 1938, 1940, 1942, 1945–46; *T. Pic.*, July 27, 1943; Orleans Parish Registrar of Voters, NOPL.

KER, MARY ELLEN SIGSBEE. See FISCHER, MARY ELLEN SIGSBEE

KERNAGHAN, CHARLES
Lithographer, active N.O. 1878.
Contemporary listings: lithographer (1878).
References: NOCD 1878.

KERNION, GEORGE LA BEDOYERE HUTCHET DE, JR. (Joseph G.)
Born LA ca. 1883; died Dallas TX May 26, 1922.
Engraver, active N.O. 1909–19.
Contemporary listings: photo–engraver, ROMANSKI Photo–Engr. Ltd. (1909); photo engraver (1910); engraver, GRELLE-EGERTON ENGRAVING CO. (1911); engraver (1912, 1915–16); photo–engraver, Grelle-Egerton Engraving Co. (1914, 1918).

References: NOCD 1907, 1909, 1911–16, 1918–19; *Item*, May 27, 1922; U.S. Census (1910), roll 521.

KERTH, GEORGE J.
Lithographer, active N.O. 1880–1902.
Contemporary listings: lithographer, 12 Commercial Pl. (1880–82); lithographer, NEW ORLEANS LITHOGRAPHING COMPANY (1883); New Orleans Lithographing Company (1884); artist, SOUTHERN LITHOGRAPHIC COMPANY (1885); lithographer (1886–90, 1893–96, 1898–1902).
Signed the masthead and illustrations in the *Mascot* (1882).
References: NOCD 1880–90, 1892–96, 1898–1902; *D. News*, May 23, 1906; *Mascot*, Feb. 18, Mar. 25, Apr. 1, 8, 15, 22, 29, May 6, 1882; Rathbone, *Mississippi Panorama*, 172.

KIBBE, MISS M. A.
Sketch artist, active N.O. 1885–86.
Exhibited: American Exposition (1885–86).
References: Creole Exhibit, 12.

KILBURN, SAMUEL S., JR.
Sketch artist, active N.O. 1858–59.
Boston wood engraver with the firm Kirk & Mallory (1852–65) who engraved illustrations for book and newspaper publishers. Kilburn may have come to N.O. to make the sketches of city views and buildings engraved for *Ballou's Pictorial Drawing Room Companion* (published 1858–59). He engraved several N.O scenes from drawings by ALFRED R. WAUD for *Every Saturday* (published 1871).
References: Groce and Wallace; THNOC 1948.9, 1953.60, 1953.78-.79, 1953.93, 1958.98.3, 1959.159-.19, 1959.159.38, 1959.183.3, 1959.204.4, 1971.108, 1974.25-.3.173, 1977.296.82.

KILIAN, DANIEL I.
Born N.O. ca. 1866; died N.O. Dec. 20, 1911.
Artist, active N.O. 1894–95; primarily printer, also photographer.
Contemporary listings: artist (1894–95).

References: NOCD 1884–86, 1888–1909, 1911; *D. Pic.*, Dec. 24, 1911.

KILLIAN, MARTIN L.
Artist, active N.O. 1908–14.
Contemporary listings: artist, 151 Baronne (1908–11); artist, 337 St. Charles (1913–14).
References: NOCD 1908–11, 1913–17; *Men of Affairs*, 104.

KING, JOHN CROOKSHANKS
Born Killwinning, Ayrshire, Scotland Oct. 11, 1806; died Boston MA Apr. 21 or 22, 1882.
Sculptor, active N.O. 1837–41.
Contemporary listings: sculptor, Royal betw. Canal and Customhouse (1838); sculptor (1841).
Exhibited: Steel's store, B. M. Norman's bookstore (1848); Norman's (1854).
Came to the U.S. (1829) and worked as a machinist for about four years before he became a sculptor. King worked in N.O. and Louisville KY before moving to Boston (1841). He executed busts and made cameo likenesses of many public figures.
References: *Comm. Bull.*, Apr. 9, 1841, Jan. 19, 1854; *Comm. Times*, Jan. 27, 1848; *D. Delta*, Apr. 27, 1848; *D. Pic.*, May 21, 1844, May 16, 1847, Apr. 27, 1882; *True Amer.*, Dec. 22, 1838; *Appleton's CAB*; Bénézit; Fielding, *Dictionary*; Foote, 25; Glenk, 89; Groce and Wallace; Louisiana Landmarks Society; William Young.

KING, LULU. *See* SAXON, LULU KING

KING, NINA ANSLEY
Born N.O. Mar. 22, 1862; died N.O. May 26, 1942.
Art craftsman, active N.O. 1901–21.
Studied: NEWCOMB COLLEGE (1889–91).
Exhibited: Art Association of New Orleans (1917).
Memberships/positions: ARTS EXHIBITION CLUB (1901).
Art craftsman at Newcomb sporadically from 1917 to 1921. Sister of N.O. author Grace King.
References: NOCD 1910–11, 1913–15, 1917 20; *Item*, Oct. 19, 1942; *T. Pic.*, May 27–28, 1942; Art Assu., *Catalogue* (1917); Arts Exhibition

Club; Orleans Parish Registrar of Voters, NOPL; Ormond and Irvine, 158; Poesch, *Newcomb Pottery*, 101.

KINGDON, ———
Engraver, active N.O. 1887.
Signed a wood engraving *Les Soeurs De Charité De La Nouvelle-Orléans*.
References: *Diamant*, Mar. 5, 1887.

KINGSLEY, ELDRIDGE
Born Carthage NY Sept. 17, 1841; died Brooklyn NY 1915 or N.Y.C. 1918.
Engraved a view of *The Three Sisters*, a row of buildings on North Rampart, (1887).
References: Bénézit; Fielding, *Dictionary*; THNOC 1957.4; William Young.

KINGSTON, JOHN
Born N.O. ca. 1855.
Painter, active N.O. ca. 1870–71.
Studied: with GEORGE DAVID COULON (ca. 1870).
Contemporary listings: painter (1871).
References: *D. Pic.*, Jan. 12, 1871.

KINSER, ———
Painter, active N.O. 1887.
Exhibited: WILLIAM J. WARRINGTON's studio (1887).
Cf. KINSER, ISAAC; KINSER, SAMUEL T.
References: *D. States*, Oct. 12, 1887.

KINSER, ISAAC
Painter, active N.O. 1888–1908.
Contemporary listings: portrait painter (1888, 1891–93); portrait painter, 341 S. Rampart (1900, 1904–1908); artist (1902).
Cf. KINSER, ———.
References: NOCD 1888, 1891–93, 1900, 1902, 1904–1908; *D. States*, Oct. 12, 1887.

KINSER, SAMUEL T.
Born ca. 1864; died N.O. Sept. 2, 1916.
Painter, active N.O. 1886–87.
Contemporary listings: portrait painter (1886); portrait painter, 294 Tulane (1887).
Cf. KINSER, ———.
References: NOCD 1886–87, 1905; *D. States*, Oct. 12, 1887; *T. Pic.*, Sept. 3, 1916; N.O. Death Certificate (1916), 167:163, NOPL.

KIRK, LAWRENCE P.
Artist, active N.O. 1898.
Contemporary listings: artist (1898).
References: NOCD 1898, 1900, 1903, 1905–1906.

KIRSCH, MATTHEW
Artist, active N.O. 1861–66.
Contemporary listings: artist, 4 Laharpe (1861, 1866).
Possibly Mat Kirsch, born ca. 1839; died Chicago IL Sept. 17, 1891.
References: NOCD 1856, 1858, 1861, 1866; *D. Pic.*, Sept. 21, 1891.

KLEMINGER, ADOLF
Painter, sketch artist, active N.O. ca. 1890.
Exhibited: ARTISTS' ASSOCIATION OF NEW ORLEANS (1890).
References: *Current Topics*, Jan. 1891, 24; *D. Pic.*, Dec. 17, 1890; AANO, *Catalogue* (1890).

KLINE, JOHN
Engraver, lithographer, active N.O. 1896–99.
Contemporary listings: engraver (1896); lithographer (1899).
References: NOCD 1892–94, 1896–1902, 1904.

KLUNG, HENRY
Died before Jan. 12, 1902.
Lithographer, engraver, active N.O. 1873–83; also printer.
Contemporary listings: lithographer, 37 Exchange Pl. (1873); D. SIMON & CO. (1874); lithographer, 79 Gravier (1875); lithographer (1876–78, 1883); lithographer and engraver, 811 Magazine (1877); lithographer, with HUGH LEWIS (1879); lithographer, NEW ORLEANS LITHOGRAPHING AND ENGRAVING CO. (1880–82).
References: NOCD 1873–83; *D. Pic.*, Jan. 13, 1902; *Demo.*, Aug. 1, 1877.

KNIGHT, GEORGE F. *See* POTTHOFF & KNIGHT

KNIRIN, CHRISTOPHER
Colorer, active N.O. ca. 1871–74.
Contemporary listings: photograph painter, with WILLIAM WATSON WASHBURN (1872); artist, with William Watson Washburn (1873–74).
Awarded: Grand State Fair, bronze medal for best colored photograph in water colors (1871).

References: NOCD 1872–74; *D. Pic.*, Dec. 3, 1871.

KNOBELOCH, CHARLES
Illustrator, active N.O. 1878–80.
Illustrated J. Curtis Waldo's *Illustrated Visitors' Guide to N.O.* (1878). References: *Bee*, June 16, 1878; *Demo.*, June 2, 1878, Sept. 1, 7, 1880; *Spanish Fort Daily Herald*, Sept. 11, 1883; Waldo.

KNOPP, FRANK
Born ca. 1865.
Sketch artist, active N.O. ca. 1897; also sign painter.
Awarded: Brownie drawing contest, first prize (1897).
Possibly Frank Knopp, Sr., born N.O.; died Fort Worth TX Dec. 24, 1935.
References: NOCD 1885, 1887–97, 1899; *D. States*, Nov. 29, 1897; *T. Pic.*, Dec. 25, 1935.

KNOTZSCH, AUGUST
Born N.O. Feb. 21, 1864; died N.O. Mar. 8, 1943.
Engraver, active N.O. 1895–1938; also printer.
Contemporary listings: engraver, with J. DOUGLAS (1895–96, 1908–11); engraver (1897); engraver (1900); steel engraver (1910); engraver, 112 Camp (1912–18).
References: NOCD 1883–1933, 1935, 1938, 1940, 1942; *T. Pic.*, Mar. 9, 1943; American Illustrating Company, 175; Orleans Parish Registrar of Voters, NOPL; U.S. Census (1900), roll 571, (1910), roll 520.

KNOTZSCH, EDWARD F.
Born N.O. ca. 1862; died N.O. Sept. 2, 1906.
Engraver, active N.O. 1895–96; also printer.
Contemporary listings: engraver, with J. DOUGLAS (1895–96).
References: NOCD 1877–78, 1880–91, 1893–1906; *D. Pic.*, Sept. 9, 1906.

KNOX, W. P.
Drew *Assylum [sic] For Destitute Orphan Boys Founded 1824. New Orleans* which was engraved, printed, and colored by John Hill.
References: Groce and Wallace; Koke, no. 159; Stauffer, 2:226; THNOC 1959.192.

KOCH, RICHARD
Born N.O. June 9, 1889; died Covington LA Sept. 20, 1971.
Painter, active N.O. 1916–19; primarily architect, also photographer.
Exhibited: ART ASSOCIATION OF NEW ORLEANS (1916–17).
Prominent architect who was noted for his restorations in association with CHARLES RICE ARMSTRONG, as the architectural firm of Armstrong and Koch (1916–33), and in partnership (1955–71) with Samuel Wilson, Jr. His restorations include the Historic New Orleans Collection, the Hermann–Grima Historic House, Gallier House, and the Cabildo. Koch was one of the founding members of the Arts and Crafts Club (1921) where he regularly served as an officer, organized exhibitions, and periodically showed his own photographic works. He was the LA director of the WPA Historic American Buildings Survey in the late 1930s and served on the City Park Commission (1930–40) and the Vieux Carré Commission (1944–54). He was a board member of the American Institute of Architects and served as president of the local chapter (1930–31). In addition, he served on the Board of Trustees of the DELGADO MUSEUM OF ART and was an associate of the National Academy of Design, N.Y.C.
References: NOCD 1909, 1911, 1916–17, 1920–33, 1935, 1938, 1940, 1942, 1945–47, 1949, 1952–56, 1958, 1960–62, 1964–69, 1971–75; Arts and Crafts Club, *Bulletin* (1929–30); *Item*, Oct. 19, 1923; *Item–Trib.*, Sept. 29, 1929, Apr. 24, 1938, May 26, 1940; *Morn. Trib.*, Dec. 29, 1926; *T. Pic.*, Mar. 15, 19, 1925, Sept. 30, 1928, Apr. 20, 1930, Dec. 5, 1932, Apr. 3, 1938, Apr. 4, Nov. 4, 1940, Sept. 21, 1971; Art Asso., *Catalogue* (1916, 1917, 1919); New Orleans Art School, *Yearbook 1926*; Orleans Parish Registrar of Voters, NOPL; Seebold, 2:190–92.

F. G. KOECKERT & CO.
Lithographers, active N.O. 1897; JOSEPH G. CURADO, FREDERICK G. KOECKERT, partners.

Contemporary listings: lithographers, 514 Natchez (1897).
Also printed sheet music covers.
References: NOCD 1897.

KOECKERT, FREDERICK G.
Born N.O. Mar. 23, 1875; died after June 12, 1924.
Commercial artist, lithographer, active N.O. 1893–1900.
Contemporary listings: artist (1893–96, 1900); F. G. KOECKERT & CO. (1897); lithographer (1898).
References: NOCD 1893–98, 1900–15, 1917–24; Orleans Parish Registrar of Voters, NOPL.

G. KOECKERT & CO.
Lithographers, engravers, active N.O. 1885–88; also printers; PETER DAVIS, GUSTAVE KOECKERT, JOHN WALLE, partners.
Contemporary listings: lithographers and engravers (1885); lithographers, 112 Gravier (1886–88).
Also printed sheet music covers.
References: NOCD 1886–88; Orleans Parish Notarial Archives, William O. Hart, Sept. 1, 1885, 5:1275; C. E. Sel, Nov. 30, 1886, 2:1625; "Polka des Negres," Sheet Music Collection, THNOC.

KOECKERT, GUSTAVE
Born Leipzig, Germany ca. 1842; died N.O. Oct. 23, 1897.
Lithographer, engraver, active N.O. 1871–96.
Contemporary listings: lithographer, with CHARLES W. CLARK (1871); map engraver, with HUGH LEWIS (1872); lithographer, with Hugh Lewis (1873, 1875, 1879); lithographer, 20 St. Charles (1874); engraver (1876–77); engraver, with Hugh Lewis (1878); treas., NEW ORLEANS LITHOGRAPHING AND ENGRAVING CO. (1880); NEW ORLEANS LITHOGRAPHING CO. (1881–84); lithographer, SOUTHERN LITHOGRAPHIC CO. (1885); KOECKERT AND DEEVES (1885); G. KOECKERT & CO. (1885–88); KOECKERT & WALLE (1889–96).
References: NOCD 1871–97; *D. Pic.*, Jan. 3, 1871, Feb. 3, 1887; *D. States*, Oct. 24, 1897; *Dixie*, Dec. 4, 1977; Friends of the Cabildo, *250 Years*, 61; Reps, 312.

KOECKERT AND DEEVES
Lithographers, active N.O. 1885; GUSTAVE KOECKERT, JOHN F. DEEVES, partners.
Contemporary listings: lithographers (1885).
References: *Daily States*, Feb. 3, 1887.

KOECKERT & WALLE
Lithographers, active N.O. 1889–96; GUSTAVE KOECKERT (1889–96), JOHN WALLE (1889–95), BERNARD J. WALLE (1896), partners.
Contemporary listings: lithographers, 112 Gravier (1889–92); lithographers, 55 Carondelet (1893–94); lithographers, 335 Carondelet (1895); lithographers, 335 and 337 Carondelet (1896).
Also printed sheet music covers.
References: NOCD 1889–96; *D. Item*, Feb. 18, 1896; "Saengerfest Waltz," Sheet Music Collection, THNOC; THNOC 1954.6.

KOEFFER, GEORGE
Artist, active N.O. 1869.
Contemporary listings: artist (1869).
References: NOCD 1869.

KOEHLE, ANTON
Born Baden, Germany ca. Aug. 2, 1822; died N.O. Mar. 17, 1891.
Sculptor, restorer active N.O. 1858–61; primarily gilder.
Contemporary listings: sculptor, 49 Royal (1858); paintings & engravings cleaned, 19 Bourbon (1861).
References: NOCD 1858, 1860–61, 1866–84, 1886–91; N.O. Death Certificate (1891), 99:88, NOPL.

KOENIG, M.
Painter, active N.O. 1871.
Painted a silk banner embroidered by Mrs. Kate Logan which was exhibited at the dry goods store of Joseph H. Wilson (1871).
References: *Times*, Mar. 4–5, 1871.

KOFFMAN, MISS _____
Artist, active N.O. 1898.
Exhibited: New Orleans Press Club (1898).
Cf. KOPMAN, KATHARINE.
References: *D. States*, Jan. 23, 1898.

KOHNKE, QUITMAN
Born Natchez MS ca. 1857; died Covington LA June 26, 1909.

Engraver, sculptor, sketch artist, painter, active N.O. 1875–1906.
Studied: with Beranger, AUGUST NOLTE, and PAUL POINCY.
Contemporary listings: engraver (1875, 1877, 1880, 1882–83); engraver, with E. A. Tyler jewelers (1876); engraver, with George E. Strong jewelers (1879, 1881); engraver, A. B. Griswold & Co. jewelers (1884–90).
Exhibited: ARTISTS' ASSOCIATION OF NEW ORLEANS (1894, 1896).
Memberships/positions: Artists' Association of New Orleans (1897); ART ASSOCIATION OF NEW ORLEANS (1905).
Noted as an amateur sculptor and a portrait and landscape painter in both oil and watercolor, as well as a portraitist in crayon. Shortly after his birth he moved with his parents to N.O. After graduating from high school, he took up the engraving trade, particularly within the jewelry business, and began to study illustrative drawing and to contribute sketches to many journals, including a political cartoon that appeared in *Figaro* (1884). In 1890 he graduated from the medical department at Tulane University, after which he worked solely as a physician. He later became a city councilman and was president of the Board of Health from 1898 until his retirement to Covington in 1906. *Cf.* K., Q.
References: NOCD 1875–1906; *Figaro*, Feb. 9, 1884, 12; *T. Demo.*, Dec. 14, 1894, June 27, 1909, AANO, *Catalogue* (1897); Art Asso., *Catalogue* (1905); Fossier, *Orleans Parish Medical Society*, 64, 226; Mount, 179; U.S. Census (1880), roll 463.

KONRAD, ADOLPH D. *See* UNIACKE & KONRAD

KOOLSBERGEN, GERARD L.
Lithographer, active N.O. 1872.
Contemporary listings: lithographer, with HUGH LEWIS (1872).
References: NOCD 1872–73.

KOPMAN, KATHARINE
Born N.O. ca. 1862–70; died Biloxi MS Mar. 11, 1950.

Art teacher, painter, designer, active N.O. 1890–1919.
Studied: with ANDRES MOLINARY, NEWCOMB COLLEGE; with DODGE MACKNIGHT; Newcomb (1895–98).
Exhibited: ARTISTS' ASSOCIATION OF NEW ORLEANS (1890–92, 1896–97, 1899, 1901–1902); Tulane University (1893); Panama–Pacific International Exposition, San Francisco (1915); Newcomb (1917).
Memberships/positions: Artists' Association of New Orleans (1890); FIVE OR MORE CLUB (1893); ART ASSOCIATION OF NEW ORLEANS (1905).
Taught drawing and design at Newcomb (1896–1919); later taught art at Louisiana College, Pineville LA and was supervisor of art, Alexandria LA grammar schools. *Cf.* KOFFMAN, MISS _____ .
References: NOCD 1898–1914, 1916–19; *Current Topics*, Jan. 1891, 24, Jan. 1892, 24, Jan. 1893, 11; Nov. 1893, 198, *D. Pic.*, Nov. 13, Dec. 17, 1890, Dec. 17, 1891, Dec. 13, 1892, Feb. 14, 1893; *Harlequin*, Dec. 6, 1899, 2, 4; *Men and Matters*, Sept. 1897, 48; *Register* (1913–14):37; *T. Demo.*, Nov. 13, 1890, Dec. 13, 1892, Dec. 3, 1901, Mar. 19, 1904; *T.Pic.*, Mar. 12, 14, 1950; *Town Talk*, July 1904, 25; AANO, *Catalogue* (1890, 1891, 1896, 1899, 1901, 1901–1902); Art Asso., *Catalogue* (1905); Fielding, *Dictionary*; LSM, *Biennial Report for 1922–23*, 108; Ogden et al., cover; Ormond and Irvine, 37, 159; Poesch, *Newcomb Pottery*, 10, 34, 101; Smithsonian Institution, *Newcomb Pottery*, 19, 21; U.S. Census (1910), roll 524.

KORNERUP, EBBE
Painter, active N.O. ca. 1910.
Exhibited: ART ASSOCIATION OF NEW ORLEANS (1910).
Memberships/positions: Royal Danish Academy.
References: Art Asso., *Catalogue* (1910).

KOSCHEL, GEORGE GUSTAVE
Born Germany ca. June 1842; died N.O. Apr. 18, 1906.
Hair worker, active N.O. 1866–71; primarily jeweler, also watchmaker.

Contemporary listings: hairworker, 89 Canal (1866); hairworker, 110 Customhouse (1867); hair jeweler, 98 Chartres (1869); hair jeweler, 109 Marais (1870–71).
References: NOCD 1866–67, 1869–80; *D. Pic.*, Apr. 19, 1906; Boyd, 180.

KOSKY, PIERRE
Born Poland ca. 1808.
Painter, active N.O. 1850.
Contemporary listings: portrait painter (1850).
References: Groce and Wallace; U.S. Census (1850), roll 236.

KRACKE, JOHN, SR.
Born N.O. Sept. 10, 1866; died N.O. Sept. 9, 1948.
Lithographer, engraver, active N.O. 1885–1935; also photographer.
Contemporary listings: lithographer, SOUTHERN LITHOGRAPHIC CO. (1885); artist, G. KOECKERT & CO. (1886–88); engraver, KOECKERT & WALLE (1889); lithographer, Koeckert & Walle (1890–91); lithographer (1893–97); engraver, WALLE & CO. (1898–99); engraver (1900).
References: NOCD 1884–91, 1893–1920, 1922–33, 1935, 1938, 1940, 1942, 1945–47; *T. Pic.*, Sept. 10, 1948; Orleans Parish Registrar of Voters, NOPL; U.S. Census (1900), roll 570.

KRAFT, GEORGE
Lithographer, active N.O. 1870–71.
Contemporary listings: lithographer (1870); lithographer, with JOHN B. KRAFT (1871).
References: NOCD 1870–71, 1873–75, 1877–88, 1890.

KRAFT, JOHN B.
Born Grunsfeld, Germany ca. Feb. 8, 1811; died N.O. Mar. 22, 1889.
Lithographer, active N.O. 1868–72; also printer.
Contemporary listings: lithographer, 533 St. Claude (1868–69); lithographer, 553 Goodchildren (1870); lithographer, 534 St. Claude (1871–72).
References: NOCD 1850–58, 1860–61, 1866–81, 1883–88; *D. Pic.*, Mar. 23–24, 1889; U.S. Census (1870), roll 523.

KRAMER, CHARLES.
Engraver, active N.O. 1872.
Contemporary listings: engraver, with Adolphe Himmel (1872).
References: NOCD 1872.

KRAUSS, WILLIAM
Lithographer, active N.O. 1868–77; also printer.
Contemporary listings: PESSOU & KRAUSS (1868); lithographer, with BENEDICT SIMON (1870, 1874–76); lithographer, with HERMANN WEHRMANN (1871); lithographer (1877).
References: NOCD 1868, 1870–71, 1873–77.

KREUZ, CHARLES
Born LA May 1876.
Artist, active N.O. 1900.
Contemporary listings: artist (1900).
References: U.S. Census (1900), roll 574.

KRUMPE, CHARLES HUNAN
Born Cincinnati OH ca. 1859; died N.O. Jan. 6, 1897.
Lithographer, active N.O. 1889.
Contemporary listings: lithographer (1889).
References: NOCD 1887–89, 1892–95; *D. Pic.*, Jan. 7, 1897; N.O. Death Certificate (1897), 112:894, NOPL.

KUMMEL, CHARLES
Died before Mar. 19, 1904.
Lithographer, active N.O. 1887–90; also publisher.
Contemporary listings: STANDARD MUSIC AND PHOTO–LITHO COMPANY (1887); lithographer, 48 Bienville (1889–90).
Lithographer and publisher of sheet music.
References: NOCD 1867–68, 1870–72, 1874–77, 1879, 1882–86, 1890–92, 1894–95, 1897–98, 1900–1903; *D. Pic.*, Mar. 20, 1904; *D. States*, Jan. 16, 1890; *T. Demo.*, Nov. 11, 1887; Map of *Parish of Plaquemines, La.* (1889), LSM.

KURSHEEDT & BIENVENU
Sculptors, active N.O. 1869; primarily marble workers; Col. Edwin I. Kursheedt (born 1838; died N.O. 1906), Joseph G. Bienvenu, partners.
Awarded: Grand State Fair, silver medal for best statuettes in plaster of

Paris (1868), bronze medal for best statuette in clay, plaster, or terra cotta (1869).

Hardware and marble works business which created monuments, tombs, and mantels (1867–88) and built the marble stairway at the U.S. Custom House (1883).

References: NOCD 1867–70, 1872–88; *D. Crescent*, Mar. 6, 1866; *D. Pic.*, Jan. 8, 1886; *Repub.*, May 12, 23, 1877; *Spanish Fort Daily Herald*, Aug. 22, 1883; Mechanics' and Agricultural Fair Asso., *Report* (1868):42, *Report*(1869):82; Morrison, *Industries*, 144.

KURZ, RUDOLPH FRIEDRICH
Born Bern, Switzerland Jan. 8, 1818; died Bern Oct. 16, 1871.
Painter, art teacher, active N.O. ca. 1846–52.
Studied: with Joseph Simon Volmar, Bern; with S. Fort, Paris; Paris (1838–42).
Portrait, animal, and landscape painter who traveled along the Mississippi and Upper Missouri rivers from N.O. to St. Louis MO and Fort Union making sketches of American Indian life (1846–52). He was the founder and first director of the Bern School of Art.

References: Bénézit; Bushnell, "Friedrich Kurz," 507–27; Curry, 38, 188; Groce and Wallace; McCracken, *Portrait*, 119–24; McDermott, *Travelers*, 27, 29, 45, 279–83; Museum of Fine Arts, 2:31–32.

KYLE, JOSEPH
Born OH 1815; died N.Y.C. 1863.
Painter, active N.O. 1852–55.
Studied: with Thomas Sully and Bass Otis, Philadelphia.
Exhibited: Pennsylvania Academy of Fine Arts, Philadelphia; Artists' Fund Society; American Art Union, N.Y.C.; National Academy of Design, N.Y.C.; Arcade (1852); Armory Hall (1855).
Memberships/positions: National Academy of Design (1849).
Painter who worked with JACOB A. DALLAS on a panorama of the Mississippi River; they exhibited an oil view of Canal St. in N.O. (1852). Kyle was one of a group of artists who contributed to the panorama illustrating John Bunyan's *The Pilgrim's Progress* exhibited at Armory Hall (1855).
References: *Courier*, Mar. 6, 1855; *D. Delta*, Mar. 5, 1855; *D Pic.*, Apr. 1, 1855; *D. Times*, Feb. 18, 1852; Bénézit; Fielding, *Dictionary*; Groce and Wallace; William Young.

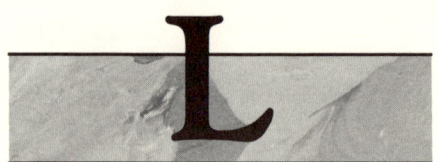

LABATUT, LOUIS, JR.
Born LA ca. 1893; died June 20,
1971.
Engraver, active N.O. 1908–49.
Contemporary listings: engraving
dept., Wm. Frantz & Co. (1908); engraver, with OTTO J. LAUTERBACH
(1909); jewelry engraver (1910); engraver, Hart Jewelry Co. (1911); engraver, T. Hausmann & Sons, Ltd.
(1912–18).
Listed as engraver for Hausmann, Inc.
until 1949.
References: NOCD 1908–1909,
1911–33, 1935, 1938, 1940, 1942,
1945–47, 1949, 1952–55, 1960–62,
1964–69, 1971; *States-Item*, June
23–24, 1971; *T. Pic.*, June 23, 1971;
U.S. Census (1910), roll 521.

LACHAPELLE, E. FERRAND
Art teacher, active N.O. ca. 1820–
22.
Contemporary listings: teacher of
drawing, Edmond Fortier's store
(1822).
References: *Courier*, July 22, 1822.

LACHAUME DE GAVAUX, JEAN LOUIS
Born N.O. 1820; died Paris, France
1882.
Painter.
Exhibited: Salon, Paris (1835–67).
Awarded: Legion of Honor, France
(1880).
A native of N.O., he was called
"Chéret" in France where he pur-
sued a career as a scenic artist and
landscape painter.
References: *Bee*, Jan. 27, 1882; Bé-
nézit.

LACHIN, ANGELO
Born Italy ca. 1859; died N.O. Jan.
25, 1938.
Sculptor, active N.O. 1909–20; also
carver, carpenter, decorator.
Contemporary listings: sculptor
(1909, 1911); sculptor, Angelo
Lachin Co. (1910); Lachin & Co.
sculptors and designers (1915–18).
Lachin immigrated to the U.S. in
1906. He continued to be listed as

decorator (1919–20); sculptor,
Lachin & Co. (1921–26); modeler,
Architectural Cast Stone Co. (1927–
32); and v. pres., Architectural Stone
Co. (1933–35). Father of JOHN M.
LACHIN and VICTOR G. LACHIN.
References: NOCD 1908–11, 1914–
33, 1935; *T. Pic.*, Jan. 26, 1938; U.S.
Census (1910), roll 520.

LACHIN, JOHN M.
Born Italy Apr. 1, 1889.
Sculptor, active N.O. 1910–32; also
carver, carpenter, decorator.
Contemporary listings: Angelo
Lachin Co. sculptors (1910); sculptor, woodwork store (1910); mgr.,
Lachin & Co. sculptors and designers
(1915–18).
Lachin immigrated to the U.S. in
1907. From 1918 to 1932 he worked
as manager at Lachin & Co. and was
an officer in Architectural Stone &
Plastering Co. through 1952. Lachin
was affiliated with Lachin & Mc-
Causland contractors (1954–62) before his retirement (1964). Son of
ANGELO LACHIN; brother of VICTOR G.
LACHIN.
References: NOCD 1908–33, 1935,
1938, 1940, 1942, 1945–47, 1949,
1952, 1954–56, 1958, 1960–62,
1964–69, 1971–79; *Morn. Trib.*,
Nov. 9, 1932; Orleans Parish Registrar of Voters, NOPL; U.S. Census
(1910), roll 520.

LACHIN, VICTOR G.
Born Venice, Italy Apr. 9, 1895.
Sculptor, active N.O. 1915–25.
Contemporary listings: Lachin & Co.
sculptors & designers (1915-17).
Lachin immigrated to the U.S. in
1907. He continued to work as a
sculptor (1921–25) and an architect
(1926) and was with the Architectural Cast Stone Company for many
years (1927–75) before his retirement (1976). Son of ANGELO LACHIN;
brother of JOHN M. LACHIN.
References: NOCD 1915–17, 1919–
33, 1935, 1938, 1940, 1942, 1945–

47, 1949, 1952, 1954–56, 1958, 1960–62, 1964–69, 1971–79; *T. Pic.*, Dec. 6, 1953; Orleans Parish Registrar of Voters, NOPL; U.S. Census (1910), roll 520.

LACHMAN, HARRY B.
Painter, active N.O. ca. 1916–20.
Exhibited: ART ASSOCIATION OF NEW ORLEANS (1916).
He exhibited at the DELGADO MUSEUM OF ART in 1920.
References: *Item*, May 23, 1916; *T. Pic.*, Feb. 14–15, 1920, Feb. 27, 1938; Art Asso., *Exhibition of Recent Paintings by Harry B. Lachman*; Art Asso., *Invitation to Private View*.

LACLOSTE, MR. _____
Painter, active N.O. 1810.
Painted decorations at the St. Philip St. Theatre (1810). *Cf.* LACLOTTE, JEAN HYACINTHE.
References· *T. Demo.*, Sept. 16, 1894.

LACLOTTE, JEAN HYACINTHE
Born Bordeaux, France 1765; died ca. 1828–29.
Painter, art teacher, active N.O 1807–15; primarily architect, engineer, decorator.
Studied: Academy of Fine Arts, Paris.
Contemporary listings: teacher of drawing with ARSENE LACARRIERE LATOUR, cor. Royal and Orleans, and scenic artist, St. Peter St. Theatre (1810); scenic artist, St. Philip St. Theatre (1811–13); teacher of drawing, St. Ann next to Orleans Theatre (1813); teacher of drawing with Louis Quemper, St. Peter (1814).
Third generation architectural engineer who was trained in France and left for LA on Aug. 22, 1804. His earliest recorded commission in N.O. was for the design of the Orleans Theatre, built in 1806–1807. Theatrical work seems to have been one of Laclotte's specialties in N.O. He designed a fireworks display (Dec. 1806) and the scenery for the closing performance at the St. Peter St. Theatre (1810). He worked as a scenic artist at the St. Philip St. Theatre (1811–13), the later year with JEAN BAPTISTE SEL. With his architectural partner Latour, he submitted plans

to the city for a public dance hall (1811), and with N.O. architect JOSEPH PILIE, he decorated the Grand Salon de Terpsichore (1814). In Feb. 1807, Laclotte first advertised as a teacher of architecture, drawing, landscapes, and flowers. He was a partner in Latour and Laclotte, engineers and architects, on Dauphine (Oct. 1810–May 1813). They also opened an art school, based on the Paris Academy of Fine Arts, where they taught landscape and portrait painting, the drawing of plans, perspectives, and ornamentation, architecture, building trades, and interior decoration. Students also accompanied the architects in field inspections of buildings in progress. After the dissolution of the partnership, Laclotte continued as an architect, scene painter, and teacher in a house next to the Orleans Theatre. During the Battle of N.O., Laclotte volunteered as an engineer in the First Louisiana Militia. From this experience, he painted what is believed to be the most accurate representation of the battle. The painting's authority was certified in July 1815 by the 13 army officers still residing in N.O. Laclotte returned to France and had the painting made into an aquatint engraving by the noted French engraver Philibert Louis Debucourt. Laclotte returned to the U.S. via N.Y.C. in fall 1817; the print was available for purchase in N.O. bookstores by Oct, 1817. By Sept. 1821 Laclotte had returned to Bordeaux where he entered into another architectural partnership. *Cf.* LACLOSTE.
References: *Courier*, Oct. 17, Nov. 12, Dec. 5, 1810, Nov. 25, 1811, May 4, 8, 1812, Feb. 3, Mar. 10, Apr. 21, June 25, July 26, Nov. 19, 1813, Oct. 12, 1814, Sept. 19, Oct. 27, 29, 31, 1817; *D. Pic.*, Jan. 8, 1860; *L'Ami des Lois*, July 27, 1813;*Gazette*, Sept. 20, 1810; *Moniteur*, Oct. 11, Dec. 27, 1806, Feb. 28, June 13, 1807, July 4, Nov. 21, 26, 1811, Apr. 28, 1812, May 22, July 28, 1813; *Collier*, "The World of Art," *T. Pic.*, Dec.

22, 1957; *T. Pic.*, Jan. 4, 1959; Arthur, *LSM Guide Book*, 66; Arthur, *Old New Orleans*, 92, 238-39; Casey, v; Comstock, "Spot News," 81–100; Cruise and Harton, 49; Delgado, *New Orleans*; Friends of the Cabildo, *Battle of New Orleans*, 2; Friends of the Cabildo, *N.O. Architecture*, 2:36; Friends of the Cabildo, *250 Years*, 41; Groce and Wallace; Kendall, *Golden Age*, 2–3; Kmen, 63, 73; Letter from City Archivist, City of Bordeaux, to Peter M. Wolf, Newcomb College, Mar. 15, 1963; Mugridge and Conover, 95; New Orleans City Council, Proceedings, July 13, 1805, Dec. 12, 1807, Oct. 2, Nov. 6, 1811, Jan. 11, 1812, NOPL; Orleans Parish Notarial Archives, Narcisse Broutin, May 16, 1810, 22:298; Rathbone, *Mississippi Panorama*, 174; THNOC 1944.5, 1946.1; Tyler, *Prints*, 1–4; Samuel Wilson, "Almonester," 198; Samuel Wilson, *Guide to Architecture*, 17, 29; Samuel Wilson, *Plantation Houses*, 18–19; Wilson and Huber, *Cabildo*, 58, 62–63; Perry Young, 37.

LACOUR, WILLIAM S.
Born NY ca. 1815; died N.O. Mar. 5, 1891.
Painter, active N.O. 1853–91; primarily sign and ornamental painter. Contemporary listings: painter, Girod betw. St. Peter and St. John (1853); painter, St. Mary near Apollo (1855); painter, 35 Apollo (1856); painter (1857); painter, Camp near Thalia (1858); painter, 881 Camp (1860); fresco painter, LACOUR & PATTERSON (1861); Lacour & Patterson (1866-74); painter, 134 Camp (1875–81); painter, William S. Lacour & Son (1882); painter, 141 Julia (1883–85); painter, 139 Julia (1886–91).
References: NOCD 1853, 1855–58, 1860–61, 1866–91; *D. City Item*, Mar. 8, 1891; N.O. Death Certificate (1891), 99:13, NOPL; U.S. Census (1860), roll 415, (1880), roll 458.

LACOUR & PATTERSON
Painters, active N.O. 1861-74 also sign and ornamental painters; WILLIAM S. LACOUR, PETER PATTERSON, partners.
Contemporary listings: fresco painters, 98 Tchoupitoulas (1861); painters, 104 Tchoupitoulas (1866–68); painters, 134 Camp (1873–74).
References: NOCD 1861, 1866–74.

LACROIX, PAUL
Born Paris, France ca. 1811; died N.O. Apr. 22, 1847.
Painter, active N.O. ca. 1830s–47; also architect.
Studied: Paris.
Master architect and artist educated in Paris where some of his finest work was done. An album of his watercolors, with some dating as early as 1823, showed miniature views of London (1830), Louvain, Belgium (1830), Cincinnati (1832), and St. James LA (1835). He married LA native Aimée Materre and lived on Rampart between Bayou and Quartier at the time of his death.
References: *Bee*, Apr. 22, 1847; Jordan, "The World of Art: Miniatures Popular in 1830s in Permanent N.O. Collection," *T. Pic.*, May 15, 1977; THNOC 1962.1.1–.9; U.S. Census (1840), roll 132.

LADD, FRANKLIN BACON
Born Augusta ME Sept. 10, 1815; died Brooklyn NY Apr. 9, 1898.
Painter, active N.O. 1841.
Contemporary listings: portrait and miniature painter, 106 Royal (1841). Exhibited: National Academy of Design, N.Y.C. (1837).
After visiting N.O. in 1841, he went back to N.Y.C. (1845), Philadelphia (1847), and Augusta ME (1853). He later settled in Brooklyn NY, where he painted portraits of several of that city's mayors.
References: *D. Pic.*, Mar. 27, 1841; Groce and Wallace.

LADIES' DECORATIVE ART LEAGUE. See TULANE DECORATIVE ART LEAGUE FOR WOMEN

LADIES' INDUSTRIAL ASSOCIATION. See SOUTHERN ART UNION

LAFOSSE, _____
Sketch artist, active N.O. ca. 1840. Signature on extant pastel portraits of Andrew Jackson that were prob-

ably made when the President visited N.O. for the 25th anniversary of the Battle of N.O. (1840). Possibly Jean Baptiste Adolphe Lafosse, born 1810; died 1879, a French miniature painter and lithographer who may have traveled in the U.S.
References: Arthur, *LSM Guide Book*, 35; Bénézit; Glenk, 49; Thieme and Becker; THNOC 1959.21.

LAGMAN, JOHN VICTOR
Born St. John Parish LA ca. 1836; died N.O. Jan. 3, 1921.
Artist, active N.O. 1898; also carpenter.
Contemporary listings: artist (1898).
References: NOCD 1888, 1890–99, 1901–1906; *T. Pic.*, Jan. 4, 1921.

LAIDLAW, JAMES B.
Painter, active N.O. 1850.
Contemporary listings: scenic artist, St. Charles Theatre (1850).
References: *D. Delta*, Oct. 11, 1850; *D. Pic.*, Oct. 14, Nov. 3, 12, 1850; Scharf, 1:982.

LAKNER, GIOVANI
Sculptor, active N.O. 1868.
Contemporary listings: sculptor (1868).
References: NOCD 1868.

LALANDE, ARSENE
Born France ca. 1824.
Hair worker, active N.O. 1858; primarily jeweler.
Contemporary listings: hair (ornamental) manufacturer, 185 Royal (1858).
References: NOCD 1851–61, 1866; U.S. Census (1860), roll 418.

LALLEMAND, ARSENE
Lithographer, active N.O 1882–84.
Contemporary listings: lithographer (1882–84).
References: NOCD 1882–88.

LAMARE, VINCENT A.
Commercial artist, active N.O. 1899; primarily printer.
Contemporary listings: artist (1899).
References: NOCD 1897–1901.

LAMB, MARIE E. (Mrs. J. Hope Lamb)
Born Mexico ca. 1866.
Painter, active N.O. 1910.
Contemporary listings: artist, painting (1910).

References: U.S. Census (1910), roll 524.

LAMBERT, JOSEPH F.
Born N.O. ca. 1868; died N.O. Apr. 30, 1933.
Lithographer, active N.O. 1886–98; also printer.
Contemporary listings: lithographer, M. F. DUNN & BRO. (1886, 1889); lithographer (1894–98).
References: NOCD 1885–87, 1889, 1891, 1894–1930; *T. Pic.*, May 2, 1933.

LAMOISE, EUGENE
Artist, active N.O. 1849.
Made an India ink sketch of Canal St. between Burgundy and Rampart during the overflow from the Sauvé Crevasse (1849).
References: *T. Demo.*, May 21, 1911; Glenk, 83.

LAMOTHE, ADRIEN
Artist, active N.O. 1885.
Contemporary listings: artist (1885).
References: NOCD 1885.

LAMOTHE, PIERRE
Engraver, active N.O. 1821; also jeweler, silversmith, goldsmith.
Contemporary listings: engraver (jeweler, silversmith), Pre. Lamothe & Son, Royal betw. St. Ann and Maine (1821).
References: *Courier*, Mar. 31, Sept. 8, 15, 1813, Apr. 1, 1816, July 2, 1817, Jan. 5, 1821; Friends of the Cabildo, *250 Years*, 38; Mackie et al., *Crescent City Silver*, 68–69, 122; Warren, 180.

LANCELIN, JEAN LOUIS
Born ca. 1788; died N.O. ca. Oct 8, 1822.
Painter, active N.O. 1819–22.
Contemporary listings: miniature and portrait painter, 92 Bourbon (1819); scenic artist, Orleans Theatre (1821).
First appeared as an actor at the Orleans Theatre after coming from the Théâtre de la Porte St. Martin (1819). Advertised as a portrait and miniature painter in Dec. 1819. Various theater benefits were held for him from 1820 until his death in 1822.
References: NOCD 1822; *Courier*, Nov. 19, Dec. 22, 31, 1819, Nov. 6, 1820, Jan. 22, 1821, Apr. 15, Oct.

11, 1822; *Gazette*, May 11, Aug. 22, 1820, Oct. 10–11, Nov. 14, 22–23, 1822; Bruns, 313; Glenk, 76; Groce and Wallace; U.S. Census (1820), roll 32.

LANDMANN, MR. ____
Engraver, active N.O. 1851.
Contemporary listings: steel engraver, 153 Dauphine (1851).
References: NOCD 1851; Friends of the Cabildo, *250 Years*, 59; Groce and Wallace.

LANDRY, PIERRE JOSEPH
Born France Jan. 9, 1770; died St. Gabriel LA Mar. 1843.
Sculptor, active N.O. ca. 1815.
Sculptor whose birthplace is variously given as Nantes, St. Malo, or St. Servan, France, Landry came to LA in 1785 and was a successful Iberville Parish planter who had no formal artistic training. His extant sculpted works date from 1812 to 1836. He served as a captain under Gen. Andrew Jackson in the Battle of N.O. (1815) and later carved a piece depicting Jackson and Louis Phillippe of France which was presented to the general by the sculptor. Later, afflicted with a tubercular infection of the knee and confined to a wheelchair, he created sculptures carved from native woods such as beech, magnolia, and walnut.
References: *Clarion* (Spring/Summer 1985):35; Friends of the Cabildo, *Newsletter* (June 1982); *T. Demo.*, Feb. 9, 1913; *T. Pic.*, Feb. 6, July 3, 1938; Collier, "The World of Art: Early Woodcarving Found—in Cabildo!" *T. Pic.*, June 12, 1955; Anglo–American Art Museum, *Louisiana Folk Art*, 18–19; Bridaham, 157–60; William Clement, 170–71; Delgado, *New Orleans*, no. 44; Friends of the Cabildo, *Battle of New Orleans*, 12; Friends of the Cabildo, *250 Years*, 41, 50; Glenk, 97; LSM, *Annual Report for 1918*, 59; LSM, *Guide Book*, 25, back cover; WPA, "Lives."

LANFER, J.
Born Austria ca. 1865.
Painter, active N.O. 1910.
Contemporary listings: artist, pictures (1910).

References: U.S. Census (1910), roll 520.

LANG, HENRY D.
Born LA Oct. 1879.
Engraver, active N.O. 1900.
Contemporary listings: engraver (1900).
References: NOCD 1901–1903; U.S. Census (1900), roll 572.

LANGBEHN, WILLIAM J.
Born Germany ca. 1868; died Chicago IL Dec. 18, 1900.
Engraver, lithographer, active N.O. 1887–90.
Studied: Tulane University (1886).
Contemporary listings: engraver, M. F. DUNN & BRO. (1887, 1890); lithographer (1888); lithographer, M. F. Dunn & Bro. (1889).
References: NOCD 1887–90; *Eve. Chronicle*, May 22, 1886; *T. Demo.*, Dec. 19, 1900.

LANGHAM, EMILY
Born Shepherd TX.
Sketch artist, painter, active N.O. 1918.
Studied: NEWCOMB COLLEGE (1918).
Exhibited: ART ASSOCIATION OF NEW ORLEANS (1918).
Awarded: national competition for war savings posters, 1st prize in Southern District.
After 1918 Langham studied at the New York School of Fine and Applied Arts and taught design in Houston TX high schools (1921–23).
References: Art Asso., *Catalogue* (1918):5; Fisk, 46.

LANGLOIS, PIERRE
Painter, active N.O. 1847.
Primarily a portrait painter.
References: Information courtesy George E. Jordan.

LANGLUME, P.
Lithographer, active N.O. 1837; also photographer.
Contemporary listings: director of the *Bee* lithography (1837).
Associated with the printing office of the N.O. *Bee*, Langlumé is known as a lithographer only through his 1837 advertisements in which he offered to print anything done in writing, such as notary acts and circular letters, as well as maps, landscapes, and

portraits (1837). His later listings were as an employee of a fancy store and a translator (1837), a trader (1843), and a daguerreotypist (1846). In 1847 he exhibited at the Baton Rouge LA fair. Langlumé's known lithographs include views of N.O. taken from the ca. 1821 drawings of FELIX ACHILLE BEAUPOIL, MARQUIS DE SAINT-AULAIRE. Langlumé was probably the Paris lithographer who exhibited at the salons between 1822 and 1824 and may have lithographed the Saint-Aulaire views in Paris before coming to N.O. Possibly Peter Langlumé, born 1780–90, who lived in East Baton Rouge Parish in 1840. References: NOCD 1837, 1843, 1846; *Bee*, Apr. 5, 14, July 11, 1837; Bénézit; Groce and Wallace; Smith and Tucker, 162; U.S. Census (1840), roll 129; William Young.

LANSOT, AIMABLE DESIRE
Born Oral, France ca. 1799; died N.O. Apr. 17, 1851.
Painter, restorer, art teacher, active N.O. 1834–51; also photographer.
Contemporary listings: miniature painter, restorer, portrait painter, 147 Royal (1834); portrait painter, miniaturist, drawing school, 147 Royal (1835); portrait painter, 192 Royal (1837); portrait and miniature painter, restorer, cor. Royal and St. Peter (1837); portrait painter, cor. Royal and St. Peter (1839); portrait painter, cor. Royal and Toulouse (1840–41); portrait painter, 163 Royal (1842); portrait painter, 63 Toulouse (1842); painter in miniature, 163 Royal (1843); painter (1845); portrait painter, 33 Toulouse (1846).
Also a landscape and genre painter, Lansot first advertised in N.O. as a portrait painter and restorer sharing a studio with JEAN JOSEPH VAUDE-CHAMP at 147 Royal (May 1834). Lansot worked in N.O. during the winter season, left the city for the country during the summer, and announced his return in newspapers in Nov. or Dec. Upon his return to the city in Dec. 1835, he again shared a studio with Vaudechamp and spe-

cialized in oil and miniature portraits. He also opened an evening drawing school for the study of the human head and landscapes. By Nov. 1839 Lansot began to advertise his ability to take portrait likenesses from the dead, for which he claimed to have five years experience. His portraits were noted for their particular attention to accessories, especially the jewelry and lace in his portraits of women. The inventory of Lansot's possessions, made soon after his death and filed with the acts of the notary, is a rare description of the contents of the studio of an antebellum N.O. portrait painter.
References: NOCD 1837, 1841–43, 1846; *Bee*, May 17–20, 1834 (advs.), May 19, 1834, Dec. 3–4, 1835, Nov. 22, 1837, Nov. 24, 1840, Feb. 12, 1841, Dec. 17, 1842; *Courier*, May 17, 20, 1834, Nov. 20, 1837, Nov. 18–19, 1839, Nov. 23–24, 1840, Dec. 15, 1841, Sept. 2, Dec. 13, 1842, May 3, 1844, Oct. 2, 1845, Nov. 2, 1846, Feb. 1, 1847, Feb. 1, 1849, Jan. 2, May 22, 1851; *Item Trib.*, Aug. 7, 1938; Bruns, 75, 113, 136, 314; Coulon MS, Scrapbook 100, LSM; Glenk, 76; Groce and Wallace; Harter and Tucker, 122; Kendall, *History*, 2:656; N.O. Death Certificate (1851), 12:697, NOPL; Orleans Parish Notarial Archives, Abel Dreyfous, May 7, 1851, 3:30; U.S. Census (1840), roll 132; Wiesendanger, 64; WPA, "American Portrait Inventory," 159.

LAPHAM, JOSEPH M.
Engraver, active N.O. 1859–60.
Contemporary listings: engraver, 85 Common (1859–60).
Possibly J.M. Lapham who worked as a landscape artist for the lithograph trade in CA (1852–58).
References: NOCD 1860; *D. Pic.*, Jan. 21, 1859; Groce and Wallace.

LAPIERRE, ALIX
Art teacher, active N.O. 1855.
Contemporary listings: teacher of drawing, 149 Royal (1855).
References: NOCD 1856; *Bee*, Dec. 1, 4, 1855.

LAPORTE, VICTOR
Artist, active N.O. 1893.
Contemporary listings: artist (1893).
References: NOCD 1893.

LAPOUYADE, ROBERT P. DE. See DE LAPOUYADE, ROBERT P.

LAROQUE, PHILIP
Painter, active N.O. 1810.
Music teacher (1822–30) who designed scenery for the St. Peter St. Theatre in 1810.
References: NOCD 1822–24, 1827, 1830, 1834; T. Demo., Sept. 16, 1894.

LA ROSA, JOHN
Born Ustica, Italy Oct. 5, 1869; died N.O. Apr. 18, 1910.
Artist, sculptor, active N.O. 1897–98; also decorator.
Contemporary listings: artist (1897–98).
Helped decorate carnival floats for the Rex, Comus, and Proteus organizations, in the employ of JOSEPH RAGUSA and GEORGE SOULIE. Also a restaurateur.
References: NOCD 1887, 1893, 1895–99, 1908, 1916; D. Pic., Apr. 18–19, 24, 1910; THNOC artists files.

LASSUS, JEAN PIERRE
Painter, sketch artist, active N.O. 1726; primarily surveyor.
Surveyor who arrived in N.O. Feb. 1725, Lassus drew a watercolor view of N.O. in 1726 entitled, Veue et Perspective de la Nouvelle Orleans. After conflicts with engineer of the colony of LA Adrien de Pauger, Lassus was dismissed as a surveyor and was reported to have sailed for France in Nov. 1728.
References: Huber and Wilson, Basilica, 7; Rowland and Sanders, 2:551; Toledano, "Marine Painters," 874; Samuel Wilson, Bienville's New Orleans, 22; Samuel Wilson, Guide to Architecture, frontispiece; Wilson and Huber, Cabildo, 2.

LATERRADE, PETER
Born LA May 1880; died N.O. Jan. 19, 1910.
Lithographer, active N.O. 1900.
Contemporary listings: lithographer (1900).

References: NOCD 1900–1904; D. Pic., Jan. 20, 23, 1910; U.S. Census (1900), roll 571.

LATHAM, JOHN
Engraver, active N.O. 1841–42; also engineer.
Contemporary listings: engraver, 213 St. Joseph (1841–42).
References: NOCD 1830, 1838, 1841–42; Groce and Wallace; U.S. Census (1840), roll 133.

LATIZAR, FERDINAND. See SALAZAR Y MENDOZA, JOSE DE

LATOUR, ARSENE LACARRIERE
Born France ca. 1770–75; died Paris 1839.
Art teacher, sketch artist, active N.O. 1810–13; primarily architect, engineer.
Contemporary listings: teacher of drawing, with JEAN HYACINTHE LACLOTTE, cor. Royal and Orleans (1810).
Left France for Santo Domingo in 1793, where he may have remained until he came to N.O. (1810). Latour entered into a partnership with Jean Hyacinthe Laclotte as engineers and architects, located first on Royal and Orleans then on Dauphine (Oct. 1810–May 1813). They also opened an art school, based on the Paris Academy of Fine Arts, and they taught landscape and portrait painting, the drawing of plans, perspective, and ornamentation, architecture, building trades, and interior decoration. Students also accompanied the architects in field inspections of buildings in progress. Recommended by N.O. lawyer Edward Livingston to Andrew Jackson in Nov. 1814, Latour was appointed principal engineer for the Seventh U.S. Military District and supervised the planning and installation of the defense systems in N.O. and along the Gulf Coast during the war of 1812. His book, Historical Memoirs of the War in West Florida and Louisiana in 1814–15 (1816), contained the first published account of the Battle of N.O. and included detailed maps of the encounters; it was considered the basic contemporary source on the

war in the southern U.S. Latour entered the Spanish service in late 1815 and, using the name John Williams, traveled extensively throughout the Spanish provinces west of LA; he delivered reports on Mexico to his superiors in Cuba in Mar. 1817. Latour stated that he planned to settle in Cuba as a farmer or professional man. Although there is no known record of his activities after 1817, it is believed that he returned to Paris where he died in 1839.

References: *Courier*, Sept. 17, Oct. 17, 1810, Mar. 10, May 3, 1813; *Gazette*, Sept. 20, 1810; *T. Demo.*, Sept. 16, 1894; Arthur, *Old New Orleans*, 92–93, 224, 238–39; Carpenter, 220–27; Edwin Davis, *Louisiana*, facing 179, 180, 181; Delery, 29; Groce and Wallace; Huber and Wilson, *Pontalba*, 19; Jumonville, 24–25; Kendall, "Old New Orleans Houses," 805; Latour; Benjamin Latrobe, *Impressions*, xiv, 23; Wilson, *Guide to Architecture*, 9, 16, 22.

LATROBE, BENJAMIN HENRY BONEVAL
Born Fulneck, England May 1, 1764; died N.O. Sept. 3, 1820.
Painter, active N.O. 1818–20; primarily architect.
Amateur artist, navigational and waterworks engineer, and one of the most important early U.S. architects. Educated at Leipzig University, Germany, and then said to have served in the Prussian Army, Latrobe returned to England (ca. 1796) and studied architecture under Samuel Pepys Cockerell (1787). He was a successful architect in England, but immigrated to the U.S. after the death of his wife. He first settled in Norfolk VA (1796); moved to Philadelphia (1798) where he became a renowned architect; and then went to Baltimore MD (1818). A leading practitioner of the Greek Revival style in the U.S., his notable buildings included the Bank of Pennsylvania (1799), the earliest U.S. public building in Greek Revival; the Philadelphia Waterworks (1799), one of the first waterworks in a U.S. city; the exterior of the VA State Capitol

(1799); and Baltimore Cathedral (1805–18). Appointed by Pres. Thomas Jefferson as Surveyor of Buildings in charge of all U.S. public buildings (1803), Latrobe supervised the completion of the south wing of the U.S. Capitol, remodeled the White House (1807), and supervised the rebuilding of Washington DC after it was burned by the British (1814). He designed the U.S. Custom House in N.O. (1807), which was later replaced (1819). He was employed to design a N.O. waterworks (ca. 1809), a task which he gave to his son Henry. Henry died of yellow fever in N.O. (1817), so Latrobe moved to N.O. to take over the project (1819). While supervising construction of the waterworks, Latrobe designed the central tower of St. Louis Cathedral (1819). He was well received in N.O. and decided to move his family to the city permanently. He returned to Baltimore (Oct. 1819) and was back in N.O. with his family in Apr. 1820. He designed the State Bank of LA (1820). Latrobe was an accomplished artist who made a number of sketches and watercolors in N.O., including *View of the Balize, at the Mouth of the Mississippi* (1819), *Market Folks* (1819), and *View from the Window of my Chamber at Tremoulet's hotel New Orleans* (1819). He died of yellow fever about five months after returning to N.O. Father of JOHN HAZELHURST BONEVAL LATROBE.

References. *L'Ami des Lois*, June 1, 1819; *Courier*, May 3, 7, 1813; *Item*, Nov. 28, Dec. 5, 9, 1951; *T. Pic.*, Dec. 2, 1951, Feb. 10, 1957, Oct. 2, 1960, Feb. 26, 1978; *Appleton's CAB*; Arthur, *Old New Orleans*, 43; Chambon, 31; Curtis, 58, 89; *DAB*; Dunlap, 2:230–34; Friends of the Cabildo, *Battle of New Orleans*, 4; Friends of the Cabildo, *N.O. Architecture*, 2:11; Groce and Wallace; Hamlin; Huber and Wilson, *Basilica*, 20–21; Benjamin Latrobe, *Engineering*; Benjamin Latrobe, *Impressions*; Benjamin Latrobe, *Journal*; Benjamin Latrobe, *Latrobe's View*; Norman, 93, 153; Samuel Wilson, "Almonester," 226; Samuel Wilson, *Guide to Architecture*, 12, 16, 22, 26, 44, 48; Samuel Wilson, *History*, 5–10; Samuel Wilson, *Plantation Houses*, 26, 36; Withey; WPA, *Louisiana*, 155.

LATROBE, JOHN HAZELHURST BONEVAL
Born Philadelphia PA May 4, 1803; died Baltimore MD Sept. 11, 1891.
Painter, sketch artist, active N.O. 1834.
Studied: with Thomas Sully.
Prominent railroad and patent attorney who was also an artist, author, inventor, and architect. Latrobe wrote and illustrated *Lucas' Progressive Drawing Book* (1827), using the pseudonym, E. Van Blon, an anagram of his middle name, Boneval. The third part of that work, entitled *Practical Perspective*, consisted chiefly of views of American scenery, including one of *The Balize, Mississippi River* which was an adapted copy of a watercolor made by his father, BENJAMIN HENRY BONEVAL LATROBE (Jan. 7, 1819). In 1834 on the way to Natchez MS, he visited N.O. going both upriver and downriver (Nov. 9–11, Nov. 29–Dec. 2). On that trip he made pencil and watercolor sketches of LA and N.O. scenes. Throughout his life he made sketches of his travels and copied family portraits in oil; a founder of the Maryland Historical Society, he was instrumental in establishing its gallery of paintings.
References: Delgado, *New Orleans*, no. 13; Kelly, 6, 49; John Latrobe; *Practical Perspective*; Rathbone, *Mississippi Panorama*, 162; Semmes; THNOC 1968.10, 1981.189.1.

LAUDUMIEY, GEORGE, SR.
Born N.O. June 1858; died N.O. May. 13, 1914.
Engraver, active N.O. 1876–1914.
Contemporary listings: engraver, with LOUIS F. GERY (1876, 1878, 1880–81); engraver (1877, 1904–1905); engraver, 84 Customhouse (1882); engraver, 55 Chartres (1883–84); engraver, 89 Customhouse (1885–89); engraver, with JOHN J. WEINFURTER (1890–92); engraver, 39 Bourbon (1893–94); engraver, 223 Bourbon (1895–98); engraver, 237 Bourbon (1899, 1902); engraver, 235 Bourbon (1900–1901); engraver, 733 Bienville (1903); engraver, 239 Chartres (1906); engraver, 222 Exchange Pl. (1907–13); engraver, 131 St. Charles (1914).
References: NOCD 1876–1914; NOBD 1898; *D. Pic.*, Mar. 14, 1914; U.S. Census (1910), roll 521.

LAUDUN, EDGAR AUGUST
Born N.O. ca. 1873; died N.O. Mar. 21, 1923.
Artist, active N.O. 1898–99.
Contemporary listings: artist (1898–99).
References: NOCD 1891–94, 1896, 1898–1901, 1903–1904, 1910, 1912–15, 1917–19, 1922–23; *T. Pic.*, Mar. 22, 1923.

LAUFER, JACOB
Born Hungary Jan. 9, 1863; died N.O. June 6, 1925.
Painter, sketch artist, active N.O. 1900–1915.
Contemporary listings: portrait painter, 317 Royal (1900–1901); portrait artist, 314 Royal (1902); portrait artist, 313 Royal (1903–1904); portrait artist, 134 Royal (1904); portrait painter, 314 Royal (1905–1909); pictures, 238 Royal (1910–15).
References: NOCD 1900–25; *D. Pic.*, Feb. 25, 1903; *T. Pic.*, June 7, 1925; *Town Talk*, July 1904, 25, Sept. 1904, 27, Feb. 1905, 46; Orleans Parish Registrar of Voters, NOPL.

LAUNITZ, ROBERT EBERHARD SCHMIDT VON DER
Born Riga, Russia Nov. 4, 1806; died N.Y.C. Dec. 13, 1870.
Sculptor, active N.O. 1852.
Studied: with Thorwaldsen.
Contemporary listings: sculptor, 31 Old Levee or 3 Commercial (1852).
Memberships/positions: National Academy of Design, N.Y.C. (1833).
Cited as an important influence in the development of monumental sculpture in the U.S., Launitz came to the U.S. in 1828 and settled in N.Y.C. He worked in both marble and gran-

ite, and executed public monuments in Savannah GA, Frankfort KY, and Troy NY, as well as mantels and gravestones. When the municipal hall for the second municipality of N.O. was constructed (1850), Launitz came to the city to create the sculpture contained in the building's pediment. The grouping depicted allegorical figures of Liberty supporting Justice and Commerce. He advertised in Jan. 1852 that he was in LA to execute several works. References: *Bee*, Jan. 27, 1852; *Appleton's CAB*; Bénézit; Friends of the Cabildo, *N.O. Architecture*, 2:204-5; Groce and Wallace; Louisiana Landmarks Society.

LAURENCE, MRS. H.
Sketch artist, painter, active N.O. 1867.
Awarded: Grand State Fair, best pencil figures and best composition in watercolor (1867).
Cf. LAWRENCE, AGLAI.
References: Mechanics' and Agricultural Fair Asso., *Report* (1867):28.

LAUTERBACH, C.
Artist, active N.O. 1872.
Contemporary listings: artist, with WILLIAM W. WASHBURN (1872).
References: NOCD 1872.

LAUTERBACH, OTTO J.
Born N.O. Mar. 10, 1877; died N.O. Sept. 1, 1956.
Engraver, active N.O. 1896–1921; also jeweler.
Contemporary listings: engraver, T. Hausmann & Sons (1896, 1898); engraver (1899–1900, 1910, 1913); engraver, with A. M. Hill (1901–1903); engraver, 130 Exchange Pl. (1904, 1906–1909, 1914–18); the Otto J. Lauterbach Engraving Concern, 637 Canal (1910); engraver, 218 Baronne (1911).
Son of TILMAN JOSEPH LAUTERBACH.
References: NOCD 1896, 1898–1904, 1906–33, 1935, 1938, 1940, 1942, 1945–47, 1949, 1952–56, 1958; *T. Pic.*, Sept. 3, 1956; Orleans Parish Registrar of Voters, NOPL; U.S. Census (1880), roll 460, (1900), roll 571, (1910), roll 520.

LAUTERBACH, TILMAN JOSEPH.
Born Cologne, Germany Jan. 1828; died N.O. Jan. 3, 1909.
Engraver, active N.O. 1872–1908; also stencil cutter.
Contemporary listings: GERY & LAUTERBACH (1872–73); engraver, 169 Common (1874); general engraver, 66 Gravier (1875); engraver, 79 Customhouse (1876); ED. SMITH & CO. (1877); engraver, with R. CHAPSKY (1878); engraver, Bienville cor. Exchange Al. (1879); engraver, 65 Exchange Pl., and lithographer (1880); engraver, 65 Exchange Al. (1881–90); engraver, 241 Exchange Al. (1895–97); engraver, 242 Exchange (1898); engraver, 241 Exchange Pl. (1898–1904, 1906–1908).
Father of OTTO J. LAUTERBACH.
References: NOCD 1872–1904, 1906–1908; NOBD 1898; *D. Pic.*, Jan. 4–5, 1909; U.S. Census, (1880), roll 460, (1900), roll 571.

LAVERGNE, ANTOINE CADET
Artist, active N.O. 1827–30.
Contemporary listings: artiste, 2 St. Julie (1827); artist, 2 St. Julie (1830).
References: NOCD 1811, 1822–23, 1827, 1830, 1832, 1834–35.

LAVIGNE, CHARLES
Born France ca. 1822; died N.O. Aug. 23, 1855.
Engraver, active N.O 1855.
Contemporary listings: engraver (1855).
References: Louisiana Charity Hospital, Death Records, NOPL.

LAVIGNE, LOUIS
Art teacher, active N.O. 1885.
Contemporary listings: professor of drawing, store of FREDERIC WILLIAM EMILE SEEBOLD (1885).
References: *Bee*, July 30, 1885.

LAW, ELIZABETH
Born Ireland ca. 1791; died N.O. Mar. 14, 1864.
Art teacher, active N.O. 1840–41.
Contemporary listings: teacher of painting and drawing (1840); academy of drawing and painting, cor. Canal and Baronne (1841).
References: NOCD 1841–43, 1846; *Bee*, Jan. 6, 11, 15, 1841; *D. Pic.*, Dec. 30, 1840, Jan. 2, 10, Mar. 3,

1841, Mar. 15, 1864; Groce and Wallace; N.O. Death Certificate (1864), 25:207, NOPL; U.S. Census (1840), roll 134.

LAWHORN, CHARLES LUTHER
Born TN.
Designer, sculptor, active N.O. 1909–18; also architect.
Contemporary listings: v. pres., ALBERT WEIBLEN Marble & Granite Co. (1909–11); designer, Albert Weiblen Marble & Granite Co. (1913, 1917–18).
Exhibited: ART ASSOCIATION OF NEW ORLEANS (1918).
As a designer for Weiblen, Lawhorn was resposible for several tombs in Metairie Cemetery and for the base of the equestrian statue of Gen. P. G. T. Beauregard by ALEXANDER DOYLE (1913).
References: NOCD 1909–11, 1913, 1917–21; T. Pic., Aug. 25, 1916, Mar. 14, 17, 1918; Art Asso., Catalogue (1918); Friends of the Cabildo, N.O. Architecture, 3:53, 57, 61, 119–21; Reeves, 110.

LAWRENCE, AGLAI (Mrs. Henry Lawrence)
Born N.O. ca. 1825.
Painter, active N.O. 1853.
Contemporary listings: amateur painter (1853).
Cf. LAURENCE, MRS. H.
References: D. Crescent, Apr. 25, 1853; U.S. Census (1850), roll 419.

LAWSON, THOMAS
Born LA ca. 1830.
Painter, active N.O. 1860.
Contemporary listings: portrait painter (1860).
References: Groce and Wallace; U.S. Census (1860), roll 420; William Young.

LAYMAN, E.
Artist, active N.O. 1838.
Contemporary listings: artist, 103 Great Men (1838).
References: NOCD 1838.

LAZARD, ALICE ABRAHAM (Mrs. Benjamin S. Lazard)
Born N.O. Nov. 1, 1893; died Highland Park IL Dec. 24, 1972.
Artist, active N.O. ca. 1917–18.

Studied: with Charles Sneed Williams, Art Institute of Chicago; with Randall Davey; NEWCOMB COLLEGE.
Exhibited: ART ASSOCIATION OF NEW ORLEANS (1917–18).
Memberships/positions: Art Association, Springfield IL; Art Club of Chicago; Art Institute of Chicago Alumni Association.
Lazard moved to the Chicago suburb of Highland Park in the early 1920s and received awards from the North Shore Art League (1948–52) and the Mile of Art Exhibition (1954).
References: T. Pic., Dec. 28, 1972; Art Asso., Catalogue (1917, 1918); Collins and Opitz; Fielding, Dictionary; Who's Who in American Art 1938–39.

LEAVITT, WILLIAM HOMER
Painter, active N.O. 1903–1907.
Studied: Ecole des Beaux Arts, Paris.
Contemporary listings: artist (1904–1905).
Exhibited: ART ASSOCIATION OF NEW ORLEANS (1904–1905).
A prominent portrait painter, Leavitt arrived in N.O. Dec. 1903. He and his wife, the daughter of William Jennings Bryan, had been touring the U.S.; they remained in N.O. until the summer of 1905 when they moved to Denver CO. Leavitt returned to spend the summer of 1907 in N.O.
References: NOCD 1905; D. Pic., Mar. 12, 1905; T. Demo., Feb. 28, 1904; Art Asso., Catalogue (1904, 1905); Fielding, Dictionary; LSM, Biennial Report for 1922–23, 108; Scrapbook 100, LSM.

LE BLANC, EMILIE MARIE DE HOA
Born N.O. June 17, 1870; died N.O. Nov. 24, 1941.
Art teacher, art craftsman, active N.O. 1897–1941.
Studied: NEWCOMB COLLEGE (1897–99, 1900–1905); Art Institute of Chicago; with Dr. D. W. Ross, Harvard University; with L'hôte, Colarossi and Grande Chaumière, Paris; with J. C. Johansen; Thurn School of Modern Art, Gloucester, England.
Contemporary listings: teacher (1900, 1904); teacher, Franklin School (1905); teacher, McDonogh

#1 (1905, 1908); teacher, Robert E. Lee School (1907–1908); artist, painter, designer, teacher, (1910); teacher, McDonogh #3 (1911–12); artist, 1225 Chartres (1912); teacher, Esplanade Ave. High School (1913–18).

Exhibited: ARTISTS' ASSOCIATION OF NEW ORLEANS (1897); ART ASSOCIATION OF NEW ORLEANS (1907, 1910–11, 1913–17); DELGADO MUSEUM OF ART (1911–12, 1915).

Awarded: Art Association of New Orleans, silver medal (1912).

Memberships/positions: Newcomb Art Alumnae; Artists' Guild; Art Association of New Orleans.

Teacher of art (1900–41) in N.O. public high schools and supervisor of drawing in N.O. elementary schools. LeBlanc was the N.O. delegate to the International Art Congress in Dresden, Germany (1912) and in Paris (1937). Sister of MARIE DE HOA LE BLANC.

References: NOCD 1900, 1904–1905, 1907–1908, 1911–33, 1938, 1940, 1942; D. Pic., Feb. 20, 1898; Item, May 3, 1915, Feb. 6, 1921; Item-Trib., Nov. 10, 1940; New Orleanian, Oct. 4, 1930, 30; States, Dec. 4, 1932; T. Pic., Mar. 3, 1930, Feb. 19, 1939, Nov. 25, 30, 1941; AANO, Catalogue (1897); Art Asso., Catalogue (1907, 1910, 1911, 1913, 1914, 1916); Art Asso., Special Exhibition; Cline, Art and Artists, 9–10; Delgado, Inaugural Exhibition; Orleans Parish Registrar of Voters, NOPL; Poesch, Newcomb Pottery, 49, 101, 109, 110; Radcliffe, 11; THNOC, Arts and Crafts Club Scrapbook; THNOC Cemetery Survey; U.S. Census (1910), roll 521; Who's Who in American Art, 1938–39; WPA, "Lives"; William Young.

LE BLANC, MARIE DE HOA

Born N.O. Nov. 23, 1874; died N.O. Apr. 16, 1954.

Painter, art teacher, art craftsman, active N.O. 1897–1949.

Studied: NEWCOMB COLLEGE (1898, 1909–14); Art Institute of Chicago; with Dr. D. W. Ross, Harvard University (1902); Ipswich MA (1902);

Europe (ca. 1904); with J. C. Johansen; with Martin Heyman, Munich; with L'hôte, Colarossi and Grand Chaumière, Paris.

Contemporary listings: artist (1900, 1916); teacher (1904, 1908, 1915); designer (1905); artist, painter, designer, teacher (1910); drawing teacher, Public Schools (1913); teacher, McDonogh #13 (1914–15); teacher, Wm. O. Rogers School (1917).

Exhibited: ARTISTS' ASSOCIATION OF NEW ORLEANS (1897); DELGADO MUSEUM OF ART (1911–12); ART ASSOCIATION OF NEW ORLEANS (1911, 1913–18).

Awarded: Louisiana Purchase Exposition, St. Louis MO, bronze medal (1904); Annual N.O. Exhibition, Newcomb College, 2nd medal (1910); Art Association of New Orleans, gold medal (1914).

Memberships/positions: Newcomb Art Alumnac; Art Association of New Orleans; Louisiana Drawing Teachers' Association.

Le Blanc was awarded $150 to travel to Harvard for the Ross lecture series (1902), was awarded $500 to travel to Europe for her superior work in the pottery department at Newcomb (1904), and was the N.O. delegate to the International Art Congress in Dresden Germany (1912). She was listed beyond 1917 as a teacher for various N.O. public schools until 1949. Sister of EMILIE MARIE DE HOA LE BLANC.

References: NOCD 1895, 1900, 1904–1906, 1908, 1910, 1912–21, 1923–33, 1938, 1940, 1942, 1945–47, 1949, 1952–55; D. Pic., Feb. 20, 1898; Harlequin, June 23, 1904; Item, May 3, 1915, Jan. 19, Feb. 6, 1921; Item-Trib., Feb. 7, 1937, Feb. 5, 1939, Oct. 20, Nov. 10, 1940; T. Demo., Mar. 19, 1904, Feb. 25, 1910, Jan. 14, 1913, Mar. 16, 1914; T. Pic., Mar. 3, 1930, Feb. 7, 1937, June 3, 1951, Apr. 18, 1954; Ball, "Newcomb Pottery Hits Big Time Again," T. Pic./States–Item, May 27, 1984; AANO, Catalogue (1897); Art Asso., Catalogue (1911, 1913, 1914,

1915, 1916, 1917, 1918); Art Asso., *Special Exhibition*; Delgado, *Catalogue*; Delgado, *Inaugural Exhibition*; Fielding, *Dictionary*; LSM, *Biennial Report for 1922-23*, 108-9; Orleans Parish Registrar of Voters, NOPL; Ormond and Irvine, 34, 83, 87, 90, 159; Poesch, *Newcomb Pottery*, 27, 41, 46-48, 51, 53-54, 58, 101, 109-11, 115-18, 126, 131; Radcliffe, 11; THNOC Cemetery Survey; U.S. Census (1910), roll 521; *Who's Who In American Art*, 1938-39.

LE BLANC, WILLIAM
Born France ca. 1822.
Sculptor, active N.O. 1849-51; also carver.
Contemporary listings: sculptor, 197 Bourbon (1849); sculptor, 31 Exchange Al. (1850-51).
References: NOCD 1849-51; *Courier*, Nov. 2, 1849; May 1, 1850; Groce and Wallace; U.S. Census (1850), roll 235; William Young.

LE BLANC, YVES
Died N.O. Aug. 25, 1826.
Silhouettist, active N.O. 1811.
Contemporary listings: profilist, 12 St. Peter (1811).
References: NOCD 1822-24; *Courier*, Nov. 11, 1811, Aug. 25, 1826.

LE BRETON, DAGMAR RENSHAW. *See* RENSHAW, DAGMAR ADELAIDE

LEBRETON, L.
Sketch artist.
Possibly came to N.O. to draw his view of Jackson Square that he lithographed (ca. 1850) in Paris. Possibly Louis Lebreton, a French painter and watercolorist who exhibited at the Paris salons of 1841-49; died 1860.
References: Bénézit; Reps, 311; THNOC 1971.45.

LEBRETHON, JULES
Sculptor, active N.O. 1859-60.
Contemporary listings: cameo cutter, 46 Camp (1859-60).
Instructor and assistant to sculptor Augustus Saint-Gaudens in N.Y.C. (1864-67).
References: NOCD 1859-60; Jordan, "LeBrethon Cameos Are Rare,"

T. Pic., Feb. 23, 1975; Groce and Wallace.

LECKIE, FRANKLIN
Painter, active N.O. 1851, 1884; also decorator.
Decorated the Varieties Theatre in 1851, and returned to N.O. in 1884 with his traveling panorama depicting the Battle of Gettysburg.
References: *Mascot*, Nov. 1, 1884.

LEDDY, MRS. ____
Painter, active N.O. 1855.
Contemporary listings: ornamental, flower, and landscape painter, Opelousas Railroad Depot (1855).
References: *D. Crescent*, July 4, 1855.

LEDOUX, ANNA
Painter, active N.O. ca. 1884-85.
Exhibited: World's Industrial and Cotton Centennial Exposition (1884-85).
References: *Bee*, Mar. 29, 1885.

LEE, CHARLES
Painter, active N.O 1888-96; also cabinetmaker.
Contemporary listings: painter (1888, 1891-92, 1894); scenic artist (1896).
References: NOCD 1887-96.

LEE, J.
Painter, active N.O. 1842; also sign and ornamental painter.
Contemporary listings: painter, 68 Gravier (1842).
Advertised as a painter of banners, imitation stained or ground glass, landscapes, portraits, dead game, fruit, and fish (1842).
References: *Lafayette City Advertiser*, Jan. 1, 8, 1842.

LEE, JAMES D., JR.
Artist, active N.O 1859-66.
Contemporary listings: artist, 142 Canal (1859-61, 1866).
References: NOCD 1859-61, 1866; Groce and Wallace.

LEE, MRS. JULIUS
Painter, active N.O ca. 1915.
Exhibited: ART ASSOCIATION OF NEW ORLEANS (1915).
References: Art Asso., *Special Exhibition*.

LEE, SAMUEL M.
Died Opelousas LA Aug. 2, 1841.
Painter, active N.O. 1835-39.

Contemporary listings: panorama painter, Banks Arcade (1835); scenic artist, with EDWARD SCHINOTTI, St. Charles Theatre (1837); principal artist, St. Charles Theatre (1838); artist, scene painter, landscape painter, St. Charles Theatre (1839). Itinerant panorama painter and scenic artist who also worked in Cincinnati OH (1837–38), Louisville KY (1838–39), and Opelousas LA (1841).
References: NOCD 1834–35; *Courier*, July 1, 1835; *D. Pic.*, Aug. 21, 1841; *True Amer.*, Mar. 28, Apr. 15, 1837, Oct. 1, Nov. 14, 1838, Apr. 15, 1839; Cist, 139; Groce and Wallace; WPA, *American Portrait Inventory*, 161.

LEEDS, LINA RAWLES
Died N.O. Aug. 3, 1891.
Painter, active N.O ca. 1885–86.
Exhibited: American Exposition (1885–86).
References: *D. Pic.*, Aug. 4, 1891; Creole Exhibit, 11.

LEESON, ANNIE
Artist, active N.O. 1874.
Contemporary listings: artist, with WILLIAM H. LEESON (1874).
References: NOCD 1874.

LEESON, WILLIAM H.
Colorer, lithographer, engraver, active N.O. 1870; primarily photographer.
Awarded: Grand State Fair, bronze medal for best colored photographs in watercolors (1870).
Listed as photographer (1865–70) and in partnership with photographer H. H. Swymmer (1868–69), and also printed sheet music covers.
References: NOCD 1866–74; *D. Pic.*, Apr. 3, 1870; *T. Deutsche Zeitung*, May 10, 1866; Dichter and Shapiro, 252; Mechanics' and Agricultural Fair Asso., *Report* (1870):47; Sheet Music Collection, THNOC; Smith and Tucker, 162.

LEFONGE, HARRY
Painter, active N.O. 1904.
Contemporary listings: assistant scenic artist, with CLARK COX, Elysium Theatre (1904).
References: *Item*, Apr. 27, 1904.

LE GRAND, MR. ____
Sculptor, painter, active N.O. 1818.
Contemporary listings: wood sculptor, Dumaine betw. Dauphine and Burgundy (1818).
Advertised in N.O. that he accepted commissions for interior painting and decoration, including the painting of murals. When he left N.O., he announced his intention to come back to the city, but there is no evidence of his return.
References: *L'Ami des Lois*, June 15, 1818.

LE GRAND, JULES
Painter, active N.O. 1857; also decorator.
Studied: Paris.
Contemporary listings: artist, fresco painter, cor. Dauphine and Customhouse (1857).
Came to N.O. from N.Y.C.
References: *Bee*, Jan. 3–Mar. 21, 1857 (advs.); Caldwell, 202–4; Groce and Wallace.

LE GRAS, EMILE
Sculptor, commercial artist, active N.O 1878–86; also decorator, carver.
Contemporary listings: artist, with THEODORE LILIENTHAL (1878); wood carver, 41 St. Peter (1883, 1886); wood carver, 40 St. Peter (1884–85).
References: NOCD 1861, 1866–79, 1881–87.

LEHMAN, THOMAS E.
Artist, active N.O. 1849.
Contemporary listings: artist, 191 St. Ann (1849).
References: NOCD 1849; Groce and Wallace.

LEHMANN, LOUISE A.
Illustrator, active N.O. 1909.
An amateur artist, she was listed as the matron at the Home for Incurables (1903–14). She drew an illustration for *Harlequin*.
References: NOCD 1903–1905, 1908, 1911, 1913–14; *Harlequin*, July 1, 1909, 12.

LEININGER, JOHN CHRISTIAN, JR.
Born LA June 1873; died Goodbee LA Mar. 10, 1931.
Engraver, active N.O 1891–1911.
Contemporary listings: engraver, with SMITH W. BENNETT (1891); engraver (1896, 1900, 1911).

References: NOCD 1891, 1896, 1900, 1911; *T. Pic.*, Mar. 12, 1931; U.S. Census (1900), roll 574.

LEMOSY, FRANCIS WILLIAM
Painter, active N.O. 1839.
Contemporary listings: historical and portrait painter, 7 Chartres (1839).
References: *D. Pic.*, Jan. 6, 1839; Groce and Wallace.

L'ENGLE, WILLIAM, JR.
Painter, active N.O. ca. 1918.
Studied: Paris.
Exhibited: ART ASSOCIATION OF NEW ORLEANS (1918).
References: *T. Pic.*, Mar. 14, 1918; Art Asso., *Catalogue* (1918).

LENON, CHARLES F.
Painter, active N.O. 1880.
Contemporary listings: portrait painter, 157 Baronne (1880).
References: NOCD 1880.

LEON, PLACIDO
Artist, active N.O. 1887.
Contemporary listings: artist (1887).
References: NOCD 1887.

LEON Y ESCOSURA, IGNACIO
Born Oviedo, Spain.
Painter, active N.O. 1885.
Studied: with Federico de Madrazo, Spain.
Exhibited: Vienna, Austria (1882); LILIENTHAL's (1885).
Spanish genre painter who eventually settled in Paris, he was also well-known in Madrid and London during his career. Leon y Escosura had planned to visit N.O. for a week, but remained for five months. He left the city in May 1885 to go back to Paris, expecting to return to N.O. during the winter of 1885 because he had been inspired by the LA landscape.
References: *Bee*, Apr. 10, May 8, 1885; Bénézit.

LEOPOLD, GODFREY
Artist, active N.O. 1885.
Contemporary listings: artist (1885).
Possibly Godfrey Leopold, died San Francisco CA Nov. 12, 1931.
References: NOCD 1885; *T. Pic.*, Nov. 14, 1931.

LEPAGE, MICHEL
Born Turin, Italy ca. 1796; died N.O. June 7, 1833.
Artist, active N.O. 1830.

Contemporary listings: artist, 121 St. Ann (1830).
References: NOCD 1830; *Bee*, June 8, 1833; Groce and Wallace; N.O. Death Certificate (1833), 3:198, NOPL; William Young.

LE PAGE DU PRATZ, ANTOINE SIMON
Born Netherlands or Belgium ca. 1689–95; died 1775.
Sketch artist, active N.O. 1718–20, 1728–34; primarily engineer, cartographer, architect.
Professional engineer who came to LA in 1718 and settled along Bayou St. John. He moved to Fort Rosalie, Natchez MS (1720) and returned to N.O. (1728) to manage a plantation of the Company of the Indies. Before leaving LA for France in 1734, he traveled extensively and made a number of drawings of the colony's flora and fauna, that were engraved for his *Histoire de la Louisiane*, published in Paris (1758).
References: Thomas Clark, 1:73–74; Friends of the Cabildo, *Louisiana Indians*, 28, 38; Groce and Wallace; Howes, 341; Le Page du Pratz; McWilliams, 214; Parke–Bernet Galleries, 104; Rader, 182; Richardson, 20; Stebbins, 7; Samuel Wilson, *Bienville*, 35.

LEPIERRE, CAPT. _____
Sculptor, active N.O. 1884.
Contemporary listings: wood carver (1884).
References: *D. Pic.*, Oct. 30, 1884, Jan. 18, 1896.

LE PRINCE, G. MARIE
Painter, active N.O. ca. 1918.
Exhibited: ART ASSOCIATION OF NEW ORLEANS (1918).
References: Art Asso., *Catalogue* (1918).

LEROUX, MR. L.
Sculptor, active N.O. 1834.
Contemporary listings: wood carver, sculptor, 112 St. Philip (1834).
References: *Bee*, Jan. 24, 1834.

LEROY, JAMES EMILE
Born N.O. Jan. 1822; died N.O. Mar. 10, 1877.
Engraver, active N.O. 1871–74.
Contemporary listings: engraver (1871, 1874).

References: NOCD 1871, 1873–77; *Bee*, Mar. 11, 1877; N.O. Death Certificate (1877), 68:524, NOPL; U.S. Census (1860), roll 421.

LE SASSIER, MISS ____
Painter, active N.O. ca. 1884–85.
Exhibited: World's Industrial and Cotton Centennial Exposition (1884–85).
Possibly Mary Le Sassier, born ca. 1867; died N.O. Dec. 9, 1887. Possibly the sister of CHARLES LE SASSIER, JR.
References: NOCD 1886–88; *D. Pic.*, Dec. 10, 1887; Woman's Department of the World's Exposition, 158.

LE SASSIER, CHARLES, JR.
Sketch artist, painter, active N.O. 1892–96.
Studied: ARTISTS' ASSOCIATION OF NEW ORLEANS.
Exhibited: Artists' Association of New Orleans (1892, 1894, 1896).
He moved to N.Y.C. sometime between 1896 and 1898. Possibly the brother of MISS LE SASSIER.
References: *Current Topics*, Jan. 1893, 10 11; *D. Pic.*, Dec 13, 1892, Jan. 12, 1898; *Down in Dixie*, July 15, 1896, 10; *T. Demo.*, Dec. 13, 1892, Dec. 14, 1894; AANO, *Catalogue* (1896); Mount, 148.

LESLIE, JOHN
Painter, artist, active N.O. 1844–45.
Contemporary listings: scenic artist, St. Charles Theatre (1844–45).
Possibly John L. Leslie, a scene and panorama painter who worked in N.Y.C. (1828–30) and OH (1840–55). He assisted HENRY LEWIS with his Mississippi River panorama (1848–49).
References: *D. Pic.*, Jan. 21, Feb. 16, 1845; *D. Tropic*, Nov. 22, 1844; Groce and Wallace; Scharf, 1:981.

LESSEPS, CHARLES DE
Born France; died N.O. 1889.
Sketch artist, painter, active N.O. ca. 1865–89.
Came to LA as a sugar planter near Bayou Lafourche but lost his plantation after the Civil War. He moved to N.O. and made miniature drawings and painted in watercolors and sepia. Brother of Numa de Lesseps who also painted in N.O.
References: Friends of the Cabildo, *250 Years*, 67, 78.

LESSEPS, NUMA DE. *See* LESSEPS, CHARLES DE

LESUEUR, CHARLES ALEXANDRE
Born Le Havre, France Jan. 1, 1778; died Sainte–Adresse, France Dec. 12, 1846.
Sketch artist, active N.O. 1828–37.
Naturalist, illustrator, painter, drawing and painting teacher, and engraver. In 1816 Lesueur came to the U.S. to aid geologist William Maclure in drawing specimens in natural history. He settled in Philadelphia as a teacher and as the curator of the Academy of Natural Sciences (1817–25). Between 1826 and 1837, he lived mainly in New Harmony IN and traveled throughout the country sketching and painting in watercolor. Lesueur made at least six trips to N.O. (1828, 1829, 1830, 1831, 1834, and 1837), the last to take ship for Le Havre, France. He sketched in and around N.O., including views of the city, street scenes, and character studies. After returning to France, he worked at the Museum of Natural History, Paris, and later at the Museum of Natural History, Le Havre.
References: Bénézit; "Charles–Alexandre Lesueur"; Detroit Institute of Arts, 23; Fielding, *Dictionary*; Groce and Wallace; Leland, 53–78; New York Historical Society, 2:891; Ord, 189–216; *Register*; Vail, 22, 76–80, 87, 102.

LETTEN, LOUISE MUELLER (Mrs. Francis J. Letten)
Born N.O. ca. 1879; died N.O. June 18, 1955.
Painter, active N.O. ca. 1915.
Exhibited: ART ASSOCIATION OF NEW ORLEANS (1915).
References: NOCD 1940, 1942, 1945–46, 1949; *T. Pic.*, June 20, 1955; Art Asso., *Special Exhibition*.

LEUSCHNER, ROBERT
Died ca. 1878.
Engraver, lithographer, active N.O. 1872–77.

Contemporary listings: lithographic engraver, MANOUVRIER & SIMON (1872); engraver, with DIONIS SIMON (1873); lithographer, with BENEDICT SIMON (1874); lithographic engraver, T. FITZWILLIAM & CO. (1877).
References: NOCD 1872–74, 1877.

LEVASSEUR, JUDAH
Artist, active N.O. ca. 1838–42.
Contemporary listings: artist, St. Ann betw. Robertson and Villere (1841).
References: NOCD 1841–42; Glenk, 76; U.S. Census (1840), roll 131.

LEVI, ISAAC
Born Germany ca. 1820.
Lithographer, active N.O. 1852.
Contemporary listings: lithographer, 11 Exchange Al. (1852).
References: NOCD 1852; Groce and Wallace.

LEVIE, JOHN E.
Born Portsmouth, England ca. 1802; died N.O. Aug. 29, 1837.
Painter, active N.O. 1835–37.
Contemporary listings: miniaturist, Old Levee (1835); artist (1837).
References: *Bee*, Dec. 31, 1835, Aug. 29, 1837; Groce and Wallace; N.O. Death Certificate (1837), 7:420, NOPL.

JOSEPH LEVY & BROS.
Lithographers, active N.O. 1883–1902; primarily stationers, printers; Joseph Levy (born 1860), Henry Levy, Sylvan Levy, partners.
Contemporary listings: lithographers, 96 Common (1883); lithographers, 520–24 Common (1902).
References: NOCD 1878, 1880–1932; *D. States*, Feb. 10, 1902; *Mascot*, Apr. 28, 1883; Orleans Parish Registrar of Voters, NOPL.

LEVY, MIRIAM FLORA
Born Franklin LA 1895; died Aug. 11, 1975.
Designer, art craftsman, active N.O. 1918–29.
Studied: NEWCOMB COLLEGE (1913–18).
Art craftsman at Newcomb (1918–29). Member of ART ASSOCIATION OF NEW ORLEANS, the Arts and Crafts Club, and the Boston Arts and Crafts Club. She designed handmade jew-

elry at Hausmann's jewelry store (1937–56).
References: *Item–Trib.*, Mar. 12, 1933; *T. Pic*, Sept. 30, 1928, Mar. 6, 1932, Mar. 14, 1933, Aug. 12, 1975; Delgado, *Bookplates*, 3; Ormond and Irvine, 160; Poesch, *Newcomb Pottery*, 101.

LEVY, SARA BLOOM
Died Nov. 3 or 5, 1955.
Art craftsman, active N.O. 1901–12.
Studied: NEWCOMB COLLEGE (ca. 1896–1902).
Known for her pottery decoration.
References: Ormond and Irvine, 160; Poesch, *Newcomb Pottery*, 101.

LEWIS, EDWARD
Painter, active N.O. 1905.
Contemporary listings: scenic artist, Elysium Theatre (1905).
References: *D. States*, Sept. 24, 1905.

LEWIS, HENRY
Born Newport or Scarborough, England Jan. 12, 1819; died Dusseldorf, Germany Sept. 16, 1904.
Painter.
Painter and panoramist who moved to the U.S. with his family. In St. Louis MO, Lewis first advertised as an artist and began making sketches along the Mississippi River for a panorama painting that was successfully exhibited in the U.S., Canada, and Europe (1849–53). Lewis was associated with LEON D. POMAREDE and with SAMUEL B. STOCKWELL in the venture, but both men left Lewis due to disagreements and painted their own panoramas. Lewis eventually settled in Dusseldorf where some of the sketches and paintings for the panorama were lithographed as illustrations in his *Das Illustrirte Mississippithal*. Although credited with creating the illustrations for the views of N.O. and LA, Lewis never traveled that far downriver. The views were based on the sketches made by one of his assistants, CHARLES ROGERS.
References: Arrington, "Henry Lewis," 239–72; Groce and Wallace; Henry Lewis; Henry McDermott, "Lewis," 332–35; Mc-

236

Dermott, *Lost Panoramas*, 81–144; Schmitz, 37–48; Squires, 244–56.

LEWIS, HUGH
Born Ireland ca. 1823.
Lithographer, engraver, sculptor, active N.O. 1869–82.
Contemporary listings: CRESCENT LITHOGRAPHY (1869); lithographer (1869); lithographer, with C. W. CLARK (1871); lithographic printing, 22 St. Charles (1871–72); lithographer, 22 St. Charles (1872–73); engraver, 20 St. Charles (1873); lithographer, 20 St. Charles (1874–79); pres., NEW ORLEANS LITHOGRAPHING AND ENGRAVING CO. (1880); New Orleans Lithographing and Engraving Co. (1881); lithographer (1882).
Awarded: Grand State Fair, diploma for best statue in stone, marble or bronze (1870).
Lewis was especially known for his printing of maps; he also received recognition for his work as an amateur sculptor (1869–70).
References: NOCD 1869–82; *D. Pic.*, July 28, 1869; *Repub.*, Nov. 9, 1873, Apr. 26, 1874; Mechanics' and Agricultural Fair Asso., *Report* (1870):47; *Murray's Planters Directory*; Phillips, 497; U.S. Census (1870), roll 520.

LEWIS, JAMES OTTO
Born Philadelphia PA Feb. 3, 1799; died N.Y.C. 1858.
Engraver, active N.O. 1823.
Contemporary listings: engraver, 104 St. Peter (1823).
Beginning as an engraver in Philadelphia (ca. 1815–19), Lewis joined an expedition going west and worked in St. Louis MO (1820–21) and N.O. (1823). He settled in Detroit MI and was employed by the U.S. government to paint Indian portraits (1823–34) that were published in Philadelphia (1835), N.Y.C., and London.
References: NOCD 1823; Fielding, *Dictionary*; Groce and Wallace; McCracken, *Portrait*, 44–46.

LEWIS, MANUSETO. *See* LUISSI, MANSUETTO

LEWIS, MILFORD C.
Lithographer, active N.O. 1878–84; also printer

Contemporary listings: lithographer, with HUGH LEWIS (1878–79); lithographer, NEW ORLEANS LITHOGRAPHING AND ENGRAVING CO. (1880–81); NEW ORLEANS LITHOGRAPHING CO. (1882); lithographer, New Orleans Lithographing Co. (1883–84).
References: NOCD 1875–84; *Mascot*, Mar. 18, 1882, 39.

LEWIS, WILLIAM P.
Sketch artist, active N.O. 1892–93; also photographer.
Contemporary listings: crayon artist, 856 Laurel (1892); artist, 856 1/2 Laurel (1893).
References: NOCD 1891–93, 1897.

LEWIS, WILLIAM T.
Born LA ca. 1846.
Engraver, active N.O. 1869–71; also stencil cutter.
Contemporary listings: engraver, 2 Old Levee (1869); engraver, with JOSEPH P. MURPHY (1870); engraver, 9 Decatur (1871).
References: NOCD 1869–72, 1874; U.S. Census (1870), roll 524.

LEWIS, MISS WILLIE
Artist, active N.O. ca. 1887; black.
Exhibited: Colored People's Fair, Spanish Fort (1887).
References: *T. Demo.*, Nov. 17, 1887.

L'HOMME, ALBERT
Artist, active N.O. 1895.
Contemporary listings: artist (1895).
References: NOCD 1895.

LIAUTAUD, BARTHELEMY ADOLPH
Died ca. 1872.
Artist, active N.O. 1859–69.
Contemporary listings: artist, 327 St. Ann (1860); artist, 312 St. Ann (1860–61, 1866, 1868–69).
References: NOCD 1859–61, 1866, 1868–70, 1873; Groce and Wallace; William Young.

LILIENTHAL, THEODORE
Born Frankfort, Germany Sept. 25, 1829.
Art dealer, painter, active N.O. 1883–86; primarily photographer.
Contemporary listings: art gallery (1883–84).
Exhibited: American Exposition (1885–86).
Coming to N.O. in 1854 after political upheavals in his native Prussia,

Lilienthal established a photographic business at 121 Poydras. From this small beginning, his reputation as a photographer grew, and his business flourished. By 1880, he was established in the Touro Buildings on Canal St. and occupied four floors for his enterprise. A portion of this space was a gallery where not only his photographs were displayed, but also paintings by local and out–of–town artists. Lilienthal furnished the photographic portraits that PAUL POINCY and VICTOR PIERSON used in their painting *Volunteer Firemen's Parade* (1872). Lilienthal held the exclusive LA and MS license for the patented Lambertype (carbon printing) process and also finished Artotypes, photographically generated images that were printed in ink.
References: NOCD 1857, 1866, 1868, 1870–94; *Bee*, June 4, 1863, Mar. 5, 1873; *Bull.*, June 9, 1875; *D. States*, Apr. 13, 1884, Feb. 19, 1890; *T. Deutsche Zeitung*, Feb. 28, 1861, May 10, 1866, Oct. 23, 1874; *Times*, Sept. 9, 25, 1876; *T. Pic.*, Oct. 2, 1977; *Almanach de la Louisiane* (1867):145; Creole Exhibit, 10; Glenk, 83; Gottheil, 5, 10; Land, 165; Lilienthal's; LSM, *Biennial Report for 1926–27*, 30, 68, 80; Morrison, *Industries*, 92–93; Smith and Tucker, 163; U.S. Census (1870), roll 524; Waldo, 133–36.

LILLIS, ANT.
Born Ireland ca. 1812.
Artist, active N.O. 1860.
Contemporary listings: artist (1860).
References: Groce and Wallace; U.S. Census (1860), roll 417.

LINDSEY, ALFRED M.
Born N.O. ca. 1867; died N.O. Nov. 21, 1910.
Sculptor, active N.O. 1894–1905; primarily carver.
Contemporary listings: wood carver (1894, 1896, 1905).
References: NOCD 1887, 1891–97, 1899, 1904–1907, 1909, 1911; *D. Pic.*, Nov. 22, 1910.

LION, JULES
Born France ca. 1810–21; died N.O. Jan. 10, 1866; black ("free man of color").

Painter, lithographer, art teacher, sketch artist, active N.O. 1837–66; also photographer.
Contemporary listings: painter, lithographer, 56 Canal (1837); painter and lithographer of portraits, 56 Canal (1838); painter and lithographer, 177 Rampart (1839); painter, lithographer, 100 and 165 Royal (1840); portrait painter, 65 Royal (1841); painter, lithographer, 44 Royal (1842–43); portrait painter, 106 Royal (1842); painter, lithographer, 3 St. Charles, and portrait painter, 44 Royal (1843); teacher of art, with DOMINIQUE CANOVA, 1 Exchange Al., and lithographer (1848); portrait painter, 108 Dauphine (1849); portraitist (1850); artist, portrait painter, cor. Dauphine and St. Philip (1851–53); drawing master/professor of drawing, Louisiana College, and painter (1852); portrait painter, 304 St. Claude (1854); lithographer (1856); artist, painter (1857); portrait painter, 439 St. Claude (1860–61); professor of drawing, Louisiana College (1865); portrait painter, 175 Frenchman (1866).
Exhibited: Salon, Paris (1831, 1833–34, 1836); hall of the St. Charles Museum (1840).
Awarded: Paris Exposition, honorable mention (1833).
In Paris, Lion exhibited in the salons, where he was awarded an honorable mention for a lithograph in 1833, and provided drawings to illustrate the journal *L'Artiste*. Renowned for his lithographs, Lion produced a series of portraits of prominent Louisianians (ca. 1837–47), which is unmatched as a comprehensive and faithful record of the leading citizens of his day. He is credited with introducing the daguerreotype process to N.O. in Mar. 1840, immediately before J. B. POINTEL DU PORTAIL. It is likely that Lion, a frequent visitor to Paris, learned the process there shortly after its invention by Louis J. M. Daguerre. This may account for the characteristically photographic qualities in his portrait and architec-

tural subjects. He also made landscape and genre drawings and provided artwork for lithographed sheet music covers. It is apparent from his signature on some work, "J. Lion, N.O., Lith. de *L'Abeille*," that he bore some affiliation with that printing establishment. Determining Lion's specific year of birth is a problem because of conflicting information: 1810 from his obituary (*Bee*, Jan. 10, 1866); ca. 1816 from the 1850 U.S. census; and 1821 from his son's birth certificate (1857).

References: NOCD 1837–38, 1841–43, 1851–56, 1858, 1860–61, 1866; *Bee*, Sept. 27, 1839, Mar. 14, 17–18, Nov. 5, 1840, Dec. 13, 1842, Jan. 3, 5, Nov. 28, 1843, Apr. 7, Nov. 30, 1848, Aug. 31, Sept. 1, 1852, Oct. 12, 1865, Jan. 10, 1866; *Comm. Bull.*, Oct. 2, 1856; *Courier*, Jan. 16, Mar. 10, 13–14, Apr. 2, 11, 1840, Apr. 8, Sept. 12, Nov. 30, 1848, Dec. 26, 1851, June 11, Dec. 28, 1852, Mar. 1, 1857; *D. Delta*, Apr. 18, 1850, July 14, 1860; *D. Pic.*, Mar. 17, 20, 22, 29, 1840, Apr. 12, 14–15, May 12–13, 14, 1841, Oct. 2, 1856; *Revue Louisianaise* 1(1846):465–66; *T. Pic.*, Mar. 24, 1940; Jordan, "Mystery Surrounds Louisiana Painting in Met Exhibit," *T. Pic.*, July 25, 1976; Jordan, "The World of Art: Sheet Music Covers," *T. Pic.*, Jan. 28, 1979; *Wkly. Delta*, Apr. 22, 1850; *Almanach de la Louisiane* (1867);following 32, 80, 119; Bénézit, 594; Bruns, 314; Coulon MS, Scrapbook 100, LSM; Dichter and Shapiro, 252; Driskell, 36, 38; Elder, following 8; Fielding, *Dictionary*; Glenk, 77, 246; Groce and Wallace; Huber and Wilson, *Basilica*, 28; Korn, 142, 308; LHS (1900); LHS (1903):10-11; Louisiana Landmarks Society; LSM, *Biennial Report for 1922-23*, 70; O'Neill, 71–73; Orleans Parish Office of the Recorder of Births, Marriages, and Deaths, Birth Certificate (Nov. 6, 1857); Perry, cover; Harry Peters, *America on Stone*, 267; Smith and Tucker, 3–4, 12, 17–21, 28, 35–36, 48, 149, 163; THNOC: 1959.13.1– 76, 1970–

.11.1–.157; U.S. Census (1850), roll 236; Wiesendanger, 66–68; Willis–Thomas, 4–5.

LION, P. P.
Artist, active N.O. 1841.
Contemporary listings: artist, 244 St. Ann (1841).
References: NOCD 1841–42; Groce and Wallace.

LIPS, JACOB JULIUS
Born Zurich, Switzerland Mar. 2, 1871; died N.O. May 14, 1934. Designer, active N.O. 1897–1932; also glazier.
Contemporary listings: proprietor, CRESCENT CITY ART STAINED GLASS WORKS (1897–1902); art glass (1918). Advertised as operating the only stained glass factory of its type in the South (1902). Lips created some of the designs himself and specialized in the manufacture of art and beveled glass, memorial and figure windows, and glass painting.
References: NOCD 1897–1932; *D. States*, Feb. 10, 1902; *T. Pic.*, May 15, 1934; Orleans Parish Registrar of Voters, NOPL.

LISSAUTE, PIERRE
Painter, art teacher, active N.O. 1822.
Contemporary listings: teacher and portrait painter, 143 Burgundy (1822).
References: NOCD 1822; Glenk, 77; Groce and Wallace.

LITTLEJOHN, CYNTHIA PUGH
Born Assumption Parish LA Oct. 8, 1890; died N.O. July 1, 1959. Painter, art teacher, art craftsman, active N.O. 1906–20.
Studied: NEWCOMB COLLEGE (1906–11, 1914–18); Columbia University (summer 1910); with ELLSWORTH WOODWARD; with A. A. Dow.
Contemporary listings: drawing teacher, N.O. public schools (1913). Exhibited: Newcomb Art Alumnae Association exhibition (1910); ART ASSOCIATION OF NEW ORLEANS (1910, 1916–18); Panama–Pacific International Exposition, San Francisco (1915).
Awarded: traveling scholarship (1908–1909).

Chiefly a pottery decorator, she also exhibited tooled leather and leaded–glass objects (1910).
References: *T. Demo.*, Jan 14, 1913; *T. Pic.*, July 2, 1959; Art Asso., *Catalogue* (1910, 1916, 1917, 1918); Fielding, *Dictionary*; Orleans Parish Registrar of Voters, NOPL; Ormond and Irvine, 86, 160; Poesch, *Newcomb Pottery*, 58, 70, 102.

LITTLEJOHN, JOSEPH FEILD
Born Glenwood County NC; died N.O. Mar. 13, 1918.
Artist, active N.O. 1896.
Contemporary listings: artist (1896).
Amateur artist who worked as a salesman (1899–1918).
References: NOCD 1896, 1899–1906, 1908; *T. Pic.*, Mar. 14, 1918.

**LIVINGSTON, MRS. ——— AND MISS
———**
Art teachers, active N.O. 1838; also needleworkers.
Contemporary listings: teachers of drawing, painting, velvet painting, cor. Rampart and Conti (1838).
References: *Comm. Bull.*, May 17, 1838.

LIVINGSTON, MAJ. EDWARD
Born Mobile AL Sept. 27, 1837; died N.O. Nov. 23, 1898.
Painter, sketch artist, active N.O. 1871–98.
Exhibited: WAGENER's (1877, 1880); A. B. Griswold & Co. silversmiths (1877); SOUTHERN ART UNION (1880–81); LILIENTHAL's (1883–84); ARTISTS' ASSOCIATION OF NEW ORLEANS (1886–92, 1897); Tulane University (1892–93).
Memberships/positions: Southern Art Union, art committee chairman and charter member (1881); Artists' Association of New Orleans, pres. (1886); New Orleans Camera Club, honorary member (1891).
Moved to N.O. soon after the Civil War, during which he served as a major in the Confederate army. A descendant of the noted Livingston family of NY, he was a successful insurance agent by profession and an amateur artist active throughout his life in art organizations.

References: NOCD 1871, 1876–98; *Art and Letters*, Dec. 1887, 228; *Bee*, May 27, 1880, May 4, 1881; *Current Topics*, Jan. 1891, 23–24, Nov. 1891, 22, Jan. 1892, 23–24, Jan. 1893, 10–11; *D. City Item*, Mar. 4, 1892; *D. Pic.*, July 28, Sept. 29, Oct. 20, Nov. 27, Dec. 2, 1877, May 26, 1881, July 26, 1885, Nov. 6, 1886, Dec. 17, 29, 1887, Dec. 17, 1889, Nov. 13, Dec. 17, 1890, Dec. 17, 1891, Mar. 3, Dec. 14, 1892, Feb. 14, 1893, Mar. 30, 1897, Nov. 24, 1898; *D. States*, Apr. 17, Oct. 8, 1880, May 26, 1881, Apr. 13, 1884, Nov. 5, 1886, Nov. 24, 1898; *Demo.*, May 12, 1881; *Harlequin*, Nov. 1, 1899, 3; *T. Demo.*, Nov. 13, 1890, Mar. 3, 1892, Feb. 15, 1893; *T. Pic.*, Jan. 25, 1937; AANO, *Catalogue* (1886, 1890, 1891, 1897); Cline, *Art and Artists*, 11; Delgado, *New Orleans*, no. 47; Glenk, 77; Kendall, *History*, 2:659; Rightor, 384; Lilienthal's, 8; Wiesendanger, 68; WPA, *New Orleans*, 104.

LOBRANO, JOSEPH J.
Born LA June 1846.
Commercial artist, sketch artist, painter, active N.O. 1877–1909.
Contemporary listings: artist (1877, 1879–80, 1882, 1887–89, 1899–1900, 1902–1904, 1909); artist, with THEODORE LILIENTHAL (1878, 1883–86); crayon artist, with EDWARD J. SOUBY (1880); crayon artist (1887, 1890, 1900); crayon artist, 21 Commercial (1891–94); artist, 630 Commercial (1895); painter, 630 Commercial (1896); portrait painter, 630 Commercial (1897–98); portrait painter, 829 Camp (1898).
Exhibited: Lilienthal's (1883–84).
References: NOCD 1877–80, 1882–1900, 1902–1904, 1906, 1909; NOBD 1898; *D. States*, Apr. 17, 1880, Dec. 30, 1887; Lilienthal's, 4; U.S. Census (1900), roll 575.

LOBRE, ALEXANDER
Artist, active N.O. 1903.
Contemporary listings: artist (1903).
References: NOCD 1903.

LOCQUET, EDWARD
Born Ghent, Belgium ca. 1829; died N.O. Mar. 11, 1859.

Sketch artist, art teacher, active N.O. 1851–53.
Contemporary listings: pencil drawings (1851); teacher of linear drawing, Boys' High School (1853).
Exhibited: J. B. Steel's store (1851).
References: NOCD 1853–60; *Bee*, Oct. 8, 1851; *Courier*, Oct. 7, 1851, Oct. 27, 1853; *D. Delta*, Mar. 12, 1859; *D. Pic.*, Mar. 12, 1859; *T. Deutsche Zeitung*, Mar. 12, 1859; Groce and Wallace; N.O. Death Certificate (1859), 20:164, NOPL.

LOEB, SIDONIA (Mrs. Lewis Crager)
Born N.O. Sept. 3, 1871; died N.O. Dec. 29, 1944.
Artist, active N.O. ca. 1886–92.
Studied: New York School of Art; ARTISTS' ASSOCIATION OF NEW ORLEANS (1886–87).
Exhibited: Artists' Association of New Orleans (1886–87); Columbian Exposition, Chicago (1893).
References: *D. Pic.*, Nov. 7, 1886, May 7, 1887, Nov. 6, 1892, Jan. 15, 1893; *T. Demo.*, Jan. 15, 1893; *T. Pic.*, Dec. 30, 1944; Orleans Parish Registrar of Voters, NOPL.

LOGAN, DIXIE WOODWARD (Mrs. William Bainbridge Logan)
Sketch artist, painter, active N.O ca. 1905–15.
Exhibited: ART ASSOCIATION OF NEW ORLEANS (1915).
Memberships/positions: Art Association of New Orleans (1905).
References: *T. Pic.*, Nov. 15, 1933; Art Asso., *Catalogue* (1905); Art Asso., *Special Exhibition.*

LOGAN, LILLY
Born N.O. Dec. 24, 1861; died N.O. Apr. 10, 1929.
Sketch artist, painter, active N.O. ca. 1885–86.
Studied: Tulane University (1886).
Exhibited: American Exposition (1885–86).
References: *Eve. Chronicle*, May 22, 1886; *T. Pic.*, Apr. 12, 1929; Creole Exhibit, 15; Orleans Parish Registrar of Voters, NOPL.

LOHR, AUGUST
Painter, active N.O. 1884–85.
Contemporary listings: panorama painter (1884–85).

Panorama painter who, with Louis Braun, executed *The Battle of Sedan* for the American Panorama Company. The painting was displayed in N.O. in a specially constructed building on St. Charles Ave. across from the gates of the World's Industrial and Cotton Centennial Exposition. Lohr was brought to the city from Munich, Germany to touch up the painting in 1884. After being artistically engaged in Milwaukee WI (1885), he returned to N.O. to arrange the foreground of the panorama *The Battle of Paris*, which was exhibited at the corner of Dauphine and Canal (Oct.–Dec. 1885).
References: *D. States*, Dec. 19, 21, 1884, Apr. 3, Dec. 19, 1885; *T. Demo.*, Oct. 30, 1885; Bénézit.

LONERGAN, JAMES
Engraver, lithographer, active N.O. 1858–61; also printer.
Contemporary listings: engraver, lithographer, James Lonergan's General Engraving and Printing Establishment, 6 Exchange Al. (1858); engraver, Exchange Pl. cor. Canal (1859–61).
References: NOCD 1859–61; *D. Pic.*, Apr. 2, 5, 1858; Groce and Wallace.

LONG, ARTHUR
Painter, active N.O. 1854.
Contemporary listings: portrait painter, 131 Customhouse (1854).
References: *Bee*, Jan. 26, 1854; Groce and Wallace.

LONNEGAN, ADA WILT (Mrs. George F. Lonnegan)
Born N.O. Dec. 20, 1879; died N.O. Oct. 15, 1963.
Sketch artist, painter, art craftsman, designer, active N.O. 1896–1906.
Studied: NEWCOMB COLLEGE (1896–1906).
Exhibited: Louisiana Purchase Exhibition, St. Louis MO (1904).
References: NOCD 1931–33, 1935, 1938, 1940, 1942, 1945–47, 1949, 1952–56, 1958, 1960–1962, 1964; *T. Pic.*, Oct. 16, 1963; Orleans Parish Registrar of Voters, NOPL; Ormond and Irvine, 161; Poesch, *Newcomb Pottery*, 20, 102.

241

LONSDALE, ADELINE
Art teacher, active N.O. 1859.
Contemporary listings: teacher of painting, St. Louis Hotel (1859).
References: D. Pic., Jan. 4, 1859.

LOOF, MR. A:
Painter, active N.O. ca. 1841.
Exhibited: King's American Exchange (1841).
References: D. Pic., Apr. 1, 1841; Groce and Wallace.

LOOMIS, OSBERT BURR
Born Windsor CT July 30, 1813.
Painter, active N.O. 1851.
Exhibited: Armory Hall (1851); National Academy of Design, N.Y.C. (until 1858).
Portrait, landscape, and panorama painter who worked in N.Y.C. and Charleston SC. In 1843 he went to Cuba and spent six years there. From his sketches, Loomis painted his Grand Moving Panorama of Cuba which he exhibited in Charleston, N.Y.C., and Cincinnati OH, and then in N.O. (Apr. 1851) at Armory Hall before taking it to the western U.S. The work was said to be on 50,000 square feet of canvas and depicted Cuba's principal cities and countryside.
References: D. Crescent, Apr. 9–17, 1851 (advs.); D. Delta, Apr. 6, 8–9, 25, 1851; Union, Apr. 9, 11, 16, 20, 1851; Groce and Wallace.

LOSSING, BENSON JOHN
Born Beekman NY Feb. 12, 1813; died Dover Plains NY June 3, 1891.
Sketch artist, active N.O. 1861.
Studied: with Joseph A. Adams.
Contemporary listings: artist (1861).
Author, engraver, and war illustrator who wrote and illustrated volumes on the Revolutionary and Civil wars and the War of 1812. Lossing came to N.O. in 1861 to sketch sites relevant to the 1815 Battle of N.O.
References: D. Delta, Apr. 13, 1861; States–Item, Feb. 18, 1974; Appleton's CAB; DAB; Fielding, Dictionary; New York Historical Society; Ver Nooy, 524–29; Wilson, Plantation Houses, 28–30.

LOSTINE, HENRY
Born Prussia ca. 1814.
Sculptor, active N.O. 1860.

Contemporary listings: sculptor (1860).
References: Groce and Wallace; U.S. Census (1860), roll 416.

LOTTA, MR. _____. See SOTTA, MR. _____

LOUISE, MANUEL
Sculptor, active N.O. 1872.
Contemporary listings: plasterer and figure maker (1872).
References: NOCD 1872.

LOUISIANA DRAWING ACADEMY
Art school, active N.O. 1824–25; JEAN BAPTISTE FOGLIARDI, proprietor.
Contemporary listings: school, Government House (1824); school, Royal betw. St. Ann and Dumaine (1824).
References: Courier, Sept. 16, Oct. 23–27, 1824 (advs.); Oct. 31, Nov. 1, 1825; WPA, Louisiana, 163.

LOUISIANA PAINTING AND SCULPTURE ACADEMY
Art school, active N.O. 1819; Mrs. Gachot, MR. TOIRY, partners.
Contemporary listings: school, Royal oppos. Seignouret's House (1819).
References: Courier, Jan. 27, 1819.

LOWE, J.
Engraver, active N.O. 1837–38.
Contemporary listings: engraver, 75 Chartres (1837); engraver, 34 Canal (1838).
References: NOCD 1837–38; Groce and Wallace.

LUBBER, ERNEST
Commercial artist, active N.O. 1882–84.
Contemporary listings: artist, with WILLIAM W. WASHBURN (1882–84).
References: NOCD 1882–84.

LUBELSKY, DAVID
Engraver, active N.O. 1893.
Contemporary listings: engraver (1893).
References: NOCD 1893.

LUCCHESI, GIUSEPPI
Born Lucca, Italy ca. 1823; died N.O. Feb. 28, 1902.
Sculptor, active N.O. 1867–1902.
Contemporary listings: statuary, 248 Burgundy (1867); statuary, 243 Burgundy (1868); plasterworker, 168 St. Peter (1870); statuary, 234 Rampart (1871); statuary, 232 N. Rampart (1873–78); sculptor, 157 Bourbon

(1879–81); sculptor, 189 Royal (1882); sculptor, 173 Royal (1883–86); plaster figures, 173 Royal (1887–94); plaster figures, 729 Royal (1895–98, 1900–1901); sculptor, 729 Royal (1899, 1902).
References: NOCD 1867–68, 1870–1902; *D. Pic.*, Mar. 1, 1902; *T. Pic.*, Apr. 16, 1962.

LUCECK, MR. G.
Born Hungary ca. 1820.
Artist, active N.O. 1860.
Contemporary listings: artist (1860).
References: Groce and Wallace; U.S. Census (1860), roll 419.

LUDLOW, FANNIE BLACKMAN. *See* BLACKMAN, FANNIE

LUGANO, INEZ SOMENZINI (Mrs. Gaspare Lugano)
Born Verreto, Italy Sept. 30, 1891; died N.O. Nov. 29, 1983.
Painter, illustrator, restorer, active N.O. 1917–78.
Studied: Collegio di San Giorgio, Pavia, Italy; Civica Scuola di Pittura, Pavia; with Professor Romeo Borgognani, Pavia.
Contemporary listings: artist, 632 Orleans (1917–18).
Exhibited: ART ASSOCIATION OF NEW ORLEANS (1918).
Miniature and portrait painter and medical illustrator who came to N.O. in 1910. During the 1920s she worked with Dr. Marcus Feingold creating drawings and paintings of various eye conditions for use as teaching aids. The project aroused her interest in painting miniature portraits, and she created a transparent technique that brought her an international reputation. Her work was exhibited throughout the U.S. and abroad.
References: NOCD 1917–18, 1920–25, 1954–56, 1958, 1960–62, 1964–69, 1971–79; Palao, "Ines Somenzini Lugano: World Renowned Artist at Maison Hospitalière," *Italian-American Digest*, Autumn 1978, 18; *Item*, Feb. 6, 1939; *Item–Trib.*, Feb. 5, 12, 1939; *States–Item*, Jan. 15, 1963; *T. Pic.*, Jan. 24, 1923, June 2, 1935, Mar. 7, 1937, Mar. 14, 1974; Jackson, "Vivant: Ines Lugan-

o's Career: Illustrations to Portraits," *T. Pic.*, Aug. 27, 1975; *T. Pic./States–Item*, Dec. 2, 1983; Art Asso., *Catalogue* (1918); Fielding, *Dictionary*; LSM, *Biennial Report for 1922–23*, 109; Orleans Parish Registrar of Voters, NOPL; THNOC artists files; *Who's Who in American Art*, 1938–39; WPA, *Louisiana*, 169.

LUGENBUHL, JULIUS J.
Painter, active N.O. 1858–59.
Contemporary listings: landscape and marine painter, 27 Royal (1858–59).
References: NOCD 1858–59; Groce and Wallace.

LUISSI, MANSUETTO (Monsuite Allauze; Manjueto Allinzi; Mansuete Alueje; M. Aluise; Manuseto Lewis; Mars Luisi)
Born Italy Dec. 1832; died N.O. Mar. 20, 1904.
Sculptor, artist, active N.O. 1867–96.
Contemporary listings: sculptor, 350 Dauphine (1867); moulder in plaster of Paris, 350–52 Dauphine (1868); sculptor, 9 Frenchmen (1868); figurist, 401 Dauphine (1871); statuemaker (1881); statuary (1884, 1889); statuettes (1886); images, 205 S. Liberty (1887); artist, 205 S. Liberty (1890); plasterer (1892, 1895, 1897); sculptor (1893); plaster figures, 710 S. Liberty (1896).
Arrived in N.O. ca. 1860; Mansuetto was listed in the NOCD under a number of name variations.
References: NOCD 1867–68, 1871, 1880–81, 1884, 1886–87, 1889–90, 1892–93, 1895–97; *D. Pic.*, Mar. 21, 1904; Caldwell, 188; N.O. Death Certificate (1904), 132:290, NOPL.

LUKES, PAUL
Painter, active N.O. 1866.
Contemporary listings: china painter (1866).
References: NOCD 1866.

LULAKOWSKI, MRS. R. (Zulakowski)
Art craftsman, sculptor, active N.O. 1888.
Contemporary listings: wood carver, painter of window shades (1888).
Exhibited: TULANE DECORATIVE ART LEAGUE FOR WOMEN (1888).

References: *D. Pic.*, Feb. 12, 1888; Tulane Decorative Art League.

LUND, N. H.
Engraver, active N.O. 1843–55; primarily jeweler, watchmaker.
Contemporary listings: engraver, 79 Gravier (1843–44); LUND & ANTZ (1853–55).
References: NOCD 1841–44, 1846, 1850–56, 1858–60.

LUND & ANTZ
Engravers, active N.O. 1853–55; also jewelers; N. H. LUND, GEORGE ANTZ, partners.
Contemporary listings: engravers, Commercial Pl. and St. Charles (1853); engravers, 92 1/2 Camp (1854–55).
References: NOCD 1853–55.

LURIA, CORINNA MORGIANA
Born N.O. Feb. 3, 1890.
Painter, art craftsman, designer, active N.O. ca. 1910–70.
Studied: NEWCOMB COLLEGE (1910–16).
Exhibited: ART ASSOCIATION OF NEW ORLEANS (1911, 1914–17); Panama–Pacific International Exposition, San Francisco (1915); Newcomb (1916).
Awarded: Newcomb, Neill medal (1913); American Electrical Association, 1st prize artists' division, national poster art contest (1916).
Listed as an artist until at least 1970 and did artwork for a sheet music cover (1947).
References: NOCD 1923, 1925–33, 1935, 1938, 1940, 1942, 1945–46, 1949; NOSD 1964–66, 1969–70, 1975–76, 1978, 1980; *Item*, Aug. 8, 1916; *New Orleanian*, Oct. 4, 1930; *States*, Sept. 23, 1942; *T. Pic.*, Jan. 2, 1915; May 12, 1929; Mar. 3, 1930; Sept. 6, Oct. 3, 1967; Art Asso., *Catalogue* (1911, 1914, 1916, 1917); Art Asso., *Special Exhibition*; Orleans Parish Registrar of Voters, NOPL; Ormond and Irvine, 161; Poesch, *Newcomb Pottery*, 102; Radcliffe, 11; "To–Morrow," Sheet Music Collection, THNOC.

LUSK, MARIE FOLGER (Mrs. James T. Lusk)
Born LA Mar. 1860; died N.O. Apr. 7, 1937.

Commercial artist, active N.O. 1900–1904.
Contemporary listings: artist (1900); teacher (1903); art dept., N.O. Carpet & Matting Co. Ltd. (1904)
References: NOCD 1903–1904; *T. Pic.*, Apr. 9, 1937; U.S. Census (1900), roll 570.

LUX, FREDERICK
Painter, active N.O. 1868; also sign painter.
Contemporary listings: fresco painter, 146 Tchoupitoulas (1868).
References: NOCD 1868.

LUX, RUDOLPH T.
Born Germany ca. 1815; died N.O. July 19, 1868.
Painter, active N.O 1856–68; also gilder, photographer.
Contemporary listings: porcelain painter, 173 Royal (1856); porcelain painter and portrait painter on china, 7 Camp (1857–58); painter on china, 1 Carondelet (1858); porcelain painter, 1 Carondelet (1859); artist (1860); porcelain painter, 10 Baronne (1860–61); porcelain china painter, 292 Canal (1861); porcelain painter, cor. N. Levee and Canal (1862); porcelain painter (1863); porcelain painter, Bienville cor. Marais (1866).
Considered the most important painter and gilder on china in N.O., Lux specialized in portraits on specially decorated cups and saucers. Between 1861 and 1863 he painted prominent military figures of the Civil War, including Gens. P. G. T. Beauregard, Benjamin F. Butler, and Nathaniel P. Banks, and Admiral David G. Farragut.
References: NOCD 1856–61, 1866; NOBD 1857–58; *D. Creole*, Feb. 25, Mar. 2, 1857; *D. Delta*, July 16, Sept. 4, 28, 30, 1862, Jan. 15, 1863; *D. Pic.*, Sept. 11, 1861, Oct. 1, 1862; *Era*, Aug. 4, Nov. 8, 1863; *T. Deutsche Zeitung*, July 16, 1862; *Times*, Oct. 6, 1863; Jordan, "The World of Art: Lux's Portraits on Porcelain Were Fashionable in 1850s," *T. Pic.*, Dec. 15, 1974; Bruns, 314; Groce and Wallace; Harter and Tucker, 122; N.O. Death Certificate

(1868), 42:643, NOPL; Rathbone, *Mississippi Panorama*, 219; U.S. Census (1860), roll 417.

LYELL, SIR CHARLES
Born Kinnordy, Scotland Nov. 14, 1797; died London, England Feb. 22, 1875.
Sketch artist, active N.O. 1841.
Noted English geologist and author who made extensive geological explorations in Europe, Canada, and the U.S. On his second tour of the U.S., he visited N.O. (Feb. 1846) and wrote an account of the city, its inhabitants, and customs, which was published in his *A Second Visit to the United States of North America* (1849). One of the book's illustrations, *Père Antoine's Date–palm*, was taken from a sketch made by Lyell in N.O.
References: *Appleton's CAB*; Arthur, *Old New Orleans*, 234–36; Bruce Chambers, 16-17; Lyell, 2:110.

LYLE, MISS N.
Sculptor, sketch artist, active N.O. ca. 1886–88.

Studied: Tulane University (1886).
Memberships/positions: TULANE DECORATIVE ART LEAGUE FOR WOMEN (1888).
Possibly Miss Nannie R. Lyle, a music teacher, listed 1890–91.
References: NOCD 1890–91; *D. Pic.*, Feb. 12, 1888; *Eve. Chronicle*, May 22, 1886; Tulane Decorative Art League.

LYNCH, FRANK
Artist, active N.O. 1897.
Contemporary listings: artist (1897).
References: NOCD 1897.

LYON, EDWIN
Born Liverpool, England ca. 1806; died Natchez MS 1853.
Sculptor, active N.O. 1846.
Contemporary listings: miniature bust modeller, 6 Carondelet (1846).
References: *Bee*, Oct. 20, Nov. 4, 1846; *Wkly. Delta*, Oct. 19, 1846; Bacot and Lambdin, 554–59.

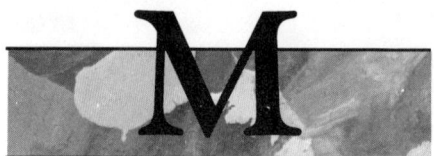

M

MAAS, DR. HELENA
Painter, active N.O. 1890.
Physician and amateur artist who painted a portrait of N.O. philanthropist John McDonogh (1890).
References: Nuhrah, 8–9; THNOC Cemetery Survey.

MABLEY, GRACE C.
Born OH ca. 1873.
Artist, active N.O. 1910.
Contemporary listings: artist, pictures (1910).
References: NOCD 1909; U.S. Census (1910), roll 520.

MCALLISTER, JAMES C.
Born Dublin, Ireland ca. 1819; died N.O. Aug. 6, 1865.
Engraver, active N.O. 1841–61; also publisher.
Contemporary listings: engraver, 29 Camp (1841); engraver, 3 Camp (1842–43); engraver, 7 Camp (1846); engraver, 11 Camp (1849–53); engraver, 19 Camp (1854); engraver, Camp cor. Gravier (1856, 1858); general engraver, 45 Camp (1857–58); engraver, 45 Camp (1858–59); engraver, 40 Camp (1859–61).
References: NOCD 1841–43, 1846, 1849–56, 1858–61; NOBD 1857–58; *Courier*, July 28, Nov. 9, 1854; *D. Crescent*, June 11, 1850, Nov. 9, 1854, *D. Pic.*, Nov. 9, 1854, Aug. 10, 1865; Groce and Wallace.

MCBRIDE, RICHARD STANLEY
Born Brooklyn NY ca. 1852–53; died N.O. Oct. 21, 1918.
Sculptor, painter, active N.O. 1870–74; also stone cutter, marble cutter, carpenter.
Contemporary listings: sculptor (1870); scenic artist (1874).
References: NOCD 1870, 1872, 1874–89, 1891, 1893–94, 1897–1907, 1909–17; *T. Pic.*, Oct. 22, 1918; U.S. Census (1870), roll 519.

MCCAFFERTY, WILLIAM
Painter, active N.O. 1826.
Primarily an actor, McCafferty was also a painter who assisted ANTOINE

MONDELLI in painting scenery at the St. Charles Theatre (1826). He later worked in Natchez MS (1828, 1831), Cincinnati OH (1829), Louisville KY (1829), St. Louis MO (1830, 1831) and Nashville TN (1831).
References: Gates, 82–83; Kendall, *Golden Age*, 42; Ludlow, 346, 350, 369, 374, 381–88; Sol Smith, 52.

MCCAFFREY, JOHN
Lithographer, active N.O. 1875–77.
Contemporary listings: apprentice, with HUGH LEWIS (1875); lithographer, with Hugh Lewis (1877).
References: NOCD 1875, 1877.

MCCALL, LOTTIE LAURIE
Born N.O. ca. 1886 or AL ca. 1891; died N.O. Oct. 14, 1965.
Painter, active N.O. ca. 1910–15.
Contemporary listings: artist (1910).
Exhibited: ART ASSOCIATION OF NEW ORLEANS (1915).
References: NOCD 1920; *T. Pic.*, May 2, 1915; Oct. 15, 1965; Art Asso., *Special Exhibition*; U.S. Census (1910), roll 520.

MCCARTER, HENRY
Born Norristown PA July 5, 1886; died Chester Springs PA 1942.
Sketch artist, active N.O. 1903.
Studied: with Thomas Eakins, Philadelphia; with Pierre Puvis de Chavannes, Leon Bonnat, Alexander Harrison, Henri de Toulouse–Lautrec, Marcel Roll, and Jean Rixens, Paris.
Awarded: Pan–American Exposition, Buffalo NY, bronze medal (1901); Louisiana Purchase Exposition, St. Louis MO, silver medal (1904); Philadelphia, Beck prize (1906); Panama–Pacific International Exposition, San Francisco (1915).
Memberships/positions: Pennsylvania Academy of Fine Arts, Philadelphia, fellowship.
Illustrator and painter who made the drawing for *The Day Before Lent in New Orleans*, published in *Harper's Weekly* (Feb. 14, 1903). He exhib-

ited paintings at the Arts and Crafts Club in N.O. in 1932.
References: *Harper's Wkly.*, Feb. 14, 1903, 255; *Item–Trib.*, Oct. 9, 1932; Bénézit; Fielding, *Dictionary.*

McCay, Windsor
Cartoonist, sketch artist, active N.O. 1910.
Contemporary listings: cartoonist, American Music Hall (1910).
Cartoonist who was best known for creating the comic strip character Little Nemo. McCay visited N.O. in 1910 to make crayon sketches at the American Music Hall.
References: *D. News*, Feb. 1, 1910; *D. Pic.*, Feb. 5, 1910.

McColl, Mrs. _____
Art teacher, active N.O. 1871.
Contemporary listings: teacher of wax work, Pelican House (1871).
References: *D. Pic.*, Mar. 22, 1871.

McConnell, Annette. See ANDERSON, ANNETTE MCCONNELL

McConnell, R. Cameron
Born Chicago IL ca. 1868.
Painter, active N.O. 1899–1900.
Studied: with Jean–Léon Gérome, Paris.
Exhibited: Salon, Paris; Berlin; Nice, France; Crystal Palace, London.
Painted portraits of several noted LA subjects, including State Supreme Court Justice Henry Carlton Miller (1899) and Judge Joseph A. Breaux when he visited N.O. on his way to Paris in 1900.
References: *D. States*, June 30, 1899, Jan. 14, 1900; Glenk, 42; LSM, *Biennial Report for 1926–27*, 29.

McConnoghey, Joseph K.
Born LA ca. 1873.
Lithographer, active N.O. 1910.
Contemporary listings: lithographer, printing office (1910).
References: U.S. Census (1910), roll 520.

McCormack, Katherine E.
Born N.O.; died N.O. Apr. 28, 1917.
Artist, active N.O. 1898–1907.
Contemporary listings: portrait painter, 68 Constance (1892); artist (1898, 1903, 1905–1907).
References: NOCD 1892, 1898, 1903, 1905–1908, 1911, 1913–17; *T. Pic.*, Apr. 29, 1917.

McCormack, Maggie (Mrs. James McCormack)
Born AL ca. 1874.
Painter, active N.O. 1910.
Contemporary listings: landscape artist (1910).
References: NOCD 1913, 1916; U.S. Census (1910), roll 524.

McCormack, Patrick Francis, Jr.
Born N.O. ca. 1869; died N.O. Apr. 10, 1892.
Lithographer, active N.O. 1889–92.
Contemporary listings: lithographer, with MICHEL CAPO (1889); lithographer, M. F. DUNN & BRO. (1890); lithographer (1892).
References: NOCD 1889–92; *D. Pic.*, Apr. 10, 1892; N.O. Death Certificate (1892), 101:671, NOPL.

McCulloch, William
Painter, active N.O. 1870.
Awarded: Grand State Fair, best animal painting (1870).
Possibly William McCulloch, born Rosshire, Scotland ca. May 1814; died N.O. Nov. 15, 1872.
References: *D. Pic.*, Nov. 16, 1872; Mechanics' and Agricultural Fair Asso., *Report* (1870):50.

McDonald, Ida Florence
Born Henry County MO June 30, 1885; died N.O. May 29, 1964.
Painter, art craftsman, designer, active N.O. 1910–35.
Studied: NEWCOMB COLLEGE (1908, 1909–11); Art Institute of Chicago.
Contemporary listings: artist (1910–11).
Exhibited: ART ASSOCIATION OF NEW ORLEANS (1911); Newcomb (1911); Louisville KY, Lexington KY, Cincinnati OH, and Jackson MS (all after 1911).
Memberships/positions: Art Club of Louisville; Louisville Art Association; Brush and Pencil Club, Lexington.
Listed as an artist (1921–22, 1924–25, 1932, 1935) and as a designer (1919). She was also a dressmaker.
References: NOCD 1911, 1914, 1918–19, 1921–25, 1928, 1930–33, 1935, 1938, 1942, 1945–47, 1949; *T. Pic.*, May 30, 1964; Art Asso., *Catalogue* (1911); Ormond and Irvine,

162; Orleans Parish Registrar of Voters, NOPL; Poesch, *Newcomb Pottery*, 102; U.S. Census (1910), roll 524.

McDONALD, LAWRENCE D.
Artist, active N.O. 1885.
Contemporary listings: artist (1885).
References: NOCD 1885.

McDONALD, MAZIE RYAN. *See* RYAN, MAZIE TERESA

McDONNELL, M. ANGELA
Painter, active N.O. 1901–28.
Exhibited: ARTISTS' ASSOCIATION OF NEW ORLEANS (1901–1902).
Landscape painter who later exhibited with the Arts and Crafts Club (1928).
References: *Item–Trib.*, Dec. 9, 1928; *T. Demo.*, Dec. 3, 1901; AANO, *Catalogue* (1901, 1901–1902).

McDOUGALL, JOHN ALEXANDER
Born Livingston NJ 1810 or 1811; died 1894.
Painter, active N.O. 1839–40.
Studied: National Academy of Design, N.Y.C.
Contemporary listings: miniature painter, Exchange Hotel (1839–40).
Exhibited: National Academy of Design, N.Y.C. (1841–49); American Art Union, N.Y.C.; Artists' Fund Society of Philadelphia.
Awarded: American Institute, N.Y.C., 1st prize for miniatures (1845, 1847–48).
Itinerant miniature and portrait painter who lived in Newark NJ, but spent some winters in N.O. (1839–40). He later became interested in photography and portraits on celluloid.
References: *D. Pic.*, Dec. 18, 1839–Feb. 1, 1840 (advs.); Bénézit; Fielding, *Dictionary*; Groce and Wallace; Wehle, *American Miniatures*, 91.

McDOWELL, H.
Engraver, active N.O. 1834.
Contemporary listings: engraver, 7 Chartres (1834).
References: Orleans Parish Notarial Archives, T. Seghers, Oct. 29, 1835, 13:634.

McELROY, WILLIAM A.
Born TN ca. 1880.
Engraver, active N.O. 1910.

Contemporary listings: engraver (1910); v. pres. and mgr., SPENCER ENGRAVING CO. (1910–11).
References: NOCD 1908, 1910–11; U.S. Census (1910), roll 520.

MACHIN, FREDERICK J.
Lithographer, active N.O. 1887–91.
Contemporary listings: lithographer, T. FITZWILLIAM & CO. (1887–88, 1891).
References: NOCD 1887–92.

MACHIN, WILLIAM T.
Born England Jan. 1827.
Lithographer, active N.O. 1885–1910; also printer.
Contemporary listings: lithographer, T. FITZWILLIAM & CO. (1885, 1889, 1903, 1910); foreman, lithographers, T. Fitzwilliam & Co. (1886–88); foreman, lithography dept. (1890); foreman, T. Fitzwilliam & Co. (1891, 1893–94); foreman (1898) and printer (1899), ART LITHOGRAPH CO.; lithographer (1900–1902, 1904, 1907–1908).
References: NOCD 1885–99, 1901–1905, 1907–10; U.S. Census (1900), roll 574.

McKEON, WILLIAM
Born Scotland ca. 1820.
Artist, active N.O. 1850.
Contemporary listings: artist (1850).
References: Groce and Wallace; U.S. Census (1850), roll 237.

McKIBBIN, MRS. _____
Sculptor, art teacher, active N.O. 1873.
Contemporary listings: artist in wax flowers, 18 Dauphine (1873).
Advertised to teach a class in her specialty (1873).
References: *D. Pic.*, Mar. 22, 1873.

MacKNIGHT, DODGE
Born Providence RI Oct. 1, 1860.
Painter, active N.O. 1899.
Studied: with Fernan and with Cormon, Paris.
Exhibited: ARTISTS' ASSOCIATION OF NEW ORLEANS (1899); ART ASSOCIATION OF NEW ORLEANS (1904).
Memberships/positions: New York Water Color Club; Boston Art Club; New Society of Artists, N.Y.C.
Impressionist landscape painter who reportedly lectured in N.O. (1899).

He lived in Mystic CT (1900), Spring Hill MA (1904), and East Sandwich MA (1929). He later exhibited at the DELGADO MUSEUM OF ART (1932). Possibly the D. R. McKnight who exhibited at the SOUTHERN ART UNION (1882).
References: D. Pic., Feb. 15, 1882, Dec. 5, 1899; Harlequin, Dec. 6, 1899, 4; Morn. Trib., Feb. 8, 1932; T. Demo., Feb. 28, 1904; Art Asso., Catalogue (1904); Bénézit; Fielding, Dictionary; Rightor, 385; Seebold 1:316.

MACKWITZ, WILLIAM
Born 1831; died St. Louis MO Aug. 6, 1919.
St. Louis wood engraver whose illustration, The New Orleans Elevator, appeared in New Orleans and the New South (1888).
References: Morrison, New Orleans, 3; "William Mackwitz," 176–79.

MCLAUGHLIN, WILLIAM W.
Born Albany NY ca. 1833; died N.O. Mar. 22, 1908.
Artist, active N.O. 1894–96; primarily gilder.
Contemporary listings: artist, 37 Union (1894); artist, 816 Union (1896).
References: NOCD 1868–71, 1873–90, 1894–97, 1900–1908; D. Pic., Mar. 29, 1908.

MCLELLAN, ERNESTINE BRES
Painter, active N.O. ca. 1911.
Exhibited: ART ASSOCIATION OF NEW ORLEANS (1911).
Memberships/positions: NEWCOMB Art Alumnae Association.
References: Art Asso., Catalogue (1911).

MCLEOD, KATE. See NICHOLS, KATE MCLEOD

MCMILLEN, PERCY
Born LA ca. 1882.
Engraver, active N.O. 1910–14.
Contemporary listings: engraver–photographs (1910); photo engraver (1912–13); photo engraving dept., Times–Democrat (1914).
References: NOCD 1912–14; U.S. Census (1910), roll 520.

MCMURTRIE, WILLIAM B.
Sketch artist, active N.O. ca. 1862.
Exhibited: Pennsylvania Academy of Fine Arts, Philadelphia (1837–44); American Art Union, N.Y.C. (1845). Portrait and landscape artist who executed a pencil drawing entitled Farragut's Fleet Before New Orleans (ca. 1862). He worked mainly in Philadelphia, as well as in CA (1849–50).
References: Groce and Wallace; National Gallery, 129–30.

MCNAUGHTON, MARY HUNTER
Painter, active N.O. ca. 1915.
Exhibited: ART ASSOCIATION OF NEW ORLEANS (1915).
References: Art Asso., Special Exhibition.

MCNEIL, ARCHIBALD
Born N.O. Nov. 7, 1875; died N.O. Mar. 3, 1931.
Lithographer, active N.O. 1896–98; primarily printer, pressman.
Contemporary listings: lithographer (1896–98).
References: NOCD 1896–1926, 1928–31; T. Pic., Mar. 4–5, 1931; Orleans Parish Registrar of Voters, NOPL.

MCREA, C.
Sketch artist, active N.O. 1869.
Awarded: Grand State Fair, 1st premium, best drawing in pastile, crayon, or pencil on stump (1869).
References: D. Pic., Apr. 13, 1869.

MADDEN, JOHN W.
Born Ireland ca. 1843–44; died N.O. Mar. 1, 1891.
Engraver, lithographer, active N.O. 1868–74; also stationer, printer, publisher.
Contemporary listings: engraver, 73 Camp (1869); L. GRAHAM & CO., and engraver, 73 Camp (1870–71); lithographer, 73 Camp (1872, 1874).
Came to N.O. ca. 1851–52 and was appointed Orleans Parish recorder of mortgages (1864). In 1874 Madden's company produced a carnival handbook and was a publisher and printer to the Rex organization. At the time of his death, he was serving in the U.S. sub-treasury.
References: NOCD 1866–91, D. Pic., Mar. 2, 1891; D. States, Mar. 2, 1891;

D. True Delta, July 14, 1865; *National Repub.*, Oct. 15, 1872; *Repub.*, Jan. 30, 1872, Feb. 11, 15, 1874; *T. Deutsche Zeitung*, Mar. 17, 1864; *Times*, June 4, 1865; Boyd, 158; THNOC 1950.62.8, 1955.41.2, 76–29–L; U.S. Census (1880), roll 458.

MAGGIE, LOUIS
Born France ca. 1816.
Artist, active N.O. 1870.
Contemporary listings: artist (1870).
References: U.S. Census (1870), roll 523.

MAGNIER, PAUL
Engraver, active N.O. 1874.
Contemporary listings: engraver (1874).
References: NOCD 1874.

MAGNY, LOUIS XAVIER
Born Avignon, France ca. 1800–10; died N.O. July 15, 1855.
Lithographer, active N.O. 1847–55.
Contemporary listings: lithographic printer, Exchange Al. (1847); lithographer, 35 St. Louis Exchange Al., and artist, lithographer, 145 Chartres (1849); lithographer, 145 Chartres; lithographer, 14 Exchange Al., and artist (1850); lithographer, 117 Exchange Pl. (1854–55).
Prominent lithographer and publisher of portraits, city views, and sheet music covers. Magny lithographed a view of St. Louis Cathedral as it appeared in the late 1840s and then again as the church was to appear following rebuilding in 1850. ALEXANDER BOULET exhibited at Magny's studio (1851). Brother of RISSO MAGNY.
References: NOCD 1849–55; *Bee*, Apr. 18, 1850, Oct. 10. 1851, July 16, 1855; *Courier*, May 31, 1847, Oct. 6, 1849, Jan. 17, Mar. 8, Apr. 17, May 8, 1850, Jan. 15, 1851; *D. Delta*, Sept. 4, 1849, Apr. 18, 1850; *Wkly. Delta*, July 30, Sept. 10, 1849, Apr. 22, 1850; "The Crescent Mazurka," "The Golden Bird of Hope," "Hymne A Pie IX," "Sauterelle," "Second Esmerelda," Sheet Music Collection, LA Coll., TU; Dichter and Shapiro, 252; Groce and Wallace; Harry Peters, *America on Stone*, 270;

THNOC 1940.3, 1957.39; U.S. Census (1850), roll 235.

MAGNY, RISSO
Born Thore, France 1798; died N.O. June 24, 1850.
Sketch artist, lithographer, active N.O. 1847–50.
Contemporary listings: artist (1850).
Accused in 1847 by JOSEPH AUGUSTE DE CHATILLON of producing a lithographic drawing from one of de Châtillon's paintings and distributing it as his own. Brother of LOUIS XAVIER MAGNY.
References: *Courier*, May 31, 1847, Jan. 17, June 24, 1850; Groce and Wallace.

MAHIER, EDITH
Painter, active N.O. ca. 1915–23.
Studied: NEWCOMB COLLEGE (ca. 1916).
Exhibited: ART ASSOCIATION OF NEW ORLEANS (1915–16).
Lived in Baton Rouge LA (1916); Art Association of New Orleans sponsored an exhibit of her work (1923).
References: *Item*, Nov. 25, 1923; Art Asso., *Catalogue* (1915, 1916).

MAIER, JOHN
Painter, active N.O. ca. 1838–39.
Portrait painter who, after working in N.O., traveled to Columbus GA.
References: Information courtesy George E. Jordan.

MAILLET, LOUIS
Born Gresille, France; died N.O. Sept. 15, 1875.
Artist, active N.O. 1869–73.
Contemporary listings: artist, Opera House (1869); artist (1873).
References: NOCD 1869, 1873; *Bee*, Sept. 16, 1875.

MAIR, C. H.
Painter, active N.O. 1834.
Contemporary listings: miniature painter, E. Johns & Co. publishers (1834).
References: *Courier*, July 12, 1834; Groce and Wallace.

MALLEVILLE, MRS. A. J. B.
Artist, active N.O. 1859.
Contemporary listings: artist, Johnson near Laharpe (1859).
References: NOCD 1859–61.

MALLORY, LEE
Painter, active N.O. 1861–62.
Painted a panorama of 20 scenes from the Civil War which were exhibited at the Academy of Music (1861–62). References: *Bee*, Jan. 20, 1862; *D. Crescent*, July 26–30, 1861 (advs.), Aug. 24, Dec. 9–10, 13, 25, 31, 1861, Jan. 13, 15, 18, 20, 27, Feb. 3, 1862; *D. Delta*, Dec. 1, 10, 17, 19, 1861, Jan. 8, 28, 1862; *D. Pic.*, Jan. 15, 1862; *D. True Delta*, July 28, Aug. 25, Dec. 1, 3, 10, 1861, Dec. 8–31, 1861 (advs.), Jan. 1, 8, 11, 18, 26, 30, Feb. 1, 1862; Coulter, 489–90; Kendall, *Golden Age*, 487.

MALONEY, WILLIAM M. (Molony)
Born Ireland ca. 1815–23; died N.O. Jan. 30, 1875.
Painter, art teacher, active N.O. 1847–74.
Contemporary listings: portrait and miniature painter, 38 St. Charles (1847); portrait and miniature painter, landscape, oil and watercolor painting lessons, 46 Canal (1848); portrait and historical painter, 46 Canal (1849); artist (1850); portrait painter, Rousseau near Jackson (1854); portrait painter, 8 St. Charles (1858–61); portrait painter, 223 Tchoupitoulas (1866); portrait painter (1872–74).
Memberships/positions: Royal Academies, London, Paris, Dublin (before 1847).
Portrait and miniature painter who also did copy and restoration work and daguerreotypes.
References: NOCD 1843, 1849–50, 1853–54, 1857–61, 1866, 1870, 1872–74; *D. Delta*, Dec. 18, 1847, Dec. 18, 1847–June 28, 1848 (advs.); *D. Pic.*, Dec. 19, 1847; Groce and Wallace; N.O. Death Certificate (1875), 62:861, NOPL; U.S. Census (1850), roll 235, (1860), roll 416.

MALTRY, FRANK, JR.
Born N.O. Nov. 4, 1884; died N.O. Sept. 3, 1959.
Engraver, active N.O. 1909–10; primarily jeweler.
Contemporary listings: engraver, T. Hausmann & Sons (1909–10); jewelry engraver (1910).

References: NOCD 1882–91, 1893–1915, 1917–33, 1935, 1938, 1940; *T. Pic.*, Sept. 4, 1959; Orleans Parish Registrar of Voters, NOPL; U.S. Census (1910), roll 523.

MALUS, ALEXANDER
Born St. Charles Parish LA Mar. 1841; died N.O. May 2, 1897.
Engraver, active N.O. 1860–97; also printer.
Contemporary listings: engraver (1860, 1870, 1877); engraver, 7 Exchange Al., and MALUS & MAURICE (1862); engraver, 28 Chartres (1864, 1868); engraver, 50 Royal (1865–67); engraver, 52 Royal (1866–67); engraver on wood, 28 Chartres (1867); engraver, 14 Chartres (1869); engraver, 18 Royal (1871); engraver, 4 Carondelet (1872); engraver 199 Ursulines (1874); engraver, 62 Royal (1875–76); engraver, 60 Chartres (1885–87); MALUS & HOFELINE (1888–97).
References: NOCD 1866–77, 1879–97; NOBD 1865; *Bee*, June 18, 1872; *D. Crescent*, Nov. 1, 1867; *D. Delta*, Jan. 5, 1862, Mar. 9–12, 1862 (advs.); *Renaissance Louisianaise*, 4(Jan. 24, 1864): 4; Groce and Wallace; *Louisiana State Gazetteer*; N.O. Death Certificate (1897), 113:740, NOPL; U.S. Census (1860), roll 419, (1870), roll 522; William Young.

MALUS, ANNA. See MALUS & HOFELINE

MALUS, LEOTINE. See MALUS & HOFELINE.

MALUS & HOFELINE
Engravers, active N.O. 1888–98; also printers; ALEXANDER MALUS, partner (1888–97), Anna Malus and Leotine Malus, partners (1898), ALBERT D. HOFELINE, partner (1888–98).
Contemporary listings: engravers, 60 Chartres (1888–94); engravers, 300 Chartres (1895–97); engravers, 305 Chartres (1898).
References: NOCD 1888–98.

MALUS & MAURICE
Engravers, active N.O. 1862; also printers; ALEXANDER MALUS, ALFRED MAURICE, partners.
Contemporary listings: engravers and printers, 10 Camp (1862).

References: *Bee*, Mar. 26, Dec. 30, 1862; *D. Delta*, Mar. 9–12, 1862 (advs.).

MANN, GUSTAV
Born Darjeeling, East India Nov. 6, 1864; died Tampico, Mexico July 18, 1921.
Painter, active N.O. ca. 1913–15.
Exhibited: Tulane University, (1913); ART ASSOCIATION OF NEW ORLEANS (1915).
Professor of physiology at Tulane (1908–ca. 1915).
References: NOCD 1910–11; *T. Demo.*, June 15, 1913; *T. Pic.*, Aug. 4–5, 1921; Art Asso., *Special Exhibition*; *Who's Who in America*, 1916–17.

J. MANOUVRIER & CO.
Lithographers, active N.O. 1860–65; JULES MANOUVRIER, JOHN BOEHLER, partners (1861).
Contemporary listings: lithographers, 30 Camp (1860, 1865); lithographers, 30 Camp and 175 Philip (1861).
References: NOCD 1861; NOBD 1865; *D. Crescent*, July 1, 1861; *D. Delta*, Jan. 6–Mar. 3, 1860 (advs.); *D. True Delta*, Jan. 6–Mar. 29, 1860 (advs.); Dichter and Shapiro, 252.

MANOUVRIER, JULES (Julius)
Born Bremen, Prussia Feb. 10, 1816; died N.O. Aug. 23, 1875.
Lithographer, engraver, active N.O. 1838–72.
Contemporary listings: lithographer, 51 Basin (1841–42); MANOUVRIER & CHAVIN (1843–44); MANOUVRIER & SNELL (1846, 1850–52); lithographer, St. Philip betw. Robertson and Claiborne (1849); lithographer, 33 Camp (1853–61); J. MANOUVRIER & CO. (1860–61, 1865); lithographer, 133 St. Mary (1866–67); MANOUVRIER & SIMON (1866–72); engraver (1870).
His lithograph of the store of E. Johns & Co. is included in the 1838 NOCD.
Also engraved sheet music covers.
References: NOCD 1838, 1841–44, 1846, 1849–61, 1866–75; NOBD 1857–58, 1865; *D. Pic.*, May 11, 1855, Aug. 23–24, 1875; "La Couronne Imperiale de l'Etoile du Nord,"

"Douze Nouvelle Danses pour le Piano," Sheet Music Collection, THNOC; Groce and Wallace; LSM artists files; Record of interments in the Lafayette Cemeteries, vol. 3, Aug. 1875, roll LM430, NOPL; U.S. Census (1860), roll 416, (1870), roll 524.

MANOUVRIER & CHAVIN
Lithographers, active N.O. 1843–44; also printers; JULES MANOUVRIER, FRANÇOIS CHAVIN, partners.
Contemporary listings: lithographers, 62 Magazine (1843–44).
References: NOCD 1843–44; Reps, 311.

MANOUVRIER & SIMON
Lithographers, engravers, active N.O. 1866–72; JULES MANOUVRIER, DIONIS SIMON, partners.
Contemporary listings: lithographers, engravers, 92 Exchange Pl. (1866–67); lithographers, 90 Exchange Pl. (1866–68); lithographers, 20 Exchange Pl. (1869); lithographers, 90 Exchange Al. (1870–72).
Also lithographed sheet music covers.
References: NOCD 1866–72; *Bee*, July 26, 1870; *Repub.*, Feb. 9, 1872; "Crispino e la Comare Waltz," Sheet Music Collection, THNOC; *Edwards' Descriptive Gazetteer*; *Louisiana State Gazetteer*.

MANOUVRIER & SNELL
Lithographers, active N.O. 1846–52; JULES MANOUVRIER, PEREZ SNELL, partners.
Contemporary listings: lithographers, 33 Camp (1846, 1850–52).
Awarded: Grand State Fair, first premium for finest specimens of lithographic engraving (1846).
Also lithographed sheet music covers.
References: NOCD 1846, 1850–52; *D. Delta*, Jan. 8, 1846; *De Bow's Review*, Feb. 1846, 166; *Wkly. Delta*, Jan. 12, 1846; Groce and Wallace; Sheet Music Collection, THNOC.

MANSFIELD, M.
Painter, active N.O. ca. 1881.
Exhibited: SOUTHERN ART UNION (1881).
References: *D. Pic.*, May 26, 1881.

MARAGLIANO, ROSA A.
Artist, active N.O. 1898–1901.
Contemporary listings: artist, 1235
Carondelet (1898–1901).
References: NOCD 1898–1901.

MARCELLIN, RAPHAEL
Engraver, active N.O. 1888.
Contemporary listings: engraver
(1888).
References: NOCD 1888.

MARCHANT, EDWARD DALTON
Born Edgartown MA Dec. 16, 1806;
died Asbury Park NJ Aug. 15, 1887.
Painter, active N.O. 1839–40.
Contemporary listings: portrait
painter, cor. Exchange Pl. and Canal
(1839–40); portrait painter, 12 Ex-
change Pl. (1840).
Exhibited: National Academy of De-
sign, N.Y.C. (1829, 1832–51).
Memberships/positions: National
Academy of Design (1833).
Painted a portrait of Andrew Jackson
from life in N.O. (1840). He also
worked in Charleston SC, N.Y.C.,
Nashville TN, and Philadelphia.
References: Comm. Bull., Jan. 14,
1840; D. Pic., Dec. 3, 1839–Jan. 19,
1840 (advs.), Dec. 4, 1839, Jan. 17,
Oct. 14, 1840; Bénézit; Bolton,
Painters in Miniature; Fielding, Dictionary; Groce and Wallace; New
York Historical Society, 770; Wil-
liam Young.

MARCOU, LUCIEN
Born Lesparre, France ca. 1816; died
N O. Nov. 29, 1871.
Sculptor, active N.O. 1858–59.
Contemporary listings: wax figure
maker, St. Ann betw. Bourbon and
Royal (1858); wax figure maker, 82
St. Ann (1859).
References: NOCD 1858–61, 1866–
72; NOBD 1858–59; Bee, Nov. 30,
1871; Groce and Wallace; U.S. Cen-
sus (1860), roll 418.

MARCOU, SAMUEL A.
Painter, art teacher, active N.O.
1908–16.
Studied: Ecole des Beaux Arts, Paris;
Royal Academy, Munich, Germany.
Contemporary listings: instructor,
ART LEAGUE OF NEW ORLEANS (1908);
artist (1911, 1916); painter (1914).

Exhibited: ART ASSOCIATION OF NEW
ORLEANS (1915).
References: NOCD 1911–12, 1914,
1916; D. Pic., June 28, 1908; Art
Asso., Special Exhibition.

MARDING, _____. See HART, W. A.

MARES, C.
Painter, active N.O. 1858.
Contemporary listings: painter on
glass, 264 Burgundy (1858).
References: NOBD 1858.

MARGRAF, FRANK
Painter, active N.O. 1896–99.
Contemporary listings: fresco artist,
418 Camp (1896–97); painter, 1731
Washington (1899).
References: NOCD 1896–97, 1899.

MARMU, CALISTE
Born France ca. 1819–20.
Painter, colorer, active N.O. 1854–
63; primarily photographer.
Contemporary listings: partner, PI-
CARD & MARMU (1854); portraits in oil,
watercolor, and pastel, 69 Royal
(1863).
References: NOCD 1858–61, 1866–
75; Bee, May 8, 1863; Courier, Dec.
20, 1854; D. Crescent, June 8, 1866;
Renaissance Louisianaise 1(Nov. 22,
1863): 9; Smith and Tucker, 164;
U.S. Census (1860), roll 421, (1870),
roll 521.

MARQUE, ALPHONSE
Died Los Angeles CA July 3 or 4,
1924.
Lithographer, active N.O. 1885; also
printer.
Contemporary listings: lithographer,
with MICHEL CAPO (1885).
References: NOCD 1882–95, 1897–
1916, 1921; T. Demo., Feb. 22,
1905; T. Pic., July 13, 20, 1924.

MARQUIGNIES, HIPPOLYTE
Painter, active N.O. 1886–97; also
sign painter, decorator.
Contemporary listings: painter
(1886, 1891); decorative painter
(1887); fresco painter, 104 Bienville
(1888); painter, 736 Conti (1896–
97).
References: NOCD 1886–88, 1891,
1893–94, 1896–1901.

MARQUIS, JOSEPH
Sculptor, active N.O. 1887.
Contemporary listings: sculptor
(1887).

References: NOCD 1882, 1885, 1887.

MARS, CHESTER P.
Born LA Apr. 1886.
Painter, active N.O. 1905–1908.
Contemporary listings: artist, SOUTHERN ART STUDIO (1905); painter (1908).
Brother of PETER JOSEPH LAWRENCE MARS.
References: NOCD 1904–1905, 1907–1908, 1911–12, 1914; U.S. Census (1900), roll 573.

MARS, PETER JOSEPH LAWRENCE
Born Houma LA Aug. 28, 1874; died 1949.
Sculptor, art teacher, painter, active N.O. 1893–1947.
Contemporary listings: artist (1893–94, 1902–1903, 1906–1908, 1910, 1912–13); sculptor (1895); artist, 2524 Dumaine (1897); portrait painter, 2524 Dumaine, and artist, 1519 Marigny (1898); artist, 610 Royal (1899); artist, AUDUBON PORTRAIT HOUSE (1900); artist, 1506 Marigny (1901, 1903–1904); artist, SOUTHERN ART STUDIO, and Peters and Mars, scenic artist, Earle Stock Company (1905); portrait painter, 124 St. Charles (1909); proprietor, MARS SCHOOL OF ART (1914–18); artist, 617 Commercial (1917); artist, 325 Camp (1918).
Mars continued to be listed as either an artist or a portrait painter in 1919–22, 1926, and 1947. Between 1923 and 1947 he taught art at Isaac Delgado Central Trades School, and in 1930 he copied Murillo's *Ascension* for the Charity Hospital Chapel. He exhibited at the Arts and Crafts Club (1932) and the New Orleans Art League (1934), from which he received an award (1942). Brother of CHESTER P. MARS.
References: NOCD 1893–95, 1897–1910, 1912–33, 1935, 1938, 1940, 1942, 1945–47, 1949; NOBD 1898; *D. News*, Jan. 24, 1906; *Morn. Trib.*, Mar. 17, 1930; *Old French Quarter News*, Jan. 16, 1942; *States*, Dec. 4, 1932; *T. Demo.*, Oct. 26, 1905; *T. Pic.*, Apr. 1, 1934; Orleans Parish Registrar of Voters, NOPL; LSM, *Biennial Report for 1920–21*, 85; THNOC Cemetery Survey; U.S. Census (1900), roll 573, (1910), roll 520.

MARS SCHOOL OF ART
Art school, active N.O. 1914–18, PETER JOSEPH LAWRENCE MARS, proprietor.
Contemporary listings: portrait painting, designing and sculptures, pastels, water and oil painting, 325 Camp (1914–16); 325 Camp (1917–18).
References: NOCD 1914–18.

MARSDEN, FRANCES M. *See* BELDEN, FRANCES MARSDEN

MARTEL, GUSTAVE E.
Painter or art dealer, active N.O. 1895.
Contemporary listings: portraits, old 330 Canal (1895); mgr., G. E. Martel Portrait Copying House (1896). Possibly a photographer.
References: NOCD 1895–96.

MARTELLI, MR. _____. *See* MONDELLI & MARTELLI

MARTIN, CHARLES E.
Designer, sculptor, active N.O. 1909–18; also decorator, architect.
Contemporary listings: designer, Boh & Co. (1909); designer (1910); sculptor, with J. H. Duffy (1912); artist (1917–18).
Head modeler of the Grunewald Cave, a nightclub (ca. 1910–20) decorated as the interior of a cave in the basement of the Grunewald Hotel.
References: NOCD 1908–13, 1915, 1917–18; Jean Duffy, 20.

MARTIN, E. HALL
Painter, active N.O. 1839.
Studied: with THOMAS SULLY.
Contemporary listings: portrait and miniature painter, 46 Canal (1839).
Exhibited: American Art Union, N.Y.C. (ca. 1847–48).
Portrait and landscape painter who worked in N.Y.C. and CA (1851).
References: *D. Pic.*, Mar. 10, 1839; Groce and Wallace; William Young.

MARTIN, F.
Painter, active N.O. 1918.
Several murals of City Park were painted by F. Martin in 1918. Possibly Francis Xavier Martin, listed as

sign painter (1915, 1920) and painter (1916–17, 1919), born N.O. ca. 1897, died N.O. Jan. 29, 1964.
References: NOCD 1915–17, 1919–22; *States–Item*, Jan. 29–30, 1964; *T. Pic.*, Jan. 30, 1964; Morton's Auction Exchange, Mar. 29, 1966.

MARTIN, J.
Painter, active N.O. ca. 1881.
Exhibited: SOUTHERN ART UNION (1881).
References: *D. Pic.*, May 26, 1881.

MARTIN, JOSEPH BERNARD
Born N.O. Aug. 19, 1854; died N.O. May 26, 1911.
Painter, active N.O. 1889; primarily grainer.
Contemporary listings: fresco painter, 202 Baronne (1889).
References: NOCD 1878, 1880–83, 1885–92, 1894–1906, 1908–11; *D. Pic.*, May 27–28, 1911; *D. States*, Aug. 7, 1886.

MARTINELLI, ADAM
Artist, active N.O. 1897.
Contemporary listings: artist (1897).
References: NOCD 1897.

MARTINELLI, LUCAS
Artist, active N.O. 1897.
Contemporary listings: artist (1897).
References: NOCD 1897.

MARTINEZ, FELIPE J.
Lithographer, active N.O. 1890.
Contemporary listings: lithographer, with MICHEL CAPO (1890).
References: NOCD 1890.

MARTINEZ, JOHN B.
Born Mexico ca. 1855; died N.O. Jan. 30, 1894.
Lithographer, active N.O. 1884–94; also printer.
Contemporary listings: lithographer, with MICHEL CAPO (1884–85, 1890–93).
Probably brother of JOSEPH A. MARTINEZ.
References: NOCD 1884–85, 1887–88, 1890–93; N.O. Death Certificate (1894), 105:854, NOPL; THNOC Cemetery Survey.

MARTINEZ, JOSEPH A.
Lithographer, active N.O. 1893.
Contemporary listings: lithographer, with MICHEL CAPO (1893).

Probably brother of JOHN B. MARTINEZ.
References: NOCD 1893; THNOC Cemetery Survey.

MASANET, _____
Engraver, active N.O. 1838; also jeweler.
Contemporary listings: engraver, 297 Royal (1838).
References: NOCD 1838.

MASON, ALMA FLORENCE (Mrs. Benjamin F. Burke)
Born N.O. July 9, 1886; died Apr. 12, 1970.
Painter, art craftsman, active N.O. 1910–21; also needleworker.
Studied: NEWCOMB COLLEGE (1904–1909).
Contemporary listings: landscape painter (1910).
Exhibited: ART ASSOCIATION OF NEW ORLEANS (1911, 1913, 1916–17); Panama–Pacific International Exposition, San Francisco (1915).
Worked as art craftsman (1910–21) specializing in pottery design and china painting.
References: NOCD 1916–17, 1955, 1960–61; Art Asso., *Catalogue* (1911, 1913, 1916, 1917, 1918); Orleans Parish Registrar of Voters, NOPL; Ormond and Irvine, 163; Poesch, *Newcomb Pottery*, 102; U.S. Census (1910), roll 524.

MASON, JOSEPH ROBERT
Born ca. 1807.
Painter, active N.O. 1821–22.
Studied: with JOHN JAMES AUDUBON, Cincinnati OH (1820) and LA (1821–22).
Student of John James Audubon in Cincinnati OH who accompanied Audubon to the South on his first expedition to paint American birds. Although only 13 years old, Mason had shown sufficient talent that Audubon hired him to paint the backgrounds for his works. The two artists left Cincinnati on Oct. 12, 1820 and arrived in N.O. on Jan. 7, 1821. Along the way and in N.O., Mason collected plants and flowers to paint, and many of these were used as backgrounds in Audubon's bird studies. They remained in N.O. until June 16,

1821 when they left for Oakley plantation near St. Francisville LA, returning to N.O. by Nov. 1821. On Mar. 16, 1822 they left for Natchez MS where they parted and Mason returned to OH. Audubon's *Birds of America* was published serially (1826–38) in Great Britain. By the late 1830s, Mason was in Philadelphia where he painted flower pictures for the botanical gardens. In later life, Mason charged that he had not been given just credit for his contribution to the published Audubon works, because his name did not appear on them.

References: Joy Jackson, "A Thirteen–Year–Old Boy was Flower Painter for Audubon," *Dixie*, Mar. 2, 1952; J. J. Audubon, *Journal*, 3; Rourke.

MASON, RUTH

Born LA ca. 1890.

Painter, active N.O. 1910.

Contemporary listings: landscape painter, 6003 Tchoupitoulas (1910).

References: U.S. Census (1910), roll 524.

MASON SMITH, MARGUERITE LACAMUS (Mrs. William Mason Smith)

Died N.O. ca. 1926.

Artist, active N.O. 1893–1915.

Studied: Paris; with Stevens, France.

Exhibited: Salon, Paris; Tulane University (1893); ARTISTS' ASSOCIATION OF NEW ORLEANS (1897, 1899, 1901); ART ASSOCIATION OF NEW ORLEANS (1910, 1915).

Memberships/positions: ARTS EXHIBITION CLUB (1901).

References: NOCD 1898, 1911; *D. Pic.*, Feb. 14, 1893, Mar. 30, 1897; *Harlequin*, Dec. 6, 1899, 4–5; *T. Demo.*, Feb. 15, 1893; AANO, *Catalogue* (1897, 1899, 1901); Art Asso., *Catalogue* (1910, 1915); Arts Exhibition Club; Grace King, *Memories*, 366–67; Information courtesy Harry T. Howard.

MASSARINI, RAYMOND H.

Born LA or TN ca. 1851–52.

Painter, designer, active N.O. 1870–1907; also sign painter, decorator, gilder.

Contemporary listings: painter (1870, 1872–74, 1876–85, 1888–98, 1902–1903, 1907); frescoes, banners, flags, and transparencies painted, 84 Customhouse (1879–80). With ACHILLE BEORCI, designed and decorated the triumphal arch at the West End railroad terminus for the French Fête (1883).

References: NOCD 1872–85, 1888–98, 1902–1905, 1907; *D. States*, July 14, 1883; *Southern Business Guide*; U.S. Census (1860), roll 419, (1870), roll 520.

MASSIE, JULIA M.

Born near Jackson MS Nov. 1869; died N.O. June 20, 1949.

Painter, art teacher, sketch artist, active N.O. 1886–1921.

Studied: ARTISTS' ASSOCIATION OF NEW ORLEANS (1886–87, 1890–91); with BROR ANDERS WIKSTROM, PAUL POINCY, ANDRES MOLINARY.

Contemporary listings: teacher, School of Art (1890); instructor, elementary class, Artists' Association of New Orleans (1891–93); artist (1900); artist, oil and watercolors (1910).

Exhibited: Artists' Association of New Orleans (1886–87, 1889, 1890–92, 1894, 1896–97, 1899, 1901–1902); Tulane University (1893); Tennessee Centennial Exposition, Nashville (1897); E. Curtis's Exchange (1902); ART ASSOCIATION OF NEW ORLEANS (1904–1905, 1907, 1910–11, 1913–18).

Awarded: Art Association of New Orleans, gold medal (1912).

Memberships/positions: Artists' Association of New Orleans (1889–90, 1896), secy. (1897).

Landscape and still life painter who moved to N.O. as a child. She was a successful art instructor at the Artists' Association (1890–91); and along with Paul Poincy, served on the Jury of Selection at the Tennessee Centennial Exposition (1897). By 1898 she was said by the *Daily States* to be one of the city's leading artists, whose works were praised "both at home and abroad." She continued to be listed as an artist (1919–20) and

exhibited as a member of the Artists' Guild (1921).
References: NOCD 1891, 1908, 1919–20; *Current Topics*, Nov. 1890, 23, Jan. 1891, 24, Jan. 1892, 24, Jan. 1893, 10, Nov. 1893, 198; *D. Pic.*, Nov. 7, 1886, May 7, 1887, Dec. 17, 1889, Nov. 13, Dec. 17, 1890, Apr. 29, May 22, Dec. 17, 1891, Dec. 14, 1892, Feb. 14, 1893, Mar. 30, 1897, Jan. 6, 1907, *D. States*, May 16–17, 1890, Apr. 29, 1891, Jan. 23, 1898; *Harlequin*, Dec. 6, 1899, 4; *Item*, Feb. 3, 6, 1921; *T. Demo.*, May 16, 1890, Feb. 15, 1893, Dec. 14, 1894, Dec. 3, 1901, Mar. 22, 24, 1902, Feb. 28, 1904, Dec. 28, 1905; *T. Pic.*, June 21, 1949; *Town Talk*, July 1904, 24; AANO, *Catalogue* (1890, 1891, 1896, 1897, 1899, 1901, 1902); AANO, *School of Art* (1892–93); Art Asso., *Catalogue* (1904, 1905, 1907, 1910, 1911, 1913, 1914, 1915, 1916, 1917, 1918); Delgado, *Catalogue of Paintings, Sculpture*; Meyerbeer (adv.); Mount, 136; Tennessee Centennial Exposition, 66; U.S. Census (1900), roll 575, (1910), roll 524.

MASSY, MARIE L.
Painter, active N.O. 1857–66.
Contemporary listings: portrait painter, 235 St. Ann (1857); portrait painter, 202 St. Ann (1860–61, 1866).
References: NOCD 1857, 1860–61, 1866; Groce and Wallace; William Young.

MASTIO, ADELINA VARGAS. *See* VARGAS, ADELINA

MATHER, FRANCIS W.
Engraver, designer, active N.O. 1889–95.
Contemporary listings: wood engraver and designer, 112–114 Poydras (1889); engraver, with SMITH W. BENNETT (1889); wood engraver, BENNETT & KOENIG (1890); engraver (1895).
References: NOCD 1889–91, 1895; *D. States*, Feb. 4–July 8, 1889 (advs.).

MATHERNE, SAMUEL T., SR.
Born N.O. Mar. 26, 1866; died N.O. Nov. 12, 1949.
Lithographer, active N.O. 1910–16.

Contemporary listings: lithographer (1910–13, 1915–16).
Worked as a lithographer for the American Can Company.
References: NOCD 1906–1908, 1910–16, 1919–28, 1930, 1932, 1935, 1938, 1940, 1942, 1946–47, 1952–55; *Item*, Nov. 14, 1949; *T. Pic.*, Nov. 13–14, 1949; Orleans Parish Registrar of Voters, NOPL; U.S. Census (1910), roll 521.

MATHEW, ADOLPH
Engraver, active N.O. 1887.
Contemporary listings: engraver (1887).
References: NOCD 1887.

MATHIEU, JEAN PIERRE
Born Ste. Marie–aux–Mines, France ca. 1804–18; died N.O. Jan. 3, 1868.
Artist, active N.O. 1859–66.
Contemporary listings: artist, 260 Main (1859); artist, 223 Main (1860–61, 1866).
References: NOCD 1859–61, 1866; Groce and Wallace; N.O. Death Certificate (1868), 38:680, NOPL; U.S. Census (1860), roll 418.

MAUBERRET, GERALDINE REGIS (Mrs. Samuel A. Byrne)
Born N.O. ca. 1882; died N.O. Dec. 24, 1963.
Art craftsman, active N.O. 1905–1906.
Studied: NEWCOMB COLLEGE (1904).
Listed as pottery artisan at Newcomb (1905–1906).
References: *States–Item*, Dec. 25–26, 1963; *T. Pic.*, Dec. 25–26, 1963; Poesch, *Newcomb Pottery*, 102.

MAURAS, JUANITA MARIE
Born N.O. Mar. 27 or 28, 1880; died N.O. Oct. 16, 1952.
Art craftsman, art teacher, bookbinder, active N.O. 1908–45; also silversmith, jeweler, needleworker.
Studied: NEWCOMB COLLEGE (1905–1908); Columbia University, N.Y.C. (1910).
Exhibited: ART ASSOCIATION OF NEW ORLEANS (1911, 1914, 1916–18); Panama–Pacific Exposition, San Francisco (1915).
Awarded: Louisiana State Fair and Mississippi State Fair, blue ribbons.

Mauras was listed as an art craftsman (1908–29); on the Newcomb art faculty (1922–45); exhibited at the Arts and Crafts Club (1924); and taught a class in metal craft and jewelry making at the Arts and Crafts Club (1925).
References: NOCD 1924, 1927–33, 1935, 1938, 1940, 1942, 1945–47, 1949, 1952–53; *D. Pic.*, Dec. 26, 1909; *Item*, Jan. 30, 1921; *T. Demo.*, Jan. 6, 1913; *T. Pic.*, Feb. 29, 1924, May 24, Dec. 6, 1925, Oct. 17, 1952; Art Asso., *Catalogue* (1911, 1914, 1916, 1917, 1918); Orleans Parish Registrar of Voters, NOPL; Ormond and Irvine, 163; Poesch, *Newcomb Pottery*, 37, 78, 96, 102.

MAURICE, ALFRED
Born N.O. ca. 1826.
Engraver, sketch artist, active N.O. 1862.
Contemporary listings: artist in drawing and engraving, MALUS & MAURICE.
References: *D. Delta*, Mar. 12, 1862; U.S. Census (1860), roll 422.

MAURIES, FERNAND
Artist, active N.O. 1872.
Contemporary listings: artist (1872).
References: NOCD 1872.

MAURY, CORNELIA FIELD
Born N.O. 1866; died after 1938.
Painter, active N.O. 1894.
Studied: St. Louis School of Fine Arts, MO; Académie Julian, Paris; with Benjamin–Constant; Jean Paul Laurens; R. Collin; Jules Lefebvre, Paris.
Exhibited: ARTISTS' ASSOCIATION OF NEW ORLEANS (1894, 1896).
Awarded: Lewis and Clark Centennial Exposition, Portland OR, bronze medal (1905).
Memberships/positions: St. Louis Association of Painters and Sculptors; St. Louis Artists' Guild; Society of Western Artists; Society of Independent Artists, St. Louis; Southern States Art League; Southern Printmakers Society.
Native of N.O. whose artistic career was in mainly St. Louis.
References: *T. Demo.*, Dec. 14, 1894; AANO, *Catalogue* (1896); Collins and Opitz; Mount, 136; Tennessee Centennial Exposition; *Who's Who in American Art*, 1938–39.

MAVERICK, SAMUEL R.
Born N.Y.C. Jan. 19, 1812; died N.O. Aug. 24, 1839.
Engraver, active N.O. ca. 1837–39; also printer.
Worked in N.Y.C. (1833) and then moved to N.O. (1837) where he was employed by engraver J. LOWE and then printer D. G. Johnson.
References: Groce and Wallace; William Young.

MAY, JOHN C.
Born ca. 1827; died St. Bernard Parish LA Oct. 8, 1892.
Artist, active N.O. 1892; also carver, carpenter, cabinetmaker.
Contemporary listings: artist (1892).
References: NOCD 1861, 1866–68, 1870–73, 1875, 1877–92; N.O. Death Certificate (1892), 102:942, NOPL.

MAYANS, RICHARD
Died before 1927.
Artist, active N.O. 1882–83.
Contemporary listings: artist (1882–83).
References: NOCD 1881–83; *T. Pic.*, Feb. 7, 1927.

MAYER, DAVID
Sketch artist, active N.O. 1897–1902.
Contemporary listings: artist (1897–98).
Drew a cover for *Men and Matters* (1902) which was engraved by the ELECTRIC ENGRAVING CO.
References: NOCD 1897–98; *Men and Matters*, June 1902, cover.

MAYERS, MR. A.
Painter, art teacher, active N.O. 1832.
Contemporary listings: painter, teacher of drawing and painting, 134 Royal (1832).
References: *Advertiser*, Dec. 24, 1832.

MAYFIELD, ROBERT BLEDSOE
Born Carlinville IL Jan. 1, 1869; died N.O. Dec. 4, 1934.
Painter, etcher, active N.O. 1892–1932.
Studied: St. Louis Academy of Fine Arts, MO; with Luc Olivier Merson,

Jules Lefebvre, Flameng, Gabriel Ferrier, Benjamin Constant; Académie Julian, Paris.
Contemporary listings: artist, *Times–Democrat* (1892–97, 1899–1907).
Exhibited: ARTISTS' ASSOCIATION OF NEW ORLEANS (1899, 1901–1902); Newspaper Artists Association, St. Charles Hotel (1903); ART ASSOCIATION OF NEW ORLEANS (1904–1905, 1910–11, 1913); St. Louis; Boston; Paris; N.Y.C.
Awarded: Art Association of New Orleans, gold medal (1908).
Memberships/positions: Art Association of New Orleans, executive committee (1904–1905, 1910–11); DELGADO MUSEUM, committee for painting and sculpture.
Listed as musical critic (1905), literary editor (1906–1907), and Sunday editor (1908–13) of the *Times–Democrat*, and associate editor of the *Times–Picayune* (1920–33). Mayfield exhibited at the Arts and Crafts Club (1924) and at the Delgado Museum of Art (1932).
References: NOCD 1892–97, 1899–1933; *D. Pic.*, Feb. 29, 1904; *Harlequin*, Dec. 6, 1899, 4; *Men and Matters*, Feb, 1896, 2, 7, Mar. 1897, 5, 7, (illustrations); *T. Demo.*, Dec. 3, 1901, July 7, 1903, Dec. 27, 1905, Feb. 25, 1910; *T. Pic.*, Nov. 30, Dec. 1, 1924, Dec. 11, 1932, Dec. 5–6, 1934, Feb. 4, 1935; AANO, *Catalogue* (1899, 1901, 1902); Art Asso., *Catalogue* (1904, 1905, 1910, 1911, 1913, 1914); Bénézit; Delgado, *Catalogue of Paintings, Sculpture*, 21; Fielding, *Dictionary*; Orleans Parish Registrar of Voters, NOPL; Wiesendanger, 69–71.

MAYR, CHRISTIAN
Born Germany ca. 1805; died N.Y.C. Oct. 19, 1851.
Painter, active N.O. 1844.
Contemporary listings: portrait painter (1844).
Exhibited: National Academy of Design, N.Y.C. (1834); Banks Arcade, and 50 Camp Street (1844).
Memberships/positions: National Academy of Design, N.Y.C. (1836).

Painter of portraits and genre who was also a designer and daguerreotypist. Mayr came from his native Germany to the U.S. ca. 1834, and traveled to Boston (1839) and Charleston SC (1840) where he remained until 1843. In 1844 he came to N.O. to exhibit some of his genre paintings. The following year he had returned to N.Y.C. where he stayed until his death.
References: *Bee*, Feb. 7, 1844; *Comm. Bull.*, Jan. 24, Apr. 2, 1844; *Courier*, Mar. 12–13, 1844 (advs.), Mar. 13, 15, 1844; *D. Pic.*, Feb. 11–18, 1844 (advs.); Groce and Wallace; Rinhart, 124.

MAZUREAU, POLYXENE. *See* REYNES, POLYXENE MAZUREAU

MEADE, THOMAS, JR.
Born N.O. ca. 1870; died N.O. Jan. 1, 1906.
Lithographer, active N.O. 1898–1903; primarily printer, bookbinder.
Contemporary listings: lithographer (1898, 1903).
References: NOCD 1886–1900, 1902–1906; *D. Pic.*, Jan. 2, 1906; *Item*, Jan. 7, 1906.

MEARA, JAMES
Engraver, active N.O. 1885.
Contemporary listings: engraver, SOUTHERN LITHOGRAPHIC CO. (1885).
References: NOCD 1885.

MEEKEN, MISS F. C.
Painter, active N.O. ca. 1889.
Exhibited: ART LEAGUE OF NEW ORLEANS (1889).
Memberships/positions: Art League of New Orleans (1889).
References: *D. Pic.*, Mar. 10, 1889.

MEEKER, JOSEPH RUSLING
Born Newark NJ Apr. 22, 1827; died St. Louis MO Sept. 27, 1887.
Painter, sketch artist.
Studied: with Charles Loring Elliot, National Academy of Design, N.Y.C. (1844); with Asher B. Durand.
Exhibited: American Art Union, N.Y.C. (1842); National Academy of Design (1867); Boston Art Club (1877); Tennessee Centennial Exposition, Nashville (1897).
Awarded: National Academy School, N.Y.C., scholarship (1845).

Noted landscape painter who grew up in Auburn NY, then moved to Buffalo NY (1849), and to Louisville KY, where he taught art and painted portraits and landscapes (1852), before he settled in St. Louis MO (1859). During the Civil War he entered the U.S. Navy (1862) and became a paymaster on a gunboat that traveled the Mississippi River. It is not verified that Meeker actually visited N.O. at that time, but he is known to have made many sketches of LA bayous and swamplands in the area (ca. 1862–65). At the end of the war, Meeker returned to St. Louis and painted popular swamp scenes based on the sketches. He also traveled in the Midwest making sketches which later became the subjects of other landscape paintings. Meeker was a leading figure in the St. Louis art community and was involved with several art organizations.
References: *St. Louis Republican*, Sept. 29, 1887; Brown; Bruce Chambers; Dixson, 10–15; Groce and Wallace; Nellie J. Meeker, document, THNOC artists files.

MEGAREY, JOHN (Henry J.)
Born 1818; died N.Y.C. May 14, 1845.
Painter, active N.O. 1841; also publisher.
Exhibited: National Academy of Design, N.Y.C. (1841–44).
Memberships/positions: National Academy of Design, N.Y.C. (1844 or 1845).
N.Y.C. publisher and portrait and landscape painter who visited N.O. to do a view of the city for his series *Views of the Cities of the United States* (1841).
References: *D. Pic.*, Apr. 14, 1841; Groce and Wallace; New–York Historical Society, 501.

MELBOURNE, HENRY CLAY
Born MD ca. 1828; died N.O. Sept. 26, 1917.
Artist, active N.O. 1893–1909; also sign painter.
Contemporary listings: artist (1893–94); painter (1896–97, 1905–1907, 1909).

Moved to N.O. ca. 1842.
References: NOCD 1890–94, 1896–98, 1900, 1902–17; *T. Pic.*, Sept. 27, 1917.

MELLEN, CORINNE CASTELLANOS (Mrs. Delos C. Mellen)
Born N.O. Nov. 1863; died N.Y.C. May 5, 1909.
Painter, active N.O. ca. 1889–94.
Exhibited: Cotton Palace (1889); ARTISTS' ASSOCIATION OF NEW ORLEANS (1889, 1891–92, 1894).
Memberships/positions: GANGLIONICS.
Well–known singer and writer who moved to N.Y.C. (ca. 1906). Daughter of DR. JOHN JOSEPH CASTELLANOS; sister of JOHN JOSEPH CASTELLANOS, JR.
References: *Current Topics*, Jan. 1892, 24, Jan. 1893, 11; *D. Pic.*, Dec. 17, 1889, Dec. 17, 1891, Dec. 13, 1892, May 6–7, 1909; *T. Demo.*, Feb. 19, 1889, Dec. 13, 1892, Dec. 14, 1894; Mount, 107–9; THNOC Cemetery Survey; Tinker, *Ecrits*, 350–51.

MENKEMELLER, MR. ———
Sketch artist, active N.O. 1910.
Pen–and–ink artist in N.O. acting with a national theatrical group (1910).
References: *D. News*, Feb. 9, 1910.

MENKEN, ADAH ISAACS
Born N.O. June 15, 1835; died Paris, France Aug. 10, 1868.
Sculptor, active N.O. ca. 1859.
Studied: with Antoine–Louis Barye, Paris; Columbus OH.
World–renowned stage actress who was also a poet and sculptor. She met French sculptor ANDRE DE BEAUVILLE during his N.O. visit and through him learned to model clay figures which she then worked in stone.
References: Joy Jackson, "New Orleans' 'Naked Lady'," *Dixie*, July 12, 1953; *T. Pic.*, Feb. 25, 1934, Jan. 25, 1937; *Appleton's CAB*; *DAB*; E. J. Harvey, 35; *Historical Sketchbook*, 307–9; Kunitz and Haycraft; Laver, 70–74; Paul Lewis; *NCAB*, 435–36; Preston.

MERIC, STANLEY A.
Born St. Louis MO Dec. 11, 1890.
Painter, active N.O. 1910–13.

Contemporary listings: scenic artist (1910); artist (1911, 1913), painter (1912).
References: NOCD 1911–13; Orleans Parish Registrar of Voters, NOPL; U.S. Census (1910), roll 520.

MERISYINE, LUCA
Sculptor, active N.O. 1880.
Contemporary listings: sculptor (1880).
References: NOCD 1880.

MERLE, VICTOR, JR.
Born LA ca. 1884.
Engraver, active N.O. 1910; primarily stencil cutter.
Contemporary listings: engraver (1910).
References: NOCD 1898, 1900–1904, 1906–19; U.S. Census (1910), roll 521.

MERRY, HARLEY C.
Painter, active N.O. 1888–92.
Contemporary listings: scenery painter, St. Charles Theatre (1888, 1892); scenery painter, Grand Opera House (1890).
References: NOCD 1898, 1900–1904, 1906–19; Mascot, Nov. 3, 1888; Oct. 11, 1890; States, Dec. 23, 1888, Oct. 16, 1892.

MERVING, CHRISTIAN
Born Germany ca. 1823.
Artist, active N.O. 1850.
Contemporary listings: artist (1850).
References: Groce and Wallace; U.S. Census (1850), roll 235.

METCALF, ELIAB
Born Franklin MA Feb. 5, 1785; died Havana, Cuba Jan. 15, 1834.
Painter, active N.O. 1819–22.
Studied: with John Rubens Smith, N.Y.C.; with Samuel Lovett Waldo and William Jewett, N.Y.C. (1815).
Contemporary listings: portrait and miniature painter, Magazine (1820); portrait and miniature painter, Magazine betw. Common and Gravier (1821); portrait and miniature painter, 25 Magazine (1822).
Exhibited: American Academy, N.Y.C. (ca. 1819–23).
Came to N.O. during the autumn of 1819. For the next several years he divided his time between N.O. and

N.Y.C.; after 1824 he lived in Havana, Cuba and N.Y.C.
References: NOCD 1822; Gazette, Jan. 27, June 13, 1820, Jan. 2, 1821; T. Pic., July 10, 1977; Barker, 279–80; Bénézit; Bolton, Painters in Miniature; Dunlap, 2:387–90; Fielding Dictionary; Glenk, 77; Groce and Wallace; Emily Jackson, Silhouette; WPA, American Portrait Inventory, 179; WPA, "Lives."

METHUA, J. GERARD
Painter, active N.O. 1877–78.
Contemporary listings: decorative painter and frescoer, St. Charles Theatre (1877); scenic artist (1878).
References: NOCD 1878; D. Pic., Oct. 14, 1877.

MEUCCI, ANTHONY
Born Rome, Italy.
Painter, art teacher, restorer, active N.O. 1818–27.
Contemporary listings: portrait and miniature painter, teacher of drawing, St. Ann betw. Dauphine and Bourbon (1818); portrait and miniature painter, teacher of drawing, academy of painting and drawing, 92 Bourbon (1818); miniature painter and retoucher, corner St. Peter and Royal (1826); miniature painter and scenic painter, Orleans Theatre (1827).
Miniature painter in oil and crayons who came to the U.S. from Rome (1818) and lived and worked in N.O. (1818, 1826–27), Charleston SC (1822), N.Y.C. (1823), and Salem MA (1825). He painted opera scenery and decorations at the Orleans Theatre (1827). Meucci left N.O., probably with his wife, NINA MEUCCI, for Havana, Cuba, and then the northern coast of South America. In 1830 he painted Simon Bolivar in Cartegena, Columbia.
References: Advertiser, Nov. 13, 1826; Argus, Nov. 13–Dec. 8, 1826 (advs.), Feb. 5, 8, Mar. 16, Apr. 11, 1827; Bee, June 6, 1831; Courier, Aug. 17, 1818, Nov. 13–16, 1818 (advs.), Feb. 2, 6, Mar. 19, May 4, 1827; Glenk, 77; Groce and Wallace; Information courtesy George F. Jordan; WPA, "Lives."

MEUCCI, NINA (Mrs. Anthony Meucci)
Born Spain.
Painter, restorer, active N.O. 1818–26.
Studied: with Anthony Meucci.
Contemporary listings: miniature painter, St. Ann betw. Dauphine and Bourbon (1818); miniature painter, 92 Bourbon (1818); miniature painter and retoucher, cor. St. Peter and Royal (1826).
References: *Advertiser*, Nov. 13, 1826; *Argus*, Nov. 13–Dec. 8, 1826 (advs.); *Courier*, Aug. 17, 1818, Nov. 13–16, 1818 (advs.); Groce and Wallace; WPA, "Lives."

MEUNIO, LOUIS
Born France ca. 1844.
Painter, active N.O. 1884.
Contemporary listings: fresco artist (1884).
Moved to N.O. from Panama (1884); worked for TOBY HART frescoing Illinois Central Railroad ticket office when he disappeared (Dec. 5, 1884) and was presumed to have committed suicide.
References: *D. Pic.*, Dec. 9, 1884; *Eve. Chronicle*, Dec. 9, 1884.

J. MEY & CO.
Lithographers, active N.O. 1857–59; also printers; JOHN F. MEY, owner.
Contemporary listings: lithographers, 102 Exchange Pl. (1857–59).
References: NOCD 1858–59; NOBD 1857–58.

MEY, JOHN F. *See also* MEY & AMENDT
Lithographer, active N.O. 1857–59; also printer.
Contemporary listings: J. MEY & CO. (1857–59); lithographer, 102 Exchange Pl. (1858).
References: NOCD 1850–56, 1858–59; NOBD 1857–58; *Courier*, Mar. 11, 1857.

MEY & AMENDT
Engravers, lithographers, active N.O. 1857; JOHN F. MEY, PHILIP AMENDT, partners.
Contemporary listings: engravers, 102 Exchange Al. (1857).
Lithographed sheet music covers (1857) and drew a map of the Dimitri estate, Harrison County MS (1857) used in a real estate transaction.
References: "C'est au Pied d'un Rosier Blanc," Sheet Music Collection, LA Coll., TU; "Les Amours de Diable," THNOC 1979–59–3–L, 1982–8–L; Orleans Parish Notarial Archives, Plan Book 6:1.

MEYER, ADOLPH
Engraver, active N.O. 1874.
Contemporary listings: engraver (1874).
References: NOCD 1860, 1869, 1874–75, 1880–83, 1885, 1888–89.

MEYER, JOSEPH FORTUNE
Born Alsace–Lorraine, France Feb. 18, 1848; died N.O. Mar. 16, 1931.
Potter, active N.O. 1878–1929.
Studied: with his father, François Meyer, Biloxi MS.
Contemporary listings: potter (1878, 1903–1904, 1907); pottery, St. Bernard betw. Solidelle and Josephine (1881); pottery, St. Bernard betw. Prieur and Johnson (1882–83); potter, NEWCOMB COLLEGE (1906, 1908, 1910–14, 1916–18).
Exhibited: ART ASSOCIATION OF NEW ORLEANS (1910).
Awarded: Louisiana Purchase Exposition, St. Louis MO, silver medal (1904).
Came to the U.S. with his family (ca. 1857) and settled in Biloxi MS. His father established a pottery works there and Meyer and GEORGE OHR were apprenticed as potters. Meyer and his father came to N.O. during the 1860s to operate a pottery and a shoe store, both of which the younger Meyer continued to run after his father's death (1870) until 1890. From about 1888, Meyer and Ohr were employed by the NEW ORLEANS ART POTTERY COMPANY, where they remained until its demise (1890). WILLIAM WOODWARD and ELLSWORTH WOODWARD asked Meyer to help set up the Newcomb pottery operation (1893) and he was hired permanently (ca. 1896). He handled all of the pottery throwing, glazing, and mechanical work; was skilled at reproducing pottery shapes and designs drawn by others; and was noted

for his experimentation with glazes. By 1905, failing eyesight limited his work to turning the pots, but he remained at Newcomb until 1927. He is credited with throwing 90% of all Newcomb pottery produced during his career, and as late as 1929 was still listed as a potter.
References: NOCD 1878, 1880–89, 1891, 1903–1904, 1906–29, 1931; *T. Pic.*, Mar. 17, 1931; Art Asso., *Catalogue* (1910); Newcomb School of Art, announcement 1913–14; Ormond and Irvine, 24, 28, 145–46; Poesch, *Newcomb Pottery*, 13, 18, 37, 41, 48, 52–53, 61, 70, 72, 74, 94; Rago, 9B.

MEYERS, CHARLES
Born TN ca. 1884.
Engraver, active N.O. 1910–13.
Contemporary listings: engraver (1910); engraver (1913).
References: NOCD 1913–14; U.S. Census (1910), roll 520.

MICEU, VIRGINIA
Painter, active N.O. 1855.
The painting of *Storm Over Niagara Falls* is inscribed on reverse "No. 9/ Virginia Miceu/March 1855/N.O."
References: Sotheby Parke Bernet, *Americana* (Apr. 1977), no. 495A.

MICHEL, CLARA E.
Born N.O. Jan. 29, 1872; died N.O. Nov. 14, 1952.
Art teacher active N.O. ca. 1913–42.
Contemporary listings: drawing teacher, N.O. Public Schools (1913). Listed as a teacher, Francis T. Nicholls Industrial School (1915–19, 1921–33); teacher (1935); teacher, L. E. Rabouin (1938, 1940, 1942).
References: NOCD 1905–1906, 1913–33, 1935, 1938, 1940, 1942, 1945–47, 1949; *T. Demo.*, Jan. 14, 1913; *T. Pic.*, Nov. 15, 1952.

MIDDLEMIST, CHARLES
Art teacher, active N.O. 1824.
Contemporary listings: professor of drawing, 172 Tchoupitoulas (1824).
References: NOCD 1824.

MIESTCHOVICH, GEORGE A.
Born LA ca. 1881; died Covington LA Jan. 8, 1964.

Painter, active N.O. 1910–42; primarily decorator.
Contemporary listings: artist, decorator (1910); artist (1911–12); painter (1914–42).
Probably a house decorator and painter.
References: NOCD 1911–12, 1914–20, 1922–27, 1930–33, 1935, 1938, 1940, 1942; *States-Item*, Jan. 10, 1964; *T. Pic.*, Jan. 9, 1964; U.S. Census (1910), roll 521.

MILLER, MR. _____
Designer, engraver, active N.O. 1865.
Contemporary listings: engraver, Vogt's jewelry store (1865).
Designed and created an Abraham Lincoln commemorative medallion (1865).
References: *Trib.*, May 7, 1865.

MILLER, ALFRED JACOB
Born Baltimore MD Jan. 2, 1810; died Baltimore June 26, 1874.
Painter, active N.O. 1836–39.
Studied: with THOMAS SULLY, Baltimore (1831–32); Ecole des Beaux Arts, Paris (1833); English Life School, Rome (1834); Florence, Italy (ca. 1834).
Contemporary listings: painter, 26 Chartres (1838).
Exhibited: Baltimore (1838); Apollo Gallery, NY (1839).
Portrait and landscape painter known for his studies of American Indians. Miller arrived in N.O. on Dec. 7, 1836; he rented a studio over L. Chittenden's Dry Goods Store on Chartres in exchange for a portrait of Chittenden, and as a result, received a number of portrait commissions. In 1837 he met Capt. William Drummond Stewart of Scotland, who hired Miller to accompany him on a trip to the Rocky Mountains and Green River WY. They left N.O. in Apr. 1837, and along the way Miller drew over 200 pencil and watercolor sketches of scenery and Indian life. In the autumn Miller was back in N.O., doing oil paintings based on his sketches. By July 1838 he had set up a studio in Baltimore MD, but a few months later was again working in

N.O. In Mar. 1839, Miller began shipping paintings from N.O. to Stewart in Scotland and he himself soon followed. He remained in Scotland until 1842 when he returned to Baltimore to resume portrait painting. In both Scotland and Baltimore he continued creating Indian paintings based on his western sketches.
References: NOCD 1838; *Appleton's CAB*; Bénézit; *Bryan's*; Corcoran Gallery, 36; Curry, 33–34; Ewers, 98–117; Fielding, *Dictionary*; Groce and Wallace; McCracken, *Portrait*, 77–80; Museum of Fine Arts, 1:237; Ross, xvi–xxiii; Tyler, *Miller*, 18–20, 36, 49, 60.

MILLER, ALLEN G.
Sketch artist, active N.O. 1903–1906.
Signed illustrations for the *Harlequin* (1903, 1905–1906) and worked for the *Times–Democrat* as editor (1909).
References: NOCD 1905, 1908–1909; *Harlequin*, Feb. 19, 1903, 12, Nov. 30, 1905, 1, Jan. 18, 1906, 6, 7.

MILLER, ALVIN PHILIP
Born N.O. Sept. 24, 1891; died N.O. Sept. 18, 1955.
Lithographer, engraver, commercial artist, active N.O. 1910–55; also printer.
Contemporary listings: lithographer (1910, 1915); engraver (1913, 1917).
Listed as lithographer (1920); artist, *Times–Picayune* (1921–23); engraver (1926); commercial artist (1929, 1931–33, 1935, 1942, 1949, 1952–55); and artist (1947).
References: NOCD 1913, 1915, 1917–23, 1926, 1929–33, 1935, 1938, 1940, 1942, 1947, 1949, 1952–55; *T. Pic.*, Sept. 19, 20, 21, 1955; Orleans Parish Registrar of Voters, NOPL; U.S. Census (1910), roll 524.

MILLER, ANNA LOUISE
Born N.O. Jan. 12, 1856; died N.O. Dec. 6, 1893.
Sketch artist, designer, active N.O. ca. 1888.
Exhibited: TULANE DECORATIVE ART LEAGUE FOR WOMEN (1888).

References: NOCD 1879–94; *D. Pic.*, Feb. 12, 1888, Dec. 7–8, 10, 1893; Tulane Decorative Art League.

MILLER, ANNA S.
Born LA Oct. 1866.
Artist, active N.O. 1900.
Contemporary listings: artist (1900).
References: U.S. Census (1900), roll 574.

MILLER, ANTHONY
Painter, active N.O. 1874–84; also sign painter.
Contemporary listings: fresco painter (1874); artist (1876–77); portrait painter (1878–79, 1884); landscape painter (1879).
Landscape and portrait artist whose portrait paintings included officers in the LA Field Artillery and the Orleans Artillery. Possibly Anthony Miller born Switzerland; died N.O. Feb. 10, 1889.
References: NOCD 1870, 1874–79, 1885–89, 1891–92; *Demo.*, Oct. 9, 1879; *D. Pic.*, Feb. 11, 17, 1889; *D. States*, Feb. 24, Aug. 2, 1884.

MILLER, CHARLES F.
Engraver, active N.O. 1879.
Contemporary listings: engraver, with JAMES S. RIVERS (1879).
References: NOCD 1879.

MILLER, DAVID R.
Born N.O. ca. 1888; died N.O. Jan. 16, 1948.
Engraver, active N.O. 1907–15.
Contemporary listings: engraver, T. Hausmann & Sons, Ltd. (1907–1909); engraver, 921 Canal (1911–15).
References: NOCD 1901–29, 1938, 1940, 1942, 1945–47; *States*, Jan. 17, 1948.

MILLER, MISS ERNESTINE A.
Sketch artist, designer, active N.O. ca. 1886–1905.
Studied: TULANE FREE DRAWING CLASS (1886).
Exhibited: TULANE DECORATIVE ART LEAGUE FOR WOMEN (1888).
Memberships/positions: Tulane Decorative Art League for Women (1888); ART ASSOCIATION OF NEW ORLEANS (1905).
Listed as teacher (1887); teacher, McDonogh School No. 18 (1888);

teacher, St. Ann Street School (1889–93); principal, Beauregard School (1894–1903); teacher (1904).
References: NOCD 1887–1904; *D. Pic.*, Feb. 12, 1888; *Eve. Chronicle*, May 22, 1886; Art Asso., *Catalogue* (1905); Tulane Decorative Art League.

MILLER, MRS. H.
Sculptor, active N.O. 1884–94.
Awarded: World's Industrial and Cotton Centennial Exposition, 1st prize (1884–85).
Created a wax sculpture of birds in a tree (1894). *Cf.* MILLER, MRS JOHN.
References: *D. Pic.*, Sept. 30, 1894.

MILLER, JAMES A.
Born N.O. ca. Oct. 13, 1871; died N.O. Mar. 30, 1905.
Potter, active N.O. 1900–1905.
Contemporary listings: potter (1900–1902, 1905); potter, Crescent Pottery Works (1903).
Assistant potter to JOSEPH FORTUNE MEYER at NEWCOMB COLLEGE (ca. 1903–1905) where he was succeeded by his brother, ROBERT MILLER.
References: NOCD 1900–1903, 1905–1906; N.O. Death Certificate (1905), 134:1131, NOPL; Poesch, *Newcomb Pottery*, 53, 94.

MILLER, MRS. JOHN
Art craftsman, active N.O. 1884.
Awarded: Louisville Exposition, KY, gold medal (1885).
Exhibited a collection of wax flowers (1884). *Cf.* MILLER, MRS. H.
References: *D. Pic.*, Oct. 28, 1885.

MILLER, JOSEPH
Painter, active N.O. 1892.
Contemporary listings: fresco painter (1892).
References: NOCD 1892.

MILLER, PHILIP
Lithographer, active N.O. 1878.
Contemporary listings: lithographer (1878).
References: NOCD 1878.

MILLER, ROBERT
Potter, active N.O. ca. 1905–16.
Contemporary listings: potter (1906–14, 1916).
Exhibited: ART ASSOCIATION OF NEW ORLEANS (1910).

Brother of JAMES MILLER whom he succeeded as assistant potter at NEWCOMB COLLEGE under JOSEPH FORTUNE MEYER (ca. 1905–10). Possibly Robert Miller listed as a painter (1904–1905, 1917).
References: NOCD 1904–14, 1916–17; Art Asso., *Catalogue* (1910); Poesch, *Newcomb Pottery*, 53, 94; Ormond and Irvine, 85, 146.

MILLER, SAMUEL T.
Born Switzerland Sept. 1840; died N.O. June 4, 1912.
Lithographer, active N.O. 1870–1912; also printer.
Contemporary listings: lithographer (1870, 1873, 1876–77, 1883, 1893–94, 1896–97, 1899–1901, 1903–1905, 1908); lithographer, with JOHN B. KRAFT (1871); lithographic printer, John B. Kraft (1872); lithographer, with HUGH LEWIS (1879); lithographer, NEW ORLEANS LITHOGRAPHING AND ENGRAVING CO. (1880–82); NEW ORLEANS LITHOGRAPHING CO. (1884); lithographer, G. KOECKERT & CO. (1886–88); lithographer, KOECKERT & WALLE (1889, 1891–92); lithographer, WALLE & CO. (1912).
References: NOCD 1866, 1870–77, 1879–94, 1896–97, 1899–1906, 1908–12; *D. Pic.*, June 5, 9, 1912; N.O. Death Certificate (1912), 155:119, NOPL; U.S. Census (1860), roll 415, (1870), roll 524, (1900), roll 574.

MILLS, CLARK
Born Onondaga County NY Dec. 1, 1815; died Washington DC Jan. 12, 1883.
Sculptor, active N.O. ca. 1830, 1855–56.
Contemporary listings: sculptor (1855–56).
Sculptor who worked primarily in Charleston SC and Washington DC. Mills reportedly lived in N.O. briefly ca. 1830, and returned (1855–56) to oversee the erection of his statue of Andrew Jackson in Jackson Square. The statue, a replica of his earlier Washington DC statue (dedicated 1853), was commissioned by the City Council and paid for with private contributions. His design was chosen

over that of ACHILLE PERELLI. Mills's statue was of pioneering importance, because such a large bronze casting had never been undertaken in the U.S. It was also a triumph of balance, since the weight of the work was supported only by the hind legs of Jackson's rearing horse.
References: *American Exponent*, Jan. 19, Feb. 2, 1856; *Bee*, May 5, 1851, June 16, July 13, Aug. 22, 1853, Jan. 17, 24, Dec. 27, 1855, Feb. 7, 1856; *Courier*, May 5, 1851, May 18, 1854, June 16, 1855, Jan. 6, 1856; *D. Delta*, July 19, 1855, Feb. 24, 1856; *D. Pic.*, Mar. 31, 1848, July 14, Aug. 23, 1853, Oct. 28, 31, 1855, Jan. 6, 1856, June 13, 1880, Jan. 19, 1883; *Appleton's CAB*; Craven, 166–74; *DAB*; Fielding, *Dictionary*; Groce and Wallace; W. O. Hart, 614–16; Jackson Monument Association.

MILLS, W.
Painter, active N.O. 1885.
Scenic artist who came to N.O. from NY to assemble a scenic painting for the North, Central, and South American Exposition (1885).
References: *T. Demo.*, Nov. 3, 1885.

MILNER, URIELLA SERENA
Born N.O. ca. Jan. 1866; died N.O. May 9, 1902.
Painter, active N.O. ca. 1892.
Exhibited: Tulane University (1892).
References: NOCD 1892–93, 1895; *D. Pic.*, Mar. 3, 1892, May 10–11, 1902; *T. Demo.*, May 10–11, 1902; N.O. Death Certificate (1902), 127:410, NOPL.

MILTMAN, G. W.
Painter, active N.O. ca. 1883.
Contemporary listings: scene painter, John Becker's concert saloon (ca. 1883).
References: *T. Demo.*, Apr. 24, 1883.

MILTON, C. M.
Lithographer, active N.O. 1888–89.
Contemporary listings: lithographer, T. FITZWILLIAM & CO. (1888–89).
References: NOCD 1888–89.

MINGEAU, FRANÇOIS
Engraver, active N.O. 1841; also stonecutter.
Contemporary listings: engraver, 148 St. Peter (1841).

References: NOCD 1841–42; Groce and Wallace.

MINTON, J.
Illustrator, active N.O. ca. 1888.
Name appeared on three illustrations in *New Orleans and the New South* (1888), a book about N.O. trade, landmarks, and organizations. The illustrations by Minton are: *The Customhouse*; *The Mint*; and *Tulane University*.
References: Morrison, *New Orleans*, 15, 41, 74.

MIRET, LEON A.
Born LA May 1873.
Painter, active N.O. 1900.
Contemporary listings: portrait painter (1900).
References: U.S. Census (1900), roll 573.

MITCHELL, _____
Cartoonist, active N.O. 1904.
Contemporary listings: cartoonist (1904).
From Memphis TN; he signed cartoons in *Harlequin* (1904).
References: *Harlequin*, June 16, 1904, 1, June 23, 1904, 5, Sept. 8, 1904, 8, Sept. 15, 1904, 1.

MODERSOHN, WILLIAM E.
Artist, active N.O. 1888; also carpenter.
Contemporary listings: artist, with FELIX OLLERT (1888).
References: NOCD 1888, 1891–94, 1896.

MOHRFELD, CHARLES CHRISTIAN
Born N.O. Sept. 15, 1868; died N.O. Apr. 12, 1944.
Lithographer, active N.O. 1889; primarily printer, pressman, also cabinetmaker.
Contemporary listings: lithographer, M. F. DUNN & BRO. (1889).
References: NOCD 1886, 1889–94, 1896–1905, 1909, 1912–15, 1917–29, 1931–33, 1935, 1938, 1940, 1942; *Item*, Apr. 13, 1944; Orleans Parish Registrar of Voters, NOPL.

MOIRE, THOMAS
Painter, active N.O. 1842.
Contemporary listings: portrait painter, 25 St. Charles (1842).
References: NOCD 1842; Groce and Wallace.

MOISE, C. H.
Painter, active N.O. ca. 1893.
Exhibited: Tulane University (1893).
Possibly Charles Henry Moise, born Charleston SC; died N.O. Mar. 5, 1898, and listed as an architect 1889–91, 1894–98.
References: NOCD 1889–91, 1894–98; *D. Pic.*, Feb. 14, 1893; *T. Demo.*, Mar. 6, 1898.

MOISE, JAMES CAMPBELL
Born Natchitoches LA Jan. 30, 1849; died N.O. Feb. 11, 1901.
Painter, active N.O. 1875–87; also draftsman.
Exhibited: Press Club (1875); George's coffee house (1875); ARTISTS' ASSOCIATION OF NEW ORLEANS (1886–87).
Portraitist in oil who was primarily a lawyer. He was Assistant Attorney General for the State of LA (1884–88) and was appointed Judge of the Orleans Parish Criminal Court (1892), a position which he held until his death. Paintings by Moise include portraits of Dr. Thomas G. Hunt, Col. F. C. Zacharie, and Lord Byron. Son of THEODORE SIDNEY MOISE.
References: NOCD 1870–76, 1885–1901; *Art and Letters* 1(Dec. 1887): 228; *D. Pic.*, June 2, 1875, Dec. 17, 29, 1887, Feb. 12, 14, 17, 1901; *D. States*, Nov. 5, 1886; *Item*, Sept. 30, 1925; *Repub.*, June 5, 1875; *States*, Feb. 16–17, 1901; *T. Demo.*, Feb. 12–14, 17, 1901; AANO, *Catalogue* (1886); *Biographical and Historical Memoirs of Louisiana*; Fortier, *Louisiana*, 3:305–7; Mount, 100–5; U.S. Census (1870), roll 519.

MOISE, THEODORE SIDNEY
Born Charleston SC Nov. 20, 1808; died Natchitoches LA July 2, 1885.
Painter, active N.O. 1841–84.
Contemporary listings: portrait painter, St. Charles, and with TREVOR THOMAS FOWLER (1842); portrait painter, Royal near Customhouse (1842–43); portrait painter, with JAMES HENRY BEARD and ROBERT BRAMMER (1843); portrait painter, Royal, and with Trevor Thomas Fowler, St. Charles near Canal (1844); artist, 51

Canal (1850–52); artist, Camp near Julia (1858–61); artist, 135 Esplanade (1868); portrait painter, 44 Carondelet (1869–71); artist (1869, 1878), portrait painter, 28 Carondelet (1873–77); artist, 28 Carondelet (1879–82); portrait painter (1880); artist, 45 Baronne (1883–84).
Exhibited: St. Charles Hotel (1843, 1872); 19 St. Charles (1851); Hall's store (1854); Grand State Fair (1870); Eyrich's store (1872); Grunewald's music store (1875); Press Club (1875); SEEBOLD's (1875, 1880).
Awarded: N.O. City Council, best portrayal of Andrew Jackson, with JACQUES AMANS (1844); Grand State Fair, best historical painting in oil, with VICTOR PIERSON (1868).
Memberships/positions: SOUTHERN ART UNION (1881).
One of the finest portrait and horse painters active in the South during Reconstruction. Moise first worked in Charleston SC in a cotton factor's office and painted portraits in oil as an amusement. He opened a studio in Charleston (1835) but in 1836 moved to Woodville MS. By 1841 he had moved to N.O. where he worked with a number of partners and painted throughout LA and nearby states. During 1845, he met ALFRED S. WAUGH in N.O. who described Moise as eccentric, ingenious, and a former partner of FORD. He spent four years working in Louisville and Frankfort KY, where he worked with Fowler and was one of the few southern artists to paint portraits of horses. He also worked for one year in NY. By 1850 he was painting in N.O. again and established a partnership with BENJAMIN FRANKLIN REINHART (1859–ca. 1861). During the Civil War, Moise joined the Confederate army, attaining the rank of major. Afterward, he resumed painting in N.O. and formed a partnership with PAUL POINCY. He painted portraits of John R. Grymes (1842), Henry Clay (1843), James Dick (1844), and Andrew Jackson (1844, with Jacques

Amans). He collaborated with Victor Pierson on a number of works, including *Life on the Metairie* (1868) and portraits of many prominent people. Father of JAMES CAMPBELL MOISE.

References: NOCD 1850–52, 1858–61, 1868–69, 1871, 1873–84; *Bee*, June 22, 1844, Nov. 16, 1881; *Bull.*, June 13, 20, Dec. 9, 1875; *Comm. Bull.*, Feb. 14, 1842, Feb. 10, 1843; *Courier*, June 20, July 28, Nov. 9, 1854; *D. Crescent*, Nov. 9, Dec. 27, 1854; *D. Delta*, June 20, 1854; *D. Pic.*, Mar. 27, 1842, Nov. 29, 1842–July 9, 1843 (advs.), Jan. 31, Apr. 6, 1843, Nov. 20, 1844, Mar. 26, Apr. 10, 1851, June 20, Nov. 9, 1854, Jan. 9, 11, Aug. 9, 1868, Feb. 21, 1869, Apr. 27, Aug. 25, 1870, Apr. 11, June 13, 29, Dec. 9, 1875, July 3, 4, 5, 1885; *D. States*, July 3, 1885; *D. Tropic*, Feb. 7, 1844; *Demo.*, Oct. 17, 1880, May 12, 1881; *Repub.*, Apr. 5, 16, 1872, June 11, 1875; *T. Demo.*, July 5, 1885; Bénézit; Boyd, 200; Fielding, *Dictionary*; Glenk, 47, 59, 69, 77, 215, 269; Groce and Wallace; Information courtesy George E. Jordan; LSM, *Biennial Report for 1920–21*, 28, 40, 61, 86, 89; Mechanics' and Agricultural Fair Asso., *Report* (1868):42; Moise, 25; "Theodore S. Moise," Scrapbook 100, LSM; U.S. Census (1870), roll 519, (1880), roll 458.

MOLINARY, ANDRES
Born Gibraltar Nov. 2, 1847; died N.O. Sept. 11, 1915.
Painter, art teacher, restorer, active N.O. 1872–1915; also photographer.
Studied: with Valles and Alvarvery, San Lucas Academy, Rome; Fine Art Academy, Seville, Spain; in East Africa and Morocco.
Contemporary listings: artist, 82 Camp (1872–73); artist, 113 Canal (1879); artist, 3 Carondelet (1880–82); art teacher (1880); professor of painting, SOUTHERN ART UNION (1881–82); artist, 43 Baronne (1885–87, 1890–94); painting instructor, ARTISTS' ASSOCIATION OF NEW ORLEANS (1886–87, 1890–91); artist

(1888–89); artist, 206 Baronne (1897–99, 1904–15); portrait painter, 206 Baronne (1898, 1900–1903).
Exhibited: WAGENER's (1880, 1883, 1885); Southern Art Union (1881); World's Industrial and Cotton Centennial Exposition (1884–85); SEEBOLD's (1884, 1886); Artists' Association of New Orleans (1886–87, 1890–92, 1894, 1901); DELGADO MUSEUM OF ART, retrospective exhibit of portraits (1915).
Memberships/positions: Southern Art Union (1880–82); Artists' Association of New Orleans, v. pres. (1886), pres. (1890); ART ASSOCIATION OF NEW ORLEANS, executive committee (1904–1905); Delgado, art committee (1911–15).
Painter who came to N.O. (1872) where his uncle, John Brunasso, was a partner in the importing firm of Fatjo and Brunasso. After traveling to Mexico and Central America, Molinary settled permanently in N.O. (1876). His family wanted him to be a civil engineer, but instead he set up an art studio with the help of Brunasso who was impressed with his work. Molinary painted portraits of many prominent people in N.O. and other southern cities, as well as landscapes and genre scenes which had been his interest before coming to N.O. He was a leading figure in the N.O. art community, and his studio was a favorite gathering place for local artists. He organized and founded several organizations including the CUP AND SAUCER CLUB, the Southern Art Union, and the Artists' Association of New Orleans. Husband of MARIE MADELEINE SEEBOLD.
References: NOCD 1871–77, 1879–82, 1885–94, 1897–1915; NOBD 1898; *Art and Letters* 1(Dec. 1887): 227; *Bee*, May 4, 27, 1880, May 4, 1881, Sept. 27, 1885; *Current Topics*, Nov. 1890, 23, Jan. 1891, 24, Jan. 1892, 22, 24, Jan. 1893, 11; *D. City Item*, Dec. 17, 1891; *D. News*, Apr. 16, 1907; *D. Pic.*, Mar. 24, May 26, 1881, Jan. 12, Feb. 6, 17, 1882, Nov. 30, 1884, July 26, 1885, Nov.

6–7, 1886, May 7, Oct. 2, Dec. 17, 29, 1887, Nov. 13, Dec. 17, 1890, May 22, Dec. 17, 1891, Dec. 13–14, 1892; *D. States*, Apr. 17, June 12, Aug. 11, 1880, May 26, June 10, 1881, Jan. 23, 1882, Apr. 13, 1884, Oct. 29, Nov. 5, 1886, Mar 31, 1889, Nov. 13, Dec. 17, 1890; *Demo.*, May 27, 1880, May 12, June 8, July 5–6, 1881; *Down in Dixie*, July 15, 1896, 10, Aug. 1, 1896, 6; *Harlequin*, Oct. 25, 1899, 9, Dec. 20, 1899, 1, 10, Nov. 5, 1903, 9; *T. Demo.*, July 17, 1883, Jan. 3, 1886, Nov. 13, Dec. 17, 1890, Dec. 14, 1894; *T. Pic.*, Sept. 12–13, 1915; *Town Talk*, date obliterated, TU, 39, July 1904, 25; AANO, *Catalogue* (1886, 1890, 1891, 1897, 1899, 1901, 1902); Anglo–American Art Museum, *Sail and Steam*, nos. 23–24; Art Asso., *Catalogue* (1904, 1905, 1907); Bénézit; Delgado, *Bulletin* 1(Apr. 1927):4; Delgado, *Catalogue of Paintings, Sculpture*, 21, 56; Delgado, *Catalogue of Paintings by Andres Molinary*; French Opera Libretto and Commercial Guide, 1890–91; Glenk, 46–47, 51, 57, 77; Mount, 134–36; Reeves, 125, 127, 131–32; Seebold, 1:26–29, U.S. Census (1880), roll 458; WICCE, *Catalogue* 36; WPA, "Lives."

MOLINARY, MARIE SEEBOLD. *See* SEEBOLD, MARIE MADELEINE

MONALUSUN, PETER
Art teacher, active N.O. 1808.
Contemporary listings: teacher of drawing (1808).
References: *Courier*, Nov. 7, 1808.

MONCHET, F. L.
Born France ca. 1782.
Painter, active N.O. 1821.
Miniature painter who arrived in N.O. from Bordeaux, France on his way to Opelousas LA (1821).
References: Rieder, *New Orleans Ship Lists*, 1:69.

MONDELLI, ANTOINE
Born Italy ca. 1799.
Painter, art teacher, designer, active N.O. 1821–54; also architect, ornamental and sign painter, decorator, gilder, glazier, art store proprietor.

Contemporary listings: painter, teacher of drawing, 21 Dumaine (1821); drawing master, scene painter, St. Charles Theatre (1822); scene painter, New American Theatre, and painter and designer, 169 Bourbon (1823); scene painter and designer, American Theatre (1824, 1830); scene painter, American Theatre, and teacher of painting and designing (1826); painter and designer, 148 Toulouse and 73 Camp (1827); scene painter, American Theatre (1828–29, 1831–32); scene painter, Camp St. Theatre (1829–30); MONDELLI & MARTELLI (1832); scenographer, 183 Chartres (1834–35); painter, 58 Camp (1835); principal artist, St. Charles Theatre (1836); scenograph painter, 58 Camp (1837); scenographer, 52 Camp (1841); scenic painter, with JOSEPH A. FOSTER, Poydras Street Theatre (1842); fanciful painter (1843); painter with LOUIS DOMINIQUE GRANDJEAN DEVELLE, Varieties Theatre (1844); scenographer, 69 Canal (1845); scenographic painter, 76 Gravier (1846); scenic artist, Olympic Theatre (1848); scenic artist, American Theatre (1848–49); scene painter, Placide Varieties (1849–50); artist, 252 St. Philip (1850–51); artist, Toulouse (1852); scenic painter, St. Charles Theatre (1852–53); artist, Toulouse cor. Bourbon (1853–54).
Chiefly a scene painter, Mondelli created scenic works in Cincinnati OH, Nashville TN, and Mobile AL, as well as in N.O. He was the architect for the St. Charles Theatre (1835), and with his partner John Reynolds, designed the U.S. Marine Hospital (1834) and made a plan for the LA State Capitol (1847) which was never executed. With DOMINIQUE CANOVA he decorated the ceiling of the bishop's church, now Our Lady of Victory (1846). Mondelli designed the cenotaph honoring Zachary Taylor in the Place d'Armes (now Jackson Square) (1847) and the one for the memorial to Henry Clay, Daniel Webster, and John C. Calhoun in Lafayette Square (1852). He

was the first teacher of LEON D. PO-MAREDE, and he assisted his pupil in painting the ceiling of St. Patrick's Church (1841). Mondelli was Pomarede's father–in–law, and they also worked together in St. Louis MO. References: NOCD 1822–24, 1827, 1830, 1832, 1834–35, 1837–38, 1841–44, 1846, 1850–57; *Advertiser*, June 20, 1826, May 14–15, 1830, May 7, 1831, Dec. 29, 1832, Feb. 26, 1834–June 7, 1835 (advs.); *Argus*, May 22, 1826; *Bee*, May 7, 1831, Oct. 30, 1834, Mar. 10, 1835, May 14, 1836; *Comm. Bull.*, Jan. 26, 1843; *Courier*, Oct. 29, 1821, May 31, 1824–June 2, 1824 (advs.), Feb. 15, 1826, Dec. 17, 1828, Apr. 2–3, 6, 9, May 19, Dec. 15, 1829, Mar. 24, May 15, 1830, May 7, 1831, May 19, 1832, Aug. 5, Oct. 1, 1835, Aug. 5–Oct. 1, 1835 (advs.), Apr. 23, 1838, May 4, 1841, Sept. 8, Dec. 6, 1842, Jan. 4, 1843, June 21, Nov. 20, 1844, June 27, 1845, Aug. 1, 1849, Feb. 11, 1850, Oct. 29, 1852, May 29, 1853; *D. Crescent*, Nov. 9, 1848, Dec. 7, 1849, July 1–2, 1850; *D. Delta*, Apr. 16, Dec. 4, 1847, Aug. 29, 1848–Oct. 5, 1848 (advs.), Sept. 28, 1848, July 24, 1849, Sept. 23, Oct. 7, 1851, Apr. 14, 1852; *D. Pic.*, Dec. 15, 1839, May 12, June 26, 1841, Mar. 15, 1842, Feb. 18, 1844–Mar. 31, 1844 (advs.), July 2–3, 9, 1845, Nov. 27, 1849, Oct. 14, 1850, Nov. 12, 1853, May 17, 1897; *Gazette*, Oct. 22, 1822, Jan. 3, Dec. 27, 1823, Jan 7, 1824; *Mercantile Advertiser*, Apr. 5, May 6, Dec. 21, 1831; *Revue Louisianaise* 1(Aug. 2, 1846): 587, 1(Aug. 16, 1846): 514; *T. Demo.*, Oct. 14, 1894; *True Amer.*, May 2, 1836–Oct. 31, 1836 (advs.); May 12, June 4, 1836; *Wkly. Delta*, Dec. 29, 1845, Jan. 8, 21–22, Nov. 25, 1849, Dec. 12, 1852; Coad and Mims, 135; Coulon MS, Scrapbook 100, LSM; Friends of the Cabildo, *N.O. Architecture*, 2:228; Groce and Wallace; *History of the Proceedings*, 16, 30; Kendall, *Golden Age*, 42, 53–54, 59, 76, 116, 121, 152; Magnaghi, 55–56; Ludlow, 265–66, 268, 272–73, 289, 291; McDermott, *Lost*

Panoramas, 9–10, 177; Norman, 125–26; U.S. Census (1850), roll 235.

MONDELLI, J. E.
Painter, active N.O. ca. 1862.
His oil portrait of Confederate Gen. "Stonewall" Jackson was confiscated by police as contraband (Dec. 1862).
References: *Bee*, Dec. 30, 1862.

MONDELLI & MARTELLI
Painters, active N.O. 1832; also ornamental and sign painters; ANTOINE MONDELLI, _____ Martelli, partners.
Contemporary listings: fresco painters, 183 Chartres (1832).
References: *Advertiser*, Dec. 29, 1832.

MONETTE, ARTHUR
Born LA ca. 1882.
Lithographer, active N.O. 1909–10; also printer.
Contemporary listings: lithographer (1909); lithographer, WALLE & CO. (1910).
References: NOCD 1909–14, 1917; U.S. Census (1910), roll 520.

MONSSEAUX, PAUL H.
Born France ca. 1808–1809; died N.O. Mar. 28, 1874.
Sculptor, active N.O. 1837–54; also marble cutter.
Contemporary listings: sculptor, Rampart near Conti (1837); sculptor, 190 St. Louis (1838); marble sculptor, 115 Rampart (1843); marble sculptor, cor. St. Louis and Franklin (1846); marble sculptor, St. Louis betw. Marais and Franklin (1850); marble sculptor, cor. St. Louis and Franklin and cor. St. Louis and Robertson (1851); marble sculptor, cor. St. Louis and Robertson (1852–53); marble sculptor, St. Louis cor. Robertson (1854).
References: NOCD 1837–38, 1841–43, 1846, 1849–61, 1866–74; *Bee*, Mar. 29, 1874; *Courier*, May 2, 1838. Groce and Wallace; Henry and Gerodias, 450; THNOC Cemetery Survey; U.S. Census (1850), roll 235, (1860), roll 419, (1870), roll 522.

MONTGOMERY, LOUIS M.
Painter, active N.O. ca. 1861–62.
While with the Washington Artillery of N.O., he painted 180 watercolor sketches of military subjects.
References: Coulter, 490–91.

MONTGOMERY, ROBERT B.

Born Ireland ca. 1832; died N.O. Jan. 30, 1882.

Sketch artist, active N.O. 1866–77.

Exhibited: WAGENER's (1866).

Awarded: Grand State Fair, diploma for best drawing with pen (1867); Grand State Fair, bronze medal for best drawing with pen (1868); Grand State Fair, bronze medal for best drawing with pen (1869); Grand State Fair, honorable mention for best drawing with a pen, certificate for best specimen of illuminated fancy lettering and drawing (1870). Primarily an instructor of penmanship at various schools (1867–82), including Soulé's Commercial College and Dolbear's Commercial College. Montgomery drew a number of fine pen–and–ink portraits that resembled steel engravings.

References: NOCD 1866–78, 1880–82; *Bee*, Jan. 17, 1866, July 21, 1867; *D. Pic.*, Jan. 9, 19, 1868, Apr. 13, Dec. 5, 1869, Oct. 21, 1877, Jan. 31, Feb. 5, 1882; *D. States*, May 11, 1881, LSM, *Biennial Report for 1922–23*, 30; Mechanics' and Agricultural Fair Asso., *Report* (1867):28, (1868):42, (1869):68, (1870):61; N.O. Death Certificate (1882), 80:214, NOPL.

MONTGOMERY, VIRGINIA T.

Born Mobile AL.

Painter, active N.O. 1887–1932.

Studied: N.Y.C.

Contemporary listings: artist, 225 Delachaise (1887); miniature painter (1894); artist (1897–98, 1910, 1913–18); artist, 1724 Delachaise (1901–1903, 1906).

Exhibited: ARTISTS' ASSOCIATION OF NEW ORLEANS (1887, 1889, 1890–92); Tulane University (1893).

Winner of the design competition for the Confederate monument in San Antonio TX (ca. 1898); listed in N.O. as an artist (1919–21, 1923–28, 1930, 1932).

References: NOCD 1887, 1889, 1897–98, 1901–1903, 1906, 1910, 1913–33, 1935, 1938, 1940; *Current Topics*, Jan. 1891, 24; Jan. 1892, 24; Jan. 1893, 10; *D. Pic.*, Dec. 17,

29, 1887, Dec. 17, 1889, Nov. 13, Dec. 17, 1890, Dec. 17, 1891, Dec. 13, 1892, Feb. 14, 1893, Sept. 9, 1894, Feb. 16, 1901; *D. States*, Jan. 23, 1898; *T. Demo.*, Nov. 13, 1890, Dec. 13, 1892, Dec. 10, 1901; *T. Pic.*, May 15, 1927; AANO, *Catalogue* (1890, 1891).

MONTULE, EDOUARD DE

Born LeMans, France 1790s.

Sketch artist, active N.O. 1817.

Awarded: Legion of Honor, France.

French traveler and writer. Montulé arrived in N.Y.C. in Nov. 1816, visiting there and Philadelphia. He sailed to the West Indies and then to N.O. During his stay in the city (Apr.–May 1817), he visited French compatriots and refugees and made excursions where he observed the inhabitants, climate, crops, Indians, and swamp life. He took a steamboat up the Mississippi River to Louisville KY and then traveled overland by stage and horseback to N.Y.C. where, on Oct. 16, 1817, he took ship for France. In 1821 his account of his American journey, as well as others, was published in two volumes as *Voyage en Amérique, en Italie, en Sicile et en Egypt, pendant les années, 1816, 1817, 1818 et 1819*. Two letters in the book, dated Apr. 25 and May 16, 1817, described N.O. and its surroundings. The book was illustrated with lithographs of Montulé's sketches, including a view of St. Louis Cathedral, one of the earliest of a N.O. scene.

References: Thomas Clark, 2:47–48; Groce and Wallace; Montulé, 1821 ed.; Montulé, 1951 ed., 9–10, 13, 70–88.

MOODY, MISS S. N.

Art teacher, active N.O. 1890–92.

Contemporary listings: teacher of drawing, Pinac Institute (1890); teacher of drawing and painting, Pinac Institute (1892).

References: *D. City Item*, June 21, 1892; *D. Pic.*, June 28, 1890; *T. Demo.*, June 28, 1890.

MOORE, FRANK B.

Born Saux Center MN Mar. 18, 1870; died Covington LA Jan. 21, 1957.

Painter, active N.O. 1896; primarily photographer.
Contemporary listings: portrait painter, 1008 Canal (1896).
References: NOCD 1896–1931, 1933, 1935, 1938, 1940, 1942, 1945–47, 1949, 1952–56, 1958; *States*, Jan. 22–23, 1957; *T. Pic.*, Jan. 22–23, 1957; Orleans Parish Registrar of Voters, NOPL.

MOORE, MRS. FRANK B.
Artist, active N.O. 1900.
Contemporary listings: artist, 147 Baronne (1900).
References: NOCD 1900.

MOORE, GEORGE
Engraver, active N.O. 1871–72.
Contemporary listings: engraver, with E. A. Tyler silversmith (1871); engraver (1872).
References: NOCD 1871–72.

MOORE, GEORGE
Sketch artist, active N.O. 1872.
Illustrator who came to N.O. to sketch the Colored National Convention for *Leslie's* (1872).
References: *Repub.*, Apr. 11, 1872.

MOORE, JOSEPH THOITS
Born North Yarmouth ME Mar. 8, 1796; died Montgomery AL Oct. 17, 1854.
Painter, active N.O. 1837.
Contemporary listings: portrait painter, 9 Royal (1837).
References: NOCD 1837; *Comm. Bull.*, Mar. 2, 1837; *Pic.*, Mar. 2, 1837; Groce and Wallace.

MOORE, LOUISE A. COOK (Mrs.
Frederick F. Moore)
Born N.O. Feb. 1854; died N.O. Mar. 5, 1941.
Painter, art teacher, colorer, active N.O. 1884–1905.
Studied: Athens GA; with WILLIAM BUCK; with FRANCISCO CASANOVA.
Contemporary listings: artist (1884, 1900, 1905); artist, art teacher, miniature portrait painter, china painter, photography painter, Royal (1894); art school, 2712 Royal (1897); portrait painter, 2712 Royal (1898).
Worked in pastels; painted views of N.O. on china and portrait miniatures.

References: NOCD 1875–77, 1881, 1884–86, 1888, 1890, 1894, 1896–98, 1904–1905; NOBD 1898; *D. Pic.*, Sept. 9, 16, 1894; *T. Demo.*, Apr. 22, 1894; *T. Pic.*, Mar. 7, 1941; U.S. Census (1900), roll 573.

MOORE, WILLIAM A.
Engraver, active N.O. 1885.
Contemporary listings: engraver, 414 S. Rampart (1885).
References: NOCD 1885.

MOREL, _____
Painter, active N.O. 1834–35.
Contemporary listings: portrait painter, cor. Dumaine and Royal (1834–35).
References: NOCD 1834–35; Groce and Wallace.

MOREL, MARY SYDNOR (Mrs. Octave J.
Morel)
Died N.O. Mar. 7, 1924.
Painter, active N.O. 1889–1903.
Contemporary listings: portrait painter (1902–1903).
Exhibited: Cotton Palace (1889); Tulane University (1892).
Mother of MAY SYDNOR MOREL.
References: *D. Pic.*, Mar. 3, 1892; *D. States*, Jan. 23, 1898; *Item*, June 3, 1903; *T. Demo.*, Feb. 19, 1889, Mar. 12, 1902; *T. Pic.*, Dec. 16, 1920, Mar. 8–9, 1924; Glenk, 77.

MOREL, MAY SYDNOR
Died N.O. Dec. 15, 1920.
Art craftsman, designer, painter; active N.O. 1911–17; also jeweler.
Studied: NEWCOMB COLLEGE (1905–17).
Exhibited: ART ASSOCIATION OF NEW ORLEANS (1911, 1917); Panama–Pacific International Exhibition, San Francisco (1915).
Awarded: Newcomb College, Home Study Prize (1908); Neill Medal (1909).
Listed as art craftsman (1912–16) and best known for her decorations of poems and Christmas cards, usually with children as subjects. She also created handmade jewelry, including a set of carnival jewels, soon after her graduation (ca. 1908–10). Confined to her home because of ill health, she was the eldest daughter of MARY SYDNOR MOREL.

References: *Item*, Dec. 16, 1920; *T. Pic.*, Dec. 16, 1920; Art Asso., *Catalogue* (1911, 1917); Ormond and Irvine, 164; Poesch, *Newcomb Pottery*, 102.

MORES, S.
Painter, active N.O. 1849–50.
Contemporary listings: portrait painter, 220 Royal (1849–50).
References: NOCD 1849–50; Groce and Wallace; William Young.

MORET, JEAN BAPTISTE
Born Carouge, Savoie, France ca. 1825; died N.O. July 16, 1876.
Lithographer, active N.O. 1868; also photographer.
Contemporary listings: lithographer (1868).
References: NOCD 1857–61, 1866–68, 1870–77; *D. Pic.*, July 23, 1876.

MORGAN, MR. ____
Painter, active N.O. 1864.
N.Y.C. artist who painted the panels of the dome of the Academy of Music in N.O. (1864).
References: *New York Clipper*, Sept. 24, 1864.

MORLAND, ____
Painter, active N.O. ca. 1881.
Exhibited: SOUTHERN ART UNION (1881).
References: *D. Pic.*, May 26, 1881.

MOROSCO, F.
Painter, active N.O. 1888.
Painted scenery for the Tivoli Theatre (1888).
References: *Lantern*, Jan. 14, 1888.

MORRIS, CHARLES
Engraver, active N.O. 1889.
Contemporary listings: engraver (1889).
References: NOCD 1888–89.

MORRIS, ELLEN HALE (Mrs. Eugene Morris).
Born ME ca. 1834; died N.O. Nov. 29, 1912.
Artist, active N.O. ca. 1887–88.
Studied: with WILLIAM JENNINGS WARRINGTON (1887).
Exhibited: William Jennings Warrington's (1887).
Memberships/positions: TULANE DECORATIVE ART LEAGUE FOR WOMEN (1888).

Moved to N.O. ca. 1862 and later exhibited needlework.
References: NOCD 1880–83, 1885, 1887–92, 1894–1902, 1904–1907, 1909; *D. Pic.*, Feb. 12, 1888, Nov. 30, Dec. 1, 1912; *T. Demo.*, Oct. 18, 1887.

MORSE, ALICE BEAUREGARD. *See* BEAUREGARD, ALICE TOUTANT

MORTON, EDWIN W.
Engraver, active N.O. 1898–1901.
Contemporary listings: engraver, Boone & Bruguière (1898–99); engraver, NEW ORLEANS STENCIL WORKS (1900–1901).
References: NOCD 1898–1901.

MORTON, WILLIAM M.
Born Scotland ca. 1877.
Engraver, active N.O. 1908–15.
Contemporary listings: photo–engraver (1908, 1910); engraver (1909); photo–engraver, newspapers (1910); foreman, GRELLE-EGERTON ENGRAVING CO. (1911–14); photo–engraver, Grelle–Egerton Engraving Co. (1915).
Immigrated to the U.S. in 1892.
References: NOCD 1908–15; U.S. Census (1910), roll 520.

MORVAN, HENRY
Painter, active N.O. 1897–1902; primarily photographer.
Contemporary listings: portrait painter, 131 S. Robertson (1897–98). Advertised enlargements in oil, watercolor, and crayon (1902).
References: NOCD 1890, 1894–1923; NOBD 1898; *D. States*, Feb. 10, 1902.

B. MOSES & CO.
Painters, active N.O. 1858–59; BERNARD MOSES, owner.
Contemporary listings: portrait painter, 46 Camp (1858–59).
References: NOCD 1858–59.

B. & G. MOSES
Painters, colorers, active N.O. 1858–69; primarily photographers; BERNARD MOSES, GUSTAVE MOSES, partners.
Contemporary listings: pictures copied in photograph and painted in oil, 46 Camp (1858).
Exhibited: Grand State Fair, best composition in oil, best colored photographs in watercolors (1869).

References: NOCD 1858–61, 1867–78, 1883–84; *D. Pic.*, Jan. 23, 1868, Apr. 11, 24, 1869; Groce and Wallace.

MOSES, BERNARD
Born Bavaria Nov. 22, 1832; died N.O. Sept. 24, 1899.
Painter, colorer, sketch artist, active N.O. 1858–98; primarily photographer, also jeweler.
Studied: Europe.
Contemporary listings: B. MOSES & CO. (1858–59); B. & G. MOSES (1858, 1869); pictures on porcelain, cor. Camp and Canal (1865); portrait painter, with S. Moses (1882); portrait painter, with GUSTAVE MOSES (1885); portrait painter, 829 Canal (1898).
Exhibited: ARTISTS' ASSOCIATION OF NEW ORLEANS (1886).
Studied portrait painting in Europe before coming to N.O. (ca. 1845–47). Although a photographer by trade, he produced a number of portraits, sketched or in oil, including a posthumous one in crayon of Paul Morphy, the famous N.O. chess player (1898). He also enlarged photo–portraits and painted them in oils (1886). He was in the photographic business with his father, Samuel Moses (1882), a pioneer N.O. photographer, and brother Gustave Moses (1858–81, 1883–84).
References: NOCD 1858–59, 1866–99; *Bee*, Aug. 15, 1865; *D. Pic.*, Apr. 11, 1869, July 26, 1885, Nov. 6, 1886, Mar. 2, 1898, Sept. 24, Oct. 1, 1899; *D. States*, Dec. 30, 1886, Sept. 25, 1899; *T. Demo*, Sept. 24, 1899; Glenk, 77; LSM, *Biennial Report for 1920–21*, 40; LSM, *Biennial Report for 1922–23*, 68; LSM, *Biennial Report for 1924–25*, 27, 48; Smith and Tucker, 165; U.S. Census (1850), roll 235, (1870), roll 522.

MOSES, GUSTAVE
Born Speyer, Bavaria July 4, 1836; died Oct. 23, 1915.
Painter, active N.O. 1858–93; primarily photographer.
Contemporary listings: B. & G. MOSES (1858–59); oil and crayon portraits, 121 Canal (1893).

Moses arrived in N.O. ca. 1845–47. He learned the art of photography from his father, Samuel Moses, one of the pioneer N.O. photographers. Gustave Moses remained a professional photographer throughout his life and was in partnership with his brother BERNARD MOSES (1858–81, 1883–84). He later went into partnership with his son WILLIAM H. MOSES as G. Moses & Son Photographic Studio and Gallery (1896–1915). Also father of HARRY LEON MOSES.
References: NOCD 1858–61, 1866–79, 1882–1916; *Current Topics*, Aug. 1894, 435, Nov. 1891, 27; *D. Orleanian*, Dec. 23, 1854; *D. Pic*, Aug. 26–Sept. 2, 1864 (advs.); *New Delta*, Apr. 12, 1891; *Times*, June 6, 1866; *T. Pic.*, Oct. 24–25, 1915; Moses; Myers, 114; Smith and Tucker, 165–66; U.S. Census (1850), roll 235, (1860), roll 418, (1910), roll 521.

MOSES, HARRY LEON
Born N.O. Mar. 28, 1877; died N.O. Feb. 19, 1935.
Artist, active N.O. 1901–10; primarily decorator, also photographer.
Contemporary listings: pyrographer (1901); artist–decorator (1910).
Exhibited: ARTISTS' ASSOCIATION OF NEW ORLEANS (1901).
Memberships/positions: NEW ORLEANS ART LEAGUE (1908).
The pyrography process involved burning designs in wood, and Moses executed detailed works in this medium, such as portraits, including a nearly life–size bust of his father. *Cf.* MOSES, L.
References: NOCD 1896–1902, 1906–33; *D. Pic.*, Dec. 17, 1891, June 28, 1908; *T. Demo.*, Dec. 29, 1901; *T. Pic.*, Feb. 20–21, 1935; AANO, *Catalogue* (1891, 1901); U.S. Census (1910), roll 521; *Who's Who in Louisiana and Mississippi.*

MOSES, L.
Painter, active N.O. ca. 1890–97.
Exhibited: ARTISTS' ASSOCIATION OF NEW ORLEANS (1890–91).
Memberships/positions: Artists' Association of New Orleans (1890, 1897).
Cf. MOSES, HARRY LEON.

References: *Current Topics*, Jan. 1891, 24, Jan. 1892, 24; *D. Pic.*, Nov. 13, 1890, Dec. 17, 1890, Dec. 17, 1891; *D. States*, Dec. 17, 1890; AANO, *Catalogue* (1890, 1891, 1897).

MOSES, WILLIAM H.
Born N.O. ca. 1871; died N.O. Sept. 24, 1923.
Painter, active N.O. 1896; primarily photographer, also architect, draftsman.
Contemporary listings: painter (1896).
Memberships/positions: ARTISTS' ASSOCIATION OF NEW ORLEANS (1896–97).
Son of GUSTAVE MOSES; brother of HARRY LEON MOSES.
References: NOCD 1887, 1890–14, 1917–23; *T. Pic.*, Sept. 25–26, 1923; AANO, *Catalogue* (1897); Moses; Mount, 178; U.S. Census (1910), roll 521.

MOSKAU, AUGUST EDWARD
Born LA ca. 1885; died after 1953.
Engraver, active N.O. 1910–17.
Contemporary listings: engraver (1910, 1913); photo–engraver, PANAMA PHOTO-ENGRAVING CO. (1914, 1916–17); photo–engraver (1915).
Listed with Panama Photo–Engraving Co. as pres.–mgr. (1931–33, 1935), and as pres. (1938, 1940, 1945–46); also listed with the company in 1942, 1947, 1949, 1952–53.
References: NOCD 1913–33, 1935, 1938, 1940, 1942, 1945–47, 1949, 1952–55; *T. Pic.*, Aug. 10, 1948; U.S. Census (1910), roll 520.

MOSS, ALICE E.
Born N.O. ca. 1854.
Sketch artist, active N.O. 1867–68.
Awarded: Grand State Fair, best drawing with pen (1867), best pen–and–ink sketch (1868).
Sister of ELLA A. MOSS.
References: *D. Pic.*, Jan. 10, 1868; Mechanics' and Agricultural Fair Asso., *Report* (1867):28, (1868):41.

MOSS, ELLA A.
Born N.O. 1844.
Sketch artist, painter, active N.O. 1867–68.

Studied: Europe; with Sohn, Dusseldorf, Germany.
Exhibited: C. H. Zimmerman's store (1867); National Academy of Design, N.Y.C. (1878).
Awarded: Grand State Fair, best crayon drawing (1867), best portrait in oil, and best pastel painting (1868).
Exhibited portraits of Andrew Jackson and Robert E. Lee (1867). She had moved to NY and opened a studio by 1877. Sister of ALICE E. MOSS.
References: *D. Pic.*, Jan. 10, 19, 1868; *Times*, Feb. 3, 1867; Bénézit; Fielding, *Dictionary*; Mechanics' and Agricultural Fair Asso., *Report* (1867):27, (1868):42.

MOTT, ELIZABETH
Sketch artist, painter, active N.O. ca. 1881–96.
Studied: with HENRIETTE WINANT, SOUTHERN ART UNION (1883); with Charles Lazarre, Delachaise, and Julian Dapres, Paris (ca. 1890–96).
Contemporary listings: artist, 17 Carondelet (1889).
Exhibited: Southern Art Union (1881); ARTISTS' ASSOCIATION OF NEW ORLEANS (1896).
Awarded: Southern Art Union, first prize for sketch from life, first prize for oil painting (1883).
Memberships/positions: Southern Art Union (1883); Artists' Association of New Orleans (1896); New York Art League.
Shared a studio with JENNIE WILDE (1889). She studied art in Europe in the 1890s and, on her return (ca. 1896), she was offered a teaching position at an institution near N.Y.C. Daughter of Robert Mott who was the first president of the Southern Art Union.
References: NOCD 1889; *D. Pic.*, May 26, 1881, May 8, 1883; *Down in Dixie*, July 5, 1896, 10; *T. Demo.*, May 8, 1883; AANO, *Catalogue* (1896); Mount, 136, 186.

MUGNIER, ANDRE
Born N.O. Mar. 1875; died N.O. Aug. 7, 1920.
Engraver, etcher, active N.O. 1893–1920; also photographer.

Contemporary listings: etcher, PHOTO–ELECTRIC–ENGRAVING CO. (1893); engraver (1896, 1900, 1907, 1909, 1911, 1916–18); engraver, PHOTO–ENGRAVING CO. (1903, 1905); photo–engraver, NEW ORLEANS ENGRAVING AND ELECTROTYPE CO. LTD. (1908, 1910, 1912–14).
Engraver for the N.O. Times–Democrat (ca. 1896–1907). Half–brother of GEORGE FRANÇOIS MUGNIER.
References: NOCD 1893–94, 1896–99, 1901–18, 1920; T. Pic., Aug. 8, 1920; Friends of the Cabildo, Mugnier; U.S. Census (1900), roll 573, (1910), roll 524.

MUGNIER, GEORGE FRANÇOIS
Born Geneva, Switzerland Jan. 1, 1857; died N.O. Apr. 12, 1938.
Engraver, commercial artist, active N.O. 1889–1923; primarily photographer, also watchmaker.
Contemporary listings: crayon artist, and artist, Exchange Place near Canal (1889); PHOTO–ELECTRIC–ENGRAVING CO. (1894); mgr., ELECTRIC ENGRAVING CO. (1895–1900); foreman, photo–engraving department Times–Democrat (1901–10); engraver (1911).
Trained as a watchmaker by his father, Jules, Mugnier was in N.O. by 1868. He abandoned this trade to open a photographic studio (1884–88). As a photographer, Mugnier recorded a vast array of subjects including views around the city and its neighborhoods, the surrounding countryside, and the sugar plantations of the lower Mississippi River. He published and sold views of the 1884 World's Industrial and Cotton Centennial Exposition held in N.O., as well as a series of stereographic cards of local subjects. Although Mugnier held many jobs throughout his life, he always continued to photograph in his spare time. Half–brother of ANDRE MUGNIER.
References: NOCD 1874, 1876–79, 1884–1923, 1930; Current Topics, Nov. 1891, 22; D. States, Mar. 9, 1889; T. Demo., Mar. 9, 1889; T. Pic., Apr. 13, 1938; Friends of the Cabildo, Mugnier; Kemp and King, 1–

5; Orleans Parish Registrar of Voters, NOPL; Washington Artillery Souvenir, 78.

MUGNIER, MARY C.
Born LA ca. 1880.
Painter, active N.O. 1907–21.
Contemporary listings: china painting, 527 Canal (1907); Keramic Studio (1908–10); artist (1912, 1917); art studio (1914); china painting (1910, 1916).
Listed as china painter (1921).
References: NOCD 1907–10, 1912–14, 1916–18, 1920–21, 1925; U.S. Census (1910), roll 523.

MULLANE, MICHAEL
Engraver, active N.O. 1877.
Contemporary listings: engraver, 182 Poydras (1877).
References: NOCD 1877.

MULLER, ADAM
Born N.O. Nov. 12, 1855; died N.O. Feb. 26, 1907.
Engraver, active N.O. 1892.
Contemporary listings: engraver (1892).
References: NOCD 1892–96, 1898–99, 1902–1903, 1905–1907; D. Pic., Feb. 27–28, Mar. 3, 1907.

MÜLLER, FRANZ
Born Hesse–Darmstadt ca. 1837; died N.O. Aug. 14, 1858.
Engraver, active N.O. 1858.
Formerly of Havana, Cuba, Müller died of yellow fever after a three–month residence in N.O.
References: Louisiana Charity Hospital, Death Records, NOPL.

MULQUEENY, MARY A.
Born LA ca. 1882.
Artist, active N.O. 1910.
Contemporary listings: artist (1910).
References: NOCD 1909–10, 1912; U.S. Census (1910), roll 521.

MULVEY, JOSEPH T.
Illustrator, active N.O. 1892.
His name appeared on a cover illustration of the Head Light (1892), for which he was listed as editor and proprietor (1890–95). Also listed as editor of the Lantern (1887–89).
References: NOCD 1876–81, 1884–85, 1887–95; Head Light, Mar. 19, 1892, cover, June 18, 1892, cover.

MURPHY, JOSEPH P.
Born Ireland ca. 1840.
Engraver, active N.O. 1867–78; also stencil cutter.
Contemporary listings: engraver, 2 Old Levee (1867–69); engraver, MURPHY & LEWIS (1869); engraver, 2 Decatur and Old Levee, and 69 Canal (1870); engraver (1874); ED. SMITH & CO. (1878).
References: NOCD 1866–75, 1877–79; *Repub.*, May 3, 1870; *Almanach de la Louisiane* (1867):166; *Louisiana State Gazetteer*, 123; U.S. Census (1870), roll 519.

MURPHY, MRS. L.
Painter, active N.O. ca. 1885–86.
Exhibited: American Exposition (1885–86).
References: Creole Exhibit, 18.

MURPHY & LEWIS
Engravers, active N.O. 1869–71; JOSEPH P. MURPHY, WILLIAM T. LEWIS, partners.
Contemporary listings: engravers, 2 Old Levee (1869); engravers, 9 Decatur (1870–71).
References: NOCD 1869; Boyd, 158

MURRAY, ROSA GRANER. *See* GRANER, ROSA RAINOLD

MUSE, EDWARD MCGEHEE
Born LA.
Illustrator, active N.O. 1902–1906.
Studied: Art Students' League, N.Y.C.
Contemporary listings: artist (1903); artist, 717 Common (1904); artist, 719 Common (1905); artist, 824 Common (1906).
His name appeared on a cover illustration of *Harlequin* (1902) and *Town Talk*.
References: NOCD 1903–1906; *Harlequin*, Feb. 6, 1902, cover; *Town Talk*, date obliterated, TU, 38.

MUZZY, C. B.
Painter, active N.O. 1858–59.
Contemporary listings: portrait and landscape painter, 198 Common (1858); landscape painter, 198 Common (1859).
References: NOBD 1858–59; Groce and Wallace.

MYNERTS, W. E.
Painter, art teacher, active N.O. 1838–40.
Contemporary listings: miniature painter, Exchange Hotel (1838); miniature painter, 80 Poydras (1840); portrait and miniature painter, teacher of fine arts, Planters Hotel (1840).
References: *Comm. Bull.*, June 2, 1838, Dec. 2, 1840; *D. Pic.*, Feb. 17, May 23, 1838, July 14–Nov. 10, 1840 (advs.); Groce and Wallace; William Young.

MYSSEN, FATHER
Painter, active N.O. 1891.
Monk from the Calceated Order, Munich, Germany who, with FATHER ANGELUS, frescoed the interior of the mortuary chapel built in St. Roch Cemetery (1891).
References: *D. Pic.*, Aug. 23, 1891.

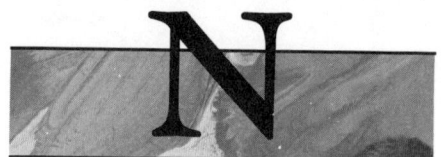

NAGLE, JAMES
Sketch artist, active N.O. 1883.
Staff artist for *Frank Leslie's Illustrated Newspaper* on an 1883 trip through the South with Mrs. Leslie and CHARLES UPHAM.
References: Stern, 111.

NAHR, EDWIN R.
Born LA June 1877.
Engraver, lithographer, active N.O. 1899–1912.
Contemporary listings: engraver, WALLE & CO., LTD. (1899, 1902, 1908–1909); lithographer (1900, 1903–1907); art dept., Walle & Co., Ltd. (1910); lithographer, Walle & Co., Ltd. (1912).
References: NOCD 1899, 1902–10, 1912; U.S. Census (1900), roll 570.

NANON, LOUIS
Painter, active N.O. 1854.
Contemporary listings: portrait painter, Canal betw. Roman and Prieur (1854).
Exhibited: Dupuy's store (1854).
Painted portraits, landscapes, and religious subjects.
References: *Bee*, Feb. 16, Dec. 8, 1854; Groce and Wallace.

NAST, THOMAS
Born Landau, Bavaria Sept. 27, 1840; died Guayaquil, Ecuador Dec. 7, 1902.
Cartoonist, active N.O. 1885.
Studied: with Theodor Kaufmann; with Alfred Fredericks; National Academy of Design, N.Y.C.
Nast, who was also an illustrator and painter, worked for *Frank Leslie's Illustrated Newspaper* (ca. 1855), *New York Illustrated News* (1859), and *Harper's Weekly* (1862–86). Nast caricatured Gen. Benjamin Butler in *Harper's* (1863) and painted *The Massacre at New Orleans* as part of his Grand Caricaturama exhibited in N.Y.C. (1867). Nast is credited with creating the political party symbols of the elephant and donkey. He visited N.O. in May 1885 and presented a cartoon to the Boston Club and the Pickwick Club while a guest of Col. W. D. Mann.
References: *D. Pic.*, May 18, 1885; *D. States*, Jan. 31, 1884; Amon Carter Museum, 82; *Appleton's CAB*; Bénézit; *Bryan's*; Fielding, *Dictionary*; Groce and Wallace; Murrell, 1:206–9, ii:18–21; THNOC 1953.63, 1974.25.25.225.

NATIONAL BANK NOTE COMPANY (OF NEW YORK)
Engravers, active N.O. 1878–79; Charles R. Benton, pres. and agent.
Contemporary listings: engravers, 10 Carondelet (1878–79).
References: NOCD 1878–81.

NATIONAL DRAWING ACADEMY
Art school, active N.O. 1853; JULES BRETTE, owner.
Contemporary listings: 13 St. Charles (1853).
References: *D. Crescent*, Apr. 18, 1853.

NATIONAL GALLERY OF PAINTINGS. *See* COOKE, GEORGE

NATIONAL PUBLISHING & PORTRAIT CO.
Art dealers, active N.O. 1892–93; William Burke, mgr.
Contemporary listings: 291 Camp (1892–93).
References: NOCD 1892–93.

NAVARRE, BISYNTHE
Born ca. 1785–1804; black ("free colored person").
Engraver, active N.O. 1841–42.
Contemporary listings: engraver, 147 Customhouse (1841–42).
References: NOCD 1841–42, 1849–53; Groce and Wallace; U.S. Census (1840), roll 132.

NAZZI, MR. ____ (Nasi)
Painter, active N.O. 1883.
Contemporary listings: scenic painter, French Opera House (1883).
References: *D. States*, Oct. 31, Nov. 2, 1883.

NEAGLE, JOHN
Born Boston MA Nov. 4, 1796 or 1799; died Philadelphia PA Sept. 17, 1865.

Painter, active N.O. ca. 1819–20.
Studied: with Pietro Ancora, Thomas Wilson, Bass Otis.
Memberships/positions: National Academy of Design, N.Y.C., honorary member (1828); Philadelphia Artists' Fund Society, pres. and founder.
Portrait painter who lived in N.O. briefly before permanently settling in Philadelphia. Son–in–law of THOMAS SULLY.
References: *Appleton's CAB*; Bénézit; *Bryan's*; Clement and Hutton; Dunlap, 3:165–71; Fielding, *Dictionary*; Groce and Wallace.

NEGUS, NATHAN
Born Petersham MA Mar. 20, 1801; died Petersham July 19, 1825.
Painter, active N.O. 1824.
Studied: with Ethan Allen Greenwood and John R. Penniman, Boston (1815).
Exhibited: Boston (ca. 1819).
Itinerant portrait painter who worked in MA, NH, VT, GA, AL, and FL.
References: Dods, 434–37; Groce and Wallace; Lay, 404.

NEILL, MARY L. SCHULTZ (Mrs. Henry M. Neill)
Born NY ca. 1835; died N.O. Apr. 7, 1901.
Painter, active N.O. 1881–83.
Studied: with HENRIETTE WINANT (1883).
Exhibited: SOUTHERN ART UNION (1882).
Awarded: exhibition of Miss Winant's pupils, Southern Art Union, honorable mention for oil painting (1883).
Memberships/positions: Southern Art Union (1881).
Moved to N.O. ca. 1866. She later began a book club and upon her death the club's members established a medal for watercolor in her name given to NEWCOMB COLLEGE art students.
References: *D. Pic.*, May 10, 1882, May 8, 1883; *Demo.*, May 12, 1881; *T. Demo.*, Apr. 8, 14, 1901; N.O. Death Certificate (1901), 124:727, NOPL; University Archives, TU.

NELDER, ALEXANDER
Born Santo Domingo ca. 1823; died ca. 1868; black ("free man of color," "mulatto").
Sculptor, active N.O. 1846–54; also marble cutter.
Contemporary listings: marble sculptor, cor. Robertson and St. Louis (1846); sculptor, 36 St. Bernard (1851–54).
Signed the marble slab on the tomb of Gen. P. G. T. Beauregard in St. Bernard Cemetery.
References: NOCD 1846, 1851–61, 1866–67, 1869; P. G. T. Beauregard Tomb, St. Bernard Cemetery, St. Bernard LA; Groce and Wallace; U.S. Census (1850), roll 238.

NENNIG, ISIDORE
Died ca. 1884.
Painter, active N.O. 1872–78.
Contemporary listings: painter (1872); artist (1878).
References: NOCD 1872–73, 1875, 1878–79, 1885; *Courier*, Aug. 26, 1852.

NEUMEYER, AUGUST C.
Born N.O. Mar. 28, 1886; died N.O. Feb. 5, 1940.
Painter, active N.O. 1896.
Contemporary listings: painter (1881, 1885–99, 1901–1902); fresco painter (1896).
References: NOCD 1881–99, 1901–1902, 1905–13, 1915–18, 1921, 1923–28, 1930–33, 1935, 1938, 1940; *T. Pic.*, Feb. 6, 1940; Orleans Parish Registrar of Voters, NOPL; THNOC Cemetery Survey.

NEUSER, L. A. WILLIAM
Born Germany Jan. 1833; died N.O. Sept. 30, 1902.
Painter, restorer, sketch artist, active N.O. 1856–1902; also copyist.
Contemporary listings: portrait, landscape, and banner painter, 76 Baronne, 3 St. Charles and 162 Carondelet (1856); painter, 160 Carondelet, and portrait painter, 162 Carondelet (1857); portrait painter, 160–162 Carondelet (1858); painter, 161 Carondelet (1859); painter, 342 St. Charles (1860–61, 1866); portrait painter, Carondelet cor. Girod (1861); portrait painter (1866–67,

1879); portrait painter, 115 Carondelet (1869–75); portrait painter, 282 Camp (1876); portrait painter, 212 Baronne (1877–78); portrait painter, 110 St. Charles (1880); portrait painter, 109 St. Charles (1881–82); portrait painter, 203 Camp (1883–84); artist, Third cor. Magazine (1885); portrait painter, 734 Magazine (1886–88); portrait painter, 351 1/2 Dryades (1889); portrait painter, 418 S. Rampart (1890–91, 1893–94); artist, 418 S. Rampart (1892); portrait painter, 1327 S. Rampart (1895–99, 1902); artist, 1327 S. Rampart (1900–1901). Exhibited: Grand State Fair (1868). Educated as a doctor, Neuser arrived in the U.S. in 1852 and was licensed to practice medicine when he came to N.O. (1853). By 1856 he had opened a studio specializing in portrait, landscape, and banner painting. He continued working in N.O. as a prolific portrait painter, until at least 1866, after which he established a studio in Baton Rouge LA. By 1869 Neuser was back in N.O. and by the time of his death (1902), was considered a master of portrait painting in the South.
References: NOCD 1853, 1856–61, 1866, 1870–1902; NOBD 1857–58; *D. Pic.*, Jan. 14, 1868, Nov. 1, 1885, Oct. 2, 1902; *Era*, Sept. 30, 1863; *Repub.*, May 27, 29, 1869, May 27, 1870; *Semi–Wkly. Creole*, Jan. 1–23, 1856 (advs.), Jan. 26, June 4, 1856; *T. Demo.*, Oct. 1–2, 1902; Glenk, 77, 105; Groce and Wallace; *Louisiana State Gazetteer*; Wiesendanger, 78.

NEVILLE, ALEX
Born France ca. 1836.
Artist, active N.O. 1860.
Contemporary listings: artist (1860).
References: U.S. Census (1860), roll 419.

NEW ORLEANS ART GLASS CO., LIMITED
Designers, active N.O. 1895–1901.
Contemporary listings: 623 Baronne (1895); 619–21 Poydras (1897–98); 115–17 Camp (1899); 217 Chartres (1900–1901).

Claimed to be the first stained glass establishment in LA; JAMES BLOOMFIELD was the designing artist. The New Orleans Art Glass Company was responsible for at least one of the stained glass windows in St. Patrick Church.
References: NOCD 1895, 1897–1901; *Men and Matters*, Sept. 1897, 55; Louisiana Industrial Exposition, 64.

NEW ORLEANS ART LEAGUE
Art school, active N.O. 1908.
Reported as a new institution teaching free–hand drawing, watercolor, and oil painting. The instructor was SAMUEL A. MARCOU. Another league with the same name was organized in 1927.
References: *D. Pic.*, June 28, 1908.

NEW ORLEANS ART POTTERY COMPANY
Art association, potters, art craftsmen, active N.O. 1885–90.
Organized by members of the TULANE DECORATIVE ART LEAGUE FOR WOMEN (1885), the officers were Samuel L. Gilmore, secy., and WILLIAM WOODWARD, treas. JOSEPH FORTUNE MEYER and GEORGE OHR were hired as potters. The pottery shared a building at 249 Baronne with the FIVE OR MORE CLUB; it erected a kiln at 247 Baronne. All work was done entirely by hand, including goods manufactured for the Cotton Palace (1889). Unsuccessful financially, the company was succeeded in 1890 by the ART LEAGUE POTTERY CLUB.
References: NOCD 1889; *D. Pic.*, Feb. 17, 1888, Jan. 5, 1890; *D. States*, June 10, 1888; *T. Demo.*, Jan. 20, 1889, Jan. 6, 1890; Ormond and Irvine, 11–14, 19, 22, 24, 36, 141; Poesch, *Newcomb Pottery*, 12–13, 17–18; THNOC 1969.11.

NEW ORLEANS DRAWING & PAINTING ACADEMY. *See* ACADEMIE DE DESSIN ET DE PEINTURE DE LA NOUVELLE ORLEANS

NEW ORLEANS ELECTROTYPING AND WOOD ENGRAVING CO.
Engravers, active N.O. 1874; CHARLES G. SCHULZ, mgr.
Contemporary listings: 82 Gravier (1874).
References: NOCD 1874.

NEW ORLEANS ENGRAVING AND
ELECTROTYPE CO., LTD.
Engravers, active N.O. 1906–47;
Andrew Vidak, pres., Joseph Steck-
ler, v. pres. and treas., Remigius J.
Slattery, mgr., FRANÇOIS BILDSTEIN,
secy. (1906–1908); Remigius J. Slattery, pres. and mgr., THOMAS G. SMITH,
v. pres., François Bildstein, secy.
(1909–10); François Bildstein, pres.
and mgr., Ludwig Platz, secy. (1911–
12); François Bildstein, pres. and
mgr. (1913–18).
Contemporary listings: 524 Gravier
(1906–18).
References: NOCD 1906–33, 1935,
1938, 1940, 1942, 1945–47.
NEW ORLEANS ENGRAVING COMPANY
Engravers, active N.O. 1873.
Contemporary listings: office of *Our
Home Journal*, 68 Camp (1873).
Engraving company which prepared
a wood engraving of Christ Church
for the *Daily Picayune* (1873). J. R.
BUCKINGHAM and ADOLPH ZENNECK
were artists affiliated with the firm
and left its employ by Jan. 15, 1873.
References: *D. Pic.*, Jan. 5, 15, 1873.
NEW ORLEANS ETCHING CLUB
Etchers, active N.O. 1886.
Menu dated Jan. 9, 1886 signed
"N.O. Etching Club, E. ERTZ–Del."
References: THNOC 1982.223.
NEW ORLEANS GALLERY OF THE FINE
ARTS. *See* COOKE, GEORGE
NEW ORLEANS LITHOGRAPHING AND
ENGRAVING CO.
Lithographers, engravers, active
N.O. 1879–82; HUGH LEWIS (1879–
81), GUSTAVE KOECKERT (1879–82),
PETER DAVIS (1879–82), MILFORD C.
LEWIS (1882), partners.
Contemporary listings: 20 St. Charles
(1879–80); 78 St. Charles (1880–
82).
Gustave Koeckert, Peter Davis, and
others later formed the NEW ORLEANS
LITHOGRAPHING COMPANY.
References: NOCD 1880–82; *Mas-
cot*, Mar. 18, 1882; *Southern Busi-
ness Guide*, 410.
NEW ORLEANS LITHOGRAPHING
COMPANY
Lithographers, engravers, active
N.O. 1883–84; also printers.

Contemporary listings: 10 Union
(1883–84).
In Mar. 1883 PETER DAVIS, GUSTAVE
KOECKERT (formerly partners in the
NEW ORLEANS LITHOGRAPHING AND
ENGRAVING CO.), and GEORGE J. KERTH
formed this partnership. They offered engraving and lithography as
their services and produced bonds,
stock certificates, diplomas, business
cards, etc. In Oct. 1883 Davis,
Koeckert, Kerth, and Charles R.
Benton formed a new partnership in
which Koeckert and Benton served
as managers. It was dissolved in Feb.
1884 at which time the New Orleans
Lithographing Company and the
SOUTHERN LITHOGRAPHIC CO. were
consolidated as the Southern Litho-
graphic Co.
References: NOCD 1883–84; *T.
Demo.*, Jan 20, 1884; *Figaro*, Feb. 2,
1884, 11, Feb. 9, 1884, 9; Orleans
Parish Notarial Archives, William O.
Hart, Mar. 5, 1883, 3:488, Oct. 1,
1883, 3:663, Feb. 6, 1884, 3:763,
Apr. 12, 1884, 4:799.
NEW ORLEANS MUSEUM OF ART. *See*
DELGADO MUSEUM OF ART
NEW ORLEANS PORTRAIT SOCIETY &
FRAME FACTORY. *See* RIVOIRE, JULIEN
EMILE
NEW ORLEANS STENCIL WORKS. *See*
CHAPSKY & TEETZEL
NEW ORLEANS WOOD ENGRAVING
COMPANY
Engravers, active N.O. 1873.
Contemporary listings: 26 Commer-
cial (1873).
References: *D. Pic.*, Jan. 15, 1873.
NEWCOMB COLLEGE (H. Sophie
Newcomb Memorial College)
Art school, active N.O. 1887–pres-
ent.
Awarded: International Exposition,
Paris, bronze medal (1900); Pan-
American Exposition, Buffalo NY,
silver medal (1901); Charleston SC,
silver medal (1902); Louisiana Pur-
chase Exposition, St. Louis MO, sil-
ver medal (1904); Lewis and Clark
Centennial Exposition, Portland OR,
bronze medal (1905); Tercentenary
Exposition, Jamestown VA, gold
medal (1907); Knoxville TN, gold

medal (1913); Panama–Pacific International Exposition, San Francisco, silver medal (1915).

Founded in 1886 as the H. Sophie Newcomb Memorial College with money from Mrs. Josephine Louise Newcomb in memory of her daughter. Affiliated with Tulane University, Newcomb was the first women's coordinate college in the country. The college opened in the fall of 1887 with classical, literary, industrial, and scientific degree programs. Among the electives at Newcomb, art classes were the most popular; art majors were classified as normal art students, who were interested in teaching, or as special students, usually part time, who could earn certificates in art after completing prescribed courses in industrial and free–hand drawing, decorative design, modeling, woodcarving, water and oil painting, and drawing. ELLSWORTH WOODWARD was Newcomb's first professor of drawing; his brother WILLIAM WOODWARD was the first professor of oil painting. GERTRUDE ROBERTS SMITH replaced William Woodward in 1887; and, until 1894, she and Ellsworth Woodward were the only instructors teaching art. In 1894 a four–year curriculum in art was organized, and a new art building was constructed on Newcomb's campus on Washington Ave. In Nov. 1908, the present campus, adjacent to Tulane University, was acquired and Newcomb moved there in 1918. From his experiences with the TULANE DECORATIVE ART LEAGUE and the NEW ORLEANS ART POTTERY COMPANY, Ellsworth Woodward developed an idea for combining the training of the fine and the industrial arts through the traditional handicraft of art pottery. All pieces were to be beautiful objects for everyday use, but thrown by hand and decorated separately. MARY GIVEN SHEERER was brought to N.O. (1894) to be head of pottery decoration. She introduced courses in china painting and a complete course in ceramic art from pottery manufacture to decoration. A two–year apprenticeship was added as a graduate program during the 1895–96 session to train women as professional pottery decorators. From 1908, certain women who worked regularly were designated as craftsmen. Pottery judged by a faculty jury to be of acceptable quality was sold, beginning in 1896 until the Newcomb Guild was officially recognized as the sales outlet for the pottery (1941). JULES GABRY was hired as potter (ca. 1894–95), followed by George Wasmuth (ca. 1895), JOSEPH FORTUNE MEYER (ca. 1896–1927), GEORGE OHR (ca. 1896), Paul Ernest Cox (1910–18), and others. The clay for the pottery came from Bayou Boguefalaya on the north shore of Lake Pontchartrain and Back Bay, Biloxi MS. Decorative motifs incised into and painted on the surfaces were inspired by local flora, such as pine, oak, magnolia, and oleander. Pottery creation was the most prolific craft in the art department. Newcomb pottery won numerous awards in the U.S. after its first international recognition at the 1900 Paris Exposition. Its success inspired others: embroideries and needlework were introduced through Smith (1902); calligraphy (1902); metalwork through MARY WILLIAMS BUTLER; bookbinding through LOTA LEE TROY (1913); and also printmaking, wood carving, weaving, and spinning. Production of Newcomb artworks, especially pottery, reached its peak after 1910 and continued at that level until after World War I, when output declined with a new generation of students and the successive retirements of Meyer (ca. 1920), Woodward (1931), Sheerer (1931), Smith (1934), and SARAH AGNES ESTELLE IRVINE (1952).

References: Brandt Dixon; John Dyer, 96–97; Paul Evans, 182–87; Ormond and Irvine; Poesch, *Newcomb Pottery*.

NICHOLS, KATE McLEOD (Mrs. Frederick G. Nichols)
Born N.O. May 12, 1843; died N.O. Nov. 14, 1927.

Painter, active N.O. 1870; also needleworker.
Awarded: Grand State Fair, certificate for best ornamental needlework with oriental painting combined (1870).
References: NOCD 1887–1914, 1921; D. Pic., Feb. 25, 1866; T. Pic., Nov. 15, 1927; Orleans Parish Registrar of Voters, NOPL; Mechanics' and Agricultural Fair Asso., Report (1870):52.

NICHOLS, PAULINE WRIGHT. See WRIGHT, PAULINE

NICHOLSON, LEONA FISCHER (Mrs. Bentley W. Nicholson)
Born St. Francisville LA Apr. 11, 1875; died 1966.
Art craftsman, art teacher, potter, active N.O. ca. 1900–55.
Studied: NEWCOMB COLLEGE (1896–97); Alfred University.
Exhibited: Louisiana Purchase Exposition, St. Louis MO (1904); Boston Society of Arts and Crafts (1907); ART ASSOCIATION OF NEW ORLEANS (1910, 1917); Panama–Pacific International Exposition, San Francisco (1915).
Awarded: Art Association of New Orleans, prize.
Memberships/positions: Boston Society of Arts and Crafts; Philadelphia Arts and Crafts Guild; Art Association of New Orleans (1905).
Artist who worked as art craftsman at Newcomb College (1908–1909, 1913–14, 1922–26, 1928–29). She often made and decorated pottery in her home studio and was the first N.O. woman to receive the title "Master Craftsman" from the Boston Society of Arts and Crafts. Nicholson was a member of the Arts and Crafts Club and a ceramics instructor and director of the Jewish Community Center (1949–65).
References: NOCD 1905, 1927, 1931, 1935, 1938, 1940, 1942, 1945–47, 1949, 1952–56, 1958, 1960–62, 1964–66; Harlequin, June 23, 1904, 8; Item, Nov. 26, 1923; T. Pic., Mar. 16, 1925, Oct. 4, 1927, Mar. 3, 1930, June 3, 1951, Jan. 14, 1962; Wurzlow, "Ceramics Teacher

Given Plaque for Long Service," T. Pic., Apr. 12, 1964; Ball, "Newcomb Pottery Hits Big Time Again," T. Pic./States–Item, May 27, 1984; Art Asso., Catalogue (1905, 1910, 1917); Delgado, Catalogue of Paintings, Sculpture, 39; Orleans Parish Registrar of Voters, NOPL; Ormond and Irvine, 38, 83–84, 86, 88, 93, 164–65; Poesch, Newcomb Pottery, 46, 50, 54, 103, 124–25, 129; Who's Who in American Art, 1938–39.

NICODEMUS, LOUISE
Painter, active N.O. 1890.
Contemporary listings: portrait painter, 33 S. Claiborne (1890).
References: NOCD 1890.

NIENEM, CHRISTIAN
Painter, active N.O. 1874.
Contemporary listings: portrait painter (1874).
References: NOCD 1874.

NIPPERT, EMILE E.
Born N.O. ca. 1871; died N.O. Mar. 22, 1918.
Painter, active N.O. 1891–1916; also decorator.
Contemporary listings: scenic painter, with FRANK COX (1891); artist (1892, 1894–96, 1909–11); artist, with Philip Werlein (1893); scenic painter, French Opera House (1896); scenic artist (1897, 1915–16); DRESSEL & NIPPERT (1899–1900); scenic painter (1900); scenic artist, Tulane and Crescent Theatres, French Opera House, and Orpheum (1902–1903); scenic artist, Tulane and Crescent Theatres (1904–1908); scenic artist and painter (1910).
Painted scenery at the French Opera House in 1896 with CLARK COX or FRANK COX and ROBERT W. BOHM; also painted tableaux for many carnival balls.
References: NOCD 1884–85, 1889–90, 1892–97, 1899–1911, 1915–16; D. Pic., Oct. 23, 1899, Oct. 26, 1902; D. States, Sept. 27, 1891; Harlequin, Feb. 14, 1900, 7; T. Demo., Sept. 22, 1896, Sept. 21, 1902; T. Pic., Mar. 24, 1918; French Opera Season 1902–1903, 11; Tulane Theatre Program, Nov. 6, 1904, TU; U.S. Census (1910), roll 520.

NOGUES, RALPH J.

Born N.O. ca. 1887; died N.O. Aug. 6, 1942.

Commercial artist, painter, active N.O. 1910–42; also sign painter, photographer.

Contemporary listings: artist and portrait painter (1910); artist, New Orleans Portrait Co. (1912).

Active as a commercial artist at the time of his death.

References: NOCD 1902–1903, 1905–12, 1914–33, 1935, 1938, 1940, 1942; *T. Pic.*, Aug. 8, 1942; U.S. Census (1910), roll 521.

NOLTE, AUGUST

Born Dhueringer, Germany Jan. 1836; died N.O. Dec. 18, 1914.

Sketch artist, painter, art teacher, active N.O. 1880–1914.

Contemporary listings: artist and portrait painter, THEODORE LILIEN-THAL's (1880); artist, with Theodore Lilienthal (1881, 1886); portrait painter, 111 Canal (1883–85); night class instructor, ARTISTS' ASSOCIATION OF NEW ORLEANS (1886–87); scenic artist (1887); artist (1888–97, 1899–1900, 1910–14); portrait painter (1901–10).

Exhibited: Theodore Lilienthal's (1880); Artists' Association of New Orleans (1886).

Memberships/positions: Artists' Association of New Orleans (1886, 1890).

Designed the frontispiece of the *Saengerfest Zeitung*, a supplement to the *Sunday German Gazette* (1889). He drew and painted portraits of many prominent individuals, including Ulysses S. Grant and Charles Morgan.

References: NOCD 1881, 1883–97, 1899–1914; *D. Pic.*, Nov. 6, 1886, May 7, 1887, Nov. 13, 1890; *D. States*, Apr. 17, May 13, June 12, 1880, Oct. 29, Nov. 5, 1886; *Eve. Chronicle*, Dec. 27, 1885; *T. Pic.*, Dec. 19, 1914; AANO, *Catalogue* (1886); North American Saenger-bund; U.S. Census (1880), roll 463, (1900), roll 574, (1910), roll 523.

NOON, T. F.

Painter, active N.O. 1837–38.

Contemporary listings: portrait painter, 31 Canal (1837–38).

Portrait and landscape painter with a primitive folk style who had worked in Portsmouth VA (1829). Possibly Thomas F. Noone, born ca. 1800–10, who lived in Jackson LA in 1840.

References: NOCD 1838; *Pic.*, Dec. 24, 1837; Glenk, 77; Information courtesy George E. Jordan.

NORIERI, AUGUST

Born N.O. Jan. or Feb. 1860; died N.O. July 11, 1898.

Sketch artist, painter, sculptor, active N.O. 1884–98.

Studied: with ANDRES MOLINARY (1880–81).

Contemporary listings: artist (1884–89, 1893); portrait painter, 9 Commercial (1891); crayon artist, 9 Commercial (1894); artist, 614 Commercial (1895–98); portrait painter, 614 Commercial (1898).

Exhibited: National Academy of Design, N.Y.C. (1885); American Exposition (1885–86); ARTISTS' ASSOCIATION OF NEW ORLEANS (1886–87, 1889–92).

Memberships/positions: Artists' Association of New Orleans (1890).

Known for his paintings of steamboats and other marine scenes, Norieri also painted portraits. He established a studio in N.O. by 1884 which continued until his death in 1898. He received little recognition for his work during his lifetime.

References: NOCD 1878, 1880–81, 1884–91, 1893–98; NOBD 1898; *Art and Letters* 1(Dec. 1887):227; *Current Topics*, Jan. 1891, 24, Jan. 1893, 11; *D. Pic.*, July 26, 1885, Nov. 6, 1886, Dec. 17, 29, 1887, Dec. 17, 1889, Nov. 13, Dec. 17, 1890, July 12, 1898; *D. States*, Dec. 17, 1890; AANO, *Catalogue* (1886, 1890, 1891); Anglo–American Art Museum, *Louisiana Landscape*, item 22; Anglo–American Art Museum, *Sail and Steam*, items 32–37; Creole Exhibit, 13; Glenk, 78, 251; Friends of the Cabildo, *Norieri*; LSM, *Annual Report for 1918*, 59; LSM, *Annual*

Report for 1919, 26–27; LSM, *Biennial Report for 1922-23*, 58; LSM, *Biennial Report for 1924-25*, 26–27, 53; LSM, *Biennial Report for 1928-29*, 35.

NORTON, WILLIAM D.
Died N.O. Dec. 30, 1918.
Lithographer, active N.O. 1889–96.
Contemporary listings: lithographer (1889); artist (1896).
References: NOCD 1885–89, 1891–92, 1894–98; *T. Pic.*, Jan. 1, 1919.

NOXON, T. C. (T. S.)
Painter, active N.O. 1855–56.
Contemporary listings: scenic artist, St. Charles Theatre (1855–56).
Possibly Thomas Noxon who was working in St. Louis MO in 1852 at People's Theatre.
References: *D. Pic.*, Nov. 11, 1855, Nov. 9, 1856; Scharf, 1:982.

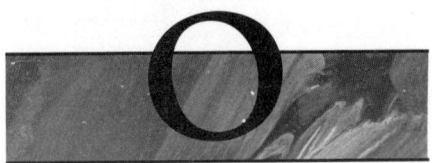

O'CONNELL, JOSEPH PAUL
Sketch artist, painter, active N.O. ca. 1876.
Exhibited: Duhamel's (1876).
References: NOCD 1877–78; *Demo.*, Apr. 16, 1876.

ODELL, T. J.
Died Monroe LA July 13, 1849.
Painter, active N.O. 1848.
Contemporary listings: 15 Camp (1848).
Exhibited: Pierson & Bonneval auctioneers (1848).
Worked in Nashville TN; painted the last portrait from life of Andrew Jackson.
References: *Comm. Bull.*, July 25, 1849; *D. Crescent*, Mar. 5, June 8, 1848; *D. Delta*, June 10, 1848; Groce and Wallace; William Young.

OESCHSNER, CHARLES
Engraver, active N.O. 1883–85.
Contemporary listings: engraver, with HARRY TODSWER (1883–84); engraver (1885).
References: NOCD 1883–85.

OFFICER, THOMAS S.
Born Carlisle PA ca. 1809–20; died San Francisco CA ca. 1859–60.
Painter.
Miniaturist and portrait painter who worked in Philadelphia (ca. 1834–45), Mobile AL (1837), Richmond VA (1845), N.Y.C. (1846–49), and San Francisco (1856–59). He is reported by Bénézit, Young, Fielding, and Appleton to have spent time in N.O. (ca. 1833, ca. 1847), but no contemporary local sources verify this.
References: *Appleton's CAB*; Bénézit; Corcoran Gallery, 35; Fielding, *Dictionary*; Groce and Wallace; Sidney Smith, 487; WPA, *American Portrait Inventory*, 192; William Young.

OGDEN, CAROLINE
Sketch artist, designer, active N.O. 1895–97.
Studied: NEWCOMB COLLEGE (1897).
References: *Men and Matters*, Sept. 1897, 48; Ogden, et al.

OGDEN, MISS Z.
Sculptor, active N.O. ca. 1889.
Contemporary listings: wood carver (1889).
Exhibited: ART LEAGUE OF NEW ORLEANS (1889).
References: *D. Pic.*, Mar. 10, 1889.

O'HARA, PATRICK H.
Artist, active N.O. 1891.
Contemporary listings: artist (1891).
References: NOCD 1891.

OHR, GEORGE E.
Born Biloxi MS 1857; died Biloxi 1918.
Potter, active N.O. 1879–90.
Studied: with JOSEPH MEYER (ca. 1879).
Contemporary listings: potter (1880–81, 1883); potter, 249 Baronne (1889).
Exhibited: Cotton Exposition, Atlanta GA (1895).
Awarded: World's Industrial and Cotton Centennial Exposition, medal (1884–85); Louisiana Purchase Exposition, St. Louis MO, medal for most original art pottery (1904).
Considered to be among the most important 19th–century art potters in the U.S., Ohr had a flamboyant personality and was noted for works of sinuous form. He came to N.O. (ca. 1876) and worked for a ship chandler until 1879 when he was apprenticed to Joseph Meyer's pottery. At the end of his apprenticeship, he spent about two years traveling and observing pottery methods in other states, then returned to Biloxi where he set up the Biloxi Art Pottery (1883). There he made countless objects, including some 600 pots which he planned to sell at the 1884–85 exposition in N.O. In 1886 he was back in N.O. where he and Joseph Meyer set up the NEW ORLEANS ART POTTERY COMPANY, which lasted until 1890. A fire destroyed his Biloxi pottery (1893), and he spent most of the next year building a new and better

one. After the fire, his works exhibited a change in the forms and in the glazing techniques, and his attitude toward the sale of his pieces became more eccentric. About 1896 Meyer was hired to work at NEWCOMB COLLEGE; Ohr also worked there briefly although there is no official record of his employment. Ohr concentrated most of his career as an artist at his Biloxi Art Pottery until he abandoned the work in 1909 when he became an automobile dealer. At the time of his death, over 6,000 pieces from his mature career remained, stored in the family warehouse.

References: NOCD 1880–81, 1883, 1889; *Gambit*, June 4, 1983; Reif, "Antiques View: A Passion for Pottery," *New York Times*, Dec. 2, 1984; Reif, "Antiques View: Rediscovering a Potter," *New York Times*, Feb. 24, 1985; Green, "Sensual Ceramics from an Outrageous Gulf Coast Eccentric," *T. Pic./States Item*, June 12, 1983; *T. Pic./States-Item*, Feb. 24, 1984; Anderson, 60–61, 63; Beffart, 6B, 8B, 9B; Blasberg, *Ohr*; Garth Clark, *Biloxi Art Pottery*; Garth Clark, "George E. Ohr," 490–97; Garth Clark, "George Ohr: Clay Prophet," 44–49, 65; Paul Cox, 116–19, 140; Ormond and Irvine, 11–14, 24, 145; Poesch, *Newcomb Pottery*, 7, 13, 18, 21, 94; William Woodward, plate 54.

OLIVER, ROBIN
Born PA ca. 1823–25.
Engraver, active N.O. 1860.
Contemporary listings: engraver (1860).
References: Groce and Wallace; U.S. Census (1850), roll 234, (1860), roll 416; William Young.

OLLERT, FELIX
Engraver, active N.O. 1887–88.
Contemporary listings: wood engraver, 46 Camp (1887); engraver, 46 Camp (1888).
References: NOCD 1888; *D. States*, Apr. 17, 1887; *South Illustrated*, Sept. 1887, 21; Morrison, *New Orleans*, 63, 110.

ORD, P.
Artist, active N.O. 1843.
Contemporary listings: artist, 3 St. Charles (1843).

References: NOCD 1843, 1846, 1849; Groce and Wallace; William Young.

O'REGAN, C.
Engraver, active N.O. 1856–59.
Contemporary listings: engraver, Exchange Pl. cor. Customhouse (1856, 1858–59).
References: NOCD 1855–56, 1858–59; Groce and Wallace; William Young.

O'REGAN, JAMES
Born Wales or Ireland ca. 1822–25.
Engraver, active N.O. 1850–77; also engineer.
Contemporary listings: engraver, 122 Canal (1850–52); engraver, Bienville cor. Exchange Pl. (1853–54); engraver, 56 Customhouse (1857); copper engraver, 56 Customhouse (1858); engraver, Exchange Pl. cor. Customhouse (1859–61, 1866–68); engraver, 86 Customhouse (1870–71); engraver, 76 Gravier (1877).
References: NOCD 1850–61, 1866–68, 1870, 1874, 1877; Boyd, 158; *Edwards' Descriptive Gazetteer 1866*, 861; Groce and Wallace; *Louisiana State Gazetteer*, 123; U.S. Census (1860), roll 421, (1870), roll 521; William Young.

ORLEANS LITHOGRAPHIC OFFICE
Lithographers, active N.O. 1836–38; WILLIAM GREENE, owner.
Contemporary listings: lithographers, Magazine oppos. Bank's Arcade (1836); lithographers, 53 Magazine (1838).
Lithographed views of *Charity Hospital*, *State House*, and *Franklin Infirmary*, which appeared in the 1838 NOCD and were from engravings by R. W. FISHBOURNE.
References: NOCD 1838: opp. 325; *Bee*, Dec. 30, 1836; *True Amer.*, July 2, 1838; Groce and Wallace; Harry Peters, *America on Stone*, 296.

O'ROURKE, MARY R.
Born N.O. Oct. 26, 1868; died N.O. Nov. 2, 1953.
Painter, active N.O. ca. 1918.
Exhibited: ART ASSOCIATION OF NEW ORLEANS (1918).
Primarily a music teacher at St. Francis de Sales School.

References: NOCD 1907–20, 1922–33, 1935, 1938, 1940, 1942, 1945–47, 1949; *T. Pic.*, Nov. 3, 1953; Art Asso., *Catalogue* (1918); Orleans Parish Registrar of Voters, NOPL.

ORR, ROBERT
Lithographer, active N.O. 1872.
Contemporary listings: lithographer, with HUGH LEWIS (1872).
References: NOCD 1872–73.

ORRANTIA, AMELIA
Born LA Apr. 1878.
Artist, active N.O. 1900.
Contemporary listings: portrait artist (1900).
References: U.S. Census (1900), roll 573.

ORSINI, LORENZO
Born LA ca. 1866.
Sketch artist, designer, active N.O. 1908–10; also architect, draftsman.
Contemporary listings: designer (1908, 1910).
Designed granite pedestal for monument to Jefferson Davis, erected 1911.
References: NOCD 1908, 1910–12; *T. Pic.*, Dec. 13, 1925; U.S. Census (1910), roll 520.

ORTTE, JAMES A.
Born N.O. July 27, 1875; died N.O. Apr. 20, 1958.
Artist, active N.O. 1910.
Contemporary listings: artist, Home Art Studio, 311 Baronne (1910).
Brother of RICHARD W. ORTTE.
References: NOCD 1910–11; *T. Pic.*, Apr. 22, 1958; Orleans Parish Registrar of Voters, NOPL.

ORTTE, RICHARD W.
Born N.O. Apr. 4, 1879.
Painter, active N.O. 1900–11; also photographer.
Contemporary listings: mgr., AUDUBON PORTRAIT HOUSE (1900); proprietor, Audubon Portrait House (1901); artist (1903); mgr., Home Art Studio, 311 Baronne (1908, 1910); portrait painter, 311 Baronne (1909); artist, portrait (1910); Home Art Studio (1911).
Worked with Otis Harris at the Home Art Studio (1911). Brother of JAMES A. ORTTE.

References: NOCD 1896–1901, 1903, 1905–17, 1919–30; Orleans Parish Registrar of Voters, NOPL; U.S. Census (1910), roll 524.

ORTTE & HENRY
Painters, active N.O. 1900; Charles H. Ortte, William F. Henry, partners.
Contemporary listings: artists, painters (portrait), 739 Baronne.
References: NOCD 1900.

OSBORNE, MR. _____
Painter, active N.O. 1841.
Contemporary listings: miniature painter, cor. Royal and Customhouse (1841).
References: *Bee*, July 27, 1841; Groce and Wallace; William Young.

OSBORNE, HENRY
Sketch artist, active N.O. 1884.
Artist for the *New York Graphic* who visited N.O. to observe and sketch carnival scenes (1884).
References: *D. States*, Feb. 24, 1884.

OSGOOD, SAMUEL STILLMAN
Born Boston MA or New Haven CT June 9, 1808; died CA 1885.
Painter, active N.O. 1853–54.
Studied: Boston; Europe (ca. 1851–53).
Contemporary listings: painter, 10 Rampart (1853); artist, cor. Camp and Canal (1853–54).
Memberships/positions: National Academy of Design, N.Y.C.
Portrait and historical painter in N.Y.C. (1835–51), Osgood had traveled to Europe before arriving in N.O.
References: *Comm. Bull.*, Feb. 22, Dec. 22, 1853; *Courier*, May 18, 1853; *D. Crescent*, Jan. 9, Feb. 20, July 15, 1850; *D. Delta*, Feb. 20, 1853, Jan. 6, 1854, Dec. 28, 1855; *D. Pic.*, May 25, 1855; Bénézit; Fielding, *Dictionary*; Groce and Wallace; LSM, *Biennial Report for 1920–21*, 86; New–York Historical Society, 580, 632; Say, 408; William Young.

OSICRAN, ISNARD
Painter, active N.O. 1905–10.
Contemporary listings: artist painter, 109 Camp (1905); portrait painter (1906); portrait painter, 111 Camp

(1909); portrait artist, 617 Canal (1910).
Painted a portrait of LA Gov. Henry W. Allen (ca. 1906).
References: NOCD 1909–10; *D. Pic.*, Sept. 14, Nov. 24, 1906; *Town Talk*, Feb. 1905; Glenk, 83, 214, 328; LSM, *Annual Report for 1919*, 69.

O'TOOLE, STEPHEN
Engraver, active N.O. 1885.
Contemporary listings: engraver, SOUTHERN LITHOGRAPHIC COMPANY (1885).
References: NOCD 1885.

OTTER, ROBERT E.
Born PA ca. 1866; died N.O. Aug. 1, 1939.
Engraver, active N.O. 1906–38.
Contemporary listings: engraver, with L. Krower (1906–10, 1912–15, 1917); engraver (1911); engraver, L. Krower & Son (1918).
After 1918 he continued as an engraver with Leonard Krower & Son and independently as well; also listed as a jeweler (1927).
References: NOCD 1906–15, 1917–33, 1938; *T. Pic.*, Aug. 2, 1939; U.S. Census (1910), roll 524.

OURLAC, JEAN NICOLAS
Born N.O. 1789; died Paris, France 1821.
Painter, active N.O. ca. 1815–17.
Studied: with Jacques–Louis David, Paris.
Ourlac left N.O. at an early age to study in Paris. He returned to the U.S. and visited N.Y.C., Baltimore, Boston, and N.O. He painted many views of American scenery based on his travels, including *Scènes du marché à la Nouvelle Orléans* (1820) and *Une vue du Mississippi près de la Nouvelle Orléans* (1821).
References: *Appleton's CAB*; Fielding, *Dictionary*; Groce and Wallace; William Young.

OWEN, GEN. ALLISON (Albion)
Born N.O. Dec. 29, 1869; died N.O. Jan. 30, 1951.
Sketch artist, painter, art teacher, active N.O. 1889–97; primarily architect.

Studied: Tulane University (graduated 1885); Massachusetts Institute of Technology (1892–94).
Exhibited: ART LEAGUE OF NEW ORLEANS (1889); Tulane University (1892); ARTISTS' ASSOCIATION OF NEW ORLEANS (1896–97).
Memberships/positions: Art League of New Orleans (1889); Artists' Association of New Orleans (1896–97); ART ASSOCIATION OF NEW ORLEANS (1905), board of directors, executive committee (1910–11).
Nationally known architect, World War I veteran, and civic leader. Owen and Collins Cerré Diboll, Sr., (born 1868; died 1936) were partners in the architectural firm, Diboll and Owen (1895–1936). Together they designed many buildings, the majority of which were in N.O., notably, New Orleans Public Library at Lee Circle, Notre Dame Seminary, and the Criminal Courts Building on Tulane Ave.
References: NOCD 1896–1933, 1935, 1938, 1940, 1942, 1945–47, 1949, *D. Pic.*, Mar. 10, 1889, Mar. 3, 1892, Mar. 30, 1897; *Eve. Chronicle*, May 22, 1886; *Men and Matters*, Sept. 1897, 46; *New Orleans Illustrated News*, July 1921, 20–21; *T. Demo.*, Mar. 5, 21, 1904; *T. Pic.*, Jan. 25, 1937, Jan. 31, 1951; AANO, *Catalogue* (1896, 1897); Friends of the Cabildo, *N.O. Architecture*, 2:229; Henry Chambers, 1:14; Dufour, *Battle of New Orleans*, 9; Mount, 136; Orleans Parish Registrar of Voters, NOPL; Thompson, "Checklist"; U.S. Census (1910), roll 524.

OWEN, GEORGE
Born England ca. 1830.
Lithographer, active N.O. 1860–66.
Contemporary listings: lithographer (1860); lithographer, 87 Palmyra (1861, 1866).
References: NOCD 1861, 1866; Groce and Wallace; U.S. Census (1860), roll 417.

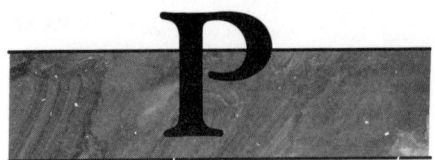

P.
Sketch artist, active N.O. 1891.
Signed a political cartoon engraved by the PHOTO-ENGRAVING CO. for the *Mascot* (1891).
References: *Mascot*, Aug. 8, 1891.

A. J. PADRON & SONS
Engravers, active N.O. 1889; also printers; Arthur Joseph Padron (born N.O.? ca. 1835; died N.O. Dec. 30, 1902), owner.
Contemporary listings: engravers, 136 Chartres (1889).
References: NOCD 1886–90; NOBD 1889; *D. Pic.*, Dec. 31, 1902.

PAGANINI, CHRISTOPHANI
Painter, art teacher, active N.O. 1830.
Contemporary listings: portrait and miniature painter, teacher, cor. Royal and St. Louis (1830).
References: *Bee*, July 20, 1830; Groce and Wallace.

PAJARAS, ALBERTO
Born Havana, Cuba Jan. 1877; died N.O. Apr. 12, 1924.
Lithographer, active N.O. 1908–24; also printer, pressman.
Contemporary listings: lithographer, with MICHEL CAPO (1908, 1914); newspaper lithographer (1910); lithographer, R. F. Grace Printing and Mnfg. Co. Ltd. (1915); lithographer (1918).
Memberships/positions: International Association of Amalgamated Lithographers of America.
Listed as lithographer (1920–24).
References: NOCD 1908, 1913–15, 1917–18, 1920–24; *T. Pic.*, Apr. 13, 1924; U.S. Census (1910), roll 521.

PALESSARD, LOUIS
Painter, active N.O. 1842–44.
Contemporary listings: portrait painter, 150 Chartres (1842–44).
References: NOCD 1842–44.

PALFREY, ELIZABETH GOELET ROGERS (Mrs. Arthur Griswold Palfrey)
Born N.O. Feb. 27, 1871; died N.O. Aug. 2, 1933.

Art craftsman, designer, painter, active N.O. 1894–1918.
Studied: with ACHILLE PERELLI; NEWCOMB COLLEGE (1895–1902).
Exhibited: ARTISTS' ASSOCIATION OF NEW ORLEANS (1894); ART ASSOCIATION OF NEW ORLEANS (1918).
Designer of bookplates and jewelry, pottery decorator, and metal worker. She reportedly was the first at Newcomb to design and execute a pierced brass lamp shade, one of the school's distinctive crafts.
References: NOCD 1903, 1905, 1907–1909, 1912, 1922, 1935; *D. Pic.*, Sept. 30, 1894; *T. Demo.*, Dec. 14, 1894; *T. Pic.*, Aug. 3, 1933; Art Asso., *Catalogue* (1918); Art Asso., *Exhibition of Bookplates*; Friends of the Cabildo, *N.O. Architecture*, 3:57, 112; Orleans Parish Registrar of Voters, NOPL; Ormond and Irvine; Poesch, *Newcomb Pottery*, 20, 37–39, 103; WPA, *Bookplates*.

PALFREY, MARY HARRISON
Born N.O. Apr. 8, 1887; died N.O. May 25, 1929.
Art craftsman, active N.O. ca. 1907–16.
Studied: NEWCOMB COLLEGE (1909, 1911–12).
Exhibited: ART ASSOCIATION OF NEW ORLEANS (1911).
Pottery decorator and jewelry designer.
References: NOCD 1911, 1920, 1925, 1928. *T. Pic.*, May 26, 1929; AANO, *Catalogue* (1911); Orleans Parish Registrar of Voters, NOPL; Poesch, *Newcomb Pottery*, 103, 126, 132.

PALMER, THERESA ZMISLOW (Mrs. A. W. L. Palmer)
Painter, active N.O. 1834–46.
Contemporary listings: portrait painter, 99 Frenchmen (1846).
References: NOCD 1846; *Courier*, May 21, 1834; Groce and Wallace.

PALTENGHI, A.
Sculptor, active N.O. 1854.
Contemporary listings: sculptor, St. Louis cor. Franklin (1854).
References: NOCD 1854–56; Groce and Wallace.

PANAMA PHOTO-ENGRAVING CO.
Engravers, active N.O. 1914–61; Henry J. Pettingill, AUGUST EDWARD MOSKAU, original partners.
Contemporary listings: photo–engraving, 612 Gravier (1914–61).
The partnership between Pettingill and Moskau dissolved by 1916. Moskau was then listed as manager (1916–21), but later formed a partnership with Cornelius H. Fitzpatrick, Milton Rue, and Albert Terry (1931–53), in which Moskau was president (1931–53). The firm's next partners were John L. Kolp, Rue, and Terry (1954–55) after which only Rue was listed as manager (1958–61).
References: NOCD 1914–29, 1931–33, 1935, 1938, 1940, 1942, 1945–47, 1949, 1952–55, 1958, 1960–61.

PARDEE, H. L.
Art teacher, active N.O. 1842.
Contemporary listings: teacher of landscape drawing, 9 Exchange Pl. (1842).
References: NOCD 1842; D. Pic., Jan. 26, 1842.

PARDO, AMBROISE
Painter, active N.O. 1803–1805.
Contemporary listings: painter (1803).
Also active as a portrait painter in LA during the 1790s.
References: NOCD 1805; Moniteur, Feb. 20, 1803; Groce and Wallace.

PARHAM, FREDERICK DUNCAN
Born N.O. Nov. 13, 1893; died N.O. Aug. 7, 1971.
Sketch artist, active N.O. 1915; primarily architect.
Exhibited: ART ASSOCIATION OF NEW ORLEANS (1915).
Prominent N.O. architect with the firms of Moise H. Goldstein (1920–ca. 1947); Goldstein, Parham & Labouisse (1952–62); and Parham & Labouisse (1963–71). He served as a member of the first Vieux Carré Commission and designed or assisted in the design of the N.O. Civic Center and City Hall (1956–59), N.O. Public Library (1958), Moisant Airport (1958–59), Clearview Shopping Center (1970), and many other public and private buildings.
References: NOCD 1915, 1920–26, 1928–33, 1935, 1938, 1940, 1942, 1945–47, 1949, 1952–56, 1958, 1960–62, 1964–69, 1971; T. Pic., Jan. 1, 1950, Aug. 9–10, 1971; Art Asso.,Special Exhibition; Orleans Parish Registrar of Voters, NOPL.

PARKER, C. R.
Painter, active N.O. 1826–48.
Contemporary listings: portrait painter, 48 Canal (1832); portrait painter, cor. Royal and Customhouse (1835); portrait painter, cor. Canal and St. Charles (1838); portrait painter, 32 St. Charles (1845–46); portrait painter, 38 St. Charles (1846); portrait painter, 71 Canal (1847–48).
Memberships/positions: Free Society of Artists, England.
Itinerant portrait painter who traveled throughout the South, including Columbus GA (1838), Natchez MS, Mobile, Montgomery, and Huntsville AL, and Charleston SC. His portraits of noted Americans were placed in the chambers of the LA State Legislature in 1826.
References: NOCD 1846; Advertiser, Feb. 3.–Apr. 11, 1832 (advs.); Argus, Dec. 2, 1826; Bee, Oct. 26, 1835, Dec. 2, 1847, Nov. 30, 1847–Feb. 22, 1848 (advs.); Comm. Times, Nov. 30, 1847 Jan. 29, 1848 (advs.), Dec. 2, 1847; D. Delta, Mar. 4–Apr. 16, 1846 (advs.), Sept. 18, 1846; D. National, Dec. 7, 1847; D. Pic., Dec. 4, 1845, Feb. 3, 1846; Jordan, "Jewelry––It's a Part of History Too," T. Pic., Nov. 14, 1976; True Amer., July 2, 1838; Bruns, 315; Glenk, 78; Groce and Wallace; Lay, 404.

PARKER, MARY VIRGINIA
Painter, art teacher, active N.O. ca. 1918–25.
Studied: Pennsylvania Academy of Fine Arts, Philadelphia; Paris.
Exhibited: ART ASSOCIATION OF NEW ORLEANS (1918).

Awarded: Pennsylvania Academy of Fine Arts, Thouron Prize for Composition (1922).
Continued exhibiting watercolors, oil paintings, and drawings at the Art Association and at the Arts and Crafts Club in the 1920s.
References: *T. Pic.*, May 31, 1922, Nov. 16–17, 1924, Mar. 4, Dec. 6, 1925; Art Asso., *Catalogue* (1918).

PARMELEE, JAMES MARCUS
Died N.O. Dec. 9, 1918.
Painter, active N.O. ca. 1915–16.
Exhibited: ART ASSOCIATION OF NEW ORLEANS (1915–16).
Father of MARCUS SUTTON PARMELEE.
References: NOCD 1878–80, 1884–96, 1914–19; *Item*, May 3, 1915; *T. Pic.*, May 2, 1915, Dec. 10, 1918; Art Asso., *Catalogue* (1916); Art Asso., *Special Exhibition*.

PARMELEE, MARCUS SUTTON
Born N.O. Apr. 2, 1894; died Metairie LA Dec. 18, 1954.
Sketch artist, commercial artist, painter, active N.O. 1915–32.
Exhibited: ART ASSOCIATION OF NEW ORLEANS (1915).
Listed as a commercial artist in 1932.
Son of JAMES MARCUS PARMELEE.
References: NOCD 1916–18, 1922–23, 1925–33, 1935, 1938, 1940, 1942, 1947, 1949, 1952–55; *Item*, Dec. 20, 1954; Art Asso., *Special Exhibition*; Orleans Parish Registrar of Voters, NOPL.

PARPAL, JOHN, JR.
Born LA Oct. 1878.
Engraver, lithographer, active N.O. 1900.
Contemporary listings: lithographer and engraver, WALLE & CO. (1900).
References: NOCD 1900–14; U.S. Census (1900), roll 572.

PASCIA, MR. _____
Sculptor, active N.O. 1849.
Contemporary listings: plaster of Paris figures, 67 Conti (1849).
References: NOCD 1849.

PASCIN (Julius Mordecai Pincas)
Born Widdin, Bulgaria Mar. 31, 1885; died Paris, France June 1, 1930.
Painter, sketch artist, active N.O. ca. 1915–17.

Studied: Vienna; Munich.
Exhibited: Salon d'Automne (ca. 1908–12); International Exhibition of Modern Art (1913); Berlin Photographic Company, N.Y.C. (1915); Macbeth Gallery, N.Y.C.
Painter and sketch artist whose full name was Julius Mordecai Pincas, and who began early in 1905 using the anagram "pascin" as his artistic signature. Often referred to as Jules Pascin, he never used the name himself. Pascin studied art in Munich and frequently had his drawings published in the satirical review *Simplicissimus*. He went to Paris in Dec. 1905, settled there, and became associated with an international group of artists known as the School of Paris. In 1914, to escape military service, he came to the U.S., arriving in N.Y.C. on Oct. 8, 1914. He spent the next six years traveling around the southern states, including FL, LA, NC, SC, and TX, and visiting the southwestern U.S. and Cuba. His N.O. sketches reveal his focus on human figures in his own cubistic style with architecture and vegetation as atmospheric backgrounds (ca. 1915–17). Pascin became a U.S. citizen in 1920; the same year he returned to Paris permanently, where he committed suicide in his studio on the eve of a prestigious one–man show.
References: *States–Item*, Dec. 30, 1974; *T. Pic.*, Apr. 22, 1973; Collier, "The World of Art: Show at Vincent Mann Gallery a Must for Serious Art Lovers," *T. Pic.*, Apr. 24, 1977; Green, "Vision: The World of Art: New Interest in Latter Day Lautrec," *T. Pic./States–Item*, Dec. 5, 1982; Bénézit; Diehl; News release, Vincent Mann Gallery, Inc., Nov. 1982; Werner.

PASQUIER, ASPES
Hairworker, active N.O. 1859–61.
Contemporary listings: hairworker, 132 Royal (1859–61).
References: NOCD 1859–61.

PASTRI, MR. S.
Painter, active N.O. 1837.
Sent a letter to the Council of the first municipality "proposing to make

a painting in oil of the city of New Orleans and its environs."
References: *Bee*, Aug. 31, 1837.

PATRICK, WILLIAM K.
Born St. Louis MO; died San Antonio TX Feb. 15, 1936.
Cartoonist, sketch artist, active N.O. 1914–19.
Studied: Crow Memorial Institute.
Contemporary listings: cartoonist, *Times–Democrat* (1914–17); cartoonist, *Times–Picayune* (1917); director, Associated Cartoonists (1917–18).
Drew most of the cartoons for the book *Club Men of Louisiana in Caricature* (printed 1917).
References: NOCD 1914–19; *T. Pic.*, Feb. 22, 1917, Feb. 16, 1936; Patrick.

PATTERSON, JOSEPH
Art teacher, active N.O. 1822.
Contemporary listings: drawing master, 30 Conti (1822).
Possibly Jos. Patterson, born Scotland; died N.O. Sept. 28, 1822.
References: NOCD 1822; *Courier*, Oct. 2, 1822; Groce and Wallace.

PATTERSON, LINDSAY
Painter, active N.O. 1850.
Contemporary listings: portrait painter, 46 Canal (1850).
References: NOCD 1850.

PATTERSON, PETER
Born Hawick, Roxburyshire, Scotland ca. 1834; died N.O. Feb. 13, 1876.
Painter, active N.O. 1860–76.
Contemporary listings: painter, Poydras near Bolivar (1860); LACOUR & PATTERSON (1861, 1867, 1869–74); painter, 437 Poydras (1866); painter, 231 Carondelet (1875–76); painter (1877).
References: NOCD 1860–61, 1866–77; *D. Pic.*, Feb. 20, 1876; N.O. Death Certificate (1876), 65:516, NOPL; U.S. Census (1860), roll 417.

PATTERSON, ROBERT L.
Born Edinburgh, Scotland ca. 1840–43; died N.O. Mar. 26, 1900.
Designer, engraver, active N.O. 1882–84; also printer.
Contemporary listings: BENNETT & PATTERSON (1882–84).

References: NOCD 1872, 1874–78, 1880–98; *D. Pic*, Mar. 28, 1900; *Mascot*, May 13, Sept. 2, 1882; N.O. Death Certificate (1900), 121:1170, NOPL.

PATTERSON, WILLIAM
Born MS.
Sketch artist, active N.O. 1849–50.
Contemporary listings: caricaturist (1849); artist (1850).
Came from Madison Parish LA in 1849 to settle in N.O.
References: *D. Delta*, July 22, 1849; Groce and Wallace; U.S. Census (1850), roll 237.

PATTERSON, WILLIAM
Lithographer, active N.O. 1889; also pressman.
Contemporary listings: lithographer, M. F. DUNN & BRO. (1889).
References: NOCD 1888–89.

PAUL, EUGENE
Born France ca. 1830.
Engraver, active N.O. 1860.
Contemporary listings: engraver (1860).
Possibly Eugene Paul, died ca. Apr. 17, 1862 in a Civil War battle as one of the 18th Regular Louisiana Volunteers; or Eugene Paul, born Paris, France ca. 1824; died N.O. July 12, 1860.
References: *Bee*, July 13, 1860; *D. Pic.*, Apr. 18, 1862; Fielding, *Dictionary*; Groce and Wallace; U.S. Census (1860), roll 421.

PAYNE, CHARLOTTE. See POLK, CHARLOTTE PAYNE

PEARCE, GEORGE E.
Born N.O. May 7, 1889; died Apr. 9, 1976.
Engraver, sketch artist, commercial artist, active N.O. 1910–55; also printer.
Contemporary listings: newspaper engraver (1910); artist (1912–13); artist, GRELLE-EGERTON ENGRAVING CO. (1914).
Drew illustrations for Stanley C. Arthur's book *Old New Orleans* (1936); exhibited with the New Orleans Art League, ART ASSOCIATION OF NEW ORLEANS, and Arts and Crafts Club from the 1920s through the 1940s; and

worked as an artist with various advertising agencies until at least 1955.
References: NOCD 1912–17, 1920–21, 1924–28, 1930–33, 1935, 1938, 1940, 1942, 1945–47, 1949, 1952–56, 1958, 1960–62, 1964–69, 1971–74; *Item–Trib.*, Dec. 4, 1927, Apr. 15, 1928; *Morn. Trib.*, Feb. 1, 1928; *T. Pic.*, Apr. 1, 1934, Oct. 27, 1937; Arthur, *Old New Orleans*; Brownson (illus.); New Orleans Art League (1926, 1949–50); Orleans Parish Registrar of Voters, NOPL; THNOC Cemetery Survey; U.S. Census (1910), roll 524.

PECK, ANN J. (Mrs. Wiley B. Peck)
Art craftsman, art teacher, active N.O. 1853–73.
Contemporary listings: wax flowers, 164 Camp (1853–54); teacher of wax flower making, cor. Camp and Orange (1855–56); wax flower work taught, Orange cor. Camp (1857); wax fruit and flowers, Camp cor. Orange (1858); wax fruit, Camp cor. Orange (1859); wax fruit, 26 Tivoli Circle (1860); teacher of ornamental branches (1871); wax work, 175 Carondelet (1872); teacher, waxworks (1873).
Possibly Ann Peck, born VA ca. 1811.
References: NOCD 1853–54, 1857–61, 1866, 1869, 1871–73; *D. Delta*, Dec. 14, 1855–Jan. 6, 1856 (advs.); U.S. Census (1860), roll 417.

PEDRETTIS, R. M.
Painter, active N.O. 1894, also decorator.
Artist with the Cincinnati OH firm F. Pedrettis Sons who came to N.O. in 1894 to submit plans for frescoes and interior decoration of the Pickwick Hotel. His designs, which were accepted, were in the French rococo style.
References: *T. Demo.*, July 29, 1894.

PEETZ, CHARLES L.
Lithographer, active N.O. 1875.
Contemporary listings: lithographer, with HERMAN WEHRMANN (1875).
References: NOCD 1875, 1879–80.

PEIRCE, ANNA M.
Born MA ca. 1846; died N.O. Jan. 3, 1913.

Painter, designer, active N.O. 1880–1900.
Contemporary listings: portrait painter (1880); artist (1891–93, 1895, 1900); art studio (1896); portrait painter, 713 St. Joseph (1898); art studio, 713 St. Joseph (1900).
Exhibited: TULANE DECORATIVE ART LEAGUE FOR WOMEN (1888); ART LEAGUE OF NEW ORLEANS (1889).
Exhibited "designs for surface decorations" at the Tulane Decorative Art League (1888). Daughter of OLIVER PEIRCE; sister of MARTHA A. PEIRCE.
References: NOCD 1891–93, 1895–97, 1899–1900; NOBD 1898; *D. Pic.*, Feb. 12, 1888, Mar. 10, 1889, Jan. 4, 1913; THNOC Cemetery Survey; Tulane Decorative Art League, 4; U.S. Census (1880), roll 464.

PEIRCE, MARTHA A.
Born Salem MA ca. 1842; died N.O. Apr. 3, 1900.
Designer, active N.O. 1888–1900.
Contemporary listings: artist (1891–93, 1895–97, 1900); art studio, 713 St. Joseph (1898–1900).
Exhibited: TULANE DECORATIVE ART LEAGUE FOR WOMEN (1888).
Exhibited "designs for surface decorations" at the Tulane Decorative Art League (1888). Daughter of OLIVER PEIRCE; sister of ANNA M. PEIRCE.
References: NOCD 1891–93, 1895–97, 1898–1900; *D. Pic.*, Feb. 12, 1888, Apr. 4, 1900; THNOC Cemetery Survey; Tulane Decorative Art League, 4; U.S. Census (1880), roll 464.

PEIRCE, OLIVER
Born Cambridge MA Sept. 13, 1807; died N.O. Dec. 16, 1893.
Artist, active N.O. 1890–91.
Contemporary listings: art studio, St. Charles cor. Howard (1890); artist (1891).
Father of ANNA M. PEIRCE and MARTHA A. PEIRCE.
References: NOCD 1857–61, 1866, 1869, 1872–73, 1875–93; *D. Pic.*, Dec. 17, 1893; THNOC Cemetery Survey; U.S. Census (1880), roll 464.

PELLISSIER, CHARLES
Born Ile–de–France ca. 1828; died
N.O. Feb. 25, 1878.
Painter, active N.O. ca. 1874–78.
Contemporary listings: portrait
painter (1878).
Came to N.O. from Belgium.
References: Louisiana Charity Hospital, Death Records, NOPL.

PELTIER, GEORGE
Artist, active N.O. 1892.
Contemporary listings: artist (1892).
References: NOCD 1892.

PEMBERTON, JOHN PETER
Born N.O. 1873; died Perpignan,
France Dec. 27, 1914.
Painter, art teacher, designer, active
N.O. 1893–1910.
Studied: with ANDRES MOLINARY, PAUL
POINCY, and WILLIAM WOODWARD;
Académie Julian, and with William
Adolphe Bougereau, Gabriel Ferrier, and Filippo Colarossi, Paris
(1895–96); Art Students' League,
N.Y.C.; New York School of Art,
N.Y.C.
Contemporary listings: teacher
(1893); instructor, Tulane Manual
Training School (1894); professor
(1895); prof., NEWCOMB COLLEGE
(1903–1908); asst. prof., Newcomb
College (1909–10).
Exhibited: Tulane University (1893);
ARTISTS' ASSOCIATION OF NEW ORLEANS (1896–97); Louisiana Historical Society (1903); ART ASSOCIATION
OF NEW ORLEANS (1905, 1907–1908);
National Association of Newspaper
Artists, Hotel Bruno (1905).
Awarded: Académie Julian, first
honor, concours
Memberships/positions: Artists' Association of New Orleans (1896); Art
Association of New Orleans, executive committee (1904–1905, 1907).
Professor of drawing until ill health
led him to retire to France.
References: NOCD 1890–95, 1900,
1903–10; D. Pic., Feb. 14, 1893,
Mar. 30, 1897, Oct. 22, 1903, Mar.
20, 1905; Harlequin, Dec. 28, 1905,
8; T. Demo., Mar. 15, 1908; T. Pic.,
Jan. 4, 1915; AANO, Catalogue
(1896, 1897); Art Asso., Catalogue
(1904, 1905, 1907, 1910); Bénézit;

Cline, Contemporary Art, 11; Glenk,
82–83; LHS (1903):15; Mount, 136,
138; Thieme and Becker; WPA, Louisiana, 167.

PENCO, ANDREW (Andrea)
Born Genoa, Italy ca. 1841; died
N.O. Feb. 14, 1889.
Painter, active N.O. 1880–88.
Contemporary listings: artist (1880);
painter (1881–84, 1886); fresco
painter (1888).
References: NOCD 1880–89; D. Pic.,
Feb. 15, 1889; N.O. Death Certificate (1889), 94:742, NOPL.

PENISTON, JOSEPH ALLARD
Born ca. June 1844; died St. Paul MN
Oct. 22, 1881.
Painter, active N.O. 1869.
Painted in N.O. a copy of a 1782 portrait by Isabey of Joseph Antoine Guy
Allard Duplantier of Voisin, France.
References: D. Pic., Oct. 24, 1881;
LSM, Biennial Report for 1920–21,
29, 72.

PENNELL, JOSEPH
Born Philadelphia PA July 4, 1857;
died Brooklyn Apr. 23, 1926.
Sketch artist, active N.O. 1882.
Studied: Pennsylvania School of Industrial Art; Pennsylvania Academy
of Fine Arts, Philadelphia.
Illustrator, etcher, lithographer, author, and teacher who came to N.O.
in Jan. 1882 and remained for four
months, creating illustrations pertaining to LA for Century Magazine
(published Jan.–Apr. 1883) and for
George Washington Cable's The Creoles of Louisiana (1885). Pennell was
also an instructor at the Art Students
League in N.Y.C. and won many
medals and awards for his work in
Europe (1900–14).
References: Preservation in Print,
Feb. 1983, 12; Beall, 342, 367, 373;
George W. Cable; Fielding, Dictionary; LSM, Biennial Report for 1926–
27, 30; Matthews; Pennell, Adventures; Pennell, Life and Letters.

PENNEY, L.
Painter, active N.O. 1839.
Contemporary listings: miniature
painter, 18 Chartres (1839).
References: D. Pic., Mar. 2–10, 1839
(advs.); Groce and Wallace.

PEPITE, JOSEPH
Painter, active N.O. 1832.
Contemporary listings: scene painter, Orleans Theatre (1832).
Cf. PEPITE, LOUIS.
References: NOCD 1832.

PEPITE, LOUIS
Born ca. 1806–20; black ("free colored male").
Painter, active N.O. 1827–35; also decorator.
Studied: with JEAN BAPTISTE FOGLIARDI.
Contemporary listings: painter, 89 Maine (1827); scene painter, Orleans Theatre (1830); scenographe and ornamental painter, 112 Royal (1834–35).
Cf. PEPITE, JOSEPH.
References: NOCD 1827, 1830, 1834–35; *Courier*, Apr. 18, 1828.

PERACHI, _____
Painter, active N.O. 1866.
With DOMINIQUE CANOVA and JEAN ROSSI, painted frescoes in the interior of the Church of St. Alphonsus and created medallions of saints and apostles (1866). *Cf.* PERELLI, ACHILLE.
References: *Times*, Sept. 9, 1866.

PERCEL, MME. _____ DE
Painter, active N.O. 1837.
Contemporary listings: portrait and miniature painter, Marty's Hotel, Chartres betw. Toulouse and St. Louis (1837).
Reported in Mar. 1837 to have arrived in N.O. from Paris.
References: *Bee*, Mar. 30, 1837; *Courier*, Mar. 28–Apr. 6, 1837 (advs.); Glenk, 78; Groce and Wallace.

PERELLI, ACHILLE
Born Milan, Italy Mar. 7, 1822; died N.O. Oct. 9, 1891.
Sculptor, painter, art teacher, sketch artist, active N.O. 1850–91; also marble cutter.
Studied: with Galli, Italy; Reale Academia di Belle Arti, Milan.
Contemporary listings: crayon portraitist, cor. Franklin and Conti (1851); sculptor, cor. Franklin and Conti (1852–54); sculptor, St. Louis cor. Franklin (1856–61); sculptor, 150 Galvez (1866); sculptor, 154 Galvez (1867); sculptor (1868, 1871, 1873); drawing master, Classical and Commercial College, and teacher, Locquet Institute (1870); teacher, A. V. Romain School (1871–72); sculptor, Gallier Court, and teacher of drawing, Institution D'Aquin (1872); teacher, De Montluzins School (1873); sculptor and painter, Gallier Court (1874); teacher, Sylvester Larned Institute (1874–75); sculptor, 181 Common (1875–80); sculptor, 26 Carondelet (1880–90); professor of drawing, SOUTHERN ART UNION (1881–84); professor of sculpture and modeling, ARTISTS' ASSOCIATION OF NEW ORLEANS (1890–91); portrait painter, 26 Carondelet (1891).
Exhibited: New Commercial Exchange (1850); Union Gallery of Fine Arts (1851); Charleville's gun store (1873); WAGENER's (1877); SEEBOLD's (1880, 1884); Southern Art Union (1881); American Exposition (1885–86); Artists' Association of New Orleans (1886–87, 1889–90); Tulane University (1890).
Awarded: Milan Academy of Art, first prize for sculpture (1847).
Memberships/positions: CUP AND SAUCER CLUB; Southern Art Union, art committee (1880–81); Artists' Association of New Orleans (1890).
Sculptor and painter who served under Garibaldi in the Italian revolution of 1848 and shortly after came to N.O. By 1851 he was known in the city as an accomplished sculptor and crayon portraitist, and he submitted a model to the Jackson Monument Committee for the equestrian statue of Andrew Jackson; although highly praised, it was rejected in favor of the design by CLARK MILLS. Perelli executed numerous busts, statues, and medallions, including busts of notables Winfield Scott (1852), P. G. T. Beauregard (1861), and Abraham Lincoln. With other artists, he suggested the selection of the site and form of improvement for the Henry Clay monument (1860), eventually erected on the neutral ground at Canal and Royal. He was

the first sculptor living in N.O. to be commissioned for significant sculptural monuments in the city. He sculpted busts of Confederate generals Robert E. Lee and Stonewall Jackson (1872), which were studies for the Monument to the Confederate Dead erected in Greenwood Cemetery (1874). In 1880 he was commissioned by the Association of the Louisiana Division of the Army of Northern Virginia to create a statue of Stonewall Jackson for the top of their tomb in Metairie Cemetery; later he executed a bronze insignia for the entrance of the tomb of the Army of Tennessee at the same location. Perelli was also renowned for his watercolors of *natures mortes*, particularly birds, fish, and small game, which were painted with lifelike intensity. He exhibited these works as well as his LA landscapes. With ANDRES MOLINARY and BRORS ANDERS WIKSTROM, he organized the Southern Art Union (1881) and took the position of professor of drawing there; he was an active member of the Artists' Association of New Orleans and also taught modeling at the Association's school. Perelli was reported by the *Daily States* (June 20, 1890) to have designed and made the first bronze bust of heroic size in N.O.: the poet Dante for the tomb of the Dante Lodge of Masons in St. Louis Cemetery III. During his career, he received numerous private and public commissions from throughout the U.S., including sculptures for the balustrade of the Capitol in Washington DC. Father of ALBINO JOSEPH PERELLI and JOHN A. PERELLI. Cf. PERACHI, _____.
References: NOCD 1851–57, 1858–61, 1866–68, 1870–91; *Art and Letters* 1(Dec. 1887):227; *Bee*, May 5, 1851, Aug. 25, 1872, May 27, 1880, May 4, 11, Nov. 16, 1881, Jan. 20, 1882, Apr. 5, 1885; *Courier*, Feb. 17, May 5, Sept. 17, 1851, Aug. 6, 1852; *Current Topics*, Nov. 1890, 23, Jan. 1891, 25, Jan. 1892, 22, 24; *D. City Item*, Oct. 10–11, 1891; *D. Crescent*, Jan. 24, 1850; *D. Delta*,

Apr. 20, Oct. 5, 1851; *D. Pic.*, Apr. 27, Oct. 30, 1852, Feb. 12, 1860, Sept. 24, 1861, Nov. 24, 1872, Feb. 17, 1874, Nov. 27, Dec. 2, 1877, Nov. 29, 1880, Mar. 24, May 26, 1881, Jan. 12, May 17, 1882, May 20, 1883, Nov. 30, Dec. 3, 1884, May 31, 1885, Nov. 6, 1886, Dec. 29, 1887, Dec. 24, 1888, Dec. 7, 17, 1889, Feb. 14, Sept. 3, Oct. 19, Dec. 17, 1890, Apr. 29, May 3, 22, 24, Oct. 10, Dec. 17, 1891; *Harlequin*, Nov. 1, 1899, 3; *Mascot*, June 10, 1882; *Repub.*, Sept. 28, 1873; *D. States*, Apr. 17, June 12, 1880, May 10, June 10, 1881, Jan. 23, 1882, Apr. 13, 1884, Nov. 5, 1886, June 20, 30, 1890, Jan. 10, Sept. 24, 26, 1891; *Demo.*, Nov. 13, 1880, Jan. 23, May 12, June 8, July 5–6, 1881; *States*, Jan. 23, 1882; *T. Demo.*, May 8, 1883, May 15, Sept. 16, Dec. 14, 1884, Apr. 7, 1887, Dec. 2, 1889, Oct. 19, 1890, Jan. 10, 1891, Feb. 5, 1892; *T. Pic.*, Oct. 3, 1948, AANO, *Catalogue* (1886, 1890); Cocke, 15; Creole Exhibit, 16–17; Groce and Wallace; Thompson, "Checklist," 286–88, U.S. Census (1860), roll 417; WPA, "Lives."

PERELLI, ALBINO JOSEPH
Born N.O. Feb. 11, 1880; died N.O. Nov. 9, 1942.
Artist, active N.O. 1910.
Contemporary listings: artist, 2511 Bayou Road (1910).
Primarily a butcher. Son of ACHILLE PERELLI; brother of JOHN A. PERELLI.
References: NOCD 1905–16, 1918–25, 1927, 1929–33, 1935, 1938, 1940, 1942; *T. Pic.*, Nov. 10, 1942; Orleans Parish Registrar of Voters, NOPL; U.S. Census (1910), roll 522.

PERELLI, JOHN A.
Born N.O. Dec. 1861; died N.O. Mar. 10, 1905.
Painter, active N.O.
Studied: Spring Hill College, AL.
Painted landscapes as a hobby. Son of ACHILLE PERELLI; brother of ALBINO JOSEPH PERELLI.
References: NOCD 1880–85, 1887–91, 1893, 1895–1905; *D. Pic.*, Mar. 11, 1905; *Item*, Mar. 11, 1905; *T. Demo.*, Mar. 11, 1905; N.O. Death

Certificate (1905), 134:951, NOPL;
WPA, "Lives."

PERETTI, ACHILLE
Born Alessandria, Piedmont, Italy
1857 or 1862; died Chicago IL Aug.
22, 1923.
Painter, sculptor, active N.O. 1884–
1923; also glazier, copier.
Studied: Art School of Rome; with
Bertini and Raffaele Casnedi, Milan;
with Morelli, Naples; with Isola and
Barabino, Geneva; with Ciseri and
Massarani, Rome; Reale Academia di
Belle Arte, Milan; Milan Academy of
Arts.
Contemporary listings: painter
(1889–90); portrait painter, 26 Carondelet (1894); portrait painter, 212
Carondelet (1895); portrait painter,
616 Orleans (1896–1900, 1907);
artist, 616 Orleans (1901–1902);
artist, 514 St. Peter (1903); portrait
painter, 514 St. Peter (1904); artist
(1906); artist, 632 St. Peter (1908–
14, 1917); artist painter, 632 St. Peter (1915–16); portrait painter, 632
St. Peter (1918).
Exhibited: ARTISTS' ASSOCIATION OF
NEW ORLEANS (1894, 1897, 1901–
1902); Tennessee Centennial Exposition, Nashville (1897).
Awarded: Academical Study, Milan,
1st silver medal.
Memberships/positions: French Association of Artists, Rome, Chicago,
and N.O.; Artists' Association of New
Orleans (1905).
Painter and sculptor who was the
third generation of a family of artists,
Peretti came to N.O. from Italy in
1884. Sometime between 1885 and
1889, he decorated the waiting room
of the Pickwick Club and created
frescoes and religious paintings for
the interiors of the Church of Our
Lady of the Gulf in Bay St. Louis MS
and for St. Stephen's Church in N.O.
St. Stephen's ornamentation included a mural showing the martyr-
dom of the saint after Raphael. Peretti became a U.S. citizen on Feb.
20, 1890, and two years later was
commissioned to fresco the interior
of St. Colombkill Church in Chicago
IL. He also painted and exhibited
portraits, landscapes, still lifes, and
miniatures and was adept at wood
carving and sculpture in plaster. He
was involved in N.O. in the interior
decoration of St. Patrick's Church
(1904); St. Vincent de Paul Church
(1907); St. Theresa's Church (1911);
New Orleans Opera Company
(1919); St. John the Baptist Church;
Holy Name of Mary Church; and St.
Louis Cathedral. Peretti was listed as
an artist and portrait painter at 632
St. Peter until his death. Cf. PERETTI,
ANTHONY.
References: NOCD 1889–90, 1894–
1904, 1906–23; D. Pic., Mar. 30,
1897, Apr. 11, 1904, June 18, 1911;
D. States, Dec. 1, 1889, Feb. 21,
1890; Harlequin, Dec. 6, 1899;
States, Mar. 14, 1920; T. Demo., Dec.
2, 1889, Sept. 9, Dec. 14, 1894, Dec.
3, 1901; T. Pic., Sept. 14, 1919, Aug.
9–11, 23, 1923, July 17, 31, 1966;
Collier, "The World of Art: Peretti's
Murals Decorate Church," T. Pic.,
Nov. 20, 1966; Collier, "Decorative
Wall Paintings Reappear From Past,"
T. Pic., Feb. 13, 1972; AANO, Catalogue (1897, 1901, 1905); Glenk,
2; 78, 87, 92; LSM, Annual Report
for 1919, 66; Mount, 192; Rightor,
383; Tennessee Centennial Exposition, 78; U.S. Census (1910), roll
521.

PERETTI, ANTHONY
Artist, active N.O. 1907.
Contemporary listings: artist, 514 St.
Peter (1907).
Cf. PERETTI, ACHILLE.
References: NOCD 1907.

PERGOLI, A.
Lithographer, active N.O. 1871.
Contemporary listings: lithographer,
with BENEDICT SIMON (1871).
References: NOCD 1871.

PERINOR, MR. _____
Painter, active N.O. 1825; 1835.
Studied: Royal School of Fine Arts,
Paris.
Contemporary listings: portrait,
landscape, and genre painter, 256
Dumaine (1825).
Exhibited: St. Philip Theatre (1825).
An entertainer in Richmond VA
(1824) prior to arriving in N.O., Per-

inor exhibited animated pictures at the Waterloo Panorama (1835).
References: *Bee*, Feb. 12, 21, 1835; *Gazette*, Apr. 5, 1825; Groce and Wallace.

PERKINS, MR. _____
Painter, active N.O. 1854.
Contemporary listings: scenic artist, Placide's Varieties (1854).
References: *D. Delta*, Nov. 18, 1854.

PERRET, PAULIN
Engraver, active N.O. 1841–42.
Contemporary listings: engraver, 11 Rampart (1841–42).
References: NOCD 1841–42; Groce and Wallace.

PERRY, ENOCH WOOD, JR.
Born Boston MA July 31, 1831; died N.Y.C. Dec. 14, 1915.
Painter, active N.O. 1860–62.
Studied: with Emanuel Leutze, Dusseldorf, Germany (1852–54); with Thomas Couture, Paris (1854–55); Rome (1856); Venice (1856–57).
Contemporary listings: artist and portrait painter (1860).
Exhibited: Melville's store, and the library of City Hall (1854); National Academy of Design, N.Y.C. (1858); E. JACOBS' (1860); Messrs. Gregor & Co. (1861); World's Industrial and Cotton Centennial Exposition (1884–85).
Memberships/positions: National Academy of Design; American Water–Color Society.
Portrait and landscape painter noted for his genre works. He came to N.O. from Boston with his family (ca. 1843) and was one of the first graduates of the city's High School. He worked as a clerk at a commission house from 1848 until about 1852 when he traveled to Europe to receive formal art instruction. He lived in various cities there: Dusseldorf, Paris, Rome, and Venice. While in Venice, Perry was named U.S. Consul (1856–57). He returned to America (ca. 1857), stopping first in Philadelphia where he opened a studio and remained for two years. In 1860 he came back to N.O. where local newspapers had reported on his career throughout the years. That same year he received a commission to paint a portrait of LA Senator John Slidell in Washington DC. While there, he painted portraits of John C. Breckinridge and Andrew Jackson, the latter, a copy of JOHN VANDERLYN's earlier work. Upon his return to N.O. (1861), he executed a portrait of Jefferson Davis and planned a life–size canvas of the signing of the LA ordinance of secession which was never completed. Following the outbreak of the Civil War, commissions were few, and Perry went to San Francisco and the Yosemite Valley. He traveled in the West, lived in N.Y.C. (1867–77), and returned to the western U.S. (ca. 1877–81), finally settling in N.Y.C. (1882) where he remained until his death.
References: *Comm. Bull.*, July 23, 1860; *D. Crescent*, July 23, 1860, Feb. 1, May 2, 1861; *D. Delta*, Dec. 22, 1853, Dec. 10, 16, 1854, July 22, Sept. 30, 1860; *D. Pic.*, Feb. 8, 1857, Apr. 29, July 22, 1860; Jan. 8, 1867; *D. True Delta*, July 22, 1860; *Repub.*, Nov. 11, 1871; *T. Pic./States–Item*, Nov. 19, 1983; *Appleton's CAB*; Cline, *Art and Artists*, 12; *DAB*; Gibbs; Glenk, 78, 138; Groce and Wallace; U.S. Census (1850), roll 234, (1860), roll 417; WICCE, *Catalogue*, 44.

PERRY, ROLAND HINTON
Born N.Y.C. Jan. 25, 1870; died Oct. 27, 1941.
Designer, active N.O. 1898.
N.Y.C. sculptor and painter who came to N.O. and submitted a design for the monument to John McDonogh to the school board committee.
References: *D. Pic.*, Aug. 1, 1897, Jan. 27, 1898; *D. States*, Jan. 24, 27, 1898; *T. Demo.*, Jan. 27, 1898; Bénézit; Fielding, *Dictionary*; William Young.

PERSAC, MARIE ADRIEN
Born Lyons, France ca. 1822–24; died Manchac LA July 21, 1873.
Painter, sketch artist, lithographer, art teacher, active N.O. ca. 1857–72; also architect, photographer, engineer.

Contemporary listings: artist and teacher of painting and drawing, 130 Canal (1865); academy of drawing and painting, 75 Camp (1869); artist, 83 Exchange Al. (1871); artist, 12 Commercial (1872).

Exhibited: Paris Exposition (1868); UTER's store (1872).

Awarded: Grand State Fair, best landscape watercolor, best composition watercolor, best crayon drawing, best stump drawing (1867), best painting in watercolors (1869), best painting in watercolors, best drawing in stump or pencil (1870), and silver medal, best painting in watercolors (1871).

Notable architectural artist who married Odile Daigre on Dec. 8, 1851 in Baton Rouge LA, lived with her family at Manchac LA, and operated an apple orchard in IN (ca. 1851, 1854) with money he inherited from his mother's estate. He was a partner with photographer William G. Vail in Baton Rouge (1856) and was later associated with PESSOU & SIMON as an artist and lithographer (ca. 1857, 1861). In 1858 N.O. publisher B. M. Norman published *Norman's Chart of the Lower Mississippi River by A. Persac*, based on the artist's descent of the river from Natchez MS to N.O., detailing all the plantation lines, names, owners, and landmarks. It was engraved, printed, and mounted by J. H. Colton & Co., of N.Y.C. Two other river sections were planned (one from Natchez to Greenville, another from Greenville to Memphis) but never executed. In 1860 he made a design with Eugene Surgi for a monument to Washington and Lafayette for Lafayette Square. He also painted watercolors of N.O. buildings and sites used in real estate transactions. He executed these first with Surgi (1860–61) and then on his own (1865–66, 1869). His extant gouache paintings of southern LA plantations, such as Shadows–on–the–Teche, Olivier, and Ile Copal, date from 1860 to 1861. Four of his lithographs were published in N.O. in *Almanach de la Louisiane* (1867):

all are scenes in the city, and one shows Persac's sign over his business address at 83 Exchange Alley. About 1870 BENEDICT SIMON published a series of lithographs of N.O. business establishments, 12 of which were signed "A. P." Persac also worked with Simon to publish a commercial map of N.O. (1871). In 1872 he collaborated with PAUL POINCY on a portrait of presidential candidate Horace Greeley. Persac died suddenly the next year while attending a family picnic at Manchac; he was buried in the old Catholic cemetery in Baton Rouge.

References: NOCD 1869, 1871–74; *Bee*, May 11, 1865, Jan. 26, 1869, July 25, 1873; *Courier*, Mar. 14, 1857; *D. Crescent*, Feb. 16, 1857; Apr. 2, 1858; *D. Pic.*, Mar. 8, 1857, Apr. 2, 1858, May 3, 1860, Apr. 11, 24, 1869, Dec. 3, 1871; *Repub.*, Aug. 18, 1872; *Times*, Mar. 27, 1865; Collier, "The World of Art: State Museum Receives Historic Persac Canvas," *T. Pic.*, Apr. 3, 1969; *Almanach de la Louisiane* (1867), frontis., illus. facing 3, 81, 120; Anglo–American Art Museum, *Louisiana Landscape*, items 2, 8–9; Anglo–American Art Museum, *Sail and Steam*, item 16; Friends of the Cabildo, *N.O. Architecture*, 4:42, 109; Gottheil; Gustafson, 1128; Harnett Kane, *Plantation Parade*, 254; J. St. Clair Favrot to Weeks Hall, Aug. 23, 1951, THNOC artists files; *Louisiana State Gazetteer*, 43; LSM negative no. 1596; Mechanics' and Agricultural Fair Asso., *Report* (1867):27; Mechanics' and Agricultural Fair Asso., *Report* (1869):88; Mechanics' and Agricultural Fair Asso., *Report* (1870):53; Orleans Parish Notarial Archives, F. D. Seghers, Sept. 30, 1873, 2:64; Orleans Parish Notarial Archives, Plan Books; Rathbone, *Mississippi Panorama*, 108–109; Reps, 311; Smith and Tucker, 149, 167; THNOC artists files; THNOC, *Waters of America*, 73; THNOC 1939.5, 1945.6, 1947.1, 1949.1.1–.32, 1950.5.84, 1958.78.1.1–.11,

1958.78.2.1–.11, 1966.5, 1967.19; U.S. Census (1860), roll 418.

PERSEVEAUX, ALPHONSE T.
Born N.O. Jan. 1, 1876; died N.O. Feb. 1, 1950.
Lithographer, active N.O. 1895–1935; also printer, pressman.
Contemporary listings: lithographer (1895–96, 1898–1902, 1904–1907, 1909–10); lithographer, WALLE & CO., LTD. (1912).
Brother of WILLIAM G. PERSEVEAUX and WALTER P. PERSEVEAUX.
References: NOCD 1895–96, 1898–1902, 1904–13, 1915–26, 1928–29, 1931–33, 1935; *States*, Feb. 2, 1950; Orleans Parish Registrar of Voters, NOPL; U.S. Census (1900), roll 572, (1910), roll 521.

PERSEVEAUX, WALTER P.
Born LA ca. Aug. 1867.
Lithographer, active N.O. 1894.
Contemporary listings: lithographer (1894).
Brother of ALPHONSE T. PERSEVEAUX and WILLIAM G. PERSEVEAUX.
References: NOCD 1887, 1889–97, 1899–1900, 1902–1908, 1910–15; U.S. Census (1900), roll 572.

PERSEVEAUX, WILLIAM G.
Born N.O. Mar. 1864; died N.O. May 3, 1926.
Lithographer, active N.O. 1887–1921; also pressman.
Contemporary listings: lithographer, M. F. DUNN & BRO. (1887, 1890); lithographer, T. FITZWILLIAM & CO. (1888–89); lithographer (1892, 1894–95, 1897, 1899–1900, 1903, 1905, 1917); lithographer, WALLE & CO. LTD. (1912).
Brother of ALPHONSE T. PERSEVEAUX and WALTER P. PERSEVEAUX.
References: NOCD 1885–97, 1899, 1902–1903, 1905, 1908–19, 1921–23; *T. Pic.*, May 4, 1926; U.S. Census (1900), roll 572.

PESCIA, NAPOLEON
Born France ca. Feb. 1845; died N.O. Nov. 23, 1907.
Painter, active N.O. 1874.
Contemporary listings: fancy painter (1874).
Primarily a house painter (1878–79, 1881–94, 1905); also listed as a wall-paperer (1895–1900, 1902–1904, 1906–1907).
References: NOCD 1874, 1878–1900, 1902–1907; *D. Pic.*, Nov. 24, 1907.

PESSOU, LOUIS LUCIEN
Born N.O. ca. 1825; died N.O. Dec. 18, 1886; black ("colored").
Lithographer, active N.O. 1853–68.
Contemporary listings: lithographer, 175 Chartres (1853); lithographer, 165 Chartres (1854); PESSOU & SIMON (1855–61, 1865–67); PESSOU & KRAUSS (1868).
References: NOCD 1853–61, 1866–77, 1879–85; *Bee*, Dec. 19, 1886; *Courier*, Nov. 6, 1851, Feb. 19, 1854, Dec. 28, 1856; *Repub.*, Sept. 23, 1871, Mar. 12, 1872; Groce and Wallace; N.O. Death Certificate (1886), 90:486, NOPL.

PESSOU & KRAUSS
Lithographers, active N.O. 1868; LOUIS LUCIEN PESSOU, WILLIAM KRAUSS, partners.
Contemporary listings: lithographers, 116 Exchange Al. (1868).
References: NOCD 1868.

PESSOU & SIMON
Lithographers, active N.O. 1855–67; also printers, publishers; LOUIS LUCIEN PESSOU, BENEDICT SIMON, partners.
Contemporary listings: lithographers, 161 Chartres (1855–56); lithographers, 23 Royal (1857–58); lithographers, 116 Exchange Al. (1857–61, 1865–67).
References: NOCD 1855–61, 1866–67; NOBD 1857–58, 1865; *Courier*, Jan. 13, 1853; *D. Crescent*, Feb. 26, June 3, Oct. 17, 1861; *D. True Delta*, Feb. 7, 1855; Groce and Wallace; Reps, 311.

PETERS, WILLIAM B.
Engraver, active N.O. 1887–88.
Contemporary listings: engraver, M. F. DUNN & BRO. (1887–88).
References: NOCD 1883–85, 1887–88.

PETERSEN, AUGUST H. M.
Born Russia, or Hamburg, Germany ca. 1819; died Aug. 8, 1882.
Engraver, active N.O. 1859–79; also stencil cutter.

Contemporary listings: engraver, Exchange Al. cor. Bienville (1858–59); engraver, Exchange Pl. (1860); engraver, successor to CHARLES BELLENOT, cor. Exchange Al. and Bienville (1866); engraver, 67 Exchange Pl. (1866–67); engraver, cor. Exchange Al. and Bienville (1866–77); engraver, 30 Commercial (1877–79). Came to N.O. ca. 1840. Father of OTTO A. A. PETERSEN.
References: NOCD 1855–56, 1858–60, 1866–79; *D. City Item*, Nov. 3, 1877; *Times*, Nov. 20, 1877; *T. Deutsche Zeitung*, Apr. 8, 1869; "Dame Blanche," back cover, Sheet Music Collection, LA Coll., TU; N.O. Death Certificate (1882), 81:241, NOPL; Groce and Wallace; *Louisiana State Gazetteer*, 123; U.S. Census (1860), roll 412, (1870), roll 521.

PETERSEN, OTTO A. A.
Born LA ca. 1857–58; died after 1940.
Engraver, active N.O. 1877–86; also stencil cutter, printer.
Contemporary listings: engraver, Exchange Al. cor. Bienville (1877); engraver, with AUGUST H. M. PETERSEN (1878–79); engraver, 14 Commercial (1880); engraver, with Isidore Gugenheim (1882); engraver, 34 Natchez (1883–85); engraver, 27 Commercial (1886).
Son of AUGUST H. M. PETERSEN.
References: NOCD 1877–88, 1890–1914, 1916–17, 1919–25, 1928–33, 1935, 1938, 1940; U.S. Census (1860), roll 412, (1870), roll 521.

PETERSON, HENRY
Painter, active N.O. 1887–89.
Contemporary listings: painter (1888–89).
Frescoed and painted the interior of Fabacher's Royal Restaurant with the assistance of EDWARD SCHARFSCHWERDT (1887).
References: NOCD 1885, 1888–89; *D. Pic.*, Sept. 4, 1887.

PETERSON, JOHN
Born LA ca. 1862.
Engraver, active N.O. 1880.
Contemporary listings: engraver (1880).

Boarded with TILMAN JOSEPH LAUTERBACH in 1880.
References: NOCD 1875–78, 1880–83; U.S. Census (1880), roll 460.

PETERVIST, R.
Painter, active N.O. 1883.
Exhibited: 10 S. Rampart (1883).
References: *Bee*, Jan. 13, 1883.

PETIT, PETER B.
Sculptor, active N.O. 1872–89; also cabinetmaker.
Studied: apprentice, with LOUIS M. BLIGNY (1872).
Contemporary listings: carver, with Louis M. Bligny (1873); carver, Roberts & Co. (1885); PETIT & BOH (1886–89).
Assisted Louis M. Bligny in carving a madonna and child in 1872. Possibly P. Petit, born ca. June 1860.
References: NOCD 1872–73, 1885–1912, 1914; Arthur, *LSM Guide*, 99; Glenk, 229; U.S. Census (1860), roll 419.

PETIT & BOH
Sculptors, active N.O. 1886–89; also cabinetmakers; PETER B. PETIT, JOHN P. BOH, partners.
Contemporary listings: woodcarvers, 88 Bienville (1886); woodcarvers (1887); sculptors and woodcarvers, Basin cor. St. Louis (1888–89).
References: NOCD 1886–1908.

PETRANECK, GEORGE
Born N.O. ca. 1867; died N.O. Apr. 13, 1901.
Lithographer, active N.O. 1884–1901; also pressman.
Contemporary listings: lithographer (1884, 1888, 1892–93, 1896–97, 1899, 1901); lithographer, T. FITZWILLIAM & CO. (1885–87, 1900); lithographer, M. F. DUNN & BRO. (1889–90).
References: NOCD 1884–93, 1896–97, 1899–1901; *D. Pic.*, Apr. 14, 1901.

PEW, JAMES
Born England ca. 1822.
Engraver, active N.O. 1850.
Contemporary listings: engraver (1850).
In Charity Hospital at the time of the 1850 U.S. census.

References: U.S. Census (1850), roll 234.

PEYROUX, ALPHONSE, JR.
Born N.O. 1874; died Bay St. Louis MS Jan. 13, 1910.
Sketch artist, active N.O. ca. 1892.
Exhibited: Tulane University (1892). Employed by the post office (ca. 1892–1907) while studying to be a dentist. He practiced dentistry for only three years until his death.
References: NOCD 1893–97, 1900–1908; *D. Pic.*, Mar. 3, 1892, Jan. 14, 1910; *T. Demo.*, Mar. 3, 1892.

PEYTON, IDA
Born N.O.; died N.O. Feb. 12, 1898.
Painter, designer, active N.O. 1884–98; also photographer.
Studied: Paris.
Contemporary listings: art studio, 147 Canal (1887–88); miniature portraits on copper (1894); artist (1898).
Exhibited: World's Industrial and Cotton Centennial Exposition (1884–85).
References: NOCD 1888–95, 1898; *D. Pic.*, Apr. 25, 1889, Sept. 9, 1894, Feb. 13, 1898; *D. States*, Oct. 23, 1887, Nov. 29, 1888; *T. Demo.*, June 7, 1885, Apr. 25, 1889; N.O. Death Certificate (1898), 115:915, NOPL; THNOC Cemetery Survey; Woman's Department of World's Exposition, 161.

PFISTER, FRANK
Engraver, active N.O. 1879.
Contemporary listings: engraver, with TILMAN JOSEPH LAUTERBACH (1879).
References: NOCD 1866–68, 1870–83, 1885–90, 1892–93, 1896–97; *D. Pic.*, Aug. 5, 1887, Feb. 24, 1900.

PFLUECKHAHN, HENRY
Lithographer, active N.O. 1869–91; also printer.
Contemporary listings: lithographer, 116 Exchange Pl. (1869); lithographic printer, with CAPT. JOHN E. BOEHLER (1870); lithographic printer (1871); lithographic printer, MANOUVRIER & SIMON (1872); lithographer, D. SIMON & CO. (1874); lithographer, with DIONIS SIMON; lithographer, T. FITZWILLIAM & CO.

(1885–86); lithographer, M. F. DUNN & BRO. (1887–88); lithographer (1889); lithographer, with MICHEL CAPO (1891).
References: NOCD 1869–77, 1879–80, 1885–89, 1891.

PHELPS, ALBERT CARRUTHERS
Born N.O. Dec. 29, 1875; died N.O. May 16, 1912.
Sketch artist, cartoonist, painter, active N.O. ca. 1897–1912.
Memberships/positions: Tulane Sketch Club, pres. (ca. 1896); ARTISTS' ASSOCIATION OF NEW ORLEANS (1897); ARTS EXHIBITION CLUB (1901). Journalist, historian, poet, and music critic, who, while working as an editor for the *New Orleans Item* from 1907–12, also contributed cartoons and illustrations. His extant drawings and watercolors date from the early 1900s and possibly as early as 1897. Phelps began to write for the *Evening Post* of N.Y.C. while a freshman at Tulane. In 1905 he wrote a history of Louisiana entitled *Louisiana, A Record of Expansion*.
References: NOCD 1896, 1898, 1907, 1909–12; *D. Pic.*, May 17, 1912; *Item*, May 17, 1912; AANO, *Catalogue* (1897); Albert Carruthers Phelps Collection, Special Collections, TU; Arts Exhibition Club, 15; Knight, 341–42; *NCAB*.

PHELPS, EDWIN FORMAN
Born Aurora NY Mar. 9, 1796; died Chadron OH 1863.
Painter, sketch artist, active N.O. ca. 1822–26.
Itinerant portrait and miniature painter who traveled down the Mississippi River to N.O. on two painting and sketching expeditions, the first from KY (1822–23) and the second from OH (1825–26). It is believed that Phelps worked with JOHN JAMES AUDUBON and English painter William Bamborough (born 1792; died 1860) during his visits to the South.
References: Collier, "The World of Art: Itinerant Artist E. Phelps Leaves Trip Journal Behind," *T. Pic.*, Oct. 9, 1977; Edwin Forman Phelps Papers,

THNOC; THNOC 1965.10.1–.2, 1967.29.

PHILASTRE, EUGENE
Born Paris, France 1828; died N.O. June 21, 1886.
Painter, active N.O. 1871–85; also decorator.
Contemporary listings: scenic painter, French Opera House (1871); scenic painter, New Orleans Opera Company (1872); scenic artist, Théâtre de l'Opéra (1880); painter (1881); scenic painter, Signor Faranta's Iron Theatre (1884); scenic painter, French Opera House (1884–85).
Fresco and scenic painter who decorated the interiors of Grunewald Hall (1873), the St. Charles Hotel, and the Crescent Hall, as well as restaurants and private residences (1875). He also did fresco work in barrooms and saloons (1875, 1885).
References: NOCD 1872, 1881; *Bee*, Dec. 12, 19, 1875, June 22, 1886; *Bull.*, Dec. 24, 1875; *D. Pic.*, May 6, 1871, Nov. 29, 1880; *D. States*, Oct. 13, 1884, Nov. 8, 1885; *Eve. Chronicle*, Oct. 11, 1884; *Repub.*, Oct. 13, 1872, Nov. 2, 1873.

PHILBRICK, GEORGE. *See* HAMMOND & PHILBRICK

PHILIASTRE, OMER
Artist, active N.O. 1874.
Contemporary listings: artist (1874).
References: NOCD 1874.

PHILIPPOTEAUX, PAUL DOMINIQUE
Born Paris, France 1846; died Paris, France July 2, 1923.
Painter, active N.O. 1885.
Studied: with his father Félix Emmanuel Philippoteaux; with Cabanel and Léon Cogniet (ca. 1862); Ecole des Beaux Arts, Paris.
Exhibited: Salon, Paris (1866–67).
Renowned French historical painter who visited N.O. in Jan. 1885 and returned in Oct. to marry native New Orleanian Marie Bechet. Among his works painted in the U.S. were a panorama of Niagara Falls, a cyclorama of the Battle of Gettysburg, and a diorama of the life of Ulysses S. Grant.
References: *D. States*, Jan. 9, Oct. 17, 1885, May 22, 1886, June 9, 1891;

Mascot, Dec. 6, 1884; *T. Demo.*, Nov. 1, 1885; *T. Pic.*, July 4, 1923; Bénézit.

PHILLIPPI, HENRIETTA
Born LA ca. 1887.
Painter, active N.O. 1910.
Contemporary listings: artist and painter (1910).
References: U.S. Census (1910), roll 519.

PHILLIPS, A. L.
Born NY ca. 1820.
Painter, active N.O. 1850–54.
Contemporary listings: DRURY & PHILLIPS (1850–51); painter, 76 Carondelet (1852); painter, 109 St. Charles (1853); PHILLIPS AND BOWEN (1854).
References: NOCD 1851–54; *D. Pic.*, Feb. 13, 1851; U.S. Census (1850), roll 237.

PHILLIPS AND BOWEN
Painters, active N.O. 1854; also sign, ship, and steamboat painters; A. L. PHILLIPS, O. F. BOWEN, partners.
Contemporary listings: transparencies and landscapes executed, 59 Poydras (1854).
References: *Semi–Wkly. Creole*, Oct. 4–Dec. 16, 1854 (advs.).

PHOTO-ELECTRIC-ENGRAVING CO.
Engravers, designers, lithographers, painters, active N.O. 1893–94; also photographers; HENRY ROMANSKI, mgr., GEORGE FRANÇOIS MUGNIER.
Contemporary listings: 12 and 14 Exchange Pl. (1893–94).
References: NOCD 1893–94; *T. Demo.*, June 4, 1893.

PHOTO-ENGRAVING COMPANY
Engravers, designers, artists, active N.O. 1890–1905; George Supot, mgr. (1893); FRANÇOIS BILDSTEIN, mgr. (1893–1902); Fred Querens, Jr., pres. (1896–98); T. G. Rapier, pres. (1902); T. A. Slattery, v. pres. (1902).
Contemporary listings: 117 Poydras (1891–93); 61 Camp (1894); 325 Camp (1895, 1905).
Established in 1890.
References: NOCD 1891–1905; *Architectural Art* 1(Oct. 1905):11; *D. States*, Feb. 10, 1902; *Mascot*, Mar. 1, 1890–Feb. 2, 1895 (illus.); *Town Talk*, Feb. 1905; Seymour.

PICARD & MARMU
Colorers, active N.O. 1854; primarily photographers; Mr. _____ Picard, CALISTE MARMU, partners.
Contemporary listings: colorers, 106 Royal (1854).
References: *Courier*, Dec. 20, 1854.

PICCHI, FREDERICK
Born Italy ca. 1795.
Sculptor, active N.O. 1856–61; also molder, gilder.
Contemporary listings: statuary, 184 Bourbon (1856), sculptor, 138 Bourbon (1860–61).
References: NOCD 1851–61; Orleans Parish Notarial Archives, Plan Book, 72:9.

PICCIRILLI, ATTILIO
Born Massa di Cararra, Italy May 16, 1866; died NY 1945.
Sculptor, active N.O. 1898.
Studied: Academy of St. Luke, Rome (before 1888).
Member of marbleworking family who came to the U.S. (1888) and settled in N.Y.C. He arrived in N.O. in Jan. 1898 to submit his design for the John McDonogh monument in Lafayette Square. His design was chosen and in Dec. he returned from N.Y.C. for the statue's unveiling. It was his first major public monument; he later created numerous others, including the national monument to the sinking of the battleship *Maine*. Brother of FURIO PICCIRILLI.
References: *D. Pic.*, Jan. 27, Dec. 30, 1898; *D. States*, Jan. 24, 28, 1898; *T. Demo.*, Jan. 27, 1898, July 1, 1899; *T. Pic.*, Apr. 4, 1936, May 2, 1937; Craven, 500–1; Dabney, 329; Fielding, *Dictionary*, 740; Gardner, *American Sculpture*, 94–95; William Young.

PICCIRILLI, FURIO
Born Massa di Cararra, Italy Mar. 14, 1868; died Rome, Italy 1949.
Sculptor, active N.O. 1898.
Studied: Academy of St. Luke, Rome (before 1888).
Marble worker who came to N.O. from N.Y.C. in January 1898 to submit his design for the John McDonogh monument in Lafayette Square, the successful design was

submitted by his brother, ATTILIO PICCIRILLI.
References: *D. States*, Jan. 24, 29, 1898; *T. Demo.*, Jan. 27, 1898; Fielding, *Dictionary*; Gardner, *American Sculpture*, 94, 102–3.

PICHON, ARTHUR
Born LA Feb. 1857.
Painter, active N.O. 1875–1922; also sign painter.
Contemporary listings: painter, (1875–80, 1883, 1885, 1887, 1890–91, 1893–1903, 1905, 1907, 1910, 1912, 1916); painter, Morgan's Louisiana & Texas Railroad & Steamship Co. (1884); portrait painter (1886); artist (1888).
References: NOCD 1875–80, 1883–91, 1893–1905, 1907, 1910–12, 1914, 1916–19, 1921–22, 1927; U.S. Census (1900), roll 573.

PICKET, THOMAS
Painter, active N.O. 1885.
Contemporary listings: fresco painter, Trisconi's Theatre (1885).
References: *Eve. Chronicle*, June 5, 1885.

PICKHIL, ALEXANDRE
Died N.O. ca. 1840–50; black.
LA portrait painter mentioned in secondary sources; there are no known contemporary listings or extant works.
References: Desdunes, 71; Groce and Wallace.

PIERCE, LOUIS R.
Lithographer, active N.O. 1894; also pressman.
Contemporary listings: lithographer (1894).
References: NOCD 1894–95, 1898–1911.

PIERCY, FREDERICK HAWKINS
Born Portsmouth, England Jan. 27, 1830; died London, England June 10, 1891.
Sketch artist, painter, active N.O. 1853.
Portrait and landscape painter who arrived in N.O. from England on Mar. 21, 1853 and then traveled throughout the Mississippi Valley and westward to Salt Lake City UT, sketching scenes and portraits under commission of the Church of Latter-Day

Saints. He returned to England in 1854, and his illustrated narrative, *Route from Liverpool to Great Salt Lake Valley* was published in 1855.
References: Baenézit; Groce and Wallace; Museum of Fine Arts, 2:37–39; Piercy; Powell, 34–39.

PIERSON, JOSEPH. *See* DAMERON–PIERSON CO. LTD.

PIERSON, VICTOR
Painter, active N.O. ca. 1865–73.
Contemporary listings: PIERSON & GENIN (1871–72); PIERSON & POINCY (1872–73).
Exhibited: WAGENER's (1868, 1870); SEEBOLD's (1884).
Awarded: Grand State Fair, gold medal, best historical painting in oil, with THEODORE SIDNEY MOISE (1868). Artist reputed to be from England or France who came to N.O. (ca. 1865) via Mexico. He was noted for horse paintings, although he also painted other animals, portraits, and hunting and outdoor scenes. While in N.O. he often worked in collaboration with other artists on large paintings, such as *On the Metairie* (1868) with Theodore Sidney Moise and *Volunteer Firemen's Parade* (1872) with PAUL POINCY and THEODORE LILIENTHAL. Pierson left N.O. (ca. 1873) and was said to have returned to Mexico.
References: NOCD 1872–73; *D. Pic.*, Jan. 9–10, 19, 23, Apr. 12, 1868, Aug. 25, 1870, Nov. 30, 1884; *Repub.*, Dec. 18, 1873, Dec. 31, 1874; Coulon MS, Scrapbook 100, LSM; Glenk, 78, 149–150; Kendall, *History*, 2:658; LSM, *Biennial Report for 1920–21*, 82; LHS (1900):item 1511; LSM, *Annual Report for 1919*, 63; LSM, *Biennial Report for 1928–29*, 34; Mechanics' and Agricultural Fair Asso., *Report* (1868):42; WPA, *Louisiana*, 166.

PIERSON & GENIN
Painters, active N.O. 1871–72; VICTOR PIERSON, JOHN GENIN, partners.
Contemporary listings: portrait painters, 24 1/2 Carondelet (1872).
Awarded: Grand State Fair, best composition and best portrait, cabinet size (1871).

References: NOCD 1872; *D. Pic.*, Dec. 3, 1871.

PIERSON & POINCY
Painters, active N.O. 1872–73; VICTOR PIERSON, PAUL POINCY, partners.
Contemporary listings: portrait painters, 24½ Carondelet (1873).
Exhibited: UTER's store (1872); 30 Camp (1873).
Collaborators on *Volunteer Firemen's Parade* (1872), an enormous canvas over 12 feet long which depicted the Mar. 4, 1872 parade forming on Canal Street, including firemen, horses, and onlookers around the statue of Henry Clay. Pierson and Poincy were aided by THEODORE LILIENTHAL, who furnished photographs of many of the men portrayed among the 126 active firemen and numerous other identifiable figures, and by THEODORE SIDNEY MOISE, who helped promote the fire companies' interest in the success and completion of the painting.
References: NOCD 1873; *Bee*, Aug. 17, 1872, Mar. 5, 1873; *D. Pic.*, Feb. 23, 1873; *Repub.*, Aug. 18, 1872, Feb. 23, Mar. 4, 1873.

PIGGOTT, JOSEPH
Painter, active N.O. 1872–87.
Studied: Italy.
Contemporary listings: scenic artist, Varieties Theatre (1872); scene painter, Milneburg New Opera House, and scenic artist, Grunewald Opera House (1885); scenic painter, Signor Faranta's Iron Theatre (1885–86); scenic artist, French Opera House (1887).
References: NOCD 1885–87; *D. Pic.*, Oct. 19, 1872, Oct. 3, 1875, Sept. 18, 1886; *D. States*, Oct. 18, 1884; *Eve. Chronicle*, Oct. 13, 1884, June 4, 1885; *Mascot*, Jan. 29, 1887; *National Repub.*, Oct. 25, 1872; *Repub.*, Feb. 4, Apr. 14, 21, May 2, 5, Oct. 19, Nov. 28, Dec. 20, 22, 1872, Jan. 3, 7, 1874; Cruise and Harton, 73, 78–80.

PILES, CONRAD. *See* PYLES, CHARLES C.

PILIE, JOSEPH (Gil Joseph)
Born Mirbalis, Santo Domingo ca. 1789; died N.O. June 29, 1846.

Painter, art teacher, designer, active N.O. 1808–34; primarily surveyor, engineer, architect, decorator.

Contemporary listings: teacher of portrait, landscape, and flower drawing, 32 North Royal (1808); designer (1811); scenic painter, St. Philip Street Theatre and Orleans Theatre (1816); scenic painter, Olympic Circus (1817).

Served periodically as N.O. city surveyor from ca. 1822 until his death. With JEAN HYACINTHE LACLOTTE, he decorated the Grand Hall of the Terpischore (1813). Pilié designed several temporary public monuments, including a triumphal arch executed by JEAN BAPTISTE FOGLIARDI, honoring the visit of Gen. Lafayette (1825); a cenotaph commemorating the deaths of Thomas Jefferson and John Adams (1826); and an obelisk for the anniversary celebration of the Battle of N.O. (1832), all of which were erected in what is now Jackson Square. For the memorial service of Gen. Lafayette held on July 26, 1834, Pilié directed the decoration of St. Louis Cathedral and also supervised the erection of a mausoleum.

References: NOCD 1811, 1822–24, 1827, 1830, 1832, 1834–35, 1837–38, 1841–44, 1846; *Bee,* June 30, 1846; *Courier,* Mar. 18, 1808, Nov. 19, 1813, Jan. 12, Oct. 25, Nov. 8, 1816, Feb. 17, 28, 1817, Aug. 18, 1826, Dec. 24, 1832, July 28, 1834; *Gazette,* Aug. 18, 1826; *Mercantile Advertiser,* May 27, 1834; *Moniteur,* Mar. 18, 1808 (advs.); Arthur, *Old New Orleans,* 137; Friends of the Cabildo, *N.O. Architecture,* 2:229; Huber and Wilson, *Basilica,* 24–25; Levasseur, 2:90–91; N.O. Death Certificate (1840), 11:16, NOPL; U.S. Census (1840), roll 132.

PINAC, ANNA V.
Born N.O. June 1863; died N.O. Jan. 11, 1929.
Art teacher, painter, active N.O. 1885–1920.
Contemporary listings: drawing teacher, Pinac Institute (1885); teacher of fancy work, Pinac Institute (1893); portrait painter (1910);

artist, 1600 Gov. Nicholls (1914, 1918).
References: NOCD 1890–91, 1901, 1907, 1909–12, 1914, 1916–20; *Bee,* July 4, 1885; *T. Demo.,* June 28, 1890, June 27, 1893; *T. Pic.,* Jan. 12, 1929; U.S. Census (1900), roll 572.

PINCAS, JULIUS MORDECAI. *See* PASCIN

PINISTRI, S.
Sketch artist, active N.O. 1833; primarily architect, engineer, also cartographer.
Made a sketch of N.O. from the west bank of the Mississippi River, which was engraved as a vignette on the map that he published, *New Orleans General Guide & Land Intelligence* (1841).
References: *Courier,* Oct. 4, 1841; *D. Pic.,* Nov. 5, 1841; Fossier, facing 49; THNOC 1960.45.

PINOLI, MR. A.
Painter, active N.O. 1838–44.
Contemporary listings: CERESA & PINOLI (1838); portrait painter, 72 Chartres (1841); portrait painter, 190 Royal (1842); portrait painter, Royal near St. Peter (1843–44).
With DOMINIQUE CANOVA painted frescoes for the interior of the rotunda of the St. Louis Exchange Hotel, which was built in 1841.
References: NOCD 1841–44; *Comm. Bull.,* Apr. 5, May 24, 1841, Jan. 10, 1842; Caldwell, 210–13; Norman, 158.

PINTO, MR. _____
Art teacher, painter, active N.O. 1831.
Contemporary listings: painting teacher, 149 Chartres (1831).
References: *Mercantile Advertiser,* Apr. 9, 1831.

PIRIN, ALBERT
Born LA Apr. 1875.
Painter, active N.O. 1900.
Contemporary listings: artist painter (1900).
References: U.S. Census (1900), roll 572.

PIROTZO, DANIEL
Born OH ca. 1877.
Engraver, active N.O. 1910.
Contemporary listings: die and stamp engraver (1910).

307

References: U.S. Census (1910), roll 524.

PITARD, ROBERT C.
Born N.O. ca. 1876.
Painter, sketch artist, active N.O. 1884–87; also copyist.
Studied: with WILLIAM J. WARRINGTON (1887).
Exhibited: American Exposition (1885–86); William J. Warrington's studio (1887).
Memberships/positions: ART ASSOCIATION OF NEW ORLEANS (1905).
Artistic child prodigy who taught himself to paint and draw in 1884 at about the age of eight by copying the works of others. He became a noted violinist at Belhaven College, Jackson MS.
References: NOCD 1893–1905; *D. Pic.*, Oct. 25, 1885, June 29, 1912; *T. Demo.*, Oct. 18, 1887; Art Asso., *Catalogue* (1905); *Who's Who in Louisiana and Mississippi.*

PITKIN, JOSEPH LOVELL
Born N.O. Nov. 1878; died Charlotte NC June 1, 1939.
Engraver, active N.O. 1900.
Contemporary listings: stationery engraver (1900).
Brother of ROBERT GRAHAM PITKIN.
References: NOCD 1898–1906, 1908–1909; *T. Pic.*, June 2, 1939; U.S. Census (1900), roll 570.

PITKIN, ROBERT GRAHAM
Born N.O. Oct. 1880; died East Islip NY June 22, 1970.
Cartoonist, active N.O. 1896–1900.
Contemporary listings: cartoonist, *Harlequin* (1899–1900).
Brother of JOSEPH LOVELL PITKIN.
References: NOCD 1898–1902; *D. States*, Nov. 29, 1897; *Harlequin*, Sept. 13, 1899–July 28, 1900, Mar. 28, 1900, Jan. 2, 1902, July 26, 1906, July 11, 1907; *States*, Nov. 15, 1896; *States–Item*, July 18, 1970; U.S. Census (1900), roll 570.

PITOT, ARMANTINE. *See* ALLAIN, ARMENTINE PITOT

PLAISTED, T. S.
Painter, active N.O. 1873–74.
Contemporary listings: scenic artist, Academy of Music (1873–74).

References: NOCD 1874; *Repub.*, Oct. 19, 1873.

PLANTOU, MME. ANTHONY
Painter, active N.O. 1819.
Studied: with Renaud; with Jacques–Louis David, Paris.
Exhibited: Girod's house (1819).
Historical, religious, landscape, portrait, and miniature painter; probably from France. She and her husband came to N.O. in 1819 to exhibit her allegorical painting, *The Treaty of Ghent*, from which her husband had prints struck. The painting was also shown in Philadelphia (1818) where she had lived, and later in Washington DC (1820) where she also painted portraits.
References: *Courier*, Jan. 20–Feb. 5, 1819 (advs.), Jan. 25, 29, Mar. 5, 1819; Bolton, *Painters in Miniature*, 130; Fielding, *Dictionary*; Groce and Wallace; Benjamin Latrobe, *Impressions*, 102–5; New Orleans City Council, Proceedings, Mar. 13, 1819, NOPL.

PLAQUE, R.
Painter, active N.O. ca. 1867.
Awarded: Grand State Fair, best southern landscape in oil, best head in oil, best composition in oil (1867).
References: Mechanics' and Agricultural Fair, *Report* (1867):27.

PLATTSMIER, JOHN T.
Born Baltimore MD ca. 1827; died N.O. Jan. 3, 1904.
Designer, active N.O. 1858; primarily architect, carpenter.
Came to N.O. ca. 1854; designed the engraving executed by JOHN V. CHILDS on a silver pitcher to honor A. B. Clark, late foreman of the Washington Fire Co. No. 20 (1858).
References: NOCD 1857, 1859–61, 1866–70, 1872, 1874–86, 1890–91, 1895–97, 1899–1904; *D. Crescent*, May 2, 1854, Oct. 25, 1858; *D. Pic.*, Jan. 10, 1904; *T. Demo.*, Jan. 4, 1904; N.O. Death Certificate (1904), 131:675, NOPL; U.S. Census (1860), roll 415.

PLAUCHE, LEDA HINCKS (Mrs. Henry Plauché)
Born N.O. Dec. 30, 1887; died N.O. Dec. 3, 1980.

Designer, commercial artist, painter, active N.O. ca. 1915–60s.
Studied: NEWCOMB COLLEGE (graduated 1907).
Exhibited: ART ASSOCIATION OF NEW ORLEANS (1917).
Mainly a self–taught artist who designed tableaux, costumes, and floats for carnival organizations. Among her first known designs were those for Nereus (1916), and she also worked for Proteus prior to 1938. At one time she was a commercial artist for Maison Blanche department store and president of the Women's Advertising Club of N.O. (1926–27). Her illustrations appeared in her own book *Old New Orleans Characters* (1931) and in Stanley Clisby Arthur's *Old New Orleans* (1937). She worked for the carnival organizations Rex (ca. 1935–65) and Atlanteans.
References: NOCD 1922, 1925–30, 1932–33, 1935, 1938, 1940, 1942, 1945–47, 1949, 1952–56, 1958, 1960, 1964, 1966–69, 1971–79; *Item*, Feb. 21, 1952; *States*, Dec. 4, 1932; *T. Pic.*, May 15, 1938; *T. Pic./States–Item*, Dec. 4, 1980; Art Asso., *Catalogue* (1917); Arthur, *Old New Orleans*, 104; Information courtesy Charles L. Mackie; La Cour, 200; Orleans Parish Registrar of Voters, NOPL; Plauché; THNOC 1981.331-.9-.15, 1982.205.53, 1982.205.79-.224.

PLICATOR, FRANK
Born N.O. ca. 1838.
Engraver, active N.O. 1860.
References. U.S. Census (1860), roll 418.

PLUMB, H. B.
Painter, active N.O. ca. 1882.
Exhibited: SOUTHERN ART UNION (1882).
References: *D. Pic.*, Mar. 19, 1882.

PLUMMER, HARRISON LORENZO
Born Haverhill MA Mar. 2, 1814.
Painter, active N.O. 1859–66.
Contemporary listings: portrait painter (1859); portrait painter, M. J. Hinton's daguerrean gallery (1866).
Exhibited: Boston Athenaeum (1837); Royal Academy, London

(1837–45); Victorin Guette's store (1859).
Portrait and genre painter who came to N.O. after working in London from 1837 to 1845.
References: *Bee*, Mar. 2, 1859; *D. Pic.*, Feb. 25, 1866; Groce and Wallace.

POHL, OTTO
Artist, active N.O. 1893–94.
Contemporary listings: artist (1893–94).
References: NOCD 1893–94.

POHLMANN, THEODORE
Lithographer, active N.O. 1882–86.
Contemporary listings: lithographer (1882, 1886); lithographer, with T. FITZWILLIAM (1883); pres., SOUTHERN LITHOGRAPHIC COMPANY (1884); supt., Southern Lithographic Co. (1885).
References: NOCD 1882–86; *Mascot*, Oct. 18, 1884.

POINCY, PAUL E.
Born N.O. Mar. 11, 1833; died N.O. Nov. 14, 1909.
Painter, art teacher, active N.O. 1859–1909.
Studied: Ecole des Beaux Arts, and with Marc–Gabriel–Charles Gleyre, Léon Cogniet, and Julien, Paris (ca. 1852–58).
Contemporary listings: portrait painter, 6 Royal (1859); artist painter (1870); artist, 186 Common (1872); PIERSON & POINCY (1872–73); portrait painter (1874); portrait painter, 28 Carondelet (1875–77); artist (1878, 1881, 1898, 1902–1903, 1907–1908); artist, 28 Carondelet (1879); artist, 166 Canal (1880); portrait painter, 737 N. Rampart (1882); portrait painter, 172 Canal (1883–87); antique class instructor, ARTISTS' ASSOCIATION OF NEW ORLEANS (1886–87, 1891–93); lecturer in perspective, Artists' Association of New Orleans (1886–87, 1892–93); portrait painter, 13 Commercial (1888–94); artist, 618 Commercial (1895–97, 1899–1901); painter (1904); artist, 2033 Dumaine (1905–1906); portrait painter, 2119 Hospital (1909).

Exhibited: SEEBOLD's (1879–80); LILIENTHAL's (1883); Artists' Association of New Orleans (1886–87, 1890–92, 1896–97, 1899, 1901); Tulane University (1892); Tennessee Centennial Exposition, Nashville (1897); Moses & Son (1901).

Memberships/positions: SOUTHERN ART UNION (1880–81); Artists' Association of New Orleans (1885–97).

Portrait, genre, landscape, and religious painter whose early education was at the Jesuit school in Grand Coteau LA and then in St. Louis MO. After studying in Paris, he returned to N.O. by Jan. 1859; he also spent time in AL that year. He opened a N.O. studio with RICHARD CLAGUE, but with the outbreak of the Civil War, Poincy entered the Confederate Army. In partnership with VICTOR PIERSON, he painted the large canvas *Volunteer Firemen's Parade* (1872). He was one of the promoters and founders of the Southern Art Union (1880), as well as one of the organizers of the Artists' Association of New Orleans (1885), where he acted as secretary and treasurer for many years and taught classes in perspective drawing. With JULIA M. MASSIE he served on the Jury of Selection at the Tennessee Centennial Exposition (1897). Poincy exhibited his works throughout the city and was considered by *Harlequin* (1899) to be one of the best portrait painters in N.O. Although he painted many notable subjects and street scenes, he preferred creating children's portraits and works with religious themes.

References: NOCD 1861, 1866–1868, 1870, 1910; *Art and Letters*, 1(Dec. 1887):227–28; *Bee*, Jan. 18, 22, 1859, May 27, 1880, May 4, Nov. 16, 1881, Sept. 27, 1885; *Current Topics*, Nov. 1890, 23, Jan. 1891, 24, Jan. 1892, 24, 26, Jan. 1893, 11; *D. Pic.*, Apr. 10, 1879, Mar. 2, 4, 1881, July 26, 1885, Nov. 7, 1886, Dec. 17, 1887, July 27, Nov. 13, 1890, Apr. 29, May 22, 24, Dec. 17, 1891, Mar. 3, 1892, Mar. 30, 1897, Nov. 15, 1909; *D. States*, May 13, 1880, Oct. 29, Nov. 5, 1886, May 16, 1890, Jan. 8, 1899; *Demo.*, May 12, 1881; *Down in Dixie*, Aug. 1, 1896, 6; *Harlequin*, Nov. 8, 1899, 10; *Lantern*, Nov. 10, 1886; *Men and Matters*, Sept. 1897, 49, 51; *T. Demo.*, July 30, 1883, Dec. 13, 1885, Nov. 13, Dec. 17, 1890, Dec. 13, 1892, Dec. 3, 29, 1901, Mar. 22, 24, 1902; *Town Talk*, Sept. 1904, 27; AANO *Catalogue* (1886, 1890, 1891, 1896, 1897, 1899, 1901); AANO, *School of Art* (1892–93); Bruns, 315; Coulon MS, Scrapbook 100, LSM; Glenk, 43, 78; Groce and Wallace; Lilienthal's, 8; LSM, *Biennial Report for 1920–21*, 69; LSM, *Biennial Report for 1932–33*, 57; Moses; Mount, 134–35; Rightor, 382–83, 385; Tennessee Centennial Exposition, 79; U.S. Census (1870), roll 523, (1900), roll 572; WPA, "Lives."

POINDEXTER, JAMES THOMAS
Born Christian County KY June 6, 1832; died Eddyville KY June 10, 1891.
Painter, active N.O. 1870–71.
Contemporary listings: portrait painter, 80 Camp (1870–71).
References: Boyd, 200; Bruns, 315; Groce and Wallace.

POINTEL DU PORTAIL, J. B.
Born France.
Painter, art teacher, lithographer, sketch artist, active N.O. 1836–40; also photographer.
Studied: with Jacques–Louis David, Léon Cogniet, and Redouté, Paris.
Contemporary listings: teacher of drawing and painting figures, landscapes, and flowers, and miniature painter, 74 Orleans (1836); portrait painter and lithographer, 33 Royal, and teacher of drawing and painting, Mme. Boyer's and 106 Royal (1837); lithographer, portrait painter, 33 Royal, and lithographer (1838); painter and lithographer (1840).
Awarded: Grand State Fair, certificate for portraits (1844).
Portrait and miniature painter who in 1856 was noted as having come from Paris. He made lithographic portraits of many notable N.O. citizens and was the lithographer at the

Bee. He was one of the earliest daguerreotypists in the city (1840). By 1844 he was living in Baton Rouge LA.
References: NOCD 1838; *Bee*, Nov. 11, 1836, Apr. 5, Nov. 22, 1837, Feb. 11, Apr. 9, 1840; *Courier*, June 11, 1838, Mar. 7, 1839; *D. Pic.*, Jan. 14, 1844; Glenk, 78, 273; Groce and Wallace; Harter and Tucker, 124; Smith and Tucker, 168; Thieme and Becker.

POLHEMUS & COOK
Painters, active N.O. 1837; also glaziers, sign and ornamental painters; J. D. L. Polhemus, Francis Cook, partners.
Contemporary listings: military standard and transparency painters, 22 Exchange Pl. (1837).
References: NOCD 1838; *Bee*, Apr. 24–Aug. 17, 1837 (advs.).

POLK, CHARLOTTE PAYNE (Mrs. Armour Cantrell Polk)
Died Mar. 17, 1963.
Art craftsman, designer, active N.O. 1895–1905.
Studied: NEWCOMB COLLEGE (1895, 1902–1905).
Exhibited: Louisiana Purchase Exhibition, St. Louis MO (1904).
Distinguished as a pottery designer. With JENNIE WILDE, she prepared enormous maps of N.O. and the Mississippi River for the St. Louis World's Fair (1904).
References: *D. States*, Dec. 6, 1903; *States-Item*, Mar. 20, 1963; Poesch, *Newcomb Pottery*, 103; Smithsonian, *Newcomb Pottery*, 14.

POLLARD, POLLARD
Born LA ca. 1883.
Painter, active N.O. 1910.
Contemporary listings: painter–pictures (1910).
References: U.S. Census (1910), roll 521.

POLLOCK, THOMAS
Engraver, active N.O. 1832–33; also printer.
Contemporary listings: engraver, 7 Chartres (1832–33).
Engraver from Edinburgh, Scotland who also worked in Boston (1834

35), Providence RI (1839), and N.Y.C. (1840–57).
References: *Bee*, Dec. 20, 1832–Jan. 7, 1833 (advs.); Groce and Wallace.

POMAREDE, EDOUARD
Born Ponpegrive, France ca. 1809; died N.O. Sept. 23, 1879.
Painter, active N.O. 1859–74; also sign painter.
Contemporary listings: portrait painter, 266 Bourbon (1859–60); portrait painter, 146 Basin (1861); portrait painter, 119 Exchange Al. (1870–71); oil painter, North Front cor. Customhouse (1874).
References: NOCD 1859–61, 1870, 1874; *Bee*, Sept. 24, 1879; Boyd, 200.

POMAREDE, LEON D.
Born Tarbes, France ca. 1807–11; died St. Louis MO Oct. 10, 1892.
Painter, art teacher, sketch artist, active N.O. 1830–69.
Studied: Paris; Germany; Italy; with Mr. Findelles; with his father–in–law, ANTOINE MONDELLI; with LOUIS DOMINIQUE GRANDJEAN DEVELLE.
Contemporary listings: oil and fresco painter and teacher of painting and drawing, Marine Hotel (1832); painter, 62 Camp (1842); miniature painter, Marais near St. Philip (1843–44); artist, 417 Constance, and scenic artist, St. Charles Theatre (1867); portrait painter, 417 Constance (1869).
Exhibited: Armory Hall (1849–50).
Awarded: Grand State Fair, silver medal for best animal painting (1868).
Panorama, landscape, miniature, scene, and religious painter, who is believed to have come to the U.S. in 1830 and have briefly lived in N.O. that year. Pomarède first advertised in N.O. (*Bee*, Jan. 1832) that he could ornament rooms in oil and fresco painting "in the most English manner." That same year, he was working in St. Louis MO where he painted one of the earliest views of the city and later decorated the cathedral with frescoes, oil paintings, and transparent window paintings (1834). Pomarède returned to N.O. in 1837

and by 1841 had married Antoine Mondelli's daughter. He had received the commission for three paintings behind the main altar of St. Patrick's Church (*Transfiguration of Christ, St. Patrick baptising the daughters of the King of Ireland,* and *Christ walking on the Sea of Galilea*): they were first shown to the public in June 1841. Although listed in N.O. in 1842–44, Pomarède had returned to St. Louis by Oct. 1843 to make the city his permanent home and had entered into a partnership with T. E. Courtenay as plain and ornamental painters. Briefly in 1848, Pomarède worked with HENRY LEWIS on his panorama of the Mississippi River, but left to make sketches and paintings for his own panorama, supposedly with the assistance of the western artist Charles Wimar. With his partner Courtenay, he opened *Pomarède's Original Panorama of the Mississippi River and Indian Life* in St. Louis in Sept. 1849, after what he claimed was four years in preparation. With plans to take the work to Europe, Pomarède also exhibited it in N.O. in Armory Hall from Nov. 1849 to Jan. 13, 1850. The panorama illustrated only the upper Mississippi, in four moving sections, with accompanying music and descriptive oration. It was also seen in several cities from Mobile AL to N.Y.C., but was destroyed by fire in Newark NJ in Nov. 1850. Pomarède spent most of the rest of his life painting religious and genre paintings and murals for churches, public buildings, and theaters. He died after a fall from scaffolding while decorating a church in Hannibal MO.
References: NOCD 1842–44, 1867, 1869; *Bee,* Jan. 23, 1832; *Comm. Bull.,* Jan. 26, 1843, Nov. 15, 1849; *Courier,* July 17, Nov. 9, 1841; Dec. 19, 1849; *D. Crescent,* Nov. 12, 1849, Aug. 3, 1850; *D. Delta,* Nov. 29, 1850; *D. Pic.,* June 26, 29, 1841, Nov. 24, 27, 28, 29, 30, Dec. 1, 4, 5, 8, 9, 11, 13, 17, 18, 20, 23, 1849, Jan. 3, 5, 9, 1850, Jan. 19, 1868, Oct. 13, 1892; *Repub.,* Aug. 25, 27, 1867; *Wkly. Delta,* Dec. 3, 1849, Jan. 14, 1850. Arrington, "Léon Pomarède"; Coulon MS, Scrapbook 100, LSM; Friends of the Cabildo, *N.O. Architecture,* 2:228; Groce and Wallace; McDermott, *Lost Panoramas,* 145–60; McDermott, "Léon Pomarède"; Mechanics' and Agricultural Fair Asso., *Report* (1868):42; Rathbone, *Mississippi Panorama,* 110.

POMMAYRAC, PIERRE PAUL EMMANUEL DE
Born Puerto Rico Apr. 25, 1807; died Paris, France July 10, 1880.
Painter, art teacher, active N.O. 1832–35.
Studied: with Gros; with Mme. Lizinka de Mirbel.
Contemporary listings: miniature painter and teacher, 91 St. Louis (1832); miniature painter, 82 St. Louis (1833–35).
Exhibited: Boimare's bookstore (1832); Salon, Paris (1835–80).
References: NOCD 1834–35; *Bee,* Dec. 20, 1832; *Courier,* Dec. 5, 1833; Bénézit; *Bryan's;* THNOC 1962.1.8.3, 1962.1.8.17, 1962.1-.8.30.

PONS, VALENTINE WILLIAM
Painter, active N.O. 1888–89.
Contemporary listings: artist (1888); artist and portrait painter, 443 Bayou Rd. (1889).
References: NOCD 1885, 1888–1900, 1902, 1904–19, 1921–22, 1924, 1927.

PONTALBA, GASTON DE
Born France ca. 1828; died Nov. 1, 1875.
Sketch artist, active N.O. 1848–51. Son of Joseph Xavier Célestin Delfau de Pontalba and Micaëla Leonarda Almonester, both born in LA of prominent families. Gaston de Pontalba was considered the most gifted of the three Pontalba sons: he was a musician as well as an artist. After his parents were divorced in 1838, he lived with his mother in Paris. Because of the 1848 revolution in France, Madame Pontalba fled with two of her sons, Gaston and Alfred, to London, then to N.O., her birthplace. Gaston recorded their trip and

stay in his diary/sketchbook *Voyage à la Nouvelle Orléans du Fev. 1848 au 7 Mai 1851.* He included several drawings of the city, mostly of the buildings around the Place d'Armes (now Jackson Square), where his mother had constructed two rows of buildings facing each other. The family moved into one of these apartments, located on the corner of Decatur and St. Peter, in the fall of 1850. Gaston and his brother were listed there in the 1850 U.S. census as landlords. The Pontalba family left N.O. on Apr. 6, 1851, to return to Paris; their N.O. property holdings were managed through local agents. Gaston pursued his art interests in Europe and published lithographic prints of drawings of French estates and chateaux.

References: Arthur, *Old Families*, 31; Huber and Wilson, *Pontalba*, 16, 26, 32, 40, 45–48; LSM, *Biennial Report for 1926–27*, 64; LSM artists files; U.S. Census (1850), roll 235.

PORTAIL, J.B. POINTEL DU. *See* POINTEL DU PORTAIL, J. B.

PORTE CRAYON. *See* STROTHER, DAVID HUNTER

PORTER, WILLIAM T.
Painter, active N.O. 1866–67.
Contemporary listings: scenic artist, Varieties Theatre (1866–67); scenic painter, Academy of Music (1867).
Worked at Pike's Opera House, Cincinnati OH before coming to N.O.
References: *D. Pic.*, Nov. 29, Dec. 10, 1867; *Repub.*, Nov. 24, 1867; *Times*, Sept. 27, Oct. 2, Nov. 11–12, Dec. 9, 13, 1866.

PORZIN, E.
Cartoonist, active N.O. ca. 1899–1900.
Name appeared with H. H. SCARTABELLI on a political cartoon dated N.O. Jan. 1, 1900 in *Harlequin.*
References: *Harlequin*, Jan. 3, 1900, 6–7.

POTTHOFF, CHARLES
Born Emden, Germany ca. 1824; died N.O. Feb. 21, 1879.
Painter, active N.O. 1854–68.
Fresco painter who decorated the ceiling of Trinity Episcopal Church,

corner Jackson and Coliseum (1854), and was in the partnership of POTTHOFF & KNIGHT (1857–68).
References: NOCD 1851–59, 1868–79; *D. Delta*, Mar. 26, 1854; *D. Pic.*, Mar. 21, 1854, Feb. 22, 1879.

POTTHOFF & KNIGHT
Painters, sculptors, active N.O. 1857–68; primarily sign and decorative painters; CHARLES POTTHOFF, George F. Knight, partners.
Awarded: Grand State Fair, honorable mention for best display of medallions in plaster (1868).
Dealers in paint and art supplies who frescoed the rear of the pulpit and ceiling of the First Presbyterian Church (1857).
References: NOCD 1855–61, 1866–70; *D. Creole*, Feb. 24, June 4, 1857; Mechanics' and Agricultural Fair Asso., *Report* (1868):43.

POUPART, J. F.
Engraver, active N.O. 1812.
Contemporary listings: engraver, Bellanger's jeweler, Royal (1812).
Possibly Jacques François Poupart, born Les Cayes, Ste.–Domingue Apr. 15, 1781; died N.O. Oct. 21, 1855.
References: NOCD 1811, 1822, 1830, 1834–35, 1838, 1841, 1843–44, 1846, 1849–58; *Courier*, July 29, 1812; Groce and Wallace; N.O. Death Certificate (1855), 17:246, NOPL; THNOC Cemetery Survey; U.S. Census (1810), roll 10.

POWELL, WILLIAM HENRY
Born N.Y.C. Feb. 14, 1823; died N.Y.C. Oct. 6, 1879.
Painter, active N.O. 1842; 1854.
Studied: with JAMES HENRY BEARD; with HENRY INMAN, N.Y.C. (ca. 1840–41); Paris; Florence, Italy.
Contemporary listings: portrait painter, 47 Common (1842).
Exhibited: National Academy of Design, N.Y.C. (1838); Armory Hall (1854).
Memberships/positions: National Academy of Design (1839).
Historical and portrait painter who moved to Cincinnati OH with his family during his childhood. Briefly in 1842 he came to N.O. and established a studio where he painted por-

traits. By 1847 he was commissioned to paint a panel, *De Soto Discovering the Mississippi* for the rotunda of the Capitol in Washington DC. In 1848 he went to Paris to complete the work, returned to the U.S. in 1853, and exhibited the panel in N.O. in 1854. After the painting was installed in the Capitol, Powell remained in Washington several years, painting portraits of government officials. Later he was commissioned by the state of OH to paint Commodore Perry at the naval battle of Lake Erie during the War of 1812, completed in 1863.

References: NOCD 1842; *Bee*, Jan. 7, 1842, May 16, 1854; *Courier*, May 26, 1854; *Crescent Monthly*, Dec. 1866, 489; *D. Crescent*, Jan. 4, 1851, Feb. 4, 1852, May 1–15, 1854, May 18, 26, 1854; *D. Delta*, Mar. 23, 1847; *D. Pic.*, Feb. 24, 1855; *Repub.*, Jan. 19, 1873; *Wkly. Delta*, Feb. 7, 1848, Jan. 12, 1852; *Appleton's CAB*; *Biographical Sketches of American Artists* (1915); Bruns, 316; *DAB*; Groce and Wallace; THNOC Artists Files.

POWERS, ALENSON G.
Born NY ca. 1815 or VA ca. 1819.
Painter, active N.O. 1848–67.
Studied: Paris (1855); Florence, Italy (1856).
Contemporary listings: artist, 13 St. Charles (1849, 1854); artist, 13 St. Charles, studio no. 14 (1850–53); portrait painter, 82 Camp (1856–59); portrait painter, Camp cor. Natchez (1857); portrait painter, 142 Canal (1859–61); portrait painter, 2 Camp (1867).
Exhibited: Hewlett's Exchange (1848); Norman's bookstore (1857); WAGENER's (1867).
Portrait and historical painter noted for his numerous portraits of N.O.'s prominent citizens. He began his career in northern OH (ca. 1842) and spent the summer of 1844 in Cincinnati as a portrait painter. In 1845 he was working in Lexington KY and by 1848 he was in Baton Rouge LA painting a portrait of Zachary Taylor. Later that year he came to N.O. when

the painting was exhibited. In 1854 it was offered for sale to the city of N.O., and in 1858 the purchase was completed. Powers remained in N.O. until June 1854 when he left for Europe to study and visit art galleries. By Dec. 1856 he had returned to N.O., but left again in June 1860 for Madison Parish LA where he worked as an artist. Powers returned to N.O. (ca. 1867); nothing is known of him after Mar. 1867.

References: NOCD 1849–54, 1857–61; *Bee.*, Nov. 3, 1848; *Comm. Bull.*, Nov. 3. 1848, Oct. 13, 1853, Dec. 22, 1856; *Courier*, Sept. 14, Nov. 2, 1852, June 27, 1854, Mar. 16, 1855; *D. Crescent*, Feb. 26, 1852, Feb. 6, 1857, Dec. 19, 1859; *D. Delta*, Nov. 7, 1848, Nov. 22, 1850, June 11, 1852, Jan. 17, Mar. 12, June 27, 1854; *D. Pic.*, Nov. 2, 1848, Nov. 14, 1850, June 27, Sept. 16, 1854, Mar. 25, 1856, Mar. 24, 1858, Jan. 4, 1859, Mar. 3, 1867; *D. Times*, Feb. 18, 1852; *D. True Delta*, Dec. 11, 1859–Jan. 25, 1860 (advs.); *Mercantile Advertiser and Daily Business Directory*, Dec. 17, 1851; *Parlor Magazine*, Jan. 1857; *Times*, Jan. 3, Feb. 3, 1867; Bruns, 316; Coulon MS, Scrapbook 100, LSM; Glenk, 78; Kendall, *Golden Age*, 334–35; New-York Historical Society, 738–39; U.S. Census (1850), roll 234, (1860), roll 413.

POWERS, J.
Born Philadelphia PA ca. 1815.
Painter, active N.O. 1860.
Contemporary listings: portrait painter (1860).
References: NOCD 1858; U.S. Census (1860), roll 421.

POWERS, S.
Born NY ca. 1820.
Artist, active N.O. 1850.
Contemporary listings: artist (1850).
References: U.S. Census (1850), roll 235.

PRADOS, MME. _____
Born N.O.
Painter, active N.O. ca. 1800–24.
Painter of miniatures credited as having produced works in N.O. ca. 1800–24 which were later exhibited

at the American Exposition (1885–86).
References: Creole Exhibit, 35–36; Coulon MS, Scrapbook 100, LSM; WPA, *American Portrait Inventory*, 209.

PRAGUE, MARY BRICE. *See* BRICE, MARY B.

PRESTON, BLANCHE PRESTON
Born Fayetteville WV.
Designer, painter, active N.O. 1910–16.
Studied: Museum of Art, Cincinnati OH; Art Students' League, N.Y.C.
Exhibited: ART ASSOCIATION OF NEW ORLEANS (1913).
Portrait, miniature, and landscape painter, who, for several years, designed parade floats for the Comus carnival organization. After 1916 she returned to WV.
References: *T. Pic.*, Nov. 26, 1939; Art Asso., *Catalogue* (1913).

PREVOT, CHARLES
Painter, active N.O. 1879.
Contemporary listings: artist and portrait painter, 195 Canal (1879).
References: NOCD 1879.

PRIOR, MR. J.
Born England ca. 1795.
Painter, active N.O. 1848.
Contemporary listings: scenic painter, Olympic Theatre (1848).
Advertised in 1848 that he had previously been the pyrotechnic and scenic artist of the St. Charles and American Theatres.
References: *D. Delta*, May 14, June 29, 1848; U.S. Census (1850), roll 234.

PROSPER. *See* FOY, RENE PROSPER

PROSSER, PERCY J.
Born England ca. 1871.
Sculptor, active N.O. 1908–27; also decorator.
Contemporary listings: modeler and plastic relief decorator, 1213 Dryades (1908); sculptor, 1213 Dryades (1909–10); sculptor, 1744 Erato (1911–18).

References: NOCD 1907–21, 1923, 1927, 1930; *Men of Affairs*, 70; U.S. Census (1910), roll 523.

PROSSER, PERCY J., JR.
Born IN ca. 1893.
Sculptor, active N.O. 1911–13; also decorator.
Contemporary listings: sculptor (1911); modeler, with PERCY J. PROSSER (1912–13).
References: NOCD 1911–26; McCarthy et al., 10; U.S. Census (1910), roll 523.

PRURNACKE, CHARLES
Artist, active N.O. 1838.
Contemporary listings: artist, 42 Great Men (1838).
References: NOCD 1838.

PUCCIO, ANTONIO
Born Palermo, Sicily.
Sculptor, designer, active N.O. 1909; primarily cabinetmaker, carpenter, carver.
Cabinetmaker in the employ of the Monteleone Hotel's cabinet shop. He was commissioned to design and carve the large, ornate, grandfather clock in the hotel's lobby (1909).
References: NOCD 1903–1906, 1909–12, 1915–16, 1919, 1921–24, 1927, 1929–32, 1935, 1938, 1940, 1942; *States–Item*, Aug. 18, 1961, Apr. 25, 1976.

PURSELL, MATTIE E. *See* SHIELDS, MATTIE E. PURSELL

PYLES, CHARLES C. (Conrad Piles)
Born LA or KY 1846; died 1881.
Painter, active N.O. 1870–81.
Contemporary listings: painter (1870, 1878, 1881); portrait painter, 371 Chartres (1872); portrait painter (1875, 1880); artist (1876–77, 1880); painter, 31 N. Rampart (1879).
References: NOCD 1869, 1871–72, 1875–81; THNOC Cemetery Survey; U.S. Census (1870), roll 523, (1880), roll 463.

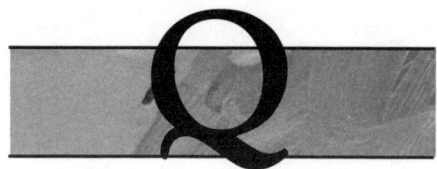

QUESTY, JACOB
Born LA ca. 1843; black ("mulatto").
Sculptor, active N.O. 1880; also marble cutter.
Contemporary listings: sculptor, with Joseph Llulla (1880).
References: NOCD 1871, 1875–77, 1880–83; U.S. Census (1870), roll 521.

QUILLIAM, JOHN
Engraver, active N.O. 1858–77.
Contemporary listings: engraver, 8 St. Charles (1858–59, 1877); engraver, 10 Camp (1867–68); engraver (1869, 1873); engraver, with JOHN DOUGLAS (1871, 1874, 1876).
References: NOCD 1858–59, 1867–69, 1871, 1873–74, 1876–77; Groce and Wallace.

QUINN, LUCILLE
Artist, active N.O. ca. 1916.
Exhibited: ART ASSOCIATION OF NEW ORLEANS (1916).
References: Art Asso., *Catalogue* (1916).

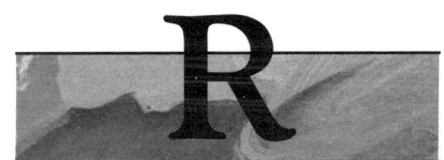

RACKLE, WILLIAM
Born Germany June 1842.
Sculptor, active N.O. 1899–1909;
also decorator, marble cutter.
Contemporary listings: sculptor
(1899–1900); stone sculptor (1900);
sculptor, 2103 Magazine (1903);
sculptor, 1217 Felicity (1908–1909).
References: NOCD 1899–1900,
1902–1904, 1906–1909; U.S. Census (1900), roll 571.

RAGUSA, JOSEPH
Born Palermo, Italy ca. 1848; died
N.O. Mar. 21, 1921.
Sculptor, designer, active N.O.
1882–1920; also builder.
Contemporary listings: sculptor
(1884, 1913, 1916); artist (1900–1904, 1906).
Came to the U.S. in 1872 and used
his ability as a sculptor in making
floats for the Rex carnival organization (1882–1920). He designed floats
in N.O. for nearly 40 years and also
created works for the Hudson–Fulton celebration in N.Y.C. (1908), the
Gasparilla Parade in FL (1912), and
the Memphis TN Centenary Celebration (1918).
References: NOCD 1878, 1884,
1900–1904, 1906–10, 1912–13,
1915–21; *Item*, Mar. 24, 1921; *T.
Pic.*, Oct. 5, 1919, Mar. 22–23, 1921;
T. Pic./States–Item, Mar. 4, 1984.

RAILEY, LAURA
Sketch artist, art teacher, active N.O.
1892–1913.
Studied: NEWCOMB COLLEGE (1892).
Contemporary listings: supervisor of
drawings, public schools (1911);
drawing teacher, New Orleans Public Schools (1913).
Exhibited: Tulane University (1892).
References: NOCD 1897–98, 1911–12, 1915–16; *D. Pic.*, Mar. 3, 1892;
T. Demo., Jan. 14, 1913.

RANCON, VICTOR
Artist, active N.O. 1824.
Contemporary listings: artist, 145
Orleans (1824)

References: NOCD 1824; Glenk, 78;
Groce and Wallace.

RANDOLPH, BEVERLY PARHAM (Mrs.
Edwin Lewis Stephens)
Born Biloxi MS; died N.O. Dec. 26,
1943.
Sketch artist, art teacher, active N.O.
1901.
Studied: NEWCOMB COLLEGE (1898,
1900–1902).
Contemporary listings: drawing
teacher (1901).
References: NOCD 1901; *Item*, Dec.
27, 1943; *States*, Dec. 27, 1943; *T.
Pic.*, Dec. 27, 1943; Ormond and Irvine, 166.

RANDOLPH, LEILA PIERCE
Born N.O. Sept. 23, 1891; died Mar.
29, 1956.
Art craftsman, active N.O. ca. 1916–17.
Exhibited: ART ASSOCIATION OF NEW
ORLEANS (1916–17).
Pottery decorator who was listed as
a teacher in 1935 and 1939.
References: *States*, Mar. 29, 1956;
Art Asso., *Catalogue* (1916, 1917);
Orleans Parish Registrar of Voters,
NOPL.

RASCHE, MARY RICHARDSON. *See*
RICHARDSON, MARY WALCOT

RASCON, CORA TOWNSEND. *See*
TOWNSEND, CORA ALICE

RATELLE, ARTHUR WILLIAM
Born N.O. Sept. 25, 1879; died N.O.
Mar. 15, 1926.
Lithographer, active N.O. 1898–1900; primarily carpenter; also surveyor.
Contemporary listings: artist, ART
LITHOGRAPH CO. (1898); lithographer–artist (1900).
References: NOCD 1896–99, 1901,
1903–11, 1913, 1917, 1919–23; *T.
Pic.*, Mar. 16, 1926; Orleans Parish
Registrar of Voters, NOPL; U.S.
Census (1900), roll 570.

RAUCH, PHILIP HENRY
Born N.O. June 19, 1887; died N.O.
June 8, 1933.

Engraver, active N.O. 1907–21. Contemporary listings: engraver (1907, 1909); engraver, M. Scooler Co. (1908); jewelry engraver (1910); engraver, with DIETRICH A. WALTER (1910–13).

Also listed as an engraver in 1920–21 and thereafter listed mostly as an optometrist.

References: NOCD 1907–13, 1920–33, 1935; *T. Pic.*, June 9, 1933; Orleans Parish Registrar of Voters, NOPL; U.S. Census (1910), roll 524.

RAUSHER, F.

Hair worker, active N.O. 1858. Contemporary listings: ornamental hair manufacturer, 204 Baronne (1858).

References: NOBD 1858.

RAUVIERE, MELANIE

Artist, active N.O. 1893. Contemporary listings: artist (1893). References: NOCD 1893.

RAWDON, WRIGHT, HATCH & EDSON

Engravers, active N.O. 1839–59; also printers; Freeman Rawdon (born ca. 1801; died 1859), Ralph Rawdon, Neziah Wright (born ca. 1804), George Whitfield Hatch (born ca. 1805; died 1867), TRACY ROBINSON EDSON, partners.

Contemporary listings: banknote engraving (1839); banknote engravers, 2 Royal (1841); banknote engravers, 10 Royal (1842, 1849–51); banknote engravers, cor. Royal and Canal (1843, 1845, 1847); engravers of banknotes, 12 Royal (1852–59).

Rawdon, Wright, Hatch & Edson was a N.Y.C. bank note engraving firm organized in 1835. There were branches of the firm in Albany NY, Boston, Cincinnati OH, and N.O. In 1858 the firm amalgamated with six other engraving companies to form the AMERICAN BANK NOTE COMPANY.

References: NOCD 1841–43, 1849–59; *Bee*, June 17, 1841, Jan. 7, 1842; *D. Pic.*, Apr. 29, 1841, Dec. 21, 1845, June 8, 1847, Mar. 17, 1850; *Comm. Bull.*, Feb. 14, 1839; *Courier*, Nov. 19, 1842; *True Amer.*, Jan. 7, 1839; Boggs; Groce and Wallace.

RAYMOND, NORMAN O. SAMUEL

Born N.O. Apr. 28, 1861; died N.O. Mar. 23, 1897.

Artist, active N.O. 1891–96. Contemporary listings: artist (1891–94, 1896).

References: NOCD 1873–74, 1884, 1886, 1891–94, 1896; *D. Pic.*, Mar. 24, 1897.

READ, J. B.

Painter, active N.O. 1845. Contemporary listings: portrait painter, Royal betw. Canal and the Post Office (1845).

References: *D. Pic.*, Nov. 21, 1845.

READ, THOMAS BUCHANAN

Born Chester County PA Mar. 12, 1822; died N.Y.C. May 11, 1872.

Painter, active N.O. 1865.

Studied: with Shobal V. Clevenger (1837).

Contemporary listings: portrait painter, 156 Canal (1865).

Poet and painter of portraits and historical events who first worked as a ship and sign painter (1837), then as a sculptor in Cincinnati OH (ca. 1839). He lived in Boston (ca. 1841), Philadelphia (1846), and Europe; he came to N.O. to set up a studio and to paint a portrait of Gen. Philip H. Sheridan (1865). Read returned to Europe and lived in Italy until 1872.

References: *D. Pic.*, July 10, 1859; *D. True Delta*, Nov. 9, 1865; *Repub.*, May 19, 1872; *Wkly. National Repub.*, June 16, 1872; *Appleton's CAB*; Bénézit; Fielding, *Dictionary*; Groce and Wallace.

REAVES, J.

Born ca. 1822.

Artist, active N.O. 1850. Contemporary listings: artist (1850). References: U.S. Census (1850), roll 234.

REBETY, VICTOR

Artist, active N.O. 1860–66. Contemporary listings: artist, 297 St. Peter (1860–61, 1866).

References: NOCD 1860–61, 1866, 1868–70, 1873; Groce and Wallace.

RECLUS, JEAN JACQUES ELISEE

Born Sainte–Foy la Grande, France Mar. or May 15, 1830; died Torhout, Belgium July 4, 1905.

Sketch artist, active N.O. 1855.

Famous geographer and writer of many volumes whose article "Frag-

ment d'un Voyage à la Nouvelle–Orléans" includes illustrations after his
own drawings. His writings were
praised for their literary and scientific merit.
References: *Appleton's CAB; Encyclopaedia Britannica*; Reclus, *The
United States*; Reclus, "Fragment
d'un Voyage."

REDKIN, RUDOLPH
Born LA ca. 1880.
Lithographer, active N.O. 1905–10.
Contemporary listings: lithographer
(1905–1906); lithographer, printers
shop (1910).
References: NOCD 1902, 1905–
1909; U.S. Census (1910), roll 520.

REED, ADINE
Painter, sketch artist, art teacher, active N.O. 1893–97.
Studied: with GEORGE DAVID COULON.
Contemporary listings: painter, artist, teacher, Canal and Bourbon
(1893); artist (1897).
Opened an art school and studio with
CARRIE TROST in 1893. Reed was later
listed in 1903–1904 and 1912 as a
music teacher.
References: NOCD 1894, 1896–98,
1900, 1903–1904, 1912, 1916,
1920–24, 1926; *T. Demo.*, June 11,
1893.

REED, WILLIAM
Painter, active N.O. 1873–85.
Contemporary listings: painter
(1873–74); artist (1885).
Cf. REID, _____.
References: NOCD 1873–74, 1885.

REEDER, CLARENCE M.
Born N.O. Sept. 13, 1894; died after
1962.
Sketch artist, commercial artist,
painter, active N.O. 1910–32; also
photographer.
Contemporary listings: sketch artist–
photogrpher (1910); artist, GRELLE-
EGERTON ENGRAVING CO. (1913); artist, *Item* (1914–18).
Exhibited: ART ASSOCIATION OF NEW
ORLEANS (1917).
Reeder worked for the *Item* (1914–
22) and the Chambers Advertising
Agency (1923–24), he was listed as
an artist or commercial artist until at
least 1932.

References: NOCD 1912–25, 1927–
28, 1932, 1960–62; Art Asso., *Catalogue* (1917); Orleans Parish Registrar of Voters, NOPL; U.S. Census
(1910), roll 520.

REEVES, FRANKLIN A.
Born NY ca. 1841; died N.O. Feb.
20, 1915.
Sculptor, active N.O. 1871–1910;
primarily marblecutter.
Contemporary listings: sculptor, with
James Hagan (1871–72); marble
sculpture (1910).
References: NOCD 1871–76, 1878–
84, 1886–1904, 1906–1916; *T. Pic.*,
Feb. 21, 1915; U.S. Census (1910),
roll 524.

REEVES, W. H.
Born England ca. 1823.
Artist, active N.O. 1850.
Contemporary listings: artist (1850).
Possibly H. Reeves listed as a printer
(1851–53).
References: Groce and Wallace; U.S.
Census (1850), roll 234.

REGAMEY, FELIX ELIE
Born Paris, France Aug. 7, 1844; died
Juan–les–Pins, France May 7, 1907.
Sketch artist, active N.O. 1880.
Studied: with his father, Louis Pierre
Guillaume Regamey; with Le Coq de
Boisbaudran.
Contemporary listings: artist (1880).
Exhibited: French Opera House
(1880).
Noted French portrait, history, and
genre painter, as well as caricaturist,
who stopped in N.O. while on a tour
of the U.S., England, and Japan.
References: *D. Pic.*, Feb. 21, 1880;
Times, Feb. 19, 1880; Bénézit.

REHN, MICHAEL
Born Germany ca. 1818.
Artist, active N.O. 1850.
Contemporary listings: artist (1850).
References: Groce and Wallace; U.S.
Census (1850), roll 235.

REICHMAN, MR. _____
Artist, active N.O. 1866.
Contemporary listings: artist (1866).
References: *Bee*, Oct. 22–27, 1866
(advs.).

REID, _____
Painter, active N.O. 1876–78.
Contemporary listings: portrait
painter (1876); painter (1878).

Exhibited: JULIO's studio (1876, 1878).

Cf. REED, WILLIAM.

References: *Demo.*, Dec. 17, 1876, Jan. 13, 1878.

REID, CHRISTIAN

Sculptor, active N.O. 1871–86.

Contemporary listings: wood carver, 150 Harmony (1871, 1874); wood carver, 244 S. Rampart (1886).

References: NOCD 1871, 1874, 1886.

REINAGLE, HUGH

Born Philadelphia PA ca. 1788–90; died N.O. May 23, 1834.

Painter, sketch artist, active N.O. 1832–34.

Studied: with John J. Holland, Philadelphia (before 1813).

Contemporary listings: portrait painter, 45 Canal (1832); scenic artist (1834).

Exhibited: National Academy of Design, N.Y.C. (1826–31); Mariner's Church (1832).

Memberships/positions: National Academy of Design, founder (1826).

Scenic designer who was the son of noted musician and composer Alexander Reinagle and possibly learned scenery painting when his father was director of a theater in Philadelphia. Reinagle moved to N.Y.C. (1807–13), and Albany NY (1815–17) where he ran a drawing academy. He returned to Philadelphia (1818) and then to N.Y.C. (1820s) where he was the chief scene painter at the Park Theatre. He was also a landscape and genre painter: one of his most noted works was *Belschazzar's Feast* which he brought to N.O. in 1832. While in the city he painted portraits and was the head scene painter at the American Theatre on Camp.

References: *Argus*, May 19, 24, 1834; *Bee*, Jan. 30, Feb. 22, 1832, Jan. 4, May 17, 24, 1834; *Appleton's CAB*; Bénézit; Dunlap, 3:72; Fielding, *Dictionary*; Friends of the Cabildo, *250 Years*, 42; Fulton and Toledano, 506; Groce and Wallace; Kendall, *Golden Age*, 76; Museum of Fine Arts, 1:264; Harry Peters, *America on Stone*, 295–96, 332; Thompson, "Checklist."

REINFORT, MARY

Born Austria ca. 1845; died Pass Christian MS Nov. 17, 1916.

Art craftsman, active N.O. 1889–1902.

Studied: NEWCOMB COLLEGE (1886–87, 1891–94).

Exhibited: ART LEAGUE OF NEW ORLEANS (1889); Tulane University (1892).

Memberships/positions: Art League of New Orleans (1889); ART LEAGUE POTTERY CLUB (1892).

Pottery decorator who moved to LA ca. 1856. She entered Newcomb (1886) as a member of the Saturday TULANE FREE DRAWING CLASS and later as a pottery designer (1901–1902).

References: NOCD 1891, 1895; *D. Pic.*, Mar. 10, 1889, Mar. 3, 1892; *T. Demo.*, Mar. 3, 1892; *T. Pic.*, Nov. 18, 1916; Poesch, *Newcomb Pottery*, 103.

REINHARDT, JACOB

Engraver, active N.O. 1892; primarily engineer.

Contemporary listings: engraver (1892).

References: NOCD 1879, 1881–94, 1896, 1898.

REINHART, BENJAMIN FRANKLIN (Reinhardt, Rinehart)

Born near Waynesburg PA Aug. 29, 1827; died Philadelphia PA May 3, 1885.

Painter, active N.O. ca. 1859–62.

Studied: Pittsburgh PA (1844); National Academy of Design, N.Y.C. (1847); Dusseldorf, Germany; Paris; Rome (1850–53).

Contemporary listings: portrait painter, Canal betw. Baronne and University Pl. (1859); portrait and historical painter, 170 Canal (1860–61, 1866); artist, Canal St. (1862).

Memberships/positions: National Academy of Design (1871).

Successful portrait, genre, and historical painter who came to N.O. in 1859 and went into partnership with THEODORE SIDNEY MOISE. Several sources indicate that he left the city in 1861 with the outbreak of the Civil

War, although he was still reported by the press to have been in the city in early 1862, when a military company was named in his honor because of the financial aid he had given to the Confederacy. Sometime afterward he went to London, where he remained as a noted portrait painter until 1868. He returned to the U.S. and worked in N.Y.C.

References: NOCD 1860–61, 1866; *D. Crescent*, Nov. 28, 1859, Nov. 18, 1861, Jan. 14, 1862; *D. Delta*, Feb. 14, 20, 1862; *D. Pic.*, Apr. 28, Aug. 4, 1867; Bénézit; Bruns, 316; Coulon MS, Scrapbook 100, LSM; Fielding, *Dictionary*; Freeman, 15, 17; Glenk, 79; Groce and Wallace; Harter and Tucker, 124; LSM, *Biennial Report for 1920–21*, 89; LSM, *Biennial Report for 1921–22*, 41; LSM, *Biennial Report for 1922–23*, 58; Seebold, 1:23; WPA, *American Portrait Inventory*; WPA, *Louisiana*, 166; William Young.

RELAREY, JOHN A.

Born LA ca. 1888.

Engraver, active N.O. 1910.

Contemporary listings: photo–engraver (1910).

Somewhat illegible surname in census; listed as photo–engraver with the "daily paper" (1910).

References: U.S. Census (1910), roll 520.

RELF, RICHARD

Born N.O. July 13, 1883.

Painter, colorer, active N.O. ca. 1900–1979; primarily photographer, also printer.

Contemporary listings: artist (1900). Noted N.O. portrait photographer whose long career ended with retirement at age 90, although he continued to color photographs and make small paintings which he gave away to his friends. At present Relf is still living in N.O.

References: NOCD 1901–11, 1913–22, 1924–33, 1935, 1938, 1940, 1942, 1945–47, 1949, 1952–56, 1958, 1960–62, 1964–69, 1971–77; Interview with Richard Relf, Feb. 20, 1979; Orleans Parish Registrar of Voters, NOPL; U.S. Census (1900), roll 573.

RENAULT, ANTOINE F. (Renaud)

Born France; died ca. 1829.

Painter, active N.O. 1803–27; also gilder.

Contemporary listings: artist, painter (1803); painter, 15 Rampart (1811); painter (1812); scenic painter (1817); painter, 106 (286) Rampart (1822); artist, 23 Amour (1823); artiste, 23 Amour (1827).

Scenic interior painter, and carriage decorator from Paris who came to N.O. in 1803 after having been in N.Y.C. (1794–ca. 1801). He created public fireworks displays which often included large, decorated ascending balloons.

References: NOCD 1811, 1822–23, 1827, 1830; *Courier*, June 22, 1808, May 15, 1809, June 29, Dec. 9, 1812, Mar. 1, June 28, 1813, Mar. 13, June 28, 1816, Jan. 8, Feb. 17, June 27, Aug. 15, Nov. 5, 1817, June 26, 1818, June 10, July 1, 1822; *Gazette*, June 7, 1805; *Moniteur*, May 7, 1803; Groce and Wallace; New Orleans City Council, Proceedings, Mar. 15, 1817, NOPL; New Orleans City Council, Records, Mar. 15, 1817; St. Louis Cathedral, Archives of the Archdiocese of N.O.; U.S. Census (1820), roll 32.

RENOIR, ALEXANDER

Engraver, hairworker, art teacher, painter, silhouettist, restorer, active N.O. 1819–32; also jeweler, museum proprietor, goldsmith, gilder.

Contemporary listings: hairworker, sculptor, engraver, restorer (1819); engraver, 46 Levee cor. Jefferson (1822); engraver, 79 Levee (1823–24); engraver, Jefferson (1827); artist, hairworker, Hewlett's Exchange (1829); silhouettes, hairworker, engraver (1829); engraver, 149 Burgundy and 175 Bourbon (1830); teacher of painting, engraving, and silhouette, 172 Bourbon (1830); hairworker, engraver, painter, painting on silhouette (1831); engraver, Toulouse betw. Royal and Bourbon (1832).

Renoir operated a museum (1820) depicting tableaux from around the world. In 1828, he conducted a similar enterprise, in conjunction with the operation of a coffeehouse. In February of that year, fire destroyed most of the contents of his museum. His advertisements of 1829 made direct solicitation of the students of Mrs. Reynolds.
References: NOCD 1822–24, 1827, 1830, 1832; *Bee*, Feb. 17, 1829, Mar. 19–30, 1829 (advs.), July 27–29, 1830 (advs.); *Courier*, Jan. 12, 22, Feb. 2, 4, 1828, July 5–15, 1831 (advs.), Aug. 15, 1831; *Gazette*, Oct. 19–Nov. 6, 1819 (advs.); *L'Ami des Lois*, July 5, 1819, June 6, 13, 1820; Groce and Wallace; New Orleans City Council, Proceedings, June 15, Aug. 21, 1819, Mar. 25, 1820, NOPL; U.S. Census (1830), roll 45; William Young.

RENSHAW, DAGMAR ADELAIDE (Mrs. Edmond Jules Le Breton)
Born N.O. Feb. 20, 1891.
Art teacher, designer, illustrator, active N.O. 1917–39.
Studied: NEWCOMB COLLEGE (1908–12, 1914).
Contemporary listings: teacher, with Miss M. Finney (1917).
Artist who illustrated *France D'Amérique* (1932) and whose works were included in an exhibition of bookplates at the DELGADO MUSEUM OF ART (1939). She was also an author and teacher of French and Italian who retired in 1956; at present she is still living in N.O. First cousin of LEA MCLEAN RENSHAW.
References: NOCD 1908, 1910–11, 1914–33, 1935, 1938, 1940, 1942, 1945–47, 1949, 1952–56, 1958, 1960–62, 1964–69, 1971–79; Harnett Kane, "Orleanians Who Write Books," *Dixie*, Apr. 30, 1950; *Item*, Nov. 1, 1953; *Item–Trib.*, May 15, 1932; *T. Pic.*, Feb. 19, 1939; Caulfeild, 242; Interview with Mrs. Edmond Le Breton, Nov. 1, 1986; Orleans Parish Registrar of Voters, NOPL; Ormond and Irvine, 166–67; WPA, "Bookplates," 3.

RENSHAW, LEA MCLEAN
Born N.O. Jan. 28, 1887; died N.O. Feb. 7, 1973.
Painter, active N.O. ca. 1901–1972.
Studied: with ELMIRE M. VILLERE (1900–1901).
Exhibited: ARTISTS' ASSOCIATION OF NEW ORLEANS, Grunewald's music store (1901).
An amateur painter, primarily of portraits, but also of still lifes and historical subjects who was a professional cotton buyer. First cousin of DAGMAR ADELAIDE RENSHAW.
References: NOCD 1902–12, 1914–16, 1918, 1920, 1922–24, 1926–33, 1935, 1938, 1942, 1945–47, 1949, 1952–56, 1958, 1960–62, 1964–69, 1971–74; *D. Pic.*, Feb. 10, 1901; *T. Demo.*, Dec. 3, 1901; AANO, *Catalogue* (1901); Interview with Mrs. Edmond Le Breton, Nov. 1, 1986; Orleans Parish Registrar of Voters, NOPL.

REPETTO, ANTONIO
Born Genoa, Italy ca. 1837; died N.O. Apr. 4, 1902.
Sculptor, art teacher, active N.O. 1876–1902.
Contemporary listings: sculptor, teacher, 123 Bourbon (1876); sculptor, 101 St. Louis (1878); sculptor (1879–80, 1889–94); sculptor, 831 Toulouse (1895, 1897–1901); sculptor, 833 Toulouse (1902).
Member of the chorus of the French Opera. Repetto's dwarfism kept him from an operatic career so he turned to sculpting and created portraits in bust, statue, and cameo, as well as vases and statues in plaster and cement. His works included statues for carnival floats and a bust of N.O. philanthropist John McDonogh, which was reproduced for each of the McDonogh schools.
References: NOCD 1878–80, 1884, 1889–95, 1897–1902; *Bee*, Apr. 16, 1876; *D. Pic.*, Mar. 31, Apr. 13, 1890, Aug. 1, 1897; *Demo.*, Aug. 10–12, 1876 (advs.); *Dixie*, Oct. 4, 1959, Nov. 29, 1959; *T. Demo.*, Feb. 11, Mar. 28, 1890; "A Modern Quasimodo," 318–20; N.O. Death Certificate (1902), 4:4, NOPL.

REYFF, LOUIS
Engraver, active N.O. 1888–91; also jeweler, watchmaker.
Contemporary listings: engraver (1888); engraver, Koch & Dreyfus (1889); engraver, with M. Scooler (1891).
References: NOCD 1888–91.

REYNES, JEANNE
Born ca. 1866; died N.O. Apr. 2, 1950.
Art teacher, active N.O. 1893.
Contemporary listings: teacher of drawing and painting, Pinac Institute (1893).
References: T. Demo., June 27, 1893; T. Pic., Apr. 4, 1950.

REYNES, POLYXENE MAZUREAU (Mrs. Joseph Reynes)
Born N.O. ca. 1808; died N.O. Mar. 2, 1879.
Painter, active N.O. 1831.
Studied: with Louis François Aubry, Paris.
Amateur miniature painter.
References: Bee, Mar. 4, 1879; Delgado, Loan Exhibition; Groce and Wallace; N.O. Death Certificate (1879), 74:520, NOPL; THNOC Cemetery Survey; WPA, "Lives."

REYNOLDS, MRS. _____. See RENOIR, ALEXANDER

REYNOLDS, HENRY W. W.
Born N.O. Feb. 1833; died June 5, 1911.
Painter, active N.O. 1860; also engineer, draftsman.
Contemporary listings: painter (1860).
Merchant who was an amateur portrait painter; in 1874 he was appointed draftsman by the N.O. City Surveyor's office. Cousin of noted painter Frederic Edwin Church.
References: NOCD 1857–61, 1866–69, 1875, 1878–79, 1881–1906, 1908; D. Crescent, Nov 8, 1860; D. Delta, Oct. 7, 16, 1860; D. Pic., Dec. 11, 1874, June 11, 1911; Repub., Dec. 11, 1874; U.S. Census (1860), roll 420.

RICARBY, GEORGE
Born England ca. 1828.
Engraver, active N.O. 1850.

Contemporary listings: engraver (1850).
Possibly George D. Rickarby listed in 1852–53.
References: NOCD 1852–53; Groce and Wallace; U.S. Census (1850), roll 235.

RICE, CHARLES EDWARD
Born N.O. Dec. 2, 1843; died N.O. Dec. 13, 1902.
Sculptor, active N.O. ca. 1891–92.
Exhibited: ARTISTS' ASSOCIATION OF NEW ORLEANS (1891–92).
Insurance broker who was an amateur artist; he was president of the Morris Building and Land Improvement Co. of N.O.
References: NOCD 1891–1902; Current Topics, Oct. 1891, 18, Jan. 1892, 22, 24, Jan. 1893, 11; D. Pic., Dec. 17, 1891, Dec. 14, 1902; D. States, Dec. 14, 1902; T. Demo., Dec. 13, 1892, Dec. 14, 1902; AANO, Catalogue (1891).

RICE, MATTHEW A.
Born N.O. Apr. 17, 1879; died N.O. Nov. 13, 1924.
Lithographer, active N.O. 1904–10; also printer.
Contemporary listings: lithographer (1904); lithographer–newspaper (1910).
References: NOCD 1899–1923; T. Pic., Nov. 14, 1924; Orleans Parish Registrar of Voters, NOPL; U.S. Census (1910), roll 523.

RICHARDS, NEWTON
Born NH Dec. 4, 1805; died N.O. Oct. 9, 1874.
Designer, sculptor, engraver, art teacher, sketch artist, active N.O. 1843–73; also marble and stone cutter.
Contemporary listings: sculptor, 146 Customhouse (1843); sculptor (1852); professor of drawing, design, engraving and artisan sketching, N.O. Polytechnic and Industrial Institute (1873).
Richards was apprenticed to Boston stoneworker Abner Joy, who eventually put Richards in charge of his N.Y.C. stoneworking business. After working in Philadelphia, Richards came to N.O. (Dec. 1831) and es-

tablished a granite and marble yard which he maintained throughout his life. He furnished stone materials for all types of architecture, particularly facades and tombs. He designed the pedestal for the monument to Andrew Jackson in Jackson Square (1852), the Chalmette Monument (1855), and numerous family and individual tombs.

References: NOCD 1838, 1841–43, 1846, 1849–61, 1866–74; *Courier*, Apr. 11, May 1, 1839, Jan. 10, 1848–Feb. 5, 1852 (advs.), Jan. 17, Nov. 13, 1849, Apr. 26, 1850, Feb. 19, 1851, Feb. 17, 1853, May 14, Aug. 4, 1854, May 4, 1856; *D. Creole*, Apr. 26–July 2, 1856 (advs.); *D. Orleanian*, Nov. 7, 1857; *D. Pic.*, Apr. 5, 1871; *T. Deutsche Zeitung*, Dec. 31, 1852; *Repub.*, June 25, 1873, Oct. 11, 1874; *T. Pic.*, Nov. 22, 1925; *Wkly. Delta*, Oct. 31, 1852; Friends of the Cabildo, *N.O. Architecture*, 2:116, 230, 3:29–30; Huber and Wilson, *Pontalba*, 40–41; THNOC Cemetery Survey; U.S. Census (1850), roll 235, (1860), roll 421, (1870), roll 519; Samuel Wilson, *Plantation Houses*, 35, 37; William Young.

RICHARDSON, F.
Art teacher, sketch artist, active N.O. 1857–61.

Contemporary listings: drawing teacher, 13 Camp (1857, 1860); F. Richardson's Drawing Academy and School of Design, 26 St. Charles (1859); Writing and Drawing Academy, 28 St. Charles (1860–61).

Drew the illustrated advertisement engraved by CHARLES J. STEVENS that appeared in the *Weekly Mirror* (1859).

References: NOCD 1856–57, 1859–61; *D. Creole*, Mar. 11, 26, 1857; *D. Pic.*, Jan. 3, 10, Feb. 12, 1860; *Wkly. Mirror*, Jan. 15–Mar. 12, 1859 (advs.).

RICHARDSON, HENRY
Painter, active N.O. 1836–42.
Contemporary listings: partner, RICHARDSON & WATSON (1836–37); painter, Gravier near Circus (1841–42).
References: NOCD 1841–42.

RICHARDSON, MARY WALCOT (Mrs. William H. Rasche)
Art craftsman, active N.O. ca. 1901–1905.
Studied: NEWCOMB COLLEGE (1897–1901).
Memberships/positions: ARTS EXHIBITION CLUB.
Listed in the 1901–1902 Newcomb catalogue as a graduate in normal art; ca. 1902–1905 she was a pottery decorator.
References: Arts Exhibition Club, 15; Ormond and Irvine, 167; Smithsonian, *Newcomb Pottery*, 14.

RICHARDSON & WATSON
Painters, active N.O. 1836–37; HENRY RICHARDSON, James A. Watson (died Providence RI Jan. 5, 1844), partners.
Contemporary listings: historical, landscape, portrait, miniature, and fancy painters, Merchants' Exchange, Royal St. (1836); portrait painters, Merchants' Exchange, and landscape and fancy painters, 14 Chartres (1837).
References: NOCD 1837; *Bee*, Dec. 2, 1836; *Comm. Bull.*, Dec. 12, 1836; *D. Pic.*, Jan. 24, 1844; *True Amer.*, Mar. 29, 1837–Apr. 8, 1837 (advs.); Groce and Wallace; THNOC artists files.

RICHTER, MR. ——
Born Berlin, Germany.
Art teacher, sketch artist, active N.O. 1851.
Contemporary listings: drawing teacher, 93 Customhouse (1851).
Advertised a new method of teaching drawing in one lesson. He seems to have traveled around the country drawing portraits of notable people. Possibly Gustav Karl Ludwig Richter, a noted German portraitist and history painter, born Berlin, Germany Aug. 31, 1823, died Berlin, Apr. 3, 1884.
References: *Bee*, Mar. 13, 1851; *D. Pic.*, Apr. 4–5, 1851; Bénézit; *Bryan's*.

RIECKE, GEORGE
Painter, active N.O. ca. 1887–1902.
Exhibited: ARTISTS' ASSOCIATION OF NEW ORLEANS (1902).

References: *Kennedy Qtrly.*, Apr. 1971; AANO, *Catalogue* (1902).

RIES, SOLOMON
Born Obernai, France ca. 1805; died N.O. Mar. 17, 1875.
Art teacher, sketch artist, active N.O. 1858.
Contemporary listings: drawing instruction (1858).
References: NOCD 1855–58, 1860–61, 1866, 1868–69, 1872–75; *Bee*, June 15–19, 1858 (advs.); *D. Pic.*, Mar. 15, 1875.

RIESS, PAUL
Born Berlin, Prussia ca. 1843; died N.O. May 31, 1926.
Sculptor, active N.O. 1882–86; primarily molder.
Studied: Berlin.
Contemporary listings: sculptor (1882); sculptor, near cor. Erato and Tchoupitoulas (1883).
Exhibited: Grunewald's music store (1882); Washington Artillery Hall (1883); American Exposition (1885–86).
Primarily a molder and caster in association with RUDOLPH THIEM who actually made the models of their works. In 1890 Riess was in charge of the casting department of the Edison Electric Co.; for many years he was a saloon keeper.
References: NOCD 1879–81, 1884–89, 1892–93, 1895–97, 1900–1902, 1905–17, 1919, 1922–25; *Bee*, Apr. 1, 1882; *D. Pic.*, Aug. 10, 1883; *D. States*, Aug. 17, 1883, June 20, 1890; *T. Pic.*, June 2, 1926; Creole Exhibit, 18.

RIGGS, KATHERINE LOUISE
Born Iberia Parish LA Oct. 23, 1859–68; died N.O. Apr. 18, 1928.
Painter, art teacher, active N.O. 1892–1928.
Contemporary listings: drawing teacher (1902); drawing teacher, N.O. Normal School (1903); art teacher (1910).
Exhibited: Tulane University (1893); ARTISTS' ASSOCIATION OF NEW ORLEANS (1892–94, 1896–97, 1899).
Memberships/positions: Artists' Association of New Orleans (1896);

ARTS EXHIBITON CLUB (1901); ART ASSOCIATION OF NEW ORLEANS (1905). Listed from 1904 until 1928 as a teacher at the N.O. Normal School. Although her birthday is consistently cited as October 23, various years are given in the U.S. census and voter registration cards (1859, 1865, 1868).
References: NOCD 1894–95, 1902–28; *Current Topics*, Jan. 1893, 10; *D. Pic.*, Feb. 14, 1893, Mar. 30, 1897; *T. Demo.*, Dec. 13, 1892, Dec. 14, 1894; *T. Pic.*, Apr. 19–20, 1928; AANO, *Catalogue* (1897); N.O. Board of Health, Registers, NOPL; Mount, 136; Orleans Parish Registrar of Voters, NOPL; Thompson, "Checklist"; U.S. Census (1910), roll 520.

RILEY, JOHN
Designer, active N.O. 1858.
Contemporary listings: fancy paper cutter, 78 St. Charles (1858).
References: NOCD 1858.

RILEY, JOHN NICHOLS
Born Algiers LA ca. 1862; died Algiers LA Mar. 17, 1932.
Sketch artist, active N.O. ca. 1896.
Executed a pen–and–ink drawing of Hughes' Hotel which appeared in *The Story of Algiers* (ca. 1896).
References: NOCD 1893–99; *T. Pic.*, Mar. 17, 1932; Seymour, 87.

RINCK, ADOLPH D.
Born France ca. 1810.
Painter, art teacher, sketch artist, active N.O. 1840–71.
Studied: Royal Academy of Berlin; with Paul Delaroche, Paris (1835–40).
Contemporary listings: portrait painter, cor. Royal and St. Peter (1840); portrait painter, Royal near St. Anthony Square (1841); portrait painter, cor. Royal and St. Anthony (1842); portrait painter, 119 Toulouse (1843–44); portrait painter and teacher of painting and drawing, 20 Bourbon (1846); portrait painter and teacher of painting and drawing, 6 Place d'Armes (1850–51); artiste (1851); painter and artist, 190 Canal (1858); portrait painter (1859), portrait painter, 7 Bourbon (1860–61);

painter (1870); portrait painter, 67 Royal (1871).

Exhibited: Salon, Paris (1835–40); lecture hall, Monsieur Bravo (1846). Portrait painter who came to N.O. prior to Dec. 9, 1840 to work during the winter. Advertisements mentioned that he was a friend of JEAN JOSEPH VAUDECHAMP. Rinck remained in the city to work during subsequent winters and went elsewhere during the summers. By 1846 his N.O. residence seems to have become permanent; he gave painting and drawing lessons while his wife, Margarette, opened a shop on the Place d'Armes. Rinck traveled frequently, including a trip to Brazil in 1851. He continued painting portraits but also bought a farm by late 1859 in Algiers LA where he could practice scientific agriculture; he wrote a pamphlet concerning his ideas on a model farm. Rinck possibly left the city during the Civil War, since there are no records of his presence in N.O. between 1861 and 1869. He was again reported to be in the city by Dec. 5, 1869, and again was proposing his idea for an educational institution where agricultural labor could be scientifically and practically taught along with the sciences and *belles lettres*. An advertisement for portrait painting on Feb. 17, 1871 was the last indication of Rinck's residence in N.O.; an extant portrait dated 1872 indicates he was still active in LA.

References: NOCD 1841–44, 1846, 1855–56, 1858; *Bee*, Dec. 9, 1840, Jan. 4–8, 1842 (advs); Jan. 21–23, 1843 (advs.), Jan. 3–10, 1846 (advs.), Oct. 29, 1846, Dec. 30, 1850, Jan. 9, 1851, Mar. 19–30, 1858 (advs.), Mar. 20, 1858, Dec. 11, 1860–Apr. 4, 1861 (advs.), Feb. 17–21, 1871 (advs.); *Courier*, June 2, 1841, Apr. 2, 1845, June 1, Oct. 28, 1846, May 1, 1851, Sept. 28, 1856; *D. Delta*, Jan. 21, 1851; *D. Pic.*, Dec. 31, 1850–Jan. 9, 1851 (advs.), Nov. 19, 1859, Dec. 5, 1869; *Revue Louisianaise*, Aug. 2, 1846, 441; Bénézit; Bruns, 316; Buchanan; Delgado, *New Orleans*; Foote, 25–26; Glenk, 79; Groce and Wallace; Harter and Tucker, 65–66, 68, 84, 102, 124; Information courtesy John Fowler; LSM, *Biennial Report for 1922–23*, 57; Montreal Museum; "Roster of Artists," Special Collections, TU; Seebold, 1:23; Thieme and Becker; U.S. Census (1870), roll 525; WICCE, *Catalogue*, 92; Wiesendanger, 87–88; WPA, *Louisiana*, 164; WPA, "Passenger Lists" (1851):52.

RIOU, E.

Painter, active N.O. 1847; also gilder. Contemporary listings: porcelain painter, Gretna LA (1847).

Riou painted and gilded porcelain and was proprietor of the Gretna Chinaware Establishment in the N.O. suburb, Gretna LA. The firm moved to 110 Chartres in N.O. prior to December 22, 1847.

References: NOCD 1850–52; *D. Delta*, Apr. 22–30, 1847 (advs.); *D. National*, Dec. 22, 1847; *D. Pic.*, Apr. 3–24, 1847 (advs.); *Wkly. Delta*, Nov. 17, 1845.

RIPLEY, ELISE

Sketch artist, active N.O. ca. 1884. Daughter of Eliza Moore Ripley, author who wrote *Social Life in Old New Orleans* (1912). Elise drew 14 pen-and-ink illustrations of N.O. used in the book.

References: Ripley, 303–25.

RISSO, CHARLES

Lithographer, active N.O. 1837–47; also publisher.

Contemporary listings: lithographer, with DOMINIQUE THEURET (1837); artist, Exchange Al. betw. Conti and St. Louis (1838); artist, Exchange Al. (1841); artist, lithographer, 145 Dumaine (1845–46); lithographer (1847).

In N.Y.C. with Risso & Browne (1832–36), the firm that lithographed a Natchez MS view by JAMES TOOLEY, JR. In 1837 Theuret referred to Risso as the "oldest lithographer in the Union" with 20 years of experience as an artist who could speak English, French, Spanish, and Portuguese.

References: NOCD 1838, 1841–42, 1846; *Courier*, Apr. 6, 1837, June 5, 1838, May 25, July 9, 1846, May 24, 27, 31, 1847; *D. Delta*, Nov. 25, 1845–Feb. 5, 1846 (advs.), May 26, 1846; Dichter and Shapiro, 252; Groce and Wallace.

RIVE, LEON
Born France ca. 1809.
Painter, active N.O. 1849–50.
Contemporary listings: portrait painter, 103 Orleans (1849–50).
References: NOCD 1849–50; *Courier*, Aug. 1, 1849; Glenk, 79; Groce and Wallace.

RIVERS, JAMES S.
Born MS; died N.O. July 1, 1885.
Lithographer, engraver, active N.O. 1876–85; primarily stationer, printer.
Contemporary listings: lithographer and engraver, 74 Camp (1876); lithographer, 74 Camp (1879).
Executed several engraved and lithographed views of the World's Industrial and Cotton Centennial Exposition (1884–85).
References: NOCD 1875–85; *D. Pic.*, July 2, 1885; *Eve. Demo.*, June 20–Sept. 20, 1876 (advs.); THNOC 1944.1, 1957.42–.43, 1957.53, 1976.13, 1980.167.

RIVOIRE, JULIEN EMILE
Sketch artist, painter, active N.O. 1885–1903; also photographer.
Contemporary listings: artist (1885); crayon portraits, artiste, 40 Toulouse (1887); crayon portraits, artiste and portrait painter, 40 Toulouse (1888); portrait painter (1889); artist in crayon and watercolor portrait painting, cor. Royal and Dumaine (1892); portrait painter, 207 Royal cor. Dumaine (1893–94); portrait painter, 933 Royal (1898); portrait painter, 157 Baronne (1903).
Exhibited: cor. Royal and Dumaine (1892).
Primarily a portrait artist, Rivoire later added photography to his skills (1894–1903). He first appeared in N.O. as the editor of the *Franco-Louisianais* newspaper, and remained in the city until ca. 1889. Upon his return to N.O. (1892), Ri-

voire exhibited his portraits at his studio at the corner of Dumaine and Royal. In 1892–93 he was the manager of the New Orleans Portrait Society & Frame Factory and later was the general manager of the ART MATERIAL & PHOTO SUPPLY CO.
References: NOCD 1888–89, 1892–1903; NOBD 1898; *Bee*, June 12, 1885, Nov. 11, 1887–Dec. 30, 1888 (advs.); *D. States*, Nov. 14, 1892; Glenk, 38; Information courtesy J. Richard Rivoire, Nov. 14, 1979.

RIVOIRI, _____
Artist, active N.O. ca. 1836.
Name appeared on a lithograph of St. Louis Cathedral (1836).
References: *T. Pic.*, Mar. 29, 1959; Fortier, *Louisiana*, 4:betw. 166 and 167.

ROBERTS, EMELINE MARIE
Painter, active N.O. ca. 1918.
Exhibited: ART ASSOCIATION OF NEW ORLEANS (1918).
References: Art Asso., *Catalogue* (1918).

ROBERTS, GERTRUDE. *See* SMITH, GERTRUDE ROBERTS

ROBERTS, HARRY
Artist, active N.O. 1891.
Contemporary listings: artist, PHOTO-ENGRAVING COMPANY (1891).
References: NOCD 1891.

ROBERTSON, ANNE MACKINNE
Born Augusta GA June 8, 1887; died N.O. Mar. 13, 1959.
Sketch artist, designer, active N.O. 1906–23.
Studied: NEWCOMB COLLEGE (1905–1907); with ELLSWORTH WOODWARD.
Contemporary listings: artist, 1313 Eighth (1909); artist (1911–12, 1916); designer (1917).
Exhibited: Newcomb Art Alumnae Association (1910); ART ASSOCIATION OF NEW ORLEANS (1910).
Awarded: Mary L.S. Neill Medal (1906); *Architectural Art and its Allies*, cover design competition, honorable mention (1906).
Came to N.O. in 1897; fine draftsman and designer who was best known for her bookplate designs and prints. Some of her bookplates were exhibited at DELGADO MUSEUM OF ART

in 1940. She was active in city planning and was named secretary of the City Planning and Zoning Commission when it was formed in 1923. She remained in that position until her retirement in 1953.
References: NOCD 1909, 1911–12, 1914, 1916–20, 1922–32, 1935, 1938, 1940, 1942, 1945–47, 1949, 1952–56, 1958; *Architectural Art*, 1(June 1906):7, 9; *D. Pic.*, Dec. 26, 1909; *States–Item*, Mar. 14, 1959; Schoenberger, "Tireless Zoning Secretary to Retire After Long Duty," *T. Pic.*, Aug. 23, 1953; *T. Pic.*, Mar. 14, 1959; Art Asso., *Catalogue* (1910); Orleans Parish Registrar of Voters, NOPL; Ormond and Irvine, 167; WPA, *Bookplates*, 3.

ROBERTSON, COL. N.
Sketch artist, active N.O. 1885.
Contemporary listings: sketch artist (1885).
Artist representing *Frank Leslie's Illustrated* who came to N.O. to sketch during the World's Industrial and Cotton Centennial Exposition (1885).
References: *D. States*, Feb. 3, 1885.

ROBINSON, HARRY A.
Painter, active N.O. 1888–1900.
Contemporary listings: artist (1888); painter (1890, 1892–94, 1897–98, 1900).
Came to N.O from Cleveland OH.
References: NOCD 1890, 1892–94, 1897–98, 1900–1901; *D. Pic.*, Feb. 29, 1888.

ROBINSON, JOHN
Engraver, active N.O. 1871.
Contemporary listings: engraver, 104 Third (1871).
References: NOCD 1867, 1871–72, 1875–77.

ROBINSON, MARCUS J.
Born N.O. Apr. 13, 1858; died N.O. Nov. 25, 1930.
Painter, active N.O. 1879–1902.
Contemporary listings: artist (1879, 1882–83, 1890–91, 1893, 1899–1900); painter (1897); portrait painter (1902).
References: NOCD 1878–79, 1882–83, 1885, 1887–93, 1897, 1899–1906, 1908–10, 1912–24, 1926–28, 1931; *T. Pic.*, Nov. 26, 1930; Orleans Parish Registrar of Voters, NOPL; U.S. Census (1900), roll 572.

ROBINSON, MAUDE
Died before 1976.
Designer, art craftsman, active N.O. 1903–10; also needleworker.
Studied: NEWCOMB COLLEGE (1903–10); Dow Summer School, Ipswich MA.
Artist who worked in several mediums, including clay and glass. She is best remembered for her leaded glass objects, especially lampshades and firescreens.
References: NOCD 1909; Ormond and Irvine, 167; Poesch, *Newcomb Pottery*, 103.

ROBIRA, LOUISE
Born Bay St. Louis MS; died N.O. Mar. 3, 1947.
Artist, active N.O. 1892.
Contemporary listings: artist (1892).
Possibly Robira who drew the undated crayon portrait *Mr. Lewis*.
References: NOCD 1892; *D. Pic.*, Oct. 25, 1892; *T. Pic.*, Mar. 5, 1947; LSM, *Biennial Report for 1924–25*, 56.

ROCHA, R. V.
Painter, active N.O. 1873.
Contemporary listings: portrait and fresco painter (1873).
References: *Repub.*, Oct. 29, Nov. 2, 1873; Thompson, "Checklist."

RODDIS, MARY AUGUSTA
Born Troy NY; died N.O. May 30, 1925.
Painter, active N.O. 1889–1910.
Contemporary listings: artist (1889–97, 1899–1902, 1905); chinaware painter (1910).
Exhibited: ARTISTS' ASSOCIATION OF NEW ORLEANS (1894).
Memberships/positions: ARTS EXHIBITION CLUB (1901).
References: NOCD 1889–97, 1899–1906, 1908, 1910, 1912, 1914–24; *T. Demo.*, Dec. 14, 1894; *T. Pic.*, May 31, 1925; Arts Exhibition Club, 15.

RODRIGUEZ, RAPHAEL
Engraver, active N.O. 1876–77.
Contemporary listings: engraver (1876–77).
References: NOCD 1876–80.

ROESSLE, SIGMUND G. (Sigmond Russell)
Born N.O. ca. 1854; died N.O. June 30, 1907.
Painter, active N.O. 1879–1906.
Contemporary listings: frescoer (1879); fresco painter and assistant scenic artist, Academy of Music (1880); painter (1882, 1891–92, 1895–99, 1901, 1906); with Edgar & Roessle (1889); scene painter (1889).
References: NOCD 1874–77, 1879–80, 1882–89, 1891–92, 1895, 1898–99, 1901, 1905–1907; *D. States*, Dec. 8, 1880; *D. Pic.*, July 1, 1907.

ROGERS, CHARLES
Sketch artist, active N.O. 1849.
Contemporary listings: scenic artist, American Theatre (1849).
Artist who made a trip down the Mississippi River to its mouth during 1849 to make sketches used for the paintings in HENRY LEWIS's monumental panorama. Rogers was possibly the scene painter who worked in San Francisco from ca. 1856–72.
References: *D. Crescent*, Nov. 1, 1849; Arrington, "Henry Lewis," 245–46, 249; Groce and Wallace; McDermott, *Lost Panoramas*, 192; McDermott, *Seth Eastman's Mississippi*, 10, 12.

ROGERS, ELIZABETH GOELET. *See* PALFREY, ELIZABETH GOELET ROGERS

ROGERS, JULIA BRINCOMBE
Painter, sculptor, active N.O. ca. 1894.
Studied: with ACHILLE PERELLI.
Contemporary listings: watercolor, woodcarving, and modeling, Canal (1894).
Exhibited: ARTISTS' ASSOCIATION OF NEW ORLEANS (1894).
Sister of ELIZABETH GOELET ROGERS PALFREY.
References: *D. Pic.*, Sept. 30, 1894; *T. Demo.*, Dec. 14, 1894.

ROGERS, WILLIAM ALLEN
Born Springfield OH May 23, 1854; died N.Y.C. Oct. 20, 1931.
Painter, active N.O. 1898.
Illustrator, cartoonist, engraver, and writer who was on the staff of *Har-*

per's Weekly where his illustrations appeared between 1879 and 1900. Rogers traveled to various parts of the U.S. and Canada and visited N.O. in Dec. 1898 to make watercolor sketches of Jackson Square, Canal St., and the Sugar Exchange, later reproduced in *Harper's* (1899–1900).
References: *D. Pic.*, Dec. 28, 1898; *Harper's Wkly.*, Dec. 30, 1899, 1323–26, Nov. 10, 1900, 1071; Bénézit; Fielding, *Dictionary*; McCracken, *Portrait*, 225.

ROHRER, JOSEPH
Born Alsace ca. 1820; died N.O. Oct. 1, 1893.
Sculptor, active N.O. 1870–92; also carver.
Contemporary listings: sculptor (1870, 1873); wood carver (1891–92).
References: NOCD 1868–70, 1872–74, 1876–78, 1880–81, 1891–92; N.O. Death Certificate (1893), 104:1100, NOPL.

ROJAS, ADOLPHE J.
Artist, active N.O. 1888; primarily photographer.
Contemporary listings: artist, with JOHN H. CLARKE (1888).
Photographer in partnership with SAMUEL A. CONNER (1895–1908).
References: NOCD 1886–88, 1891–1909, 1911, 1913–16.

ROLLAND, WILLIE (William Rowland)
Born MS Feb. 5, 1872.
Designer, active N.O. 1900.
Contemporary listings: artist and designer (1900).
References: NOCD 1900; U.S. Census (1900), roll 570.

ROMAN, MARIE DESIREE
Born St. James Parish LA June 12 or 16, 1867; died N.O. Aug. 26, 1950.
Art craftsman, art teacher, sketch artist, active N.O. ca. 1885–1939.
Studied: with Arthur Dow, Ipswich MA (1904); NEWCOMB COLLEGE (1885–87, 1889–91, 1896–1905).
Contemporary listings: drawing teacher (1890); teacher (1893–1901).
Awarded: New England scholarship (1904).

Member of the first graduating class of Newcomb where she received a diploma in normal art (1890). She was the clerk of pottery and sales agent at Newcomb from 1903 until her retirement in 1939. Sister of MARIE JEANNE AMELIE ROMAN; niece of LA author Alcée Fortier.
References: NOCD 1886, 1888, 1890, 1893–1903, 1906–33, 1935, 1938, 1940, 1942, 1945–47, 1949; *Harlequin*, June 23, 1904, 8; *Register*, Oct. 1, 1914; *T. Demo.*, Mar. 19, 1904; *T. Pic.*, Aug. 28, 1950; Cochran, 165; Ormond and Irvine, 167–68; Poesch, *Newcomb Pottery*, 27, 104.

ROMAN, MARIE JEANNE AMELIE
Born St. James Parish LA Dec. 2, 1873; died N.O. July 17, 1955.
Art craftsman, art teacher, sketch artist, painter, active N.O. 1895–1939.
Studied: NEWCOMB COLLEGE (1895–1901); with Arthur W. Dow, Ipswich MA (1901); with John Carlsen, Woodstock NY (1914); with Julien, Towdonze and Baschet, Paris (1909).
Exhibited: ARTISTS' ASSOCIATION OF NEW ORLEANS (1897); Louisiana Purchase Exposition, St. Louis, MO (1904); ART ASSOCIATION OF NEW ORLEANS (1917–18).
Memberships/positions: Artists' Association of New Orleans; Louisiana Art Teachers' Association, treas. (1903–1904).
Member of the first Newcomb class in pottery decoration for the academic year 1895–96. After graduating from Newcomb, she joined the school's art faculty where she remained until her retirement in 1939. Sister of MARIE DESIREE ROMAN; niece of Alcée Fortier.
References: NOCD 1901–21, 1923–33, 1935, 1938, 1940, 1942, 1945–47, 1949, 1954–55; *Harlequin*, June 23, 1904, 8; *T. Demo.*, Dec. 8, 1901; *T. Pic.*, July 18–19, 1955; AANO, *Catalogue* (1897); *American Art Annual*, 1903–1904; Art Asso., *Catalogue* (1917, 1918); Cline, *Contemporary Art*, 11; Cochran, 165; Ormond and Irvine, 167; Poesch,

Newcomb Pottery, 27–29, 49, 103–4.

ROMANELLE, P.
Sculptor, active N.O. 1865.
Signed the sculpture depicting a mother and infant on the Rodd family tomb in Cypress Grove Cemetery commemorating the death of the young Albert Hall Rodd.
References: Friends of the Cabildo, *N.O. Architecture*, 3:127.

ROMANSKI, HENRY J.
Born Zytomir, Poland Feb. 21 or 26, 1861; died N.O. Dec. 25, 1944.
Engraver, illustrator, designer, active N.O. ca. 1892–1942.
Contemporary listings: mgr., PHOTOELECTRIC ENGRAVING CO. (1893–94); artist, *States* (1895–1900); proprietor, SOUTHERN BUREAU OF ENGRAVING (1895); illustrator and engraver, and staff artist, *Daily States* (1901); Romanski Photo Engraving Co., Ltd. (1902–1904); pres. and mgr., Romanski Photo Engraving Co. (1905–18); artist, engraver (1896, 1910).
Exhibited: ARTISTS' ASSOCIATION OF NEW ORLEANS (1897).
Memberships/positions: Artists' Association of New Orleans (1896); ART ASSOCIATION OF NEW ORLEANS (1905).
Came to the U.S. from Poland ca. 1887 and became a lithographer, illustrator, and photoengraver in N.Y.C. Romanski came to N.O. ca. 1892 to find employment as a photoengraver. In 1895 he formed an engraving company with HENRY GRELLE known as the Southern Bureau of Engraving. In 1901 he advertised alone as a book and newspaper illustrator and general designer. In 1902 he opened the Romanski Photo–Engraving Company located at 402 Camp (1902–1909), 825–827 Perdido (1910–26), 320–322 Exchange Pl. (1927–33), 628–630 Poydras (1935), and 440 St. Charles (1938–42).
References: NOCD 1893–1933, 1935, 1938, 1940, 1942, 1945–46; *D. Pic.*, Mar. 30, 1897; *D. States*, Jan. 8, 1896, Dec. 6, 1905; *Harlequin*, Dec. 6, 1900, 2, Sept. 1, 1904, 9; *T. Pic.*, Dec. 27, 1944; *Town Talk*, July

1904; AANO, *Catalogue* (1897); Art Asso., *Catalogue* (1905); Augustin, *The Vigil of a Soul*, 13, 17, 25, 33, 39, 43, 47, 53; Orleans Parish Registrar of Voters, NOPL; Mount, 140–42; "Panama Exposition March," Sheet Music Collection, THNOC; U.S. Census (1910), roll 519; Wiesendanger, 89.

ROMEGAR, _____. *See* SALAZAR Y MENDOZA, JOSE DE

ROMEGAS, JEAN BAPTISTE
Born Marseille, France Mar. 2, 1800; died Marseille Oct. 12, 1867.
Painter, active N.O. ca. 1838.
Exhibited: Salon, Paris (1838–42); St. Louis Exchange (ca. 1838).
Awarded: Paris, bronze medal (ca. 1838).
Exhibited his award–winning landscape in N.O. ca. 1838. Romegas did not receive the acclaim he anticipated in N.O., and after staying a few months, moved to Mexico.
References: *D. Pic.*, May 17, 1897; Bénézit; Coulon MS, Scrapbook 100, LSM; Fulton and Toledano, "Landscape Painting," 504.

RONDEAU, ZILLAH
Died Chatawa MS Aug. 24, 1902.
Sketch artist, art teacher, painter, active N.O. 1882–98.
Contemporary listings: teacher of drawing, china–painting and water–colors, Christian Woman's Exchange, artist and china painter (1882); art teacher (1884); artist (1891, 1898); portrait painter, 1424 Amelia (1895).
Exhibited: Louisiana Purchase Exposition, St. Louis MO (1904).
References: NOCD 1878–79, 1891, 1895, 1898; *D. States*, Nov. 12, 1882; *T. Demo.*, May 28, 1882, Feb. 11, 1884; Comité de l'Exposition, 25; LSM *Annual Report for 1919*, 28.

ROONEY, RICHARD
Engraver, active N.O. 1885.
Contemporary listings: engraver (1885).
Also listed as a clerk (1881, 1883, 1893), collector (1886–87), laborer (1888–89, 1894), driver, Police Jail (1890–91), deputy sheriff (1898, 1900).

References: NOCD 1881, 1883, 1885–91, 1893–94, 1898, 1900.

ROSADO, LUCY ALFONSO ALFARO (1. Mrs. Augustin Alexander Alfaro; 2. Mrs. Joseph T. Rosado)
Born N.O. 1894; died N.O. 1978.
Sculptor, active N.O. ca. 1908–1940s.
Granddaughter of FRANCISCO VARGAS, SR., and daughter of CONCEPCION VARGAS, she worked in the family's waxworking business. She was particularly adept at creating costumes for the wax figures of black street vendors, and she conceived the idea of making a washerwoman character (ca. 1940). Her son, August Alfaro, sculpted and molded figures with her and carried on the wax modeling tradition.
References: NOCD 1929, 1932, 1976–77; *Item–Trib.*, Feb. 16, 1941; Interviews with August Alfaro, May 17, 1984, Mar. 26, 1986.

ROSE, SEAVER E. B.
Born N.O. Oct. 22, 1887; died after 1925.
Painter, active N.O. 1906–23; also sign painter.
Contemporary listings: scenic artist (1906–1908, 1910); artist (1909–10); scenic painter (1911, 1916); painter (1913, 1917).
References: NOCD 1906–13, 1916–20, 1923, 1925; Orleans Parish Registrar of Voters, NOPL; U.S. Census (1910), roll 520.

ROSENBERGER, G.
Lithographer, active N.O. 1884.
Contemporary listings: lithographer, SOUTHERN LITHOGRAPHIC COMPANY (1884).
References: NOCD 1884.

ROSS, HENRY W.
Designer, active N.O. 1885–88.
Contemporary listings: ornamental glass, 6 Perdido (1885–88); stained glass maker (1885).
References: NOCD 1884–88; *T. Demo.*, Jan. 1, 1885.

ROSS, MARIE MEDORA
Born St. James Parish LA ca. 1844; died N.O. Sept. 7, 1920.
Art craftsman, painter, sketch artist, active N.O. 1891–1906.

Studied: NEWCOMB COLLEGE (1885–87, 1889–93, 1895–97, 1901–1905).
Exhibited: Tulane Hall (1892–93); ARTISTS' ASSOCIATION OF NEW ORLEANS (1892, 1897).
Memberships/positions: FIVE OR MORE CLUB (1893).
Member of the first Newcomb class in pottery decoration for the academic year 1895–96.
References: NOCD 1893, 1896–98, 1903; *Current Topics*, Jan. 1892, 24; *D. Pic.*, Dec. 17, 1891, Mar. 3, 1892, Feb. 14, 1893; *Eve. Chronicle*, May 22, 1886; *Item*, Sept. 7, 1920; *T. Demo.*, Mar. 3, 1892; AANO, *Catalogue* (1891, 1897); Ormond and Irvine, 43, 168; Poesch, *Newcomb Pottery*, 104, 110, 125.

ROSS, ROBERT
Born N.O. ca. 1805; died at sea July 11, 1840.
Painter, active N.O. 1830–40.
Contemporary listings: portrait painter, Perdido cor. St. Paul (1830); portrait and miniature painter, cor. Chartres and Canal (1831); portrait painter, 3 Canal (1832); portrait painter (1840).
Died of consumption aboard the vessel *Orozimbo* en route to N.O. from Europe, where he had gone to study the fine arts.
References: NOCD 1830, 1832; *Advertiser*, Jan. 25, 1831; *Bee*, July 28, 1840; Groce and Wallace; William Young.

ROSSI, JEAN BAPTISTE
Painter, active N.O. 1859–68.
Contemporary listings: artist, 244 St. Peter (1859–60); artist, 187 St. Peter (1861, 1866); journeyman painter, (1868).
Painted the frescoes on the ceiling of St. Alphonsus Church (1866) with DOMINIQUE CANOVA and PERACHI; assisted by ALEXANDER BOULET in painting the frescoes on the ceiling of St. Louis Cathedral, depicting Faith, Hope, and Charity, the four evangelists, St. Cecilia, and St. Louis (1851).
References: NOCD 1859–61, 1866, 1868; *Courier*, July 25, 1851, Jan.

13, 1853; *Times*, Sept. 9, 1866; Caldwell, 209; Groce and Wallace.

ROSSMORE, MR. _____
Born England.
Painter, active N.O. 1883.
Contemporary listings: plaque painter (1883).
References: *D. States*, Dec. 11, 1883.

ROTH, ANDREW
Born Bavaria ca. 1835; died N.O. June 29, 1896.
Painter, active N.O. 1867–77; primarily photographer.
Contemporary listings: portrait painter, 368 Victory (1867, 1869); portrait painter, 368 Old Levee (1868); portrait painter, 368 Decatur (1870–71); portrait painter, 11 Frenchman, (1877).
References: NOCD 1866–96, 1899; *D. Pic.*, Jan. 7, 1877, Nov. 9, 1913; Boyd, 200; N.O. Death Certificate (1896), 111:528, NOPL; Smith and Tucker, 169; U.S. Census (1870), roll 522.

ROTHHAAS, JACOB
Art teacher, sketch artist, painter, active N.O. 1835; primarily architect, surveyor.
Studied: Royal Academy of Arts, Munich.
Contemporary listings: teacher of drawing, painting of portraits and miniatures (1835).
Architecture and art teacher who began his career ca. 1823, and in 1835 was reported to have been working for three years as an architect and surveyor in N.Y.C. and N.O.
References: *Bee*, Nov. 12, 18, 1835; Groce and Wallace.

ROTTMAN, JULIUS
Born Westphalz, Prussia ca. 1829; died N.O. Aug. 11, 1858.
Lithographer, active N.O. 1858.
References: Louisiana Charity Hospital, Death Records, NOPL.

ROUSSEL, C.
Painter, active N.O. ca. 1813.
Signed a watercolor of the *Corsair Alligator*, under the command of Capt. Sam Griggs, N.O.
References: THNOC 1939.7.

ROUSSEL, MARIE (Mrs. de Calcinara)
Painter, active N.O. ca. 1894–95.
Contemporary listings: painter, artist (1894).
Landscape painter who in 1895 began a French language periodical called *La Revue* which lasted only three months. Following her marriage, she went to Galveston TX and then to Mexico where, in 1899, she resumed her publication renamed *La Revue Internationale, hebdomadaire, politique et littéraire*.
References: NOCD 1895; *D. Pic.*, Aug. 31, 1894; *T. Demo.*, Jan. 1, 1894; Tinker, *Ecrits*, 424–25.

ROUSSEVE, WILLIAM
Lithographer, active N.O. 1898.
Contemporary listings: lithographer (1898).
References: NOCD 1898.

ROWLAND, WILLIAM. *See* ROLLAND, WILLIE

RUBE, CHAPERON AND JAMBON
Sketch artists, active N.O. 1889.
Artists who drew a color sketch dated 1889 for the curtain of the French Opera House.
References: LSM, *Biennial Report for 1928–29*, 70.

RUDIE, MICHEL
Painter, active N.O. 1908–1909.
Contemporary listings: artist, painter (1908); artist (1909).
Exhibited: art store, Canal (1908).
The N.O. police removed Rudie's painting, *Artist and his Muse*, from a Canal St. art store because it depicted nudity. The painting was later found inoffensive by the city attorney and returned.
References: NOCD 1909; *Item*, Sept. 3–5, 22, 1908.

RUDOLPH, HAROLD
Born ca. 1850; died 1883 or 1884.
Painter, active N.O. 1873–83 or 1884.
Contemporary listings: portrait painter, over SEEBOLD's (1873–74); portrait painter, 166 Canal and 8 St. Charles (1874); painter (1875–77); portrait painter, Orleans cor. Exchange Passage (1877); painter (1883).
Exhibited: Seebold's (1873, 1883).

Portrait painter who came to N.O. sometime before Dec. 14, 1873. His portraits were lauded by both the *New Orleans Republican* and *Daily Picayune* as among the best ever produced in the city. Following the suicide (1877) of his brother–in–law and partner, BRUTUS DUCOMMAN, also a portrait painter, Rudolph turned increasingly to painting landscapes.
References: NOCD 1871, 1874, 1877; *D. Pic.*, Aug. 16, 1874, Sept. 29, 1877, Nov. 30, Dec. 3, 1884; *Repub.*, Dec. 14, 1873, May 17, 1874, June 5, 1875, Feb. 22, 1876; *T. Demo.*, July 30, 1883; Anglo–American Art Museum, *Louisiana Landscape*, 32–33; Anglo–American Art Museum, *Sail and Steam*, item 21; Fulton and Toledano, "Landscape Painting," 506, 509; Glenk, 79; LSM, *Biennial Report for 1920–21*, 65; LSM, *Biennial Report for 1924–24*, 59; LSM, *Biennial Report for 1932–33*, 41; Rathbone, *Mississippi Panorama*, 114; Seebold, 1:314; Thompson, "Checklist"; Wiesendanger, 90.

RUMPLER, WILLIAM
Born Frankfort, Germany 1824.
Painter, active N.O. 1853–66.
Studied: with Jakob Becker.
Contemporary listings: artist, 7 Gleise's Row, Poydras (1853); portrait painter, 122 Royal (1858); painter, 138 Carondelet (1859–61, 1866).
Portrait and landscape painter.
References: NOCD 1853, 1858–61, 1866; Bruns, 316; Glenk, 79; Groce and Wallace; Harter and Tucker, 124; LSM, *Biennial Report for 1932–33*, 43.

RUPPELL, MRS. ADAM. *See* WHITE, LILY F.

RUSH, IRA G.
Born OH ca. 1822.
Painter, active N.O. 1850.
Contemporary listings: portrait painter (1850).
Cf. RUSH, J. G.
References: Groce and Wallace; U.S. Census (1850), roll 237.

RUSH, J. G.
Painter, active N.O. 1846–47.
Contemporary listings: J & G Rush & Co., painters, 58 Customhouse (1846); painter, 173 Bienville (1847).

Cf. RUSH, IRA G.
References: NOCD 1846; *D. Delta*, Mar. 3, 1847.

RUSSELL, SIGMOND. *See* ROESSLE, SIGMUND G.

RUSSELL, VIRGINIA FLORIAN. *See* FLORIAN, VIRGINIA JOSEPHINE

RUSSO, CHRISTOPHER, JR.
Born N.O. May 24, 1893; died N.O. July 12, 1936.
Engraver, active N.O. 1910–23.
Contemporary listings: engraver for jewelers (1910); engraver, with L. Krower (1912); engraver, Wm. Frantz & Co. (1915–16).
Listed as an engraver in 1920, 1921, and 1923. In 1924 he began working for N.O. Public Service and appeared to have abandoned his engraving career.
References: NOCD 1910, 1912, 1915–16, 1920, 1922–33, 1935; *T. Pic.*, July 14, 1936; Orleans Parish Registrar of Voters, NOPL; U.S. Census (1910), roll 520.

RYAN, MAZIE TERESA (Mrs. Donald Eugene McDonald)
Born N.O. Sept. 1880; died Pass Christian MS July 31, 1946.
Art craftsman, active N.O. 1900–14; also decorator.
Studied: NEWCOMB COLLEGE (1896–1906); with George W. Maynard, National School of Design, Columbia University, N.Y.C.
Contemporary listings: artist (1900).
Exhibited: Louisiana Purchase Exposition, St. Louis MO (1904); Society of Keramic Arts, National Arts Club, N.Y.C.; ART ASSOCIATION OF NEW ORLEANS (1911).
References: *T. Pic.*, Aug. 2, 1946; Art Asso., *Catalogue* (1911); Robert Clark, 145; Ormond and Irvine, 168; Poesch, *Newcomb Pottery*, 37, 40, 48–49, 104, 117, 121, 124, 130; Smithsonian, *Newcomb Pottery*, 14, 20; U.S. Census (1900), roll 570.

RYAN, MICHAEL D.
Painter, active N.O. 1885–88.
Contemporary listings: painter (1885); fresco painter (1888).
References: NOCD 1885; *D. States*, Oct. 24, 1888.

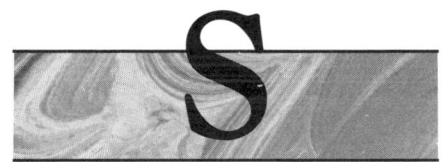

SACKETT, H. A.
Silhouettist, active N.O. 1888.
Contemporary listings: silhouettist,
Robinson's Dime Museum (1888).
References: *D. Pic.*, Dec. 14, 1888.

SAENZ, MANUEL
Painter, active N.O. 1842.
Contemporary listings: miniature
painter, 84 St. Peter (1842).
Memberships/positions: Madrid
Academy of Painting; Valladolid So-
ciety of Arts, Spain.
References: *Courier*, Oct. 10, 1842;
Groce and Wallace.

ST. AMAND, _____. *See* SALAZAR Y MEN-
DOZA, JOSE DE

**SAINT-AULAIRE, FELIX ACHILLE DE
BEAUPOIL, MARQUIS DE**
Born Verceil, France 1801.
Painter, active N.O. 1820.
Studied: with Jean–François Gar-
neray and one of his sons, Paris.
Exhibited: Salon, Paris (1827, 1838).
Marine and landscape painter and li-
thographer who arrived in N.O. on
Feb. 22, 1820. While in the city he
produced a number of street scenes.
He then went to KY and OH, after
which he returned to France. He
lithographed several of his U.S. views
himself, while others were done by
P. LANGLUME.
References: Bénézit; Delgado, *New
Orleans*, item 57; Groce and Wal-
lace; Huber et al., 92–93; Rathbone,
Westward, 278; Rieder, *New Or-
leans Ship Lists*, 1:12.

ST. CLAIR, ANDREW
Painter, active N.O. 1884–86; also
decorator.
Contemporary listings: WEST & ST.
CLAIR (1884–85); fresco and deco-
rative painter, 420 St. Charles
(1886).
References: NOCD 1885–87; *Eve.
Chronicle*, Sept. 10, 20, 1884; *Mas-
cot*, May 16, 1886.

ST. GEES, J. F.
Sculptor, engraver, active N.O.
1817–18; also stone cutter, carver.

Contemporary listings: ST. GEES & IS-
NARD (1817); sculptor and engraver
(1818).
Commissioned by the N.O. City
Council (1818) to erect an obelisk on
the grounds of Christ Church, Canal
St. to the memory of William C. C.
Claiborne, LA's first American gov-
ernor. *Cf.* ST. GES, MR. _____.
References: *Courier*, Oct. 10, 1817,
Mar. 13, 1818; *L'Ami des Lois*, Mar.
13, 1818; *States*, Nov. 25, 1894;
Groce and Wallace; Mayor's Office,
Messages, Sept. 12, Oct. 3, 10, 1818,
NOPL; New Orleans City Council,
Proceedings, Jan. 31, Sept. 21, Oct.
3, Dec. 16, 1818, NOPL.

ST. GEES & ISNARD
Sculptors, engravers, active N.O.
1817; also stone cutters, carvers; J.
F. ST. GEES, JEAN JACQUES ISNARD, part-
ners.
Contemporary listings: sculptors and
engravers, St. Peter (1817).
References: *Courier*, Oct. 10, 1817.

ST. GES, MR. _____
Art teacher, active N.O. 1816.
Contemporary listings: drawing mas-
ter, Madame Felix's school (1816).
Came to N.O. from France ca. 1816.
Cf. ST. GEES, J. F.
References: *L'Ami des Lois*, June 7,
1816; Groce and Wallace.

ST. PE, EMMANUEL (Emile)
Born LA ca. 1890.
Engraver, active N.O. 1908–17.
Contemporary listings: engraver, T.
Hausmann & Sons (1908–17).
References: NOCD 1908–18; U.S.
Census (1910), roll 521.

ST. ROMAN, MISS _____
Painter, active N.O. ca. 1868.
Awarded: Grand State Fair, honorable mention for best miniature
painting on ivory (1868).
References: Mechanics' and Agricultural Fair Asso., *Report* (1868):6.

SALAZAR, MANUEL
Artist, active N.O. 1878–86; also
photographer.

Contemporary listings: artist, with WILLIAM WATSON WASHBURN (1878–86).

References: NOCD 1878–86, 1888.

SALAZAR Y MAGAÑA, FRANCISCA DE (Mrs. Pedro Gordillo)
Born Mérida, Yucatan, Mexico before 1781.
Painter, active N.O. 1802.
Studied: with her father, JOSE DE SALAZAR Y MENDOZA.
Portrait painter and copyist whose family came to N.O. in 1782. She was commissioned to copy her father's portrait of N.O. Bishop Peñalver y Cárdenas (1802).
References: Groce and Wallace; Harter and Tucker, 124; LSM, *Salazar*.

SALAZAR Y MENDOZA, JOSE FRANCISCO XAVIER DE
Born Mérida, Yucatan, Mexico mid–1700s; died N.O. Aug. 15, 1802.
Painter active N.O. ca. 1782–1802.
Contemporary listings: painter (1791).
Earliest known portrait painter of the 18th century in Spanish colonial LA. He came to N.O. as an accomplished artist in 1782 with his wife, daughter, FRANCISCA DE SALAZAR Y MAGAÑA, and son, José. Some sources contend that he was assisted by his son and/or daughter, or that he may have had a brother with whom he worked; he fathered two additional sons while living in N.O., but little more is known about his life. Salazar has been erroneously identified as several different artists with the names "Latizar," "Romegar," and "St. Amand." His extant works are the only identifiable portraits made in N.O. during the Spanish colonial period: these include paintings of prominent people such as Andrés Almonester y Roxas (1796) and Bishop Luís de Peñalver y Cárdenas (1801).
References: *T. Demo.*, May 8, 1904; Collier, "The World of Art: Paintings May Be Work of Salazar," *T. Pic.*, Apr. 23, 1967; *T. Pic.*, July 11, 1971; Jordan, "The World of Art," *T. Pic.*, Dec. 15, 1974; Jordan, "Mystery of Clarice is Solved," *T. Pic.*, Dec. 29, 1974; Jordan, "Madame John's is Alive," *T. Pic.*, May 11, 1975; Jordan, "Jewelry–It's a Part of History Too," *T. Pic.*, Nov. 14, 1976; Bénézit; Bruns, 316; Burson, 247–48; Coulon MS, Scrapbook 100, LSM; Delgado, *New Orleans*, items 58–62; Fielding, *Dictionary*; Friends of the Cabildo, *250 Years*, 17, 29–30; Glenk, 79; Groce and Wallace; Harter and Tucker, 125; Information courtesy the Frick Art Reference Library; Information courtesy George E. Jordan; LSM, *Salazar*; Montero de Pedro, 142–44; Spanish Census of New Orleans, Nov. 6, 1791, NOPL; THNOC artists files; THNOC 1981.213, 1984.14.

SALOMON, WILLIAM
Born N.O. Dec. 25, 1822; died N.O. Dec. 5, 1881.
Engraver, active N.O. 1841–59; also printer, goldsmith.
Contemporary listings: engraver, 82 Chartres (1841–42); engraver, 100 Chartres (1846); engraver, 85 Chartres (1849); engraver, 76 Chartres (1850); engraver, 75 Chartres (1853–55); engraver, 6 Chartres (1856); engraver, Melpomene near Basin (1858–59).
Engraver and copperplate printer who was ordered out of N.O. for refusing to take the oath of allegiance to the U.S. after the occupation of the city during the Civil War. He went to MS and AL, then joined the Confederate army. Following the war, he returned to N.O. and was a cotton weigher until his death.
References: NOCD 1841–44, 1846, 1849–50, 1853–56, 1858–61, 1868, 1870–72, 1875–79; *D. Pic.*, Dec. 6, 11, 1881; Fortier, *Louisiana*, 3:389–90; Groce and Wallace; U.S. Census (1850), roll 237.

SALVADOR, RICHARD
Sculptor, active N.O. 1860–66.
Contemporary listings: sculptor, 204 Bourbon (1860–61, 1866).
References: NOCD 1860–61, 1866.

SALVIOLI, ATTILIO
Born Italy.
Sculptor, active N.O. 1900–1903; also decorator.

Contemporary listings: sculptor (1901); artist, 605 Bourbon (1902); sculptor, 326 Chartres (1903).

Decorator of marble, plaster, and stone who began learning his art ca. 1877 and established himself in N.O. in 1900. He preferred cemetery work, and his work appears on numerous tombs and monuments in N.O.

References: NOCD 1901–1903; *D. States*, Feb. 10, 1902.

SALZMANN, JEAN CHRISTIAN
Born Erfurt, Germany June 21, 1758; died N.O. Sept. 29, 1840.
Engraver, active N.O. 1827–40; also goldsmith.
Contemporary listings: engraver, 41 Levee (1827); engraver, 6 Customhouse (1830); engraver, 80 Customhouse (1832, 1834–35); engraver (1840).
Moved to N.O. ca. 1810.
References: NOCD 1824, 1827, 1830, 1832, 1834–35, 1838, 1841; *Bee*, Sept. 30, 1840; Groce and Wallace; N.O. Death Certificate (1840), 8:620, NOPL; U.S. Census (1830), roll 45, (1840), roll 132.

SAMOURI, CLAUDE
Engraver, active N.O. 1849–51.
Contemporary listings: engraver, Dumaine betw. Royal and Bourbon (1849–51).
References: NOCD 1849–51; Groce and Wallace.

SANCAN, JUSTIN
Born France ca. 1830.
Painter, active N.O. 1850–54.
Contemporary listings: artist (1850), portrait painter, 80 Camp (1854).
References: NOCD 1854; Groce and Wallace; U.S. Census (1850), roll 235.

SANCHEZ, MANUEL D.
Born N.O. Nov. 14, 1883; died N.O. Dec. 13, 1958.
Lithographer, active N.O. 1909–10.
Contemporary listings: lithographer (1909); lithographer–theatre (1910).
Worked at a number of jobs throughout his life, but was primarily a bartender.
References: NOCD 1902–1903, 1906–1907, 1909, 1911, 1913–31,

1942, 1945–47, 1949, 1952–56; *T. Pic.*, Dec. 14–15, 1958; Orleans Parish Registrar of Voters, NOPL; U.S. Census (1910), roll 520.

SANDERS, WOODFORD J.
Born Richmond VA or MS June 1870; died N.O. Nov. 1, 1923.
Painter, sketch artist, active N.O. 1881–1920; also photographer.
Contemporary listings: portrait painter (1881, 1897, 1900); portrait painter, 418 Dryades (1882–83); portrait painter, 103 Canal (1890); artist (1892–96, 1898–99, 1901, 1904, 1907–1908); artist, 918 Canal and artist–crayon works (1910).
Listed as portrait painter (1919–20).
References: NOCD 1881–83, 1885–86, 1890–1901, 1903–1904, 1906–1908, 1910, 1912–13, 1918–22; *T. Pic.*, Nov. 2, 1923; LSM, *Biennial Report for 1926–27*, 29; U.S. Census (1900), roll 574, (1910), roll 520.

SANSUM, EDITH M.
Born Evanston IL Jan. 29, 1867; died N.O. Sept. 26, 1934.
Sketch artist, art teacher, painter, active N.O. 1884–1901.
Studied: with ZILLAH RONDEAU (1884); ARTISTS ASSOCIATION OF NEW ORLEANS (1886, 1890).
Contemporary listings: elementary class teacher, Artists' Association of New Orleans (1890–93).
Exhibited: Zillah Rondeau's studio (1884); Artists' Association of New Orleans (1886–87, 1890–94, 1901); Amateur Art League (1891); Tulane University (1892–93).
Awarded: BLACK AND WHITE CLUB, Pinckney–Smith medal for best collection of sketches; Artists' Association of New Orleans, medal for landscape in oil.
Memberships/positions: Artists' Association of New Orleans (1890, 1896), secy., (1893); Black and White Club, pres. (1890).
Created landscapes and still lifes.
References: NOCD 1891, 1893, 1909, 1916, 1918, 1920–25, 1927–33; *Art and Letters*, 1(Dec. 1887):227–28; *Current Topics*, Jan. 1893, 10, Nov. 1893, 198; *D. Pic.*, Nov. 7, 1886, Nov. 13, Dec. 17,

1890, Apr. 29, May 22, 1891, Mar. 3, 1892; *D. States*, May 16, 1890; *T. Demo.*, Feb. 11, 1884, Nov. 13, Dec. 17, 1890, Dec. 13, 1892, Feb. 15, 1893, Dec. 14, 1894; *T. Pic.*, Sept. 27, 1934; AANO, *Catalogue* (1890, 1891, 1901); AANO, *School of Art* (1892–93); Cline, *Contemporary Art*, 11; Mount, 142; Orleans Parish Registrar of Voters, NOPL; U.S. Census (1900), roll 575.

SARAZIN, MR. ———
Sketch artist, active N.O. 1880.
Contemporary listings: crayonist, with WILLIAM WATSON WASHBURN (1880).
References: *D. States*, Apr. 17, 1880.

SARRE, HENRY W.
Born Strasburgh, Prussia Jan. 21, 1829; died N.O. July 3, 1872.
Painter, active N.O. 1858–72; also photographer.
Contemporary listings: decorative painter (1858–60); decorative painter, Sarre & Bencke (1861); portrait painter, 201 Tchoupitoulas (1866–67); painter (1870); picture painter (1871); artist (1872).
Painted decorations for the German theater (1866).
References: NOCD 1858–61, 1870–72; *T. Deutsche Zeitung*, May 10, Aug. 28, 1866, July 4, 1872; *Louisiana State Gazetteer*; THNOC Cemetery Survey.

SASSMAN, JOHN C.
Engraver, active N.O. 1807–22; primarily jeweler, goldsmith, silversmith.
Contemporary listings: engraver, St. Peter (1807); engraver, 37 Bourbon (1807, 1809); engraver, Conti (1812); engraver, Foucher betw. Levee and Magazine (1813); engraver, Customhouse betw. Royal and Bourbon (1817); engraver, 29 Levee or 58 Bourbon (1822).
References: NOCD 1809, 1811, 1822–24; NOBD 1807; *Courier*, Oct. 19, 1807, July 20, 1812, June 1, 1814, Nov. 5, 1817; *Gazette*, June 5, 1807, Oct. 15, 1822; *L'Ami des Lois*, Aug. 26, 1813; *Moniteur*, Oct. 17, 1807; Groce and Wallace.

SATURDAY DRAWING CLASSES. *See* TULANE FREE DRAWING CLASSES

SAUCIER, CHARLES EBERLE
Born N.O. October 4, 1872; died N.O. June 8, 1922.
Engraver, lithographer, active N.O. 1888–94; also draftsman.
Contemporary listings: engraver, T. FITZWILLIAM & CO. (1888, 1890–92); lithographer, T. Fitzwilliam & Co. (1889); engraver (1893); lithographer (1894).
References: NOCD 1888–1918, 1920–24; *T. Pic.*, June 9, 11, 1922; Orleans Parish Registrar of Voters, NOPL.

SAUERBREY, ADOLPH
Born Bavaria ca. 1834–35; died N.O. Apr. 16, 1909.
Sculptor, active N.O. 1869–1907; also carver, marble cutter.
Contemporary listings: sculptor (1869–70, 1875, 1879, 1884, 1888, 1893, 1904, 1907); sculptor, with PAUL H. MONSSEAUX (1872); sculptor, with PROSPER FLORVILLE FOY (1880, 1889).
Moved to N.O. ca. 1849.
References: NOCD 1870–73, 1875–81, 1884–85, 1887–89, 1893–96, 1900–1904, 1906–1907; *D. Pic.*, Apr. 17–18, 1909; *Repub.*, Aug. 1, 1869; N.O. Death Certificate (1909), 146:562, NOPL; U.S. Census (1870), roll 523, (1880), roll 463.

SAULBERGER, GOTLIED
Born Switzerland ca. 1877.
Painter, active N.O. 1910.
Contemporary listings: fresco painter (1910).
Came to the U.S. in 1882.
References: U.S. Census (1910), roll 523.

SAUNIER, GASTON
Born LA Mar. 1849.
Painter, active N.O. 1887–89; also engineer.
Contemporary listings: painter (1885, 1890–92); fresco painter (1887, 1889).
References: NOCD 1885, 1887, 1889–92, 1895–97, 1901; U.S. Census (1900), roll 573.

SAUVE, CELESTA
Born France ca. 1823.
Artist, active N.O. 1860.

Contemporary listings: artist (1860).
References: Groce and Wallace; U.S.
Census (1860), roll 421.

SAUVE, PAUL
Born Jefferson Parish LA. ca. 1849;
died N.O. Nov. 17, 1907.
Engraver, lithographer, active N.O.
1881–82; primarily stationer,
printer.
Contemporary listings: engraver, lithographer, 74 St. Charles (1881–
82).
References: NOCD 1869–1901,
1903–1906; Land, 182; N.O. Death
Certificate (1907), 142:513, NOPL.

SAWKINS, JAMES G.
Painter, active N.O. 1831–34.
Contemporary listings: portrait and
miniature painter, 58 Royal and cor.
Chartres and St. Louis (1831); por-
trait and miniature painter, 22
Chartres (1834).
In 1831 Sawkins was reported in
N.O. with a studio adjoining that of
JOSEPH HENRY BUSH.
References: *Advertiser*, Jan. 13–May
19, 1834 (advs.); *Mercantile Adver-
tiser*, Mar. 17, Nov. 15–24, 1831
(advs.); Groce and Wallace.

SAXON, LULU KING (Mrs. Walter Lyle
Saxon)
Born LA ca. 1855; died N.O. Feb.
21, 1927.
Painter, sketch artist, active N.O.
1884–1922.
Studied: with ANDRES MOLINARY (ca.
1884); with BROR ANDERS WIKSTROM
and F. ARTHUR CALLENDER; ARTISTS'
ASSOCIATION OF NEW ORLEANS (1887,
1890, 1893).
Exhibited: World's Industrial and
Cotton Centennial Exposition (1884–
85); Artists' Association of New Or-
leans (1887, 1889–97, 1899, 1901–
1902); Tulane University (1892); ART
ASSOCIATION OF NEW ORLEANS (1910,
1915).
Awarded: Artists' Association of New
Orleans, gold medal (1888).
Memberships/positions: Artists' Association of New Orleans (1897); Art
Association of New Orleans (1910).
Landscape artist who was also a
writer, poet, amateur actress, singer,
and musician. She exhibited paint-

ings she had made in Russia prior to
World War I at the Arts and Crafts
Club (1922).
References: *Current Topics*, Jan.
1891, 24–25, Jan. 1892, 23–26, Jan.
1893, 11, Nov. 1893, 198; *D. Pic.*,
May 7, 1887, Dec. 17, 1889, Dec.
17, 1890, Dec. 17, 1891, Dec. 13,
1892, Mar. 30, 1897; *D. States*, May
16, 1890, Jan. 23, 1898, Jan. 8, 1899;
Down in Dixie, Aug. 1, 1896, 18–19;
Harlequin, Dec. 6, 1899, 5; *Item*,
June 16, 1922; *T. Demo.*, Nov. 13,
1890, Mar. 3, 1892, Dec. 14, 1894;
T. Pic., June 11, 1922, Feb. 22, 1927;
AANO, *Catalogue* (1890, 1891,
1896, 1897, 1899, 1901, 1902); Art
Asso., *Catalogue* (1910); Art Asso.,
Special Exhibition; Board of Health
Register, NOPL; Mount, 19–22.

SAXTON, GERARD
Painter, active N.O. 1908–1909.
Contemporary listings: portrait
painter, 1201 Dryades (1908); artist
(1909).
Exhibited: SEEBOLD's gallery (1908).
NY portrait and landscape painter
who executed several commissions
in N.O.
References: NOCD 1908–1909; *T.
Demo.*, Mar. 19, 1908.

SCARTABELLI, H. H.
Cartoonist, active N.O. 1900.
Name appeared with E. PORZIN on a
political cartoon dated N.O. Jan. 1,
1900 in *Harlequin*.
References: *Harlequin*, Jan. 3, 1900,
6–7.

SCHAEFFER, WILLIAM
Painter, active N.O. 1869–70.
Contemporary listings: scenic artist,
Varieties Theatre (1869–70).
References: NOCD 1870; *Repub.*,
Oct. 1, 1869.

SCHARDT, MR. A.
Art teacher, active N.O. 1855–56.
Studied: Munich.
Contemporary listings: drawing
teacher, Schardt's Institution (1855–
56).
References: *Bee*, May 21, 1855–July
2, 1856 (advs.).

SCHARFSCHWERDT, EDWARD
Painter, active N.O. 1887–88; also
decorator.

339

Contemporary listings: fresco painter (1887); painter (1888).

Assisted HENRY PETERSON in the frescoing and painting of the Royal Restaurant (1887).

References: NOCD 1887–88; *D. Pic.*, Sept. 4, 1887.

SCHARPE, CHRISTIAN

Born Bremen, Germany Mar. 1818; died N.O. Mar. 26, 1872.

Lithographer, engraver, active N.O. 1868–72.

Contemporary listings: lithographer (1868, 1872); lithographer, with BENEDICT SIMON (1870); lithographer, with CHARLES W. CLARK (1871). Commissioned with GUSTAVE KOECKERT to engrave an official map of the state of LA (1871).

References: NOCD 1868, 1870–72; *D. Pic.*, Jan. 3, 1871, Mar. 27, 1872; *T. Deutsche Zeitung*, Mar. 27, 1872.

SCHELL, FRANCIS H.

Sketch artist, active N.O. 1862–64. Born Philadelphia PA 1834; died Germantown PA Mar. 31, 1909.

Sketch artist and illustrator who worked as a lithographer in Philadelphia as early as 1850. He became a special artist for *Frank Leslie's Illustrated Newspaper* during the Civil War, and his first known war drawings were engraved and published Apr. 30, 1861. In 1862–63 he accompanied Gen. Nathaniel Banks's expedition to N.O., Baton Rouge, and Bayou Teche LA; he was with Banks's army during the Red River campaign and also witnessed Adm. David Farragut's running past the batteries at Port Hudson LA (1863). Among the many drawings he created of life in N.O. during his assignment were *The Demand for the Surrender of New Orleans* (1862) and *General Banks Addressing the Louisiana Planters at the St. Charles Hotel, New Orleans, La.* (1863). After the war, Schell became the superintendent of *Leslie's* art department and later formed a 30–year partnership with lithographer Thomas Hogan.

References: *Leslie's*, Feb. 21, 1863; Beall, 107, 130; Bénézit; Groce and Wallace; Sears, 375–76; THNOC

1951.10, 1959.27.17; William Young.

SCHERNBECK, JOHN C.

Born N.O. Apr. 1854; died N.O. Jan. 21, 1909.

Painter, active N.O. 1881–1908; also decorator.

Contemporary listings: painter, New Orleans Railroad Co. (1881, 1885–86, 1888–89); painter (1882–84, 1890–93, 1897–98, 1901, 1905); fresco painter (1887, 1894–96, 1904, 1908).

References: NOCD 1881–98, 1900–1902, 1904–1909; *D. Pic.*, Jan. 22, 23, 1909.

SCHILDER, _____

Sketch artist, cartoonist, active N.O. 1917.

Name appeared with WILLIAM K. PATRICK on illustrations in *Club Men of Louisiana in Caricature* (1917).

References: Patrick.

SCHINDLER, LOUIS

Engraver, active N.O. 1888.

Contemporary listings: engraver (1888).

References: NOCD 1888.

SCHINOTTI, EDWARD

Painter, active N.O. 1835–46; also gilder, glazier.

Contemporary listings: scenic painter, St. Charles Theatre (1835, 1837); scenic painter, cor. Camp and Girod (1841–43); portrait painter, 8 Royal and 168 Camp (1846).

Scenic and ornamental artist who also painted military flags and banners. At the St. Charles Theatre he worked with ANTOINE MONDELLI (1835, 1837) and with SAMUEL M. LEE (1837).

References: NOCD 1841–42, 1846, 1849–50; *D. Pic.*, Dec. 4, 1864; *Lafayette City Advertiser*, Jan. 1, 1842–Aug. 12, 1843 (advs.); *True Amer.*, Mar. 28, Apr. 15, 1837; Groce and Wallace; Hoole, 82–84; Kendall, *Golden Age*, 121, 146, 151–52; Sol Smith, 101–5.

SCHIPFER, FREDERICK

Died ca. 1894.

Lithographer, active N.O. 1884–90. Contemporary listings: artist (1884); lithographer, T. FITZWILLIAM & CO. (1885); lithographer, M. F. DUNN &

BRO. (1886); lithographer (1887, 1890).
References: NOCD 1884–87, 1890, 1892, 1895.

SCHLESSINGER, J.
Painter, active N.O. 1881.
Contemporary listings: portrait painter (1881).
References: NOCD 1881.

SCHMICH, LOUIS
Engraver, active N.O. 1885–87.
Contemporary listings: engraver, T. FITZWILLIAM & CO. (1885); artist, T. Fitzwilliam & Co. (1886–87).
References: NOCD 1885–87.

SCHMIDT, EUGENE
Lithographer, active N.O. 1872–74; also printer.
Contemporary listings: lithographer, with HERMANN WEHRMANN (1872); lithographer (1874).
References: NOCD 1872–74.

SCHMIDT, FREDERIC
Lithographer, active N.O. 1850–66; also jeweler, printer.
Contemporary listings: lithographic printer, 160 Barracks (1850–53); lithographic printer, 137 Goodchildren (1854); lithographer, 60 Union (1857); lithographer, 64 Union (1860); lithographer, 95 Union (1861); lithographer (1866).
References: NOCD 1843, 1850–61, 1866–67, 1869; Groce and Wallace.

SCHMIDT, FREDERICK G.
Artist, active N.O. 1885.
Contemporary listings: artist, SOUTHERN LITHOGRAPHIC COMPANY (1885).
References: NOCD 1884–85.

SCHMIDT, GABRIEL
Lithographer, active N.O. 1867.
Contemporary listings: lithographer, 563 St. Claude (1867).
References: NOCD 1861, 1867–68.

SCHMIDT, IMANUEL ALBERT
Born Hamburg, Germany ca. 1838; died N.O. Oct. 19, 1892.
Engraver, active N.O. 1870–89; primarily taxidermist.
Contemporary listings: engraver (1870–72, 1874, 1889); engraver, with SALOMON SCHMIDT (1873); engraver, AMERICAN BANK NOTE COMPANY (1874)

Listed as manager of the American Bank Note Company (1877–80).
References: NOCD 1859–60, 1868–83, 1885, 1889; D. City Item, Oct. 19, 1892; D. Pic., Oct. 23, 30, 1892; N.O. Death Certificate (1892), 102:1025, NOPL.

SCHMIDT, PAUL
Sculptor, active N.O. 1905; primarily carver.
Contemporary listings: woodcarver (1905).
References: NOCD 1901, 1903, 1905–1908, 1910–11.

SCHMIDT, PETER
Born Baden, Germany Jan. 1829; died N.O. Oct. 4, 1866.
Painter, illustrator, active N.O. 1858–66.
Contemporary listings: portrait painter (1858); portrait painter, 163 Royal (1859); portrait painter, 133 Royal (1860–61); portrait painter, 82 Royal (1866–67).
Signature appeared on a sheet music cover lithographed by PESSOU & SIMON (1861).
References: NOCD 1858–61, 1866–67; NOBD 1858–59; T. Deutsche Zeitung, Oct. 5, 1866; Coulon MS, Scrapbook 100, LSM; Glenk, 79; Groce and Wallace; LSM, Annual Report for 1920–21, 65; N.O. Death Certificate, (1866), 35:80, NOPL; U.S. Census (1860), roll 418; "War to the Yankees!" Sheet Music Collection, LA Coll., TU.

SCHMIDT, PETER CHARLES
Born N.Y.C. Mar. 1, 1879; died N.O. Dec. 1, 1048.
Engraver, active N.O. 1898–1948.
Contemporary listings: engraver, with WILLIAM JOHN SCHMIDT (1898, 1901–1902, 1905, 1908, 1910, 1912); engraver (1899, 1903–1904, 1913); engraver, 528 Gravier (1907); owner, SCHMIDT BROTHERS (1914–18).
Listed with Schmidt Brothers (1919–49). Brother of William John Schmidt.
References: NOCD 1898–99, 1901–1908, 1910–33, 1935, 1938, 1940, 1942, 1945–47, 1949; T. Pic., Dec. 5, 1948; Orleans Parish Registrar of

Voters, NOPL; U.S. Census (1910), roll 520.

SCHMIDT, SALOMON (Carl August Salomon)
Born Baden, Saxony July 5, 1806; died N.O. July 22, 1876.
Engraver, active N.O. 1842–76; also printer.
Contemporary listings: engraver 109 Carondelet (1843–44, 1846); engraver, cor. Royal and Canal (1849–50); engraver, RAWDON, WRIGHT, HATCH & EDSON (1851–56); engraver, 12 Royal (1857); bank note engraver, 12 Royal (1858–60); engraver, AMERICAN BANK NOTE COMPANY (1865); engraver, 36 Natchez (1866); bank note engraver, American Bank Note Company (1867–68); engraver (1870, 1875–77).
Engraver who came to N.O. ca. 1840. He engraved the two successive mastheads that appeared in the *Daily Picayune* (Nov. 8, 1842–Nov. 12, 1849 and Nov. 13, 1849–Oct. 15, 1851). As a bank note engraver, he served as an agent for Rawdon, Wright, Hatch & Edson (1851–56) and manager of the American Bank Note Co. (1860–76).
References: NOCD 1843–44, 1846, 1849–61, 1866–77; NOBD 1865; *D. Delta*, Nov. 15, 1849; *D. Pic.*, Nov. 8, 1842, Nov. 13, 1849 (masthead); *Repub.*, Sept. 26, 1867; Groce and Wallace; N.O. Death Certificate (1876), 66:763, NOPL; THNOC Cemetery Survey; U.S. Census (1850), roll 236, (1860), roll 418, (1870), roll 521.

SCHMIDT, W. B.
Lithographer, active N.O. 1884.
Contemporary listings: lithographer, SOUTHERN LITHOGRAPHIC COMPANY (1884).
References: NOCD 1884.

SCHMIDT, WILLIAM JOHN
Born N.Y.C. Aug. 26, 1872; died N.O. May 30, 1931.
Engraver, active N.O. 1896–1931.
Contemporary listings: steel and copper plate engraver, 418 Camp (1896–97); engraver, 325 Camp (1898–1903); engraver, 407 Carondelet (1904–1905); engraver, 528

Gravier (1906–1907); engraver, 430 Gravier (1908–12); engraver, 325 Camp (1913); SCHMIDT BROTHERS (1914–18).
A physician who stopped practicing medicine to become an engraver and was listed with Schmidt Brothers (1919–26, 1931). Brother of PETER CHARLES SCHMIDT.
References: NOCD 1896–1931; *Item–Trib.*, May 31, 1931; *T. Pic.*, May 31, 1931; Orleans Parish Registrar of Voters, NOPL; U.S. Census (1900), roll 575.

SCHMIDT BROTHERS
Engravers, active N.O. 1914–75; also printers; PETER CHARLES SCHMIDT, WILLIAM JOHN SCHMIDT, partners.
Contemporary listings: engravers, 325 Camp (1914–18).
Later listed as engravers at various addresses (1919–75).
References: NOCD 1914–33, 1935, 1938, 1940, 1942, 1945–47, 1949, 1952–56, 1958, 1960–62, 1964–69, 1971–75.

SCHMIT, WILHELM
Born Holland ca. 1808; died N.O. Oct. 15, 1852.
Sculptor, active N.O. 1852.
Contemporary listings: sculptor (1852).
References: Louisiana Charity Hospital, Death Records, NOPL.

SCHMUTZ, RUDOLPH F.
Born LA Mar. 1856; died after 1923.
Sculptor, active N.O. 1900; primarily carver, engineer.
Contemporary listings: woodcarver (1900).
References: NOCD 1882–87, 1889–97, 1901–1905, 1907–21, 1923–24; U.S. Census (1870), roll 521, (1900), roll 573.

SCHNEIDAU, MARETTA D.
Painter, active N.O. ca. 1901.
Exhibited: ARTISTS' ASSOCIATION OF NEW ORLEANS (1901).
Landscape and still life painter.
References: AANO, *Catalogue* (1901).

SCHNEIDER, EDWARD LOUIS
Born N.O. ca. 1883–85; died N.O. Mar. 7, 1952.

Painter, designer, active N.O. ca. 1895–1949.
Contemporary listings: artist (1905, 1910); artist, 1423 Burgundy (1912). Began working as a scene painter at the French Opera House (ca. 1895), and became a float designer and builder for several carnival parades. Later listed as artist (1920, 1922, 1929, 1947); scenic artist (1921, 1931–33, 1938, 1949); and painter (1930).
References: NOCD 1905, 1912, 1920–22, 1929–33, 1935, 1938, 1947, 1949; *Item–Trib.*, Dec. 10, 1939; *States*, Mar. 7, 1952; U.S. Census (1910), roll 521.

SCHNYDER, ALBERT
Born Switzerland Mar. 1861; died N.O. Feb. 18, 1940.
Painter, active N.O. 1885–1940; also decorator.
Contemporary listings: SCHNYDER BROTHERS (1885–1901); fresco painter (1900); fresco painter, 1434 Camp (1902–1904); A. Schnyder & Co. (1905–1909); fresco painter, 1023 Delachaise (1910); painter, 1023 Delachaise (1911–14); painter, 3424 Annunciation (1915–17). Later listed as painter (1919–23, 1925, 1927–29, 1932, 1935, 1938, 1940); and fresco painter (1932).
References: NOCD 1885–1923, 1925–30, 1932, 1935, 1938, 1940; *T. Pic.*, Feb. 19, 1940; U.S. Census (1900), roll 570.

SCHNYDER, JOSEPH
Painter, active N.O. 1885–1900.
Contemporary listings: SCHNYDER BROTHERS (1885–1900).
References: NOCD 1885–1900.

SCHNYDER BROTHERS
Painters, active N.O. 1885–1901; ALBERT SCHNYDER, JOSEPH SCHNYDER, partners.
Contemporary listings: fresco painters, 163 Gravier (1885); fresco painters, 83 Carondelet (1886); fresco painters, 24 1/2 Carondelet (1887); painters, 244 Carondelet (1888–89); fresco painters, 51 Prytania (1890–91); painter, Prytania (1892); painters, 400 Camp (1893); painters, 424 Camp (1894), paint

ers, 1430 Camp (1895–96); fresco painters, 1430 Camp (1897–98); fresco painters, 1432 Camp (1899); fresco painters, 1434 Camp (1900–1901).
References: NOCD 1885–1901.

SCHOEBEL, JOSEPH
Born N.O. Aug. 4, 1866; died N.O. Apr. 20, 1941.
Lithographer, active N.O. 1885–1939; also pressman, printer.
Contemporary listings: lithographer, T. FITZWILLIAM & CO. (1885–87, 1891, 1902, 1910, 1912–13); lithographer (1893, 1900). Later listed as lithographer (1921, 1923, 1926–27, 1930–31) and lithographic printer (1922, 1939).
References: NOCD 1884–91, 1893, 1895–98, 1901–1903, 1907–1908, 1910–13, 1923–26, 1931, 1938, 1940; *T. Pic.*, Apr. 21, 1941; Orleans Parish Registrar of Voters, NOPL; U.S. Census (1900), roll 571, (1910), roll 521.

SCHREIBER, JOHN
Painter, active N.O. 1836–37.
Painted watercolors of N.O. buildings used in real estate transactions (1836–37).
References: Friends of the Cabildo, *N.O. Architecture* 4:38.

SCHRENK, JOHN
Born Wettenberg, Germany ca. 1836; died N.O. Mar. 30, 1916.
Engraver, lithographer, active N.O. 1885–93; also printer.
Contemporary listings: lithographer, SOUTHERN LITHOGRAPHIC COMPANY (1885); artist, T. FITZWILLIAM & CO. (1890); engraver, T. Fitzwilliam & Co. (1891); lithographer (1892–93). Also music teacher. Father of JOHN SCHRENK, JR.
References: NOCD 1860–61, 1866–69, 1871–74, 1879–83, 1885, 1887, 1890–95, 1897, 1900, 1905–1907, 1909, 1912–17; *T. Pic.*, Mar. 31, Apr. 1, 1916.

SCHRENK, JOHN, JR.
Born N.O. ca. 1866; died N.O. Sept. 24, 1951.
Engraver, lithographer, active N.O. 1894–97.

Contemporary listings: lithographer (1894–95, 1897); engraver (1896). Also music teacher. Son of JOHN SCHRENK.

References: NOCD 1894–13, 1915–31, 1933, 1935, 1938, 1940, 1942, 1945–47, 1949; *T. Pic.*, Sept. 26, 1951.

SCHRIEFFER, REUBEN P.
Born LA ca. 1876; died N.O. Sept. 8, 1944.
Engraver, active N.O. 1894–1933; also jeweler, photographer.
Contemporary listings: photo–engraver, PHOTO–ENGRAVING COMPANY (1894); photo–engraver (1897, 1908); photo–engraver, *Times-Democrat* (1901–1907, 1912–14); photo–engraver, ROMANSKI Photo–Engraving Company (1909–11); engraver, *Times-Picayune* (1915, 1917); engraver (1916); photo–engraver, *Times-Picayune* (1918).
Later listed as photoengraver, *Times-Picayune* (1919–20, 1922, 1925, 1929–33); engraver, *Times-Picayune* (1921, 1926–27); and engraver (1923–24, 1928).
References: NOCD 1892–94, 1896–97, 1899–1933, 1935, 1938, 1940, 1942; *T. Pic.*, Sept. 9, 1944; U.S. Census (1910), roll 520.

SCHROEDER, BERNARD
Engraver, active N.O. 1874; also printer.
Contemporary listings: engraver, with Robert Chapsky (1874).
References: NOCD 1870, 1872, 1874–75.

SCHROEDER, DAVID R.
Born LA ca. 1829.
Engraver, active N.O. 1850–54.
Contemporary listings: engraver (1850, 1854); engraver, Live Oak cor. Austerlitz (1853).
References: NOCD 1853–54; U.S. Census (1850), roll 232.

SCHULER, WILLIAM WASHINGTON
Born N.O. May 1859; died N.O. May 31, 1892.
Lithographer, active N.O. 1880–82; also printer.
Contemporary listings: lithographer (1880); lithographer, NEW ORLEANS LITHOGRAPHING AND ENGRAVING CO. (1881); lithographer, NEW ORLEANS LITHOGRAPHING COMPANY (1882).
References: NOCD 1881–82, 1884, 1888–89, 1892; *D. Pic.*, June 1, 1892; N.O. Death Certificate, (1892), 101:1130, NOPL; U.S. Census (1880), roll 459.

SCHULTZ, ARTHUR G.
Born Louisville KY ca. 1872–74; died N.O. Dec. 15, 1943.
Engraver, active N.O. 1901–30.
Studied: Europe.
Contemporary listings: engraver, T. Hausmann & Sons (1901–1902, 1904–1905, 1907–14); engraver (1903, 1906); general engraver, 206 Baronne (1916); engraver, 830 Canal (1917–18).
Later listed as engraver (1919–27, 1929–30).
References: NOCD 1901–14, 1916–27, 1929–31, 1933, 1935, 1938, 1940, 1942; *T. Pic.*, Dec. 16–17, 1943; U.S. Census (1910), roll 524.

SCHULTZ, MARY L. *See* NEILL, MARY L. SCHULTZ

SCHULZE, CHARLES G.
Born Prussia ca. 1844; died after 1921.
Engraver, active N.O. 1866–85; also stencil cutter.
Studied: with his father, Guben, Germany.
Contemporary listings: engraver, 139 Poydras (1866–67); engraver, 18 Commercial (1867–68); engraver, 66 Gravier (1869–71); NEW ORLEANS ELECTROTYPING AND WOOD ENGRAVING CO. (1874); engraver, 1 Bank (1875); engraver, 38 Natchez (1876); wood engraver, 98 Poydras (1880); wood engraver, 22 Natchez (1881); engraver, 25 Natchez (1884–85).
First worked as an engraver in Guben with his father, then moved to London and to Birmingham, England to practice his craft. In 1862 he came to the U.S. and set up an engraving business in St. Louis MO, but in Sept. 1865 he moved to N.O. seeking a warmer climate. Schulze engraved a silver medal to commemorate the World's Industrial and Cotton Centennial Exposition (1884).

References: NOCD 1867–78, 1880–94, 1896–1919, 1921–22; *Eve. Chronicle*, Dec. 19, 1884; *Repub.*, Jan. 14, 1871; *Lousiana State Gazetteer*; Morrison,*Industries*, 136–37; U.S. Census (1870), roll 521.

SCHWAN, PHI.
Born Germany ca. 1831.
Artist, active N.O. 1850.
Contemporary listings: artist (1850).
References: Groce and Wallace; U.S. Census (1850), roll 235.

SCHWODE, ANDREA
Born Bavaria ca. 1825.
Painter, active N.O. 1860.
Contemporary listings: portrait painter (1860).
References: Groce and Wallace; U.S. Census (1860), roll 418.

SCOTT, EDWARD
Born Germany ca. 1811.
Engraver, lithographer, active N.O. 1850–54.
Contemporary listings. stone engraver (1850); lithographer, 37 Goodchildren (1854).
References: NOCD 1853–56, 1858; Groce and Wallace, U.S. Census (1850), roll 238.

SCUDDER, ALICE RAYMOND (Mrs. Ray G. Coates)
Born N.O. 1879; died Mar. 5, 1957.
Painter, art craftsman, active N.O. 1904–16.
Studied: NEWCOMB COLLEGE (1899–1903, 1907–10, 1914–15); with F. Luis Mora; with William M. Chase; New York School of Applied Design for Women.
Exhibited: ART ASSOCIATION OF NEW ORLEANS (1904–1905, 1907, 1911, 1913, 1915–16).
Awarded: Mary L. S. Neill water color competition, honorable mention.
Memberships/positions: Art Association of New Orleans (1904–1905, 1907, 1911, 1913); Art Exhibition Club (1901); American Federation of Arts.
Landscape painter in watercolor and pastel; also listed as pottery worker (1905).
References: Art Asso., *Catalogue* (1904, 1905, 1907, 1911, 1913, 1915, 1916); Arts Exhibition Club, 15; Bénézit; Fielding, *Dictionary*; Ormond and Irvine, 168; Poesch, *Newcomb Pottery*, 104.

SEBRON, HYPPOLITE VICTOR VALENTIN
Born Caudebec, France Aug. 21, 1801; died Paris, France Sept. 1, 1879.
Painter, sketch artist, active N.O. ca. 1850–53.
Studied: with Louis Jacques Mandé Daguerre; with Léon Cogniet.
Contemporary listings: painter (1851); portrait and sketch painter, 124 St. Louis (1852).
Exhibited: Salon, Paris (1831–78); Royal Bazaar, London (1833); Commercial Reading Room (1847); Faivre's music store (1852); World's Exposition, Paris (1855); National Academy of Design, N.Y.C. (1854).
French diorama, landscape, and portrait painter who, despite having only one arm, enjoyed a long and successful career. Sebron was noted for exterior and interior views taken from his extensive travels through Europe (1831–48), the U.S. (1849–55), and Europe and Asia (1867–77). Sebron first painted historical, religious, and scenic dioramas in France in collaboration with his teacher, L. J. M. Daguerre, the famous inventor of the first widely–accepted photographic process. They improved on the visual effect of popular dioramas by painting transparent and opaque colors on both sides of the works and creating special lighting that transformed day scenes to night and made figures appear and disappear. They created five dioramas between 1834 and 1839 and exhibited them throughout Europe and the U.S. through their agents. One of their works, a four–part diorama with scenes in Italy, Switzerland, and France, arrived in N.O. in Jan. 1843 during its tour of the U.S., but was destroyed by a fire in the museum that housed it. Another of their collaborations, a painting called *The Departure of the Israelites*, was exhibited in N.O. and offered for sale in Mar. 1847. When Sebron came to the

U.S. (1849–55), he worked mostly in N.Y.C. and N.O. He passed through N.O. on his way west, and on his return trip, was noted in the city from Dec. 1851 to May 1852. During his stay, he painted and lithographed portraits and exhibited a view of Niagara Falls and one of the levee at N.O. The levee view, based on an 1850 oil sketch, was exhibited in N.O. during May 1852. Sebron returned to N.Y.C. by 1854 and then went on to France. At the 1855 Paris exposition, he exhibited the N.O. levee view under the title *Bateaux à Vapeur Geants* (dated 1853). The painting was eventually purchased (1868) by the N.O. department store owner, D. H. Holmes, who exhibited it at the World's Industrial and Cotton Centennial Exposition in N.O. (1884–85) and donated it to Tulane University (1892). Two known paintings suggest that Sebron either returned to LA after his first visits or painted more LA scenes in Europe: a watercolor of N.O. steamboats (dated 1858) and *Lake of Alligators–Louisiana* (1868).

References: *Bee*, Jan. 30–31, 1843, Dec. 15, 1851, May 11, 1852; *Comm. Times*, Mar. 25, 31, 1847; *Courier*, Jan. 31, 1843, Feb. 14, May 12, 1852; *D. Delta*, Mar. 21, 1847, Feb. 1, May 4, 13, 1852; *D. Pic.*, Mar. 27, 1892; Bénézit; *Bryan's*; Champlin; Gernsheim, 33–34, 45; Groce and Wallace; Poesch, *Art of the Old South*, 287–90; THNOC 1958.14; WICCE, *Catalogue*, 92.

SEEBOLD, FREDERIC WILLIAM EMILE
Born Lachem, Hanover Sept. 15, 1833; died N.O. June 25, 1921.
Art dealer, engraver, active N.O. ca. 1865–1920; also stationer, printer, art store proprietor.
Contemporary listings: art dealer, 166 Canal (1877–78); engraver and fine art dealer, 166 Canal (1890); art dealer and engraver, 130 Carondelet (1913–17); art dealer and engraver, 119–21 Carondelet (1918).
Arriving in N.O. (ca. 1861), Seebold served in the Civil War and then opened an art store (ca. 1865). He

was the first print dealer to introduce the photogravure process to N.O. (1877). Seebold became one of the foremost art connoisseurs in the city and assisted many struggling artists. From 1879 to 1916, almost every notable artist who visited N.O. dined at his home; his gallery became a meeting place for painters such as RICHARD CLAGUE, EVERETT B. D. JULIO, and HAROLD RUDOLPH and for writers and musicians as well. He was responsible for organizing the Art Gallery at the World's Industrial and Cotton Centennial Exposition (1884–85) and was a founding member of the SOUTHERN ART UNION, the ARTISTS' ASSOCIATION OF NEW ORLEANS, and the ART ASSOCIATION OF NEW ORLEANS. Seebold continued to be listed as an art dealer in his later years (1919–20). Father of HERMAN BOEHM DE BACHELLE SEEBOLD and MARIE MADELEINE SEEBOLD.

References: NOCD 1866–99, 1901–22; *Current Topics*, Oct. 1890 (adv.); *D. Pic.*, July 9, 1865, Sept. 29, 1877, Dec. 21, 1890; *D. States*, Mar. 14, 1883; *Item*, June 25, 1921; *T. Pic.*, June 26, 1921; Lily Jackson, "Their Legacy: An Artistic Spirit," *T. Pic./States–Item*, Oct. 9, 1983; Clement Evans, 10:577; Seebold, 1:312–22, 2:216–21.

SEEBOLD, HERMAN BOEHM DE BACHELLE
Born N.O. Aug. 5, 1875; died N.O. Dec. 11, 1950.
Sketch artist, painter, active N.O. 1906–1907.
Primarily a physician, he drew illustrations for an issue of the *Illustrated Sunday Magazine* of the *Daily Picayune* (1906). Seebold created watercolor and pencil illustrations of French Quarter buildings and courtyards (1906) for his articles published in the *New Orleans American* in 1915, and he also authored *Old Louisiana Plantation Homes and Family Trees*. Son of FREDERIC WILLIAM EMILE SEEBOLD; brother of MARIE MADELEINE SEEBOLD.
References: NOCD 1907–22, 1924, 1926, 1935, 1938, 1940, 1942,

1945–47, 1949; *American*, May 16, 23, 1915; *D. Pic.*, June 16, 1907; Kane, "Orleanians Who Write Books," *T. Pic.*, Apr. 30, 1950; *T. Pic.*, Dec. 12, 1950; Lily Jackson, "Their Legacy: An Artistic Spirit," *T. Pic./ States–Item*, Oct. 9, 1983; Glenk, 83; *NCAB*; Seebold; *Who's Who in Louisiana and Mississippi*.

SEEBOLD, MARIE MADELEINE (Mrs. Andres Molinary)

Born N.O. Aug. 13, 1866; died N.O. Aug. 19, 1948.

Painter, restorer, designer, art teacher, active N.O. ca. 1885–1943. Studied: with GEORGE DAVID COULON and PAUL POINCY (ca. 1877); ARTISTS' ASSOCIATION OF NEW ORLEANS (1887); with BROR ANDERS WIKSTROM, Andres Molinary, SOUTHERN ART UNION; with William Chase, N.Y.C.; Chicago Art Institute; Museum of Art, Philadelphia.

Exhibited: Atlanta Exposition (1881); American Exposition (1885–86); Artists' Association of New Orleans (1887, 1889–92, 1894, 1896–97, 1899, 1901–1902), Cotton Palace (1889); Tulane University (1892–93); World's Columbian Exposition, Chicago (1893); Tennessee Centennial Exposition, Nashville (1897); E. Curtis's Exchange (1902); ART ASSOCIATION OF NEW ORLEANS (1904–1905, 1907, 1910, 1913–18).

Awarded: Brownie drawing contest, St. Charles Theatre, first ladies' prize (1897); Waco TX, first prize (1914); Artists' Association of New Orleans, prize.

Memberships/positions: Artists' Association of New Orleans; Art Association of New Orleans (1904, 1914).

Still life painter known for her compositions of fruits and of flowers who also created portraits, landscapes, and genre works. She started painting at an early age and was 11 years old when her art instruction began. Her father, FREDERIC WILLIAM EMILE SEEBOLD, encouraged her to be an artist, and she studied not only in N.O., but also in N.Y.C. for about five years. She was first known to have exhibited in N.O. in 1885, and by 1887

her paintings were shown in the city regularly. Seebold was the second woman to be accepted as a member of the Artist's Association of New Orleans and was the protégé of longtime teacher and colleague Andres Molinary, whom she married (1915) shortly before his death in the same year. From him she learned the art of restoration, and she cleaned and repaired old paintings for many residents of N.O. Seebold also designed invitations, programs, and backdrops for various carnival organizations and painted china and terra cotta as well. After 1918, she continued to exhibit with the Art Association of New Orleans (1919–39) where she held a number of positions, culminating with membership on the board of directors (1931). She also exhibited at the Arts and Crafts Club (1922–26) and was a member of the Southern States Art League. She conducted art classes at the DELGADO MUSEUM OF ART and gave private lessons in her home. Seebold stopped painting about five years before her death. Sister of HERMAN BOEHM DE BACHELLE SEEBOLD

References: NOCD 1920–26, 1928–31, 1940, 1942, 1945–46; *Art and Letters* 1(Dec. 1887):227; *D. Pic.*, May 7, Dec. 29, 1887, Dec. 17, 1889, Nov. 13, 1890, Mar. 3, Dec. 13, 1892, Mar. 30, 1897; *D. States*, Apr. 4, Dec. 5, 1897, July 3, 1898; *Harlequin*, Dec. 6, 1899, 5; *Item*, Apr. 2, 1930, Aug. 20, 1948; *Morn. Trib.*, Oct. 20, 1926, Oct. 5, 1927; *States*, Aug. 20, 1948; *T. Demo.*, Feb. 19, 1889, Nov. 13, 1890, Feb. 15, 1893, Dec. 14, 1894, Mar. 24, 1902; *T. Pic.*, June 5, 1918, June 11, 1922, May 2, 1926, Aug. 20, Nov. 27, 1948; Lily Jackson, "Their Legacy: An Artistic Spirit," *T. Pic./States–Item*, Oct. 9, 1983; *Woman's World*, Dec. 20, 1890; AANO, *Catalogue* (1890, 1891, 1896, 1897, 1899, 1901, 1902); Art Asso., *Catalogue* (1904, 1905, 1907, 1910, 1913, 1914, 1915, 1916, 1917, 1918, 1919, 1921, 1922, 1927, 1929, 1930, 1931, 1933, 1934, 1935, 1936, 1938, 1939); Art Asso., *Spe-*

cial Exhibition; Creole Exhibit, 15; Fielding, *Dictionary*; Mount, 29–31; Seebold, 2:220–21; Tennessee Centennial Exposition; *Who's Who in American Art*, 1938–39; WPA, "Lives."

SEGHERS, DOMINIQUE EDOUARD
Born N.O. Aug. 1848; died N.O. July 20, 1911.
Painter, active N.O. 1874–86; primarily surveyor, draftsman, architect.
Painted watercolors of N.O. buildings used in real estate transactions (1874–86).
References: NOCD 1869–70, 1872–1911; *D. Pic.*, July 11, 1911; Friends of the Cabildo, *N.O. Architecture*, 2:111; N.O. Death Certificate (1911), 152:774, NOPL; Orleans Parish Notarial Archives, Plan Books; U.S. Census (1870), roll 521.

SEILE, SIGMOND
Engraver, active N.O. 1884.
Contemporary listings: engraver, with George Bozant, 3 Chartres.
References: NOCD 1884.

SEILE, SIMON BENNO
Born Austria ca. 1840.
Engraver, active N.O. 1868–84; also jeweler.
Contemporary listings: engraver, Merchants' and Auctioneers' Exchange (1868); engraver (1869); engraver, 69 Chartres (1870–71); engraver, 70 St. Charles (1873–78); engraver, 161 Common (1879); engraver, 183 Gravier (1881); engraver, with G. Bozant (1884).
References: NOCD 1868–69, 1873–81, 1884; Boyd, 158; U.S. Census (1870), roll 521.

SEITZ, JACOB
Lithographer, active N.O. 1889–91.
Contemporary listings: lithographer, M. F. DUNN & BRO. (1889); lithographer, T. FITZWILLIAM & CO. (1891).
References: NOCD 1886–87, 1889–91.

SEL, JEAN BAPTISTE
Born Santo Domingo ca. 1780–90; died N.O. Jan. 28, 1832.
Painter, art teacher, active N.O. 1811–30.

Contemporary listings: miniature and portrait painter, 38 Conti (1811); drawing teacher, Orleans College (1813); drawing teacher, school of Messrs. Pre, Lambert, and J. Davezac (1814); miniature and portrait painter, 43 Maine (1822); miniature and portrait painter, 119 Maine (1823, 1827); miniature and portrait painter, 115 Maine (1824, 1830).
Miniature and portrait painter in oils who came to N.O. ca. 1800. In 1813 Sel and JEAN HYACINTHE LACLOTTE executed a painting which was part of the scenery for the play *Clémence & Waldimar* at the Théâtre St.–Philippe. His works included portraits of Placide Bossier (1824) and François Xavier Martin (ca. 1830). *Cf.* SELLE, MR. _____.
References: NOCD 1811, 1822–24, 1827, 1830; *Courier*, May 10, July 26, 1813, Feb. 10, 1817, July 27, 1821, Jan. 28, 1832; *L'Ami des Lois*, Oct. 22, 1814; *Moniteur*, July 29, 1813; Glenk, 40, 61, 79; Groce and Wallace; Harter and Tucker, 125; LSM, *Annual Report for 1918*, following 56; U.S. Census (1830), roll 45.

SELLE, MR. _____
Art teacher, active N.O. 1810.
Contemporary listings: drawing teacher, Mrs. Martin's school for young ladies and Mr. J. Martin's school for young gentlemen, 32 Toulouse (1810).
Cf. SEL, JEAN BAPTISTE.
References: *Courier*, Nov. 28, Dec. 3, 5, 1810.

SELLE, F. W.
Born Germany ca. 1790.
Engraver, active N.O. 1820.
Contemporary listings: engraver (1820).
Arrived in N.O. from Bremen (1820).
References: Rieder, *New Orleans Ship Lists*, 1:9–10.

SELOVER, ALVIN T.
Engraver, active N.O. 1867–70.
Contemporary listings: engraver, St. Charles Rotunda, and near the corner of Chartres and Canal (1867); engraver (1870).

Primarily a professional card writer and teacher of penmanship.
References: NOCD 1867, 1870–72, 1877, 1879–80, 1886–87, 1889–91, 1894, 1897; *Repub.*, Apr. 28, 1867, Apr. 9, Dec. 17, 1876.

SEMMES, THOMAS JENKINS
Born Georgetown DC Dec. 16, 1824; died N.O. June 23, 1899.
Designer, active N.O. ca. 1862.
Attorney who moved to N.O. in 1850 and was elected LA Attorney–General (1859). He was selected to serve in the state's secession convention (Jan. 1861) and designed the Great Seal of the Confederate States of America, dated Feb. 22, 1862.
References: NOCD 1852–61, 1867–1904; *D. Crescent*, Feb. 1, 1861; *D. Pic.*, Oct. 2, 1887, Jan. 6, 1889; *T. Demo.*, June 23–24, 26, July 2, 1899, June 12, 1904; *DAB*; Jewell; M'Caleb, 160; *NCAB*; THNOC 1957.129.1.

SENN, JOHN
Born Switzerland ca. 1825; died N.O. Apr. 22, 1883.
Painter, active N.O. 1870–72; also sign and decorative painter.
Contemporary listings: fresco painter, 38 Exchange Al. (1870); fresco painter, 39 Exchange Al. (1871–72).
References: NOCD 1860–61, 1866, 1869–83; THNOC Cemetery Survey.

SERVANT, EMELIE E.
Born France ca. 1841.
Art craftsman, art teacher, active N.O. 1860–63.
Contemporary listings: artificial flower maker (1860); teacher and maker of artificial flowers, 161 Royal (1863).
References: NOCD 1866; *Bee*, Apr. 11, 1863; U.S. Census (1860), roll 418.

SEVIN, CLIFFORD L.
Born LA ca. 1892.
Engraver, active N.O. 1907–17.
Contemporary listings: engraver (1907–1909, 1915–16); engraver, with Leonard Krower (1910–12); photo–engraver, ROMANSKI Photo–Engraving Co., Ltd. (1913); en-

graver, with DAVID R. MILLER (1914); engraver, D. H. Holmes Co., Ltd. (1917).
References: NOCD 1907–18; U.S. Census (1910), roll 519.

SEWELL, MR. _____
Painter, active N.O. 1838.
Contemporary listings: scene painter, Camp Street Theatre (1838).
References: *True Amer.*, Oct. 23, 1838.

SHAKESPEARE, MRS. _____
Painter, active N.O. ca. 1884–85.
Exhibited: Woman's Department, World's Industrial and Cotton Centennial Exposition (1884–85).
Pottery painter.
References: Woman's Department of World's Exposition, 222.

SHANDANK, WILLIAM
Born LA ca. 1846.
Painter, active N.O. 1875–80.
Contemporary listings: fresco painter (1875, 1880).
References: NOCD 1875; U.S. Census (1880), roll 458.

SHANNON, AILLEEN PHILLIPS
Painter, sketch artist, active N.O. ca. 1915.
Exhibited: ART ASSOCIATION OF NEW ORLEANS (1915).
References: Art Asso., *Catalogue* (1915).

SHANNON, LOUISE BAILEY. *See* BAILEY, LOUISE MARIE

SHARP, MR. _____
Painter, active N.O. 1838.
Contemporary listings: portrait painter, 22 Chartres (1838).
References: *Comm. Bull.*, May 12, 1838; Groce and Wallace.

SHARP, BEMIS (Mrs. Frank W. Hart)
Born N.O. Apr. 11, 1884; died Aug. 20, 1979.
Art craftsman, active N.O. 1913–26; also needleworker.
Studied: NEWCOMB COLLEGE (1902–1907), Pennsylvania Academy of Fine Arts, Philadelphia.
Exhibited: ART ASSOCIATION OF NEW ORLEANS (1913).
Memberships/positions: Art Association of New Orleans (1913).
Later exhibited at the Arts and Crafts Club (1926).

References: NOCD 1915, 1956, 1958, 1960–62, 1964–69, 1971–79; *T. Pic.*, Oct. 20, 1926; Art Asso., *Catalogue* (1913); Orleans Parish Registrar of Voters, NOPL; Poesch, *Newcomb Pottery*, 104.

SHAW, MR. _____

Painter, art teacher, active N.O. 1832.

Contemporary listings: botanical and ornamental painting teacher, Mr. Dolbear's Writing Academy (1832). Advertised as being from Boston.

References: *Advertiser*, Mar. 24–Apr. 16, 1832 (advs.); *Bee*, Mar. 26, 1832; *Courier*, Mar. 24, 1832; *Emporium*, Sept. 28, 1832; Groce and Wallace.

SHAW, STEPHEN WILLIAM

Born Windsor VT Dec. 15, 1817; died San Francisco CA Feb. 12, 1900.

Painter, active N.O. 1848–49.

Contemporary listings: portrait painter, Canal (1848); portrait painter (1849).

Exhibited: J. B. Steel's store (1848); Hewlett's Exchange (1849).

Though most widely regarded for portraits, Shaw painted scenes of Mexico during the U.S. occupation (1847). As a result, he was commissioned to paint a portrait of Gen. Persifor F. Smith, a New Orleanian who served in the Mexican War. The painting was to hang in the council chamber of the second municipality, and after some reluctance, the portrait was accepted, and Shaw was paid his fee (1849). Shaw moved to CA that year and established himself as a portrait painter in San Francisco; he was said to have executed over 200 portraits of the Masons of CA and other western notables.

References: *Comm. Times*, Aug. 1, 1848; *D. Crescent*, Jan. 24, Feb. 7, 1849; *D. Pic.*, Jan. 10, 1849; *Wkly. Delta*, Feb. 12, 26, 1849; Groce and Wallace.

SHAW, WILLIAM R.

Born N.O. Feb. 26, 1860; died N.O. May 2, 1950.

Sketch artist, active N.O. ca. 1886–98; primarily sign painter.

Studied: Tulane University (1886).

Drew pencil and ink scenes of N.O., LA, and MS (ca. 1886–98). Listed as a sign painter throughout his career (1880–1949).

References: NOCD 1880–1922, 1924–33, 1935, 1938, 1940, 1942, 1945–47, 1949; *Eve. Chronicle*, May 22, 1886; *T. Pic.*, May 4, 1950; Orleans Parish Registrar of Voters, NOPL; THNOC 1964.12, 1983-.170.1–.72; U.S. Census (1880), roll 458.

SHEEN, ANN EVELYN (Mrs. Daniel A. Carney)

Painter, art craftsman, active N.O. ca. 1911–14.

Studied: NEWCOMB COLLEGE (1911); Art Students League, N.Y.C.; with John Carlson.

Exhibited: Newcomb College (1911).

Awarded: ART ASSOCIATION OF NEW ORLEANS, silver medal (1914).

References: *T. Demo.*, Mar. 16, 1914; Art Asso., *Catalogue* (1914); Ormond and Irvine.

SHEERER, MARY GIVEN

Born Covington KY May 21, 1865; died Dec. 3, 1954.

Art teacher, art craftsman, potter, painter, active N.O. 1894–1931.

Studied: Cincinnati Art Academy, OH; Art Students League, N.Y.C.; with Denman Ross, Harvard University; with Arthur W. Dow, Ipswich MA (1908); with Hugh Breckenridge and Daniel Garber, Pennsylvania Academy of Fine Arts, Philadelphia (1913–14); with Frank Duveneck; with Anna M. Riis; with Kenyon Cox; with Henry Siddons Mowbray.

Contemporary listings: instructor of china painting and ornamental pottery (1897).

Exhibited: ARTISTS' ASSOCIATION OF NEW ORLEANS (1894, 1897, 1899); Louisiana Purchase Exposition, St. Louis MO (1904); ART ASSOCIATION OF NEW ORLEANS (1905, 1915–18); Panama–Pacific International Exposition, San Francisco (1915).

Memberships/positions: Cincinnati Woman's Art Club; Crafters' Club; Cincinnati Museum Association; Art Association of New Orleans, board of directors (1905).

Hired in 1894 from the Cincinnati School of Art to organize the NEW-COMB COLLEGE pottery department, Sheerer was the stimulus for the artistic and commercial success of its pottery wares. She held successive positions at Newcomb as instructor of china painting (1894), assistant professor in the art department (1895–1903), professor of pottery and china decoration (1903–1909), and professor and assistant director of pottery (1909–31). Sheerer became a nationally recognized authority on ceramics through her work at Newcomb. She stressed the cooperative influences of art and industry in crafts production and encouraged her students toward individual design and execution in their work. Sheerer was a member of the Arts and Crafts Club and a founding member of the Artists' Guild. She was a member and art chairman of the American Ceramic Society and was its delegate to the International Exposition of Modern Decorative and Industrial Art in Paris (1925). Sheerer was made a fellow of the society and professor emeritus of ceramics at Newcomb upon her retirement in 1931; she returned to Cincinnati shortly thereafter.
References: NOCD 1897–1908, 1910–13, 1915–21, 1923–31, 1935, 1942, 1945–46; *D. Pic.*, Feb. 10, 1901; *Harlequin*, Dec. 6, 1899, 5; June 23, 1904, 7; *Item*, Jan. 16, 1921, Nov. 25, 1923; *Item-Trib.*, May 15, 1932; *Men and Matters*, Sept. 1897, 48; *Morn. Trib.*, Dec. 1, 1926; *T. Demo.*, Dec. 14, 1894, Dec. 28, 1905; *T. Pic.*, May 28, 1924, Dec. 6, 1925, Mar. 22, 30, 1931; AANO, *Catalogue* (1897, 1899); Art Asso., *Catalogue* (1905, 1915, 1916, 1917, 1918); Robert Clark, 144; Orleans Parish Registrar of Voters, NOPL; Ormond and Irvine, 169; Poesch, *Newcomb Pottery*, passim; WPA "Lives."

SHEPARD, ERIN E. (Effie)
Died N.O. Dec. 8, 1917.
Art craftsman, art teacher, active N.O. 1900–14.

Studied: NEWCOMB COLLEGE (1900–1909).
Contemporary listings: art craftsman (1910–13); professor, Tulane University (1912); teacher, Newcomb (1914).
Exhibited: ART ASSOCIATION OF NEW ORLEANS (1910–11, 1914); Newcomb Art Alumnae Christmas show (1910, 1913).
Awarded: Mary L. S. Neill medal for watercolor painting (1905).
Memberships/positions: Art Association of New Orleans (1905).
References: NOCD 1912, 1914; *T. Pic.*, Dec. 9, 1917; Art Asso., *Catalogue* (1905, 1910, 1911, 1914); Ormond and Irvine, 169; Poesch, *Newcomb Pottery*, 104–5.

SHERLOCK, _____
Artist, active N.O. 1823.
Contemporary listings: artist, 81 Camp (1823).
References: NOCD 1823; Groce and Wallace.

SHIELDS, MATTIE E. PURSELL (Mrs. James Shields)
Died N.O. Oct. 6, 1921.
Art craftsman, active N.O. ca. 1888.
Exhibited: TULANE DECORATIVE ART LEAGUE FOR WOMEN (1888).
References: NOCD 1889–92, 1895–1909, 1911–20; *D. Pic.*, Feb. 12, 1888, July 15, 1892; *T. Pic.* Oct. 7, 1921; Tulane Decorative Art League, 4.

SHIELDS, THOMAS H.
Born N.Y.C. ca. 1818–19; died N.O. Aug. 13, 1876.
Engraver, active N.O. 1836–52; also printer.
Contemporary listings: engraver, 3 Camp (1838–39); engraver, 90 St. Charles (1839); engraver, 48 Canal (1840–41); engraver, 5 Camp (1840–44); SHIELDS & COLLINS (1842, 1848–50); SHIELDS & HAMMOND (1845); engraver, 9 Camp (1846, 1849); engraver, 7 Camp (1847); engraver, 17 St. Charles (1850–52).
Came to N.O. ca. 1836 where he advertised a general practice for engraving and printing and executed masthead designs for the *Daily Picayune* (1851–79), *La Patria* (1849),

and *La Union* (1851). He later became a wholesaler of painters' supplies. Active in politics, Shields made badges commemorating Henry Clay (1844) and Zachary Taylor (1847). He served as a member of the Board of Aldermen for the second municipality and served several terms as a state legislator. He was a member of the N.O. City Council (1868–70) and served on the board of directors of the N.O. public school system for 25 years. During the Civil War, Shields was a member of the Home Guard. References: NOCD 1841–44, 1846, 1849–61, 1866–68, 1870–76; *Bee*, Dec. 1, 1847; *Courier*, Nov. 26, 1858; *D. Crescent*, Nov. 13–30, 1850 (advs.); *D. Pic.*, Dec. 2, 1838–Aug. 13, 1839 (advs.), Nov. 21–Dec. 11, 1839 (advs.), Mar. 18–July 14, 1840 (advs.), Nov. 1, 1840–Jan. 5, 1844 (advs.), Jan. 2, 1841, Aug. 12, 1842, July 15, 1843, Jan. 5, 1844, Dec. 16, 1845, Dec. 3, 1848, Aug. 20, 1876; *D. Tropic*, Sept. 25, 1844; *Patria*, Jan. 7, 1849; *T. Deutsche Zeitung*, Mar. 31, 1860; Groce and Wallace; Kendall, *History*, 3:1027–28; N.O. Death Certificate (1876), 66:878, NOPL; THNOC Cemetery Survey; U.S. Census (1840), roll 132, (1850), roll 237.

SHIELDS & COLLINS
Engravers, active N.O. 1842–50; also printers; THOMAS H. SHIELDS, CHARLES COLLINS, partners.
Contemporary listings: engravers, 5 Camp (1842); engravers, 34 Camp (1848–49); engravers, 11 Camp (1850).
References: NOCD 1842, 1849–50; *D. Crescent*, Dec. 5, 1849; *D. Pic.*, Dec. 3, 1848–Mar. 24, 1849 (advs.); *Wkly. Delta*, July 2, 1849; Groce and Wallace.

SHIELDS & HAMMOND
Engravers, active N.O. 1845; also printers; THOMAS H. SHIELDS, JOHN T. HAMMOND, partners.
Contemporary listings: engravers, 2 Camp (1845).
References: *Courier*, June 23, 1845; *D. Pic.*, Feb. 2–12 (advs.), Dec. 16, 1845; Norman; Stauffer, 1:246.

SHULER, C.
Painter, active N.O. ca. 1883.
Exhibited: LILIENTHAL'S (1883).
References: Lilienthal's, 6.

SHUMWAY, HENRY COLTON
Born Middletown CT July 4, 1807; died N.Y.C. May 6, 1884.
Painter, active N.O. 1859–60.
Studied: National Academy of Design, N.Y.C. (ca. 1828–30).
Contemporary listings: miniature painter, cor. St. Charles and Common (1859–60).
Memberships/positions: National Academy of Design (1832).
Miniature painter who visited N.O. during Dec. 1859 and Jan. 1860. After the Civil War, when photography had reduced the demand for miniature paintings, he was chiefly occupied in tinting photographs in N.Y.C.
References: *Bee*, Dec. 5, 1859, Jan. 2, Jan. 6, 1860; *D. Pic.*, Dec. 14, 1859; Bolton, *Painters in Miniature*; Fielding, *Dictionary*; Groce and Wallace.

SIDNEY, HENRY CHARLES
Born N.O. ca. 1842; died N.O. Oct. 30, 1905.
Engraver, active N.O. 1869; primarily stencil cutter, sign and ornamental painter.
Contemporary listings: engraver, 8 Natchez (1869).
References: NOCD 1867–69, 1873, 1876–77, 1881, 1901, 1904–1905; *T. Demo.*, Oct. 31, Nov. 5, 1905; N.O. Death Certificate (1905), 136:743, NOPL.

SIEBRECHT, EDWARD
Sculptor, active N.O. 1886.
Contemporary listings: sculptor, with FLORVILLE FOY (1886).
References: NOCD 1886.

SILICEO, LOUIS
Painter, active N.O. 1889.
Contemporary listings: portrait painter (1889).
References: NOCD 1889.

SIM, WILLIAM
Engraver, active N.O. 1830.
Contemporary listings: engraver, 78 Magazine (1830).
References: NOCD 1830, 1837.

SIMMS, MRS. FRANK
Painter, active N.O. ca. 1891–1901.
Exhibited: ARTISTS' ASSOCIATION OF
NEW ORLEANS (1891).
Memberships/positions: ARTS EXHI-
BITION CLUB (1901).
References: *Current Topics*, Jan.
1892, 24; AANO, *Catalogue* (1891);
Arts Exhibition Club, 17.

SIMON, BENEDICT
Born Todtmoos, Baden, Germany ca.
1824; died N.O May 29, 1878.
Lithographer, active N.O. 1850–78;
also, publisher.
Contemporary listings: lithographer
(1850, 1860); lithographer, 175
Chartres (1853); lithographer, 165
Chartres (1854); PESSOU & SIMON
(1855–61, 1865–67); lithographer,
116 Exchange Pl. (1869); lithographer, Conti cor. Exchange Al. (1870–
72); lithographer, 47 Conti (1873–
77); lithographer, 49 Conti (1878).
After arriving in N.O. ca 1849, Simon became one of the city's earliest
and finest color lithographers of local
views. He was particularly known for
a series of 32 N.O. buildings drawn
by MARIE ADRIEN PERSAC and E. VIDAL
(ca. 1869–78).
References: NOCD 1853–61, 1866–
67, 1869–78; NOBD 1865; *Bee*, May
30, 1878; *Courier*, Mar. 11, 1857;
Groce and Wallace; N.O. Death Certificate (1878), 71:117, NOPL; U.S.
Census (1850), roll 235, (1860), roll
421; William Young; THNOC
1949.1.1–.8.

D. SIMON & CO.
Lithographers, active N.O. 1874;
DIONIS SIMON, HENRY KLUNG, part-
ners.
Contemporary listings: lithogra-
phers, 166 Common (1874).
References: NOCD 1874.

SIMON, DIONIS
Born Baden, Germany ca. 1830; died
N.O. June 30, 1876.
Lithographer, active N.O. 1857–76.
Contemporary listings: lithographer,
72 Exchange Al. (1857); lithogra-
pher, 72 Exchange Pl., and lithog-
rapher, 102 Exchange Al. (1858–59);
TOLTI & SIMON (1860); lithographer
(1860, 1870, 1874); lithographer,

115 Exchange Pl. (1861); MANOU-
VRIER & SIMON (1866–72); lithographer, 90 Exchange Al. (1873); D. SI-
MON & CO. (1874); lithographer, 79
Exchange Al. (1875–76).
Also lithographed sheet music covers.
References: NOCD 1858–61, 1866–
76; *Courier*, Mar. 11, 1857; *D. Creole*, Mar. 26, 1857; Groce and Wallace; N.O. Death Certificate (1876),
66:606, NOPL; "The Southern Gal-
axy," Sheet Music Collection,
THNOC; U.S. Census (1860), roll
421, (1870), roll 521.

SIMON, EUGENE
Born N.O. ca. 1850; died N.O. Oct.
17, 1914.
Sketch artist, painter, active N.O.
1879–89; primarily photographer.
Advertised ink, crayon, oil, and wa-
tercolor portraits in his studio (1879–
89).
References: NOCD 1870–1914; *Bee*,
Dec. 21, 1879; *D. States*, Jan. 8,
1881, Jan. 5, 1887, Mar. 17, 1889;
T. Pic., Oct. 18, 1914; N.O. Death
Certificate (1914), 161:796, NOPL.

SIMON, GUSTAVE
Born N.O. ca. 1860–61; died N.O.
Sept. 18, 1934.
Engraver, lithographer, active N.O.
1877–83.
Contemporary listings: engraver
(1877); lithographer, with DAVID
WEIL (1878–79); lithographer
(1880); lithographer, with HERMANN
WEHRMANN (1881–83).
References: NOCD 1872–74, 1876–
1890, 1894–1904, 1906–25, 1928–
29; *T. Pic.*, Sept. 21, 1934; U.S. Cen-
sus (1880), roll 460.

SIMONS, RUDOLPH
Engraver, active N.O. 1875–78.
Contemporary listings: engraver,
ZENNECK & BUCKINGHAM (1875); en-
graver (1877); engraver, with
ADOLPH ZENNECK (1878).
References: NOCD 1875, 1877–78.

SIMPSON, ANNA FRANCES CONNOR
Born N.O. Aug. 14, 1880; died N.O.
June 26, 1930.
Art craftsman, active N.O. 1897–
1930.

Studied: NEWCOMB COLLEGE (1902–1908).
Exhibited: ART ASSOCIATION OF NEW ORLEANS (1910–11, 1913, 1916–18); Newcomb (1911, 1913); Panama–Pacific International Exposition, San Francisco (1915).
Awarded: Brownie drawing contest, St. Charles Theatre, second prize (1897).
Primarily known for her pottery decoration but also skilled in needlework and printmaking. She was later listed as artist (1925) and professional designer (1927). Simpson was awarded the Southern States Art League, San Antonio TX, silver medal for best pottery (1929). An exhibition of her work was held at the Museum of Fine Arts in Houston TX, six months after her death.
References: NOCD 1916, 1918, 1922, 1925; D. States, Dec. 5, 1897; T. Pic., June 27, 1930; Morn. Trib., June 27, 1930; Art Asso., Catalogue (1910, 1911, 1913, 1916, 1917, 1918); Orleans Parish Registrar of Voters, NOPL; Ormond and Irvine, 169; Poesch, Newcomb Pottery, 105.

SINGER, ROBERT LEE
Born N.O. Mar. 23, 1865; died N.O. Mar. 17, 1907.
Painter, active N.O. 1880–1907; also decorator.
Contemporary listings: painter (1880, 1885–86, 1891–94, 1900–1902, 1904–1905); J. SUZEN & CO. (1896); fresco painter, 867 Baronne (1897–99); fresco painter (1907).
References: NOCD 1881–86, 1891–1902, 1904–1905, 1907; D. News, Mar. 18, 1907; D. Pic., Mar. 19, 24, 1907; THNOC Cemetery Survey; U.S. Census (1880), roll 458.

SIROTI, FELIX
Painter, active N.O. 1858–59; also glazier.
Contemporary listings: painter on glass, 355 Bourbon (1858–59).
References: NOCD 1858; NOBD 1858–59.

SKINNER, GEORGE H.
Born London, England ca. 1829; died N.O. Jan. 7, 1896.
Painter, active N.O. 1860–94.

Contemporary listings: painter (1860–61, 1866, 1888, 1890, 1893); ornamental painter (1870); artist (1871–72, 1874–77, 1879, 1891, 1894); artist–painter (1880).
References: NOCD 1860–61, 1866, 1870–77, 1879, 1888, 1890–91, 1893–94, 1896; D. Pic., Jan. 8, 12, 1896; U.S. Census (1870), roll 522, (1880), roll 462.

SLATTERY-SMITH CO., LTD.
Commercial artists, engravers, active N.O. 1911–15; Remigius J. Slattery, pres. and mgr., THOMAS G. SMITH, v. pres., George F. Bartley, secy. (1911); JOSEPH AIENA, secy. (1912, 1914–15), v. pres. (1913–15); W. K. Desposito, secy. (1913).
Contemporary listings: artists and photo–engravers, 302 Camp (1911–12); photo–engravers and commercial artists, 302 Camp (1913–15).
References: NOCD 1911–15.

SLOCOMB, CORA ANNE (Mrs. Samuel B. Slocomb)
Born ca. 1810; died N.O. Mar. 15, 1884.
Sculptor, painter, active N.O. ca. 1868.
Awarded: Grand State Fair, honorable mention for best statuette in marble (1868).
References: NOCD 1838, 1841–44, 1846, 1849–56, 1858–61, 1866–67, 1869–81; Bee, Mar. 16, 1884; D. Pic., Jan. 19, 1868, Mar. 17, 1884; Mechanics' and Agricultural Fair Asso., Report (1868):41.

SMEDLEY, HENRY
Engraver, active N.O. 1868.
Contemporary listings: engraver (1868).
References: NOCD 1866, 1868.

SMEDLEY, WILLIAM THOMAS
Illustrator, active N.O. ca. 1892–93.
Born Chester County PA Mar. 26, 1858; died Bronxville NY Mar. 26, 1920.
Illustrator for Harper's Weekly and Harper's New Monthly Magazine for which he did several illustrations of N.O. (1892–93).
References: Harper's Wkly., Mar. 19, 1892, 265; "Acquisitions," 30; Biographical Sketches of American Art-

ists (1912); Fielding, *Dictionary*; Ralph, 364–73.

SMITH, MRS. _____

Art craftsman, art teacher, active N.O. 1838–39.

Contemporary listings: teacher and maker of wax flowers, 52 Tchoupitoulas (1838); teacher and maker of wax flowers, 172 Royal (1839).

Exhibited: Redun's and Casey's store (1838).

Awarded: American Institute, silver medal.

References: *Courier*, Dec. 30, 1839; *D. Pic.*, Dec. 7, 1838.

SMITH, BENJAMIN F., JR.

Born South Freedom ME 1830; died 1927.

Sketch artist, active N.O. ca. 1852. Drew, with JOHN WILLIAM HILL, and lithographed *New Orleans from St. Patrick's Church 1852* and *New Orleans from the Lower Cotton Press 1852*. Both were printed and published by Smith Bros, N.Y.C.

References: *D. Delta*, June 3, 1852; *D. Pic.*, Apr. 27, 1852, Groce and Wallace; Reps, 312; THNOC 1947.20, 1954.3.

SMITH, MRS. C. D.

Artist, active N.O. 1891.

Contemporary listings: artist, with Edward H. Peters, N.O. Enterprise Portrait Co. (1891).

References: NOCD 1891.

SMITH, CHARLES

Born LA ca. 1837.

Artist, active N.O. 1850.

Contemporary listings: artist (1850). Son of CHARLES L. SMITH; brother of JAMES and WILLIAM SMITH.

References: U.S. Census (1850), roll 234.

SMITH, CHARLES H.

Born MA Sept. 1859; died Chicago IL Feb. 4, 1918.

Engraver, lithographer, commercial artist, active N.O. 1884–1912.

Contemporary listings: lithographer (1884, 1896, 1898); engraver (1885, 1891, 1900–1902, 1912); artist, T. FITZWILLIAM & CO. (1886–89).

References: NOCD 1884–91, 1893–98, 1901 1903, 1908–1909, 1912; *T. Pic.*, Feb. 5, 1918; U.S. Census (1900), roll 575.

SMITH, CHARLES L.

Born NY ca. 1812.

Painter, active N.O. 1840–67; also decorator.

Contemporary listings: scenic artist, American Theatre (1842, 1847); scenic artist, National Theatre (1846); scenic artist, St. Charles Theatre (1848–50); scenic artist (1852, 1857); scenic artist, Gaiety Theatre (1855); painter (1857–61, 1866–67); scenic artist, Varieties Theatre (1858, 1863).

Exhibited: Dan Rice's Amphitheatre (1852); Armory Hall (1857).

Well-known scenic artist for N.O. theaters, Smith was first mentioned in the city as designing the sets for the 1840 opening season of the new American Theatre, where he continued to work for several years (1840–42, 1850, 1854). In 1842 he decorated the interior of the new St. Charles Theatre, after the building had been destroyed by fire. He worked there as scenic artist from 1848 to 1850. In Apr. 1852, Smith had completed painting 10,000 square feet of canvas with scenes for his *Moving Panorama of Texas and California*, based mostly on the 1849–52 sketches that Lt. James G. Benton made on duty in San Antonio TX. The panorama's premiere exhibition was in N.O. at Dan Rice's Amphitheatre on St. Charles, and on May 13, 1852, it left to be shown at the principal upriver cities. In June 1857 Smith's panoramas, *Creation of the World* and *Commodore Perry's Expedition to Japan*, were first shown at Armory Hall. Father of CHARLES, WILLIAM, and JAMES SMITH.

References: NOCD 1843–44, 1846, 1853, 1855–61, 1866–67; *Bee*, May 1, 1852, June 4–6, 1857; *D. Creole*, June 4, 1857; *D. Crescent*, Nov. 20, 1848, Oct. 1, Nov. 8, 1849, Jan. 25, 1850, June 5, 1857, Nov. 12, 1858; *D. Delta*, Oct. 30, 1846, Apr. 30, May 13, 1852, Dec. 5, 1858; *D. National*, Nov. 6, 1847; *D. Pic.*, Feb. 13, 1842, Apr. 30, 1852, Oct. 29, 1855; *Era*,

Mar. 3, 1863; *Wkly. Delta*, Oct. 1, 1849; Groce and Wallace; Kendall, *Golden Age*, 190, 197, 210, 249, 252, 376; Pinckney, 68–69; U.S. Census (1850), roll 234.

SMITH, CLAUDE
Commercial artist, active N.O. 1892–93.
Contemporary listings: SMITH BROTHERS (1892); artist (1893).
References: NOCD 1892–96, 1898, 1901–1905.

SMITH, DAVID
Died N.O. Mar. 2, 1841.
Painter, active N.O. 1841.
Contemporary listings: portrait painter (1841).
References: *D. Pic.*, Mar. 4, 1841; Groce and Wallace; William Young.

ED. SMITH & CO.
Engravers, active N.O. 1878; also stencil cutters; Edward Smith (born VA ca. 1843–44; died N.O. Oct. 26, 1907), JOSEPH P. MURPHY, partners.
Contemporary listings: engravers, 12 Natchez (1878).
References: NOCD 1877–78; *D. Pic.*, Oct. 27, 1907; U.S. Census (1880), roll 459.

SMITH, EDITH PAUL (Mrs. Charles Smith)
Born N.O. June 1876.
Sculptor, painter, active N.O. 1896–1903.
Studied: with ACHILLE PERELLI.
Contemporary listings: sculptor and portrait painter, 644 Commercial (1896); sculptor, 622 Commercial (1897); portrait painter, 4425 Constance (1898); sculptor, 4425 Constance (1898–1900); sculptor, 4430 Magazine (1901–1902); sculptor (1903).
References: NOCD 1895–1903, 1908; NOBD 1898; *D. Pic.*, Mar. 28, 1897, Jan. 11, 1903; *D. States*, Dec. 20, 1897; *Men and Matters*, Sept. 1897, 52; *T. Demo.*, May 28, 1908; U.S. Census (1900), roll 575.

SMITH, EMMA J. B.
Born ca. 1846; died N.O. Aug. 30, 1889.
Painter, art teacher, active N.O. ca. 1884–89.

Contemporary listings: artist (1886–87, 1889); portrait painter, 787 Magazine (1886).
Exhibited: World's Industrial and Cotton Centennial Exposition (1884–85).
Advertised drawing classes and portraits in oil, pastel, or crayon, and in china painting.
References: NOCD 1886, 1887; *D. Pic.*, Aug. 31, 1889; Business card, Commercial File, THNOC; N.O. Death Certificate (1889), 95:854, NOPL; Woman's Department of World's Exposition, 160.

SMITH, FREDERICK
Born Germany ca. 1812.
Engraver, lithographer, active N.O. 1849–50.
Contemporary listings: lithographer, Derbigny near Customhouse (1849); stone engraver (1850).
References: NOCD 1849–53; U.S. Census (1850), roll 238.

SMITH, G. W.
Artist, active N.O. ca. 1868.
Awarded: Grand State Fair, silver medal for best pencil drawing (1868).
References: *D. Pic.*, Jan. 19, 1868; Mechanics' and Agricultural Fair Asso., *Report* (1868):43.

SMITH, GERTRUDE ROBERTS (Mrs. Frederich Smith)
Born Cambridge MA May 11, 1869; died Asheville NC Feb. 24, 1962.
Painter, art teacher, art craftsman, active N.O. 1887–1934; also needleworker.
Studied: with Miss White, Boston; Massachusetts Normal Art School; Chase School, N.Y.C.; with Julian, Paris; Colarossi Academy, Paris.
Exhibited: TULANE DECORATIVE ART LEAGUE FOR WOMEN (1888); ART LEAGUE OF NEW ORLEANS (1889); ARTISTS' ASSOCIATION OF NEW ORLEANS (1889–92, 1894, 1897, 1899, 1901–1902); Tulane University (1890, 1892–93); ART ASSOCIATION OF NEW ORLEANS (1905, 1907, 1910–11, 1913–15, 1917–18); Panama–Pacific International Exposition, San Francisco (1915).
Awarded: Louisisana Purchase Exposition, St. Louis MO (1904); Art

Association of New Orleans, gold medal.

Memberships/positions: Art League of New Orleans; Art Association of New Orleans, founder, executive committee (1911); Society of Western Artists (1905, 1910, 1914).

Appointed to the NEWCOMB faculty in Oct. 1887, Smith and ELLSWORTH WOODWARD were the college's only art instructors through 1894. Smith became assistant professor of drawing and painting (1889–1906), then professor of watercolor painting and textile decoration (1907–1934) until her retirement. In 1902 she introduced embroidery and needlework into the art curriculum. Smith was a founder of the Brush and Pen Club, the Artists Guild of New Orleans (pres., 1921), the Arts and Crafts Club (board of directors, 1926; executive board, 1928–30), and a member of the Southern States Art League, and the Boston Arts and Crafts Club. She frequently exhibited with the organizations, especially watercolor scenes of her extensive travels. In 1921 she was awarded the DELGADO MUSEUM OF ART purchase prize. After her retirement, Smith maintained a residence in Andrews NC until 1952, when she moved to Asheville.

References: NOCD 1888–89, 1891–1933, 1935, 1940, 1942, 1945–46; *Current Topics*, Jan. 1891, 24, Jan. 1892, 24, Jan. 1893, 10; *D. City Item*, Dec. 17, 1891; *D. Pic.*, Feb. 12, 1888, Mar. 10, Dec. 17, 1889, Feb. 14, Nov. 13, 1890, Mar. 3, Dec. 13, 1892, Feb. 14, 1893, Mar. 30, 1897, Dec. 26, 1909; *D. States*, Dec. 17, 1891, Jan. 23, 1898; *Harlequin*, Dec. 6, 1899, 5; *Item*, Jan. 16, 19, 30, Feb. 3, 1921; *Morn. Trib.*, Oct. 20, 1926, May 4, 1927; *States–Item*, Mar. 9, 1962; *T. Demo.*, Dec. 17, 1890, Dec. 14, 1894, Dec. 8, 1901; *T. Pic.*, Jan. 2, 1923, Oct. 6, 1924, Apr. 8, Oct. 11, 1925, Sept. 30, 1928, Mar. 6, 1932, Mar. 9, 1962; AANO, *Catalogue* (1890, 1891, 1897, 1899, 1901, 1902); Art Asso., *Catalogue* (1905, 1907, 1910, 1911, 1913,

1914, 1915, 1917, 1918); Art Asso., *Special Exhibition*; Delgado, *Catalogue of Paintings, Sculpture*; Mount, 191; New Orleans Art School, *Bulletin*; New Orleans Art School, *Year Book*; Ormond and Irvine, 46, 170; Poesch, *Newcomb Pottery*, passim; *Who's Who in American Art*, 1938–39.

SMITH, GLENDOWER E.
Painter, active N.O. 1890–95.
Contemporary listings: portrait painter, 169 St. Charles (1890); SMITH BROTHERS (1892); portrait painter, 158 Julia (1893); artist (1895).
References: NOCD 1890, 1892–93, 1895.

SMITH, J.
Engraver, active N.O. 1830.
Contemporary listings: engraver on wood, 108 Levee (1830).
References: NOCD 1830.

SMITH, JAMES
Born LA ca. 1831.
Artist, active N.O. 1850.
Contemporary listings: artist (1850). Son of CHARLES L. SMITH, brother of CHARLES and WILLIAM SMITH.
References: U.S. Census (1850), roll 234.

SMITH, JOHN
Engraver, active N.O. 1886.
Contemporary listings: engraver (1886).
References: NOCD 1886.

SMITH, JOHN ROWSON
Born Boston MA May 11, 1810; died Philadelphia PA Mar. 21, 1864.
Painter, active N.O. 1835–59.
Studied: with his father, John Rubens Smith, Brooklyn NY and Philadelphia.
Contemporary listings: artist, American Theatre (1835); artist, 256 Camp (1838); scenic artist, Varieties Theatre (1859).
Itinerant scenic artist who was said to have been an assistant to ANTOINE MONDELLI at the St. Charles Theatre (1835), visited the city (1837), and worked as a scene painter at the American Theatre (1840–41). During one of his N.O. visits, he made drawings of the city and of other parts

of LA used in his panorama of the Mississippi River which was a popular success during U.S. and European tours in the 1840s. He claimed that it was the first moving panorama, and it was credited with having stimulated immigration to the Mississippi Valley. Smith continued as a scene painter during the 1850s in the North, particularly in N.Y.C. He often worked in the South during winters, but with the outbreak of the Civil War, he left Mobile AL, where he was working, and returned to the North by ship from N.O.

References: NOCD 1838, 1841–42; *Bee*, Apr. 22, 1835; *D. Crescent*, Nov. 11, 1859; Barker, 447–49; *DAB*; Groce and Wallace; Kendall, *Golden Age*, 121; Ludlow, 469, 482, 531, 543; McDermott, *Lost Panoramas*, 47–67; Odell, 4:611, 5:1, 114, 329, 6:467, 7:487; Scharf, 1:970.

SMITH, JOSEPH C.
Artist, active N.O. 1896.
Contemporary listings: artist (1896).
References: NOCD 1896.

SMITH, LOUIS
Lithographer, active N.O. 1885.
Contemporary listings: lithographer (1885).
References: NOCD 1885.

SMITH, MARGUERITE MASON. *See* MASON SMITH, MARGUERITE LACAMUS

SMITH, MARSHALL JOSEPH, JR.
Born Norfolk VA Dec. 1, 1854; died Covington LA Oct. 20, 1923.
Painter, active N.O. 1870–1906; also draftsman.
Studied: with ADOLPHE J. JACQUET (ca. 1866); VA (1869); with RICHARD CLAGUE (ca. 1870–73); with THEODORE SIDNEY MOISE (1874); with J.O. de Montalent, Accademia dei Medici, Rome (1874); with Prof Rensùr, Royal Bavarian Academy of Fine Arts, Munich, Germany (1876).
Contemporary listings: artist, 30 Carondelet (1889); artist (1891–96, 1898–1903, 1906).
Exhibited: SEEBOLD's (1874); SOUTHERN ART UNION (1881); ARTISTS' ASSOCIATION OF NEW ORLEANS (1889–90); Tulane University (1893); G. MOSES gallery (1902).

Memberships/positions: Southern Art Union, charter member.
Smith was brought as a child to N.O., where he received his first art lessons from Jacquet. After attending school in VA (1867–69), he returned to N.O. to work as a clerk and to continue to pursue his interest in art. Smith became the favorite pupil of the city's foremost landscape painter, Richard Clague, who greatly influenced his painting style. After Clague's death, Smith studied in Moise's studio, and his paintings were exhibited in the city. In Oct. 1874, he left N.O. to study art in Rome and Munich and traveled in Italy, Germany, France, and England where he met many distinguished artists, writers, and musicians. He returned to the U.S. in Apr. 1876 via the Philadelphia Centennial Exposition and was supposed to have opened a studio in Atlanta GA in late 1876. By 1878, Smith had returned to N.O. to work as a clerk in his father's insurance business and later became an insurance agent, his occupational listing through 1888. During that time, he remained active artistically, painting and exhibiting coastal LA landscapes showing fishermen's shanties and moss–laden oak trees. He was a founder of both the Southern Art Union (1880) and the carnival organization Proteus (1882), for which he designed many parades and tableaux. By 1889 Smith had opened a studio on Carondelet and by 1891 he had moved his studio to Carrollton where he remained through 1906 when he apparently left the city, perhaps for Covington, the place of his death.
References: NOCD 1871, 1879–89, 1891–1904, 1906; *Bee*, May 4, 1881, Nov. 16, 1881; *D. Pic.*, Sept. 25, 1875, Mar. 16, 1876, Sept. 30, 1877, May 26, 1881, Dec. 17, 1889, Dec. 17, 1890, Feb. 14, 1893; *D. States*, Oct. 8, 1880; *Demo.*, May 27, 1880, May 12, 1881; *Repub.*, May 17, 1874; *T. Demo.*, Jan. 5, 1890; *T. Pic.*, Oct. 21, 1923; Anglo–American Art Museum, *Louisiana Landscape*, item 19A, 19B; Cline, *Contemporary Art*,

12; Hardy, 481; Moses, items 41, 50, 54, 62, 76, 85; Mount, 118–21; U.S. Census (1900), roll 576.

SMITH, MARY SUMMEY. *See* SUMMEY, MARY WILLIAMSON

SMITH, THOMAS G.
Born LA Apr. 1875.
Engraver, artist, active N.O. 1894–1911; also photographer, printer.
Contemporary listings: photo–engraver, PHOTO–ENGRAVING COMPANY (1894, 1899); artist (1897); engraver, Photo–Engraving Company (1898, 1901, 1903); engraver (1900, 1905–1906); foreman, NEW ORLEANS ENGRAVING AND ELECTROTYPE CO., LTD. (1907); photo–engraver, New Orleans Engraving and Electrotype Co., Ltd. (1908); v. pres., New Orleans Engraving and Electrotype Co., Ltd. (1909–10); photo–engraver (1910–11); v. pres., SLATTERY–SMITH CO., LTD. (1911–12).
References: NOCD 1894, 1896–99, 1901, 1903, 1905–12; U.S. Census (1900), roll 570, (1910), roll 524.

SMITH, WILLIAM
Born LA ca. 1834.
Artist, active N.O. 1850.
Contemporary listings: artist (1850).
Son of CHARLES L. SMITH; brother of CHARLES and JAMES SMITH.
References: U.S. Census (1850), roll 234.

SMITH BROTHERS
Artists, active N.O. 1892; CLAUDE SMITH, GLENDOWER E. SMITH, partners.
Contemporary listings: artists, 180 St. Charles (1892).
References: NOCD 1892.

SMITH-MONRO, CORA TOWNSEND. *See* TOWNSEND, CORA ALICE

SMITHSON, JOSEPH
Artist, active N.O. 1892–94.
Contemporary listings: artist (1892–94).
References: NOCD 1892–94, 1896.

SMITHSON, MRS. WILLIE
Painter, active N.O. ca. 1894.
Exhibited: ARTISTS' ASSOCIATION OF NEW ORLEANS (1894).
References: T Demo., Dec. 14, 1894.

SMYTH, WILLIAM G.
Engraver, active N.O. 1895.
Contemporary listings: engraver (1895).
References: NOCD 1895.

SMYTHE, MRS. M. B.
Artist, active N.O. ca. 1883–87.
Studied: with HENRIETTE WINANT (1883); ARTISTS' ASSOCIATION OF NEW ORLEANS (1886–87).
Exhibited: Artists' Association of New Orleans (1886–87).
Awarded: SOUTHERN ART UNION, first prize for drawing from cast (1883).
References: *Art and Letters*, 1(Dec. 1887):227–28; *D. Pic.*, May 8, 1883, Nov. 6–7, 1886, May 7, Dec. 29, 1887; *T. Demo.*, May 8, 1883.

P. SNELL & BECKER
Lithographers, engravers, active N.O. 1841; also draftsmen, printers; PEREZ SNELL, GEORGE J. BECKER, partners.
Contemporary listings: lithographers and engravers, 44 Canal and 36 Camp (1841).
References: NOCD 1841; *D. Pic.*, Jan. 19, 1841; Groce and Wallace.

SNELL, PEREZ
Born ca. 1790–1800.
Lithographer, active N.O. 1835-52; also printer.
Contemporary listings: lithographer, 12 Circus (1835); lithographer, Canal near Bourbon (1837); lithographer and engraver, 36 Camp and 44 Canal, and P. SNELL & BECKER (1841); SNELL & FISHBOURNE (1842); lithographer, 36 Camp (1843–44); MANOUVRIER & SNELL (1846, 1850–52).
References: NOCD 1835, 1837, 1841–44, 1846, 1850–52; *D. Pic.*, May 18, 1841; *De Bow's Review*, Feb. 1846, 166; *Wkly. Delta*, Jan. 12, 1846; Groce and Wallace; U.S. Census (1840), roll 133.

SNELL & FISHBOURNE
Engravers, lithographers, active N.O. 1842; PEREZ SNELL, R. W. FISHBOURNE, partners.
Contemporary listings: engravers and lithographers 36 Camp (1842).
References: NOCD 1842, Groce and Wallace.

SOELLNER, CHARLES FREDERICK
Painter, active N.O. before 1894.
Advertised on his business card as a
portrait artist in crayon, watercolor,
oil, and pastel at 158 N. Rampart in
N.O. and in Lexington MO.
References: Commercial File,
THNOC.

SOLENSKI, MR. _____
Painter, active N.O. 1885.
Contemporary listings: portrait
painter (1885).
References: D. Pic., July 26, 1885.

SONNTAG, WILLIAM LOUIS
Born Pittsburgh PA Mar. 2, 1822;
died N.Y.C. Jan. 22, 1900.
Painter, active N.O. 1888.
Memberships/positions: National
Academy of Design, N.Y.C. (1860).
Noted painter of idealized American
landscapes who signed a painting in
N.O. of sailing ships at anchor (1888).
Father of WILLIAM LOUIS SONNTAG, JR.
References: Bénézit; Fielding, Dic-
tionary; LSM, Annual Report for
1919, 27.

SONNTAG, WILLIAM LOUIS, JR.
Born NY 1870.
Sketch artist, active N.O. 1894.
His drawings of New Orleans To–day
were published in N.Y.C. by Once A
Week (1894). Son of WILLIAM LOUIS
SONNTAG.
References: Once a Week, Mar. 17,
1894, 8, May 12, 1894, 9; Bénézit;
THNOC 1984.87.

SOROE, CHARLES F.
Born N.O. ca. 1874; died N.O. Jan.
13, 1910.
Lithographer, active N.O. 1887–
1905; also printer, pressman.
Contemporary listings: lithographer,
G. KOECKERT & CO. (1887); lithographer (1889, 1894, 1903–1905);
foreman, WALLE & CO., LTD. (1899,
1901).
References: NOCD 1887, 1889,
1894, 1896–1910; N.O. Death Certificate (1910), 148:537, NOPL.

SOROE, JOHN F.
Lithographer, active N.O. 1904–24;
also printer.
Contemporary listings: lithographer
(1904–1905); lithographer, WALLE &

CO., LTD. (1912); Walle & Co., Ltd.
(1918).
Later listed as lithographer (1919,
1921–22, 1924).
References: NOCD 1894, 1898–
1919, 1921–22, 1924.

SOROE, THEODORE
Born N.O. ca. 1878; died N.O. Dec.
17, 1909.
Lithographer, active N.O. 1899–
1905; also pressman.
Contemporary listings: lithographer
(1899, 1901, 1903–1905).
References: NOCD 1899–1910; D.
Pic., Dec. 19, 1909; N.O. Death Cer-
tificate (1909), 148:265, NOPL.

SOSA, VIVENCIO
Born U.S. ca. 1876.
Engraver, painter, active N.O. 1910–
22; also photographer.
Contemporary listings: engraver
(1910); painter, 1121 N. Rampart
(1911); proprietor, SOSA'S ART STU-
DIO (1913, 1916).
Advertised portraiture (1922).
References: NOCD 1911–13, 1915–
16, 1918, 1921–29; U.S. Census
(1910), roll 521.

SOSA'S ART STUDIO
Painters, active N.O. 1913–16; also
photographers; VIVENCIO SOSA, proprietor.
Contemporary listings: 826 Common (1913); 725 Common (1916).
Advertised portrait and landscape
painting in oil (1913) and commercial art works (1916).
References: NOCD 1913, 1916.

SOTTA, MR. _____
Born France.
Painter, active N.O. 1840–42; also
copyist.
Contemporary listings: portrait
painter, Chartres oppos. Jefferson
(1840); portrait painter, 125 St. Louis
(1842).
Exhibited: Salon, Paris (1833, 1838).
The artist's name has sometimes been
misinterpreted as "Lotta."
References: NOCD 1842; Courier,
Mar. 20, 1840; Bénézit; Glenk, 77;
Groce and Wallace; Harter and
Tucker, 125; LSM, Biennial Report
for 1922–23, 58; William Young.

SOUBY, EDWARD J.
Born LA June 24, 1844; died N.O
June 10, 1907.
Sketch artist, active N.O. 1880–84;
primarily photographer.
Drew crayon portraits (1880, 1884).
References: NOCD 1870–93, 1895–
98, 1900–1906; *Bee*, Jan. 11, 1871;
D. Pic., Nov. 25, 1884, June 11,
1907; *D. States*, Feb. 3, Apr. 17, June
12, 1880; *Demo.*, Mar. 15, 1876; *Republic*, Nov. 30, Dec. 21, 1873; Morrison, *Industries*, 91; N.O. Death
Certificate (1907), 141:224, NOPL;
U.S. Census (1870), roll 524; Waldo,
207–8.

SOUFERT, MR. _____
Sculptor, active N.O. 1849.
Executed a cameo likeness of Gen.
Taylor in 1849.
References: *D. Pic.*, Jan. 24, 1849;
Groce and Wallace.

SOULIE, GEORGE S.
Born Paris, France Dec. 1844; died
ca. 1910.
Commercial artist, sculptor, painter,
active N.O. ca. 1872–1910; also
decorator.
Studied with his father, Paris.
Contemporary listings: fresco artist
(1874–75); sculptor (1880, 1910);
artist (1885–86, 1888, 1891–96,
1898–1900, 1908–10); sculptor,
Coliseum betw. Valmont and Leontine, and 38 Exchange Al., and papier maché artist (1885); artist, 2405
Calliope (1907).
Immigrated to N.O. ca. 1872 from
his native Paris where he learned the
craft of sculpting in plaster and papier maché from his father. Among
his first commissions in N.O. were
the side altars for St. Louis Cathedral
(1873) and the decorative figures for
the 1873 parade of the carnival organization Comus, the first parade
with floats made entirely in N.O.
With EUGENE PHILASTRE, he frescoed
and decorated the interior of Crescent Hall. Soulié constructed an 18–
foot–tall replica of the Statue of Liberty (1885) for the Bastille Day celebrations of that year. His son HENRY
A. SOULIE eventually succeeded him
in his practice.

References: NOCD 1874–75, 1880–
99, 1907–10; *Bee*, Dec. 9, 17, 1873,
Aug. 11, 1874, Dec. 12, 19, 1875,
Jan. 27, 1885; *Bull.*, Dec. 24, 1875;
D. Pic., July 15, 1885, Aug. 11, 1895;
D. States, June 22, 1885; *Repub.*,
Dec. 2, 1873; Caldwell, 205–6; La
Cour, 200–1; U.S. Census (1900),
roll 575, (1910), roll 519; Perry
Young, 127.

SOULIE, HENRY A.
Born LA Feb. 1881; died N.O. Jan.
31, 1958.
Commercial artist, active N.O. 1900–
55; also decorator.
Contemporary listings: artist (1900,
1902–10, 1912–13, 1915–16); artist–carnival decorator (1910).
In partnership with HARRY WILLIAM
CRASSONS (1923–40), he built and
decorated floats for parades for carnival organizations, continuing the
work begun by his father, GEORGE
SOULIE. He continued to be listed as
an artist (1942, 1945–49, 1952–55).
References: NOCD 1902–10, 1912–
30, 1932, 1935, 1938, 1940, 1942,
1945–47, 1949, 1952–55, 1958;
Item, Feb. 1, 1958; La Cour, 201;
U.S. Census (1900), roll 575, (1910),
roll 524.

SOUTHERN ART COMPANY
Painters, active N.O. 1908; JOHN
BLOHORN, HENRY J. STANG, partners.
Contemporary listings: portrait
painters, 204 Camp (1908).
References: NOCD 1908.

SOUTHERN ART STUDIO
Art dealers, artists, active N.O.
1905–1906; CHARLES TUGENDHAFT,
proprietor.
Contemporary listings: 124 St.
Charles (1905–1906).
References: NOCD 1905–1906.

SOUTHERN ART UNION AND WOMAN'S
INDUSTRIAL ASSOCIATION
Art association, active N.O. 1880–
86; Marion A. Baker, secy. (1882),
John Crickard, secy. (1880), William
Preston Johnston, pres. (1885–86),
Mrs. Scott McGehee, secy. (1886),
Mrs. D. A. McGelrac, secy. (1886),
W. S. Mitchell, secy. (1882–83),
Robert Mott, pres. (1880–84), H. M.
Neill, v. pres. (1880), J. H. Oglesby,

v. pres. (1886), Mrs. J. H. Oglesby, treas. (1886), Milton C. Randall, treas. (1880, 1882–83), secy.–treas. (1881), Adolph Schrieber, v. pres. (1881), MARSHALL JOSEPH SMITH, JR., v. pres. (1886), Adam Thomson, v. pres. (1883), Gideon Townsend, v. pres. (1880–83).

Contemporary listings: 203 Canal (1881–82, 1884–86); 201 Canal (1883).

A chartered association of professional and amateur artists that had its headquarters in N.O.; it was open to membership from all southern states. It was originally formed in May 1880 as the Southern Art Union to promote interest in art through a permanent exhibition gallery and an art school. The women's department was added in Apr. 1881 for the display and sale of handiwork and household decorations made by women. The Union's first meetings were held in the St. Charles Hotel; permanent headquarters were opened at 203 Canal in May 1881 with an exhibition of members' works. In June 1881, the association opened a school of design with instruction in drawing by ACHILLE PERELLI, in oil painting by ANDRES MOLINARY, and in watercolor by MISS J. TUZO. It later received donations of books for a lending library. After losing members to the newly formed ARTISTS' ASSOCIATION OF NEW ORLEANS, the Union voted to disband in June 1886 and to give its property to Tulane University.

References: NOCD 1882–86; *Bee*, May 4, 26–27, 1880, May 4, Nov. 16–29 (advs.), 1881; *D. Pic.*, Mar. 20, 23–24, Apr. 12, May 22, 26, 28, 1881, Feb. 15, 18, Apr. 23, May 2, 1882, May 8, 1883, Apr. 27, 29, 1884, July 26, 1885, June 6, 1886; *D. States*, Apr. 29, May 22, 27, June 12, 1880, Apr. 20, May 26–27, June 7, 10, 1881, Jan. 23–31, 1882 (advs.), Apr. 29, 1883, June 6, 1886; *Demo.*, May 6, 13, 27, 1880, May 12, June 8, 1881; *Times*, May 6, 13, 27, 1880; *T. Demo.*, Apr. 15, May 8, 1883, Sept. 16, Oct. 31, Dec. 14, 1884.

SOUTHERN BUREAU OF ENGRAVING
Engravers, designers, painters, active N.O. 1895.

Contemporary listings: engravers, designers, portrait painters, 323 Baronne (1895).

References: NOCD 1895.

SOUTHERN LITHOGRAPHIC COMPANY
Lithographers, engravers, designers, artists, active N.O. 1883–85; also printers; THEODORE POHLMANN, pres. (1883–84), mgr. (1884), supt. (1885); WILLIAM B. STANSBURY, secy. (1883–85); Marcellin Gillis, pres. (1884–85); Isidore Newman, pres. (1884); Richard Weightman, secy. (1884).

Contemporary listings: 36 and 38 Natchez and 22, 24, 26, 28, and 30 Bank Pl. (1884); 38 Natchez (1885). Incorporated June 18, 1883, and then consolidated in Feb. 1884 with the NEW ORLEANS LITHOGRAPHING COMPANY as the Southern Lithographic Company of New Orleans.

References: NOCD 1884–85; *D. Pic.*, Aug. 11, 1883; *D. States*, Feb. 3, 23, 1884; *Figaro*, Dec. 8, 1883, 4, Feb. 2, 1884, 11, Feb. 9, 1884, 9, Apr. 5, 1884, cover, 10, Apr. 19, 1884, 10, Apr. 26, 1884, 8; *Item*, Aug. 2, 1905; Orleans Parish Notarial Archives, Andrew Hero, Jr., June 18, 1883, 48:10348, Samuel Flower, Dec. 31, 1883, 2:104, Feb. 1, 1884, 3:14, Feb. 7, 1884, 3:16, May 30, 1884, 3:52, William O. Hart, Apr. 12, 1884, 4:799.

SPENCER ENGRAVING CO. LTD.
Engravers, active N.O. 1910–11; L. C. Spencer, pres., J. M. Reeser, secy.–treas. (1910).

Contemporary listings: 302 Camp (1910–11).

References: NOCD 1910–11.

SPOFFORD, MISS E.
Painter, active N.O. ca. 1884–85; also needleworker.

Exhibited: World's Industrial and Cotton Centennial Exposition (1884–85).

Probably daughter of MRS. O. M. SPOFFORD.

References: Woman's Department of World's Exposition, 159, 166.

SPOFFORD, MRS. O. M.
Painter, active N.O. ca. 1884–85.
Exhibited: World's Industrial and Cotton Centennial Exposition (1884–85).
Probably mother of MISS E. SPOFFORD.
References: WICCE, *Catalogue*, 52; Woman's Department of World's Exposition, 159, 166.

SPRUOR, JOHN
Lithographer, active N.O. 1856–66.
Contemporary listings: lithographer, Coliseum betw. Eighth and Ninth (1856); lithograph grinder, Constance cor. Washington (1859–61, 1866).
References: NOCD 1856–61, 1866; Groce and Wallace.

STANDARD MUSIC AND PHOTO-LITHO COMPANY *See also* WEHRMANN & CO.
Lithographers, active N.O. 1886–87; also publishers; Augustus Craft, ODBERT V. GREEND, CHARLES KUMMEL, HERMANN WEHRMANN, partners.
Contemporary listings: lithographic establishment, 48 Bienville (1886–87).
The firm was founded in 1886 with Craft, Greend, and Wehrmann as partners. Craft later sold his interest to Kummel, and subsequently Wehrmann and Greend petitioned for the firm's dissolution (1887). The company continued publishing sheet music until at least 1891.
References: *T. Demo.*, Nov. 11, 1887; Sheet Music Collection, THNOC.

STANG, HENRY J.
Painter, active N.O. 1908–1909; also decorator.
Contemporary listings: SOUTHERN ART COMPANY (1908); painter (1909).
References: NOCD 1908–1909, 1911.

STANLEY, MR. R. E.
Painter, active N.O. 1872; also sign painter.
Contemporary listings: fresco painter, 43 Exchange Al. (1872).
Scenic artist for Tally's Opera House, Shreveport LA (1874).
References: NOCD 1870, 1872; *Repub.*, Apr. 9, 1874.

W. B. STANSBURY & CO.
Lithographers, active N.O. 1884–85; also printers, publishers; William B. Stansbury (born ca. 1856; died Aug. 1, 1905), William Mead Montgomery, partners.
Contemporary listings: lithographers, 38 Natchez (1884–85).
References: NOCD 1884–86; *Item*, Aug. 2, 1905; *T. Demo.*, Aug. 2–3, 1905.

STANTON, GIDEON TOWNSEND
Born Morris MN July 14, 1885; died N.O. Nov. 23, 1964.
Painter, active N.O. 1907–50.
Studied: with Samuel Edwin Whiteman, Charcoal Club, Baltimore MD.
Exhibited: ART ASSOCIATION OF NEW ORLEANS (1907–11, 1913–18).
Awarded: Art Association of New Orleans, silver medal (1911).
Memberships/positions: Art Association of New Orleans (1914), board of directors (1912–18), executive committee (1913–18), secy. (1913–17).
Came to N.O. ca. 1888 where he worked primarily as a stock broker. Stanton exhibited frequently at the Art Association of New Orleans (1919–41), Arts and Crafts Club (1922–35), New Orleans Art League (1927–50), and the Artists' Guild (1921). He also exhibited in Atlanta GA, Baltimore MD, NY, and ME. His later awards included the Art Association of New Orleans president's prize (1925) and the New Orleans Art League first prize in oil (1932) and second prize (1947). He was actively involved in several N.O. art groups. With the Art Association of New Orleans, Stanton was a member of the board of directors (1919–20, 1924–25, 1928, 1930–32), and president (1926–27). Other memberships included the New Orleans Art League, charter member (1927); Artists' Guild (1921); Southern States Art League; American Federation of Arts, Washington DC; and St. Augustine (FL) Art Association. He served on the boards of the DELGADO MUSEUM OF ART and the Arts and Crafts Club, and was the LA State

Director for the WPA Federal Art Project (1935–38).
References: NOCD 1905–32, 1938, 1940, 1942, 1945–47, 1949, 1952–56, 1958, 1960–62, 1964–67; *Arts and Antiques*, Nov. 1938, 7–9; *Item*, Jan. 16, Feb. 6, 18, 1921, Jan. 27, 1922, June 30, 1949, Dec. 3, 1950; *Item-Trib.*, May 22, Dec. 4, 1927, Feb. 10, 1935, Nov. 20, 1938; *Morn. Trib.*, Oct. 19, 1927, Feb. 1, 1928; *States*, Dec. 4, 1927, Dec. 4, 1932; *States-Item*, Nov. 23, 1964; *T. Pic.*, Dec. 3, 1923, Mar. 4, Oct. 25, 1925, Dec. 6, 1927, May 12, 1929, Mar. 3, 1930, Mar. 6, Dec. 11, 1932, Nov. 23, 1935, Apr. 5, 12, 1936, Feb. 5, 1941, Jan. 7, 1947, Dec. 3, 1950, Nov. 24, 1964; Art Asso., *Catalogue* (1907, 1910, 1911, 1913, 1914, 1915, 1916, 1917, 1918, 1919, 1921, 1922, 1924, 1925, 1926, 1927, 1929, 1930, 1931, 1932); Art Asso., *Special Exhibition*; New Orleans Art League (1949–50); Barbara Walker, 4–5; Who's Who in American Art, 1940–41; *Who's Who in the South and Southwest*; WPA, "Lives."

STANTON, PHINEAS, JR.
Born Sept. 23, 1817; died Quito, Ecuador Sept. 5, 1867.
Painter, active N.O. 1847, 1853.
Contemporary listings: artist and portrait painter, St. Charles oppos. the St. Charles Hotel, and 38 Chartres (1847); portrait painter, Crescent Bldgs. (1853).
Exhibited: Norman's bookstore (1847).
Portrait and miniature painter who was probably born in Wyoming NY. He worked in N.Y.C. (1841, 1845, 1859–60), Charleston SC (1844), and N.O. (1847, 1853), and died in Ecuador during an expedition sponsored by Williams College and the Smtihsonian Institution, on which he served as artist.
References: *Bee*, Apr. 16, 1847; *D. Delta*, June 22, 1847; *D. Pic.*, Apr. 1, 1847, Jan. 26, 1853; Groce and Wallace; WPA, *American Portrait Inventory*, 241.

STAUFFER, MRS. W. C.
Painter, active N.O. ca. 1881–87.
Exhibited: ARTISTS' ASSOCIATION OF NEW ORLEANS (1887).
Memberships/positions: SOUTHERN ART UNION (1881).
References: *Art and Letters* 1(Dec. 1887):227–28; *D. Pic.*, Mar. 23, 1881, Dec. 29, 1887.

STEEL & CO.
Lithographers, active N.O. 1870–71; also stationers, printers; Thomas Steel, William A. Weed, partners.
Contemporary listings: lithographers, 72 Camp (1870).
References: NOCD 1870–71.

STEELE, MRS. _____
Painter, active N.O. 1845.
Contemporary listings: miniature painter, St. Charles Hotel (1845).
From western NY, she worked in St. Louis MO (Jan. 1845) and Davenport IA (July 1845) and painted portrait miniatures in N.O. during the interim. *Cf.* STEELE, MRS. DANIEL.
References: *D. Pic.*, Mar. 11, 1845; Waugh, 3–4.

STEELE, DANIEL
Born Auburn NY Dec. 8, 1801; died N.O. July 24, 1839.
Painter, active N.O. 1839.
Contemporary listings: portrait and miniature painter, 112 Customhouse (1839).
Husband of MRS. DANIEL STEELE.
References: *Comm. Bull.*, July 31, 1839; *D. Pic.*, June 25, Aug. 2, 1839; Groce and Wallace; *History of the Yellow Fever*, 61; Information courtesy George E. Jordan.

STEELE, MRS. DANIEL
Painter, art teacher, active N.O. 1839.
Contemporary listings: portrait and miniature painter and teacher of miniature painting, 112 Customhouse and miniature painter, 93 Julia (1839).
Wife of DANIEL STEELE. *Cf.* STEELE, MRS. _____.
References: *D. Pic.*, June 25, Aug. 2, 1839; Groce and Wallace.

STEMPEL, FREDERICK WILLIAM, JR.
Born N.O. Dec. 14, 1887; died N.O. July 26, 1959.

Painter, commercial artist, active N.O. 1905–19; also sign painter.
Contemporary listings: portrait painter, 1821 Dryades (1905); portrait painter (1906); artist, with Junius Garlick (1908); artist (1909–13); landscape painter (1910).
Exhibited: ART ASSOCIATION OF NEW ORLEANS (1915).
Memberships/positions: NEW ORLEANS ART LEAGUE (1908).
Later listed as artist (1919); for the remainder of his career (1920–55), he was listed in various service occupations.
References: NOCD 1905–1906, 1908–33, 1935, 1938, 1940, 1942, 1945–47, 1949, 1952–56, 1958; *D. Pic.*, June 28, 1908; *T. Pic.*, July 28, 1959; Art Asso., *Special Exhibition*; Cruise and Harton, 98, 117–18; U.S. Census (1910), roll 521.

STEMPEL, HENRY
Painter, active N.O. 1861–66.
Studied: Munich, Germany (1867).
Contemporary listings: portrait painter, 8 St. Charles (1861, 1866).
Exhibited: C. H. Zimmerman's (1867).
References: NOCD 1861, 1866; *Times*, Feb. 3, 1867.

STEPHENS, BEVERLY PARHAM
RANDOLPH. *See* RANDOLPH, BEVERLY PARHAM

STETSON & ARMSTRONG
Lithographers, active N.O. 1870; primarily printers, stationers; Henry G. Stetson (born ca. 1806; died July 27, 1886), Johnson L. Armstrong (born ca. 1825), partners.
Lithographed a view of the steamboat *Robert E. Lee* in 1870; listed as booksellers (1867), stationers (1867–73), blank book manufacturers (1870–72), and printers (1870–72).
References: NOCD 1859, 1867–68, 1870–73; *D. Pic.*, July 31, 1886; LSM, *Biennial Report for 1926–27*, 31.

STEVENS, CHARLES J.
Born NY ca. 1822.
Engraver, designer, active N.O. 1851–60; also printer.
Contemporary listings: engraver, designer, 3 Camp (1851); engraver, 3

Camp and 86 Canal (1852); engraver, 126 Canal and 11 Camp (1853); engraver, 9 Camp and 26 Camp (1854); engraver, 26 Camp (1855–58); engraver, 7 Camp (1858–60).
Worked with THOMAS H. SHIELDS before opening his own establishment in Dec. 1851. He also engraved sheet music covers.
References: NOCD 1852–60; NOBD 1858–59; *Bee*, Sept. 12, 1859; *Carrollton Star*, Mar. 24, 1855 (masthead); *D. Creole*, Jan. 1, 1857; *D. Crescent*, Nov. 20, Dec. 25, 1854, Mar. 29, 1855; *D. Delta*, Sept. 18, 1852, Mar. 16, 1856; *D. Pic.*, Dec. 24, 1851–Jan. 17, 1852 (advs.), Jan. 19, 1853, Nov. 7, Dec. 3, 1854, Dec. 27, 1854–Jan. 21, 1855 (advs.); May 18, 1855, Oct. 25, 1857, Dec. 20, 1859; *D. Times*, Apr. 28, 1857 (masthead); *D. True Delta*, Sept. 18, 1852, Dec. 11, 1859, Jan. 5, 1860; Groce and Wallace; Sheet Music Collection, THNOC; U.S. Census (1860), roll 421.

STEWART, JAMES
Born KY ca. 1832.
Artist, active N.O. 1860.
Contemporary listings: artist (1860).
References: U.S. Census (1860), roll 417.

STEWART, WILLIAM J.
Engraver, active N.O. 1885.
Contemporary listings: engraver, SOUTHERN LITHOGRAPHIC COMPANY (1885).
References: NOCD 1885.

STIFFT, MICHAEL
Born Poland ca. 1822.
Engraver, active N.O. 1860–77; also jeweler, watchmaker.
Contemporary listings: engraver (1860); engraver, 163 Baronne (1866); engraver, 184 Poydras (1874); engraver, 84 Carondelet (1876–77).
References: NOCD 1866, 1868, 1870–74, 1876–77; Groce and Wallace; U.S. Census (1860), roll 417.

STOCKTON, SAM
Painter, active N.O. 1853.
Scenic artist from Mobile AL who came to N.O. briefly to work on scenery. *Cf.* STOCKWELL, SAMUEL B.

References: *D. Crescent*, Feb. 14, 1853.

STOCKWELL, SAMUEL B.
Born Boston, MA 1813; died Savannah GA Sept. 23, 1854.
Painter, active N.O. 1843–49.
Contemporary listings: scenic artist, St. Charles Theatre (1843, 1845–46). Worked with HENRY LEWIS on a panorama of the Mississippi River (1848), but the partnership dissolved and Stockwell completed his own which he exhibited in N.O. (1848–49). *Cf.* STOCKTON, SAM.
References: *Courier*, Jan. 2–31, 1849 (advs.); *D. Crescent*, Nov. 24, 1848; *D. Delta*, Oct. 5, 1848; *D. Orleanian*, Jan. 8, 1849; *D. Pic.*, Apr. 9, Dec. 16, 1843, Nov. 5, 1845, Mar. 24, 1846, Dec. 3, 1848; *Wkly. Delta*, Jan. 12, 1846, Dec. 3, 18, 1848, Feb. 5, 1849; Arrington, "The Story of Stockwell's Panorama"; Groce and Wallace; Ludlow, 561, 578, 601, 607, 611, 640; McDermott, *Lost Panoramas*, 68–80.

STOEKLE, RUDOLPH
Engraver, active N.O. 1886.
Contemporary listings: lithographic engraver, M. F. DUNN & BRO. (1886).
References: NOCD 1886.

STRADELL, MARY A.
Artist, active N.O. 1887.
Contemporary listings: artist (1887).
References: NOCD 1887.

STRAUS, MEYER
Painter, active N.O. 1869–72.
Contemporary listings: scenic artist, Academy of Music (1870–72).
Exhibited: WAGENER & MEYER'S (1869).
Primarily a scenic painter who also painted landscapes, Straus was in San Francisco by 1884. N.O. auctioneers Onorato & Stuart sold his Pacific coast scenes at Grunewald Hall (1891).
References: NOCD 1872; *Bee*, Dec. 19, 1869; *D. Pic.*, Sept. 10, 1870, Apr. 7, 1872, Dec. 17, 1891; *Old Print Shop Portfolio*, Apr. 1958, item 29; *Repub.*, Jan. 15, 22, Apr. 18, Sept. 24, Dec. 10, 1871, Jan. 2, 18, Apr. 14, 1872.

STRETTON, MR. H.
Art teacher, active N.O. 1851.
Contemporary listings: drawing and painting teacher (1851).
Exhibited: Hewitt's Exchange (1851).
References: *D. Pic.*, Nov. 20, 1851.

STRINGER, ADDISON M.
Sketch artist, active N.O. 1880–87.
Contemporary listings: artist in crayon and pastel and portrait artist, 143 St. Charles (1880); artist, 143 St. Charles (1881); artist (1882–87).
References: NOCD 1867, 1869, 1881–87; *Demo.*, Mar. 4, 7, 1880; *States–Item*, Oct. 20, 1965; *Louisiana State Gazetteer*, 168.

STROMEYER, J.
Painter, active N.O. ca. 1883.
Exhibited: LILIENTHAL'S (1883).
References: Lilienthal's, 7.

STROTHER, DAVID HUNTER
Born Martinsburg VA (now WV) Sept. 26, 1816; died Charleston WV Mar. 8, 1888.
Sketch artist, active N.O. 1858.
Visited N.O. in 1858 to sketch for his series of articles, *A Winter in the South*, for *Harper's Monthly*. Strother wrote and illustrated under the name "Porte Crayon."
References: *D. Crescent*, Nov. 30, 1858; *D. Pic.*, Mar. 10, 1888; *Harper's Wkly.*, Mar. 24, 1888, 203; *Appleton's CAB*; *DAB*; Groce and Wallace; Museum of Fine Arts, 1:280.

STROUD, ARTHUR
Born N.O. ca. 1861; died N.O. Apr. 27, 1893.
Sculptor, active N.O. 1880; primarily marble and stone carver.
Contemporary listings: sculptor (1880).
References: NOCD 1876–77, 1879–87, 1891–93; *T. Demo.*, Apr. 27, 1893; U.S. Census (1880), roll 463.

STROUD, IDA WELLS
Born N.O. Oct. 19, 1869.
Painter, active N.O. 1896–1902.
Studied: Pratt Institute; Art Students League, N.Y.C.; with William Merritt Chase.
Exhibited: ARTISTS' ASSOCIATION OF NEW ORLEANS (1896–97, 1902).
Memberships/positions: Artists' Association of New Orleans (1896–97);

National Association of Women Painters & Sculptors; New York Water Color Club; Essex County Water Color Club.

Later active in Newark NJ (ca. 1929–36) as an instructor in painting, drawing, and design at the Newark School of Fine and Industrial Arts.

References: *D. Pic.*, Mar. 30, 1897; AANO, *Catalogue* (1896, 1897, 1902); Collins and Opitz; Fielding, *Dictionary*; Mount, 136; *Who's Who in American Art*, 1936–37; William Young.

STRUVE, ROBERT L.

Born N.O. ca. May 7, 1864; died N.O. Feb. 18, 1900.

Painter, active N.O. ca. 1881–1900. Contemporary listings: painter (1886); scenic painter (1887–88, 1900); scenic artist, Avenue Theatre (1887, 1889); scenic artist, People's Theatre (1891); scenic artist, Academy and St. Charles Theatres (1894–95), scenic artist, St. Charles Theatre (1896); scenic artist, Academy of Music (1897); scenic artist, C. B. Jefferson, Klaw & Erlanger (1898); scenic artist, 339 Baronne (1899).

Exhibited: ARTISTS' ASSOCIATION OF NEW ORLEANS (1894).

Served as assistant to ANTONIO R. BAGNETTO and HARRY H. DRESSEL before becoming associated with ROBERT W. BOHM (1886–1900). They painted scenery for N.O. and Mobile theaters, and floats and other artwork for carnival parades, including the 1900 electrical parade of the Nereus organization.

References: NOCD 1881, 1884, 1886–88, 1890, 1893–1900; *D. Pic.*, Feb. 19, 1900; *D. States*, May 5, 7, 1889, Feb. 19, 1900; *Lantern*, Nov. 10, 1886; *Mascot*, Sept. 19, 1891, 4; *T. Demo.*, May 10, 1887, Dec. 14, 1894, Feb. 19, 1900.

STUARD, JOSEPH

Engraver, active N.O. 1907.

Contemporary listings: engraver (1907).

References: NOCD 1907.

STUBENRAUCH, CATHERINE (Mrs.
FRANCIS STUBENRAUCH)

Hairworker, active N.O. 1866; also jeweler.

Contemporary listings: hairworker, 14 Chartres (1866).

Announced in May 1866, after her husband's death, the continuation of his hairworking and jewelry business.

References: NOCD 1867–69; *Bee*, May 10, 1866.

STUBENRAUCH, FRANCIS

Born Goutersheim, Germany Aug. 1818; died N.O. Feb. 8, 1866.

Hairworker, active N.O. 1852–66; also jeweler.

Contemporary listings: hairworker, 53 Royal (1852–56); artist in hair, 27 Chartres (1857–59); hairworker, 27 Chartres (1860–61); hairworker, 14 Chartres (1866).

Noted hairworker who made flowers, bouquets, bracelets, and monuments of hair, and who in 1858–59 listed as references the N.O. silversmiths Hyde and Goodrich and E. A. Tyler. His wife, CATHERINE STUBENRAUCH, briefly continued the business after his death.

References: NOCD 1852–61, 1866; NOBD 1858–59; *D. Crescent*, Jan. 12, 1857; *State Repub.*, Mar. 24, 1855; *Times*, Feb. 9, 1866; *T. Deutsche Zeitung*, Feb. 9, 1866; N.O. Death Certificate (1866), 31:244, NOPL.

STUMPF, ANSELM

Born Baden, Germany Sept. 1832; died N.O. May 28, 1900.

Painter, active N.O. 1866–1900; also sign painter.

Contemporary listings: painter (1866–68, 1871–72, 1875–77, 1879–81, 1885–86, 1888, 1892–93, 1895–99); fresco painter, 374 St. Louis (1870); fresco painter (1873–74, 1878); frescoer (1889–90).

Father of JOHN ERNEST STUMPF.

References: NOCD 1866–68, 1870–93, 1895–1900; *D. Pic.*, May 29, 1900; U.S. Census (1870), roll 521, (1880), roll 461.

STUMPF, JOHN ERNEST

Born N.O. May 15, 1857; died N.O. Dec. 24, 1939.

Painter, active N.O. 1874–1930. Contemporary listings: fresco painter (1874, 1878, 1891); painter (1876–

77, 1879–88, 1892–93, 1895–1918); frescoer (1889–90).
Later listed as a painter (1919–20, 1924–25, 1927, 1930). Son of AN-SELM STUMPF.
References: NOCD 1874, 1876–93, 1895–1920, 1922, 1924–25, 1927, 1930–33, 1935, 1938, 1940; *T. Pic.*, Dec. 26, 1939; Orleans Parish Registrar of Voters, NOPL; U.S. Census (1870), roll 521, (1880), roll 461.

SUITS, STANLEY B.
Born NY ca. 1853; died N.O. Dec. 20, 1903.
Artist, active N.O. 1895–96; also decorator.
Contemporary listings: artist (1895–96).
References: NOCD 1890, 1894–96, 1899; *D. Pic.*, Dec. 21, 1903.

SULLIVAN, VIRGINIA J.
Art teacher, painter, sculptor, active N.O. 1856–57; also needleworker.
Contemporary listings: teacher of Grecian painting and glass and china decoration, cor. Julia and Magazine (1856–57); teacher of wax works (1857).
Teacher of china and glass decoration, embroidery, leather embossing, and waxwork, who for publicity, raffled off examples of her own work.
References: *D. Creole*, Jan. 1, 1857; *D. Crescent*, Dec. 31, 1856, Mar. 14, 1857; *D. Pic.*, Jan. 28, 1857; *D. True Delta*, Jan. 3, 1857.

SULLY, GEORGE WASHINGTON
Born Norfolk VA Oct. 1816; died Covington LA 1890.
Painter, active N.O. ca. 1835–41.
A cotton broker by profession, Sully moved to N.O. ca. 1835 after spending the previous several years in FL where he made numerous sketches (1832–34, 1839). While in N.O., he painted watercolor scenes of sites in the city (ca. 1835–41). By 1862 Sully and his family had moved to Covington LA. Nephew of THOMAS SULLY, father of N.O. architect Thomas Sully.
References: NOCD 1841–44, 1846, 1849–51; Bruce Chambers, 13, 15, 63; Ellsworth.

SULLY, MARY STUART
Born N.O. ca. 1842; died N.O. Dec. 17, 1915.
Painter, art teacher, active N.O. 1884–96.
Studied: with WILLIAM JENNINGS WARRINGTON (1887).
Contemporary listings: teacher of china decoration, W. J. Warrington's (1887).
Exhibited: World's Industrial and Cotton Centennial Exposition (1884–85); W. J. Warrington's (1887); ARTISTS' ASSOCIATION OF NEW ORLEANS (1887).
Awarded: Dallas State Fair, TX, first prize for watercolors and two first prizes for china painting (1888).
Also a teacher of watercolor and china painting (1887–96); she was a successful writer before becoming an artist.
References: NOCD 1913–16; *Art and Letters*, 1(Dec. 1887):227; *D. Pic.*, Dec. 17, 1887; *D. States*, Oct. 12, 1887, Jan. 8, 1888; *T. Demo.*, Oct. 13, 1887; *T. Pic.*, Dec. 18, 1915; Mount, 152; N.O. Death Certificate (1915), 165:260, NOPL; THNOC Cemetery Survey; Woman's Department of World's Exposition, 160.

SULLY, T. O., JR.
Illustrator, active N.O. ca. 1879–80.
Signed a wood engraving in *Illustrated Visitor's Guide to New Orleans* (1879), "T. O. Sully, Jr., New Orleans La."
References: NOCD 1880; Waldo.

SULLY, THOMAS
Born Horncastle, Lincolnshire, England June 19, 1783; died Philadelphia PA Nov. 5, 1872.
Painter.
Brought to the U.S. at age nine, Sully became America's most celebrated and influential portrait painter and art teacher during his active years in Philadelphia (1808–72). Although he traveled throughout the U.S. and Europe during his career, Sully was not documented in N.O. and his portraits of Louisianians were probably made during the sitters' visits to Philadelphia or when Sully visited other cities. His career was frequently re-

ported in N.O. newspapers. Sully sketched Andrew Jackson from life shortly after the Battle of N.O. and later made a number of paintings of the general. One of these, a three-quarter length portrait, was engraved in 1819 by James Barton Longacre. Uncle of GEORGE WASHINGTON SULLY.

References: *L'Ami des Lois*, Apr. 23, 1819; *Bee*, Jan. 10, 1840, Mar. 1, 1841, Mar. 19, 1842; *Courier*, Dec. 28, 1839, Jan. 13, 1840, Sept. 6, 1843; *D. Crescent*, May 1, 1850, May 7, 1856; *D. Delta*, Oct. 29, 1852; *D. Pic.*, Jan. 16, 1839, Jan. 3, 1840, Mar. 2, 1841, Sept. 3, 1843, Aug. 20, 1845, Sept. 18, 1857; *D. Tropic*, Feb. 22, 26, 1845; *Gazette*, Apr. 15, 1819; *States–Item*, Mar. 24, 1960, Mar. 19, 20, 1973; *T. Pic.*, July 31, 1938, Apr. 15, 1971, Dec. 26, 1976; *True Amer.*, June 12, Dec. 18, 28, 1839; Anglo–American Art Museum, *Catalogue*; Bénézit; Bishop, 12, 235; Bruns, 317; Corcoran Gallery, 27; Dawson, 193; Fabian; Fielding, *Dictionary*; Glenk, 47; Groce and Wallace; Marquis James, *Border Captain*, 340; Marquis James, *Portrait of a President*, 98, 260; Kendall, *History* 2:654–55; Lipton, 42–43; Looney, 383; LSM, *Biennial Report for 1920–21*, 36, 77; LSU, *Louisiana Paintings*, item 41; Mugridge and Conover, 96; Stauffer, 2:331; Wiesendanger, 96; WPA, "Lives."

SUMMERS, LEON
Artist, active N.O. 1898–99.
Contemporary listings: artist (1898–99).
References: NOCD 1898–99.

SUMMERS, LILLY R.
Born N.O. ca. 1873; died N.O. Mar. 25, 1920.
Artist, painter, active N.O. 1890–99.
Studied: with ANDRES MOLINARY; ARTISTS' ASSOCIATION OF NEW ORLEANS (1890).
Exhibited: Artists' Association of New Orleans (1890, 1894, 1897, 1899); Atlanta Exposition (1896).
Memberships/positions: Artists' Association of New Orleans (1896–97).

References: *D. Pic.*, Mar. 30, 1897; *D. States*, May 16, 1890; *T. Demo.*, Dec. 14, 1894; *T. Pic.*, Mar. 27, 1920; AANO, *Catalogue* (1897, 1899); Mount, 211.

SUMMEY, MARY WILLIAMSON (Mrs. Cleveland S. Smith)
Born SC ca. 1887; died May 26, 1980.
Art craftsman, active N.O. 1909–20.
Studied: NEWCOMB COLLEGE (1906–1909).
Contemporary listings: art craftsman, Newcomb (1909–13, 1918); pottery decorator (1910).
Exhibited: ART ASSOCIATION OF NEW ORLEANS (1910–11).
Later listed as art craftsman, Newcomb (1919–20).
References: Art Asso., *Catalogue* (1910, 1911); Ormond and Irvine, 170; Poesch, *Newcomb Pottery*, 105; U.S. Census (1910), roll 524.

SURGI, HENRY G.
Engraver, active N.O. 1891–99.
Contemporary listings: engraver, PHOTO–ENGRAVING COMPANY (1891–95); engraver (1896, 1899).
References: NOCD 1880, 1882–1904, 1906–1907, 1909, 1911, 1913, 1915.

J. SUZEN & CO.
Painters, active N.O. 1896; JOSEPH SUZEN, ROBERT LEE SINGER, partners.
Contemporary listings: fresco painters, 867 Baronne (1896).
References: NOCD 1896.

SUZEN, JOSEPH
Painter, active N.O. 1894–96.
Contemporary listings: fresco painter (1894); J. SUZEN & CO. (1896).
References: NOCD 1894, 1896.

SWART, ELMER E.
Painter, active N.O. 1904–1905.
Contemporary listings: scenic artist, Grand Opera House (1904–1905).
References: *Item*, Nov. 13, 1904, Feb. 25, Mar. 12, 1905; *States*, Apr. 16, 1905.

SWITZER, MAURICE
Born N.O. ca. 1871; died NY Apr. 8, 1929.
Illustrator, active N.O. 1895–97.
Memberships/positions: ARTISTS' ASSOCIATION OF NEW ORLEANS (1897).

Illustrated the *Owl* in 1895–96. Left N.O. in 1900 for NY where he had a successful advertising career.
References: NOCD 1893, 1896; *Morn. Trib.*, Apr. 9, 1929; *Owl*, Dec. 1895–Nov. 1896, illus.

SYLVESTER, FREDERICK OAKES
Born Brockton MA Oct. 3, 1869; died St. Louis MO Feb. 24, 1915.
Painter, art teacher, active N.O. 1891–93.
Studied: Massachusetts Normal Art School (1892).
Contemporary listings: artist (1892).
Exhibited: ARTISTS' ASSOCIATION OF NEW ORLEANS (1891); Tulane University (1892).
Awarded: Louisiana Purchase Exposition, St. Louis MO, bronze medal (1904); Lewis and Clark Centennial Exposition, Portland OR, silver medal (1905).
Memberships/positions: Society of Western Artists, v. pres. (1906); St. Louis Artists' Guild, pres.
Head of the department of drawing and painting at NEWCOMB COLLEGE (1893).
References: NOCD 1892; *D. Pic.*, Mar. 3, 1892; *D. States*, Mar. 3, 1915; *T. Demo.*, Mar. 3, 1892; AANO, *Catalogue* (1891); Rathbone, *Mississippi Panorama* 117–18.

SYMMS, GEORGE GARDNER
Born OH ca. 1840.
Painter, active N.O. 1876–83.
Contemporary listings: portrait painter (1876, 1878–81); portrait painter, 239 Chippewa (1877); artist (1882–83).
References: NOCD 1869–83; Glenk, 79; LSM, *Biennial Report for 1928–29*, 34, 67; U.S. Census (1880), roll 463.

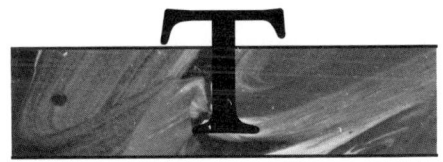

TALEN, WALDEMAR APPOLONIUS
Born Ober, Finland Apr. 1812; died
N.O. Jan. 16, 1882.
Sculptor, active N.O. 1856–68; also
carpenter, architect, carver, draftsman.
Contemporary listings: A. DEFRASSE &
CO. (1856); sculptor, Magazine cor.
Calliope (1858–59); carver in wood,
282 Magazine (1867–68).
First noted in N.O. in 1841, Talen
worked on the carving of the doors
and counters of the New Orleans
Savings Institution (ca. 1873), the
carved figure of Mr. Pickwick at the
Pickwick Club (ca. 1870), and the
working drawings for the "AP" mon-
ogram on the ironwork of the Pontalba buildings.
References: NOCD 1856, 1858–61,
1866–83; *D. Pic.*, May 18–27, 1841
(advs.), Jan. 17, 1882; *Repub.*, Mar.
5, 1875; Civil District Court, Succession of Waldemar Appolonius Talen,
1882, docket 5102, NOPL; Groce
and Wallace; Huber and Wilson,
Pontalba, 40–41; Jewell, 267; Miceli, 79; WPA, "Lives."

TANQUERY PORTRAIT SOCIETY
(Tanquerey Crayon Portrait
Society)
Sketch artists, active N.O. 1887–91.
Contemporary listings: crayon por-
traits, 203 Canal (1887).
References: NOCD 1888–91; *D. Pic.*,
Dec. 4, 1887.

TAUZIN, THEOPHILE E.
Born Natchitoches Parish LA.
Painter, active N.O. 1898–1902.
Studied: with Lassassaign, Natchi-
toches; Dallas TX.
Contemporary listings: artist, 815
Carondelet (1898); artist (1899–
1900, 1902); portrait painter (1900).
Awarded: Dallas Fair, 1st prizes.
References: NOCD 1898–1900,
1902; *Harlequin*, Apr. 28, 1900, 10;
Jeffersonian, Feb. 22, 1847.

TAYLOR, MRS. H. L.
Painter, active N.O. ca. 1891.
Exhibited: ARTISTS' ASSOCIATION OF
NEW ORLEANS (1891).
Possibly Mrs. Harry L. Taylor, born
Louise Hincks, from Evanston IL;
died N.O. June 23, 1936.
References: *Current Topics*, Jan.
1892, 24; *D. Pic.*, Dec. 17, 1891;
AANO, *Catalogue* (1891).

TEBAULT, SALLIE BRADFORD BAILEY
(Mrs. Christopher Hamilton
Tebault, Sr.)
Born Baldwin County GA Feb. 10,
1843; died 1926.
Painter, sculptor, active N.O. ca.
1866–1926.
Studied: Academy of Fine Arts, Phil-
adelphia (ca. 1864–66).
Exhibited: Columbian Exposition,
Chicago (1893); Atlanta Exposition.
Amateur artist who went to school
near Baltimore and then in Philadel-
phia, before leaving the academy to
move to N.O. to marry a physician.
She exhibited painted china, land-
scape paintings with carved borders,
portraits, and most notably, sculp-
ture. She worked during her leisure
hours in a studio in her home at 623
North.
References: NOCD 1918–24, 1926;
T. Pic., Sept. 5, 1934; Orleans Parish
Registrar of Voters, NOPL; Mount,
180.

GEORGE E. TEETZEL & CO. *See also*
CHAPSKY AND TEETZEL, TEETZEL AND
CHAPSKY
Engravers, active N.O. 1876–78;
primarily stencil cutters.
Contemporary listings: engravers, 81
Gravier (1876); engravers, 76 Gra-
vier (1878).
References: NOCD 1870–78; *Re-
pub.*, Aug. 2, 1872, Jan. 29, 1874.

TEETZEL AND CHAPSKY. *See also*
CHAPSKY AND TEETZEL, GEORGE E.
TEETZEL & CO.
Engravers, active N.O. 1877; also
stencil cutters; George E. Teetzel,

Max Chapsky (ca. 1853–78), partners.
Contemporary listings: engravers, 76 Gravier (1877).
References: NOCD 1877.

TEIJELO, GUSTAVE
Born Cadiz, Spain ca. 1862; died N.O. Sept. 24, 1898.
Lithographer, active N.O. 1884–97; also printer, photographer.
Contemporary listings: lithographer (1884–87, 1890–94, 1896–97); lithographer, T. FITZWILLIAM & CO. (1885, 1888–89, 1891).
Reported to have come to N.O. ca. 1874.
References: NOCD 1884–94, 1896–98; *D. Pic.*, Sept. 25, 1898.

TEJADA, M. S. DE, JR.
Painter, active N.O. 1843–44.
Contemporary listings: miniature painter, 84 St. Peter (1843–44).
References: NOCD 1843–44.

TENNANT, THOMAS R.
Born Leeds, England.
Painter, active N.O. ca. 1886–87.
Exhibited: SEEBOLD'S (1886); ARTISTS' ASSOCIATION OF NEW ORLEANS (1886–87).
Memberships/positions: Artist's Association of New Orleans (1886).
Primarily a sales clerk in N.O. (1876–92) who exhibited as an amateur painter. He later moved to St. Louis MO. His daughter, Allie Victoria Tennant, achieved fame as a TX sculptor.
References: NOCD 1876–81, 1883–90, 1892; *Art and Letters* 1(Dec. 1887):227; *D. Pic.*, Nov. 6, 1886, Dec. 29, 1887; *D. States*, Nov. 5, 1886; *T. Demo.*, Jan. 3, 1886; AANO, *Catalogue* (1886); Fisk, 220.

TERRY, MISS _____
Sketch artist, painter, active N.O. ca. 1882–89.
Studied: SOUTHERN ART UNION (1882).
Exhibited: Southern Art Union (1882); Cotton Palace (1889).
Awarded: Southern Art Union, third prize for best specimen of crayon drawing (1882).
References: *D. Pic.*, May 2, 1882; *T. Demo.*, Feb. 19, 1889.

TESSIN, GERMAIN
Born France ca. 1829.
Sculptor, active N.O. 1860.
Contemporary listings: sculptor (1860).
References: Groce and Wallace; U.S. Census (1860), roll 418.

TETTUS, W.
Painter, active N.O. 1886.
Contemporary listings: scenery, Bidwell's New St. Charles Theatre (1886).
References: *Mascot*, Dec. 24, 1886.

TEXIER, ALFRED M.
Died ca. 1890.
Sketch artist, active N.O. ca. 1884–85.
Contemporary listings: pen and ink artist (1885).
Exhibited: World's Industrial and Cotton Centennial Exposition (1884–85).
Amateur artist of landscapes, marine scenes, and profiles, who was a N.O. cotton broker and merchant.
References: NOCD 1857–61, 1866, 1868, 1872–80, 1882–90; *D. Pic.*, Aug. 20, 1893; *Eve. Chronicle*, Feb. 11, 1885.

THALMAN, JOSEPH
Born Germany Jan. 1870.
Painter, active N.O. 1900.
Contemporary listings: artist–portrait (1900).
References: U.S. Census (1900), roll 570.

THEURET, DOMINIQUE
Born France ca. 1812.
Lithographer, active N.O. 1837–54.
Contemporary listings: lithographer, with CHARLES RISSO, Orleans betw. Royal and Bourbon (1837); lithographer, 264 St. Louis (1849–50); lithographer, 11 Exchange Al. (1850–51); lithographer, Exchange Al. (1852); lithographer, Exchange Pl. (1853–54).
According to his advertisements, Theuret ran a general lithographic practice and could do work in English, French, Spanish, and Portuguese. He produced, with P. SNELL, a lithographed plan of Houston TX and printed the libretto for Verdi's

Jerusalem in French and in English (ca. 1850).
References: NOCD 1837, 1849–54; *Courier*, Apr. 6–8, 1837 (advs.), Nov. 29, Dec. 2, 1850; Groce and Wallace; Orleans Parish Notarial Archives, Plan Book 23:1; U.S. Census (1850), roll 235; Verdi, cover.

THIBAULT, MISS E. A.
Born N.O.
Painter, sketch artist, active N.O. 1882–84.
Studied: SOUTHERN ART UNION (1882).
Contemporary listings: sketch artist (1882); painter (1884).
Exhibited: Southern Art Union (1882).
Contributed a painting of a horse's head to a benefit which was used to raise money for the construction of the new armory for the Continental Guards (1884).
References: *D. Pic.*, May 2, 1882; *D. States*, Feb. 10, 1884.

THIBAUT, HENRY W.
Painter, active N.O. 1904–1908; also photographer.
Contemporary listings: portrait painter (1904); artist (1907–1908).
References: NOCD 1898, 1900–14.

THIEL, EMMA C. NEPHLER (Mrs. Charles A. Thiel)
Born Baton Rouge LA ca. 1849; died N.O. Nov. 20, 1927.
Painter, active N.O. ca. 1896.
Amateur painter who was married to a businessman and was noted for her public and charitable works.
References: NOCD 1905–23; *T. Pic.*, Nov. 22, 1927; Mount, 88–89; N.O. Board of Health Records, NOPL.

THIEM, RUDOLPH
Born Germany.
Sculptor, active N.O. ca. 1882–86.
Studied: Berlin.
Contemporary listings: sculptor (1882); sculptor, near cor. Erato and Tchoupitoulas (1883).
Exhibited: Grunewald's music store (1882); Washington Artillery Hall (1883); American Exposition (1885–86).
Sculptor from Berlin who was in partnership with PAUL RIESS. Thiem modeled statues in clay, which were then cast in white bronze by Riess, and electroplated with copper. In 1883 they produced a full-length portrait of Gen. Robert E. Lee.
References: *Bee*, Apr. 1, 1882; *D. Pic.*, Aug. 10, 1883; *D. States*, Aug. 17, 1883; Creole Exhibit, 18.

THOM, JAMES
Born Dumfries, Ayrshire, Scotland ca. 1799–1802; died N.Y.C. Apr. 17, 1850.
Sculptor, active N.O. 1834–35.
Contemporary listings: sculptor (1835).
Exhibited: British Institute, London (1815); 53 Camp (1834); Pennsylvania Academy of Fine Arts, Philadelphia (1850–70).
Sculptor first noted in the U.S. when he exhibited in N.O. (Feb.–Mar. 1834) a group of four life–size statues illustrating the Robert Burns poem "Tam O'Shanter." Thom arrived again in N.O. for a few days in Oct. 1835 en route from London to N.Y.C. where a cargo of his sculptures had arrived. By 1836 he had settled in NJ and later lived in N.Y.C.
References: *Bee*, Mar. 19, 1834; *Courier*, Feb. 27–Mar. 22, 1834 (advs.), Feb. 28, Mar. 10, Mar. 22, 1834, Oct. 7, 1835; *Mercantile Advertiser*, Feb. 27–May 5, 1834 (advs.), Apr. 8–May 5, 1834 (advs.); Bénézit; Groce and Wallace.

THOMAS, AMAND
Born Alsace, France ca. 1828–30; died N.O. Sept. 9, 1899.
Artist, active N.O. 1860.
Contemporary listings: French artist (1860).
References: *D. Pic.*, Sept. 10, 1899; *T. Demo.*, Sept. 10, 1899; U.S. Census (1860), roll 418.

THOMAS, GEORGE
Born Germany ca. 1815.
Engraver, active N.O. 1844.
Contemporary listings: stencil plate and wood engraver, cor. Camp and Canal (1844).
References: *D. Pic.*, Jan. 28–Mar. 1, 1844 (advs.); Groce and Wallace.

THOMAS, JAMES S.
Born NY Apr. 1834.
Engraver, active N.O. 1900; also stencil cutter.

Contemporary listings: engraver (1900).
References: NOCD 1899–1904; U.S. Census (1900), roll 570.

THOMAS, JOSEPH
Born France ca. 1829; died N.O. Sept. 4, 1847.
Sculptor, active N.O. 1847.
Contemporary listings: sculptor (1847).
Arrived in N.O. early in 1847 from Le Havre, France, and died of yellow fever.
References: Louisiana Charity Hospital, Death Records, NOPL.

THOMAS, KATE (Mrs. F. B. Thomas)
Born Ireland ca. 1842; died N.O. July 23, 1883.
Commercial artist, active N.O. 1876–80.
Contemporary listings: artist, with W. W. WASHBURN (1876); artist (1880).
References: NOCD 1876, 1879–80, 1884; N.O. Death Certificate, July 23, 1883, 83:261, NOPL.

THOMAS, LOUIS
Art dealer, active N.O. 1895.
Contemporary listings: IDEAL ART CO. (1895).
References: NOCD 1895.

THOMAS, LOUISA
Commercial artist, active N.O. 1884.
Contemporary listings: artist, with W. M. Sherburne (1884).
References: NOCD 1884.

THOMAS, STEPHEN SEYMOUR
Born Nacogdoches or San Augustine TX Aug. 20, 1868; died Feb. 29, 1956.
Painter, active N.O. 1894.
Studied: Art League of New York; Académie Julian; Ecole des Beaux Arts, Paris.
Exhibited: World's Industrial and Cotton Centennial Exposition (1884–85); Salon, Paris (1890, 1892–95, 1901, 1904); Columbian Exposition, Chicago (1893); Tulane University (1894); International Exposition, Paris (1900).
Awarded: Salon, Paris, honorable mention (1895); International Exposition, Paris, bronze medal (1900); Salon, Paris, third class medal (1901),

second class medal (1904); Chevalier da la Légion D'Honneur (1905).
Primarily a portraitist who exhibited at the N.O. exposition, but did not visit the city until 1894 when he exhibited at Tulane and painted a portrait intended for the 1894 Paris salon.
References: *T. Demo.*, Feb. 11, 1894; Bénézit; Fielding, *Dictionary.*

THOMAS, WARREN W.
Artist, painter, active N.O. 1879–80.
Contemporary listings: artist, 117 Customhouse (1879); THOMAS & COMFORD (1880).
References: NOCD 1879–80.

THOMAS & COMFORD
Painters, active N.O. 1880; WARREN W. THOMAS, Edward P. Comford, partners.
Contemporary listings: painters, 146 Sixth (1880).
References: NOCD 1880.

THOMPSON, AARON B.
Sketch artist, active N.O. 1874.
His drawings depicting the Battle of Liberty Place were reproduced as wood engravings in *Frank Leslies' Illustrated Newspaper* (Oct. 3, 1874).
References: Landry, 82; THNOC 1979.206.

THOMPSON, CEPHAS
Born Middleboro MA July 1, 1775; died Middleboro Nov. 6, 1856.
Painter, active N.O. 1815–16.
Contemporary listings: portrait painter, St. Louis (1815–16).
Mostly self-taught, Thompson spent winters until 1825 painting portraits and cutting silhouettes in southern cities: Baltimore MD (1804), Charleston SC (1804, 1818, 1822), Richmond VA (1809–10), and N.O. After 1825 he remained in Middleboro until his death. Father of JEROME B. THOMPSON.
References: *L'Ami des Lois*, Dec. 11, 1815–Jan. 3, 1816 (advs.); *Appleton's CAB*; Corcoran Gallery, 20; Groce and Wallace; Kelly, 5, 61.

THOMPSON, FLORENCE TRUE
Born N.O. July 4, 1877; died Feb. 24, 1957.
Art teacher, active N.O. 1913.

Contemporary listings: drawing teacher (1913).

Continued to be listed as a teacher in various N.O. public schools until 1942.

References: NOCD 1913–33, 1935, 1938, 1940, 1942, 1945–47, 1949, 1952–56; *T. Demo.*, Jan. 14, 1913; *T. Pic.*, Feb. 24, 1957; Orleans Parish Registrar of Voters, NOPL; U.S. Census (1900), roll 575.

THOMPSON, JEROME B.
Born Middleboro MA Jan. 30, 1814; died Glen Gardner NJ May 1, 1886.
Painter, active N.O. 1839.
Studied: England (1852–54).
Contemporary listings: portrait painter, 33 Royal (1839).
Exhibited: American Academy of Fine Arts, N.Y.C., National Academy of Design, N.Y.C. (1835); 29 Camp (1839).
Memberships/positions: National Academy of Design (1851).
Portrait, landscape, and genre painter who traveled extensively seeking commissions and was in N.O. during Dec. 1839 to solicit portrait commissions and exhibit his work. In 1844 Thompson moved to N.Y.C. where he specialized in sentimental genre scenes, many of which were lithographed. Son of CEPHAS THOMPSON.
References: *True Amer.*, Dec. 2, 23, 25, 31, 1839; Bénézit; Edwards; Groce and Wallace.

THORAME, JEAN PIERRE
Art teacher, active N.O. 1822–35.
Contemporary listings: professor of painting, Orleans College (1822); drawing master, 187 St. Louis (1823); drawing and painting academy, cor. of St. Peter and Dauphine, No. 131 (1824); drawing master, 192 Dauphine (1827, 1830); drawing master, cor. Bourbon and St. Peter (1832, 1834–35).
Cf. TORAM, MR. _____
References: NOCD 1822–23, 1827, 1830, 1832, 1834–35; *Courier*, Sept. 27, 1824; Groce and Wallace; Record Group 10, 810/19, 826/6, LSM.

THORN, JAMES. *See* THOM, JAMES

THORNTON, MARY MINOR TURNER (1. Mrs. J. C. De Camp; 2. Mrs. James B. Thornton)
Born N.O. Dec. 1826; died N.O. Jan 25, 1911.
Art teacher, active N.O. ca. 1866–72.
Contemporary listings: instruction in painting, coloring of photographs, leather and wax work, drawing, penmanship, and ornamental and fancy work, 2 Old Magazine (1866).
Listed as a teacher at the Magnolia School (1870, 1872) and at the Poydras Female Orphan Asylum.
References: NOCD 1860–61, 1870, 1872–74, 1879, 1881–85, 1887–88, 1893, 1898–99; *D. Pic.*, Jan. 26, 1911; *Times*, Mar. 11–20, 1866 (advs.); N.O. Death Certificate (1911), 151:396, NOPL.

THORPE, THOMAS BANGS
Born Westfield MA Mar. 1, 1815; died N.Y.C. Sept. 20, 1878.
Painter, active N.O. 1836–54, 1862–63.
Studied: with John Quidor, N.Y.C.
Contemporary listings: painter (1842, 1846, 1848–49); portrait painter (1850–51).
Exhibited: American Academy of Fine Arts, N.Y.C. (ca. 1833); St. Charles Hotel (1842); J. B. Steel's bookstore (1848, 1850); Phoenix House (1850); Lyceum Library (1851).
Noted newspaper editor and writer as well as amateur artist, Thorpe came to LA in 1836 and remained until 1854. He edited the *Concordia Intelligencer* (1843), the N.O. *Commercial Times* (1845), the N.O. *Daily Tropic* (1846), the Baton Rouge LA *Conservator* (1847), and the Batesville LA *Eagle* (1850). An early supporter of Zachary Taylor for president, Thorpe painted a full–length potrait of him, executing Taylor's face from life and using daguerreotype views of his own body to complete the image. The work was purchased by the LA State Legislature. He returned to N.O. in 1862 as a colonel under Benjamin Butler during the

Union occupation of the city and again in 1863.
References: NOCD 1846; *Bee*, Jan. 3, 1846, Mar. 3, 1851; *Comm. Times*, May 25, 1848; *D. Crescent*, Jan. 12, 18, 28, 29, 1850, Jan. 4, 1851, May 12, 1860; *D. Pic.*, Sept. 7, 1842, Jan. 14, 1844, Feb. 24, Apr. 1, 1846, Sept. 9, 1877, Oct. 31, 1884; *Leslie's*, May 24, 1862; *Wkly. Delta*, Nov. 26, 1849; Allibone, 3:2412; *Appleton's CAB*; Bruns, 317; Edwin Davis, *Plantation Life*, 66; Duyckinck, 2:612–15; Friends of the Cabildo, *250 Years*, 42–43, 61; Groce and Wallace; Kunitz and Haycraft, 749–50; U.S. Census (1850), rolls 229, 234; Wiesendanger, 97–98; WPA, "Lives."

THROOP, ORRAMEL HINCKLEY
Born Oxford NY June 12, 1798.
Engraver, active N.O. 1821, 1831–35; also printer, publisher.
Studied: with G. Fairman of Murray, Draper, Fairman & Co. Bank Note Engravers, Philadelphia.
Contemporary listings: Throop and Duncan, engravers and copper plate printers, 27 Royal (1821); engraving and copperplate printing, cor. of Chartres and Bienville (1831); engraver and publisher, 46 Bienville, and engraver and printer, 92 Chartres (1832); engraving, 112 Chartres, 27 Chartres, and 57 Chartres (1834); engraver and printer, 57 Conti (1834–35).
General engraver and copperplate printer who also worked in N.Y.C. (1825). He engraved landscapes and vignettes, as well as maps, charts, address cards, and various business forms. He also did decorative engraving on wood and metal.
References: NOCD 1832, 1834–35; *Advertiser*, Mar. 26, 1831, Nov. 17, 19, 21–25, 1834 (advs.); *Bee*, Jan. 20, Mar. 22, June 1, 1832, Jan. 14, 1834; *Courier*, June 1, 1832; *Emporium*, Sept. 27–28, 1832; *Gazette*, Mar. 7, 9, 1821; *Mercantile Advertiser*, Jan. 24, 1831, Jan. 28–Feb. 11, 1834 (advs.); *Old Print Shop Portfolio*, Feb. 1966; Bénézit; "La Chatelaine," "Madame Arraline Brooks,"

Sheet Music Collection, THNOC; Dunlap, 2:24, 258, 469; Fielding, *Dictionary*; Groce and Wallace; Mayor's Office, Messages, June 16, 1821, 9:170; New Orleans City Council, Proceedings, June 20, 1821, NOPL; Throop, 615.

THULSTRUP, THURE DE. *See* DE THULSTRUP, THURE

TIERNAN, MICHAEL
Born Ireland ca. 1832.
Artist, active N.O. 1850.
Contemporary listings: artist (1850).
References: Groce and Wallace; U.S. Census (1850), roll 235.

TIMOTHY, HENRY
Born LA ca. 1884.
Lithographer, active N.O. 1910.
Contemporary listings: lithographer–cannery (1910).
References: U.S. Census (1910), roll 521.

TIRRELL, GEORGE
Painter, active N.O. 1874–75.
Contemporary listings: principal scenic artist, Varieties Theatre (1874); scenic artist, Varieties Theatre (1875).
References: NOCD 1875; *D. Pic.*, Nov. 1, 1874; *Repub.*, Nov. 15, 1874; Kendall, *Golden Age*, 446.

TISDALE, JOHN B.
Born ca. 1822.
Painter, active N.O. 1845.
Came with ALFRED S. WAUGH from Mobile AL to N.O. in Jan. 1845 where they shared a studio on St. Charles until they left the city in May of that year. They traveled by steamboat to MO, where they hoped to join John C. Fremont's expedition to the Rocky Mountains but were refused. Tisdale later returned to Mobile, where he was active in local government and where he was presumed to have died.
References: Groce and Wallace; Waugh, xii–xiii, 1–10.

TODSWER, HARRY
Born MD ca. 1846.
Engraver, active N.O. 1880–85.
Contemporary listings: glass engraver, 47 Baronne (1880–85).
References: NOCD 1879–86; U.S. Census (1870), roll 525.

TOIRY, MR. _____
Art teacher, active N.O. 1819.
Contemporary listings: professor, LOUISIANA PAINTING AND SCULPTURE ACADEMY (1819).
Cf. TOIRY, PIERRE.
References: *Courier*, Jan. 27, 1819.

TOIRY, PIERRE
Painter, active N.O. 1830.
Contemporary listings: portrait painter, 111 St. Louis (1830).
Cf. TOIRY, MR. _____.
References: NOCD 1823, 1830.

TOLIAS, T. J.
Born LA Sept. 1873; black.
Artist, active N.O. 1900.
Contemporary listings: artist (1900).
References: U.S. Census (1900), roll 570.

TOLING, JAMES
Artist, active N.O. 1896.
Contemporary listings: artist (1896).
References: NOCD 1896.

TOLTI, GIOVANNI (Jean)
Born Italy ca. 1822; died N.O. Aug. 23, 1860.
Lithographer, engraver, active N.O. 1849–60.
Contemporary listings: lithographer, 11 Exchange Al. (1849); lithographer (1850); TOLTI & CARNAHAN (1856–59); TOLTI & SIMON (1860).
Also illustrated sheet music covers.
References: NOCD 1853–60; *Bee*, Dec. 20, 1849, Oct. 10, 1851, Aug. 24, 1860; N.O. Death Certificate (1860), 21:113, NOPL; Reinders, illus. facing 225; U.S. Census (1850), roll 235, (1860), roll 421.

TOLTI & CARNAHAN
Engravers, lithographers, active N.O. 1856–59; also printers, publishers; GIOVANNI TOLTI, CHARLES CARNAHAN, partners.
Contemporary listings: engravers, lithographers, 119 Exchange Pl. (1856–57); lithographers, 119 Exchange (1858); lithographers, 119 Exchange Pl. (1859).
Also lithographed sheet music covers.
References: NOCD 1856–59; *D. Crescent*, May 10, 1856; "Les Amours du Diable," Sheet Music Collection, THNOC.

TOLTI & SIMON
Lithographers, active N.O. 1860; GIOVANNI TOLTI, DIONIS SIMON, partners.
Contemporary listings: lithographers, 115 Exchange Pl (1860).
References: NOCD 1860; "Oratorial Grand March," Sheet Music Collection, NOPL; Commercial File, THNOC.

TOOLEY, JAMES, JR.
Born Aug. 8, 1816; died Aug. 10, 1844.
Painter, active N.O. 1839.
Contemporary listings: miniature painter, 5 Camp (1839).
Active in both Natchez MS (ca. 1833–35, 1843–44) and Philadelphia (1842–43), Tooley sketched a view of Natchez that was the basis of a lithograph by RISSO & Browne of N.Y.C.
References: *D. Pic.*, Nov. 30, 1839; Groce and Wallace; Stokes and Haskell, 81; THNOC 1971.41.

TORAM, MR. _____
Art teacher, active N.O. 1833–34.
Contemporary listings: drawing teacher, Madame Vernles's Boarding School (1833–34).
Cf. THORAME, JEAN PIERRE.
References: *Bee*, July 3–Aug. 26, 1833 (advs.); *Courier*, June 21, 1833, July 23–Nov. 4, 1833 (advs.), May 1, 1834; Mobley, 853.

TORO, FRANCIS
Born Spain ca. 1833.
Lithographer, painter, active N.O. 1870–77.
Contemporary listings: painter (1870); lithographer (1874, 1876–77).
References: NOCD 1871–72, 1874, 1876–78; U.S. Census (1870), roll 523.

TORRE, PETER, JR.
Born N.O. ca. 1880–83; died N.O. Apr. 4, 1953.
Sketch artist, active N.O. 1905; primarily architect, draftsman.
Submitted the winning design in a T–Square Club emblem competition (1905). Torre was a draftsman (1906–1907), an architectural colorist (1909), and then an architect

with the firm Nolan & Torre (1910–31). He later became president of the N.O. Fruit Importing Co. (1922) and continued in that position from 1932 to 1953.

References: NOCD 1903–1907, 1909–33, 1935, 1938, 1940, 1942, 1945–47, 1949, 1952–53; *Architectural Art*, 1(Aug. 1905):14; *T. Pic.*, Apr. 6, 1953; U.S. Census (1910), roll 522.

TORREY, CHARLES C.
Born Beverly or Salem MA July 9, 1799; died Nashville TN Feb. 9, 1827.
Engraver, active N.O. 1823.
Contemporary listings: engraver, 102 Royal (1823).
References: NOCD 1823; Bénézit; Fielding, *Dictionary*; Groce and Wallace.

TOUPS, V. P.
Artist, active N.O. 1899.
Contemporary listings: artist (1899).
References: NOCD 1899.

TOWNSEND, CORA ALICE (1. Mrs. José Martin Rascon; 2. Mrs. Bannister Smith–Monro)
Born NY ca. 1853; died Arcachon, France Mar. 26, 1898.
Painter, active N.O. 1889–91; also woodcarver.
Studied: NEWCOMB COLLEGE (1887).
Exhibited: ARTISTS' ASSOCIATION OF NEW ORLEANS (1889–91).
Memberships/positions: Artists' Association of New Orleans (1890).
Amateur painter of still lifes of fruits and flowers. Member of a prominent N.O. family and daughter of the famous southern poet Mary Ashley Townsend, she resided in Europe most of her life after her second marriage (ca. 1895).
References: *Current Topics*, Jan. 1891, 25, June 1891, 22; *D. Pic.*, Dec. 17, 1889, Nov. 13, Dec. 17, 1890, Mar. 28, 1898; *T. Demo.*, Oct. 18, 1891, Mar. 27, 1898; AANO, *Catalogue* (1890); Meyer, *Townsend*; Ormond and Irvine, 170.

TOWNSLEY, JOHN L.
Lithographer, active N.O. 1893–1900; also printer.

Contemporary listings: lithographer (1893–97, 1899–1900).
Possibly John Lawson Townsley, born MS Nov. 12, 1874; died Fort Worth TX Sept. 4, 1959.
References: NOCD 1893–1901, 1903; *T. Pic.*, Sept. 6, 1959; THNOC Cemetery Survey.

TOYE, FRANK E. W.
Born N.O. Oct. 10, 1860; died N.O. Nov. 8, 1917.
Commercial artist, painter, active N.O. 1879–1915.
Contemporary listings: artist (1879, 1882–84, 1888, 1902, 1906); painter (1880–81, 1885, 1887, 1891, 1893, 1895–96, 1898–1901, 1905, 1908–11, 1915); fresco painter (1904); scenic painter (1910).
Painted carnival floats in various American cities, including those of the Rex organization in N.O.
References: NOCD 1878–85, 1887–88, 1890–91, 1893–1902, 1904–1906, 1908–18; *T. Pic.*, Nov. 9, 1917; U.S. Census (1900), roll 572.

TRAYOR, FRANK
Engraver, active N.O. 1876.
Contemporary listings: engraver, with FREDERICK HOLYLAND (1876).
References: NOCD 1876.

TREAT, ARABELLA ELISE. *See* BELDEN, ARABELLA ELISE TREAT

TREZEVANT, MARYE BROOKS (Dick)
Born Memphis TN Nov. 9, 1872; died Pass Christian MS June 20, 1930.
Cartoonist, active N.O. 1897–1904; also photographer.
Studied: Tulane University (ca. 1898); with Howard Chandler Christy, N.Y.C. (1900).
Exhibited: ARTISTS' ASSOCIATION OF NEW ORLEANS (1899); Press Artists' League, N.Y.C. (1900).
Memberships/positions: Art Students' League, N.Y.C. (1900).
Newspaper journalist and editor who came to N.O. in 1897 and contributed cartoons to the *Daily States* (1897–1902) and to *Harlequin* (1899–1904). The cartoons were sometimes signed "TREZ" or "ZERT," the latter being the abbreviation of his last name spelled backwards. Trezevant later became a press agent

(1899), an artist with the *Mail and Express* (1900) in N.Y.C., and general manager of the Progressive Union, a civic organization in N.O. (1906–1914). At the time of his death, he was retired from the Whitney Bank of N.O.
References: NOCD 1898–99, 1901–1903, 1905–17, 1929; *D. News*, Sept. 7, 1906; *D. States*, Nov. 6, 1897, Oct. 2, 1899, Feb. 10, Apr. 22, 24–25, 1902 (illus.), Feb. 15, 1904; *Harlequin*, June 28, 1899–Aug. 25, 1904, July 26, Oct. 11, 1899, Jan. 10, 17, June 16, 1900, Apr. 16, 30, June 4, 1903, Nov. 5, 1903, Aug. 11, Sept. 8, 22, 1904, Mar. 8, 1906; *T. Pic.*, June 21, 1930; AANO, *Catalogue* (1899); Fortier, *Louisiana*, 3:437–38; Orleans Parish Registrar of Voters, NOPL; Patrick, 278.

TRIMBLE, WILLIAM J.
Born LA ca. 1854.
Artist, active N.O. 1903–17.
Contemporary listings: artist (1903–1905); theater lobby artist (1910); artist, Orpheum Theatre (1917).
References: NOCD 1900–17, 1920; U.S. Census (1910), roll 524.

TRINCHARD, JUNIUS BRUTUS
Sculptor, active N.O. 1841–43; primarily marblecutter.
Contemporary listings: marble sculptor, Rampart near St. Louis (1841); marble sculptor (1843).
References: NOCD 1824, 1827, 1830, 1832, 1841–43, 1846.

TROBRIAND, PHILIPPE RÉGIS DENIS DE KEREDEN DE. *See* DE TROBRIAND, PHILIPPE REGIS DENIS DE KEREDEN

TROST, CARRIE (Caroline)
Born N.O. Jan. 2, 1878; died N.O. Nov. 22, 1953.
Art teacher, painter, active N.O. 1893–1931.
Studied: with GEORGE DAVID COULON.
Contemporary listings: art studio, with ADINE REED, Canal and Bourbon (1893); art studio, with Adine Reed, 4 Bourbon (1894); artist (1896–97, 1899–1900, 1903, 1905–1906); art teacher (1902); drawing teacher, N.O. Public Schools (1913).
Exhibited: Tulane University (1893).

Later listed as artist (1924–25, 1931) and teacher (1927).
References: NOCD 1892–94, 1896–97, 1899–1903, 1905–1906, 1911–15, 1917, 1922–27, 1929–33, 1938, 1940, 1942, 1949, 1952–53; *D. Pic.*, Feb. 14, 1893; *Item*, Nov. 23, 1953; *T. Demo.*, June 11, 1893; Orleans Parish Registrar of Voters, NOPL.

TROST, HENRY, JR.
Born N.O. Apr. 9, 1863; died N.O. July 17, 1890.
Lithographer, active N.O. 1887–90.
Contemporary listings: lithographer, M. F. DUNN & BRO. (1887–90).
References: NOCD 1884, 1887–91; *D. Pic.*, July 18, 1890; *T. Demo.*, July 3, 1891.

TROUARD, MR. D.
Sculptor, active N.O. 1848–50.
Contemporary listings: sculptor (1848, 1850).
Exhibited: Bourse Saint Louis and Bertrand's drug store (1848).
Self–taught French sculptor who created portrait busts of blacks in terra cotta and by 1850 wanted to return to Paris to study.
References: *Bee*, Dec. 28, 1850; *Courier*, July 6, 1848; *Times*, Sept. 28, 1866.

TROWBRIDGE, N. C.
Born MA ca. 1830.
Artist, active N.O. 1860.
Contemporary listings: artist (1860).
References: U.S. Census (1860), roll 417.

TROY, LOTA LEE
Born Pleasant Garden NC Nov. 14, 1874; died Dec. 10, 1963.
Art teacher, bookbinder, designer, painter, active N.O. 1909–46.
Studied: Greensboro College NC (1888–1902); with Arthur Dow, Walter Roach, and William Mason, Columbia University, N.Y.C.; Chicago Art Institute.
Contemporary listings: asst. prof., NEWCOMB COLLEGE (1910); prof., Newcomb (1911–18).
Exhibited: ART ASSOCIATION OF NEW ORLEANS (1914).
Memberships/positions: Louisiana Education Association, art division

chairman (1910–12); Louisiana Art Teachers Association, pres. (1913). Came to Newcomb in 1909 as an instructor in normal art and later was assistant director (1928–1931), acting director (1931–1935), and director (1935–1940). During her tenure, Troy specialized in bookbinding and design, though she also taught drawing, watercolor, and art education.

References: NOCD 1910–33, 1935, 1938, 1940, 1942, 1945–46; *Morn. Trib.*, Feb. 8, 1928; *T. Pic.*, June 5, 1931; Art Asso., *Catalogue* (1914); Cattell et al., 1018; Looney, 392; Ormond and Irvine, 130, 136, 143, 150, 153, 159, 160, 162, 171; Poesch, *Newcomb Pottery* 77, 83–85; *Who's Who in American Art*, 1938–39.

TROYE, EDWARD

Born near Lausanne, Switzerland July 12, 1808; died Georgetown KY July 25, 1874.

Painter, active N.O. 1844–57.

Contemporary listings: portrait painter, 38 St. Charles (1844).

Exhibited: St. Charles Exchange (1845); City Hotel (1853); Odd Fellows' Hall (1857).

Animal, portrait, and landscape painter who arrived in the U.S. in 1831 and established himself as the foremost American painter of horses and cattle. Troye traveled widely, particularly throughout KY, and in Nov. 1836, worked at Magnolia plantation near Natchitoches LA. During Nov.–Dec. 1844, he advertised in N.O. as a portrait painter; and in Jan. 1845, his painting of a race horse, *Peytona*, was on display at the St. Charles Exchange. His N.O. stay led to several commissions during 1845 in LA and MS. One patron was the wealthy N.O. lawyer and sugar planter Duncan Kenner, for whom Troye painted six horse portraits at his racing stables and breeding farm on Ashland plantation near Darrow LA. Troye returned to N.O. en route to Havana, Cuba, during the fall of 1847. While teaching painting at Spring Hill College, Mobile AL

(1849–55), he probably had the opportunity to visit N.O. and may have accompanied his painting which was exhibited in Jan. 1853. In 1855 Troye toured the Middle East to paint five large canvases of scenes in the Holy Land. He considered the works to be the most important of his career and hoped that they would establish him in the art world as a serious artist. The works were intended for the gallery of a private collector and not for public viewing, but they were given two special public exhibitions: in N.O. during Apr.–May 1857 and in N.Y.C. in Mar. 1858. The final years of his life were spent in KY.

References: *Bee*, Apr. 2, 1857, Apr. 15–May 2, 1857 (advs.), May 2, 1857; *Comm. Bull.*, Apr. 25, May 2, 1857; *Courier*, Jan. 19, 1853, Apr. 3, 15, 1857; *D. Creole*, Apr. 15, 1857; *D. Crescent*, Apr. 15, 20, May 2, 1857; *D. Orleanian*, Apr. 2, 1857; *D. Pic.*, Nov. 28, Dec. 12, 1844, Jan. 8, 1845, Apr. 14, 18, 1857, Dec. 3, 1869; *D. Times*, May 2, 1857; *DAB*; Groce and Wallace; LSM, *Biennial Report for 1920–21*, 89; Mackay–Smith.

TRUDEAU, DR. JAMES DE BERTY

Born Jefferson Parish LA Sept. 14, 1817; died N.O. May 25, 1887.

Painter, sculptor, active N.O. 1840, 1856–87.

Exhibited: American Exposition (1885–86).

Born on his family's sugar plantation near N.O. and educated as a physician in Europe and the U.S., Trudeau began to practice medicine in N.Y.C. in 1837. That year he also read his first paper on birds to the Academy of Natural Science, Philadelphia, and soon became a friend of JOHN JAMES AUDUBON. Trudeau assisted his friend's research by acquiring books and examining collections of birds during his trips to Europe (1838) and in the U.S. He also made watercolor drawings (ca. 1837–38) of bird eggs collected by Audubon from his Labrador expedition, and Audubon named the Trudeau tern after him. By May 1840 Trudeau had returned to N.O. to join Victor Tixier on an expedition to St. Louis MO and the Osage Indian country; he returned to N.O. by Aug. of that year. Trudeau resumed his medical practice in N.Y.C. (1843–52). By 1856 he was established in N.O. for the rest of his life as a physician and as an amateur artist known for his work with pencil and brush and his humorous statuettes of N.O. citizens from the past. References: NOCD 1857, 1861, 1867–77, 1879–85, 1887; *Bee*, May 26, 1887; *States–Item*, Aug. 15, 1961; *T. Demo.*, Aug. 28, 1892; Kneece, "Museum Finds Priceless Art," *T. Pic.*, Aug. 14, 1961; Arthur and de Kernion, 95–96; Creole Exhibit, 23, 26, 36; Ewan, 259–63; Herrick, 184–86; McDermott and Salvan, 9–12; N.O. Death Certificate (1887), 91:257, NOPL; Tinker, *Ecrits*, 475.

TRUDEAU, JUST. (Juste)
Born N.O. 1826; died N.O. Dec. 2, 1875.
Sculptor, artist, active N.O. 1849–68.
Contemporary listings: sculptor (1849–50, 1866); artist, 205 Greatmen (1851–54); sculptor, with HORTAIRE GUENARD, 234 Camp (1851).
Exhibited: Bank of Louisiana (1866); Stapleton & Co., and E. A. Tyler's jewelry store (1867); International Exposition, Paris (1867).
Self–taught sculptor who worked in clay and made plaster casts from the clay models.
References: NOCD 1846, 1850–56, 1858–61, 1867–68, 1871–72, 1874–75; *Bee*, Aug. 24, 1850, Dec. 3, 1875; *Courier*, June 27, 1849; *Crescent Monthly*, Nov. 1866, 409; *D. Crescent*, Jan. 8, 1867; *D. Pic.*, Jan. 30, 1867; *Spectator*, Feb. 14, 1851; *Times*, Sept. 28, Nov. 17, 1866, Jan. 27, 1867; Gottheil, 5; Groce and Wallace; LSM, *Biennial Report for 1832–33*, 68; N.O. Death Certificate (1875), 65:76, NOPL; THNOC Cemetery Survey; U.S. Census (1850), roll 238.

TRUEHOLZ, MR. _____
Painter, active N.O. 1854.
Contemporary listings: portrait and historical painter, Mechanics' Institute (1854).
References: *D. Crescent*, Dec. 27, 1854; *D. Pic.*, Dec. 27, 1854.

TRYON, H.
Painter, active N.O. 1871–72.
Contemporary listings: scene painter, New Varieties Theatre (1871–72).
References: *Times*, Nov. 23, 1871.

TUCKER, JIMMIE
Sketch artist, painter, active N.O. ca. 1887–89.
Studied: with WILLIAM JENNINGS WARRINGTON (1887); ACADEMY OF FINE ARTS (1889).
Exhibited: W. J. Warrington's studio (1887); Academy of Fine Arts (1889).
References: *D. Pic.*, Jan. 22, 1889; *T. Demo.*, Oct. 13, 1887.

TUGENDHAFT, CHARLES
Born Austria Apr. 19, 1872; died Covington LA May 4, 1937.
Painter, active N.O. 1905–1908.
Contemporary listings: proprietor, SOUTHERN ART STUDIO (1905); artist (1907); portrait painter, 638 Canal (1908).
References: NOCD 1905, 1907–17, 1919, 1921–25; *T. Pic.*, May 5, 1937; Orleans Parish Registrar of Voters, NOPL.

TULANE DECORATIVE ART LEAGUE FOR WOMEN (Ladies' Decorative Art League)
Art association, active N.O. 1885–99.
First organized in the fall of 1885 as the Ladies' Decorative Art League to continue the work of the Woman's Department of the World's Industrial and Cotton Centennial Exposition (1884–85). Its purpose was to foster native talent by exhibiting and teaching decorative arts; it was also a commercial venture and sold its members' creations. Classes were taught by ELLSWORTH WOODWARD and WILLIAM WOODWARD. Located at 249 Baronne, the league worked in conjunction with the NEW ORLEANS ART POTTERY COMPANY by providing designs. In 1886 the Tulane Decorative

Art League for Women developed out of the classes of the Ladies' Decorative Art League. The major forms of instruction were art pottery, woodcarving, design, wallpaper, and art embroidery. The FIVE OR MORE CLUB had its headquarters on the third floor of the league's building. In 1899 the league disbanded, and its functions were assumed by NEWCOMB COLLEGE.

References: *D. Pic.*, Feb. 12, 1888; *D. States*, Dec. 23, 1888; *Men and Matters*, Sept. 1897, 49–50; Kendall, *History*, 2:661; Ormond and Irvine, 11–14, 19, 22; Poesch, *Newcomb Pottery*, 12–13, 28; Smithsonian, *Newcomb Pottery*, 4; Stevens, 2; Tulane Decorative Art League.

TULANE FREE DRAWING CLASSES
Art school, active N.O. 1885–94.
Free art classes organized by WILLIAM WOODWARD for Tulane University and its associated high school. Woodward had given similar art instruction at the World's Industrial and Cotton Centennial Exposition (1884–85) and set up the Tulane classes when the fair closed. Beginning Nov. 1, 1885, night classes were held twice weekly in a building on Lafayette and Dryades. Intended for working men who could not attend the regular day classes, courses included free-hand drawing, mechanical drawing, and school methods. Saturday drawing classes for teachers were added on Jan. 1, 1886. In 1887 a women's decorative art class began meeting two nights a week. At the completion of a session, students were given certificates, awarded prizes, and their work was shown at an exhibition. The classes ceased in 1894 when Tulane moved to the present campus on St. Charles.

References: *Eve. Chronicle*, May 22, 1886; *T. Demo.*, Jan. 6–7, 1886, Oct. 13, 1887, Oct. 6, 1894; Poesch, *Newcomb Pottery*, 12, 13.

TUPPER, MARY BALLARD. *See* BALLARD, MARY

TURBERG, PIERRE F. *See* FEUSIER & TURBERG

TUREAUD, MISS or MRS. F.
Painter, active N.O. ca. 1890–93.
Exhibited: ARTISTS' ASSOCIATION OF NEW ORLEANS (1890, 1892).

Memberships/positions: Artists' Association of New Orleans (1890, 1893).

References: *Current Topics*, Jan. 1891, 25, Jan. 1893, 11; *D. Pic.*, Nov. 13, Dec. 17, 1890, Dec. 13, 1892; *T. Demo.*, Dec. 13, 1892; AANO, *Catalogue* (1890); Wiesendanger, 101.

TURLER, JOSEPH
Born Germany ca. 1810; died N.O. Feb. 2, 1856.
Lithographer, active N.O. 1856.
Contemporary listings: lithographer (1856).
References: Louisiana Charity Hospital, Death Records, NOPL.

TURNER, HELEN MARIA
Born Louisville KY Nov. 13, 1858; died N.O. Jan. 31, 1958.
Painter, art teacher, active N.O. ca. 1880–93, 1926–49.
Studied: TULANE FREE DRAWING CLASSES (1886); ARTISTS' ASSOCIATION OF NEW ORLEANS (1886–93); with BROR ANDERS WIKSTROM and ANDRES MOLINARY; with Kenyon Cox, William Merritt Chase, and Douglas Volk, Art Students League, N.Y.C. (1895–99); with Douglas Volk, Cooper Union Women's Art School, N.Y.C. (1898–1901, 1904–1905); Columbia University, N.Y.C. (ca. 1899–1904).
Exhibited: Artists' Association of New Orleans (1886–87, 1889–96); New York Water Color Club (1897); Pennsylvania Academy of Fine Arts, Philadelphia (1898, 1913); Society of American Artists (1900, 1904); American Society of Miniature Painters (after 1900); Pennsylvania Society of Miniature Painters (after 1900); National Academy of Design, N.Y.C. (1906); Gimbel Brothers department store, N.Y.C. (1912); MacBeth Gallery (1916); Milch Gallery (1917); Exhibition of Contemporary American Paintings, Corcoran Gallery, Washington DC (1917); City Museum of St. Louis, MO (1917); Rehn, Ferargil and Grand Central Art Galleries, N.Y.C. (after 1917); City Club, N.Y.C.

Awarded: Cooper Union, N.Y.C., bronze medal (1899); New York Woman's Art Club, Elling prize for landscape (1910); Association of Painters and Sculptors, National Arts prize (1913); National Academy of Design, Julia A. Shaw Memorial Prize (1913); National Association of Women Painters and Sculptors, John G. Agar prize (1913); Art Institute of Chicago, honorable mention (1913); Panama–Pacific International Exposition, San Francisco (1915).

Memberships/positions: Artists' Association of New Orleans (1893, 1896); Art Students League, N.Y.C. (1897); National Academy of Design, associate (1913), academician (1921); National Arts Club, N.Y.C.; American Artists Professional League; New York Water Color Club.

Portrait, landscape, and still life painter who first came to N.O. with her family in 1866. Turner began painting at age 22 and exhibited regularly at the Artists' Association between 1886 and 1896. In 1893 she left N.O. to become an art instructor at St. Mary's Institute, a girls school in Dallas TX. In 1895 she moved to N.Y.C. where in 1902 she began to teach in the art school of the YWCA, a position she held until retiring in 1919. Between 1906 and 1941 she lived during the summers in Cragsmoor NY where a community of artists had been established. In October 1926 she returned to N.O. to teach the class in draped model drawing at the Arts and Crafts Club. She exhibited in N.O. throughout the 1930s, but her production dwindled when she developed cataracts; her last painting was done in 1949.

References: NOCD 1928, 1931–33, 1935, 1938, 1940, 1942, 1954–55; *Current Topics*, Jan. 1891, 25, June 1891, 23, Jan. 1892, 24, Jan. 1893, 10, Nov. 1893, 198; *D. Pic.*, Nov. 7, 1886, May 7, 1887, Dec. 17, 1889, Nov. 13, Dec. 17, 1890, Apr. 29, May 22, Dec. 17, 1891, Dec. 13, 1892; *D. States*, May 16, Dec. 17, 1890; *Eve. Chronicle*, May 22, 1886; *Item*, Feb. 8, Apr. 8, 1949, Jan. 31, 1958; *Item–Trib.*, Feb. 5, 1928, Aug. 3, 1930, Mar. 12, 1933; *Morn. Trib.*, Oct. 6, 1926, Jan. 26, 1927, Sept. 1, 1930, Apr. 27, 1931; *Review*, May 27, 1891; *States*, Feb. 7, 1949, Jan. 31, Feb. 1, 1958; *T. Demo.*, Nov. 13, Dec. 17, 1890, Dec. 13, 1892, Dec. 14, 1894; *T. Pic.*, Oct. 18, 1925, Oct. 19, 1926, Jan. 22, 1931, Mar. 14, 1933, Jan. 21, 1934, Sept. 13, Nov. 1, 1936, Jan. 25, Feb. 7, 1937, Jan. 22, 1939, Dec. 12, 1948, Feb. 6, 1949; Collier, "Orleans Artist Delighted With 99th Birthday Party," *T. Pic.*, Nov. 14, 1957; *T. Pic.*, Feb. 1, 1958; *Town Talk*, July 1904, 25; AANO, *Catalogue* (1890, 1891, 1896); AANO, *Charter*; Bénézit; Cragsmoor Free Library; Mount, 136; *NCAB*; New Orleans Art School; Orleans Parish Registrar of Voters, NOPL; *Who's Who in American Art*, 1936–37; *Who's Who in South and Southwest*.

TURNER & COHEN

Colorers, art dealers, active N.O. 1866–67; primarily photographers; Austin Augustus Turner, Warren A. Cohen, partners.

Contemporary listings: photographic colorers and proprietors, fine art gallery (1866); fine art gallery, 57 Camp (1867).

Awarded: Grand State Fair, best porcelain painting (1867).

References: NOCD 1867; *Bee*, Oct. 22, 1866; *D. Pic.*, July 7, Nov. 13, 1866; Mechanics' and Agricultural Fair, *Report* (1867):27; Smith and Tucker, 138–40.

TUTTLE, CHARLES F.

Born OH ca. 1841–42; died Nov. 26, 1893.

Engraver, active N.O. 1869–93; also decorator.

Contemporary listings: wood engraver, 19 Commercial Pl. (1869); wood engraver, 61 Camp (1870–71); engraver (1874, 1887–88, 1892); wood engraver (1875); engraver, 199 Baronne (1876); engraver, 62 St. Philip (1877); engraver, 168 Camp (1879); wood engraver, 127 Caron-

delet (1879–80); engraver, 107 St. Charles (1880); BOEHLER & TUTTLE (1881); wood engraver, 163 Baronne (1885).
References: NOCD 1870, 1874–77, 1879–81, 1885–88, 1891–92; NOBD 1889; *Southern Monthly*, Aug. 1869, 86, front and back covers; Boyd, 8; N.O. Death Certificate (1893), 105:298, NOPL; U.S. Census (1870), roll 519, (1880), roll 459.

TUTTLE, H. MORRIS
Painter, active N.O. 1909–10.
Contemporary listings: scenic artist, Dauphine Street Theatre (1909–10).
References: *D. News*, Aug. 20, 1909.

TUVE & LECOURT
Engravers, active N.O. 1831; also printers.
Contemporary listings: engravers, cor. Bourbon and St. Philip (1831).
References: *Mercantile Advertiser*, Aug. 6, 1831.

TUZO, MISS J.
Art teacher, painter, active N.O. 1881–82.

Contemporary listings: teacher of watercolor and porcelain painting, SOUTHERN ART UNION (1881); teacher of watercolor, china, silk, and satin painting, Southern Art Union (1882). Exhibited: Southern Art Union (1882).
Reported to have been from NY when she became a part of the Southern Art Union's faculty (1881).
References: *Bee*, Oct. 29, 1881, Nov. 16, 1881–Jan. 20, 1882 (advs.); *D. Pic.*, Nov. 15, 1881–Jan. 12, 1882 (advs.), Feb. 15, 1882; *States*, Jan. 23, 1882.

TYLER, EDMOND GODDARD
Born ca. May 1858; died Suspension Bridge NY Aug. 3, 1882.
Painter, active N.O. ca. 1868.
Awarded: Grand State Fair, honorable mention for best painting in watercolors (1868).
References: *D. Pic.*, Jan. 9, 14, 19, 1868, Aug. 5, 1882; Mechanics' and Agricultural Fair Asso., *Report* (1868):41.

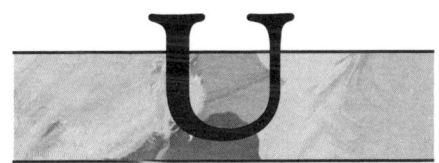

ULLRICH, EDMUND W.
Born Ironton OH Apr. 22, 1889; died N.O. Oct. 13, 1951.
Painter, active N.O. 1913–18.
Contemporary listings: artist (1913).
Exhibited: ART ASSOCIATION OF NEW ORLEANS (1914–15, 1918).
Memberships/positions: Art Association of New Orleans (1914).
Later listed as manager of Pittsburgh Plate Glass Co. (1914–18) and president of the E. W. Ullrich Glass Co., Inc. (1920–32).
References: NOCD 1912–33, 1938, 1940, 1942, 1945–46, 1949, 1952–53; *T. Pic.*, Oct. 14, 1951; Art Asso., *Catalogue* (1914, 1918); Art Asso., *Special Exhibition*; Orleans Parish Registrar of Voters, NOPL.

ULRICH, FREDERICK
Lithographer, active N.O. 1875; also silversmith, gilder, cabinetmaker.
Contemporary listings: lithographer, with DIONIS SIMON (1875).
References: NOCD 1866–73, 1875–84.

UNIACKE, MRS. WILLIAM E., JR.
Painter, active N.O. ca. 1901–1904.
Contemporary listings: portrait painter (1904).
Exhibited: ARTISTS' ASSOCIATION OF NEW ORLEANS (1901).
References: *T. Domo*, Dec. 3, 1901, May 24, 1904; AANO, *Catalogue* (1901).

UNIACKE, WILLIAM E., JR.
Born Summit MS June 1861; died N.O. Apr. 19, 1912.
Painter, active N.O. 1878–1911; primarily sign and ornamental painter.
Contemporary listings: painter (1878); painter, WILLIAM E. UNIACKE, SR. (1879–92, 1894); painter, 122 Exchange Pl. (1895–1907, 1909–11); fresco painter, 122 Exchange Pl. (1902).
Successor in 1887 to the firm of his father, William E. Uniacke, Sr., he was also the Orleans Parish criminal

sheriff (1897–99). His son William L. Uniacke continued as a painter in the firm of Uniacke & Ollie.
References: NOCD 1878–1912; *D. Pic.*, Apr. 19–21, 1912; *D. States*, Feb. 10, 1902; N.O. Death Certificate (1912), 154:940, NOPL.

UNIACKE, WILLIAM E., SR.
Born County Cork, Ireland ca. 1829; died N.O. Dec. 28, 1894.
Painter, active N.O. 1852–87; primarily sign and ornamental painter, gilder.
Contemporary listings: Uniacke & Nugent, painters, 109 Poydras (1852); painter, 109 Poydras (1853–56); painter, 16 Exchange Pl. (1860–61); painter, 14 Exchange Pl. (1866–67, 1869, 1876–93); UNIACKE & KONRAD (1870–75).
Came to N.O. in 1847. In 1887 he was succeeded by his son WILLIAM E. UNIACKE, JR.
References: NOCD 1852–56, 1860–61, 1866–94; *Bee*, Sept. 27, 1859; *D. Crescent*, Jan. 5, 1855, Jan. 7, 1867; *D. Item*, Dec. 29, 1894; *D. Pic.*, Dec. 30, 1894; *D. States*, Feb. 10, 1902; *D. True Delta*, Aug. 1–2, 1865 (advs.); Land, 97; N.O. Death Certificate (1894), 107:768, NOPL.

UNIACKE & KONRAD
Painters, active N.O. 1870–75; also sign painters, gilders; WILLIAM E. UNIACKE, SR., Adolph D. Konrad, partners.
Contemporary listings: fresco and banner painters, 14 Exchange Pl. (1870–71); painters, 14 Exchange Pl. (1872–75).
Awarded: Grand State Fair, diploma for best anatomical drawing (1870).
References: NOCD 1871–75; Mechanics' and Agricultural Fair, *Report* (1870):67; THNOC 85–82–L.

UNION GALLERY OF ART. *See* GALVANI, CHARLES

UPHAM, CHARLES
Sketch artist, illustrator, active N.O. ca. 1883–91.

Staff artist for *Frank Leslie's Illustrated Newspaper* who first came to N.O. in 1883 on a trip through the South with Mrs. Leslie and another staff artist, JAMES NAGLE. Upham returned to N.O. to make drawings for illustrations in *Leslie's* of the World's Industrial and Cotton Centennial Exposition (published Dec. 1884–Jan. 1885) and probably again in 1891 for views of the French Market (published April 4, 1891).
References: Stern, 111; THNOC 1982.92, 1982.104–.106, 1983.196.

URQUHART, ALICE ROSALIE
Born NY Sept. 27, 1854; died N.O. Feb. 21, 1922.
Art craftsman, art teacher, illustrator, active N.O. 1886–1922.
Studied: NEWCOMB COLLEGE (1887, 1890–93, 1896–97, 1900–1908).
Contemporary listings: teacher (1898–1904, 1908, 1915, 1917, 1920); artist (1905–1906, 1913, 1916).
Exhibited: Tulane University (1890, 1892–93); ARTISTS' ASSOCIATION OF NEW ORLEANS (1890–92, 1894, 1896, 1901); Columbian Exposition, Chicago (1893); Newcomb Art Alumnae Association (1909–10, 1913–14); Newcomb (1911); Atlanta GA.
Memberships/positions: FIVE OR MORE CLUB (1892–93).
One of the first women in the crafts program at Newcomb whose training led to a part–time career. After receiving her diploma from Newcomb, Urquhart continued as a graduate art student (1901–1903), as a student in the pottery design class (1900–1908), and as an art craftsman (1908–17). During these years, she produced a variety of crafts that were sold locally, including decorated pottery, metalwork, bookplates, hand–painted postcards, and pictorial calendars, her own innovation. Her most noted paintings were watercolors of landscapes and still lifes. Seven of her pastel drawings were used as illustrations in the book *Diary of a Refugee* (1910), a Civil War account. For most of her life, Urquhart was listed as a teacher and for a few years (1899–1904) taught with her sister ELISE URQUHART.
References: NOCD 1894–95, 1897–1906, 1908, 1913, 1915–17, 1920, 1922; *Current Topics*, Jan 1891, 25, Jan. 1892, 24, Jan. 1893, 10; *D. Pic.*, Feb. 14, Dec. 17, 1890, Dec. 17, 1891, Mar. 3, Dec. 13, 1892, Feb. 14, 1893, Sept. 1, 1895, Dec. 26, 1909; *D. States*, Dec. 17, 1890; *Harlequin*, June 23, 1904, 8; *Item*, Feb. 21, 1922; *T. Demo.*, Mar. 3, Dec. 18, 1892, Dec. 14, 1894, Feb. 22, 1914; AANO, *Catalogue* (1890, 1891, 1896, 1901); Coulter, *Travels*, 91; Fearn; Jumonville, 171; Mount, 210; Ormond and Irvine, 84, 86, 90-91, 170-71; Poesch, *Newcomb Pottery*, 13, 34, 40, 66-67, 105, 121, 128, 143; U.S. Census (1910), roll 524.

URQUHART, MISS E.
Artist, active N.O. ca. 1890.
Studied: ARTISTS' ASSOCIATION OF NEW ORLEANS (1890).
Exhibited: Artists' Association of New Orleans (1890).
Cf. URQUHART, ELISE; URQUHART, EMMA J.
References: *D. States*, May 16, 1890.

URQUHART, ELISE
Born LA ca. 1858; died N.O. Nov. 8, 1912.
Art teacher, active N.O. 1910.
Contemporary listings: artist (1910).
Listed as a teacher (1899–1912), she was principal of her own private school at 4913 St. Charles, where her sister, ALICE ROSALIE URQUHART, also taught. *Cf.* URQUHART, MISS E.
References: NOCD 1894–95, 1898–1906, 1908, 1912–13; *D. Pic.*, Nov. 9, 17, 1912; N.O. Death Certificate (1912), 156:223, NOPL; U.S. Census (1910), roll 524.

URQUHART, EMMA J.
Born 1865; died Dec. 8, 1929.
Art craftsman, active N.O. ca. 1901–17.
Studied: NEWCOMB COLLEGE (1901–1909).
Primarily a pottery decorator. *Cf.* URQUHART, MISS E.
References: NOCD 1920; Ormond and Irvine, 171; Poesch, *Newcomb Pottery*, 105.

UTER, LAURENT
Born Lorraine, France ca. 1814; died
N.O. Jan. 24, 1891.
Art dealer, engraver, active N.O. ca.
1868–91; also gilder, publisher.
Contemporary listings: 159 Main
(1843); 78 Toulouse (1849–50); 87
Chartres (1851–59); 77 Chartres
(1860–61); 49 Royal (1866–70); engraver, 49 Royal (1869); 135 Canal
(1871–74); 38 Royal (1875–81); 47
Royal (1882–91).
First listed in N.O. in 1843, Uter became an importer of French mirrors
by 1854 and a framemaker by 1855.
After the Civil War, he also imported
engravings and artwork made in
France. In 1868 Uter advertised the
sale of a series of four lithographs
issued by A. L. Boimare, a publisher
in Paris who had worked in N.O.
1823–60. The lithographs, dedicated to Gen. P. G. T. Beauregard,
were subjects in LA history and were
to be accompanied by a text in French
and English. Uter's store periodically
exhibited paintings for sale by N.O.
artists and was a major outlet of the
work of JOHN GENIN. Uter eventually
became one of the largest art dealers
in the city and sold oil paintings, art
prints, frames, and artists' supplies;
he continued his business until his
death.
References: NOCD 1843, 1849–58,
1860–61, 1866–91, 1895; D. Pic.,
Sept. 29, 1868; D. States, Mar. 27,
1888; Repub., May 20, 1874; Boimare; Information courtesy Florence
M. Jumonville; N.O. Death Certificate (1891), 98:160, NOPL; THNOC
1970.1; U.S. Census (1860), roll 421.

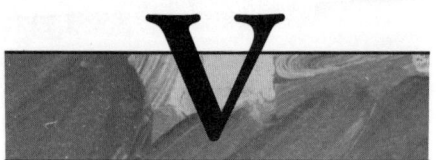

V

VALENCIA, ANTONIO H.
Lithographer, active N.O. 1884–87.
Contemporary listings: lithographer
(1884, 1887); lithographer, with M.
CAPO (1885).
References: NOCD 1884–85, 1887;
"Tchomboli," Sheet Music Collection, LA Coll., TU.

VALENTINE, _____
Painter, active N.O. 1839.
Exhibited: Plough's Museum, St.
Charles (1839).
With JOSEPH LOUIS FIRMIN CERVEAU
exhibited their dioramas including
the *Fairy Grotto*.
References: *Courier*, June 7, 1839.

VALFRAMBERT, MARZILIE
Art teacher, sketch artist, active N.O.
1822–23.
Contemporary listings: teacher of
drawing, convent of the Ladies of St.
Ursula (1822).
References: NOCD 1823; *Courier*,
May 6–8, 1822 (advs.), Nov. 1, 1822;
Groce and Wallace.

VALLEE, JEAN FRANÇOIS DE
Born France.
Painter, active N.O. ca. 1808–18.
Came to the U.S. in 1785 to open a
cotton mill near Alexandria VA. After it failed, Valleé became an itinerant miniature and portrait painter
and silhouettist who worked in
Charleston SC (1790s, 1803, 1805–
1806), Philadelphia (1794, 1797–
98), N.O., and Boston (1826, 1828).
Valleé's work in N.O. included a
miniature of Andrew Jackson painted
at his request after the Battle of N.O.
(1815). It was presented by Jackson
to N.O. lawyer Edward Livingston as
a token of friendship and esteem. *Cf.*
VALLEE, P. R.
References: Bolton, *Painters in Miniature*, 166; Carolina Art Association; Fielding, *Dictionary*; Groce and
Wallace; Emily Jackson, *Silhouette*,
53, 150; James, *Border Captain*,
betw. 280–81; LSM, *Annual Report
for 1919*, 28, 58; LSM, *Biennial Report for 1920–21*, 37; LSM, *Biennial
Report for 1932–33*, 36; Orleans Parish School Board, 26; THNOC
1975.143.1, 1983.55; WPA,
"Lives"; WPA, *Miniatures*, 5–6.

VALLEE, P. R.
Painter, art teacher, sketch artist, active N.O. 1810–12.
Contemporary listings: miniature
painter, house of Mr. Pedesclaux, cor.
St. Peter and Royal (1810); miniature painter, teacher of drawing and
miniature painting, 15 Royal, house
of Mr. Devaise (1812).
Painter of portraits in miniature. *Cf.*
VALLEE, JEAN FRANCOIS DE.
References: *Courier*, Sept. 5, 1810,
Oct. 10–17, 1810 (advs.); Feb. 26–
Apr. 10, 1812 (advs.); Friends of the
Cabildo, *250 Years*, 37; Glenk, 79;
Groce and Wallace; Huber et al., 90;
Thompson, "Checklist"; WPA,
"Lives."

VALLIERE, ADELE
Artist, active N.O. 1841.
Contemporary listings: artist, Treme
betw. Main and St. Ann (1841).
References: NOCD 1841–42.

VALSON, HENRY J.
Sculptor, active N.O. 1869.
Contemporary listings: sculptor,
Water betw. 3rd and 4th (1869).
References: NOCD 1869.

VAN BETS, JOHN L. M.
Artist, active N.O. 1893.
Contemporary listings: artist (1893).
References: NOCD 1893.

VAN BLON, E. *See* LATROBE, JOHN
HAZELHURST BONEVAL

R. V. VAN DALSON & CO.
Painters, active N.O. 1845; also sign
painters, gilders, glaziers.
Contemporary listings: heraldry
painting, 15 Circus betw. Common
and Gravier (1845).
References: *D. Tropic*, May 17–July
1, 1845 (advs.).

VANDERDOES, ALEXIE
Artist, active N.O. 1830.
Contemporary listings: artist, 141 St.
Peter (1830).
References: NOCD 1830, 1832.

VANDERHOOF, CHARLES A.
Died Locust Point NJ Apr. 1, 1918.
Etcher.
Painter and writer who improved the
process of drypoint etching. He
worked mostly for *Century Magazine*, as well as for *Harper's Weekly*,
and later became an etcher and book
illustrator. He produced an etched
view of N.O. depicting cotton being
loaded at N.O. wharves (ca. 1885–
90).
References: Johnson and Buel, 2:xii,
207; Kelly, 8, 63, 138; Sears, 392–
94; THNOC 1947.18.

VANDERLYN, JOHN
Born Kingston NY Oct. 15, 1775;
died Kingston Sept. 23, 1852.
Painter, copyist, active N.O. 1821,
1828.
Studied: with Jacques–Louis David,
Paris; with François Andre Vincent,
Paris (1796); Columbian Academy of
Archibald Robertson, NY; with Gilbert Stuart (ca. 1796); Paris (1796–
1801).
Exhibited: Salon, Paris (1800, 1804,
1810); Wadsworth Athenaeum, Boston (after 1804); N.Y.C. (1815);
American Academy, N.Y.C. (1816);
Baltimore MD (1820); cor. St. Louis
and Royal (1821); Philadelphia PA
(1821); Savannah GA (1822);
Charleston SC (1822–23); Boston
(1826); Chartres, and cor. of Royal
and St. Ann (1828); Rampart and Orleans (1828); Havana, Cuba (1829).
Portrait, historical, and landscape
painter who studied and worked in
the U.S. and Europe, particularly
Paris and Rome. While in Europe, he
painted his two most important
works, *Marius Amid the Ruins of Carthage* and *Ariadne*. The latter, the first
important painting of a nude figure
by an American artist, created a
scandal when first exhibited in N.Y.C.
after Vanderlyn's return to the U.S.
in 1815. From Mar. to May 1821, he
was in N.O. exhibiting his paintings,
including his two masterpieces, and
painting portraits at his studio on
Royal and St. Louis. According to
N.O. businessman Edward Fenno,
the exhibition was not profitable.

JOHN JAMES AUDUBON was also in N.O.
in the spring of 1821. He showed a
portfolio of his bird drawings to Vanderlyn, who wrote a letter of com-
mendation (Mar. 20). Audubon com-
mented favorably on Vanderlyn's
portrait of Andrew Jackson (Apr. 27).
Although primarily a portrait painter,
Vanderlyn was one of the first American artists to paint and exhibit panoramas in the U.S. In Jan. 1828, he
returned to N.O. with *Ariadne* and
on Mar. 7 opened his famous panorama, the *Palace and Garden of Versailles*, first exhibited in N.Y.C. in
1819. Displayed in a specially constructed building in the public square
on Rampart and Orleans, it was probably the first large panorama seen in
N.O. It is said that while in the city,
Vanderlyn tried unsuccessfully to
raise funds for a panorama of the Battle of N.O. It has been claimed that
Vanderlyn returned to N.O. in the
1840s to paint portraits and that he
exhibited the Versailles panorama at
Oak Alley plantation in St. James
Parish LA (1847).
References: *Bee*, Feb. 25, Mar. 6,
1828; *Courier*, Mar. 9–Apr. 2, 1821
(advs.), June 8–10, 1824 (advs.), Jan.
28, Mar. 8, Apr. 5, 30, 1828, Aug.
3, 1843, Feb. 28, 1855; *Comm. Bull.*,
Oct. 11, 1852; *D. Crescent*, June 5,
1851; *D. Delta*, Oct. 30, 1845; *D.
Pic.*, Aug. 3, 1843, Oct. 1, 1845, Feb.
24, 1855; *D. True Delta*, Oct. 5,
1852; *Gazette*, Apr. 5, 1821, Oct. 3,
1820; *Wkly. Delta*, Nov. 3, 1845,
Oct. 19, 1846; Alexander Adams,
235–36; Arthur, *Audubon*, 277–81;
J. J. Audubon, *Journal*, 143–46, 154;
Bolton, *Draughtsmen*, 93–94; Cline,
Storms, 126; Edward Fenno to James
Fenno, Mar. 5, 1821, Edward Fenno
Papers, William L. Clements Li-
brary; Fielding, *Dictionary*; Fowble,
111–12, 120; Glenk, 63, 79; Groce
and Wallace; Holzer, 1030–39;
McGinnis, 40–87; Museum of Fine
Arts, 1:291.

VAN DER WEYDE, GERTRUDE
Painter, active N.O. ca. 1891–92.
Studied: NEWCOMB COLLEGE (1892).

Exhibited: ARTISTS' ASSOCIATION OF NEW ORLEANS (1891–92); Tulane University (1892).
References: *Current Topics*, Jan. 1892, 24, Jan. 1893, 10; *D. City Item*, Dec. 17, 1891; *D. Pic.*, Dec. 17, 1891; *T. Demo.*, Mar. 3, Dec. 13, 1892.

VAN HAELEN, JOHN B.
Died ca. 1896.
Painter, active N.O. 1870–91.
Contemporary listings: painter (1870, 1877, 1879–81); fresco painter (1876, 1878, 1889–91).
References: NOCD 1870, 1876–87, 1889–93, 1897.

VAN LOO, PIERRE
Born Ghent, Belgium ca. 1827; died N.O. Feb. 2, 1858.
Painter, active N.O. 1858.
Contemporary listings: artist, Orleans Theatre (1858).
References: *Bee*, Feb. 3, 1858; *Courier*, Feb. 3, 1858; Groce and Wallace.

VAN PALLANDT, ADOLPHE
Artist, active N.O. 1889.
Contemporary listings: artist (1889).
References: NOCD 1889.

VAN THORSEN, PETER H.
Born N.O. ca. 1851; died N.O. Feb. 5, 1908.
Painter, active N.O. 1880–1908; also decorator.
Contemporary listings: painter (1880–84, 1886, 1888, 1891–98, 1900–1905, 1907–1908); fresco painter (1880, 1885, 1887, 1889–90).
References: NOCD 1880–1905, 1907–1908; *D. Pic.*, Feb. 6, 9, 1908; N.O. Death Certificate (1908), 143:105, NOPL; U.S. Census (1880), roll 458.

VAN VOOTH, MEPHO
Painter, active N.O. 1888–89.
Contemporary listings: fresco painter, 254 Magazine (1888); fresco painter (1889).
References: NOCD 1888–89.

VANNUCHI, MR. S. (Von Vannuchi)
Born Italy ca. 1800–1803.
Sculptor, active N.O. 1852–62.
Contemporary listings: wax works (1854); Vannuchi's Museum, 52 St.

Charles (1855); Vannuchi's Museum, 107 St. Charles (1855–61); Vannuchi's Museum, St. Charles (1862).
Exhibited: Charleston SC (1845); N.Y.C. and Philadelphia (1847); Commercial Hall (1852–53).
Proprietor of Vannuchi's Wax Museum (1855–62) where his wax figures were exhibited in tableaux representing current events.
References: NOCD 1855, 1858–61; NOBD 1858–59; *Bee*, Jan. 3, 1853, Nov. 15, 1856, Jan. 24–Feb. 24, 1862 (advs.), Jan. 25, 1862; *Courier*, Mar. 4, 1856; *D. Crescent*, Nov. 17, 1852, Oct. 18, Nov. 14, 1855, Oct. 27, 1856, Nov. 3, 1858; *D. Creole*, Feb. 26, 1857; *D. Delta*, Nov. 22, 1854, Dec. 9–Dec. 14, 1855, Apr. 17, 1856, Mar. 12, 1861; *D. Orleanian*, Nov. 23–24, Dec. 21, 1852; *D. Pic.*, Sept. 20, 1855, Nov. 8–9, 1855 (advs.), Nov. 9–11, 1855, Oct. 28–Nov. 18, 1857 (advs.), Nov. 10, 1857, Feb. 4–Feb. 21, 1858 (advs.), Oct. 25, 1859, Feb. 7, 1860; *D. True Delta*, Dec. 9, 1855, Feb. 29, 1856, Nov. 8, 1860–Mar. 8, 1861 (advs.), Mar. 7, 1861; *T. Demo.*, Sept. 24, 1913; Groce and Wallace; U.S. Census (1860), roll 417.

VARGAS, ADELINA (Mrs. Alexander Mastio)
Born Mexico City, Mexico ca. 1869; died N.O. Mar. 25, 1945.
Sculptor, active N.O. ca. 1879–1934.
Contemporary listings: sculptor, 2103 Magazine (1906–1907).
Assisted her father, FRANCISCO VARGAS, SR., and family in the business of making wax sculptures. She was particularly adept at dressing the wax figures and worked on the clothing for their Mexican peasant dolls displayed at the World's Industrial and Cotton Centennial Exposition (1884–85). She first suggested the modeling of black characters to represent N.O. street vendors and working class people. Beginning ca. 1900, they became popular to the exclusion of the earlier Mexican and religious figures. Half–sister of FRANCISCO JR., JESUS, CONCEPCION, and MARIA VARGAS.

References: NOCD 1906–1907; *T. Pic.*, Dec. 1, 1915; Mar. 26, 1945; Interviews with August Alfaro, May 17, 1984, Mar. 26, 1986; U.S. Census (1880), roll 462.

VARGAS, CONCEPCION (Mrs. Carlos Alfonso)

Born Mexico 1858; died N.O. 1933. Sculptor, active N.O. ca. 1879–1933. Contemporary listings: sculptor, 2103 Magazine (1906–1908); artist, 1054 Camp (1909); artist, 525 Howard (1912–15).

Daughter of FRANCISCO VARGAS, SR. who worked in the family's wax modeling business. Her speciality was creating wax flowers, fruits, vegetables, and foods as still–life sculptures and as accessories for their wax figures. She assisted in creating examples of Mexican peasant life displayed at the World's Industrial and Cotton Centennial Exposition (1884–85) and also helped with other special commissions. Vargas continued wax sculpting all her life. Mother of LUCY ALFONSO ALFARO ROSADO; grandmother of August Alfaro who carried on the family tradition; sister of JESUS and FRANCISCO VARGAS, JR.; half–sister of ADELINA and MARIA VARGAS.

References: NOCD 1906–15; *T. Demo.*, June 12, 1887; Interviews with August Alfaro, May 17, 1984, Mar. 26, 1986.

FRANCISCO VARGAS & SON

Sculptors, active N.O. 1878, 1886; FRANCISCO VARGAS, SR., JESUS VARGAS, partners.

Contemporary listings: artists, 165 Marais (1878); sculptors, 120 Royal (1886).

References: NOCD 1878, 1886.

FRANCISCO VARGAS & SONS

Sculptors, active N.O. 1882–85; FRANCISCO VARGAS, SR., FRANCISCO VARGAS, JR., JESUS VARGAS, partners.

Contemporary listings: wax works, 124 Royal (1882–85).

References: NOCD 1882–85; *D. Pic.*, Jan 13, 1884.

VARGAS, FRANCISCO, JR.

Born Mexico ca. 1849–58. Sculptor, active N.O. ca. 1875–85.

Contemporary listings: sculptor (1880); FRANCISCO VARGAS & SONS (1882–85).

Said to have moved to Los Angeles CA and probably lived there the rest of his life. Son of FRANCISCO VARGAS, SR.; brother of JESUS and CONCEPCION VARGAS; half–brother of ADELINA and MARIA VARGAS.

References: NOCD 1880, 1882–85; Interviews with August Alfaro, May 17, 1984, Mar. 26, 1986.

VARGAS, FRANCISCO, SR.

Born Mexico City, Mexico Sept. ca. 1824–25; died N.O. Nov. 30, 1915. Sculptor, art teacher, active N.O. ca. 1875–1915.

Contemporary listings: FRANCISCO VARGAS & SON (1878, 1886); sculptor (1880, 1899–1908, 1910–16); FRANCISCO VARGAS & SONS (1882–85); sculptor, 120 Royal (1887–89); sculptor, 112 Royal (1890–94); sculptor, 603 Royal (1895–96); sculptor, 537 Royal (1897–98); sculptor, 511 Royal (1909).

Exhibited: World's Industrial and Cotton Centennial Exposition (1884–85); Pan–American Exposition, Buffalo NY (1901); Louisiana Purchase Exposition, St. Louis MO (1904).

Sculptor who came to the U.S. from Puebla, Mexico, where he had learned the art of wax modeling from a Jesuit priest. He went by covered wagon to Galveston TX, N.O. (ca. 1875), N.Y.C., Buffalo NY, and back to N.O. (1878). Vargas sculpted large works in plaster and clay, small ones in wax (1875–1915) and advertised lessons in wax scupture at 124 Royal (ca. 1882–85). His family business created figures and still lifes using beeswax over wood armatures which were painted and decorated with bits of fabric dipped in wax. He made plaster molds of the small figures to expedite production and maintained over 150 character types and poses. With assistance from his family, he received and executed numerous special commissions, including Mexican figures for the N.O. exposition (1884–85) and an over 30-foot high interpretation of "King Cotton" for

the St. Louis exposition (1904), which featured a life–size image of the MS commissioner of agriculture sitting on a cotton bale throne. Vargas was married three times and was the father of JESUS, FRANCISCO JR., and CONCEPCION VARGAS by his first wife; ADELINA VARGAS by his second wife; and Alta Gracia and MARIA VARGAS by his third wife, GUADALOUPE LUNA VARGAS. His children, his grand-daughter, LUCY ROSADO, and his great–grandson, August Alfaro, continued the family waxworking business.
References: NOCD 1878, 1880, 1882–99, 1901–16; *D. Pic.*, June 18, 1911; *Item–Trib.*, Feb. 16, 1941; *T. Demo.*, June 12, 1887; *T. Pic.*, Dec. 1, 1915; Interviews with August Alfaro, May 17, 1984, Mar. 26, 1986; N.O. Death Certificate (1915), 165:37, NOPL; THNOC 1967. 22, 1980.125.1; U.S. Census (1880), roll 462, (1900), roll 573.

VARGAS, GUADALOUPE LUNA (Mrs. FRANCISCO VARGAS, SR.)
Born Mexico City, Mexico Dec. 1852–54; died N.O. June 20, 1924.
Sculptor, active N.O. 1918.
Contemporary listings: sculptor (1918).
Third wife of Francisco Vargas, Sr.; mother of MARIA VARGAS. She was possibly Francisca Vargas listed in 1919 as a sculptor.
References: NOCD 1917–21, 1923–24; *T. Pic.*, June 21, 1924; Interviews with August Alfaro, May 17, 1984, Mar. 26, 1986; U.S. Census (1880), roll 462, (1900), roll 573.

VARGAS, JESUS
Born Mexico ca. 1849.
Sculptor, active N.O. 1878–89.
Contemporary listings: FRANCISCO VARGAS & SON (1878, 1886); wax worker (1880); FRANCISCO VARGAS & SONS (1882–85); sculptor (1888–89).
Son of FRANCISCO VARGAS, SR. who supposedly drowned in the N.O. area; brother of FRANCISCO, JR., and CONCEPCION VARGAS; half–brother of ADELINA and MARIA VARGAS.
References: NOCD 1878, 1882–86, 1888–89; Interviews with August

Alfaro, May 17, 1984, Mar. 26, 1986; U.S. Census (1880), roll 462.

VARGAS, MARIA (Mrs. Brooks)
Born LA Aug. 1879.
Sculptor, active N.O. 1914.
Contemporary listings: sculptress (1914).
Daughter of FRANCISCO VARGAS, SR. and GUADALOUPE LUNA VARGAS, who moved to El Paso TX and then returned to N.O. Half–sister of FRANCISCO, JR., JESUS, CONCEPCION, and ADELINA VARGAS.
References: NOCD 1910–12, 1914, 1917–19; Interviews with August Alfaro, May 17, 1984; Mar. 26, 1986; U.S. Census (1880), roll 462, (1900), roll 573.

VARILLAT, LEONCE
Sculptor, active N.O. 1873.
Contemporary listings: sculptor (1873).
References: NOCD 1873.

VARNOUT, MR. _____. *See also* DE-VELLE, LOUIS DOMINIQUE GRAND-JEAN
Painter, active N.O. 1861.
Contemporary listings: scenery painter, Opera House (1861).
References: *D. Crescent*, Jan. 28, 1861; *D. Delta*, Jan. 30, 1861.

VASNIER, J. B.
Engraver, active N.O. 1830.
Contemporary listings: stone engraver, 116 Moreau (1830).
References: NOCD 1830.

VASSELAIS, CHARLES DE LA. *See* DE LA VASSELAIS, CHARLES

VAUDECHAMP, JEAN JOSEPH
Born Rambervillers (Vosges), France 1790; died France 1866.
Painter, active N.O. 1831–39.
Studied: with Anne–Louis Girodet, Paris (before 1812).
Contemporary listings: portrait painter, 147 Royal (1832, 1834–35); portrait painter (1833, 1836); portrait painter, 163 Royal (1837).
Exhibited: Salons, Paris (1817, 1819, 1822, 1824, 1827, 1831, 1835, 1838, 1840–42, 1844–46, 1848).
Awarded: Salon, Paris, third class medal (1843).
Considered the foremost portrait painter in N.O. during the 1830s,

Vaudechamp spent most of his life in Paris and often exhibited portraits and historical subjects in the salons. He also worked in N.O. in the 1830s, usually arriving by Nov. or Dec. to spend the winters painting the city's prominent citizens. Trained in the art studio of Girodet, he painted in the formal academic tradition of the prevailing neoclassical style. His sitters were usually portrayed in a partially turned, half–length pose and the paintings have a finished surface. Vaudechamp is documented in N.O. through extant paintings and newspaper advertisements for every year between 1831 and 1839, except the winter of 1834–35. Dunlap claimed that Vaudechamp was so successful that, after working in N.O. between 1831 and 1834, he went home with $30,000. Vaudechamp was perhaps instrumental in bringing another French portrait painter, JACQUES AMANS, to N.O.: they exhibited at the same Paris salons, traveled to N.O. on the same ships (1836, 1837), and occupied studios in the same block of Royal (1837). Vaudechamp may have returned to N.O. after 1839 since ADOLPH RINCK advertised in Dec. 1840 as a friend of the artist, and a portrait in LA of an unidentified sitter is signed by Vaudechamp and dated 1845.
References: NOCD 1834–35, 1837; *Bee*, Dec. 28, 1833, Jan. 3, 1834, Dec. 4, 1835, Nov. 30–Dec. 1, 1836 (advs.), Dec. 9, 1840; *Courier*, Nov. 28, 1832, Dec. 26, 1833, June 16, 1834, Mar. 21, 1837; Bénézit; *Bryan's*; Dunlap, 2:471, 3:339; Farwell, 371–75; Fielding, *Dictionary*; Glenk, 45–46, 55, 80; Groce and Wallace; LSM, *Annual Report for 1918*, 27, 59; LSM, *Annual Report for 1919*, 27, 61; LSM, *Biennial Report for 1920–21*, 91; LSM, *Biennial Report for 1924–25*, 27, 56; LSM, *Vaudechamp*; Salam, 22–29, 39–41, 94–97, 124–72; THNOC 1981-.376.1; WPA, "Lives"; WPA, "Passenger Lists," (1835):36.

VAUGHT, MARY A. BAYNE (Mrs. D. Albert S. Vaught)
Born ca. 1854; died N.O. Aug. 28, 1921.
Designer, active N.O. 1898.
Designed a scroll (1898) depicting LA's role in the Civil War. Executed by MARIE MADELEINE SEEBOLD, the scroll was placed in the Louisiana Room of the Richmond VA museum.
References: NOCD 1901–1908; *D. States*, July 3, 1898; *T. Pic.*, Aug. 29, 1921.

VAUQUELIN, HENRY F.
Designer, active N.O. 1869; primarily sign and ornamental painter.
Created an illuminated tableau for Ionia Conclave second grand annual ball, with JULES VEQUE (1869).
References: NOCD 1867–77; *Repub.*, Nov. 28, 1869.

VAURIGAUD, A. F.
Art teacher, active N.O. 1882.
Contemporary listings: professor of linear drawing, SOUTHERN ART UNION (1882).
References: *Bee*, Jan. 20, 1882; *D. Pic.*, Jan. 12, 1882.

VEAZIE, H. P.
Painter, active N.O. 1899.
Signed two paintings of teal ducks, made in N.O. (1899).
References: NOCD 1909–10; *T. Demo.*, June 13, 1910.

VEILER, JOSEPH
Sculptor, active N.O. 1838–49.
Contemporary listings: sculptor, 228 Dauphine (1838); sculptor, 230 Dauphine (1841); sculptor, 214 Dauphine (1843–44); sculptor, 214 Dauphine (1849).
References: NOCD 1838, 1841–44, 1849; Groce and Wallace; U.S. Census (1840), roll 132.

VELASQUEZ, _____
Art teacher, sketch artist, active N.O. 1869.
Contemporary listings: teacher of drawing, landscape and portraiture, 394 St. Charles (1869).
References: *Repub.*, Feb. 17, 1869.

VENNE, MR. JUS.
Born ME ca. 1818.
Artist, active N.O. 1850.

Contemporary listings: artist, Tremont Hotel (1850).
References: Groce and Wallace; U.S. Census (1850), roll 234.

VENTADOUR, FANNY. *See* CRAIG, FANNY ESHLEMAN

VEQUE, JULES
Born N.O. ca. 1838; died N.O. Aug. 4, 1882.
Designer, active N.O. 1869; also glazier.
Created an illuminated tableau for Ionia Conclave second grand annual ball, with HENRY F. VAUQUELIN (1869). Listed as painter, probably indicating house painter (1869–71, 1873–78, 1880–82).
References: NOCD 1869–71, 1873–78, 1880–82; *Bee*, Aug. 5, 1882; *Repub.*, Nov. 28, 1869.

VER BRYCK, WILLIAM
Born N.Y.C. 1823; died 1899.
Painter, active N.O. 1870–71.
Contemporary listings: portrait painter, 132 Canal (1870–71).
References: *Times*, May 28, 1871; Bénézit; Boyd, 200; Groce and Wallace.

VERDEREAU, MME. HENRY
Painter, art teacher, active N.O. 1807–13.
Contemporary listings: drawing teacher, cor. St. Philip and Levee (1807); painter, St. Philip (1811); painter, cor. St. Philip and Levee (1813).
Painter of feather fans and also teacher of embroidery and crochet.
References: *Courier*, Apr. 10, 1811; June 30, 1813; *Moniteur*, Nov. 7, 1807.

VERNELLE, BERNARD
Painter, active N.O. 1849–53.
Contemporary listings: portrait painter, 254 Royal (1849–51); portrait painter, Orleans betw. St. Claude and Treme (1852–53).
References: NOCD 1849–53; Glenk, 80; Groce and Wallace.

VERNET, CHARLES
Born France ca. 1820.
Artist, active N.O. 1850.
Contemporary listings: artist (1850).
References: Groce and Wallace; U.S. Census (1850), roll 235.

VIAU, JOSEPH MARC-ANTOINE (Vicaire)
Born Marseilles, France ca. 1809; died N.O. June 29, 1847.
Sculptor, active N.O. 1846; primarily stone cutter, marble cutter.
Contemporary listings: marble sculptor and engraver, 181 Bourbon (1846).
References: NOCD 1842–44, 1846; *Bee*, Jan. 30–Feb. 10, 1841 (advs.), June 30, 1847; Friends of the Cabildo, *N.O. Architecture*, 3:131–32.

VIAVANT, MME. ____
Sketch artist, active N.O. 1885–86.
Exhibited: American Exposition (1885–86).
Possibly Mrs. Emma Viavant, died Covington LA Oct. 19, 1900.
References: NOCD 1891, 1893, 1895–1900; *T. Demo.*, Oct. 21, Oct. 28, 1900; Creole Exhibit, 12.

VIAVANT, GEORGE LOUIS
Born N.O. 1872; died N.O. 1925.
Painter, sketch artist, active N.O. 1891–1921.
Studied: SOUTHERN ART UNION, with ACHILLE PERELLI (ca. 1884–93).
Contemporary listings: painter, Dolhonde (1891); artist, 2437 Columbus (1899); artist–picture (1910).
Exhibited: ART ASSOCIATION OF NEW ORLEANS (1914).
Awarded: World's Industrial and Cotton Centennial Exposition, blue ribbon for landscape (1884–85).
Watercolor painter of *natures mortes*, or works depicting dead animals. In 1884 at the age of 12, he began studying at the Southern Art Union and in that same year, he won an award at the N.O. exposition. In 1899, Viavant moved with his family to a rural area in the eastern sector of N.O. There he concentrated on painting wildlife and landscapes. His daughter Ruby (born N.O. 1904; died N.O. 1925) showed much promise as a painter; however, she died at the age of 21. A few months after her death, Viavant also died.
References: NOCD 1890–91, 1893–96, 1899; *New Orleans*, Dec. 1984, 31, 77; *T. Pic./States-Item*, Jan 9, 1983; Art Asso., *Catalogue* (1914); Bénézit; Bruce Chambers, 63, 70;

Fielding, *Dictionary*; Scrapbook 100:63, LSM; U.S. Census (1910), roll 522; Wiesendanger, 101; WPA, *Louisiana*, 167.

VICAIRE, JOSEPH. *See* VIAU, JOSEPH MARC–ANTOINE

VICTOR, MR. ____
Painter, active N.O. 1828.
Contemporary listings: painter, Orleans Theatre (1828).
References: *Courier*, Mar. 14, 1828.

VIDAL, ____
Art teacher, sketch artist, active N.O. 1855–56.
Contemporary listings: drawing instructor, 189 Common (1855–56).
References: *Courier*, Aug. 31, 1855–Jan. 4, 1856 (advs.).

VIDAL, E.
Lithographer, active N.O. ca. 1869–78.
Contemporary listings: lithographer, 8 St. Louis (ca. 1869–78).
References: THNOC 1949.1.4, 1949.1.9, 1949.1.23.

VILLERE, ELMIRE M.
Artist, active N.O. 1899–1905.
Contemporary listings: artist (1899–1905).
Exhibited: Louisiana Purchase Exposition, St. Louis MO (1904).
Memberships/positions: ART ASSOCIATION OF NEW ORLEANS (1905).
Listed as a teacher (1894, 1898, 1907–1908); she assisted JENNIE WILDE in the execution of two large maps depicting N.O. and the Mississippi River which were exhibited at the St. Louis exposition (1904).
References: NOCD 1894, 1898–1905, 1907–1908; *States*, Dec. 6, 1903; Art Asso., *Catalogue* (1905).

VINCENT, LESASSIER
Sculptor, active N.O. 1837.
Contemporary listings: sculptor, 122 Rampart (1837).
References: NOCD 1837.

VIVARILLI, G.
Sculptor, active N.O. 1872; also carver, carpenter.
Contemporary listings: woodcarver, 282 Magazine (1872).
References: NOCD 1872; *Repub.*, Mar. 5, 1872.

VOIGHTLIN, ____
Painter, active N.O. 1892.
Contemporary listings: scenery, Grand Opera House (1892).
References: *States*, Nov. 2, 1892.

VOLCKMANN, VIOLA ADELAIDE (Mrs. Andrew Buhler)
Painter, active N.O. 1889.
Exhibited: Academy of Fine Arts (1889).
References: *D. City Item*, Jan. 13, 1892; *D. Pic.*, Jan. 22, 1889; *T. Demo.*, Jan. 13, 1892.

VOLLRATH, GEORGE J.
Born N.O. ca. 1863; died N.O. Nov. 1, 1915.
Lithographer, active N.O. 1889–90; also printer, engineer.
Contemporary listings: lithographer, M. F. DUNN AND BRO. (1889–90).
Also listed as a laborer (1893–1916).
References: NOCD 1884–87, 1889–94, 1896–1916; *T. Pic.*, Nov. 2, 1915.

VON BEUST, ANTON
Born Germany.
Painter, active N.O. 1894.
Created watercolor sketches of N.O. and vicinity copied as vignettes in a promotional printed calendar for a cigar company.
References: *D. Pic.*, Dec. 16, 1894; *T. Demo.*, Oct. 9, 1894; Bénézit; THNOC 1963.4.

VONDERHEIDEN, CHARLES (R., E. or B.)
Commercial artist, active N.O. 1909–17; primarily photographer.
Contemporary listings: artist, with SAMUEL A. CONNER (1909); artist (1914, 1916); artist, with A. H. Hitchler (1917).
References: NOCD 1907–20.

VON EHREN, SUSUS FREDERICK (Frederick S. Aaron; Susa F. Ahren; Frederick S., Susis T. or Suter F. Ehren)
Born N.O. ca. 1865–67; died N.O. Mar. 22, 1957.
Commercial artist, lithographer, engraver, active N.O. 1885–1952.
Contemporary listings: artist, SOUTHERN LITHOGRAPHIC CO. (1885); lithographic artist, G. KOECKERT & CO. (1886); artist, G. Koeckert & Co. (1887); artist, G. Koeckert & Co., and

lithographer (1888); engraver, KOECKERT & WALLE (1889); artist, Koeckert & Walle (1890–92); lithographer (1894, 1897, 1901–1902); artist (1895–96, 1905, 1912–13); artist, WALLE & CO. (1899, 1911); engraver, Walle & Co. (1900, 1902, 1907, 1914–16); artist, and lithographer (1904); lithographic artist, Walle & Co. Ltd. (1906); artist and engraver, Walle & Co. Ltd. (1908); Walle & Co. Ltd. (1909); artist and art dept., Walle & Co. Ltd.(1910).
References: NOCD 1885–92, 1894–97, 1899–1902, 1904–16; *Morn. Trib.*, July 25, 29, 1932; *States*, Mar. 23, 1957; *T. Pic.*, July 17, 24, 31, 1932, Mar. 23–24, 1957; Bartlett, "From Yesterday's Grocery Shelf," *T. Pic.*, Dec. 4, 1977; U.S. Census (1910), roll 521.

VON EYE, JOHN
Lithographer, active N.O. 1899–1914.
Contemporary listings: lithographer (1899, 1901–1902, 1908, 1910, 1914).
References: NOCD 1887–88, 1899, 1901–1902, 1908, 1910, 1914.

VON HOHENBERG, BARON. *See* WURTTEMBERG, FRIEDRICH WILHELM HERZOG PAUL

VON KIRSCH, HERR
Painter, active N.O. 1859.
Contemporary listings: portrait and landscape painter, Jacob's art gallery (1859).
References: *D. Pic.*, Dec. 17, 1859.

VON SMITH, AUGUSTUS A. *See* BRAMMER & VON SMITH

VON WAGNER, MRS. ANNIE R. (Mrs. Wiley P. Von Wagner)
Art teacher, sketch artist, active N.O. 1871.
Contemporary listings: drawing teacher, Girls' High Schools (1871). Primarily a music teacher.
References: NOCD 1873–74, 1876, 1878–85, 1887, 1889–95; *Repub.*, July 9, 1871.

VON WESTERNHAGEN, WILHELM
Painter, active N.O. 1875.
Contemporary listings: portrait painter (1875).
References: NOCD 1875.

VUAGNIERE, A.
Art teacher, sketch artist, active N.O. 1851–58.
Contemporary listings: drawing master, 217 Bayou (1851–56, 1858).
References: NOCD 1851–56, 1858.

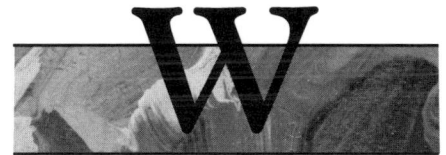

WAGENER, FRANK
Born Cologne, Germany ca. 1827; died N.O. Jan. 21, 1890.
Art dealer, active N.O. 1866–87.
Contemporary listings: Importer of English, French and German engravings, lithographs, and oil paintings, 51 Camp (1866–69); WAGENER & MEYER (1869–72); pictures, 113 Baronne (1874–76); pictures, 152 Canal (1877–80); with THEODORE LILIENTHAL (1881–82); art dealer, 51 Baronne (1882–84); art dealer, 69 Baronne (1885–86); pictures, 74 Carondelet (1887).
Memberships/positions: SOUTHERN ART UNION (1880–81).
References: NOCD 1861, 1866–88, 1890; *Bee*, May 27, 1880, May 4, 1881; *D. Pic.*, May 26, 1881, June 21, 1885; *D. States*, Jan. 20, 1882; *Demo.*, May 12, 1881; *T. Demo.*, July 17, 1883; Mechanics' and Agricultural Fair Asso., *Report* (1867) 27; N.O. Death Certificate (1890), 96:547, NOPL.

WAGENER & MEYER
Art dealers, active N.O. 1869–72; FRANK WAGENER, Louis Meyer, partners.
Contemporary listings: assortment of pictures, lithographs and paintings, 166 Canal (1869); art gallery and importer of French, German, English engravings, lithographs and oil paintings, 164–66 Canal (1870).
Awarded: Grand State Fair, best historical painting (1871).
Primarily manufacturers and importers of mirrors and picture frames, their stock included oil paintings, engravings, marble and clay statuary, and shades, cords, and tassels. They often exhibited the artworks of N.O. artists, particularly of EVERETT B. D. JULIO, FRANÇOIS BERNARD, RICHARD CLAGUE. The firm went bankrupt in Dec. 1872.
References: NOCD 1870–72; *Bee*, Dec. 19, 1869, Jan. 18, 1870, Jan.

22, 1871; *Comm. Bull.*, Jan. 21, 1871; *D. Pic.*, Jan. 20, Sept. 25, Nov. 6, 1870, Dec. 3, 1871; *Repub.*, Dec. 28, 1872; *Times*, Mar. 12, 1871.

WAILENBERG, GEORGE W.
Born Germany ca. 1869.
Painter, active N.O. 1910.
Contemporary listings: artist, oil painting (1910).
References: U.S. Census (1910), roll 522.

WAKEFIELD, JAMES ANTOINE
Painter, active N.O. ca. 1915.
Exhibited: ART ASSOCIATION OF NEW ORLEANS (1915).
References: Art Asso., *Special Exhibition*.

WALDHAUSER, EMILE
Born Hungary ca. 1859; died N.O. Mar. 16, 1908.
Lithographer, engraver, active N.O. 1886–1908.
Contemporary listings: lithographer, M. F. DUNN & BRO. (1886), engraver, M. F. Dunn & Bro. (1887–88, 1890–91); lithographer (1889, 1892–95, 1897–98, 1901, 1904, 1907–1908); engraver, ART LITHOGRAPH CO. (1899); engraver (1902, 1905); engraver, H. WEHRMANN & SONS (1903); lithographic engraver (1906).
References: NOCD 1886–99, 1901–1908; *D. Pic.*, Mar. 17, 1908.

WALDO, JAMES CURTIS
Born Meredosia IL Dec. 10, 1835; died N.O. Aug. 28, 1901.
Engraver, active N.O. 1876–83; primarily publisher.
Contemporary listings: photo–engraver, 46 Camp (1878–79); photo–engraver, 61 Camp (1880–82); photo–engraver, 8 St. Charles (1883).
Writer, poet, and journalist who opened his own publishing and photoengraving business in N.O. in 1876. He published numerous articles and pamphlets concerning N.O., such as his *Illustrated Visitor's Guide to New Orleans* (1879), illustrated by SMITH

W. BENNETT and CHARLES KNOBE-LOCH.
References: NOCD 1867–1901; *D. Pic.*, May 2, 1883, Aug. 29, 1901; *D. States*, Aug. 29, 1901; *Demo.*, June 2, 1878, Sept. 1, 1880; *T. Demo.*, Aug. 29, 1901; Fortier, *Louisiana*, 3:584–85; Jumonville, 78–79; Morrison, *Industries*, 40, 47, 54; THNOC 1982.198; Waldo.

WALKER, ELOISE P.
Born LA Oct. 1864.
Painter, active N.O. ca. 1889–1910.
Contemporary listings: portrait painter (1890–91); retoucher, with Charles T. Yenni (1892–93); artist, with Charles T. Yenni (1894–1910); artist (1910).
Exhibited: ARTISTS' ASSOCIATION OF NEW ORLEANS (1889).
References: NOCD 1890–1910; *D. Pic.*, Dec. 17, 1889; U.S. Census (1900), roll 574.

WALKER, KATHERINE
Painter, active N.O. 1886–92.
Studied: NEWCOMB COLLEGE (1886–92).
Exhibited: ARTISTS' ASSOCIATION OF NEW ORLEANS (1891–92).
References: *Current Topics*, Jan. 1892, 24, Jan. 1893, 10; *D. Pic.*, Dec. 17, 1891, Dec. 14, 1892; AANO, *Catalogue* (1891); Poesch, *Newcomb Pottery*, 105.

WALKER, SAMUEL
Born England ca. 1811.
Painter, active N.O. 1860–61.
Studied: with William Etty.
Contemporary listings: portrait painter, 175 Canal (1860–61).
Probably the itinerant artist who exhibited at the Royal Academy, London (1850–52), was in Brooklyn and N.Y.C. (1853–54) when exhibiting at the National Academy of Design, and exhibited at the Pennsylvania Academy of Fine Arts, Philadelphia (1865–68).
References: NOCD 1860–61; *D. Delta*, Feb. 3, 1861; Glenk, 80; Groce and Wallace; Looney, 15; U.S. Census (1860), roll 417.

WALKER, THOMAS B.
Art teacher, active N.O. 1849.
Contemporary listings: professor of drawing and sketching, Fulton betw. Philip and Sorapuru (1849).

Also listed as the superintendant of the male orphan asylum on Jackson (1850–53).
References: NOCD 1849–53.

WALKER, WILLIAM AIKEN
Born Charleston SC Mar. 23, 1838; died Charleston Jan. 3, 1921.
Painter, art teacher, active N.O. 1876–1905.
Exhibited: South Carolina Institute Fair (1850); Courtenay's Book Store, Charleston (1858–59); Baltimore (1870); Montgomery's (1876); SOUTHERN ART UNION (1880); Blessing's (1883, 1885); LILIENTHAL's (1883); SEEBOLD's (1884); American Exposition (1885–86); Savannah GA (after 1885); ARTISTS' ASSOCIATION OF NEW ORLEANS (1885–1905); Tulane University (1892); Columbian Exposition, Chicago (1893); Louisiana Purchase Exposition, St. Louis MO (1903).
Memberships/positions: Wednesday Club, Baltimore (1865); Artists' Association of New Orleans (1890, 1893, 1897, 1899); CUP AND SAUCER CLUB.
Genre and landscape painter who first exhibited a painting at age 12 in his native city of Charleston. By 1860 Walker had begun painting the fish and game that he caught. He served the Confederacy as a draftsman during the Civil War, afterward settling in Baltimore as an artist, traveling extensively throughout the South during most winters, and maintaining a summer studio in Arden NC. Walker's first visit to N.O., which he came to regard as his second home, was during the spring of 1876; he returned almost annually (1878–80, 1883, 1888–89, 1893–97, 1900–1901, 1903, and 1905) to a studio at what is presently 1521 Toledano. Sometime in the 1890s, he began to stay in the French Quarter; in 1905 his address was on St. Louis between Royal and Bourbon. Walker was active in N.O. art and social circles; most contemporary genre and landscape painters were his friends. He was particularly close to N.O. artist EVERETT B. D. JULIO, and together they

tried to form an art league in the city. When Julio died in 1879, Walker began a five–year period of what is considered to be his most consistent work: images of southern blacks and of plantation life, executed mostly in N.O., FL, and NC. He preferred either single, frontally posed figures with a landscape or levee background or rural scenes with a family working near a cabin. Two of his large paintings executed in 1883, *The Levee–New Orleans* and *A Cotton Plantation on the Mississippi*, were reproduced by CURRIER AND IVES in 1884 as chromolithographs. In N.O. Walker often set up on the street at the corner of Royal and Dumaine where he painted and sold his work. He also exhibited with the city's art organizations: he showed in every Artists' Association exhibition from 1885 through 1905. During the spring and early summer, he usually visited Biloxi MS. Walker preferred rural life and with the growth of the city, he left N.O. permanently after 1905.
References: *Art and Letters*, 1(Dec. 1887):228; *Current Topics*, Jan. 1891, 25, Jan. 1892, 24, Jan. 1893, 11; *D. Pic.*, Nov. 30, Dec. 3, 1884, July 26, Oct. 25, 1885, Nov. 7, 1886, Dec. 17, 1887, Dec. 17, 1889, Nov. 13, Dec. 17, 1890, Mar. 3, Dec. 13, 1892; *D. States*, Nov. 5, 1886; *Repub.*, Feb. 22, 1876; *T. Demo.*, July 17, 1883, Dec. 14, 1894; AANO, *Catalogue* (1886, 1890–91, 1897); Artists' Association, Vertical File, LA Coll., TU; Bruce Chambers, 25, 27, 44–47, 63; Creole Exhibit, 15; Groce and Wallace; Kelly, 9, 66; Lilienthal's, 5–6, 9; LSM, *Biennial Report for 1920–21*, 29; Norton Art Gallery, 38; Trovaioli and Toledano; Wiesendanger, 104–5.

WALLACE, ALEXANDER
Lithographer, active N.O. 1887–89; also photographer.
Contemporary listings: lithographer, G. KOECKERT & CO (1887); lithographer, KOECKERT & WALLE (1889).
References: NOCD 1886–90.

WALLACE, D. J.
Born KY ca. 1829.
Painter, active N.O. 1850–58; also sign and ornamental painter.
Contemporary listings: artist (1850); painter, D. J. Wallace & Co. (1853–54); painter (1856); D. J. WALLACE & HARRIS (1857); painter (1858).
References: NOCD 1853–58; *D. Creole*, July 17, 1856; *D. Pic.*, Jan. 19, 1854; *D. True Delta*, July 13, 1856; U.S. Census (1850), roll 237.

D. J. WALLACE & HARRIS
Painters, active, N.O. 1856–57; also sign and ornamental painters; D. J. WALLACE, William Harris, partners.
Contemporary listings: fancy, transparency and banner painters, 105 St. Charles (1856–57).
References: NOCD 1857; *D. Creole*, Sept. 4, 1856, Oct. 17, 1856–Feb. 4, 1857 (advs.).

WALLACE, DAVID
Born IL Apr. 1875.
Lithographer, active N.O. 1900.
Contemporary listings: lithographer (1900).
References: U.S. Census (1900), roll 575.

WALLACE, HARRY DUFF
Born 1875; died 1952.
Designer, sketch artist, active N.O. 1903–47.
Contemporary listings: artist, 1103 Napoleon (1903); designer, Louisiana Glass and Mirror Works, Ltd. (1904–1906); designer (1907, 1909, 1917); designer, Central Glass Co., Ltd. (1908); proprietor, WALLACE GLASS COMPANY (1910–11); glass (1914, 1916).
Exhibited: ART ASSOCIATION OF NEW ORLEANS (1915).
Listed in various sales capacities for trucking and automotive companies (1918–47). He made at least one etching and continued to draw; he designed *Carnival Playing Cards New Orleans* (ca. 1925).
References: NOCD 1903–22, 1924–33, 1935, 1938, 1940, 1942, 1945–47, 1949, 1952; *States*, Apr. 17, 1927; *Town Talk*, July 1904, cover; Art Asso., *Special Exhibition*; THNOC 1950.64.42–.45, 1978.184, 1980-

.163, 1982.206; THNOC Cemetery Survey.

WALLACE GLASS COMPANY

Art craftsmen, active N.O. 1910–11; HARRY DUFF WALLACE, proprietor.

Contemporary listings: art glass makers, 420 Chartres (1910–11).

References: NOCD 1910–11; *Architectural Art* 6(Nov. 1910):27.

WALLASTER, JOHN G.

Born Chicago IL ca. 1868; died N.O. Nov. 27, 1936.

Lithographer, active N.O. 1893–1905.

Contemporary listings: lithographer (1893); manager, AMERICAN LITHOGRAPHIC CO. OF N.Y. (1895–99); lithographic art goods, 131 Camp (1900–1905).

References: NOCD 1893–1931; *T. Pic.*, Nov. 28, 1936.

WALLE, BERNARD JOHN. *See* WALLE & CO.

WALLE, FRANK LEONARD CHARLES

Born N.O. Dec. 29, 1882; died N.O. Feb. 22, 1938.

Lithographer, engraver, artist, active N.O. 1899–1933.

Contemporary listings: artist (1899); lithographer (1901, 1911–13); engraver, WALLE & CO., LTD. (1902); lithographer (1910).

Later listed as a lithographer (1920, 1926, 1933); engraver (1927).

References: NOCD 1899, 1901–23, 1925–27, 1930–33; *T. Pic.*, Feb. 23, 1938; Orleans Parish Registrar of Voters, NOPL; U.S. Census (1910), roll 521.

WALLE, FRANK P.

Born N.O. ca. 1864–65; died N.O. June 23, 1920.

Lithographer, active N.O. 1887–1920.

Contemporary listings: lithographer, G. KOECKERT & CO. (1887–88); lithographer, KOECKERT & WALLE (1889–1892); lithographer (1893, 1905, 1910–11).

Father of JOHN A. WALLE.

References: NOCD 1884,1886–1914, 1920; *T. Pic.*, June 24, 1920; U.S. Census (1910), roll 521.

WALLE, JOHN. *See* WALLE & CO.

WALLE, JOHN A.

Born LA ca. 1892.

Lithographer, active N.O. 1910–55.

Contemporary listings: lithographer (1910, 1916–18).

Son of FRANK P. WALLE.

References: NOCD 1916–33, 1935, 1940, 1942, 1945–47, 1954–56, 1958, 1960–62, 1964–69, 1971; U.S. Census (1910), roll 521.

WALLE & COMPANY (Walle & Co. Ltd.)

Lithographers, active N.O. 1897–1929; also printers, stationers; John Walle (born Baden, Germany ca. 1841), his son Bernard John Walle (born N.O. Nov. 28, 1869; died N.O. May 4, 1929), Frederick W. Young, partners.

Contemporary listings: lithographers, 220 Camp (1897–98); lithographers, 523 Gravier (1899, 1902, 1907–18); lithographers, 525 Gravier (1906).

Incorporated in 1897 after the dissolution of KOECKERT & WALLE. In 1900 Frederick W. Young became a partner, and the company was incorporated as Walle & Co. Ltd. They began creating the invitations of the carnival organization of Rex in 1902 and lithographed the carnival bulletins of Momus (1902–17), Rex (1904–17), Comus (1905–17), and Proteus (1912–16). They used chromolithography extensively, particularly in the creation of labels for numerous commercial products manufactured in N.O. and the South. SUSUS FREDERICK VON EHREN was the primary artist for the labels. Walle & Co. was credited as one of the first printing companies in the nation to master a four–color printing process. With the death of Bernard J. Walle in 1929, the company was dissolved but reorganized as Walle & Co. Inc. and continues at present as Walle Corporation.

References: NOCD 1897–1929; NOBD 1897–98; *D. Pic.*, Apr. 3, 1912; *T. Demo.*, Sept. 26, 1905; *T. Pic.*, May 5, 1929, Dec. 4, 1977; AANO, *Catalogue* (1899, 1902);

James Adams; La Cour, 210; Orleans Parish Registrar of Voters, NOPL.

WALTER, CHARLES
Lithographer, active N.O. 1878.
Contemporary listings: lithographer, with BENEDICT SIMON (1878).
References: NOCD 1871, 1877–78.

WALTER, DIETRICH ALBERT
Born ca. 1864; died N.O. Dec. 25, 1916.
Engraver, active N.O. 1886–92; also jeweler, watchmaker.
Contemporary listings: engraver, with Maurice Scooler (1886–88); engraver, Frantz & Opitz (1889–92).
References: NOCD 1886–95, 1897–1916; *T. Pic.*, Dec. 26, 1916; LSM, *Biennial Report for 1932–33*, 68; N.O. Death Certificate (1916), 167:1172, NOPL.

WALTER, EDWARD
Artist, active N.O. 1892.
Contemporary listings: artist (1892).
References: NOCD 1892.

WALTER, JOHN
Sculptor, active N.O. 1846.
Contemporary listings: sculptor, 214 Dauphine (1846).
References: NOCD 1846, 1849–53.

WALTER, PETER C.
Born N.O. Apr. 18, 1886.
Lithographer, active N.O. 1906–32; also printer, pressman, photographer.
Contemporary listings: lithographer (1906, 1909, 1912, 1917); lithographer, WEHRMANN'S SONS (1908, 1910–11, 1913–14).
Later listed as a pressman (1918); printer (1919, 1921, 1928–29); lithographer (1920, 1922–25, 1927, 1930–32); photographer (1926).
References: NOCD 1902–1903, 1906–32; Orleans Parish Registrar of Voters, NOPL; U.S. Census (1910), roll 521.

WANG, FRED M., JR.
Born N.O. ca. 1872; died N.O. Jan. 31, 1900.
Artist, active N.O. 1886–90.
Studied: ARTISTS' ASSOCIATION OF NEW ORLEANS (1886–87).
Exhibited: Artists' Association of New Orleans (1886–87, 1890).

Memberships/positions: BLACK AND WHITE CLUB (1887).
References: *D. Pic.*, Nov. 6–7, 1886, May 7, 1887; *D. States*, May 16, 1890; *T. Demo.*, Feb. 1, 1900; Stern's Auction Co., Oct. 24, 1911.

WANGERHEIM, ALBERT
Sketch artist, active N.O. 1877; also photographer.
Exhibited: W. E. SEEBOLD's (1877).
References: NOCD 1878; *Demo.*, Sept. 25, 1877.

WARBURG, DANIEL (Warbourg)
Born N.O. 1836; died Sept. 16, 1911; black ("mulatto," "free man of color").
Sculptor, active N.O. 1852–1911; primarily marble cutter.
Known primarily as Daniel Warburg, although his full name was Joseph Daniel Warburg. He took over the shop of his brother, EUGENE WARBURG, when the latter left for Europe (1852), and continued a marble cutting business. Father of JOSEPH DANIEL WARBURG, JR.
References: NOCD 1854–61, 1866–68, 1871–73, 1875–76, 1878–1906, 1910–11; Desdunes, 70–71; Friends of the Cabildo, *N.O. Architecture*, 3:92–93; Korn, 181, 321; O'Neill, 77–78; U.S. Census (1850), roll 235.

WARBURG, EUGENE (Warbourg)
Born N.O. ca. 1825–26; died Rome, Italy Jan. 12, 1859; black ("mulatto," "free man of color").
Sculptor, active N.O. ca. 1850–52; also marble cutter.
Studied: with PHILIPPE GARBEILLE; Paris.
Contemporary listings: sculptor (1850); sculptor, St. Louis betw. Basin and Franklin (1851–52).
Exhibited: Hall's gilding establishment (1850).
Known as Eugene Warburg, although his full name was Joseph Eugene Warburg. He began his career by opening a studio–shop at 89 St. Peter, receiving numerous commissions for busts and tombstones from prominent New Orleanians and members of the clergy. Because of the worsening racial situation for a free black in the South, he left for

Europe, sailing Nov. 1852. He studied sculpture in Paris and then worked as a sculptor throughout Europe: Belgium (1856); England (1856), under the patronage of the Duchess of Sutherland; Florence (1857); and Rome (1857), where he remained until his death. Brother of DANIEL WARBURG.
References: NOCD 1850–53; *Bee*, Dec. 13, 1850, Mar. 9, 1859; *D. Crescent*, Dec. 26, 1857; *D. Pic.*, Dec. 26, 1857; Desdunes, 69–70; Korn, 181–82; O'Neill, 74–77; Perry; THNOC Cemetery Survey (Builder/Carver Index); U.S. Census (1850), roll 235.

WARBURG, JOSEPH DANIEL JR.
Born N.O. ca. 1867; died Biloxi MS Aug. 14, 1921; black ("mulatto").
Sculptor, active N.O. 1889–91; primarily marble cutter.
Contemporary listings: sculptor (1889–91).
Active as a marble and stone cutter (1879–1916), Warburg ornamented tombs throughout N.O.'s cemeteries, many with his father, DANIEL WARBURG.
References: NOCD 1879–94, 1896–1905, 1907–10, 1912–17; *T. Pic.*, Aug. 16, 1921; Desdunes, 70; O'-Neill, 77–78.

WARDLAW, MRS. J. D.
Sculptor, art craftsman, active N.O. ca. 1888–90.
Exhibited: TULANE DECORATIVE ART LEAGUE FOR WOMEN (1888); ART LEAGUE POTTERY CLUB (1890).
Exhibited a carved wooden bookcase (1888) and decorated pottery (1890).
References: *D. Pic.*, Feb. 12, 1888, Feb. 14, 1890; Tulane Decorative Art League.

WARRELL, MR. _____
Art dealer, active N.O. 1834.
Contemporary listings: proprietor, gallery of paintings, cor. Bienville and Chartres (1834).
Cf. WARRELL, JAMES.
References: *Mercantile Advertiser*, Apr. 18, 1834.

WARRELL, JAMES
Born ca. 1780; died before 1854.
Painter, active N.O. 1825–27.

Contemporary listings: portrait painter, cor. St. Charles and Canal (1825–26); portrait painter, 49 Canal (1827).
Portrait and historical painter and scenic artist who began painting professionally in 1808. In 1817 he and his brother–in–law opened the Virginia Museum in Richmond, which existed until 1936. Although he spent much of his life in Richmond and Petersburg VA, he was also an itinerant scenic artist. Warrell painted portraits in N.O. (1825–27) and Natchez MS (1828), and was in N.Y.C. periodically between 1829 and 1839.
Cf. WARRELL, MR. _____.
References: NOCD 1827; *Ariel*, Feb. 2, 1828; *Courier*, Mar. 10, 1826; *Gazette*, Feb. 21, 1825; Glenk, 80; Groce and Wallace.

WARRINGTON, WILLIAM JENNINGS
Born Atlanta GA Oct. 3, 1850; died N.O. Jan. 22, 1941.
Painter, sketch artist, art teacher, active N.O. ca. 1887–89.
Contemporary listings: art teacher, painter, 154 Carondelet (1887–88); director, ACADEMY OF FINE ARTS (1889).
After working as an artist for four years, Warrington moved from GA in 1870 to N.O. to live in his family's home on Royal (present 1140 Royal). In 1873 he established there a refuge for homeless men and boys, which was incorporated in 1920 as Warrington House. He received the 1926 *Times–Picayune* Loving Cup for his community service as a social worker and philanthropist. Warrington was also involved in the city's cultural organizations: first director of the New Orleans Conservatory of Music; member of the Musical Review (1883–85); and an organizer of the ARTISTS' ASSOCIATION OF NEW ORLEANS. As an amateur artist, Warrington was noted for portraits, landscapes, and hand–painted cards; his portrait of LA historian and author Charles Gayarre was privately commissioned for the State of LA. Warrington was also active for a few years (1887–89) as a teacher and director

of an art school in his Royal Street home. His students' works, as well as paintings from other collections, were frequently shown at public exhibitions there.
References: NOCD 1883–85, 1888–89, 1916–33, 1935, 1938, 1940; *D. Pic.*, Jan. 11, 1883, Sept. 4, 1887; *D. States*, Oct. 1–2, 8, 12, Dec. 8, 1887; *Item–Trib.*, Jan. 20, 1939; *T. Demo.*, Oct. 8, 13, 1887; *T. Pic.*, Oct. 23, 1921, Jan. 23, 1941; *Wkly. States*, Sept. 9, 1887; Hodding and Betty Carter, 178–79; Glenk, 43; Kendall, *History*, 2:659, 3:1098.

WASHBURN, MARY HELEN (Minnie)
Born N.O. May 6, 1862; died N.O. June 24, 1934.
Painter, sketch artist, active N.O. 1894–98.
Studied: with ANDRES MOLINARY; ARTISTS' ASSOCIATION OF NEW ORLEANS.
Exhibited: Artists' Association of New Orleans (1894, 1896–97); New Orleans Press Club (1898).
Memberships/positions: Artists' Association of New Orleans (1896–97).
Portrait painter from life or photographs who also painted scenes of N.O. and still lifes of flowers. After 1898, her primary occupation was teaching.
References: NOCD 1894–95, 1899, 1908–16, 1918–19, 1922–23, 1929, 1933; *D. Pic.*, Mar. 30, 1897; *D. States*, Jan. 23, 1898; *T. Demo.*, Dec. 14, 1894; *T. Pic.*, June 25, 1934; AANO, *Catalogue* (1896, 1897); LSM, *Biennial Report for 1922–23*, 62; LSM, *Biennial Report for 1924–25*, 62; Scrapbook 100, LSM; Mount, 136–37; Orleans Parish Registrar of Voters, NOPL; THNOC Cemetery Survey.

WASHBURN, WILLIAM WATSON
Born Peterboro NH Nov. 1825; died N.O. Nov. 15, 1903.
Colorer, art dealer, restorer, active N.O. 1870–85; primarily photographer.
Awarded: Grand State Fair, first premium for best photographs (1866, 1868).
Major 19th–century N.O. daguerreotypist and photographer who

maintained a studio in the city from 1849 until his death. He specialized in photographing visiting celebrities.
References: NOCD 1850, 1852–61, 1866–1903, *Bee*, Sept. 24, 1863, Mar. 8, 13, 1870, Mar. 25, 1873; *D. Crescent*, Dec. 25, 1854; *D. Pic.*, Nov. 22, 1849, Mar. 29, 1854, Oct. 28, 1855, Mar. 1, 1868, July 22, 1877; *Our Home Journal*, Jan. 21, 1871, 27; *Repub.*, Sept. 7, 1873; *Times*, Oct. 22, 1871; *T. Demo.*, Nov. 16, 18, 1903; *Wkly. Mirror*, Mar. 5, 1859; Land, 94; Morrison, *Industries*, 152; Smith and Tucker, 47–48, 66–68, 85, 115, 140–41, 148, 170–71.

WASSON, J. B.
Born LA ca. 1838.
Lithographer, active N.O. 1885; primarily stationer, printer.
Contemporary listings: lithographer, 46 Carondelet (1885).
References: NOCD 1856–58, 1861, 1866–68, 1870–85; Morrison, *Industries*, 175; U.S. Census (1880), roll 463.

WATERS, W. H.
Artist, active N.O. 1868; also sign and ornamental painter.
Contemporary listings: artist, Orleans House, 143 Common (1868).
References: NOCD 1850–61, 1866–68, 1871–74.

WATSON, JAMES A. *See* RICHARDSON & WATSON

WAUD, ALFRED RODOLPH
Born London, England Oct. 2, 1828; died Marietta GA Apr. 6, 1891.
Sketch artist, illustrator, active N.O. 1866, 1871–72.
Studied: School of Design, Somerset House, London; Royal Academy, London.
Exhibited: National Academy of Design, N.Y.C. (ca. 1858).
After completing his training, Waud traveled to N.Y.C. in 1850 where he worked as an illustrator both there and in Boston. Hired for a time by the *New York Illustrated News* (1860–62), he left to become "Special Artist" for *Harper's Weekly*, traveling with the Army of the Potomac throughout the Civil War and making sketches of battle scenes and mil-

itary installations that were published as illustrations in the magazine. In 1866 *Harper's* sent Waud to the South via the Ohio and Mississippi rivers to record Reconstruction, writing his own commentaries to accompany the drawings. He continued to accept assignments from *Harper's* until 1876, except for a stint in 1871 with *Every Saturday*, a Boston journal, when he traveled up the Mississippi. Called away from the journey in Oct. 1871 to cover the Chicago fire, Waud returned to the river to finish the trip, which supplied illustrations for four chapters in *Picturesque America*. Throughout his career, he continued to work on travel books, histories, geographies, textbooks, novels, and for periodicals, but he was most noted for publications on the Civil War. Major collections of his original drawings and manuscript material are in the Library of Congress and the Historic New Orleans Collection. Brother of WILLIAM WAUD.
References: Alfred R. Waud Papers, THNOC; Groce and Wallace; Hamilton, passim; Montgomery, 2:833–40; Mugridge and Conover, 166–67; Museum of Fine Arts, 1:35, 300, 2:64, 87–90; Ray; Samuel et al., 66–71; Sears, 394–96; Taft, 54–62, 296–98; THNOC 1965.11–.90, 1977-.137.2–.39; THNOC, *Waud*.

WAUD, WILLIAM
Born England; died Jersey City NJ Nov. 10, 1878.
Sketch artist, illustrator, active N.O. 1862.
Trained as an architect in England, where he assisted in the design of London's Crystal Palace, Waud came to the U.S. in 1856 and settled in N.Y.C. He became an illustrator with *Frank Leslie's Illustrated Newspaper*: on assignment to cover the Civil War, he sailed aboard a ship in the federal fleet which captured N.O.; his drawings of the battle were published in 1862. He continued as an illustrator, joining the staff of *Harper's Weekly* in 1864. Brother of ALFRED R. WAUD.

References: *Illustrated London News*, Apr. 15, 1861, 634; Groce and Wallace; Hamilton, 1:218–19, 2:145–46; Mugridge and Conover, 166–67; Museum of Fine Arts, 2:91; National Gallery of Art, 107; Ray, passim; Samuel et al., 66; Sears, 396; THNOC 1977.137.1.1–.73.

WAUGH, ALFRED S.
Born Ireland; died St. Louis MO Mar. 18, 1856.
Painter, active N.O. 1845.
Studied: with Smythe, Royal Dublin Academy (1827).
Itinerant portrait sculptor and painter, and profilist, writer, and lecturer who came to the U.S. after studying in Ireland and worked in Baltimore MD (1833), Raleigh NC (1838), and Pensacola FL (1843). In 1844 he left Mobile AL with JOHN B. TISDALE for a tour of the U.S. to make colored profile portraits. They arrived in N.O. on Jan. 20, 1845, and stayed at the Verandah Hotel for two days before opening a studio in a house on St. Charles next to GEORGE COOKE's National Gallery of Paintings. They met other artists in the city: THEODORE SIDNEY MOISE, THOMAS CANTWELL HEALY, MRS. STEELE, MR. FORD, and MATTHEW WILSON. Since their profile business only met expenses, Waugh and Tisdale left N.O. on May 8, 1845 for St. Louis, where they hoped to join J. C. Frémont's expedition to the Rocky Mountains. In 1846, Waugh went to Santa Fe NM, and by 1848 had settled in St. Louis.
References: Groce and Wallace; Waugh, xi–xii, 1–5.

WAUGH, HENRY W.
Born ca. 1835; died England ca. 1865.
Sketch artist, painter, active N.O. 1858–59.
Studied: Rome (1860–65).
Landscape and scenery painter who sketched and painted a series of N.O. and Mississippi River views (1858–59) while touring the country as a theatrical troupe clown.
References: Groce and Wallace; Museum of Fine Arts, 1:300–1.

WEBB, J.
Engraver, active N.O. 1832; also jeweler.
Contemporary listings: engraver, 55 Julia (1832).
References: NOCD 1832, 1834–35.

WEBER, PAUL R.
Born LA June 1875.
Engraver, active N.O. 1892–1900.
Contemporary listings: engraver (1892, 1894, 1897); engraver, Walter & Winter (1893); engraver, Frantz & Opitz (1896); engraver, T. Hausmann & Sons (1898–1900).
References: NOCD 1892–94, 1896–1900; U.S. Census (1900), roll 573.

WEEKS, JOHN
Born Germany Feb. 1855.
Painter, active N.O. 1891–1900.
Contemporary listings: portrait painter (1891); artist (1892, 1895–96, 1899–1900); artist, with T. J. Brennan, photographer (1898).
References: NOCD 1891–93, 1895–96, 1898–1900; U.S. Census (1900), roll 570.

WEHRMAN, H.
Lithographer, active N.O. 1868
Awarded: Grand State Fair, honorable mention for best lithography on stone (1868).
Cf. WEHRMANN, HENRY; WEHRMANN, HERMANN.
References: D. Pic., Jan. 19, 1868; Mechanics' and Agricultural Fair Asso., Report (1868):42.

WEHRMANN, ADOLPH
Born N.O. Nov. 3, 1870; died N.O. Aug. 30, 1920
Lithographer, active N.O. 1899–1920.
Contemporary listings: lithographer, with HENRIETTA TERMIER WEHRMANN (1899); lithographer (1900–1901, 1910); lithographer, H. WEHRMANN & CO. (1902); H. WEHRMANN & SONS (1903–1905); WEHRMANN'S SONS (1906–18).
Son of HERMANN WEHRMANN and Henrietta Termier Wehrmann.
References: NOCD 1888, 1892–93, 1899, 1901–20; T. Pic., Aug. 31, 1920; THNOC Cemetery Survey; U.S. Census (1880), roll 460, (1900), roll 571, (1910), roll 521.

WEHRMANN, CHARLOTTE MARIE CLEMENTINE BOHNE (Mrs. HENRY WEHRMANN)
Born Paris, France Apr. 1, 1830; died N.O. Mar. 30, 1911.
Engraver, active N.O. ca. 1852–85.
Studied: Paris.
Contemporary listings: engraver (1860).
Exhibited: World's Industrial and Cotton Centennial Exposition (1884–85).
Awarded: Grand State Fair, silver medal for best musical engraving (1867).
She and Henry Wehrmann married in 1848 and arrived in N.O. in 1849. When her husband established his lithographic firm, she began engraving sheet music. Together they printed over 8,000 individual compositions and were commissioned by all the N.O. music houses. She also engraved the plates of the first compositions published by her son, HENRY W. WEHRMANN; also mother of VALENTINE WEHRMANN.
References: NOCD 1906–11; D. Pic., Mar. 31, 1911; Kendall, "New Orleans' Musicians," 147–49; Mechanics' and Agricultural Fair Asso., Report (1867):28; Soniat du Fossat, 78; U.S. Census (1860), roll 418.

WEHRMANN, FREDERICK
Born N.O. Jan. 16, 1874; died N.O. Jan. 11, 1918.
Lithographer, active N.O. 1895–1918.
Contemporary listings: lithographer (1895, 1897, 1901, 1910); lithographer, with HENRIETTA TERMIER WEHRMANN (1899–1900); lithographer, H. WEHRMANN & CO. (1902); H. WEHRMANN & SONS (1903–1905); WEHRMANN'S SONS (1906–18).
Son of HERMANN WEHRMANN and Henrietta Termier Wehrmann.
References: NOCD 1895, 1897, 1899–1918; T. Pic., Jan. 12, 1918; THNOC Cemetery Survey; U.S. Census (1880), roll 460, (1910), roll 520.

H. WEHRMANN & CO.
Lithographers, active N.O. 1902; HERMANN WEHRMANN, Hermina Wickbold, partners.

Contemporary listings: lithographers, 327 Chartres (1902).
Succeeded by H. WEHRMANN & SONS (1903–1905) and WEHRMANN'S SONS (1906–18).
References: NOCD 1902.

H. WEHRMANN & SONS (WEHRMANN & SONS)
Lithographers, active N.O. 1903–1905; ADOLPH WEHRMANN, FREDERICK WEHRMANN, HERMANN WEHRMANN, partners.
Contemporary listings: lithographers, 327 Chartres (1903–1905).
Successor to H. WEHRMANN & CO. (1902); name changed to WEHRMANN'S SONS (1906–18) after the death of Hermann Wehrmann.
References: NOCD 1903–1905.

WEHRMANN, HENRIETTA TERMIER
(Mrs. HERMANN WEHRMANN)
Born Luchtringen on the Weser, Westphalia, Germany Oct. 4, 1834; died N.O. June 22, 1901.
Lithographer, active N.O. 1893–1901.
Contemporary listings: lithographer, 75 Chartres (1893–94); lithographer, 327 Chartres (1895–1901).
Mother of ADOLPH and FREDERICK WEHRMANN.
References: NOCD 1879–1901; *D. Pic.*, June 23, 1901; Land, 81; THNOC Cemetery Survey; U.S. Census (1880), roll 460, (1900), roll 571.

WEHRMANN, HENRY
Born Germany May 18, 1827; died N.O. Sept. 13, 1905.
Engraver, lithographer, active N.O. 1852–1905; also printer.
Contemporary listings: music engraver, 9 Treme (1852); music engraver, Treme betw. St. Louis and Toulouse (1853); music engraver, Treme near Toulouse (1854); music engraver, Camp near Girod (1855–56); music engraver, 78 Toulouse (1856); engraver, 170 Burgundy (1857); music engraver, 170 Burgundy (1858–59); music engraver, 142 Burgundy (1860); engraver, 142 Burgundy (1861); engraver (1868, 1876–77, 1887, 1892, 1894–95); lithographer (1869–70).

Husband of CHARLOTTE MARIE CLEMENTINE BOHNE WEHRMANN; father of HENRY W. and VALENTINE WEHRMANN. *Cf.* WEHRMAN, H.
References: NOCD 1852–61, 1866, 1868–79, 1881–88, 1890–98, 1900–1905; *Bee*, Mar. 4, 1856; *Courier*, Feb. 24, 1852; *Item*, Sept. 14, 1905; *T. Demo.*, Sept. 14, 1905; Kendall, "New Orleans' Musicians," 147–49; N.O. Death Certificate (1905), 136:337, NOPL; Harry Peters, *America on Stone*, 398; Sheet Music Collection, LA Coll., TU; "Souvenir de la Nouvelle Orleans," Sheet Music Collection, LSM; U.S. Census (1860), roll 418.

WEHRMANN, HENRY W.
Born N.O. Dec. 27, 1871; died N.O. Oct. 21, 1956.
Painter, sketch artist, active N.O. 1896–1903.
Accomplished musician and composer, who according to Mount was a fine draftsman who sketched portraits of his favorite composers (1896). In 1903 his studio at 1726 St. Mary was noted as being adorned with paintings and drawings he had made. Son of HENRY WEHRMANN and CHARLOTTE MARIE CLEMENTINE BOHNE WEHRMANN.
References: NOCD 1892–1928, 1930–33, 1935, 1938, 1940, 1942, 1945–47, 1949, 1952–56; *D. Pic.*, Mar. 2, 1903; *Harlequin*, Dec. 27, 1899, 1, 11; *T. Pic.*, Feb. 22, 1920, Oct. 22, 1956; Mount, 90–92; Peeler, 35, 48; *Who's Who in America*, 1918–19.

WEHRMANN, HERMANN
Born Minden, Germany July 11, 1840; died N.O. Oct. 26, 1905.
Lithographer, engraver, active N.O. 1867–1905; also printer.
Contemporary listings: lithographer (1870, 1889, 1892–97, 1901); lithographer, 38 Exchange Al. (1871); lithographer, 87 Exchange Al. (1872, 1878–79); engraver and lithographer, 87 Exchange Pl. (1873, 1876–77); engraver and lithographer, 90 Exchange Al. (1874); lithographer, 90 Exchange Al. (1875); lithographer, 71 Chartres (1880–83); li-

thographer, 75 Chartres (1884–86, 1890–91); WEHRMANN & CO. (1887); lithographer, with HENRIETTA TERMIER WEHRMANN (1898–1900); H. WEHRMANN & CO. (1902); H. WEHRMANN & SONS (1903–1905).
Reported to have established his lithographing firm in N.O. in 1867. Husband of Henrietta Termier Wehrmann; father of ADOLPH and FREDERICK WEHRMANN. *Cf.* WEHRMAN, H.
References: NOCD 1870–1905; *Repub.*, Nov. 9, 1873; *T. Demo.*, Oct. 27, 1905; Braun; Land, 81; Sheet Music Collection, LA Coll., TU; THNOC Cemetery Survey; U.S. Census (1870), roll 521, (1880), roll 460, (1900), roll 571; *Washington Artillery Souvenir*, 76.

WEHRMANN, VALENTINE
Born N.O. Dec. 1850; died N.O. May 24, 1887.
Sketch artist, active N.O. 1868–84.
Awarded: Grand State Fair, best crayon drawing by boy 16 years of age (1868).
Primarily a merchant and an amateur artist who created in ink a souvenir for the Orpheon Française, a French musical association (1884). Son of HENRY WEHRMANN and CHARLOTTE MARIE CLEMENTINE BOHNE WEHRMANN.
References: NOCD 1871, 1873–88; *D. Pic.*, Jan. 19, 1868; *Eve. Chronicle*, Sept. 5, 1884; *T. Demo.*, Sept. 5, 1884; Mechanics' and Agricultural Fair Asso., *Report* (1868):43; N.O. Death Certificate (1887), 91:252, NOPL; U.S. Census (1860), roll 418.

WEHRMANN & CO. *See also* STANDARD MUSIC AND PHOTO–LITHO COMPANY
Lithographers, active N.O. 1887; also publishers; HERMANN WEHRMANN, ODBERT V. GREEND, partners.
Contemporary listings: zinco–lithographers, 48 Bienville (1887).
References: NOCD 1887; *T. Demo.*, Nov. 11, 1887.

WEHRMANN'S SONS
Lithographers, active N.O. 1906–18; ADOLPH WEHRMANN, FREDERICK WEHRMANN, partners.

Contemporary listings: lithographers, 327 Chartres (1906–18).
Successor of H. WEHRMANN & CO. (1902) and H. WEHRMANN & SONS (1903–1905), the firm continued after the deaths of the partners, until 1923.
References: NOCD 1906–18.

WEIBLEN, ALBERT
Born Metzingen, Württemberg, Germany Nov. 9, 1857; died N.O. May 1, 1957.
Designer, active N.O. ca. 1885–1957; also stone carver.
Studied: Stuttgart, Germany.
Contemporary listings: foreman, KURSHEEDT & BIENVENU (1888); marble yard, 233 Baronne (1889–94); marble yard, 824 Baronne (1895–1907); pres., A. Weiblen Marble & Granite Co. (1908–57).
Weiblen came to the U.S. ca. 1883 and worked in Chicago, San Francisco and Cleveland. He settled in N.O. in 1885 where he was employed by KURSHEEDT & BIENVENU, first as a helper and then as foreman. In 1887 he bought the company, later incorporating it as the Albert Weiblen Marble and Granite Works, which was responsible for the majority of the work in Metairie Cemetery. In 1910 Weiblen established the Stone Mountain Granite Corporation in GA, which was responsible for the early work on the monumental carving on Stone Mountain. In other cities, he also designed and built numerous monuments, tombs, fountains, and wading pools.
References: NOCD 1888–1913, 1915–33, 1935, 1938, 1940, 1942, 1945–47, 1949, 1952–56; *D. Pic.*, Feb. 19, 1911; *T. Pic.*, Dec. 6, 13, 1925, Feb. 28, Mar. 14, 28, 1926, May 2, 1957; Friends of the Cabildo, *N.O. Architecture*, 3:39–40, 61–62, 103, 110–13; Gandolfo, 39, 51, 53, 65, 74, 93–95; Glenk, 98; Orleans Parish Registrar of Voters, NOPL; Reeves, 110, 113; Voss.

WEIBRACH, LUDWIG
Born Switzerland ca. 1821; died N.O. Jan. 23, 1855.
Painter, active N.O. 1855.

Portrait painter from ME who worked in N.O. for three weeks until his death.

References: Louisiana Charity Hospital, Death Records, NOPL.

WEIL, DAVID

Born Alsace, France ca. 1832; died N.O. June 29, 1900.

Lithographer, active N.O. 1870–85. Contemporary listings: lithographer (1870); lithographer, 113 Chartres (1871); lithographer, 9 St. Louis (1872); lithographer, 80 Exchange Al. (1873–82); lithographer (1885).

References: NOCD 1871–85; *D. Pic.*, June 30, 1900; *T. Demo.*, June 30, July 1, 1900; U.S. Census (1870), roll 521.

WEINBERGER, AMELIE

Painter, active N.O. ca. 1915–16.

Exhibited: ART ASSOCIATION OF NEW ORLEANS (1915–16).

References: Art Asso., *Catalogue* (1916); Art Asso., *Special Exhibition*.

WEINFURTER, JOHN JULIUS, JR.

Born N.O. July 22, 1876; died N.O. Nov. 3, 1938.

Engraver, active N.O. 1894–1900; also jeweler.

Contemporary listings: engraver (1894–99); steel engraver (1900).

Although not listed as an engraver, he continued with Weinfurter's Jewelers until his death.

References: NOCD 1894–1933, 1935, 1938; *T. Pic.*, Nov. 4–5, 1938; Orleans Parish Registrar of Voters, NOPL; THNOC Cemetery Survey; U.S. Census (1900), roll 571.

WEINMAN, R.

Lithographer, active N.O. 1854–57. Contemporary listings: lithographer, 130 Exchange Pl. (1854); lithographer, 115 Exchange Pl. (1855–58).

Noted for a lithographic cartoon of N.O. philanthropist John McDonogh. Weinman advertised the sale of his business due to poor health (Dec. 1856–Jan. 1857).

References: NOCD 1854–58; *Bee*, Dec. 30, 1856–Jan. 13, 1857 (advs.); *D. Pic.*, Aug. 28, 1904; Groce and Wallace.

WEINZETTEL, HENRY C.

Born N.O. Nov. 24, 1878; died June 12, 1960.

Engraver, active N.O. 1899–1960; also jeweler.

Contemporary listings: engraver (1899, 1906); engraver, Frantz Bros. and Co. (1900–1902); engraver, William Frantz and Co. (1903–1905, 1909–18); engraving department, William Frantz and Co. (1908).

Continued as an engraver until 1954.

References: NOCD 1899–1933, 1935, 1938, 1940, 1942, 1947, 1949, 1952–56, 1958, 1960; *T. Pic.*, June 14, 1960; Orleans Parish Registrar of Voters, NOPL; U.S. Census (1900), roll 571.

WEIS, GEORGE

Sculptor, active N.O. 1830; also carver, gilder.

Contemporary listings: sculptor, Customhouse betw. Royal and Chartres (1830).

References: NOCD 1827, 1830; *Courier*, Nov. 24, 1830; Groce and Wallace.

WEIS, SAMUEL WASHINGTON

Born Natchez MS Aug. 8, 1870; died Chicago IL Apr. 6, 1956.

Sketch artist, painter, active N.O. ca. 1915–36.

Exhibited: ART ASSOCIATION OF NEW ORLEANS (1915, 1917).

Memberships/positions: ARTISTS' ASSOCIATION OF NEW ORLEANS, v. pres. (1901–1903), 2nd v. pres. (1904–11).

Amateur artist who was a cotton broker with Julius Weis & Co. and was secretary–treasurer of the Art Association of New Orleans (1936). He spent some years of his later life in Chicago and its suburbs, where he was affiliated with several art clubs.

References: NOCD 1892–1915, 1917–1922, 1924–27, 1933, 1935, 1938, 1945–46; *States*, Apr. 12, 1936; *T. Pic.*, Oct. 25, 1936, Apr. 8, 1956; AANO, *Catalogue* (1901, 1902); Art Asso., *Catalogue* (1904, 1905, 1907, 1910, 1911, 1917); Art Asso., *Special Exhibition*; Fielding, *Dictionary*; Orleans Parish Registrar of Voters, NOPL; Reeves, 127, 130.

WEISS, HUGO A.

Artist, active N.O. 1898.

Contemporary listings: artist, WALLE & CO. (1898).

References: NOCD 1898.

WEISS, ROBERT
Born Berlin, Prussia ca. 1843.
Sculptor, active N.O. 1898; primarily coppersmith, tinsmith.
Studied: Potsdam, Germany (1857).
Designed and made by hand the copper eagle on top of the *Daily Picayune* building, Camp (1893), and was listed as proprietor of Southern Cornice and Ornamental Works (1893–1909).
References: NOCD 1872–1917; *D. Pic.*, Feb. 20, 1898; Dabney, 380, 460.

WELLS, SABINA ELLIOTT
Born 1876; died 1943.
Art craftsman, potter, painter, active N.O. 1902–1904.
Studied: NEWCOMB COLLEGE (1902–1904).
Exhibited: Louisiana Purchase Exposition, St. Louis MO (1904); Newcomb (1909); ART ASSOCIATION OF NEW ORLEANS (1910, 1914); Panama–Pacific International Exposition, San Francisco (1915).
Wells came to N.O. from Charleston SC to study art at Newcomb. She left to work at a pottery in Baltimore MD and later returned to Charleston to practice her craft. She continued to send pottery and oil paintings to exhibitions in N.O.
References: *D. Pic.*, Dec. 26, 1909; *Harlequin*, June 23, 1904, 8; Ball, "Newcomb Pottery Hits Big Time Again," *T. Pic./States-Item*, May 27, 1984; Art Asso., *Catalogue* (1910, 1914); Ormond and Irvine, 171; Poesch, *Newcomb Pottery*, 106; Smithsonian, *Newcomb Pottery*, 16, 18–19.

WELSCH, _____
Artist, active N.O. 1837.
Contemporary listings: artist, Orleans Theatre (1837).
References: NOCD 1837; *Courier*, July 2, 1838; Groce and Wallace.

WELSCHANS, WILLIAM
Born Germany ca. 1826; died N.O. Dec. 6, 1903.
Sculptor, active N.O. 1860–90; primarily carver, cabinetmaker.
Contemporary listings: sculptor (1860); woodcarver (1873, 1890).

References: NOCD 1866, 1868, 1872–75, 1883–84, 1886–87, 1890, 1899–1900, 1902–1903; *D. Pic.*, Dec. 7, 13, 1903; U.S. Census (1860), roll 421.

WERNTER, FERDINAND
Sculptor, active N.O. 1870; also stone carver.
Contemporary listings: wood and stone carver, 109 Rampart (1870).
References: NOCD 1870.

WEST, HARRY C.
Born PA ca. 1854; died N.O. Apr. 15, 1892.
Engraver, active N.O. 1889.
Contemporary listings: engraver (1889).
References: NOCD 1889; *D. Pic.*, Apr. 17, 1892; *T. Demo.*, Apr. 16, 1892.

WEST, WILLIAM EDWARD
Born Lexington KY Dec. 10, 1788; died Nashville TN Nov. 2, 1857.
Painter, active N.O. ca. 1816–17.
Studied: with THOMAS SULLY, Philadelphia (ca. 1808–1809); Florence, Italy (ca. 1819–24).
Exhibited: Royal Academy, London (1826–33); London (1834–37).
Memberships/positions: National Academy of Design, N.Y.C. (1832).
Portrait painter who studied and worked in Philadelphia (1807–16) and has usually been credited for the design of the print, *Battle of New Orleans and the Death of Major General Packenham, January 8, 1815*. It was first printed and published in Philadelphia by Joseph Yeager and published again in that city in July 1817 by McCarty & Davis. In early 1817, West was in N.O. where he painted several portraits but, prompted by a yellow fever epidemic in the summer of 1817, left the city for Natchez MS where he worked from 1817 to 1819. At the end of 1819, he sailed from N.O. for Europe where he worked as a successful portrait painter from 1820 to 1838 in Florence, Paris, and London. West continued his career in the U.S. when he returned briefly to Baltimore and then to N.Y.C. (1840–52).

References: *Argus*, July 19, 1826; *Appleton's CAB*; Barker, 540–41; Bénézit; Bolton, *Draughtsmen*; Bolton, *Painters in Miniature*; Bruns, 317; Bruce Chambers, 8; Corcoran Gallery, 29–30; *DAB*; Delgado, *New Orleans*, nos. 74, 75; Drepperd, "Selling," 220–21; Fielding, *Dictionary*; Flanary, 1010–15; Groce and Wallace; Harter and Tucker, 125; Information courtesy George E. Jordan; Sara Lewis; Mugridge and Conover, 95–96; Pennington; Rathbone, *Mississippi Panorama*, 189; Selter, 89; Tyler, 4–6; WPA, *Louisiana*, 162.

WEST, WILLIAM J.
Painter, active N.O. 1878–1905.
Contemporary listings: painter, with TOBY HART (1878); painter (1879, 1886, 1898–1905); painter, DRESSEL & EVANS (1881); DRESSEL & WEST (1883); painter, 104 St. Charles (1884); WEST & ST. CLAIR (1884–85); painter, 481 Chippewa (1887); painter, 479 Chippewa (1888–89); painter, 273 Third (1890); painter, 477 St. Thomas (1893); painter, 271 Third (1894); painter 1912 First (1895–97).
References: NOCD 1878–79, 1881, 1883–90, 1892–1907; *D. States*, Apr. 22, 1883.

WEST & ST. CLAIR
Painters, active N.O. 1884–85; WILLIAM J. WEST, ANDREW ST. CLAIR, partners.
Contemporary listings: artists (1884); painters, 265 Camp (1885).
References: NOCD 1885; *Eve. Chronicle*, Sept. 10, 20, 1884.

WESTFELDT, MARTHA JEFFERSON GASQUET (Mrs. George Gustaf Westfeldt)
Born N.O. Feb. 22, 1884; died N.O. Apr. 15, 1960.
Art craftsman, bookbinder, potter, active N.O. 1916–25.
Studied: NEWCOMB COLLEGE; Alfred University, NY.
Exhibited: ART ASSOCIATION OF NEW ORLEANS (1916–18).
Civic leader and art patron who also practiced the art of pottery making. During World War II she gave the profits from her novelty shop at 633

Royal to the French resistance. Her husband's uncle was PATRICK MCLOSKEY WESTFELDT.
References: *Item*, Jan. 16, Aug. 14, 1921; *Item–Trib.*, Mar. 12, 1933; *T. Pic.*, Oct. 25, 1925, May 4, 1927, Mar. 14, 1933, Apr. 17, 1960; Art Asso., *Catalogue* (1916–18); Ormond and Irvine, 154; Radcliffe, 11.

WESTFELDT, PATRICK MCLOSKEY
Born N.Y.C. May 25, 1854; died Charlotte NC June 2, 1907.
Painter, active N.O. 1887–1905.
Studied: England; with Carl Hecker and William Prettyman.
Exhibited: ARTISTS' ASSOCIATION OF NEW ORLEANS (1887, 1890–92, 1894, 1896–97, 1899–1903); Tulane University (1892–93); ART ASSOCIATION OF NEW ORLEANS (1904–1905, 1907, 1910); National Water Color Society, N.Y.C. (1897).
Memberships/positions: Artists' Association of New Orleans (1885–1903), pres. (1890, 1899–1900), treas. (1901–1903); Art Association of New Orleans, executive committee (1904–1907).
Commission merchant and importer with Westfeldt Bros., and watercolorist, mainly of landscapes. His nephew was married to MARTHA JEFFERSON GASQUET WESTFELDT.
References: NOCD 1881–1907; *Art and Letters*, 1(Dec. 1887):228; *Current Topics*, Jan. 1891, 25, Nov. 1891, 22, Jan. 1892, 24, Jan. 1893, 11; *D. Pic.*, Mar. 3, 1892, Feb. 14, 1893, Mar. 30, 1897; *Harlequin*, Dec. 6, 1899, 5; *Men and Matters*, Sept. 1897, 43, 51, Dec 1897, frontis.; *T. Demo.*, Dec. 14, 1894, Dec. 28, 1905, June 3, 1907; *Town Talk*, Sept. 1904, 27; AANO *Catalogue* (1890–91, 1896–97, 1899–1903); Art Asso., *Catalogue* (1904–1905, 1907); Bénézit; Fielding, *Dictionary*.

WHARTON, THOMAS KELAH
Born Hull, England Apr. 17, 1814; died N.O. May 24, 1862.
Sketch artist, active N.O. 1844–62; primarily architect.
Contemporary listings: sketch artist (1848).

Exhibited: National Academy of Design, N.Y.C. (1834–35).

After immigrating to OH with his parents (1830), Wharton moved to N.Y.C. (1832) where he practiced architecture and painted and exhibited landscapes. In Holly Springs MS (1845), he designed his first major building for N.O., Christ Church at Canal and Dauphine. Wharton eventually moved to N.O. where he worked for the U.S. Treasury Department in various administrative and supervisory positions in the construction of the U.S. Custom House (Nov. 1848–Jan. 1861). He also worked on private architectural projects in the city and, for a short period during 1859–60, was a partner in the architectural firm of Wharton & Reid. A talented sketch artist, Wharton made drawings of the progress and changes in the building of the Custom House and of scenes around the city and illustrated his N.O. diary (1853–62).

References: NOCD 1850–61, 1866–68; D. Pic., May 25, 1862; D. True Delta, May 25, 1862; Repub., May 30, 1875; Wkly. Delta, Jan. 31, 1848, Jan. 9, 1853; Hodding and Betty Carter, 93; Groce and Wallace; Reinders, 16–18; Stokes and Haskell, 142–43; U.S. Census (1860), roll 415; Thomas K. Wharton diary, New York Public Library; Samuel Wilson, History, 41–50, 52–54, 56–57.

WHEELER, ANNA NORTON (Mrs. Arthur S. Wheeler)

Born ca. 1869; died ca. Apr. 17, 1962.

Artist, active N.O. ca. 1891.

Exhibited: ARTISTS' ASSOCIATION OF NEW ORLEANS (1891).

References: Current Topics, Jan. 1892, 24; D. Pic., Dec. 17, 1891; T. Pic., Apr. 18, 1962; AANO, Catalogue (1891).

WHEELER, NATHAN W.

Born MA ca. 1789–94; died N.O. May 8, 1849.

Painter, active N.O. 1815–44.

Studied: with Benjamin West.

Contemporary listings: artist, Chartres (1815); soldier artist (1844). Miniature painter in Boston MA (1809) and Portsmouth NH (Apr. 1810) who fought in the Battle of N.O. In May 1815 he advertised his portrait of Andrew Jackson which was engraved and published in N.Y.C. in 1816. It was reported in 1844 that Wheeler was working on an historical painting, probably of the Battle of N.O. He was listed in N.O. as a merchant (1822–24) and at the time of his death was identified as a distiller and artisan artist.

References: Courier, Jan. 25, 1844; Gazette, May 6, 18, 1815 (advs.); Item–Trib., July 17, 1938; Glenk, 42; Groce and Wallace; LSM, Biennial Report for 1928–29, 73; N.O. Death Certificate (1849), 11:1444, NOPL.

WHITE, CHARLES HENRY

Born Hamilton, Ontario Apr. 14, 1878, died Nice, France Sept. 1918.

Etcher, active N.O. 1906.

Studied: Art Students League, N.Y.C.; Paris; with JOSEPH PENNELL, James Whistler, and Benjamin Constant.

Produced six etchings for his article, "New Orleans," for Harper's Monthly (Dec. 1906).

References: Harper's Monthly, Dec. 1906, 121–30; Beall, 523; Weitenkampf, American Graphic Art, 26.

WHITE, K.

Painter, active N.O. ca. 1900.

Executed watercolors of N.O. carnival scenes on a Mardi Gras dinner menu for the St. Charles Hotel (1900).

References: Harlequin, Mar. 7, 1900, 3.

WHITE, LILY F. (Mrs. Adam Ruppell)

Painter, active N.O. ca. 1915.

Contemporary listings: teacher, Laurel School (1910–14).

Exhibited: ART ASSOCIATION OF NEW ORLEANS (1915).

References: NOCD 1910–14; Art Asso., Special Exhibition.

WHITNEY, MORGAN

Born N.O. 1869; died N.O. July 19, 1913.

Painter, active N.O. 1891–1901; also photographer.

Studied: with Albert Herter, Ecole des Beaux Arts, Paris.

Exhibited: ARTISTS' ASSOCIATION OF NEW ORLEANS (1891, 1901); Tulane University (1893).

Memberships/positions: ART ASSOCIATION OF NEW ORLEANS (1905).

Member of a prominent N.O. family and brother of the founder of the Whitney National Bank, Whitney was an amateur painter and photographer of N.O. and the surrounding area. Also a connoisseur, he amassed a notable collection of artworks, bought in part during frequent visits to Europe.

References: NOCD 1890–1900, 1902–13; *Current Topics*, Jan. 1892, 24; *D. Pic.*, Dec. 17, 1891, Feb. 14, 1893, July 20, 1913; *T. Demo.*, Dec. 3, 1901; Collier, "The World of Art," *T. Pic.*, Mar. 7, 1976; AANO, *Catalogue* (1891, 1901); Art Asso., *Catalogue* (1905); Delgado, *Morgan Whitney Collection*; N.O. Death Certificate (1913), 158:203, NOPL.

WICKBOLD, HERMINA. *See* H. WEHRMANN & CO.

WIENER, B. C.

Painter, active N.O. 1871.

Awarded: Grand State Fair, best flower painting (1871).

References: *D. Pic.*, Dec. 3, 1871.

WIGG, JOHN

Painter, active N.O. 1889.

Contemporary listings: portrait painter, 105 N. Liberty (1889).

References: NOCD 1889.

WIGLEY, ALBERT E.

Born Birmingham, England ca. 1875; died N.O. July 24, 1934.

Engraver, active N.O. 1901–14.

Contemporary listings: engraver, with C. E. Adler (1901, 1906, 1913–14); engraver (1902, 1905–1906, 1909–10).

Listed as manager of C. E. Adler (1915–18) and president of William Frantz & Co., Inc., jewelers (1920–33).

References: NOCD 1901–1902, 1904–1906, 1908–33; *T. Pic.*, July 26, 1934.

WIKSTROM, BROR ANDERS

Born Stova Lassana, Sweden Apr. 14, 1854; died N.Y.C. Apr. 27, 1909.

Painter, art teacher, etcher, designer, illustrator, active N.O. 1883–1909.

Studied: Royal Academy of Fine Arts, Stockholm (before 1883); with Prof. Persens (before 1883); with Julien and Colarossi, Paris (before 1883).

Contemporary listings: sketching instructor, ARTISTS' ASSOCIATION OF NEW ORLEANS (1886); artist, 13 Commercial (1887, 1894); artist (1888, 1893); portrait painter, 13 Commercial (1888, 1890–92); painting, etching, and sketching instructor, Artists' Association (1891); artist and portrait painter, 618 Commercial (1896–1909).

Exhibited: SEEBOLD's (1886); Artists' Association of New Orleans (1886–87, 1890–92, 1894, 1896–99, 1901–1902); Tennessee Centennial Exposition, Nashville (1897); ART ASSOCIATION OF NEW ORLEANS (1904–1905); E. Curtis' Exchange (1902); Louisiana Historical Society (1903); Louisiana Purchase Exposition, St. Louis MO (1904).

Memberships/positions: Artists' Association of New Orleans, founder, treas. (1890), pres. (1892, 1895–96), secy. (1899–1903); Art Association of New Orleans, board of directors (1904–1908), executive committee (1904–1905, 1909); art commissioner to Europe for Nashville Exposition (ca. 1904).

Went to sea as a boy and was said to have earned the rank of captain. Because he was becoming nearsighted, he decided to change careers and pursue his interest in art. After studying in Stockholm, Wikstrom became a magazine illustrator. When engaged in 1881 to illustrate a story on life at sea, he decided to draw the scenes on voyages between Holland and N.Y.C. The trips influenced his decision to remain in the U.S., and he stayed in FL for about a year. His earliest recorded works in N.O. were cartoons on the covers of the *Mascot* in Sept. 1883 and *Figaro* in Jan. 1884.

He returned to N.O. during the World's Industrial and Cotton Centennial Exposition (1884–85) and remained to assist an unidentified fellow countryman, probably CHARLES BRITON, in designing and creating N.O. carnival pageants. Wikstrom continued with the work after his colleague's death and developed into the city's most noted carnival designer during the 1880s and 1890s, particularly for the Rex and Proteus organizations. He was actively involved in the arts and helped to organize the ARTISTS' ASSOCIATION OF NEW ORLEANS, taught in its art school, and participated on its art juries. In 1892 he became the association's president and was corresponding secretary in 1901. Wikstrom was the founder and chief financial supporter of the short-lived literary and artistic journal *Art and Letters* (1887) and also contributed his etchings as illustrations. He was often listed as a portrait painter, but also painted historical and genre subjects and LA landscapes. His marine paintings, usually taken from sketches made during his annual summer vacations sailing in Sweden or on trips to other parts of Europe and the Caribbean, were highly sought after during his life. At the time of his death, Wikstrom was working temporarily in N.Y.C. on the design for a parade for a Hudson–Fulton celebration.

References: NOCD 1887–88, 1890–1900; NOBD 1898; *Architectural Art*, 4(Apr. 1909):3; *Art and Letters*, 1(Feb. 1887)–1(Dec. 1887):illustrations, 1(Dec. 1887):228; *Current Topics*, Nov. 1890, 23, Jan. 1891, 25, Jan. 1892, 24–25, Jan. 1893, 11; *D. City Item*, Dec. 13, 1892; *D. Pic.*, Nov. 7, 1886, Oct. 2, 17, Dec. 17, 1887, Feb. 18, Mar. 1, 1888, July 27, Nov. 13, Dec. 17, 1890, Apr. 29, May 22, Dec. 17, 1891, Nov. 27, Dec. 13, 14, 1892, Mar. 30, 1897, Dec. 18, 1903, Apr. 28, 29, 30, May 2, 1909, Jan. 31, 1910; *D. States*, Oct. 29, Nov. 5, 1886, Apr. 29, 1891, Jan. 8, 1899; *Down in Dixie*, July 15, 1896, 10, Aug. 1, 1896, 6 7, 19;

Harlequin, Nov. 1, 1899, 1,10, Dec. 6, 1899, 5, Dec. 10, 1903, 3, Dec. 28, 1905, 8; *Lantern*, 1886, 6; *Mascot*, Sept. 1, 8, 29, 1883, covers; *Men and Matters*, Sept. 1897, 47–51; *Processional* (Mardi Gras, 1938):5; *T. Demo.*, Jan. 3, 1886, Nov. 13, Dec. 17, 1890, Dec. 13, 18, 1892, Dec. 14, 1894, Dec. 3, 1901, Mar. 22, 24, 1902, Mar. 12, 1905, Apr. 28, 1909; *T. Pic.*, Jan. 25, 1937; Collier, "The World of Art: Unsigned Watercolor Attributed to Early N.O. Carnival Designer," *T. Pic.*, July 18, 1965; *Town Talk*, Feb. 1905, 46; AANO, *Catalogue* (1886, 1890, 1891, 1896, 1897, 1899, 1901, 1902); AANO, *Charter, Constitution, and By-Laws*; Art Asso., *Catalogue* (1904, 1905, 1907); Art Asso., *Memorial Exhibition*; Bénézit; Comité de l'Exposition française; Delgado, *Catalogue of Paintings, Sculpture*, 57; Glenk, 80; Levy, 1903–1904, 197; Mount, 134–36; Tennessee Centennial Exposition, 5, 106; WPA, "Lives"; Perry Young, illustrations.

WILCOX, JOHN
Painter, active N.O. 1882–93.
Contemporary listings: asst. scenic artist, Grand Opera House (1882–84); asst. artist, St. Charles Theatre (1889); asst. artist, Academy of Music and St. Charles Theatre (1890); scenic artist, Academy of Music (1893).
References: NOCD 1882–84, 1889–90, 1893.

WILCOX, MISS S. C.
Art teacher, active N.O. 1856.
Contemporary listings: teacher, 286 Camp (1856).
Advertised classes in "Grecian Painting."
References: *D. Crescent*, Jan. 12, 1856; *D. Delta*, Jan. 12–13, 1856.

WILDE, EMILY
Born LA.
Commercial artist, active N.O. 1910–17.
Contemporary listings: decorative artist (1910); artist, with Miss J. Wilde (1913); artist, 136 Carondelet (1914–15); artist (1917).
Sister of JENNIE WILDE.

References: NOCD 1913–17, 1920; U.S. Census (1910), roll 524.

WILDE, JENNIE (Virginia Wilkinson Wilde)

Born Augusta GA Apr. 10, 1865; died Measden, England Sept. 11, 1913. Painter, commercial artist, designer, art teacher, active N.O. 1882–1913. Studied: with HENRIETTE WINANT, SOUTHERN ART UNION (1882–83); Southern Art Union (ca. 1885); with J. Carroll Beckwith, Art League of New York (1886).

Contemporary listings: Mott & Wilde (1889); teacher, Southern Academic Institute (1889–90, 1892); artist, 17 Carondelet (1890–91); artist (1892–93); teacher, Home Institute (1893–97); teacher, Guillot Institute (1895); studio, 219 Camp (1898–1902); artist, 136 Carondelet (1903–1904, 1907–13); artist, Heath Schwartz & Co. (1905); artist, Schwartz Eustis Co. (1906); decorative artist (1910).

Exhibited: ARTISTS' ASSOCIATION OF NEW ORLEANS (1889–92, 1901); Tulane University (1892).

Awarded: Southern Art Union, honorable mention for sketch from life (1883).

Memberships/positions: Art League of New York (1886–1913); FIVE OR MORE CLUB (1892); Artists' Association of New Orleans (1896); ART ASSOCIATION OF NEW ORLEANS (1905).

Teacher with the Southern Academic Institute (1886–92), and with the Home Institute (1893–97), before she opened her own studio as a commercial artist. Wilde became the designer of pageants for certain N.O. carnival organizations, particularly Comus for which she worked exclusively the last 10 years of her life. She executed the mural paintings for the interior of the Church of Notre Dame on Jackson Avenue (1903). Also a well-known author and poet, Wilde was considered at her death N.O.'s most distinguished woman artist. Sister of EMILY WILDE.

References: NOCD 1886, 1889–1913; *Current Topics*, Nov. 1890, 23, Jan. 1891, 25, Jan. 1892, 24, Jan. 1893, 10–11; *D. Pic.*, May 8, 1883, Dec. 17, 1889, July 27, Dec. 17, 1890, Mar. 29, Dec. 17, 1891, Mar. 3, 6, 1892, Aug. 23, 1894, Jan. 31, 1903, Oct. 7, 13, 1913; *D. States*, Dec. 17, 1890, Jan. 23, 1898, Dec. 6, 1903; *Down in Dixie*, July 15, 1896, 10; *Harlequin*, Oct. 25, 1899, 9; *Men and Matters*, Sept. 1897, 50–52; *Review*, Apr. 8, 1891; *T. Demo.*, May 8, 1883, Oct. 24, 1886, Mar. 3, Dec. 13, 1892, Oct. 8, Oct. 13, 1913; AANO, *Catalogue* (1890, 1891, 1901); Art Asso., *Catalogue* (1905); Fielding, *Dictionary*; Glenk, 191, 279; Grace King, *Memories*, 352–53; Mount, 26–29; U.S. Census (1910), roll 524.

WILDER, J. F.

Painter, active N.O. ca. 1871.

Contemporary listings: painter (1871).

Awarded: Grand State Fair, best landscape painting and best animal painting (1871).

References: *D. Pic.*, Dec. 3, 1871.

WILKINS, JAMES F.

Painter, art teacher, active N.O. 1842–43.

Studied: Royal Academy, London (1835–36).

Contemporary listings: miniature painter, 34 St. Charles (1842); portrait and miniature painter, teacher, 32 St. Charles (1843).

Exhibited: Royal Academy, London (1835–36).

Memberships/positions: Society for the Study of Historical, Poetical and Rustic Figures, Paris.

References: NOCD 1842; *D. Pic.*, Jan. 27, 1843; Friends of the Cabildo, *250 Years*, 37; Groce and Wallace; McDermott, *Lost Panoramas*, 16; Wilkins.

WILKINSON, STEPHANIE. *See* BIGOT, STEPHANIE WILKINSON

WILLEM, MICHEL

Artist, active N.O. 1891, also engineer.

Contemporary listings: artist, with Ed. H. Peter (1891).

Also listed as clerk (1883, 1886, 1888), and as collector (1885) with T. LILIENTHAL. Possibly Michel Wil-

lem, born N.O. ca. 1867; died N.O. August 28, 1928.
References: NOCD 1882–88, 1891–93; *T. Pic.*, Aug. 29, 1928.

WILLIAMS, MR. ____
Engraver, active N.O. 1884.
Contemporary listings: ornamental glass engraver, John Gauche's Sons (1884).
References: *D. Pic.*, Nov. 28, 1884.

WILLIAMS, BLANCHE BLANCHARD. *See* BLANCHARD, BLANCHE

WILLIAMS, DANIEL
Born London, England ca. 1827–30; died N.O. Oct. 17, 1855.
Engraver, active N.O. ca. 1852–55; also printer.
Contemporary listings: engraver, with JOHN DOUGLAS, SR., 17 St. Charles (1855).
References: *Bee*, Oct. 18, 1855; *D. Crescent*, Oct. 19, 1855; *D. Delta*, Oct. 18, 1855; *T. Deutsche Zeitung*, Oct. 19, 1855.

WILLIAMS, DAVID M.
Born Louisville KY Sept. 1, 1838; died N O. Mar. 23, 1882.
Engraver, active N.O. 1872–80; primarily marble cutter, stone cutter.
Contemporary listings: engraver (1872, 1880).
References: NOCD 1861, 1866–67, 1870, 1872–82; THNOC Cemetery Survey; U.S. Census (1870), roll 524, (1880), roll 463.

WILLIAMS, E.
Artist, active N.O. 1849; primarily carver.
Contemporary listings: artist, cor. Customhouse and Dauphine (1849).
References: NOCD 1837–38, 1841–43, 1846, 1849–56; Groce and Wallace.

WILLIAMS, JAMES W.
Born England ca. 1787.
Painter, active N.O. 1843–45.
Contemporary listings: miniature painter, 3 St. Charles (1843); miniature painter, 38 St. Charles (1845).
Exhibited: Pennsylvania Academy of Fine Arts, Philadelphia (1829–44).
References: *D. Pic.*, Feb. 9 12, 1843 (advs.); Dec. 9, 1845; Groce and Wallace.

WILLIAMS, LOUISA A.
Born GA.
Painter, sculptor, active N.O. 1896–1902.
Studied: with Prof. Hart, N.Y.C.; with William Ordway Partridge, N.Y.C.; with Moody and Fisher, Washington DC; Baltimore Conservatory.
Exhibited: Grunewald's music store (1896); Canal St. (1902); Charleston Exposition.
Artist from Augusta GA who specialized in animal paintings. She maintained a studio in Baltimore MD (ca. 1901) where she created and sold a number of sculptures and other works.
References: NOCD 1897, 1901; *D. States*, Feb. 20, 1896, May 11, 29, 1902.

WILLIAMS, THOMAS
Art teacher, painter, active N.O. ca. 1834–42.
Contemporary listings: professor of drawing and painting (1834–36); professor of drawing and painting, portrait and landscape painter, 5 Camp (1838–39).
References: NOCD 1838, 1842; *Courier*, Oct. 9, 1834–Apr. 6, 1835 (advs.); *D. Pic.*, Dec. 6, 1838–Aug. 22, 1839 (advs.); Groce and Wallace.

WILLIAMS, TRUE
Engraver, illustrator, active N.O. 1872.
Contemporary listings: engraver, *Our Home Journal* (1872); illustrator, *New Orleans Weekly* (1872).
References: *Our Home Journal*, Jan. 27, 1872, 56; *Repub.*, Dec. 15, 1872.

WILLIAMSON, FRANK G.
Commercial artist, active N.O. 1898–1900.
Contemporary listings: artist (1898); artist, Bucklin Advertising Concern (1900).
References: NOCD 1898, 1900.

WILLIAMSON, JAMES H.
Painter, active N.O. 1873–74.
Contemporary listings: artist (1873); painter (1874).
References: NOCD 1873–74.

WILLIAMSON, SUSANA (Mrs. C. H. Williamson)
Born Ireland ca. 1812; died N.O. Oct. 12, 1854.

Art teacher, active N.O. 1854.
Contemporary listings: drawing teacher (1854).
References: NOCD 1851; *D. Crescent*, Jan. 4–10, 1854 (advs.); *D. Pic.*, Oct. 13, 1854; U.S. Census (1850), roll 232.

WILLY, JOHN H.
Lithographer, active N.O. 1899–1901.
Contemporary listings: lithographer (1899, 1901).
References: NOCD 1898–1901.

WILMERSDORF, JAKE
Born IL ca. 1874.
Painter, active N.O. 1910.
Contemporary listings: painter (1910).
References: U.S. Census (1910), roll 520.

WILSON, FRANK H.
Born N.O. Feb. 22, 1844; died Indianapolis IN July 14, 1900.
Sketch artist, active N.O. 1876.
Secretary of the Shakespeare Club who designed the lithograph for the cover of the *Illuminated Programme* for the Varieties Theatre (1876). He worked as a clerk (1870, 1872), bookkeeper (1871, 1873–77), and manager for JOHN W. MADDEN, until he moved to Plattsmouth NE (1880) where he lived the rest of his life. He was on a business trip in Indianapolis when he died.
References: NOCD 1868, 1870–80; *D. Pic.*, July 22, 1900; *Repub.*, Apr. 30, 1876.

WILSON, J. G.
Painter, active N.O. 1838–42.
Contemporary listings: portrait painter, 411 Magazine (1838).
Possibly John Graham Wilson, born ca. 1818; died N.O. Feb. 14, 1879.
References: NOCD 1838, 1842; *D. Pic.*, Feb. 15–16, 1879; Glenk, 80; Groce and Wallace.

WILSON, JOHN
Painter, active N.O. 1883.
Contemporary listings: scenic artist, Grand Opera House (1883).
References: NOCD 1883.

WILSON, JOHN T.
Born England ca. 1831.
Painter, active N.O. 1880–89; also photographer.

Contemporary listings: artist (1880, 1887, 1889); artist, 152 Poydras (1881); portrait painter, 256 Canal (1883); portrait painter, (1884, 1886); portrait painter, 1465 Tchoupitoulas (1885).
References: NOCD 1881, 1883–89; U.S. Census (1880), roll 461.

WILSON, MATTHEW
Born London, England July 17, 1814; died Brooklyn NY Feb. 23, 1892.
Painter, active N.O. 1845.
Studied: with HENRY INMAN; with Edouard Dubufe, Paris (1835).
Contemporary listings: portrait painter, St. Charles oppos. St. Charles Hotel (1845).
Memberships/positions: National Academy of Design, N.Y.C. (1843).
A miniature and portrait painter, Wilson came to the U.S. from London in 1832, settling in Philadelphia. He visited N.O. for a short period and executed several portraits (1845). Wilson was commissioned by the GA legislature to paint a copy of JOHN VANDERLYN's portrait of Andrew Jackson in Charleston SC (Aug. 1847). During the Civil War, he spent time in Washington DC where he painted images of prominent statesmen, including the last portrait of Abraham Lincoln. He settled permanently in Brooklyn NY after the Civil War.
References: *D. Delta*, Aug. 12, 1847; *D. Pic.*, Feb. 12, 1845; *D. Tropic*, Mar. 10, 14, Apr. 10, May 15, July 31, 1845; *Appleton's CAB*; Bénézit; Bolton, *Painters in Miniature*, 174; Fielding, *Dictionary*; Friends of the Cabildo, *250 Years*, 37; Groce and Wallace; Waugh, 3.

WILTZ, EMILE (Jean Baptiste Emile)
Born N.O. 1812; died N.O. July 26, 1891.
Painter, active N.O. 1841–42.
Contemporary listings: portrait painter, 146 Toulouse (1841–42).
Served as parish tax collector (1843), alderman in the first municipality, chairman of the committee on public education, and translator for the LA Senate (1844).

References: NOCD 1837, 1841–43, 1846, 1849–51; *Courier*, Mar. 15, May 11, 15, July 12, 1843, Apr. 6, 1846, Mar. 8, 1849, Mar. 25, 1850, Mar. 18, 1854; *D. City Item*, July 27, Aug. 1, 1891; *D. Pic.*, July 27, Aug. 2, 1891; *T. Demo.*, July 27, 1891; Groce and Wallace; N.O. Death Certificate (1891), 99:1148, NOPL.

WILTZ, LEONARD, JR.
Born N.O. ca. 1815–18; died N.O. Apr. 14, 1861.
Sculptor, active N.O. 1843–46; primarily marble cutter.
Contemporary listings: marble sculptor, 100 Dauphin (1843); marble sculptor, 96 Dauphin (1846).
References: NOCD 1837, 1841–43, 1846, 1849–53, 1855–56, 1858; *Bee*, Apr. 15, 1861; Groce and Wallace; N.O. Death Certificate (1861), 21:519, NOPL; U.S. Census (1850), roll 238.

WINANT, HENRIETTE
Art teacher, active N.O. 1882–84.
Studied: N.Y.C.
Contemporary listings: teacher, SOUTHERN ART UNION AND WOMAN'S INDUSTRIAL ASSOC., 203 Canal (1882–84); teacher, 212 Prytania (1884).
Graduate of N.Y.C. art schools who taught in N.O. (1882–84) and returned to her home in the North for the summers.
References: NOCD 1884; *D. Pic.*, Nov. 11, 1882, May 8, 11, 1883, Apr. 27, 1884; *D. States*, Apr. 29, 1883; *T. Demo.*, May 8, 1883, Oct. 31, Nov. 23, 1884.

WINTER, J A
Born Germany ca. 1821.
Painter, active N.O. 1850.
Contemporary listings: portrait painter (1850).
References: Groce and Wallace; U.S. Census (1850), roll 238.

WINTERHALDER, JOSEPH
Born Germany ca. 1820; died N.O. Nov. 1, 1867.
Painter, active N.O. 1851–57.
Contemporary listings: portrait and landscape painter, 121 Greatmen (1849, 1852–54); portraits, Port near Greatmen (1855–56); portrait painter, 46 Port (1857).

Itinerant portrait and landscape painter who was the brother of Franz X. Winterhalder, a noted portrait painter in Paris and England. Joseph Winterhalder was first recorded in the U.S. in Montgomery AL (1849) and was said to have been on his way to N.O., then CA. He settled in N.O. by 1851 and married Margaret Mohr. He changed occupations by 1858 and gave up painting to become a baker for the rest of his life. Father of LOUIS ADOLPH WINTERHALDER.
References: NOCD 1852–61, 1866–67; *Courier*, Apr. 27, 1853; Groce and Wallace; N.O. Death Certificate (1867), 41:492, NOPL; Second District Court, Succession of Joseph Winterhalder, 1867, 30101, NOPL; William Young.

WINTERHALDER, LOUIS ADOLPH
(Ludwig)
Born N.O. July 31, 1862; died N.O. Mar. 19, 1931.
Commercial artist, painter, cartoonist, active N.O. 1882–1931.
Studied: with ANDRES MOLINARY; with ACHILLE PERELLI; with WILLIAM H. BUCK.
Contemporary listings: artist, the *Mascot* (1883); artist (1887); artist, with FELIX OLLERT (1888); designer, with Charles A. Orleans (1889); designer, Hallowell Granite Co. (1890); special artist, *Picayune* (1892–95); artist, *Picayune* (1896–1914, 1916); cartoonist (1915, 1917–18).
Exhibited: SOUTHERN ART UNION (1882); Academy of Fine Arts, Chicago.
Born Ludwig Adolph Winterhalder and credited with drawing the first political cartoon published in a N.O. newspaper (*Daily Picayune*, Apr. 18, 1896). He also illustrated the covers of the *Daily Picayune Carrier's Address* and created the paper's cartoon character, the "weather frog." Son of JOSEPH WINTERHALDER.
References: NOCD 1883, 1887–90, 1892–1928, 1930–31; *D. Pic.*, May 2, 1882, Apr. 18, 1896, Aug. 16, Dec. 6, 1903; *D. Pic. Carrier's Address*, 1897, 1900, 1901, 1902, 1903, 1907; *Mascot*, Sept. 9, 1882–

Mar. 3, 1883; *Morn. Trib.*, Mar. 20, 1931; *T. Demo.*, Jan. 29, May 14, 1893; *T. Pic.*, Mar. 20, 1931, Jan. 25, 1937, April 26, 1958, Mar. 20, 1960; Dabney, 308, 310; Fielding, *Dictionary*; LSM, *Biennial Report for 1922-23*, 112; Mount, 144; Orleans Parish Registrar of Voters, NOPL; *Picayune's Guide* (1897, 1900, 1906); Second District Court, Succession of Joseph Winterhalder, 1867, 30101, NOPL; THNOC 1985.71.1-.79; U.S. Census (1900), roll 573.

WISE, JAMES
Painter, active N.O. 1843.
Contemporary listings: miniature painter, cor. Royal and Customhouse (1843).
Miniature painter who also worked in Charleston SC (1844-45), VA, MO, and possibly San Francisco (1856-60).
References: *D. Pic.*, Apr. 18-May 3, 1843 (advs.); Friends of the Cabildo, *250 Years*, 37; Groce and Wallace.

WISER, ANGELO
Born PA ca. 1841.
Painter, active N.O. 1871-72.
Contemporary listings: scenic artist and fresco painter, St. Charles Theatre (1871); scenic artist, St. Charles Theatre (1872).
References: NOCD 1871; *National Repub.*, Nov. 3, 1872; *Repub.*, Oct. 15, 1871, Jan. 26, Apr. 9, 1872; *Times*, Oct. 8, 1871; Groce and Wallace; National Gallery of Art, 107.

WISLY, MR. ____
Born LA Mar. 3, 1875.
Artist, active N.O. 1900.
Contemporary listings: artist (1900).
References: U.S. Census (1900), roll 570.

WOGAN, CAROLINE S. *See* DURIEUX, CAROLINE

WOISERI, JOHN L. BOQUETA DE. *See* BOQUETA DE WOISERI, JOHN L.

WOLF, JACOB J., JR.
Born N.O. June 5, 1888.
Commercial artist, engraver, active N.O. 1907-60.
Contemporary listings: engraver (1907); artist, NEW ORLEANS ENGRAVING AND ELECTROTYPE CO., LTD. (1908-1909); artist, Spencer En-

graving Co. and landscape artist (1910); engraver, 618 Commercial (1911-12); artist, Crockett Agency (1913-16); artist, Chalmers Agency Inc. (1917-18).
Continued with Chambers Agency Inc. as an artist (1919) and as art director (1920-31), and as art director with Walker Saussy Advertising until he retired ca. 1973.
References: NOCD 1907-25, 1927-28, 1930-31, 1933, 1935, 1938, 1940, 1942, 1945-47, 1949, 1952-56, 1958, 1960-62, 1964-69, 1971-75; *Creole Tourist's Guide*, cover; U.S. Census (1910), roll 521.

WOLF, SARAH K.
Died N.O. Feb. 2, 1953.
Painter, active N.O. ca. 1890-94.
Studied: with Mrs. F. Moore (1894).
Exhibited: Mrs. F. Moore's studio (1894).
Praised in the *Daily Picayune* for a 116-piece set of china she had painted some years before with scenes of LA and other places. Because of its delicacy, she had refused to send it to the Columbian Exposition, Chicago, in 1893. She also painted in oil and watercolor on silk, velvet, and canvas.
References: NOCD 1897; *D. Pic.*, Aug. 19, 1894; *T. Demo.*, Apr. 22, 1894; *T. Pic.*, Feb. 3, 1953.

WOLFE, JOHN C.
Artist, active N.O. 1891.
Contemporary listings: artist (1891).
Possibly John Wolfe, born N.O. June 1844; died N.O. Apr. 17, 1904.
References: NOCD 1891; *D. Pic.*, Apr. 18, 24, 1904; *T. Demo.*, Apr. 18, 24, 1904; N.O. Death Certificate (1904), 132:557, NOPL; THNOC Cemetery Survey.

WOLFE, JOSEPH C.
Painter, active N.O. 1884-88.
Contemporary listings: artist (1884, 1886); painter (1888).
References: NOCD 1884, 1886, 1888.

WOLTZE, G.
Painter, active N.O. 1889.
Signed two watercolors, *Hauling Cotton at the Levee* and *Street Scene*,

New Orleans, the latter inscribed "New Orleans, 1889."
References: *Old Print Shop Portfolio*, (Oct. 1946).

WOMAN'S INDUSTRIAL ASSOCIATION. *See* SOUTHERN ART UNION

WOOD, MR. _____
Colorer, active N.O. 1857.
Contemporary listings: photograph colorer, Clarke & Hedrick (1857).
References: *D. Delta*, Mar. 31, 1857.

WOOD, DANIEL
Born NH ca. 1821.
Artist, active N.O. 1850.
Contemporary listings: artist (1850).
References: Groce and Wallace; U.S. Census (1850), roll 234.

WOOD, ELLA MIRIAM
Born Birmingham AL Feb 18, 1888; died N.O. Dec. 7, 1976.
Painter, art teacher, active N.O. 1911–71.
Studied: NEWCOMB COLLEGE (1905–1908, 1910–11); Pennsylvania Academy of Fine Arts, Philadelphia (ca. 1909); with Charles W. Hawthorne, Cape Cod Outdoor School of Painting, Provincetown MA; with HENRY MCCARTER; with Daniel Garber; with William Chase, N.Y.C.
Contemporary listings: artist (1913, 1916–17).
Exhibited: ART ASSOCIATION OF NEW ORLEANS (1911, 1913–14, 1916–17).
Awarded: Newcomb College, Fannie Estelle Holley Memorial Medal for proficiency in watercolor painting (1907–1908); Mississippi State Fair, purchase prize (1913).
Memberships/positions: Art Association of New Orleans.
Portrait and mural painter who was listed as an artist from 1920 to 1971. Wood exhibited at the Arts and Crafts Club (1924, 1926–27), where she was an instructor (1924–25), the Art Association of New Orleans (1932, 1939), and the DELGADO MUSEUM OF ART (1935, 1940).
References: NOCD 1913, 1916–17, 1920–24, 1928–30, 1932–33, 1938, 1940, 1942, 1945–47, 1949, 1952–56, 1958, 1960–62, 1964–69, 1971–72, 1974–77; *Item*, Jan. 16, June 12, 1921, Sept. 10, 1950; *Item-Trib.*, Feb. 5, 1939; *Morn. Trib.*, Sept. 18, Oct. 20, 1926, Nov. 9, 1927, Sept. 27, 1929, Nov. 11, 1932; *New Orleans Life*, Nov. 1925, 27; *States*, Nov. 27, 1927, Jan. 22, 1931; *T. Pic.*, Feb. 29, June 1, Oct. 5–6, 1924, May 24, 1925, Oct. 20, 1926, Jan. 13, 1935, Sept. 5, 1937, Mar. 15, 1938, Sept. 10, 1950; Collier, "The World of Art: Portraitist Paints Three Generations," *T. Pic.*, Aug. 23, 1964; *T. Pic.*, Dec. 9, 1976; Art Asso., *Catalogue* (1911, 1913, 1914, 1916, 1917); Bénézit; Collins and Opitz; Fielding, *Dictionary*; Glenk, 47, 337; LSM, *Annual Report for 1918*, 33; LSM, *Annual Report for 1919*, 37; LSM, *Biennial Report for 1920–21*, 9, 50; LSM, *Biennial Report for 1922–23*, 18, 112; Ormond and Irvine, 172; Poesch, *Newcomb Pottery*, 106; Sutton, 96.

WOOD, MRS. K. E.
Art craftsman, active N.O. 1888.
Exhibited: TULANE DECORATIVE ART LEAGUE FOR WOMEN (1888).
Memberships/positions: Tulane Decorative Art League for Women (1888).
References: *D. Pic.*, Feb. 12, 1888; Tulane Decorative Art League.

WOOD, TRIST (Julien Bringier Trist)
Born June 10, 1868; died N.O. Nov. 7, 1952.
Cartoonist, art teacher, sketch artist, active N.O. 1880–1935.
Studied: Tulane University.
Contemporary listings: teacher (1893); artist (1894–95); artist, *Times-Democrat* (1907–1908); cartoonist, *Item* (1913–18).
Artist from a prominent N.O. family who began sketching early, sending a drawing to the mayor of the city (1880) and making drawings in Mexico (1882). Wood studied and taught art at Tulane and then, for the next 15 years, he lived in Europe as a student, art critic, and author, and was the editor of the *Quartier Latin*, a periodical for Americans in Paris. After returning to N.O., he was primarily a newspaper cartoonist, one of the first in the city, working for the *Times-Democrat* (ca. 1907–12)

and the *Daily Item* (ca. 1912–25). After a few years of retirement, Wood joined the staff of a succession of newspapers supported by LA politician Huey Long from 1930 to 1940: *Louisiana Progress, American Progress, Daily Progress,* and *Progress.* He continued to contribute cartoons to N.O. newspapers, including the *Item–Tribune* (ca. 1932–35), and in later years spent most of his time researching family genealogies.
References: NOCD 1886, 1890–95, 1897, 1906–1908, 1910–25, 1927–28, 1930, 1932–33, 1935, 1938, 1940, 1942, 1945–47, 1949, 1952–53; *D. States,* May 17, 1880; *Demo.,* May 18, 1880; *T. Demo.,* May 17, 1908; *T. Pic.,* Nov. 8, 1952; Chase, 32–35, 53–58; Trist Wood Papers, THNOC; WPA, *Louisiana,* 170.

WOODHOUSE, HARRY V.
Born DE ca. 1874.
Artist, active N.O. 1910.
Contemporary listings: artist (1910).
References: NOCD 1910; U.S. Census (1910), roll 519.

WOODSIDE, MR. _____
Painter, active N.O. 1837–50.
Painted a river scene of N.O. to ornament a fire engine built for the Louisiana Hose Company (1837). Another engine, manufactured in Baltimore MD for the Lafayette Fire Company of N.O. (1850), was decorated by Woodside with figures of Thomas Jefferson, Gen. Lafayette, John Rodgers, and the signers of the Declaration of Independence.
References: *Bee,* Mar. 28, 1837; *D. Delta,* Jan. 25, 1850.

WOODWARD, ELLEN
Born LA ca. 1889.
Art teacher, active N.O. 1910.
Contemporary listings: drawing teacher (1910).
Daughter of WILLIAM WOODWARD.
References: U.S. Census (1910), roll 524.

WOODWARD, ELLSWORTH
Born Seekonk MA July 14, 1861; died N.O. Feb. 28, 1939.
Art teacher, painter, etcher, sculptor, active N.O. 1885–1939.

Studied: Rhode Island School of Design, Providence (1878–80); Munich, Germany (ca. 1884); with Samuel Richards and Richard Fehr, Munich; with Carl Marr, Munich (1891–92).
Contemporary listings: professor, Tulane University (1886, 1888–89); professor of drawing, Tulane University (1887); professor, NEWCOMB COLLEGE (1890–1918).
Exhibited: ARTISTS' ASSOCIATION OF NEW ORLEANS (1887, 1890, 1892, 1896–97, 1899, 1901–1902); TULANE DECORATIVE ART LEAGUE FOR WOMEN (1888); ART LEAGUE OF NEW ORLEANS (1889); Tulane University (1890, 1892–93); Tennessee Centennial Exposition, Nashville (1897); Newcomb College (1899, 1905); Louisiana Historical Society (1900); E. Curtis' Exchange (1902); ART ASSOCIATION OF NEW ORLEANS (1904–1905, 1907, 1913–18); Fine Arts Club (1909).
Awarded: Newcomb College, first medal, and Art Association of New Orleans, gold medal (1910); Mississippi Art Association, gold medal; Society of Arts and Crafts of Boston, bronze medal of honor.
Memberships/positions: Providence Art Club (ca. 1880); Art League of New Orleans (1889); Artists' Association of New Orleans (1896); ARTS EXHIBITION CLUB, executive committee, (1901); Art Association of New Orleans (1904–18), executive committee (1904–1905, 1913–14, 1916–18), board member (1910–11, 1913–14, 1916–18), v. pres. (1913–14, 1916–18); American Federation of Arts (1913); College Art Association (1913); International Union of Fine Arts and Letters, Paris (1913); Louisiana Art Teachers' Association (1913); Minnesota State Art Society (1913); Society of Western Artists (1913); Royal Society for Encouragement of Art, Manufacturing and Commerce, London (1913); Philadelphia Art Guild; Providence Watercolor Club; Society of Arts and Crafts of Boston; National Society of Craftsmen.

Portrait, landscape, and genre painter who began drawing early, studied art in the progressive MA school system, at the Rhode Island School of Design, and in Munich. Woodward moved to N.O. in 1885 to take the position of assistant professor of painting and drawing at Tulane under his brother WILLIAM WOODWARD. Ellsworth Woodward remained at Tulane until the opening of Newcomb in 1887 when he became the school's first professor of art and then the head of the art department from 1890 until he retired as director emeritus in June 1931. At Newcomb, Woodward introduced the college's successful art pottery program and expanded the art department curriculum to include a variety of programs, such as embroidery, metalwork, and china painting. In his retirement, Woodward remained active as an artist and began making etchings from the sketches he had made during his earlier travels. He was active in the formation and administration of many art organizations: founder of the Tulane Decorative Art League for Women, of NEW ORLEANS ART POTTERY, and of the Arts Exhibition Club; a founder and first president of the Art Association; an active participant in the founding of the DELGADO MUSEUM OF ART and later a member and president of the museum board and acting director; a founder and president of the Southern States Art League. Woodward was frequently honored for his contributions to the arts and was awarded an honorary Doctor of Laws degree by Tulane (1933). In 1934, he was appointed by Pres. Franklin D. Roosevelt to the directorship of the Gulf States Public Works of Art Project which provided assistance to unemployed artists. Woodward's special talent was watercolor painting, and in 1936 the Fine Arts Club of N.O. established a prize in his name for the best watercolor shown at Art Association exhibitions. He continued to exhibit throughout his life at the Art Association, and in 1937 his work was displayed at the Library of Congress. Husband of MARY BELLE JOHNSON WOODWARD.

References: NOCD 1886–1933, 1935, 1938; *Art and Letters*, 1(Dec. 1887):228; *Current Topics*, Jan. 1891, 25, Jan. 1893, 11; *D. Pic.*, Mar. 10, 1889, Feb. 14, Nov. 13, Dec. 17, 1890, Mar. 3, 1892, Feb. 14, 1893, Mar. 30, 1897, Dec. 3, 1899, Dec. 5, 1909, Jan. 19, 1913; *D. States*, Dec. 17, 1890; *Down in Dixie*, July 15, 1896, 10; *Harlequin*, June 23, 1904, 7; *Item*, May 21, 23, Aug. 27, 1916, Jan. 16, Feb. 6, Apr. 10, 16, June 12, 1921, Mar. 18, Nov. 25, 1923, Mar. 28, 1929, Feb. 28, 1939; *Item–Trib.*, May 15, 1927, June 7, 1931, Mar. 12, 1933, Feb. 5, 12, May 7, 1939; *Morn. Trib.*, Sept. 18, Oct. 11, 1926, Apr. 6, May 11, Oct. 5, 1927, Feb. 8, 29, Oct. 29, 1928, June 5, 1929, Nov. 13, Dec. 7, 10, 1932, Jan. 20, 27, Mar. 10, 1933; *New Orleanian*, Aug. 1931, 18–21, 31; *New Orleans Life*, May 1927, 26; *States*, Dec. 11, 1932, May 5, 1935, July 6, 1948; *T. Demo.*, Nov. 13, 1890, Mar. 22, 24, 1902, Feb. 28, 1904, Dec. 28, 1905, Jan. 6, 1907, Feb. 25–26, 1910, Jan. 6, 1913; *T. Pic.*, Feb. 16, 1919, Dec. 9, 1923, Feb. 29, 1924, Mar. 4, Apr. 8, May 18, 1925, July 11, 1926, May 5, 1929, Feb. 16, Mar. 3, 1930, Jan. 22, Apr. 11, June 5, 1931, Mar. 6, June 12, July 17, 24, 31, 1932, Mar. 14, May 6, 1933, Mar. 16, 1934, Feb. 9, Mar. 15, Apr. 12, Oct. 25, 1936, Jan. 25, Feb. 7, Mar. 7, 1937, Apr. 3, 17, 1938, Jan. 22, Feb. 5, 14, Feb. 19, Mar. 1–2, 1939; *Tulane News Bulletin*, 13(May 1933):140–41; AANO, *Catalogue* (1890, 1896–97, 1899, 1901–1902); Art Asso., *Catalogue* (1904–1905, 1907, 1910, 1911, 1913–19, 1921–22, 1924–39); Art Asso., *Charter* (1916); Art Asso., *Membership*; Arts Exhibition Club; Barkemeyer; Bénézit; Fielding, *Dictionary*; Glenk, 80, 214; Heidelberg; LSM, *Biennial Report for 1924–25*, 49; LSU, *Louisiana Artists*; Mount, 136, 159–60; Orleans Parish Registrar of Voters, NOPL; Ormond and Irvine, 11–14,

141–42; Poesch, *Newcomb Pottery*, passim; Reeves, 126–28, 130, 134; Tennessee Centennial Exposition; Tulane, *Two Southern Impressionists*; Tulane Decorative Art League; *Who's Who*, 1936–37; *Who's Who in American Art*, 1936–37, 1938–39.

WOODWARD, L. I.
Painter, active N.O. ca. 1889.
Exhibited: ARTISTS' ASSOCIATION OF NEW ORLEANS (1889).
References: *D. Pic.*, Dec. 17, 1889; Morton's Auction Exchange, Aug. 1973, 31.

WOODWARD, LOUISE AMELIA GIESEN (Mrs. WILLIAM WOODWARD)
Born N.O. ca. 1862; died Biloxi MS Oct. 29, 1937.
Painter, sculptor, potter, active N.O. 1888–1912.
Contemporary listings: potter, sculptor (1889); painter (1892).
Exhibited: TULANE DECORATIVE ART LEAGUE FOR WOMEN (1888); ART LEAGUE OF NEW ORLEANS (1889); ARTISTS' ASSOCIATION OF NEW ORLEANS (1891–92, 1896–97, 1902); Newcomb Art School (1892); Tulane University (1892–93); DELGADO MUSEUM OF ART (1912).
Memberships/positions: Art League of New Orleans (1889); Artists' Association of New Orleans (1896); ARTS EXHIBITION CLUB (1901).
References: *Current Topics*, Jan. 1892, 24, Jan. 1893, 11; *D. City Item*, Dec. 17, 1891; *D. Pic.*, Mar. 10, 1889, Dec. 17, 1891, Mar. 3, 1892, Feb. 14, 1893, Mar. 30, 1897; *T. Demo.*, Mar. 3, Dec. 13, 1892; *T. Pic.*, Oct. 30–31, 1937; AANO, *Catalogue* (1891, 1896, 1897, 1902); Arts Exhibition Club; Delgado, *Catalogue* (1911–12, 1912–13); Delgado, *Catalogue of Paintings, Sculpture*, 40; Mount, 136; Thompson, "Checklist"; Tulane Decorative Art League.

WOODWARD, MARY BELLE JOHNSON (Mrs. ELLSWORTH WOODWARD)
Born N.Y.C. Apr. 11, 1862; died N.O. Jan. 1, 1943.
Painter, sculptor, active N.O. 1886–1939.
Studied: Tulane University (1886); NEWCOMB COLLEGE (1887–91).
Exhibited: TULANE DECORATIVE ART LEAGUE FOR WOMEN (1888); ART ASSOCIATION OF NEW ORLEANS (1905).
Memberships/positions: Tulane Decorative Art League for Women (1888); Newcomb Art Alumnae Association, secy. (1895); ARTS EXHIBITION CLUB (1901); Art Association of New Orleans (1905, 1913, 1916).
References: NOCD 1920–21, 1938, 1940, 1942, 1945–46; *D. Pic.*, Feb. 12, 1888; *Eve. Chronicle*, May 22, 1886; *T. Pic.*, Jan. 2, 1943; *Tulane News Bulletin*, 13(May 1933): 140; Art Asso., *Catalogue* (1905, 1938, 1939); Art Asso., *Charter* (1916); Art Asso., *Membership*; Arts Exhibition Club; Orleans Parish Registrar of Voters, NOPL; Ormond and Irvine; Tulane Decorative Art League.

WOODWARD, WILLIAM
Born Seekonk MA May 1, 1859; died N.O. Nov. 17, 1939.
Art teacher, painter, sketch artist, etcher, potter, active N.O. 1885–1923; also architect.
Studied: Rhode Island School of Design, Providence (1877–83); Massachusetts Normal Art School, Boston (1883–86, 1885–86 via correspondence); with G. R. C. Boulanger, J. J. Lefebvre, Académie Julian, Paris (1886).
Contemporary listings: professor, Tulane University (1886, 1888–1903); professor of drawing, Tulane University (1885, 1887); professor of drawing and painting, Tulane University (1904–1905); professor, NEWCOMB COLLEGE (1904–1909, 1911–18); professor, Newcomb College and professor of art (1910).
Exhibited: American Exposition (1885–86); Columbian Expositon, Chicago (1893); ARTISTS' ASSOCIATION OF NEW ORLEANS (1887, 1889–92, 1896–97, 1899, 1901–1902); TULANE DECORATIVE ART LEAGUE FOR WOMEN (1888); ART LEAGUE OF NEW ORLEANS (1889); Tulane University (1890, 1892–93); ART LEAGUE POTTERY CLUB (1892); Tennessee Centennial Exposition, Nashville (1897); Newcomb (1899); E. Curtis' Exchange (1902); ART ASSOCIATION OF

NEW ORLEANS (1904–1905, 1907, 1910–11, 1913–18); National Association of Newspaper Artists (1905); Panama–Pacific International Exposition, San Francisco (1915).

Awarded: Rhode Island Industrial Exhibition, medal for three oil paintings (1881); Art Association of New Orleans, silver medal for second best oil painting (1909).

Memberships/positions: Providence Art Club (ca. 1880); Tulane Decorative Art League for Women, founder, pres., and art director; Art League of New Orleans, and NEW ORLEANS ART POTTERY, treas. (1889); Art League Pottery Club, pres. (1890); Columbian Exposition, Louisiana Art Exhibits Committee, chairman (1893); Louisiana Drawing Teachers' Association, pres. (1896); Artists' Association of New Orleans (1896), pres. (1897); ARTS EXHIBITION CLUB, v. pres. (1901); Art Association of New Orleans, founder, first v. pres. (1904–1905, 1907, 1913), executive committee (1904–1905, 1907, 1910–11, 1913–14, 1916–18), board member (1913–14, 1916–18); Louisiana Art Teachers' Association, pres. (1905, 1910, 1911); Third International Congress for the Advancement of Drawing and Art Teaching, London, American Official Committee, v. pres. (1908); American Federation of Arts, Washington DC, original board member; College Art Association of America; Mississippi Art Association.

Portrait, still life, landscape, and cityscape painter who became interested in art after visiting the Centennial Exposition in Philadelphia (1876). Following training in RI and MA, Woodward moved to N.O. (1884) as associate professor of art at the newly formed Tulane College and High School (later Tulane University) and taught there until his retirement in 1922. He organized and taught the TULANE FREE DRAWING CLASSES (ca. 1885–94) for teachers and working people. He helped organize Newcomb College in 1887,

brought his brother ELLSWORTH WOODWARD to N.O. as Newcomb's first art teacher, and taught drawing at the Newcomb Summer Normal School (1908–21). Trained also as an architect, William Woodward assisted in designing the early buildings on the Tulane campus (1894) and was the founder of the Tulane School of Architecture (1907). An important early preservationist, he protested the proposed destruction of the Cabildo (1895). From 1895 to 1915, he made numerous paintings of the French Quarter and its buildings in order to record their appearance; in 1936 he became associated with the newly founded Vieux Carré Commission in helping to preserve the district's historic architectural characteristics. Both of the Woodward brothers were active in organizing and promoting the arts in the South and were founders and officers of art organizations in N.O. In 1921, while painting a mural in the United Fruit Company building, William Woodward fell from the scaffolding, damaged his spine, and was confined to a wheelchair for the rest of his life. As a result, he retired from teaching (1922) and settled in Biloxi MS (1924) where he continued to paint and where he built "The Studio," his home and art gallery. Finding it increasingly difficult to paint, Woodward turned to drypoint etching and invented "fiberloid," a simplified etching process. He created prints based on his earlier Vieux Carré paintings and published a selection in 1938 to promote preservation efforts. Husband of LOUISE AMELIA GIESEN WOODWARD.

References: NOCD 1886–1921, 1924–31, 1933, 1935; *Architectural Art*, 4(Aug. 1908):8, 4(June 1909):3–4; *Art and Letters*, 1(Dec. 1887):227; *Current Topics*, Jan. 1891, 25, Jan. 1892, 24–25, Jan. 1893, 11; *D. City Item*, Dec. 17, 1891; *D. Pic.*, Oct. 29, Nov. 8, 1885, Dec. 17, 1887, Dec. 12, 1888, Mar. 10, Dec. 17, 1889, Feb. 14, Dec. 17, 1890, Mar. 3, Dec. 13, 1892, Feb. 14, 1893, Mar. 30,

1897, Dec. 3, 1899, Mar. 20, May 28, 1905, Mar. 12, 1909; *D. States*, Dec. 17, 1890; *Down in Dixie*, July 15, 1896, 10; *Harlequin*, Oct. 25, 1899, 9, Jan. 31, 1900, 1–2; *Illustrated News*, July 1921, cover, 21; *Item*, Feb. 6, Apr. 10, 16, Dec. 18, 1921; *Item–Trib.*, Mar. 12, 1933, Apr. 17, 1938; *Men and Matters*, Sept. 1897, 42–55; *Morn. Trib.*, Oct. 20, 1926; *New Orleans Life*, May 1927, 26; *T. Demo.*, Jan. 6, 1890, Mar. 3, 1892, Mar. 24, 1902, Feb. 28, 1904, Jan. 6, 1907, Feb. 25, 1910; *T. Pic.*, Feb. 29, 1924, Apr. 8, 1925, Oct. 20, Dec. 12, 1926, May 5, 1929, Mar. 3, 1930, Mar. 14, 1933, Mar. 8, 1936, Jan. 25, 1937, Apr. 10, May 8, 1938, Nov. 18–19, 1939; *Town Talk*, July 1904, 25, Feb. 1905, 46; AANO, *Catalogue* (1890, 1891, 1896, 1897, 1899, 1901, 1902); Art Asso., *Catalogue* (1904, 1905, 1907, 1910, 1911, 1913, 1914, 1916, 1917, 1918, 1919, 1921, 1922, 1924, 1925, 1927, 1928, 1929, 1930, 1931, 1932, 1933, 1934, 1935, 1936, 1937, 1938, 1939); Art Asso., *Charter* (1916); Art Asso., *Exhibition of Paintings by Woodward*; Art Asso., *Membership*; Art Asso., *Special Exhibition*; Arts Exhibition Club; Bénézit; Creole Exhibit, 10, 15; Delgado, *Catalogue of Paintings, Sculpture*, 25, 57; Fielding, *Dictionary*; Glenk, 80; Heidelberg; LSM, *Biennial Report for 1922–23*, 113; Mount, 93–97, 136; Ormond and Irvine, 11–14, 142–43; Poesch, *Newcomb Pottery*, 9–14, 17, 76; Reeves, 126, 130, 132; Rightor, 386–87; Tennessee Centennial Exposition; Tulane Decorative Art League; Tulane, *Two Southern Impressionists*; U.S. Census (1910), roll 524; *Who's Who in American Art*, 1938–39; William Woodward; WPA, *New Orleans*, 105.

WOODWORTH, ROBERT
Engraver, active N.O. 1870; also stencil cutter.
Contemporary listings: engraver, with AUGUST H. M. PETERSON (1870).

Possibly R. B. Woodworth, died N.O. May 5, 1884.
References: NOCD 1867, 1870–73; *D. Pic.*, May 16, 18, 1884.

WORCESTER, ALBERT
Born West Campton NH 1878.
Painter, etcher, active N.O. 1918.
Studied: with Luc Olivier Merson and J. P. Laurens, Paris.
Contemporary listings: painter (1918).
Exhibited: ART ASSOCIATION OF NEW ORLEANS (1918); DELGADO MUSEUM OF ART (1919).
Active in Detroit MI, Worcester came to N.O. to exhibit three paintings of landscape and genre scenes (1918). He was commissioned that year to execute a large canvas symbolizing the motto of the Benevolent Protective Order of the Elks.
References: NOCD 1918; *T. Pic.*, Mar. 14, 1918, Jan. 19, 1919; Art Asso., *Catalogue* (1918); Bénézit; Fielding, *Dictionary*.

WRAIGHT, KATHERINE SEVERANCE
Art craftsman, active N.O. ca. 1911–17.
Studied: NEWCOMB COLLEGE, (1902–1906, 1916–17).
Exhibited: ART ASSOCIATION OF NEW ORLEANS (1911).
References: Ormond and Irvine, 173; Poesch, *Newcomb Pottery*, 106.

WRIGHT, JAMES HENRY
Born NY 1813; died Brooklyn NY 1883.
Painter, active N.O. 1836.
Contemporary listings: portrait and miniature painter, 3 Royal (1836).
Exhibited: National Academy of Design, N.Y.C.; American Art Union.
From 1842, Wright worked in and around N.Y.C.
References: *Bee*, July 6, 1836; Bénézit; Fielding, *Dictionary*; Groce and Wallace.

WRIGHT, PAULINE (Mrs. Irby C. Nichols)
Born Senatobia MS Dec. 7, 1889; died Baton Rouge LA June 13, 1983.
Painter, art teacher, active N.O. 1911–18.
Studied: NEWCOMB COLLEGE (1911); Art Institute, Chicago (1916).

Exhibited: ART ASSOCIATION OF NEW ORLEANS (1913, 1915–17).

After graduating from Newcomb, Wright taught art for a year at Millsaps College, Jackson MS. The following year she returned to Newcomb to teach until her marriage in 1918 when she moved to Baton Rouge LA where her husband taught at L.S.U. In that city, as one of a few professional artists, she worked privately and in the community.

References: NOCD 1915–18; Art Asso., *Catalogue* (1913, 1915, 1916, 1917); Information courtesy Nina Nichols Pugh, Sept. 19, 1986.

WULFF, AUGUSTE

Born Germany Jan. 1853.

Commercial artist, active N.O. 1876–1900.

Contemporary listings: painter, with J. W. Norris (1876); painter, (1877); artist, Diebold Lock and Safe Co. (1878); painter, with A. Roy (1880); artist, Roy and Timbrell (1882–83); artist, with A. Roy (1884–86); painter, A. Roy & Co. (1887); artist (1900).

Immigrated to the U.S. in 1872.

References: NOCD 1875–78, 1880, 1882–87; U.S. Census (1900), roll 570.

WUNDERLICH, ALBERT

Born N.O.; died Lansdowne PA Dec. 13, 1943.

Engraver, active N.O. 1884.

Contemporary listings: engraver (1884).

Also listed as a clerk at T. LILIENTHAL (1885–86).

References: NOCD 1884–86; *T. Pic.*, Dec. 18–19, 1943.

WUNDERLICH, GEORGE

Painter, active N.O. 1867–83.

Contemporary listings: fairy landscape artist (1867); painter (1883).

Exhibited: LILIENTHAL's (1883).

References: *Repub.*, Dec. 15, 1867; Lilienthal's, 8.

WÜRTTEMBERG, PRINCE PAUL OF

(Herzog Friedrich Wilhelm Paul, Duke of Württemberg)

Born Karlsruhe, Silesia June 25, 1797; died Mergentheim, Germany Nov. 24, 1860.

Sketch artist, active N.O. 1822–52.

Topographical artist and scientific explorer who was originally educated for a military career but left the army to study the natural sciences. During trips through North America, Württemberg visited N.O. in 1822, 1829 (under the alias Baron von Hohenberg), 1850, and 1852. It was during the first trip that he made a sketch for the lithograph, *The Balize, Louisiana*.

References: *Courier*, Dec. 1, 1829; *Wkly. Delta*, Sept. 16, 1850; *Appleton's CAB*; Groce and Wallace; Rathbone, *Westward*, 31, 34, 261, 279–80; Reps, 313; Taft, 280; Stokes and Haskell, 65.

WYNNE, PETER H.

Born Dublin, Ireland May 1858; died N.O. July 31, 1907.

Artist, painter, active N.O. ca. 1896–1907.

Contemporary listings: artist (1897–99); WYNNE & FRANK (1900); painting artist (1900); artist (1901–1903, 1907).

Exhibited: ARTISTS' ASSOCIATION OF NEW ORLEANS (1896).

References: NOCD 1897–1903, 1905–1907; *D. Pic.*, Aug. 1, 4, 1907; AANO, *Catalogue* (1896); Mount, 136; N.O. Death Certificate (1907), 141.745, NOPL; U.S. Census (1900), roll 573.

WYNNE & FRANK

Artists, active N.O. 1900; PETER H. WYNNE, CHARLES L. FRANK, partners.

Contemporary listings: artists, 1038 St. Charles (1900).

References: NOCD 1900.

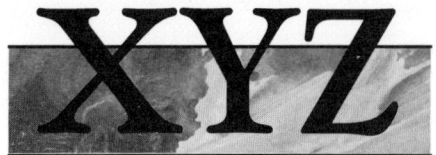

XIQUES, ANTONIA
Born N.O.; died N.O. May 5, 1930.
Artist, active N.O. 1889–91.
Contemporary listings: artist (1889–91).
References: NOCD 1889–91; *T. Pic.*,
May 6, 1930.
YEAGER, JOSEPH. *See* WEST, WILLIAM
EDWARD
YOUNG, JOHN
Sculptor, active N.O. 1870.
Contemporary listings: woodcarver
(1870).
References: NOCD 1870.
YOUNG, MAY
Painter, active N.O. 1890.
Contemporary listings: painter
(1890).
Exhibited: Werlein's music store
(1890).
Possibly May E. Young, died February 14, 1912, buried in St. Joseph
Cemetery I.
References: *D. Pic.*, Feb. 2, 1890;
THNOC Cemetery Survey.
YOUNGBLOOD, WILLIAM
Born LA Nov. 1881.
Artist, active N.O. 1900.
Contemporary listings: artist (1900).
Primarily a clerk and window dresser.
References: NOCD 1894, 1896–1915; U.S. Census (1900), roll 573.
ZAINEY, EUGENE V.
Born LA ca. 1891.
Engraver, active N.O. 1910.
Contemporary listings: engraver,
photographs (1910).
References: U.S. Census (1910), roll
520.
ZAMORA, M. J.
Artist, active N.O. ca. 1890.
Memberships/positions: ARTISTS' ASSOCIATION OF NEW ORLEANS (1890).
References: *D. Pic.*, Nov. 13, 1890.
ZAPARY, FRANCISCO
Born Italy.
Painter, active N.O. 1825; also architect.
Contemporary listings: painter
(1825).

Architect and painter who was paid
$1,855 for decorating the interior of
St. Louis Cathedral and its three altars during Nov.–Dec. 1825.
References: Financial Reports of St.
Louis Cathedral, 1823–34, Archives
of the Archdiocese of N.O.; St. Louis
Cathedral Marriage Register, 1821–30, 4:74, Archives of the Archdiocese of N.O.; Wilson and Huber,
Basilica, 22.
ZAVYTOWSKY, A.
Born Poland ca. 1826.
Artist, active N.O. 1850.
Contemporary listings: artist (1850).
References: Groce and Wallace; U.S.
Census (1850), roll 234.
ZELINSKEY, ARTHUR
Artist, active N.O. 1886.
Contemporary listings: artist (1886).
References: NOCD 1886.
ZENNECK, ADOLPH
Born Stuttgart, Württemberg 1851;
died N.O. Aug. 31, 1887.
Engraver, commercial artist, active
N.O. 1873–84.
Contemporary listings: engraver,
NEW ORLEANS ENGRAVING COMPANY
(1873); ZENNECK & BUCKINGHAM
(1873–75); wood engraver, 26 Commercial (1874, 1876–78); engraver,
26 Commercial (1879); wood engraver, 61 Camp (1880); BENNETT &
ZENNECK (1880–81); wood engraver,
68 Camp (1882–83); artist, *Mascot*
(1884).
Started his career as an apprentice
to a wood engraver; emigrated to the
U.S. (ca. 1870), worked two years in
N.Y.C. for several publications, including *Frank Leslie's*, and then came
to N.O. At the time of his death, Zenneck was managing editor and half
owner of the *Mascot*; he was shot and
killed by a disgruntled subject of a
Mascot story.
References: NOCD 1874–85, 1887;
D. Pic., Jan. 15, Feb. 1, 9, Dec. 21,
1873, Nov. 29, 1874, Jan. 14, 1885,
Sept. 1, 1887, Feb. 2, 1888; *D. States*,

Oct. 2, 1882, Jan. 2, 1883, May 29, 1885, Aug. 19, 1887; *Demo.*, Sept. 17, 1876; *Eve. Chronicle*, Jan. 13, 1885; *Herald*, Dec. 14, 1873; *Lantern*, Aug. 20, 1887, 8; *Mascot*, Aug. 20, Sept. 3, 10, 1887; *Our Home Journal*, Jan. 4, 1873; *T. Demo.*, Sept. 1, 4, 6, 1887; Wilds, "In 1885 We Were Here," *T. Pic.*, Mar. 20, 1977; *Wkly. Budget*, July 4, 1875; *Wkly. States*, Aug. 19, 1887; Landry, 97, 106, 110; Morrison, *New Orleans*, 135; Tinker, *Lafcadio Hearn*, 88; Weitenkampf, *Political Caricature*, 155–56.

ZENNECK & BUCKINGHAM
Engravers, designers, active N.O. 1873–75; ADOLPH ZENNECK, J. L. R. BUCKINGHAM, partners.
Contemporary listings: designers and engravers on wood, 26 Commercial (1873); 26 Commercial (1874); wood engravings, 26 Commercial (1875).
References: NOCD 1875; *D. Pic.*, Jan. 16, 19, 26, Feb. 9, 16, 23, Mar. 2, 9, 30, Apr. 27, 1873, Nov. 6, Dec. 9, 1874; *Repub.*, Jan. 16, 1873, Feb. 15, 1874; THNOC 1965.97; Tinker, *Creole City*, 327.

ZICON, MR. I.
Lithographer, active N.O. 1837.
Contemporary listings: lithographer, *Bee* (1837).
References: *Bee*, Apr. 5, 1837.

ZIELINSKI, A[UGUST] OR H.
Painter, active N.O. 1884; also topographical engineer.
References: NOCD 1886; Catalogue sheet 12601, LSM.

ZIMMER & DROZ
Lithographers, engravers, active N.O. 1833; Mr. Zimmer, A. DROZ, partners.
Contemporary listings: lithographers, 152 Chartres (1833).
References: *Bee*, Jan. 26, May 22, June 3, 1833; *Courier*, Jan. 25, 1833; Friends of the Cabildo, *250 Years*, 59; Groce and Wallace.

ZIMMERMAN, GEORGE
Engraver, active N.O. 1881–87.
Contemporary listings: engraver, with FREDERICK HOLYLAND (1881); engraver, Frantz & Opitz (1882–87).
References: NOCD 1881–87.

ZINK, FREDERICK F.
Born LA ca. 1882.
Painter, active N.O. 1906–11.
Contemporary listings: painter (1906–11); fresco painter (1910).
Later listed as an insurance agent (1912–42).
References: NOCD 1903–30, 1932–33, 1935, 1938, 1940, 1942; U.S. Census (1910), roll 523.

ZULAKOWSKI, MRS. R. *See* LULAKOWSKI, MRS. R.

BIBLIOGRAPHY

SECONDARY SOURCES

AANO. Artists' Association of New Orleans. *Catalogue of the Annual Exhibition.* New Orleans, 1886–1903. Published annually.

————. *Catalogue of the Paintings By Members of the Artists' Association of New Orleans, At Auction Sale, By E. Curtis, Under the Free Library, Lafayette Square, Saturday, April 10th, 1897, at 2 o'clock.*

————. *Charter, Constitution and By-Laws.* New Orleans, 1893.

————. *School of Art, Season of 1886–1887.* New Orleans, [1886].

————. *School of Art, Session of 1892–1893.* New Orleans, [1892].

"Acquisitions." *Archives of American Art Journal* 18(1978):30.

Adams, Alexander B. *John James Audubon.* New York: G. P. Putnam's Sons, 1966.

Adams, James H., Jr. "A Brief History of Walle & Co." A paper presented at Southeastern Louisiana University, Hammond LA, May 1976. (Typewritten.)

Alexander, Edward Porter. *Catterel Ratterel (Doggerel).* New York: G. P. Putnam's Sons, 1890.

Alexander, James E. *Transatlantic Sketches.* 2 vols. London: Richard Bentley, 1833.

Allibone, S. Austin. *A Critical Dictionary of English Literature and British and American Authors.* 3 vols. Philadelphia: J. B. Lippincott, 1877.

Almanach de la Louisiane. New Orleans: Francis Bouvain, 1866.

Almanach de la Louisiane. New Orleans: Francis Bouvain, 1867.

Almanach de la Renaissance pour 1870. New Orleans: Emile LeFranc, 1870.

American Art Annual. 37 vols. Washington DC: American Federation of Arts, 1898–1948.

American Illustrating Company. *Pen and Sunlight Sketches of Greater New Orleans.* New Orleans: American Illustrating Company, [1912].

American Institute of Architects, New Orleans Chapter, and Louisiana Landmarks Society. *A Century of Architecture in New Orleans, 1857–1957.* New Orleans, 1957.

"American Paintings in the Collection of James H. Ricau." *Antiques*, Nov. 1964, 579–82.

Amon Carter Museum of Art. *The Image of America in Caricature & Cartoon.* Fort Worth TX: Amon Carter Museum, 1975.

Amoss, Jim. "An Art Carried On." *States-Item*, Feb. 11, 1976.

Anderson, Alexandra. "George Ohr's 'Mud Babies.'" *Art in America*, Jan.–Feb. 1979, 60–63.

Anglo-American Art Museum. *American Folk Art, 1730–1968.* Baton Rouge: Anglo-American Art Museum, 1968.

————. *Catalogue.* Baton Rouge: Louisiana State University Office of Publications, 1971.

————. *Louisiana Folk Art.* Baton Rouge: Louisiana State University, 1972.

————. *The Louisiana Landscape, 1800–1969.* Baton Rouge: Louisiana State University Office of Publications, 1969.

————. *Sail and Steam in Louisiana Waters.* Baton Rouge: Louisiana State University Office of Publications, 1971.

BIBLIOGRAPHY

Appleton's Cyclopaedia of American Biography, edited by James Grant Wilson and John Fiske. 6 vols. New York: D. Appleton, 1887–89.

Archives of American Art. "Louisiana Collections." Oct. 10, 1984. (Typewritten.)

Arrington, Joseph Earl. "Henry Lewis' Moving Panorama of the Mississippi River." *Louisiana History* 6(Summer 1965):245–49.

———. "Leon D. Pomarede's Original Panorama of the Mississippi River." *Bulletin of the Missouri Historical Society* 34(Apr. 1953):261–73.

———. "Samuel A. Hudson's Panorama of the Ohio and Mississippi Rivers." *Ohio Historical Quarterly* 66(Oct. 1957):355–74.

———. "The Story of Stockwell's Panorama." *Minnesota History* 33(Autumn 1953):284–90.

Art Association of New Orleans. *Catalogue of the Annual Exhibition.* New Orleans, 1904–57. Published annually.

———. *Catalogue of Oil Paintings by Charles W. Hutson.* New Orleans, 1931.

———. *Charter, By–Laws, and Roll of Members.* New Orleans: Art Association of New Orleans, 1916.

———. *Charter, By–Laws, and Roll of Members.* New Orleans: Art Association of New Orleans, 1928.

———. *Exhibition of Bookplates from the Collection of Mrs. Arthur Griswold Palfrey and Miss Jane Grey Rogers.* New Orleans: Delgado Museum of Art, 1917.

———. *Exhibition of Paintings by Professor William Woodward.* New Orleans: Art Association of New Orleans, 1918.

———. *Exhibition of Recent Paintings by Harry B. Lachman.* New Orleans: Delgado Museum of Art, 1920.

———. *Exhibition of Silversmithing by Rosalie Roos Wiener; Block Prints by Henrietta Bailey and Sadie E. A. Irvine; Watercolors by Elizabeth B. Raymond.* New Orleans: Delgado Museum of Art, 1934.

———. *Invitation to a Private View of Paintings and Sketches by Mr. Harry B. Lachman at the Delgado Museum of Art.* New Orleans, 1916.

———. *Membership.* New Orleans: Art Association of New Orleans, 1913.

———. *Memorial Exhibition of the Works of Bror Anders Wikstrom.* New Orleans: Isaac Delgado Museum of Art, 1912.

———. *Paintings by Charles W. Hutson.* New Orleans, 1948.

———. *Special Exhibition of Local Work Without Jury.* New Orleans, 1915.

Arthur, Stanley Clisby. *Audubon: An Intimate Life of the American Woodsman.* New Orleans: Harmanson, 1937.

———. *Louisiana State Museum: A Guide Book.* New Orleans: Board of Curators, 1944.

———. *Old New Orleans: A History of the Vieux Carré.* New Orleans: Harmanson, 1936.

Arthur, Stanley Clisby, and George Campbell Hutchet de Kernion. *Old Families of Louisiana.* Reprint. Baton Rouge: Claitor's, 1971.

Arts and Humanities Council of Greater Baton Rouge and the Baton Rouge Gallery. *Caroline Durieux Retrospective.* Baton Rouge, 1981.

Arts Exhibition Club. *Charter, By–Laws and Roll of Members.* New Orleans, 1901.

Audubon, John James. *The Birds of America.* 7 vols. New York: J. J. Audubon, 1840–44.

———. *Journal of John James Audubon Made during his Trip to New Orleans in 1820–1821.* Edited by Howard Corning. Boston: The Club of Odd Volumes, 1929.

———. *Letters of John James Audubon 1826–1840.* Edited by Howard Corning. Boston: The Club of Odd Volumes, 1930.

Audubon, John W. *Audubon's Western Journal: 1849–1850*. Edited by Frank H. Hodder. Cleveland: Arthur H. Clark, 1906.

Augustin, George. *The Vigil of A Soul*. New Orleans, 1899.

Bacot, H. Parrott. "Pietro Gualdi: A Nineteenth–Century Italian Architect in New Orleans." *Journal of the Society of Architectural Historians* 33(Oct. 1974):242.

Bacot, H. Parrott, and Bethany B. Lambdin. "Edwin Lyon, an Anglo–American Sculptor in the Lower Mississippi River Valley." *Antiques*, Mar. 1977, 554–59.

Baigell, Matthew. *Dictionary of American Art*. New York: Harper & Row, 1982.

Baker, W. S. *American Engravers and Their Works*. Philadelphia: Gebbie & Barrie, 1875.

Ball, Millie. "Newcomb Pottery Hits Big Time Again." *Times–Picayune*, May 27, 1984.

Banks, William Nathaniel. "George Cooke, Painter of the American Scene." *Antiques*, Sept. 1972, 449–54.

Bannon, Lois Elmer, and Taylor Clark. *Handbook of Audubon Prints*. Gretna LA: Pelican, 1980.

Banvard, John. *Description of Banvard's Panorama of the Mississippi River, Painted on Three Miles of Canvas: Exhibiting a View of Country 1200 Miles in Length, Extending from the Mouth of the Missouri River to the City of New Orleans; Being by Far the Largest Picture Ever Executed by Man*. Boston: J. Putnam, 1847.

Barkemeyer, Estelle. "Ellsworth Woodward: His Life and His Work." M.A. thesis, Tulane University, 1942.

Barker, Virgil. *American Painting: History and Interpretation*. New York: Macmillan, 1950. Reprint. New York: Bonanza, 1960.

Baroncelli–Javon, J. G. de. *Une colonie française, en Louisiane*. New Orleans: Geo. Muller, 1909.

Bartlett, Larry. "From Yesterday's Grocery Shelf." *Times–Picayune*, Dec. 4, 1977.

————. "On the Gallery." *Times–Picayune*, Mar. 9, 1980.

Beall, Karen F., comp. *American Prints in the Library of Congress: A Catalog of the Collection*. Baltimore: Johns Hopkins, 1970.

Beffart, Mark. "Ohr's Contorted Pottery Distinctive." *Antique Monthly*, Apr. 1983, 6B–9B.

Bénézit, Emmanuel, ed. *Dictionnaire Critique et Documentaire des Peintres, Sculpteurs, Dessinateurs et Graveurs*. Rev. ed. 8 vols. Paris: Librairie Gründ, 1966.

Biddle, Edward, and Mantle Fielding. *The Life and Works of Thomas Sully 1783–1872*. Philadelphia: Wickersham, 1921.

Bilodeau, Francis W., and Mrs. Thomas J. Tobias, comps. and eds. *Art in South Carolina 1670–1970*. Columbia: South Carolina Tricentennial Commission, 1970.

Biographical and Historical Memoirs of Louisiana. Vol. 1. Chicago: Goodspeed, 1892. Reprint. Baton Rouge: Claitor's, 1975.

Biographical and Historical Memoirs of Northwest Louisiana Comprising a Large Fund of Biography of Actual Residents, and an Interesting Historical Sketch of Thirteen Counties. Nashville: Southern, 1890.

"Biographical and Professional Record of Arthur H. Feitel." New Orleans. (Typewritten.)

Biographical Sketches of American Artists. Lansing: Michigan State Library, 1912.

Biographical Sketches of American Artists. 3d ed. Lansing: Michigan State Library, 1915.

Bishop, Robert. *Folk Painters of America*. New York: E. P. Dutton, 1979.

BIBLIOGRAPHY

Bisland, Mary. "King Carnival in New Orleans." *Cosmopolitan*, Feb. 1890, 469–78.

Blanchard, Olivia. "Death Mask of Napoleon at the Cabildo, New Orleans." *Louisiana Historical Quarterly* 8(Jan. 1925):71–83.

Blasberg, Robert W. *George E. Ohr and His Biloxi Art Pottery*. Port Jervis NY: J. W. Carpenter, 1973.

———. "The Sadie Irvine Letters: A Further Note on the Production of Newcomb Pottery." *Antiques*, Aug. 1971, 250–51.

Blumenthal, Henry. *American and French Culture, 1800–1900: Interchanges in Art, Science, Literature, and Society*. Baton Rouge: Louisiana State University Press, 1975.

Boatner, Mark Mayo III. *The Civil War Dictionary*. New York: David McKay, 1959.

Boggs, Winthrop S. *Ten Decades Ago, 1840–1850: A Study of the Work of Rawdon, Wright, Hatch and Edson of New York City*. American Philatelic Society, 1949.

Boimare, Antoine Louis, ed. *Texte Explicatif pour Accompagner La Première Planche Historique Relative A La Louisiane*. New Orleans: L. Uter, 1868.

Bolton, Theodore. *Early American Portrait Draughtsmen in Crayons*. New York: Da Capo, 1970.

———. *Early American Portrait Painters In Crayons*. New York: Kennedy Graphics, Da Capo, 1970.

———. *Early American Portrait Painters in Miniature*. New York: Frederic Fairchild Sherman, 1921.

———. "Henry Inman, Portrait Painter." *Creative Art* 12(Feb. 1933):116–23.

Bolton, Theodore, and George C. Groce, Jr. "John Wesley Jarvis: An Account of His Life and the First Catalogue of His Work." *The Art Quarterly* 1(1938):299–321.

Bonner, Judith Hopkins. "George David Coulon: A Nineteenth Century French Louisiana Painter." *The Southern Quarterly* 20(Winter 1982):41–61.

———. "George David Coulon: A Nineteenth Century French Louisiana Painter and His Family." M.A. thesis, Tulane University, 1983.

Booth, Andrew B., comp. *Records of Louisiana Confederate Soldiers and Louisiana Confederate Commands*. 3 vols. New Orleans, 1920.

Boyd, Andrew. *Louisiana and Mississippi Directory, 1870–1871*. New Orleans: Andrew Boyd, 1870.

Boyer, Lillian Frances. "The Etchings of Ellsworth Woodward: A Catalogue Raisonné." M.A. thesis, Louisiana State University, 1982.

Brandywine River Museum. *The Illustrations of W. T. Smedley (1858–1920)*. Chadds Ford PA: Brandywine River Museum, 1981.

Braun, J. F., comp. *Plan Book of the Fourth District*. New Orleans: H. Wehrmann, 1874.

Bremer, Fredrika. *Homes of the New World: Impressions of America*. 2 vols. 1853. Reprint. New York: Greenwood, 1968.

Bridaham, Lester Burbank. "Pierre Joseph Landry, Louisiana Woodcarver." *Antiques*, Aug. 1957, 157–60.

Brooklyn Museum. *The American Renaissance, 1876–1917*. New York: Pantheon, 1979.

Brown, C. Reynolds. *Joseph Rusling Meeker: Images of the Mississippi Delta*. Montgomery AL: Montgomery Museum of Fine Arts, 1981.

Brownson, Leo, ed. *New Orleans Short Stories*. New Orleans, n.d.

Bruns, Mrs. Thomas Nelson Carter, comp. *Louisiana Portraits*. New Orleans: National Society of the Colonial Dames of America in the State of Louisiana, 1975.

Bryan's Dictionary of Painters and Engravers, edited by Michael Bryan. Rev. ed., edited by George C. Williamson. 5 vols. London: George Bell and Sons, 1903–1905.

Buchanan, Charles S. "Adolph Rinck, Portraitist." *The Historic New Orleans Collection Newsletter* 3(Spring 1985):4.

Buechner, Howard A. *Daniel Anton Buechner: Master Lithographer of Old New Orleans (1856–1937)*. Metairie LA: Thunderbird, 1983.

————. *Drysdale (1870–1934): Artist of Myth and Legend*. Metairie LA: Thunderbird, 1985.

Burson, Caroline Maude. *The Stewardship of Don Esteban Miró, 1782–1792*. New Orleans: American, 1940.

Bushnell, David I., Jr. *Drawings by A. DeBatz in Louisiana, 1732–1735*. Smithsonian Miscellaneous Collections, vol. 80, no. 5. Washington DC, 1927.

————. "Friedrich Kurz, Artist–Explorer." *Annual Report of the Board of Regents of the Smithsonian Institution*. Washington DC, 1928.

Byrnes, James B. "Edgar Degas' New Orleans Paintings." *Antiques*, Nov. 1965, 664–69.

Cable, George W. *The Creoles of Louisiana*. London: John C. Nimmo, 1885.

Cable, Mary. *Lost New Orleans*. Boston: Houghton Mifflin, 1980.

Cahalane, Victor H. Introduction to *The Imperial Collection of Audubon Animals*. New York: Bonanza, 1967.

Caldwell, Joan G. "Italianate Domestic Architecture in New Orleans, 1850–1880." Ph.D. dissertation, Tulane University, 1975.

Carolina Art Association. *An Exhibition of Miniatures Owned in South Carolina and Miniatures of South Carolinians Owned Elsewhere Painted Before the Year 1860*. Carolina Art Association, 1936.

Carpenter, Edwin H., Jr. "Arsene Lacarriere Latour." *Hispanic American Historical Review* 18(1938):221–27.

Carrick, Alice Van Leer. *A History of American Silhouettes: A Collector's Guide, 1790–1840*. Rutland VT: C.E. Tuttle, 1968.

Carter, Hodding, and Betty Werlein Carter. *So Great a Good: A History of the Episcopal Church in Louisiana and of Christ Church Cathedral, 1805–1955*. Sewanee TN: University Press, 1955.

Carter, Samuel. *Blaze of Glory: The Fight for New Orleans, 1814–1815*. New York: St. Martin's, 1971.

Casey, Powell A. *Louisiana in the War of 1812*. Baton Rouge, 1963. (Typewritten.)

Castellanos, Henry C. *New Orleans As It Was*. New Orleans: L. Graham & Son, 1895.

Cattell, J. McKeen, Jacques Cattell, and E. E. Ross, eds. *Leaders in Education*. New York: Science Press, 1941.

Catton, Bruce. "A Southern Artist on the Civil War." *American Heritage*, Oct. 1958, 117–20.

Caulfeild, Ruby Van Allen. *The French Literature of Louisiana*. New York: Columbia University, Institute of French Studies, 1929.

Chambers, Bruce W. *Art and Artists of the South: The Robert P. Coggins Collection*. Columbia: University of South Carolina Press, 1984.

Chambers, Henry. *A History of Louisiana*. 3 vols. Chicago: American Historical Society, 1925.

Chambon, Celestin M. *The St. Louis Cathedral and Its Neighbors*. 2d ed. Edited by James J. A. Fortier. New Orleans: Louisiana State Museum, 1938.

Champlin, John Denison, Jr., ed. *Cyclopedia of Painters and Paintings*. Port Washington NY: Kennikat Press, 1969.

Chancellor, John. *Audubon: A Biography*. New York: Viking, 1978.

BIBLIOGRAPHY

"Charles–Alexandre Lesueur (1778–1846)." *Bulletin Trimestriel de la Société Géologique de Normandie et des Amis du Muséum du Havre*, 1978.

Chase, John. "One Political Cartoonist Remembers Another—Trist Wood." *New Orleans*, Aug. 1970, 32–58.

Churchill, Frank G. *Pen Drawings of Old New Orleans*. New Orleans: Robert H. True, 1916.

Cist, Charles. *Cincinnati in 1841*. Cincinnati: Charles Cist, 1841.

The City of New Orleans. The Book of the Chamber of Commerce and Industry of Louisiana and Other Public Bodies of the "Crescent City." New Orleans: George W. Engelhardt, 1894.

Clapp, William W., Jr. *A Record of the Boston Stage*. Boston: James Munroe, 1853.

Clark, Garth. *The Biloxi Art Pottery of George Ohr*. Jackson: Mississippi Department of Archives and History, 1978.

———. "George E. Ohr." *Antiques*, Sept. 1985, 490–7.

———. "George Ohr: Clay Prophet." *Craft Horizons*, Oct. 1978, 44–49, 65.

Clark, Robert Judson, ed. *The Arts and Crafts Movement in America, 1896–1916*. Princeton NJ: Princeton University Press, 1972.

Clark, Thomas D., ed. *Travels in the Old South*. 3 vols. Norman: University of Oklahoma Press.

Classified Business Directory of Louisiana. Louisiana Mercantile Guide to Cities and Suburbs of the State of Louisiana. Compiled by M. S. Baxter. New Orleans: L. Graham & Son, Ltd., 1899.

Clement, Clara Erskine. *Women in the Fine Arts from the Seventh Century B.C. to the Twentieth Century A.D.* Boston: Houghton, Mifflin, 1904. Reprint. Hacker Art Books, 1974.

Clement, Clara Erskine, and Laurence Hutton. *Artists of the Nineteenth Century and Their Works*. 2 vols. in 1. St. Louis: North Point, 1969.

Clement, William Edwards, with Stuart O. Landry. *Plantation Life on the Mississippi*. 2d ed. New Orleans: Pelican, 1961.

Clements, George H. "A Painter's Comparison of Europe and America." *Art and Letters* 1(Aug. 1887):146–50.

Cline, Isaac M. *Art and Artists in New Orleans During the Last Century*. Reprinted from *Biennial Report, Louisiana State Museum*. New Orleans, 1922.

———. *Contemporary Art and Artists in New Orleans*. Reprinted from *Biennial Report, Louisiana State Museum*. New Orleans: Louisiana State Museum, 1924.

———. *Storms, Floods and Sunshine*. New Orleans: Pelican, 1951.

Coad, Oral Sumner, and Edwin Mims, Jr. *The American Stage*. Vol. 14 of *The Pageant of America*, edited by Ralph Henry Gabriel. New Haven CT: Yale University Press, 1929.

Cochran, Estelle M. Fortier. *The Fortier Family and Allied Families*. [San Antonio], 1963.

Cocke, Edward J. *Monumental New Orleans*. New Orleans: La Fayette, 1968.

Cohn, Isidore, with Hermann B. Deutsch. *Rudolph Matas: A Biography of One of the Great Pioneers in Surgery*. Garden City NY: Doubleday, 1960.

Coleman, J. Winston, Jr. *Three Kentucky Artists: Hart, Price, Troye*. Lexington: University Press of Kentucky, 1974.

The Collection of American Silhouette Portraits Cut by August Edouart. Introduction by Arthur S. Vernay. New York: William H. Benthuysen, 1913.

"The Collection: Paintings by G. P. A. Healy." *Chicago History* 10(Fall 1981):164–66.

Collier, Alberta. "Decorative Wall Paintings Reappear from Past." *Times–Picayune*, Feb. 13, 1972.

———. "Gallery Sets First Fall Exhibition." *Times–Picayune*, Sept. 19, 1965.

————. "Orleans Artist Delighted with 99th Birthday Party." *Times–Picayune*, Nov. 14, 1957.

————. "Portrait is Gift of Mrs. Francis." *Times–Picayune*, June 6, 1971.

————. "A Romantic Classicist." *Dixie*, Oct. 27, 1974.

————. "Work of Artistic, Historical Value." *Times–Picayune*, Aug. 20, 1967.

————. "The World of Art." *Times–Picayune*, Dec. 3, 1950, Mar. 13, 1955, Nov. 11, 1956, Dec. 22, 1957, Sept. 22, 1968, May 21, 1970, Sept. 23, 1973, Mar. 7, 1976.

————. "The World of Art: Ceiling Art Work Found in Old House." *Times–Picayune*, July 28, 1968.

————. "The World of Art: Delgado Adds 14 Oils to Its Collection." *Times–Picayune*, Mar. 14, 1971.

————. "The World of Art: Early Woodcarving Found—in Cabildo!" *Times–Picayune*, June 12, 1955.

————. "The World of Art: Historic Civil War Painting Restored." *Times–Picayune*, Aug. 4, 1968.

————. "The World of Art: Historic New Orleans Collection Adds 1850 Era Marine Painting." *Times–Picayune*, July 20, 1975.

————. "The World of Art: Historic N.O. Collection Has Develle 'Red Store' on View." *Times–Picayune*, Aug. 26, 1973.

————. "The World of Art: Hunt for Doughty Works is Begun in New Orleans." *Times–Picayune*, Jan. 3, 1972.

————. "The World of Art: Itinerant Artist E. Phelps Leaves Trip Journal Behind." *Times–Picayune*, Oct. 9, 1977.

————. "The World of Art: Major Art Event of the Year: 'Cotton Exchange' on View." *Times–Picayune*, June 8, 1975.

————. "The World of Art: Museum Gets Four Fine Paintings." *Times–Picayune*, Nov. 11, 1956.

————. "The World of Art: Museum May Get Portrait of Jackson." *Times–Picayune*, Nov. 8, 1970.

————. "The World of Art: Newcomb to Feature Two Artists." *Times–Picayune*, Nov. 4, 1956.

————. "The World of Art: 'Operation Paintings' Project Cited." *Times–Picayune*, June 21, 1964.

————. "The World of Art: Paintings May Be Work of Salazar." *Times–Picayune*, Apr. 23, 1967.

————. "The World of Art: Peretti's Murals Decorate Church." *Times–Picayune*, Nov. 20, 1966.

————. "The World of Art: Portraitist Paints Three Generations." *Times–Picayune*, Aug. 23, 1964.

————. "The World of Art: Revival in Portraiture Noted." *Times–Picayune*, Aug. 3, 1958.

————. "The World of Art: Show at Vincent Mann Gallery a Must for Serious Art Lovers." *Times–Picayune*, Apr. 24, 1977.

————. "The World of Art: State Museum Receives Historic Persac Canvas." *Times–Picayune*, Apr. 3, 1969.

————. "The World of Art: State Museum's Gualdi Painting Has Near Twin in New Hampshire." *Times–Picayune*, July 13, 1975.

————. "The World of Art: Unsigned Watercolor Attributed to Early N.O. Carnival Designer." *Times–Picayune*, July 18, 1965.

Collins, Jim, and Glenn B. Opitz, eds. *Women Artists in America: Eighteenth Century to the Present (1790–1980)*. Rev. ed. Poughkeepsie NY: Apollo, 1980.

Comité de l'Exposition française de la Louisiane. *Exposition Française de la Louisiane*. New Orleans: L. Graham, 1904.

Comstock, Helen. "A Directory of Source Books, 1608–1860." *Antiques*, Feb. 1961, 174–76.

———. "Spot News in American Historical Prints 1805–1821." *Antiques*, Jan. 1962, 100.

Comus Diamond Jubilee, 1857–1931. New Orleans: Carnival Press, 1931.

Conrad, Glenn R., trans & comp. *The First Families of Louisiana*. Vol. 1. Baton Rouge, Claitor's, 1970.

Cooke, George. "Commerce and the Fine Arts." *DeBow's Review* 1(Mar. 1846):269–75.

Copley Gallery. *Paintings of New Orleans and Colorado by Luis Graner, The Spanish Painter*. Boston: Copley Gallery, 1917.

Corcoran Gallery of Art. *American Painters of the South*. Washington DC: Corcoran Gallery of Art, 1960.

Coulon, George A. *350 Miles in a Skiff Through the Louisiana Swamps*. New Orleans, 1888.

Coulter, E. Merton. *The Confederate States of America, 1861–1865*. Vol. 7 of *A History of the South*. Baton Rouge: Louisiana State University Press, 1950.

———. *Travels in the Confederate States: A Bibliography*. Norman: University of Oklahoma Press, 1948.

Cox, Paul E. "Potteries of the Gulf Coast." *Ceramic Age*, Apr. 1935, 116–17, 119, 140.

Cox, Richard. *Caroline Durieux: Lithographs of the Thirties and Forties*. Baton Rouge: Louisiana State University Press, 1977.

Cragsmoor Free Library. *Helen M. Turner (1858–1958): A Retrospective Exhibition*. Cragsmoor NY: Cragsmoor Free Library, 1983.

Craven, Wayne. *Sculpture in America*. New York: Thomas Y. Crowell, 1978.

Creole Art Gallery. *Synopsis Catalogue*. New Orleans: Malns and Hofeline, 1892.

Creole Exhibit. *Official Catalogue of the Creole Exhibit Art Gallery, American Exposition, 1885–86*. New Orleans: W. B. Stansbury, 1886.

"The Creole Sketchbook of A. R. Waud." *American Heritage*, Dec. 1963, 33–48.

The Creole Tourists' Guide and Sketch Book. New Orleans: Creole Publishing, [1909].

Cruise, Boyd, and Merle Harton. *Signor Faranta's Iron Theatre*. New Orleans: The Historic New Orleans Collection, 1982.

Curry, Larry. *The American West: Painters from Catlin to Russell*. New York: Viking, 1972.

Cursiter, Stanley. *Scottish Art to the Close of the Nineteenth Century*. New York: Chanticleer, 1949.

Curtis, Nathaniel Cortlandt. *New Orleans: Its Old Houses, Shops and Public Buildings*. Philadelphia: J. B. Lippincott, 1933.

Cutler, Jervis. *A Topographical Description of the State of Ohio, Indiana Territory, and Louisiana*. Boston: Charles Williams, 1812.

DAB. *Dictionary of American Biography*, edited by Allen Johnson. 20 vols. New York: Charles Scribner's Sons, 1928–36.

Dabney, Thomas Ewing. *One Hundred Great Years: The Story of the Times–Picayune from Its Founding to 1940*. Baton Rouge: Louisiana State University Press, 1944.

Darby, William. *A Geographical Description of the State of Louisiana . . . with an Account of the Character and Manners of the Inhabitants. Being an Accompaniment to the Map of Louisiana*. Philadelphia: John Melish, 1816.

Davidson, Marshall B. *The American Heritage History of American Antiques from the Revolution to the Civil War*. New York: American Heritage, 1968.

———. "The 'American Woodsman.'" *American Heritage*, Dec. 1959, 12–23, 94–99.

———. *Life in America*. Bicentennial ed. 2 vols. Boston: Houghton Mifflin, 1974.

Davidson, Marshall B., and the Editors of *American Heritage*. *The American Heritage History of the Artists' America*. New York: American Heritage, 1973.

Davies, Marcia. "Louisiana Art." *Men and Matters*, Sept. 1897, 40–55.

Davis, Edwin Adams. *Louisiana, a Narrative History*. 3d ed. Baton Rouge: Claitor's, 1971.

———. *Plantation Life in the Florida Parishes of Louisiana, 1836–1846, as Reflected in the Diary of Bennet H. Barrow*. New York: AMS, 1967.

———. *The Story of Louisiana*. 4 vols. New Orleans: J. F. Hyer Publishing Co., 1960–63.

Davis, Ellis Arthur, ed. *The Historical Encyclopedia of Louisiana*. Louisiana Historical Bureau, [1940].

Dawson, Sarah Morgan. *A Confederate Girl's Diary*. Boston: Houghton Mifflin, 1913.

Degas, Edgar Germain Hilaire. *Letters*. Edited by Marcel Guerin. Oxford: Bruno Cassirer, 1947.

"Degas' American Cousins." *Life*, July 2, 1965, 1–7.

Délégation aux Célébrations Nationales, Délégation à l'Action Artistique de la Ville de Paris, et Fondation MacDonald Stewart. *Naissance de la Louisiane*. Paris, 1982.

Delery, Simone de la Souchere. *Napoleon's Soldiers in America*. Gretna LA.: Pelican, 1972.

Delgado Museum of Art. *Catalogue*. New Orleans, [ca. 1911–12].

———. *Catalogue*. New Orleans, [ca. 1912–13].

———. *Catalogue of Paintings by Andrés Molinary*. New Orleans, 1915.

———. *Catalogue of Paintings, Sculpture and Other Objects of Art in the Isaac Delgado Museum of Art*. New Orleans, 1932.

———. *Charles W. Hutson, 1840–1936: A Retrospective Exhibition*. New Orleans.

———. *Inaugural Exhibition Collected and Arranged for the Isaac Delgado Museum of Art by the Art Association of New Orleans*. New Orleans, 1911.

———. *Loan Exhibition of Works of New Orleans Artists Prior to 1900*.

———. *The Morgan Whitney Collection of Chinese Jades and Other Hard Stones*. New Orleans, 1914.

———. *New Orleans: Its People and Its Environs*. New Orleans: Delgado Museum of Art, [1962].

———. *The World of Miss Josephine Crawford*. New Orleans: Delgado Museum of Art, 1965.

De Mare, Marie. *G. P. A. Healy, American Artist: An Intimate Chronicle of the Nineteenth Century*. New York: David McKay, 1954.

Denson & Nelson's New Orleans and Mississippi Valley Business Directory and River Guide for 1866 and '67. St. Louis: P. M. Pinckard, 1866.

Desdunes, Rodolphe Lucien. *Our People and Our History*. Translated and edited by Sister Dorothea Olga McCants. Baton Rouge: Louisiana State University Press, 1973.

Detroit Institute of Arts. *The French in America, 1520–1880*. Detroit: Detroit Institute of Arts, 1951.

De Ville, Roy V., Jr. "A Brief Study of Richard Clague, Jr.: A Nineteenth Century New Orleans Painter." *Louisiana Studies* 10(Fall 1971):202–5.

Dichter, Harry, and Elliot Shapiro. *Early American Sheet Music: Its Lure and Its Lore, 1768–1889*. New York: R. R. Bowker, 1941.

Dickson, Harold F. *John Wesley Jarvis, American Painter, 1780–1840*. New York: The New-York Historical Society, 1949.

Dictionary of American Portraits, edited by Hayward and Blanche Cirker. New York: Dover, [1968].

Dictionary of National Biography, edited by Sir Sidney Lee and Sir Leslie Stephen. 22 vols. London: Oxford University Press, 1885–1901.

Dictionnaire Général des Artistes de L'Ecole Française, edited by Emile Bellier de la Chavignerie and Louis Auvray. 5 vols. New York: Garland, 1979.

Diehl, Gaston. *Pascin.* Translated by Rosalie Siegal. New York: Crown, 1968.

Dixon, Brandt V. B. *A Brief History of H. Sophie Newcomb Memorial College, 1887–1919.* New Orleans: Hauser, 1928.

Dixon, Richard Remy. *Elements of Victory: An Address.* New Orleans, 1963.

Dixson, Kathryn Vogt. "Joseph Rusling Meeker: The Land of Evangeline and Beyond." *Gateway Heritage* 3(Winter 1982–83):10–15.

Dods, Agnes M. "Nathan and Joseph Negus, Itinerant Painters." *Antiques,* Nov. 1959, 434–37.

Donaldson, Susan Van D'Elden. "The Artist and His Scene: Pastoralism and Romanticism in Modern Southern Literature and Painting." M.A. thesis, Brown University, 1983.

Dover, Cedric. *American Negro Art.* Greenwich CT: New York Graphic Society, 1960.

Downs, Arthur Channing Jr. "Portraits By Theodore A. Gould, Brooklyn, 1850." *Antiques,* Feb. 1977, 388.

"The Drawings of Alfred R. Waud." *Bulletin of the Missouri Historical Society,* Jan. 1963, 163–64.

Drepperd, Carl W. *Early American Prints.* New York: Century, 1930.

———. "Selling Jackson's Great Victory." *Antiques,* Nov. 1940, 220–21.

———. "Three Battles of New Orleans." *Antiques,* Aug. 1928, 129–31.

Driskell, David C. *Two Centuries of Black American Art.* New York: Los Angeles County Museum of Art/Alfred A. Knopf, 1976.

Duffy, Jean H. "The Cave." *Architectural Art and Its Allies* 6(Feb. 1911):20.

Duffy, John, ed. *The Rudolph Matas History of Medicine in Louisiana.* 2 vols. Baton Rouge: Louisiana State University Press, 1958–62.

Dufour, Charles L. "A La Mode: Former Orleanian's Poems Full of Color and Imagery, If Obscure." *States-Item,* June 16, 1966.

———. *Battle of New Orleans.* New Orleans: Friends of the Cabildo, 1965.

———. *Krewe of Proteus: The First Hundred Years.* New Orleans: Krewe of Proteus, 1981.

———, ed. *St. Patrick's of New Orleans, 1833–1958. Commemorative essays for the 125th Anniversary.* New Orleans: St. Patrick's Parish, 1958.

Dufour, Charles L., and Leonard V. Huber. *If Ever I Cease to Love: One Hundred Years of Rex, 1872–1971.* New Orleans, 1970.

Dunbar, Prescott N. "The Diamond Jubilee History Exhibition: Part II, The Professional Directors." *Arts Quarterly* 8(Summer 1986):27–32.

———. "The Growth of the Art Collection: The First Donors." *Arts Quarterly* 8(Spring 1986):26–31.

Dunlap, William. *History of the Rise and Progress of the Arts of Design in the United States.* New York, 1834. Rev. ed., edited by Alexander Wyckoff. 3 vols. New York: Benjamin Blom, 1965.

Duyckinck, Evert A., and George L. Duyckinck. *Cyclopedia of American Literature.* 2 vols. New York: Charles Scribner, 1856.

Dwight, Edward H. "Art in Early Cincinnati." *Cincinnati Art Museum Bulletin* 3(Aug. 1953):6.

Dyer, Brainerd. *Zachary Taylor.* Baton Rouge: Louisiana State University Press, 1946.

Dyer, Frederick H. *A Compendium of the War of Rebellion.* Dayton OH: National Historical Society, 1979.

Dyer, John P. *Tulane: The Biography of a University, 1834–1964.* New York: Harper and Row, 1966.

Edwards, Lee M. "The Life and Career of Jerome Thompson." *The American Art Journal* 14(Autumn 1982):4–30.

Edwards' Descriptive Gazetteer and Commercial Directory of the Mississippi River, from St. Cloud to New Orleans. St. Louis MO: Edwards, Greenough & Deved, 1866.

Elder, Mrs. S. B., comp. and ed. *Life of the Abbe Adrien Roquette.* New Orleans: L. Graham, 1913.

Ellsworth, Linda V. "George Washington Sully." *Antiques*, Mar. 1983, 600–5.

Encyclopaedia Britannica. 15th ed. 30 vols. Chicago: Encyclopaedia Britannica, 1943–74.

Evans, Clement A., ed. *Confederate Military History.* 12 vols. Atlanta: Confederate Publishing, 1899.

Evans, Paul. *Art Pottery of the United States: An Encyclopedia of Producers and Their Marks.* New York: Charles Scribner's Sons, 1974.

Ewan, Joseph. "James Trudeau and the Recent Discovery of a Collection of Paintings of Eggs of North American Birds." *Tulane Studies in Zoology* 9(Apr. 16, 1962):259–63.

Ewers, John C. *Artists of the Old West.* Enl. ed. Garden City NY: Doubleday, 1973.

Fabian, Monroe H. *Mr. Sully, Portrait Painter: The Works of Thomas Sully (1783–1872).* Washington DC: Smithsonian Institution, 1983.

Fagg, Daniel. "Henry Byrd in Arkansas." Batesville, Arkansas, 1981. (Typewritten.)

Fairbanks, Jonathan. "A Decade of Collecting Decorative Arts and Sculpture at the Museum of Fine Arts, Boston." *Antiques*, Sept. 1981, 590.

Fairman, Charles E. *Art and Artists of the Capitol of the United States of America.* Washington DC, 1927.

Farwell, Lynne. "John Joseph Vaudechamp and New Orleans." *Antiques*, Sept. 1968, 371–75.

Fearn, Frances, ed. *Diary of a Refugee.* New York: Moffat, Yard, 1910.

Feldman, Sandra K. *William Penhallow Henderson: The Early Years: 1901–1916.* New York: Hirschl & Adler Galleries, Inc., 1982.

Fielding, Mantle. *American Engravers upon Copper and Steel.* Supplement to *American Engravers upon Copper and Steel* by David McNeely Stauffer. Philadelphia, 1917. Reprint. New York: Burt Franklin, 1964.

———. *Mantle Fielding's Dictionary of American Painters, Sculptors, & Engravers.* 1926. 4th ed., rev. and enl., edited by Glenn B. Opitz. Poughkeepsie NY: Apollo, 1983.

Fine, Elsa Honig. *The Afro–American Artist: A Search for Identity.* New York: Hacker Art Books, 1982.

Fischer Galleries. *Exhibition of 55 Oil Paintings by Joseph Jefferson.* Washington DC: Fischer Galleries, 1900.

Fisk, Frances Battaile. *A History of Texas Artists and Sculptors.* Abilene TX, 1928.

Flanary, Sara E. Lewis. "William Edward West in New Orleans and Mississippi." *Antiques*, Nov. 1983, 1010–15.

Fleming, Mary Boyd. "The Last Meeting of Lee and Jackson: The Southern Painter, Julio, and His Most Celebrated Work, a Touching Scene Typical of the South in the Great Civil War." *The Journal of American History* 5(Third Qtr. 1911):409–11.

Flexner, James Thomas. *America's Old Masters.* Rev. ed. New York: Dover, 1967.

———. *The Light of Distant Skies, 1760–1835.* New York: Dover, 1969.

———. *That Wilder Image: The Painting of America's Native School from Thomas Cole to Winslow Homer.* New York: Bonanza, 1962.

Floyd, William Barrow. *The Barrow Family of Old Louisiana.* Lexington KY: William B. Floyd, 1963.

———. *Jouett–Bush–Frazer: Early Kentucky Artists.* Lexington: William B. Floyd, 1968.

Foote, Henry Wilder. *Theodore Clapp.* Reprinted from the proceedings of the Unitarian Historical Society. Boston, [1933].

Ford, Alice. *Audubon, By Himself.* Garden City NY: The Natural History Press, 1969.

Fortier, Alcée. *A History of Louisiana.* 4 vols. New York: Manzi, Joyant, 1904.

———. *Louisiana: Comprising Sketches of Parishes, Towns, Events, Institutions, and Persons, Arranged in Cyclopedic Form.* 3 vols. Madison WI: Century Historical Association, 1914.

Fossier, A. E. *History of the Orleans Parish Medical Society 1878–1928.* New Orleans, 1930.

Fossier, Albert A. *New Orleans: The Glamour Period, 1800–1840.* New Orleans: Pelican, 1957.

Foster, John. "Degas' New Orleans Period." *Dixie,* May 2, 1965.

Fowble, E. McSherry. "Without a Blush: The Movement Toward Acceptance of the Nude as an Art Form in America, 1800–1825." *Winterthur Portfolio,* 1974, 103–21.

Freeman, Samuel T., & Co. *The Dr. I. M. Cline Collection of New Orleans, Louisiana: Early American Portraits by Eminent American Artists.* Philadelphia, 1927.

Fremaux, Leon J. *New Orleans Characters.* New Orleans: Peychaud & Garcia, 1876.

French Opera. Season 1902–3. New Orleans, [1902].

Friends of the Cabildo. *Audubon Exhibit.* New Orleans: Friends of the Cabildo, 1960.

———. *August Norieri, 1860–1898.* New Orleans: Louisiana State Museum, 1970.

———. *Battle of New Orleans.* New Orleans, 1965.

———. *Louisiana Indians: 12,000 Years.* New Orleans: Louisiana State Museum, 1966.

———. *Mugnier: The Look of New Orleans, 1880–1910.* New Orleans, 1975.

———. *New Orleans Architecture.* 6 vols. Gretna LA: Pelican, 1971–80.

———. *250 Years of Life in New Orleans: The Rosemonde E. and Emile Kuntz Collection and the Felix H. Kuntz Collection.* New Orleans: Louisiana State Museum, 1968.

Frost, Orcutt William, Jr. "The Early Life of Lafcadio Hearn." Ph.D. dissertation, University of Illinois, 1954.

Fulkerson, H. S. *Random Recollections of Early Days in Mississippi.* Vicksburg MS: Vicksburg Printing and Publishing, 1885.

Fulton, W. Joseph, and Roulhac B. Toledano. "New Orleans Landscape Painting of the Nineteenth Century." *Antiques,* Apr. 1968, 504–10.

———. "Portrait Painting in Colonial and Ante–bellum New Orleans." *Antiques,* June 1968, 788–95.

Gallegly, Joseph S. *Footlights on the Border: The Galveston and Houston Stage Before 1900.* The Hague, Netherlands: Mouton, 1962.

———. "Plays and Players at Pillot's Opera House." *Southwestern Historical Quarterly* 66(July 1962):43–58.

Galvani, Charles. *Catalogue of the Collection of Paintings, and Other Works of Art, Belonging to James Robb, Esq. Washington Avenue, New Orleans.* New Orleans, 1859.

Gandolfo, Henri A. *Metairie Cemetery: An Historical Memoir.* New Orleans: Stewart Enterprises, 1981.

Gardner, Albert TenEyck. *American Sculpture: A Catalogue of the Collection of the Metropolitan Museum of Art.* New York: Metropolitan Museum of Art, 1965.

————. *Yankee Stonecutters: The American School of Sculpture, 1800–1850*. New York: Columbia University Press, 1945.

Gates, William Bryan. "The Theatre in Natchez." *Journal of Mississippi History* 3(Apr. 1941):71–129.

Gayarré, Charles. "A Louisiana Sugar Plantation of the Old Regime." *Harper's New Monthly Magazine*, Mar. 1887, 606–62.

Gebhard, David, and Deborah Nevins. *200 Years of American Architectural Drawing*. New York: Watson–Gupill, 1977.

Gernsheim, Helmut, and Alison Gernsheim. *L. J. M. Daguerre: The History of the Diorama and the Daguerreotype*. New York: Dover, 1968.

Gibbs, Linda Mary Jones. "Enoch Wood Perry, Jr.: A Biography and Analysis of His Thematic and Stylistic Development." M.A. thesis, University of Utah, 1981.

Gilchrist, Agnes Addison. *William Strickland: Architect and Engineer, 1788–1854*. Enl. ed. New York: Da Capo, 1969.

Glasgow, Vaughn L. "G.P.A. Healy and His Louisiana Portraits." *Antiques*, June 1977, 1204–9.

Glenk, Robert. *Handbook and Guide to the Louisiana State Museum*. New Orleans, 1934.

Gottheil, Edward. *Reports of the Chief Commissioner to the Paris Exposition*. New Orleans: A. L. Lee, 1868.

Grand Celebration in Honor of the Passage of the Ordinance of Emancipation . . . Also the Proceedings of the American Arts Association of New Orleans, and the Distribution of Prizes. New Orleans: H. P. Lathrop, 1864.

Grant, Ulysses S. *The Papers of Ulysses S. Grant*. Edited by John Y. Simon. 14 vols. to date. Carbondale: Southern Illinois University Press, 1967–.

Graves, Algernon. *The Royal Academy of Arts: A Complete Dictionary of Contributors and their work from its foundation in 1769 to 1904*. 8 vols. in 4. Reprint. New York: Burt Franklin, 1972.

Green, Roger. "Architectural Trailblazers." *Times–Picayune/States–Item*, Feb. 11, 1984.

————. "Sensual Ceramics From an Outrageous Gulf Coast Eccentric." *Times–Picayune*, June 12, 1983.

————. Vision: The World of Art: New Interest in Latter Day Lautrec." *Times–Picayune*, Dec. 5, 1982.

Greenville County Museum of Art. *Eight Southern Women*. Greenville SC: Greenville County Museum of Art, 1986.

Groce, George C., and David H. Wallace. *The New–York Historical Society's Dictionary of Artists in America, 1564–1860*. New Haven CT: Yale University Press, 1957.

Gross, Mrs. Ben J. "Mitchell Genealogy." *New Orleans Genesis* 15(June 1976):267–74.

Guren, Jay, and Richard Ugan. *Carnival Panorama: New Orleans Mardi Gras Medals and Krewes, 1884–1965*. New Orleans: Anderson, 1966.

Gustafson, Eleanor H. "Museum Accessions." *Antiques*, June 1977.

Hachard, Marie Madeleine. *The Letters of Marie Madeleine Hachard, 1727–28*. Translated by Myldred Masson Costa. New Orleans, 1974.

Hale, Walter. "George W. Cable's New Orleans." *The Bookman* 13(Apr. 1901):136–47.

Hall, Capt. Basil. *Forty Etchings From Sketches Made With the Camera Lucida, in North America, in 1827 and 1828*. Edinburgh: Cadell, 1829.

Hamilton, Sinclair. *Early American Book Illustrators and Wood Engravers, 1670–1870*. 2 vols. Princeton NJ: Princeton University Press, 1968.

Hamlin, Talbot. *Benjamin Henry Latrobe*. New York: Oxford University Press, 1955.

BIBLIOGRAPHY

Hammersmith, Paul. "Autobiographical Notes." Oct. 12, 1936. (Typewritten.)

Hanners, John. "The Adventures of an Artist: John Banvard (1815–1891) and His Mississippi Panorama." Ph.D. dissertation, Michigan State University, 1979.

———. "John Banvard's Mississippi Panorama." *American History Illustrated*, Nov. 1982, 32–39.

Hardy, Stella Pickett. *Colonial Families of the Southern States of America*. Baltimore: Genealogical Publishing, 1968.

Harkey, Ira B., Jr. "The End of the Make–Believe House." *Times–Picayune*, Dec. 12, 1941.

Harper, J. Russell. "Paul Kane's Frontier." *Antiques*, Mar. 1971, 391–99.

Hart, Charles Henry. "The Last of the Silhouettists." *The Outlook*, Oct. 6, 1900, 329–35.

Hart, W. O. "Clark Mills." *Louisiana Historical Quarterly* 3(Jan. 1920):614–16.

Harter, John Burton, and Mary Louise Tucker. *The Louisiana Portrait Gallery*. New Orleans: Louisiana State Museum, 1979.

Harvey, Cathy Chance. "Lyle Saxon: A Portrait in Letters, 1917–1945." Ph.D. dissertation, Tulane University, 1980.

Harvey, E. T. *Recollections of a Scene Painter*. Cincinnati: E. T. Harvey, 1916.

Harwood, Michael, and Mary Durant. "In Search of the Real Mr. Audubon." *Audubon* 87(May 1985):58–118.

Hearn, Lafcadio. *Creole Sketches*. Edited by Charles Woodward Hutson. Boston: Houghton Mifflin, 1924.

Heidelberg, Michelle Favrot. "William Woodward." M.A. thesis, Tulane University, 1974.

Helfer, Harold. "Shades of the Past: An Exhibit of Shadowy Characters Gives Silhouettes Renewed Respect." *Aloft*, 64–68.

Hemperly, Marion R., comp. "Federal Naturalization Oaths, Savannah, Georgia, 1790–1860." *Georgia Historical Quarterly* 51(Dec. 1967):454–87.

Henry, Adolphe, and Victor Gerodias. *The Louisiana Coast Directory of the Right and Left Banks of the Mississippi River, from its Mouth to Baton Rouge*. New Orleans: E. C. Wharton, 1857.

Herrick, Francis Hobart. *Audubon the Naturalist*. 2d ed., 2 vols. in 1. New York: D. Appleton–Century, 1938.

Hirschl & Adler Galleries. "American Art From the Gallery's Collection." New York, 1980.

Hirschl & Adler Galleries, Inc., to George E. Jordan. Feb. 22, 1983. (Typewritten.)

Historical Epitome of the State of Louisiana, with an Historical Notice of New–Orleans, Views and Descriptions of Public Buildings, &c.. New Orleans, 1840.

Historical Sketch Book and Guide to New Orleans and Environs. Edited and compiled by writers of the New Orleans Press. New York: Will H. Coleman, 1885.

A History of the Proceedings in the City of New Orleans, on the Occasion of the Funeral Ceremonies in Honor of Calhoun, Clay and Webster, Which Took Place on Thursday, Dec. 9th, 1852. New Orleans, 1853.

History of the Yellow Fever in New Orleans, During the Summer of 1853. By a Physician of New Orleans Who Was Present During the Fatal Epidemic of 1853. Philadelphia: C. W. Kenworthy, 1854.

"History on Canvas." *Chicago History* 1(Spring 1947):185–87, cover.

Holzer, Edith, and Harold Holzer. "Portraits in City Hall, New York." *Antiques*, Nov. 1976, 1030–39.

Hoole, W. Stanley. *The Ante–Bellum Charleston Theatre*. Tuscaloosa: University of Alabama Press, 1946.

Hornblow, Arthur. *A History of the Theatre in America.* 2 vols. Philadelphia: J. B. Lippincott, 1919.

Howard University. *Ten Afro–American Artists of the Nineteenth Century.* Washington DC, 1967.

Howes, Wright, comp. *U.S.IANA (1650–1950).* Rev. and enl. ed. New York: R. R. Bowker, 1962.

Huber, Leonard V., and Guy F. Bernard. *To Glorious Immortality: The Rise and Fall of the Girod Street Cemetery, New Orleans' First Protestant Cemetery, 1822–1957.* New Orleans: Alblen, 1961.

Huber, Leonard V., and Clarence A. Wagner. *The Great Mail: A Postal History of New Orleans.* State College PA: American Philatelic Society, 1949.

Huber, Leonard V., and Samuel Wilson, Jr. *Baroness Pontalba's Buildings.* New Orleans: New Orleans Chapter of the Louisiana Landmarks Society and Friends of the Cabildo, 1964.

Huber, Leonard V., and Samuel Wilson, Jr. *The Basilica on Jackson Square: The History of the St. Louis Cathedral and Its Predecessors, 1727–1965.* New Orleans: St. Louis Cathedral, 1965.

Huber, Leonard V., Samuel Wilson, Jr., and Garland F. Taylor. *Louisiana Purchase: An Exhibition.* New Orleans: Louisiana Landmarks Society, 1953.

Huber, Victor. "Autobiographical Sketch and Mementoes." Edited by Leonard V. Huber. New Orleans, 1960. (Typewritten.)

Hughes, Glenn. *A History of the American Theatre 1700–1950.* London: Samuel French, 1951.

Inventory of Original Works of Art in the New Orleans Public Schools As of Tuesday, May 20, 1969. Art Section, Division of Instruction, Department of Curriculum Services, June 1969. (Typewritten.)

Ireland, Le Roy. *The Works of George Inness.* Austin: University of Texas Press, 1965.

Jackson, Emily Nevill. *Ancestors in Silhouette, Cut By August Edouart.* New York: John Lane, 1921.

———. *The History of Silhouettes.* London: The Connoisseur, 1911.

———. *Silhouette: Notes and Dictionary.* London: Methuen, 1938.

Jackson, Joy. "New Orleans' 'Naked Lady.' " *Dixie,* July 12, 1953.

———. "A Thirteen–Year–Old Boy Was Flower Painter for Audubon." *Dixie,* Mar. 2, 1952.

Jackson, Lily. "Their Legacy: An Artistic Spirit." *Times–Picayune,* Oct. 9, 1983.

———. "Vivant: Ines Lugano's Career: Illustrations to Portraits." *Times–Picayune,* Aug. 27, 1975.

Jackson Monument Association *Report of the Commissioners.* Baton Rouge: Advocate, 1856.

Jacobsen, Anita. *From Sail to Stream: The Story of Antonio Jacobsen, Marine Artist.* Staten Island NY: Manor, 1972.

James, Marquis. *Andrew Jackson, The Border Captain.* New York: Literary Guild, 1933.

James, Marquis. *Andrew Jackson, Portrait of a President.* Indianapolis NY: Bobbs–Merrill, 1937.

Janis, Sidney. *They Taught Themselves: American Primitive Painters of the 20th Century.* New York: Dial, 1942.

Jefferson, Eugénie Paul. *Intimate Recollections of Joseph Jefferson.* New York: Dodd, Mead, 1909.

Jefferson, Joseph. "The Autobiography of Joseph Jefferson." *The Century,* May–Oct. 1890.

Jewell, Edwin L., ed. *Jewell's Crescent City Illustrated: The Commercial, Social, Political and General History of New Orleans.* New Orleans, 1873.

BIBLIOGRAPHY

Johns, Emile. *Album Louisianais: Hommage aux Dames de la Nouvelle Orléans.* Paris: F. Pleyel, ca. 1832–34.

Johnson, J., and A. Greutzner, comps. *The Dictionary of British Artists, 1880–1940.* Woodbridge, England: Antique Collectors Club, 1976.

Johnson, Robert Underwood, and Clarence Clough Buel, eds. *Battles and Leaders of the Civil War.* 3 vols. New York: Century, 1884–87.

Johnson, Una E. *American Woodcuts, 1670–1950: A Survey of Woodcuts and Wood-Engravings in the United States.* Brooklyn NY: Brooklyn Museum, 1950.

Jones, Karen M. "Accessions." *Antiques,* Feb. 1975, 254.

Jordan, George E. "Artist Recorded Charms of New Orleans." *Times–Picayune,* July 31, 1977.

——. "Carlin is Noted for Details." *Times–Picayune,* Mar. 30, 1975.

——. "Clague Seen in Retrospective." *Times–Picayune,* Nov. 25, 1974.

——. "Crawford Bequest." *Times–Picayune,* Apr. 2, 1978.

——. "Drysdale Bayou Painting Adorns T. Roosevelt's Sagamore Hill." *Times–Picayune,* Oct. 31, 1976.

——. "Interest in Guard History Saves Fine Old Painting." *Times–Picayune,* Oct. 7, 1976.

——. "Jewelry—It's a Part of History Too." *Times–Picayune,* Nov. 14, 1976.

——. "LeBrethon Cameos Are Rare." *Times–Picayune,* Feb. 23, 1975.

——. "Madame John's is Alive." *Times–Picayune,* May 11, 1975.

——. "Mystery of Clarice is Solved." *Times–Picayune,* Dec. 29, 1974.

——. "Mystery Surrounds Louisiana Painting in Met Exhibit." *Times–Picayune,* July 25, 1976.

——. "Old Sketch Books Recall Early N.O. Artist." *Times–Picayune,* Apr. 4, 1976.

——. "Painting Has Puzzle to It." *Times–Picayune,* July 11, 1976.

——. "Rare Pastie 'Silhouettes' Come to New Orleans." *Times–Picayune,* Oct. 26, 1975.

——. "Request: La. Artists of 1800s." *Times–Picayune,* Jan. 12, 1975.

——. "The World of Art." *Times–Picayune,* Dec. 15, 1974.

——. "The World of Art: Carnival Visitors' Works Were Fashionable in 1850s." *Times–Picayune,* Feb. 5, 1978.

——. "The World of Art: Lux's Portraits on Porcelain." *Times–Picayune,* Dec. 15, 1974.

——. "The World of Art: Miniatures Popular in 1830s in Permanent N.O. Collection." *Times–Picayune,* May 15, 1977.

——. "The World of Art: Rare 'Pasties' Visiting New York." *Times–Picayune,* Nov. 27, 1977.

——. "The World of Art: Sheet Music Covers." *Times–Picayune,* Jan. 28, 1979.

Josephy, Alvin M., Jr., ed. *The American Heritage Book of Indians.* New York: American Heritage, 1961.

Jumonville, Florence M., ed. *Bound to Please.* New Orleans: The Historic New Orleans Collection, 1982.

Kane, Harnett. "Orleanians Who Write Books." *Dixie,* Apr. 30, 1950.

——. *Plantation Parade: The Grand Manner in Louisiana.* New York: William Morrow, 1945.

Kane, Paul. *Paul Kane's Frontier: Including Wanderings of an Artist Among the Indians of North America.* Edited by J. Russell Harper. Austin: University of Texas Press, 1971.

Kelly, James C. *The South on Paper: Line, Color and Light.* Spartanburg SC: Robert M. Hicklin Jr., 1985.

Kemp, John R., and Linda Orr King, eds. *Louisiana Images, 1880–1920: A Photographic Essay by George François Mugnier.* Baton Rouge: Louisiana State Museum by Louisiana State University Press, 1975.

Kendall, John Smith. *The Golden Age of the New Orleans Theater*. Baton Rouge: Louisiana State University Press, 1952.

————. *History of New Orleans*. 3 vols. Chicago: Lewis, 1922.

————. "New Orleans' Musicians of Long Ago." *Louisiana Historical Quarterly* 31(Jan. 1948):130–49.

————. "Old Days on the New Orleans Picayune." *Louisiana Historical Quarterly* 33(July 1950):317–42.

————. "Old New Orleans Houses and Some of the People Who Lived in Them." *Louisiana Historical Quarterly* 20(July 1937):796–820.

————. "Who Killa de Chief?" *Louisiana Historical Quarterly* 22(Apr. 1939):492–530.

Kenny, Michael. *Catholic Culture in Alabama*. New York: America, 1931.

Kimball & James' Business Directory, for the Mississippi Valley: 1844. Cincinnati: Kendall & Barnard, 1844.

King, Edward. *The Great South*. Baton Rouge: Louisiana State University Press, 1972.

————. *The Southern States of North America: A Record of Journeys in Louisiana, Texas, the Indian Territory, Missouri, Arkansas, Mississippi, Alabama, Georgia, Florida, South Carolina, North Carolina, Kentucky, Tennessee, Virginia, West Virginia and Maryland*. London: Blackie & Son, 1875.

King, Grace. *Creole Families of New Orleans*. New York: Macmillan, 1921.

————. *Memories of a Southern Woman of Letters*. New York: Macmillan, 1932.

————. *New Orleans: The Place and the People*. New York: Macmillan, 1895.

Klitgaard, Kaj. *Through the American Landscape*. Chapel Hill: University of North Carolina Press, 1941.

Kmen, Henry A. *Music in New Orleans. The Formative Years 1791–1841*. Baton Rouge: Louisiana State University Press, 1966.

Kneece, Jack. "Museum Finds Priceless Art." *Times-Picayune*, Aug. 14, 1961.

Knight, Lucian Lamar, ed. *Library of Southern Literature*. Vol. 15. Atlanta: Martin and Hoyt, 1907.

Koke, Richard J. *A Checklist of the American Engravings of John Hill (1770–1850)*. New York: New-York Historical Society, 1961.

Korn, Bertram Wallace. *The Early Jews of New Orleans*. Waltham MA: American Jewish Historical Society, 1969.

Kouwenhoven, John A. *Adventures of America, 1857–1900: A Pictorial Record from Harper's Weekly*. New York: Harper and Brothers, 1938.

Krebs, Albert. "Degas à la Nouvelle-Orléans." *Rapports France-Etats-Unis* 65(Aug. 1952):63–72.

Kubly, Vincent F. *The Louisiana Capitol: Its Art and Architecture*. Gretna LA: Pelican, 1977.

Kunitz, Stanley J., and Howard Haycraft, eds. *American Authors, 1600–1900*. New York: H. W. Wilson, 1938.

La Cour, Arthur Burton, with Stuart Omer Landry. *New Orleans Masquerade: Chronicles of Carnival*. New Orleans: Pelican, 1952.

Lafayette Natural History Museum and Planetarium. *Annotated Checklist. Audubon's World: A Window into Nature*. Lafayette LA: Lafayette Natural History Museum and Planetarium, 1985.

Land, John E. *Pen Illustrations of New Orleans, 1881–82*. New Orleans: Jno. E. Land, 1882.

Landry, Stuart O. *The Battle of Liberty Place*. New Orleans: Pelican, 1955.

Larsen, Ellouise Baker. *American Historical Views on Staffordshire China*. 3d ed. New York: Dover, 1975.

Latour, Arsène Lacarrière. *Historical Memoir of The War in West Florida and Louisiana in 1814–15, with an Atlas*. Philadelphia: John Conrad, 1816.

BIBLIOGRAPHY

Latrobe, Benjamin H. *The Engineering Drawings of Benjamin Henry Latrobe.* Edited by Darwin H. Stapleton. New Haven CT: Yale University Press, 1980.
————. *Impressions Respecting New Orleans: Diary and Sketches, 1818–1820.* Edited by Samuel Wilson, Jr. New York: Columbia University Press, 1951.
————. *The Journals of Benjamin Henry Latrobe, 1799–1820.* Edited by Edward C. Carter II, John C. Van Horne, and Lee W. Fornwalt. New Haven CT: Yale University Press, 1980.
————. *Latrobe's View of America, 1795–1820: Selections from the Watercolors and Sketches.* Edited by Edward C. Carter II, John C. Van Horne, and Charles E. Brownell. New Haven CT: Yale University Press, 1985.
Latrobe, John H. B. *Southern Travels: Journal of John H. B. Latrobe, 1834.* Edited by Samuel Wilson, Jr. New Orleans: The Historic New Orleans Collection, 1986.
Laughlin, Clarence John. *Ghosts Along the Mississippi.* New York: Bonanza, 1959.
Laussat, Pierre Clément de. *Memoirs of My Life.* Translated by Sr. Agnes–Josephine Pastwa. Edited by Robert D. Bush. Baton Rouge: Louisiana State University Press for the Historic New Orleans Collection, 1978.
Laver, James. *Manners and Morals in the Age of Optimism 1848–1914.* New York: Harper and Row, 1966.
Lay, Mrs. Orville, comp. *Alabama Portraits Prior to 1870.* Mobile: National Society of the Colonial Dames of America in the State of Alabama, 1969.
Le Breton, Dagmar Renshaw. *Chahta–Ima: The Life of Adrien–Emmanuel Rouquette.* Baton Rouge: Louisiana State University Press, 1947.
Lee, Cuthbert. *Contemporary American Portrait Painters.* New York: W. W. Norton, 1929.
Le Gardeur, Rene J., Jr. *The First New Orleans Theatre, 1792–1803.* New Orleans: Leeward, 1963.
Leland, Waldo G. "The Lesueur Collection of American Sketches in the Museum of Natural History at Havre, Seine–Inferieure." *Mississippi Valley Historical Review* 10(June 1923):53–78.
Lemann, Bernard. "New Orleans Prefab, 1867." *Journal of the Society of Architectural Historians* 22(Mar. 1963):38.
Le Page du Pratz, Antoine Simon. *The History of Louisiana.* Paris, 1774. Reprint, edited by Joseph G. Tregle, Jr. Louisiana State University Press, 1975.
Levasseur, A. *Lafayette in America in 1824 and 1825.* 2 vols. Philadelphia: Carey and Lea, 1829.
Levy, Florence N., ed. *American Art Annual.* Vol. 3. Boston: Noyes, Platt, 1900.
————. *American Art Annual.* Vol. 4. New York: American Art Annual, 1903.
Levy, Lester S. *Grace Notes in American History: Popular Sheet Music from 1820–1900.* Norman: University of Oklahoma Press, 1967.
Lewis, Henry. *Making a Motion Picture in 1848: Henry Lewis' Journal of a Canoe Voyage from the Falls of St. Anthony to St. Louis.* Edited by Bertha L. Heilbron. Saint Paul: Minnesota Historical Society, 1936.
Lewis, Paul. *Queen of the Plaza: A Biography of Adah Isaacs Menken.* New York: Funk & Wagnalls, 1964.
Lewis, Sarah Elizabeth. "The Pre–European Career of William Edward West (1788–1857) in New Orleans and Mississippi." M.A. thesis, Virginia Commonwealth University, 1981.
LHS. Louisiana Historical Society. *A Catalogue of the Colonial Exhibit.* New Orleans, 1903.
————. *Catalogue of the Exhibit.* New Orleans: Palfrey–Dameron, [1900].
Libbie, C. F., & Co. *Catalogue of the Dr. Charles E. Clark Collection of American Portraiture.* Boston, 1901.

Lilienthal's Art Gallery. *Collection of Paintings by Leading New Orleans Artists.* New Orleans, 1883.

Lindsey, Alton A. *The Bicentennial of John James Audubon.* Bloomington: Indiana University Press, 1985.

Lipman, Jean, and Alice Winchester. *Primitive Painters in America, 1750-1950: An Anthology.* New York: Dodd, Mead, 1950.

Lipton, Leah. "William Dunlap, Samuel F. B. Morse, John Wesley Jarvis, and Chester Harding: Their Careers as Itinerant Portrait Painters." *American Art Journal* 13(Summer 1981):34-50.

Lister, Raymond. *Silhouettes: An Introduction to Their History and the Art of Cutting and Painting Them.* London: Sir Isaac Pitman and Sons, 1953.

"Literary and Artistic Celebrities." *The Anglo American Magazine* 6(May 1855):401-6.

Little, Nina Fletcher. "Indigenous Painting in Maine, 1825-1865." *Antiques,* Apr. 1963, 456.

London, Hannah R. *Miniatures and Silhouettes of Early American Jews.* 2 vols. in 1. Rutland VT: Charles E. Tuttle, 1970.

Longaker, Jon D. "Painting In the South—A Double Portrait." In *Art and Music In the South,* edited by Francis B. Simkins. Farmville VA: Longwood College, 1961.

Looney, Ben Earl. "Historical Sketch of Art in Louisiana." *Louisiana Historical Quarterly* 18(Apr. 1935):382-96.

Louisiana Art Commission Galleries. *Artists Who Flourished in the Past.* Baton Rouge: Louisiana Art Commission Galleries, 1965.

Louisiana College. *Catalogue.* Parish of St James, 1855.

Louisiana Crafts Council. *Sadie Agnes Estelle Irvine Memorial Show, 1906-1960.* New Orleans, [1971].

Louisiana Industrial Exposition. *Official Souvenir and Program of the Louisiana Industrial Exposition and Peace Jubilee.* New Orleans. Daily Item, 1899.

Louisiana Landmarks Society. *James Gallier, Architect.* New Orleans: Louisiana Landmarks Society, 1950.

Louisiana State Gazetteer and Business Man's Guide, for 1866 and 1867. New Orleans: Palmer, Buchanan, & Smith, [1866].

Loyola University. *Caroline Durieux.* New Orleans, 1977.

LSM. Louisiana State Museum. *Annual Report.* New Orleans, 1918, 1919.

———. *Audubon in Louisiana.* New Orleans: Louisiana State Museum, 1966.

———. *Biennial Report.* New Orleans, 1916-17, 1920-21, 1922-23, 1924-25, 1926-27, 1928-29, 1930-31, 1931-32, 1932-33.

———. *G. P. A. Healy: Famous Figures and Louisiana Patrons.* New Orleans: Louisiana State Museum, 1976.

———. *Guide Book.* New Orleans: Louisiana State Museum, 1956.

———. *Jose Salazar.* New Orleans: Louisiana State Museum, 1981.

———. *Vaudechamp: Jean Joseph Vaudechamp, 1790-1866.* New Orleans: Louisiana State Museum, 1967.

LSU. Louisiana State University. *Caroline Durieux: 43 Lithographs and Drawings.* Baton Rouge: Louisiana State University Press, 1949.

———. *Louisiana Artists from the Collection of Dr. and Mrs. James W. Nelson.* Baton Rouge: J.-B. Printing, 1968.

———. *Louisiana Paintings of the Nineteenth Century.* Baton Rouge, 1959.

Ludlow, Noah M. *Dramatic Life As I Found It.* St. Louis, 1880. Rev. ed. New York: Benjamin Blom, 1966.

Lyell, Sir Charles. *A Second Visit to the United States of North America.* 2d ed., 2 vols. London: John Murray, 1850.

MacBeth, Jerome R. "Portraits by Ralph E. W. Earl." *Antiques,* Sept. 1971, 390-93.

BIBLIOGRAPHY

M'Caleb, Thomas, ed. *The Louisiana Book: Selections from the Literature of the State*. New Orleans: R. F. Straughan, 1894.

McCarthy, Dennis, Gilbert Sutton, Gilbert Edge, and Roy Aymond. *Our Prominent Citizens As We See Them*. New Orleans: Morris, 1921.

McCracken, Harold. *George Catlin and the Old Frontier*. New York: Dial, 1959.

———. *Portrait of the Old West*. New York: McGraw–Hill, 1952.

McDermott, John Francis. "Alfred S. Waugh's 'Desultory Wanderings in the Years 1845–46.' " *Bulletin of the Missouri Historical Society* 6(Apr. 1950):303.

———. *The Art of Seth Eastman: A Traveling Exhibition of Paintings & Drawings Circulated By The Smithsonian Institution*. Washington DC, 1959.

———. "Audubon's Earliest Oil Portraits." *Antiques*, Nov. 1958, 434–35.

———. *George Caleb Bingham, River Portraitist*. Norman: University of Oklahoma Press, 1959.

———. "Henry Lewis and His Views of Western Society." *Antiques*, Apr. 1952, 332–35.

———. "Leon Pomarede, 'Our Parisian Knight of the Easel.' " *Bulletin of the City Art Museum of St. Louis* 34(Winter 1949):8–18.

———. "Likeness by Audubon." *Antiques*, June 1955, 499–501.

———. *The Lost Panoramas of the Mississippi*. Chicago: University of Chicago Press, 1958.

———. "Mrs. Trollope's Illustrator: Auguste Hervieu in America (1827–1831)." *Gazette des Beaux-Art*, Mar. 1958, 169–90.

———. *Seth Eastman's Mississippi: A Lost Portfolio Recovered*. Urbana: University of Illinois Press, 1973.

———. *Seth Eastman: Pictorial Historian of the Indian*. Norman: University of Oklahoma Press, 1961.

———, ed. *Travelers on the Western Frontier*. Urbana: University of Illinois Press, 1970.

McDermott, John Francis, ed., and Albert J. Salvan, trans. *Tixier's Travels on the Osage Prairies*. Norman: University of Oklahoma Press, 1940.

McGinnis, Karin Hertel. "Moving Right Along: Nineteenth Century Panorama Painting in the United States." Ph.D. dissertation, University of Minnesota, 1983.

McGlauflin, Alice Coe, ed. *Dictionary of American Artists, 19th & 20th Century*. Poughkeepsie NY: Glenn Opitz/Apollo, 1929.

Mackay–Smith, Alexander. *The Race Horses of America, 1832–1872: Portraits and Other Paintings by Edward Troye*. Saratoga Springs NY: National Museum of Racing, 1981.

Mackie, Carey T., H. Parrott Bacot, and Charles L. Mackie. *Crescent City Silver*. New Orleans: The Historic New Orleans Collection, 1980.

———. "Hyde and Goodrich and Its Successors: Nineteenth–Century New Orleans Silver Manufacturers." *Antiques*, Aug. 1982, 293–303.

McLanathan, Richard. *The American Tradition in the Arts*. New York: Harcourt, Brace & World, 1968.

McMullan, T. N., ed. *Louisiana Newspapers, 1794–1961*. Baton Rouge: Louisiana State University Library, 1965.

McNay Art Institute. *A Seth Eastman Sketchbook, 1848–1849*. Austin: University of Texas Press, 1961.

McWilliams, Richebourg Gaillard, ed. and trans. *Fleur de Lys and Calumet: Being the Penicaut Narrative of French Adventure in Louisiana*. Baton Rouge: Louisiana State University Press, 1953.

Madwell, Charles Jr. "Continuation of the Records of the Girod Street Cemetery." *New Orleans Genesis* 13(Sept. 1974):391–400.

Magnagbi, Russell M. "Louisiana's Italian Immigrants Prior to 1870." *Louisiana History* 27(Winter 1986):43–68.

Mallett, Daniel T. *Mallett's Index of Artists*. New York: R. R. Bowker, 1935. Reprint. New York: Peter Smith, 1948.

———. *Supplement. Mallett's Index of Artists*. New York: R. R. Bowker, 1940. Reprint. New York: Peter Smith, 1948.

Marlor, Clark S. *A History of the Brooklyn Art Association with an Index of Exhibitions*. New York: James F. Carr, 1970.

Matthews, E. C. *Joseph Pennell's Sketches of Old New Orleans*. New Orleans: Hope, 1966.

Mechanics' and Agricultural Fair Association of Louisiana. *Report of The First Grand Fair*. New Orleans: Commercial Bulletin Job Office, 1867.

———. *Report of the Second Grand Fair*. New Orleans: J. H. Keefe, 1868.

———. *Report of the Third Grand Fair*. New Orleans: Commercial Bulletin, 1869.

———. *Report of Their Fourth Grand State Fair*. New Orleans: Steel, 1870.

Megroz, R.L. *Profile Art through the Ages*. New York: Philosophical Library, 1949.

Men of Affairs in Progressive New Orleans, 1908. New Orleans, 1908.

Metropolitan Museum of Art. *American Paintings and Historical Prints from the Middendorf Collection*. New York: Metropolitan Museum of Art, 1967.

Meyer, Audrey May. *Mary Ashley Townsend [Xariffa] (1832–1901): Poet Laureate of Louisiana*. New Orleans, 1938.

Meyerbeer, Giacomo. *L'Africaine*. Libretto. Edited by M. Variol. New Orleans, [1890].

Miceli, Augusto P. *The Pickwick Club of New Orleans*. New Orleans: Pickwick, 1964.

Mississippi Museum of Art. *To Live Upon Canvas: The Portrait Art of Thomas Cantwell Healy*. Jackson: Mississippi Museum of Art, 1980.

Mississippi State Historical Museum. *The Biloxi Art Pottery of George Ohr*. Jackson: Mississippi Department of Archives and History, 1978.

———. *Made By Hand: Mississippi Folk Art*. Jackson: Mississippi Department of Archives and History, 1980.

Mobley, James. "The Academy Movement in Louisiana." *Louisiana Historical Quarterly* 30(July 1947):738–978.

"A Modern Quasimodo." *Louisiana Historical Quarterly* 2(July 1919):318–20.

Moise, Harold. *The Moise Family of South Carolina*. Columbia SC: R. L. Bryan, 1961.

Montero de Pedro, José. *Españoles en Nueva Orleans y Luisiana*. Madrid: Ediciones Cultura Hispanica, 1979.

Montgomery, Walter, ed. *American Art and American Art Collections*. 2 vols. Boston: E. W. Walker, 1889. Reprint. New York: Garland, 1978.

Montreal Museum of Fine Arts. *The Painter and the New World: A Survey of Painting from 1564 to 1867*. Montreal, Canada, 1967.

Montulé, Edouard de. *A Voyage to North America and the West Indies in 1817*. London: Sir Richard Phillips, 1821.

———. *Travels in America 1816–1817*. 1821. Translated by Edward D. Seeber. Bloomington: Indiana University Press, 1951.

Moore, Lillian. "New York's First Ballet Season." *Bulletin of the New York Public Library* 64(Sept. 1960):478–90.

Morrison, Andrew. *The Industries of New Orleans*. New Orleans: J. M. Elstner, 1885.

———. *New Orleans and the New South*. New Orleans: Graham, 1888.

Morse, John D., ed. *Prints in and of America to 1850*. Winterthur Conference Report 1970. Charlottesville: University Press of Virginia for Henry Francis du Pont Winterthur Museum, 1970.

BIBLIOGRAPHY

Morton's Auction Exchange. *Catalogue.* Mar. 29, 1966, Aug. 29, 1967, Aug. 1973, Mar. 13, 1979, Oct. 29–30, 1982, Dec. 10–11, 1982, May 1983, May 20, 1983.

Moses, G. *A Catalogue of the Pictures Comprising the Collection of Gustave Moses, Will H. Moses, Harry L. Moses.* New Orleans: C. T. Hodges, 1902.

Mottelay, Paul F., and T. Campbell–Copeland, eds. *The Soldier in Our Civil War.* New York: Stanley Bradley, 1890.

Mount, May W. *Some Notables of New Orleans: Biographical and Descriptive Sketches of the Artists of New Orleans, and Their Work.* New Orleans: May W. Mount, 1896.

Mugridge, Donald H., and Helen F. Conover. *An Album of American Battle Art, 1755–1918.* Washington DC: Library of Congress, 1947.

Murray, Peter, and Linda Murray. *Dictionary of Art and Artists.* New York: Frederick A. Praeger, 1965.

Murray's 1871–1872 Planters' Directory of Louisiana. Compiled by William L. Murray. New Orleans: Wm. L. Murray, 1871.

Murrell, William. *A History of American Graphic Humor.* 2 vols. New York: Cooper Square, 1967.

Museum of Fine Arts. *M. & M. Karolik Collection of American Water Colors & Drawings, 1800–1875.* 2 vols. Boston: Museum of Fine Arts, 1962.

Myers, William E. *The Israelites of Louisiana.* New Orleans: W. E. Meyers, 1904.

National Gallery of Art. *The Civil War: A Centennial Exhibition of Eyewitness Drawings.* Washington DC, 1961.

NCAB. *National Cyclopaedia of American Biography.* 32 vols. New York: James T. White, 1893–1936.

Neal, John. "Our Painters." *Atlantic Monthly,* Dec. 1868, 641–50.

Nelson, Nathalie G. "Genealogical Data on (Napo)leon Joseph Fremaux." Nov. 30, 1971. (Typewritten.)

Nevins, Allan. "The Troubled Career of Lafcadio Hearn." *Mentor* 13(Mar. 1925):47–50.

Nevins, Allan, and Frank Weitenkampf. *A Century of Political Cartoons: Caricature in the United States from 1800 to 1900.* New York: Charles Scribner's Sons, 1944.

New Orleans Art League. *Fifteenth Annual Membership Exhibition.* New Orleans, [1926].

———. *Twenty–Third Annual Membership Exhibition.* New Orleans, 1949–50.

New Orleans Art School. *Bulletin.* New Orleans, 1929–30, 1930–31.

———. *Year Book.* New Orleans, 1926.

New Orleans Museum of Art. *Handbook of the Collection.* Edited by Betty N. McDermott. New Orleans: New Orleans Museum of Art, 1980.

———. *1977 Artists Biennial.* New Orleans, 1977.

New–York Historical Society. *Catalogue of American Portraits in the New–York Historical Society.* 2 vols. New Haven CT: Yale University Press, 1974.

Newcomb College. *A Retrospective Exhibition: Angela Gregory, 1925, and a Collection of the Works of Selina E. Bres Gregory.* New Orleans, 1981.

Newcomb School of Art. *Announcement.* New Orleans, 1913–14.

Norman, B. M. *Norman's New Orleans and Environs.* New Orleans: B. Norman, 1845. Facsimile reproduction, edited by Matthew J. Schott. Baton Rouge: Louisiana State University Press, 1976.

North American Saengerbund. *Official Text–book and Programmes of the Twenty–Sixth Saengerfest.* New Orleans: Crescent, 1890.

Norton Art Gallery. *Louisiana Landscapes and Genre Painings of the 19th Century.* Shreveport LA: Norton Art Gallery, 1981.

Norvell, Lillian. "Ellsworth Woodward." *New Orleanian,* Aug. 1931, 18–21.

Nott, C. William. "John Jarvis." *New Orleanian,* Sept. 6, 1930, 28–29, 44.

Nouvelle Biographie Générale. Paris: Firmin Didot Frères, Fils, 1858.

Novak, Barbara. *American Painting of the Nineteenth Century: Realism, Idealism, and the American Experience.* New York: Praeger, 1969.

Nuhrah, Arthur George. *Memorials and Portraits of John McDonogh.* New Orleans: Gulf, 1951.

O'Connor, Thomas, ed. *History of the Fire Department of New Orleans.* New Orleans, 1895.

Odell, George C. D. *Annals of the New York Stage.* 15 vols. New York: Columbia University Press, 1927–49.

Ogden, Caroline, Frances Jones, Frances Howe, and Katherine Kopman. *The New Orleans Calendar.* New Orleans: Electric Engraving & Printing, 1895.

O'Neill, Charles Edwards. "Fine Arts and Literature; Nineteenth Century Louisiana Black Artists and Authors." In *Louisiana's Black Heritage,* edited by Robert R. Macdonald, John R. Kemp, and Edward F. Haas. New Orleans: Louisiana State Museum, 1979.

Ord, George. "A Memoir of Charles Alexander Lesueur." *American Journal of Science and Arts* 8(Sept. 1849):189–216.

Orleans Parish School Board. *The New Orleans Book.* New Orleans: Searcy & Pfaff, 1919.

Ormond, Suzanne, and Mary E. Irvine. *Louisiana's Art Nouveau: The Crafts of the Newcomb Style.* Gretna LA: Pelican, 1976.

Orr, Linda Carol. "Francisco Bernard: Louisiana Portrait and Landscape Artist." M.A. thesis, Louisiana State University, 1971.

Overdyke, W. Darrell. *Louisiana Plantation Homes.* New York: Architectural Book Publishing, 1965.

"Paintings of Note." *Chicago History* 1(Winter 1947–48):286–88.

Palao, Mike. "Ines Somenzini Lugano: World Renowned Artist At Maison Hospitaliere." *Italian–American Digest,* Autumn 1978.

Parke–Bernet Galleries, Inc. *The Celebrated Collection of Americana Formed by the Late Thomas Winthrop Streeter.* New York: Parke–Bernet Galleries, Inc., 1966.

Patrick, W. K. *Club Men of Louisiana in Caricature.* East Aurora NY: Roycrofters, 1917.

Peat, Wilbur D. *Pioneer Painters of Indiana.* Indianapolis: Art Association of Indianapolis, 1954.

Peeler, A. J. *The Standard Blue Book of the United States of America, 1917.* Vol. 9. Deluxe ed. New York: A. J. Peeler, 1916.

Pennell, Joseph. *The Adventures of an Illustrator Mostly in Following His Authors in America and Europe.* Boston: Little, Brown, 1925.

———. *The Life and Letters of Joseph Pennell.* Edited by Elizabeth Robins Pennell. 2 vols. Boston: Little, Brown, 1929.

Pennington, Estill Curtis. *William Edward West, 1788–1857: Kentucky Painter.* Washington DC: National Portrait Gallery, 1985.

Perry, Regenia A. *Selections of 19th–Century Afro-American Art.* New York: Metropolitan Museum of Art, 1976.

Peters, Harry T. *America on Stone: The Other Printmakers to the American People.* Garden City NY: Doubleday, Doran, 1931.

———. *California on Stone.* Garden City NY: Doubleday, Doran, 1935.

———. *Currier & Ives: Printmakers to the American People.* 2 vols. Garden City NY: Doubleday, Doran, 1929–31.

Peters, Martha Ann. *The St. Charles Hotel, 1835–1860.* M.A. thesis, Tulane University, 1949.

Peterson, Roger Tory. Introduction to *The Art of Audubon.* New York: Times Books, 1979.

BIBLIOGRAPHY

Phillips, P. Lee. *A List of Maps of America in the Library of Congress*. Washington DC: Government Printing Office, 1901.

Photographic Album of the City of New Orleans, Comprising the Principal Business Houses and Views of the City. New Orleans: Hofeline & Adams, 1887.

Picayune's Guide to New Orleans. Rev. and enl. New Orleans: The Picayune, 1897.

Picayune's Guide to New Orleans. Rev. and enl. 4th ed. New Orleans: The Picayune, 1900.

Picayune's Guide to New Orleans. Rev. ed. 7th ed. New Orleans: The Picayune, 1906.

Picayune's Guide to New Orleans. 11th ed. New Orleans: The Picayune, 1913.

Piercy, Frederick Hawkins. *Route from Liverpool to Great Salt Lake Valley*. New Orleans: F. H. Hawkins, 1845. Facsimile reproduction, edited by Matthew J. Schott. Cambridge: Belknap Press of Harvard University Press, 1962.

Pinckney, Pauline A. *Painting in Texas: The Nineteenth Century*. Austin: University of Texas Press, 1967.

Pitot, James. *Observations on the Colony of Louisiana from 1796 to 1802*. Translated by Henry C. Pitot. Baton Rouge: Louisiana State University Press for the Historic New Orleans Collection, 1979.

Plauché, Léda. *Old New Orleans Characters*. New Orleans: Green Orchid, 1931.

Poesch, Jessie. *The Art of the Old South: Painting, Sculpture, Architecture, and the Products of Craftsmen, 1560–1860*. New York: Alfred A. Knopf, 1983.

————. *Newcomb Pottery: An Enterprise for Southern Women, 1895–1940*. Exton PA: Schiffer, 1984.

Post, Marie Caroline. *The Life and Memoirs of Comte Régis de Trobriand*. New York: E. P. Dutton, 1910.

Powell, Mary M. "Three Artists of the Frontier." *Bulletin of the Missouri Historical Society*, Oct. 1948, 34–39.

Practical Perspective. Baltimore: Fielding Lucas, Jr., 1827.

Pratt, John Lowell, ed. *Currier and Ives: Chronicles of America*. New York: Promontory, 1974.

Preston, Wheeler. *American Biographies*. New York: Harper & Brothers, 1940.

Radcliffe, Anthony. "Some Artists of Louisiana." *Southern Magazine*, June 1937, 11–12, 35.

Rader, Jesse L. *South of Forty: From the Mississippi to the Rio Grande*. Norman: University of Oklahoma Press, 1947.

Rago, Dave. "Newcomb Origins in 1884 Exposition." *Antique Monthly*, Apr. 1983, 9B.

Ralph, Julian. *Dixie; or, Southern Scenes and Sketches*. New York: Harper & Brothers, 1896.

Rand, Clayton. *Stars in Their Eyes: Dreamers and Builders in Louisiana*. Gulfport MS: Dixie, 1953.

Rathbone, Perry T. "Mississippi Panorama." *Art News*, Oct. 1949, 39–40, 53–54.

————. *Mississippi Panorama*. St. Louis: City Art Museum, 1949. Rev. ed., 1950.

————, ed. *Westward the Way: The Character and Development of the Louisiana Territory As Seen By Artists and Writers of the Nineteenth Century*. St. Louis MO: City Art Museum of St. Louis, 1954.

Ray, Frederic E. *Alfred R. Waud: Civil War Artist*. New York: Viking, 1974.

Reclus, Elisée. *The United States*. Vol. 3 of *The Earth and Its Inhabitants: North America*. Edited by A. H. Keane. New York: D. Appleton, 1893.

————. "Fragment D'Un Voyage A La Nouvelle Orléans." *Le Tour Du Monde*, 1860, 177–92.

Reeves, Sally K. Evans, and William D. Reeves. *Historic City Park New Orleans*. New Orleans: Friends of City Park, 1982.

Register, James. *New Orleans is My Name.* Shreveport LA: Mid–South, 1971.

Reif, Rita. "Antiques View: A Passion for Pottery." *New York Times*, Dec. 2, 1984.

———. "Antiques View: Rediscovering a Potter." *New York Times*, Feb. 24, 1985.

Reinders, Robert C. *End of an Era: New Orleans, 1850–1860.* New Orleans: Pelican, 1964.

Reps, John W. *Views and Viewmakers of Urban America: Lithographs of Towns and Cities in the United States and Canada, Notes on the Artists and Publishers, and a Union Catalog of Their Work, 1825–1925.* Columbia: University of Missouri Press, 1984.

Rewald, John, James B. Byrnes, and Jean Sutherland Boggs. *Edgar Degas: His Family and Friends in New Orleans.* New Orleans: Isaac Delgado Museum of Art, 1965.

Richardson, E. P. *Painting in America.* New York: Thomas Y. Crowell, 1965.

Rickels, Patricia K. *1776–1976: 200 Years of Life and Change in Louisiana.* Lafayette LA: Lafayette Natural History Museum Association, 1977.

Rieder, Milton P., Jr., and Norma Gaudet Rieder, comps. and eds. *The Crew and Passenger Registration Lists of the Seven Acadian Expeditions of 1785.* Metairie LA, 1965.

———, eds. *New Orleans Ship Lists.* Vol. 1. 1820–1821. Metairie LA, 1966.

Rightor, Henry, ed. *The Standard History of New Orleans, Louisiana.* Chicago: Lewis, 1900.

Rinhart, Floyd, and Marion Rinhart. *American Daguerreian Art.* New York: Clarkson N. Potter, 1967.

Ripley, Eliza. *Social Life in Old New Orleans.* New York: D. Appleton, 1912.

Ritchan. "Hair Portraiture." *Connoisseur*, Dec. 1932, 392–93.

Roehl, Marjorie. "Follow–Up: City's Monuments Showing Their Age." *Times–Picayune*, Oct. 30, 1983.

Ross, Marvin C. *The West of Alfred Jacob Miller.* Norman: University of Oklahoma Press, 1968.

Rossini, Gioachino Antonio. *Guillaume Tell Libretto.* Edited by M. Variol. New Orleans, [1890].

Rowland, Dunbar, and Albert Godfrey Sanders, eds. and trans. *Mississippi Provincial Archives: French Dominion.* 3 vols. Jackson: Mississippi Department of Archives and History, 1927–32.

Rudolph, Marilou Alston. "George Cooke and His Paintings." *Georgia Historical Quarterly* 44(June 1960):117–53.

Rutledge, Anna Wells. *Artists in the Life of Charleston. Transactions of the American Philosophical Society*, n.s. 39. Philadelphia, 1949.

———. *Catalogue of Paintings and Sculpture in the Council Chamber, City Hall, Charleston, South Carolina.* Charleston: City Council, 1943.

———. "Paintings in the Council Chamber of Charleston's City Hall." *Antiques*, Nov. 1970, 794–99.

Saarinen, Aline. *The Proud Possessors: The Lives, Times, and Tastes of Some Adventurous American Art Collectors.* New York: Random House, 1958.

St. Charles Hotel. *New Orleans: The Paris of America.* New Orleans: Alfred S. Amer, 1928.

St. Charles Hotel. *Souvenir of New Orleans, "The City That Care Forgot."* New Orleans: Alfred S. Amer, 1917.

Salam, Cara Lu. "French Portraitists: New Orleans, 1830–1860." M.A. thesis, Louisiana State University, 1967.

Samuel, Martha Ann Brett, and Ray Samuel. *The Great Days of the Garden District and the Old City of Lafayette.* New Orleans. Parents' League of Louise S. McGehee School, 1961.

Samuel, Ray, Leonard V. Huber, and Warren C. Ogden. *Tales of the Mississippi*. New York: Hastings House, 1955.

Saxon, Lyle, comp. *Gumbo Ya–Ya*. Boston: Houghton Mifflin, 1945.

Scharf, J. Thomas. *History of St. Louis City and County*. 2 vols. Philadelphia PA: Louis H. Everts, 1883.

Schmitz, Marie L. "Henry Lewis: Panorama Maker." *Gateway Heritage* 3(Winter 1982–83):36–48.

Schoenberger, Podine. "Tireless Zoning Secretary to Retire After Long Duty." *Times–Picayune*, Aug. 23, 1953.

Schwarz & Son, Frank S. *American Paintings, $2,000 and Under*. Philadelphia.

Scully, Arthur, Jr. *James Dakin, Architect: His Career in New York and the South*. Baton Rouge: Louisiana State University Press, 1973.

Sears, Stephen W., ed. *The American Heritage Century Collection of Civil War Art*. New York: American Heritage, 1974.

Seebold, Herman de Bachelle. *Old Louisiana Plantation Homes and Family Trees*. 2 vols. New Orleans: Pelican, 1941. Reprint. Gretna LA: Pelican, 1971.

Selter, H. Foure. *L'Odysee americaine d'une famille française*. Baltimore, 1936.

Semmes, John E. *John H. B. Latrobe and His Times, 1803–1891*. Baltimore: Norman Remington, 1917.

Semple, Henry Churchill, ed. *The Ursulines in New Orleans and Our Lady of Prompt Succor: A Record of Two Centuries, 1727–1925*. New York: P. J. Kenedy & Sons, 1925.

Seymour, William H. *The Story of Algiers, 1718–1896*. Gretna LA: Pelican, 1971.

Sheldon, G.W. *American Painters: With One Hundred and Four Examples of Their Work Engraved on Wood*. Enl. ed. New York: Benjamin Blom, 1972.

Simms, George A. *Notable Men of New Orleans*. New Orleans: George Simms, 1905.

Smith, E. Herndon. "Florian." Mobile Public Library. (Typewritten.)

Smith, Edgar Newbold. *American Naval Broadsides: A Collection of Early Naval Prints (1745–1815)*. New York: Philadelphia Maritime Museum, 1974.

Smith, Margaret Denton, and Mary Louise Tucker. *Photography in New Orleans: The Early Years, 1840–1865*. Baton Rouge: Louisiana State University Press, 1982.

Smith, Sidney Adair. "The Arts in Mobile." *Antiques*, Sept. 1977, 482–91.

Smith, Sol. *Theatrical Management in the West and South for Thirty Years*. New York: Harper & Brothers, 1868.

Smithsonian Institution. *Newcomb Pottery: An Enterprise for Southern Women, 1895–1940*. Washington DC: Smithsonian Institution, 1984.

———. *The Civil War: A Centennial Exhibition of Eyewitness Drawings*. Washington DC, 1961.

Soards, Lon, comp. *Soards' Blue Book of New Orleans, for 1890–91*. New Orleans: L. Soards, 1890.

"Sol Smith and Theatre Folk, 1836–1865." *Missouri Historical Society* 5(July–Sept. 1938):101–5.

Soniat du Fossat, Mrs. Eugene. *Biographical Sketches of Louisiana's Governors, from d'Iberville to Foster*. 2d ed. Baton Rouge: The Advocate, 1893.

Sotheby Parke Bernet. *American Folk Art from the Collection of Peter Tillou*. New York: Sotheby Parke Bernet, 1985.

———. *The American Heritage Society Auction of Americana*. New York: Sotheby Parke Bernet, 1977.

———. *Americana*. New York: Sotheby Parke Bernet, 1977.

Southeast Arkansas Arts and Science Center. *F. T. Anderson: Man Out of Time*. Pine Bluff AR: Southeast Arkansas Arts and Science Center, 1984.

The Southern Business Directory and General Commercial Advertiser. Charleston, 1854.

Southern Business Guide, 1879–80. New York: United States Central Publishing, 1880.

Spring Hill College. *Spring Hill College, Mobile Alabama, 1830–1905.* Mobile: Commercial Printing, [1906].

Squires, Monas N. "Henry Lewis and His Mammoth Panorama of the Mississippi River." *Missouri Historical Review* 27(Jan. 1933):244–56.

Starke, Aubrey. "Richard Henry Wilde and the Establishment of the University of Louisiana." *Louisiana Historical Quarterly* 17(Oct. 1934):605–24.

Stauffer, David McNeely. *American Engravers Upon Copper and Steel.* 2 vols. New York, 1907. Reprint. New York: B. Franklin, 1964.

Stebbins, Theodore E., Jr. *American Master Drawings and Watercolors: A History of Works on Paper from Colonial Times to the Present.* New York: Harper & Row, 1976.

Stephens, Stephen DeWitt. *The Mavericks: American Engravers.* New Brunswick NJ: Rutgers University Press, 1950.

Stern, Madeleine B. *Purple Passage: The Life of Mrs. Frank Leslie.* Norman: University of Oklahoma Press, 1953.

Stern's Auction Co. *Catalogue.* New Orleans, 1911, 1916, 1925.

Stevens, Harriet. "The History of Ceramics at Newcomb College." Senior thesis, Tulane University, 1948.

Stokes, I. N. Phelps, and Daniel C. Haskell. *American Historical Prints: Early Views of American Cities, Etc., from the Phelps Stokes and Other Collections.* New York: New York Public Library, 1932.

Sutton, Cantey Venable, ed. *History of Art in Mississippi.* Gulfport MS: Dixie, 1929.

Swift, Samuel. "The Pictorial Representation of Architecture; the Work of Jules Guerin." *The Brickbuilder* 18(Sept. 1909):177–84.

Taft, Robert. *Artists and Illustrators of the Old West, 1850–1900.* New York: Charles Scribner's Sons, 1953.

Tallant, Robert. *The Romantic New Orleanians.* New York: E. P. Dutton, 1950.

Tennessee Centennial and International Exposition. *Catalogue: Fine Arts Department, Tennessee Centennial.* Nashville: Brandon, 1897.

Testut, Charles. *Portraits Littéraires de la Nouvelle-Orléans.* New Orleans, 1850.

Thieme, Ulrich, and Felix Becker. *Allgemeines Lexikon Der Bildenden Künstler.* 37 vols. Leipzig: E. A. Seemann, 1907–55.

THNOC. The Historic New Orleans Collection. *Alfred R. Waud: Special Artist on Assignment.* New Orleans: The Historic New Orleans Collection, 1979.

———. *Caroline Durieux: Retrospective Exhibition.* New Orleans: The Historic New Orleans Collection, 1976.

———. *The Waters of America: 19th-Century American Paintings of Rivers, Streams, Lakes, and Waterfalls.* New Orleans: The Historic New Orleans Collection, 1984.

Thompson, Maurice. *My Winter Garden: A Nature Lover Under Southern Skies.* New York: Century, 1900.

Thompson, Thomas P. *Louisiana Writers.* New Orleans, 1904.

Thompson, W. Ruth Farr. "A Biographical Checklist of Artists in New Orleans in the Nineteenth Century." B.S. thesis, Louisiana State University, 1961.

Thorpe, Russell Walton. "The Waldo Portraits of Our Seventh President." *Antiques*, May 1948, 364–65.

Throop, Walter Fay, and Beryl Estelle Burch Throop. *The Throop Tree.* La Mirada CA: Throop, 1971.

Thurber Art Galleries. *Special Showing and Sale of Works by Robert W. Grafton.* Chicago: Thurber Art Galleries, 1917.

Thwaites, Reuben Gold, ed. *Early Western Travels 1748–1846.* Cleveland OH: Arthur H. Clark, 1906.

BIBLIOGRAPHY

Tinker, Edward Larocque. *Creole City: Its Past and Its People*. New York: Longmans, Green, 1953.

———. *Les ecrits de langue française en Louisiane aux XIXe siecle*. Paris: Librairie Ancienne Honore Champion, 1932.

———. *Lafcadio Hearn's American Days*. New York: Dodd, Mead, 1924.

———. *Pen, Pills & Pistols: A Louisiana Chronicle*. Franco–American Pamphlet Series, 2. New York: American Society of the French Legion of Honor, 1934.

Toledano, Roulhac B. "Marine Painters in New Orleans." *Antiques*, Dec. 1968, 874–78.

———. *Richard Clague, 1821–1873*. New Orleans, 1974.

Trollope, Frances. *Domestic Manners of the Americans*. London, 1832. Reprint, edited by Donald Smalley. New York: Vintage, 1960.

Trovaioli, August P., and Roulhac B. Toledano. *William Aiken Walker: Southern Genre Painter*. Baton Rouge: Louisiana State University Press, 1972.

Tucker, Mary Louise, "Jacques G. L. Amans: Portrait Painter in Louisiana, 1836–1856." M.A. thesis, Tulane University, 1970.

Tuckerman, Henry T. *Book of the Artists*. New York: James F. Carr, 1966.

Tulane Decorative Art League for Women. *Catalogue for the Opening Exhibition of Work*. New Orleans, 1888.

Tulane University. *Two Decades of Newcomb Pottery: Pieces from the Period of 1897 to 1917*. New Orleans, 1963.

———. *Two Southern Impressionists*. New Orleans, 1985.

Turner, Arlin. *George W. Cable: A Biography*. Durham NC: Duke University Press, 1956.

Tyler, Ron. *Alfred Jacob Miller: Artist on the Oregon Trail*. Fort Worth TX: Amon Carter Museum, 1982.

———. *Prints of the American West*. Fort Worth: Amon Carter Museum, 1983.

United Confederate Veterans, Louisiana Division. *Roster of Camps with Officers and List of Delegates to State and General Convention, Held in New Orleans, April 7th, 8th, and 9th, 1892*. New Orleans: A. W. Hyatt, [1892].

Vail, R. W. G. *The American Sketchbooks of Charles Alexander Lesueur, 1816–1837*. Worcester MA, 1938.

Van Ravenswaay, Charles. "The Forgotten Arts and Crafts of Colonial Louisiana." *Antiques*, Sept. 1953, 192–95.

Verdi, Giuseppe. *Jerusalem Libretto*. New Orleans, 1850.

Ver Nooy, Amy. "Benson J. Lossing, Nineteenth–Century Historian and Wood Engraver." *Antiques*, Apr. 1968, 524–29.

Villiers du Terrage, Marc. *Histoire de la Fondation de la Nouvelle–Orléans (1717–1722)*. Paris: Imprimerie Nationale, 1917.

Virginia Museum of Fine Arts. *Painting in the South: 1564–1980*. Compiled by David S. Bundy. Richmond: Virginia Museum of Fine Arts, 1983.

Voss, Louis. *History of the German Society of New Orleans*. New Orleans: German Society of New Orleans, 1927.

Wachenheim, Maxine T. "The Stylistic Development of Tombs in the Cemeteries of New Orleans." *Southwestern Louisiana Journal* 3(Fall 1959):258–81.

Waitz, Julia LeGrand. *The Journal of Julia LeGrand: New Orleans, 1862–1863*. Edited by Kate Mason Rowland and Mrs. Morris L. Croxall. Richmond VA: Everett Waddey, 1911.

Waldo, J. Curtis. *Illustrated Visitors' Guide to New Orleans*. New Orleans: Waldo, 1879.

Walker, Barbara C. "A Kind of Archeology or Why Dig That Up?" *Regional Dimensions* 2(1984):1–16.

Walker, Norman. "The New Orleans Carnival." *Harper's Weekly*, Mar. 12, 1898, 249–54.

Walmsley, Carroll B. *A Catalogue of the Collection of Dr. (and the late) Mrs. I. M. Cline . . . Which Will Be Sold By Auction by Carroll B. Walmsley on the Premises Starting on Tuesday, July 17, 1928 . . .* New Orleans, 1928.

Walpole Society. *Prints Pertaining to America.* Charlottesville VA: Walpole Society, 1963.

Waring, Joseph Frederick. *Cerveau's Savannah.* Savannah: Georgia Historical Society, 1973.

Warner, Charles Dudley. "The Acadian Land." *Harper's New Monthly Magazine,* Feb. 1887, 334–54.

——. "New Orleans." *Harper's New Monthly Magazine,* Jan. 1887, 186–206.

Warner, Ezra J. *Generals in Gray: Lives of the Confederate Commanders.* Baton Rouge: Louisiana State University Press, 1959.

Warren, David B. *Bayou Bend: American Furniture, Paintings, and Silver from the Bayou Bend Collection.* Houston: The Museum of Fine Arts, 1975.

Washington Artillery Souvenir. [New Orleans], ca. 1894.

Waugh, Alfred S. *Travels in Search of the Elephant: The Wanderings of Alfred S. Waugh, Artist, in Louisiana, Missouri, and Santa Fe, in 1845–1846.* Edited and annotated by John Francis McDermott. St. Louis: Missouri Historical Society, 1951.

Weddell, Alexander Wilbourne. *Portraiture in the Virginia Historical Society.* Richmond: Virginia Historical Society, 1945.

Wehle, Harry B. *American Miniatures, 1730–1850, and A Biographical Dictionary of the Artists.* Garden City NY: Garden City, 1937.

Weitenkampf, Frank. *American Graphic Art.* Rev. and enl. New York: Macmillan, 1924.

——. *Political Caricature in the United States.* New York: New York Public Library, 1953.

Werner, Alfred, ed. *Pascin: 110 Drawings.* New York: Dover, 1972.

Whitney Museum of American Art. *200 Years of American Sculpture.* New York: David R. Godine, 1976.

Who's Who In America: A Biographical Dictionary of Notable Living Men and Women of the United States. Chicago: A. N. Marquis, 1899–. Published biennially.

Who's Who in American Art, edited by Dorothy B. Gilbert. 4 vols. Washington DC: American Federation of Arts, 1936–47.

Who's Who in Louisiana and Mississippi. New Orleans: Times–Picayune, 1918.

Who's Who in the South and Southwest. Chicago: Marquis–Who's Who, 1956.

Who Was Who in America: Historical Volume 1607–1896. Chicago: A. N. Marquis, 1963.

Who Was Who in America: Historical Volume 1607–1896. Rev. ed. Chicago: A. N. Marquis, 1967.

WICCE. World's Industrial and Cotton Centennial Exposition. *Catalogue of the Art Collection.* 2d ed. New Orleans, 1884–85.

——. *A Guide to the Principal Cities in the South, including St. Louis, Cairo, Memphis, Vicksburg, Mobile, and New Orleans.* Chicago: Rand, McNally, 1885.

Wickiser, Ralph, Caroline Durieux, and John McCrady. *Mardi Gras Day.* New York: Henry Holt, 1948.

Wiesendanger, Martin, and Margaret Wiesendanger. *19th Century Louisiana Painters and Paintings from the Collection of W. E. Groves.* New Orleans: W. E. Groves, 1971.

Wilds, John. "In 1885 We Were Here." *Times–Picayune,* Mar. 20, 1977.

Wilkerson, Marcus Manley. *Thomas Duckett Boyd: The Story of a Southern Educator.* Baton Rouge: Louisiana State University Press, 1935.

Wilkins, James F. *An Artist on the Overland Trail.* Edited by John Francis McDermott. San Marino CA: Huntington Library, 1968.

BIBLIOGRAPHY

"William Mackwitz, Wood Engraver." *Bulletin of the Missouri Historical Society* (Jan. 1952):176–79.

Williams, Hermann Warner. *The Civil War: The Artists' Record*. Boston: Beacon, 1961.

Willis–Thomas, Deborah. *Black Photographers, 1840–1940*. New York: Garland, 1985.

Wilson, Alexander. *Wilson's American Ornithology*. New York: H. S. Samuels, 1852.

Wilson, Francis. *Joseph Jefferson: Reminiscences of a Fellow Player*. New York: Charles Scribner's Sons, 1906.

Wilson, Samuel, Jr. "Almonester: Philanthropist and Builder in New Orleans." In *The Spanish in the Mississippi Valley, 1762–1804*, edited by John Francis McDermott. Urbana: University of Illinois Press, 1974.

———. *Bienville's New Orleans: A French Colonial Capital, 1718–1768*. New Orleans: Friends of the Cabildo, 1968.

———. *The Capuchin School in New Orleans, 1725*. New Orleans: Archdiocesan School Board, 1961.

——— "Colonial Fortifications and Military Architecture in the Mississippi Valley." In *The French in the Mississippi Valley*, edited by John Francis McDermott. Urbana: University of Illinois Press, 1965.

———. *A Guide to Architecture of New Orleans, 1699–1959*. New York: Reinhold, 1959.

———. *A History of the U.S. Customhouse in New Orleans*. New Orleans, 1982.

———. "Louisiana Drawings by Alexandre De Batz." *Journal of the Society of Architectural Historians* 22(May 1963): 75–89.

———. *Plantation Houses on the Battlefield of New Orleans*. New Orleans: Battle of New Orleans, 150th Anniversary Committee of Louisiana, 1965.

———. "Religious Architecture in French Colonial Louisiana." *Winterthur Portfolio 8*. Charlottesville: University Press of Virginia, 1973.

———. *The Vieux Carré, New Orleans: Its Plan, Its Growth, Its Architecture*. New Orleans, 1968.

Wilson, Samuel, Jr., and Leonard V. Huber. *The Cabildo on Jackson Square*. New Orleans: Friends of the Cabildo, 1970.

Wilson, Samuel, Jr., and Leonard V. Huber. *The St. Louis Cemeteries of New Orleans*. New Orleans: St. Louis Cathedral, 1963.

Winter, William. *Life and Art of Joseph Jefferson*. New York: MacMillan, 1894.

Withey, Henry F., and Elsie Rathburn Withey. *Biographical Dictionary of American Architects (Deceased)*. Los Angeles: Hennessey & Ingalls, 1970.

Woman's Department of the World's Exposition. *Report and Catalogue*. Boston: Rand, Avery, 1885.

Wood, Christopher. *The Dictionary of Victorian Painters*. 2d ed. Woodbridge, England: Antique Collectors' Club, 1978.

Wood, James Playsted. *Magazines in the United States*. 2d ed. New York: Ronald, 1956.

Wood, Allen T. *Wood's Directory, Being a Colored Business, Professional and Trades Directory of New Orleans, Louisiana, 1912*. New Orleans: Allen T. Wood, 1912.

———. *Wood's Directory: Being A Colored Business, Professional and Trades Directory of New Orleans, Louisiana 1914*. New Orleans: Allen T. Wood, 1914.

Woodward, David, ed. *Five Centuries of Map Printing*. Chicago: University of Chicago Press, 1975.

Woodward, William. *French Quarter Etchings of Old New Orleans*. New Orleans: Magnolia, 1938.

The World in Miniature; or Diamond Atlas of Every Nation and Country Both Ancient and Modern. New Orleans: William F. Stuart, 1861.

WPA. Works Progress Administration. *American Portrait Inventory: 1440 Early American Portrait Artists (1663–1860)*. Newark NJ, 1940.
———. "Bookplates." New Orleans. Delgado Museum of Art, 1940. (Typewritten.)
———. *Illinois: A Descriptive and Historical Guide*. Chicago: A. C. McClurg, 1939.
———. "Lives, New Orleans Artists." New Orleans. Isaac Delgado Museum of Art. (Typewritten.)
———. *Louisiana: A Guide to the State*. New York: Hastings, 1941.
———. *Miniatures and Fans*. New Orleans: Delgado Museum of Art, 1937.
———. *New Orleans City Guide*. Boston: Houghton Mifflin, 1938. Reprint. Introduction by the Historic New Orleans Collection. New York: Pantheon, 1983.
———. "N.O. Artists Directory, 1805–1940." 13 vols. New Orleans. Isaac Delgado Museum of Art. (Typewritten.)
———. "Notes on Art Objects in City Hall, New Orleans." New Orleans. Isaac Delgado Museum of Art. (Typewritten.)
———. "Passenger Lists Taken From Manifests of the Customs Service Port of New Orleans, 1813–37, 1834–38, 1850–61." New Orleans. (Typewritten.)
Wunderlich, Rudolf. "Important American Still Life and Portrait Paintings." *Kennedy Quarterly* 3(Dec. 1862).
Wurzlow, Helen. "Ceramics Teacher Given Plaque for Long Service." *Times–Picayune*, Apr. 12, 1964.
Yeager, Allison. "John Antrobus, Artist, Poet." Knob Noster MO. (Typewritten.)
Young, Perry. *The Mistick Krewe: Chronicles of Comus and His Kin*. New Orleans: Carnival, 1931.
Young, William, ed. *A Dictionary of American Artists, Sculptors and Engravers*. Cambridge MA: William Young, 1968.

DIRECTORIES

NOBD   New Orleans Business Directory
NOCD   New Orleans City Directory
NOSD   New Orleans Suburban Directory

NOCD 1805. *New Orleans in 1805. A Directory and a Census*. Facsimile ed. New Orleans: Pelican Gallery, 1936.
NOBD 1807. *Calendrier de Commerce de la Nouvelle-Orléans* . Compiled by Barthelemy Lafon. New Orleans: Jean Renard.
NOCD 1809. *Annuaire Louisianais*. Compiled by Barthelemy Lafon. New Orleans: Barthelemy Lafon, 1808.
NOCD 1811. *Whitney's New-Orleans Directory, and Louisiana & Mississippi Almanac*. New Orleans: Thomas H. Whitney, 1810.
NOCD 1822. *The New-Orleans Directory and Register*. Compiled by John Adems Paxton. New Orleans: John Adems Paxton, 1822.
NOCD 1823. *The New-Orleans Directory and Register*. Compiled by John Adems Paxton. New Orleans: John Adems Paxton, 1823.
NOCD 1824. *A Supplement to the New-Orleans Directory of the Last Year*. Compiled by John Adems Paxton. New Orleans, 1824.
NOCD 1827. *The New Orleans Directory and Register*. Compiled by John Adems Paxton. New Orleans, 1827.
NOCD 1830. *The New-Orleans Directory and Register*. Compiled by John Adems Paxton. New Orleans: John Adems Paxton, 1830.
NOCD 1832. *The New-Orleans Annual Advertiser, for 1832, Annexed to the City Directory*. New Orleans: Stephen E. Percy, 1832.

BIBLIOGRAPHY

NOCD 1834. *Michel's New Orleans Annual and Commercial Register*. New Orleans: Gaux & Sollée, 1833.

NOCD 1835. *New Orleans Directory*.

NOCD 1837. *The New Orleans Guide, or General Directory*. New Orleans, 1837.

NOCD 1838. *Gibson's Guide and Directory of the State of Louisiana, and the Cities of New Orleans & Lafayette*. New Orleans: John Gibson, 1838.

NOCD 1841. *New-Orleans Directory*. New Orleans: E. A. Michel, 1840.

NOCD 1842. *New-Orleans Directory*. New Orleans: Pitts & Clarke, 1842.

NOCD 1843. *Michel & Co. New-Orleans Annual and Commercial Directory*. New Orleans: Justin L. Sollée, 1842.

NOCD 1844. *New-Orleans Annual and Commercial Directory*. J. J. Calberthwaite, 1844.

NOCD 1846. *Michel & Co. New Orleans Annual (Directory) and Commercial Register*. New Orleans: E. A. Michel.

NOBD 1849. *The New-Orleans Pictorial Advertiser*. New Orleans: Cook, Young.

NOCD 1849–52. *Cohen's New Orleans and Lafayette Directory*. New Orleans, 1849–52. Published annually.

NOCD 1853–55. *Cohen's New Orleans Directory*. New Orleans, 1852–55. Published annually.

NOCD 1856. *Cohen's New Orleans and Southern Directory*. Compiled by B. W. Cohen. New Orleans: Daily Delta.

NOCD 1856. *Kerr's General Advertiser, and Directory*. Compiled by R. Crockett Kerr. New Orleans: Sherman, Wharton, 1856.

NOCD 1857. *Mygatt & Co.'s Directory*. Compiled by W. H. Rainey. New Orleans, 1857.

NOBD 1857–58. *New Orleans Merchants' Diary and Guide*. Compiled by Wallace A. Brice. New Orleans: Wallace A. Brice, 1857.

NOCD 1858. *Gardner & Wharton's New Orleans Directory*. Compiled by Charles Gardner. New Orleans: Edward C. Wharton.

NOBD 1858. *A. Mygatt & Co.'s New Orleans Business Directory*. Compiled by W. H. Rainey. New Orleans: A. Mygatt, 1858.

NOBD 1858–59. *Crescent City Business Directory*. New Orleans: Price–Current.

NOCD 1859–61. *Gardner's New Orleans Directory*. Compiled by Charles Gardner. New Orleans: Charles Gardner, 1858–61. Published annually.

NOBD 1860. *Gardner's Commercial and Business Registry of New Orleans*. New Orleans: Isaac T. Hinton, 1860.

NOBD 1860–61. *Hellier's New Orleans Business Directory*. New York: Hellier, 1860.

NOBD 1865. *Duncan & Co.'s New Orleans Business Directory*. Compiled by William A. Baker. New Orleans: Duncan.

NOCD 1866–69. *Gardner's New Orleans Directory*. Compiled by Charles Gardner. New Orleans: Charles Gardner, 1866–68. Published annually.

NOCD 1867. *Graham's Crescent City Directory*. Compiled by L. Graham. New Orleans: L. Graham.

NOCD 1870–73. *Edwards' Annual Directory*. New Orleans: Southern Publishing Company, 1869–73. Published annually.

NOCD 1874–1933, 1935. *Soards' New Orleans City Directory*. New Orleans: L. Soards, 1874–1935.

NOBD 1889. *Business Guide of New Orleans and Vicinity*. Baltimore: Wm. A. Flamm, 1889.

NOBD 1897–98. *Smith's Business Directory of New Orleans*. Compiled by Frank W. Smith. New Orleans, 1897–98. Published annually.

NOBD 1913. *Soards' New Orleans Trade Guide*. New Orleans: Soards Directory Co., 1913.

NOCD 1938, 1940, 1942, 1945–47, 1949, 1952–56, 1958, 1960–62, 1964–69, 1971–79. *Polk's New Orleans City Directory*. New Orleans: R. L. Polk, 1938–79.

NOSD 1959, 1963–66, 1968–76, 1978, 1980. *Polk's New Orleans Suburban Directory*. New Orleans: R. L. Polk, 1959–80.

PERIODICALS: New Orleans

Advertiser. See Louisiana Advertiser
American, 1914–17.
American Exponent, 1856.
L'Ami des Lois, 1809–19.
Architectural Art and Its Allies, 1905–11.
Argus, 1824–34.
Art and Letters, 1887.
Arts and Antiques, 1938.
Bee (L'Abeille), 1827–1923.
Bull Frog, 1841.
Bulletin, 1874–77.
Carnival Joker, 1909.
Carrollton Star, 1855.
Carrollton Sun, 1859–60.
Commercial Bulletin, 1832–71.
Commercial Times, 1845–49.
Courier. See Louisiana Courier
Crescent Monthly, 1866–67.
Current Topics, 1890–94.
Daily City Item, 1877–92.
Daily Creole, 1856–57.
Daily Crescent, 1848–69.
Daily Delta, 1845–63.
Daily Democrat, 1876.
Daily Item, 1877–1958.
Daily National, 1847.
Daily News, 1886–1911.
Daily Orleanian, 1847–58.
Daily Picayune, 1838–1914.
Daily Picayune Carrier's Address, 1897–1907.
Daily Southern Star, 1865–66.
Daily States, 1880–1918.
Daily Times, 1851–57.
Daily Tropic, 1842–47.
Daily True Delta, 1849–66.
De Bow's Review, 1846–64.
Delgado, *Bulletin*, 1927–29.
Democrat, 1875–81.
Le Diamant, 1887.
Dixie, 1946–86.
Down in Dixie, 1896.
Elite, 1899–1900.
Emporium, 1832.
Era, 1863–65.
Evening Chronicle, 1883–88.
Evening Democrat, 1876.

BIBLIOGRAPHY

Figaro, 1883–84.
Friends of the Cabildo, *Newsletter*, 1982–86.
Gambit, 1983.
Gazette. See Louisiana Gazette
Green Room, 1870.
Harlequin, 1899–1909.
H.B. Stevens' Illustrated Monthly, 1888–89.
Head Light, 1892.
Herald, 1873.
Illustrated News, 1919–22.
Italian–American Digest, 1978.
Item, 1877–1958.
Item–Tribune, 1925–41.
Jeffersonian, 1845–47.
Jolly Joker, 1889–1900.
Lafayette City Advertiser, 1841–43.
Lantern, 1886–88.
Lorgnette, 1841–43.
Louisiana Advertiser, 1820–42.
Louisiana Courier (Le Courrier de la Louisiane), 1807–60.
Louisiana Gazette, 1804–26.
Louisiana Review, 1888–94.
Louisiana Spectator, 1849–53.
Louisiana State Republican, 1850–55.
Louisiana Whig, 1824–35.
Mascot, 1882–95.
Men and Matters, 1894–1904.
Mercantile Advertiser, 1820–34.
Mercantile Advertiser and Daily City Business Directory, 1851.
Miscellany, 1848.
Moniteur de la Louisiane (Louisiana Monitor), 1794–1814.
Morning Tribune, 1924–37.
National, 1855–58.
National Republican, 1871–72.
New Delta, 1891.
New Orleanian, 1930–31.
New Orleans, 1984.
New Orleans Life, 1925–27.
Old French Quarter News, 1942–51.
Our Home Journal, 1871–73.
Owl, 1895–96.
Parlor Magazine, 1857.
Patria, 1846–49.
Picayune, 1837.
Pioneer, 1908.
Present Age, 1870–72, 1881.
Preservation in Print, 1983.
Processional, 1938.
Register (Bulletin of Tulane University of Louisiana), 1913–14.
Renaissance Louisianaise, 1861–71.
Republican, 1867–78.
Review. See Louisiana Review
Revue Louisianaise, 1846–47.
Semi–Weekly Creole, 1853–56.
South Illustrated, 1886–87.

Southern Monthly Magazine, 1869.
Spanish Fort Daily Herald, 1883.
Spectator. See Louisiana Spectator
State Republican. See Louisiana State Republican
States, 1880–1958.
States–Item, 1958–80.
Tagliche Deutsche Zeitung, 1848–1907.
Times, 1863–81.
Times–Democrat, 1881–1914.
Times–Picayune, 1914–80, 1986.
Times–Picayune/States–Item, 1980–86.
Town Talk, 1904–1905.
True American, 1835–39.
Tribune de la Nouvelle Orleans (New Orleans Tribune), 1864–70.
Tulane News Bulletin, 1920, 1933.
Union, 1835.
La Union, 1851.
Weekly Budget, 1872–75.
Weekly Delta, 1845–63.
Weekly Mirror, 1858–59.
Weekly National Republican, 1871–72.
Weekly Pelican, 1886–89.
Weekly States, 1882–1907.
Weekly Times–Democrat, 1881–1914.
Whig. See Louisiana Whig
Woman's World, 1890.

PERIODICALS: Other

Ballou's Pictorial Drawing Room Companion, 1851–59.
Baton Rouge Advocate, 1861.
Baton Rouge State–Times, 1981.
Chicago Tribune, 1883.
Clarion (Museum of American Folk Art), 1985.
Detroit Free Press, 1878, 1907.
Detroit News, 1907.
Every Saturday, 1871.
Frank Leslie's Illustrated Newspaper, 1862–81.
Harper's New Monthly Magazine, 1887–1906.
Harper's Weekly, 1861–1903.
Illustrated London News, 1849, 1961.
Kennedy Quarterly, 1959–71.
Milwaukee Journal, 1934.
Natchez Ariel, 1828.
New York Clipper, 1863–64, 1883, 1885.
New York Times, 1888, 1893, 1933, 1984–85.
Old Print Shop Portfolio, 1946–85.
Once A Week, 1894.
Philadelphia Aurora General Advertiser, 1804.
Print Collector, 1970.
Richmond Standard, 1881.
St. Louis Republican, 1887.
Time, 1941.

BIBLIOGRAPHY

SPECIAL COLLECTIONS

Archives of the Archdiocese of New Orleans
Priests Biographical File
St. Louis Cathedral. Burial Records
St. Louis Cathedral. Financial Records
St. Louis Cathedral. Marriage Register
St. Louis Cemetery. Interment Records

William L. Clements Library, University of Michigan
Edward Fenno Papers

LSM. Louisiana State Museum
Artists files
Catalogue sheets
Coulon manuscript, Scrapbook 100
Document file
Map of "Parish of Plaquemines, La." (1889)
Pictorial material
Record Group 10
Registrars files
Scrapbooks 39A, 50, 53, 60, 95, and 100
Sheet music collection
W.P.A. tombstone inscription file

Missouri Historical Society
Nellie J. Meeker, document concerning Joseph R. Meeker

New York Public Library
Thomas K. Wharton diary

NOPL. New Orleans Public Library
Louisiana Division
Census of the City of New Orleans(1804)
City Archives Collection
Civil District Court. Records
Lafayette Cemeteries. Records of Interments
Louisiana and New Orleans Scrapbooks
Louisiana Biography and Obituary Index
Louisiana Charity Hospital. Death Records
Louisiana News Index
Mayor's Office. Messages
New Orleans City Council. Letters, Petitions, and Reports
New Orleans City Council. Proceedings of Council Meetings
New Orleans Health Department. Death Certificates
New Orleans Health Department. Death Index
Orleans Parish Registrar of Voters. Registration cards
Second District Court. Records
Sheet music collection
Spanish Census of New Orleans (1791)

Orleans Parish Notarial Archives
Notarial act volumes
Plan books

THNOC. The Historic New Orleans Collection
Curatorial Division
Artists files

Map collection
Pictorial materials
Manuscripts Division
Alexander–McClure Family Papers
Arts and Crafts Club Papers
Bringier Family Papers, Hermitage Foundation Papers
Commercial file
Josephine Crawford Papers
Jean Genin receipt
Performing Arts Collection
Edwin Forman Phelps Papers
James Robb Papers
Survey of Historic New Orleans Cemeteries: The Historic New Orleans Collection/Save Our Cemeteries Joint Project
United States Census for the State of Louisiana, 1810–1880, 1900–1910. Washington DC: National Archives. (Microfilm.)
Alfred R. Waud Papers
Trist Wood Papers
Research Library
Sheet music collection

TU. **Howard–Tilton Memorial Library, Tulane University**
Louisiana Collection
Art vertical file
Louisiana scrapbooks
Sheet music collection
Maxwell Music Library
Sheet music collection
Special Collections/University Archives
Prosper Foy Papers
New Orleans Artists' Roster (Copy of the W.P.A. "Lives, New Orleans Artists" and "N.O. Artists Directory." The collection also contains early drafts of entries, including three entries which do not appear in the final typescript at the New Orleans Museum of Art.)
Albert Carruthers Phelps Collection
Sheet music collection
William Ransom Hogan Jazz Archive
Sheet music collection

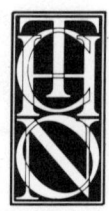

Board of Directors